BOOK OF MORMON
REFERENCE COMPANION

BOOK OF MORMON REFERENCE COMPANION

DENNIS L. LARGEY
GENERAL EDITOR

ASSOCIATE EDITORS
MARILYN ARNOLD, TERRY B. BALL,
LARRY E. DAHL, DONALD W. PARRY,
DAVID R. SEELY, AND CLYDE J. WILLIAMS

GRAPHICS EDITOR
RICHARD N. HOLZAPFEL

DESERET BOOK COMPANY
SALT LAKE CITY, UTAH

Visit us at deseretbook.com

Library of Congress Cataloging-in-Publication Data

The Book of Mormon reference companion / Dennis L. Largey, general editor.
p. cm.
Includes bibliographical references and index.
ISBN 1-57345-231-9 (alk. paper)
1. Book of Mormon. I. Largey, Dennis L. II. Title.

BX8627.B64 2003
289.3'22—dc21 2003008517

Printed in China 68875-6251
Palace Press International, Hong Kong

10 9 8 7 6 5 4 3 2 1

Contents

PREFACE

EIGHTEEN MONTHS AFTER BECOMING A MEMBER of The Church of Jesus Christ of Latter-day Saints, I went on a mission to Ireland at the age of twenty-two. In the Salt Lake City mission home, just three days prior to my departure, it became apparent to me that I lacked a very important missionary tool. I knew through prayer that The Church of Jesus Christ of Latter-day Saints is true, so I knew the Book of Mormon must be true. But the Book of Mormon had not been a part of my conversion, and I hadn't read it. I realized that to be the missionary I desired to be, I needed to read the book and receive my own spiritual confirmation of its truth. Armed with such a testimony, I would be able to invite investigators of the Church to read and pray about it—if I had done it, they could do it. I started reading that day and finished my first reading about a month later. I knelt by my bed in Dublin, Ireland, and reported to the Lord that I had read the Book of Mormon and desired spiritual confirmation of its truthfulness. The Lord answered my prayers in a strong, clear, definite manner. I knew by the power of the Holy Ghost that the Book of Mormon was true. I couldn't wait to go out that afternoon and bear my testimony of the Book of Mormon.

The Book of Mormon is exhibit A, so to speak, for the truth of the restoration of the gospel and the Church through the Prophet Joseph Smith. A testimony of the Book of Mormon is inseparably linked to a testimony of Joseph Smith, the restoration of the true Church of Jesus Christ in the latter days, and the truth that living prophets walk the earth today. I am grateful for the opportunity that working on the *Book of Mormon Reference Companion* has given me to examine so many important Book of Mormon subjects and teachings. I know that the Book of Mormon is a true account of ancient peoples who lived in the Americas. The characters were real people: they lived, they died, and they left a true record of their times and teachings. The truth of the historicity of Book of Mormon accounts is attested to by witnesses who not only saw and handled the plates that Joseph Smith translated by the gift and power of God but who also saw the sword of Laban, the Liahona, and the Urim and Thummim, sacred objects spoken of in the book's narrative and passed down through Nephite history.

Above all else, the Book of Mormon is, as its subtitle declares, Another Testament of Jesus Christ. In an increasingly skeptical world, the Book of Mormon serves as a second witness of cherished biblical truths—Jesus Christ was born of the virgin Mary, he taught the truth, he performed miracles, he suffered and died for the sins of the world, and he was resurrected on the third day. Jesus the Messiah is the literal son of God, he loves all people, and he lives today. As promised, Christ will come a second time, he will defeat Satan, and he will reign as Lord of Lords. In effect, to have a testimony of the Book of Mormon is to have a testimony of the reality of Jesus Christ and his redemptive mission.

I know, as both the Bible and the Book of Mormon teach, that Jesus Christ is the Only Begotten Son of God in the flesh, the Savior of the world, and that salvation comes only through him. I know, as one Book of Mormon prophet testified, "there is no flesh that can dwell in the presence of God, save it be through the merits, and the mercy, and grace of the Holy Messiah" (2 Ne. 2:8). Jesus Christ is the central character in the Book of Mormon—the record is a testimony of him.

—Dennis L. Largey
General editor

Acknowledgments

THIS VOLUME IS THE PRODUCT OF THE EFFORTS of many people. I would like to give special recognition to the following and express my gratitude to them.

Contributors. One hundred eleven authors wrote the articles in this volume. Approximately two hundred short articles on people and places were written by a team of authors assembled specifically to accomplish this task. Special appreciation for that service is extended to Carl W. Griffin, Frank F. Judd Jr., Jared W. Ludlow, Kerry M. Muhlestein, and Eric E. Vernon. Authors' initials do not follow the short entries written by these individuals.

Associate editors. The associate editors—Marilyn Arnold, Terry B. Ball, Larry E. Dahl, Donald W. Parry, David R. Seely, and Clyde J. Williams—possess a love for the Book of Mormon and an expertise in it that have made the production of this volume possible. I am deeply grateful for their efforts and endurance over the course of the project.

Graphics editor and staff. Richard N. Holzapfel generously used his wide knowledge in gathering the images, securing permissions for their use, and writing selected captions. The graphics staff—Craig Garrick, Karyn Hunter, and Rachel Seely—rendered valuable assistance. I also appreciate the excellent work of D. Kelly Ogden and Andrew Livingston, who created the biblical maps, and of Stephen Hales, who created the concept for the alphabetical division pages and devised the table entitled "Structure of the Book of Mormon." The map "Lehi's Journey: Possible Route" was created by S. Kent Brown, D. Kelly Ogden, and Andrew Livingston. The genealogical chart showing the posterity of Jared is adapted from one created by Lynn F. Price.

Office staff. The following individuals checked references and quotations, performed style editing, and offered helpful suggestions: Katie Anderson, Shalene Barfuss, Jennifer Blum, Melissa Boyer, Sarah Jean Carter, Vanessa Christianson, Rachel Cope, Reina Gould, Kristene Largey, Amy McLaughlin, Melissa Nelson, Kimberly Peterson, Angela Rasmussen, and Steven Sandberg.

Reviewers. Reviews and suggestions on various aspects of this volume and critiques of articles, in addition to those made by the associate editors, were given by David Bohn, Kent Brown, John Clark, Peter Crawley, Larry Draper, Richard Draper, Larry EchoHawk, Chad Foulger, David Galbraith, Dana Griffen, Kimball Hansen, Juan

Henderson, Paul Hoskisson, Kent Jackson, Boyd Jarman, Clark Johnson, Daniel Ludlow, Robert Matthews, Robert Millet, Alan Miner, Monte Nyman, Robert Parsons, Dana Pike, Larry Porter, John Pratt, Rex Reeve Jr., Vern Sommerfeldt, Calvin Stephens, Charles Tate, Bruce Warren, John Welch, and Fred Woods.

Special assistants. Gratitude must be expressed to Bart Bailey for his legal help in constructing contracts for contributors; to Judy Tolman for reading nearly all of the entries and for looking up and checking every reference; to D. Kelly Ogden for reading the entire manuscript and offering important suggestions; and to Robert L. Millet for his support, advice, and encouragement. Appreciation is extended to Suzanne Brady, senior editor at Deseret Book, for her kind and patient assistance throughout the course of this project as well as for her excellent work with the completed manuscript; to Richard Erickson, art director; Scott Eggers, designer; and Laurie Cook, typographer.

About This Volume

The *Book of Mormon Reference Companion* (*BMRC*) contains more than nine hundred entries covering Book of Mormon peoples, places, doctrines, books, historical topics, general topics of interest, and important words and phrases in the text. Its name reflects its intended use—a companion, to give Book of Mormon readers help when needed. Because it was written by experienced scholars and teachers, having this reference companion at hand is like having a teacher beside you as you read and study. It is a book that can be helpful to the seasoned reader as well as to the investigator or new convert reading the Book of Mormon for the first time.

Patterned after encyclopedic Bible dictionaries, the *BMRC* has been designed so that the first sentence contains a concise explanation of the topic addressed, providing basic knowledge as introductory information, followed by helpful elaborations that are augmented by multiple examples and references.

Style and Format

Typical of religious reference texts, the *BMRC* contains an alphabetical listing of topics in a split-column format with topic headings for ease in finding desired subjects. *See also* cross-referencing at the end of entries and SMALL CAPITALS and *see* references within entries direct readers to related articles. For example, in the article on Laban, the phrase "PLATES OF BRASS" appears in small capitals to alert readers to a more detailed discussion of this topic than is given in the article on Laban. Words and phrases that represent titles of entries appear in small capitals the first time they are used in an article.

Book of Mormon characters and places with the same names are designated by a superscript indicating the particular person or place to which the article refers. For example, there are two Almas, four Nephis, four Lehis, and two Bountifuls. The *BMRC* follows the practice of the index to the Book of Mormon regarding superscription except in the case of biblical characters that are not found in the Book of Mormon. When an article frequently repeats the name of the same character, only the first use contains the identifying superscript. Superscripts have also been omitted in most cases for the well-known prophets Mormon and Isaiah and individuals identified by other means, such as Alma the Elder, Mormon's son Moroni, or captain Moroni.

Characters

This volume contains a concise yet comprehensive view of the life of every Book of Mormon personality and includes entries on biblical characters mentioned in the text, such as Abraham, Jeremiah, Melchizedek, and Zedekiah. At the end of entries addressing the more prominent Book of Mormon characters (e.g., Lehi[1], Nephi[1], Jacob[2], Alma[1], Alma[2], and Abinadi, etc.) is a summary of major teachings. Readers can review at a glance the significant doctrinal contributions of these prominent teachers and prophets. Because the *BMRC* contains entries on every character in the Book of Mormon, names have not been included in the small-capitals cross-referencing system; readers should assume that every Book of Mormon name has an entry in the *BMRC* that will give further information. Likewise, most biblical personalities mentioned in the Book of Mormon have a corresponding article, even though their names do not appear in small capitals. Biblical characters found only in Isaiah quotations (e.g., Ahaz, Pekah, Uriah, etc.) do not have separate articles. These persons are briefly discussed in the reviews of the Isaiah chapters in which they appear.

Places

The *BMRC* contains a concise treatise on every Book of Mormon land, city, valley, hill, or river. Statements about geography are limited to the information, if any, provided by the Book of Mormon itself. Also included are articles on locations related to Lehi's journey to the promised land, including Jerusalem, Shazer, Nahom, and Bountiful. Because all place names in the Book of Mormon have an entry on that location that contains more information, place names are not included in the small-capitals cross-referencing system. Biblical place names found only in Isaiah quotations (e.g., Laish, Nob, Shinar, Edom) do not have separate articles. These places are briefly addressed in the reviews of the Isaiah chapters in which they appear.

Bible maps referred to in the text are maps in the Latter-day Saint edition of the King James Version of the Bible published in 2000 or later.

Doctrinal topics

This volume contains articles on nearly every major doctrine of the gospel. The doctrinal entries are centered on what the Book of Mormon teaches about the particular subject. In some cases, where the Book of Mormon gives only a partial view of the doctrine, readers are directed to other scriptures for additional information.

Books of the Book of Mormon

Each of the fourteen books of the Book of Mormon, plus Words of Mormon, has an entry in the *BMRC* outlining the contents of the book, identifying its authorship and the sources for its contents, and discussing its major themes and messages. These entries provide an overview of the book and point out important items that readers should understand.

Historical entries

Numerous articles written by Latter-day Saint historians for the *BMRC* document the fascinating story of the coming forth of the Book of Mormon. For example, entries include discussions of the visits of Moroni to Joseph Smith, the translation of the gold plates, the witnesses to the Book of Mormon, the printing and publication of the Book of Mormon, and early Book of Mormon conversion stories. Quotations from early documents retain original spellings, indicated by [*sic*].

Historical background

From the first page, readers of the Book of Mormon are exposed to an Old World setting: Lehi's family left Jerusalem in 600 B.C. Many find the reading challenging because they lack the basic knowledge of the Old Testament that is presupposed throughout the Book of Mormon. The *BMRC* provides this background information and explanation of terms so that readers may more easily learn the valuable lessons the writers of the Book of Mormon intended them to have. For example, the *BMRC* contains articles dealing with the Abrahamic covenant, the history of the house of Israel, and the city of Jerusalem, among other topics.

General topics

Scattered alphabetically throughout the volume are entries addressing a variety of Book of Mormon subjects and issues. Examples of subjects include olive trees, what the Book of Mormon says about the Bible, Jaredite civilization, the Book of Mormon as literature, warfare in the Book of Mormon, and Book of Mormon themes and purposes.

Words and phrases

The *BMRC* analyzes the meaning of selected words and phrases as they appear in various contexts. Examples include articles on "fruit," "Messiah," "tabernacle," "familiar spirit," "condescension of God," and "blotted out." Readers may locate articles on phrases by looking up the first word of the phrase.

Reviews of Isaiah chapters

This volume contains a review of each of the twenty-one chapters of Isaiah found in the Book of Mormon. Each review is divided into four parts. First, a clear explanation is given of the historical context from which Isaiah spoke, as well as an explanation in plain language of what the chapter is about. Second, an outline of the chapter shows how the details correspond to themes and subjects Isaiah addressed in the chapter. Third, explanations of words, phrases, people, and places within the chapter are arranged as they appear, verse by verse. Thus a reader can receive immediate help while reading Isaiah by referring to this volume for commentary on important verses. Fourth, the latter-day applicability of the chapter content is addressed. Several chapter reviews include tables showing differences between selected verses in Isaiah in the Book of Mormon and Isaiah in the King James Version of the Bible. Such tables also contain a brief commentary on the differences.

Appendixes

The *BMRC* has three appendixes to further assist readers in their study and appreciation of the Book of Mormon.

Appendix A contains two sections. The first, Readings, matches topics in the *BMRC* with reading blocks in the Book of Mormon (for example, 1 Ne. 1–7; 1 Ne. 8–15; etc.). The second, Subject Groupings, directs readers to *BMRC* articles that relate to a particular theme (for example, entries on the fall of Adam and Eve, repentance, baptism, and the Atonement are listed under "Doctrines").

Appendix B contains selected statements from LDS Church leaders about the Book of Mormon—its place, role, and significance in the Lord's kingdom.

Appendix C contains selected excerpts of definitions from Webster's 1828 *American Dictionary of the English Language,* featuring words or phrases that may have changed in meaning or usage since the original publication of the Book of Mormon or that may be unfamiliar to modern readers.

Contributors

JLA Joseph L. Allen—The Book of Mormon Archaeological Foundation; Orem, Utah

PAA Philip Andrew Allred—Religious Education; Brigham Young University–Idaho, Rexburg, Idaho

RLA Richard Lloyd Anderson—Ancient Scripture, emeritus; Brigham Young University, Provo, Utah

RDA Ronald Dean Anderson—Religious Education; Brigham Young University–Idaho, Rexburg, Idaho

MA Marilyn Arnold—English, emeritus; Brigham Young University, Provo, Utah

MVB Milton V. Backman—Church History and Doctrine, emeritus; Brigham Young University, Provo, Utah

TBB Terry B. Ball—Ancient Scripture; Brigham Young University, Provo, Utah

KDB K. Douglas Bassett—Church Educational System; Orem, Utah

ALB Alexander L. Baugh—Church History and Doctrine; Brigham Young University, Provo, Utah

RAB Reed Amussen Benson—Ancient Scripture, emeritus; Brigham Young University, Provo, Utah

SB Susan Easton Black—Church History and Doctrine; Brigham Young University, Provo, Utah

RLB Randy L. Bott—Church History and Doctrine; Brigham Young University, Provo, Utah

DEB Douglas E. Brinley—Church History and Doctrine; Brigham Young University, Provo, Utah

SKB S. Kent Brown—Ancient Scripture; Brigham Young University, Provo, Utah

DQC Donald Q. Cannon—Church History and Doctrine; Brigham Young University, Provo, Utah

JRC Jack R. Christianson—Church Educational System; Orem, Utah

JC John E. Clark—Anthropology; Brigham Young University, Provo, Utah

RAC Robert A. Cloward—Church Educational System; Cedar City, Utah

ROC Richard O. Cowan—Church History and Doctrine; Brigham Young University, Provo, Utah

RHC Richard H. Cracroft—English; Brigham Young University, Provo, Utah

LED Larry Evans Dahl—Church History and Doctrine, emeritus; Brigham Young University, Provo, Utah

GLD Guy L. Dorius—Church History and Doctrine; Brigham Young University, Provo, Utah

RDD Richard D. Draper—Ancient Scripture; Brigham Young University, Provo, Utah

DJF Daniel Justin Fairbanks—Botany and Range Science; Brigham Young University, Provo, Utah

RCF Robert C. Freeman—Church History and Doctrine; Brigham Young University, Provo, Utah

CF Camille Fronk—Ancient Scripture; Brigham Young University, Provo, Utah

AKG Arnold K. Garr—Church History and Doctrine; Brigham Young University, Provo, Utah

HDG Henry Dean Garrett—Church History and Doctrine; Brigham Young University, Provo, Utah

TLG Ted L. Gibbons—Church Educational System; Orem, Utah

KWG Kenneth W. Godfrey—Church Educational System, emeritus; Logan, Utah

CG Carl Wayne Griffin—Institute for the Study and Preservation of Ancient Religious Texts (ISPART); Brigham Young University, Provo, Utah

CWG C. Wilfred Griggs—Ancient Scripture; Brigham Young University, Provo, Utah

RLH Randall L. Hall—Church Educational System; Orem, Utah

WJH William J. Hamblin—History; Brigham Young University, Provo, Utah

HKH H. Kimball Hansen—Physics and Astronomy, emeritus; Brigham Young University, Provo, Utah

BMH Brian Michael Hauglid—Ancient Scripture; Brigham Young University, Provo, Utah

AHH Andrew H. Hedges—Church History and Doctrine; Brigham Young University, Provo, Utah

WMH Wilford M. Hess—Botany and Range Science; Brigham Young University, Provo, Utah

RNH Richard Neitzel Holzapfel—Church History and Doctrine; Brigham Young University, Provo, Utah

GAH George A. Horton Jr.—Ancient Scripture, emeritus; Brigham Young University, Provo, Utah

PYH Paul Y. Hoskisson—Ancient Scripture; Brigham Young University, Provo, Utah

VMH Valerie M. Hudson—Political Science; Brigham Young University, Provo, Utah

RH Ray Lynn Huntington—Ancient Scripture; Brigham Young University, Provo, Utah

KPJ Kent P. Jackson—Ancient Scripture; Brigham Young University, Provo, Utah

PVJ Paul Vere Johnson—Church Educational System; Salt Lake City, Utah

SAJ Stanley A. Johnson—Ancient Scripture; Brigham Young University, Provo, Utah

DKJ Daniel K. Judd—Ancient Scripture; Brigham Young University, Provo, Utah

FJ Frank F. Judd Jr.—Ancient Scripture; Brigham Young University, Provo, Utah

NEL Neal Elwood Lambert—English, emeritus; Brigham Young University, Provo, Utah

DLL Dennis L. Largey—Ancient Scripture; Brigham Young University, Provo, Utah

DHL Daniel H. Ludlow—Ancient Scripture, emeritus; Brigham Young University, Provo, Utah

JWL Jared Warner Ludlow—History and Religion; Brigham Young University–Hawaii, Laie, Hawaii

VLL Victor L. Ludlow—Ancient Scripture; Brigham Young University, Provo, Utah

CKM Craig K. Manscill—Church History and Doctrine; Brigham Young University, Provo, Utah

WJM W. Jeffrey Marsh—Ancient Scripture; Brigham Young University, Provo, Utah

RJM Robert J. Matthews—Ancient Scripture, emeritus; Brigham Young University, Provo, Utah

JFM Joseph Fielding McConkie—Ancient Scripture; Brigham Young University, Provo, Utah

BRM Byron R. Merrill—Ancient Scripture; Brigham Young University, Provo, Utah

KHM Keith H. Meservy—Ancient Scripture, emeritus; Brigham Young University, Provo, Utah

RLM Robert L. Millet—Ancient Scripture; Brigham Young University, Provo, Utah

CBM Cheryl Brown Mitchell—Linguistics and English Language; emeritus; Brigham Young University, Provo, Utah

MMM Maren M. Mouritsen—Ancient Scripture, emeritus; Brigham Young University, Provo, Utah

KMM Kerry Miles Muhlestein—Los Angeles, California

RJN Robert James Norman—Church Educational System; Salt Lake City, Utah

VGN V. Garth Norman—Ancient America Foundation and Archaeological Research Consultants; American Fork, Utah

MSN Monte Stephen Nyman—Ancient Scripture, emeritus; Brigham Young University, Provo, Utah

DDO Dallin D. Oaks—Linguistics and English Language; Brigham Young University, Provo, Utah

DKO D. Kelly Ogden—Ancient Scripture; Brigham Young University, Provo, Utah

CJO Craig James Ostler—Church History and Doctrine; Brigham Young University, Provo, Utah

DP Melvin Deloy Pack—Asian and Near Eastern Languages, emeritus; Brigham Young University, Provo, Utah

TBP Todd Brian Parker—Ancient Scripture; Brigham Young University, Provo, Utah

AKP Alan K. Parrish—Ancient Scripture; Brigham Young University, Provo, Utah

DWP Donald W. Parry—Asian and Near Eastern Languages; Brigham Young University, Provo, Utah

DCP Daniel C. Peterson—Institute for the Study and Preservation of Ancient Religious Texts (ISPART); Brigham Young University, Provo, Utah

WRP William Revell Phillips—Geology, emeritus; Brigham Young University, Provo, Utah

DMP Dana M. Pike—Ancient Scripture; Brigham Young University, Provo, Utah

LCP Larry C. Porter—Church History and Doctrine, emeritus; Brigham Young University, Provo, Utah

MHR Martin H. Raish—McKay Library; Brigham Young University–Idaho, Rexburg, Idaho

RCR Rex C. Reeve Jr.—Ancient Scripture, emeritus; Brigham Young University, Provo, Utah

MDR Michael D. Rhodes—Ancient Scripture; Brigham Young University, Provo, Utah

MOR Matthew O. Richardson—Church History and Doctrine; Brigham Young University, Provo, Utah

SDR Stephen David Ricks—Asian and Near Eastern Languages; Brigham Young University, Provo, Utah

CCR Chauncey C. Riddle—Philosophy, emeritus; Brigham Young University, Provo, Utah

SER Stephen E. Robinson—Ancient Scripture; Brigham Young University, Provo, Utah

RDR Richard Dilworth Rust—English; University of North Carolina, Chapel Hill, North Carolina

DRS David Rolph Seely—Ancient Scripture; Brigham Young University, Provo, Utah

JHS Jo Ann H. Seely—Provo, Utah

TES Thomas E. Sherry—Church Educational System; Corvallis, Oregon

ACS Andrew Charles Skinner—Ancient Scripture; Brigham Young University, Provo, Utah

RJS Royal Jon Skousen—Linguistics and English Language; Brigham Young University, Provo, Utah

BLS Brian L. Smith—Church Educational System; Orem, Utah

KS Kip Sperry—Church History and Doctrine; Brigham Young University, Provo, Utah

GS Gaye Strathearn—Ancient Scripture; Brigham Young University, Provo, Utah

TLS Terrence L. Szink—Ancient Scripture; Brigham Young University, Provo, Utah

JST John Sears Tanner—English; Brigham Young University, Provo, Utah

CDT Charles D. Tate Jr.—English and Ancient Scripture, emeritus; Brigham Young University, Provo, Utah

JCT John C. Thomas—Religious Education; Brigham Young University–Idaho, Rexburg, Idaho

MCT M. Catherine Thomas—Ancient Scripture, emeritus; Brigham Young University, Provo, Utah

BLT Brent L. Top—Church History and Doctrine; Brigham Young University, Provo, Utah

RT Rodney Turner—Ancient Scripture, emeritus; Brigham Young University, Provo, Utah

JAT John A. Tvedtnes—Institute for the Study and Preservation of Ancient Religious Texts (ISPART); Brigham Young University, Provo, Utah

BAV Bruce A. Van Orden—Church History and Doctrine; Brigham Young University, Provo, Utah

EEV Eric E. Vernon—New Haven, Connecticut

JWW John W. Welch—J. Reuben Clark Law School; Brigham Young University, Provo, Utah

DMW David M. Whitchurch—Ancient Scripture; Brigham Young University, Provo, Utah

ALW Alan L. Wilkins—Organizational Behavior; Brigham Young University, Provo, Utah

CJW Clyde James Williams—Ancient Scripture; Brigham Young University, Provo, Utah

KJW Keith J. Wilson—Ancient Scripture; Brigham Young University, Provo, Utah

FEW Fred E. Woods—Church History and Doctrine; Brigham Young University, Provo, Utah

DAW Dennis A. Wright—Church History and Doctrine; Brigham Young University, Provo, Utah

HCW Herbert Curtis Wright—Lee Library, emeritus; Brigham Young University, Provo, Utah

EDS. Editors

Abbreviations

Old Testament

Gen.	Genesis
Ex.	Exodus
Lev.	Leviticus
Num.	Numbers
Deut.	Deuteronomy
Josh.	Joshua
Judg.	Judges
Ruth	Ruth
1 Sam.	1 Samuel
2 Sam.	2 Samuel
1 Kgs.	1 Kings
2 Kgs.	2 Kings
1 Chr.	1 Chronicles
2 Chr.	2 Chronicles
Ezra	Ezra
Neh.	Nehemiah
Esth.	Esther
Job	Job
Ps.	Psalms
Prov.	Proverbs
Eccl.	Ecclesiastes
Song.	Song of Solomon
Isa.	Isaiah
Jer.	Jeremiah
Lam.	Lamentations
Ezek.	Ezekiel
Dan.	Daniel
Hosea	Hosea
Joel	Joel
Amos	Amos
Obad.	Obadiah
Jonah	Jonah
Micah	Micah
Nahum	Nahum
Hab.	Habakkuk
Zeph.	Zephaniah
Hag.	Haggai
Zech.	Zechariah
Mal.	Malachi

New Testament

Matt.	Matthew
Mark	Mark
Luke	Luke
John	John
Acts	Acts
Rom.	Romans
1 Cor.	1 Corinthians
2 Cor.	2 Corinthians
Gal.	Galatians
Eph.	Ephesians
Philip.	Philippians
Col.	Colossians
1 Thes.	1 Thessalonians
2 Thes.	2 Thessalonians
1 Tim.	1 Timothy
2 Tim.	2 Timothy
Titus	Titus
Philem.	Philemon
Heb.	Hebrews
James	James
1 Pet.	1 Peter
2 Pet.	2 Peter
1 Jn.	1 John
2 Jn.	2 John
3 Jn.	3 John

Jude	Jude
Rev.	Revelation

Book of Mormon

1 Ne.	1 Nephi
2 Ne.	2 Nephi
Jacob	Jacob
Enos	Enos
Jarom	Jarom
Omni	Omni
W of M	Words of Mormon
Mosiah	Mosiah
Alma	Alma
Hel.	Helaman
3 Ne.	3 Nephi
4 Ne.	4 Nephi
Morm.	Mormon
Ether	Ether
Moro.	Moroni

Doctrine and Covenants

D&C	Doctrine & Covenants

Pearl of Great Price

Moses	Moses
Abr.	Abraham
JS–M	Joseph Smith–Matthew
JS–H	Joseph Smith–History
A of F	Articles of Faith

Other References

CR	Conference Report
FARMS	Foundation for Ancient Research and Mormon Studies
JST	Joseph Smith Translation of the Bible
KJV	King James Version of the Bible
NIV	New International Version of the Bible
NRSV	New Revised Standard Version of the Bible
RSV	Revised Standard Version of the Bible

General

A.D.	anno domini (in the year of our Lord)
B.C.	before Christ
ca.	about, approximately
cf.	compare, confer
ed.	edition, editor
eds.	editors
e.g.	for example
et al.	and others
etc.	and so on
ff.	and following
i.e.	that is
n or n.	note
n.p.	no publisher
qtd.	quoted
[*sic*]	thus, in this manner
s.v.	under the word
v.	verse
vv.	verses
//	parallel passage(s)

Repositories of Documents and Photos

LDS Family and Church History Archives	Family and Church History Department, The Church of Jesus Christ of Latter-day Saints, Salt Lake City, Utah.
CCA	Community of Christ, Library-Archives, Independence, Missouri.
DNMF	Det Nationalhistoriske Museum pa Frederiksborg; Hillerod, Denmark.
DUP	International Society, Daughters of Utah Pioneers, Salt Lake City, Utah.
FARMS	Foundation for Ancient Research and Mormon Studies, Brigham Young University, Provo, Utah.
HBLL	L. Tom Perry Special Collections, Harold B. Lee

	Library, Brigham Young University, Provo, Utah.
MCHA	Museum of Church History and Art, The Church of Jesus Christ of Latter-day Saints, Salt Lake City, Utah. All images © Intellectual Reserve, Inc.
MFAB	Museum of Fine Arts, Boston, Massachusetts.
MOA	Museum of Art, Brigham Young University, Provo, Utah.
VRL	Visual Resource Library, The Church of Jesus Christ of Latter-day Saints, Salt Lake City, Utah. All images © Intellectual Reserve, Inc.
WWF	© Wilford Wood Foundation, Bountiful, Utah. All rights reserved.

Maya

Turkish

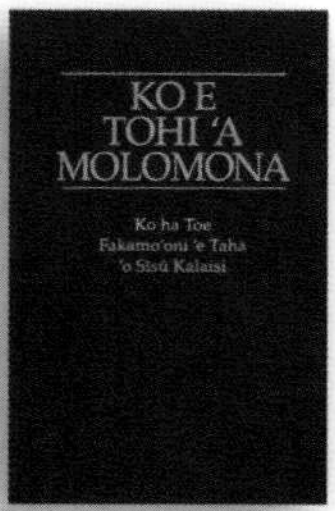

Tongan

Korean

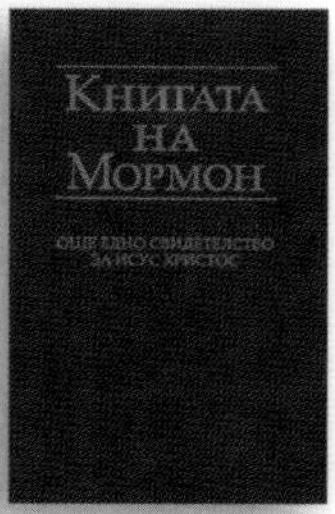

Bulgarian

Hmong

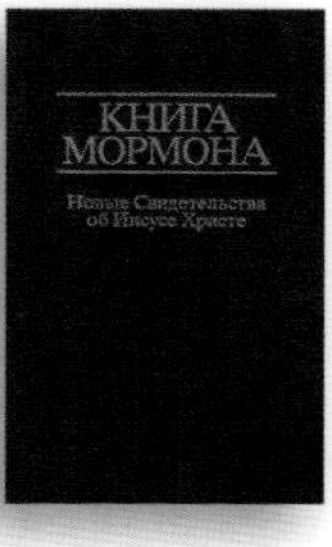

Russian

Spanish

Arabic

Afrikaans

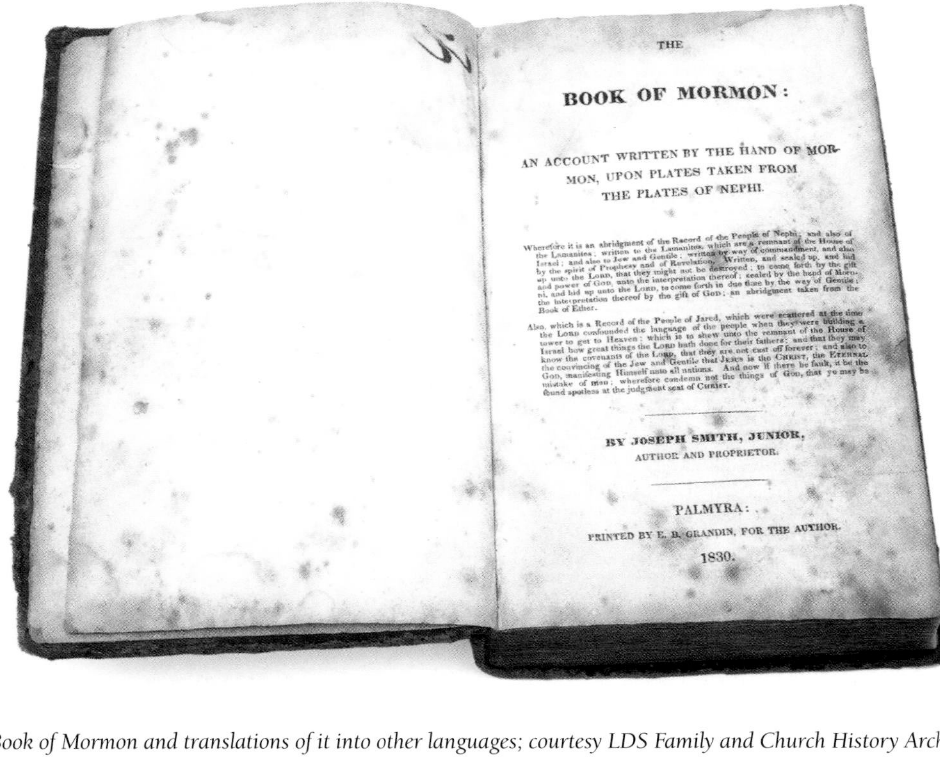

THE

BOOK OF MORMON:

AN ACCOUNT WRITTEN BY THE HAND OF MORMON, UPON PLATES TAKEN FROM THE PLATES OF NEPHI.

Wherefore it is an abridgment of the Record of the People of Nephi; and also of the Lamanites; written to the Lamanites, which are a remnant of the House of Israel; and also to Jew and Gentile; written by way of commandment, and also by the spirit of Prophesy and of Revelation. Written, and sealed up, and hid up unto the LORD, that they might not be destroyed; to come forth by the gift and power of GOD, unto the interpretation thereof; sealed by the hand of Moroni, and hid up unto the LORD, to come forth in due time by the way of Gentile; the interpretation thereof by the gift of GOD; an abridgment taken from the Book of Ether.

Also, which is a Record of the People of Jared, which were scattered at the time the LORD confounded the language of the people when they were building a tower to get to Heaven; which is to shew unto the remnant of the House of Israel how great things the LORD hath done for their fathers; and that they may know the covenants of the LORD, that they are not cast off forever; and also to the convincing of the Jew and Gentile that JESUS is the CHRIST, the ETERNAL GOD, manifesting Himself unto all nations. And now if there be fault, it be the mistake of man; wherefore condemn not the things of GOD, that ye may be found spotless at the judgment seat of CHRIST.

BY JOSEPH SMITH, JUNIOR,
AUTHOR AND PROPRIETOR.

PALMYRA:
PRINTED BY E. B. GRANDIN, FOR THE AUTHOR.
1830.

1830 Book of Mormon and translations of it into other languages; courtesy LDS Family and Church History Archives.

The Book of Mormon: An Overview and Introduction

The Book of Mormon is a book of holy scripture comparable to the Bible. An important member of the scriptural canon of the Latter-day Saints and one of the Church's standard works, it is a record of God's dealings with his ancient people in the western hemisphere. The Book of Mormon was written upon metal plates in a language known as "reformed Egyptian" (Morm. 9:32). It is largely an abridgment of records kept from generation to generation by faithful followers of Jesus Christ who lived in the ancient Americas, until finally it was buried in the earth to come forth in the latter days. Because its central character is the Lord and Savior, it is another testament of Jesus Christ.

The Bible foretold the coming forth of the Book of Mormon. The Book of Mormon is the "stick of Joseph" that would one day be joined with the "stick of Judah," the two records thereby becoming one (Ezek. 37:15–19; cf. 1 Ne. 13:41; 2 Ne. 3:12). The Book of Mormon is a significant part of the "marvellous work and a wonder" prophesied by Isaiah, the restoration of the gospel of Jesus Christ in the last days (Isa. 29:13–14). Further, the people of the Book of Mormon are the "other sheep" of whom Jesus spoke in his earthly ministry (John 10:14–16; 3 Ne. 15:13–21).

A Religious History

The Book of Mormon is not, strictly speaking, a secular history, although it contains many historical elements. Rather, it is a religious or spiritual history, the "saga of a message, a testament" (Packer, 282). Jacob[2], one of the record's principal writers, was instructed that he "should not touch, save it were lightly, concerning the history of this people." Instead, he was to focus on "preaching which was sacred, or revelation which was great, or prophesying" (Jacob 1:2, 4). Thus the most important messages of the Book of Mormon are doctrinal—they pertain to the ministry of the Lord Jesus Christ and what men and women must do to be saved.

In speaking of the Book of Mormon, Elder Russell M. Nelson observed: "I have read it many times. I have also read much that has been written about it. Some authors have focused upon its stories, its people, or its vignettes of history. Others have been intrigued by its language structure or its records of weapons, geography, animal life, techniques of building, or systems of weights and measures. Interesting as these matters may be, study of the Book of Mormon is most rewarding when one focuses on its *primary* purpose—to testify of Jesus Christ. By comparison, all other issues are incidental. . . . When Mormon abridged these records, he noted that he could not write a 'hundredth part' of their proceedings. Thus, *historical* aspects of the book assume *secondary* significance" (69).

The Book of Mormon chronicles the Lord's dealings with two major civilizations on the American continent. The first group, called the Jaredites, arrived in the New World at about the time of the tower of Babel, when the Lord chose to confound the languages of the people (Gen. 11:1–9; Ether 1:33). The book of Ether, within the Book of Mormon, is a brief account, an abridgment, of the rise and fall of this mighty nation. It recounts how God revealed himself to the prophets among this group, how the people were prospered both temporally and spiritually when they kept the commandments of God, and how, through spurning the holy word and rejecting the prophets, the nation was eventually destroyed by war.

Most of the Book of Mormon deals with a group of Hebrews (in this case descendants of the tribe of Joseph[1], son of Jacob[1]) who left Jerusalem[1] in the first year of the reign of king Zedekiah (ca. 600 B.C.), having been divinely warned concerning the coming overthrow of the kingdom of Judah by the Babylonians. Led by Lehi[1], the people traveled until they reached a seashore and eventually set sail for a "promised land," a land "choice above all other lands," the land now called America. The record of this people highlighted the early dissension between Nephi[1], a righteous and obedient leader of his people, and his rebellious and murmuring brothers, Laman[1] and Lemuel. Eventually the internal conflicts resulted in a total break of the migrants into two separate bodies of people—the followers of Nephi (Nephites) and the followers of Lemuel and Laman (Lamanites). As the history unfolded, prophet after prophet arose to call the people to repentance and declare the message of salvation. The Nephites were told repeatedly of the coming of Jesus the Messiah, and the prophet-leaders constantly sought to turn the hearts of the people to Christ. The Book of Mormon is essentially a story of the repeated rise and fall of the Nephite nation (not unlike the accounts of the children of Israel contained in 2 Kings), as the people chose either to obey God or to yield to the enticings of riches and pride.

An account of the visit and brief ministry of Jesus Christ to people in America following his death, resurrection, and ascension in the Old World is found in 3 Nephi 11 through 28. Jesus organized a church in the New World and established standards for a Christian community. An era of peace and unity followed for almost two hundred years as the people cared for each other's temporal and spiritual needs. The misuse of material blessings, however, eventually led to pride and class distinctions, which in turn led to the return of former struggles between good and evil. The story of the Book of Mormon culminates in a final battle between the Nephites and the Lamanites in which the Nephites were exterminated.

Both the sacred and the secular history of the people from the time of Nephi had been kept by the prophets (many of whom were also civic leaders) on metal plates.

The final task of completing, compiling, and abridging the collection of plates remained for the prophet-leader Mormon (for whom the book/collection is named) and his son Moroni[2]. Moroni concluded the record around A.D. 421. This same Moroni appeared to Joseph Smith in September 1823 and delivered the plates to him in 1827. Joseph Smith translated the plates into English through the gift and power of God.

The Book of Mormon has been described as "a record of a fallen people" (D&C 20:9). In one sense, the Book of Mormon delivers sobering evidence of what did and can happen to a civilization that ignores prophetic warnings and refuses to worship the God of the land, Jesus Christ (Ether 2:9–12). Further, the message of Book of Mormon prophets parallels that of biblical prophets—attesting that unless men and women repent of their sins and come unto Christ through the Atonement, they will forever remain in their lost, fallen, and unredeemed condition. The Book of Mormon contains the fulness of the gospel of Jesus Christ (D&C 20:9). That is, it teaches and emphasizes the gospel or glad tidings—that Christ came into the world and offered himself as a ransom for the sins of mankind (3 Ne. 27:13–15; D&C 76:40–42). This it does more clearly and powerfully than any other book. Its pages document the story of a people who had this fulness and were blessed when they were faithful, but who experienced the judgments of God when they turned away from it.

Written for Latter-day People

"Most books contained in libraries of the world," Elder Russell M. Nelson pointed out, "were authored for contemporary readers. . . . Not so with the Book of Mormon. It was written *anciently* for *our day*" (69–70). There is little indication in the Bible, for example, that the prophet-writers delivered and preserved their messages for any day other than their own. There is no doubt that Isaiah, Jeremiah[1], Ezekiel, Daniel, Malachi, Peter, Paul, John, and others spoke of the distant future, that by the power of the Spirit they saw and described the doings of peoples of another time and place. But their words were given to the people of their own time. Though their words have and will yet find application and fulfillment for future times, one never reads of a particular prophet from the stick of Judah addressing himself directly to those who will one day read his pronouncements.

How very different is the Book of Mormon. It was prepared and preserved by men with seeric vision who wrote and spoke to future readers; they saw and knew and addressed specific issues that people in the last days would confront. "Behold, I speak unto you as if ye were present," Moroni stated, "and yet ye are not. But behold, Jesus Christ hath shown you unto me, and I know your doing" (Morm. 8:35). Later Moroni added, "Behold, I speak unto you as though I spake from the dead; for I know that ye shall have my words" (Morm. 9:30). In the words of President Ezra Taft Benson, the Book of Mormon "was written for our day. The Nephites never had the book," meaning the complete collection that became the Book of Mormon; "neither did the Lamanites of ancient times. It was meant for us. Mormon wrote near the end of the Nephite civilization. Under the inspiration of God, who sees all things from the beginning, he abridged centuries of records, choosing the stories, speeches, and events that would be most helpful to us. . . . If they [the keepers of the plates] saw our day and chose those things which would be of greatest worth to us, is not that how we should study the Book of Mormon? We should constantly ask ourselves, 'Why did the Lord inspire Mormon (or Moroni or Alma) to include that in his record? What lesson can I learn from that to help me live in this day and age?'" (CR, 1986, 5).

Elder Nelson further stated that the Book of Mormon "can help with personal problems in a very real way. Do you want to get rid of a bad habit? Do you want to improve relationships in your family? Do you want to increase your spiritual capacity? Read the Book of Mormon! It will bring you closer to the Lord and His loving power" (71). Those who desire to know how to handle wayward children, how to deal justly yet mercifully with transgressors, how to bear pure testimony, how to teach and preach in such a manner that people cannot go away unaffected, how to detect the enemies of Christ and how to withstand those who seek to destroy faith, how to discern and expose secret combinations that seek to destroy the works of Christ, how to deal properly with persecution, and how to establish Zion—can find answers in the Book of Mormon.

If one desires to know how to avoid pride and the perils of the prosperity cycle; how to avoid priestcraft and acquire and embody charity, the pure love of Christ; how sins may be remitted and how to know one has been forgiven; how to retain a remission of sins from day to day; how to come unto Christ, receive his holy name, partake of his goodness and love, and be sanctified by his Spirit; and how to prepare for the second coming of the Son of Man—then one must search and study the Book of Mormon. This volume of holy writ is without peer. It is the most relevant and pertinent book available to mankind today.

Latter-day Saints love the Bible. They cherish the Doctrine and Covenants, glory in its plain and pure doctrinal pronouncements and clarifications, and feel a deep sense of gratitude and thanksgiving for this "capstone" of our religion (Benson, CR, 1987, 105). The Pearl of Great Price is exactly what its name implies; it is worth more than silver and gold. It is an inspired collection of unique Latter-day Saint doctrines and messages. It bears a powerful witness of Christ's eternal gospel, of the Restoration in the last days, and of the divine calling of the Prophet Joseph Smith. And yet the Book of Mormon is different from the other books of scripture—it has a special spirit all its own. President Benson taught: "It is not just that the Book of Mormon teaches us truth, though it indeed does that. It is not just that the Book of Mormon bears testimony of Christ, though it indeed does that, too. But there is something more. There is a power in the book which will begin to flow into your lives the moment you begin a serious study of the book. You will find greater power to resist temptation. You will find the power to avoid deception. You will find the power to stay on the strait and narrow path. The scriptures are called 'the words of life' (see D&C 84:85), and nowhere is that more true than it is of the Book of Mormon. When you begin to hunger and thirst after those words, you will find life in greater and greater abundance" (*Witness*, 21–22). This surely is what the Prophet Joseph Smith meant when he taught that a person could "get nearer to God by abiding by its precepts, than by any other book" (194).

The Book of Mormon is far more than a theological treatise, more than a collection of great doctrinal sermons. It is not just a book which helps readers feel good; it is a heavenly document that has been given to help men and women be good. It is as if the Nephite prophet-leaders were beckoning and pleading from the dust: "We sought for the Lord. We found him. We applied the gospel of Jesus Christ and have partaken of its sweet fruits. We know the joy of our redemption and have felt to sing the song of redeeming love. And now, O reader, come unto Christ and do thou likewise!"

The Book of Mormon does more than teach with plainness and persuasion the effects of the Fall and the absolute necessity for an atonement; it cries out that unless one acknowledges his fallen state, puts off the natural man, applies the atoning blood of Christ, and is born again, he can never be with or become like the Lord. The challenge, therefore, is not just to read and study the Book of Mormon, but to accept it and apply its doctrines and philosophy.

Serious Consequences

Too much effort has been expended over too many centuries, too much blood has been shed, too many prayers have ascended to the Lord, too great a price has been paid for the Book of Mormon record to be destroyed, or discarded, or ignored (e.g., Enos 1:12–18; Morm. 6:6; D&C 135:6). God himself has borne solemn witness of the Book of Mormon. To Oliver Cowdery, who was raised up to serve as scribe in the translation of the gold plates, the Lord affirmed, "I tell thee these things as a witness unto thee—that the words or the work which thou hast been writing are true" (D&C 6:17; cf. 18:2). And through Joseph Smith he revealed, "As your Lord and your God liveth it is true" (D&C 17:6). "Do eternal consequences rest upon our response to this book?" President Ezra Taft Benson asked. He answered, "Yes, either to our blessing or our condemnation" (CR, 1975, 97).

"The plain fact," Elder Bruce R. McConkie stated, "is that salvation itself is at stake in this matter. If the Book of Mormon is true—if it is a volume of holy scripture, if it contains the mind and will and voice of the Lord to all men, if it is a divine witness of the prophetic call of Joseph Smith—then to accept it and believe its doctrines is to be saved, and to reject it and walk contrary to its teachings is to be damned" (CR, 1983, 104).

Such language may sound harsh or divisive. To some it may be even offensive. And yet this is exactly what the Book of Mormon itself declares (e.g., 1 Ne. 14:7; 2 Ne. 33:10–15; 3 Ne. 21:11; Moro. 10:24–29). The Book of Mormon demands a decision. It forces an issue. One cannot simply dismiss it with a wave of the hand and a turn of the head; it must be explained. Thus, as Elder McConkie observed: "These are deep and solemn and ponderous matters. We need not think we can trifle with sacred things and escape the wrath of a just God. Either the Book of Mormon is true, or it is false. . . . It is not and cannot be simply another treatise on religion; it either came from heaven or from hell. And it is time for all those who seek salvation to find out for themselves whether it is of the Lord or of Lucifer" (CR, 1983, 105–6). As far as members of the Church are concerned, President Ezra Taft Benson declared boldly: "Every Latter-day Saint should make the study of this book a lifetime pursuit. Otherwise he is placing his soul in jeopardy and neglecting that which could give spiritual and intellectual unity to his whole life" (CR, 1975, 97).

Conclusion

Ancient prophecy decreed that truth would spring forth out of the earth in the last days; that truth, the Book of Mormon, would bear testimony of Jesus Christ as well as the Lord's resurrection from the dead and the resurrection of all men and women (Ps. 85:11; Moses 7:62–64). In addition, the Book of Mormon is destined to assist in a significant way in gathering Israel from the four corners of the earth, establishing Zion, and preparing a people for the second coming and millennial reign of the Savior. Indeed, the Book of Mormon has a very bright future. Looking ahead, President Benson said: "I have a vision of homes alerted, of classes alive, and of pulpits aflame with the spirit of Book of Mormon messages. I have a vision of home teachers and visiting teachers, ward and branch officers, and stake and mission leaders counseling our people out of the most correct of any book on earth—the Book of Mormon. I have a vision of artists putting into film, drama, literature, music, and paintings great themes and great characters from the Book of Mormon. I have a vision of thousands of missionaries going into the mission field with hundreds of passages memorized from the Book of Mormon so that they might feed the needs of a spiritually famished world. I have a vision of the whole Church getting nearer to God by abiding by the precepts of the Book of Mormon. Indeed, I have a vision of flooding the earth with the Book of Mormon" (CR, 1988, 4–5).

The Book of Mormon is the word of God. The Lord God is its author. It is truly, as Joseph Smith the Prophet explained, the "keystone of our religion"—the keystone of our witness of Christ, the keystone of our doctrine, the keystone of our testimony (Benson, CR, 1986, 4). It has been delivered by a gracious Lord to a generation that desperately needs it; it was sent forth with the Bible to confound false doctrines, lay down contentions, and establish peace among the people of God (2 Ne. 3:12). It speaks peace and joy to the soul. It can and should serve as a quiet, steadying influence in the lives of those who know of its truthfulness. Often longings for another time and place, those vague but powerful feelings that one has "wandered from a more exalted sphere" (Snow), are satisfied and soothed when reading the Book of Mormon. Reading it is like coming home. It is a gift of God that he expects his children to receive, understand, and experience.

See also The Coming Forth of the Book of Mormon, 9; The Structure of the Book of Mormon, 17; Book of Mormon: Another Testament of Jesus Christ; Book of Mormon, condemnation for treating lightly; Book of Mormon, as keystone scripture; Book of Mormon, as most correct book; Book of Mormon, selected purposes of; Book of Mormon, selected themes of.

BIBLIOGRAPHY

Benson, Ezra Taft. *A Witness and a Warning*. Salt Lake City: Deseret Book, 1988.
———. Conference Report, April 1975.
———. Conference Report, October 1986.
———. Conference Report, April 1987.
———. Conference Report, October 1988.

McConkie, Bruce R. Conference Report, October 1983.

Nelson, Russell M. Conference Report, October 1999.

Packer, Boyd K. *Let Not Your Heart Be Troubled.* Salt Lake City, Utah: Bookcraft, 1991.

Smith, Joseph. *Teachings of the Prophet Joseph Smith.* Selected by Joseph Fielding Smith. Salt Lake City: Deseret Book, 1976.

Snow, Eliza R. "O My Father." *Hymns of The Church of Jesus Christ of Latter-day Saints.* Salt Lake City: The Church of Jesus Christ of Latter-day Saints, 1985. No. 292.

RLM

THE COMING FORTH OF THE BOOK OF MORMON

THE COMING FORTH OF THE BOOK OF MORMON was foretold by prophets of the Old Testament period as well as Book of Mormon prophets (e.g., Enoch [Moses 7:60–62], Ezekiel [Ezek. 37:15–19], Isaiah [Isa. 29], Nephi[1] [2 Ne. 25:21–22], Mormon [Morm. 5:12–14], and Moroni[2] [Morm. 8:14–18]). The story begins with an angelic visitation in 1823 to Joseph Smith and ends with the publication of the Book of Mormon in 1830.

On Sunday evening, 21 September 1823, in the Smith family log home in Manchester, New York, seventeen-year-old Joseph Smith supplicated the Lord for "forgiveness" and to know his "state and standing before [God]." While he was calling upon the Lord, a light appeared in his room. That light, Joseph reported, "continued to increase until the room was lighter than at noonday, when immediately a personage appeared at my bedside, standing in the air, for his feet did not touch the floor." Joseph testified, "He called me by name, and said unto me that he was a messenger sent from the presence of God to me, and that his name was Moroni; that God had a work for me to do; and that my name . . . should be both good and evil spoken of among all people" (JS–H 1:29–33).

The reconstructed Smith family log home, Palmyra, New York (dedicated 27 March 1998); courtesy VRL. In 1982, archaeological work identified the location of the original house. The home, which measured approximately 18.5 x 28 feet, was completed in 1819. It was in the family home that the angel Moroni first visited Joseph Smith.

The angel told Joseph of an ancient record written on GOLD PLATES and an instrument called the URIM AND THUMMIM that was prepared "for the purpose of translating the book" (JS–H 1:35). As Moroni conversed with Joseph, "the place

Moroni Delivering the Golden Plates; *painting by Gary L. Kapp; courtesy Gary L. Kapp.*

where the plates were deposited" was shown him in vision. When this extraordinary visitation ended, "the room was again left dark." But before dawn the messenger appeared twice more to Joseph Smith. During the second visit he repeated all that he had said at the first appearance and added information about judgments that would come on the earth. During the third visit he again repeated "the same things as before; and added a caution" to Joseph to withstand Satan's temptations to use the plates for monetary gain (JS–H 1:36–46).

Arising from the sleepless night, Joseph walked from the house to the field and began the "necessary labors of the day." He soon discovered, however, that he was too exhausted to assist in the fields that day. While returning to the house, he was again visited by the angel Moroni, who "related . . . all that he had [said] . . . the previous night," and instructed Joseph to tell his father what he had seen and heard. Obediently, Joseph returned to the fields and told his father, Joseph Smith Sr., who assured him that the visitations were of God, and told Joseph "to go and do as commanded by the messenger." Young Joseph then went directly to the hill he had seen in vision the night before, "a hill of considerable size, and the most elevated of any in the neighborhood," about three miles southeast of the family farm. There, he reported, "under a stone of considerable size, lay the plates, deposited in a stone box." He was forbidden by the messenger to remove the contents from the box, because "the time for bringing them forth had not yet arrived" (JS–H 1:48–53).

Four years passed before Joseph received the gold plates and the Urim and Thummim, years in which he was instructed by the Lord and visited by heavenly personages. Every September he went to the hill in Manchester, New York, where the angel Moroni instructed him. Joseph wrote that during this period he was visited by "angels of God unfolding the majesty and glory of the events that should transpire in the last days" (Smith, *Church,* 4:537).

As heavenly truths were unfolded to Joseph, he shared the inspired insights with his family. His mother remembered that "he would describe the ancient inhabitants of this continent, their dress, mode of traveling, and the animals upon which they rode; their cities, their buildings, with every particular; their mode of warfare; and also their religious worship. This he would do with as much ease, seemingly, as if he had spent his whole life among them." His mother wrote: "I presume our family presented an aspect as singular as any that ever lived upon the face of the earth—all seated in a circle, father, mother, sons and daughters, and giving the most profound attention to a boy" (Smith, *Joseph,* 83, 82). They were attentive because of their conviction that Joseph spoke the truth. When his brother William was asked, "Did you not doubt Joseph's testimony sometimes?" he replied, "No, we all had the most implicit confidence in what he said. He was a truthful boy. Father and mother believed him; why should not the children? . . . No sir, we never doubted his word for one minute" (*News*).

Believing in Joseph, the family readily came to his defense. One evening as Joseph entered the Smith home his father asked, "Joseph, why are you so late? has anything happened to you? we have been much distressed about you these three hours." Joseph replied, "I have taken the severest chastisement that I have ever had in my life." Father Smith, surmising that the mob element in the area was harassing his son, retorted, "I would like to know what business anybody has to find fault with you!" Joseph countered, "Stop, father, stop, it was the angel of the Lord." The angelic messenger told him that he "had not been engaged enough in the work of the Lord; that the time had come for the record to be brought forth; and that [he] must be up and doing and set [himself] about the things which God had commanded [him] to do" (Smith, *Joseph,* 100).

As Joseph prepared himself to receive the plates and the Urim and Thummim, he charged his family never to mention outside the family circle the heavenly truths he shared, for "the world was so wicked that when they came to a knowledge of these things they would try to take our lives" (Smith, *Joseph,* 82). Nonetheless, news of Joseph's angelic visitations and preparations spread to the community. The family remained calm as neighbors strained to hear fanciful accounts and responded with mockery and ridicule. The family did not falter, Mother Smith insisted, "although persecuted by the preachers, who declared there was no more vision, the canon of scripture was full, and no more revelation was needed" (Barrett, 72). The Smiths, she continued, "were now confirmed in the opinion that God was about to bring to light something upon which we could stay our minds, or that would give us a more perfect knowledge of the plan of salvation and the redemption of the human family. This caused us greatly to rejoice, the sweetest union and happiness pervaded our house, and tranquility reigned in our midst" (Smith, *Joseph,* 82–83).

Tranquility did not endure. In October 1825, young Joseph left his parents' home to accept employment digging for a lost silver mine in the Ouaquaga Mountains in Harmony Township, Pennsylvania. The treasure hunt proved fruitless, halting less than a month after it began, and Joseph's reputation suffered from his association with the scheme. By declaring him a money digger, many citizens of Pennsylvania and New York handily dismissed his account of an angel, plates, and interpreters as absurd. To them it sounded like the typical fantastic imaginings that were widespread in the northeastern United States during the nineteenth century.

As insinuations increased against Joseph, only a handful of people believed in his recitations. Among them was Emma Hale of Harmony, Pennsylvania, whom he met while boarding with the Isaac Hale family. The happiness of meeting his future bride was tempered by the cold reception of Emma's father, who opposed her marriage to a man who claimed to have been visited by an angel (JS–H 1:58). Nevertheless, Joseph and Emma were married 18 January 1827 in South Bainbridge, New York, by Esq. Zachariah Tarbell. Soon after their marriage, Joseph and Emma moved to Manchester, where Emma was welcomed into the Smith home and where they lived for several months.

On 22 September 1827, the angel Moroni again met Joseph Smith at the hill Cumorah. As Joseph climbed the hill to the place where the plates were deposited, Emma waited in the wagon below the hill, and Mother Smith prayed at home, "for the anxiety of my mind would not permit me to sleep. . . . [I] feared lest Joseph might meet with another disappointment" (Smith, *Joseph,* 102). But Joseph was not disappointed.

"Having gone as usual . . . to the place where [the plates] were deposited," Joseph said, he was met by "the same heavenly messenger [who] delivered [the plates] up to me with this charge: that I should be responsible for them; that if I should let them go carelessly, or through any neglect of mine, I should be cut off; but that if I would use all my endeavors to preserve them, . . . they should be protected" (JS–H 1:59).

Emma Smith (1804–1879); courtesy CCA.

When he and Emma returned to the house with news of the unearthed treasure, the Smith family rejoiced. As word of gold treasure spread through the Manchester-Palmyra area, however, the plates became the object of much curiosity and unseemly desire. Cash and property were offered for a glimpse of what people referred to as "Joe's Gold Bible." When Joseph refused the offers, schemes were contrived to get the plates from him.

Keeping the plates safe proved difficult for Joseph. A birch log, hearth stones, floor boards, flax, and a barrel of beans were used at various times to conceal them. But little could stop the spirit of mobocracy from taking hold. As the frenzy over the "Gold Bible" mounted, Joseph left the area, turning to his father-in-law Isaac Hale in Harmony, Pennsylvania, for refuge. Hale initially welcomed his son-in-law and daughter into his home in the winter of 1827, and there Joseph "commenced copying the characters off the plates" (JS–H 1:62). When Isaac Hale discovered that Joseph had a chest containing secret materials, however, the hospitality ended. Hale, like the treasure hunters of Palmyra and Manchester, was determined to see the plates.

Joseph's refusal deepened a family rift and led to his and Emma's leaving the Hale home and taking up residence in a small farmhouse nearby, once owned by Emma's brother Jesse. This was their home for two and a half years. Those years saw both joy and tragedy. There Joseph dictated 116 pages of manuscript to Martin Harris between April and June 1828. On June 15, 1828, Emma gave birth to a son, only to lose him to death a few hours later. Within the next few weeks, through the carelessness of Martin Harris, the 116 manuscript pages were lost, and the plates and the Urim and Thummim were taken from Joseph. "In a few days," however, the plates and interpreters were returned to the Prophet. Though he again had the plates and the Urim and Thummim, Joseph explained, "I did not, however, go immediately to translating, but went to laboring with my hands upon a small farm which I had purchased of my wife's father, in order to provide for my family" (Smith, *Church,* 1:23, 28).

At some point while in their house in Harmony, Emma acted, for a brief period, as scribe for Joseph. She later said of that experience, "The Book of Mormon is of divine authenticity—I have not the slightest doubt of it. I am satisfied that no man could have dictated the writing of the manuscripts unless he was inspired; for, when acting as his scribe, [Joseph] would dictate to me hour after hour; and when returning after meals, or after interruptions, he would at once begin where he had left off, without either seeing the manuscript or having any portion of it read to him. This was a usual thing for him to do. It would have been improbable that a learned man could do this; and, for one so ignorant and unlearned as he was, it was simply impossible" (Smith, *Saints' Advocate,* 52).

Oliver Cowdery, the principal scribe of the Book of Mormon, joined Joseph in Harmony in early April, 1829, and the translation proceeded in earnest. Oliver later testified, "These were days never to be forgotten—to sit under the sound of a voice dictated by the *inspiration* of heaven, awakened the utmost gratitude of this bosom! Day after day I continued, uninterrupted, to write from his mouth, as he translated, with the Urim and Thummim . . . the history, or record, called The book of Mormon" (Cowdery, 14). Yet amid these joyous days, rumors were spreading. According to his mother, "Evil-designing people were seeking to take away his [Joseph's] life, in order to prevent the work of God from going forth to the world" (Smith, *Joseph,* 147). Amidst growing persecution, Joseph and Emma, along with Oliver Cowdery, moved temporarily from Harmony to Fayette, New York, being welcomed into the Peter Whitmer Sr. log home. Here the translation continued, with Joseph and Oliver "work[ing] from morning till night" (Porter, 238).

As the work neared completion, three witnesses (Oliver Cowdery, Martin Harris, and David Whitmer) were shown the plates by the angel Moroni, Joseph also being present. Returning from this experience, Joseph said to his parents, "Father, mother, you do not know how happy I am: the Lord has now caused the plates to be shown to three more besides myself . . . they will have to bear witness to the truth of what I have said, . . . and I feel as if I was relieved of a burden which was almost too heavy for me to bear, and it rejoices my soul, that I am not any longer to be entirely alone in the world" (Smith, *Joseph,* 152). Shortly after the Three Witnesses were shown the plates by the angel Moroni, Joseph was permitted to show the plates to eight other men (Christian, Jacob, Peter Jr., and John Whitmer; Hiram Page; Joseph Sr., Hyrum, and Samuel Smith). These eight witnesses avowed, "We did handle [them] with our hands; and we also saw the engravings thereon, all of which has the appearance of ancient work, and of curious workmanship." The testimonies of the Three Witnesses and the Eight Witnesses are published in the Book of Mormon. Concerning what happened to the plates after the translation was completed, Joseph Smith explained, "They remained safe in my hands, until I had accomplished by them what was required at my hand. When, according to arrangements, the messenger called for them, I delivered them up to him" (JS–H 1:60).

As the translation neared completion, Joseph began preparations for publishing the Book of Mormon. After obtaining a copyright 11 June 1829, from R. R. Lansing, clerk of the northern district of New York, he sought a publisher. His initial efforts to secure the printing services of Egbert B. Grandin of Palmyra, New York, were not successful. Grandin was reported to have declined "to entertain the proposal to print at any price, believing the whole affair to be a wicked imposture and a scheme to defraud" (Tucker, 51). Joseph then approached printers in Rochester, New York, one of whom, Elihu Marshall, agreed to publish the book. Perhaps because of cost and distance, however, Joseph decided to approach E. B. Grandin one more time. Wavering in what had been an earlier adamant refusal, Grandin sought advice from prominent community leaders. Verbal assurance that his business reputation would not be harmed and an offer by Martin Harris, a well-to-do farmer in Palmyra, to secure payment of publication costs led the Palmyra printer to agree to publish the Book of Mormon manuscript.

The contract to print the Book of Mormon called for five thousand copies to be printed at a cost of $3,000, a large printing project at the time, especially for a village printer like Grandin. Outside of Boston, New York, and Philadelphia, a normal book edition ran five hundred to one thousand copies. To meet his contractual agreement of five thousand copies, Grandin ran his presses fourteen hours a day, six days a week for seven months.

Initially, the printing of the Book of Mormon was slow because additional type ordered by Grandin did not arrive from Albany until late November 1829. Grandin had anticipated printing all five thousand copies of the Book of Mormon (amounting to nearly three million pages) by early February 1830, but the delay in getting the type pushed the completion date to late March. On 26 March 1830, Grandin announced the Book of Mormon was published and ready for sale at his bookstore, even though not all of the copies were bound.

See also Book of Mormon, printing and publication of; Book of Mormon, translation of; Cumorah, hill; Grandin, Egbert Bratt; Metals, ancient writing on; Moroni[2], visits of, to Joseph Smith; Smith, Joseph, Jr.; Stone boxes, burial of documents in; Witnesses of the Book of Mormon.

BIBLIOGRAPHY

Barrett, Ivan J. *Young Joseph.* RIC Publishing, 1981.

Cowdery, Oliver. *Messenger and Advocate* 1 (October 1834).

Deseret Evening News, 20 January 1894.

Porter, Larry C. "A Study of the Origins of The Church of Jesus Christ of Latter-day Saints in the States of New York and Pennsylvania, 1816–1831." Ph.D. dissertation, Brigham Young University, 1971.

Smith, Lucy Mack. *History of Joseph Smith by His Mother.* Edited by Preston Nibley. Salt Lake City: Bookcraft, 1958.

Smith, Joseph. *History of The Church of Jesus Christ of Latter-day Saints.* Edited by B. H. Roberts. 7 vols. 2d ed. rev. Salt Lake City: The Church of Jesus Christ of Latter-day Saints, 1932–51.

Smith, Joseph, III. *Saints' Advocate* 2 (2 October 1879).

Tucker, Pomeroy. *Origin, Rise, and Progress of Mormonism.* New York: D. Appleton and Company, 1867.

SB

The Structure of the Book of Mormon

From the angel Moroni Joseph Smith received the plates from which the Book of Mormon was translated. These plates consisted of the small plates of Nephi, and the plates of Mormon.

The first six books of the Book of Mormon—1 Nephi, 2 Nephi, Jacob, Enos, Jarom, and Omni—constitute the unabridged small plates of Nephi, the writings of nine Nephite authors covering a portion of Nephite history from 600 B.C. to around 130 B.C. Although containing some historical detail, the small plates were primarily religious records reserved for recording the teachings of Nephite prophets. The next section is called the Words of Mormon and is dated A.D. 385. Mormon added these few words to tell readers of his discovery of the small plates of Nephi and to provide information about the reign of king Benjamin. This addendum serves as a bridge connecting the historical narratives found on the small plates of Nephi and the plates of Mormon.

The plates of Mormon were fashioned by Mormon for the purpose of containing his abridgment of the records of his ancestors—ancient American prophets and scribes who recorded both their secular and religious history. The plates of Mormon contained Mormon's abridgment of the large plates of Nephi. The books of Mosiah, Alma, Helaman, 3 Nephi, 4 Nephi, and Mormon chapters one to seven constitute the work Mormon did on the plates of Mormon. This portion of the Book of Mormon covers a period from around 130 B.C. to A.D. 385. These books bear the marks of an abridgment as Mormon tells the Nephite story, using selections from the large plates that coincide with the religious purposes of the record. Mormon also interjected himself into his narrative, pointing out important lessons and conclusions readers should glean (e.g., Alma 30:60; 46:8–9; Hel. 12).

Mormon's son Moroni made significant additions to the plates of Mormon. His additions include (1) the material found in Mormon 8 and 9; (2) the abridgment of the plates of Ether (the book of Ether), which tells the story of the Jaredites, another group of people divinely led to the Americas in ancient times; (3) the material in the book that bears his name; (4) the title page; and (5) the part of the plates that were sealed, which Joseph Smith was instructed not to translate. Moroni finished his work about A.D. 421.

The accompanying table shows the structure of the Book of Mormon as described. Also shown is the book of Lehi—the 116 pages of manuscript lost by Martin Harris during the translation of the Book of Mormon. The book of Lehi was Mormon's abridgment of the large plates of Nephi, apparently covering the period from Lehi's departure from Jerusalem to king Benjamin. Joseph Smith was instructed not to retranslate this segment (D&C 10:30) and that the material found on the plates of Nephi (the small plates), a somewhat parallel account covering approximately the same time period, should instead be sent forth as part of the Book of Mormon (D&C 10:30, 45).

See also Book of Mormon, lost manuscript of (116 pages); Gold plates; Lehi, book of; Sealed portion of the gold plates; Words of Mormon.

DLL

Structure of the Book of Mormon

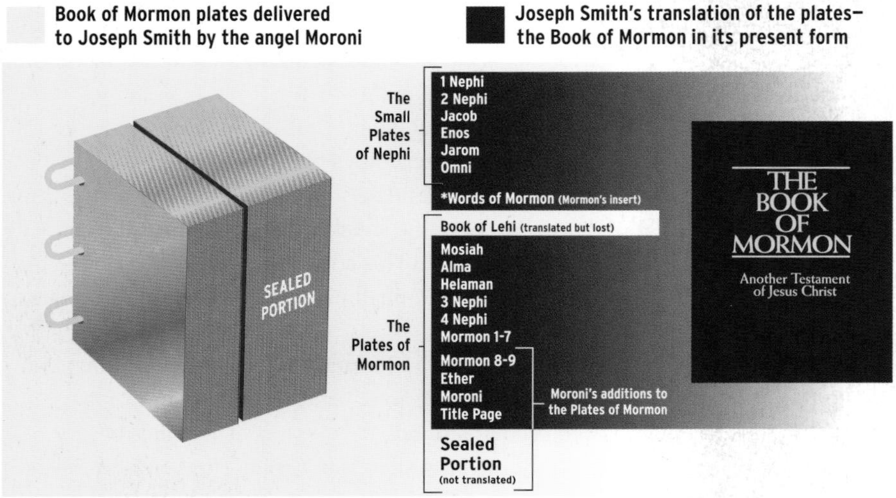

* It is unclear whether Mormon inscribed Words of Mormon in space remaining on the small plates of Nephi or on an additional plate or plates he inserted into his record.

And it came to pass that they all went forth and smote them, saying the same words, even until the last; and when the last had spoken unto them the power of God was upon Alma and Amulek, and they rose and stood upon their feet. And Alma cried, saying: How long shall we suffer these great afflictions, O Lord? O Lord, give us strength according to our faith which is in Christ, even unto deliverance. ALMA 14: 25-26

Aaron[1] Brother of the prophet Moses and the individual after whom the Aaronic Priesthood was named. Aaron is not mentioned by name in the Book of Mormon, but his role as Moses' SPOKESMAN is referred to in a prophecy given by Joseph of Egypt which Lehi[1] quoted when blessing his youngest son Joseph[2]. The Lord said to Joseph[1] that he would "raise up a Moses . . . and I will give judgment unto him in writing. Yet I will not loose his tongue, that he shall speak much . . . and I will make a spokesman for him" (2 Ne. 3:17; cf. Ex. 4:10–16). The Joseph Smith Translation of the Bible, which also contains this prophecy, reads: "And I will make a spokesman for him, and his name shall be called Aaron" (JST Gen. 50:35).

DLL

Aaron[2] *See* Jared[1], posterity of.

Aaron[3] A son of king Mosiah[2]. As an unbeliever, he had tried with his brothers and Alma the Younger to destroy the Nephite Church (Mosiah 27:8–10; ca. 100 B.C.). His conversion began with the appearance of an angel "with a voice of thunder, which caused the earth to shake" (Mosiah 27:11–18). In great "anguish of soul because of their iniquities" (Mosiah 28:4), and desiring "to repair all the injuries which they had done to the church," Aaron and his brothers began to preach the gospel, bringing "many to the knowledge of the truth, yea, to the knowledge of their Redeemer" (Mosiah 27:35–36). Like his brothers, Aaron "could not bear that any human soul should perish" (Mosiah 28:3), and after "many days" and "inquir[ing] of the Lord" king Mosiah finally granted their persistent plea to preach among the Lamanites in the land of Nephi (Mosiah 28:5–8). All of the brothers refused to be named the next king, choosing instead to continue preaching the gospel (Mosiah 28:10; 29:1–6). In Alma's reunion with Aaron and his brothers some fourteen years later, Alma rejoiced that "they were still his brethren in the Lord" and that "they had waxed strong in the knowledge of the truth" because of their diligent scripture study, and faithfulness in fasting and prayer: "Therefore they had the spirit of prophecy, and the spirit of revelation, and when they taught, they taught with power and authority of God" (Alma 17:2–3).

When Aaron and his brethren separated to preach in different Lamanite locations (Alma 17:17–18), he went to the land of Jerusalem[2] where the Amalekites contended with him and refused to listen as he preached from the scriptures about the atonement of Christ (Alma 21:1–10). Traveling next to Ani-Anti, Aaron met Muloki, Ammah, and others (Alma 21:11). Together they journeyed to Middoni and continued their preaching but with little success. While in Middoni, the Lamanites imprisoned Aaron and several others. After enormous suffering, Aaron and his companions were delivered by God through the instrumentality of Aaron's brother Ammon[2] and king Lamoni (Alma 21:14; cf. 20). Following their deliverance, the missionaries preached in Amalekite synagogues and among the Lamanites, converting many (Alma 21:15–19). From Middoni Aaron was led by the Spirit to the land of Nephi, where he met and taught Lamoni's father, king over all the Lamanites (Alma 22:1).

As recorded in a choice scriptural account, Aaron taught Lamoni's father with great power about the Creation, the fall of Adam, and the plan of redemption through the atonement of Christ (Alma 22:1–18). So convincing were Aaron's words that the once haughty king was miraculously humbled and moved to desire eternal life. He vowed he would sacrifice his sins and everything he possessed, including his kingdom, to gain it. This mighty king then bowed and prayed fervently to the God he had never known but now wished with all his being to know. Then, overcome by the Spirit, the king lost consciousness and was thought dead by members of his household. Aaron raised the converted king, the king ministered to them, and all in the household were converted (Alma 22:17–23). The king issued a proclamation granting Aaron and his brethren the right to preach with freedom and safety throughout all the land (Alma 22:27; 23:1–4). Consequently, multitudes of Lamanites were converted, and the Church was widely established in Lamanite lands and cities (Alma 23:4–12).

After a consultation among the king, Aaron,

and others, it was determined that the Lamanite converts, to distinguish themselves from their brethren, would be called "Anti-Nephi-Lehies" (Alma 23:16–17). A period of martyrdom soon followed, in which many ANTI-NEPHI-LEHIES were slaughtered by their brethren (Amalekites, Amulonites, and Lamanites) who were angered over their conversions. Aaron and his brothers were instrumental in relocating the people to Nephite lands to avoid further bloodshed. After these murders, the Lamanites themselves suffered greatly as a result of continuing battles with the Nephites and the atrocities committed against them by such dissenters as the Amulonites. Aaron's earlier preaching among the Lamanites became a blessing for these humbled Lamanites, for, as Mormon noted, "many of [the Lamanites], after having suffered much loss and so many afflictions, began to be stirred up in remembrance of the words which Aaron and his brethren had preached to them in their land; therefore they began to disbelieve the traditions of their fathers, and to believe in the Lord" (Alma 25:6).

Aaron and his brothers rejoiced over the success the Lord had granted them among the Lamanites (Alma 25:17). When Ammon recounted these blessings, Aaron mildly rebuked him for what he thought was boasting (Alma 26:10). Undaunted, Ammon assured Aaron that he was boasting not in himself but in God (Alma 26:12). After leaving the land of Nephi, Aaron continued his missionary labors with his brothers, one mission being to the Zoramites[2] where many accepted their teachings (Alma 31:6–7; 35:6). Mormon paid Aaron and others a high tribute by comparing them to Moroni[1] (Alma 48:17–18). It appears that the record's final reference to Aaron notes his preaching and ministering to the Church among the Nephites in 72 B.C. (Alma 49:30).

Summary of major teachings

1. "There is a God" (Alma 22:8).

2. The CREATION. God "created all things both in heaven and in earth," and "God created man after his own image" (Alma 22:10, 12).

3. The FALL OF ADAM AND EVE. Transgression caused the fall of man (Alma 22:13). Mortals are in a "carnal state," unable to "merit anything" of themselves (Alma 22:13–14).

4. Redemption through Christ—the ATONEMENT and RESURRECTION. "There could be no redemption for mankind save it were through the death and sufferings of Christ, and the atonement of his blood" (Alma 21:9). Christ's "sufferings" enable forgiveness of sin through faith and repentance (Alma 22:14). Christ "breaketh the bands of death, that the grave shall have no victory" (Alma 22:14).

5. Obtaining a HOPE for eternal life. If mortals repent of their sins, "bow down before God, and call on his name in faith," they can receive a hope for eternal life (Alma 22:15–18).

See also Lamoni, father of; Missionary service; Mosiah[2], sons of.

WJM

Aaron[4] Lamanite king who with his 44,000 soldiers was defeated by Mormon (ca. A.D. 330). This was apparently Mormon's first victory as a young commander (Morm. 2:9). Some years later the two sides entered into a treaty ceding the land northward to the Nephites and the land southward to the Lamanites (Morm. 2:28–29). After ten years of peace, Aaron sent an epistle to Mormon, warning of Lamanite preparations for battle (Morm. 3:4). In a letter to his son Moroni[2], Mormon spoke of the "awful brutality" of Aaron's army (Moro. 9:17).

Aaron, city of After being rejected by the people in the city of Ammonihah, Alma[2] "took his journey towards the city which was called Aaron" (Alma 8:13; ca. 82 B.C.). During this journey an angel of the Lord appeared to Alma and instructed him to return to the city of Ammonihah to preach again to the people (Alma 8:14–16). A "city of Aaron" is mentioned later in the book of Alma (50:14), raising the question of whether it is the same city or another one.

Aaronic Priesthood *See* Priesthood among the Nephites.

Abel A son of Adam and Eve. Abel was murdered following a plot between Satan and Cain, "that if he would murder his brother Abel it should not be known unto the world" (Hel. 6:27; cf. Moses 5:16–33).

Abinadi Courageous prophet and first Nephite recorded in the Book of Mormon to die as a martyr (ca. 150 B.C.). In this and in other ways, Abinadi served as a type of Christ as well as a messenger of him. Abinadi preached repentance and prophesied destruction to king Noah[3] and to the people of Zeniff in the land of Lehi-Nephi and was arrested for his teachings and rebuke.

Confronting the wicked royal establishment single-handedly, Abinadi boldly explained the purpose of the LAW OF MOSES, identified the Redeemer as God, and declared details about the RESURRECTION not previously taught in the Book of Mormon. He spoke in exquisitely colorful language sparked with fiery metaphor and concrete bluntness. So far as is known, Abinadi converted only one man, yet that one, Alma[1], became the progenitor of a posterity that kept the sacred records and served the Nephites as their ecclesiastical (and sometimes their political) leaders for the remainder of their history. Abinadi's history and teachings, preserved by Alma, influenced the entire second half of Nephite history.

The man Abinadi

Abinadi is first mentioned, though not by name, in Mosiah 7:26–28. King Limhi, son of Noah, told his people why Abinadi was martyred: "Because he said unto them that Christ was the God, the Father of all things, and said that he should take upon him the image of man . . . and that God should come down among the children of men, and take upon him flesh and blood, and go forth upon the face of the earth . . . they did put him to death."

Nothing is known of Abinadi's parentage or life, whether he was old or young, large or small. Yet, his teachings and manner when confronting the priests of Noah—baiting, challenging, and questioning them—tell much about his courage, agility of mind, knowledge of the gospel, and strength of character.

The people of Zeniff were Nephites who had left Zarahemla about 200 B.C. to reclaim the land of their ancestry (Omni 1:27; Mosiah 7:1, 21). Although Zeniff was a good man, his son and successor, Noah, was not. Under Noah's reign both the government and the people moved rapidly into a wicked lifestyle supported by high taxes (Mosiah 11:2–15, 19). Neither Noah and his priests nor the people they ruled wanted to hear the dire warnings uttered by Abinadi, the Lord's spokesman (Mosiah 11:20–25). Abinadi escaped their wrath once, but after two years he returned and again publicly preached repentance. His later teachings, however, were no longer warnings of consequences that could be averted through repentance; they had become unconditional pronouncements from the Lord of impending destruction, illustrating that the consequences of postponed repentance are frighteningly severe: "In my fierce anger will I visit them. . . . This generation, because of their iniquities, shall be brought into bondage, . . . smitten on the cheek, . . . driven by men, and shall be slain; and the vultures of the air, and the dogs, yea, and the wild beasts, shall devour their flesh" (Mosiah 12:1–2). Abinadi prophesied specifically of king Noah: "The life of king Noah shall be valued even as a garment in a hot furnace; for he shall know that I am the Lord" (Mosiah 12:3). He warned that Noah should be "as a dry stalk of the field, which is run over by the beasts and trodden under foot," and as a fully ripe thistle blown in the wind (Mosiah 12:11–12). Still quoting the Lord, Abinadi prophesied famine, pestilence, terrible storms, and heavy burdens for the people. "Except they repent," he said, they would be "utterly destroy[ed] . . . from off the face of the earth" (Mosiah 12:4–8). It would be impossible to misunderstand Abinadi's message, as it is full of high-intensity verbs, descriptive adjectives, and colorful nouns.

Abinadi was arrested, and his captors elaborated on his pronouncements spoken against the people and against Noah. In self-justification they denied Abinadi's ability to speak for God and insisted on their own and the king's innocence (Mosiah 12:12–14). Noah ordered that Abinadi be cast into prison and then brought before himself and his priests for questioning. The intent of the priests was to "cross him, . . . but he answered them boldly, and withstood all their questions, yea, to their astonishment . . .

and did confound them in all their words" (Mosiah 12:19). In this dramatic encounter, Abinadi's defense was aggressive, confident, and marvelous. He vigorously discussed with the priests the prophecies of Isaiah, the TEN COMMANDMENTS, and the law of Moses. With hot denunciation he scalded their pretense at being teachers of the law. Mosiah 12 and 13 offer an impressive glimpse of this exchange. The priests were simply helpless to contain him.

At last, Noah ordered Abinadi slain, contending that "he is mad" (Mosiah 13:1). But "the people of king Noah durst not lay their hands on him, for the Spirit of the Lord was upon him; and his face shone with exceeding luster, even as Moses' did while in the mount of Sinai. . . . And he spake with power and authority from God" (Mosiah 13:5–6).

Abinadi could not be harmed until he had delivered the remainder of his message: that Christ is God and would be born on earth to redeem mankind. He cited Moses and Isaiah specifically and all the prophets generally in support of these teachings (Mosiah 13:33–35; 14). He particularly emphasized Christ's divinity and his power over death. His teachings about who Christ is and what he would do constitute five and one-half pages in the present Book of Mormon (in English).

Noah and his priests deemed Abinadi "worthy of death" because he had said "God himself should come down among the children of men" (Mosiah 17:7–8), something they could twist and construe as blasphemy, which was punishable by death under the law of Moses (Lev. 24:16). Unnerved by Abinadi's unwavering testimony before his accusers, Noah was about to release him, but the priests appealed to the king's vanity by reminding him that Abinadi had reviled even him (Mosiah 17:11–12). Thereupon Noah ordered Abinadi put to death. They "bound him, and scourged his skin with faggots, yea, even unto death" (Mosiah 17:13). He sealed the truth of his words by his death, becoming "the first [among the Nephites] that suffered death by fire because of his belief in God" (Alma 25:11).

Alma[1], one of the priests of Noah, believed Abinadi and pleaded with the king in his behalf. Forced to flee, Alma escaped and hid for many days, and "did write all the words which Abinadi had spoken" (Mosiah 17:1–4). Readers of the Book of Mormon have Alma to thank for the record of Abinadi's inspiring story and words. The record bears out the truth of his prophecies, including those that foresaw Noah's own death by fire (Mosiah 12:3; 19:20) and the bondage of his people (Mosiah 11:21).

Although Alma wrote "all" of Abinadi's words, Mormon did not include all of them in the abridged account in Mosiah 11–17. Mosiah 12:18–19 states that Abinadi answered all the questions of the priests, yet the record deals only with questions about Isaiah 52:7–10. Furthermore, the prophet Mormon later spoke of the "sorceries, and witchcrafts, and magics" in the land, "fulfilling . . . all the words of Abinadi" (Morm. 1:19). The Book of Mormon record contains no such prophecy of Abinadi.

Abinadi's life can be seen as a type or a foreshadowing of several details of the life of Christ. Abinadi, like Christ, faced questioning by corrupt priests whose efforts were to "cross him, that thereby they might have wherewith to accuse him" (Mosiah 12:17–19; cf. Matt. 26:59–66). Both Abinadi and Christ answered questions to the astonishment of their audience (Mosiah 12:19; cf. Matt. 22:46; Luke 2:47). The charge against Abinadi was for teaching that "God himself should come down among the children of men, and take upon him the form of man" (Mosiah 13:34; 17:7–8). The charge against Christ was that he "being a man, makest [himself] God" (John 10:33; Matt. 26:63–65). King Noah, like Pilate, was willing to let him go, yet the voice of the crowd objecting, "He has reviled the king," would not permit it (Mosiah 17:11–12; cf. John 19:4–15). Neither Abinadi nor Christ was taken and executed until his mortal mission was completed (Mosiah 13:2–3; cf. John 10:18; 19:11; Matt. 26:53–54).

Ever present in Abinadi's ministry is the awareness that he was a special witness for the Lord Jesus Christ. He spoke in great plainness and with much energy, and his words were fulfilled to the letter (Mosiah 20:21; Alma 25:9–12; Morm. 1:19). If he had been less fierce and less blunt, he might not have been taken seriously, and his words might not have pierced Alma's soul. Abinadi was the very man the Lord needed in that time and place.

Summary of major teachings

1. The law of Moses—what it was, why it was given, and its relationship to the ATONEMENT (Mosiah 13:29–31; 16:14). Salvation, Abinadi declared, "doth not come by the law alone" (Mosiah 13:28) but "through the redemption of God" (Mosiah 13:32).

2. God himself will make the Atonement. Abinadi left no doubt that the God of Israel himself would be the Redeemer who would come to earth as the Son of God (Mosiah 13:28, 32, 33, 34–35; 15:1, 2–4, 5–7, 8, 23; 16:4, 15; cf. 1 Ne. 19:10; 2 Ne. 9:5; 10:3; Mosiah 3:5–10). Abinadi was so effective in making this point that the charge against him by the priests was, "Thou art worthy of death. For thou hast said that God himself should come down among the children of men" (Mosiah 17:7–8).

3. The first resurrection. Earlier prophets had taught of the resurrection, but Abinadi was the first in the Book of Mormon to describe and use the phrase "first resurrection" (Mosiah 15:21). His discourse on the subject begins in Mosiah 15:20 and extends through Mosiah 16:11, a total of two complete pages. He stated explicitly that without Christ there could not have been a resurrection (Mosiah 16:6–8).

Abinadi's teachings are in harmony with expanded knowledge about the resurrection that the Prophet Joseph Smith gained through revelation; however, Abinadi's record does not tell it all. What he did not say, at least in what was recorded, is that those who die after the time of Christ, who are righteous, will also be in the first resurrection. The first resurrection that Abinadi spoke of consisted of the righteous who lived from the time of Adam to the time of Christ. Those who have lived since the time of Christ know of a continuation of the first resurrection, stretching from Jesus' time to the Second Coming and on through the Millennium (D&C 63:49–52; 76:63–65; 88:97–98; McConkie, 640). Additionally, Abinadi taught that little children and those who die in "ignorance, not having salvation declared unto them" will "have a part in the first resurrection"; on the other hand, those who "die in their sins" by willfully rebelling against God, although eventually resurrected, will be excluded from the first resurrection (Mosiah 15:24–26; cf. D&C 137:7–8).

4. The JUDGMENT. One's personal and individual accountability to God (Mosiah 16).

5. Other important subjects. Abinadi's teachings include an explanation of the role of Jesus Christ as Father and Son (Mosiah 15:1–7), an identification of the "seed" of Christ as all those who believe and obey the Messiah (Mosiah 15:10–13), and his marvelous use of Isaiah 52 and 53 in speaking of the Redeemer (Mosiah 14–15).

See also Isaiah chapter reviews, Mosiah 14 // Isaiah 53; Jesus Christ, role of, as Father and Son; Noah[3], priests of; Seed of Christ.

BIBLIOGRAPHY

McConkie, Bruce R. *Mormon Doctrine.* 2d ed. Salt Lake City: Bookcraft, 1966.

RJM

Abinadom A Nephite historian (between 279 and 130 B.C.), son of Chemish (Omni 1:10), father of Amaleki[1] (Omni 1:12), and a direct descendant of Jacob[2]. He participated in war with the Lamanites and wrote only briefly on the plates, reasoning that he knew of no revelation or prophecy to add to what had been written by his predecessors (Omni 1:10–11).

RDA

Abish A Lamanite woman who was a servant to king Lamoni (Alma 19:13–31; ca. 90 B.C.). Abish was converted to Christ as a result of a vision her father received, but she chose to keep her beliefs secret. She was present at the marvelous conversions and resultant joy of king Lamoni, his wife the queen, and the king's servants. When all had fallen to the ground, "overpowered by the spirit" (Alma 19:13), Abish recognized the opportunity for many to witness the power of God. She rushed "from house to house" (Alma 19:17) with the news of what had occurred, but to her disappointment the assembled group contended about the meaning of the spectacle before them and about the presence of Ammon[2], a Nephite. To avert further discord, Abish took the queen by the hand "that perhaps she might raise her from the ground" (Alma 19:29). The queen arose and in turn raised her husband. After rebuking the people, the king taught the words of Ammon, which resulted in many conversions.

Ablom Jaredite "place" by the seashore to which king Omer fled with his family after his kingdom was overthrown by the secret combinations of Akish. The Lord had warned Omer in a dream of this danger (Ether 9:1–3).

Abominations, mother of *See* Mother of abominations.

Abraham Abraham, son of Terah and father of Ishmael and Isaac (Gen. 11:26; 16:15; 21:3), is a major figure in the Bible and in the Book of Mormon. He grew up in Ur of the Chaldees (Gen. 11:26–28; Abr. 1:1; 2:1) but moved to Haran and then to the land of Canaan at the command of the Lord (Gen. 12:1–6; Abr. 2:1–15). He and his wife Sarah also resided in Egypt for an unspecified time (Gen. 12:10–13:1; Abr. 2:21). His original name was Abram. The name Abraham, given to him by the Lord (Gen. 17:5), means "father of a multitude." Although the Book of Mormon says little about Abraham's life, it ties his name to important actions of the past that are to influence eternally his descendants and others.

A few details of Abraham's life appeared on the plates of brass and find mention in the Book of Mormon: his meeting with Melchizedek to whom he paid tithes (Alma 13:15; Gen. 14:18–20); his offering of Isaac "in the wilderness," which was "a similitude of . . . [God's] Only Begotten Son" (Jacob 4:5; Gen. 22:9–14); his association with the miraculous powers of God (Morm. 9:11); his vision of the coming Messiah (Hel. 8:17); and his redemption by the Lord (2 Ne. 27:33). Furthermore, Abraham has already entered the kingdom of God (e.g., Alma 5:24; 7:25; D&C 132:29). For Nephites and Lamanites, of course, Abraham was their ancestor, their "father," and Sarah was "she that bare you" (2 Ne. 8:2; cf. Alma 13:15). The most notable covenant made between the Lord and Book of Mormon peoples is "the covenant which [God] made with Abraham" (3 Ne. 20:27; cf. 1 Ne. 15:18; 17:40; 22:9). It is a covenant that will stand eternally as a proof of the Lord's enduring goodness and mercy (2 Ne. 29:14). The title "God of Abraham" (e.g., 1 Ne. 6:4; 19:10) reflects this covenant. Associated with this title are God's acts as deliverer of the Hebrew slaves (Alma 29:11; 36:2) and his redemptive role as Savior (1 Ne. 19:10).

See also Abrahamic covenant.

SKB

Abrahamic covenant The Lord established a covenant with Abram (subsequently renamed Abraham; Gen. 17:5) when he instructed him to leave Haran and go to the land of Canaan. Promises to Abraham in that covenant include the following:

1. Promise of land. "But I, Abraham, and Lot, my brother's son, prayed unto the Lord, and the Lord appeared unto me, and said unto me: Arise, and take Lot with thee; for I have purposed to take thee away out of Haran, and to make of thee a minister to bear my name in a strange land which I will give unto thy seed after thee for an everlasting possession, when they hearken to my voice" (Abr. 2:6; cf. Gen. 12:7; 13:15; 15:9–14).

2. Promise of posterity. "I will make of thee a great nation, and I will bless thee above measure, and make thy name great among all nations." The Lord told Abraham that not only his literal blood descendants but "as many as receive this Gospel shall be called after thy name, and shall be accounted thy seed" (Abr. 2:9–10; cf. Gen. 12:2; 18:18).

3. Promise of priesthood blessings. "Behold, I will lead thee by my hand, and I will take thee, to put upon thee my name, even the Priesthood of thy father, and my power shall be over thee" (Abr. 1:18).

4. Promise of gospel blessings for all families of the earth. Abraham's seed "shall bear this ministry [the Lord's name; Abr. 2:6] and Priesthood unto all nations; And I will bless them through thy name; for as many as receive this Gospel shall be called after thy name, and

shall be accounted thy seed, and shall rise up and bless thee, as their father; And I will bless them that bless thee, and curse them that curse thee; and in thee (that is, in thy Priesthood) and in thy seed (that is, thy Priesthood), for I give unto thee a promise that this right shall continue in thee, and in thy seed after thee (that is to say, the literal seed, or the seed of the body) shall all the families of the earth be blessed, even with the blessings of the Gospel, which are the blessings of salvation, even of life eternal" (Abr. 2:9–11).

Book of Mormon references to the Abrahamic covenant come mostly in the form of reminders to the descendants of Lehi[1] that they are Abraham's seed and therefore heirs of the blessings and responsibilities associated with the covenant established millennia earlier between God and Abraham, with reassurances that God's promises concerning Abraham's seed would indeed be fulfilled (1 Ne. 17:40; 22:8–12; 2 Ne. 29:14; 3 Ne. 16:11; 20:27; Morm. 5:20; Ether 13:11). "The making known of the covenants of the Father of heaven unto Abraham" was a part of the "marvelous work" of restoration God accomplished in the latter days through the Prophet Joseph Smith (1 Ne. 22:8–11).

Book of Mormon references to specific terms of the Abrahamic covenant include the following: covenant people of the Lord being "gathered together to the lands of their inheritance" (1 Ne. 22:12); through Abraham's seed "shall all the kindreds of the earth be blessed" (1 Ne. 22:9); the descendants of Abraham, including and specifically identifying Lehi's children, in the last days will be brought to a knowledge of the fulness of the gospel and their covenant relationship with the Lord (3 Ne. 16:11; 20:25–41; Morm. 5:20; Ether 13:11); a call for the covenant people of the Lord to measure up to their responsibilities in the Abrahamic covenant, to "Awake, awake, put on thy strength . . . put on thy beautiful garments . . . shake thyself from the dust . . . loose thyself from the bands of thy neck" (2 Ne. 8:24–25; cf. Isa. 51–52; D&C 113:7–10).

All who enter into the Abrahamic covenant through baptism are "numbered among" or "numbered with" the house of Israel—meaning they are counted as Abraham's seed and thus are partakers of the blessings and responsibilities of the covenant (1 Ne. 14:2; 2 Ne. 10:18; 3 Ne. 21:6, 22; 30:2; Morm. 7:10; cf. Gal. 3:26–29).

See also Adoption; Covenant(s); Israel, covenants unto; Israel, numbered among.

SDR

Abridgment An abbreviated, condensed, or shorter version of some larger work or text. The title page of the Book of Mormon declares that "it is an abridgment of the record of the people of Nephi, and also of the Lamanites" and "an abridgment taken from the book of Ether also, which is a record of the people of Jared."

The "record of the people of Nephi, and also of the Lamanites" was written on two sets of plates: the large PLATES OF NEPHI, which were abridged by Mormon on the PLATES OF MORMON; and the small plates of Nephi, which Mormon did not abridge (W of M 1:3–5). Authors of the small plates of Nephi also mention shortening their records (Jacob 3:13) or abridging the records of others (1 Ne. 1:16–17). As Mormon abridged the more detailed account of Nephite and Lamanite history from the large plates of Nephi, he sometimes added his own commentary and interpretation to help readers recognize and understand important truths and doctrines (e.g., Alma 24:27; 30:60; Hel. 3:24–30; 6:34–35; 3 Ne. 29:30). Mormon also, after writing a more detailed history of events in his day on the large plates of Nephi, abridged his own writings and included them on the plates of Mormon (Morm. 2:18; 5:9).

The "abridgment taken from the Book of Ether" mentioned on the title page of the Book of Mormon was made by Moroni[2] after the death of Mormon, his father (Ether 1:1–5). The book of Ether, which consisted of twenty-four plates, contained the larger history of the Jaredites. As he abridged the Jaredite history, Moroni, like his father, added some of his own commentary and insights for readers (e.g., Ether 4:3–19; 5:1–6; 12:6–41).

Book of Mormon abridgers were limited in their writing to not even "a hundredth part" of their peoples' history (Jacob 3:13; W of M 1:5; Hel. 3:14; 3 Ne. 5:8; 26:6; Ether 15:33). Their inspired abridgment reflects deliberate attention to their predetermined purposes, as well as their intended latter-day audience. Concerning Mormon's work President Ezra Taft Benson wrote, "Under the inspiration of God, who sees all things from the beginning, [Mormon] abridged centuries of records, choosing the stories, speeches, and events that would be most helpful to us" (19).

The Book of Mormon promises more than the abridged records that have been revealed if those who receive the abridged records repent and exercise faith (3 Ne. 26:9–11; Ether 4:5–7).

BIBLIOGRAPHY

Benson, Ezra Taft. *A Witness and a Warning*. Salt Lake City: Deseret Book, 1988.

CBM

Abyss A vast, immeasurable void often associated with HELL, darkness, and misery. The term signifies a state far from God and his light. God's power redeems repentant individuals from the abyss of rebellion and apostasy as well as that of ignorance and false traditions (Mosiah 27:29; Alma 26:3).

RDD

According to the flesh A phrase generally denoting the conditions and laws that govern in MORTALITY (e.g., 1 Ne. 19:6; 22:18, 27; 2 Ne. 2:8, 27; 9:53; 10:2; 31:7). Alma[2] used the phrase more specifically, emphasizing that cognitive understanding, even revealed understanding, was not sufficient for Christ to accomplish the Atonement. He had to actually *experience* "according to the flesh" the suffering, pain, afflictions, and temptations of every kind in order "that he may know according to the flesh [by his own experience] how to succor his people according to their infirmities" (Alma 7:11–13; cf. Heb. 2:16–17; 4:15).

See also Condescension of God.

LED

Accountability Being responsible, or answerable, for one's deeds, words, and thoughts. For mortals to be accountable to God, several conditions must exist. First, laws must be given (2 Ne. 2:13; Alma 42:17–22). Second, there must be a knowledge of good and evil (2 Ne. 2:5); and third, there must be AGENCY, the freedom to choose between good and evil (2 Ne. 2:26–27). God has caused these conditions to exist as part of the plan of salvation. Thus all are accountable to God for the choices they make: "Whosoever perisheth, perisheth unto himself; . . . for behold, ye are free; . . . God hath given unto you a knowledge and he hath made you free" (Hel. 14:30).

Little children and those who are "without the law" are "alive in Christ." Because they are not accountable, the "power of redemption cometh on all them" (Moro. 8:22; cf. 8:10).

Alma[2] taught that at the Day of Judgment people will be held accountable not only for their works but also for their words and thoughts (Alma 12:14). Moreover, those with the responsibility of guiding others, such as parents and leaders, will be held responsible, or accountable, if they fail to teach. Jacob[2] explained that he and his brother Joseph[2] were "taking upon us the responsibility, answering the sins of the people upon our own heads if we did not teach them the word of God with all diligence" (Jacob 1:19; cf. 2 Ne. 4:5–6).

Because everyone sins and because "no unclean thing can inherit the kingdom of God" (Alma 40:26), all accountable individuals are prevented from returning to live with God. But as part of the plan of salvation, God has provided the atonement of Jesus Christ to "answer the ends of the law" for all who will repent (2 Ne. 2:7; cf. Mosiah 3:20–22).

See also Alive in Christ; Children, baptism of little; Ignorance, died in; Law, without the.

PVJ

Accursed *See* Appendix C.

Adam The first man upon this earth, the progenitor of the entire human family, and a preeminent leader in the plan of salvation. The Book of Mormon references to Adam highlight his roles as the father of mankind and facilitator of the Fall (2 Ne. 2:19–25; Mosiah 3:11, 16; Alma 12:22–23; 42:5; Hel. 14:16; Morm. 9:12). He is identified in the scriptures as Michael, "the prince of all," the archangel, and "the ancient of days" (D&C 27:11; 88:112). His mission spans not only mortality but premortality and the afterlife as well.

In premortality Adam boldly led the forces of righteousness against Satan in defense of Christ (Rev. 12:7). There he received the priesthood and was designated as the father of the human family (Smith, 157–58; D&C 78:16). He was created in the image of God as the "first man" and placed in the Garden of Eden with his wife Eve (Moses 1:34; Gen. 1:27; 2:8). Adam knowingly partook of the forbidden fruit, thus giving all mankind the chance to experience mortality (2 Ne. 2:25). He fathered sons and daughters during his lifetime and knew much adversity as a parent (Moses 5:2, 13, 16, 25–37). In the afterlife Adam will continue to lead his posterity in the cause of Christ (Smith, 157, 122). As the Millennium concludes he will once again fight Satan and defeat his forces (D&C 88:111–15).

See also Curse of Adam, the; Fall of Adam and Eve, the; Forbidden fruit; Tree of knowledge of good and evil; Tree of life.

BIBLIOGRAPHY

Smith, Joseph. *Teachings of the Prophet Joseph Smith*. Selected by Joseph Fielding Smith. Salt Lake City: Deseret Book, 1976.

KJW

Adam, curse of *See* Curse of Adam, the.

Adieu *See* Anachronisms, alleged.

Admonish *See* Appendix C.

Adoption To become a member of the family of Jesus Christ and to be included in the lineage of Abraham, Isaac, and Jacob through entrance into gospel covenants (for example, baptism). The word *adoption* is not used in the Book of Mormon, but the concept or doctrine is plainly taught. King Benjamin instructed his people that "because of the covenant which ye have made ye shall be called the children of Christ, his sons, and his daughters; for behold, this day he hath spiritually begotten you; for ye say that your hearts are changed through faith on his name; therefore, ye are born of him and have become his sons and his daughters" (Mosiah 5:5, 7; cf. 27:25). The adopted children of God thus become "heirs of God, and joint-heirs with Christ" (Rom. 8:17).

Gentiles who receive the gospel of Jesus Christ and are baptized are adopted into the lineage of Abraham and are "accounted" his seed (Abr. 2:10; Gal. 3:27–29). Nephi[1] referred to this adoption when he said that "as many of the Gentiles as will repent are the covenant people of the Lord" (2 Ne. 30:2; cf. 3 Ne. 16:13; 21:6; 30:2). The doctrine of adoption was also expressed in Zenos' allegory of the wild and tame olive trees when the branches of the wild olive tree, or the Gentiles, were grafted into the tame olive tree, or house of Israel (Jacob 5:7, 9–10, 17).

See also Abrahamic covenant; Grafting; Israel, numbered among.

RH

Adultery *See* Chastity.

Affliction *Afflict* derives from the Latin word meaning "to strike or cast down" (*affligere*). Thus, affliction signifies a condition of being downcast in body, mind, or spirit. In Book of Mormon usage, although "affliction" sometimes serves as a generic term for every sort of suffering, tribulation, adversity, calamity, distress, grief, trouble, trial, and sorrow—as in the phrase "all manner of afflictions" (Alma 4:13; 34:40)—the term typically retains its root association with the notion of being brought low or humbled by misery.

The Book of Mormon, like other scripture, often depicts affliction as evidence of divine chastisement: "And thus we see that except the Lord doth chasten his people with many afflictions . . . they will not remember him," wrote Mormon, articulating the text's providential view of history (Hel. 12:3; cf. Mosiah 1:17). Throughout the Book of Mormon, God calls to his people through the voice of affliction and thereby readies them for repentance (cf. Alma 32:6). This pattern conforms to the Lord's promise that he will "consecrate thine afflictions for thy gain" (2 Ne. 2:2; cf. D&C 98:3) and to his great plan for educating fallen humanity by means of "opposition in all things" (2 Ne. 2:11).

Yet affliction does not necessarily ensure spiritual growth, which depends on whether individuals or nations choose to be humbled or to be hardened by suffering. Mormon underscored this lesson near the end of the book of Alma, when he noted that "many had become hardened, because of the exceedingly great length of the war; and many were softened because of their afflictions, insomuch that they did humble themselves before God, even in the depth of humility" (Alma 62:41). Suffering sensitizes some but embitters and inures others until they become "past feeling" (Moro. 9:20).

As divine chastisement, affliction may signal the sinful state of individuals or communities. Yet this is not always the case. The Book of Mormon corroborates the lesson of Job that suffering is not a sure sign of sinfulness, for the righteous, too, are often afflicted. Indeed, in an encounter between the righteous Anti-Nephi-Lehis and the wicked Lamanites, only "righteous people" were killed: "There was not a wicked man slain among them" (Alma 24:26–27). Similarly, the Book of Mormon depicts memorable martyrdoms by fire of innocent women and children as well as of the prophet Abinadi (Alma 14:8–11; Mosiah 17). Many of the righteous in the Book of Mormon were persecuted by their brethren, causing them to "wade through much affliction" (Hel. 3:34). In so doing they trod in the footsteps of Christ, the only perfect man, who nevertheless had to suffer "pains and afflictions and temptations of every kind" (Alma 7:11; cf. Mosiah 3:7; 14:4, 7).

Himself oppressed and afflicted (Mosiah 14:7 // Isa. 53:7), the Lord expressed special concern for the afflicted. He assured the people of Alma in bondage that he would "ease [their] burdens," for "I, the Lord God, do visit my people in their afflictions" (Mosiah 24:14). Likewise, Jacob[2] testified that the Lord would "console you in your afflictions, and . . . plead your cause" (Jacob 3:1). And Nephi[1], quoting Isaiah, reminded readers that the Lord has "mercy upon his afflicted," whom he loves more than does a mother her nursing child and whom he has graven on the palms of his hands (1 Ne. 21:13–16 // Isa. 49:13–16). True to his character as one who keeps company with the afflicted, the resurrected Savior bade the multitude at Bountiful[2] to bring forward those who were "afflicted in any manner": "Bring them hither and I will heal them, for I have compassion upon you" (3 Ne. 17:7).

Likewise the Book of Mormon admonishes the followers of Christ to minister to the afflicted (Jacob 2:19; Alma 1:27; Morm. 8:39). Indeed, it teaches that if they "visit not the sick and afflicted," their prayers are vain (Alma 34:28) and they risk losing the remission of their sins (Mosiah 4:26).

And to those who suffer affliction, the Book of Mormon prescribes patience, consistent with the counsel of all scripture: "Have patience, and . . . bear with all manner of afflictions" in the "firm hope that ye shall one day rest from all your afflictions" (Alma 34:40–41; cf. 17:11; 26:27).

JST

After the manner of the flesh An expression used once in the scriptures (1 Ne. 11:18), "after the manner of the flesh" refers to Mary's being the mother of Christ's mortal body.

See also Conceive by the power of the Holy Ghost; Condescension of God.

LED

Against *See* Appendix C.

Agency The word *agency* denotes an abstract concept useful in describing that which a human being has when he or she "acts or has power to act" (Funk and Wagnalls). Perhaps the finest account of agency in the literature of this world is the discourse of father Lehi[1] to his son Jacob[2] in 2 Nephi 2. Although the word *agency* itself is not used in Lehi's discourse, the concept of agency is clearly conveyed by "free," "act for themselves," and "free to choose." Lehi made three main points.

First, he defined agency as "man . . . act[ing] for himself" (2 Ne. 2:16). But he noted that man can act for himself only if he knows both good and evil (2 Ne. 2:5; cf. 9:25–27) and is "enticed by the one or the other" (2 Ne. 2:16). Thus, the necessary components of agency are as follows: (1) an intelligent being, one who can choose for himself when given the opportunity; (2) that intelligent being must have a knowledge of alternatives for action; and (3) that intelligent being must have the power to act on a choice freely made.

Adam in the Garden of Eden was an intelligent being, but because he had a limited knowledge of good and evil, he was thus not yet fully an agent, even though he had power to act. By the Fall, Adam and Eve became more fully aware of both good and evil, thus gaining added agency (2 Ne. 2:16–25).

For every person of normal intelligence, agency is a matter of degree. The level of knowledge of good and evil and the amount of power to act on one's choices determine the degree of agency. God increases or decreases that power to act according to each person's own will and choices (Hel. 14:30–31), but everyone of normal intelligence has enough knowledge and power to choose between Christ and the devil and to be held accountable for the choice made (2 Ne. 2:26–27; cf. Moro. 7:12–19).

Second, Lehi pointed out to Jacob that gaining agency was a blessing to Adam and Eve only because of the atonement of Christ (2 Ne. 2:26–27; cf. 9:6–19). Had there been no atonement, the sins each person committed would bind him or her to Satan forever, having no recourse. Both temporally and spiritually, sin would have destroyed agency and the future possibility of happiness under the strict demands of the law of justice (2 Ne. 2:5). Under the law of justice, every sin results in punishment and captivity; only choosing good is rewarded with happiness and freedom (Alma 40:12–13; 41:3–4). Applying the law of justice alone, only perfection succeeds or can survive; there is no room for experimentation, learning, and repentance. But the atonement of Jesus Christ brings mercy into the picture. The Savior satisfied the demands of justice both by being perfect and just himself, committing no sin during his mortal probation, and then single-handedly paying the demands of justice for the sins of every mortal who comes to this earth (2 Ne. 2:6–8). This act of grace and mercy allows human beings to experience both good and evil, to learn well which one they really desire to pursue, and then to have the freedom to repent of the evil choices they have made and receive eternal rewards as if they had made only good choices. Thus, father Lehi exulted concerning mankind, "And because that they are redeemed from the fall they have become free forever, knowing good from evil; to act for themselves and not to be acted upon, save it be by the punishment of the law at the great and last day, according to the commandments which God hath given" (2 Ne. 2:26).

Third, father Lehi affirmed that the essence of agency is not about physical freedom, to go here or there, to do this or that; rather, the essence of agency is morality—to be able to choose good or evil. This is important to know because many persons in this world count physical agency as the only real and desirable freedom. They do not understand that moral agency, the choice between good and evil, is the root problem of mankind and also the key to success in the physical realm. The world glories in what it calls truth and greatly desires political and physical liberty; indeed, those are good things. But to ignore the basic importance of choosing between good and evil is to misunderstand what mortality is all about. Lehi clearly understood the overwhelming importance of moral choice and pointed his sons to the great truth that they were free to make a choice between two critical alternatives: to choose to do good and thus receive liberty and eternal life; or to choose to do evil, which brings captivity and death, the misery engendered by Satan, who is the enemy of all mankind (2 Ne. 2:27–29). Agency thus has one principal focus: by choosing good or evil in all of the many decisions of daily life, men and women are establishing for themselves a character and a future. Their character determines how much blessing from God they can stand (Morm. 9:3–5), and that determines their future (Alma 41:2–4; cf. D&C 88:22–28).

The agency of each mortal is made possible by the atonement of Christ, is delivered to mankind through the fall of Adam, and consists of the opportunity to make daily choices between good and evil, which choices determine each mortal's eternal reward.

See also Accountability.

BIBLIOGRAPHY

Funk and Wagnalls Standard Encyclopedic Dictionary. Chicago: J. G. Ferguson Publishing Company, 1970. S.v. "Agency."

CCR

Agosh, plains of Site of a great battle during the last wars of the Jaredites. Lib[2] pursued Coriantumr[2] and his people to the plains of Agosh, where Coriantumr gave battle to Lib. Coriantumr slew Lib there, but Lib's brother, Shiz, continued the battle until Coriantumr fled (Ether 14:15–17).

Agriculture in the Book of Mormon The Book of Mormon civilizations depended on well-developed agriculture. More than sixty passages refer to agriculture in the Book of Mormon, most of them incidental to historical accounts but some of them allegorical.

Lehi[1] and his company carried seeds of both grain and fruit species on their migration to the promised land (1 Ne. 8:1; 18:6). In spite of eight years in the wilderness, time during which many seeds may lose their ability to germinate, the seeds brought from Jerusalem "did grow exceedingly" when cultivated in the promised land (1 Ne. 18:24). The Jaredites also carried seeds to the promised land along with domestic and wild ANIMALS, including flocks, fowl, fish, and honeybees (Ether 1:41; 2:1–3).

Several specific cultivated plants are mentioned in the Book of Mormon. The Nephite civilization had corn, wheat, barley, neas, and sheum (Mosiah 9:9). In the Bible, the word *corn* typically refers to a cereal grain of some type, such as wheat or barley (e.g., Isa. 28:28); however, the corn mentioned in Mosiah 9:9 was probably maize (called corn in the United States) because wheat and barley are mentioned separately in the same verse. Indeed, maize was among the most important staple foods of ancient American civilizations and was found throughout the Americas at the time of European contact. The single reference to neas and sheum in Mosiah 9:9 provides no additional information about these plants other than their agricultural importance. Olive is mentioned several times prior to the allegory of the olive tree in Jacob 5 but never in a context of cultivation in the New World. After the allegory of the olive tree, there is no further reference to the olive in the Book of Mormon. Grape is not specifically mentioned, although there are several references to wine. King Noah[3] planted vineyards and built wine-presses. Indeed, people cultivated grapes in both the Old and New Worlds prior to European contact. No fiber-producing plants are specifically mentioned. LINEN, which is derived from flax (a plant of Old World origin), is mentioned on several occasions in the Book of Mormon (Mosiah 10:5; Alma 1:29; Ether 9:17). Cotton is a domesticated native of both the Old and New Worlds, but there is no reference to it in the Book of Mormon.

Agriculture includes animal husbandry, and several domesticated animals are mentioned in the Book of Mormon. Nephites had cattle, goats, wild goats, horses, and donkeys (1 Ne. 18:25; Enos 1:21; Alma 18:9; 20:6). Sheep were often mentioned allegorically in sermons among the Nephites, and flocks were mentioned frequently. Among the Jaredites, cattle, sheep, swine, goats, donkeys, fowl, fish, honeybees, elephants, cureloms, and cumoms are specifically mentioned (Ether 2:1–3; 9:17–19). The modern equivalents of cureloms and cumoms are not known. Animals were also used for sacrifice and burnt offerings in accordance with the law of Moses (1 Ne. 7:22; Mosiah 2:3).

Nearly all the domesticated animals specifically mentioned in the Book of Mormon originated in the Old World and were important in Judah during Lehi's day. For the most part they are not native to the American continents. Although it is clear that the Jaredites brought domesticated animals with them from the Old World to the Americas (Ether 1:41; 2:1–3), there is no indication that Lehi's group carried such animals on their voyage. In fact, there are evidences that they did not do so. For example, during their time in the wilderness, Lehi's group hunted wild animals for meat, and they were unable to obtain food when the bow of Nephi[1] was broken, suggesting that they had no domestic animals with them that they could use for food. Yet, upon their arrival in the promised land, they found domestic animals, including "the cow and the ox, and the ass and the horse, and the goat" (1 Ne. 18:25). Possibly some of these animals remained in the promised land as remnants of the Jaredite civilization.

The Book of Mormon portrays prosperous agriculture as a consequence of righteousness and associates famine, plundering, and subsistence on wild beasts with wickedness. Enos 1:20–21 depicts righteous Nephites as an agrarian society, whereas the Lamanites were "wild, and ferocious, and a blood-thirsty people, . . . feeding upon beasts of prey; dwelling in tents, and wandering about in the wilderness." In several instances in the Book of Mormon, the wicked obtained their subsistence by plundering the agricultural production of the righteous (Mosiah 9:14; 10:2–4, 21; 11:15–17; 21:17–21; Alma 17:25–28, 39; 3 Ne. 4:2–6, 18–20, 24). Famine was not uncommon, and more than once the Lord used famine to humble his people (Mosiah 12:4–7; Hel. 11:4–17; 12:2–3; Ether 9:28–35).

Agricultural production and distribution of food are also associated with war in the Book of Mormon. The Nephite grain fields were trodden down and their flocks and herds slaughtered during war (Alma 3:1–2; 4:2); the distribution of provisions is often mentioned as an important aspect of war (Alma 54:2; 55:34; 57:6–10; 58:3–8; 60:3, 9, 19, 34; 61:16–18; 62:13; 3 Ne. 3:22; 4:2–6, 18–20, 24).

Several passages on agriculture in the Book of Mormon are allegorical rather than historical. Prophets have often taught by analogy using customs and practices familiar to their audience to explain sacred principles. The olive tree allegory of Zenos in Jacob 5, which was given to people familiar with olive culture, uses detailed aspects of olive culture as symbols of the scattering and gathering of Israel. The sermon of Alma[2] on faith, comparing faith to a seed that sprouts and grows, was given to impoverished people, many of whom were farmers (Alma 32:21–25). Isaiah's writings quoted in the Book of Mormon regularly rely on agricultural metaphors (2 Ne. 12–24). The spiritual lessons involving agriculture in the Book of Mormon remain pertinent today.

DJF

Aha *See* Zoram[2].

Ahah *See* Jared[1], posterity of.

Akish Jaredite king, wicked son of Kimnor, and husband of the daughter of Jared[2]. Akish was used by Jared and his daughter in their scheme to restore Jared to the throne he had lost to his father, Omer. The daughter of Jared, influenced by ancient records that contained secret plans to "obtain kingdoms and great glory," proposed to her father that he send for Akish, and after she had danced before him and pleased him, he would desire her for his wife. Moreover, if Akish then asked Jared for permission to marry her, Jared should grant the request if Akish would murder his father (Ether 8:8–10). Akish agreed and "gathered in unto the house of Jared all his kinsfolk" and administered to them secret oaths, binding the group together in their plot to assassinate Omer the king (Ether 8:13–15). The Lord warned Omer in a dream, and he with his family departed from the land (Ether 9:3). Jared was crowned king, and Akish married Jared's daughter as planned, but Akish's ambition exceeded his desire to simply marry Jared's daughter. He used the same "secret society" organized to kill Omer to kill his father-in-law, Jared, and thereby he became the next king (Ether 9:4–6).

Akish was a cruel man, one time imprisoning a son because of jealousy and starving him to death (Ether 9:7). His people and his own sons mirrored his wickedness. Offering them money, Akish's sons lured "the more part of the people after them" (Ether 9:11), which division initiated a long war that ended in the destruction of all the people "save it were thirty souls, and they who fled with the house of Omer" (Ether 9:12).

See also Jared[2], daughter of.

DLL

Akish, wilderness of Jaredite region into which the armies of Coriantumr[2] pursued Gilead (the brother of Shared) and his forces. The ensuing battle at Akish left many thousands dead. Coriantumr "did lay siege to the wilderness," but Gilead gained the upper hand by escaping during the night, killing some of Coriantumr's drunken troops, and placing himself on

Coriantumr's throne in the land of Moron. After two years in the wilderness gathering "strength to his army," Coriantumr traveled to the land of Moron to give battle to Lib[2], who had succeeded Gilead to the throne after Gilead's assassination. Eventually Lib prevailed and drove Coriantumr back to the wilderness of Akish (Ether 14:3–14).

Alive in Christ Phrase which characterizes the life of persons blessed by the benefits of the ATONEMENT of Jesus Christ. Being reborn to a "life which is in Christ" (2 Ne. 25:27), they have been reawakened to things of righteousness. Figuratively, they are eating the "bread of life" (John 6:28–59) and drinking the "living water" Christ offers (John 4:5–14). These benefits are available to accountable people through faith and obedience to the laws and ordinances of the gospel (2 Ne. 25:25; A of F 4). For those who are not accountable (i.e., children and those without the law), these benefits are automatic through "his mercy"; such people "are not capable of committing sin" and thus are "under no condemnation" (Moro. 8:8, 12, 19, 22; D&C 137:7).

See also Accountability; Law, without the.

RLM

All is well in Zion An attitude or state of mind reflecting spiritual complacency. Satan pacifies and lulls away unwary Saints into a state of apathy, which allows him to lead them "carefully down to hell" (2 Ne. 28:21). Elder Dallin H. Oaks applied the expression to material prosperity: "When we place our trust in our property, we have 'carnal security.' In that state of mind we are inclined to say that all must be well with us and with Zion *because* we are prospering, thus relying on worldly success as a mark of divine favor. He who does this is an easy mark for being led 'carefully down to hell'" (79). The Lord warns specifically against the attitude that "all is well" (2 Ne. 28:25).

See also Pacify.

BIBLIOGRAPHY

Oaks, Dallin H. *Pure in Heart.* Salt Lake City: Bookcraft, 1988.

CJW

All things common A living arrangement, based on the principles of consecration and stewardship, in which a community of Saints shares and works together as one toward the establishment of Zion, "every man seeking the interest of his neighbor, and doing all things with an eye single to the glory of God" (D&C 82:19). "All things common" did not mean that everyone pooled all resources and shared everything in common, all having equal amounts. It means that every person and family had an equality according to their needs (cf. Acts 2:45; 4:32, 35; D&C 51:3). The early Saints in the Old World, united by the power of the Holy Ghost, had all things common among them (Acts 2:44; 4:31–32). After the Savior had visited and taught the Nephites, the people had all things common among them, a practice that continued for almost two hundred years (3 Ne. 26:19; 4 Ne. 1:3). When the Nephites turned from righteousness, however, they divided into classes and no longer had all things common (4 Ne. 1:25).

HDG

Allegory An extended narrative in which the characters, events, or setting of the story correspond symbolically to individuals, events, or ideas outside the allegory itself. An allegory is usually longer and more complex than a parable; but like a parable, an allegory uses common figures to present a lesson, doctrine, idea, prophecy, or principle in terms familiar to its audience. Zenos' allegory in Jacob 5 is one of the most magnificent examples of this genre in all sacred literature. It begins, "I will liken thee, O house of Israel, like unto a tame olive-tree, which a man took and nourished in his vineyard" (Jacob 5:3). Then, using techniques of olive tree cultivation—pruning, cultivating, grafting, harvesting, and even burning—the allegory outlines the history of the relationship of the people of Israel with their Lord (the "Lord of the vineyard") down to the time of the final gathering in the last days.

See also Zenos, allegory of.

NEL

Allegory of Zenos *See* Zenos, allegory of.

ALMA[1]

Alma[1] First in a line of great prophets, convert of Abinadi, descendant of Nephi[1], born ca. 173 B.C. Alma is first mentioned in the record as a "young man" and a priest in the court of the wicked king Noah[3]. There he heard the prophetic words of Abinadi, believed, and was forced to flee for his life. In hiding, Alma wrote the words of Abinadi (Mosiah 17:1–4; 18:1–3), repented of his transgressions, and taught privately among the people. The believers gathered secretly near the waters of Mormon, and there Alma, "having authority from the Almighty God" (Mosiah 18:13; Alma 5:3), preached, baptized, and organized the faithful into the church of Christ (Mosiah 18:3–18; Smith, 4:160–64).

Warned by the Lord of impending discovery, Alma and his people fled deeper into the wilderness where, in Helam, they built their own community and prospered both spiritually and materially (Mosiah 18:31–34; 23:1–20). Discovered by a Lamanite army, they were put under severe taskmasters; however, with the Lord's miraculous help, Alma was able to lead his people to Zarahemla (Mosiah 23:21–39; 24:10–25).

In Zarahemla, king Mosiah[2] "granted unto Alma that he might establish churches throughout all the land" (Mosiah 25:19). For almost thirty years, Alma effectively directed the Church there through times of spiritual success and prosperity as well as times of iniquity and apostasy (Mosiah 26:37–39).

Perhaps the most heart-wrenching challenge during his leadership came from within the Church itself through the destructive opposition of an unfaithful "rising generation," among whom were four of the sons of king Mosiah and Alma's own son and namesake, Alma the Younger. Nevertheless, after an experience similar to what Paul would experience later in New Testament times (Acts 9:1–22), Alma's son was converted (Mosiah 27:11–24), in part because the Lord heard the "prayers of his servant, Alma, . . . for he has prayed with much faith concerning [Alma[2]]" (Mosiah 27:14). In the years following, Alma the Elder lived to see his once wayward son chosen by the people as their first chief judge, and, perhaps even more gratifying for the now aged father, to confer upon his own son the office of high priest over "all the affairs of the church" (Mosiah 29:42). Alma the Elder died in Zarahemla at age eighty-two, in 91 B.C.

There are at least three major elements to Alma's life that make him one of the great figures of the Book of Mormon:

1. He was a splendid example of faith. He grew up in a society corrupted by evil leaders, and he himself had to repent of certain "sins and iniquities" (Mosiah 18:1). Yet in spite of his circumstances, Alma believed the prophetic words of Abinadi, and courageously put his life at risk for what he had heard. As the Lord told Alma several decades later, "Blessed art thou, Alma . . . because of thy exceeding faith in the words alone of my servant Abinadi" (Mosiah 26:15).

2. He was a great builder of the Church. Alma was considered the founder of the Church at Mormon and at Zarahemla. He "consecrated all their priests and all their teachers" and saw that the people were watched over and nourished "with things pertaining to righteousness" (Mosiah 23:16–18). Mosiah 26 presents an impressive example of revelation guiding the Church as the prophet Alma "went and inquired of the Lord what he should do concerning this matter" of transgressors within the Church (Mosiah 26:13). The Lord responded with important instruction and doctrine that clarified the work of the ministry for Alma and for latter-day peoples.

Furthermore, Alma established a covenant Church. He organized not a loose association of interested people but rather a committed congregation bound to one another and to their God in a covenant relationship, the points of which set the standard for a true Christian community (Mosiah 18:8–10). Additionally, Alma established the Church on a firm system of clear commandments by which the people could be guided and blessed in their economic and social relationships, as well as in their spiritual lives (Mosiah 18:18–30). The principles and doctrines he taught, as "delivered" by his "mouth," were in turn taught by all the teachers and priests in the various congregations of the Church (Mosiah 25:21–22). This helped the Church to remain pure in its teachings.

3. Alma was a remarkable father. He stood at

the head of an extraordinary, continuous line of prophets and leaders: Alma[2], Helaman[2], Helaman[3], Nephi[2], Nephi[3], Nephi[4], and other successors. Alma might well be called the father of prophets. Although the record does not speak extensively of Alma's practice as a father, several important matters of character stand out and may help explain his remarkable influence on the succeeding generations of his posterity.

To begin with, he was a man of great meekness and devotion, always mindful of doing the right thing, "for he feared that he should do wrong in the sight of God" (Mosiah 26:13). He was mighty in prayer, pouring out "his whole soul to God" regarding the Church and those around him (Mosiah 26:14). In a time of family crisis, too, he gathered his associates around him to fast and to pray, seeking the Lord's help in behalf of his son Alma (Mosiah 27:22). He sought and acted upon the mind and will of the Lord in all things.

Alma's foundation was his profound faith in and love for Jesus Christ, and his son clearly knew that about his father. Even in the terrible pit of his hell-like suffering, even in his agonized longing for annihilation, Alma's son could not forget the words of his father, and the remembrance of that testimony became the turning point in the son's repentance process. Years later, Alma[2] would continue to hold up the example of his father's testimony in his own teaching and ministry (Alma 5:11–13), and, as he handed on the responsibility of the plates to his son Helaman[2], Alma[2] also passed on the story of the saving effect of his father's testimony and teaching: "I remembered also to have heard my father prophesy unto the people concerning the coming of one Jesus Christ, a Son of God, to atone for the sins of the world" (Alma 36:17). The testimony of Alma[1] helped save not only Alma[2] but a host of descendants for generations to come.

Summary of major teachings

1. Principles of the gospel, including "repentance, and redemption, and faith on the Lord" (Mosiah 18:7, 19–20; 25:21–22).

2. Specifics of the baptismal covenant and blessings for obedience (Mosiah 18:8–10).

3. Obligations of Church membership, including unity, love, assembly, observance of the Sabbath day, thanksgiving to God, giving willingly of one's substance, and the responsibility of the priests to support themselves (Mosiah 18:21–29; 23:15).

4. Cautions concerning the dangers of being ruled by kings, for "ye shall not esteem one flesh above another, or one man shall not think himself above another" (Mosiah 23:7), and warnings concerning whom to trust: "Trust no one to be your teacher nor your minister, except he be a man of God, walking in his ways and keeping his commandments" (Mosiah 23:14).

See also Baptism; Church discipline; Church of God (Christ) in ancient America; Priesthood among the Nephites.

BIBLIOGRAPHY

Smith, Joseph Fielding. *Answers to Gospel Questions.* 5 vols. Salt Lake City: Deseret Book, 1963.

NEL

Alma[2] Son of Alma[1], a dynamic Nephite prophet, first chief judge, and high priest of the Church. Alma[2] was perhaps the most eminent Nephite personality of his age (ca. 100–73 B.C.). Also known as Alma the Younger, he exerted a defining influence on political and religious matters in his society. In addition, from his hand the Book of Mormon preserves some of its most important doctrinal discourses.

The names of Alma's mother and siblings are unknown. He himself might have been born in the colony established by his father in the land of Helam (Mosiah 23:1–20) or even earlier, for he seems to have included himself when mentioning the flight of the colonists from that region: "By the power of [God's] word . . . we were brought into this land [of Zarahemla from Helam]" (Alma 5:5).

Although Alma's father became the high priest of the Church in Zarahemla, a position of high trust (Mosiah 26:7–8), Alma turned against his father's teachings and, together with the four sons of king Mosiah[2], secretly sought "to destroy the church of God." The record describes the youthful Alma as "a very wicked and an idolatrous man," a flatterer who stole "away the hearts of the people" and led them into iniquity,

Alma Arise; *painting by Walter Rane; courtesy MCHA. As Alma and the sons of Mosiah "were going about rebelling against God, behold, the angel of the Lord appeared unto them; and he descended as it were in a cloud; and he spake as it were with a voice of thunder, which caused the earth to shake upon which they stood"* (Mosiah 27:11).

ALMA[2]

which opened them to the power of Satan, "murder[ing]" their souls (Mosiah 27:8–10; Alma 36:11–14).

Alma's conversion to Christ is one of the most dramatic and inspiring events related in the Book of Mormon. Obviously, Alma had exceptional personal power and capability and, when applied to righteous purposes, he became a tremendous force for good among the Nephites. In response to the prayers of his father and members of the Church (Mosiah 27:14), an angel appeared to him and his four royal youthful companions, an event that not only turned them from their wicked ways but also led them to seek to "repair" the damage they had caused (Mosiah 27:32–37; Alma 36:24–27). In the account it becomes evident that Alma possessed considerable ability—"he was a man of many words"—and, because the narrative focuses chiefly on him, it is probably safe to assume that he was the leader among the five friends (Mosiah 27:8–10).

Although the appearance of the angel led the youths to reverse directions spiritually, Alma observed that his final, true conversion came only after he had "fasted and prayed many days" (Alma 5:46), a clarification of the relationship between miraculous events and genuine conversion.

Alma's political career was relatively short-lived, lasting just eight years (Alma 4:20), but his service was significant. Following the political reforms of king Mosiah[2], which abolished the Nephite monarchy in favor of elected officials (Mosiah 29:38–39), Alma became the first chief judge, the head of state (Mosiah 29:42). Alma faced the severe difficulties that often accompany the inaugural years of new political systems. In his first year, he presided over the trial and execution of a man named Nehor. This man had committed murder to assert his corrupt religious belief in priestcraft and in the false doctrine of redemption for all mortals, regardless of their works (Alma 1:1–16). Nehor's philosophy did not die with him, however, and subsequent events, including the persecution of believers, touched off further crises.

The rebellion of the Amlicites may or may not have raised a question of public confidence in Alma's leadership, but it certainly threatened the survival of an elective form of government. The followers of Amlici were determined to return Nephite society to kingship. Although Alma won needed public support to retain office and to maintain the fledgling democracy, Amlici and his followers continued to stir the pot of contention until civil war broke out not five years after Alma assumed office (Alma 2:1–14). Alma must have been strong physically as well as spiritually, for he personally led to victory the forces loyal to his government, slaying Amlici himself and thus preserving national unity. His army achieved victory, even though a large band of Lamanite warriors had joined forces with the Amlicites (Alma 2:15–38).

Following this bloody and costly conflict in which Alma himself was wounded, he faced another military crisis when a Lamanite army invaded the land of Zarahemla (Alma 3:20–23). The forces Alma sent repelled the invaders, and the ensuing peace opened a two-year period of prosperity during which thousands of people united themselves to the Church (Alma 4:1–5). But this spiritual surge ended almost as quickly as it had begun, blunted by months of contentions and other manifestations of pride within the Church. Concluding that his only hope for reclaiming his people lay "in bearing down in pure testimony against them" (Alma 4:19), Alma resigned as chief judge to devote his full time to his responsibilities as head of the Church (Alma 4:15–20). He continued faithfully in that service until he disappeared some ten years later. His "death or burial" remained a mystery to his people, but many believed "that he was taken up by the Spirit, or buried by the hand of the Lord, even as Moses" (Alma 45:18–19).

Alma's extraordinary ministry spanned probably more than two decades (ca. 100–92 B.C. to 73 B.C.). At the death of his father in 91 B.C., Alma had succeeded to the office of high priest in "the high priesthood of the holy order of God" (Alma 4:20), evidently only months before also assuming his demanding government post (Mosiah 29:42, 45). After turning over his political responsibilities to his appointed successor Nephihah (Alma 4:16–18, 20), Alma entered his most productive years, his labors in the ministry

ALMA[2]

of Christ, which generated an inspiring written legacy of his work and teachings.

In his effort to reverse the rising tides of apostasy and spreading religious indifference, Alma's strategy was brilliant in its simplicity and demanding in its execution. Preaching initially at home, he first centered his efforts on Church members living close by and then sought to extend gospel influences among people living on the Nephite frontier. At each turn, miracles accompanied his efforts, and eventually a small circle of friends and family joined him in the work (Alma 31:6–7).

Alma's superb sermon on conversion and commitment to Christ (Alma 5) represents his missionary labors in and around Zarahemla (Mosiah 25:23). Alma's words movingly urge a personal conversion to Christ and his gospel, a change of heart in which the spiritually reborn receive Christ's "image in [their] countenances" (Alma 5:14, 19). After establishing "the order of the church in . . . Zarahemla" (Alma 6: 4, 1), Alma turned his attention to other congregations.

Alma traveled to Gideon, then the one sizeable town on the east bank of the Sidon river (Alma 6:7), a settlement of people who had escaped captivity with Alma's father almost forty years earlier. Alma's splendid recorded sermon at Gideon breathes a spirit of mutual love and respect (Alma 7). At its heart shines his prophecy about the coming mortal ministry of the Savior. Alma emphasized the Savior's unfathomable compassion and mercy, noting that he would suffer "pains and afflictions and temptations of every kind," that he would "take upon him the pains and the sicknesses of his people," and that he would "take upon him death" and "the sins of his people" and deliver them (Alma 7:11–13). Returning home, Alma prepared himself to travel to Nephite settlements in the west and north (Alma 8:1–3, 6), a journey that would test his faith and skills like none other.

After a successful sojourn among inhabitants of the land of Melek, Alma traveled "three days' journey" northward to the city of Ammonihah, a stronghold of monarchical sentiment where he, a former head of state, was treated rudely, almost treasonously, and sent away. He departed, "weighed down with sorrow," but an angel turned him back to the city, where he met a man named Amulek who first took him in (Alma 8:14ff.) and then became his faithful companion in the ministry, both in Ammonihah (Alma 9–15) and elsewhere. Their preaching in that city, though it had limited effect, won some souls, the most notable of whom was a prominent lawyer named Zeezrom, who at first opposed Alma and Amulek. In fact, the doctrinal challenges from Zeezrom (and later Antionah) elicited significant statements from Amulek about redemption, resurrection, and related teachings (Alma 11:21–45), and notable insights from Alma about "the mysteries of God," including the Final Judgment and its aftermath (Alma 12:1–18), the plan of salvation (Alma 12:20–37), and the priesthood order in the kingdom of God (Alma 13).

Those cast out of Ammonihah for believing the missionaries, Zeezrom among them, relocated to the city of Sidom (Alma 15:1, 3–12). Their wives and children and others who remained were ensnared in a rampage of slaughter that the captive Alma and Amulek were forced to witness (Alma 14:8–11). Finally, through divine intervention the two missionaries escaped when the earth shook causing the walls of their prison to fall upon and kill the perpetrators of the citywide persecution (Alma 14:24–29). Later, as Alma had prophesied (Alma 9:4, 18), Ammonihah was utterly destroyed in a single day by a marauding Lamanite army (Alma 10:21–23; 16:1–3, 9–11; 25:1–2).

Following Alma's extended western mission, he traveled south to the land of Manti, where he happened upon his friends of old, the sons of king Mosiah[2], who were just returning from a fourteen-year mission among the Lamanites (Alma 17:1, 4). The reunion was sweet to the five friends, for they rejoiced to learn that each had remained strong in the faith (Alma 17:2–3; 27:16–20).

Years later, Alma participated in another memorable legal case, this time of a man named Korihor. Korihor was an anti-Christ whose preaching was permitted; according to Nephite law he could not be punished for his beliefs

(Mosiah 27:23; Alma 30:6–12). Alma was not the civil judge, but Korihor pressed his atheistic views until Alma invoked a divine response, which left Korihor deaf, mute, and a beggar. He eventually suffered death at the hands of some Nephite separatists who followed an apostate named Zoram[3] (Alma 30:50–60).

About a year before his supposed death, Alma and select companions preached among ZORAMITES[2] in the land of Antionum (Alma 31–35). From this missionary enterprise came some of the most significant doctrinal declarations found in scripture. One of the most impressive is Alma's teaching about the process of planting the word of Christ in one's heart and thereby passing from nonfaith to faith and then to knowledge. In that magnificent sermon, he metaphorically likened the personal "planting" and nourishing of the word of Christ to the planting and nourishing of a seed (Alma 32).

Next to Alma's public exertions stand his efforts to teach and influence individuals privately. One person who benefited from such was Amulek. After particularly disheartening reverses for Amulek, Alma took him to his own home "and strengthened him in the Lord" (Alma 15:16, 18). In a similar yet more visible vein, chiefly because Alma's words are preserved, is his memorable counsel to his three sons (Alma 36–42).

To his son Helaman[2] (Alma 36–37), Alma bore his witness, decades before Jesus was born, about the effects of the Atonement in his own life, beginning the moment that the angel had appeared to him and his four friends. By Alma's account, in an agony of despair for his soul, the thought of "the coming of one Jesus Christ" entered his mind, and he "cried . . . O Jesus, thou Son of God, have mercy on me" (Alma 36:17–18). The ensuing relief and joy was "exquisite and sweet," allowing him to stand and "manifest . . . that I had been born of God" (Alma 36:21, 23). This experience left its traces on all his later sermons and writings.

To his son Shiblon, Alma spoke as he had to Helaman, though in briefer terms, recounting his frightening experience when the angel had called him to repentance (Alma 38:7–8). Alma also bore his testimony that, as a result of that experience, he had "been born of God" and that Shiblon would "be delivered out of [his] trials, and [his] troubles" and would "be lifted up at the last day" (Alma 38:5–6). With a final appeal that Shiblon remain humble, Alma ended his instruction to this son (Alma 38:11–14).

To his wayward son Corianton, Alma spoke frankly about sexual misconduct, about the state of the soul between death and resurrection, about the eternal connection between justice and mercy, and about life as a probationary state essential to the plan of salvation (Alma 39–42).

If the record contains one phrase that defines Alma, it is that spoken of him by the angel who visited Amulek. Alma, the angel said, was "a holy man, . . . a chosen man of God" (Alma 10:7, 9).

Summary of major teachings

1. Jesus Christ. Alma was a witness in his generation of the coming of Jesus Christ and his redemptive mission: "I know that Jesus Christ shall come, yea, the Son, the Only Begotten of the Father, full of grace, and mercy, and truth. And behold, it is he that cometh to take away the sins of the world" (Alma 5:48, 50; 7:11–13; 9:26–27; 39:15–19).

2. ATONEMENT. At the top of Alma's teachings stands deliverance through the atonement of Jesus Christ: "All mankind were fallen, and they were in the grasp of justice; yea, the justice of God, which consigned them forever to be cut off from his presence. . . . The plan of mercy could not be brought about except an atonement should be made; therefore God himself atoneth for the sins of the world, to bring about the plan of mercy, to appease the demands of justice, that God might be a perfect, just God, and a merciful God also" (Alma 42:14–15). Christ's atonement also encompasses his taking upon himself people's pains, sicknesses, and infirmities, "that he may know according to the flesh how to succor his people according to their infirmities" (Alma 7:11–12).

3. RESURRECTION. Alma taught that departed souls experience a period of time "between death and the resurrection" (Alma 40:11) which offers rest and peace to the righteous and a "fearful looking for the fiery indignation of the wrath

of God" among the wicked (Alma 40:14). In addition, at the time of the resurrection, there will be a "restoration" of "evil for evil [and] . . . good for that which is good" according to one's actions in mortality (Alma 40:11–41:15; 42:27–28). *See* Restoration, plan of.

4. Plan of salvation. Alma taught that the "plan of redemption" included the fall of Adam, mortality as a "probationary state," and the Atonement that "had been prepared from the foundation of the world" (Alma 12:22–37; 42:1–31). *See* Fall of Adam and Eve, the; Plan.

5. God's judgment. As one of a cluster of subjects about postmortal matters, the Judgment leads to a "spiritual death" for the wicked whose "torments shall be as a lake of fire and brimstone" (Alma 12:12–18). *See* Judgment, the; Spiritual death.

6. Spiritual rebirth. Alma spoke of this experience as being "born of God" or "born again" (Mosiah 27:24–25; Alma 5:49) or as "a mighty change" of heart (Alma 5:12, 26). He testified that all mankind must be BORN AGAIN (Alma 27:25) or they "cannot inherit the kingdom of heaven" (Alma 7:14). He connected it to indescribable joy (Alma 36:20–21).

7. HUMILITY. Alma was one who was "compelled to be humble." After his conversion, he tried to invite people to come to Christ without such compulsion (Alma 5:27; 32:12–16).

8. FAITH. Alma's teachings on faith rested on how one comes to faith, how one nurtures faith, and only incidentally on what faith is (Alma 32:17–43).

9. REPENTANCE. Alma was his own best example of the value of repentance leading to a remission of sins, having suffered for his sins until he learned that repentance is available only through Jesus Christ and that destruction is its alternative (Mosiah 27:24–29; Alma 9:12–18; 36:16–22; 38:8). To repent fully, one must confess his or her sins before those whom the offender has wronged (Alma 39:13).

10. Melchizedek Priesthood. Alma is an important source for much of what is known about both Melchizedek and the priesthood named after him (Alma 13:3–19). Additionally, Alma taught of the foreordination of priests, men who had been "called and prepared from the foundation of the world according to the foreknowledge of God" (Alma 13:3–5). *See* Chosen; Priesthood among the Nephites.

11. ACCOUNTABILITY according to the "light and knowledge" one possesses. Alma foretold the restoration of the Lamanites to the truth and taught that it would be "more tolerable" for the Lamanites in the Day of Judgment than for the Nephites if the Nephites failed to repent (Alma 9:15–18). The Nephites, so greatly blessed by the Lord, would be "utterly" destroyed if they transgressed contrary to the light and knowledge that they possessed (Alma 9:18–24). *See* Lamanites, Book of Mormon message concerning.

12. The Good Shepherd invites all to come unto him. "Behold," Alma proclaimed, "he sendeth an invitation unto all men, for the arms of mercy are extended towards them, and he saith: Repent, and I will receive you. Yea, he saith: Come unto me and ye shall partake of the fruit of the tree of life; yea, ye shall eat and drink of the bread and the waters of life freely" (Alma 5:33–42, 57–62).

See also Alma, book of; Chastity.

SKB

Alma, book of The largest book in the Book of Mormon, abridged from the large PLATES OF NEPHI by Mormon from the records of Alma[2] (Alma 1–44), Helaman[2] (Alma 45–62), and Shiblon (Alma 63). It covers the period from approximately 91 B.C. to 52 B.C. In making the abridgment, Mormon at times entered the original discourses into his narrative, at times he condensed and summarized, and at times he provided transitional commentary. The book of Alma chronicles forty years of Nephite history—years of growth, internal contention, and war. The book also contains some of the most important doctrinal discourses in the Book of Mormon. In many ways, in its teachings, prophecies, revelations, and political upheavals, the book of Alma is a microcosm of the larger Book of Mormon. Its primary thrust is the anticipation of the coming Christ and the preparation of the Nephites for that coming. At the same time, like the whole of the Book of Mormon, it is written for latter-day peoples in anticipation of Christ's second coming.

ALMA, BOOK OF

Content and message

The major themes of the book of Alma are about the mission of Christ—his teachings, his atonement, his resurrection, and the significance of those teachings and events. Juxtaposed against these themes are episodes in which anti-Christs attacked the Church and its doctrines, contending that there would be no coming Redeemer. Another theme is the divinely established creed of human liberty, the preservation of which justifies righteous warfare. Still other themes include conversion to Christ, the importance of covenants, and the preciousness of the record.

Generally, the book of Alma separates into (1) events and sermons connected with missionary efforts to solidify and strengthen the existing Church among the Nephites, (2) events and teachings connected with highly successful missionary efforts among the Lamanites, and (3) wars fought against Nephite dissenters and their Lamanite allies. But even more compelling than the dynamic external events that provide the book's structural design are its

OUTLINE OF ALMA

I. The beginning of the reign of judges (Mosiah 29:38–47; Alma 1)
   A. The challenge of Nehor and PRIESTCRAFT, and of Amlici, who wishes to be king (2–3)
   B. Growth and iniquity in the Church; the departure of Alma[2] from the judgeship for full-time service in the ministry (4)

II. Alma's missionary labors and teachings (5–16)
   A. The success of Alma's teachings of Christ in Zarahemla, Gideon, and Mulek (5–8:5)
   B. Rejection of Alma and Amulek's teachings in Ammonihah, including the challenge of Zeezrom and the destruction of Ammonihah (8:6–16)

III. The simultaneous missionary labors of the sons of Mosiah[2], resulting in the great Lamanite conversion (17–28)
   A. Ammon[2] and the conversion of Lamoni and his people (17–20)
   B. Aaron[3] and the conversion of Lamoni's father and his people (21–23)
   C. The covenant of converted Lamanites (Anti-Nephi-Lehies) against taking up arms against their enemies (24–27)
   D. Defeat of Lamanite armies (28)

IV. The teaching and testifying of Alma and Amulek (29–35)
   A. Alma's desire to preach repentance (29)
   B. The challenge of the anti-Christ Korihor (30)
   C. The challenge of the apostate Zoramites[2]; great sermons on faith and redemption (31–35)

V. Alma's counsel to his sons (36–42)
   A. To Helaman[2]: testimony of Christ and instruction regarding the records now entrusted to him (36–37)
   B. To Shiblon: testimony of Christ and personal counsel (38)
   C. To Corianton: chastisement for misbehavior and instruction in doctrines of resurrection, restoration, and atonement (justice and mercy) (39–42)

VI. Nephite wars, civil and national, in the cause of freedom, with Moroni[1] as commander of Nephite armies (43–63)
   A. The threat presented by Zarahemnah (44)
   B. The departure of Alma after charging Helaman with keeping the records and prophesying the end of the Nephite nation (45)
   C. The threat of the KING-MEN and Amalickiah, who incited the Lamanites, and of his successor Ammoron; Moroni's defense; the reestablishment of peace and order (46–62)
   D. Shiblon, followed by Helaman[3], responsible for records; emigrations north by sea (63)

ALMA, BOOK OF

doctrinal sermons and teachings. The inclusion of these teachings contributes to a major Book of Mormon purpose, the restoration of "plain and precious" truth (1 Ne. 13:25–41). It is an understatement to say that the power of the book's language attests to the truth of its teachings.

The early chapters of the book of Alma detail challenges to Alma[2], both as chief judge and prophet. Specifically, a man named Nehor defiantly introduced priestcraft, and the ambitious Amlici incited his followers to rebel and make him king. Furthermore, the "church began to fail in its progress" because of the wickedness and pride of Church members (Alma 4:8–15). These conditions led Alma to relinquish the judgeship in order to teach the gospel full time, "that he might pull down, by the word of God, all the pride and craftiness and all the contentions which were among his people" (Alma 4:19).

Chapter 5 is a representation of Alma's teachings to the people of Zarahemla. Its message is the need for mortals to be reborn spiritually, in this life, as children of Christ. In Gideon, Alma foretold the birth of Christ to Mary and taught again the necessity of spiritual rebirth (Alma 7). Alma then taught in the land of Mulek and "the people came to him. . . . And they were baptized throughout all the land" (Alma 8:4–5). Traveling to Ammonihah, Alma met Amulek whom the Lord had prepared as a companion. The two met much opposition in Ammonihah, some of it spoken by the lawyer Zeezrom as he sought to confound Amulek. But Amulek confounded him with testimony of Christ and with discourse on temporal death and resurrection (Alma 11). Then Alma entered the discussion, explaining the reality of spiritual death as well as temporal death in the context of "the plan of redemption" (Alma 12:25). He further taught of "the high priesthood of the holy order of God" (Alma 13:6) and other important truths, for which teachings and blunt denunciation of the people's iniquities he and Amulek were punished and imprisoned.

Chapters 17 through 28 drop back in time to recount the missionary activities of the sons of Mosiah, principally Ammon[2] and Aaron[3], among the Lamanites. Their efforts resulted in the soul-stirring conversions of king Lamoni and his father and subsequently of a great many Lamanites. These converts later became known as the people of Ammon. After the narrative returns to Alma in chapter 29, doctrinal discourses are the principal content of the book until its attention shifts to Moroni[1] and the battles for religious and personal freedom. Alma's desire was to "declare unto every soul . . . repentance and the plan of redemption" (Alma 29:2), and he had many opportunities to do so.

Taken together, the contents of Alma 30–34 could be viewed as a unified gospel discourse that addresses "the great question" Amulek raised climactically in Alma 34:5, "whether the word be in the Son of God, or whether there shall be no Christ." Varied in approach and yet uniquely focused on a single theme, these chapters testify powerfully "that the word is in Christ unto salvation" (Alma 34:6). In the anti-Christ Korihor and the apostate Zoramites, Alma confronted people who contended that there was no Christ (Alma 30–31). He testified to the arrogant Korihor that "all things denote there is a God" (Alma 30:44), and he began teaching the reality of Christ to the poorer Zoramites through the metaphor of planting and nourishing the seed of faith in Christ (Alma 32). Alma then turned to the witness of three ancient prophets—Zenos, Zenock, and Moses—all of whom "testified of the Son of God" (Alma 33:17–19). At the conclusion of Alma's sermon, Amulek added his resounding witness "that I do know that Christ shall come" (Alma 34:8). Amulek then expanded his testimony to include a magnificent discourse on the "infinite atonement" and the necessity of repentance.

Chapters 36–42 record Alma's counsel to his three sons, Helaman[2], Shiblon, and Corianton. In his instructions to Helaman, Alma related the details of his own conversion as a young man (Alma 36) and then charged him with care of the records (Alma 37). In doing so, Alma made a stunning comparison. He described the Liahona (the compass that directed Lehi and his family in the wilderness; 1 Ne. 16:10–16) as a type for the "words of Christ" (Alma 37:38–45). Alma commended Shiblon for his faithfulness, recounted his own conversion, and cautioned him against such things as pride, idleness, and praying as the

Zoramites (Alma 38). When Alma turned to Corianton, he first chastised him for his wanton behavior and then addressed questions Corianton had raised. He spoke of the resurrection and of a spirit world to which the dead go to await judgment (Alma 40). He also introduced the doctrine of restoration, and explored its inexorable connection with "the justice of God" (Alma 41:2). Those who have desired good, Alma explained, will "be restored unto that which is good" (Alma 41:3). He encapsulated the principle in one sentence: "The meaning of the word restoration is to bring back again evil for evil, or carnal for carnal, or devilish for devilish—good for that which is good; righteous for that which is righteous; just for that which is just; merciful for that which is merciful" (Alma 41:13). Speaking then of humankind's need to be reclaimed from spiritual death, Alma affirmed that law and justice are essential and that an atonement is therefore necessary. On condition of a person's repentance, mercy answers the demands of justice through the Savior's atoning sacrifice (Alma 42).

Although the final third of the book of Alma is given largely to descriptions of war, civil and national, the overriding theme of these chapters, like that of the whole of the Book of Mormon, is the reality of the living and coming Christ. Humility and faithfulness, through the Lord's strengthening hand, led to victory, peace, and prosperity. Character and personality also come to the forefront in these chapters. Most notable among the figures of this period is Moroni[1]—a brilliant military strategist, a patriot and devotee of liberty, a fiery commander, and a faithful servant of God. He is the moving force at this juncture in Nephite history, and the narrative underlines his character and function by setting him against contrasting figures of both evil and good. His evil adversaries were the ruthless and ambitious Amalickiah and Ammoron, whom he more than matched in intelligence, prowess, and will. His great friends were the faithful Helaman[2] and Pahoran[1]; but they, too, in their gentleness, contrasted with the swift-acting Moroni. Pahoran's response to Moroni's condemning and threatening letter is a classic in meekness and maturity (Alma 61).

A highlight of these chapters is the sweet "father-son" relationship between Helaman and the 2,060 youthful warriors who fought under his command. These youth, children of the converted Lamanites (the people of Ammon) who buried their weapons and covenanted never to take them up again, volunteered to serve in the cause of freedom and faith. All were severely wounded, but not one was killed (Alma 57:25; 58:39).

The Nephite nation narrowly escaped annihilation in these dangerous years. Only through the Lord's strengthening might and the faith and fortitude of such people as Moroni, Helaman, Pahoran, Lehi[3], and Teancum was peace restored.

See also Stripling warriors; Warfare, principles governing; Warfare in the Book of Mormon.

MA

Alma, valley of Located a day's journey from the city of Helam, the valley of Alma was so named because Alma[1] led his people there after their miraculous escape from Lamanite bondage. On arriving in the valley, they gave thanks to God for their deliverance and then departed for Zarahemla (Mosiah 24:20–25). The Lord had warned Alma that the Lamanites were in pursuit and promised to stop them in the valley.

Alms Voluntary offerings given to the poor. In the Book of Mormon the term is used only by Christ in the sermon at the temple in Bountiful[2] (3 Ne. 13:1–4). Here, as in the similar account in Matthew's Gospel (Matt. 6:1–4), Christ indicated that alms should be given out of an inner desire to help one's neighbors rather than as an attempt to be seen or considered righteous by others. The prophet Jacob[2] spoke of almsgiving when he listed several purposes for the use of wealth. He taught his people, "And after ye have obtained a hope in Christ ye shall obtain riches, if ye seek them; and ye will seek them for the intent to do good," which he defined as "to clothe the naked, and to feed the hungry, and to liberate the captive, and administer relief to the sick and the afflicted" (Jacob 2:19). Such teaching was reiterated by king Benjamin (Mosiah 4:26) and practiced by the Ammonites (Alma 35:9).

GS

Alpha and Omega The first and last letters of the Greek alphabet used as a title for the Savior (e.g., 3 Ne. 9:18; D&C 19:1; 35:1; Rev. 1:8, 11; 21:6; 22:13). The title reflects the eternal and all-encompassing nature of the Lord's existence, work, and glory. All life, all light, all progress, all salvation come in and through him.

RDD

Altar of stones A structure constructed by Lehi[1] in the wilderness upon which he offered a sacrifice of thanksgiving (1 Ne. 2:7). Lehi appears to have followed the pattern set by other ancient prophets and leaders: Noah[1] built an altar after surviving the Flood (Gen. 8:20); Abraham built altars in several places where he had important spiritual experiences (Gen. 12:7–8; 13:18; 22:9); and Moses, Joshua, David, and Elijah, among others, also built altars (Ex. 17:15, 24:4; Josh. 8:30; 2 Sam. 24:18; 1 Kgs. 18:30–32). According to the law of Moses, an altar made of stones was to be made of unhewn stones (Ex. 20:25; Deut. 27:5).

Lehi built his altar and offered sacrifice upon it by virtue of the Melchizedek Priesthood, not by the authority of the Aaronic Priesthood; he was a descendant of Joseph[1] (1 Ne. 5:14) rather than of Levi[1] or Aaron[1]. And because he was a prophet, he held the Melchizedek Priesthood (Smith, 181).

BIBLIOGRAPHY

Smith, Joseph. *Teachings of the Prophet Joseph Smith.* Selected by Joseph Fielding Smith. Salt Lake City: Deseret Book, 1976.

TLS

Amaleki[1] Son of Abinadom, descendant of Jacob[2], and the last of nine Nephite scribes to write on the small plates of Nephi (ca. 130 B.C.). Amaleki noted that he "was born in the days of Mosiah[1]" (Omni 1:23), but he does not say where he was born nor specify which "days of Mosiah" he meant—those in the land of Nephi or those in the land of Zarahemla. If he was born in the land of Nephi, he was numbered among those who left the land with Mosiah and would have witnessed firsthand the events he wrote about.

Amaleki lived to see the death of king Mosiah and the coronation of his son Benjamin (Omni 1:23). He experienced war between his people and the Lamanites, as did his predecessors, and under the righteous king Benjamin the Nephites were able to prevail (Omni 1:24). In his later years, having "no seed" to perpetuate the family responsibility for keeping the small plates of Nephi, he entrusted them to the care of king Benjamin (Omni 1:25).

The writings of Amaleki make at least three contributions. First, as a historical link, they are the source of all that is known about king Mosiah (Omni 1:12–23); they document the merger between Nephites and the people of Zarahemla (Omni 1:19), and they tell of two attempts by Nephite groups to regain an inheritance in the land of Nephi—the first a failure and the second a qualified success (Omni 1:27–30; cf. Mosiah 9:1–4). Second, Amaleki's recording of God's commandment for righteous Nephites to depart out of the land of Nephi verified the fulfillment of a prophecy uttered by Jacob[2] more than three hundred years before (Omni 1:12; Jacob 3:4). Third, Amaleki's writing is consistent with the commandment given by his ancestor Nephi[1] that the small plates were to persuade readers to "come unto" Christ (Omni 1:25–26; cf. 1 Ne. 6:4, 6; Jacob 1:1–3; 7:27). Amaleki sealed his plea to come unto Christ and his testimony of how to accomplish it with a promise attested by a sacred oath: "As the Lord liveth ye will be saved" (Omni 1:26).

Perhaps Amaleki's testimony to readers regarding the sources of good and evil (Omni 1:25) provided the seeds of inspiration for Mormon's more extended discourse on this subject (Moro. 7:12–17).

See also Omni, book of.

DLL

Amaleki[2] *See* Ammon[1].

Amalekites Nephite apostates who lived in the land of Nephi among the Lamanites and who were noted for their "more wicked and murderous disposition than the Lamanites" (Alma 43:6; 21:1–2; ca. 90 B.C.). The Book of Mormon does not supply any information concerning the origin of this group, but it does record some important details about their activities. The Amalekites, with the Lamanites and Amulonites, "built a great city, which was called Jerusalem" (Alma 21:2). Many of them followed after the "order of the Nehors," and synagogues were built where they assembled to worship their God (Alma 21:4–6). They rejected the tradition of their Nephite fathers concerning the coming of Christ, not believing that anyone could know of "things to come," and they believed "that God will save all men" (Alma 21:6–8). The gospel was preached among them by Aaron[3] with little success (Alma 23:14).

As with the Amulonites and Lamanites, the Amalekites were angered over the conversions of their Lamanite brethren, the ANTI-NEPHI-LEHIES, and attacked them and slaughtered more than a thousand. Stung with remorse because they had killed their unarmed brethren, many Lamanites repented, "threw down their weapons," and joined the "people of God"; however, "there were none who were Amalekites" (Alma 24:1–2, 20–30). Presumably part of the Lamanite contingent who were "more angry" because they had killed their own brethren, the Amalekites "swore vengeance upon the Nephites" and helped destroy the wicked Nephite city of Ammonihah in one day (Alma 25:1–2; 16:1–10). In this act of destruction the words of Mormon were verified: "It is by the wicked that the wicked are punished" (Morm. 4:5).

A few years later the Amalekites were mentioned in connection with Lamanite-Nephite wars. Because of their murderous disposition, Zerahemnah, the leader of the Lamanite armies, appointed them as chief captains to lead the Lamanites to battle against the Nephites. This was done to preserve hatred and inspire ferocity among the Lamanite troops. The Amalekites, unlike the Lamanites, were more fully clothed on the battlefield (Alma 43:6–7, 20).

The Amalekites exemplify the tragic state of a people who had become "more hardened" in their lives because they had fallen into "sin and transgression" after having been "enlightened by the Spirit of God" and blessed with "great knowledge of things pertaining to righteousness" (Alma 24:30; cf. D&C 82:3).

CKM

Amalickiah Nephite traitor who through deception and murder became commander of the Lamanite armies and then king of the Lamanites (ca. 73 B.C.). A Nephite by birth, Amalickiah was a descendant of Zoram[1] (Alma 49:25; 54:23). He used flattery and played on the ambitions of others to obtain a substantial following, particularly among the lower judges of the land (Alma 46:4–5). He made significant inroads in his effort to destroy the Church and the foundation of liberty among the Nephites (Alma 46:7, 10). His rebellion led Moroni[1] to rend his coat and rally faithful Nephites in defense of liberty and religious freedom (Alma 46:11–36). Later, in the face of Moroni's success, Amalickiah and his followers fled and joined the Lamanites (Alma 46:29; 47:1), inciting their anger against the Nephites and beginning a sinister quest for power among them, a quest that ended in his becoming king of the Lamanites (Alma 47).

Amalickiah's hunger for power over Nephites and Lamanites alike stood in stark contrast to the objective of captain Moroni, who was preparing his people to be faithful and to expend every effort toward preserving their freedom (Alma 48:1–10). The life of Amalickiah and his followers teaches the sobering lesson of how much "more hardened and impenitent, and more wild, wicked and ferocious" are those who have dissented from the truth (Alma 47:36).

Amalickiah sent his Lamanite armies against the rebuilt city of Ammonihah and the city of Noah (Alma 49) in 72 B.C., and they were soundly defeated; not one Nephite was killed (Alma 49:23). This so angered Amalickiah that he swore with an oath that he would drink the blood of Moroni (Alma 49:27; 51:9–10), a rash threat that fortunately was never fulfilled.

Remarkably, during the time of Amalickiah's military campaign, the Nephites enjoyed some of the happiest times to that point in their history (Alma 50:17–23). Their happiness appears to have been short-lived, however, because rebellious Nephites who called themselves king-men weakened the nation to such an extent that Amalickiah and the Lamanites were able to take possession of many Nephite cities (Alma 51). Following one particularly sore battle, in the final days of the twenty-fifth year of the reign of the judges (ca. 67 B.C.), Teancum, a Nephite captain, crept by night into the camp of the fatigued Lamanites and put a javelin through the heart of Amalickiah, ending his diabolical career (Alma 51:33–37; 52:1).

Reading of these events, one can understand why Mormon wrote, "We . . . see the great wickedness one very wicked man can cause to take place among the children of men" (Alma 46:9). Amalickiah's life followed the pattern one would expect of SATAN were he given a mortal probation. Like Lucifer, Amalickiah rebelled against the gospel plan in his thirst for glory and power, and he led others away from the truth (Alma 45:23–24; 46:1, 4, 7, 10; 48:2; cf. 2 Ne. 24:12–14; D&C 29:36; 76:25, 28). It was Amalickiah's intent, as it was Lucifer's, to destroy the liberty of men (Alma 46:10; cf. Moses 4:3). They both sought to make war against the righteous (Alma 48:3; cf. D&C 76:29–30), and in the end both rewarded their followers with sorrow, misery, and suffering (cf. 2 Ne. 2:27; Alma 30:60). The life of Amalickiah exposes the pattern followed by many who are the enemies of Christ.

CJW

Amalickiahites Nephite dissenters who were followers of Amalickiah (Alma 46:28–29; 73 B.C.). They joined Amalickiah in rebellion against Helaman[2] and his brethren, and supported him in his bid to become king (Alma 45:23–46:11). Outnumbered by the people of Moroni[1] and somewhat "doubtful concerning the justice" of their cause (Alma 46:29), most Amalickiahites fell to the forces of Moroni before they could escape to the land of Nephi. Moroni compelled them to enter "the covenant of freedom" or be executed (Alma 46:35).

Amaron Nephite record keeper who received the small PLATES OF NEPHI from his father Omni and eventually conferred them upon his brother Chemish. Observing the judgments of God upon wicked Nephites who had been destroyed, Amaron's brief contribution was his testimony that the Lord "would not suffer that the words should not be verified, which he spake unto our fathers, saying that: Inasmuch as ye will not keep my commandments ye shall not prosper in the land" (Omni 1:4–8).

Amen An adverb or interjection meaning truly or surely, derived from the Hebrew root *aman* meaning to confirm or support. It is spoken at the conclusion of testimonies (e.g., 1 Ne. 9:6), sermons (e.g., 1 Ne. 15:36), prayers (e.g., 3 Ne. 13:9–13), and blessings (e.g., 2 Ne. 3:25).

TBB

Amgid Jaredite king who reigned at a time when the Jaredite kingdom was divided. After many years of fighting with his rival, king Com[2], Amgid was deposed, and Com gained "power over the remainder of the kingdom" (Ether 10:32).

See also Jared[1], posterity of.

Aminadab "A Nephite by birth, who had once belonged to the church of God but had dissented from them" (Hel. 5:35) and then had gone over to live with the Lamanites. When Nephi[2] and Lehi[4] came preaching to the Lamanites in the land of Nephi (ca. 30 B.C.), they were cast into prison (Hel. 5:20–21). Aminadab was present when a cloud of darkness overshadowed the Lamanites and Nephite dissenters in the prison (Hel. 5:22–35). He turned, and through the cloud he saw the uplifted faces of Nephi and Lehi, seemingly conversing with an unseen heavenly being. Aminadab cried to the multitude to look, and then he explained that Nephi and Lehi were conversing with angels (Hel. 5:36–39). The darkness, Aminadab told the Lamanites, would be removed if they would repent and pray "until ye shall have faith in Christ" (Hel. 5:40–41). Glorious manifestations followed their prayer and conversion to Christ (Hel. 5:42–48).

BAV

Aminadi Nephite holy man, a descendant of Nephi[1] and an ancestor of Amulek. According to Amulek, Aminadi "interpreted the writing which was upon the wall of the temple, which was written by the finger of God" (Alma 10:2–3). This is reminiscent of the biblical account of Daniel

(Belteshazzar), who interpreted the writing on the palace wall for king Belshazzar during the Babylonian captivity (Dan. 5:1–29).

Amiss *See* Appendix C.

Amlici An adherent of the apostate religion of Nehor (ca. 87 B.C.), who sought to become king of the Nephites and to destroy the Church of God (Alma 2:4). After drawing "away much people after him" (Alma 2:2), Amlici and his followers forced a vote to see if the Nephites wanted him as their king. Much to the relief of the righteous Nephites, the vote was negative. Dissatisfied with the outcome, Amlici rallied his followers, called Amlicites. They consecrated him as their king and marked themselves on their foreheads like the Lamanites (Alma 3:4), probably in an unintended fulfillment of prophecy (2 Ne. 5:23). When they sought to seize control of the Nephite government by force of arms, Amlici and his followers were defeated and fled from the Nephites. The next day, however, the Amlicites received additional help from "a numerous host of the Lamanites," and together they began marching towards Zarahemla, destroying everything in their path (Alma 2:24–26). Under the command of Alma[2], the Nephite army was able to head off the combined Lamanite and Amlicite army near the river Sidon and in a sorely contested battle defeat them (Alma 2:27–28). In the course of the battle Alma fought with Amlici face to face and with the Lord's strength was able to slay him with the sword (Alma 2:29–31).

PYH

Amlicites Followers of Amlici, a "cunning" man who wanted to become king of the Nephites (87 B.C.). When the people rejected his bid, his followers took up the sword to force the Nephites to accept him as their king. In the initial battle the defeated Amlicites fled but were joined by a large Lamanite army and renewed the fight. Though outnumbered, the Nephites defeated the combined Amlicite-Lamanite army, and Alma[2] killed Amlici. The surviving Amlicites fled with the retreating Lamanite army toward the wilderness, but the Nephites vigorously pursued them. Many of the defeated Amlicites died in the wilderness of their wounds and were devoured by ravenous beasts (Alma 2).

The Amlicites had marked their foreheads with red "after the manner of the Lamanites" (Alma 3:4), fulfilling the Lord's declaration that a mark would be "set" on those who fight against the Nephites (Alma 3:13–18). Mormon added his lesson: the Amlicites "brought upon themselves the curse" as "doth every man that is cursed bring upon himself his own condemnation" (Alma 3:19).

PYH

Ammah A Nephite missionary who labored among the Lamanites (ca. 90–77 B.C.), presumably a member of the original group that left Zarahemla with the sons of Mosiah[2] (Alma 17:8). Ammah and his companion Muloki taught in the village of Ani-Anti, where they were joined by Aaron[3] (Alma 21:11–12). Having no success there, they traveled to the land of Middoni, where they were cast into prison and cruelly mistreated (Alma 20:29; 21:13–14). When God instructed Ammon[2] to go to Middoni because his brethren were imprisoned there (Alma 20:2), Lamoni, a converted Lamanite king, accompanied Ammon and influenced Antiomno, king of Middoni, to release them (Alma 20:4, 28, 30).

There is no further reference to Ammah or his missionary efforts after his release from prison.

Ammaron Historian who maintained the sacred record of the Nephites beginning about A.D. 306 and who also hid all the Nephite records for safekeeping in a hill called Shim (4 Ne. 1:47–49; Morm. 1:3). Ammaron was descended from a line of historians, including his great-grandfather Nephi[3], one of the twelve disciples of Jesus in the New World. Ammaron's grandfather Nephi[4], father Amos[1], and brother Amos[2] likewise served as record keepers, and all were sources for 4 Nephi. At the time he "hid up the records unto the Lord," Ammaron instructed ten-year-old Mormon to retrieve the PLATES OF NEPHI when he was "about" twenty-four and to continue the history (Morm. 1:2–3; 2:17; 4:23).

BAV

Ammon[1] Leader of an expedition (ca. 121 B.C.) sent by Mosiah[2] from Zarahemla to the land of Lehi-Nephi to ascertain the fate of Nephite colonists there (Mosiah 7:1–5; cf. 9; Omni 1:27–30). There he and his companions (Amaleki[2], Helem, and Hem) were captured and imprisoned by guards of king Limhi (Mosiah 7:6–12; 21:23). When he told Limhi of his mission, he and his companions were freed, and the people rejoiced to learn that Zarahemla had not been destroyed, as they had thought (Mosiah 7:13–14; 21:24–26). Ammon related the history of Zarahemla to Limhi's people (Mosiah 8:2–3) and read the record of king Limhi's colony (Mosiah 8:5–6). During this time Ammon heard Limhi's account of finding the Jaredite record written on twenty-four gold plates (Mosiah 8:6–12) and explained the gift of seership to Limhi (Mosiah 8:13–18; 21:28). Ammon sorrowed over the trials of Limhi and his people (Mosiah 21:29–30) but declined to baptize them because he felt unworthy (Mosiah 21:33). He planned to liberate the people of Limhi from bondage (Mosiah 21:36–22:2) and was eventually able to lead them back to Zarahemla (Mosiah 22:11–13). Mormon noted that Ammon was a "strong and mighty man," a descendant of Zarahemla (Mosiah 7:3).

KPJ

Ammon[2] One of four sons of Mosiah[2] (Mosiah 27:34). Once numbered among the unbelievers, Ammon sought secretly to destroy the Church (Mosiah 27:8–10). In the midst of Ammon's rebellion, an angel appeared to him, his brothers, and Alma[2], which resulted in their sincere repentance (Mosiah 27:11–12). With his brothers and Alma, Ammon "suffered much anguish of soul" because of his early behavior (Mosiah 28:4) and began preaching the word of God in an effort to repair the damage he had done (Mosiah 27:35). He sought his father Mosiah's blessing to serve a mission to the Lamanites, and the Lord promised to protect him (Mosiah 28:5–7).

A courageous and devoted man, Ammon served fourteen years as "chief," or leader, among the missionaries (Alma 17:18). He traveled to the land of Ishmael where he was taken captive and brought before king Lamoni. He gained great favor with the king, largely because of his selfless desire simply to be the king's servant (Alma 17:25). When Ammon demonstrated great power defending the king's flock against a band of marauders, king Lamoni was ready to assume he was the Great Spirit, but Ammon corrected him (Alma 18:2–4, 11, 17, 19). Astonished at Ammon's faithfulness (Alma 18:10) and his ability to discern his thoughts, Lamoni granted Ammon permission to "speak boldly" and offered Ammon anything he desired if he would just reveal how he could know his thoughts and "by what power" he was able to defeat the men who scattered his flocks (Alma 18:20–21).

Asking only that the king hearken to his words (Alma 18:22), Ammon taught him of the Creation, the fall of man, and the plan of redemption (Alma 18:24–40). In response, Lamoni cried "unto the Lord, saying: O Lord, have mercy . . . upon me, and my people." The king then fell to the earth as though dead (Alma 18:41–42). Ammon knew, however, that Lamoni "was under the power of God" and was experiencing a spiritual transformation (Alma 19:6). When Lamoni revived at the time "Ammon had appointed" and testified to the queen, "I have seen my Redeemer," she too was overcome by the Spirit. Ammon was "also overpowered with joy," and the three "sunk to the earth" (Alma 19:11, 13–14).

Abish, a "Lamanitish woman" who had previously been "converted unto the Lord," saw this event as a missionary opportunity and spread the news so people would gather and "believe in the power of God" (Alma 19:16–17). Unfortunately, contention resulted as people debated over the meaning of their fallen king, queen, their servants, and Ammon, the Nephite. Ammon's life was miraculously spared when an angry brother of someone whom Ammon had slain in defending the king's flocks tried to kill Ammon as he lay on the ground; instead, the assailant "fell dead" (Alma 19:22). The Lord's promise to Mosiah was again verified concerning the promise of divine protection (Alma 19:23). The debate amongst the people continued, many believing Ammon was the "Great Spirit" and others saying he was a "monster" (Alma

AMMON[2]

19:25–26). A sorrowful Abish revived the queen, who then raised the king. Lamoni ministered to his people, and many believed and were baptized (Alma 19:28–31, 35). This was the beginning of the great Lamanite conversion.

After Ammon "establish[ed] a church among [the Lamanites]" (Alma 19:35; 20:1), the Lord directed him to journey to Middoni because his brother Aaron[3] and others were imprisoned there. En route, he and king Lamoni met the father of Lamoni, who was angered at seeing his son with a Nephite and attempted to kill Lamoni for refusing to obey his command to slay Ammon. When Ammon interceded, Lamoni's father attempted to kill Ammon. In the ensuing scuffle, Lamoni's father was wounded. Seeking Ammon's mercy, he offered to grant him his desire, "even to half of the kingdom," if he would spare his life. Ammon's only requests were for the release of his brethren from prison and for Lamoni to retain his kingdom and operate independently, "according to his own desires." When the humbled king saw "the great love [Ammon] had for his son Lamoni" and also "that Ammon had no desire to destroy him," he was "astonished" and granted Ammon's requests (Alma 20:2–27). The power of Ammon's love and generosity and the "greatness of [his] words" (Alma 22:3) softened the king's heart and caused him to want to hear the gospel (Alma 20:27).

After freeing his brothers from prison in Middoni, Ammon returned to the land of Ishmael, where he taught Lamoni's people (Alma 21:23). Lamoni's father was later converted, and freedom to preach the gospel throughout all Lamanite lands was granted (Alma 23:4). Ammon and his brethren had "great success" as thousands were converted and "brought to believe in the traditions of the Nephites" (Alma 23:5). Thus their original mission goals to "bring [the Lamanites] to the knowledge of the Lord their God, and convince them of the iniquity of their fathers; and . . . [to] cure them of their hatred towards the Nephites, that they might . . . rejoice in the Lord" were being realized (Mosiah 28:2).

These converts took the name of ANTI-NEPHI-LEHIES and vowed never to take up arms again (Alma 23). Hated now by their Lamanite brothers and apostate Nephites, these converts were extremely vulnerable, which prompted Ammon and his brethren to hold a council to determine their defense (Alma 24:5). They refused to resist any aggression against them; consequently 1,005 of their people were slain. In an effort to avert further bloodshed, Ammon and his brethren proposed to take the ANTI-NEPHI-LEHIES to Zarahemla, and Ammon prayed to know if this was the Lord's desire. He was instructed to return to Zarahemla with his brothers and the Anti-Nephi-Lehies (Alma 27:1–12). On their journey they encountered Alma[2], and Ammon was so overcome with joy in the reunion and "in the joy of his God" that he "fell . . . to the earth" (Alma 27:16–17).

That Ammon was a man of great enthusiasm and feeling is evident from the record. The joy of his brothers and Alma at their meeting was said to be "truly great" but not so much as "to exceed their strength" (Alma 27:19). So exuberant was Ammon over the missionaries' success among the Lamanites that on one occasion Aaron mildly rebuked him for boasting. Undaunted, Ammon replied, "I do not boast in my own strength, nor in my own wisdom; . . . I will rejoice in my God. . . . I will not boast of myself, but I will boast of my God, for in his strength I can do all things" (Alma 26:11–12).

The Nephites granted the Anti-Nephi-Lehies the land of Jershon for their home, "and they were called . . . the people of Ammon" (Alma 27:26). As high priest to these converts, Ammon banished Korihor the anti-Christ (Alma 30:20–21). Later he served another mission with Alma to the Zoramites[2] (Alma 31:6).

Ammon's great faith is well documented. The account of his activities in the book of Alma demonstrates his use of sacred records to convince many thousands of the incorrect traditions of their fathers and to bring them to repentance and a lasting knowledge of God. Mormon called Ammon a man of God, comparing captain Moroni to him (Alma 48:18), and Moroni[2] testified that it was Ammon's faith that "wrought so great a miracle among the Lamanites" (Ether 12:15).

Ammon's teachings are not recorded in detail,

but it is clear that he taught the gospel extensively and powerfully among the Lamanites, presumably the same things he taught Lamoni: the "Great Spirit" of their tradition was the true God of heaven (Alma 18:24–32). He taught from the sacred Nephite records and the "holy scriptures" (Alma 18:36), "he expounded unto them the plan of redemption," and "he also made known unto them concerning the coming of Christ." Indeed, "all the works of the Lord did he make known unto them" (Alma 18:39). Through Ammon, too, the modern reader can appreciate a model for effective missionary work and learn the meaning and source of true joy (Alma 19:12–14; 27:17–18).

Summary of major teachings

1. The existence of God (Alma 18:28).
2. God created his children from the beginning (i.e., premortal existence); he "looketh down" on them, and "he knows all the thoughts and intents of [their] hearts" (Alma 18:32).
3. "Man in the beginning was created after the image of God" (Alma 18:34).
4. God's spirit gives knowledge and power according to faith, righteous desires, and the purposes of God (Alma 18:35).
5. The Creation, "the fall of man," and "the plan of redemption" (Alma 18:36, 39).
6. The coming of Jesus Christ (Alma 18:39).

See also Missionary service; Mosiah[2], sons of.

JRC

Ammon, people of *See* Anti-Nephi-Lehies.

Ammonihah, land of and city of Nephite locale remembered primarily for its "great city" whose inhabitants boasted, "God could not destroy, because of its greatness." Yet the city suffered complete annihilation in a single day at the hands of the Lamanites (Alma 9:4; 16:9–10; 81 B.C.). A three-day journey from Melek and bordered on the west by wilderness, the city of Ammonihah was located in the same environs as the city of Noah (Alma 8:5–6). According to tradition, the land and city were named after their first possessor, of whom the record is silent (Alma 8:7).

Ammonihah was the fourth and most difficult city Alma[2] encountered on his journey to strengthen the Church and reconvert apostate Nephites (Alma 8–16). Rejected and abused during his initial efforts, Alma left Ammonihah, only to be stopped by an angel who instructed him to return (Alma 8:14–16). He was guided to Amulek, a prominent citizen of Ammonihah whom God had prepared to be Alma's companion and a second witness of his teachings (Alma 9:2, 6; 10:12). After their preaching, which included a verbal duel with the lawyer Zeezrom, Alma and Amulek were bound, subjected to a brief trial (Alma 14:4–5), and forced to witness the martyrdom by fire of women and children "whosoever believed or had been taught to believe in the word of God" (Alma 14:8). Subsequent to the imprisonment and miraculous deliverance of Alma and Amulek, the city of Ammonihah was destroyed by the Lamanites, who were angered over their own slaughtering of the converted ANTI-NEPHI-LEHIES (Alma 25:1–2). So strong was the stench of death that Ammonihah was left barren "for many years." It became known as the DESOLATION OF NEHORS because many of its inhabitants had been adherents to the false doctrines of Nehor (Alma 1:2–19; 16:11).

By 71 B.C. Ammonihah had been rebuilt "in part" and fortified by captain Moroni with high ridges of dirt to shield the city from Lamanite stones and arrows (Alma 49:1–3). Lamanite armies were "astonished" at these preparations and withdrew their aggressive plans (Alma 49:4–9).

The city's significance to the Book of Mormon can be measured by the importance of the doctrines that were taught there: ACCOUNTABILITY for light and knowledge (Alma 9), details concerning the RESURRECTION (Alma 11), the JUDGMENT, the FALL OF ADAM AND EVE, the purpose of life, the plan of redemption (Alma 12), the PREMORTAL EXISTENCE, foreordination, and priesthood (Alma 13). The Ammonihah narrative contains the verification of many truths taught throughout the Book of Mormon and elsewhere in scriptures: deliverance comes through faith in Jesus Christ (Alma 14:25–29; cf. 1 Ne. 1:20; Alma 36:2); a FULNESS OF INIQUITY brings a fulness of God's wrath (Alma 16:9–10; 49:3; cf.

Ether 2:8–12); the judgments of God follow the casting out of the righteous (Alma 10:23; 14:7–8; 16:3; cf. Hel. 13:14); a warning voice must precede destruction (Alma 10:20–23; cf. 2 Ne. 25:9); martyrs receive a celestial reward (Alma 14:11; cf. Rev. 6:9–11); and the justice of God punishes sinners and vindicates the innocent (Alma 60:13; cf. 3 Ne. 9:9–11). In addition, the account gives readers a view of the Nephite economy, which was based on a system of weights and measures (Alma 11:4–19), as well as a brief glance at their legal system.

DLL

Ammonihahites Apostate Nephites living in the city of Ammonihah, which bordered the land of Zarahemla. In fulfillment of prophecy, "every living soul of the Ammonihahites was destroyed, and also their great city" in a Lamanite attack (Alma 16:9).

Ammonites *See* Anti-Nephi-Lehies.

Ammoron A descendant of Zoram[1], Ammoron was a Nephite traitor who defected to the Lamanites and became their king after the death of his brother Amalickiah (Alma 52:3; 66 B.C.). Glimpses of Ammoron's personality can be viewed in his forceful response to the threatening epistle of Moroni[1] in which Ammoron declared himself a "bold Lamanite" (Alma 54:16–24), who intended to avenge his brother's death. References to Ammoron are solely in context with the affairs of the Lamanite-Nephite wars (Alma 52:12; 54; 56:18; 57:1, 17; 59:7; 62:33). Ever devious, he also proposed a one-sided prisoner exchange to Helaman[2] (Alma 57:1–3). Ammoron, like his brother Amalickiah, was slain by Teancum (Alma 62:36).

Amnigaddah *See* Jared[1], posterity of.

Alma and Amulek; *painting by Gary L. Kapp; courtesy Gary L. Kapp. Through faith in Jesus Christ, Alma and Amulek are delivered from an Ammonihah prison: "And the earth shook mightily, and the walls of the prison were rent in twain, so that they fell to the earth; and the chief judge, and the lawyers, and priests, and teachers, who smote upon Alma and Amulek, were slain by the fall thereof"* (Alma 14:27).

Amnihu, hill A hill east of the river Sidon and near Zarahemla where the Amlicites fought "with great strength" against Alma[2] and the Nephites (Alma 2:15–17; 87 B.C.).

Amnor One of the spies sent out by Alma[2], along with Limher, Manti, and Zeram, to watch the camp of the Amlicites, a Nephite group engaged in rebellion (ca. 87 B.C.). They returned with the alarming report that the Amlicites had united with a host of Lamanites and were marching upon the Nephites above the land of Zarahemla (Alma 2:22–25).

Amnor *See* Nephite weights and measures.

Amoron A Nephite who during the final conflict between the Nephites and Lamanites reported to Mormon concerning Lamanite atrocities in Sherrizah (Moro. 9:7–10).

Amos[1] Son of Nephi[4] and record keeper in his father's stead (ca. A.D. 110–194). In Amos' days "there was still peace in the land"; however, "a small part of the people . . . revolted from the church and [took] upon them the name of Lamanites." Amos passed the records to his son Amos[2] (4 Ne. 1:19–21).

Amos[2] Son of Amos[1], who followed his father as Nephite record keeper (ca. A.D. 194–306). Over the course of his life, Amos witnessed the complete moral collapse of the Nephite nation as had been prophesied by his predecessors (4 Ne. 1:21–47; cf. 2 Ne. 26:10; Alma 45:10–12).

Amulek A descendant of Nephi[1] (Alma 10:2–3) and a prominent citizen of Ammonihah, a good and generous man who after conversion became a powerful teacher of the word of Christ (ca. 82–74 B.C.). An industrious, wealthy man with "many kindreds and friends" (Alma 10:4), Amulek confessed that despite witnessing the Lord's "mysteries and his marvelous power," (Alma 10:5) he had hardened his heart. "I was called many times," he said, "and I would not hear; therefore I knew concerning these things, yet I would not know; therefore I went on rebelling against God" (Alma 10:6).

Amulek continued his worldly lifestyle until the day an angel of the Lord appeared, instructing him to return home and there "receive" and give nourishment to "a prophet of the Lord" (Alma 10:7–9). This prophet was Alma[2]. For this kindness Alma blessed Amulek and his house (Alma 8:22; 10:7, 11; cf. Matt. 10:40–41). Amulek was spiritually awakened during Alma's stay as the prophet and an angel taught him the gospel of Jesus Christ (Alma 10:9–10; 11:31). After many days, the word of the Lord came to Alma and Amulek to "go forth and prophesy unto this people, saying—Repent ye, for . . . except ye repent I will visit this people in mine anger" (Alma 8:29). The two men labored in Ammonihah where, filled with the Spirit (Alma 8:30), Amulek astonished his fellow townsmen with his testimony (Alma 10:12). A group of lawyers led by Zeezrom tried to trap Amulek in his words (Alma 10:16) and bribe him to deny his faith in the existence of God (Alma 11:22). Amulek perceived their thoughts through the Spirit (Alma 10:17; 12:3) and skillfully withstood Zeezrom and the others, eventually silencing them with the truth concerning Christ, redemption from sin, resurrection (which he also termed "restoration"), and judgment (Alma 11:38–46).

Although the teachings of Alma and Amulek led some people in Ammonihah to repent, most rejected what they heard, arresting Alma and Amulek and taking them before the chief judge. These missionaries were then cruelly forced to witness the burning of their converts. Greatly distressed at the horrible spectacle, Amulek desired that they "stretch forth [their] hands" and save the martyrs from the consuming fire through "the power of God." Alma replied that the Spirit constrained him from doing so, assuring Amulek that the slain would be received into glory. Moreover, their blood would "stand as a witness against" the wicked inhabitants of Ammonihah (Alma 14:8–11).

Brought again before the chief judge, Amulek and Alma kept silent while the wicked magistrate struck them repeatedly and then cast them into prison. There they were mocked, stripped naked, spit upon, bound with strong cords, and denied food and water. Finally, after many days of suffering, Alma called upon the Lord for deliverance. In response, "the walls of the prison were rent in twain, so that they fell to the earth; and the chief judge, and the lawyers, and priests, and teachers, who smote upon Alma and Amulek, were slain by the fall thereof" while the two missionaries walked out unhurt (Alma 14:14–28).

Alma and Amulek were then commanded by the Lord to go to the land of Sidom. Here they were reunited with many who had believed their message in Ammonihah and with Zeezrom, who had been consumed by guilt over his wickedness (Alma 15:1–3). Zeezrom was subsequently healed and baptized. After establishing the Church at Sidom, Alma and Amulek went to the land of Zarahemla where Alma took Amulek "to his own house, and did administer unto him in his tribulations, and strengthened him in the Lord," because Amulek had been "rejected by those who were once his friends and also by his father and his kindred" (Alma 15:16–18). Amulek had sacrificed everything—home, family, friends, wealth—for his faith.

Alma and Amulek then resumed "preaching repentance to the people" (Alma 16:13–15). Approximately four years later, Amulek joined Alma and a number of other missionaries in an effort to reclaim the apostate Zoramites[2]. Later, Amulek went into the land of Jershon where he ministered among the people of Ammon (Alma 35:1).

Summary of major teachings

1. Jesus Christ. The son of God is the "very Eternal Father of heaven and of earth, and all things which in them are; he is the beginning and the end, the first and the last" (Alma 11:39).

2. The Atonement. "Christ shall come" and "atone for the sins of the world" (Alma 34:8). All mankind are fallen and lost and "must unavoidably perish . . . except it be through the atonement" of Christ (Alma 34:9). Christ came to redeem believers; the wicked "remain as though there had been no redemption made," except being saved from temporal death (Alma 11:40–42). The Atonement must be "infinite and eternal" to "suffice for the sins of the world." A sacrifice of man or animal would not do. The Law of Moses and its sacrifices all pointed to Christ—the "great and last sacrifice . . . yea, infinite and eternal" (Alma 34:10–14). The Atonement brings mercy which "can satisfy the demands of justice" for those who have "faith unto repentance." Without Christ's mercy one is left to suffer the demands of justice (Alma 34:15–16).

3. The Resurrection. All people will be resurrected—the "wicked and the righteous," "the spirit and the body shall be reunited again in its perfect form . . . even as [they] now are" (Alma 11:43–44). After the resurrection there is no more death, the spirit and the body will "never" be divided again, "the whole [i.e., the spirit and the resurrected body combined] becoming spiritual and immortal" (Alma 11:45). *See* Spiritual.

4. The Judgment. All people will be brought before Jesus Christ, God the Father, and the Holy Spirit to be judged according to their works; they shall have "a bright recollection of all [their] guilt" (Alma 11:43–44; Jacob[2] added that "the righteous shall have a perfect knowledge of their enjoyment, and their righteousness"; 2 Ne. 9:14).

5. Repentance. "Repent, for the kingdom of heaven is at hand" (Alma 10:20). "No unclean thing can inherit the kingdom of heaven"; therefore, Christ cannot save his people "in their sins" (Alma 11:37; cf. Hel. 5:10–11). Mortal life is given "to prepare to meet God"(Alma 34:32). Procrastinating repentance is dangerous because there will come a time when "there can be no labor performed" and the "same spirit [i.e., the 'Spirit of the Lord' or the 'spirit of the devil'] which doth possess your bodies at the time that ye go out of this life . . . will have power to possess your body in that eternal world" (Alma 34:32–35). *See* Night of Darkness.

6. Christian characteristics and practices. Mortals can and should pray over temporal as well as spiritual concerns, and prayer is not limited to formal places of worship (Alma 34:17–27, 39). Prayers have efficacy only if the disciple also reaches out in true charity to the poor, the sick, and the needy (Alma 34:28–29). Moreover disciples must "work out [their] salvation with fear before God," be humble, "live

in thanksgiving daily," and be patient in afflictions (Alma 34:37–38).

7. Conditions for destruction. If the "voice of this people should choose iniquity," and "cast out the righteous from among [them]," they qualify for destruction, "except [they] repent" (Alma 10:19–23; cf. Hel. 13:12–14; Ether 2:8–11).

RLH

Amulon Leader of the wicked priests of king Noah[3] (Mosiah 23:32). Amulon was among the proud, lazy, immoral, and idolatrous priests chosen by king Noah to rule the Nephite colony in the land of Nephi following Zeniff's death (Mosiah 11:5–6; ca. 160 B.C.). Amulon was one of the evil leaders who influenced the people to become wicked and caused the Lord to send the prophet Abinadi to prophesy that unless they repented, they would be taken into bondage (Mosiah 11:20–25). As a priest of Noah, Amulon would have been part of the audience that heard Abinadi's doctrine and stinging rebuke and also would have been one of the voices urging Abinadi's execution (Mosiah 17:12).

Amulon was among those who left their families at king Noah's command to flee from the attacking Lamanites. He escaped Noah's fate of being burned to death by fleeing with the other priests into the wilderness, thus evading those who were angry with Noah because of his command to desert their families (Mosiah 19:20–21). While in the wilderness, Amulon and the other priests continued to cause sorrow among the people. Their abduction of twenty-four Lamanite daughters incited the wrath of the Lamanites against the Nephites in the land of Nephi, whom they supposed were guilty of the kidnapping (Mosiah 20:1–7). Eventually Amulon and his group settled in a "place which they called Amulon" and began to "till the ground" (Mosiah 23:31).

On another occasion Amulon escaped destruction when Lamanite soldiers, lost in the wilderness while searching for Limhi's people who had escaped from the land of Nephi, stumbled upon them. It was the pleading of their Lamanite wives (the Lamanite daughters they had previously abducted) that softened the hearts of the Lamanites and prevented their destruction (Mosiah 23:30–34). "Amulon and his brethren" joined the Lamanites and the search for the land of Nephi continued (Mosiah 23:35). En route, they discovered the people of Alma[1] in the land of Helam, and the Lamanites took them into bondage. Amulon gained "favor in the eyes of the king of the Lamanites." He was granted to be "a king and a ruler" over Alma's people in the land of Helam, and he and his priests were "appointed teachers" in various Lamanite lands (Mosiah 23:39; 24:1, 4). Amulon knew Alma as a former priest of king Noah's court and was angry at him because of his defection from their group. He punished and persecuted Alma's people, even threatening execution if they were found praying (Mosiah 24:8–11).

In later generations the descendants of Amulon (Amulonites) retained their specific identity even though they integrated with the Lamanites. They were noted for their wickedness, extreme hatred, and impenetrable hearts (Alma 21:3; 23:14; 24:1–2, 20–22, 28–30). As prophesied by Abinadi, the "seed of Amulon" were scattered, hunted, and slain (Mosiah 17:16–17; Alma 25:7–12).

KJW

Amulon, land of An area between the lands of Nephi and Zarahemla settled by the priests of Noah[3] and presumably named after their leader, Amulon. The Lamanites who had become lost in the wilderness while chasing the people of Limhi found the corrupt priests of Noah in Amulon. Following a plea for mercy on the part of Amulon and their Lamanite wives, the Lamanites softened their hearts toward the priests. The priests joined the Lamanites in their search for the land of Nephi. Later, the king of the Lamanites appointed Amulon and his fellow priests as teachers over the Lamanites living in the land of Amulon (Mosiah 23:30–35; 24:1; between 145 and 121 B.C.).

Amulonites Descendants and followers of the wicked priests of king Noah[3] whose leader was Amulon. The Amulonites, many of whom were followers "after the order of the Nehors" (Alma 21:4), were noted both for their own hardness of heart and for "caus[ing] the Lamanites that they should harden their hearts" and increase in wickedness (Alma 21:3; 23:14). After their defection to the Lamanites (Mosiah 23:30–24:4), some of the children of the Amulonites renounced their fathers and took upon them "the name of Nephi" that they might be "numbered among" the Nephites (Mosiah 25:12). Later, the Amulonites with the Lamanites helped build the city of Jerusalem[2] (Alma 21:2).

The large-scale conversions of the Lamanites by the sons of Mosiah[2] angered the Amulonites, and they, with the Amalekites and other Lamanites, attacked their converted brethren, the ANTI-NEPHI-LEHIES. Their brutal attack was not resisted (Alma 24:21–22). The faith of those being killed, as well as their own feelings of compassion for their slain brethren and the guilt for their murders, caused many of the attacking Lamanites to repent and become converted (Alma 24:23–25). Not a single Amulonite was among the new converts, however (Alma 24:29). Drawing a lesson from these events, Mormon taught the principle "that after a people have been once enlightened by the Spirit of God, and have had great knowledge of things pertaining to righteousness, and then have fallen away into sin and transgression, they become more hardened, and thus their state becomes worse than though they had never known these things" (Alma 24:30).

The final reference to the Amulonites noted their continuing wars with the Nephites in which "almost all the seed of Amulon and his brethren . . . were slain by the hands of the Nephites" (Alma 25:3–4). The remainder escaped into the wilderness. There, "having usurped . . . power and authority over the Lamanites" the seed of Amulon burned many Lamanite believers to death (Alma 25:5). The executions so angered the Lamanites that they commenced to hunt and kill the seed of Amulon (Alma 25:8). This series of events fulfilled Abinadi's prophecy, uttered while he was being burned to death at the hands of Noah's priests, that the seed of the priests of Noah would cause others to also suffer death by fire and that they too would be scattered, hunted, and suffer a similar fate (Mosiah 17:15–18; Alma 25:9–12).

See also Noah[3], priests of.

KJW

Anachronisms, alleged Since the earliest days of the Church, critics of the Book of Mormon have pointed to certain alleged anachronisms—claims that ideas, words, events, persons and objects are historically out of place—as evidence that the Book of Mormon is false. Those who have a conviction that the Book of Mormon is an authentic and true record have little difficulty finding sound arguments to dismiss any presumed anachronisms that might undermine the text's credibility. This point can be illustrated by evaluating examples from three categories of alleged anachronisms: linguistic, cultural, and doctrinal.

Alleged linguistic anachronisms

Allegations of linguistic anachronisms concern words in the Book of Mormon. For example, the book of Jacob ends with the French word for farewell, "adieu" (Jacob 7:27). It would be impossible for French to have been in the original language of the text, as the book of Jacob dates between 544 and 420 B.C., and French did not even exist until A.D. 700. Further, critics charge that the use in the Book of Mormon of terms with Greek origin such as "Christ" (e.g., 2 Ne. 25:26) and "Alpha and Omega" (e.g., 3 Ne. 9:18) are anachronistic, for if the Nephites had really been Hebrews they would never have used such terms.

These criticisms may best be answered by understanding the character of typical nineteenth-century English. The earliest forms of English, like the oldest forms of French, did not even develop until the first millennium A.D. By the nineteenth century A.D., however, English was a rich, flexible, nuanced, and highly expressive language that had borrowed words from many other languages. Thus, in the case of "adieu," Joseph Smith must have felt the sense of the original Nephite term could be expressed quite nicely by the use of this French word, a word used commonly by English-speaking Americans of Joseph Smith's day. Indeed, Webster's 1828 *Dictionary* defines "adieu" as "an elliptical form

ANACHRONISMS, ALLEGED

of speech, for *I commend you to God*" and also "farewell; an expression of kind wishes at the parting of friends."

The term "Christ" is also a very acceptable rendering of the Hebrew term "Messiah" into nineteenth-century English. The root meaning of both of these words is the same—the "anointed"—Christ from the Greek *christos,* and MESSIAH from the Hebrew *mashiach.* "Messiah" also appears frequently in the Book of Mormon, sometimes in combination with "Christ" (e.g., 2 Ne. 25:16, 18–19). The use of "Alpha and Omega" as a rendering of a Hebrew (or other Afro-Asiatic) phrase reflects the expressiveness of English as a language spoken predominantly by those with the religious vocabulary of Christians. In fact, "Alpha and Omega" is found in the book of Revelation to render the Hebrew of Isaiah's words "first" and "last" (Isa. 41:4; 44:6; 48:12); in Revelation 22:13 it is a self-designation of Christ. *See* Alpha and Omega.

Thus in translating the original language of the Book of Mormon, Joseph Smith used the English words and terms of his day that would be best understood by his contemporaries, without concern that some might appear anachronistic. His major concern in translating was understanding. God does the same, for he "speaketh unto men according to their language, unto their understanding" (2 Ne. 31:3; cf. D&C 1:24). Other alleged linguistic anachronisms, such as the use of the words "synagogue," "baptism," and the name "Timothy," can be similarly explained using the same principles. *See* Names in the Book of Mormon; Synagogue(s).

Alleged cultural anachronisms

Critics of the Book of Mormon have noted certain cultural features of the Book of Mormon that supposedly do not square with its presumed setting in Mesoamerica. For example, according to these critics, the Book of Mormon describes ancient Americans involved in massive armed conflicts, with armies of hundreds of thousands engaged in single battles, but they claim ancient Americans were sedentary and peaceful. Other critics claim that the use of the word "horse" is a striking anachronism, because no horses existed in Mesoamerica until the time of Columbus.

The cultural criticism of the Book of Mormon because of the presumed peacefulness of ancient Mesoamericans is becoming more and more difficult to maintain in the light of more recent research. According to one scholar, "It has been held that the Maya pursued a peaceful existence. From the beginning of the Classical Era, however, the treading of victors on captives is represented and such scenes carved in stone increase in number and complexity with the passage of time" (Lothrop, 107; qtd. in Sorenson, 132). Professor John Sorenson has also identified many fortified Mesoamerican sites indicative of a warring people that date to Book of Mormon times. As for the second claim, there have been several archaeological discoveries of what appears to be pre-Columbian horses in the New World (Sorenson, 295–96; Welch, 98–100). It is also possible that Book of Mormon authors, with their ancient Near Eastern background, may have described some ANIMALS (possibly of the deer family) as horses, though their taxonomy varies markedly from horses known today (Welch, 98), much the same as the Greeks, who, when they first visited the Nile in Egypt, became acquainted with a large animal that they described as "hippopotamus," meaning "river horse." Similar arguments can be used to dismiss other alleged cultural anachronisms, such as the mention in the Book of Mormon of "silk," "barley," and "steel." *See* Agriculture in the Book of Mormon; Archaeology; Linen; Metals of the Book of Mormon; Silk.

Alleged doctrinal anachronisms

An example of a presumed anachronism in doctrine is the early reference to the unpardonable sin (e.g., Jacob 7:19; Alma 39:6; cf. 2 Ne. 31:14). Some see this as problematic because the doctrine of an unpardonable sin is not taught in the Bible until New Testament times, well after Lehi and his family left Jerusalem (e.g., Matt. 12:31; Mark 3:29; Luke 12:10; cf. Heb. 10:26; 1 Jn. 5:16–17). In response, it should be noted that the unpardonable sin is defined as "deny[ing] the Holy Ghost when it once has had place in you" (Alma 39:6). It is evident from the text of the Book of Mormon that the descendants of Lehi knew of and received the witness of the Holy Ghost (e.g., 1 Ne. 10:17–19, 22; 2 Ne. 31:13, 18; Jacob 6:8; Alma 9:21). They thus had knowledge sufficient to commit such a sin and to be warned against committing it.

See also Book of Mormon, language of the translated text of.

BIBLIOGRAPHY

Lothrop, Samuel K. *Treasures of Ancient America.* Cleveland, Ohio: World Publishing, 1964.

Sorenson, John. *An Ancient American Setting for the Book of Mormon.* Salt Lake City: Deseret Book, 1985.

Webster, Noah. *An American Dictionary of the English Language.* 1828.

Welch, John W., ed. *Reexploring the Book of Mormon.* Salt Lake City and Provo: Deseret Book and FARMS, 1992.

SDR

And it came to pass A phrase used frequently in the scriptures to join consecutive events in historical narrative. In the Old Testament, the phrase "and it came to pass" reflects the Hebrew expression *wa-ye hee,* which means "and it was." In the Book of Mormon, as in the Old Testament, it is often followed by a time phrase: "Now it came to pass that not many days after the battle" (Alma 3:20), or, "And it came to pass that in the same year" (Alma 50:37).

MDP

And thus we see A phrase often used by Book of Mormon record keepers to emphasize a principle, precept, or consequence that can be learned from the event(s) or behavior(s) just discussed. It signals the reader that something important will immediately follow. Simply put, by using the phrase "and thus we see," the writer is saying, "If you missed the point of what you just read, I will now explain the message you should have received."

Because Book of Mormon record keepers could not include even "a hundredth part" of their history, the use of this literary device served as a significant tool helping them to summarize, conclude, encapsulate, and highlight important concepts (Jacob 3:13; W of M 1:5; 3 Ne. 5:8; Ether 15:33).

A well-known example is found in the passage where Nephi[1] explained the operation of the Liahona and then concluded, "And thus we see that by small means the Lord can bring about great things" (1 Ne. 16:29). A more comprehensive example is Mormon's use of the phrase when explaining the Nephites' prosperous circumstances: "And thus we see how merciful and just are all the dealings of the Lord, to the fulfilling of all his words unto the children of men; yea, we can behold that his words are verified, even at this time, which he spake unto Lehi, saying: Blessed art thou and thy children; and they shall be blessed, inasmuch as they shall keep my commandments they shall prosper in the land. But remember, inasmuch as they will not keep my commandments they shall be cut off from the presence of the Lord. And we see that these promises have been verified to the people of Nephi" (Alma 50:19–21). Mormon pointed out that the history of the Nephites has borne out the Lord's promise originally given to Lehi[1] (2 Ne. 1:9, 20; cf. 1 Ne. 2:20–21).

The accompanying table gives representative examples of messages or conclusions introduced by the phrase "and thus we see."

REFERENCE	AND THUS WE SEE	CONTEXT	WRITER
1 Ne. 17:3	"that the commandments of God must be fulfilled"	Lehi's family was nourished and strengthened in their journey to the promised land because of their obedience (1 Ne. 17:1–4)	Nephi[1]
Alma 24:19	those who are "brought to believe and to know the truth . . . would suffer even unto death rather than commit sin"	After conversion, the Anti-Nephi-Lehies refused to shed blood (Alma 23–24)	Mormon

continued

continued

REFERENCE	AND THUS WE SEE	CONTEXT	WRITER
1 Ne. 17:3	"that the commandments of God must be fulfilled"	Lehi's family was nourished and strengthened in their jouney to the promised land because of their obedience (1 Ne. 17:1–4)	Nephi[1]
Alma 24:19	those who are "brought to believe and to know the truth . . . would suffer even unto death rather than commit sin"	After conversion, the Anti-Nephi-Lehies refused to shed blood (Alma 23–24)	Mormon
Alma 30:60	"the end of him who perverteth the ways of the Lord; and thus we see that the devil will not support his children at the last day"	Korihor the anti-Christ was "struck dumb," became a beggar, and was "trodden down" and killed as he went among the Zoramites[2] (Alma 30:6–59)	Mormon
Alma 42:4	"that there was a time granted unto man to repent"	After the Fall, men were given time to repent before they die (Alma 42:2–5)	Alma[2]
Alma 42:14	"that all mankind were fallen, and they were in the grasp of justice; yea, the justice of God, which consigned them forever to be cut off from his presence"	Redemption from the Fall comes through the atonement of Christ. Mercy appeases justice when one repents (Alma 42:9–15)	Alma[2]
Alma 50:19	"how merciful and just are all the dealings of the Lord, to the fulfilling of all his words"	The prosperous circumstances of the Nephites in the twenty-first year of the reign of judges (Alma 50:17–22; cf. 1 Ne. 2:20)	Mormon
Hel. 6:35	"that the Spirit of the Lord began to withdraw . . . because of the wickedness and the hardness of their hearts"	Increasing wickedness among the Nephites in the sixty-seventh and sixty-eighth year of the reign of judges (Hel. 6:31–41)	Mormon
Hel. 12:3	"that except the Lord doth chasten his people . . . they will not remember him"	Famine brings the Nephites to repentance, but they quickly return to iniquity (Hel. 11:7–12:2)	Mormon
Ether 14:25	"that the Lord did visit them [the Jaredites] in the fulness of his wrath, and their wickedness and abominations had prepared a way for their everlasting destruction"	The immense destructions attending the final battles of the Jaredite civil war (Ether 10:2–14:24)	Moroni[2]

Casual readers recognize these phrases indicating important lessons, especially toward the latter part of Mormon's abridgment (Alma 26:37–Hel. 15:9), but careful review reveals more than two hundred fifty occurrences in the Book of Mormon of variant "and thus we see" forms, including the following:

"And now . . . ye see"
"And now . . . we see"
"And thus we can behold"
"And thus . . . we see"
"And thus it is"
"And we see"
"And when ye shall see"
"For I see"
"For . . . we see"
"Look . . . and see"
"Nevertheless . . . we see"
"Now we see"
"Now . . . we see"

"Seeing we know"
"Thus we may see"
"Thus we see"
"Thus . . . we see"
"We may see
"We see"
"We shall see"
"When ye see these"
"Ye see"
"Ye shall see"
"Ye should see"

Other less obvious phrases that serve the same purpose of indicating a principle, precept, or a cause-and-effect relationship include such words as "and," "behold," "cause," "for," "know," "remember," "say" or "saying," "see," "seeth," or "seeing," "therefore," "thus," and "wherefore." The word *because* is perhaps the most commonly used key word indicating a cause-and-effect relationship, but it is found in other contexts also.

In addition Book of Mormon writers used a host of other phrases to point out significant spiritual lessons that can be learned from the historical narrative, including the following:

"And the reason why"
"And this to the intent"
"As I said . . . before"
"Because of this"
"But behold"
"But now"
"For behold"
"He showeth"
"I . . . show unto you"
"I will show"
"I would show"
"It was on account of"
"It shall be made manifest"
"It showeth"
"Now all this was done"
"Now behold"
"This cometh unto you"
"Thus shall be"
"We . . . discern"
"Ye behold"

In some instances, these "and thus we see" phrases announce the results before the causes are explained.

"And thus we see" does not appear in other volumes of scripture, but such words as "behold," "therefore," "wherefore," "because," and sometimes, "thus saith the Lord," often function as cause-and-effect conjunctions. It becomes apparent that most writers of holy writ used some form of the "and thus we see" model (e.g., Deut. 9:6; 32:39; Josh. 23:15; Judg. 2:16; 1 Sam. 24:13; John 3:16; Acts 10:34–35; 1 Cor. 10:11; Heb. 3:19–4:2).

In all cases, the full context of the "and thus we see" model must be understood in order to recognize the antecedents from which conclusions are drawn. It may be only a few verses or it may be hundreds of pages. The following are examples from the book of Alma indicating complete blocks of preceding context: Alma 1:31 (31 verses, from Alma 1:1); Alma 9:14 (174 pages, from 2 Ne. 1:20); Alma 11:37 (4 verses, from Alma 11:34); and Alma 19:36 (6 verses, from Alma 19:31).

In addition to the lessons learned from carefully considering the "and thus we see" passages in the Book of Mormon, readers can be inspired to "see" other principles and lessons beyond those highlighted by the authors in the text. Further, since all scripture is included for a purpose, in instances where no conclusions are given by the author, readers can seek their own insights by beginning with the "and thus we see" statement and then stating their own conclusion. Most principles or precepts can be converted into this format. For example, an individual could make personal application of 1 Nephi 3:7 by converting it to "And thus we see, the Lord will give [me] no commandment save he will prepare a way for [me] to accomplish it."

GAH

Angels, ministry of Angels are messengers from the Lord, sent to proclaim the plan of salvation to man: "The office of their ministry is to call men unto repentance, and to fulfil and to do the work of the covenants of the Father, which he hath made unto the children of men, to prepare the way among the children of men, by declaring the word of Christ unto the chosen vessels of the Lord, that they may bear testimony of him. And by so doing, the Lord God prepareth the way that the residue of men may have faith in Christ, that the Holy Ghost may have place in their hearts, according to the power thereof; and after this manner bringeth to pass the Father, the covenants which he hath made unto the children of men" (Moro. 7:31–32; cf. Alma 13:21–26; Hel. 13:7; 16:14). This pattern of angels teaching chosen vessels who in turn bear testimony and teach others was established in the very beginning of earth's history with Adam (Moses 5:6–8) and was followed repeatedly in Book of Mormon times. For example, Nephi[1] (1 Ne. 11–14), king Benjamin (Mosiah 3), Alma[2] (Mosiah 27), Nephi[2], and Lehi[4] (Hel. 5) all conversed with angelic personages. Mormon and Moroni[2] were visited and taught by the three Nephite disciples who had been translated (3 Ne. 28:26; Morm. 8:11). Angels minister not only to chosen vessels (i.e., prophets) but also to others "of strong faith and a firm mind in every form of godliness" (Moro. 7:29–30), including men, women, and children (Alma 32:23).

The ministry of angels is not limited to the righteous. An angel visited the brothers of Nephi[1] and Alma[2] and the four sons of Mosiah[2] in their wickedness (1 Ne. 3:29–31; 17:45; Mosiah 27). Amulek, who was basically a good man but casual about his relationship with God and who had resisted repeated calls from heaven, also received an angelic visitation (Alma 10:4–10).

Ministering angels are sent to mankind because of God's love and mercy (Alma 24:14) that the "power and deliverance of Jesus Christ" might be made known, that mankind might not perish but rather accept the blessings of the Atonement through faith, repentance, and baptism, and the gift of the Holy Ghost (Alma 9:25–29; cf. 10:20–21; 12:28–30; Hel. 5; Moro. 7:21–25). Nephi testified that "angels speak by the power of the Holy Ghost; wherefore, they speak the words of Christ" (2 Ne. 32:3), and Mormon affirmed that if angels cease to appear to the children of men it is because of unbelief (Moro. 7:36–38).

Concerning the way angels communicate to people on earth, Elder Dallin H. Oaks wrote, "Nephi described three manifestations of the ministering of angels when he reminded his rebellious brothers that (1) they had 'seen an angel,' (2) they had 'heard his voice from time to time,' and (3) also that an angel had 'spoken unto [them] in a still small voice' though they were 'past feeling' and 'could not feel his words' (1 Ne. 17:45). . . . Most angelic communications are felt or heard rather than seen" (39).

See also Ministering spirits; Tongue of angels.

BIBLIOGRAPHY

Oaks, Dallin H. "The Aaronic Priesthood and the Sacrament." *Ensign* 28 (November 1998): 37–40.

LED

Anger, wrath Strong emotions of displeasure, usually focused against the teachings, actions, or traits of another. "Anger" is used in the Book of Mormon to describe the feelings of those opposed to God's prophets and their teachings (1 Ne. 1:20; 2 Ne. 33:5) or as a goal of Satan or dissenters to "stir" up anger in others (2 Ne. 28:20; Alma 27:2, 12; 43:8; 47:1; Hel. 4:4). The term is also used to describe the displeasure of God (2 Ne. 15:25; Hel. 13:30, 39) and his righteous servants (2 Ne. 1:26; Alma 44:17). The use of the word "wrath" appears to be used synonymously with anger and is used most often to represent an attribute of God and not man (2 Ne. 19:19; 23:9, 13; Ether 9:20).

Nephi[1] lamented over his negative experience with anger and committed to regain his peace: "Why am I angry because of mine enemy? Awake, my soul! No longer droop in sin. . . . Do not anger again because of mine enemies" (2 Ne. 4:27–29). On the other hand, the Lord warned the people of king Noah[3] of His righteous anger: "Wo be unto this people, for I have seen their abominations, and their wickedness, and their whoredoms; and except they repent I will visit them in mine anger" (Mosiah 11:20). Nephi's anger was to be repented of because it was centered on himself and disrupted his spiritual strength; God's selfless anger is controlled and exercised in harmony with eternal principles pertaining to the plan of redemption. Therefore, he corrects and judges mankind appropriately, for "he doeth not anything save it be for the benefit of the world" (2 Ne. 26:24; cf. Hel. 12:2). Elder Neal A. Maxwell explained, "God's anger is kindled not because we have harmed him, but because we have harmed ourselves" (85). Those who have "harmed themselves" by rejecting the truth and rebelling against God, Nephi[2] declared, "are heaping up for [themselves] wrath against the day of judgment," rather than "laying up for [themselves] treasures in heaven" (Hel. 8:25).

Mankind's self-centered anger is clearly contrary to the Lord's will. During the Savior's visit to the Nephites after his resurrection, he explained that the devil "stirreth up the hearts of men to contend with anger, one with another. Behold, [Christ declared] this is not my doctrine, to stir up the hearts of men with anger, one against another; but this is my doctrine, that such things should be done away" (3 Ne. 11:29–30). Jesus also warned of an important consequence of being angry with one another: "Whosoever is angry with his brother shall be in danger of his judgment" (3 Ne. 12:22).

BIBLIOGRAPHY

Maxwell, Neal A. *Sermons Not Spoken*. Salt Lake City: Bookcraft, 1985.

DKJ

Angola, city of The Nephite city to which Mormon's troops retreated, afraid to do battle with a powerful Lamanite army (ca. A.D. 327–328). Despite great efforts to fortify Angola against a Lamanite offensive, the Nephites were driven from the city (Morm. 2:2–4).

Ani-Anti, village of Lamanite locale in the land of Nephi (Alma 21:11). Aaron[3], Muloki, Ammah, and other missionaries preached and "contended" there, but the inhabitants were not receptive (Alma 21:11–12).

Animals Twelve animals are specifically identified in the Book of Mormon: ass, cow, dog, goat, wild goat, horse, sheep, ox, swine, elephant, "curelom," and "cumom" (e.g., 1 Ne. 18:25; Ether 9:18–19). Other related terms include calf, cattle, fowl, lamb, and the fatling (Sorenson, *Ancient*, 289). Metaphorical references to animals also occur. For instance, "ye are his sheep . . . suffer no ravenous wolf to enter among you" (Alma 5:60); "the people had turned from their righteousness, like the dog to his vomit, or like the sow to her wallowing in the mire" (3 Ne. 7:8); "they shall be driven before like a dumb ass" (Mosiah 12:5); "they were struck with great fear, and fled from the presence of Alma and Amulek even as a goat fleeth with her young from two lions" (Alma 14:29).

Several types of animals are referred to in the account of the Jaredite migration to the new world and shortly after their arrival (perhaps ca. 2200 B.C.; *see* Chronology, Book of Mormon). It appears that the Jaredites brought some animals indigenous to the Old World with them to the New World. Before their departure, the record states, "they had prepared all manner of food, that thereby they might subsist upon the water, and also food for their flocks and herds, and whatsoever beast or animal or fowl that they should carry with them" (Ether 6:4). Later the record states that cattle, oxen, cows, sheep, swine, goats and other kinds of animals "were useful for the food of man," and that horses, asses, elephants, cureloms, and cumoms "were useful unto man" (Ether 9:18–19).

When the Nephites reached the promised land, they discovered many animals (1 Ne. 18:25) and sometime between 588 and 570 B.C. they began to raise their own "flocks, and herds, and animals of every kind" (2 Ne. 5:11). Later, Enos reported that the Nephites raised "flocks of herds, and flocks of all manner of cattle of every kind, and goats, and wild goats, and also many horses" (Enos 1:21; between 544 and 421 B.C.).

Problems emerge when one tries to identify animals in the Book of Mormon with North American or Mesoamerican animals. At present there is not enough evidence to conclusively demonstrate the presence of some of the animals mentioned in the Book of Mormon in North America or Mesoamerica during the Book of Mormon periods. But the cases of the horse and the elephant are instructive. For many years scholars maintained that the horse became extinct in the western hemisphere long before the time when the Jaredites or the Nephites arrived in the Americas. But recently several discoveries have been made of what appears to be pre-Columbian horses (Sorenson, *Ancient*, 295–96; Welch, 98–100). Likewise, the elephant

BOOK OF MORMON NAME	CANDIDATE ANIMAL ON THE SCENE
Elephant	Mastodon, Mammoth
"Curelom"	Sloth, Bison, Tapir, Mastodon, or Mammoth
"Cumom"	Same possibilities as "curelom"
Cow	Deer, Brocket, Bison
Horse	Deer, Tapir, Horse
Ox	Tapir, Bison
Ass	Tapir
Sheep	Paca or Agouti
Goat	Brocket, Deer
Swine	Peccary
Dog	Dog

mentioned in Jaredite times (Ether 9:19) may be a reference to the mastodon. Long believed to be extinct before the period of the Jaredites, evidence has emerged that the mastodon was still to be found in Mexico around 2500 B.C. (Sorenson, *Ancient,* 297–98). In time the evidence will vindicate the claims of the Book of Mormon.

A noted Book of Mormon scholar, John Sorenson, working on the model of Mesoamerica as the primary geographical location for much of the Book of Mormon, has postulated that part of the puzzle may be the terminology used in the Book of Mormon. Tracing the development of terminology for animals through the ages he noted, the "terminology the Nephite volume uses to discuss animals follows a different logic than the scheme familiar to most of us whose ancestors came out of western Europe" (Sorenson, *Ancient,* 289). For instance, Sorenson pointed out, several early Mesoamerican figures show individuals riding deer and postulates that the deer may have served as a "sort of 'horse' for riding" (*Ancient,* 295–6). The Jaredite term "elephant" seems to square well with the terms "mastodon" and "mammoth" (Sorenson, *Ancient,* 297–98). And the terms "flocks and herds" usually applied to sheep and goats in the ancient Near East can easily be equated with deer and pigs that were commonly used for food in Mesoamerica. Sorenson created the accompanying table to present tentative possible identifications between Book of Mormon and Mesoamerican animals that are attested in Book of Mormon times (*Ancient,* 299).

Sorenson concluded that "considering all we now know about animal use in Mesoamerican cultures, it is fair to state that most of what the Book of Mormon says about animals is plausible. Some of the book's statements remain hard to square with present knowledge, but the picture is considerably more acceptable to scientists than a few years ago" (*Ancient,* 292).

See also Agriculture in the Book of Mormon; Archaeology.

BIBLIOGRAPHY

Sorenson, John L. *An Ancient American Setting for the Book of Mormon.* Salt Lake City and Provo: Deseret Book and FARMS, 1985.

———. "Digging into the Book of Mormon." *Ensign* 14 (October 1984): 19–20.

Welch, John W., ed. *Reexploring the Book of Mormon.* Salt Lake City and Provo: Deseret Book and FARMS, 1992.

BMH

Anoint To place oil, usually olive oil, on the head or other prominent part of a person or building. The Hebrew term *mashiach* (Messiah) and the Greek term *christos* (Christ) derive from the verb "to anoint" in their respective languages.

Among both Nephites and Jaredites, anointing was practiced when enthroning kings (e.g., Jacob 1:9; Ether 6:22).

Anointing is also mentioned in a passage from Isaiah that prophesies the future gathering of the Israelites and their protection. As Isaiah spoke of the Lord's punishing the Assyrians and other oppressors of Israel, he used words that might have foreshadowed the work of the MESSIAH, literally the "anointed one": "The yoke [of Assyria] shall be destroyed because of the anointing" (2 Ne. 20:27 // Isa. 10:27). In this passage the phrase "because of the anointing" literally translates from the Hebrew as "because of oil," suggesting anointing.

ANTHON TRANSCRIPT

In biblical accounts, anointing was a part of the ceremony of divine investiture for prophets (e.g., 1 Kgs. 19:16), priests (e.g., Ex. 28:41), kings (e.g., 1 Sam. 15:1), and sanctuaries (Ex. 30:22–29). In addition, it was an element in certain blessings (Ps. 23:5; James 5:14).

Anciently, the olive tree was the source of oil for anointing and other dietary and medicinal purposes in the Mediterranean area (Judg. 9:8–9; Zech. 4:1–3, 11–14). The source of oil among Book of Mormon peoples for such functions, if oil was used, remains unknown.

BIBLIOGRAPHY

Szikszai, Stephen. "Anoint." *Interpreter's Dictionary of the Bible.* Edited by George Arthur Buttrick. New York: Abingdon, 1962. 1:138–39.

SKB

Anthon transcript A piece of paper containing "reformed Egyptian" characters copied from the plates from which the Book of Mormon was translated, which transcription Martin Harris took to New York and showed to Professor Charles Anthon and others.

One significant and controversial event to occur during the translation of the Book of Mormon was the visit of Martin Harris to Charles Anthon in New York City in February 1828. Charles Anthon (1797–1867) was a professor of classical studies and literature at Columbia College from 1820 until his death and was a distinguished scholar of Greek and Latin. Although Anthon and other contemporaries wrote conflicting accounts describing the conversation between Anthon and Harris, Latter-day Saints assert that the actions of Martin Harris support his basic renditions of that event. A document preserved by members of the Reorganized Church of Jesus Christ of Latter Day Saints (now Community of Christ), called the Anthon transcript, probably the original or a copy of the document which Martin Harris requested Charles Anthon and other scholars to evaluate, also supports Harris's accounts.

On several occasions, Joseph Smith wrote or dictated accounts of the Martin Harris trip to New York and his meeting with Charles Anthon. Except for incidents in which he participated, these accounts were based on information he had learned from Martin Harris himself. According to Joseph Smith, "the Lord appeared" to Martin Harris in a vision and showed him the remarkable work that was about to come forth (Smith, *Papers*, 9). Immediately following this vision, Harris traveled to Joseph Smith's home in Harmony, Pennsylvania, and advised Joseph that the Lord had shown him that he must go to New York City with some of the "characters" (Smith, *Papers*, 9). Subsequently, Joseph Smith copied characters from the Book of Mormon plates and provided Martin Harris with a translation of

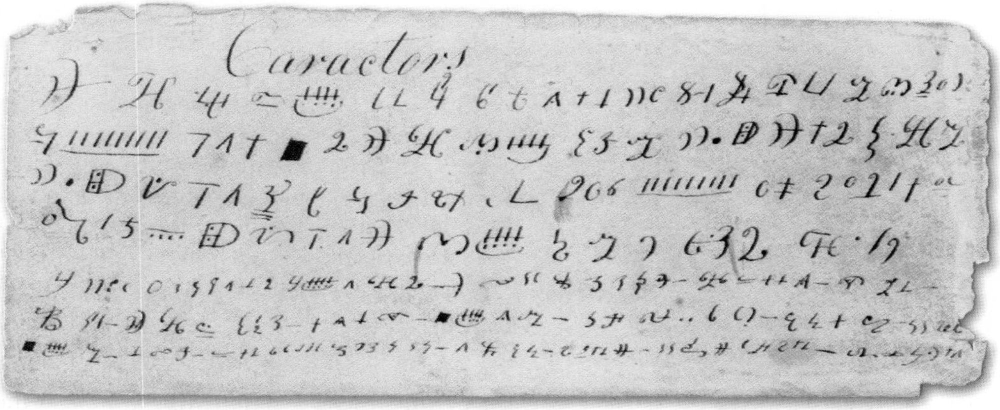

The Anthon transcript; courtesy CCA. Traditionally thought to be the piece of paper containing the translated Book of Mormon characters taken by Martin Harris to New York City to show Professor Charles Anthon and Dr. Samuel Mitchill.

ANTHON TRANSCRIPT

those characters (Smith, *History,* 1:20; Smith, *Papers,* 9, 285). Martin Harris then traveled to New York City and showed the characters and translation to Professor Anthon, "a gentleman celebrated for his literary attainments."

According to Martin Harris, Professor Anthon stated that the characters appeared to be genuine Egyptian, Chaldaic, Assyriac, and Arabic. During this meeting, Anthon gave Martin Harris a certificate specifying that the paper contained true characters and that the translation was apparently correct. After Anthon learned from Martin Harris about the coming forth of the Book of Mormon by divine means and that a portion of the plates was sealed and not to be translated, he promptly asked to reexamine the certificate. Anthon then tore the certificate to pieces and said, as predicted by Isaiah, "I cannot read a sealed book" (Smith, *Papers,* 9, 285–86; Isa. 29:11; Smith, *History,* 1:20; cf. JS–H 1:63–65).

Charles Anthon (1797–1867); courtesy LDS Family and Church History Archives.

Samuel Latham Mitchill (1764–1831); courtesy VRL.

Martin Harris further reported that during his visit to New York City, he showed the characters to another scholar, "Dr. Mitchel," Samuel Latham Mitchill, who had studied classics, received medical and scientific training, was a professor of natural history, chemistry, and agriculture at Columbia, and had served as a vice-president of Rutgers Medical College. He was recognized as a "living encyclopedia." Mitchill, Martin Harris reported, sanctioned what Professor Anthon said respecting both the characters and the translation (Kimball, 333–34; Smith, *Papers,* 286–87; see Smith, *History,* 1:20 n, regarding variations in the reports of the sequence of events in Martin Harris's visits to Anthon and Mitchill).

Charles Anthon wrote two letters published by critics in which he denied some of the claims of Martin Harris. The first letter, written in 1834, was included in E. D. Howe's *Mormonism Unvailed* (1834). The second letter, written to T. W. Coit, dated April 3, 1841, appeared in John A. Clark's *Gleanings by the Way* (1842). After writing in 1834 that he lost "no time in making a reply" to his evaluation of the "Mormonite inscription," he wrote in 1841 that "no one, until the present time, has ever requested from me a statement in writing" (233). In 1834 Anthon declared that he declined giving an opinion of the characters in writing. In 1841 Anthon contradicted himself by writing that after being requested to give an opinion in writing, "without any hesitation," he prepared a document stating that marks on the paper contained "merely an imitation of various alphabetical characters" that had no meaning.

Although there are contradictions in the two letters written by Anthon, there is a general harmony regarding a description of the characters he examined. In both letters Anthon stated that a "farmer" or "countryman" showed him various alphabetic characters arranged in

ANTHON TRANSCRIPT

columns. He described these characters as an unusual medley of Greek, Hebrew, and Roman letters decked with strange marks, the whole becoming a rude representation of the Mexican "zodiac" or "calendar" stone. In his letter to E. D. Howe in 1834 he denied that he pronounced the characters as "reformed Egyptian hieroglyphics." In these letters Anthon did not comment on the reliability of the translation of the characters he examined. In fact, in 1834, he suggested that the young man who was deciphering the characters with "spectacles" had not brought forth a translation—another basic claim of Anthon that does not harmonize with the ensuing actions of Martin Harris (such as serving as scribe for Joseph Smith and supporting financially the publication of the Book of Mormon). In 1834 Anthon stated that he warned the "farmer" that he was involved in a scheme designed to cheat him. In 1841 Anthon wrote that the "countryman" left convinced that this hoax was designed to defraud him of his property and indicated that he would not "embark in the speculation of printing the golden book" (Howe, 270–72; Clark, 233–38; these letters are reproduced in Backman, 215–23, in parallel columns to aid readers in identifying their similarities and differences; Kirkham, 414–22).

Many contemporaries bore witness that Martin Harris returned from New York City convinced that Joseph's testimony regarding the coming forth of the Book of Mormon was reliable (Anderson, 6, 108). In 1831, before joining the Restored Church, William W. Phelps wrote that Harris was known as an honest and sincere farmer who maintained a strong testimony of Joseph Smith's divine calling. Following his trip to New York, Phelps added, Harris informed others that Anthon declared the characters to be "ancient short-hand Egyptian" (Howe, 273).

According to an account published in the Hillsborough *Gazette* (Ohio), 29 October 1831, written by reporter James Gordon Bennett, Martin Harris was a "maiden convert" who raised the money needed to print the Book of Mormon. According to Bennett, before the publication of that work, Harris traveled to New York City with manuscripts and showed the characters on these papers to a "Doctor Mitchell," who compared them with hieroglyphics discovered by Champollion in Egypt and determined that the characters were from a "language of a people" who formerly existed in the East (qtd. in Kirkham, 169–70).

Writings of the Episcopal minister of Palmyra, Reverend John A. Clark, also support some of the basic claims of Martin Harris. Reverend John A. Clark recalled that before Martin Harris went to New York City he showed him a transcript that contained "three or four lines of characters." After returning from his consultation with Professor Anthon, Clark added that Harris again met with him. Clark reported that Martin Harris had become "a perfect believer" and "had no more doubt of Smith's commission." He also confirmed that Harris became a scribe for Joseph Smith and later mortgaged his farm to pay for the publication of the Book of Mormon (Clark, 228–29; Kirkham, 161–62, 168; Backman, 209–13; Kimball, 342–46).

The Anthon transcript provides further evidence to support the testimony of Martin Harris that Joseph Smith had a record containing genuine ancient characters. In his *Address to All Believers in Christ* (1887), David Whitmer declared that he had in his possession "the original paper containing some of the characters transcribed from one of the golden plates, which paper Martin Harris took to Professor Anthon, of New York" (Whitmer, 11). This manuscript was given to the Reorganized Church of Jesus Christ of Latter Day Saints by heirs of David Whitmer fifteen years after Whitmer's death. Although this manuscript does not include a translation of the text, it appears to be a copy of characters taken from the Book of Mormon plates.

A comparison of the seven lines of characters from the Anthon transcript with known "reformed" or hieratic and demotic Egyptian shows a remarkable parallel. Although this transcript is undoubtedly not an exact reproduction of characters on the Book of Mormon record (for only a most skilled scribe could copy all details of complex characters) and much of the Book of Mormon was written in a "reformed Egyptian" (Morm. 9:32), nearly all the characters on that document are remarkably similar to recognizable Egyptian cursive characters. There is also a similarity in form of these characters and Chaldaic, Assyriac, and Arabic forms of writing. Consequently, the Anthon transcript supports the thesis that scholars who had in their libraries preliminary data on Egyptian script, such as Anthon and Mitchill, could have recognized that the characters shown to them by Martin Harris appeared as ancient Egyptian script, or "shorthand" Egyptian (Crowley, 76–78; see also FARMS "Martin Harris' Visit with Charles Anthon").

Although the characters on the Anthon transcript appear as genuine ancient script, they probably were not copied from a few lines or from one page of the metal plates. Scholars have not provided a translation of the characters on that transcript that resemble a portion of the Book of Mormon text. If the Anthon transcript is what it is said to be, then Joseph Smith probably gave Martin Harris samples of characters recorded on the Book of Mormon plates and a translation of individual rather than a combination of characters.

Since Anthon examined a document that contained characters similar to ancient script, he may have initially assumed that because the characters appeared genuine, the translation might be correct. Scholars in the United States, however, had a very limited understanding of Egyptian in 1828. After the discovery of the Rosetta Stone (1799), scholars in Europe began to publish texts providing some information on the translation of Egyptian script. Dictionaries and grammars, however, were in an initial stage of development. Even though Charles Anthon and Samuel L. Mitchill could not read Egyptian in 1828, they were undoubtedly aware that scholars in Europe were making good progress in the understanding of that language (Crowley, 58–60, 125; Kimball, 331–32). Anthon was apparently interested in obtaining a copy of an ancient record, desired to be involved in its translation, and probably did not want to admit his limitations.

Various historical records support the thesis that Charles Anthon informed Martin Harris that the characters which he examined resembled ancient script and admitted that he could not read a sealed book. Meanwhile, the publication of the Book of Mormon fulfills Isaiah's prophecy that while the learned would fail to read the "words of a book," the "book" would be given to one unlearned, resulting in a marvelous work and wonder (Isa. 29:11–14).

See also Book of Mormon, translation of.

BIBLIOGRAPHY

Anderson, Richard Lloyd. *Investigating the Book of Mormon Witnesses*. Salt Lake City: Deseret Book, 1981.

Backman, Milton V. Jr. *Eyewitness Accounts of the Restoration*. Salt Lake City: Deseret Book, 1986.

Clark, John A. *Gleanings by the Way*. Philadelphia: W. J. & J. K. Simon, 1842.

Crowley, Ariel L. "The Anthon Transcript." *Improvement Era* 45 (January-March 1942): 14–15, 58–60, 76–80, 124–25, 150–51, 182–83; and 47 (September 1944): 542–43, 576–83.

FARMS Staff. "Martin Harris' Visit with Charles Anthon: Collected Documents on the Anthon Transcript and Shorthand Egyptian." Provo, Utah: FARMS, 1990.

Howe, E. D. *Mormonism Unvailed*. Painesville: E. D. Howe, 1834.

Kimball, Stanley B. "The Anthon Transcript: People, Primary Sources, and Problems." *BYU Studies* 10:3 (1970): 325–52.

Kirkham, F. W. *A New Witness for Christ in America*. Vol. 1. Provo: Utah Printing Co., 1967.

Smith, Joseph. *History of The Church of Jesus Christ of Latter-day Saints*. Edited by B. H. Roberts. 2d ed. rev. 7 vols. Salt Lake City: The Church of Jesus Christ of Latter-day Saints, 1932–51.

———. *The Papers of Joseph Smith*. Vol. 1, *Autobiographical and Historical Writings*. Edited by Dean C. Jessee. Salt Lake City: Deseret Book, 1989.

Whitmer, David. *An Address to All Believers in Christ*. Richmond, Mo.: David Whitmer, 1887.

MVB

Anti-Christ A group or individual who seeks to lead people away from Christ by denying Christ (e.g., Jacob 7:2; Alma 30:6, 12; Alma 31:16, 29), or offering an alternative to Christ and his plan of salvation (e.g., Jacob 7:7; Alma 1:4; 15:15; 30:16–17). Antichrists in the Book of Mormon include three prominent individuals: Sherem (Jacob 7:1–23), Nehor (Alma 1:2–16), and Korihor (Alma 30:6–30), as well as several groups of people, such as the Ammonihahites, the Amalekites and Amulonites, and the Zoramites[2]. Typically, flattery, false logic, and deception are employed to deny Christ (Jacob 7:2, 4). Sherem and Korihor argued that there could be no Christ because no one could know the future in which a Christ would come (Jacob 7:7, 9; Alma 30:13, 15). Korihor taught that there is no need for a redeeming Christ because there is no such thing as sin or an afterlife (Alma 30:17–18). Nehor's doctrine negated personal accountability because God intended to save all men (Alma 1:4). Korihor ridiculed belief in Christ as a foolish tradition and a sign of mental instability (Alma 30:13, 14, 16, 23). Sherem taught that prophets who teach of Christ pervert the truth (Jacob 7:7), and Korihor added that they did so to take advantage of the people (Alma 30:27–28, 31). Nehor's anti-Christ teachings were accepted by the Ammonihahites (Alma 15:15), as well as by the Amalekites and Amulonites (Alma 24:28–29). The Zoramites likewise accepted anti-Christ doctrines, professing that "there shall be no Christ" and that belief in Christ was a "foolish" tradition (Alma 31:16–17, 29).

Anti-Christs attempted to deceive not only the people in general but even prophets and men of great faith (Jacob 7:5; Alma 1:7; 30:30). When unsuccessful at dissuading the prophets, Korihor and Sherem demanded a sign to prove Christ; Nehor resorted to violence. Before their deaths, both Korihor and Sherem confessed their deceptions and claimed that they had themselves been deceived by Satan (Jacob 7:18; Alma 30:53).

TBB

Anti-Nephi-Lehi The name given to the brother of king Lamoni (Alma 24:3). The name is perhaps a throne name taken by Lamoni's brother when he became leader of the ANTI-NEPHI-LEHIES (cf., e.g., Jacob 1:11). When Ammon[2] and his missionary companions saw the Lamanite preparations to destroy their new Lamanite converts, the Anti-Nephi-Lehies, they traveled to the land of Ishmael to hold a council with Lamoni and Anti-Nephi-Lehi to determine how they might defend themselves (Alma 24:5). The name "Anti" of "Anti-Nephi-Lehi" may be a reflex of the Egyptian *nty* "he of, the one of." Thus, rather than having the sense "against," it has the meaning "the one of Nephi and Lehi."

SDR

Anti-Nephi-Lehies Anti-Nephi-Lehies, or people of Ammon[2] (Ammonites), is the name given to the thousands of Lamanites from seven Lamanite lands and cities (Alma 23:8–13) who were converted to the Lord through the efforts of Ammon, the son of Mosiah[2], and his fellow missionaries. The Anti-Nephi-Lehies were utterly firm in their testimony and afterward "never did fall away" from the truth (Alma 23:6). Their conversion was a source of bitter irritation to the apostate Amalekites and Amulonites, who in turn provoked the unconverted Lamanites to rebellion against the Anti-Nephi-Lehies and their king. The latter had himself been converted to the Lord and had renamed his son and successor Anti-Nephi-Lehi (Alma 24:1–5). The Anti-Nephi-Lehies, however, refused to "take up arms against their brethren; nay, they would not even make any preparations for war" (Alma 24:6). The Lamanites—in concert with renegade Amalekites and Amulonites—attacked and killed 1,005 of the Anti-Nephi-Lehies (Alma 24:22). So affected were the Lamanites by the willingness of their brethren, the Anti-Nephi-Lehies, to die rather than to take up arms to defend themselves, that many of them, "more than the number who had been slain," were converted to the Lord (Alma 24:26).

The troubles of the Anti-Nephi-Lehies, however, were still not at an end. They were obliged to leave their homes in Lamanite lands and move to Jershon, a territory protected by the Nephites. They offered to become the slaves of the Nephites, but the Nephites refused (Alma 27:4–9). Although their sacred pledge prevented the Anti-Nephi-Lehies (whom the Nephites called the people of Ammon) from standing with their protectors in battle, they provided substantial support to the Nephite armies (Alma 27:21–26). In the war between the Lamanites and Nephites near the end of the book of Alma, the Anti-Nephi-Lehies would have broken their oath in order to assist the Nephites against the Lamanites had not Helaman[2] dissuaded them (Alma 56:6–9). He instead accepted service from their sons, who had not taken the oath to lay down their arms. Together they formed a defensive force. These "sons of Helaman," as they were called, fought bravely in numerous conflicts with the Lamanites, and although many were wounded, none died from their wounds.

See Anti-Nephi-Lehi for a discussion of the origin of their name, meaning "those of Nephi and Lehi," which they took upon themselves after their conversion (Alma 23:17).

See also Stripling warriors.

SDR

Antiomno Lamanite king in the land of Middoni and a friend of king Lamoni (Alma 20:4; ca. 90 B.C.). After Ammon[2] was instructed by the Lord that his brethren were imprisoned in Middoni, both Ammon and Lamoni journeyed to Middoni to deliver them. King Lamoni proposed to use his friendship with king Antiomno as means to persuade him to release the prisoners (Alma 20:2–7, 28–30).

Antion *See* Nephite weights and measures.

Antionah A chief ruler in Ammonihah (ca. 82 B.C.) who, in his questioning of Alma[2], implied that Alma's teachings contradicted scripture (Alma 12:20–21). Antionah questioned the possibility of immortality because God had placed cherubim before the tree of life to prevent Adam and Eve from living forever.

Antionum Nephite military leader killed with his ten thousand troops in the last battle between the Nephites and Lamanites (Morm. 6:14; A.D. 385).

See also Cumorah, battle of.

Antionum, land of Land east of Zarahemla, "which lay nearly bordering upon the seashore, which was south of the land of Jershon, which also bordered upon the wilderness south, which wilderness was full of the Lamanites" (Alma 31:3). Here Alma[2] and his brethren preached the gospel to the Zoramites[2] (Alma 31–34; ca. 74 B.C.). Those who believed were expelled and took refuge in Jershon, while the remainder united with the Lamanites and began plans for war against Jershon and the Nephites (Alma 35:6, 10–11). The Lamanite-Zoramite coalition had intended to mount an invasion from Antionum into Jershon but changed plans when they saw the innovative preparations of the army of Moroni[1] (Alma 43:15, 18–22).

Antiparah, city of Nephite city taken by the Lamanites and garrisoned with their strongest army (Alma 56:13–14, 34; ca. 64 B.C.). Helaman[2] and 2,000 stripling Ammonite youth decoyed the Lamanite troops from the city and, together with the forces of Antipas, defeated them (Alma 56:31–54). When the Nephites prepared to go against Antiparah itself, the remaining Lamanites fled (Alma 57:3–4).

Antipas, mount The mount upon which deserting Lamanites who refused to go to war against the Nephites gathered to resist efforts to "compel them to arms" (Alma 47:3; ca. 72 B.C.). The traitorous Amalickiah met with the rebellious Lamanite leader Lehonti in the night at the foot of the mount. There, pretending alliance with Lehonti, he agreed to surrender his army to Lehonti as part of his plan to take over the Lamanite kingdom (Alma 47:8–19).

Antipus Nephite army officer (ca. 66 B.C.) whom Moroni[1] appointed to command the Nephite forces in a portion of Nephite lands including the city of Judea. His men suffered many losses to the Lamanites until joined by Helaman[2] and his 2,000 stripling warriors. Because of these reinforcements, Ammoron ordered the Lamanites not to attack the city (Alma 56:9–18).

Later Antipus and Helaman enacted a successful strategy to trap the Lamanites outside of their stronghold in Antiparah. The armies of Antipus and Helaman defeated the Lamanites, but in the course of the battle Antipus, wearied from "the speed of [his] march" in pursuit of the Lamanites, lost his life (Alma 56:21–57).

BAV

Antum, land of Nephite land where the hill Shim was located. It was to this hill that Ammaron instructed Mormon to go to obtain the plates of Nephi in order to engrave the history of his people (Morm. 1:2–4). The land of Antum was near the city Jashon (Morm. 2:17).

Apostasy "An abandoning of what one has believed in" (*Webster's*). Although the word *apostasy* is not used in the text, the Book of Mormon has much to say about the nature, causes, and effects of apostasy. Indeed, the stories of two of its great civilizations, the Jaredites and the Nephites, end in massive, and fatal, national apostasies.

The nature of apostasy

The Book of Mormon teaches that apostasy occurs in at least two ways: (1) Drifting or falling away; losing one's zeal for or commitment to the gospel; losing one's way (1 Ne. 8:23), often in almost imperceptible degrees. The phrase "dwindle in unbelief" is used to represent such a process (2 Ne. 1:10; 26:15, 17, 19; Alma 50:22; 4 Ne. 1:34; Morm. 9:20). (2) Knowingly and openly rebelling. Indeed, those who sin knowingly, "in open rebellion," are especially condemned (Mosiah 2:36–39; Jacob 6:8–10; Mosiah 3:12; 15:26–27; Hel. 7:24; 3 Ne. 6:18; Morm. 1:16), and are frequently the most bitter of apostates, far more so than those whose apostasy stems from backsliding parents or inherited false traditions (Alma 24:30; 43:6–8; 47:36; 60:32).

Causes of apostasy

A primary cause of apostasy is simply giving in to the tendencies of one's carnal nature: "Because of the fall our natures have become evil continually" (Ether 3:2); "carnal, sensual, and devilish" (Alma 42:10); "without God in the world" (Alma 41:11); and even "an enemy to God" (Mosiah 3:19). Thus to dwindle in unbelief or rebel against God is a "natural" tendency of fallen man and requires constant and careful monitoring (Mosiah 4:30; Alma 34:39; 3 Ne. 18:15, 18). The seeds of faith must be continually nourished if they are to survive and if apostasy of either kind is to be avoided (Alma 32:28, 38–40).

Common factors repeatedly spoken of in the Book of Mormon that lure people into apostasy include (1) pride and the quest for status (1 Ne. 11:34–36; 22:23; 2 Ne. 24:12–14; 26:20, 29; Alma 1:6, 16, 22–24; 31:15–29; Hel. 3:1, 33–36; 7:21, 26; Morm. 8:28, 36); (2) an exaggerated trust in human learning or wisdom (2 Ne. 9:28–29, 42–43; 26:20; 28:4, 15, 26; 3 Ne. 6:12–16); and (3) material wealth/prosperity and ease (1 Ne. 13:7–8; 2 Ne. 9:30, 42; Alma 4:6–12; 5:53–55; 11:24; Hel. 3:36; 4:12; 6:16–17; 12:2; 3 Ne. 6:10–16; 4 Ne. 1:24–26; Morm. 8:37–40).

Effects or consequences of apostasy

Unrighteousness deadens one to the influence of the Spirit, making it very difficult to respond to the messages of the prophets (1 Ne. 1:4–6, 13, 19–20; 15:3; 2 Ne. 27:1, 5; 32:4–7; Ether 11:7, 13, 22). Because of their sins, the wicked frequently find the preaching of the gospel almost unendurably painful (1 Ne. 16:2; Mosiah 13:7–8), so they create false religions with which they can feel more comfortable (1 Ne. 13:4–9, 26–29, 32, 34; 2 Ne. 28:8–9; Alma 1:2–6; 30:17–18, 53). In some instances, wickedness leads the Lord to withdraw his warning prophets and his Spirit from among the people (3 Ne. 16:10; Morm. 1:13–14, 16–17; 8:10; Ether 4:3; 11:13; 13:13). Those who fail to understand through sheer unwillingness (2 Ne. 32:4, 7–8) or because they cannot muster even enough faith to "experiment upon [the] words" (Alma 32:27, 33, 36) withhold from themselves the blessings of heaven, including the gifts of the Spirit (Alma 12:9–11; 13:4; Morm. 9:7–8, 20; Ether 12:12, 35; Moro. 7:37–38; 10:24). This isolation from the Spirit can put them into a terrible downward spiral, as their incomprehension allows them to drift into wickedness, which, in turn, makes it even harder for them to understand (Alma 33:20).

The Book of Mormon speaks too of those who, infuriated at the word of God, persecute those who preach it or live it (2 Ne. 28:20, 28; 33:5; Mosiah 26:38; 27:1, 32; Alma 8:13; 14:7, 14–25; Hel. 10:15; 14:10). In some cases, people become so filled with anger and hate that they seek to murder the prophets and those who follow them (1 Ne. 2:1, 13; 17:44; Mosiah 17:3, 11–13; 24:11; Alma 1:7–9, 12, 25; 14:2–4, 8; 3 Ne. 1:9; 4 Ne. 1:30–34; Ether 13:22; Moro. 1:1–2). Indeed, it was such wickedness that motivated the people of Jerusalem to reject and crucify their God (1 Ne. 19:9, 13–14; 2 Ne. 10:3, 5).

See also Dissenters.

BIBLIOGRAPHY

Webster's New World Dictionary. 3d ed. New York: Simon and Schuster, 1988.

DCP

Apostles, the Twelve Modern revelation designates apostles as "special witnesses of the name of Christ in all the world" (D&C 107:23). Jesus called the Twelve Apostles during his mortal ministry in the Holy Land. Both Lehi[1] and Nephi[1] had visions of the Savior and his apostles as they "went forth upon the face of the earth" (1 Ne. 1:9–11; 11:29). The Book of Mormon teaches that the Twelve would testify of Christ (1 Ne. 13:24), that by their "hand" a book containing the "fulness of the gospel" would go forth to the Gentiles (1 Ne. 13:24–26), and that after the death of Jesus Christ they would be persecuted by their own people of the house of Israel (1 Ne. 11:34–36). Moreover, the Twelve would have the responsibility of judging the twelve tribes of Israel, as well as the twelve Nephite disciples, whom Jesus called during his ministry in America (1 Ne. 12:9; Morm. 3:18–19).

The Book of Mormon also reveals important information regarding a specific member of the Twelve Apostles, John the Beloved, who was commissioned to write about the end of the world (1 Ne. 14:19–23) and who desired to remain upon the earth to continue his apostolic ministry and bring souls unto Christ (3 Ne. 28:6–10).

See also Disciples, twelve Nephite; John the Beloved/Revelator; Records of the Twelve Apostles.

RH

Apparel, costly *See* Costly apparel.

Appease To SATISFY, reconcile, placate, or propitiate. Alma[2] taught his son Corianton that the plan of mercy, made operative through the atonement of Christ, can appease or satisfy the demands or requirements of God's justice through repentance. In this way God is both just and merciful (Alma 42:15, 22–24; cf. Alma 34:15–16; 2 Ne. 2:5–7; 1 Jn. 2:2).

See also Justice, law of; Law, answer the ends of.

DLL

Archaeology Archaeology studies material remains left by past civilizations and peoples. Since the publication of the Book of Mormon in 1830, Latter-day Saint scholars have realized the value of archaeology for substantiating the record's claims. If definitive physical evidence of Book of Mormon events can be recovered in the New World, then it should be possible to identify the locations of some Book of Mormon lands and cities and to determine the identities of Book of Mormon peoples (i.e., their current archaeological labels as New World peoples and cultures). Being able to place Book of Mormon events in a real-world setting and environment might then lead to an increased understanding of the sacred text.

For the archaeologist, the task of finding convincing confirmatory physical evidence for the authenticity of scriptural accounts such as the Bible or the Book of Mormon is formidable. Recovery of evidence to support any ancient account depends upon three fortuitous circumstances: (1) the chance preservation of materials in corrosive climates (e.g., cloth does not preserve well in the tropics); (2) the actual discovery of any such preserved but rare evidence—the classic needle-in-a-haystack problem (e.g., imagine trying to find a solitary artifact in an ancient ruin 20 feet deep and 5,000 acres in extent); and (3) the ability to recognize and interpret correctly the evidence for what it once was—the classic motel-of-mysteries syndrome (where it is imagined that a future archaeologist would misinterpret modern bathroom fixtures as royal regalia and ceremonial objects). This third difficulty is common in biblical archaeology. For example, it is a well-known fact that many biblical scholars deny that king David was an historic individual; he and his deeds are relegated by many to the realm of ancient folklore. Further, skeptical scholars have found no convincing evidence that Jerusalem was an important capital during the tenth century B.C. or that Israel was a united kingdom of the dimensions claimed in the Bible. Recently, this controversy appeared resolved with the discovery of the Tel Dan Stela (a carved stone monument) which carries an inscription from this time period mentioning the "house of David." But scholars are currently arguing over the translation of the inscription, the meaning of the translation, and the possibility that the stone monument is a modern forgery. Thus, while some now find the archaeological evidence for king David compelling, others find reason to doubt it. Comparable debates continue over the historicity of other biblical people, such as the Patriarchs, and such biblical events as the Exodus and the conquest of Canaan (Shanks, 32–52).

Similar controversies exist among researchers seeking to interpret evidence with potential ties to the Book of Mormon. For example, STELA 5, known as the "Lehi Stone" in LDS circles, is considered by many as the single best New World artifact attesting to the historicity of the Book of Mormon account. This carved stone slab from southern Mexico dates to about 200 B.C. to 300 B.C. and portrays a complicated scene of humans and supernatural beings seated or standing around a magnificent fruit tree. Some Book of Mormon researchers associate the stela with Lehi[1]'s vision of the tree of life. Others believe that although the tree may represent a tree of life, the interpretation of the other images remains an open and difficult question. The latter argue that since no written inscription accompanies the carved scene, positive interpretation is impossible. Similar difficulties hamper efforts to prove the presence in the New World of other items or ANIMALS mentioned in the Book of Mormon, such as horses, elephants, silk, iron, steel, and gold plates.

Most debates about archaeological evidence concern specific items and forget that massive clues may be as important as minute ones. For example, the best current case for the Book of Mormon is the overall configuration of geographical, historical, and cultural evidence. Based upon clues in the text and modern GEOGRAPHY and archaeological findings, researchers have proposed a number of different locations for Book of Mormon lands and peoples, locations that range from New York to northern South America, and many places in between. The strongest case to date has been made for Middle America (Palmer; Sorenson, *Ancient;* Washburn). The physical geography of southern Mexico and Guatemala, including the relative locations of mountains, hills, rivers, plains, the best farm land, waste lands, oceans, and so forth, have been shown to match reasonably well with the Book of Mormon narrative (Sorenson, *Ancient*).

Similarly, many of the cultural elements, practices, metaphors, and allusions in the latter part of the Book of Mormon appear to be Mesoamerican. These include such things as writing and record keeping, cannibalism, large-scale warfare, human sacrifice, conquest of cities by capturing the central "tower" or pyramid (Moro. 9:7), combat weaponry, cotton armor (Alma 49:6), metaphors for the countenance of god in statuary (Alma 5), representations of trees growing out of human hearts (Alma 32), a directional system of four quarters, pagan beliefs of gods inhabiting an underworld (Alma 18:31), and many other items (see Sorenson, *Images*). Moreover, the chronology of the rise and fall of civilized peoples, the relative locations of these civilizations, and the extreme fluctuations in populations recorded in the Book of Mormon correspond reasonably well with those reconstructed archaeologically in the last thirty years for Middle America (Sorenson, *Ancient*).

Perhaps much of the difficulty in trying to find physical evidence that validates the Book of Mormon or the Bible lies in the very impossibility of gauging the heavens by earthly standards, of using mundane objects to validate spiritual truths. It is well to remember that no amount of historical verification of biblical details could ever provide sufficient logical grounds for believing in Jesus Christ. Earthly logic should simply surrender in such confrontations. The holy grail or Christ's burial shroud could never suffice to prove his existence or divine Sonship. Such conclusions are precluded by the naturalistic assumptions of science that guide archaeological research. At best, physical evidence of the Bible's historic claims can strengthen the faith of the believer, but it cannot be the initial or primary basis for his or her belief. This must come from another source. The same is true of the Book of Mormon. Initial and continuing faith and testimony come from prayerful study of its spiritual message.

In this light, the existence of the Book of Mormon is the most convincing proof of its own authenticity. For open-minded inquirers, the materiality of the book and the remarkable consistency of its narrative are sufficient grounds for taking the book seriously and considering its truthfulness. But the ultimate question of truthfulness is a spiritual one requiring faith in the possibility of a spiritual answer from a divine source. Sincere inquirers, Latter-day Saints or otherwise, need to test the promise of the prophet Moroni[2] and read the book, ponder, and pray. There is no adequate, secular shortcut to the difficult process of personal revelation. Believers who put stock in physical evidences confuse the real basis of their belief. Testimony from the earth follows that from the heavens. This principle was well summarized by President Gordon B. Hinckley: "The evidence for [the Book of Mormon's] truth, for its validity in a world that is prone to demand evidence, lies not in archaeology or anthropology, though these may be helpful to some. It lies not in word research or historical analysis, though these may be confirmatory. The evidence for its truth and validity lies within the covers of the book itself. The test of its truth lies in reading it" (52).

See also Transoceanic crossings, pre-Columbian.

BIBLIOGRAPHY

Hinckley, Gordon B. "The Cornerstone of Our Faith." *Ensign* 14 (November 1984): 50–53.

Palmer, David A. *In Search of Cumorah*. Bountiful, Utah: Horizon Publishers, 1981.

Shanks, Hershel. "Biblical Minimalists Meet Their Challengers Face to Face." *Bible Review* 8 (June 1997): 32–52.

Sorenson, John L. *An Ancient Mesoamerican Setting for the Book of Mormon*. Salt Lake City: Deseret Book, 1985.

———. *Images of Ancient America: Visualizing Book of Mormon Life*. Provo, Utah: FARMS Research Press, 1998.

Washburn, J. Nile. *Book of Mormon Lands and Times*. Bountiful, Utah: Horizon Publishers, 1974.

JC

Archeantus A Nephite who along with other "choice men" lost his life in an intense battle with the Lamanites in the latter part of the fourth century A.D. (Moro. 9:2). Mormon's singling out Archeantus in his epistle to Moroni[2], along with Luram and Emron by name, may have indicated his military importance to the Nephites, personal friendship, or both.

Aright *See* Appendix C.

Armor A specialized type of military equipment designed to protect the body from wounds. Armor has been widely used throughout history in most regions of the world. The Book of Mormon uses eight terms for armor: breastplates, shields, armor, head-plates, arm-shields, animal skins, thick clothing, and bucklers (a type of a shield). A comparison of the descriptions of armor in the Book of Mormon with pre-Columbian archaeological evidence indicates that most armor was made of animal skins, cloth, wood, or stone. The only reference to metal armor in the Book of Mormon is to a Jaredite breastplate (Mosiah 8:10), which may roughly correspond to iron mirror-like breastplates known to have been used by the Olmecs. The Book of Mormon states that non-Nephite peoples had inferior types of armor until the first century B.C. (Alma 3:5; 43:19–37), when they seem to have begun to adopt Nephite-style armor (Alma 49:6). The standard system of armor described in the Book of Mormon consisted of a basic cloak or vest of thick fabric or animal skin, a breastplate, a headplate, and a shield, which broadly corresponds with artistic and archaeological evidence of pre-Columbian armor from Mesoamerica. Book of Mormon armor also differs from the biblical descriptions of armor. Although coats of mail or scale (small overlapping pieces of metal sewn onto a leather jacket), greaves (leg armor), and helmets are conspicuous in biblical accounts of warfare (1 Sam. 17:5–6), they are absent from the Book of Mormon. Likewise, scale or mail armor and greaves are not found in early classic artistic and archaeological records in the New World.

See also Fortifications; Warfare in the Book of Mormon; Weapons.

BIBLIOGRAPHY

Hamblin, William J. "Armor in the Book of Mormon." *Warfare in the Book of Mormon*. Edited by Stephen D. Ricks and William J. Hamblin. Salt Lake City: Deseret Book, 1990.

WJH

Arms of safety A metaphor for salvation in Christ that is found in scripture only in Alma 34:16. When the guilty exercise faith unto repentance, the suffering of Christ satisfies the demands of justice in their case, and the mercy of Christ "encircles them in the arms of safety." The outstretched arms are, of course, those of Jesus himself (Morm. 5:11; 6:17), who stands always ready to cleanse and embrace the repentant. They are also referred to as "the arms of mercy" (Mosiah 16:12; Alma 5:33) and "the arms of [Christ's] love" (2 Ne. 1:15; D&C 6:20).

SER

Article of Faith 8. *See* Book of Mormon, and Article of Faith 8.

Articles of Faith, Book of Mormon references pertaining to Book of Mormon references that relate to doctrines in the Articles of Faith are shown in the accompanying table.

CJW

BOOK OF MORMON REFERENCES PERTAINING TO ARTICLES OF FAITH

ARTICLE OF FAITH	KEY CONCEPTS	B OF M REFERENCES
1. We believe in God, the Eternal Father, and in His Son, Jesus Christ, and in the Holy Ghost.	• The Godhead	• 2 Ne. 31:12–13; Alma 11:44; 3 Ne. 11:31–32, 35–36; Morm. 7:7; Ether 5:4; Moro. 4:3; 5:2
	• God the Eternal Father	• Mosiah 2:34; 3 Ne. 9:15; 12:45, 48; 26:2; 28:10–11
	• Son Jesus Christ	• 1 Ne. 10:17; 11:21; 2 Ne. 25:12–13; Alma 5:48; 9:26
	• Holy Ghost	• 1 Ne. 12:18; 3 Ne. 19:13, 20–22; 29:6; Moro. 10:4–5
2. We believe that men will be punished for their own sins, and not for Adam's transgression.	• Punished for own sins	• 1 Ne. 15:32–36; 2 Ne. 9:45–46; 10:23; 28:23; Mosiah 2:32–33; Alma 3:26–27; 12:14; 41:3–4; Hel. 14:15–19
	• Adam's transgression	• 2 Ne. 2:25–26; Mosiah 3:11; Morm. 9:12
3. We believe that through the Atonement of Christ, all mankind may be saved, by obedience to the laws and ordinances of the Gospel.	• Atonement	• 2 Ne. 2:6–9; 9:7–10; Jacob 4:11–12; Mosiah 3:7–18; 4:2, 6–7; 13:28; Alma 21:9; 34:8–14; 36:16–21; 42:7–15; 3 Ne. 11:10–11
	• Obedience to gospel laws and ordinances	• 1 Ne. 22:31; 2 Ne. 31:7, 10; Mosiah 4:6–7; 5:8; Alma 37:35; 3 Ne. 11:33; Ether 4:18

continued

continued

ARTICLE OF FAITH	KEY CONCEPTS	B OF M REFERENCES
4. We believe that the first principles and ordinances of the Gospel are: first, Faith in the Lord Jesus Christ; second, Repentance; third, Baptism by immersion for the remission of sins; fourth, Laying on of hands for the gift of the Holy Ghost.	• Faith in Jesus Christ • Repentance • Baptism by immersion • Gift of the Holy Ghost	• 1 Ne. 7:12; 2 Ne. 9:23; Enos 1:8; Alma 32:21–43; Ether 12:6–22 • 1 Ne. 10:18; Mosiah 3:21; Alma 9:12; 34:31–35; Hel. 12:23; 3 Ne. 9:22; 27:16; Moro. 6:2; 8:25 • 2 Ne. 31:5, 11–12; Mosiah 18:14; 3 Ne. 11:23–27; Moro. 6:1–4 • 2 Ne. 31:12; Alma 9:21; 3 Ne. 18:36–37; 19:9; Moro. 2:2
5. We believe that a man must be called of God, by prophecy, and by the laying on of hands by those who are in authority, to preach the Gospel and administer in the ordinances thereof.	• Called of God • Laying on of hands / Authority	• 2 Ne. 6:2; Mosiah 23:10; Alma 6:8; 8:4; 18:34; Hel. 11:18; 3 Ne. 19:4 • Mosiah 18:12–13; 21:33; 23:16–17; Alma 5:3; 6:1; 3 Ne. 11:21–25; 12:1; Moro. 2:1–3; 3
6. We believe in the same organization that existed in the Primitive Church, namely, apostles, prophets, pastors, teachers, evangelists, and so forth.	• Church organization	• 2 Ne. 5:26; Jarom 1:11; Mosiah 23:16–17; 25:18–24; 26:6, 22; Alma 4:7; Morm. 9:18; Ether 12:41; Moro. 2; 3; 6
7. We believe in the gift of tongues, prophecy, revelation, visions, healing, interpretation of tongues, and so forth.	• Gifts of the Spirit	• Omni 1:25; Alma 9:21; 17:3; 3 Ne. 29:6; Morm. 9:7–10, 24; Moro. 10:9–17
8. We believe the Bible to be the word of God as far as it is translated correctly; we also believe the Book of Mormon to be the word of God.	• Bible • Book of Mormon	• 1 Ne. 13:20–26, 40–41; 2 Ne. 29:12–13; Morm. 7:8–9 • 1 Ne. 13:34–36, 39–41; 2 Ne. 3:12, 19–23; 26:16–17; 27; 29; Morm. 7:8–9
9. We believe all that God has revealed, all that He does now reveal, and we believe that He will yet reveal many great and important things pertaining to the Kingdom of God.	• All God has revealed • Does now reveal • Will yet reveal	• 1 Ne. 3:19–20; Jacob 4:8 • 2 Ne. 5:5–6; Jacob 1:5–6; Hel. 11:23 • 2 Ne. 27:11; 30:17; Alma 5:44; 26:22; Morm. 9:7–9
10. We believe in the literal gathering of Israel and in the restoration of the Ten Tribes; that Zion (the New Jerusalem) will be built upon the American continent; that Christ will reign personally upon the earth; and, that the earth will be renewed and receive its paradisiacal glory.	• Gathering of Israel • Zion built in America • Christ reigns personally • Earth's paradisiacal glory	• 1 Ne. 19:15–16; 22:3–12; 2 Ne. 29:14; 30:7; Jacob 5; 3 Ne. 5:24–26; 20:11–41; 21:26–29 • 3 Ne. 20:22; 21:23–25; Ether 13:4–8 • 1 Ne. 22:24; 2 Ne. 12:11–21; 3 Ne. 20:22; 21:25 • 2 Ne. 14:3–4; 21:6–9; 30:12–18; Ether 13:9

ARTICLE OF FAITH	KEY CONCEPTS	B OF M REFERENCES
11. We claim the privilege of worshiping Almighty God according to the dictates of our own conscience, and allow all men the same privilege, let them worship how, where, or what they may.	• Freedom to worship	• Mosiah 27:2–4; Alma 1:21; 21:22; 30:11; 50:39; 51:6; 3 Ne. 21:4
12. We believe in being subject to kings, presidents, rulers, and magistrates, in obeying, honoring, and sustaining the law.	• Subject to government leaders • Obeying and honoring the law	• Mosiah 2:11, 30–31; 6:3–7; 29:1–6, 11–13, 44; Alma 1:14 • Mosiah 29:15, 25–26; Alma 62:10; 3 Ne. 6:4
13. We believe in being honest, true, chaste, benevolent, virtuous, and in doing good to all men; indeed, we may say that we follow the admonition of Paul—We believe all things, we hope all things, we have endured many things, and hope to be able to endure all things. If there is anything virtuous, lovely, or of good report or praiseworthy, we seek after these things.	• Honest, true, chaste . . . • Believe, hope, endure • Seek after virtuous, lovely, and good things	• Jacob 2:28; Mosiah 2:17–18; 3:19; Alma 34:27–29; 3 Ne. 12 • 2 Ne. 31:15–16, 20; Omni 1:25; Ether 12:4, 32; Moro. 7:41, 45 • Omni 1:25; Alma 37:34; 41:13–15; Ether 4:11–12; Moro. 7:13–28

Artificer *See* Appendix C.

Assyria A country located on the Tigris River in what is now northern Iraq. Assyria is mentioned in the Isaiah passages quoted in the Book of Mormon (e.g., 2 Ne. 17:17, 20). The history of Assyria covers approximately two millennia (mid-third to mid-first millennia B.C.), but it was in the Neo-Assyrian period, the mid-ninth through late seventh centuries B.C., that it became the largest empire in the ancient Near East (Middle East) to that time (Bible Map 5). During this period the Assyrians had a major effect on Israelite history. *Ashur* (sometimes spelled *Assur* or *Ashshur*) was the original form of the name *Assyria* and was the name of the land, the chief god, and the first capital city of the Assyrians. Nineveh, already an ancient city by the time of Jonah's visit in the eighth century, did not become the Assyrian capital until 701 B.C. Neo-Assyrian administrative and military capabilities were highly developed and unrivaled in their day. The Assyrians often deported members of the upper classes of conquered peoples to other portions of their empire in order to dissipate rebellious energies.

The Bible notes that the second son of Shem was named "Asshur" (Gen. 10:22), although nothing more is known of him nor of any explicit connection with the historical Assyrians. The Assyrians, whose language and culture was Semitic, are mentioned many times in the Bible, especially in 2 Kings and Isaiah. The first nonbiblical attestation of an Israelite king occurs in the annals of king Shalmaneser III (859–824 B.C.), who claims to have suppressed an anti-Assyrian coalition led by the Aramean nations of Damascus and Hamath that included Ahab, king of Israel, in 853. Although the encounter is not recorded in the Bible, Assyrian sources indicate that Ahab contributed 2,000 chariots and 10,000 infantry to the coalition (Pritchard, 279). This action began more than two centuries of interaction between the Assyrians and the Israelites, in which the nations of Israel and later JUDAH were often tribute-paying vassals to the Assyrians. Two events that had a major influence on Israelites deserve mention: (1) Hoshea, the last king of Israel (732–722 B.C.), rebelled against the Assyrian Empire, for which the Assyrians attacked Israel and besieged its capital, Samaria, for three years (2 Kgs. 17:5; 18:9). The Assyrian conquest of Israel by Shalmaneser V in 722 was followed by the accession of a new Assyrian king, Sargon II (722–705 B.C.), who claimed to have deported 27, 290 Israelites in 721 B.C. (Pritchard, 285; no number of deportees is given in the Bible). These people became popularly known as the "lost ten tribes" (2 Kgs. 17:6, 23; 18:11; cf. 1 Ne. 22:3–4). The nation of Israel was subdivided and converted into provinces of the Assyrian Empire. (2) Two decades later, in 701 B.C., Sennacherib (705– 681 B.C.) became the first Assyrian king to attack Judah,

ASSYRIAN EMPIRE AT THE TIME OF ISAIAH

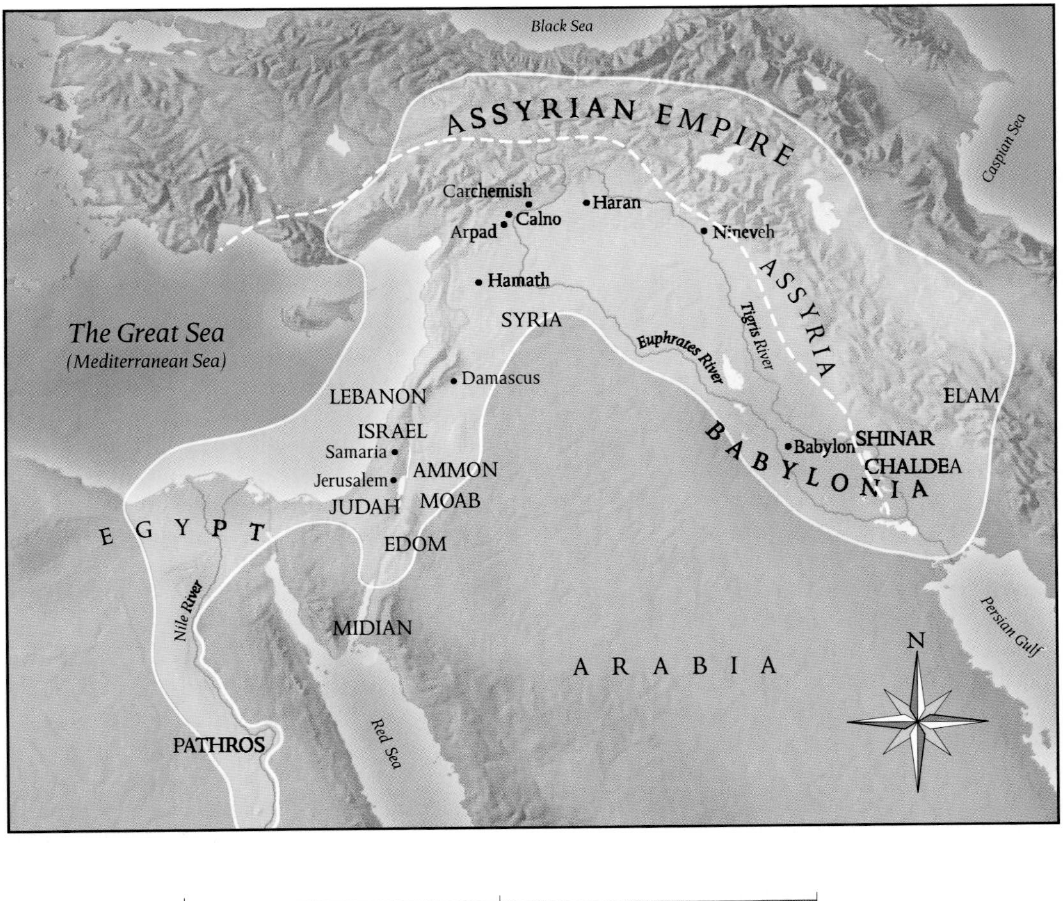

including besieging Jerusalem. The Bible recounts Hezekiah's and Isaiah's faith in Jehovah and Jerusalem's miraculous deliverance (2 Kgs. 18:13–19:37 // Isa. 36–37). While Jerusalem was spared, the Assyrians destroyed dozens of other cities in Judah and claimed to have deported thousands of Judahites. Judah became a vassal of the Assyrians for about six decades. Some other references to Assyrian interaction with Israelites include 2 Kings 15:19–20, 29–30; Isaiah 7–8 // 2 Nephi 17–18; 2 Kings 16:7–10 (see also Assyrian inscriptions that refer to Israelite kings in Pritchard, 276–305). The mighty Assyrian Empire had run its course by 640 B.C. The final disintegration occurred quickly, with Nineveh falling to the Medes and Babylonians in 612 B.C. The last Assyrian resistance was suppressed in Haran in 609 B.C. Assyria was annexed into the Neo-Babylonian Empire, and Babylonia became the dominant power in the Near East a short time before Lehi's prophetic call ca. 600 B.C.

Not surprisingly, all eleven references to "Assyria" and "Assyrian" in the Book of Mormon occur in the Isaiah passages that Nephi[1] included in 2 Nephi. In one of these, Isaiah prophesied to Ahaz, king of Judah (735–715 B.C.), that Assyria would crush an anti-Assyrian coalition in which Damascus and Israel were participating (2 Ne. 18:4 // Isa. 8:4). In several other passages, Isaiah clearly indicated that "the Lord shall bring upon [Judah] . . . the king of Assyria," as a consequence of too many Israelites breaking their covenants (2 Ne. 17:17 // Isa. 7:17; 2 Ne. 17:20 // Isa. 7:20; 2 Ne. 18:6–8 // Isa. 8:6–8). Isaiah also prophesied that in their ignorant pride the Assyrians would neither recognize nor appreciate that Jehovah, not their god Assur, allowed them success in their conquests. Thus, their season of power would pass (2 Ne. 20:12 // Isa. 10:12; 2 Ne. 20:24–26 // Isa. 10:24–26). In a prophecy concerning the latter-day gathering of Israel, Isaiah indicated that, "the Lord shall set his hand again the second time to recover the remnant of his people, which shall be left, from Assyria, and from Egypt, and from Pathros," and so on (2 Ne. 21:11 // Isa. 11:11). Isaiah naturally used the names of the countries and regions of his day to designate the areas and directions from which future Israelites would be gathered.

See also Babylon, Babylonia; Chronology, Bible; Isaiah chapter reviews (2 Ne. 17 // Isa. 7; 2 Ne. 18 // Isa. 8; 2 Ne. 20 // Isa. 10); Israel, historical background of; Israel, kingdom of; Israel, lost tribes of; Israel, scattering of; Second time.

BIBLIOGRAPHY

Pritchard, James B., ed. *Ancient Near Eastern Texts.* 3d ed. Princeton: Princeton University Press, 1969.

DMP

Astronomy The study of objects and matter outside of the earth's atmosphere, such as the sun, the moon, and the stars. Passages from the Book of Mormon suggest that the Nephites had some understanding of astronomy and how objects in the solar system moved. For example, they apparently had a more accurate understanding of the nature of the earth's movement than did their Greek contemporaries who at that time predominantly believed in a stationary earth. Alma[2], testifying to Korihor about the existence of God, explained, "Yea, and all things denote there is a God; yea even the earth . . . and its motion, yea, and also all the planets which move in their regular form do witness that there is a Supreme Creator" (Alma 30:44). Likewise, Mormon, testifying of God's omnipotence, declared, "And thus, according to his word the earth goeth back, and it appeareth unto man that the sun standeth still; yea, and behold, this is so; for surely it is the earth that moveth and not the sun" (Hel. 12:15).

In addition, the Book of Mormon prophets recorded astronomical events associated with the birth and the death of Christ. Samuel the Lamanite prophesied that at Christ's birth there would be a night of no darkness, and also that a new star would appear (Hel. 14:3–6). In 3 Nephi 1:15–21 a description of the fulfillment of these prophecies is given. Interestingly, in both accounts the sentence order and wording imply that the new star was *not* the cause of there being no darkness that night. The event is very difficult for astronomers to explain by any natural phenomena, and no account of any comparable incident is given by any New Testament writer nor by any other contemporary historical record from the eastern hemisphere. This apparently was a remarkable sign given in the Nephite regions of the world only, though the new star could perhaps be the same observed by the wise men in the New Testament account (Matt. 2:1–2).

Samuel the Lamanite also prophesied that at Christ's death there would be a three-day period of darkness. Third Nephi 8:19–23 gives an account of the fulfillment of this prophecy. Though it is stated that the sun, moon, and stars were not visible during that time (3 Ne. 8:22), it is likely the event was more the result of things occurring on the earth than in the heavens. Perhaps the darkness resulted from the catastrophes on the land that accompanied Christ's death, such as earthquakes, upheavals, tempests, whirlwinds, and fires (3 Ne. 8:5–18), all of which could have created great quantities of light-obscuring dust and smoke. No comparable event is found in the New Testament record, suggesting that the three days of darkness was another remarkable and unique sign to the Book of Mormon people.

In addition to references to literal astronomical matters (events, objects, principles), there are also some figurative or metaphorical references. For example, in a vision Lehi[1] saw Christ, whose "luster was above that of the sun at noon-day," and his disciples, whose "brightness did exceed that of the stars" (1 Ne. 1:9–10). Mormon described the Nephites as being "swept off by [the Lamanites] even as a dew before the sun" (Morm. 4:18).

HKH

Asunder *See* Appendix C.

Atonement, the The supreme accomplishment of Jesus Christ in setting "at one" those who had been estranged, making possible a reconciliation of man and God. The Atonement required the Redeemer's complete sinlessness, the shedding of his blood, excruciating spiritual and bodily pain, and his physical death.

The Atonement provides a just recompense for broken law in consequence of Adam's transgression and also of mankind's individual sins, which have subjected the human family to spiritual and physical death without the capacity to free themselves. The demands of eternal justice are so exacting that fallen, finite mortals have not the ability to make the payment. Without INTERCESSION, every human being would be consigned to permanent dissolution of the physical body, and every human spirit would become a devil, forever miserable.

Because only a god could work out the needed infinite atonement, the God of Israel, who is Jesus Christ, took upon himself flesh and blood through birth to a mortal mother on this earth in order that he would be in a condition to pay the price of man's redemption. Yet, being literally the Only Begotten Son of God in the flesh, Jesus also received "power . . . from the Father" (Hel. 5:11) to do what mortal man could not do.

The effects of the Atonement are two-fold: (1) unconditional rescue of all mankind from the spiritual and physical deaths inherited through the fall of Adam (this means that every person will be resurrected from the dead and be restored to the presence of God for judgment; Alma 42:23); (2) redemption from personal sins only on conditions of individual repentance.

Christ's atonement permits MERCY to be accorded to man without offending justice, and thus man is delivered from what otherwise would have been a totally devastating and everlastingly miserable condition during and after mortal life.

The atonement of Jesus Christ is the focus of all the prophets in the Book of Mormon. Man's absolute dependence upon the Atonement is especially well-defined, along with the solemn declaration that only Christ could provide it. The Atonement was neither a simple nor a single act. Its accomplishment was multidimensional, and every requirement had to be firmly in place. Neither is the Atonement an abstract philosophical exercise; it is functional in the lives of people, planned and prepared from the foundation of the world, and is the very center and core of God's great plan of redemption.

All mankind is fallen

Many prophets spoke of the two kinds of death that resulted from the fall of Adam. For example, Alma[2] taught that "our first parents were cut off both temporally and spiritually from

ATONEMENT

the presence of the Lord; . . . the fall had brought upon all mankind a spiritual death as well as a temporal" (Alma 42:7, 9). Samuel the Lamanite spoke the same doctrine: "All mankind, by the fall of Adam being cut off from the presence of the Lord, are considered as dead, both as to things temporal and to things spiritual" (Hel. 14:16; cf. 2 Ne. 9:6–7; Alma 12:23– 24).

Man is unable to save himself

That fallen, mortal mankind does not have the capacity to save itself is emphatically declared by Book of Mormon prophets. Nephi[1]: "My soul delighteth in proving unto my people that save Christ should come all men must perish" (2 Ne. 11:6). Aaron[3]: "Since man had fallen he could not merit anything of himself" (Alma 22:14). Abinadi: "Thus all mankind were lost; and behold, they would have been endlessly lost were it not that God redeemed his people from their lost and fallen state" (Mosiah 16:4; cf. 1 Ne. 10:6; Mosiah 15:19; Alma 12:22; 34:9, 15).

Jesus was without sin

That Jesus was holy, totally obedient "unto the Father . . . in keeping his commandments" (2 Ne. 31:7), and that he "yieldeth not to the temptation" (Mosiah 15:5), and thus was sinless, is categorically stated by several prophets and implied by all of them (2 Ne. 2:3; Mosiah 3:7; 14:9; Alma 7:11–12; Heb. 4:15; 1 Pet. 1:19; 2:21–24). The Redeemer of others must be without sin himself.

Jesus is God

Jesus Christ is more than mortal. His status is defined by the prophets as God who partook of flesh and blood, literally the Son of God according to the mortal flesh. He was God before he came to earth and while he was on earth. Nephi[1]: "The very God of Israel . . . the God of Abraham, and of Isaac, and the God of Jacob" will come to earth and be "crucified" and "be buried in a sepulchre" (1 Ne. 19:7, 10). King Benjamin (citing the words of an angel): "The Lord Omnipotent . . . shall come down from heaven among the children of men, and shall dwell in a tabernacle of clay. . . . And he shall be called Jesus Christ, the Son of God, . . . and his mother shall be called Mary. . . . [Yet the world] shall consider him a man . . . and shall crucify him" (Mosiah 3:5–9). Abinadi (as cited by Limhi): "God should come down among the children of men, and take upon him flesh and blood" (Mosiah 7:27; cf. 13:28, 34). Also, the Lord showed the brother of Jared[1] that he (the Lord) would take upon himself flesh and blood (Ether 3:9).

Jesus received special power from the Father

That Jesus was the Only Begotten Son of God in the flesh (meaning biologically) is evident in many passages, expressly stated by an angel to Nephi (1 Ne. 11:13–21) and affirmed by Alma (Alma 9:26). Because Jesus in his flesh is the direct offspring of the Father, he had "power given unto him from the Father" (Hel. 5:11; John 5:26; 10:18) to make the infinite Atonement. Amulek expressed the absolute insistence that Christ be more than a mortal man: "For it is expedient that there should be a great and last sacrifice; yea, not a sacrifice of man, neither of beast, neither of any manner of fowl; for it shall not be a human sacrifice; but it must be an infinite and eternal sacrifice. Now there is not any man that can sacrifice his own blood which will atone for the sins of another . . . therefore there can be nothing which is short of an infinite atonement which will suffice for the sins of the world" (Alma 34:10–12).

The Atonement would have been incomplete without the shedding of Jesus' blood (Mosiah 3:15; Alma 5:21; 21:9; 24:13; 34:9–12; 3 Ne. 18:11; Moro. 5:1–2; Heb. 9:22). But the shedding of his blood was not confined to his crucifixion. Benjamin explained that Jesus' "blood cometh from every pore" because of "his anguish for the wickedness and the abominations of his people" (Mosiah 3:7). This denotes severe spiritual pain, leading to the conclusion that Jesus suffered more from his struggles in Gethsemane than from the cruel nails of the cross (Luke 22:42–44; D&C 19:16–19).

Jesus made intercession for all men

Jesus literally took upon himself the transgressions and sins, even the sicknesses of the people. Abinadi: "God breaketh the bands of death, . . . giving the Son power to make intercession for the children of men" (Mosiah 15:8). Abinadi cited the entire text of Isaiah 53 as descriptive of Christ's intercession (Mosiah 14). Amulek: Christ "shall take upon him the transgressions of those who believe on his name" (Alma 11:40; 34:8; 2 Ne. 9:21). Alma rejoiced in the knowledge that the most important of all events was the coming of the Redeemer, who would be the Son of God, who would "take upon him the pains and the sicknesses of his people" (Alma 7:7–11). Jesus himself said, "I have come unto the world to bring redemption unto the world, to save the world from sin. Therefore, whoso repenteth . . . for such I have laid down my life, and have taken it up again" (3 Ne. 9:21–22). He later stated, "I have drunk out of that bitter cup which the Father hath given me, and have glorified the Father in taking upon me the sins of the world" (3 Ne. 11:11).

Little children are saved by the Atonement

The Book of Mormon leaves no doubt about the status of little children. They are saved by the atonement of Christ. If there had been no atonement, children could not be saved, even though they are sinless, because they (as all mankind) have inherited spiritual and physical death through the fall of Adam (Mosiah 3:11, 16, 19). Jacob[2] explained with precision that because all mankind are subject to the Fall, were it not for the atonement of Christ, bodies would die, decay, and never return from mother earth, and spirits would become devils, forever miserable (2 Ne. 9:6–10). Nevertheless, there is an atonement, and therefore the status of those who die as little children is glorious: They are saved. Mormon exclaimed that "little children are whole, for they are not capable of committing sin; wherefore the curse of Adam is taken from them in [Christ] . . . and also all they that are without the law. For the power of redemption cometh on all them that have no law" (Moro. 8:8, 22; cf. Mosiah 3:18; 15:24–25). As Mormon indicated, the Atonement provides not only for little children but for those who are not little children and for those who live and die "without the law." Although the Book of Mormon does not explain just how the Atonement provides for those who die without the law, latter-day revelation makes clear that such persons will have the opportunity to hear and receive the law (the GOSPEL) in the postmortal spirit world and enjoy its fruits in the eternities to come (D&C 137:7–10; 138:29–37, 58–59).

Both mercy and justice are attributes of the same God

The Atonement allows the operation of both mercy and justice. Abinadi: The Son of God has "power to make intercession for the children of men . . . standing betwixt them and justice; having . . . taken upon himself their iniquity and their transgressions, having redeemed them, and satisfied the demands of justice" (Mosiah 15:8–9). Amulek: The "infinite and eternal" sacrifice by the Son of God will "bring about the bowels of mercy, which overpowereth justice, and bringeth about means unto men that they may have faith unto repentance. And thus mercy can satisfy the demands of justice, and encircles them in the arms of safety, while he that exercises no faith unto repentance is exposed to the whole law of the demands of justice" (Alma 34:14–16). Alma: "God himself atoneth for the sins of the world, to bring about the plan of mercy, to appease the demands of justice, that God might be a perfect, just God, and a merciful God also" (Alma 42:15).

The Atonement was retroactive

Many blessings related to the Atonement were available even before the Son of God came in the flesh, because of the perfect assurance that he would indeed come at the appointed time and make the necessary sacrifice of his blood and his life. Such things as priesthood (Alma 13:1–16), baptism (Mosiah 18:5–10), visions, revelations, visits of angels, and all the gifts of the Spirit (Alma 9:21), including the remission of sins, were fully operative before Christ came. King Benjamin: "And the Lord God hath sent his holy prophets among all the children of men, to declare these things to every kindred, nation, and tongue, that thereby whosoever should believe that Christ should come, the same might receive remission of their sins, and rejoice with exceedingly great joy, even as though he had already come among them" (Mosiah 3:13; e.g., Enos 1:2–8; Alma 36:16–21). Resurrection from the dead, however, was reserved until after Jesus rose from the dead (2 Ne. 2:8).

The Atonement reaches every creature

The Book of Mormon does not discuss the Atonement as it relates to animals, yet a connection might be drawn from 2 Nephi 2:22–26 and Mosiah 27:30. The subject is mentioned in other scriptural texts and prophetic commentary, inferring positive benefits of the Atonement for all forms of life (D&C 29:23–25; 77:1–3; Rev. 5:8–9, 13; Smith, 289–94).

Christ's atonement is the only way

The Atonement is unique. There is no optional plan, no other Redeemer, nor could there be, for it was planned from "the foundation of the world" (Mosiah 4:6–7; Ether 3:14). Benjamin: "There shall be no other name given nor any other way nor means whereby salvation can come unto the children of men, only in and through the name of Christ, the Lord Omnipotent" (Mosiah 3:17). "Neither are there any conditions whereby man can be saved except the conditions which I have told you" (Mosiah 4:8). Helaman[3]: "There is no other way nor means whereby man can be saved, only through the atoning blood of Jesus Christ" (Hel. 5:9; cf. Mosiah 5:8; D&C 18:23; Moses 6:52; Acts 4:12).

Praise God

Experiencing even the smallest part of the gift of God available because of the Atonement draws forth spontaneous praise and gratitude. Such persons are "filled with joy, . . . peace of conscience" (Mosiah 4:3), and "hope" (Moro. 7:41). They "sing the song of redeeming love" (Alma 5:26; 26:13) and have a desire to "shout praises unto the Holy One of Israel" (2 Ne. 31:13). Numerous accounts tell of men and women praising God for his marvelous blessings because of his Son (1 Ne. 1:8, 14; 2 Ne. 4:30; 9:8–20; 33:6; Alma 19:29–30; 26:8, 13–22, 35; 33:11; 36:17–22; 3 Ne. 11:17). Such blessings are available to all, for "unto him that has faith unto repentance is brought about the great and eternal plan of redemption" (Alma 34:16).

See also Alive in Christ; Appease; Book of Mormon: Another Testament of Jesus Christ; Children, salvation of little; Fall of Adam and Eve, the; Jesus Christ; Jesus Christ, role of, as Father and Son; Justice, law of; Justification; Reconciled unto Christ; Resurrection, the; Sanctification; Satisfy.

BIBLIOGRAPHY

Smith, Joseph. *Teachings of the Prophet Joseph Smith.* Selected by Joseph Fielding Smith. Salt Lake City: Deseret Book, 1976.

RJM

Awful monster Jacob[2] identified physical death and spiritual death, consequences of the fall of Adam and Eve, as an awful monster to which all mankind would be everlastingly subjected if it were not for Christ's infinite atonement (2 Ne. 9:10, 19; cf. Rev. 20:12–15).

BLT

Wherefore, do the things which I have told you I have seen that your Lord and your Redeemer should do; for, for this cause have they been shown unto me, that ye might know the gate by which ye should enter. For the gate by which ye should enter is repentance and **baptism** by water; and then cometh a remission of your sins by fire and by the Holy Ghost. 2 NEPHI 31:17

Babel, tower of A monumental tower built a few generations after the great flood by people whose pride and false worship prompted the Lord to confound their language and scatter some of them abroad (Gen. 11:1–9). In the Book of Mormon it is called "the tower" or "the great tower" (Ether 1:5, 33; Mosiah 28:17). Several points in the account in Genesis 11 indicate this episode occurred in the region of Mesopotamia (modern Iraq). "Shinar," where the tower was built (Gen. 11:2), is a Hebrew term designating central and southern Mesopotamia (Bible Map 9). The tower was most likely a Mesopotamian stepped temple-tower known as a ziggurat, which consisted of multiple platforms and had a temple on the top as well as one at the bottom. Ziggurats were typically located in major cities and were made of mud bricks; bitumen (KJV, "slime") was often used as mortar (Gen. 11:3). Although their symbolism is not completely understood, the ziggurats focused attention heavenward and are thought to have represented, among other things, a holy mountain, representing the connection between heaven and earth, as true temples are meant to do. The attempt to build "a tower, whose top may reach unto heaven" (Gen. 11:4; cf. Title Page; Hel. 6:28) indicates not that these people were foolishly attempting to climb to heaven but rather that they wanted to build a prominent tower that rose high into the sky (Hebrew *shamayim* means "sky" and "heaven"). Unfortunately, there are no contemporary historical accounts of this episode, and the brevity of the biblical account leaves many questions unanswered. For example, the people involved are never named, nor can a precise date be given. The city in which the tower was being built is generally accepted as Babylon (known to exist by at least 2400 B.C.), based on Genesis 11:9: "Therefore is the name of it called Babel [Hebrew *babel*]; because the Lord did there confound [*balal*] the language of all the earth." *Babel* is the standard Hebrew name for Babylon; the Babylonian word is *bab-ili,* sometimes *bab-ilani,* "gate of the god(s)." Postbiblical Jewish traditions that Nimrod built the tower developed from the note in Genesis that Nimrod founded several cities in Mesopotamia, including Babylon (Gen. 10:9–10). One Babylonian tradition credits the god Marduk with founding and naming the city.

All six references to the tower of Babel in the Book of Mormon occur in relation to the Jaredites, whom the Lord directed to leave the area of the tower and to travel to the Americas (Ether 1:38–43). The tower was mentioned in a Jaredite inscription (Omni 1:22) and in Ether's record of the Jaredite people (Mosiah 28:17). Moroni[2] said that as he edited Ether's record, he dispensed with the portion that dealt with the creation of the earth "even to the great tower" (Ether 1:3) but provided a partial account of what was available "from the tower down until [the Jaredites] were destroyed" (Ether 1:5). Although the Book of Mormon references corroborate the basic account in the Bible, they do not provide any significant additional historical information. One consequence of constructing the tower was that "the Lord confounded the language of the people" (Title Page; Omni 1:22; Mosiah 28:17; Ether 1:33; cf. Gen. 11:7, 9). As one result of this confounding, some "people . . . were scattered abroad upon the face of all the earth" (Mosiah 28:17; Ether 1:33; cf. Gen. 11:8–9). Helaman 6:28 contains the theological observation, not specified in the Bible, that Satan motivated the people to build this tower.

See also Jaredite civilization.

DMP

Babylon, Babylonia Babylonia was a kingdom in southern Mesopotamia (now Iraq) in the Tigris and Euphrates valleys (Bible Map 9). From its capital city, Babylon, it ruled much of the Near East during two time periods particularly important to the scriptures. The Old Babylonian empire, primarily under king Hammurabi (1792–1750 B.C.), was roughly contemporary with Abraham, Isaac, and Jacob[1] and influenced much of the cultural milieu in which they lived. The much-later Neo-Babylonian empire (626–539 B.C.) was the Babylon of the days of the biblical prophets Jeremiah[1], Ezekiel, and Daniel and of the Book of Mormon prophets Lehi[1] and Nephi[1] (Bible Map 6). In Old Testament history it is important as the empire that God used to bring about his judgments against the biblical kingdom of Judah.

The Neo-Babylonian empire rose to international power with the fall of Assyria (ca. 609 B.C.), quickly conquering most of the areas previously controlled by its predecessor. Under the leadership of their king Nebuchadnezzar (605–562 B.C.), the Babylonians overpowered many nations, from which they extorted tribute with the threat of conquest and destruction. Nations that could not or would not pay tribute were subjected to SIEGE and, almost inevitably, conquest and the deportation of many of their citizens, usually to Babylonia.

Lehi and other prophets foretold that Judah and its capital, Jerusalem, would be destroyed by the Babylonians and its people taken captive (e.g., 1 Ne. 1:4, 13; 10:3; Jer. 21:1–10). In 597 B.C. Nebuchadnezzar took Jerusalem and deported part of its population, including the future prophets Ezekiel and Daniel. This was the beginning of what is called the Exile. In 586 B.C. the rebellion of Judah under its last king, Zedekiah, led to a brutal siege and the complete destruction of Jerusalem and Solomon's temple, followed by the deportation of many

BABYLONIAN EMPIRE AT THE TIME OF LEHI

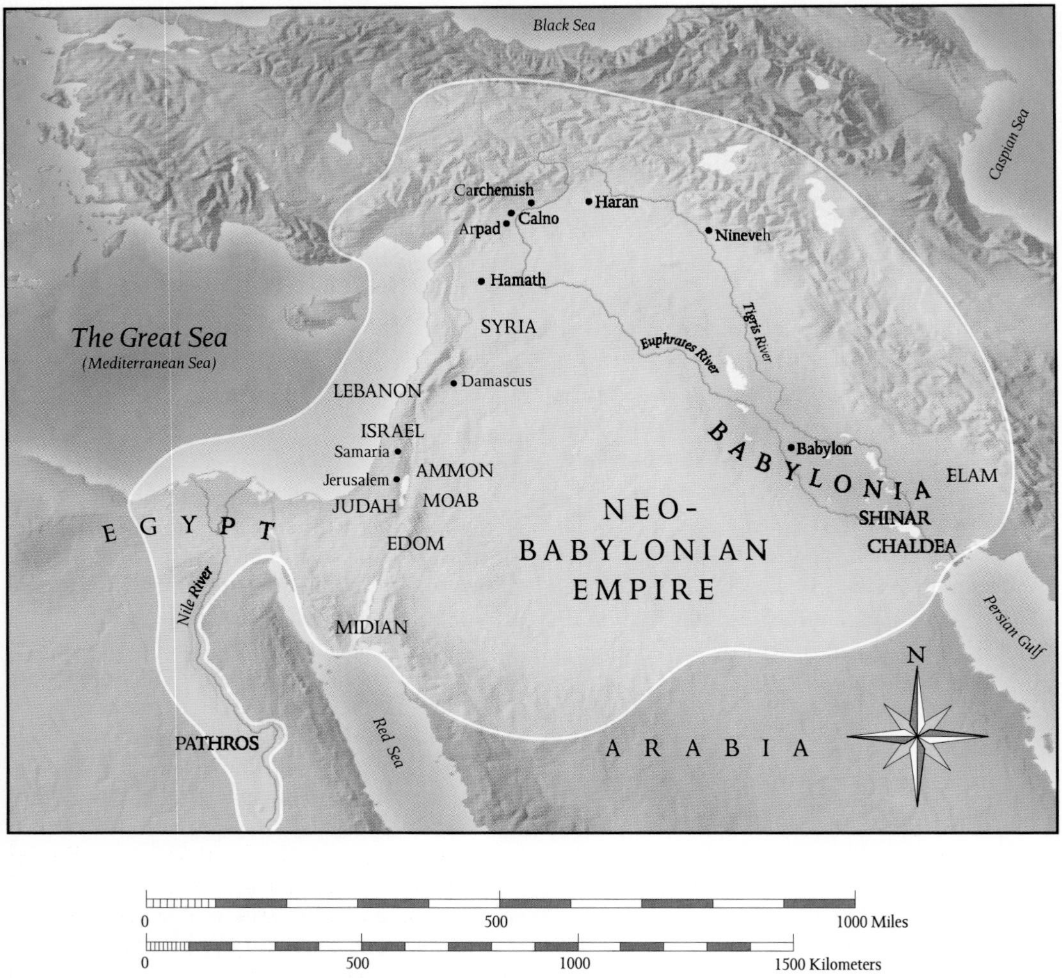

more of Judah's citizens. It was this destruction that Lehi and his family were directed to escape. Some years after his departure, Lehi learned through revelation that the prophecies had been fulfilled (2 Ne. 1:4; cf. 25:10). The Book of Mormon also tells that the people of Zarahemla, the Mulekites, left Jerusalem at the time Zedekiah was taken captive (Omni 1:15).

Most Book of Mormon references to Babylon are in quotations from the writings of Isaiah on the plates of brass. In the prophecies of Lehi's contemporary Jeremiah, the Lord called king Nebuchadnezzar "my servant" because he was raised up to perform God's will against His people (Jer. 25:9; 27:6). Isaiah—like Jeremiah (Jer. 50–51) and Habakkuk, another contemporary of Lehi (Hab. 2:2–12)—prophesied that Babylon would also be subjected eventually to the Lord's judgment as a result of its sins (1 Ne. 20:14; cf. 2 Ne. 25:15).

Because of the wealth, cultural influence, and political power that characterized Babylon in ancient times, its name was sometimes used by biblical prophets to represent the things of the world. In a striking prophecy of Isaiah recorded in 2 Nephi 23–24 (cf. Isa. 13–14), the end of the world and the end of Babylon are used as metaphors for each other. Babylon's demise would come "as a destruction from the Almighty" (2 Ne. 23:6), "cruel both with wrath and fierce anger, to lay the land desolate" (2 Ne. 23:9). The agents of the fall of ancient Babylon were invaders from Persia, who in 539 B.C. conquered Babylon and supplanted its international dominance with their own. Isaiah delivered a bitter taunt against the king of Babylon and his universal counterpart Satan, the ultimate king of Babylon, who at the end of the world would be cast into spirit prison with all the other fallen wicked souls (2 Ne. 24:3–23) while the Lord's people would enjoy millennial rest (2 Ne. 24:1–3, 7).

Isaiah's warning to flee Babylon (1 Ne. 20:20) is thus a call to forsake the things of the world and gather with other Saints to the refuge of Zion (2 Ne. 24:32; cf. 8:11). This message is repeated several times in the latter-day revelations of the Doctrine and Covenants (e.g., 133:7, 14).

See also Babylonian captivity; Chronology, Bible; Isaiah chapter reviews (2 Ne. 23 // Isa. 13).

KPJ

Babylonian captivity The sojourn of the Jews in BABYLON, beginning early in the sixth century B.C. and commonly called the Exile. The Book of Mormon refers to the Babylonian captivity in only a few places. Lehi[1] and Nephi[1] prophesied that after their departure from Jerusalem the city would be destroyed and many of its people would "be carried away captive into Babylon" (1 Ne. 1:13; 10:3; cf. 17:43). Jacob[2] learned by revelation that the prophecy had been fulfilled (2 Ne. 6:8; cf. 25:10). Nephi also prophesied that Babylon would fall and the Jews would return to again "possess the land of Jerusalem" (2 Ne. 25:11). But there they would reject their Savior and eventually be "scattered by other nations" (2 Ne. 25:15). In the last days, after the Jews accept Christ and his gospel, they will be restored again to their promised land (2 Ne. 10:7–8; 3 Ne. 20:30–33).

Following the example of the Assyrians, whose empire his father had helped overthrow, Nebuchadnezzar, king of Babylon (605–562 B.C.), adopted a policy of forcibly relocating conquered peoples, particularly the upper classes. The mass deportations and relocations were probably based on a belief that persons removed from their homelands and struggling to provide for daily needs elsewhere would be easier to control. A sense of national identity would be weakened in a new land, and national gods were frequently viewed as having power only in their home states, being thus unable to help their people in a foreign environment.

The Babylonian exile originated from two mass deportations from the kingdom of Judah. In 597 B.C., Nebuchadnezzar's army invaded the land and forced Jerusalem to surrender. Nebuchadnezzar took into exile the Judahite king Jehoiachin, along with craftsmen, soldiers, aristocrats, and other potential leaders (2 Kgs. 24:10–14). The young future prophets Ezekiel and Daniel were among those taken at that time, and soon they proclaimed the Lord's word among their fellow expatriates (e.g., Ezek. 1:1–3).

Nebuchadnezzar placed Jehoiachin's uncle, Zedekiah, on the throne in Jerusalem. When Zedekiah rebelled and ceased paying tribute to his Babylonian overlord (contrary to the counsel of the prophet Jeremiah[1]; Jer. 38:17–18), Nebuchadnezzar's armies returned for a SIEGE that led in 586 B.C. to the complete destruction of Jerusalem, including Solomon's temple. During the next few years, Nebuchadnezzar took many more Jerusalemites to Babylonia in a second large-scale deportation (2 Kgs. 25:1–17; Jer. 52:27–30).

During the Exile, Babylonia became a spiritual and intellectual capital of Judahite life. In their new environment, the people reinterpreted their religion in light of new realities: exile from their promised land, the demise of their Davidic rulers, worship without a temple, and eventually religion without prophets. Over the next few centuries, Judaism was born, with such distinctive characteristics as rabbis and rabbinical schools, worship in synagogues, and veneration of the law. The term "Jews" in the modern sense is properly used to designate the people of Judah from the point of the Exile onwards.

After conquering Babylon in 539 B.C., king Cyrus of Persia announced to the Babylonian Jews that they could return to their ancestral homeland. Some moved to Judah, now in the Persian empire, but most by then were second- or third-generation citizens of Babylon and chose not to uproot themselves to go to a land that they had never known. Those who did return rebuilt Jerusalem and its temple (Ezra 1–6; Neh. 1–7). By the time of Jesus, Jerusalem with its temple had become the Jews' spiritual capital, but two-thirds of the world population of Jews lived outside the land of Israel, and the center of intellectual life was to a large degree in Mesopotamia. Thousands of Jews still lived in Mesopotamia (now Iraq) into the twentieth century A.D.

See also Chronology, Bible; Israel, historical background of; Israel, scattering of; Jerusalem[1], destruction of, at 586 B.C.; Jews, history of.

KPJ

Bade *See* Appendix C.

Bands of death A phrase referring to the concept that death would hold all people captive forever if Jesus Christ had not triumphed over it through the Atonement and the Resurrection. The Atonement broke the bands of spiritual death, and the Resurrection broke the bands of physical death for all humankind (Alma 11:41–44). Alma[2] applied this expression to his forefathers who had broken the bands of spiritual death through their conversion to Christ (Alma 5:7–10, 13).

CDT

Baptism An essential gospel ordinance for salvation and a commandment of God. Baptism is required of all who desire to come unto Christ, have reached the years of accountability, and are capable of sinning (Ether 4:18; 2 Ne. 31:10–14; 3 Ne. 30:2; Moro. 8:10). Baptism for the remission of sins brings rebirth and is an integral part of the "doctrine of Christ" (2 Ne. 31:17–21; Alma 7:14; 3 Ne. 11:31–38; cf. Moses 6:59–60). It must be preceded by the demonstration of faith in Jesus Christ and repentance, followed by the reception of the Holy Ghost (2 Ne. 31:13, 17; 3 Ne. 27:16, 19–20). Proper baptism is by immersion in water by one who has priesthood authority from God (3 Ne. 11:21–27; Mosiah 18:13–14; 21:33). Nephi[1] taught that repentance and baptism are the gate by which individuals enter the path that leads to eternal life (2 Ne. 31:17). Notwithstanding his perfection, Christ himself was baptized to show humility and obedience to the Father, and thus he set the example for mankind, "fulfil[ing] all righteousness" (2 Ne. 31:5–9; Morm. 7:10).

Baptism is an ordinance by which individuals covenant with God that they are willing to keep his commandments and to take upon themselves the name of Christ. Those desiring baptism must be repentant and worthy (Moro. 6:1–2), demonstrate a willingness "to serve God with all their hearts" (Mosiah 21:35), and have "a determination to serve him to the end" (Moro. 6:3; Mosiah 18:13). Having taken upon themselves the name of Jesus Christ through baptism, they then belong to the church of

A baptism into The Church of Jesus Christ of Latter-day Saints, Nigeria, 1984; courtesy Gladys Stum.

Christ (2 Ne. 31:13; Mosiah 25:18; Moro. 6:4). Like those who gathered with Alma at the Waters of Mormon, they desire "to come into the fold of God, and to be called his people, and are willing to bear one another's burdens, that they may be light; . . . to mourn with those that mourn; . . . and comfort those that stand in need of comfort, and to stand as witnesses of God at all times and in all things, and in all places" (Mosiah 18:8–9).

Baptism was the first principle Jesus Christ, as a resurrected being, taught to Book of Mormon peoples. He gave authority to baptize, taught how baptism must be performed, commanded that there be no disputation concerning baptism, and then declared baptism to be part of the gospel "rock" upon which one must be built to prevail against the "gates of hell" (3 Ne. 11:21–40).

The clarity of teaching concerning baptism in the Book of Mormon restores to the world the knowledge that baptism is an essential ordinance for salvation and that this Christian ordinance was taught and practiced centuries before Christ's earthly ministry (2 Ne. 9:23; Alma 5:62; 15:6–12; Hel. 5:19; 3 Ne. 7:24–25; cf. Moses 6:52, 64–66). This clarity also fulfills an important Book of Mormon purpose, for by restoring truths about baptism, it simultaneously confounds variant false doctrines concerning its practice or neglect (2 Ne. 3:12).

See also Born again; Children, baptism of little; Fulfill all righteousness; Gospel, the.

CJO

Baptism of fire Immersion in the purifying power of the HOLY GHOST, usually following baptism in water (2 Ne. 31:13–14; but see also Hel 5:43–45 and Alma 19:6, where no baptism by water is mentioned). This process cleanses one of sin as if by fire, bringing the remission of sins (3 Ne. 12:2), peace of conscience, and joy (Mosiah 4:3). This baptism is required for entering into the kingdom of God (Moses 6:59–60, 65–66; John 3:5). It is often accompanied by gifts of the Spirit and other spiritual manifestations (Mosiah 5:3). It is associated with being born of the Spirit and receiving the mighty change (Mosiah 5:1–5). Although the baptism of fire can be a subtle and gradual process, several dramatic instances are recorded (e.g., Mosiah 4:2–3; Alma 19:6; Hel. 5:43–45; 3 Ne. 19:13). Jesus promised that "whoso cometh unto me with a broken heart and a contrite spirit, him will I baptize with fire and with the Holy Ghost" (3 Ne. 9:20).

See also Born again.

MCT

Baptism of little children *See* Children, baptism of little.

Barges Vessels used by the Jaredites for transportation over water. The use of barges for travel is mentioned two different times in the book of Ether. First, the Jaredites built barges to cross the various bodies of water they encountered as they moved across the Asian continent to the sea (Ether 2:6). Second, they constructed barges "after the manner of barges which [they had] hitherto built" to cross the ocean (Ether 2:16). These barges were enclosed, watertight, and peaked at each end (Ether 2:16–17). Their design also included a means of supplying fresh air for the passengers (Ether 2:19–20). To provide light for the barges, the brother of Jared[1] asked the Lord to touch and make "shine forth in darkness" sixteen small, "white and clear" stones that he had molten out of a rock (Ether 3:1–4). The Lord complied with the request and in the process revealed himself to the brother of Jared (Ether 3:6–16). These ocean-going barges were said to be "tight" like the ark of Noah[1] (Ether 6:7). Interestingly, the description of these barges matches quite closely the *magur* boat that Utnapishtim (Noah) built in the ancient Babylonian account of the Flood (Nibley, 343–48).

BIBLIOGRAPHY

Nibley, Hugh. *An Approach to the Book of Mormon*. Salt Lake City: Deseret Book, 1988.

MDR

Barren *See* Appendix C.

Baseness *See* Appendix C.

Beam A large weight-bearing piece of wood. Christ taught that before condemning minor sins in others, one should "first cast out the beam in [one's] own eye" (3 Ne. 14:1–5 // Matt. 7:1–5). Instructing a council of high priests and elders, the Prophet Joseph Smith applied Jesus' words when he said that "no man is capable of judging a matter, in council, unless his own heart is pure; and that we frequently are so filled with prejudice, or have a beam in our own eye, that we are not capable of passing right decisions" (Smith, 69).

See also Mote.

BIBLIOGRAPHY

Smith, Joseph. *Teachings of the Prophet Joseph Smith*. Selected by Joseph Fielding Smith. Salt Lake City: Deseret Book, 1976.

GS

Bear(eth) record To testify or witness. The phrase "bear/beareth record" occurs thirty-two times in the Book of Mormon (e.g., 1 Ne. 10:10; 12:7; Hel. 8:14) and seven times in the King James Version of the New Testament, where it is used to translate the Greek word *martureō*, meaning to give evidence, testify, or be a witness (e.g., John 8:14; 2 Cor. 8:3; 1 Jn. 5:7).

CDT

Begotten To have sired or to have produced. The term is used most frequently to describe the unique, divine parentage of Jesus' physical body—the Only Begotten of the Father in the flesh (Alma 5:48). The children of God are "spiritually begotten" of Christ when they covenant to do his will, keep his commandments, and are born of the Spirit (Mosiah 5:5–7).

See also Children of Christ.

TBB

Beguiled *See* Appendix C.

Behooveth *See* Appendix C.

Belief, believe The acceptance of, or trust and confidence in, some idea, doctrine, person, tenet, and so forth. *Belief* is often used synonymously with FAITH, but in the truest sense of the word, *faith* refers to a special kind of belief, for one may believe something that is not true (e.g., Mosiah 10:12–17), but true faith is a "hope for things which are not seen, which are true" (Alma 32:21; cf. 1 Ne. 15:11; Alma 37:40). Alma[2] taught that belief, and especially faith, should not be confused with having a "perfect knowledge" of something, "for if a man knoweth a thing he hath no cause to believe, for he knoweth it" (Alma 32:17–18, 21; cf. Ether 3:19).

In the Book of Mormon, the terms *belief* and *believe* most often refer to acceptance, trust, and confidence in God, his son Jesus Christ, and the true gospel. Prophets taught that possessing such belief is imperative. Nephi[1] testified that "the right way is to believe in Christ and deny him not" (2 Ne. 25:28–29). King Benjamin admonished his people to "believe in God . . . that he created all things. . . . And again, believe that ye must repent of your sins and forsake them" (Mosiah 4:9–10). Alma[2] pleaded with the Zoramites[2] to "believe in the Son of God, that he will come to redeem his people" (Alma 33:22; cf. Omni 1:25–26; Alma 32:22; Morm. 7:5; 9:27). The resurrected Christ himself commanded those gathered at the temple in Bountiful[2] to "believe in me, and . . . repent of your sins" (3 Ne. 12:19; cf. 11:32). Indeed, the Book of Mormon itself was written "for the intent that ye may believe" (Morm. 7:9) and to convince "Jew and Gentile that JESUS is the CHRIST, the ETERNAL GOD" (Title Page).

This belief comes as one desires to know and believe the things of God (Alma 32:27; e.g., 1 Ne. 11:1), petitions God for understanding (e.g., 1 Ne. 2:16), studies the scriptures (e.g., 1 Ne. 19:23; 2 Ne. 25:23; 33:4, 10; Mosiah 1:5; Morm. 3:20–21), and hearkens to the teachings of God's prophets and missionaries (e.g., Jarom 1:11; Mosiah 3:13; 17:2; 18:3–4). Such a humble and searching attitude allows the "Spirit of the Lord" to "change" and "soften" one's heart (Mosiah 5:2; 1 Ne. 2:16) and enables belief to grow and faith to be developed (Alma 32:26–43; Moro. 7:16, 32). Sometimes trials and afflictions, as well as signs and wonders, can foster belief in an individual (e.g., Alma 25:6; Hel. 14:28; 16:3–5), but prophets have taught and illustrated that one is more blessed if one believes "without being compelled to be humble" by hardships (Alma 32:16) or overwhelmed by signs (e.g., Jacob 7:13–16; Alma 30:48–52; cf. 32:17–18).

Belief in Christ and his gospel leads one to faith, repentance, and baptism (e.g., Mosiah 18:3–16; Alma 15:6–12; 23:5–7; Hel. 14:13). Many beautiful blessings follow. The "arm" of the Lord is "extended to all" who so believe and act (Alma 19:36), and they become part of "a delightsome people" (2 Ne. 30:7). God will grant "whatsoever [they] ask that is right, in faith, believing that [they] shall receive" (Mosiah 4:21; cf. Enos 1:15; Alma 22:16; 3 Ne. 18:20; Moro. 7:26), and he will direct them (e.g., Alma 37:40). As they continue to believe, the Lord will "pour out his Spirit upon" them (Hel. 6:36; 3 Ne. 7:21), signs will follow them (Morm. 9:24–25), and "greater things" will be made manifest to them (3 Ne. 26:9; Ether 4:13–15; cf. 1 Ne. 15:11; Ether 3:26). God will be merciful unto them (Alma 32:22), and they will receive the Holy Ghost (3 Ne. 12:2; 19:21). Christ will manifest himself unto them "by the power of the Holy Ghost" (2 Ne. 26:13; cf. 25:14; Ether 3:15) and take their transgressions upon him (Alma 11:40; cf. Hel. 14:13; 3 Ne. 19:28). As they continue to believe and do the will of the Lord, they will "rejoice, and be filled with the love of God, and always retain a remission of [their] sins" (Mosiah 4:9–12). According to the will of God, many will be preserved and protected because of their belief (e.g., 2 Ne. 6:14–15; Alma 57:26), though some may be allowed to suffer in mortality for the same reason (e.g., Mosiah 17:15; Alma 14:7–11; 15:1; 4 Ne. 1:29). Ultimately, all who stay true to their belief in Christ and act accordingly will come forth in the "first resurrection" (Mosiah 15:22) and find that the "gate of heaven is open unto" them (Hel. 3:28; cf. 2 Ne. 9:18), for they will be saved and redeemed through Christ (2 Ne. 2:9; 25:13; Alma 19:13; 26:35; 34:15; Hel. 14:2). Then, as "sons of God" (3 Ne. 9:17; cf. Mosiah 15:11), they will enjoy the blessings of eternal life (Alma 11:40; Hel. 14:8; Ether 3:14).

See also Unbelief.

TBB

Benjamin, king Son of the first Mosiah and second king of the combined Nephite and Mulekite peoples in Zarahemla (ca. 120 B.C.). Benjamin was a great spiritual and political leader, and the aging and childless record keeper, Amaleki[1], entrusted all the records and other sacred materials to his care. Amaleki knew Benjamin "to be a just man before the Lord" (Omni 1:25), and indeed he was. Tireless in serving his people, Benjamin quelled both internal and external contentions, punishing false Christs and false prophets and leading his armies against attacking Lamanites. In concert with the prophets of his day, Benjamin established peace "by laboring with all the might of his body and the faculty of his whole soul" (W of M 1:13–18). Mormon captured the essence of king Benjamin in a few words: he "was a holy man, and he did reign over his people in righteousness" (W of M 1:17).

Benjamin was conscientious in the education of his sons, and he impressed upon them the importance of the records in his care. When the time came for him to appoint a successor, he gave special instructions to the son who was to succeed him, Mosiah[2].

Benjamin is known to modern readers principally for a stirring farewell address delivered to a huge outdoor gathering at the temple. Benjamin assembled his people by issuing "a proclamation throughout all the land" (Mosiah 2:1). He had two primary reasons for calling them together: (1) to name a new king (Mosiah 1:10), and (2) to ask his people to covenant to take upon themselves the name of Christ (Mosiah 1:11–12). The sermon Benjamin delivered on that occasion is his only recorded discourse, but it reveals much about him. In response to their king's proclamation, the people pitched tents around "the temple to hear the words which king Benjamin should speak unto them" (Mosiah 2:1) before announcing his successor. So vast was the throng that all could not hear, even though he spoke from a tower. His words, therefore, were written and distributed among the multitude (Mosiah 2:8).

Unconcerned about personal power or riches, Benjamin was a remarkably effective leader, a selfless man of solid integrity, a model king. Not only did he establish peace in his nation but he also managed to maintain it, largely by hard work and unflinching faith. Benjamin exemplified all that is best in human character.

Significantly, Benjamin did not regard himself as a person of royal blood, and he opened his address by assuring his listeners that he was only a mortal like them, "subject to all manner of infirmities in body and mind." He merely happened, he said, to have been the one chosen by the people and by the Lord "to serve you with all the might, mind and strength which the Lord hath granted unto me" (Mosiah 2:11). Modest but not reticent, Benjamin reminded his people that he had never abused his authority but rather had exercised it solely in administering righteous justice. Moreover, he had not taxed the citizens for his support, he said, but had "labored with mine own hands that I might serve you" (Mosiah 2:14).

One of Benjamin's principal themes, his own personal creed, surfaces repeatedly in the early part of his address: SERVICE to other mortals and to God. And that theme he deftly merged with three related themes: gratitude, indebtedness to God, and HUMILITY. Pointing out that his own service to his listeners had in fact "been in the service of God," he insisted that if he "merit[ed] any thanks from you, O how you ought to thank your heavenly King!" (Mosiah 2:19). Everything you are, he told his people, was owing "to that God who has created you, and has kept and preserved you." Benjamin added that even if his listeners "should serve [God] with all your whole souls yet ye would be unprofitable servants" (Mosiah 2:20–21). All the Lord asks, Benjamin said, appealing to his people's individual and collective consciences, is that his people "keep his commandments" (Mosiah 2:22). And when they do, he reminded them, the Lord would bless them all the more. Consequently, "ye are still indebted unto him, and are, and will be, forever and ever; therefore, of what have ye to boast?" (Mosiah 2:24). Being less than "the dust of the earth" (Mosiah 2:25), you and I have no cause to boast, Benjamin said plainly.

Benjamin's address was clearly intended to reach and change both the minds and hearts of his people. He wanted them to humble themselves, and he warned them against listening to the evil one instead of to their new king and their God. He also urged them to repent and to remember the torment that awaits the unrepentant transgressor. The heart of Benjamin's message, however, begins in Mosiah 3, where he delivered with great power the Lord's words given him by an angel for the instruction of his people. The words beautifully prophesy of the coming Savior—his birth in the flesh, his ministry, his death, suffering for sin, and resurrection. Only through Christ's name, Benjamin insisted, could SALVATION "come unto the children of men" (Mosiah 3:17).

Reiterating the theme of humility he had introduced earlier, Benjamin spoke the angel's words of counsel, admonishing his people to put off "the natural man" who "is an enemy to God," yield "to the enticings of the Holy Spirit," become saints "through the atonement of Christ the Lord," and become "as a child, submissive, meek, humble, patient, full of love" (Mosiah 3:19). The people responded to the Lord's words just as Benjamin had hoped they would, for "they had viewed themselves in their own carnal state, even less than the dust of the earth." They pleaded "with one voice" that "the atoning blood of Christ" be applied to them, that they might be forgiven of their sins, that their "hearts may be purified" (Mosiah 4:2). In a glorious scriptural moment, "the Spirit of the Lord came upon them, and they were filled with joy, having received a remission of their sins, and having peace of conscience, because of the exceeding faith which they had in Jesus Christ who should come" (Mosiah 4:3).

Recognizing the magnitude of what had occurred, Benjamin stressed what his people would have to do to retain a remission of their sins, wrought through the Savior, the source of their salvation. He returned again to the themes of humility and humanity's indebtedness to God. He enjoined his hearers to "always retain in remembrance, the greatness of God, and your own nothingness, and his goodness and long-suffering towards you, unworthy creatures, and humble yourselves even in the depths of humility, calling on the name of the Lord daily" (Mosiah 4:11). Benjamin's counsel recorded in the remainder of chapter 4 centers on care of the needy, and he linked a retention of the remission of sins to personal generosity. One should neither judge nor deny the beggar, he declared, "For behold, are we not all beggars? Do we not all depend upon the same Being, even God, for all the substance which we have . . . ?" (Mosiah 4:19). Again, Benjamin reminded his people of their debt to God.

Having finished the main part of his message, Benjamin turned to another important matter. If the people believed his words, then he wished them to make a covenant of lifelong obedience to God. They affirmed that their hearts had been changed, that they had "no more disposition to do evil, but to do good continually" (Mosiah 5:2), and that they were "willing to enter into a covenant with [their] God" (Mosiah 5:5). Having done this, Benjamin said, they had become the "spiritually begotten" "children of Christ," their hearts having been "changed through faith on his name" (Mosiah 5:7). They were then to "take upon [them] the name of Christ" (Mosiah 5:8, 10), a solemn responsibility.

Benjamin's work at this point was nearly finished. He had led his people to experience both temporal peace and spiritual redemption, a task which few monarchs have achieved. He then ordered that the names of everyone "who had entered into a covenant with God to keep his commandments" be taken, and he learned that every person, other than small children, "had entered into the covenant and had taken upon them the name of Christ" (Mosiah 6:1–2). Finally, the aging king "consecrated his son Mosiah to be a ruler and a king over his people," and gave "him all the charges concerning the kingdom" (Mosiah 6:3). Three years later, Benjamin died, but he was long remembered as a righteous, good king.

Summary of major teachings

1. Service to others the same as service to God (Mosiah 2:17, 11–19).

2. Humanity's indebtedness to God (Mosiah 2:20–25; 4:19).

3. Two contrasting eternal states: "never-ending torment," a consequence for those who "list to obey the evil spirit" and who remain and die in their sins; and "never-ending happiness," a consequence for those who "keep the commandments of God" (Mosiah 2:32–41; 3:24–27).

4. The coming of Jesus Christ, "the Creator of all things from the beginning"; his ministry, suffering for sin, crucifixion, and resurrection (Mosiah 3:1–16).

5. The conditions for salvation, "only in and through the name of Christ" (Mosiah 3:17; 4:5–8; 5:8).

6. The fruits of spiritual rebirth (Mosiah 3:19; 4:12–16; cf. 4:2–3; 5:2–5).

7. Taking the name of Christ with a covenant of obedience (Mosiah 5:6–13).

See also Atonement, the; Book of Mormon: Another Testament of Jesus Christ; Born again; Happiness; Hell.

BIBLIOGRAPHY

King Benjamin's Speech: "That Ye May Learn Wisdom." Edited by John W. Welch and Stephen D. Ricks. Provo, Utah: FARMS, 1998.

MA

Beset *See* Appendix C.

Besom *See* Appendix C.

Besought *See* Appendix C.

Bestead *See* Appendix C.

Bestir *See* Appendix C.

Bethabara The place where John the Baptist was baptizing "beyond Jordan" (1 Ne. 10:9; John 1:28), apparently meaning at the natural fording place on the east side of the river opposite Jericho, in the province called Peraea (Greek "beyond Jordan"). In Hebrew, *Beth-avara* means "place of crossing."

DKO

Betwixt *See* Appendix C.

Bible, what it says about the Book of Mormon The role of the Book of Mormon in the Lord's work is so vital that the Lord inspired biblical prophets to discuss its use and the conditions under which it would be preserved and come forth.

The antediluvian patriarch Enoch foresaw the coming forth of the Book of Mormon. In a prophecy recorded in Joseph Smith's translation of Genesis, the Lord promised Enoch: "Righteousness will I send down out of heaven; and *truth will I send forth out of the earth,* to bear testimony of mine Only Begotten; his resurrection from the dead . . . and righteousness and truth will I cause to sweep the earth as with a flood, to gather out mine elect from the four quarters of the earth, unto a . . . New Jerusalem" (Moses 7:62; italics added). Latter-day Saints understand that the righteousness to be sent from heaven includes revelations and priesthood keys given to the Prophet Joseph Smith as part of the Restoration, and the truth sent forth out of the earth to be the Book of Mormon (Mormon 8:16). Missionaries, with Bible and Book of Mormon in hand, could then spread truth like a flood over the earth to gather scattered Israelites back to the Lord. Similar prophecies of truth springing from the earth are found in Psalms 85:9–11 and Isaiah 45:8.

Because the Nephites and Lamanites were descendants of Joseph[1], Latter-day Saints also see a foreshadowing of the Book of Mormon peoples in the final blessing the patriarch Jacob[1] gave his son Joseph. Joseph was told that he would be "a fruitful bough," or have many descendants, some of whom would "run over

JORDAN VALLEY

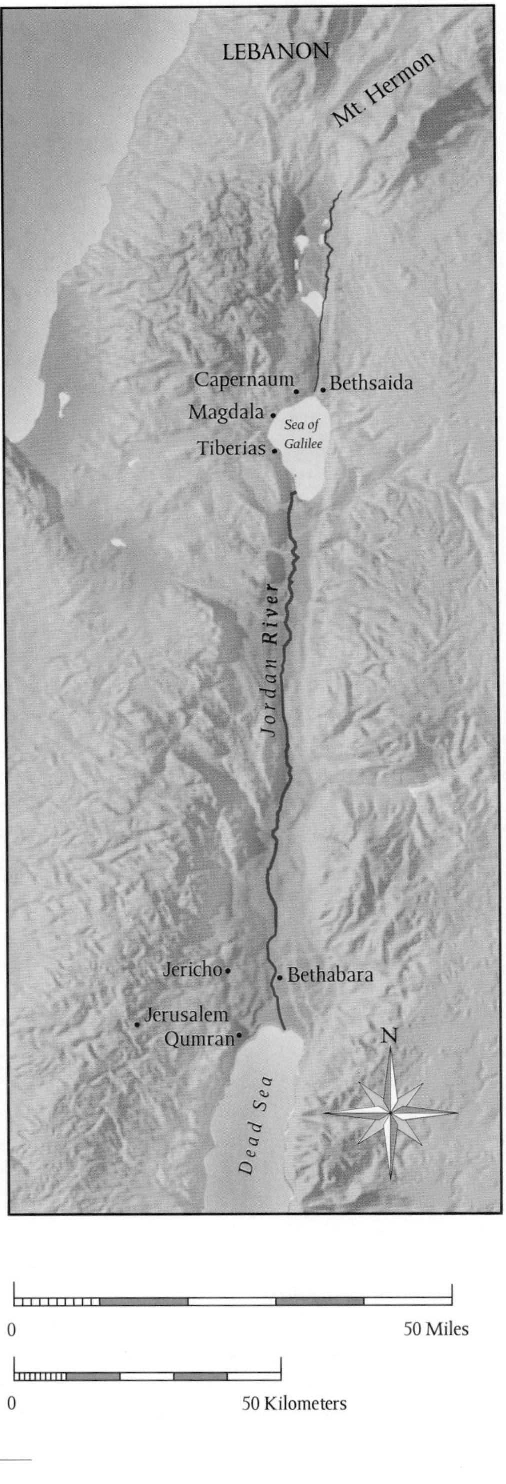

BIBLE, WHAT IT SAYS ABOUT THE B OF M

the wall" by a "well," referring to Lehi[1] and his descendants crossing the ocean to journey to the new promised land (Gen. 49:22, 26). Later, in Egypt, Joseph foretold of the records of these descendants. He prophesied that a CHOICE SEER (Joseph Smith) would eventually be raised up by the Lord to bring forth the records. These writings would testify of the truth of the biblical records already available to the world and restore many plain and precious truths that had been taken out of the Bible (JST Gen. 50: 25–31; 1 Ne. 13:23–29, 38–42). The Bible and the Book of Mormon would then "grow together" to confound false doctrines, lay down contention, establish peace among their descendants, and bring the people to the knowledge of the Lord's covenants (JST Gen. 50:31–36; 2 Ne. 3:6–15).

Isaiah saw the peculiar circumstances under which the Book of Mormon would be preserved and come forth. He knew that the Nephites would be annihilated (Isa. 29:3–4; 2 Ne. 26:15). But he also knew that though they would be "brought down" into the dust "even that they are not," they would "speak out of the ground, and [their] speech shall be low out of the dust, and [their] voice shall be, as of one that hath a familiar spirit, out of the ground, and [their] speech shall whisper out of the dust" (Isa. 29:4; 2 Ne. 26:16). FAMILIAR SPIRIT is a metaphor that Isaiah used to describe how the "words of those which have slumbered in the dust" would "speak as if it were from the dead" (2 Ne. 27:9, 13; cf. Morm. 8:23, 26, 30; Moro. 10:27).

Furthermore, Isaiah prophesied an event that occurred during the translation of the Book of Mormon: "And the vision of all is become unto you as the words of a book that is sealed, which men deliver to one that is learned, saying, Read this, I pray thee: and he saith, I cannot; for it is sealed: And the book is delivered to him that is not learned, saying, Read this, I pray thee: and he saith, I am not learned" (Isa. 29:11–12; cf. 2 Ne. 27:15–19). This prophecy was fulfilled when Martin Harris took some of the translated characters ("the words of a book") from the unsealed part of the gold plates to show them to Professor Charles Anthon (the "learned"), "a gentleman celebrated for his literary attainments." After Professor Anthon rejected Harris's story of the divine origin of the characters he had examined, he requested of Harris "that if [he] would bring the plates to him he would translate them." Harris told Anthon that "part of the plates were sealed," and Anthon replied, "I cannot read a sealed book" (JS–H 1:62–65). In the more complete account of this incident, found in the Book of Mormon, to the man "not learned" (Joseph Smith) the Lord would say, "The learned shall not read them, for they have rejected them . . . ; wherefore thou shalt read [translate] the words which I shall give unto thee" (2 Ne. 27:20).

As an integral part of the "marvellous work," these "words of a book" (the Book of Mormon) would come forth in a day of apostasy and cause "the wisdom of . . . wise men" to perish and the "understanding of . . . prudent men" to be hid (Isa. 29:13–14). Ears formerly confounded by conflicting interpretations of the Bible would "hear the words of the book," and eyes formerly blinded to the fulness of gospel truth would "see out of obscurity, and out of darkness." Meek people would increase their joy in the Lord and the poor in spirit would "rejoice in the Holy One of Israel" (Isa. 29:18–19 // 2 Ne. 27:29–30). Those who "erred in spirit [would] come to understanding, and they that murmured [would] learn doctrine" (Isa. 29:24 // 2 Ne. 27:35; see 2 Ne. 26–27 for inspired analysis of Isa. 29).

Ezekiel foresaw that God would prepare two witnesses (the Bible and Book of Mormon) to gather scattered Israelites back into full fellowship with him and back to the lands their forefathers had possessed (Ezek. 37:15–28). He combined two writing boards ("sticks") to illustrate their common role and identified them as Judah's and Joseph's records (Ezek. 37:15–20). After the records of Judah and Joseph had been joined, God would then gather "the children of Israel from among the [Gentiles] . . . and bring them into their own land: and . . . make them one nation . . . and they shall be no more two nations" (Ezek. 37:21–22; 3 Ne. 20:46; 21:1–7; 29:1).

Jesus also testified of Book of Mormon peoples when he told Judean disciples that he must visit OTHER SHEEP who would hear his voice (John 10:15–16). When he visited Lehi's

> 18 ¶ And in that [a]day shall the deaf hear the words of the [b]book, and the [c]eyes of the blind shall see out of [d]obscurity, and out of darkness.

Isaiah 29:18

> 15 ¶ The word of the LORD came again unto me, saying,
> 16 Moreover, thou son of man, take thee one [a]stick, and [b]write upon it, For [c]Judah, and for the children of Israel his companions: then take another stick, and [d]write upon it, For [e]Joseph, the [f]stick of Ephraim, and *for* all the house of Israel his companions:
> 17 And join them one to another into one stick; and they shall become [a]one in thine hand.

Ezekiel 37:15–17

descendants after his resurrection, he told them that they were the "other sheep" to whom he had referred (3 Ne. 15:16–24). The record they made of his teachings provides another vital witness of Christ and his gospel (3 Ne. 8–30).

The last biblical witness is that of John the Revelator, who saw another angel "fly in the midst of heaven, having the everlasting gospel to preach unto them that dwell on the earth" (Rev. 14:6–8). Latter-day Saints identify this angel as Moroni[2], caretaker of Joseph's records and holder of "the keys of the record of the stick of Ephraim" (D&C 27:5). Moroni heralded the Restoration and prepared Joseph Smith for his role in bringing forth God's great latter-day work.

These many references to the Book of Mormon in the Bible show the major role it would play in God's work of gathering his children back to him and back to their lands of inheritance.

See also Anthon transcript; Crying from the dust; Ephraim, stick of/Joseph, stick of; Isaiah chapter reviews (2 Ne. 26:6, 15–18; 27 // Isa. 29); Marvelous work, marvelous work and a wonder.

KHM

Birds Birds are often mentioned in the Book of Mormon in the context of metaphors and similes. For example, Christ likened his desire to gather the people to himself and nourish them to a "hen" who gathers her "chickens" under her wings (3 Ne. 10:4–6; cf. Matt. 23:37). The hen can raise her wings to offer protection, but her chicks must choose to come to her. Isaiah rehearsed the proud boast of the king of Assyria, who claimed he had gathered the riches of peoples he conquered as one gathers eggs from an abandoned nest (2 Ne. 20:14 // Isa. 10:14). Isaiah also referred to bitterns (2 Ne. 24:23 // Isa. 14:23) and owls (2 Ne. 23:21 // Isa. 13:21) to characterize desolate places. The scriptures teach that the Holy Ghost descended "in the form of a dove" at Jesus' baptism (1 Ne. 11:27; 2 Ne. 31:8; cf. Luke 3:22). The Jaredite barges floated like "a fowl upon the water" (Ether 2:16).

Birds are also referred to in a literal sense. They are mentioned as sacrificial animals (Alma 34:10) and as creations of God (2 Ne. 2:15) that are fed by him (3 Ne. 13:26). Jaredites trapped and transported birds with them in their journeys (Ether 2:2; 6:4). Abinadi warned that the wicked people of Noah[3] would be slain and left for vultures to feed upon (Mosiah 12:2), a fate also experienced by the Lamanites and Amlicites who fought against Alma[2] (Alma 2:38).

FJ

Birthright Certain privileges, blessings, and responsibilities to which a child is entitled by virtue of his or her birth. It is likely that Lehi[1] and his descendants initially followed Old Testament birthright practices of the sixth and seventh centuries B.C. The full nature of those birthright practices is unknown, but apparently they would have been based, at least partially, on Mosaic law and would have dealt primarily with rights belonging to the firstborn son of a family. Evidently, the firstborn's rights included the right to be shown deference by his siblings throughout his life (e.g., Gen. 43:33) and to inherit a double portion of the family holdings (Deut. 21:17). This would help him care for his mother and unmarried sisters when the father passed away. The firstborn also was given the right to preside over the family after the death of the father, though this right could be bartered away, as happened to Esau (Gen. 25:29–34), or forfeited by unrighteousness, as happened to Reuben (Gen. 35:22; 49:3–4; 1 Chr. 5:1).

Although the word *birthright* does not appear in the Book of Mormon, it is the concept of birthright that Laman[1] and Lemuel seemed to use to justify their primary complaint against Nephi[1]—that he, their younger brother, was usurping their right as "elder brethren" to rule and teach (1 Ne. 16:37; similarly, Nephi's forefather, Joseph of Egypt, had older brothers who complained about the meaning of his dreams: "Shalt thou indeed reign over us? or shalt thou indeed have dominion over us?"; Gen. 37:8). Lehi[1] warned Laman and Lemuel that if they did not hearken to the voice of the Lord and chose to rebel against Nephi's teachings, they would indeed lose their opportunity to receive his "first blessing" (2 Ne. 1:24, 27–29; cf. 1 Ne. 2:22–23; 7:8). After Lehi's death, Laman and Lemuel agreed: Nephi would not "be our ruler; for it belongs unto us, who are the elder brethren, to rule over this people" (2 Ne. 5:3). Angered over Nephi's status, they plotted to kill him, but being warned of the Lord, Nephi fled with those who were eager to serve God (2 Ne. 5:5–6, 19–20). Consequently, Laman and Lemuel became the undisputed rulers over their families and followers. They were called Lamanites. They taught their children that Nephi had stolen their birthright; therefore, they must hate and kill Nephites (Enos 1:20; Mosiah 10:12–17; Alma 43:7–8). The question of who had the legal right to rule became a major issue that divided Nephites and Lamanites throughout most of their history.

The notion that the eldest son had the right to rule after the death of his father was perhaps also preserved in the Nephite and Jaredite practice of often appointing a king's or chief judge's son, likely the eldest, to reign after his father (e.g., Omni 1:23; Mosiah 1:2, 9–10; 11:1; 19:26; 29:6–7, 42; Alma 50:39; Ether 6:25).

KHM

Bittern *See* Appendix C.

Blasphemy, blaspheme Blasphemy is of two types: (1) speaking or acting offensively to or about the divine, and (2) claiming the attributes or prerogatives of Deity. Korihor was guilty of the first type in his defiant defense before Alma[2] (Alma 30:30). The anti-Christ Sherem wrongfully accused Jacob[2] of the second form when he contended that the prophet was assuming the divine prerogative by mistakenly converting the law of Moses into the worship of Christ, whose coming, Sherem declared, Jacob could not foreknow (Jacob 7:7). Jarom viewed refraining from blasphemy as an aspect of piety (Jarom 1:5).

TBB

Blindness, spiritual Failure to see with the inner eye or mind. The spiritually blind person lacks the faculty of spiritual discernment and is destitute of the light of the Holy Spirit. Such a person, therefore, is unable to understand the things of God or to judge between right and wrong. Spiritual blindness takes many forms and is not limited to any one group of people or any one time period. Among Book of Mormon peoples it afflicted Nephites, Lamanites, and Jaredites alike. And in the larger world, its effects are seen among both Jews and Gentiles (1 Ne. 7:8; 13:27–32; 17:30; Jacob 4:14; Ether 15:19). Spiritual blindness is perpetuated by wicked and designing people who seek to "blind the eyes" and "harden the hearts" of others by perverting the holy scriptures (1 Ne. 13:27, 32). It is visited upon the "stiffnecked" who despise "the words of plainness," seeking things that a mortal "could not understand," and "looking beyond the mark" (Jacob 4:14). Spiritual blindness results from yielding to Satan (Alma 10:25), rejecting the Spirit of God (Alma 13:4), and listening to "lying words" (Alma 14:6). Ultimately, the spiritually blind will be "brought down into captivity, and also into destruction, both temporally and spiritually, according to the captivity of the devil" (1 Ne. 14:7; cf. 15:24; 2 Ne. 9:32).

The Book of Mormon treats hardness of hearts, deafness of ears, stiffness of necks, and blindness of minds as synonymous spiritual debilities (Jarom 1:3). Each characterizes the natural or fallen man and evidences the power of the evil one among humankind. Yet, the Book of Mormon promises that the Lord will not leave his children in a state of spiritual blindness (1 Ne. 14:7). The work of individuals can achieve much to this end. Nephi[3], for example, hoped to reverse the effects of spiritual blindness by "testify[ing], boldly, repentance and remission of sins through faith on the Lord Jesus Christ" (3 Ne. 7:16). Scripture is another means for leading mortals out of spiritual blindness, as Nephi[1] and Isaiah foresaw. Specifically, the coming forth of the Book of Mormon would restore sight to the spiritually blind who become attuned to its message: "And in that day shall the deaf hear the words of the book, and the eyes of the blind shall see out of obscurity and out of darkness" (2 Ne. 27:29 // Isa. 29:18; 1 Ne. 13:32, 34–36, 39–40).

By implication, the way to avoid spiritual blindness and to escape its damning grip is to avoid the actions and influences that produce it. The Lord promised that mortals who "hold fast" to the iron rod—that is, to the word of God—cannot be overpowered "unto blindness" (1 Ne. 15:24).

See also Hard-heartedness; Pride; Stiffnecked, stiffneckedness.

RNH

Blood, innocent *See* Innocent blood.

Blood, shedding of Inasmuch as blood is both the substance and symbol of mortal life, the phrase "shedding of blood" is a scriptural description of the taking of life. The phrase usually refers to the taking of human life or to the slaying of sacrificial animals.

The sacrificial shedding of the blood of animals was a symbolic representation of the "shedding of the blood of Christ" (Moro. 10:33), who "atoneth for the sins of the world" (Alma 42:15). Amulek taught that the shedding of the blood of beasts would end with the "great and last sacrifice" of the Son of God (Alma 34:13; cf. 3 Ne. 9:19–20; Smith, 172).

Most of the references to the "shedding of blood" in the Book of Mormon refer to the loss of human life during conflict: "The Nephites were taught to defend themselves against their enemies, even to the shedding of blood if it were necessary; . . . and never to raise the sword except it were against an enemy, except it were to preserve their lives" (Alma 48:14). The Book of Mormon condemns those who "delight in . . . the shedding of . . . blood" (Mosiah 11:19; cf. Morm. 4:11) and praises men such as Mosiah[2], Moroni[1], and the righteous Nephites whose desires were for life and not death (Mosiah 29:40; Alma 48:16, 23).

See also Blood crying from the ground; Murder.

BIBLIOGRAPHY

Smith, Joseph. *Teachings of the Prophet Joseph Smith.* Selected by Joseph Fielding Smith. Salt Lake City: Deseret Book, 1976.

DKJ

Blood crying from the ground Blood shed by murderers that has not been avenged. Nephi[1] prophesied that during the destruction that would accompany the death of Christ, the wicked who had murdered the prophets and the Saints would perish, "wherefore the cry of the blood of the saints [would] ascend up to God from the ground against them" (2 Ne. 26:3; cf. D&C 136:36). The voice of Christ later bore witness that such punishment had indeed been rendered to the guilty so "that the blood of the prophets and the saints shall not come any more unto me against them" (3 Ne. 9:5, 7–9, 11).

The Lord declared to Noah[1], "Whoso sheddeth man's blood, by man shall his blood be shed: for in the image of God made he man" (Gen. 9:6). The Lord gave this command again as part of the Mosaic law, with the explanation that the unpunished murderer "defileth the land: and the land cannot be cleansed of the blood that is shed therein, but by the blood of him that shed it" (Num. 35:30–34). If a murderer could not be found, city elders were to offer sacrifice and testify that they had neither shed the blood nor seen who did it. Then they were to plead, "Be merciful, O Lord . . . and lay not innocent blood unto thy people of Israel's charge. And the blood shall be forgiven them" (Deut. 21:1–9).

Additionally, those in the last days who teach false doctrines, support secret combinations, and do works of darkness will also find that the blood of Saints will cry out against them (2 Ne. 28:10; Morm. 8:27).

See also Blood, shedding of; Murder.

KHM

Blotted out Removed. According to the Lord's word that "the names of the wicked shall not be mingled with the names of my people" (Alma 5:57), transgressors who fail to humble themselves, confess their sins, and repent, have their names removed, or blotted out, from the records of the Church (Mosiah 26:36; Alma 1:24; 6:3). The corollary to "not [being] numbered among the people of Christ" is excommunication (Moro. 6:7). The removal of the names of rebellious and unrepentant Church members from Church records is a formal measure reflecting a loss that has already taken place in the heart. King Benjamin taught that the name of Christ received by those who enter the gospel covenant "never shall be blotted out, except it be through transgression" (Mosiah 1:12; cf. 5:7–8, 11). In an ultimate sense, the names of the wicked are blotted out of the Lord's book of life. The book of life contains the names of those who will receive an inheritance at the Lord's right hand (Alma 5:57–58; cf. Rev. 3:5; 22:19).

See also Church discipline.

DLL

Boaz, city of After their final defeat at the city of Desolation, the Nephites fled to the city of Boaz, where they defeated the Lamanites once but were defeated and expelled in a second attack (ca. A.D. 375). Here Nephite women and children were sacrificed to idols (Morm. 4:19–21).

Body of my spirit Meaning "my spirit body," this phrase is found twice and only in Ether 3:16. Christ's premortal appearance to the brother of Jared[1] shows that he was then a person with a spirit body. Humans are created in the image of that body, and Christ would later take on a body of flesh (Ether 3:15–16; cf. Moses 1:6).

KPJ

Bondage *See* Book of Mormon, selected themes of, bondage and deliverance.

Book of Mormon Aspects of the Book of Mormon are addressed under the following:

Book of Mormon, ancient Near Eastern roots of

Book of Mormon: Another Testament of Jesus Christ

Book of Mormon, and Article of Faith 8

Book of Mormon, canonization of

Book of Mormon, condemnation for treating lightly

Book of Mormon, copyright of. *See* Grandin, Egbert Bratt

Book of Mormon, early conversions through

Book of Mormon, editions of

Book of Mormon, figures of speech in

Book of Mormon, as keystone scripture

Book of Mormon, language of the translated text of

Book of Mormon, as literature

Book of Mormon, lost manuscript of (116 pages)

Book of Mormon, manuscripts of

Book of Mormon, as most correct book

Book of Mormon, names in. *See* Names in the Book of Mormon

Book of Mormon, opposition to

Book of Mormon, poetry in

Book of Mormon, printing and publication of

Book of Mormon, pronouncing guide of

Book of Mormon, prophecy in. *See* Prophecy in the Book of Mormon

Book of Mormon, selected purposes of

Book of Mormon, selected themes of

Book of Mormon, title page of

Book of Mormon, translation of

Book of Mormon, translations of, other than English

Book of Mormon, what it says about itself

B OF M, ANCIENT NEAR EASTERN ROOTS

Book of Mormon, what it says about the Bible
Book of Mormon, witnesses of. *See* Witnesses of the Book of Mormon

Book of Mormon, ancient Near Eastern roots of Inasmuch as the Book of Mormon is a record of peoples who migrated from the Old World (the Mediterranean and Mesopotamian regions) and lived in the western hemisphere, the imprint of the ancient Near Eastern cultures from which the peoples originated can still be found within the record. This observation would be as predictable as for one to note that contemporary American culture bears identifiable traces of its (primarily) European origins.

A brief overview of the international currents flowing around the world of Lehi[1] can help explain the presence of Hebrew, Egyptian, Babylonian, and even Greek cultural elements in the records of Lehi and his successors.

When Lehi and his party left the Jerusalem area in 600 B.C., the eastern Levant was experiencing an unusual degree of international ferment. Babylonia, which replaced the Assyrian empire in the seventh century B.C. as the major power in Mespotamia, achieved its zenith between 626 and 539 B.C. The splendor of its capital, Babylon, was legendary. Literary similarities between Hebrew and Babylonian writings have long been recognized (although there is some debate as to which primarily influenced the other), and they attest to cultural exchange between the two peoples. Such exchanges are to be expected, because Babylonian political powers extended westward toward Egypt, resulting in the capture of Jerusalem soon after the departure of Lehi's group.

The Phoenicians facilitated cultural exchanges during this period as well. With important coastal trading cities at Ugarit, Tyre, and Sidon, they established commercial centers throughout the Mediterranean region from ca. 1200 B.C. and for many centuries provided links between the peoples of Canaan/Israel/Judah and those to the west, notably Greeks, Etruscans, and native peoples of north Africa, Spain, and Sicily. Greek traditions attribute their written language to an adaptation of the Phoenician alphabet.

The Greeks also traveled widely. The first Greek philosophers, who date from ca. 600 B.C., were uniformly credited with obtaining wisdom from Egypt and elsewhere in the East. Greeks are known to have been in Egypt since before 660 B.C., and their contacts with Jews in the Holy Land, which lies between Greece and Egypt, can be demonstrated in archaeology and literature of the same time period.

Likewise, Egypt had a long history of interaction with the people of Canaan/Israel. Though weakened at the end of the New Kingdom (ca. 1070 B.C.), Egypt still harbored international aspirations, and under the Kushite pharaoh Piankhi, who ruled over a unified Egypt in the name of the god Amun in 727 B.C., Egyptian armies marched into Canaan. The Assyrians retaliated, attacking Egypt as far south as Thebes in 664/663 B.C. After the fall of the Assyrian empire, the Babylonians were exercising ambitious designs against Egypt when they conquered Jerusalem.

These international influences of Lehi's world can be observed in much of the Book of Mormon, particularly in the writings of the small plates (1 Ne.–Omni). Examples of such influences include, of course, Lehi's own Israelite culture in such diverse areas as names (e.g., Lehi, Sariah, Laban, Ishmael, Lemuel), visions and related topics (e.g., angels, symbols such as a heavenly book, the tree of life, rivers of life or death, and the effect of visions upon recipients), and HEBRAISMS in the linguistic pattern of the writings. The subject of opposites as the basis for existence (2 Ne. 2) is well-known as the dominant theme of pre-Socratic Greek philosophy at the time of Lehi. Egyptian elements are also present, such as the names of Nephi, Sam, Ammon, and Paanchi. Well-known aspects of virtually all the cultures contemporary with Lehi, such as COLOPHONS (author's self-identifying statement at the beginning or ending of works), CHIASMUS (reverse parallelism in literature), kingship, and festival traditions, are also part of the Lehi-Nephi record. Descriptions of travel in the desert (1 Ne.) correspond well to records and traditions from the same region and time—for example, rivers of water at some times of the year but dry at others, movable hills (sand dunes), and stable valleys (with plants and grasses).

Another instance in which ancient Near Eastern texts may parallel the Book of Mormon can be seen in apocryphal accounts of the ministry of the resurrected Lord in the Old World recently discovered and published during the twentieth century. Many of these can be found in *New Testament Apocrypha* (Schneemelcher). Those found in upper Egypt in 1946 can be read in the *Nag Hammadi Library in English* (Robinson). These texts can be compared with the account of the resurrected Christ's appearance and ministry as recorded in 3 Nephi. Some examples of similarities between these accounts include the sacredness of the records, the role of the temple and temple imagery, the reality of the Resurrection, and the covenants, ordinances, and special doctrines given by the resurrected Savior. Although no one argues that the apocryphal writings from the ancient Near East are uncontaminated and completely accurate, many argue that some elements of these works derive from authentic records and first-century sources (see Turner and McQuire). As more is learned in years to come concerning the ministry of the resurrected Jesus, the Book of Mormon record may be better appreciated in the context of that ancient Near Eastern event.

Not as much is known of the ancient Near East in the third millennium B.C., when the Jaredite migration to the western hemisphere took place, as when the later Lehite migration occurred. Nevertheless, the same observation about the imprint of cultural origins in the abridged and translated account of the book of Ether can still be made. The dominant literary genre of that period of ancient Near Eastern cultures is the epic, and the Jaredite record corresponds in nearly every way to that genre (even the poetic form of many epics may have been in the original Jaredite record, before Moroni[2] produced a prose translation). The significant activities of ancient Near Eastern cultures of the time (Sumer, Ebla, and Egypt, to name some examples) included metalworking, textile manufacture, and commercial trade, all of which were important aspects of Jaredite society. Even the great battles and wars, with the resulting extinction of peoples, are common to both the ancient Near East and the Jaredite record.

See also Names in the Book of Mormon.

BIBLIOGRAPHY

Nibley, Hugh. *An Approach to the Book of Mormon*. Vol. 6 of *The Collected Works of Hugh Nibley*. Edited by John W. Welch, Darrell L. Matthews, and Stephen R. Callister. Salt Lake City: Deseret Book, 1988.

———. *Lehi in the Desert; The World of the Jaredites; There Were Jaredites*. Vol. 5 of *The Collected Works of Hugh Nibley*. Edited by John W. Welch, Darrell L. Matthews, and Stephen R. Callister. Salt Lake City: Deseret Book and FARMS, 1988.

———. *Since Cumorah*. 2d ed. Vol. 7 of *The Collected Works of Hugh Nibley*. Edited by John W. Welch. Salt Lake City: Deseret Book, 1988.

Robinson, James M., ed. *The Nag Hammadi Library in English*. San Francisco: HarperCollins, 1990.

Schneemelcher, Wilhelm, ed. *New Testament Apocrypha*. 2 vols. Translated by R. M. Wilson. Louisville, Ky.: John Knox Press, 1991–93.

Turner, John, and Anne McGuire. *The Nag Hammadi Library After Fifty Years*. Leiden: E. G. Brill, 1997.

CWG

Book of Mormon: Another Testament of Jesus Christ Subtitle added to the Book of Mormon in 1982, highlighting one of the central purposes of the Book of Mormon: "The convincing of the Jew and Gentile that JESUS is the CHRIST, the ETERNAL GOD, manifesting himself unto all nations" (Title Page; cf. 2 Ne. 26:12; Hart, 3). In a world where the biblical account of Christ's divine status and mission is increasingly under attack in both academic and popular circles, the Book of Mormon's witness is a cardinal addition to the witness of the Bible.

An angel told Nephi[1] that the Book of Mormon would "establish the truth" of the Bible (1 Ne. 13:40). Some may wonder why the truth of the Bible concerning JESUS CHRIST needs to be "established" (2 Ne. 29:3–10) because the New Testament includes accounts of Christ's birth, baptism, teachings, miracles, ATONEMENT, and RESURRECTION. The Lord proclaimed: "Know ye not that there are more nations than one? . . . Know ye not that the testimony of two nations is a witness unto you that I am God, that I remember one nation like unto another? Wherefore, I

B OF M: ANOTHER TESTAMENT

speak the same words unto one nation like unto another" (2 Ne. 29:7–8). Adding the witness of the Book of Mormon to that of the Bible fulfills the scriptural proclamation that "in the mouth of two or three witnesses shall every word be established" (2 Cor. 13:1; cf. Deut. 19:15; D&C 6:28; 2 Ne. 29:7–9). In addition, Nephi learned that although the Bible originally "contained the fulness of the gospel of the Lord," eventually "many plain and precious things" would be taken away (1 Ne. 13:24–28). These losses would cause "an exceedingly great many [to] stumble" (1 Ne. 13:29). Nephi also learned that the Savior would manifest himself unto his posterity, and they would "write many things which [he would] minister unto them, which shall be *plain and precious*" (1 Ne. 13:35; italics added), thereby compensating for the losses to the Bible.

During the past two centuries, scholars have increasingly employed humanistic methods in biblical study that remove the idea of divine influence as the source of scripture. These methods have attacked the credibility of the biblical account of Jesus' birth, his miracles, his crucifixion, and his resurrection (cf. Ostling, 37–42). Stripping Jesus of his divinity, some scholars have variously depicted him as a Cynic philosopher (Mack), a peasant revolutionary (Crossan), a magician (Smith), a Galilean rabbi (Chilton), a Pharisee (Falk), or an eschatological prophet (Sanders)—anything but the Son of God (cf. Mosiah 3:8). Biblical passages that support Jesus' divinity are understood by those scholars as the incursions of later Christians (Mack, 245–58). Of these scholarly debates one writer observed, "Every new book, every new theory seems to wear away some long-cherished relic in this battle between faith and knowledge. Those who would come to Jesus' rescue must ask, Is it too late? Can that which has been rejected be restored?" (Biema, 54). The Book of Mormon witness confirms cherished Christian truths taught in the Bible, restores to skeptics the validity of those truths, and stands independent of the shifting sands of secular scholarly opinion.

There are at least six major ways that the Book of Mormon stands as another testament of Jesus Christ: (1) it confirms the historical events in Christ's life; (2) it confirms doctrinal truths about Christ and his various roles; (3) it expands the reader's knowledge of the Atonement; (4) it clarifies biblical passages about Christ; (5) it confirms the validity of Old Testament messianic prophecy used in the New Testament; and (6) it includes numerous examples of what can happen when individuals or communities accept the invitation to "come unto [Christ]" (3 Ne. 21:27; Moro. 10:32–33).

First, the Book of Mormon confirms the historicity of the major events of Christ's life. Nephi[1] (1 Ne. 11), king Benjamin (Mosiah 3:5–10), and Alma the Younger (Alma 7:10–13) all received revelations that foretold Christ's mortal ministry. Nephi gave the most detailed description of Christ's life, which includes Christ's miraculous birth, his baptism by John, his preaching, his calling of the Twelve Apostles, his miracles, and his crucifixion. Of particular interest is the testimony of several Book of Mormon prophets and the Father himself of Jesus' divine sonship, a doctrine that has been rejected in centuries past (e.g., Ebionites [see Irenaeus, 3.21.1]; Celsus, in A.D. second century [see Origen, 6.47]; the Adoptionists, in A.D. eighth century [see Cross]), and continues to come under attack by some modern scholars such as Hick and others (Hick). The Book of Mormon confirms the biblical account by repeatedly attesting that Jesus is the "Son of the Eternal Father," his "Only Begotten" and "Beloved Son" (1 Ne. 11:21; 2 Ne. 25:12; Alma 5:48; 9:26; 3 Ne. 11:7).

Likewise, the Book of Mormon adds its witness to the biblical teaching of Christ's resurrection: He was crucified and resurrected three days later and, as a result, all mankind will also be raised from the dead (2 Ne. 25:13; Alma 11:42; 40:4–5; cf. Luke 24:36–39; Acts 24:15; 1 Cor. 15:21–22). The importance of the confirming witness of the Book of Mormon is apparent, given that even in antiquity questions arose about the reality and nature of Christ's and all mankind's resurrected bodies. Paul addressed some of these concerns in his letter to the Corinthian Saints (1 Cor. 15), but under the influence of Platonic philosophy the debate continued down through the centuries and into modern times (e.g., Ignatius, 3; Tertullian; Origen,

B OF M: ANOTHER TESTAMENT

5:14–19; Woodward, 61–70). In contrast, the Book of Mormon is unequivocal in its testimony of Christ's physical resurrection, which is most profoundly taught in the account of the resurrected Christ's visit to the Americas (3 Ne. 11:1–28:12). There twenty-five hundred people witnessed the physical nature of his resurrected body by "going forth one by one . . . [so that they] did see with their eyes and did feel with their hands, and did know of a surety and did bear record, that it was he, of whom it was written by the prophets, that should come" (3 Ne. 11:14–17; cf. Luke 24:36–43; John 20:19–29). The Book of Mormon, therefore, adds twenty-five hundred witnesses of Christ's resurrection to the more than five hundred eyewitnesses noted in the New Testament (1 Cor. 15:5–8). Because of Christ's atonement and physical resurrection, Jacob[2] taught that all mankind can have confidence that "in our bodies we shall see God" (2 Ne. 9:4; cf. Job 19:26).

Second, the Book of Mormon confirms doctrinal truths about Christ and his various roles. It teaches that he was "prepared from the foundation of the world to redeem [his] people" (Ether 3:14; cf. 2 Ne. 10:3; 1 Pet. 1:19–20), that he is the creator of this world (Mosiah 3:8; Ether 4:7; cf. John 1:1–3; Col. 1:16; Heb. 1:1–2), that he represents the Father in all things (3 Ne. 27:13; Mosiah 15:2, 7; cf. John 5:43; 10:25), that he is the "Eternal Judge" (Moro. 10:34; 3 Ne. 27:14; cf. John 5:22, 30), that salvation comes through his "merits, and mercy, and grace" (2 Ne. 2:8; 10:24; 25:23; Acts 15:11; Eph. 2:8), that there is no other name whereby salvation cometh (Mosiah 3:17; 5:8; cf. Acts 4:12), and that "all those who shall believe on his name shall be saved in the kingdom of God" (2 Ne. 25:13; 2:9; cf. John 3:16). Furthermore, Jesus is the rock (Hel. 5:12; cf. 1 Cor. 10:4), the Redeemer (Alma 19:13; cf. Luke 1:68), the Savior (1 Ne. 10:4; cf. Luke 2:11), the true vine (1 Ne. 15:15; cf. John 15:1–5), the Lamb of God (1 Ne. 13:40; cf. John 1:29), the Mediator (2 Ne. 2:27–28; cf. 1 Tim. 2:5), Alpha and Omega (3 Ne. 9:18; cf. Rev. 1:8), and the good shepherd (Alma 5:37–41, 57, 59–60; cf. John 10:11,14).

Third, the Book of Mormon expands understanding of key biblical doctrines within the context of the whole plan of salvation, especially Christ's atonement. The Atonement was not a belated contingency plan devised because of the Fall. It was "prepared from the foundation of the world" (Mosiah 4:6; 15:19; 18:13; Alma 42:26; Ether 3:14; cf. 1 Pet. 1:19–20; Rev. 13:8) to enable mankind to learn and grow by exercising agency (2 Ne. 2:16) while still providing a way to be redeemed from the effects of the Fall and personal sins (Mosiah 3:11; Alma 22:14; Hel. 14:15–18; Rom. 5:1–21; 1 Cor. 15:21–22). Additional Book of Mormon teachings that expand understanding of the Atonement include the following: why Christ is the "great and last sacrifice" and why no human sacrifice could satisfy the demands of both justice and mercy (Alma 34:10–16); why Christ sweat blood in the garden of Gethsemane (Mosiah 3:7; cf. D&C 19:16–19)—the account in Luke does not explicitly connect this occurrence with suffering for sin (Luke 22:44); the consequences of the Fall had there been no Atonement (2 Ne. 9:7–10); and how the Atonement provides for "those . . . who have died not knowing the will of God concerning them, or who have ignorantly sinned" (Mosiah 3:11) or who "are not capable of committing sin" (Moro. 8:8, 20, 22; cf. Mosiah 3:16; 15:24–25). All of these teachings contribute to a depth of understanding of the Atonement that is not possible from the Bible alone. In this way, the Book of Mormon is another testament of Christ's atonement.

Fourth, the Book of Mormon clarifies biblical passages about Christ and his earthly mission. Three such instances are Jesus' conception, his baptism, and his "other sheep." Matthew 1:18 says that Mary "was found with child of the Holy Ghost." From early Christian times, some have misunderstood this passage to mean that the Holy Ghost was Jesus' father (e.g., *Gospel of Philip* II, 3, 55:24; McConkie, 1:82–83). Through Alma the Younger, the Book of Mormon clarifies the Matthean passage: She would be "overshadowed and conceive *by the power* of the Holy Ghost" (Alma 7:10; italics added). Concerning Jesus' baptism, Matthew recorded the Savior's insistence on being baptized so as to "fulfil all righteousness" (Matt. 3:15), but he did not explain how Jesus' baptism accomplished

B OF M: ANOTHER TESTAMENT

that purpose. In the Book of Mormon, Nephi[1] provided a concise and eloquent explanation: "He showeth unto the children of men that . . . he humbleth himself before the Father, and witnesseth unto the Father that he would be obedient unto him in keeping his commandments. . . . And again, it showeth unto the children of men the straitness of the path, and the narrowness of the gate, by which they should enter, he having set the example before them" (2 Ne. 31:7, 9). Similarly, the Book of Mormon provides increased understanding of Jesus' declaration about the "other sheep . . . which are not of this fold" (John 10:16). Biblical commentators invariably interpret this passage in terms of the mission to the Gentiles (e.g., Brown, 396), but Jesus specifically told the Book of Mormon people that "the Gentiles should not at any time hear my voice" (3 Ne. 15:23–24) and that the OTHER SHEEP refers to the blood of Israel in

The Bible and Book of Mormon Testify of Christ; *painting by Greg K. Olsen; courtesy VRL.*

B OF M: ANOTHER TESTAMENT

the Americas and to the lost tribes (3 Ne. 15:24–16:1). Without the aid of the Book of Mormon, the importance of Christ's mission to covenant Israel would be skewed.

Fifth, the Book of Mormon testifies that the mortal ministry of Jesus Christ was the fulfillment of prophecy given in Old Testament times. Although it is difficult to appreciate this concept when relying solely on the Old Testament, Lehi[1] taught that many of the Old Testament prophets testified of the coming of the Messiah (1 Ne. 10:5). Lehi's son Jacob[2] testified that "none of the prophets have written, nor prophesied, save they have spoken [of] this Christ" (Jacob 7:11; cf. Mosiah 13:33; Hel. 8:16–20). The Book of Mormon helps its readers appreciate the Old Testament's witness of Christ. It confirms that many of the TYPES and prophecies which New Testament authors drew from the Old Testament were harbingers of Christ's mortal ministry. The LAW OF MOSES was given "and all things which have been given of God from the beginning of the world . . . are [for] the typifying of [Christ]" (2 Ne. 11:4). Some of these types and prophecies include the raising of the BRAZEN SERPENT (Num. 21:7–9; John 3:14–15; Alma 33:17–22; Hel. 8:13–15), the coming of a prophet like Moses (Deut. 18:15–19; Acts 3:19–26; 1 Ne. 22:20–21; 3 Ne. 20:23–27), a virgin bearing a son named IMMANUEL (Isa. 7:14; Matt. 1:23; 2 Ne. 17:14), and the suffering servant (Isa. 53; Mark 9:12; Rom. 4:25; Mosiah 13:33–15:1). In this way the Book of Mormon "establish[es] the truth" (1 Ne. 13:40) of the New Testament's use of the Old Testament.

Sixth and finally, the Book of Mormon is another testament of Jesus Christ because it records numerous examples of people who made Jesus Christ the central focus of their lives. The Book of Mormon records that after lifetimes of faithful commitment to Christ, Lehi[1], Nephi[1], Jacob[2], and the brother of Jared[1] personally experienced His redemption (2 Ne. 1:15; 2:3; 33:6; Ether 3:13). Enos, Ether, and Moroni[2] viewed the Judgment positively because they had similar experiences (Enos 1:27; Ether 15:34; Moro. 10:34). The Book of Mormon also records the transformation that is possible for individuals and communities who turn to Christ after periods of spiritual rebellion. Alma the Elder (Mosiah 16:13–17:2), Alma the Younger (Mosiah 27:10–24; Alma 36; cf. Paul's experience in Acts 9:1–20), Zeezrom (Alma 15:5–12), king Lamoni (Alma 19:13), the ANTI-NEPHI-LEHIES (Alma 24:7–19; 27:27–28), and other groups of Lamanites and dissenters (Hel. 5:17–52) were all spiritually transformed because of Christ. On a larger scale, 4 Nephi 1:1–18 shows what can happen when an entire community does likewise. The Book of Mormon, therefore, not only teaches the doctrines of Christ but also shows what happens when those doctrines are internalized. Nephi[1] declared that "we talk of Christ, we rejoice in Christ, we preach of Christ, [and] we prophesy of Christ . . . that our children may know to what source they may look for a remission of their sins" (2 Ne. 25:26). He knew of the transforming power in the lives of both individuals and communities who "come unto Christ, and [are] perfected in him" (Moro. 10:32). The Book of Mormon bears eloquent witness of that same truth.

The Book of Mormon, therefore, is another testament of Jesus Christ because it confirms the biblical witness that Jesus is the Christ, clarifies and expands the doctrines associated with that witness, and teaches that "there shall be no other name given nor any other way nor means whereby salvation can come unto the children of men, only in and through the name of Christ, the Lord Omnipotent" (Mosiah 3:17).

See also Book of Mormon, selected purposes of, to the convincing of the Jew and Gentile that Jesus is the Christ; Book of Mormon, selected purposes of, to prove to the world that the holy scriptures are true; Book of Mormon, what it says about the Bible; Gospel, the.

BIBLIOGRAPHY

Biema, David Van. "The Gospel Truth?" *Time,* April 8, 1996.

Brown, Raymond E. "The Gospel According to John I-XII: A New Translation with Introduction and Commentary." Vol. 29 of *The Anchor Bible.* New York: Doubleday, 1966.

Chilton, Bruce D. *A Galilean Rabbi and His Bible: Jesus' Use of the Interpreted Scripture of His Time.* Wilmington: Glazier, 1984.

Cross, F. L., and E. A. Livingstone, eds. *The Oxford Dictionary of the Christian Church*. Oxford: Oxford University Press, 1997. S.v. "Adoptianism."

Crossan, John Dominic. *The Historical Jesus: The Life of a Mediterranean Jewish Peasant*. San Francisco: Harper, 1991.

Falk, Harvey. *Jesus the Pharisee: A New Look at the Jewishness of Jesus*. New York: Paulist Press, 1985.

The Gospel of Philip.

Hart, John L. "Subtitle Testifies of Jesus Christ." *Church News*, October 16, 1982.

Hick, John, ed. *The Myth of God Incarnate*. London: SCM Press, 1977.

Holland, Jeffrey R. *Christ and the New Covenant*. Salt Lake City: Deseret Book, 1997.

Ignatius. *To the Smyraeans*.

Irenaeus. *Against Heresies*.

Mack, Burton L. *The Lost Gospel: The Book of Q & Christian Origins*. San Francisco: Harper, 1993.

McConkie, Bruce R. *Doctrinal New Testament Commentary*. 3 vols. Salt Lake City: Bookcraft, 1965–73.

Origen. *Against Celsus*.

Ostling, Richard N. "Who Was Jesus?" *Time*, August 15, 1988.

Packer, Boyd K. Conference Report, October 1982.

Sanders, E. P. *Jesus and Judaism*. Philadelphia: Fortress Press, 1985.

Smith, Morton. *Jesus the Magician*. New York: Harper & Row, 1978.

Tertullian. *The Resurrection of the Flesh*.

Woodward, Kenneth L. "Rethinking the Resurrection." *Newsweek*, April 8, 1996.

GS

Book of Mormon, and Article of Faith 8 "We believe the Bible to be the word of God as far as it is translated correctly; we also believe the Book of Mormon to be the word of God" (A of F 8). This statement of belief declares that both the Bible and the Book of Mormon are held as canon by The Church of Jesus Christ of Latter-day Saints.

The sacred writings contained in the Bible were compiled over many centuries. Consequently, the Bible has sustained changes through the human processes involved in its compilation, transmission, and translation (Smith, 10–11; cf. 1 Ne. 13:26–29). Still, as Paul testified to Timothy, the Bible was "given by inspiration . . . for instruction in righteousness" (2 Tim. 3:16).

The Book of Mormon is an inspired account recorded by ancient peoples who left the eastern biblical lands and journeyed to the western hemisphere. The Lord communicated with them through prophets who recorded their revelations as well as some of their history on metal plates. These sacred writings were translated "by the gift and power of God" through a modern prophet, Joseph Smith (Smith, 17). This same prophet declared that the Book of Mormon is an inspired translation and "the most correct of any book on earth" (Introduction). In addition to the Bible, the Book of Mormon stands as another testament of Jesus Christ and his work to redeem humankind. Within its pages the Lord describes the importance of having both the Bible and the Book of Mormon testaments: "Know ye not that the testimony of two nations is a witness unto you that I am God, that I remember one nation like unto another?" (2 Ne. 29:8; cf. 1 Ne. 13:41; 2 Ne. 12). Thus the Book of Mormon and the Bible properly understood become one in the same hand (Ezek. 37:16–17).

See also Book of Mormon: Another Testament of Jesus Christ; Book of Mormon, as most correct book; Plain and precious things, loss of and restoration of.

BIBLIOGRAPHY

Smith, Joseph. *Teachings of the Prophet Joseph Smith*. Selected by Joseph Fielding Smith. Salt Lake City: Deseret Book, 1976.

KJW

Book of Mormon, canonization of The process by which the Book of Mormon became "a canon of scripture, meaning . . . [an] authoritative [guide] in matters of faith, doctrine, and conduct" for the Latter-day Saints (McConkie, 405). This process included several declarations from the Lord about the truthfulness of the Book of Mormon, as well as the sustaining vote of the Church. In a revelation given through the Prophet Joseph Smith in June 1829, the Lord declared to Oliver Cowdery, David Whitmer, and Martin Harris that the Book of Mormon was "true" (D&C 17:6). These three men subsequently saw the plates from which Joseph translated the book, heard a voice from heaven declare that these plates were "translated by the gift and power of God," and, in fulfillment of divine command, formally testified to the world, "We know of a surety that the work is true" (Smith, 1:57). Less than a year later, the Lord again endorsed the Book of Mormon by affirming that it "contains . . . the fulness of the gospel of Jesus Christ to the Gentiles and to the Jews also" and by stating that "those who receive [the gospel as contained therein] in faith, and work righteousness, shall receive a crown of eternal life" (D&C 20:9, 14). These divine declarations, included in the "Articles and Covenants of the Church" (D&C 20), were read 9 June 1830 at the first conference of the Church and were "received by unanimous voice of the whole congregation, which consisted of most of the male members of the Church" (Cannon and Cook, 1). Later statements by the Prophet Joseph Smith affirm the position of the Church that the Book of Mormon is official scripture: "Take away the Book of Mormon and the revelations," Joseph taught in 1834, "and where is our religion? We have none" (Smith, 2:52). In 1841, Joseph declared the Book of Mormon to be "the most correct of any book on earth, and the keystone of our religion" (Smith, 4:461). In 1842 Joseph Smith responded to a request from John Wentworth for a sketch of the history and beliefs of the Latter-day Saints. In his response, the prophet included the thirteen statements of belief that have since become known as the Articles of Faith and which have been canonized as scripture. The eighth article reads, "We . . . believe the Book of Mormon to be the word of God" (Smith 4:541).

See also Book of Mormon, and Article of Faith 8.

BIBLIOGRAPHY

Cannon, Donald Q., and Lyndon W. Cook, eds. *Far West Record: Minutes of The Church of Jesus Christ of Latter-day Saints, 1830–1844*. Salt Lake City: Deseret Book, 1983.

McConkie, Bruce R. *A New Witness for the Articles of Faith*. Salt Lake City: Deseret Book, 1985.

Smith, Joseph. *History of The Church of Jesus Christ of Latter-day Saints*. Edited by B. H. Roberts. 7 vols. 2d ed. rev. Salt Lake City: The Church of Jesus Christ of Latter-day Saints, 1932–51.

AHH

Book of Mormon, condemnation for treating lightly In the presence of six elders, on 22 September 1832, the Prophet Joseph Smith received a revelation on priesthood. In that revelation the Lord declared: "Your minds in times past have been darkened because of unbelief, and because you have treated lightly the things you have received—Which vanity and unbelief have brought the whole church under condemnation. And this condemnation resteth upon the children of Zion, even all. And they shall remain under this condemnation until they repent and remember the new covenant, even the Book of Mormon and the former commandments which I have given them, not only to say, but to do according to that which I have written" (D&C 84:54–57).

In June 1832 the first issue of the Church's first periodical, *The Evening and the Morning Star*, greeted the public. On page 6 editor William W. Phelps focused on the Book of Mormon, declaring that to bear testimony of its truth "is our duty." He also commented on Genesis 49:22–26 regarding Joseph[1] as a "fruitful bough . . . whose branches run over the wall . . . unto the utmost bound of the everlasting hills" and tied this scripture with the coming forth of the Book of Mormon. Ezekiel 37:16–19 was called to the readers' attention, and for the first time in print the world was told that the two sticks spoken of by that ancient prophet were the Bible and the Book of Mormon. Subsequent issues of the *Star* printed parts of the books of Jacob, Moroni, and Ether. Phelps quoted liberally from the Book of Mormon in many articles and from the revelations of Joseph Smith as well. Thus the Church's only periodical proclaimed the importance of the "keystone" of The Church of Jesus Christ of Latter-day Saints. Phelps, in fact, intended to publish the entire Book of Mormon on the pages of the *Star*.

The diaries of William E. McLellin, too, provide evidence that Latter-day Saint missionaries in 1832 used and bore testimony of the truthfulness of the Book of Mormon. Serving as a companion to Samuel Smith, the Prophet's brother, during the winter and spring of 1832, McLellin frequently mentioned the book. He wrote that on 2 December 1831, Smith, in a

B OF M, CONDEMNATION FOR TREATING

meeting of deists, gave a history of the Book of Mormon, and two days later McLellin spoke for an hour and a half on its importance (Shipps and Welch, 63–64). A number of other diary entries also reveal McLellin's heavy use of the Book of Mormon.

Perhaps some of the early missionaries were not as committed to using the Book of Mormon as was McLellin. Elder Neal A. Maxwell stated: "Quite understandably too, among early Church members the use of the Bible was much greater than the use of the Book of Mormon. Even Joseph, who had been schooled in the Bible, had scarcely had time to translate and begin to assimilate the Book of Mormon, let alone to articulate extensively regarding the gems in that book of whose truthfulness he testified" (28). Even so, many early Saints acknowledged that the Book of Mormon was an important factor in their conversion. Only twelve days before Doctrine and Covenants 84 was revealed, George A. Smith, the Prophet's cousin, was baptized in New York, having been converted after reading the Book of Mormon (Smith, 1:285).

If many of the elders and the Church's only periodical were emphasizing the Book of Mormon and nonbelievers were converted by reading it, why did the Lord declare that the whole Church was under condemnation for treating it and the former commandments "lightly"? And why, 165 years later, was the Church still considered to be under the same condemnation? In 1987, President Ezra Taft Benson said, "This condemnation has not been lifted, nor will it be until we repent" (*Teachings*, 64). What then is needed? The words of prophets and apostles from the beginning of this dispensation to the present clearly identify the remedy.

In April 1856 general conference, Elder Orson Pratt declared his belief that the condemnation resulted from the failure of the Saints to search the scriptures, especially their neglect of the Book of Mormon (Young, 3:346–7). Almost ten years later, Elder Heber C. Kimball said, "the Book of Mormon is the ensign which God has lifted up to the nations in the last days, and we are not justified when we in our feelings neglect or forsake it" (Young, 11:147). A century later,

Ezra Taft Benson (1899–1994); portrait by Kund Edsberg; courtesy VRL.

Elder Marion G. Romney promised Church members that if they would prayerfully read from the Book of Mormon with their children, faith, reverence, mutual respect, consideration, love, charity, and wisdom would increase in every home (110–13). In 1988 Elder Richard G. Scott added another witness: "I witnessed that it is not sufficient that we should treasure the Book of Mormon, nor that we testify that it is of God. We must know its truths, incorporate them into our lives, and share them with others" (89). In 1994, Elder Dallin H. Oaks shared his "clear impressions" that the condemnation of "the early Church" and the Church "in our own day" is the result of the Saints' neglecting "the Book of Mormon's witness of the divinity and mission of Jesus Christ and our covenant relationship to him" and for their not remembering "the former commandments," that is, the Old and New Testaments and the revelations given to them through the Prophet Joseph Smith, in which that covenant relationship is clearly explained (61–63; D&C 84:57).

Probably more than any other Church leader, President Ezra Taft Benson, toward the end of his ministry, spoke of the condemnation and how it might be lifted. Among his statements are the following: "We have not been using the Book of Mormon as we should. Our homes are not as strong unless we are using it to bring our children to Christ" (*Teachings*, 60); "Let us not remain under condemnation, with its scourge and judgment, by treating lightly this great and marvelous gift the Lord has given to us. Rather, let us win the promises associated with treasuring it up in our hearts" (CR, October 1986, 7); "The Book of Mormon must be reenthroned in the minds and hearts of our people. We must honor it by reading it, by studying it, by taking its precepts into our lives and transforming them into lives required of the true followers of Christ" (CR, October 1986, 103); "The Lord inspired His servant Lorenzo Snow to reemphasize the principle of tithing to redeem the Church from financial bondage. . . . Now, in our day, the Lord has revealed the need to reemphasize the Book of Mormon to get the Church and all the children of Zion out from under condemnation—the scourge and judgment. . . . I promise you that from this moment forward, if we will daily sup from its pages and abide by its precepts, God will pour out upon each child of Zion and the Church a blessing hitherto unknown—and we will plead to the Lord that He will begin to lift the condemnation" (CR, April 1986, 100); "Moses never entered the promised land. Joseph Smith never saw Zion redeemed. Some of us may not live long enough to see the day when the Book of Mormon floods the earth and when the Lord lifts His condemnation. But, God willing, I intend to spend all my remaining days in that glorious effort" (CR, October 1988, 5).

Given these many witnesses, it is clear that the way to have the condemnation lifted is to study, ponder, feast upon, and bear witness of the scriptures, emphasizing the Book of Mormon and its witness of Christ, and then *obey* the truths taught therein. The Saints must do as the faithful Nephites did. Nephi[1] explained, "We talk of Christ, we rejoice in Christ, we preach of Christ, we prophesy of Christ, and we write according to our prophecies, that our children may know to what source they may look for a remission of their sins" (2 Ne. 25:26). They must also accept the invitation of Moroni[2] to "come unto Christ, and be perfected in him" (Moro. 10:32). The Book of Mormon has power to motivate people to desire and earnestly strive for that lofty goal, "not only to say, but to do according to that which [God has] written" (D&C 84:57).

See also Book of Mormon, as keystone scripture.

BIBLIOGRAPHY

Benson, Ezra Taft. Conference Report, April 1986.

———. Conference Report, October 1986.

———. Conference Report, October 1988.

———. *Teachings of Ezra Taft Benson*. Salt Lake City: Bookcraft, 1987.

The Evening and the Morning Star, June 1832.

Maxwell, Neal A. *But for a Small Moment*. Salt Lake City: Bookcraft, 1987.

Oaks, Dallin H. "Another Testament of Jesus Christ." *Ensign* 24 (March 1994): 60–67.

Romney, Marion G. Conference Report, April 1960.

Scott, Richard G. Conference Report, October 1988.

Shipps, Jan, and John W. Welch, eds. *Journals of William E. McLellin: 1831–1836*. Chicago: University of Illinois, 1994.

Smith, Joseph. *History of The Church of Jesus Christ of Latter-day Saints*. Edited by B. H. Roberts. 7 vols. 2d ed. rev. Salt Lake City: The Church of Jesus Christ of Latter-day Saints, 1932–51.

Young, Brigham. *Journal of Discourses*. 26 vols. London: Latter-day Saints' Book Depot, 1854–86.

KWG

Book of Mormon, copyright of *See* Grandin, Egbert Bratt.

Book of Mormon, early conversions through Reading the Book of Mormon led to the conversion of thousands in the early days of the Restoration. Although the *Palmyra Freeman* newspaper (1829–30) mistakenly reported that the "'Golden Bible' was almost invariably treated as it should have been—with contempt" (Bushman, 111), as soon as the Book of Mormon was published, it set the country in an uproar. Friends and strangers embraced what Joseph Smith was calling the word of God.

Solomon Chamberlin, one of the earliest believers, wrote: "About the time that Joseph Smith found the gold record, I began to feel that the time was drawing near, that the Lord would

B OF M, EARLY CONVERSIONS THROUGH

in some shape or other bring forth His church. I made some inquiry through the country where I traveled if there was any strange work of God, such as had not been on the earth since the days of Christ. I could hear of none." Then Chamberlin wrote of being drawn to the Palmyra area and spending the night at a farmhouse in the vicinity: "In the morning the people of the house asked me if I had heard of the gold Bible [Book of Mormon]. When they said 'gold Bible,' there was a power like electricity went from the top of my head to the end of my toes. This was the first time I ever heard of the gold Bible" (Chamberlin).

Chamberlin indicated that a few days later he went to the shop of E. B. Grandin, where printing had begun on the Book of Mormon. "As soon as they had printed 64 pages," he said, "I took them with their leave, and pursued my journey to Canada, and I preached all that I knew concerning Mormonism" (Chamberlin).

Believers like Solomon Chamberlin shared the gospel with friends, pastors, congregations, and strangers who in turn shared the gospel message with near neighbors and distant relatives. Among those who shared their testimonies was the sister of Joseph Smith, Katherine Salisbury: "Many times when I have read its sacred pages, I have wept like a child, while the Spirit has borne witness with my spirit to its truth" (Salisbury, 260).

Noah Packard, who read the Book of Mormon to his wife, wrote that on the second reading, "The Lord poured out His spirit upon me and the scriptures were opened to our understanding, and we were convinced that the Book of Mormon was a true record" (Autobiography). Zina Huntington declared that when she first saw the book, "My whole soul was filled with joy. Without opening it I clasped it to my heart and exclaimed, 'O Truth, Truth, Truth!' I knew it had been brought forth by an angel's hand and the feeling that possessed me was one of supreme ecstasy" (qtd. in Talmage, 256). She shared her joy with relatives. Sidney Rigdon exclaimed after reading the Book of Mormon, "Flesh and blood hath not revealed it unto me, but my Father which is in heaven" (Smith,

Katherine Smith Salisbury (1813–1900); drawing by William Whitaker; courtesy Buddy Youngreen.

Zina Diantha Huntington Young (1821–1901); courtesy LDS Family and Church History Archives.

History, 1:125). He shared his conviction with friends in Ohio.

Young and old, rich and poor, farmer and educator welcomed news of the Book of Mormon. Warren Foote, for example, rejected "the religious teachings of the various sects" and was unmoved by "their revivals and shouting meetings." He added, "I could not believe that the Church of Christ was divided into creeds and sects, and I resolved that I would not have anything to do with any of them, but frequently prayed to the Lord in secret to guide me in the

B OF M, EARLY CONVERSIONS THROUGH

Parley P. Pratt (1807–1857), ca. 1852; photograph by Marsena Cannon; courtesy LDS Family and Church History Archives.

Brigham Young (1801–1877), ca. 1850; portrait by William W. Major; courtesy DUP.

right way" (qtd. in Jenson, 1:376). After comparing the Book of Mormon with the Bible, Foote was converted.

Another who embraced the gospel through reading the Book of Mormon was Parley P. Pratt. He wrote: "I opened it with eagerness, and read its title page. I then read the testimony of several witnesses in relation to the manner of its being found and translated. After this I commenced its contents by course. I read all day; eating was a burden, I had no desire for food; sleep was a burden when the night came, for I preferred reading to sleep. As I read, the spirit of the Lord was upon me, and I knew and comprehended that the book was true, as plainly and manifestly as a man comprehends and knows that he exists. My joy was now full. . . . I esteemed the Book, or the information contained in it, more than all the riches of the world" (Pratt, 20, 22).

Yet another convert was Jared Carter, who learned about the Book of Mormon on a business trip of several weeks' duration. He wrote that "after reading awhile in the Book of Mormon and praying earnestly to the Lord that he would show me the truth of the book, I became immediately convince[d] that it was a revelation of God and it had such an influence on my mind that I had no mind to persue [*sic*] my business" (Carter). Jacob Hamblin enjoyed a similar experience. He wrote: "The impressions I received at the time cannot be forgotten. The spirit rested upon me and bore testimony of its truth, and I felt like opening my mouth and declaring it to be a revelation from God" (Little, 196).

Not all of those who accepted the Book of Mormon did so immediately. Brigham Young, for example, spent nearly two years examining the book, testing its teachings for himself, before he was baptized. He later explained: "When the book of Mormon was first printed, it came to my hands in two or three weeks afterwards. Did I believe, on the first intimation of it? . . . 'Hold on,' says I. The mantle of my traditions was over me, to that degree, and my prepossessed feelings so interwoven with my nature, it was almost impossible for me to see at all. . . . 'Wait a little while; what is the doctrine of the book, and of the revelations the Lord has given? Let me apply my heart to them;' and after I had done this, I considered it to be my right to know for myself, as much as any man on earth. I examined the matter studiously for two years before I made up my mind to receive that book. I knew it was true, as well as I knew that I could see with my eyes, or feel by the touch of my fingers. . . . Had

B OF M, EARLY CONVERSIONS THROUGH

not this been the case, I never would have embraced it to this day. . . . I wished time sufficient to prove all things for myself" (Young, 3:91). Once convinced of the truthfulness of the Book of Mormon, Brigham Young never looked back.

By the 1840s, interest in acquiring the Book of Mormon had grown so rapidly that demand seriously outran supply (Robinson). Indeed, word about the book was spreading by means of converts like William Huntington, who "believed it with all his heart and preached it almost every day, to his neighbors and everybody he could see, or had the privilege to chat with" (Jenson, 1:369). Such enthusiasm for sacred truths spread the prophetic words of the Book of Mormon throughout the United States, Canada, and the British Isles during Joseph Smith's lifetime. As eager converts found peace and hope of eternal joy within the pages of this new scripture, many recorded their gratitude and testimony.

Journals and family stories reveal the depth of each author's conviction, sacrifice, and willingness to be numbered among the believers. In fact, Daniel Spencer's investigation of the Book of Mormon reportedly led him to close his business establishment for two weeks and refuse "to do business with any one, and shut himself up to study; and there alone with his God he weighed in the balances of his clear head and conscientious heart the divine message [contained in the Book of Mormon] and found it not wanting." He is said to have exclaimed, "My God, the thing is true, and as an honest man I must embrace it; but it will cost me all I have got on earth" (qtd. in Jenson, 1:287).

As believers like Daniel Spencer grew in testimony, they declared a strong witness of the Book of Mormon's sacred significance and were often placed in a position of defending that witness. Their faithful defense echoed the sentiments of Joseph Smith, who wrote from Liberty Jail: "Hell may pour forth its rage like the burning lava of Mount Vesuvius, or of Etna . . . yet shall 'Mormonism' stand. Water, fire, truth and God are all realities. Truth is 'Mormonism.' God is the author of it. . . . It was by Him we received the Book of Mormon" (Smith, *Scriptural,* 159).

Lucy Mack Smith (1775–1856), ca. 1853; illustration by Frederick H. Piercy; courtesy LDS Family and Church History Archives.

Among those who defended the truthfulness of the Book of Mormon was the family of Joseph Smith. Joseph Smith Sr. was jailed for refusing to burn a copy of the Book of Mormon. "I thought to myself," he wrote, "I was not the first man who had been imprisoned for the truth's sake" (qtd. in Smith, *Joseph,* 185). When Lucy Mack Smith was confronted by Deacon Beckwith and other religionists of Palmyra encouraging her to not say "anything more upon the subject" of the Book of Mormon, she said, "Deacon Beckwith, if you should stick my flesh full of faggots, and even burn me at the stake, I would declare, as long as God should give me breath, that Joseph has got that Record, and that I know it to be true" (Smith, *Joseph,* 161). Hyrum Smith was also bold in his testimony: "I [have] been abused and thrust into a dungeon, and confined for months on account of my faith, and the testimony of Jesus Christ. However I thank God that I felt a determination to die, rather than deny the things [plates] which my eyes had seen, which my hands had handled, and which I had borne testimony to" (qtd. in Smith, *History,* 4:46 n).

The accounts of these early believers and defenders focus on the Book of Mormon as the key to their discovering truth. Conversion to

BOOK OF MORMON, EDITIONS OF

Mormonism began with a quest for truth that was ultimately realized in the Book of Mormon.

BIBLIOGRAPHY

Black, Susan Easton, ed. *Stories from the Early Saints: Converted by the Book of Mormon.* Salt Lake City: Bookcraft, 1992.

Bushman, Richard L. *Joseph Smith and the Beginnings of Mormonism.* Urbana and Chicago: University of Illinois Press, 1984.

Carter, Jared. Journal (ca. 1833). Church Archives.

Chamberlin, Solomon. Autobiography (ca. 1858). Church Archives.

Jenson, Andrew. *Latter-day Saints Biographical Encyclopedia.* 4 vols. 1901–36. Reprint, Salt Lake City: Western Epics, 1971.

Little, James A. *Jacob Hamblin.* 1881. Reprinted in *Three Mormon Classics,* compiled by Preston Nibley, 197–349. Salt Lake City: Bookcraft, 1988.

Packard, Noah. *Autobiography.* Harold B. Lee Library. Brigham Young University, Provo, Utah.

Pratt, Parley P. *Autobiography of Parley P. Pratt.* Edited by Parley P. Pratt Jr. 1874. Reprint, Salt Lake City: Deseret Book, 1985.

Robinson, Ebenezer. *The Return* 2 (1890): 257–62. Church Archives.

Salisbury, Katherine. "Dear Sisters." *Saints' Herald* (1 May 1886): 260.

Smith, Joseph. *History of The Church of Jesus Christ of Latter-day Saints.* Edited by B. H. Roberts. 7 vols. 2d ed. rev. Salt Lake City: The Church of Jesus Christ of Latter-day Saints, 1932–51.

———. *Scriptural Teachings of the Prophet Joseph Smith.* Selected by Joseph Fielding Smith. Scriptural annotations and introduction by Richard C. Galbraith. Salt Lake City: Deseret Book, 1993.

Smith, Lucy Mack. *History of Joseph Smith by His Mother.* Edited by Preston Nibley. Salt Lake City: Bookcraft, 1958.

Talmage, Mary Booth. "Past Three Score Years and Ten." *Young Woman's Journal* 12 (June 1901): 255–57.

Young, Brigham. *Journal of Discourses.* 26 vols. London: Latter-day Saints' Book Depot, 1854–86.

SB

Book of Mormon, editions of The first three editions of the Book of Mormon were produced under the general supervision of Joseph Smith. The first edition (1830) consisted of five thousand copies and was published by E. B. Grandin of Palmyra, New York. This edition was chiefly set from the printer's manuscript, except for Helaman 13 through the end of Mormon, which were set from the original manuscript. The typesetter, John Gilbert, generally followed the request that the "grammatical errors" in the original text not be corrected. Nonetheless, Gilbert was responsible for the spelling, punctuation, capitalization, and paragraphing in the first edition.

The second edition was published in 1837 by the Church in Kirtland, Ohio. For this edition, Joseph Smith went through the printer's manuscript and altered the grammar of the text to reflect standard English rather than Joseph's native upstate New York English.

The third edition was published in 1840 by Shepard and Stearns in Cincinnati, Ohio, with the assistance of Ebenezer Robinson. For this edition, Joseph Smith made a few additional emendations and grammatical changes. He also restored a handful of phrases that had been lost when the printer's manuscript was produced during the printing of the 1830 edition. In addition, a stereotype of this edition was produced and taken to Nauvoo, from which a number of printings were made from 1840 to 1842.

The next three editions of the Book of Mormon (1841, 1849, and 1852) were printed in England (Liverpool and London). The 1841 edition is basically a resetting of the 1837 edition, with a few accidental changes. The 1849 edition was produced under the direction of Orson Pratt and involved a few grammatical corrections. The 1852 edition, printed and edited under the direction of Franklin Richards, is particularly interesting because in the second printing of this edition a number of in-press corrections were made by reference to the 1840 edition (the last edition Joseph Smith himself worked on). Nonetheless, these corrections took place in only some of the signatures for that edition, so not all of Joseph Smith's changes in the 1840 edition appear in the corrected 1852 text. A stereotype was made of the corrected plates and was used until 1879 for subsequent LDS printings of the Book of Mormon. Richards also numbered the paragraphs, thus producing the first (although primitive) versification for the text.

For the 1879 LDS edition, Orson Pratt created the chapter and versification system that

BOOK OF MORMON, EDITIONS OF

has been followed in all subsequent LDS editions. He divided the original chapters into smaller chapters. The original longer chapters (still followed by the Community of Christ, formerly the RLDS Church) are based on narrative cohesiveness. Pratt's chapter system is based on themes, and each chapter is small enough that no chapter reaches one hundred verses. In addition, Pratt added footnotes to the text. His footnotes give scriptural cross-references and provide commentary on the geography and other subjects.

Pratt published this edition in Liverpool, England. Two stereotypes were produced: one remained in England, and the other was sent to Salt Lake City. Printings from these stereotypes were produced up to about 1920, despite their deterioration over time.

Other editions based on the 1879 edition were produced near the turn of the century.

1888: A large-print edition printed in Salt Lake City for the *Juvenile Instructor;* this was the only edition prior to 1920 to provide dates in the text.

1902: A missionary edition published by Burd and Fletcher of Kansas City, Missouri.

1905: A missionary edition published by Henry C. Etten of Chicago, Illinois, for German Ellsworth, president of the Northern States Mission; a stereotype was produced and used for many additional printings (for at least ten years); for the third (1907) printing of this edition, a number of changes were made in the stereotype, some of which were based on the 1906 Salt Lake edition (described below).

1906: This large-print Salt Lake edition was published by the *Deseret News;* it was set not from the previous 1888 large-print edition but from a later printing of the 1879 edition; this edition introduced a few grammatical changes into the text, which the LDS textual tradition has retained.

1907: The first pocket-size edition, published by the Deseret Sunday School Union in Salt Lake City.

1911: A large-print edition published by Henry C. Etten of Chicago for German Ellsworth; this edition followed the 1907 corrected plates of the 1905 Chicago missionary edition and was used as the copy text for the 1920 edition; the year 1911 is a guess because the edition itself gives no date.

Modern LDS editions

The current LDS edition derives from the 1920 edition edited under the direction of a committee of general authorities headed by George F. Richards with Anthony W. Ivins, James E. Talmage, Melvin J. Ballard, and Joseph Fielding Smith (and perhaps Anthon H. Lund) as committee members. The 1920 edition continued the basic format of the 1879 edition but placed the text in double columns and restricted the footnotes to scriptural references. The committee placed dates at the bottom of the text (following the 1888 edition) and wrote chapter summaries placed at the head of each chapter as well as in a "Synopsis of Chapters" at the end of the book. They added an index as well as a guide to the pronunciation of names. This edition also included introductory material that lists the various plates, explains the origin of the Book of Mormon (from Joseph Smith's 1839 account), and provides a table of contents (which gives the "names and order of books").

The current LDS edition (1981) is a revision of the 1920 edition but follows its general format. The same kinds of introductory material, footnotes, dating system, chapter summaries, and indexes are found; in addition, the footnotes also frequently refer to the Topical Guide at the back of the 1979 LDS edition of the King James Version of the Bible. All of these ancillary materials were thoroughly revised for this edition, which was produced under the direction of Thomas S. Monson, Boyd K. Packer, and Bruce R. McConkie, three members of the Quorum of the Twelve Apostles. The text restored some of the original readings (that is, wordings) found in the two Book of Mormon manuscripts, plus a few readings found in the 1840 edition, the last edition that Joseph Smith edited.

The RLDS textual tradition

The RLDS (now Community of Christ) editions of the Book of Mormon are derived from the 1840 Cincinnati/Nauvoo edition. This edition was used as copy text for the 1858 "Jas. O. Wright" edition published in New York City; a couple of years later, the same printed sheets

B OF M, FIGURES OF SPEECH IN

(except for a changed introduction) were bound into volumes for Zadoc Brook ("Elder in the Church of Christ"). Copies of the Wright/ Brook edition were used by RLDS Church members for about twenty years until this edition was exhausted. In 1874 the RLDS Church published its own edition, based on both the 1840 Cincinnati/Nauvoo and 1858 Wright/Brook editions. The earliest bound volumes correctly give Plano, Illinois, as the place of publication. Later bound volumes list Lamoni, Iowa, as the place of publication. In 1892 the RLDS Church published a large-print, double-column edition based directly on their 1874 edition.

In 1903 the RLDS Church purchased the printer's manuscript of the Book of Mormon from the grandson of David Whitmer and then used it extensively to restore many original readings of the text in their 1908 edition. In 1953 the authorized text of the 1908 edition was lightly edited, with most changes involving questions of grammar. In 1966 the RLDS Church also published a modernized version of the text, one that attempted to remove all archaic language. The Community of Christ distributes the 1908/1953 "authorized edition" and the 1966 modernization.

See also Book of Mormon, manuscripts of; Book of Mormon, printing and publication of; Book of Mormon, pronouncing guide of; Book of Mormon, translations of, other than English.

BIBLIOGRAPHY

Skousen, Royal. "John Gilbert's 1892 Account of the 1830 Printing of the Book of Mormon." *The Scholar as Witness: Essays in Honor of Richard Lloyd Anderson.* Edited by Stephen D. Ricks, Donald W. Parry, and Andrew H. Hedges. Provo: FARMS, 1999.

Stocks, Hugh G. "The Book of Mormon, 1830–1879: A Publishing History." Master's thesis. UCLA, 1979.

———. "The Book of Mormon in English, 1870–1920: A Publishing History and Analytical Bibliography." Ph.D. dissertation. UCLA, 1986.

RJS

Book of Mormon, figures of speech in Figures of speech are a nonliteral means of expressing ideas through images or changes in standard word order. For instance, Psalm 23 is based on a vivid and beautiful comparison of the Lord to a caring shepherd who, David said, "maketh me to lie down in green pastures: he leadeth me beside the still waters . . . [and] in the paths of righteousness" (Ps. 23:2–3). The most common pictorial figures of speech are metaphors (comparison of apparently unlike terms), similes (comparison between things showing an aspect of significant similarity through the use of "like" or "as"), personification (treating inanimate things as persons), ALLEGORY (a form of extended metaphor in which the literal level refers to another level of meaning), and allusions (indirect references to historical events or the like). Rhetorical figures of speech (departures from the customary uses of language) include apostrophe, repetition, antithesis, PARALLELISM (including CHIASMUS), hyperbole, and paradox.

Figures of speech help bring abstract concepts alive and heighten expressions in memorable ways. For instance, the Lord through Isaiah, quoted by Nephi[1], tells Israel, "I did it because I knew that thou art obstinate, and thy neck is an iron sinew, and thy brow brass" (1 Ne. 20:4). Of course the neck is figuratively, not literally, an iron sinew. This metaphor is apt in showing the stiffneckedness, or pride, of Israel. Lehi[1] used figurative language to make vivid his desires for his oldest sons, Laman[1] and Lemuel: "O that thou mightest be like unto this river, continually running into the fountain of all righteousness! . . . O that thou mightest be like unto this valley, firm and steadfast, and immovable in keeping the commandments of the Lord!" (1 Ne. 2:9–10). Mormon also used striking similes in lamenting the spiritual decline of his people: The Nephites, he said, "are led about by Satan, even as chaff is driven before the wind, or as a vessel is tossed about upon the waves, without sail or anchor, or without anything wherewith to steer her; and even as she is, so are they" (Morm. 5:18). Following are additional examples of some of the figures of speech found in the Book of Mormon.

Metaphor: Many of the attributes of Christ are presented metaphorically, e.g., he is the "true shepherd" (Hel. 15:13), the "fountain of all righteousness" (Ether 12:28), and his love is the tree of life (1 Ne. 11:21–25).

Simile: The Nephites began to be swept off by the Lamanites "even as a dew before the sun" (Morm. 4:18; cf. Mosiah 12:12; Alma 14:29).

Simile curse: "Even as this scalp has fallen to the earth, which is the scalp of your chief, so shall ye fall to the earth except ye will deliver up your weapons of war and depart with a covenant of peace" (Alma 44:14).

Personification: "And her gates shall lament and mourn" (2 Ne. 13:26).

Allegory: "I will liken thee, O house of Israel, like unto a tame olive-tree" (Jacob 5:3). *See* Zenos, allegory of.

Allusion: "Let us be strong like unto Moses; for he truly spake unto the waters of the Red Sea and they divided hither and thither, and our fathers came through, out of captivity, on dry ground" (1 Ne. 4:2).

Metonymy (use of a name of one thing in the place of something closely related): "That I might rid my garments of your sins, I come up into the temple this day that I might declare unto you the word of God" (Jacob 2:2).

Synecdoche (a part signifying the whole or the whole signifying a part): "Many hearts died, pierced with deep wounds" (Jacob 2:35).

Apostrophe (an address to someone not present; e.g., the Zoramite[2] invocation on the Rameumptom): "Holy, holy God; we believe that thou art God, and we believe that thou art holy" (Alma 31:15).

Repetition (here, poetical parallelism): "Yea, let all thy doings be unto the Lord . . . ; yea, let all thy thoughts be directed unto the Lord; yea, let the affections of thy heart be placed upon the Lord forever" (Alma 37:36).

Antithesis: "Inasmuch as they shall keep my commandments they shall prosper in the land. But . . . inasmuch as they will not keep my commandments they shall be cut off from the presence of the Lord" (Alma 50:20).

Chiasmus (a crossing or rhetorical balance with the parts reversed): "All is well in Zion; yea, Zion prospereth, all is well" (2 Ne. 28:21).

Hyperbole (exaggeration): "O that I were an angel, . . . that I might go forth and speak with the trump of God, with a voice to shake the earth" (Alma 29:1; cf. 2 Ne. 26:5).

Paradox (apparently contradictory but true): "If they humble themselves before me, and have faith in me, then will I make weak things become strong unto them" (Ether 12:27).

See also Book of Mormon, as literature; Liken.

RDR

Book of Mormon, as keystone scripture A keystone "is the central stone in an arch. It holds all the other stones in place, and if removed, the arch crumbles" (Benson, 18). The Prophet Joseph Smith referred to the Book of Mormon as the "keystone of our religion" (Smith, 194). According to President Ezra Taft Benson, there are three ways in which the Book of Mormon serves as the keystone (18–19). First, it is "the keystone in our witness of Christ." The scriptural volume sets forth more powerfully than any other book the vital saving work of Jesus the Savior and places him at center stage in all of human history. A primary purpose of the book is to convince Jew and Gentile that Jesus is the Christ, the Eternal God (Title Page; 2 Ne. 26:12). It is in every way another testament of Jesus Christ.

Second, the Book of Mormon is "the keystone of the doctrine of the resurrection" (Benson, 18). The Book of Mormon contains the "fulness of the gospel of Jesus Christ" (D&C 20:9). The doctrines of the Creation, Fall, and Atonement are foundational to all that is presented by Nephite prophets. Further, the principles of the gospel—faith, repentance, baptism, the gift of the Holy Ghost, enduring to the end, resurrection, and eternal judgment (2 Ne. 31; 3 Ne. 27)—are taught consistently and powerfully by the Lord's legal administrators in ancient America. In short, the book delivers a timeless witness of the doctrine of Christ—who he is and what he has done to make immortality and eternal life available to all of God's children.

Third, the Book of Mormon "is the keystone of testimony" (Benson, 19). If the Book of Mormon is true, then Joseph Smith was a prophet called and empowered by God, Joseph Smith received knowledge and divine authority from heavenly messengers, The Church of Jesus Christ of Latter-day Saints is the kingdom of God on earth today. The book provides a test for its own truthfulness: those who read, ponder, and pray with sincerity and real intent may come to know, by the power of the Holy Ghost, that the Book of Mormon is true. No less a being than God himself has borne witness of the Book of Mormon: "And he [Joseph Smith] has translated the book, even that part which I have commanded him, and as your Lord and your God liveth it is true" (D&C 17:6; cf. 6:17; 18:2).

The Church of Jesus Christ of Latter-day Saints was not organized until after the Book of Mormon was translated. The Book of Mormon was and is both fundamental and foundational. The Lord therefore explained that in the Book of Mormon "are all things written concerning the foundation of my church, my gospel, and my rock" (D&C 18:4). The Book of Mormon is the heart and core of The Church of Jesus Christ of Latter-day Saints. "Take away the Book of Mormon and the revelations," Joseph Smith stated, "and where is our religion? We have none" (71).

BIBLIOGRAPHY

Benson, Ezra Taft. *A Witness and a Warning*. Salt Lake City: Deseret Book, 1988.

Smith, Joseph. *Teachings of the Prophet Joseph Smith*. Selected by Joseph Fielding Smith. Salt Lake City: Deseret Book, 1976.

MSN

Book of Mormon, language of the translated text of The title page of the Book of Mormon identifies it as a translation, and readers of the book recognize it as such; however, some may not always consider certain important implications related to the book's identity as a translated text. For example, there are those who have wondered why the book of Jacob in the Book of Mormon ends with the French word "adieu," given that the French language didn't exist in its current form at the time Jacob[2] wrote his farewell. By recognizing that the Book of Mormon is a translation, however, they realize that the French origin of the word "adieu" is unimportant. In fact, the English words found in the Book of Mormon didn't exist in Nephi's time, either, but that makes no difference. The translation was rendered into a language that modern speakers of English can understand. Even though "adieu" was originally a French

Close-up of the keystone of the arch from eastern Monumental Gate, Palmyra (Tadmor), Syria; courtesy William J. Hamblin. The keystone, sometimes called the "headstone," is the central wedge-shaped stone at the top of an arch that locks its parts together.

term, like so much other vocabulary in English, it was, as Daniel C. Peterson pointed out, very much a part of the English language in Joseph Smith's day. *The Oxford English Dictionary* shows its occurrence in English texts at least as far back as the 1300s (Peterson, 146–47). Why did Joseph translate using this term instead of *good-bye* or *farewell?* It is not known for certain, but perhaps it had something to do with its level of formality or its historical meaning. As *good-bye* once conveyed "God be with you," *adieu* conveyed a meaning like "(I commend you) to God."

That the Book of Mormon is a translation may also explain why the Isaiah passages in the Book of Mormon are so similar in wording to the Isaiah passages in the King James Version of the Bible. Although the Book of Mormon was written before the King James translation, Joseph Smith's translation occurred centuries after the King James translation. And as Hugh Nibley pointed out, "When 'holy men of God' quote the scriptures it is always in the received standard version of the people they are addressing" (*Prophetic*, 215). As an illustration of this he explained, "When Jesus and the Apostles and, for that matter, the Angel Gabriel quote the scriptures in the New Testament, do they recite from some mysterious Urtext? Do they quote the prophets of old in the ultimate original? Do they give their own inspired translations? No, they do not. They quote the Septuagint, a Greek version of the Old Testament prepared in the third century B.C. Why so? Because that happened to be the received standard version of the Bible accepted by the readers of the Greek New Testament" (Nibley, *Prophetic*, 215).

The source languages for the Book of Mormon

One factor that must be considered in relation to any translation is the nature of the original language from which a particular text is translated. Knowing something about the original language from which a text is translated can sometimes provide insights into particular linguistic features of the translation. In one respect, readers are severely limited in their knowledge about the original language of the Book of Mormon because the translation was made directly into English from gold plates which are no longer available for examination. But as Brian D. Stubbs showed, the record itself provides some information about the original language of the plates. At the beginning of the book the first prophet-writer, Nephi[1], explained that his record was in a language that "consists of the learning of the Jews and the language of the Egyptians" (1 Ne. 1:2). About a thousand years later Moroni explained that if the plates had been larger they would have written in Hebrew (a Hebrew which he admitted had undergone change), but instead the plates had been written in characters called "reformed Egyptian." Moroni explained that this reformed Egyptian had been "altered by us, according to our manner of speech" (Morm. 9:32–33). Although many questions remain unanswered, Nephi and Moroni mentioned Hebrew and Egyptian, which can serve as a starting point for comparison (Stubbs, 179–80).

Some scholars have examined the Book of Mormon, noting the kinds of language features that could be preserved even through a translation. Hugh Nibley explained that Book of Mormon names constitute a class of "untranslated words" (*Prophetic*, 97). Scholars have found that the Book of Mormon contains many names consistent with a Near Eastern origin. For example, John Gee noted the likely Egyptian origins to the name Nephi (189–91). Hugh Nibley commented on the Egyptian parallels of such Book of Mormon names as Paankhi (Paanchi), Korihor, and Hermounts (*Since Cumorah*, 168–71). He also showed that the Book of Mormon name Alma (used as a man's name) does not appear to be derived from Latin as many outside critics of the Book of Mormon have mistakenly thought but rather was an ancient Hebrew name that has since been attested (Review, 121). *See* Names in the Book of Mormon.

Sometimes the grammar of a translation can provide a clue about the source language. John A. Tvedtnes and Brian D. Stubbs have shown in separate articles that the language of the Book of Mormon contains features characteristic of Hebrew. For example, Tvedtnes showed that the book's use of expressions like "dreamed a

B OF M, LANGUAGE OF THE TRANSLATED

dream" and "judge righteous judgments," in which a noun is formed from the same root of the preceding verb, is reminiscent of the way that these ideas would be expressed in Hebrew (57). *See* Hebraisms.

In addition to names and grammatical patterns, other language features related to poetic expression seem to have been preserved through translation and are consistent with an ancient Near Eastern background. For example, John W. Welch identified startlingly complex patterns of CHIASMUS in the text. Chiasmus is a Hebrew poetic device that arranges ideas in a mirror image.

The English translation of the Book of Mormon

A prominent feature of the Book of Mormon translation is its use of early modern English, which resembles the language of the King James Version of the Bible. For example, both books use the archaic inflectional suffixes *-est* and *-eth* as in "sayest" and "maketh"; they both use archaic pronoun forms "thee," "thou," "thy," and "thine"; and they both tolerate the formation of questions and negatives in ways that are no longer used in modern English, i.e., "What sayest thou?" (John 8:5; cf. Alma 56:44) and "they knew not whither they had fled" (Mosiah 21:31; cf. 1 Sam. 30:22).

It has been noted that an existing standard version could have influenced the form in which particular passages with comparable biblical passages were translated. But what of the rest of the book, which was translated into early modern English similar to the language of the King James Version of the Bible? Any answer to this question involves a consideration of the translation process.

Joseph Smith translated the Book of Mormon by the gift and power of God, but it is not known precisely how the text was revealed to him in the translation process. More specifically, was the translation revealed to Joseph Smith in ideas that he wrote down in his own language (loose control over the translation process), or was it instead revealed to him word for word (tight control)? Or was it a combination of the two possibilities? Royal Skousen shows that there is some manuscript evidence to support the view of tight control of the translation process. In fact, Skousen's research into the manuscript history found some evidence suggesting that when Joseph Smith translated the Book of Mormon he had specific words provided to him ("Translating," 90–91).

Skousen points out that those who advocate the view that Joseph received the translation as concepts and ideas rather than word for word seem to do so, at least in part, because they are aware that the earliest text of the Book of Mormon contained what have been regarded as grammatical errors. But as Skousen points out, the Lord speaks to people "after the manner of their language" (D&C 1:24), and readers should not necessarily expect that he would reveal things to Joseph Smith in the standard English of a later time ("Original Language," 30–32).

Understanding something about Joseph Smith's dialect might yield insights into the language of the translation. This is true whether the Book of Mormon text was revealed to Joseph through concepts which he put into his own language, or whether it was revealed word for word to him in his own language, or some combination of the two. Unfortunately, there are virtually no extant personal writings by him at the time he translated the Book of Mormon. Joseph's own dialect of English at that time must therefore be inferred through an examination of some of his later writings or through the available writings of his local contemporaries.

Documents from the general time and area of Joseph Smith's boyhood attest to the presence in the local dialect(s) of some linguistic forms that would seem archaic to people today and that are similar to the language of the King James Bible. Indeed, one could find some lingering use of the pronoun forms "thee," "thou," "thy," and "thine," as well as the archaic *-eth* and *-est* verb inflectional suffixes. Other characteristics found in the King James Bible as well as in the upstate New York area of Joseph Smith's time include "for" in front of verb infinitives (i.e., "for to come") and the use of such forms as "a going."

It is common for rural communities to be conservative in preserving some older forms of speech. Furthermore, some religious groups often deliberately preserve older language forms.

By these measures, Palmyra and its surrounding area thus represented a prime region for the presence of many older linguistic forms, because it was not only decidedly rural but contained a substantial number of members of the Society of Friends (Quakers) whose speech, even in normal everyday settings, was highly influenced by older forms of English.

The presence of Friends in the Palmyra area during Joseph Smith's boyhood was more substantial than many might expect. Indeed, Milton V. Backman Jr. showed that of the various religions in the area at the time of Joseph's first vision, the Friends were the most highly represented (68, 84). And because Joseph Smith hired himself out to farms in the area around his home, it is likely that he encountered a great deal of the "plain" speech that characterized the early Friend communities and which would have had some resemblances to the language of the King James Bible.

It is difficult but ultimately unnecessary from the standpoint of Joseph Smith's dialectal environment to establish whether the presence of such linguistic forms among speakers in this area is attributable to retained older dialectal forms or to a conscious effort by some religious-minded people to use such forms in their language. Either way, these elements were in the speech of at least some of the people around Joseph Smith, and his ability to use these forms would not have to have been exclusively determined by any direct contact with the Bible. All of this is not to say that Joseph used such archaic forms in his own regular speech. His speech, like that of everyone else, would have had multiple registers that probably varied, depending on whether he was addressing a church congregation, relating a story to small children, or telling a joke to a group of friends. But it seems that he likely had a religious register containing features associated with the language of the King James Bible.

The language of Joseph Smith's translation of the Book of Mormon appropriately matches the religious register associated with the biblical translations then available throughout the English-speaking world. The language of the Book of Mormon translation was likely influenced by Joseph's own language. This would seem to be the case whether the Lord revealed the translation word for word to Joseph after the manner of Joseph's own language, or whether he revealed it to Joseph through ideas Joseph expressed in his own words. But regardless of how the translation was revealed to Joseph Smith, the result was a remarkable one. Important truths are clothed in a language that is powerful and at times beautifully poetic.

See also Anachronisms, alleged; Book of Mormon, as literature; Book of Mormon, poetry in; Book of Mormon, translation of; Book of Mormon, translations of, other than English.

BIBLIOGRAPHY

Backman, Milton V., Jr. *Joseph Smith's First Vision: Confirming Evidences and Contemporary Accounts*. 2d ed. Salt Lake City: Bookcraft, 1980.

Gee, John. "A Note on the Name Nephi." *Journal of Book of Mormon Studies* 1:1 (Fall 1992): 189–91.

Nibley, Hugh. "Review of *Bar-Kochba*." *Brigham Young University Studies* 14:1 (Autumn 1973): 115–26.

———. *Since Cumorah*. 2d ed. Vol. 7 of *The Collected Works of Hugh Nibley*. Edited by John W. Welch. Salt Lake City: Deseret Book, 1988.

———. *The Prophetic Book of Mormon*. Vol. 8 of *The Collected Works of Hugh Nibley*. Salt Lake City: Deseret Book and FARMS, 1989.

Peterson, Daniel C. "Is the Book of Mormon True? Notes on the Debate." *Book of Mormon Authorship Revisited: The Evidence for Ancient Origins*. Edited by Noel B. Reynolds. Provo, Utah: FARMS, 1997.

Skousen, Royal. "The Original Language of the Book of Mormon: Upstate New York Dialect, King James English, or Hebrew?" *Journal of Book of Mormon Studies* 3:1 (Spring 1994): 28–38.

———. "Translating the Book of Mormon: Evidence from the Original Manuscript." *Book of Mormon Authorship Revisited: The Evidence for Ancient Origins*. Edited by Noel B. Reynolds. Provo, Utah: FARMS, 1997.

Stubbs, Brian D. "Book of Mormon Language." *Encyclopedia of Mormonism*. Edited by Daniel H. Ludlow et al. 4 vols. New York: Macmillan, 1992.

Tvedtnes, John A. "Hebraisms in the Book of Mormon: A Preliminary Survey." *Brigham Young University Studies* 11:1 (Autumn 1970): 50–60.

DDO

Book of Mormon, as literature As with other notable works of literature, the Book of Mormon expresses significant ideas and experiences in lively, beautiful, and memorable ways.

BOOK OF MORMON, AS LITERATURE

For example, in his epic *Paradise Lost,* Milton justifies the ways of God to man with exalted blank verse (unrhymed iambic pentameter); the Book of Mormon does so with Hebraic poetry. In his autobiography, *Walden,* Thoreau builds with wit and wisdom on such archetypes as purification and exploration. Similar themes in the Book of Mormon are presented through a wide range of literary genres and characteristics, including narrative (story), imagery (appeals to the senses), figurative language, a variety of rhetorical devices, the epic mode, and typology, all intended "to please the eye and to gladden the heart" (D&C 59:18) as well as to instruct. Written by various prophets, the Book of Mormon comes from the Lord, who "hath made every thing beautiful in his time" (Eccl. 3:11). As that "which is of God," it "inviteth and enticeth to do good" (Moro. 7:13).

Literary elements in the Book of Mormon are not ornamental. Rather, they are an integral part of the book: its form and content are inseparable. Because everyone loves a story, it is appropriate that some of the most memorable lessons in the Book of Mormon are taught through narratives. Metaphors in which Israel is represented as an olive tree, Christ as a shepherd, and the love of Christ as a tree of life rely on lively images to stimulate the book's audience to engage all their senses—figuratively to touch, to taste, to see, and to smell in order to apprehend spiritual truths. The writers of the book reach a wide range of persons through employing such familiar patterns as the hero's journey and quest, the exodus, and the meeting of heaven and earth on a holy mountain or at a temple. Prophecy is conveyed through poetry; indeed, it is one of the characteristics of a prophet to speak poetically. In that regard, the entire Book of Mormon could be said to have a divine poetic structure, for nearly every important action, event, or character type is repeated or contrasted. For instance, Nephi[1]'s being released from his constraining bands (1 Ne. 18:20) is repeated by Alma[2]'s calling on the Lord for himself and Amulek and receiving power to break their bands (Alma 14:26). The prophets Alma and Amulek threatened within a prison are paralleled by Nephi[2] and Lehi[4] in prison (Hel. 5:21 ff.). The anti-Christ Korihor's encounter with Alma[2] (Alma 30) is closely reminiscent of Sherem's encounter with Jacob[2] (Jacob 7:1–20). And righteous king Benjamin and wicked king Noah[3] are pointedly contrasted. This kind of recurrence as found in the Bible is called by literary scholar Robert Alter a type-scene. Alter considers it an important organizing convention in the Bible. Even more so in the Book of Mormon, repeated events appear purposefully to reinforce and define each other; further, they point to an inspired design for the whole book. Most prominently, the transoceanic voyage of the Jaredites parallels the journey of Lehi[1] and his family to the promised land, with the effect of being a second witness of God's power in delivering his children.

Attention to how a number of gospel principles are presented in the Book of Mormon illustrates the integration of literary qualities and content. These examples show how truth, goodness, and beauty are combined.

The principle of faith is beautifully and memorably illustrated in the account of the brother of Jared[1] seeking for and receiving the Lord's direction and help in preparing barges and then in lighting them. This narrative is not simply retold but given dramatic force by the dialogue between the Lord and the brother of Jared: "And the Lord said unto him: Arise, why hast thou fallen? And he saith unto the Lord: I saw the finger of the Lord, and I feared lest he should smite me; for I knew not that the Lord had flesh and blood. And the Lord said unto him: Because of thy faith thou hast seen that I shall take upon me flesh and blood; and never has man come before me with such exceeding faith as thou hast" (Ether 3:7–9).

Mormon illustrated faith by presenting the extended narrative of Helaman[2] and his Lamanite "sons" (Alma 53–57). Alma[2] taught the Zoramite poor the nature of faith through an extended metaphor of the seed being planted in one's heart and becoming a tree that eventually bears fruit (Alma 32). Figuratively, spiritual knowledge comes through feasting on the words of Christ (2 Ne. 32:3), through tasting the light (Alma 32:35) or the fruit of the tree of life, "which is most precious, which is sweet above

BOOK OF MORMON, AS LITERATURE

all that is sweet, and which is white above all that is white, yea, and pure above all that is pure" (Alma 32:42). Earlier, Alma had presented the concept of faith poetically in this appeal to the people of Zarahemla, quoting the Lord's words: "Come unto me and ye shall partake of the fruit of the tree of life; yea, ye shall eat and drink of the bread and the waters of life freely; yea, come unto me and bring forth works of righteousness, and ye shall not be hewn down and cast into the fire" (Alma 5:34–35).

Hope is effectively presented in powerful sermons by such prophets as Benjamin (Mosiah 3–4), Alma[2] (Alma 7; 32), and Mormon (Moro. 7). In the classic sermon on faith, hope, and charity recorded by his son Moroni[2], Mormon affirmed through a figure of speech the necessity of goodness as a basis for hope: "For behold, a bitter fountain cannot bring forth good water; neither can a good fountain bring forth bitter water; wherefore, a man being a servant of the devil cannot follow Christ; and if he follow Christ he cannot be a servant of the devil" (Moro. 7:11). This goodness leads to faith, which is necessary for "hope through the atonement of Christ and the power of his resurrection, to be raised unto life eternal" (Moro. 7:41). Mormon concluded with an appeal to his "beloved brethren" to demonstrate the pure love of Christ so they could have the hope that when Christ appears, "we shall be like him, for we shall see him as he is" (Moro. 7:48). This appeal had special application to Moroni, who in his closing testimony at the end of the Book of Mormon spoke of his own hope, founded on faith and love: "I soon go to rest in the paradise of God, until my spirit and body shall again reunite, and I am brought forth triumphant through the air, to meet you before the pleasing bar of the great Jehovah" (Moro. 10:34). In the larger rhythms of the Book of Mormon, this testimony of hope echoes the closing testimony of Nephi[1], who said, "You and I shall stand face to face before his bar" (2 Ne. 33:11, 15); of Jacob[2], who expected to meet his brethren "before the pleasing bar of God" (Jacob 6:13); and of Mormon, who said his audience "must stand before the judgment-seat of Christ, to be judged according to your works" (Morm. 6:21).

Besides being developed in the well-designed sermons of Benjamin and Mormon, charity is illustrated in the Book of Mormon through extensively presented "type" scenes. Cast into a Lamanite prison, Nephi[2] and Lehi[4] were encircled by fire and visited by angels; subsequently, the observing Lamanites were encircled by fire and enabled to "speak forth marvelous words" and to hear the voice of God declare in a mild and "pleasant voice": "Peace, peace be unto you, because of your faith in my Well Beloved" (Hel. 5:45–47). Some sixty-five years later, Jesus demonstrated his love in blessing the little children, who then were encircled by fire and ministered to by angels. Soon thereafter, Jesus loosened the tongues of the children, "and they did speak unto their fathers great and marvelous things, even greater than he had revealed unto the people" (3 Ne. 26:14).

The need to recognize and confront evil is demonstrated in dramatically developed parallel scenes. The anti-Christ Sherem was revealed as a learned and charismatic man who with his "perfect knowledge of the language of the people" (Jacob 7:4) assumed he could turn even the prophet Jacob[2] away from the truth, addressing him familiarly and condescendingly, "Brother Jacob, I have sought much opportunity that I might speak unto you" (Jacob 7:6). In the dialogue that followed, Jacob exposed Sherem's deviousness and demonstrated his own loyalty to God. Similarly, Korihor appealed to the natural man by denigrating the "foolish traditions" of the Nephite fathers and "foolish ordinances and performances" (Alma 30:23) of the priests until he was exposed in a dramatic confrontation with Alma[2].

Another pair of scenes shows grippingly the evil of secret combinations built up to get power and gain. These combinations are said to have brought the downfall of the Nephite and Jaredite societies and will, as is prophesied, have the potential to bring destruction upon the people living in the last days (Ether 8:21–23). Mormon and Moroni[2] warned against these murderous societies, and the warnings are brought to life by parallel stories that bear some resemblance to parables, illustrating the nature and consequences of Gadiantonism. The record speaks at

BOOK OF MORMON, AS LITERATURE

length about Kishkumen and Gadianton and their society who, bound by secret oaths, attempted to murder the chief judge. A similar extended account describes the conspiring of Akish and the daughter of Jared[2] as well as the subsequent wickedness of Akish in beheading his father-in-law and starving his son to death (Ether 8–9).

Repentance is illustrated in the repeated story of the conversion (literally, turning around) of Alma the Younger, son of the head of the Church—who would in turn become the chief high priest. John W. Welch has shown how the ancient literary technique of CHIASMUS sets forth Alma's faith and repentance in an exceptionally memorable way. Welch demonstrates how the entirety of Alma 36 is a chiasm (which means, literally, a crossing, with the subject of the first part mirrored in the last part, that of the second part found in the next-to-last part, and so forth). The crossing point comes when, as Alma said, he perceived himself to be "encircled about by the everlasting chains of death" and called on Jesus for mercy. At that point, as Alma later told his son, his pains were replaced by "joy as exceeding as was my pain" (Alma 36:18, 20).

As Welch has also demonstrated, chiastic repetitions appear frequently in Benjamin's great sermon on the need for covenant making and the process of doing so. This sermon also lends itself readily to an examination of Benjamin's rhetorical methods, which can be recognized by applying the ideas of classicist George A. Kennedy. King Benjamin actually used the three modes of artistic proof that Kennedy sets forth: *ethos, pathos,* and *logos*. Benjamin's *ethos* (evidence of his credibility) comes especially in his affirming that he received his words from an angel (Mosiah 3:2–3; 4:1). *Pathos* (appeal to emotions) is developed through a figure of speech—Benjamin said that evil people at the judgment day will "have drunk out of the cup of the wrath of God" (Mosiah 3:26)—and through a rhetorical turn on the word *beggars:* "Ye will not suffer that the beggar putteth up his petition to you in vain. . . . For behold, are we not all beggars?" (Mosiah 4:16, 19). *Logos* (logical argument) is found in Benjamin's series of propositions and consequences, of which the following is an example: "If I, whom ye call your king . . . do merit any thanks from you, O how you ought to thank your heavenly King!" (Mosiah 2:19).

A frequently repeated charge in the Book of Mormon is the admonition to endure to the end, which is shown, significantly, through the journey motif. Literary treatments of the hero's quest (e.g., Joseph Campbell's *Hero with a Thousand Faces*) and epic patterns (e.g., E. M. W. Tillyard's *English Epic and Its Background*) assist the reader to see more clearly the epic elements in the Book of Mormon. Nephi[1] was heroic in obtaining the plates of brass as he was in obtaining food after breaking his bow and in building a ship. His story is like other epics in that it tells of the founding of a race or people. Other heroes in the Book of Mormon include Ammon[2], who fought off the robbers at the waters of Sebus (Alma 17:26–39); captain Moroni, who conquered Zerahemnah (Alma 44:1–19); Amalickiah (Alma 46:30–33) and the forces of Ammaron (Alma 55:20–23; 62:33–38) and others; and Mormon, leader of the Nephite armies in his "sixteenth year" (Morm. 2:2). The travels of both the Lehites and the Jaredites to the promised land are of epic magnitude, involving vast spaces, large-scale migrations, and the aid of supernatural powers. In his *Anatomy of Criticism,* literary critic Northrop Frye finds two epic frameworks in the Bible, the epic of return and the epic of wrath. The return is to redemption; the wrath is evidenced in a cycle of humanity repressed by permanent exile, war, or destruction. One can readily apply Frye's views to the Book of Mormon. The epic of wrath is the story of unrepentant Nephites and Jaredites bringing about their own destruction; the epic of return is found in the prophets' long-term view of the ultimate redemption of righteous Israel and the record assisting in this redemption coming "out of the dust" (Moro. 10:27).

Literarily, Christ is often presented in the Book of Mormon through typology—God-given events or God-directed persons serving as likenesses of Christ or his gospel. The Liahona, for example, was a type of Christ. As Alma[2] said to his son, "Is there not a type in this thing? For just as surely as this director did bring our fathers, by following its course, to the promised land, shall the words of Christ, if we follow their course, carry us beyond this vale of sorrow into a far better land of promise" (Alma 37:45). Nephi[1] was like Christ in being resisted as the rightful spiritual ruler, in being a factor in the stilling of a turbulent sea, in fulfilling his father's mission, and in guiding his people to a promised land. King Benjamin typified Christ in that he was a mortal representation of a heavenly king. Abinadi, too, exemplified Christ, as an innocent person who is cast into prison for three days, whose blood is shed for his testimony, and who at his death says, "O God, receive my soul" (Mosiah 17:19). The three-day deathlike trances and spiritual rebirths of Alma[2] and king Lamoni were TYPES of Christ's death, burial, and resurrection.

As with the Liahona, so the Book of Mormon is "of curious workmanship" (1 Ne. 16:10). A literary approach to that inspired record helps reveal the various ways by which human beings, like Nephi[1], can delight "in the things of the Lord" (2 Ne. 4:16). Just as Zion is challenged to put on its "beautiful garments" (2 Ne. 8:24; Isa. 52:1), so in the way it is presented the Book of Mormon might be considered to have beautiful garments. Through its literary dimensions, the book calls on Israel to "awake, and arise from the dust" and to "come unto Christ" (Moro. 10:30–32).

See also Book of Mormon, figures of speech in; Book of Mormon, poetry in; Parallelism.

BIBLIOGRAPHY

Alter, Robert. *The Art of Biblical Narrative.* New York: Basic Books, 1981.

———. *The World of Biblical Literature.* New York: Basic Books, 1992.

Frye, Northrop. *The Great Code: The Bible and Literature.* New York: Harcourt Brace Jovanovich, 1982.

Kennedy, George A. *Classical Rhetoric and Its Christian and Secular Tradition from Ancient to Modern Times.* Chapel Hill, N.C.: University of North Carolina Press, 1980.

———. *New Testament Interpretation through Rhetorical Criticism.* Chapel Hill, N.C.: University of North Carolina Press, 1984.

Rust, Richard Dilworth. *Feasting on the Word: The Literary Testimony of the Book of Mormon.* Salt Lake City: Deseret Book, 1997.

Thomas, Mark D. *Digging in Cumorah: Reclaiming Book of Mormon Narratives.* Salt Lake City: Signature Books, 1999.

RDR

Book of Mormon, lost manuscript of (116 pages) The manuscript pages of the book of Lehi translation, "an account abridged from the plates of Lehi, by the hand of Mormon" (Smith, *History,* 1:56), lost (stolen) through the carelessness of Martin Harris. After serving as scribe for Joseph Smith's dictation of the book of Lehi from April 12 to June 14, 1828 in Harmony, Pennsylvania, Martin Harris sought permission to show the manuscript to his wife and other relatives residing in Palmyra, New York.

Joseph Smith inquired of the Lord, through the Urim and Thummim, for permission for Martin to show the manuscript to his relatives but was initially denied. Martin coaxed Joseph to inquire again, but the answer from God was the same. On asking a third time, Joseph was granted permission on condition that Martin show the manuscript only to his wife Lucy, his brother Preserved Harris, his father and mother, and his wife's sister, Abigail Cobb (Smith, *History,* 1:21).

After making a solemn covenant of obedience to the conditions, Martin took the 116-page manuscript to Palmyra. During the ensuing three weeks, he broke the covenant by showing the manuscript to a close friend and then to others and "set at naught the counsels of God, and has broken the most sacred promises which were made before God, and has depended upon his own judgment and boasted in his own wisdom" (D&C 3:13). Through his carelessness, the manuscript was stolen from his home. According to Pomeroy Tucker (45–46), a prominent resident of Palmyra, New York, and Lucy Mack Smith, the mother of Joseph Smith, Martin Harris's wife played a key role in the theft of the manuscript. "There is no doubt but Mrs. Harris took it from the drawer [where Martin had placed it], with the view of retaining it until another translation should be given," wrote Lucy Smith, "then to alter the original translation, for the purpose of showing a discrepancy between them, and thus make the whole appear to be a deception" (Smith, *Joseph,* 131).

Telling Joseph Smith about the lost manuscript proved difficult for Martin Harris. Soon after he entered the Smith home in Manchester, where Joseph had arrived the night before, he was asked, "Martin, . . . are you sick?" Martin "pressed his hands upon his temples, and cried out in a tone of deep anguish, 'Oh, I have lost my soul! I have lost my soul!'"

"Have you lost that manuscript? Have you broken your oath, and brought down condemnation upon my head as well as your own?" Joseph asked. "Yes; it is gone," declared Martin, "and I know not where." Joseph told Martin to return to his home and look again. "I have ripped open beds and pillows; and I know it is not there," said Martin.

"Oh, my God!" replied Joseph. "All is lost! all is lost! What shall I do?" Joseph blamed himself for the loss of the 116 manuscript pages: "It is I who tempted the wrath of God. I should have been satisfied with the first answer which I received from the Lord." It seemed no one could comfort him. "Sobs and groans, and the most bitter lamentations filled the house," wrote his mother. "I well remember that day of darkness, both within and without. To us, at least, the heavens seemed clothed with blackness, and the earth shrouded with gloom" (Smith, *Joseph*, 128–29, 132).

Joseph left Manchester in July 1828 and returned to Harmony. There he received from an angel the Urim and Thummim, which had been taken from him when Martin lost the manuscript (Smith, *Church*, 1:21; D&C 10:1–3). Through the Urim and Thummim, Joseph Smith was chastised for losing the manuscript: "How oft you have transgressed the commandments and the laws of God, and have gone on in the persuasions of men" (D&C 3:6). Joseph reported that "after I had obtained the above revelation [D&C 3], both the Urim and Thummim were taken from me again; but in a few days they were returned to me."

When Joseph inquired of the Lord, he received Doctrine and Covenants 10 (Smith, *History*, 1:23). Joseph was thus called again to the work of translating the Book of Mormon, but in compliance with the Lord's instructions, he did not retranslate the book of Lehi (D&C 10:30). Joseph was told that if he were to translate the same again, his enemies would publish an altered version of that which they had stolen and "say that he has lied in his words, and that he has no gift" (D&C 10:16–18). As a result, Satan "would stir up the hearts of this generation, that they might not receive this work" (Smith, *History*, 1:56).

The Lord comforted Joseph over the loss of the manuscript by telling him that "an account of those things that you have written, which have gone out of your hands, is engraven upon the plates of Nephi. . . . Therefore, you shall translate the engravings which are on the plates of Nephi, down even till you come to the reign of king Benjamin, or until you come to that which you have translated . . . you shall publish it as the record of Nephi; and thus I will confound those who have altered my words" (D&C 10:38, 41–42; the plates of Nephi refer to 1 Nephi through the book of Omni).

The 116 manuscript pages have never been published. To date they remain lost.

See also The Coming Forth of the Book of Mormon, 9; Book of Mormon, manuscripts of; Book of Mormon, translation of; Lehi, book of.

BIBLIOGRAPHY

Smith, Joseph. *History of The Church of Jesus Christ of Latter-day Saints*. Edited by B. H. Roberts. 7 vols. 2d ed. rev. Salt Lake City: The Church of Jesus Christ of Latter-day Saints, 1932–51.

Smith, Lucy Mack. *History of Joseph Smith by His Mother.* Edited by Preston Nibley. Salt Lake City: Bookcraft, 1956.

Tucker, Pomeroy. *Origin, Rise, and Progress of Mormonism.* New York: D. Appleton and Company, 1867.

SB

Book of Mormon, manuscripts of There are two manuscripts of the Book of Mormon. The first one is the original manuscript, which the scribes wrote down as Joseph Smith dictated the text. The second manuscript is the printer's manuscript, which (for the most part) was taken to the printer and used to set the type for the 1830 edition.

The original manuscript

The original manuscript was written from 1828 through June of 1829. The first 116 pages

BOOK OF MORMON, MANUSCRIPTS OF

were lost by Martin Harris and, according to Joseph Smith's statement (in the preface to the 1830 edition), contained the book of Lehi. These pages also may have included the initial part of the book of Mosiah, because the original first two chapters of that book were apparently lost (Skousen, "Methodology," 138–39). There is some evidence that Joseph Smith translated the small plates of Nephi (from 1 Nephi through the Words of Mormon) last—that is, after finishing the book of Moroni.

For about 15 percent of the current Book of Mormon text (from Helaman 13 through Mormon 9), the original manuscript was taken to the printer's shop and used to set the type for the 1830 edition. The scribes responsible for producing the printer's manuscript probably fell behind in their copy work and allowed the original manuscript to be used by the printer until the scribes caught up with their copying (Skousen, "Piecing," 23–24).

The original manuscript was used by Joseph Smith to restore a handful of accidentally deleted phrases in the 1840 edition. For the 1981 edition, the original manuscript was used to restore the original reading (that is, wording) in about twenty places.

In October 1841 Joseph Smith placed the original manuscript in the cornerstone of the Nauvoo House.

Over forty years later (in 1882), Lewis Bidamon, the second husband of Emma Smith, removed the original manuscript from the cornerstone. The manuscript had been severely damaged by water seepage and mold; 1 Nephi was basically intact, as were the middle portions (from Alma 22 through Helaman 3). Apparently, only smaller fragments remained from the rest of the manuscript. Over the next six years, Bidamon handed out intact sheets, mostly to members of The Church of Jesus Christ of Latter-day Saints.

Most of these sheets now reside in the archives of the Church. Smaller fragments (from fifty-eight pages of the manuscript) were kept back by Bidamon and were purchased from his son in 1937 by Wilford Wood, a collector from Bountiful, Utah. In 1991 these fragments were conserved and photographed.

Cornerstone of the Nauvoo House, Nauvoo, Illinois; photograph by George Edward Anderson on 4 May 1907; courtesy LDS Family and Church History Archives. Joseph Smith put the original manuscript of the Book of Mormon into the cornerstone of the Nauvoo House, 2 October 1841.

In all, 25 to 30 percent of the original manuscript is extant. The remaining fragments are hard to read and in many places require ultraviolet photography to bring out the text.

Oliver Cowdery was the scribe for nearly all the extant portions of the original manuscript. Two unknown scribes are responsible for most of the first half of 1 Nephi, and Joseph Smith's hand is found for twenty-eight words in Alma 45.

The original manuscript was written from oral dictation. The chapter numbers are not part of the original text but were added whenever Joseph Smith saw a break in the text. Joseph also spelled out Book of Mormon names whenever the scribe was unable to figure out the spelling directly from the dictation. Joseph Smith dictated up to thirty words at a time, and there are very few signs of any editing or of Joseph changing his mind about the translation. Also, there is no original punctuation in the manuscript except for a few dashes in the summaries found at the beginning of most books.

The accuracy of the manuscript depended on Joseph Smith and his scribe carefully checking

BOOK OF MORMON, MANUSCRIPTS OF

the text for errors. The original manuscript is not letter-for-letter perfect but apparently contains only a few errors.

The text as found in the original manuscript is very consistent in usage, even though the language is a mixture of biblical style English and Joseph Smith's upstate New York English. In addition, a number of non-English HEBRAISMS (expressions characteristic of the Hebrew language) have been identified in the original text.

The printer's manuscript

The printer's manuscript is a copy made from the original manuscript, and for about 85 percent of the Book of Mormon this manuscript was the copy used by the 1830 printer for setting the type.

This copy was not made all at once but instead was produced as the printer needed copy. Many of the pages of this manuscript are covered with the punctuation and other printing-related marks made by the compositor (that is, typesetter), John Gilbert. Most of these punctuation marks are in pencil.

Three scribes are responsible for the printer's manuscript: Oliver Cowdery (who did about 85 percent of the manuscript), an unknown scribe (who did about 15 percent), and Hyrum Smith, who occasionally substituted (but only briefly) for the unknown scribe. Hyrum is responsible for less than 1 percent of the text. The copying is quite accurate, with an average of about three changes per manuscript page. Only a small proportion of these changes make any difference in meaning.

The printer's manuscript was the copy used by Joseph Smith for making changes in the 1837 edition of the Book of Mormon. His corrections (almost all of which are grammatical in nature) are in heavy black ink and are found throughout the manuscript.

Oliver Cowdery took the printer's manuscript with him when he was excommunicated from

Second Nephi 25:16–18 from the original manuscript; photograph by David W. Hawkinson; courtesy WWF. The original manuscript is the manuscript that the scribes wrote as Joseph Smith dictated the text of the Book of Mormon. This particular text of 2 Nephi 25:16–18, is in the handwriting of Oliver Cowdery. Only 28 percent of this manuscript is extant.

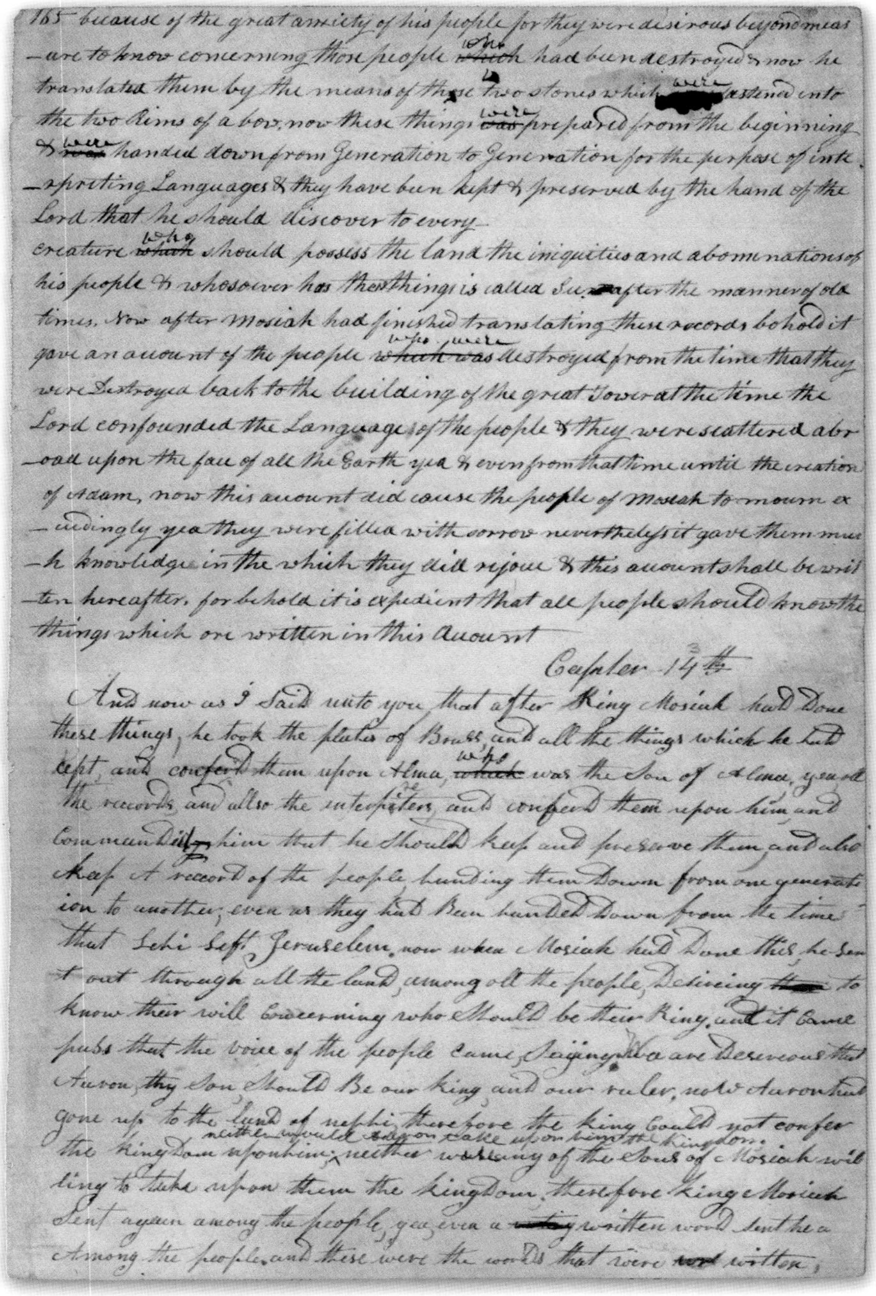
165 because of the great anxiety of his people for they were desirous beyond meas
-ure to know concerning those people who had been destroyed & now he
translated them by the means of those two stones which were fastened into
the two Rims of a bow, now these things were prepared from the beginning
& were handed down from Generation to Generation for the purpose of inte
-rpreting Languages & they have been kept & preserved by the hand of the
Lord that he should discover to every
creature who should possess the land the iniquities and abominations of
his people & whosoever has these things is called Seer after the manner of old
times, Now after Mosiah had finished translating these records behold it
gave an account of the people who were destroyed from the time that they
were Destroyed back to the building of the great Tower at the time the
Lord confounded the Language of the people & they were scattered abr
-oad upon the face of all the Earth yea & even from that time until the creation
of Adam, now this account did cause the people of Mosiah to mourn ex
-ceedingly yea they were filled with sorrow nevertheless it gave them muc
-h knowledge in the which they did rejoice & this account shall be writ
-ten hereafter, for behold it is expedient that all people should know the
things which are written in this account

Chapter 14th

And now as I Said unto you that after King Mosiah had Done
these things, he took the plates of Brass and all the things which he had
kept and conferred them upon Alma, who was the Son of Alma, yea all
the records and also the interpreters, and conferred them upon him and
Commanded him that he Should keep and preserve them and also
keep A record of the people handing them Down from one generat
ion to another, even as they had Been handed Down from the time
that Lehi left Jerusalem, now when Mosiah had Done this, he Sen
t out through all the land, among all the people, Desiring to
know their will concerning who Should be their King, and it Came
pass that the voice of the people came, Saying We are Desirous that
Aaron, thy Son Should Be our king and our ruler, now Aaron had
gone up to the land of nephi, therefore the king Could not confer
neither would Aaron take upon him the kingdom
the kingDom upon him, neither were any of the Sons of Mosiah wil
ling to take upon them the kingDom, therefore king Mosiah
Sent again among the people, yea even a written word Sent he a
Among the people, and these were the words that were written,

Mosiah 28:12–29:4 from the printer's manuscript; photograph by Nevin J. Skousen; courtesy CCA. This page shows the hand of each of the scribes and correctors who worked on the printer's manuscript. The top half is in the hand of scribe 2, not yet identified. Hyrum Smith was the scribe for the bottom half. Oliver Cowdery proofread the page against the original manuscript; the long interlinear insertion near the bottom of the page is his. The 1830 typesetter (John Gilbert) penciled in some punctuation marks. For the 1837 Kirtland edition, Joseph Smith made some grammatical changes in heavy black ink.

Printer's manuscript of the Book of Mormon; courtesy CCA. This manuscript is the copy of the original manuscript that the scribes made and took to the Palmyra printer for setting the 1830 edition. The printer's manuscript is made up of twenty-one gatherings, shown here in a stack. Each leaf measures about 13 by 8 inches. Except for three lines at the bottom of the first leaf, the manuscript is completely extant.

the Church in 1838. After Oliver's death in 1850, the manuscript was kept by David Whitmer, his brother-in-law. After Whitmer's death in 1888, the manuscript was held by a grandson of Whitmer, who sold the manuscript in 1903 to the Reorganized Church of Jesus Christ of Latter Day Saints (now known as Community of Christ).

The printer's manuscript is fully extant except for about three lines of text on the first leaf of the manuscript.

See also Book of Mormon, lost manuscript of (116 pages); Book of Mormon, printing and publication of; Book of Mormon, translation of; Gilbert, John Hulburd.

BIBLIOGRAPHY

Skousen, Royal. "Piecing Together the Original Manuscript." *BYU Today* 46 (May 1992): 18–24.

———. "Critical Methodology and the Text of the Book of Mormon." *Review of Books on the Book of Mormon* 6:1 (1994): 121–44.

———. "John Gilbert's 1892 Account of the 1830 Printing of the Book of Mormon." *The Scholar as Witness: Essays in Honor of Richard Lloyd Anderson*. Edited by Stephen D. Ricks, Donald W. Parry, and Andrew H. Hedges. Provo, Utah: FARMS, 1999.

———. "The Original Language of the Book of Mormon: Upstate New York Dialect, King James English, or Hebrew?" *Journal of Book of Mormon Studies* 3:1 (1994): 28–38.

———. "Translating the Book of Mormon: Evidence from the Original Manuscript." *Book of Mormon Authorship Revisited: The Evidence for Ancient Origins*. Edited by Noel B. Reynolds. Provo, Utah: FARMS (1997): 61–93.

RJS

Book of Mormon, as most correct book Joseph Smith declared "the Book of Mormon was the most correct of any book on earth" (194). The Lord himself has sworn with an oath that this scriptural record is true (D&C 17:6; cf. 6:17; 18:2). Several times in modern revelation Deity has proclaimed that the Book of Mormon contains the "fulness of the gospel" (D&C 20:9; 27:5; 35:12, 17; 42:12). The Book of Mormon certainly contains the will of the Lord, the mind of the Lord, the word of the Lord, the voice of the Lord, and the power of God unto salvation—the gospel (Rom. 1:16). Because it has not passed through generations of transmitters and translations, the Book of Mormon has retained plain and precious truths and the covenants of the Lord (1 Ne. 13:24–29, 39–41).

Hugh Nibley has asked, "What is a 'correct' book? One with properly cut margins, appropriate binding, a useful index, accurately numbered pages? Not at all; these are mere mechanical details, as are also punctuation, spelling, and even grammar—those matters about which the critics of the Book of Mormon have made such a to-do. . . . The most correct book in the world is the one that will be found to contain the fewest untrue statements after all the books in the world have been checked and compared. Of course no one can know today which book that will be, unless one knows it by revelation" (7–8).

The Book of Mormon is not just another treatise on religion prepared by men, even good men. It is God-inspired. Its prophet-writers were directed by God, and its message is an inspiring invitation to come unto Christ and be saved. It was translated and brought forth by the gift and power of God under the direction of an angel of God (JS–H 1:27–54; D&C 20:6–10).

BIBLIOGRAPHY

Nibley, Hugh. *Since Cumorah*. 2d ed. Vol. 7 of *The Collected Works of Hugh Nibley*. Edited by John W. Welch. Salt Lake City: Deseret Book, 1988.

Smith, Joseph. *Teachings of the Prophet Joseph Smith*. Selected by Joseph Fielding Smith. Salt Lake City: Deseret Book, 1976.

MSN

Book of Mormon, names in *See* Names in the Book of Mormon.

Book of Mormon, opposition to The gold plates from which the Book of Mormon was translated were providentially preserved during their preparation and compilation by ancient writers (Enos 1:13; W of M 1:6–11; Alma 37:1–12). Several specific passages in the book refer to the plates being hidden or deposited in antiquity "that they might not be destroyed" (Morm. 2:17; 1:3–4; 6:6; Title Page). Nephi[1] was aware of some of the opposition the book would encounter in the latter days after its publication. He recorded a revelation wherein the Lord foretold the reaction of many Gentiles to this new scripture: "And because my words shall hiss forth—many of the Gentiles shall say: A Bible! A Bible! We have got a Bible, and there cannot be any more Bible" (2 Ne. 29:3). Nephi warned against this error (2 Ne. 28:27, 29–30) and included the Lord's response to those who would reject the Book of Mormon based upon the belief that there could be no more scripture other than what is known as the Bible (2 Ne. 29:4–14). Moroni[2], apparently anticipating opposition to the Nephite record, warned: "He that condemneth, let him be aware lest he shall be in danger of hell fire" (Morm. 8:17).

From the time that Joseph Smith obtained the plates from the angel Moroni in 1827 until the time he returned them in 1829, Joseph Smith encountered various efforts to take the plates from him (Hedges). Moroni warned the young prophet about such opposition. Joseph told his family that "when we get the plates they will want to kill us for the sake of the gold" (Proctor, 111).

On the night he obtained the plates, Joseph Smith hid them in an old birch log instead of taking them home in his first effort to thwart those interested in taking the plates (Proctor, 142–44). The Prophet told people about the encounters with the heavenly messenger. As word spread that he had the plates, a group of ten or twelve men planned to locate them. At this time Joseph Smith decided to carry the plates home for safekeeping. As he made his way through the woods, in an effort to avoid anyone on the road, he was attacked three separate times before arriving at the Smith farm exhausted and with a dislocated thumb (Proctor, 144).

During the next days, weeks, and months, Joseph moved the plates several times, in some cases just ahead of those attempting to find them (Proctor, 149–51). At some point during this stressful period, Joseph decided that another location must be found where he could begin the work of translating the ancient record. With the help of a local farmer, Martin Harris, Joseph and his wife Emma traveled to Harmony, Pennsylvania, to the home of Emma's parents, Isaac and Elizabeth Hale (JS–H 1:61–62).

Anticipating trouble, Joseph Smith left two days earlier than had been noised about. He took extra precautions by placing the plates in a barrel of beans for the trip (Proctor, 154). While in Harmony, Pennsylvania, he enjoyed a brief

BOOK OF MORMON, OPPOSITION TO

respite from the opposition he faced in the Palmyra-Manchester area. When Martin Harris and his wife arrived in Harmony, Lucy Harris immediately ransacked the house in an effort to find the plates. Joseph Smith hid them again in the woods nearby (Proctor, 156–57). Martin took his wife back to Palmyra.

Martin Harris rejoined Joseph in Harmony, where on April 12, 1828, he acted as Joseph's scribe during the translation (Smith, *History,* 1:20–21). Within a short time, he and Joseph completed 116 pages of translation, a section of the ancient record known as the book of Lehi. Disregarding earlier counsel from the Lord, Joseph Smith allowed Harris to take the 116 pages to Palmyra. Harris thought that members of his family, who were opposed to his involvement with the Prophet, would be convinced of the divinity of the work once they saw the translation. Unfortunately, the manuscript entrusted to Martin was stolen by conspirators (Smith, *History,* 1:21; D&C 10:8).

The loss of the 116 pages was a severe blow to Joseph Smith, yet, the Lord reminded him, "the works, and the designs, and the purposes of God cannot be frustrated, neither can they come to naught" (D&C 3:1). Shortly thereafter, the Prophet learned of a scheme carried out by these same conspirators. They had altered the words of the stolen translation so that when he retranslated the material, they could demonstrate that he was unable to translate the same material with exactly the same words, thereby casting doubt on Joseph's claims of inspiration in the translation work (D&C 10:1–43).

After the loss of the 116 pages, when Joseph Smith was allowed to continue the work of translating the Book of Mormon, he worked with his wife, Emma, and his brother Samuel H. Smith (Smith, *Papers,* 10). Not until Oliver Cowdery arrived in April 1829, however, did the work progress on a steady basis. They also encountered increased opposition in Harmony, Pennsylvania (JS–H 1:75). Despite protection offered by his father-in-law, Joseph Smith and Oliver Cowdery decided they needed to complete the work unfettered, so they moved to Fayette, New York, where Peter and Mary Whitmer furnished them lodging and some protection. Here they finally completed the translation of the Book of Mormon (Smith, *History,* 1:48–49).

Joseph Smith eventually returned the plates to the angel Moroni, having successfully protected them against those opposed to the work. He summarized this period later in 1839: "The most strenuous exertions were used to get [the plates] from me. Every stratagem that could be invented was resorted to for that purpose" (JS–H 1:60).

And while the plates were in the custody of the angel Moroni, opposition continued. At first, Egbert B. Grandin, the Palmyra publisher, refused on religious grounds to print the volume. Eventually Grandin's concerns were overcome, and the work began. But soon Joseph Smith encountered additional difficulty as he attempted to publish the ancient record. Abner Cole (alias Obadiah Dogberry) who used the Grandin press on weekends to publish *The Reflector,* began printing segments of the Book of Mormon before it was published by Joseph Smith. And while Cole was not antagonistic towards Joseph Smith at first, he nevertheless was guilty of pirating selected portions of the book. If this action had been allowed to continue, it could have negatively affected sales of the Book of Mormon. But when asked to desist by Oliver Cowdery and Hyrum Smith, Cole refused. Joseph Smith returned from Harmony and reminded Cole of the copyright, and Cole stopped his illegal activity (Bushman, 108–9).

During this critical period, a large group of citizens hoped to thwart Joseph's efforts to publish the book when they met together and resolved not to purchase the Book of Mormon. Despite the mortgage agreement with Harris, Grandin hesitated to continue in the face of an extensive boycott of the volume. Joseph Smith was again summoned from Harmony, and he gave the necessary assurances. Grandin then continued his work. Finally, the book was made available to the public on 26 March 1830.

The publication of the Book of Mormon, however, did not stop continued opposition to the work. First, the promised boycott delayed efforts to place the book in the hands of potential converts and greatly curtailed efforts to

BOOK OF MORMON, OPPOSITION TO

recover the cost of printing. Martin Harris was forced to sell 151 acres on 7 April 1831 to satisfy the debt for the book's publication. Second, arguments were advanced to counter Joseph Smith's explanation of its origin (Midgley). Abner Cole, the editor of the Palmyra *Reflector,* provided one of the earliest alternative explanations. He asserted that the Book of Mormon was simply of human origin—that is, Joseph Smith wrote the book himself (*Reflector*). Arriving at the same conclusion in February 1831 was Alexander Campbell, an important Protestant clergyman ("Delusions").

Most early opponents thought, as did Cole and Campbell, that Joseph Smith wrote the Book of Mormon. But they underestimated the book's religious power and narrative complexity. By 1834, after a more careful analysis of the book and an increasing number of converts, opponents to the Book of Mormon proposed another explanation for its existence. These detractors, including Philastus Hurlburt and Eber D. Howe, insisted that Joseph Smith had help in writing the book. They argued that he very likely was assisted by someone else, probably Sidney Rigdon (Howe, 290). Alexander Campbell eventually repudiated his original assessment of authorship, acknowledging that Joseph Smith could not have written the book himself, as Joseph was uneducated.

Most of those espousing this argument, especially Hurlburt and later Campbell, believed that Joseph Smith and Sidney Rigdon produced the book together as a conscious fraud and also argued that they used additional sources, including the work of Solomon Spaulding (a theory now generally rejected) or Ethan Smith, author of *View of the Hebrews* (Howe, 100, 278; Brodie, 46).

Most nineteenth-century arguments against the book's ancient origin generally implied fraudulent motives by the supposed authors. In 1902 Isaac Woodbridge Riley proposed a psychological explanation (Riley). Although this naturalistic explanation held that Joseph Smith indeed wrote the book, some have argued that, because they believed the Prophet was subject to epileptic fits during his youth and to other pathological mental conditions later in life, he was not a fraud per se. Following the publication of the book, others argued there was yet another explanation. They believed some type of otherworldly influence, including Satanic power, best explained the existence of the Book of Mormon (Midgley, 103).

During the last decade of the twentieth century, a new explanation has been offered by some who believe the book to be a product of the nineteenth century. These critics detach the book from its ancient origin but nevertheless claim that the book may have some religious value as a kind of religious fiction or parable (Metcalfe, 1–20, 53–80, 165–230).

Latter-day Saints accept the Prophet Joseph Smith's statement that the Book of Mormon was an ancient record "found through the ministration of an holy angel, and translated into our own language by the gift and power of God" (Smith, *History,* 1:315). As a result, thoughtful responses to these and other claims against the Book of Mormon have been put forth in an effort to defend the ancient origin of the book. Many of these responses are found in such sources as the *Ensign* magazine, *Brigham Young University Studies,* BYU Religious Studies Center, and the Foundation for Ancient Research and Mormon Studies (FARMS; see especially *Review of Books on the Book of Mormon,* beginning in 1989, published by FARMS). Additionally, Terryl L. Givens's *By the Hand of Mormon: The American Scripture That Launched a New World Religion* (2002) provides a detailed analysis of the various expressions of opposition to the book's authorship (155–84).

Because the truth concerning the Book of Mormon is inseparably linked to the truth concerning the work and claims of Joseph Smith, including the reality of modern revelation and the restoration of the Church of Jesus Christ in modern times, debates continue to rage concerning its origin. It is an important tenet of The Church of Jesus Christ of Latter-day Saints that personal discovery of the truthfulness of the Book of Mormon comes through divine special revelation, that the book came forth by revelation, and its divine origin can only ultimately be confirmed by revelation to sincere readers. The prophet Moroni, the last Nephite author, concluded his work on the plates with a promise to all readers of the Book of Mormon: "Behold, I would exhort you that when ye shall read these things, if it be wisdom in God that ye should read them, that ye would remember how merciful the Lord hath been unto the children of men, from the creation of Adam even down until the time that ye shall receive these things, and ponder it in your hearts. And when ye shall receive these things, I would exhort you that ye would ask God, the Eternal Father, in the name of Christ, if these things are not true; and if ye shall ask with a sincere heart, with real intent, having faith in Christ, he will manifest the truth of it unto you, by the power of the Holy Ghost" (Moro. 10:3–4).

See also The Coming Forth of the Book of Mormon, 9; Anachronisms, alleged; Book of Mormon, lost manuscript of (116 pages); Book of Mormon, printing and publication of; Shakespeare and the Book of Mormon; Spaulding theory; *View of the Hebrews*.

BIBLIOGRAPHY

Brodie, Fawn M. *No Man Knows My History: The Life of Joseph Smith*. New York: Vintage, 1995.

Bushman, Richard L. *Joseph Smith and the Beginnings of Mormonism*. Urbana and Chicago: University of Illinois Press, 1984.

Campbell, Alexander. "The Mormon Bible." *Millennial Harbinger* 3 (June 1839): 265–68.

"Delusions." *Millennial Harbinger* 2/2 (7 February 1831): 85–96; as cited in Francis W. Kirkham, *New Witness for Christ in America: The Book of Mormon*. Revised and enlarged. Independence, Mo.: Zion's Printing and Publishing Company, 1947. 296.

Givens, Terryl L. *By the Hand of Mormon: The American Scripture That Launched a New World Religion*. New York: Oxford University Press, 2002.

Hedges, Andrew W. "'All My Endeavors to Preserve Them': Protecting the Plates in Palmyra, 22 September—December 1827." *Journal of Book of Mormon Studies* 8:2 (1999): 14–23.

Howe, Eber D. *Mormonism Unvailed*. Painesville, Ohio: Printed and published by the author, 1834; as cited in Francis W. Kirkham, *New Witness for Christ in America: The Book of Mormon*. Revised and enlarged. Independence, Mo.: Zion's Printing and Publishing Company, 1947. 300.

Midgley, Louis C. "Who Really Wrote the Book of Mormon? The Critics and Their Theories." *Book of Mormon Authorship Revisited: The Evidence for Ancient Origins*. Provo: FARMS (1977): 101–39.

Metcalfe, Brent Lee, ed. *New Approaches to the Book of Mormon: Explorations in Critical Methodology*. Salt Lake City: Signature Books, 1993.

The Reflector. January 7, 1831, through March 19, 1831; as cited in Francis W. Kirkham, *New Witness for Christ in America: The Book of Mormon*. Revised and enlarged. Independence, Mo.: Zion's Printing and Publishing Company, 1947. 296.

Riley, I. Woodbridge. *The Founder of Mormonism: A Psychological Study of Joseph Smith, Jr.* New York: Dodd, Mead, 1902; as cited in Francis W. Kirkham, *New Witness for Christ in America: The Book of Mormon*. Revised and enlarged. Independence, Mo.: Zion's Printing and Publishing Company, 1947. 350.

Smith, Joseph. *History of The Church of Jesus Christ of Latter-day Saints*. Edited by B. H. Roberts. 7 vols. 2d ed. rev. Salt Lake City: The Church of Jesus Christ of Latter-day Saints, 1932–51.

———. *Papers of Joseph Smith*. Vol. 1, *Autobiographical and Historical Writings*. Edited by Dean C. Jessee. Salt Lake City: Deseret Book, 1989.

Smith, Lucy Mack. *The Revised and Enhanced History of Joseph Smith by His Mother*. Edited by Scot Facer Proctor and Maurine Jensen Proctor. Salt Lake City: Bookcraft, 1996.

RNH

Book of Mormon, poetry in Book of Mormon poetry, written originally by people familiar with the Hebrew language, is like that of the Old Testament. That is, its defining characteristic is PARALLELISM. The most basic kinds of parallelism in second or subsequent lines of Hebrew poetry are (1) use of a synonym or synonymous expression (usually with intensification or amplification), (2) contrast of an opposing thought, (3) completion of the thought, and (4) repetition of the idea in a reverse order (also called CHIASMUS—literally, a crossing).

These four kinds of parallelism are observable in a notable example of poetry in the Book of Mormon, the so-called "psalm of Nephi" (2 Ne. 4:15–35). Nephi[1] began his highly poetic psalm with the first kind of parallelism, a synonymous declaration:

> For my soul delighteth in the scriptures,
> and my heart pondereth them. (V. 15)

The second kind of parallelism, contrast, is found in the end words of the following lines:

Behold, he hath heard my cry by day,
and he hath given me knowledge by
visions in the night-time. (V. 23)

Nephi completed these thoughts by revealing the consequences of the Lord's works. Nephi also contrasted those consequences:

He hath filled me with his love,
even unto the consuming of my flesh.
He hath confounded mine enemies,
unto the causing of them to quake before
me. (Vv. 21–22)

And he reversed the order of "soul" and "heart" as he repeated those words:

Awake, my *soul!* No longer droop in sin.
Rejoice, O my *heart,* and give place no
more for the enemy of my *soul.* . . .
Rejoice, O my *heart,* and cry unto the
Lord, and say:
O Lord, I will praise thee forever;
yea, my *soul* will rejoice in thee, my God,
and the rock of my salvation. (Vv. 28,
30; italics added)

Although the Book of Mormon is formatted entirely as prose, its poetry is more apparent when presented in lines, as above.

Typically, the purpose of the poetry is an exaltation of thought, as the examples above illustrate. This heightening is especially appropriate for prophetic utterances—with the poetry emphasizing "the testimony of Jesus," which is "the spirit of prophecy" (Rev. 19:10). For example, in the close of his record Nephi looked down through time and exclaimed,

I glory in plainness;
I glory in truth;
I glory in my Jesus,
for he hath redeemed my soul from hell.

He then continued,

I have charity for my people. . . .
I have charity for the Jew. . . .
I also have charity for the Gentiles. (2 Ne.
33:6–9)

Nephi had a model of a great poet in the prophet Isaiah, in whose words, Nephi said, "my soul delighteth" (2 Ne. 11:2). The same is true of Nephi's brother Jacob[2], who, after alluding to Isaiah's poetic invitation to "come . . . to the waters" of life (Isa. 55:1–2), added his own eloquent plea:

come unto the Holy One of Israel,
and feast upon that which perisheth
not. . . .

He continued in that poetic vein:

Behold, my beloved brethren,
remember the words of your God;
pray unto him continually by day,
and give thanks unto his holy name by
night.
Let your hearts rejoice. (2 Ne. 9:51–52)

Alma[2] quoted from the Old World poet Zenos with lyrically intensified ideas:

Thou art merciful, O God,
for thou hast heard my prayer,
even when I was in the wilderness;
yea, thou wast merciful
when I prayed concerning those who
were mine enemies,
and thou didst turn them to me.
Yea, O God, and thou wast merciful unto
me
when I did cry unto thee in my field;
when I did cry unto thee in my prayer,
and thou didst hear me. (Alma 33:4–5)

Alma's writings are often poetic, including, and perhaps especially, those he attributed directly to the Lord. For example, a shift is detectable when Alma turned from prose to the Lord's poetry in the following passage:

Now as to this thing I do not know. . . . But behold, the Spirit hath said this much unto me, saying:

Cry unto this people, saying—
Repent ye, and prepare the way of the
Lord,
and walk in his paths, which are straight;
for behold, the kingdom of heaven is at
hand,

B OF M, PRINTING AND PUBLICATION OF

and the Son of God cometh upon the
face of the earth. (Alma 7:8–9)

Poetry, Robert Frost said, is metaphor—"saying one thing in terms of another" (Frost, 87). While not all of the poetry in the Book of Mormon employs figurative language, much of it does. The reference in Alma's poetry above to walking in the Lord's straight paths is a common scriptural metaphor. An expansion of this metaphor is Nephi[1]'s desire in his psalm that the Lord not shut the gates of His righteousness, "that I may walk in the path of the low valley, that I may be strict in the plain road" (2 Ne. 4:32; cf. 33:9). Isaiah used a simile, and Jacob repeated it when he said that "the earth shall wax old like a garment" (2 Ne. 8:6). In a poetic expression, Lehi[1] desired that Laman might be "like unto this river, continually running into the fountain of all righteousness" (1 Ne. 2:9). Synecdoche (a part standing for the whole) is found in Abinadi's expansion of Isaiah's statement: "How beautiful upon the mountains are the feet of him that bringeth good tidings" (Mosiah 15:14–18; Isa. 52:7). And Moroni[2] followed Isaiah in personifying Zion as a woman who should put on her beautiful garments (Moro. 10:31).

Akin to music, poetry in the Book of Mormon speaks to the soul, not just the mind. Like the prose in the Book of Mormon, it partakes of qualities of divine inspiration.

See also Book of Mormon, figures of speech in; Book of Mormon, as literature; Nephi[1]'s psalm.

BIBLIOGRAPHY

Frost, Robert. "The Constant Symbol." *Robert Frost: An Introduction*. Edited by Robert A. Greenberg and James G. Hepburn. New York: Holt, Rinehart and Winston, 1961.

RDR

Book of Mormon, printing and publication of With the completion of the Book of Mormon translation at the Peter Whitmer Sr. farm in Fayette, Seneca County, New York, toward the end of June 1829, and having secured the copyright on 11 June 1829, Joseph Smith, Oliver Cowdery, Hyrum Smith, and Martin Harris sought the services of Egbert B. Grandin of Palmyra to publish the resultant manuscript. Negotiations began in June 1829. A momentary delay was experienced when Grandin initially refused on moral and religious grounds to print the volume. Eventually, Grandin's primary concerns were finally satisfied, and he consented to publish the work.

Grandin asked that John H. Gilbert, an experienced printer, assist him in estimating the cost. Gilbert stated, "A few pages of the manuscript were submitted as a specimen of the whole, and it was said there would be about 500 pages" (ultimately there were 590 pages from the title page to the two-page testimonials of the Three and Eight Witnesses at the back of the 1830 edition). Gilbert further explained, "The size of the page was agreed upon, and an estimate of the number of ems [an 'em' is the unit measure of type, the width of the letter *M*] in a page, which would be 1000, and that a page of manuscript would make more than a page of printed matter, which proved to be correct." The resulting contract specified that Grandin would print and bind in leather five thousand copies for the sum of $3,000 (Gilbert, "Memorandum," 1–2).

Payment for the job was secured in a mortgage agreement between Martin Harris and E. B. Grandin on 25 August 1829. Harris was to pay the sum of $3,000 for the requisite copies within eighteen months "from the date hereof." Should he fail to do so, his land would be sold at "public auction or vendue" to meet the demand (Wayne County Mortgages, 3:325). The press was situated in E. B. Grandin's printing shop on the third story of the west bay of the newly constructed (1827–28) "Thayer & Grandin's Row" (later "Exchange Row," 1831). Grandin rented his quarters from his brother Philip Grandin and his partners Joel and Levi Thayer. The binding process was to be conducted by Egbert Grandin's partner, Luther Howard, on the second story of that same bay. Copies could then be made available for sale in Grandin's Palmyra Bookstore on the first level (Enders; Lowe).

In an 1847 publication, Frederick Follett quoted Pomeroy Tucker as contending that "the largest printing job ever done in it [Wayne County], was the first edition of Jo Smith's 'book of Mormon,' or the 'Golden Bible.' This was

B OF M, PRINTING AND PUBLICATION OF

done at the office of the 'Wayne Sentinel,' by E. B. Grandin . . . in 1829–30" (Follett, 64). The printing of five thousand copies was unusually large as press runs were ordinarily from five hundred to two thousand copies (Ord, 66).

Preparations were made by Grandin to ready his printing shop. He went to New York and purchased five hundred pounds of new small pica font (12 point). Apparently, by early November 1829, it was again necessary to acquire even more type, which resulted in a period of delay (*New York Herald,* 25 June 1893; Gilbert, "Memorandum" 3; Cowdery). The paper was "manufactured at Shortsville, [New York,] by Case & Brown [Milliken said, "Case, Abbey, & Co."; see Milliken, *History,* 1:415]—size 22"x32" ("Mormon Bible Again," *Wayne County Journal,* 19 April 1877).

To print and bind five thousand copies of the book required an increase in the number of workers at the press. Grandin made the necessary contacts and also advertised for an "APPRENTICE TO the PRINTING BUSINESS" in August 1829 (Grandin). At the same time Luther Howard gave notice that "a GOOD Boy is wanted in the Book Bindery" (Howard).

Among the known members of the printing shop crew assembled by Grandin at one juncture or another during the printing operation were Pomeroy Tucker, "foreman of the office," reader of the proof sheets, and a brother-in-law to Grandin; John H. Gilbert, chief compositor (one who sets type, makes up pages and forms, and does some presswork); William Van Camp, compositor; Daniel Hendrix, periodic compositor and proofreader; Jacob H. Bortles, presswork; Thomas McAuley, or "Whistling Tom," presswork; and Franklin P. Rogers, a nine-year-old boy and youngest brother of Grandin's wife, Harriet, who was reported to have assisted in the typesetting process (Porter, "Book of Mormon," 53–54; Franklin P. Rogers obituary, newspaper, n.n., n.p., 11 November 1904, courtesy Don Enders; Maxson). Lucy Smith said that "a young Mr. Robinson son of our friend Dr. [Gain C.] Robinson," was also involved in the printing shop. Gain Robinson's eligible sons would have been Caius Cassius, Clark, Charles Rollin, or Erasmus Darwin (Smith, "Preliminary," 112; cf. Smith, *Joseph,* 158; Robinson Family file). J. N. T. Tucker, practical printer and a cousin to Pomeroy Tucker, claimed that he was there, but John H.

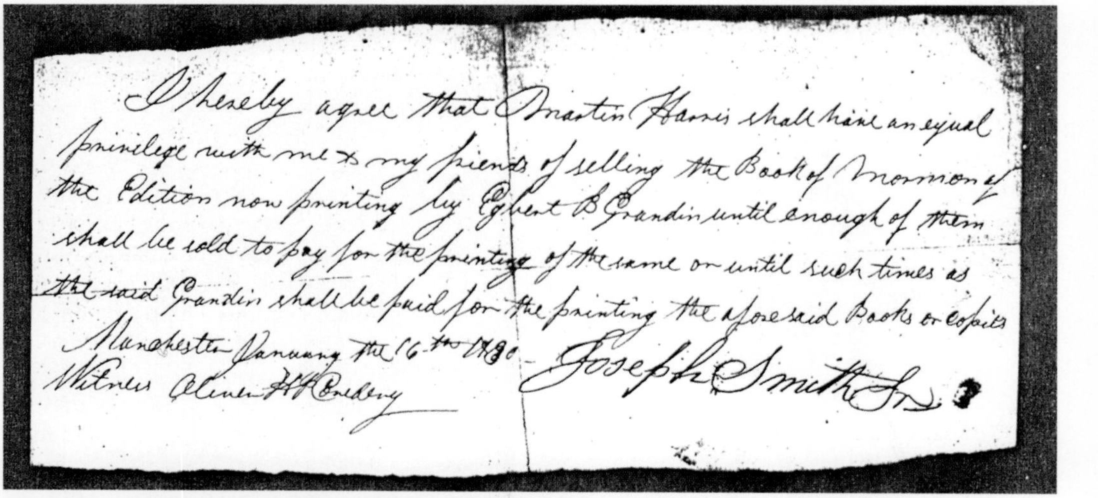
I hereby agree that Martin Harris shall have an equal privilege with me & my friends of selling the Book of Mormon of the Edition now printing by Egbert B Grandin until enough of them shall be sold to pay for the printing of the same or until such times as the said Grandin shall be paid for the printing the aforesaid Books or copies
Manchester January the 16th 1830 — Joseph Smith Jr
Witness Oliver H P Cowdery

A promissory note between Joseph Smith Jr. and Martin Harris dated 16 January 1830; courtesy VRL. Martin Harris secured the publication of the Book of Mormon in August 1829, when he promised to pay E. B. Grandin $3,000 within eighteen months. The agreement between Martin Harris and Joseph Smith allowed Harris to recover the cost of publication from future sales of the book after its publication in March 1830. Yet, a boycott by local citizens proved so successful that sales did not materialize. Martin Harris was forced to sell his property to pay the debt to Grandin. It is not known for a certainty if Harris ever recovered the cost of printing the book.

B OF M, PRINTING AND PUBLICATION OF

Gilbert thought that he was not present (J. N. T. Tucker, 79; cf. Gilbert letter to Cobb, 16 March 1879); A. [Amos?] S. Sanford was reportedly another employee (Enders); Luther Howard operated the bookbindery. One of Howard's assistants was sixteen-year-old Albert Chandler, who recalled, "I was an apprentice in the bookbindery connected with the *Sentinel* office. I helped to collate and stitch the Gold Bible" (Linn, 48). There were probably other persons hired who are as yet unnamed.

John H. Gilbert affirmed that the Book of Mormon "was printed on a 'Smith' Press, single pull, and old fashioned 'Balls' . . . were used" ("Memorandum," 3). The Smith Patented Improved Press was purchased by Grandin in early 1829.

This type of press was manufactured by Robert Hoe & Company from 1822 to 1835 (*Guide*, 60). Small printing offices did not ordinarily have composition rollers. Using a hand press required more time. Also, "the type of one form had to be distributed before another could be set up." Tucker felt that this factor accounted "for the tardiness of the work," approximately seven months' printing time (56).

About the middle of August 1829, the printer was ready to begin typesetting. Martin Harris was notified. Hyrum Smith then brought the first installment from the larger "printer's manuscript," a second copy made from the original by Oliver Cowdery for backup and use at the press, numbering 24 pages. He had them buttoned under his vest and coat for security.

After a short period Gilbert requested that the whole manuscript be left with him so he could take it home at night and go over the sheets for punctuation, which was finally allowed ("Memorandum," 2–3). The pages were closely written and legible, but Gilbert said that every chapter was virtually one solid paragraph as there was "not a punctuation mark from beginning to end" (letter to Cobb, 10 February 1879; "Memorandum," 3). Gilbert's claim of no punctuation is not entirely true because Oliver did add some punctuation, as an examination of the original translation copy shows. Pomeroy Tucker asserted that Gilbert "was given a limited discretion in correcting, which was exercised in the particulars of syntax, orthography, punctuation, capitalizing, paragraphing, etc." (53). Royal Skousen noted, however, that Gilbert was not permitted to make corrections in syntax and that any such corrections "did not occur except by accident" (Skousen, interview).

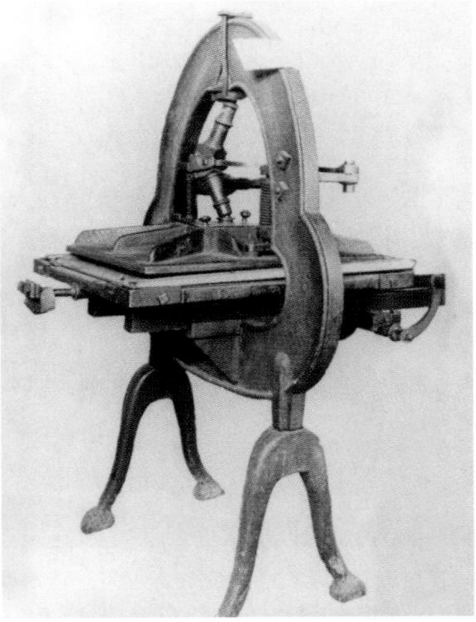

The Smith Patented Improved Press manufactured by Robert Hoe and Company; courtesy VRL.

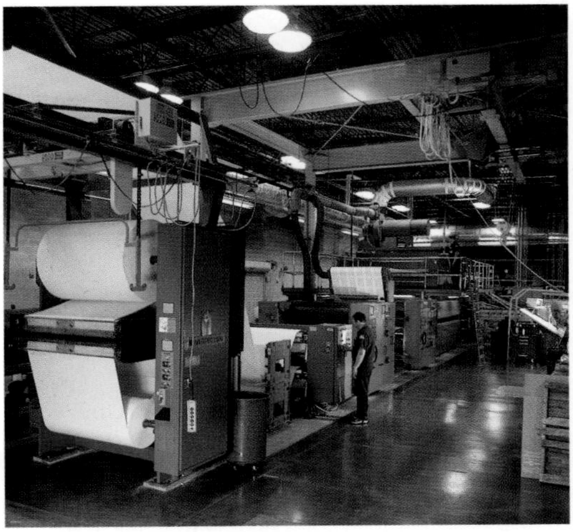

Printing press at the Church Printing Center, Salt Lake City, Utah, 2001; photograph by Kelly A. Larsen; courtesy VRL. This press produces between 5 and 5.5 million copies of the Book of Mormon a year.

B OF M, PRINTING AND PUBLICATION OF

The principal part of the typesetting was done from the "printer's manuscript"; however, Royal Skousen has found "strong evidence that for 72 pages the original manuscript rather than the printer's manuscript was used as the printer's copy" ("Piecing," 23).

The Prophet remained in Palmyra through September 1829. Assured that the details of the publication had been arranged, he returned to Emma and his home in Harmony, Pennsylvania, on 4 October (Smith, *Letter*). Oliver Cowdery was left to oversee their interests in the proofing and printing of the work with the assistance of Hyrum Smith and Martin Harris. Gilbert specified that "Oliver Cowdery was not engaged [hired] as compositor on the work—was not a printer. He was a frequent visitor to the office, and did several times take up a 'stick' and set a part of a page—he may have set 10 or 12 pages, all told" (letter to Cobb, 10 February 1879). Gilbert also stipulated: "Cowdery held and looked over the manuscript when most of the proofs were read. Martin Harris once or twice, and Hyrum Smith once, Grandin supposing that these men could read their own writing as well, if not better, than anyone else; and if there are any discrepancies between the Palmyra edition and the manuscript these men should be held responsible" ("Memorandum" 4).

Gilbert described the actual printing process: "The Bible [Book of Mormon] was printed 16 pages at a time, so that one sheet of paper made two copies of 16 pages each, requiring 2500 sheets of paper for each form of 16 pages. There were 37 forms of 16 pages each,—570 [590] pages in all" ("Memorandum," 3). A further explanation specified that "the 'matter' was 'paged' so that 32 pages could be printed at a time on one of Hoe's 'Smith' six-column hand presses. After the sheets had been run through once and properly dried, they were reversed and printed on the other side. The bookbinder then folded them by hand and severed them with an ivory paper cutter. The result was that the 2,500 large sheets made 5,000 small sheets with 16 pages printed on each side" (*New York Times*, 26 February 1888, 16). The 37 forms of 16 pages each, having printing on both sides, made up eighteen and a half signatures in each book.

The third floor of the restored Grandin Printing complex in Palmyra New York (dedicated 26 March 1998); courtesy VRL. Single sheets of paper, after they were printed on one side, were hung to dry before they could be printed on the reverse side.

Every form required 2,500 sheets of paper, for a total of 47,500 sheets of paper to print the consignment. It is estimated that the printer made 95,000 pulls of the lever during the seven months it took to print the volume (*Guide*, 59).

An early infringement of the Book of Mormon copyright came in late 1829 and early 1830 while the work was still at the Grandin press. Abner Cole, using the pseudonym of Obadiah Dogberry Jun., was editor of a small weekly Palmyra newspaper called the *Reflector.* The sheet was printed in the *Wayne Sentinel* office evenings and on Sundays, which provided ease of access to printed pages of the Book of Mormon. Availing himself of the opportunity, Cole stated in the 9 December 1829 number, "as much curiosity has been excited in this section of the country on the subject, and as the work itself will not be ready for delivery for some months to come,—at the solicitation of many of our readers we have concluded to commence publishing extracts from it on or before the commencement of the second series" (57). In the 2 January 1830 number of the *Reflector,* Cole printed a portion of "The First Book of Nephi. His Reign and Ministry, Chapter I," containing the copy found in the first eleven paragraphs of the 1830 edition

B OF M, PRINTING AND PUBLICATION OF

of the Book of Mormon (1 Ne. 1:1–2:3, in 1981 ed.). And in the 13 January issue he printed the next four paragraphs (1 Ne. 2:4–15) from 1 Nephi 1. This was followed on 22 January by copy from the book of Alma, chapter 20 (Alma 43:22–40).

Hyrum Smith, in company with Oliver Cowdery, became aware of Cole's actions and requested that he desist. Cole, even with the threat of copyright violation, refused to comply. Joseph Smith Sr. went to Harmony, Pennsylvania, to inform Joseph Smith Jr. of the situation. The Prophet and his father returned to New York to stop the pilfering. Cole, a lawyer and former justice of the peace, finally acknowledged his vulnerability when Joseph again confronted him with his intrusion on the copyright. Lucy Smith said, "He made us no further trouble" in that regard (*History*, 166; Lowe). But Cole continued to satirize the Book of Mormon and the Mormons in succeeding issues (Rich, 315–20).

Lucy Smith said that "a party of restless religionists" (*Joseph*, 158) sponsored a boycott of the Book of Mormon during the printing process. They organized into a committee and appointed persons to wait on E. B. Grandin and urged "the necessity of his putting a stop to the printing" (*Joseph*, 167). The Prophet was again summoned from Harmony, Pennsylvania, to allay Grandin's fears (Smith, *Joseph*, 158, 167). The boycott eventually proved effective in curtailing sales of the work within the community.

The forthcoming availability of the first printed copies of the volume to the public was announced in the 19 March 1830 *Wayne Sentinel:* "We are requested to announce that the 'BOOK OF MORMON' will be ready for sale in the course of next week." On 26 March 1830, the *Wayne Sentinel* published the title page of the Book of Mormon with the notice that "The above work, containing about 600 pages, large Duodecimo, is now for sale, wholesale and retail, at the Palmyra Bookstore." Initially copies sold for $1.75, but this price was soon adjusted to $1.25 because of lagging sales (Howe, 13). Pomeroy Tucker remembered that "the book . . . fell dead before the public. . . . It found no buyers, or but very few" (60–61). Lucy Smith had previously observed, "The inhabitants of the surrounding country perceived that the work still progressed [and] . . . they resolved, as before, never to purchase one of our books, when they should be printed." The threatened boycott was now put in force (*Joseph*, 166–67). The Prophet, Oliver Cowdery, Martin Harris, David Whitmer, Samuel Smith, Joseph Smith Sr., Don Carlos Smith, and others made a determined effort to place the scripture in the hands of the public. They experienced considerable antagonism but also enjoyed positive results from their labors (Porter, "Field," 73–89; Smith, *Joseph*, 169–76).

Unable to pay off the contractual agreement with proceeds from the sale of the Book of Mormon, Martin Harris arranged a private sale of 150¼ acres of his Palmyra farm to Thomas Lakey on 7 April 1831. Lakey was to reimburse Martin in a series of payments extending to October 1832 (Wayne County, New York, Deed Book, 10:515–16). A third party speeded up the process, however. John Graves had arrived in the Palmyra area from England in 1831, accompanied by his wife, Jane, and daughter, Mrs. Christina Graves Grainger, a widow. Mrs. Grainger had brought with her $3,000 in gold coins. On 28 January 1832 John Graves purchased the Harris farm from Thomas Lakey, paying $3,300. Thomas Lakey pocketed the additional $300 markup and paid Martin Harris the required $3,000 in gold, which was passed on to E. B. Grandin to retire the debt owed for the printing of the Book of Mormon (Gunnell, 37–39, 97–100; Tuckett, 49–50; Patton, 1–6; Wayne County, New York, Deed Book, 11:128–29).

Through the negotiations of President Milton A. Barlow with Mr. and Mrs. Paul I. Cherry, the space in the three-story building once occupied by E. B. Grandin and also an adjoining bay to the east (just under 3,500 square feet) was purchased by The Church of Jesus Christ of Latter-day Saints on 15 December 1978. The agreement allowed the Church to take occupancy on 1 March 1979 (*Church News*, 18 November 1978; *Church News*, 4 April 1998; Wayne County, New York, Deed Book, 725:387). Following two and one-half years of exacting reconstruction, President Gordon B. Hinckley dedicated the "Book of Mormon Historic Publication Site" in services conducted at the Palmyra Ward meetinghouse on the commemorative date of 26 March 1998, 168 years after the publishing of the Book of Mormon (*Church News*, 28 March 1998; *Church News*, 4 April 1998).

See also The Coming Forth of the Book of Mormon, 9; Book of Mormon, editions of; Book of Mormon, manuscripts of; Gilbert, John Hulburd; Grandin, Egbert Bratt.

BIBLIOGRAPHY

Church News. 18 November 1978; 28 March 1998; 4 April 1998.

Cowdery, Oliver. Letter to Joseph Smith, Manchester, New York. 6 November 1829.

Enders, Donald L. Personal interview. 28 January 1998. Church Archives.

Follett, Frederick. *History of the Press of Western New-York*. Rochester: Jerome & Brother, Daily American Office, 1847.

Gilbert, John H. Letter to James T. Cobb. Palmyra, New York, 10 February 1879. New York Public Library.

———. Letter to James T. Cobb. Palmyra, New York, 16 Mar 1879. New York Public Library. Gilbert stated that "J. N. T. Tucker was a cousin of Pomeroy Tucker, but did not work in the office at the time the Mormon Bible was printed, but did subsequently a short time, if my memory serves me."

———. "Memorandum, made by John H. Gilbert Esq, Sept 8th. 1892." King's Daughters' Free Library. Palmyra, New York.

"Gold Bible." *The Reflector* (9 December 1829): 57.

Grandin, Egbert B. *Wayne Sentinel*. 28 August 1829.

Guide to Exhibits at the Book of Mormon Historic Publication Site. Salt Lake City: The Church of Jesus Christ of Latter-day Saints, 1998. Courtesy of Donald L. Enders, Church Archives.

Gunnell, Wayne Cutler. "Martin Harris—Witness and Benefactor to the Book of Mormon." Master's thesis. Brigham Young University, 1974.

Howard, Luther. *Wayne Sentinel*. 25 September 1829.

Howe, E. D. *Mormonism Unvailed*. Painesville, Ohio: E. D. Howe, 1834.

Linn, William Alexander. *The Story of the Mormons*. New York: Macmillan, 1902.

Lowe, Robert O. Personal interview. 18 July 1998. Palmyra, New York, village and town historian.

Maxson, Anna L. Great-great granddaughter of E. B. Grandin. Personal correspondence. Toledo, Ohio, 3 June 1998.

Milliken, Charles F. *A History of Ontario County, New York and Its People*. 2 vols. New York: Lewis Historical Publishing Co., 1911.

New York Herald. 25 June 1893. 13.

New York Times. 26 February 1888. 16.

Ord, Gayle Goble. "The Book of Mormon Press." *Ensign* 2 (December 1972): 66–70.

Patton, Minor T. "How it was that my great-grandmother's gold paid for the printing of the first edition of the Book of Mormon." Typescript, Church Archives.

Porter, Larry C. "The Book of Mormon: Historical Setting for Its Translation and Publication." *Joseph Smith: The Prophet, the Man*. Edited by Susan Easton Black and Charles D. Tate Jr. Provo, Utah: Religious Studies Center, Brigham Young University, 1993.

———. "The Field Is White Already to Harvest: Earliest Missionary Labors and the Book of Mormon." *The Prophet Joseph: Essays on the Life and Mission of Joseph Smith*. Edited by Larry C. Porter and Susan Easton Black. Salt Lake City: Deseret Book, 1988.

Rich, Russell R. "The Dogberry Papers and the Book of Mormon." *Brigham Young University Studies* 10:3 (1970): 315–20.

Robinson Family file. King's Daughters' Free Library. Palmyra, New York.

Skousen, Royal. Personal interview. 13 July 1992. Provo, Utah.

———. "Piecing Together the Original Manuscript." *BYU Today* 46 (May 1992): 18–24.

Smith, Joseph. Letter to Oliver Cowdery. Palmyra, New York, 22 October 1829, Church Archives.

Smith, Lucy Mack. *History of Joseph Smith by His Mother, Lucy Mack Smith*. Edited by Preston Nibley. Salt Lake City: Bookcraft, 1958.

———. "Preliminary Manuscript." 1845. Church Archives.

Tucker, J. N. T. "Mormonism—Some Curious Facts." *The Signs of the Times*. Boston, 1842.

Tucker, Pomeroy. *Origin, Rise, and Progress of Mormonism*. New York: D. Appleton and Company, 1867.

Tuckett, Madge Harris, and Belle Harris Wilson. *The Martin Harris Story*. Provo, Utah: Press Publishing Ltd., 1983.

LCP

Book of Mormon, pronouncing guide of

The pronouncing guide of the Book of Mormon features 344 proper names with accompanying phonetic forms that aid the reader in determining correct pronunciation according to current Church practice among English speakers (e.g.,

Ether: ē´ther; Zarahemnah: zĕr-a-hĕm´nä). Many of the names—Eve, Abraham, Babylon—are Old World, but most belong to Book of Mormon places and people.

President Joseph F. Smith noted in 1903 that variant pronunciation methods for proper names existed among Church members, so he appointed a committee of scholars "to decide upon a method of pronunciation of Book of Mormon names" (*Deseret Evening News,* 3). The committee's recommendations were accepted by the First Presidency, and the 1921 edition of the Book of Mormon featured a "Pronouncing Vocabulary" that gave "a simple and consistent pronunciation of practically every proper name, and of some other words, of Book of Mormon origin" (*Relief Society Magazine,* 97). President Anthony W. Ivins of the First Presidency presented the guide to the Saints at the April 1921 general conference, and the guide was used for six decades.

Before the publication of the 1981 edition of the Book of Mormon, Soren Cox of Brigham Young University's English department, at the invitation of Church authorities, examined and then revised the guide to reflect pronunciation among present-generation Latter-day Saints. The "general American dialect" was selected as the model for pronunciation rules.

The pronouncing guide does not reflect the way that the Book of Mormon peoples pronounced their own names and places, which were most likely based upon one or more Semitic languages (Nibley, 25–42, 242–46).

BIBLIOGRAPHY

"Book of Mormon Students Meet." *Deseret Evening News,* 25 May 1903.

First Presidency: Heber J. Grant, Anthon H. Lund, and Charles W. Penrose. "New Issue of the Book of Mormon." *Relief Society Magazine* 8 (February 1921).

Nibley, Hugh. *Lehi in the Desert; The World of the Jaredites; There Were Jaredites.* Vol. 5 of *The Collected Works of Hugh Nibley.* Edited by John W. Welch, Darrell L. Matthews, and Stephen R. Callister. Salt Lake City: Deseret Book and FARMS, 1988.

DWP

Book of Mormon, prophecy in *See* Prophecy in the Book of Mormon.

Book of Mormon, selected purposes of
Selected purposes of the Book of Mormon are identified under the following:

To be a sign of the Father's work

To confound false doctrine

To the convincing of the Jew and Gentile that Jesus is the Christ

To latter-day people, that we might learn to be more wise

To prove to the world that God inspires men and calls them to his work in the latter days

To prove to the world that the holy scriptures are true

To restore plain and precious truths of the Gospel. *See* Plain and precious things, loss of and restoration of

To reveal the enemies of Christ

To show unto the remnant of the House of Israel what great things the Lord hath done for their fathers

To be a sign of the Father's work

The Book of Mormon is one of the signs of the times. It is an announcement that the restoration of the fulness of the gospel of Jesus Christ has taken place in the last days. Its presence is a sign that The Church of Jesus Christ (Zion) has been reestablished and that the work of gathering, called "the work of the Father," is underway (3 Ne. 21:7). The risen Lord explained to the Nephites that "when these things" (the Book of Mormon) would come forth to the world, people would know that God's great work of gathering (3 Ne. 21:1–7; Ether 4:17) had commenced: the prophesied return of his chosen people, first to Christ and his gospel, and second "to the lands of their inheritance" (2 Ne. 6:11; 10:7; 3 Ne. 5:24–26). Mormon thus declared that when the teachings of the Book of Mormon would begin to be made known, "then ye may know that the covenant which the Father hath made with the children of Israel, concerning their restoration to the lands of their inheritance, is already beginning to be fulfilled" (3 Ne. 29:1).

See also Israel, gathering of.

RLM

To confound false doctrine

Millennia ago the Lord told Joseph of Egypt that one day the Bible and the Book of Mormon would "grow together, unto the confounding of false doctrines" (2 Ne. 3:12). Alone, the Bible is subject to an almost endless array of interpretations. From it has come a "war of words and tumult of opinions" (JS–H 1:10). Speaking of his search to know which church he should join, Joseph Smith said that the teachers of religion "understood the same passages of scripture so differently as to destroy all confidence in settling the question by an appeal to the Bible" (JS–H 1:12).

Resolution of this doctrinal contention comes in the union of the Bible and the Book of Mormon. Joseph of Egypt knew that the seed of his father would be scattered throughout all the nations of the earth and that they would lose the knowledge of God and the covenants he had made with their fathers. Nevertheless, he was given the promise that the fruit of his loins would write a scriptural record, as would the fruit of the loins of Judah, and that when these two testimonies were brought together, they would confound false doctrines, lay down contention, establish peace among his descendants, and bring them once again to the knowledge of their fathers and the covenants of the Lord (JST Gen. 50:31). Lehi quoted this prophecy, which is no longer found in the Old Testament, in a blessing he gave to his son Joseph[2], and thus it is preserved in the Book of Mormon (2 Ne. 3).

The Book of Mormon responds directly and authoritatively to almost every important issue that divides modern Christendom. Consider the following examples:

1. REVELATION has not ceased. The Bible is not the final word of God (2 Ne. 29:6–13). MIRACLES and SPIRITUAL GIFTS are always available to the true followers of Christ (Morm. 9:15–25; Ether 12:12–16; Moro. 7:19–39).

2. People in Old Testament times knew of Christ and worshipped the Father in his name (Jacob 4:4; 7:11; Mosiah 13:33; Hel. 8:16–20). Jesus Christ, the literal Son of God "after the manner of the flesh" in the meridian of time (1 Ne. 11:14–21), is Jehovah, the God of ancient Israel, who gave and later fulfilled the law of Moses (3 Ne. 15:1–10). Before his mortal birth, he was a personage of spirit in the form of a man (Ether 3:6–17).

3. There is one true "doctrine of Christ" (2 Ne. 31:2), or GOSPEL, to which all who desire a fulness of salvation must ultimately subscribe (2 Ne. 31).

4. The fall of Adam and Eve was an anticipated, purposeful, integral part of God's plan of salvation for his children (2 Ne. 2:22–27). *See* Fall of Adam and Eve, the.

5. All mankind will be resurrected to die no more, and all except the willful followers of Satan will be saved from HELL (2 Ne. 9:10–27; Alma 11:41; 12:15–18). *See* Resurrection, the.

6. SALVATION comes by GRACE, but not by grace alone. Full access to God's grace comes only to those who are obedient to the laws and ordinances of the gospel (2 Ne. 2:8; 10:24; 25:23; 31:2–21; 3 Ne. 27:13–21; A of F 3).

7. Although BAPTISM is clearly a requirement for salvation for all accountable persons (3 Ne. 11:21–41), "little children need no repentance, neither baptism"; they are "whole," they are "alive in Christ, even from the foundation of the world" (Moro. 8:5–15, 19–21). *See* Children, baptism of little.

8. Unconditional election, or predestination to salvation or damnation, is a false notion (Alma 31:13–35). Foreordination to certain mortal opportunities and blessings, based on premortal faithfulness, is a true doctrine (Alma 13). *See* Chosen.

Thus the Book of Mormon, in fulfillment of the Savior's own words, makes it possible for the Gentiles (and all who honestly seek) to "know of the true points of my doctrine, that they may be numbered among my people, O house of Israel" (3 Ne. 21:6).

JFM

To the convincing of the Jew and Gentile that Jesus is the Christ

An important purpose of the Book of Mormon is declared on its TITLE PAGE. Book of Mormon prophets testified powerfully that Jesus is the Christ and desired that those who read their message become convinced of this truth (e.g.,

B OF M, SELECTED PURPOSES OF

1 Ne. 6:4; 19:23; 2 Ne. 25:29; 33:4, 10–11; Jacob 4:4; Mosiah 3:17; Alma 5:48; 30:39; 34:8). Nephi[1] wrote that the Book of Mormon would be given to the Jews for the purpose of "convincing them of the true Messiah" (2 Ne. 25:18–19). "And," Nephi continued, "as I spake concerning the convincing of the Jews, that Jesus is the very Christ, it must needs be that the Gentiles be convinced also that Jesus is the Christ, the Eternal God" (2 Ne. 26:12). In the final chapter of the Book of Mormon, Moroni[2] invited his readers to "come unto Christ . . . that by his grace ye may be perfect in Christ" (Moro. 10:32). President Ezra Taft Benson stated that the Book of Mormon "is a keystone in bearing witness to the world that Jesus is the Christ" (5). This emphasis on Christ is attested by the addition of "Another Testament of Jesus Christ" to the title of the Book of Mormon.

In understanding this purpose, it is helpful to analyze its various parts. The word pair "Jew and Gentile" in the topic phrase is another way of saying that the message of the Book of Mormon is for all mankind. The Lord "inviteth them all to come unto him and partake of his goodness; and he denieth none that come unto him, black and white, bond and free, male and female; and he remembereth the heathen; and all are alike unto God, both Jew and Gentile" (2 Ne. 26:33). Those who were not Jews by lineage or geography were considered GENTILES, and the Lord made it clear that all would be given the opportunity to learn of the Savior: "And the time cometh that he shall manifest himself unto all nations, both unto the Jews and also unto the Gentiles" (1 Ne. 13:42).

"The Eternal God" is one of the titles the Book of Mormon gives to JESUS CHRIST, underscoring that he is the God of Israel (known in the Old Testament as Jehovah; 3 Ne. 15:5) as well as "the God of the whole earth" (3 Ne. 11:14). His creations are endless, and his redemptive reach is infinite (Moses 1:3–4, 33; 2 Ne. 9:7–10; Alma 34:10–14). The prophet Abinadi affirmed Christ's roles as Father and Son: "The Father, because he was conceived by the power of God; and the Son, because of the flesh; thus becoming the Father and Son—And they are one God, yea, the very Eternal Father of heaven and of earth" (Mosiah 15:3–4). Amulek taught that Jesus Christ "is the very Eternal Father of heaven and of earth, and all things which in them are; he is the beginning and the end, the first and the last; and he shall come into the world to redeem his people; and he shall take upon him the transgressions of those who believe on his name; and these are they that shall have eternal life, and salvation cometh to none else" (Alma 11:39–40).

That Jesus Christ would manifest "himself unto all nations" is one of the truths taught in the Book of Mormon (Title Page). The Savior explained to the Nephites when he appeared to them after his resurrection that "I have other sheep, which are not of this land, neither of the land of Jerusalem" and, he continued, "I have received a commandment of the Father that I shall go unto them, and that they shall hear my voice . . . ; therefore I go to show myself unto them" (3 Ne. 16:1, 3). Nephi declared that the Lord would manifest himself through a witness of the Spirit to those nations who would not receive a personal visit: "And . . . he manifesteth himself unto all those who believe in him, by the power of the Holy Ghost; yea, unto every nation, kindred, tongue, and people" (2 Ne. 26:13; cf. 3 Ne. 15:21–23).

See also Book of Mormon: Another Testament of Jesus Christ; Gentiles, Book of Mormon message concerning; Jesus Christ, role of, as Father and Son; Jews, Book of Mormon message concerning.

BIBLIOGRAPHY

Benson, Ezra Taft. "The Book of Mormon—Keystone of Our Religion." *Ensign* 16 (November 1986): 4–7.

JHS

To latter-day people, that we might learn to be more wise

The Book of Mormon prophets, blessed with the gift to know of the circumstances of the last days (e.g., Morm. 8:34–35; 2 Ne. 26:14), included in their writings those items they knew would have great relevance to a latter-day audience: parts of Nephite history and prophecy that would help readers "learn to be more wise" than the Nephites had been (Morm. 9:31). President Ezra Taft Benson taught: "The Nephites never had the book; neither did the Lamanites of

B OF M, SELECTED PURPOSES OF

ancient times. It was meant for us. . . . Under the inspiration of God, who sees all things from the beginning, [Mormon] abridged centuries of records, choosing the stories, speeches, and events that would be most helpful to us" (19). Thus, the Book of Mormon imparts the collective wisdom of past prophets "crying from the dust," warning readers against making the same mistakes that destroyed two great civilizations.

For example, readers are forewarned concerning the teachings and sophistries of anti-Christs (Jacob 7; Alma 1; 30) and apostates (Alma 31; 47), pride and its destructive influence (Hel. 4:12; 12:5; 3 Ne. 6:10; cf. D&C 38:39), prosperity and materialism (Hel. 12:1–2; 4 Ne. 1:24, 43), the mocking of sacred things (1 Ne. 8:27; Hel. 4:12; 4 Ne. 1:27), adultery and whoredoms (Jacob 2:23; Alma 1:32; 16:18), false doctrines (2 Ne. 28; Alma 1:4; 30:13–18; 31:15–17), secret combinations (Hel. 2:13; 6:22–30; Ether 8:20–26), priestcrafts (2 Ne. 26:29; Morm. 8:32–33), perverted forms of worship (Alma 31:11–23), rejection of the prophets (Hel. 13:24; Ether 9:29–30), and destruction because of iniquity and failure to serve God (Morm. 6:17, 22; Ether 2:9–12).

Conversely, readers are also presented with wisdom that, if applied, can help them avoid the failings of the Nephites: the necessity of building a foundation on Christ and the blessings that come from doing so (Hel. 5:12; cf. Morm. 5:17–18), having a broken heart and a contrite spirit (2 Ne. 2:7; 4:32; 3 Ne. 12:3), placing trust in God and not in man (2 Ne. 28:31; Mosiah 23:14), having a personal testimony (Alma 5:45–48; 30:39, 44), meeting together often (3 Ne. 18:22; Moro. 6:5–6), keeping the commandments (Jarom 1:9; 3 Ne. 14:24–27), exercising faith (Alma 14:26; 32; Alma 57:21, 26), following the prophets (2 Ne. 25:9; 26:8; 3 Ne. 12:1), and so forth.

The ultimate wisdom imparted by Book of Mormon prophets lies in the true doctrine they taught. After pleading for his audience to "cleave unto God" and not harden their hearts and reject Christ, his prophets, his words, and the Holy Ghost, the prophet Jacob[2] spoke of the severe consequences for so doing. He then concluded with the challenge, "O be wise; what can I say more?" (Jacob 6:5–12).

See also Book of Mormon, selected purposes of, to reveal the enemies of Christ; Book of Mormon, selected themes of, cycles of prosperity and destruction; Book of Mormon, selected themes of, freedom to choose happiness or misery; Crying from the dust.

BIBLIOGRAPHY

Benson, Ezra Taft. *A Witness and a Warning*. Salt Lake City: Deseret Book, 1988.

BRM

To prove to the world that God inspires men and calls them to his work in the latter days

According to the Doctrine and Covenants, a purpose of the coming forth of the Book of Mormon is to prove that "God does inspire men and call them to his holy work in this age and generation, as well as in generations of old" (D&C 20:11). Thus the Book of Mormon itself, which came forth and was translated by revelation and inspiration given to the Prophet Joseph Smith, is a witness that God does indeed continue to inspire and direct his children in this latter-day dispensation.

MSN

To prove to the world that the holy scriptures are true

A primary purpose of the Book of Mormon is to prove "to the world that the holy scriptures are true" (D&C 20:11), that is, to confirm and bear witness of the essential truthfulness of the Bible. Descendants of Lehi[1] quoted and paraphrased scripture from the PLATES OF BRASS that parallel biblical books and passages, and they alluded to biblical peoples and incidents throughout the Nephite record.

The Book of Mormon bears witness to the historicity of many prominent Old Testament figures and testifies of the hand of God in their lives. Adam and Eve, Cain and Abel, Noah, the tower of Babel, Melchizedek, Abraham, Isaac, Jacob[1], Joseph of Egypt, Moses, parting the Red Sea, lifting up the brazen serpent, the conquest of Canaan, Samuel[1], David, and Solomon are all mentioned. Lehi pointed out that the plates of brass contained the five books of Moses (1 Ne.

B OF M, SELECTED PURPOSES OF

5:11). Joseph of Egypt prophesied that the Lord would "give judgment unto [Moses] in writing" (2 Ne. 3:17). Jesus declared, "The law is fulfilled that was given unto Moses" (3 Ne. 15:4–5). The plates of brass contained a record of the Jews from the beginning to the commencement of the reign of Zedekiah, king of Judah, as well as many of the prophecies of the holy prophets. The Book of Mormon prophets quoted extensively from Isaiah. Verification of Job's testimony of a literal resurrection (Job 19:25–27) is given in 2 Nephi 9:4. The Book of Mormon refers to the oracles of Jeremiah[1] and even attests that his prophecies have been fulfilled (1 Ne. 5:13; Hel. 8:20). The Savior quoted and therefore authenticated the words of Malachi (3 Ne. 24:1).

Nephi[1] saw in vision that originally the Bible "contained the fulness of the gospel of the Lord, of whom the twelve apostles bear record" (1 Ne. 13:24, 38–39, 41) and that the Book of Mormon was given to establish the truth of the record of the twelve apostles of the Lamb (1 Ne. 13:40). For example, Nephi saw the city of Nazareth and then beheld a virgin bearing a child in her arms, even "the Son of the Eternal Father" (1 Ne. 11:13–21). Nephi, Benjamin, and Alma[2] beheld the mortal ministry of Jesus (1 Ne. 11:24, 28, 31–33; Mosiah 3:5–10; Alma 7:11–13). Lehi[1] and Nephi prophesied of the ministry of John the Baptist (1 Ne. 10:7; 11:27: 2 Ne. 31:4). When the Savior appeared to the Nephites, he delivered most of what is known as the Sermon on the Mount, as recorded primarily by Matthew (5–7), with some variations in the message to suit the needs and circumstances of the Nephites (3 Ne. 12–14; 15:1). Jesus' teachings also restored some plain and precious parts that had been lost (e.g., cf. 3 Ne. 12:3, 6 with Matt. 5:3, 6). In addition, the Book of Mormon bears specific witness to the authorship of the Apocalypse, or book of Revelation. Nephi was forbidden to record many things pertaining to the last days, because he was told that an apostle of the Lamb of God by the name of John would record it (1 Ne. 14:20–27; Ether 4:16).

Above and beyond all else, the Book of Mormon confirms and amplifies the overarching and undergirding message of the Bible: that Jesus is the Christ, the Son of the living God (Title Page; 2 Ne. 26:12; Matt. 16:13–17; John 20:31), and that his is the only name by which salvation can come to the children of men (Mosiah 3:17; Acts 4:12). Truly, as Mormon explained, one of the grand reasons the Book of Mormon has been preserved is "for the intent that ye may believe" the Bible (Morm. 7:9).

See also Book of Mormon, what it says about the Bible; Old Testament, historical narrative referred to.

MSN

To restore plain and precious truths of the gospel

See Plain and precious things, loss of and restoration of.

To reveal the enemies of Christ

President Ezra Taft Benson taught that two purposes of the Book of Mormon are "testifying of Christ and revealing His enemies" (Benson, 7). The enemies of Christ, whether people, teachings, philosophies, practices, temptations, or sins, oppose the doctrine of Christ and the revealed plan of salvation. By exposing the purposes and plans of Christ's enemies, the Book of Mormon warns latter-day people "that [they] may learn to be more wise" than the Nephites had been (Morm. 9:31). For example, the stories of Korihor, Sherem, and Nehor warn readers against latter-day anti-Christs and teachers who echo their false teachings and specious arguments. Nephi[1] enumerated various false doctrines that would be taught in the latter days and warned against them. He also detailed several of the many tactics SATAN uses to take people captive in his efforts to destroy them (2 Ne. 28). Readers are taught concerning the evils of PRIESTCRAFT and SECRET COMBINATIONS and are warned that these practices will be part of latter-day society (Morm. 8:32–41; Ether 8:19–26). Jacob[2]'s condemnation of PRIDE and immorality and his discourse on their consequences address in plain language these two sins that are rampant in modern times. IDOLATRY, HYPOCRISY, HARDHEARTEDNESS, and STIFFNECKEDNESS are examples of other attitudes and behaviors the Book of Mormon reveals which alienate people from God and can be classified as enemies of Christ.

See also All is well in Zion; Antichrist; Book of Mormon, selected purposes of, to confound false doctrine; Book of Mormon, selected purposes of, to latter-day people, that we might learn to be more wise; Book of Mormon, selected themes of, freedom to choose happiness or misery; Chastity; Flatter, flattery; Flaxen cord; Worship; Zoramites[2].

BIBLIOGRAPHY

Benson, Ezra Taft. *A Witness and a Warning*. Salt Lake City: Deseret Book, 1988.

DLL

To show unto the remnant of the House of Israel what great things the Lord hath done for their fathers

The first stated purpose of the Book of Mormon found in the second paragraph of the title page is to teach the covenants of the Lord to readers who are of the house of Israel. It first fulfills this purpose by reviewing the past, showing some of the great things the Lord did for earlier generations of Israelites as he established and fulfilled covenant promises with them (e.g., 1 Ne. 16–18; Mosiah 24–25; 3 Ne. 10, 17–18). Second, the Book of Mormon teaches present generations important principles and elements of covenants (e.g., 1 Ne. 20–21; 3 Ne. 15–16, 20, 29). And third, it contains important prophecies and covenants which predict a hopeful future (e.g., 1 Ne. 22; 2 Ne. 10; 3 Ne. 21–22; Moro. 10).

The second stated purpose of the Book of Mormon, to convince "Jew and Gentile that JESUS is the CHRIST, the ETERNAL GOD, manifesting himself unto all nations," is connected with this covenant foundation found in the Book of Mormon (Title Page). Jesus' sacrifice and God's covenants are inseparably linked, for without Christ's atonement, the ultimate eternal promises of Heavenly Father's covenants with his children could never be fulfilled (2 Ne. 9; Mosiah 3–6, 18). Thus, the Book of Mormon teaches what God expects of his children in a covenant relationship and also testifies how Christ brings the blessings of the covenant into their lives.

See also Book of Mormon, selected purposes of, to the convincing of the Jew and Gentile that Jesus is the Christ; Israel, concept of; Israel, covenants unto.

VLL

Book of Mormon, selected themes of

Selected themes of the Book of Mormon are identified under the following:

Becoming convinced of sin
Bondage and deliverance
Come unto Christ
Cycles of prosperity and destruction
Freedom to choose happiness or misery
Obedience
Remember, remembrance
Restoration of the house of Israel. *See* Israel, gathering of

Becoming convinced of sin

The Lord converts people by convincing them of their sins in order to redeem them: "I will work a great . . . work among the children of men," he said through Nephi[1], "either to the convincing of them [of their sins] unto peace and life eternal, or unto the deliverance of them to the hardness of their hearts and the blindness of their minds" (1 Ne. 14:7). Through Joseph Smith he declared, "I will work a marvelous work among the children of men, unto the convincing of many of their sins" for two reasons: (1) so "that they may come unto repentance," and (2) so "that they may come unto the kingdom of my Father," neither being possible without a revealed witness of one's personal sinfulness (D&C 18:44).

The most conspicuous Nephite missionaries were convinced of their sins before becoming missionaries. Alma[2] was convinced of his sins and converted by an angel, who told him, "I come to convince thee of the power and authority of God" (Mosiah 27:14–15).

The sons of Mosiah[2] became missionaries *because* they were convinced of their sins. "Who could have supposed," they asked, "that our God would have . . . snatched us from our awful, sinful, and polluted state? . . . Why did he not consign us to an awful destruction . . . and

B OF M, SELECTED THEMES OF

doom us to eternal despair? Oh, my soul, almost . . . fleeth at the thought. . . . But in his great mercy [he] hath brought us over that everlasting gulf of death and misery, even to the salvation of our souls" (Alma 26:17–20). Then, as missionaries of "sound understanding," they "searched the scriptures diligently," convinced people of their sins, and brought "many . . . before the altar of God, to . . . confess their sins before him" (Alma 17:2–4).

The sons of Mosiah labored especially among the Lamanites to "convince them of the iniquity of their fathers," to cure their "hatred towards the Nephites," to bring them "to rejoice in the Lord," to see them "become friendly" to their brethren, and to reduce contentions among them (Mosiah 28:1–2). While Aaron[3] and his companions were teaching the Lamanites, "the Lord began to bless them, insomuch that . . . they did convince many of their sins" by showing that "the traditions of their fathers . . . were not correct" (Alma 21:14–17; cf. 23:1–3; 26:23–24, 31; 37:9).

Anti-Nephi-Lehi, a Lamanite king converted by Mosiah's sons, thanked God for sending the Nephites "to convince us of . . . [our false] traditions. . . . I also thank my God," he said, that "we have been convinced of our sins, and of the many murders which we have committed. And . . . that he hath granted unto us that we might repent of these things, and . . . he hath forgiven us of those our many sins and murders . . . and taken away the guilt from our hearts" (Alma 24:7–10).

Alma[2] taught Helaman[2] that the scriptures "convinced many of the error of their ways," for without these holy records "Ammon and his brethren could not have convinced so many . . . Lamanites of the incorrect tradition of their fathers; yea, these records and their words brought them unto repentance" (Alma 37:8–10). Helaman[2] in turn declared "the word of God with much power unto the convincing of many people of their wickedness, which did cause them to repent of their sins" (Alma 62:45). Nephi[2] and Lehi[4] continued Helaman's practice of preaching with "power and authority," arousing "great astonishment," and converting "eight thousand . . . Lamanites . . . [who were] baptized unto repentance, and . . . convinced of the wickedness of the traditions of their fathers." Their message delivered, "the Lamanites were convinced . . . because of the greatness of the evidences which they had received. And as many as were convinced did lay down their weapons of war, and also their hatred and the tradition of their fathers" (Hel. 5:18–19, 50–51).

Christ allowed the Three Nephites to remain on earth until his return. "Ye shall live to behold all the doings of the Father unto the children of men," he told them, and "ye shall not have pain . . . , neither sorrow save it be for the sins of the world . . . for ye have desired . . . [to] bring the souls of men unto me, while the world shall stand." They were to "minister . . . unto all nations" and to "bring out of them unto Jesus many souls . . . because of the convincing power of God which is in them" (3 Ne. 28:7–9, 29).

Converting God's children by convincing them of sin and redeeming them from it is thus the Lord's great, marvelous, wonderful, and eternal work.

HCW

Bondage and deliverance

A fundamental theme of the Book of Mormon, developed by many examples at both the temporal and spiritual levels, to teach faith in God's power to deliver man from all bondages, even the most impossible of all—the fall of man. This theme is introduced at the beginning of the Book of Mormon where Nephi[1] announced his intent to show that the tender mercies of the Lord are over all who have faith "to make them mighty even unto the power of deliverance" (1 Ne. 1:20).

All bondages and deliverances of repentant people reflect the redeeming power of Jesus Christ from the Fall. The promise, oft repeated, is that if the Lord's people will keep his commandments, they will "prosper in the land"; otherwise they will find themselves cut off from the Lord's presence (2 Ne. 1:20) and thus in bondage.

The Book of Mormon narrative poses a series of dilemmas from which only the Lord can deliver. Two ideas recur: "and none shall deliver them, except it be the Lord the Almighty God"

(Mosiah 11:23) and the righteous are delivered from the hands of enemies (e.g., Alma 9:10; 3 Ne. 4:33). The enemies are usually in the form of men but represent the unseen powers of darkness and the battle between good and evil. Bondage is the consequence of iniquity (Mosiah 7:20), but the righteous can be brought into bondage to serve the purposes of the Lord in order to try the faith and patience of his people (Mosiah 23:21–24) and to show forth his power (1 Ne. 18:11; Alma 8:31; 14:14–28).

Two main types of bondage are illustrated: temporal and spiritual, the temporal usually arising out of a spiritual bondage. Frequent reference is made to the bondage and deliverance of the house of Israel in Egypt as a reminder of the Lord's love and power through the atonement and to rekindle faith for deliverance from a present dilemma (1 Ne. 17:24; Alma 36:28). Reference to Nephite bondage to Lamanites recurs repeatedly to illustrate the principles of deliverance (Mosiah 7:15; Mosiah 21:15). Many received deliverance from personal bondage, from affliction, sin, or spiritual darkness (1 Ne. 7:17; 2 Ne. 4:27, 31; Mosiah 27:29; Alma 15:3; 10–11; Hel. 5:41–42). Two examples of bondage and deliverance, juxtaposed in Mosiah 22–24, provide an instructive contrast. In the first account, the people of Limhi find themselves in bondage to the Lamanites. Their suffering brought them to humility and mighty prayer. But "the Lord was slow to hear their cry because of their iniquities; nevertheless the Lord did hear their cries, and began to soften the hearts of the Lamanites that they began to ease their burdens" (Mosiah 21:15) as they progressed in their repentance. Finally their plan for deliverance operated successfully but mostly under natural conditions (Mosiah 22). The second account deals with the people of Alma[1] who have sacrificed to receive the gospel and have been cleansed by baptism. Their bondage came about not to punish but to sanctify them (Mosiah 23:21). Alma 36 brings the two main types of bondage together in beautiful symmetry, commencing and concluding with references to temporal bondage (Alma 36:2, 28)—including the Israelite exodus from Egypt with its foreshadowing of the atonement in the efficacious blood of the first-born lamb—and then, as the centerpiece, the account of Alma's personal redemption from spiritual bondage through the Lord Jesus Christ (Alma 36:16–23).

Instructions for deliverance from bondage abound. Mosiah[2] reminded his people that deliverance came from the Lord because they humbled themselves and cried mightily to him, "and thus doth the Lord work with his power in all cases among the children of men" (Mosiah 29:20). Alma[2] taught Shiblon that the degree of deliverance depends on one's TRUST in God's teaching that, as much as one shall put his trust in God, even so much is one delivered out of his trials, troubles, and afflictions, and "lifted up at the last day" (Alma 38:5; cf. Mosiah 21:15–16). Limhi gave his people a formula for deliverance: "But if ye will turn to the Lord with full purpose of heart, and put your trust in him, and serve him with all diligence of mind, if ye do this, he will, according to his own will and pleasure, deliver you out of bondage" (Mosiah 7:33). The Book of Mormon is an instruction manual for deliverance.

See also Exodus, the.

MCT

Come unto Christ

A central theme and powerful injunction of the Book of Mormon is the invitation to come unto Christ. The record declares or implies repeatedly that inasmuch as "there is no other name given whereby salvation cometh" (Mosiah 5:8), all people must come unto Christ to receive eternal life (1 Ne. 13:40).

The theme "come unto Christ" is established early in the Book of Mormon narrative. Extolling the Lord's virtues, Lehi[1] exclaimed, "Because thou art merciful, thou wilt not suffer those who come unto thee that they shall perish!" (1 Ne. 1:14). At the beginning of his writing on the small plates, Nephi[1] declared that his intent would be to "persuade men to come unto the God of Abraham, and the God of Isaac, and the God of Jacob, and be saved" (1 Ne. 6:4). A careful search of Nephi's words reveals the various ways by which he sought to accomplish his objective of bringing people to Christ. For example, Nephi included in his narrative LEHI[1]'S

B OF M, SELECTED THEMES OF

DREAM, depicting the path all people must travel to come unto Christ and partake of the fruit of the tree of life (1 Ne. 8). Further, Nephi's writings prophetically address the Lord's latter-day plan to bring three groups—Lehi's descendants (1 Ne. 15:12–16), the Jews (2 Ne. 25:9–20), and the Gentiles (1 Ne. 15:13, 17; 22:8; 2 Ne. 27)—out of apostasy and back to Christ and the true gospel. In Nephi's last writings he taught plainly the "doctrine of Christ," emphasizing the necessity of following the Savior's example (2 Ne. 31). Only by following him can mortals be "reconciled unto Christ" (2 Ne. 33:9). As Nephi had written earlier, "And we talk of Christ, we rejoice in Christ, we preach of Christ, we prophesy of Christ, and we write according to our prophecies, that our children may know to what source they may look for a remission of their sins" (2 Ne. 25:26).

When Nephi passed the small plates to his younger brother Jacob[2], he also gave him a commandment concerning what they should contain (Jacob 1:1–2; cf. 1 Ne. 6:6). Jacob thus knew that his writings must include material "most precious" (Jacob 1:2), of great spiritual worth, and like Nephi's writings, they must also be persuasive in bringing people to Christ (1 Ne. 6:4). Jacob's first effort to keep his commitment to his brother as steward of the sacred records was to record the diligent efforts among the Nephites to "persuade them to come unto Christ" (Jacob 1:7). Perhaps Jacob's greatest contribution to the "come unto Christ" theme was his decision to include the allegory of Zenos (Jacob 5). Jacob stated that he quoted the allegory in an effort to explain how the Jews could come back to Christ after they had rejected him (Jacob 4:17–18).

When Jacob in turn passed the plates to his son Enos, he repeated the commandment Nephi had given him concerning the record, and Enos promised obedience (Jacob 7:27). Enos kept his commitment by describing his own conversion to Christ and the subsequent remission of his sins (Enos 1:2–8).

The final writer on the small plates of Nephi was Amaleki[1]. He used the last available space on the plates to reiterate the primary message of those who had written before him: "And now, my beloved brethren, I would that ye should come unto Christ, who is the Holy One of Israel, and partake of his salvation, and the power of his redemption" (Omni 1:26).

Mormon's abridgment of the large plates of Nephi, beginning with Mosiah, continued the theme Nephi initiated in the small plates. Implicit in the messages and doctrinal teachings of such leaders and prophets as king Benjamin, Abinadi, Alma[2], Ammon[2], and Aaron[3] is the call to come unto Christ. Their teachings were preparatory to the personal invitation issued by Christ himself as he spoke to their descendants out of the darkness just before his appearance in the New World: "Yea, verily I say unto you, if ye will come unto me ye shall have eternal life. Behold, mine arm of mercy is extended towards you, and whosoever will come, him will I receive; and blessed are those who come unto me" (3 Ne. 9:14; A.D. 34).

The "come unto Christ" theme pervades the Book of Mormon, even to the end. Mormon's son Moroni, the last Nephite prophet to serve as guardian of the sacred writings of the Nephite people, closed his own discourses, and thus the entire Book of Mormon, with the same message his predecessors had proclaimed: "And again I would exhort you that ye would come unto Christ. . . . Yea, come unto Christ, and be perfected in him" (Moro. 10:30, 32).

In addition to the pleadings of the prophets, the Book of Mormon contains conversion stories of individuals and groups, stories that effectively teach how people can come unto Christ. For example, the account of Enos depicts his struggle with REPENTANCE, his persistence in PRAYER, and his receiving FORGIVENESS through FAITH in Christ (Enos 1:2–8). Later, king Benjamin's people recognized their fallen state and cried in HUMILITY for forgiveness through the ATONEMENT (Mosiah 4:1–3). The people of Alma[1] at the waters of Mormon expressed great desire "to come into the fold of God" through entering into the covenant of BAPTISM (Mosiah 18:8–11). The conversion stories of Alma[2], the sons of Mosiah[2], and the ANTI-NEPHI-LEHIES emphasize repentance and spiritual rebirth (Mosiah 27, 28; Alma 21:18–23; 22–27; 36). When king Lamoni's father expressed willingness to sacrifice everything to know God, Aaron[3] told him to

B OF M, SELECTED THEMES OF

do just two things—repent and pray (Alma 22:15–18). In these and other conversion stories, along with teachings of the prophets and instruction from the Savior himself, the reader finds a whole catalog of attributes and practices that set mortals on the path to Christ. These include the following:

Humility, a broken heart, and a contrite spirit (3 Ne. 9:20; 12:3, 19; Morm. 2:14)

Sincerity of heart (3 Ne. 18:32; Morm. 9:27; cf. 2 Ne. 31:13; Alma 22:15)

Gaining knowledge of Christ "and the very points of his doctrine" (1 Ne. 15:14)

Faith in Christ and his gospel (Enos 1:8; Ether 4:19; Moro. 7:34)

Repentance (1 Ne. 10:18; 2 Ne. 28:32; Alma 22:16; 3 Ne. 12:19; 21:20; Morm. 3:2; Ether 4:18; Moro. 7:34)

Prayer, a cry for mercy (1 Ne. 8:8; Mosiah 4:2; Alma 18:41; 36:18)

Reconciliation with others (3 Ne. 12:23–24)

Baptism (3 Ne. 27:20; 30:2; Morm. 3:2; Ether 4:18)

Continued obedience (2 Ne. 31:19–20; 3 Ne. 12:20; cf. A of F 3)

In essence, to accept the invitation, even the commandment, to come unto Christ (3 Ne. 12:19) requires personal application of the Atonement by "obedience to the laws and ordinances of the Gospel" (A of F 3).

The Lord promises great blessings to those who accept the invitation to come unto him. For sinners who "return and repent," he promises forgiveness (3 Ne. 18:32), a blessing that brings peace and great joy (e.g., Mosiah 4:3; Alma 19:6; 36:18–21). For disciples who believe in him, the Lord promises one day to show them "greater things, the knowledge which is hid up because of unbelief" (Ether 4:13–14). A valuable, though sometimes painful consequence of coming to Christ, is the promise the Lord gave to Moroni[2] that "if men come unto me I will show unto them their weakness," and they will be humbled thereby. The Lord pledges that his "grace is sufficient" for the humble and that through humility and faith he will make "weak things become strong" (Ether 12:27).

For Alma[2], so important was the matter of coming unto Christ that he viewed it as the solution to the world's problems and expressed his burning desire to assist in the remedy: "Yea, I would declare unto every soul, as with the voice of thunder, repentance and the plan of redemption, that they should repent and come unto our God, that there might not be more sorrow upon all the face of the earth" (Alma 29:2). Book of Mormon prophets consistently taught that the ultimate blessing of coming unto Jesus Christ is SALVATION (Hel. 5:9; 3 Ne. 9:14; Ether 8:26; Moro. 7:34; cf. Alma 5:35). Jesus said, "Come unto me and be ye saved" (3 Ne. 12:20). Perhaps no one expressed more eloquently than Jacob[2] the blessings promised to those who accept Christ. In a charged discourse, he urged his people to "turn away from your sins; shake off the chains of him that would bind you fast; come unto that God who is the rock of your salvation. . . . Hearken diligently unto me . . . and come unto the Holy One of Israel, and feast upon that which perisheth not, neither can be corrupted, and let your soul delight in fatness" (2 Ne. 9:45, 51; cf. Omni 1:26). Christ indicated, too, that the blessings that follow coming unto him are freely offered: "Come unto me and ye shall partake of the fruit of the tree of life; yea, ye shall eat and drink of the bread and the waters of life freely" (Alma 5:34; cf. 2 Ne. 26:25). And Nephi[1] taught that the invitation to come unto Christ is extended to all people: "He inviteth them all to come unto him and partake of his goodness; and he denieth none that come unto him, black and white, bond and free, male and female; and he remembereth the heathen; and all are alike unto God, both Jew and Gentile" (2 Ne. 26:33).

See also Born again.

DLL

Cycles of prosperity and destruction

The rise and fall of civilizations resulting from their obedience or disobedience to God's commandments constitutes one of the most poignant and consistent themes in the Book of Mormon. Many of the great prophet-writers witnessed these cycles of apostasy and described the waxing and waning of their respective societies. Mormon's abridgment of the Nephite records and Moroni's abridgment of the Jaredite records highlight the basic elements of this cycle. All periods of Nephite history display the common elements of the cycle, which include the following:

- The enjoyment of prosperity owing to the blessings of the Lord.
- The development of pride among the people because of their prosperity.
- The gradual increase of wickedness and concomitant loss of spiritual power as well as divine protection.
- The ensuing judgments of God because of wickedness, including increased suffering from war, bondage, or natural calamity due to the vulnerability which comes when God's help or intervention is absent.
- A return to humility and repentance on the part of the people because of their miserable and lowly circumstances, which brings again the blessings of the Lord, including prosperity.
- And the cycle is repeated.

B OF M, SELECTED THEMES OF

Two complete and yet succinct descriptions of the cycle of prosperity and destruction are offered in Helaman 11 and 4 Nephi. As Helaman 11 opens, the Nephites, who had enjoyed great prosperity and security (Hel. 8:6), had become immersed in wickedness and warfare. Nephi[2], son of Helaman[3], successfully importuned the Lord to send a famine to replace war as a means of causing the people to remember God (Hel. 11:4). The calamity produced its desired effect (Hel. 11:7), and the people humbled themselves and repented (Hel. 11:9, 15). The Gadianton robbers were eliminated, the Lord prospered the people, prophets were revered again (an important detail of the cycle), and there was peace in the land (Hel. 11:10, 17–18, 21). The cycle began its downward spiral as dissenters from the Nephites went to the Lamanites and "stirred" them to anger and to war (Hel. 11:24). Gadianton robbers reappeared and flourished, causing "great destruction" to come upon the people (Hel. 11:26–32; cf. 4 Ne. 1:42–46). Mormon concluded that "this great evil . . . came unto the people because of their iniquity" (Hel.

CYCLES OF PROSPERITY AND DESTRUCTION

Jesus Christ Visits the Americas; *painting by John Scott; courtesy VRL.*

B OF M, SELECTED THEMES OF

11:34). Although their afflictions caused them to again remember their God, it was only temporary. As the people grew stronger in pride and thus stronger in wickedness, they ripened "again for destruction" (Hel. 11:37).

Fourth Nephi describes the same cycle of apostasy, including the basic elements found in Helaman 11. The people enjoyed peace and prosperity because of the Lord (4 Ne. 1:4, 7, 14–15, 18). The downward spiral began as a small group rebelled against the true Church (4 Ne. 1:20). Pride growing out of prosperity caused social division and abandonment of the law of consecration (4 Ne. 1:23–25). The appearance and then flourishing of secret combinations brought great misery and sorrow upon the people (4 Ne. 1:42–46). Fourth Nephi also illustrates three important truths associated with the cycle of prosperity and destruction: first, Christ is the source of all true and lasting prosperity and peace (4 Ne. 1:15–18, 23); second, pride not only hastens the downward spiral of the cycle of apostasy by destroying social unity (4 Ne. 1:24–28) but also affects every segment of society sooner or later (4 Ne. 1:43–45); and, third, the righteous suffer at the hands of the wicked when a society embarks on its downward slide (4 Ne. 1:31–34). Ultimately, 4 Nephi teaches that when a group of people becomes so wicked that their sufferings no longer engender in them humility and repentance, destruction is imminent. Mormon described this condition among his people, the descendants of those mentioned at the end of 4 Nephi. For them the "day of grace," or opportunity to repent, had finally passed (Morm. 2:10–15).

A study of the cycles of prosperity and destruction in the Book of Mormon reveals that God is merciful and long-suffering. When his children make choices that cut them off from his blessings and will ultimately lead to their destruction—although he allows them the agency to make such choices—he actively seeks their repentance and redemption (e.g., 2 Ne. 25:9; Hel. 11:4; 13:17; 3 Ne. 6:20; D&C 43:25).

For other summaries of the cycle of prosperity and destruction, see Alma 4:1–12; 3 Nephi 5–8; and Ether 9–10, illustrated in the accompanying table.

ACS

Freedom to choose happiness or misery

The Book of Mormon repeatedly teaches the truth that humankind is free to choose the path that leads either to eternal life and happiness or to eternal death and misery. Lehi[1] proclaimed to his son Jacob[2] that people are "free to choose liberty and eternal life, through the great Mediator of all men, or to choose captivity and death, according to the captivity and power of the devil" (2 Ne. 2:27). He then challenged his sons to "choose eternal life . . . and not choose eternal death" (2 Ne. 2:28–29). Similarly, Samuel the Lamanite told wicked Nephites to "remember . . . that whosoever perisheth, perisheth unto himself . . . for behold, ye are free; ye are permitted to act for yourselves; for behold, God hath given unto you a knowledge and he hath made you free. . . . and he hath given unto you that ye might choose life or death; and ye can do good and be restored unto that which is good . . . or ye can do evil, and have that which is evil restored unto you" (Hel. 14:30–31). Alma[2] iterated this doctrine when he taught that people either "stand or fall; for behold, they are their own judges, whether to do good or do evil" (Alma 41:7). King Benjamin contrasted these two opposing eternal states in his address to his people, testifying that sin brings "never-ending torment," while obedience brings "never-ending happiness" (Mosiah 2:36–41).

Throughout the Book of Mormon, readers can learn about Christ and the path to happiness, or Satan and the path to misery. The Book of Mormon contains stories of individuals and groups who make choices that put them on one path or the other, and then it shows the consequences that result from these choices. Behaviors, attitudes, practices, and people representative of the two paths are contrasted so readers can clearly see what leads away from Christ as opposed to what leads to him. For example, while the dream of Lehi[1] teaches about the path to the tree of life, a symbol of "the love of God" (1 Ne. 11:21–22, 25), it also teaches

B OF M, SELECTED THEMES OF

and warns about the "great and spacious building," a symbol for "the pride of the world" (1 Ne. 8:26–28; 11:35–36). As those who build their foundation on Christ cannot fall (Hel. 5:12), those who reside in the large building with no foundation will certainly fall (1 Ne. 8:26; 11:35–36).

Many such contrasts fill the pages of the Book of Mormon: humility versus pride (Alma 4); sacred covenants versus secret combinations (Mosiah 18; Ether 8); priesthood versus priestcraft (Alma 1); the teachings of the prophets Jacob[2] and Alma[2] versus the teachings of the anti-Christs Sherem and Korihor (Jacob 7; Alma 30); the character and actions of the Nephite chief captain Moroni versus the character and actions of the dissenter Amalickiah (Alma 48); the deceit of the Gadianton chief robber Giddianhi versus the integrity of chief judge and prophet Lachoneus[1] (3 Ne. 3); the characteristics and principles governing Zion versus the evil beliefs and practices that can destroy Zion (4 Ne.).

The Lord's promise throughout the record is that if the Nephites kept the commandments, they would prosper in the land, and if they did not, he would cut them off (2 Ne. 1:20). The Book of Mormon contains a record of the literal fulfillment of the Lord's promise: its people were blessed or cursed as they obeyed or disobeyed. The righteousness and wickedness of the Nephites make up two histories, dual narrative threads, that illustrate the reality and consistency of the consequences of making right and wrong choices.

Righteousness afforded the Nephites safety from their enemies, deliverance from their captors, refuge from destruction, and a knowledge of the mysteries of God through the power of the Holy Ghost. Conversely, disobedience brought difficulty, as with the Lord's disabling of the Liahona (1 Ne. 18:12–14, 21). It also brought sorrow, suffering, the imposition of bondage (Mosiah 27:16; Alma 9:22; 36:29), and eventual destruction. It was unquestionably the choice for wickedness that brought the wrath of the Lord upon Lehi's descendants prior to Christ's ministry among them (3 Ne. 8–9) and then again some three and a half centuries later (Morm. 1–6).

With the negative consequences of sin and the positive consequences of obedience convincingly illustrated, the Book of Mormon does much to persuade readers to choose the path to eternal life and happiness rather than the path to eternal death and misery.

See also Book of Mormon, selected purposes of, to latter-day people, that we might learn to be more wise; Book of Mormon, selected purposes of, to reveal the enemies of Christ; Book of Mormon, selected themes of, come unto Christ; Book of Mormon, selected themes of, cycles of prosperity and destruction.

DLL

Obedience

In a gospel sense, obedience is the conscious and willing adherence to the will and commandments of God. Such obedience is a theme that reverberates throughout the Book of Mormon. At times, the word itself (Jacob 7:27), along with its variant forms *obey* and *obedient*, are used (1 Ne. 2:3; 4:18; 22:30–31; 2 Ne. 1:27; 5:31; 31:7; 33:15; Jacob 2:4; 4:5; 5:72; Mosiah 2:32–33, 37; 5:8; Alma 3:26–27; 57:21). In addition, such phrases as "keep the commandments" (2 Ne. 3:2; Jarom 1:10; Mosiah 2:41; Alma 36:1; 3 Ne. 6:14), "follow after righteousness" (2 Ne. 8:1), "follow the voice of the good shepherd" (Alma 5:57), "follow Christ" (Moro. 7:11), and "hearken unto my words" (Hel. 7:23; 13:21; 3 Ne. 21:22; 23:5) are used frequently and underscore the importance of this divine principle. Alma[2] equated wisdom with keeping the commandments when exhorting his son Helaman to "learn wisdom in thy youth" (Alma 37:35).

Obedience is more than mere compliance. It requires a willing and committed heart, leading to total fidelity and exactness in observance of God's laws (Jacob 5:72, 74; Omni 1:26; Mosiah 3:19; Alma 7:23; 58:40; cf. D&C 64:22, 34). The plan of happiness, as set forth in the Book of Mormon, includes agency as an integral part of Heavenly Father's plan; without freedom of choice, obedience cannot be exercised (2 Ne. 2:5, 11–13, 16, 27; Alma 42:7; Hel. 14:30–31).

B OF M, SELECTED THEMES OF

For example, the scriptures clearly depict the resolve of Lehi[1] and Nephi[1] to follow every command of the Lord. Even when confronted with difficult circumstances, their actions bespeak their determination to submit their will to God's (1 Ne. 1:18; 2:2–4; 3:7; 4:1, 7–18; 16:8; 17:8, 15, 50; 18:3–4).

Obedience brings the blessings of heaven

Obedience to the commandments brings forth blessings (1 Ne. 14:1–2; 16:8; Mosiah 2:24). Lehi and Nephi were promised that through obedience, they and their posterity would receive a land of promise in which they would prosper (1 Ne. 2:20; 13:30; 2 Ne. 1:5, 9). This promise and its fulfillment are repeated throughout the Book of Mormon (Jarom 1:9; Omni 1:6; Mosiah 1:7; 2:22, 31; Alma 9:13, 22; 36:1, 30; 37:13; 38:1; 48:25; 50:20; 3 Ne. 5:22). King Benjamin urged all to contemplate "the blessed and happy state of those that keep the commandments of God. For behold, they are blessed in all things, both temporal and spiritual" (Mosiah 2:41). Mormon wrote that deliverance from one's enemies is contingent upon obedience and that the faithful are happy, even during times of war (Alma 50:22–23). Other scriptures make it clear that true happiness can come only through obedience to God (2 Ne. 5:10, 27; Alma 41:10; Hel. 13:38). Nephi[2], the son of Helaman[3], was promised that through his "unwearyingness" the Lord would make him "mighty in word and in deed, in faith and in works," and "that all things shall be done unto thee according to thy word, for thou shalt not ask that which is contrary to my will" (Hel. 10:4–5). The sure and ultimate blessing of obedience is eternal life, salvation in the kingdom of God (2 Ne. 31:13, 20; Alma 9:28).

Divine assistance

The Lord promises his assistance to those who faithfully strive to do his will. Nephi[1] testified of this truth when he said to his father, "I will go and do the things which the Lord hath commanded, for I know that the Lord giveth no commandments unto the children of men, save he shall prepare a way for them that they may accomplish the thing which he commandeth them" (1 Ne. 3:7). Nephi's testimony was verified in his obtaining the brass plates of Laban, a perilous task accomplished only through the Lord's help (1 Ne. 4).

Additionally, the two thousand stripling warriors under Helaman[2] were preserved in battle by the power of God "because of their exceeding faith in that which they had been taught to believe" (Alma 57:21–26). They did "observe to keep his statutes, and his judgments, and his commandments continually" (Alma 58:40).

Blessings of obedience versus the consequences of disobedience

Just as obedience brings the blessings of heaven, so does disobedience result in unhappy consequences. The blessed lives of Jacob[2] (Jacob 1–7), Abinadi (Mosiah 11–17), Alma[2] (Mosiah 27–Alma 17), and the converted Lamanites (Alma 17–29) contrast sharply with the sad ends of Sherem (Jacob 7:1–23), Noah[3] (Mosiah 11–12; 17–19), Amulon (Mosiah 23–24), and Amlici (Alma 2–3). Each personality and event helps the reader better understand the attendant consequences, both positive and negative, for those who seek out and follow the Lord versus those who lack faith and disregard his commandments. The lives of Laman[1] and Lemuel, Lehi's sons, illustrate that disobedience and rebellion lead to tragedy, both temporal and spiritual. The scriptures use such terms as "stiffneckedness," "murmur," "hard in their hearts," and "rebel" to describe their attitudes and demeanor toward the pleading of Lehi and Nephi that they turn their hearts to the Lord (1 Ne. 2:11, 21–23; 15:3). Their refusal to heed the commandments of God resulted in wars, contentions, and their being cut off from God's presence (2 Ne. 5:20). The Book of Mormon clearly teaches and illustrates that those who disobey God's commandments cannot secure salvation unless they repent (Mosiah 3:12; 7:30–33; 15:26; Alma 5:57; 7:15–16; 9:12–13; 34:32–34).

A perfect example of obedience

There can be no greater example of obedience, no greater testimony of its importance, than that provided by the Savior himself. Nephi[1] quoted the Lord and then invited his readers to follow Jesus' example: "And [Jesus] said unto the

B OF M, SELECTED THEMES OF

children of men: Follow thou me. Wherefore, my beloved brethren, can we follow Jesus save we shall be willing to keep the commandments of the Father?" Nephi continued his discourse by declaring that "unless a man shall endure to the end, in following the example of the Son of the living God, he cannot be saved" (2 Ne. 31:10, 16; cf. Hel. 12:23; 3 Ne. 12:20; 15:1; 18:14–16; John 14:15). Thus, mortals avail themselves of the promised blessings of the Lord only through obedience to his commandments (1 Ne. 17:3; 2 Ne. 30:1–2; D&C 130:20–21).

See also Commandment(s); Righteous, the/ righteousness.

DMW

Remember, remembrance

To remember (and its opposite, to forget) is one of the most important and distinctive themes of the Book of Mormon. The word *remember,* or a form of it, appears nearly two hundred times in the Book of Mormon. From Nephi[1] to Moroni[2], Book of Mormon prophets constantly urge, counsel, and command the people to remember their Lord, their forebears, their history, their blessings, their promises, their covenants, their own experiences, and their deliverance from captivity. In addition to sending prophets, the Lord on occasion sends pestilence and famine to stir his people to remembrance. He also allows wars, captivity, and destruction to occur for the same purpose (Enos 1:23; Mosiah 27:16; Alma 4:2–3; Hel. 11:4–7; 12:3).

But the act of "remembering" means much more than simply calling to mind things from the past. Rather, as in the Bible, this remembering implies a course of action as well as a train of thought; it implies a way of living, not just an item of intellection. For instance, Nephi, in one of his entreaties to Laman[1] and Lemuel, clearly intends "remembering" to be a corollary with "doing" when he says, "Ye are swift to do iniquity but slow to remember the Lord your God" (1 Ne. 17:45). And in the sacramental prayer, remembering is parallel with keeping the commandments: "Always remember him, and keep his commandments which he hath given them" (Moro. 4:3). To do the one is to do the other.

When in the end of the Book of Mormon, Moroni exhorts the reader to "remember how merciful the Lord hath been unto the children of men, from the creation of Adam even down until the time that ye shall receive these things, and ponder it in your hearts" (Moro. 10:3), his "remember" signifies a study of sacred history—the mercies of God to the children of men—as the "how" of "remembering." In this case "remembering" means to read and ponder.

And as "remembering" is associated with right actions, so, in Book of Mormon usage, "forgetting" is often associated with disobedience or the breaking of covenants. The Lamanite prophet Samuel chastised the Nephites of his time for failing to "remember the Lord" and his blessings and instead "always remember[ing their] riches" (Hel. 13:22). Mormon editorialized: "Thus we see how quick the children of men do forget the Lord their God, yea, how quick to do iniquity, and to be led away by the evil one" (Alma 46:8).

One of the clearest explanations of the intent and process of "remembering" in the Book of Mormon itself is in the injunction of Helaman[3] to his sons Nephi[2] and Lehi[4]: "Behold, my sons, I desire that ye should remember to keep the commandments of God. . . . Behold, I have given unto you the names of our first parents who came out of the land of Jerusalem; and this I have done that when you remember your names ye may remember them; and when ye remember them ye may remember their works; and when ye remember their works ye may know how that it is said, and also written, that they were good. Therefore, my sons, I would that ye should do that which is good, that it may be said of you, and also written, even as it has been said and written of them" (Hel. 5:6–7). In addition to these things, Helaman enjoined his sons to remember that mortals can be saved only through the atonement of Christ, that they cannot be redeemed in their sins but only from them, and that lives built on Christ will withstand the buffetings of Satan (Hel. 5:9–12).

The Lord will, from time to time, command certain practices or establish a process as a means to remember. As Abinadi explained, "Therefore there was a law given [to Israel], yea, a law of performances and of ordinances, a law which they were to observe strictly from day to day, to keep them in remembrance of God and their duty towards him" (Mosiah 13:30).

An important outcome of such "remembering" is the establishment of communities of memory—families, congregations, and peoples who share a common knowledge about the significant matters of their past, present, and future, and who act together according to those sacred remembrances. Remembrance then provides the means for understanding events and gives direction and guidance for the community and the individuals in it. Thus in times of crisis, Book of Mormon figures frequently drew upon their own sacred history for direction and assurance. Nephi[1], for instance, continually invited the wayward Laman and Lemuel back into their family's God-directed effort by reminding them of the great miracles God had already performed for their family and their forebears (e.g., 1 Ne. 17:23–51). So also Alma[2], in testifying to his son Helaman[2], charged him to remember God's hand in their family history and its parallel with Israel's deliverance: "[God] led [Israel] by his power into the promised land; yea, and he has delivered them out of bondage and captivity from time to time. Yea, and he has also brought our fathers out of the land of Jerusalem; and he has also, by his everlasting power, delivered them out of bondage and captivity, from time to time even down to the present day; and I have always retained in remembrance their captivity; yea, and ye also ought to retain in remembrance, as I have done, their captivity" (Alma 36:28–29). This is the "remembering" that binds father to son and is the means by which the associated community of believing people is projected into its divinely appointed future.

BIBLIOGRAPHY

Midgley, Louis. "The Ways of Remembrance." *Rediscovering the Book of Mormon: Insights You May Have Missed Before.* Edited by John L. Sorenson and Melvin J. Thorne. Salt Lake City: Deseret Book and FARMS, 1991.

Yerushalmi, Yosef Hayim. *Zakhor: Jewish History and Jewish Memory.* New York: Schocken Books, 1989.

NEL

Restoration of the house of Israel

See Israel, gathering of.

Book of Mormon, title page of Readers of the Book of Mormon are introduced to this sacred scripture through the title page, a brief statement translated by Joseph Smith and published at the beginning of the book. Joseph Smith described the location of the title page among the plates of Mormon: "The title-page of the Book of Mormon is a literal translation, taken from the very last leaf, on the left hand side of the collection or book of plates . . . [it] is not by any means a modern composition, either of mine or of any other man who has lived or does live in this generation" (1:71).

The title page of the Book of Mormon explains the background of most of the sources of the book and lists some of the principal purposes of the book. Concerning the Book of Mormon sources, the title page itself indicates that it "is an abridgment of the record of the people of Nephi" and "an abridgment taken from the Book of Ether also, which is a record of the people of Jared." The title page does not mention the small plates of Nephi.

As to the purposes of the Book of Mormon, the title page indicates that the book is (1) "to show unto the remnant of the House of Israel what great things the Lord hath done for their fathers" so that (2) "they may know the covenants of the Lord, . . . and also" (3) "to the convincing of the Jew and Gentile that JESUS is the CHRIST, the ETERNAL GOD, manifesting himself unto all nations." The title page declares to the reader that the Book of Mormon record was "written by way of commandment [of the Lord], and also by the spirit of prophecy and of revelation."

The title page was officially recorded and published twice before the Book of Mormon itself was printed, bound, and made available to the public. When Joseph Smith applied for a copyright of the Book of Mormon on 11 June 1829, R. R. Lansing, the clerk of the Northern District of New York, recorded the title page with the notation, "Joseph Smith Junior of the said District, hath deposited in this Office the title of a Book . . . to wit." The title page was also printed on 26 June 1829 in the *Wayne Sentinel*, a newspaper published at the same press (Grandin's) that was also responsible for setting the type and publishing the first edition of the

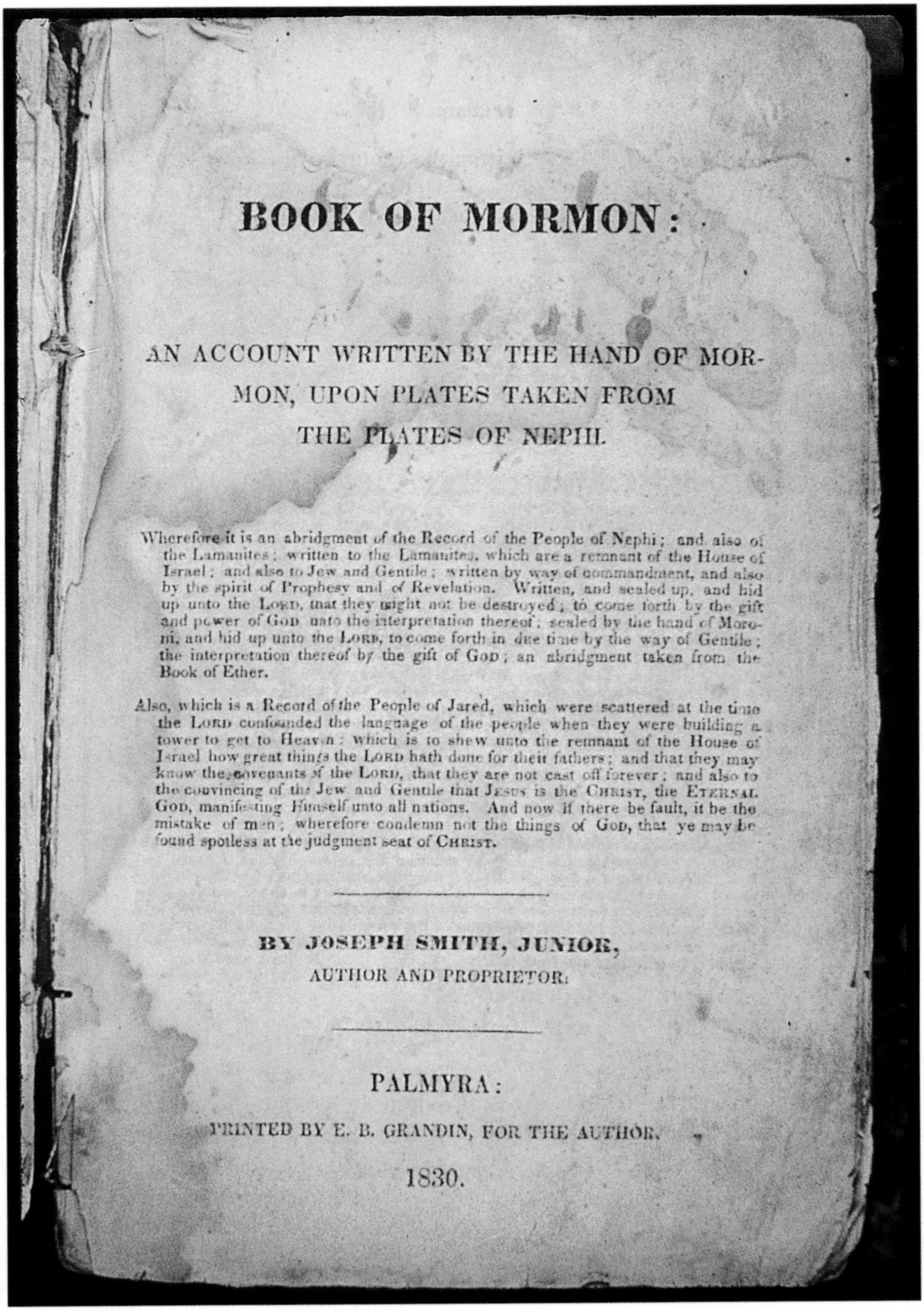

BOOK OF MORMON:

AN ACCOUNT WRITTEN BY THE HAND OF MORMON, UPON PLATES TAKEN FROM THE PLATES OF NEPHI.

Wherefore it is an abridgment of the Record of the People of Nephi; and also of the Lamanites; written to the Lamanites, which are a remnant of the House of Israel; and also to Jew and Gentile; written by way of commandment, and also by the spirit of Prophesy and of Revelation. Written, and sealed up, and hid up unto the LORD, that they might not be destroyed; to come forth by the gift and power of GOD unto the interpretation thereof; sealed by the hand of Moroni, and hid up unto the LORD, to come forth in due time by the way of Gentile; the interpretation thereof by the gift of GOD; an abridgment taken from the Book of Ether.

Also, which is a Record of the People of Jared, which were scattered at the time the LORD confounded the language of the people when they were building a tower to get to Heaven: which is to shew unto the remnant of the House of Israel how great things the LORD hath done for their fathers; and that they may know the covenants of the LORD, that they are not cast off forever; and also to the convincing of the Jew and Gentile that JESUS is the CHRIST, the ETERNAL GOD, manifesting Himself unto all nations. And now if there be fault, it be the mistake of men; wherefore condemn not the things of GOD, that ye may be found spotless at the judgment seat of CHRIST.

BY JOSEPH SMITH, JUNIOR,

AUTHOR AND PROPRIETOR.

PALMYRA:

PRINTED BY E. B. GRANDIN, FOR THE AUTHOR.

1830.

1830 title page of the Book of Mormon; courtesy MCHA.

BOOK OF MORMON, TRANSLATION OF

Book of Mormon. In both of these instances, the title page was written as one paragraph. In the first edition of the Book of Mormon, the title page was published as two paragraphs, a style followed in subsequent English editions but with a change where the paragraphs divide.

It is generally understood that Moroni[2] wrote the title page.

See also Book of Mormon, selected purposes of, to the convincing of the Jew and Gentile that Jesus is the Christ; Book of Mormon, selected purposes of, to show unto the remnant of the House of Israel what great things the Lord hath done for their fathers; Gilbert, John Hulburd.

BIBLIOGRAPHY

Lansing, R. R. See Joseph Smith, copyright entry in Court of the United States for the Northern District of New York, September 1826 to May 1831, 116:107, Copyright Office, The Library of Congress, Washington, D.C.

Smith, Joseph. *History of The Church of Jesus Christ of Latter-day Saints*. Edited by B. H. Roberts. 7 vols. 2d ed. rev. Salt Lake City: The Church of Jesus Christ of Latter-day Saints, 1932–51.

DHL

Book of Mormon, translation of On 22 September 1827 Joseph Smith received from the angel Moroni the plates used in the translation of the Book of Mormon. Approximately twenty-one months later, after completing the translation, he returned the plates to Moroni. Although Joseph Smith had the plates for nearly two years, almost all the work of translation of the current text of the Book of Mormon was accomplished in the equivalent of about two months of actual working days, nearly all of it being done between April 7 and June 30, 1829.

Many forces interfered with Joseph Smith's efforts to translate the Book of Mormon. As soon as it was learned he had the plates, "the most strenuous exertions were used to get them from" him (Smith, 1:18). To keep them safe, Joseph hid the plates in various locations in and near his parents' home in Manchester, New York, where he was living. His life continued to be disrupted by threats and evening raids. Joseph Smith was warned by Moroni that others would try to steal the record and was told to show the plates to no one, except those who were specifically designated (Smith, 1:52–58; Bushman, 82–84).

Because Joseph Smith was unable to work on the translation in Manchester, he decided to move with his wife, Emma Hale Smith, to her father's home in Harmony, Pennsylvania. Hiding the plates in a barrel of beans, Joseph and Emma traveled by wagon from Manchester to Harmony in December 1827. Shortly after arriving, Joseph purchased a thirteen-acre farm, including a home, in Harmony. The translation probably began in that small frame building, which consisted of two rooms at ground level, one room upstairs, and a full basement (Porter, 133–37; Bushman, 85–86).

In addition to the challenge of moving and securing property in Pennsylvania, Joseph Smith was faced with the responsibility of supporting himself and his wife, Emma. Joseph Smith had met his wife while working for Josiah Stowell, who had sent him to Harmony, Pennsylvania, in search of buried treasure. Instead of finding precious metals, however, Joseph met Emma, whom he married in January, 1827. Meanwhile, he had become acquainted with others who lived in that part of the country, and some of his friends, such as Joseph Knight, assisted him in 1828 and 1829 by providing work and necessary supplies so he could continue with the translation of the Book of Mormon (Porter, 181–86, 196). The work of translation was also hindered by the problem of locating satisfactory scribes.

Scribes

On a number of occasions while living in Harmony, Emma served as scribe, including the two winters of 1827–28 and 1828–29. The translation during those periods was sporadic, however. Consistent work did occur during a two-month period after the arrival of Martin Harris in mid-April 1828. Martin Harris was a prominent citizen of Palmyra who had assisted Joseph Smith financially. After receiving heavenly assurances of the validity of Joseph Smith's calling and making a visit to Charles Anthon and others in New York, Martin became increasingly convinced that Joseph Smith had the power to translate (Bushman, 86–89). For two months, Martin Harris wrote as Joseph Smith dictated to him words that he translated from the plates. Although Martin Harris later became one of the Three Witnesses of the Book of Mormon, he was not permitted to see the plates in 1828. A curtain separated the two men while translating. By the middle of June of that year, 116 foolscap pages of text, translated from the book of Lehi, had been produced. Martin took these pages to Palmyra, where they were lost.

The loss of the 116 manuscript pages created another period during which very little translating was accomplished. In the summer of 1828 both Joseph Smith and Martin Harris were chastised, and the angel, who was the custodian of the record, took the plates and URIM AND THUMMIM (sacred instrument used in the translation process) from Joseph Smith for a time. The translation did not resume until after 22 September 1828, and the work was intermittent for another six months.

Although Emma Hale Smith and probably her brother Reuben assisted Joseph in recording a portion of the manuscript during the winter of 1828–29, substantial work on the manuscript did not begin again until early April 1829. On 5 April 1829, Oliver Cowdery arrived in Harmony, and two days later he began writing as Joseph Smith dictated to him. Oliver Cowdery had learned about Joseph Smith's religious experiences while teaching school in western New York. He traveled to Pennsylvania and offered the young prophet his services (Smith, 1:32, 35).

Although Joseph Smith experienced relative peace in Harmony, Pennsylvania, for more than a year, increasing persecution caused Joseph to move in early June 1829 from Harmony to Fayette, New York, a journey of about four days by horse and wagon. Within a month of the move, Joseph and Oliver completed the translation of the Book of Mormon in an upstairs room in the Peter Whitmer log farmhouse. During the last weeks of the translation, John Whitmer also served temporarily as a scribe. Other members of the Whitmer family might also have assisted Joseph in preparing the manuscript of the Book of Mormon in June 1829. Pages from early chapters of the original manuscript contain the handwriting of several individuals who have not yet been identified (Jessee, 276–78).

Process of translation

Although very little is known about the process of translation, accounts by Joseph Smith and the scribes who assisted him provide some insights into that process. Joseph Smith deliberately did not expound on this subject. During a conference in Ohio in 1831, he said that "it was not intended to tell the world all the particulars of the coming forth of the book of Mormon, & also said that it was not expedient for him to relate these things" (Cannon and Cook, 23). Joseph Smith repeatedly declared, however, that he translated the Book of Mormon "through the medium of the Urim and Thummim . . . by the gift and power of God" (Smith, 4:537). The Three Witnesses to the Book of Mormon affirmed this same truth when they testified that the voice of God declared to them that the plates "[were] translated by the gift and power of God" (The Testimony of Three Witnesses). Oliver Cowdery wrote, "Day after day I continued, uninterrupted, to write from his mouth, as he translated, with the *Urim* and *Thummim,* or, as the Nephites would have said, 'Interpreters,' the history, or record, called 'The book of Mormon'" (*Messenger and Advocate,* 1:14). Years later Oliver Cowdery stated that he wrote nearly all the Book of Mormon as it was dictated to him by Joseph Smith (Anderson, 8:278).

When Emma Smith was interviewed in 1879 by her son regarding her knowledge of the translation, she declared that she "wrote day after day" for "your father," "often sitting at the table close by him." He dictated to her, she continued, "hour after hour." Emma insisted that her husband did not have a book or manuscript from which to read, saying, "If he had had anything of the kind he could not have concealed it from me." Emma explained that "the plates often lay on the table without any attempt at concealment, wrapped in a small linen table cloth, which I had given him." She further said that once she felt the plates as they lay on the table, "tracing their outline and shape. They seemed to be pliable like thick paper, and would rustle with a metalic [*sic*] sound when the edges were moved by the thumb, as one does sometimes thumb the edges of a book" (Bidamon, 289–90; Bushman, 96).

Different theories emerge as scholars, using various statements by Joseph Smith's contemporaries, attempt to explain in greater detail the process of translation (Ricks, 3–6). One popular theory proposes that Joseph Smith saw words or sentences as he translated and was more of a transmitter than translator. Royal Skousen, professor of English and linguistics at Brigham Young University, conducted an intensive thirteen-year study of both the printer's manuscript and what remains of the original manuscript of the Book of Mormon, and he argues that the evidence from the manuscripts strongly supports this point of view (Skousen). Others suggest that Joseph Smith used interpreters or a SEER STONE to enhance his capacity to understand but that he had the responsibility of transforming ideas into English words. Another idea is that Joseph sometimes saw words (such as names of people and places) and at other times received thoughts, making Joseph Smith both a transmitter and a translator. Concerning such particulars of the translation work, Elder Neal A. Maxwell acknowledged, "We simply do not know the details. We do know that this faith-filled process was not easy, however. This fact was clearly demonstrated in Oliver Cowdery's own attempt at translation. Oliver failed because he 'did not continue as [he] commenced,' and because, lacking faith and works, he 'took no thought save it was to ask' (D&C 9:5, 7). . . . Whatever the details of the process, it required Joseph's intense, personal efforts along with the aid of the revelatory instruments" (39).

Order of translation

The precise order of the translation is also a subject that leads to some speculation. The first part of the Book of Mormon to be translated was the book of Lehi (see Joseph Smith's explanation in the Preface to the first edition of the Book of Mormon), contained in the 116 pages that were lost by Martin Harris in the summer of 1828. The book of Lehi, evidently, was Mormon's abridgment of the Nephite record (large plates of Nephi) down to the reign of king Benjamin, or the point in history where the current book of Mosiah begins (W of M 1:3). "In the winter of 1829 Joseph and Emma took up the translation where he and Martin had broken off the previous June, that is, around the first part of the Book of Mosiah." After Oliver Cowdery arrived in April 1829, "Joseph and Oliver kept on in sequence. . . . In June, probably after the rest of the book was done, he and Oliver began work on I Nephi" (Bushman, 99). That means the first six books of the Book of Mormon, i.e., 1 Nephi, 2 Nephi, Jacob, Enos, Jarom, and Omni were translated last. These six books, known as the "small plates" of Nephi, were found by Mormon at the time he was abridging

CHRONOLOGY OF THE TRANSLATION OF THE BOOK OF MORMON

22 Sept 1827	Obtained Book of Mormon plates
Dec 1827	Moved to Harmony, Pennsylvania
winter 1827-1828	Emma Smith served as scribe
Apr to Jun 1828	Martin Harris served as scribe (about two months)
Jun 1828	Loss of 116 pages of Book of Mormon and temporary power to translate
Sep 1828	Translation resumes
Winter 1828-1829	Emma Smith, Reuben Hale, and Samuel H. Smith served as scribes
Apr to Jun 1829	Oliver Cowdery served as scribe (less than three months)
early Jun 1829	Translation continued in Peter Whitmer home, Fayette, New York
Jun 1829	John Whitmer served as scribe temporarily
11 Jun 1829	Copyright of Book of Mormon obtained
Jun 1829	Book of Mormon translation finished

the Nephite record known as the "large plates" of Nephi. Mormon was inspired to pass on to his son Moroni[2] the unabridged small plates with his abridgment of the large plates. Providentially, the small plates covered the same period of time in Nephite history as did the book of Lehi. Joseph Smith was told by the Lord, therefore, not to retranslate the book of Lehi but to translate the small plates in its stead (1 Ne. 9:1–6; W of M 1:1–11; D&C 10:6–47).

Oliver Cowdery as translator

Oliver Cowdery was not only the principal scribe in the translation of that record but was the only scribe who was granted the opportunity to translate. After a brief experience at translating, Oliver was informed by revelation through the Prophet Joseph Smith that it was not expedient for him to translate at that time (D&C 9:1, 5, 10).

The time factor in translating the Book of Mormon

Original manuscripts of the Book of Mormon containing the handwriting of Oliver Cowdery substantiate statements of Joseph and Oliver regarding Oliver's being the principal scribe. Therefore, the estimate that the Book of Mormon was dictated in approximately sixty days is based on the number of working days available to these men between early April and late June 1829. Subsequently, from the number of words on printed pages in the published editions of the Book of Mormon, Joseph would have dictated on an average of about eight pages per day (Welch, 38–39; Jessee, 278).

See also The Coming Forth of the Book of Mormon, 9; Book of Mormon, lost manuscript of (116 pages); Book of Mormon, manuscripts of.

BIBLIOGRAPHY

Anderson, Richard Lloyd. "Reuben Miller, Recorder of Oliver Cowdery's Reaffirmations." *Brigham Young University Studies* 8:3 (1968): 277–93.

———. "By the Gift and Power of God." *Ensign* 7 (September 1977): 79–85.

Bidamon, Emma Hale Smith. "Statement to Joseph Smith III," February 4–10, 1879. *Saint's Herald* [Plano] (1 October 1879): 289–90.

Bushman, Richard L. *Joseph Smith and the Beginnings of Mormonism*. Chicago: University of Illinois Press, 1984.

Cannon, Donald Q., and Lyndon W. Cook, eds. *Far West Record: Minutes of The Church of Jesus Christ of Latter-day Saints, 1830–1844*. Salt Lake City: Deseret Book, 1983.

Cowdery, Oliver. *Messenger and Advocate* 1 (October 1834): 14.

Jessee, Dean C. "The Original Book of Mormon Manuscript." *Brigham Young University Studies* 10 (Spring 1970): 259–78.

Maxwell, Neal A. "By the Gift and Power of God." *Ensign* 27 (January 1997): 34–41.

Porter, Larry C. "A Study of the Origins of The Church of Jesus Christ of Latter-day Saints in the States of New York and Pennsylvania, 1816–1831." Provo, Utah: Brigham Young University, 1971.

Ricks, Stephen D. "Joseph Smith's Translation of the Book of Mormon." Provo, Utah: FARMS, 1986.

Skousen, Royal "How Joseph Smith Translated the Book of Mormon: Evidence from the Original Manuscript." *Journal of Book of Mormon Studies* 7 (1998): 22–31.

Smith, Joseph. *History of The Church of Jesus Christ of Latter-day Saints*. Edited by B. H. Roberts. 7 vols. 2d ed. rev. Salt Lake City: The Church of Jesus Christ of Latter-day Saints, 1932–51.

Welch, John W., and Tim Rathbone. "The Translation of the Book of Mormon: Basic Historical Information." Provo, Utah: FARMS, 1986.

MVB

Book of Mormon, translations of, other than English The Book of Mormon (2 Ne. 29:2, 7) and modern revelation (D&C 124:128) proclaim that the message of the ancient Nephite record would eventually spread to every nation upon the earth. On 8 March 1833 the Lord told Joseph Smith that every person would "hear the fulness of the gospel in his own tongue, and in his own language" (D&C 90:11). In an effort to fulfill this mandate, by the beginning of the twenty-first century, the Church has translated the Book of Mormon, in selections or in full, into more than one hundred languages, including American Sign Language, so that approximately 87 percent, or several billion of the earth's inhabitants, can read from the book in their own language ("Taking," 26).

Historical overview

During the first two decades after the establishment of the Church, missionary efforts were concentrated mainly in the United States, the British Isles, and English-speaking Canada.

The few exceptions include Elder Orson Hyde's 1841 mission to Jerusalem, which took him through Europe, where he published several missionary tracts, including one in Dutch in 1841 and another in German in 1841; Dan Jones's missionary activity in Wales in the mid-1840s, during which he printed tracts in Welsh; and limited missionary efforts in the South Pacific beginning in the early 1840s.

In a dramatic and far-reaching step toward declaring the gospel worldwide, Church leaders announced in the fall 1849 general conference that missionary work would commence on the European continent. Missionaries soon arrived in Scandinavia, France, Switzerland, Germany, and Italy.

In 1850, Elder Peter O. Hanson, one of the first missionaries to Denmark, finished working on a translation of the Book of Mormon in Danish that he had commenced while in Nauvoo in the 1840s. This translation resulted in the first non-English edition of the Book of Mormon. It was initially issued to about two hundred subscribers in one-sheet installments (a sixteen-page gathering) as the sheets came off the press between January and May 1851. On May 22, the final sheet of the final gathering was printed, completing the edition of three thousand copies. Less than a year later saw the appearance of the Book of Mormon in French (published in Paris in January 1852), Italian (published in London in April 1852), Welsh (published in Merthyr-Tydfil in April 1852, although selections were available in 1851), and German (published in Hamburg in May 1852).

About the same time these early translation projects were going on in Europe, another group of elders from Utah had landed in Hawaii. Shortly thereafter, George Q. Cannon baptized Jonathan H. Napela, and together they began work on translating the Book of Mormon into Hawaiian (January 1852 through January 1854). The publication of the Hawaiian edition was completed in January 1856, in San Francisco, under the title: *Ka Buke a Moramona*, though the date printed in the book is 1855. (Occasionally, as was the case with the Hawaiian edition, the date printed on the title page of a book may be the year earlier than the date a book was actually issued. This is due to delays at the print shop or bindery. For the purposes of this article, the date that appears in the book is cited as the date of publication rather than the date it may have been issued.) Other Pacific-island language editions appeared in Maori (1889), Samoan (1903), Tahitian (1904) and Tongan (1946).

An important translation milestone in Latin America occurred when Meliton G. Trejo began translating the Book of Mormon into Spanish in 1874. While Elder Parley P. Pratt's 1850s mission to South America witnessed at least one Spanish-language missionary tract publication in January 1852, Trejo's work resulted in the first publication of "Book of Mormon selections," in which only portions of the book were printed rather than the complete book. This technique of printing selections for some foreign languages became a common tool beginning in the late 1970s to more quickly provide at least excerpts of the Book of Mormon in more languages. The Spanish edition was printed as a 96-page booklet entitled *Trozos Selectos del Libro de Mormon* and was issued in colored paper covers in August 1875 (printed in Salt Lake City by the Deseret News Company).

Missionary work in Brazil did not begin until the twentieth century with the first decade of proselyting done in the German language among people from Europe who had emigrated to Brazil. Eventually, a Portuguese translation of the Book of Mormon was begun in 1937 as missionary efforts began to reach out to non-Europeans. The resulting first Portuguese-language edition of the Book of Mormon was printed by Emprêsa Gráfica in São Paulo, Brazil, in 1939. The printing was probably completed in January or February 1940, as copies did not arrive at the mission office until 15 March 1940.

The importance of providing access to the Book of Mormon in the language of the people was recognized by President James E. Faust, an early missionary in Brazil, who said: "One year we converted only three people. In 1994 in this same country 43,247 souls were converted. . . . What is the difference between then and now? Why was it so hard in the beginning and so fruitful now? In large measure it was because the only scripture we had was the Bible. . . . Only after the Book of Mormon was published in Portuguese did the great harvest of converts come" (7).

In 1901, President Lorenzo Snow called Elders Heber J. Grant, Horace S. Ensign, Louis A. Kelsch, and Alma O. Taylor to establish a mission in Japan. Later, in January 1904, Horace S. Ensign, who was then serving as mission president, asked all the elders to "use their spare moments in translating any part they might desire and preserve those translations that in some future time they might be gathered and compared, revised, and eventually absorbed into the translation of that most sacred book" (Taylor Diary, 11 January 1904). Taylor himself began translating the Book of Mormon on January 18, 1904 (Diary, 18 January 1904). During the next several years, with the help of fellow missionaries and Japanese natives, he completed his efforts and released a Japanese-language edition of the Book of Mormon in October 1909. Other non-Roman alphabet translations followed during the twentieth century, including Turkish (1906), Armenian (1937), Korean (1967), Thai (1976), Russian (1980), and Ukrainian (1997). Central and eastern European translations of the Book of Mormon began with the Czech edition in 1933. With the help of Catholic priest Marion Grgyc, Krešimir Cosic made a Croatian translation, which was eventually published in April 1979. This same year (1979) Hungarian selections were published, followed by Bulgarian selections in 1980 and Romanian selections in 1981. Hungarian, Bulgarian, and Romanian have since been published as full-text translations. Also in the early 1980s a full-text translation of the Book of Mormon was published in Polish (Salt Lake City, 1981).

In 1965 "the First Presidency and the Quorum of the Twelve directed the establishment of the Church's Translation Division" (Williams, 26). Located at Church headquarters in Salt Lake City and at auxiliary offices located throughout the world, personnel include trained linguists and contractual, or "on call" translators (usually native members recommended by local ecclesiastical leaders who assess the spiritual worthiness and gospel understanding of prospective translators).

The translation of Church materials includes not only translating words but also conveying "the correct meaning and doctrine" ("Department," 1). Scripture translations undergo a step that non-scriptural materials do not. This step is called an ecclesiastical review. The review is conducted by a committee called by General Authorities and set apart to review the finished translation to "assure its doctrinal acceptability before it is printed." The members of the committee are "native speakers in the language of the translation with ability in English and a wealth of ecclesiastical and doctrinal background and experience" ("Translated," 10).

The 1980s and 90s witnessed an unprecedented expansion in non-English translations of the Book of Mormon. Increased efforts were made to make the book available to more people in Eastern Europe, Central Africa, Asia, and the West Indies. "In 2000, the Book of Mormon was made available in 18 new language editions, the highest for any year since it was first published" in March 1830 ("Taking," 26). Of particular significance was the release of the Book of Mormon in simplified Chinese characters in 2001. Missionary work in Taiwan had flourished during the last decades of the twentieth century and the beginning of the twenty-first, but the previous translation of the Book of Mormon in Chinese using traditional characters (December 1965) could be read only by those living in Taiwan and Hong Kong and by the older generation in mainland China.

The one hundred millionth copy of the Book of Mormon was printed by the Church on 29 February 2000, making it one of the most-published books in the world. With some 6,800 living languages in the world, the Church continues its efforts to take the gospel to the people of the earth by translating the Book of Mormon so they will "hear the fulness of the gospel in [their] own tongue, and in [their] own language" (D&C 90:11).

See also Book of Mormon, editions of.

BIBLIOGRAPHY

"Department Updates: Translation Department." The Church of Jesus Christ of Latter-day Saints, Human Resources Department. *Insights & Perspectives* (April 1993).

Faust, James E. "First Presidency Message: Joseph Smith and the Book of Mormon." *Ensign* 26 (January 1996): 2–7.

Jacobs, L. R. *Mormon Non-English Scriptures, Hymnals, & Periodicals, 1830–1986*. Salt Lake City: n.p., 1991.

"Taking the Scriptures to the World." *Ensign* 31 (July 2001): 24–31.

Taylor, Alma O. Diary. Family and Church History Department Archives, The Church of Jesus Christ of Latter-day Saints, Salt Lake City, Utah.

"Translated Scriptures Penetrate Many Climes in Quest to Fill Earth." *Church News* (March 31, 2001).

Williams, Sandra. "In His Own Language." *Tambuli* 12 (August 1988): 25–28.

RNH

Book of Mormon, what it says about itself

The Book of Mormon contains a veritable treasury of prophetic statements about its unique role in God's plan. Its pages contain information about its coming forth and the opposition its existence would generate among other Christians; it identifies those for whom the book was written; it specifies its contents and purposes; it explains what use should be made of the book and the implications of those actions; and it speaks of many witnesses that have been and would yet be borne of this sacred record.

Coming forth of the Book of Mormon

The Book of Mormon provides specifics concerning the timing of its entry into the world. Christ declared that the great "sign" of the commencement of the latter-day gathering of Israel and the establishment of Zion would be the coming forth of his words spoken to the Nephites (i.e., the Book of Mormon). The Book of Mormon would be a sign to its recipients that "the work of the Father hath already commenced unto the fulfilling of the covenant which he hath made unto the people who are of the house of Israel" (3 Ne. 21:1–7). Both Mormon and Moroni[2] reaffirmed these teachings (3 Ne. 29:1–5; Ether 4:17).

The plates were to be "hid up unto the Lord that they may come forth in his own due time. . . . when he shall see fit" (Morm. 5:12–13; Title Page). To preserve the Book of Mormon records until this time, the Lord caused that the plates not decay or tarnish but "retain their brightness" (Alma 37:4–7). Nephi[1] foretold several key historical events that would precede the book's coming forth. He taught that the "words of the righteous [Nephites]" would not be brought "out of the ground" until after his seed and the seed of his brethren the Lamanites had "dwindled in unbelief " and had been "smitten by the Gentiles" who would come among them (2 Ne. 26:15–17). Moroni saw the day in which the Book of Mormon would come forth and described it as a day when people would deny miracles, secret combinations would prevail, the power of God would be denied, churches would be defiled, and people would be full of pride—loving money, apparel, and material things (Morm. 8:34–37; cf. 2 Ne. 28:2–14). Furthermore, it would go forth in a day when there would be tempests, earthquakes, wars, and "great pollutions" upon the earth (Morm. 8:26–33, 36–37). Many would be "drunken with iniquity and all manner of abominations" (2 Ne. 27:1, 4–6).

The Book of Mormon also refers to the power by which it was translated. Because the Nephite records were written in an otherwise unknown language called reformed Egyptian (rather than Hebrew, which required more space), the Lord "prepared means for [their] interpretation" (Morm. 9:32–34). Only by the gift and power of God would one be able to translate and bring forth the record (Title Page; 1 Ne. 13:35; 2 Ne. 27:20; Morm. 8:15). Moroni acknowledged that the Book of Mormon plates were of great worth, but no one would be allowed to have them to "get gain." God willed that the bringing forth of the sacred records "be done with an eye single to his glory, or the welfare of the ancient and long dispersed covenant people of the Lord." Moreover, "whoso shall bring it to light, him [Joseph Smith] will the Lord bless. . . . And blessed be he that shall bring this thing to light," Moroni continued, for "it shall be brought out of the earth, and it shall shine forth out of darkness, and come unto the knowledge of the people; and it shall be done by the power of God" (Morm. 8:14–16).

Drawing from Isaiah's writings, Nephi described one event that would take place during the process of translating the Book of Mormon. He declared that the "book [plates] shall be delivered unto a man [Joseph Smith]"

B OF M, WHAT IT SAYS ABOUT ITSELF

(2 Ne. 27:9). He would take some of the words which were not sealed and "deliver these words unto another [Martin Harris]," who would in turn show the characters and the translation of them to the "learned [Charles Anthon]" (2 Ne. 27:9, 15; JS–H 1:63–65). For "the glory of the world and to get gain," the "learned" would request that the book be brought to him so he could read its words. After being told "I cannot bring the book, for it is sealed," the learned would say, "I cannot read it." Then to the man who was "not learned [Joseph Smith]" the Lord would say, "The learned shall not read them, for they have rejected them, and I am able to do mine own work; wherefore thou shalt read the words which I shall give unto thee" (2 Ne. 27:15–20).

Opposition to the Book of Mormon

The Book of Mormon informs its readers that it would come forth despite much opposition. Speaking of the latter days, the Savior taught that the Father would do "a great and a marvelous work" (3 Ne. 21:9) among the Gentiles but that many would not believe this work, though his servant (Joseph Smith) would declare it to them. Because of opposition his servant would be "marred." One likely way in which the Prophet Joseph Smith was "marred" and then "heal[ed]" (3 Ne. 21:10) by the Lord was the manner in which the Lord prepared for the loss of the 116-page manuscript by Martin Harris, showing that God's "wisdom is greater than the cunning of the devil" (D&C 10:43) Continuing, the Savior declared that the Father would cause his (Jesus') words to be brought forth to the Gentiles by his servant (Joseph Smith) and that those who did not believe his words "shall be cut off from among my people who are of the covenant" (3 Ne. 21:11; cf. 1 Ne. 22:8; 2 Ne. 3:11; 25:17). Nephi[1], Mormon, and Moroni[2] indicated that the Lord would seal or hide up the record so that the wicked or unbelieving would not be able to destroy it (2 Ne. 26:17; Morm. 6:6; Title Page). The Lord promised Nephi that his words would be preserved to "go from generation to generation as long as the earth shall stand" so that the seed of Joseph[1] would "never perish" (2 Ne. 25:21–22).

Moroni feared that the Gentiles would "mock" (Ether 12:23, 25) and "condemn" (Morm. 8:12; 9:31) the Book of Mormon because of its writers' "weakness in writing" (Ether 12:23), their "imperfections" (Morm. 9:31), or "because of the placing of our words" (Ether 12:25; cf. Morm. 8:12, 17; 9:31; Ether 12:23). Concerning these skeptics of the Book of Mormon, the Lord declared, "Fools mock, but they shall mourn," and the meek, he foretold, would "take no advantage of your weakness" (Ether 12:26).

Nephi was shown that others would oppose the Book of Mormon because they would feel the Bible was sufficient, containing the complete word of God, and none other was needed (2 Ne. 29:3–10; cf. 28:27–30). Yet, the Lord indicated that he "command[s] all men" to "write the words" which he speaks unto them, that he would speak to all nations, and that they would eventually have each other's writings (2 Ne. 29:11–13).

For whom the Book of Mormon was written

The Book of Mormon was written to the Lamanites, the Jews, and the Gentiles (Title Page). The record would first go to the Gentiles, who would in turn take it to the posterity of Lehi[1] and to the Jews (1 Ne. 13:34, 39; 2 Ne. 30:3–7; 3 Ne. 16:4–5). Such Nephite record keepers as Nephi[1], Enos, and Mormon knew and wrote concerning these promises (1 Ne. 13:39; Enos 1:13, 15; Morm. 5:9–15; cf. D&C 3:19–20). The invitation of the Book of Mormon to "come unto Christ" is to all the world (2 Ne. 26:25; 3 Ne. 9:22).

What the Book of Mormon contains

The writers and compilers of the Book of Mormon were careful to explain what it would and would not contain. The title page indicates that the book is an abridgment of the records of the "people of Nephi, and also of the Lamanites," and of the people of Jared[1] who were scattered at the time of the tower of Babel. Mormon indicated he was including the small PLATES OF NEPHI in his record because they contained many revelations and prophecies of the coming of Christ (W of M 1:4, 6). Undoubtedly Mormon was impressed with the small plates because Nephi[1] and Jacob[2] included only things

B OF M, WHAT IT SAYS ABOUT ITSELF

that were sacred and "pleasing unto God" (1 Ne. 6:4–6; Jacob 1:2–4). The Lord himself declared that the Book of Mormon would contain those words "which are expedient in my wisdom [to] go forth" (2 Ne. 3:18–19; 3 Ne. 26:2). The record was written and compiled under the inspiration of God and contains the words of Christ and the plainness of the gospel (2 Ne. 33:6, 10–11; 1 Ne. 13:35–36).

Mormon and Moroni[2] explained repeatedly that they wrote the "things which have been commanded [them] of the Lord" (3 Ne. 26:12; 30:1; Morm. 5:9; Ether 4:5; 8:26). Because of the sheer volume of information, Mormon indicated he could not write even the "hundredth part of the things of [his] people" (W of M 1:5; Hel. 3:14; 3 Ne. 5:8).

Some revelations and teachings are not in the Book of Mormon because of the Lord's specific instructions. Nephi was commanded not to include large parts of the vision he had concerning the latter days (1 Ne. 14:25–28). Mormon was commanded not to write more detail concerning the destruction of his people (Morm. 5:9). He was also instructed not to include portions of the Savior's teachings so that the Lord might "try [the] faith" of those who would read the Book of Mormon. If they would "believe these things," then "greater things" would be "made manifest unto them" (3 Ne. 26:8–11). The Book of Mormon plates contained a sealed portion, which included an account of a vision or revelation from God revealing "all things from the foundation of the world unto the end thereof" (2 Ne. 27:7, 10; Ether 3:25–27). This account would not be received until the Gentiles repented of their iniquities and exercised faith in the Lord, "even as the brother of Jared" (Ether 4:3–7; 5:1; cf. 2 Ne. 27:8).

Purposes of the Book of Mormon

One reason the Book of Mormon record was kept was so the Lord could "show forth his power unto future generations" (Alma 37:14, 17–18). This record would "show unto the remnant of the House of Israel what great things the Lord hath done for their fathers" and make known "the covenants of the Lord" (Title Page). The book is evidence of the fulfillment of the Lord's covenant with Abraham that the Lord "would remember his seed forever" in all the nations of the earth (2 Ne. 29:7, 11, 14; 1 Ne. 22:8–11). Moroni wrote that the records were preserved that others "may learn to be more wise" than they (the Nephites) had been (Morm. 9:31; Mosiah 12:8; cf. D&C 38–39). The coming forth of the Book of Mormon to the latter-day descendants of Lehi for the purpose of bringing them back to the gospel fulfills the promise the Lord made to ancient Nephite prophets, and it relieves them of their responsibility to future generations (2 Ne. 26:15; Enos 1:13, 15–17; 3 Ne. 5:14; Morm. 9:35; cf. D&C 3:19–20).

The restoration of plain and precious truths lost from "the gospel of the Lamb" is another important purpose of the Book of Mormon (1 Ne. 13:34, 40). Moreover, the Book of Mormon was written to help convince others of the truthfulness of the Bible, rather than to detract from it (1 Ne. 13:39–40; 2 Ne. 3:11; 29:8–9; Morm. 7:8–9). Nephi[1] was shown that when the Book of Mormon came forth it would become one with the Bible (1 Ne. 13:38–41; cf. 2 Ne. 3:12). The Lord explained the importance of two witnesses in accomplishing his work: "The testimony of two nations is a witness unto you that I am God, that I remember one nation like unto another. . . . And when the two nations shall run together the testimony of the two nations shall run together also" (2 Ne. 29:8). Joseph of Egypt prophesied that the Book of Mormon and the Bible would "grow together" to confound false doctrines, lay down contention, establish peace among the descendants of Joseph[1] and bring them to a knowledge of their

> **4 And I know that the Lord God will consecrate my prayers for the gain of my people. And the words which I have written in weakness will be made strong unto them; for it [a]persuadeth them to do good; it maketh known unto them of their fathers; and it speaketh of Jesus, and persuadeth them to believe in him, and to endure to the end, which is life [b]eternal.**

2 Nephi 33:4

fathers and the covenants of the Lord (2 Ne. 3:12; 30:3–4). The Book of Mormon would help the spiritually deaf and blind to hear and see and come to understanding (2 Ne. 27:29, 35). The Book of Mormon was given to help set forth the gospel of Jesus Christ, to bring people to a "knowledge of their Redeemer and the very points of his doctrine, that they may know how to come unto him and be saved" (1 Ne. 15:14; 22:11; 2 Ne. 30:5; Morm. 7:8). It is to be a "standard" for the house of Israel (2 Ne. 29:2). Most important, the Book of Mormon was written to convince all mankind that Jesus is the Christ, the Son of God, the true Messiah, and that by coming unto Christ and following him all can be saved (Title Page; 1 Ne. 6:4, 6; 13:40; 2 Ne. 25:17–18; 33:4, 10–11; Morm. 5:14; 7:10).

What use should be made of the Book of Mormon

The prophet Moroni made it clear that it is mankind's opportunity to come to know that the book is true. He promised that any who would read the record, ponder its message, and ask God with faith and real intent would be given a witness of its truthfulness "by the power of the Holy Ghost" (Moro. 10:3–5; cf. Ether 4:11–12). By believing and following the principles given in the Book of Mormon, the faithful can eventually obtain the greater knowledge and revelations withheld from the book (3 Ne. 26:8–9; Morm. 8:12). Those who condemn or fail to respect the words of the book will find that they will stand condemned at the last day (2 Ne. 33:14; 3 Ne. 26:10; Morm. 8:17). Indeed, all nations who possess the Book of Mormon will be judged "according to the words which are written" (2 Ne. 25:22; 29:11–12; W of M 1:11).

Witnesses within the Book of Mormon

The Book of Mormon bears witness of itself. Mormon, the principal compiler, bore a powerful witness when he declared, "I know the record which I make to be a just and a true record" (3 Ne. 5:16–18). Other Book of Mormon prophets bore similar witness (e.g., 1 Ne. 1:3; Mosiah 1:6; Ether 4:4; 5:2–6). The Book of Mormon promises that three special witnesses and a "few" others would be privileged to see the plates and "testify to the truth of the book and the things therein" (2 Ne. 27:12–13). Moroni affirmed that the Book of Mormon would show forth "the power of God and also his word, of which the Father, and the Son, and the Holy Ghost bear record" (Ether 5:4). On at least two occasions the Book of Mormon records that at the Judgment Day, God himself will declare the truthfulness of this record (2 Ne. 33:11; Moro. 10:27). Moroni indicated that the book will stand as a witness against the world and its wickedness (Ether 5:4).

See also Bible, what it says about the Book of Mormon; Book of Mormon, opposition to; Book of Mormon, selected purposes of; Book of Mormon, title page of; Crying from the dust; Isaiah chapter reviews (2 Ne. 26:6, 15–18; 27 // Isa. 29); Marvelous work, marvelous work and a wonder; Moroni[2]'s promise.

CJW

Book of Mormon, what it says about the Bible The Book of Mormon is the single most compelling tangible witness for the validity of the Bible available in the world today. Although one may reject the claim that the Book of Mormon is inspired scripture, it cannot be factually demonstrated that it contradicts or undermines the Bible on any given common point. Rather, the Book of Mormon confirms the Bible's basic historicity and doctrinal correctness. Through revelation the prophet Nephi[1] learned that "the book of the Lamb of God"—the original sources of the present Bible—went "forth from the Jews in purity unto the Gentiles" (1 Ne. 13:23–25, 28). Nephi was informed, however, that "many parts which are plain and most precious" of the gospel of Christ would subsequently be deleted from "the book" by the "great and abominable church" (1 Ne. 13:26, 28). This modified record—now the Bible—would thereafter cause "the nations of the Gentiles" to "stumble exceedingly" because the unmistakable "plainness" of the original "book of the Lamb of God" would be lost (1 Ne. 13:28–29, 34). Nevertheless, much of the original gospel, "which shall be plain and precious," is now restored to the world in the Book of Mormon: Another Testament of Jesus Christ and

B OF M, WHAT IT SAYS ABOUT THE BIBLE

a divine witness of the inspired contents of the Bible (1 Ne. 13:34–40).

Many Old Testament personalities are quoted or paraphrased in the Book of Mormon, including Joseph[1] (2 Ne. 3:6–21), Micah (3 Ne. 20:16–19; 21:19–20), Malachi (3 Ne. 24–25), and Isaiah, the primary prophetic witness for Christ in the Old Testament. Isaiah is quoted at length by Nephi, Jacob[2], Abinadi, and Christ himself (1 Ne. 20; 21; 2 Ne. 7; 8; 12–24; Mosiah 14; 3 Ne. 22). These four add their confirming witnesses to that of Isaiah and make plain the heart of his Christ-centered message.

The Book of Mormon partially parallels the Bible in that it begins in the Old Testament period with emphasis on messianic prophecy therein and then complements the New Testament account of the Savior's mortal ministry to the Jews with an account of his postresurrection ministry to Israel in America (1 Ne. 1:19; 10:4–6; 3 Ne. 11–29).

It affirms the historicity of important Old Testament persons and events now regarded as myth and legend by many Bible scholars. The list includes the Creation (1 Ne. 5:11; Ether 1:3), Adam and Eve (2 Ne. 2:19–25; 9:21), the reality of the devil (2 Ne. 28:19–22), the fall of Adam (2 Ne. 9:6; Alma 12:22), Noah[1], the ark, and the great flood (Alma 10:22; 3 Ne. 22:9; Ether 6:7; 13:2), the tower of Babel (Title Page; Ether 1:3), the Abrahamic covenant (2 Ne. 29:14; 3 Ne. 20:27), Abraham's offering of Isaac (Jacob 4:5), Israel's sojourn in and deliverance from Egypt (1 Ne. 17:23–25), and ancient Israel's justification in claiming and inhabiting the land of Canaan (1 Ne. 17:32–35).

Relative to Moses, the Book of Mormon confirms the miraculous division of an arm of the Red Sea (1 Ne. 4:2; 17:26–27), manna being given and the rock being struck (1 Ne. 17:28–29), Moses' authorship of the original five books of Moses (1 Ne. 5:11), the divine origin of the law of Moses (2 Ne. 3:17; 3 Ne. 15:4–5), the Christ-centered objective of the law (2 Ne. 25:24–30; Mosiah 13:28–32), the incident of the BRAZEN SERPENT (1 Ne. 17:41; 2 Ne. 25:20; Alma 33:19), and, finally, Moses' testimony of Christ (Deut. 18:15, 18; 1 Ne. 22:20–21; Mosiah 13:33; Alma 33:19; 3 Ne. 20:23).

The Book of Mormon greatly enhances understanding of ancient Israel's actual knowledge of the Redeemer. Missing from the current Old Testament are the words of four prophets whose writings appear on the brass plates (Zenos, Zenock, Neum, and Ezias). They plainly foretold Christ's scourging, crucifixion, death, and burial (1 Ne. 19:10–17; Alma 33:13–19; Hel. 8:19–20). Their witness joins that of Isaiah (Mosiah 14). Indeed, Moses and all the other prophets testified that "God himself should come down among the children of men . . . that he should bring to pass the resurrection of the dead" (Mosiah 13:33–35; cf. 3 Ne. 20:24). Clearly, ancient Israel's knowledge of the Messiah and his mission was more precise and extensive than is suggested by the present Old Testament.

Jesus' divinity is rejected by a number of New Testament scholars who argue that the four Gospels are vague and contradictory as to his true identity. The Book of Mormon, on the other hand, offers consistent and extensive testimony of his godhood (e.g., 1 Ne. 19:12–13; Mosiah 13:33–34; 15:1–5). It joins Matthew and Luke in testifying of his holy conception and birth (1 Ne. 11:13–21; Mosiah 3:8; Alma 7:10). It declares that he was indeed a miracle worker, healing the sick and casting out "unclean spirits" (1 Ne. 11:31; cf. Mosiah 3:5–6).

> **23 And he said: Behold it proceedeth out of the mouth of a Jew. And I, Nephi, beheld it; and he said unto me: The [a]book that thou beholdest is a [b]record of the [c]Jews, which contains the covenants of the Lord, which he hath made unto the house of Israel; and it also containeth many of the prophecies of the holy prophets; and it is a record like unto the engravings which are upon the [d]plates of brass, save there are not so many; nevertheless, they contain the covenants of the Lord, which he hath made unto the house of Israel; wherefore, they are of great worth unto the Gentiles.**

1 Nephi 13:23

Jesus confirms the authenticity and unity of the Sermon on the Mount in Matthew (3 Ne. 12–14). He establishes the sermon's gospel setting and adds significant phrases to the Beatitudes. He also indicates that some of his counsel was directed exclusively to the Nephite Twelve (3 Ne. 13:25–34).

The Book of Mormon joins the New Testament in affirming Christ's sufferings and atonement for the sins of all mankind—the very key to salvation (2 Ne. 9:7, 21; Mosiah 3:7; Alma 7:11–12; 34:8–16; 42:15). And it is a co-witness with the New Testament of Jesus' physical resurrection, recounting his appearance to thousands of Israelites in America in the same resurrected body beheld by his Jewish disciples (3 Ne. 11:8–17; cf. Ether 3:17).

The Book of Mormon attests to the lives of other New Testament individuals, including Mary (1 Ne. 11:13, 20; Mosiah 3:8; Alma 7:10), John the Baptist (1 Ne. 10:7–10), John the Beloved (1 Ne. 14:19–27; 3 Ne. 28:4–6; Ether 4:16), and the other Judean apostles (1 Ne. 11:29; 12:9; 13:24).

Finally, the fulness of the gospel of Jesus Christ is found in both the New Testament and the Book of Mormon. Yet, the principles and ordinances of the gospel—including the critical role of the Holy Ghost—are somewhat scattered in the former. Only in the latter are they presented in a clear, concise, unified manner (2 Ne. 31–32; 3 Ne. 27:13–22).

Israel's division into two kingdoms, Ephraim and Judah, produced two books of scripture, two "sticks"—the stick of Joseph, the Book of Mormon, and the stick of Judah, the Bible (Ezek. 37:15–22; 2 Ne. 3:12). As the two ancient kingdoms are to become one unified kingdom under Christ, so are these two volumes of scripture to be united in a common witness of him as the Holy One of Israel (2 Ne. 21:11–13 // Isa. 11:11–13; cf. 2 Ne. 29:8). The Book of Mormon is for "the convincing them [the descendants of Joseph[1]] of my word [the Bible], which shall have already gone forth among them" (2 Ne. 3:11). Thus the Bible and the Book of Mormon "shall grow together, unto the confounding of false doctrines and laying down of contentions" (2 Ne. 3:12). "For behold, this [the Book of Mormon] is written for the intent that ye may believe that [the Bible]; and if ye believe that ye will believe this also" (Morm. 7:9; cf. 2 Ne. 33:10–11). Clearly, these sacred volumes are not competitors for the truths of salvation but joint witnesses of it.

See also Book of Mormon: Another Testament of Jesus Christ; Book of Mormon, selected purposes of, to prove to the world that the holy scriptures are true; Old Testament, historical narrative referred to; Plain and precious things, loss of and restoration of.

RT

Book of Mormon, witnesses of *See* Witnesses of the Book of Mormon.

Books, judged out of Certain books will be used both as a standard and as a witness in the Final Judgment. The word of God contained in the scriptures constitutes a standard or measure by which humankind will be judged (2 Ne. 29:11; 33:14–15; W of M 1:11; John 12:48; D&C 41:12). Other books kept on earth and in heaven, containing records of people's works, will stand as witnesses for or against them at the Judgment. For example, the resurrected Savior instructed his disciples in the New World to record the works of their people, for out of such "books" they would be judged (3 Ne. 27:24–25). He further explained that "all things" are written by the Father and will be used to judge the world (3 Ne. 27:26). Joseph Smith explained that the chronicles kept on earth and in heaven include records of the saving ordinances performed for individuals, provided those ordinances are properly performed and recorded (D&C 128:7–9; cf. Rev. 20:12). In speaking of some of the books out of which the world would be judged, President Spencer W. Kimball offered the following insight: "The Book of Life (see Revelation 20:12) will show the earthly activities of all of us, and the book of the angels will give the entire story of every man and what he did in the light and in the shadows, in the open and in the corners, all that is said in the secret places and from the housetops, all that was thought and expressed, whether good or bad. There will be no escape. The honest judge will give full value to all for their good works and will not overlook the other" (46).

See also Judgment, the.

BIBLIOGRAPHY

Kimball, Spencer W. *The Teachings of Spencer W. Kimball.* Edited by Edward L. Kimball. Salt Lake City: Bookcraft, 1982.

TBB

Born again Born of God, born of water and of the Spirit, "baptism of fire and of the Holy Ghost," "changed from [a] carnal and fallen state, to a state of righteousness, being redeemed of God, becoming his sons and daughters; and thus [becoming] new creatures" (2 Ne. 31:13–14; Mosiah 27:25–26). To be born again is to pass from darkness to light, to have the clouds of doubt and cynicism dispelled, to have the mind illuminated (Alma 19:6; Hel. 5:19–47). It is to put off skepticism and acquire a believing heart (1 Ne. 2:16–17; Mosiah 5:2; Alma 18:23; 22:7; cf. D&C 46:13–14; 90:24). It is to demonstrate a willingness to enter into a covenant with God and "to be obedient to his commandments in all things" (Mosiah 5:5). To be born again is to receive new insights, new desires, new feelings—to have "great views of that which is to come" (Mosiah 5:3). The Spirit of the Lord brings an aversion toward sin (2 Ne. 9:49; Jacob 2:5; Alma 13:12); those who are born of the Spirit, therefore, undergo a "mighty change," not merely an enhancement of self-discipline. They have "no more disposition to do evil, but to do good continually" (Mosiah 5:2). It is not that the reborn are free from sin but rather that they do not want to sin. They may step momentarily into the darkness, but they repent quickly and do not continue to sin (JST 1 Jn. 3:9; D&C 109:21). As newborn disciples of Christ, they bear the image of their master in their COUNTENANCE (Alma 5:14).

The Book of Mormon plainly teaches the nature and plight of fallen man and the vital need to be born again. "Ye must repent, and be born again," Alma[2] declared, "for the Spirit saith if ye are not born again ye cannot inherit the kingdom of heaven" (Alma 7:14). This doctrine is as old as the world (Moses 6:51–68).

The natural or fallen or unredeemed man is subject to SPIRITUAL DEATH: he is separated from God (Alma 12:16, 32; 40:26, 42:9). There must of necessity be a rebirth of one's nature. This new birth is symbolic of death and resurrection. The old person of sin must be put to death, and the new creature must rise to a newness of life (Mosiah 27:24–26; Rom. 6:3–5).

In harmony with all scripture, the Book of Mormon affirms the necessity of baptism, both by water and by the Spirit, as the entrance to this new life (2 Ne. 31:10–19; John 3:3–5). The Prophet Joseph Smith taught that "being born again, comes by the Spirit of God through ordinances" (162). For most, spiritual rebirth begins with baptism, but the process of growth, development, and spiritual refinement continues throughout life as one cultivates the influence of the Holy Ghost.

Rebirth is inseparably connected with forgiveness of sin and requires sincere humility, repentance, and prayer. After "mighty prayer" Enos learned that his sins had been forgiven; his "guilt was swept away," and he was made whole through his faith in Christ (Enos 1:1–8; cf. Matt. 9:22). Similarly, the people of Zarahemla in king Benjamin's time, having come to a knowledge of their fallen condition, called upon God for forgiveness through the Atonement. After their plea for mercy, the Holy Ghost came upon them, and their forgiveness brought joy and "peace of conscience" (Mosiah 4:1–3). These essential attitudes and behaviors are also demonstrated in the stories of Alma the Younger (Alma 36:16–21) and king Lamoni's father (Alma 22:15–18).

Forgiveness of sin brings reconciliation with God and reinstatement in the royal family. Those who have come unto Christ and who have taken upon themselves his name through entering the covenant of baptism are the "seed" of Christ (Mosiah 15:10–13): they are born again into a new family as sons and daughters of Jesus Christ; they are expected to live with fidelity and devotion so as to bring honor to that holy name (Mosiah 5:1–8; Alma 5:38–39; D&C 18:23–25).

Another fruit of the new birth is a greater feeling for people, a deeper love and compassion, a growing desire to serve others (Moro. 8:25–26). After Enos had received forgiveness, he "began to feel a desire for the welfare of [his] brethren." His compassion even extended to his enemies the Lamanites (Enos 1:9–11). Similarly, after he had partaken of the fruit of the tree of life, Lehi[1] "began to be desirous that [his] family should partake of it also" (1 Ne. 8:12). Like the converted sons of Mosiah[2], the reborn Saint cannot "bear that any human soul should perish." Thus he or she labors to bring others to "taste of the exceeding joy" they have tasted (Mosiah 28:3; Alma 36:24).

Not all of those who are born of the Spirit will have identical experiences with those in the Book of Mormon who were reborn. Rebirth does not generally entail a one-time, dramatic change. "Being born again is a gradual thing," Elder Bruce R. McConkie explained, "except in a few isolated instances that are so miraculous they get written up in the scriptures. As far as the generality of the members of the Church are concerned, we are born again by degrees, and we are born again to added light and added knowledge and added desires for righteousness as we keep the commandments" (399). Though the dramatic experiences described in scripture "are real and powerful, they are the exception more than the rule. For every Paul, for every Enos, and for every King Lamoni, there are hundreds and thousands of people who find the process of repentance much more subtle, much more imperceptible. Day by day they move closer to the Lord, little realizing they are building a godlike life" (Benson, "Mighty Change," 5). Indeed, even if a person has had a powerful life-changing experience, he or she must press forward (2 Ne. 31:19–20) in faith thereafter, praying and pleading for the ongoing witness, the cleansing power, and the direction of the Holy Spirit. Alma[2] had been stopped in his tracks through the intervention of an angel, but his testimony was grounded not alone in this dramatic encounter but also in quiet, personal, spiritual experience over time and through significant effort (Alma 5:45–47).

Truly, one of the grand purposes of the gospel of Jesus Christ is to make a heaven of earth and of men and women, gods. That transition from frailty and fallenness to dynamic discipleship comes through the atoning blood of Jesus Christ and by means of the enlivening powers of the Spirit of God. "The Lord works from the inside out," President Ezra Taft Benson observed. "The world works from the outside in. The world would take people out of the slums. Christ takes the slums out of people, and then they take themselves out of the slums. The world would mold men by changing their environment. Christ changes men, who then change their environment. The world would shape human behavior, but Christ can change human nature" (Benson, CR, 5).

See also Children of Christ.

BIBLIOGRAPHY

Benson, Ezra Taft. "A Mighty Change of Heart." *Ensign* 19 (October 1989): 2–5.

———. Conference Report. October 1985.

McConkie, Bruce R. "Jesus Christ and Him Crucified." *Speeches of the Year, 1976*. Provo, Utah: Brigham Young University Publications, 1976.

Smith, Joseph. *Teachings of the Prophet Joseph Smith*. Selected by Joseph Fielding Smith. Salt Lake City: Deseret Book, 1976.

RLM

Born of God *See* Born again.

Bountiful[1], land of The last settlement where Lehi[1] and his party resided prior to sailing to the western hemisphere. After leaving Jerusalem, Lehi's group traveled in a south-southeast direction near the borders of the Red Sea (1 Ne. 2:5; 16:13–14). Eventually the travelers changed course to a near eastward direction (1 Ne. 17:1), until they arrived at a location bordering the sea, which they named Bountiful because of the abundance of fruit and wild honey (1 Ne. 17:5). At this location Nephi[1] and his brothers followed divine instructions to construct a ship that would carry them to the New World (see 1 Ne. 17; 18:1–8). Because of its location and abundant vegetation, the present-day Dhofar region of southern Oman is the most likely area for the party's Bountiful. *See* map, page 514.

See also Lehi[1], journey of, to the promised land.

BIBLIOGRAPHY

Aston, Warren P. "The Arabian Bountiful Discovered?" *Journal of Book of Mormon Studies* (July 1998): 4–11.

RH

Bountiful[2], land of and city of Land located south of the land of Desolation and north of the land of Zarahemla (Alma 22:28–31). It ran "from the east unto the west sea" and was apparently near the narrow neck of land (Alma 22:32–33; 63:5). As the name implies, the land was probably a fertile area. It abounded with wildlife and was part of the land the Jaredites preserved as "a wilderness, to get game" (Ether 10:21; Alma 22:31).

Many significant events took place in the land of Bountiful. Moroni[1] fortified the land in an effort to keep the Lamanites from surrounding the Nephites (Alma 52:9). Hagoth launched his ships on the western border of the land Bountiful into the west sea (Alma 63:4–6). The Nephite chief judge Lachoneus[1] gathered the Nephites along the northeastern border of the land of Bountiful, to defend themselves against the forces of the Gadianton robbers lead by Giddianhi (3 Ne. 3:23). Perhaps most significantly, the resurrected Savior made his first appearance to the Book of Mormon peoples at the temple in the land Bountiful (3 Ne. 11:1–10).

The city of Bountiful, first mentioned ca. 65 B.C., was within the same environs as the city of Mulek near the borders of the east sea (Alma 52:16–17, 22; 51:26).

Around 64 B.C., during the Nephite-Lamanite wars, the city of Bountiful was heavily fortified as the Nephites caused the Lamanite prisoners "to labor until they had encircled the city of Bountiful round about with a strong wall of timbers and earth, to an exceeding height" (Alma 53:4). About 30 B.C., Nephi[2] and Lehi[4], the sons of Helaman[3], began preaching the gospel at the city Bountiful "and from thenceforth to the city of Gid; and from the city of Gid to the city of Mulek" (Hel. 5:14–15). It is likely that the temple in the land Bountiful was located in the city of Bountiful.

JLA

Bowels *See* Appendix C.

Branch, branches There are several meanings of this term.

1. Groups of people. Often referring to Israelites who were scattered or separated from their Israelite kinsmen. For example, the prophet Lehi[1] compared the house of Israel to an olive tree whose branches would be broken off and scattered upon all the face of the earth. These scattered branches would be gathered and grafted back into the olive tree in the latter days (1 Ne. 10:14; 15:12–16). The Nephites referred to themselves as a branch or remnant, because they had been broken off from the larger body of Israelites living at Jerusalem and transplanted, or grafted, to a new land (1 Ne. 15:12; 19:24; 2 Ne. 3:5; Alma 26:36; cf. Jacob 5).

2. Undesirable cutting. Isaiah referred to the time when the king of Babylon would be "cast out of [his] grave like an abominable branch" (2 Ne. 24:19).

3. A title for Christ. The Savior is a descendant of the house of Israel through a branch of the Davidic line (2 Ne. 21:1–5; cf. Jer. 23:5–6; 33:15–17).

4. Posterity. Malachi warned that the wicked at the Second Coming would be left with "neither root nor branch" (3 Ne. 25:1).

RH

Brass plates *See* Plates of brass.

Brazen serpent The brazen, or brass, serpent that the Lord instructed Moses to manufacture and attach to a pole as a visual antidote against bites by the serpents that the Lord had sent to afflict Israelites for their murmuring in the wilderness (Num. 21:4–9). The Lord promised, "Every one that is bitten, when he looketh upon it, shall live" (Num. 21:8). In citing events associated with the EXODUS, Nephi[1] recalled both the "poisonous serpents" that had invaded the camp of the Israelites as well as "the serpent which

[Moses] did raise up before them" (2 Ne. 25:20; cf. 1 Ne. 17:41). Nephi highlighted the brazen serpent incident, along with the Lord's guidance of the Israelites and his gift of water from a rock, as indisputable evidences of Jehovah's power to save temporally as well as spiritually. Nephi swore with an oath "that as these things are true, and as the Lord God liveth, there is none other name given under heaven save it be this Jesus Christ . . . whereby man can be saved" (2 Ne. 25:20). Hereby, Nephi drew attention to the link between Moses' actions and Jesus' atonement.

Alma[2] (Alma 33:19) and Nephi[2], son of Helaman[3], both saw the raised brass serpent as a prophetic metaphor for Jesus' crucifixion. In Nephi's words, "Yea, did [Moses] not bear record that the Son of God should come? And as he lifted up the brazen serpent in the wilderness, even so shall he be lifted up who should come. And as many as should look upon that serpent should live, even so as many as should look upon the Son of God with faith . . . might live, even unto that life which is eternal" (Hel. 8:14–15; cf. Alma 37:46; John 3:14–15).

See also Fiery flying serpents; Types.

SKB

Bridle *See* Appendix C.

Brimstone Generally identified as sulfur, an extremely flammable material, which when burned emits both an intense heat as well as a noxious odor. Brimstone, together with the phrase "lake of fire," is used throughout the scriptures as a metaphor to denote the divine punishment awaiting the wicked (e.g., 2 Ne. 28:23; Jacob 6:10; Alma 12:17). The "lake of fire and brimstone" is identified with "endless torment" and "the second death" (2 Ne. 9:19; Jacob 3:11). Explaining this imagery Joseph Smith taught, "The torment of disappointment in the mind of [a wicked] man is as exquisite as a lake burning with fire and brimstone" (Smith, 357).

See also Lake of fire and brimstone.

BIBLIOGRAPHY

Smith, Joseph. *Teachings of the Prophet Joseph Smith.* Selected by Joseph Fielding Smith. Salt Lake City: Deseret Book, 1976.

RH

Brimstone, lake of fire and *See* Lake of fire and brimstone.

Broken heart and contrite spirit The broken heart is figurative of the voluntary sacrifice of one's own will to the Lord. Under the law of Moses, the broken heart was to accompany the animal sacrifice (cf. Ps. 51:17–19); the Lord did away with the animal sacrifice after the law of Moses was fulfilled (3 Ne. 9:17–20), but the broken heart and contrite spirit remained as requirements for the Lord's people. The broken heart is often found in the context of repentance (Moro. 6:2; D&C 20:37) and also sorrowing for sin (Morm. 2:13–14), though it is apparently not necessarily a state of sorrow. The word in the Greek text of the Old Testament (Ps. 51:17) *suntribo,* meaning "broken," as in the term "broken heart," means to be shattered, smashed, or ground down to pieces, signifying that the will of the natural man yields to the Lord's reshaping as he becomes a new creature in Christ (Mosiah 3:19; Rom. 6:6; 2 Cor. 5:17; Bauer, 801). "Contrite" shares similar meanings and connotes remorse for sin. Thus the term "broken heart and contrite spirit" suggests a repentant state of malleability, a sensitivity to one's fallen and dependent condition (cf. Ether 3:2; Alma 38:14), and a willingness to submit to the Lord's purposes (Mosiah 3:19; 4:2; Alma 22:15–18). Joy, consolation, and sanctification come by yielding one's heart unto God (Hel. 3:35). The Atonement answers "the ends of the law, unto all those who have a broken heart and a contrite spirit; and unto none else" (2 Ne. 2:6–7). The broken heart is a prerequisite for baptism by both water (Moro. 6:2) and Spirit (3 Ne. 9:20). Nephi[1] prayed that his broken heart and contrite spirit would close the gates of hell and keep the gates of heaven open before him (2 Ne. 4:32). The broken heart precedes rending the veil of unbelief and increased spiritual knowledge

(Ether 4:15). The Savior was anointed to "bind up the brokenhearted" (Isa. 61:1–4).

See also Humility; Lowliness of heart; Meekness.

BIBLIOGRAPHY

Bauer, Walter. *A Greek-English Lexicon of the New Testament and Other Early Christian Literature.* Translated by William F. Arndt and F. Wilbur Gingrich. Chicago: University of Chicago Press, 1957.

MCT

Brother of Jared[1] *See* Jared[1], brother of.

Bucklers *See* Appendix C.

Burnt offerings *See* Sacrifices.

By and by *See* Appendix C.

Wherefore, my beloved brethren, if ye have not charity, ye are nothing, for charity never faileth. Wherefore, cleave unto charity, which is the greatest of all, for all things must fail—But charity is the pure love of Christ, and it endureth forever; and whoso is found possessed of it at the last day, it shall be well with him. MORONI 7: 46-47

Cain A son of Adam and Eve. Mormon identified Satan as the originator of secret oaths and covenants among the Nephites and chronicled Lucifer's works of darkness from the beginning. It was Satan who plotted with Cain, promising that if he murdered his brother Abel his crime would remain a secret (Hel. 6:25–30; cf. Moses 5:16–33).

Calendar systems among the Nephites *See* Chronology, Book of Mormon.

Calling and election made sure Being sealed up to eternal life, or having one's exaltation assured. All God's children are invited or called to receive salvation. Those who "hear [his] voice and harden not their hearts" are identified by the Lord as "mine elect" (D&C 29:7) and are promised, or called and elected to, salvation "through the Atonement of Christ . . . by obedience to the laws and ordinances of the Gospel" (A of F 3). Though some may interpret statements by Peter (1 Pet. 1:2) and Paul (Rom. 9; 2 Thes. 2:13) as teaching that certain persons are unconditionally elected by God to salvation or damnation, the Prophet Joseph Smith declared that "unconditional election of individuals to eternal life was not taught by the Apostles. God did elect or predestinate that all those who would be saved, should be saved in Christ Jesus, and through obedience to the Gospel" (189). Hence, even though there were some who, on the basis of premortal faithfulness, were "chosen . . . before the foundation of the world" (Eph. 1:4) for special blessings and opportunities on earth and to receive eternal life, they and all others who make their calling and election sure do so by enduring obedience to the gospel of Jesus Christ. Nephi[1] taught, "If ye shall follow the Son, with full purpose of heart, acting no hypocrisy and no deception before God, but with real intent, repenting of your sins, witnessing unto the Father that ye are willing to take upon you the name of Christ, by baptism . . . then cometh the baptism of fire and of the Holy Ghost." Though they had now entered the "gate" and were "in this strait and narrow path which leads to eternal life," Nephi explained that all was not done: "Wherefore, ye must press forward with a steadfastness in Christ, having a perfect brightness of hope, and a love of God and of all men. Wherefore, if ye shall press forward, feasting upon the word of Christ, and endure to the end, behold, thus saith the Father: Ye shall have eternal life" (2 Ne. 31:13–20). King Benjamin exhorted his followers to "be steadfast and immovable, always abounding in good works, that Christ, the Lord God Omnipotent, may seal you his, that you may be brought to heaven, that ye may have everlasting salvation and eternal life" (Mosiah 5:15). Such promises of eternal life resulting from complete faithfulness to God abound in the Book of Mormon (e.g., Jacob 6:11; Mosiah 18:8–10; Alma 7:14–16; 11:40; Hel. 5:7–8; 8:15; 3 Ne. 9:14; 15:9; Moro. 7:41; 9:25). Hosts of faithful Saints will thus secure their eternal salvation or make their calling and election sure, being encouraged and sustained by the power of the Holy Ghost as they continue in righteousness to the end of their mortal lives (D&C 88:3–4; Mosiah 4:6–7; 26:23; Alma 5:13; 27:27).

An important dimension of this principle and an appropriate use of the terms "calling and election made sure," "sealed up unto eternal life," and "the more sure word of prophecy" is that some people, while yet in mortality, are *told* that their salvation is assured: "The more sure word of prophecy means a man's knowing that he is sealed up unto eternal life, by revelation and the spirit of prophecy, through the power of the Holy Priesthood" (D&C 131:5). Although none of these three expressions is found in the Book of Mormon, the principle is clearly evident. Alma[1] was promised, "Thou art my servant; and I covenant with thee that thou shalt have eternal life" (Mosiah 26:20). The Lord also promised king Mosiah[2] that he would protect his four missionary sons and that "they shall have eternal life" (Mosiah 28:7). Though there are no such direct statements regarding others, it seems likely that many Book of Mormon prophets, and perhaps other Saints were accorded this same blessing—Nephi[1], who saw the Lord and was taught by Jesus and the Father (2 Ne. 11:2; 31:10–12, 14–15); Jacob[2], who had "heard and seen" (Jacob 7:12; see also v. 5; 2 Ne. 2:3; 11:3); Enos, who proclaimed, "I know that in him I shall rest" (Enos 1:27); Alma[2], who was taught of the Lord and knew that he would be raised up to dwell with him at the last day (Mosiah 27:25; Alma 36:28); Nephi[2], who was instructed of the Lord, given power to seal on earth and in heaven, and told that "all things shall be done unto thee according to thy word" (Hel. 10:3–10; an interesting promise in light of D&C 50:26–29); Moroni[2], who talked with the Savior face to face and looked forward with great confidence to being "brought forth triumphant through the air" to meet his readers "before the pleasing bar of the great Jehovah" (Moro. 10:34; Ether 12:38–39).

One does not need to see the Savior or hear his voice to have his calling and election made sure. But having one's calling and election made sure opens the way for then receiving Jesus as the Second Comforter (Smith, 149–50), when the person is prepared, and when it is expedient. Such is perhaps the case with the prophets listed above. Whether one makes his calling and election sure through faithfulness to gospel covenants to the end of mortality without being told that such is the case, or whether one receives the more sure word of prophecy and thereby knows while yet in the flesh that his salvation is assured, the Lord's promise is sure: "Look unto me, and endure to the end, and ye shall live; for unto him that endureth to the end will I give eternal life" (3 Ne. 15:9).

See also Chosen; Endurance to the end; Salvation.

BIBLIOGRAPHY

Smith, Joseph. *Teachings of the Prophet Joseph Smith.* Selected by Joseph Fielding Smith. Salt Lake City: Deseret Book, 1976.

LED

Capital punishment The Book of Mormon states that "the law requireth the life of him who hath murdered" (Alma 34:12). Death was also the penalty required by the law of the land for "whomsoever . . . would not enter into a covenant to support the cause of freedom" (Alma 46:35; 62:9). Although it appears that capital punishment was practiced largely with a punitive intent, Alma[2] stated that there was a preventative purpose as well: "Now, if there was no law given—if a man murdered he should die—would he be afraid he would die if he should murder?" (Alma 42:19). There were specific legal guidelines for carrying out capital punishment. Mormon explained, "Now behold, this was contrary to the laws of the land, that any man should be put to death except they had power from the governor of the land" (3 Ne. 6:24). Jaredite and Nephite records contain examples of people who practiced capital punishment unrighteously (e.g., Ether 10:6; 3 Ne. 1:9; 6:23; Moro. 1:2).

Concerning the question of whether the practice of capital punishment ended with the coming of Christ among the Nephites and the fulfillment of the law of Moses, President Charles W. Penrose wrote: "This divine law for shedding the blood of a murderer has never been repealed. It is a law given by the Almighty and not abrogated in the Christian faith. It stands on record for all time—that a murderer shall have his blood shed. He that commits murder must be slain. 'Whoso sheddeth man's blood, by man shall his blood be shed'" (23). The Lord instructed the Prophet Joseph Smith that capital punishment is an appropriate judgment for those guilty of MURDER: "And again, I say, thou shall not kill; but he that killeth shall die" (D&C 42:19). But he made the application of capital punishment subject to the laws of civil government: "And it shall come to pass, that if any persons among you shall kill they shall be delivered up and dealt with according to the laws of the land" (D&C 42:79).

BIBLIOGRAPHY

Penrose, Charles W. *Blood Atonement: As Taught by Leading Elders of The Church of Jesus Christ of Latter-day Saints.* Salt Lake City: Deseret News, 1916.

DKJ

Captivity of the devil Bondage to the will and power of Satan, or his agents (1 Ne. 13:5–9; 14:3–4). The devil's intent is "that all men might be miserable like unto himself" (2 Ne. 2:18, 27). He desires to subject the children of men to his will, binding them with his "awful" (2 Ne. 1:13–23) and "everlasting chains" (2 Ne. 28:19–23), the "chains of hell" (Alma 12:11), carrying them "away captive down to the eternal gulf of misery and woe," even "down to everlasting destruction" (Alma 12:6). To accomplish his goal, the devil may begin with gentle nudges, gradually increasing his influence and power over his victims. Nephi[1] testified that "he leadeth them by the neck with a flaxen cord, until he bindeth them with his strong cords" (2 Ne. 26:22). By stirring people up to anger against that which is good, lulling them away into carnal security, and flattering them by telling them there is no hell, Satan "whispereth in their ears, until he grasps them with his awful chains, from whence there is no deliverance," thus leading "them away carefully down to hell" (2 Ne. 28:20–23). The most wicked and rebellious of mankind, those who suffer "a second death, which is a spiritual death," shall be "chained down to an everlasting destruction" (Alma 12:16–18). Their "final state" is that the devil will "seal [them] his" and have "all power over [them]" permanently (Alma 34:35). Those who have suffered themselves to become somewhat but not fully captivated by the devil can "shake off the awful chains" (2 Ne. 1:13) by learning the word of God, believing in Jesus Christ, and repenting of their sins (2 Ne. 1:13–23; 9:45; 15:13; 28:19; Alma 5:6–13; 12:10–11; 13:30; 26:13–15; 36:18).

The suffering of those in bondage to the devil, whether temporary or permanent, is described in the Book of Mormon as "bitter" and "exquisite" torment of the soul (Alma 36:12–21), as "weeping, and wailing, and gnashing of teeth, and this because of their own iniquity, being led captive by the will of the devil" (Alma 40:13). Yet, the devil cannot force his captivity upon a person, for "men are free according to the flesh; and all things are given them which are expedient unto man. And they are free to choose liberty and eternal life, through the great Mediator of all men, or to choose captivity and death, according to the captivity and power of the devil" (2 Ne. 2:27).

See also Hell; Lake of fire and brimstone; Satan; Spiritual death.

LED

Carnal, sensual, and devilish A disposition contrary to the nature of God wherein "the children of men" are "quick to do iniquity" and "slow to do good, . . . quick to hearken unto the words of the evil one, and to set their hearts upon the vain things of the world," seeking to satisfy the appetites and passions of the mortal mind and body (Alma 46:8; Hel. 12:4). Such persons are described in the Book of Mormon as "without God in the world," and even "enem[ies] to God" (Alma 41:11; Mosiah 16:5). This condition came upon mankind because of the Fall (Mosiah 16:3; Alma 9–10), and continues "unless he yields to the enticings of the Holy Spirit, and putteth off the natural man and becometh a saint through the atonement of Christ the Lord" (Mosiah 3:19). The Lord told Alma[2] that all who inherit the kingdom of God "must be born again; yea, born of God, changed from their carnal and fallen state, to a state of righteousness, being redeemed of God . . . becom[ing] new creatures" (Mosiah 27:25–26). Those who are thus born of the Spirit are no longer carnal, sensual, and devilish; they "have no more disposition to do evil, but to do good continually" (Mosiah 5:2).

See also Born again; Fall of Adam and Eve, the; Natural man.

LED

Cast off Expression for SPIRITUAL DEATH, synonymous with being cast out of the Lord's presence (Hel. 12:25). The term conveys a graphic image used by several prophets (Lehi[1], Nephi[1], Isaiah, Alma[2], Ammon[2], and Mormon) in their exhortations to avoid the kind of behavior which would inevitably prevent one from receiving eternal life (1 Ne. 8:36–37; 10:21; 2 Ne. 7:1; Mosiah 27:27; Alma 22:6; Hel. 12:25). Ancient Israelites may have associated the term with the notion of being cast into the fire, which was promised to the wicked (Jacob 5:7; Ps. 140:10; Matt. 3:10). Because no unclean thing can dwell with God, and therefore "must be cast off forever" (1 Ne. 10:21), only those who "cast off [their] sins" (Alma 13: 27) or repent will enjoy his presence (2 Ne. 30:2; Alma 22:15).

ACS

Cauls *See* Appendix C.

Cement *See* Gems, stones, and rocks.

Cezoram Nephite chief judge between 30 and 26 B.C. He became the chief magistrate when Nephi[2] retired from the office to dedicate himself to full-time preaching. Cezoram presided at a time when "they who chose evil were more numerous than they who chose good" (Hel. 5:1–4). Four years after taking office, Cezoram was assassinated by members of the wicked secret society, the Gadianton robbers. That same year Cezoram's son, also elected as chief judge, was likewise murdered by the Gadiantons (Hel. 6:15–19).

BAV

Cezoram, son of Nephite chief judge (ca. 26 B.C.) who was murdered by the Gadianton robbers (Hel. 6:15, 18–19). He had been appointed by the people to replace his father Cezoram, who was murdered by the Gadiantons earlier that year.

Charity "The pure love of Christ" (Moro. 7:47). Charity is spoken of in two contexts—the love of God for his children, and the love God's children should have for one another.

Necessity of charity

Charity is the "greatest of all" the gifts of the Spirit (Moro. 7:46; 1 Ne. 15:36; cf. 1 Cor. 13:2, 8). Those without charity cannot inherit the celestial kingdom (Ether 12:34; Moro. 10:21). Without charity people are nothing, like dross which the refiners cast out because it is of no worth (2 Ne. 26:30; Alma 34:29; Moro. 7:44, 46; 1 Cor. 13:1–2). Those "possessed" with charity become the covenant sons and daughters of God and will be like Christ (Moro. 7:47–48), and will be "lifted up at the last day and enter into his rest" (Alma 13:29).

The "first and great commandment" is to love God with all one's heart, soul, and mind (Matt. 22:36–38), or, as Moroni[2] stated, "with all your might, mind and strength" (Moro. 10:32). "And the second is like unto it, Thou shalt love thy neighbour as thyself" (Matt. 22:39; cf. Mosiah 23:15). Nephi[1] was of such a mind, declaring that he had charity for everyone—his people, the Jews, and the Gentiles (2 Ne. 33:7–9). The Lord has made it clear that loving one another is an important measure of discipleship, a principle implicit in the Book of Mormon but stated directly in the New Testament: "By this shall all men know that ye are my disciples, if ye have love one to another" (John 13:34–35).

Fruits of charity

"Perfect love casteth out all fear" (Moro. 8:16) and brings happiness (1 Ne. 8:10). The natural response to experiencing this love is an overwhelming desire to invite others (family, friends, and even enemies) to partake of it also (1 Ne. 8:13–17; Enos 1:9, 11; Mosiah 28:3; Alma 36:24). Those possessed of charity "always abound in good works" (Alma 7:24). They help bear the burdens of the kingdom of God in mortality, and they sustain and support other laborers in Zion (2 Ne. 26:30). They suffer long, are kind, envy not, are not puffed up, seek not their own desires, are not easily provoked, think no evil, rejoice not in iniquity but rejoice in truth, bear all things, believe all things, hope all things, and endure all things (Moro. 7:45). These virtues are foreign to the natural man but attainable for those who have put off the natural man and have become Saints through the ATONEMENT of Jesus Christ and their personal repentance and obedience (Mosiah 3:19).

Ultimately, charity enables one to be like Christ, and to be purified as he is pure (Moro. 7:48). Charity forever changes those who receive it: "Love is one of the chief characteristics of Deity, and ought to be manifested by those who aspire to be the sons of God. A man filled with the love of God, is not content with blessing his family alone, but ranges through the whole world, anxious to bless the whole human race" (Smith, 4:227).

How charity is obtained

Charity, love for God and for one another, is a gift from God. No mortal can love the Savior or his fellow men with the intensity that God does unless God reveals that love to him (G. Richards, 139; Ballard, 76; L. Richards, 28). Mormon instructed his "brethren" to "pray unto the Father with all the energy of heart, that ye may be filled with this love, which he hath bestowed upon all who are true followers of his Son" (Moro. 7:48; cf. 8:26). Alma[2] counseled his son, Shiblon, "Bridle all your passions, that ye may be filled with love" (Alma 38:12).

Furthermore, the gift of charity is bestowed upon those who apply the Atonement. Mormon described an important sequence: "And the first fruits of repentance is baptism; and baptism cometh by faith unto the fulfilling the commandments; and the fulfilling the commandments bringeth remission of sins; and the remission of sins bringeth meekness, and lowliness of heart; and because of meekness and lowliness of heart cometh the visitation of the Holy Ghost, which Comforter filleth with hope and *perfect love,* which love endureth by diligence unto prayer, until the end shall come, when all the saints shall dwell with God" (Moro. 8:25–26; italics added). Elements of this sequence—FAITH, which brings REPENTANCE and BAPTISM; repentance and baptism, which bring FORGIVENESS; forgiveness, which brings MEEKNESS and LOWLINESS OF HEART; meekness and lowliness of heart, which invite the HOLY GHOST; and the Holy Ghost, who bestows charity upon the spiritually reborn—are beautifully demonstrated in the lives of Enos (Enos 1:2–11), Alma[2] (Alma 36:16–24), the sons of Mosiah[2] (Mosiah 28:1–4), and the ANTI-NEPHI-LEHIES (Alma 24:7–19). Thus charity follows faith and HOPE: "And what is it that ye shall hope for?" Mormon inquired: "Behold I say unto you that ye shall have hope through the atonement of Christ and the power of his resurrection, to be raised unto life eternal, and this because of your faith in him according to the promise. Wherefore, if a man have faith he must needs have hope; for without faith there cannot be any hope. And again, behold I say unto you that he cannot have faith and hope, save he shall be meek, and lowly of heart. If so, his faith and hope is vain, for none is acceptable before God, save the meek and lowly in heart; and if a man be meek and lowly in heart, and confesses by the power of the Holy Ghost that Jesus is the Christ, he must needs have charity" (Moroni 7:41–44).

Christ's atoning sacrifice, the ultimate expression of charity

Charity is the "everlasting love" (Moro. 8:17) that gave Jesus Christ the desire and ability to do his Father's will—"even unto the laying down of [his] life for the world, that [he might] take it again to prepare a place for the children of men" (Ether 12:33–34; 1 Ne. 19:9; Mosiah 15:8–9; Alma 42:15; 3 Ne. 27:13–15; Moses 1:39). Elder Jeffrey R. Holland wrote: "The greater definition of 'the pure love of Christ' . . . is not what we as Christians try but largely fail to demonstrate toward others but rather what Christ totally succeeded in demonstrating toward us. *True* charity has been known only once. It is shown perfectly and purely in Christ's unfailing, ultimate, and atoning love for us. It is Christ's love for us that 'suffereth long, and is kind. . . . It is his love for us that is not 'puffed up . . . , not easily provoked, thinketh no evil.' It is Christ's love for us that 'beareth all things, believeth all things, hopeth all things, endureth all things.' It is as demonstrated in Christ that 'charity never faileth.' It is that charity—his pure love for us—without which we would be nothing, hopeless, of all men and women most miserable. Truly, those found possessed of the blessings of his love at the last day—the Atonement, the Resurrection, eternal life, eternal promise—surely it shall be well with them" (336).

Charity, "most joyous to the soul"

In Lehi[1]'s dream, the tree of life and its fruit represented the love of God for his children as manifested through the birth, life, ministry, and atonement of Jesus Christ (1 Ne. 8:10; 11:22, 25). Lehi described this fruit (love) as being most desirable of all things. He said that "it was most sweet, above all that I ever before tasted," and "white, to exceed all the whiteness that I had ever seen . . . desirable above all other fruit" (1 Ne. 8:11–12). Nephi[1] added that the beauty of the tree, or the love of God, "was far beyond, yea, exceeding of all beauty . . . precious above all. . . . and the most joyous to the soul" (1 Ne. 11:8–9, 23).

See also Born again.

BIBLIOGRAPHY

Ballard, M. Russell. "The Blessings of Sacrifice." *Ensign* 22 (May 1992): 75–77.

Holland, Jeffrey R. *Christ and the New Covenant.* Salt Lake City: Deseret Book, 1997.

Richards, George F. Conference Report, October 1946.

Richards, LeGrand. Conference Report, October 1955.

Smith, Joseph. *History of The Church of Jesus Christ of Latter-day Saints.* Edited by B. H. Roberts. 7 vols. 2d ed. rev. Salt Lake City: The Church of Jesus Christ of Latter-day Saints, 1932–51.

WJM

Chasten *See* Appendix C.

Chastity Sexual purity, "abstinence before marriage and fidelity following marriage" (Hinckley, 47). Mormon described chastity as being "most dear and precious above all things" (Moro. 9:9). The Lord has said, "For I, the Lord God, delight in the chastity of women. And whoredoms are an abomination before me" (Jacob 2:28). Alma[2] taught his son Corianton that sexual impurity was "most abominable above all sins save it be the shedding of innocent blood or denying the Holy Ghost" (Alma 39:5). Alma's counsel to Corianton provides several specific principles of prevention and redemption pertaining to the law of chastity. Corianton could have avoided his immoral encounter with the harlot Isabel had he followed the example of his brothers (Alma 39:1, 10), been more attentive to the counsel of his father (Alma 39:2), and refrained from boasting in his own strength and wisdom and then leaving his ministry to go to the land of Siron (Alma 39:2–3). Recognizing that Corianton had been influenced by others who were guilty of unchastity, Alma countered Corianton's rationalization by stating, "Yea, she did steal away the hearts of many; but this was no excuse for thee, my son. Thou shouldst have tended to the ministry wherewith thou wast entrusted" (Alma 39:4; cf. 2 Sam. 11:1). Corianton was counseled to repent and forsake his sins and to "go no more after the lusts of your eyes" and to "cross yourself" (Alma 39:9), which means to "deny [oneself] all ungodliness, and every worldly lust" (JST Matt. 16:26). Alma concluded by instructing his son to "turn to the Lord with all your mind, might, and strength" and return to those whom he had led away and "acknowledge your faults and that wrong which ye have done" (Alma 39:13; cf. Mosiah 7:33). It appears that Corianton accepted his father's counsel and repented of his unchastity, for the record later notes Corianton's faithful service in the kingdom (Alma 49:30; 48:18).

After warning against the dangers of pride, the prophet Jacob[2] stated that he must "speak . . . concerning a grosser crime" (Jacob 2:22). He then warned, "This people . . . seek to excuse themselves in committing whoredoms . . . [but] there shall not any man among you have save it be one wife; and concubines he shall have none" (Jacob 2:23, 27). Jacob then related the Lord's words concerning the devastation experienced by the innocent wives of the unchaste husbands: "For behold, I, the Lord, have seen the sorrow, and heard the mourning of the daughters of my people in the land of Jerusalem, yea, and in all the lands of my people, because of the wickedness and abominations of their husbands" (Jacob 2:31). In addition to the sufferings experienced by the wives of the unchaste husbands, Jacob also included a description of consequences suffered by the children: "Ye have broken the hearts of your tender wives, and lost the confidence of your children, because of your bad examples before them; and the sobbings of their hearts ascend up to God against you. . . . Many hearts died, pierced with deep wounds" (Jacob 2:35). The Savior taught that not only are unchaste actions an abomination, so too are unchaste thoughts and feelings: "Behold, it is written by them of old time, that thou shalt not commit adultery; but I say unto you, that whosoever looketh on a woman, to lust after her, hath committed adultery already in his heart. Behold, I give unto you a commandment, that ye suffer none of these things to enter into your heart; For it is better that ye should deny yourselves of these things, wherein ye will take up your cross, than that ye should be cast into hell" (3 Ne. 12:27–30).

See also Cross yourself.

BIBLIOGRAPHY

Hinckley, Gordon B. "Reverence and Morality." *Ensign* 17 (May 1987): 45–48.

DKJ

Check *See* Appendix C.

Chemish Nephite scribe, a descendant of Jacob[2], and a son of Omni [between 279 and 130 B.C.). Chemish received stewardship of the small PLATES OF NEPHI from his brother Amaron. Chemish noted that Amaron wrote his entry on the day that he was given the plates and that he and his brother kept the record because of the commandments of their fathers (e.g., Jacob

1:1–3). Chemish contributed one verse to the small plates before passing them to his son Abinadom (Omni 1:9).

See also Omni, book of.

Cherubim and a flaming sword Guardian sentinels placed to prevent Adam and Eve from partaking of the TREE OF LIFE after their fall. "A *cherub* is an angel of some particular order or rank to whom specific duties and work are assigned" (McConkie, 124). *Cherubim* is the Hebrew plural of *cherub*. The beings who guarded the tree of life were "faithful personages belonging to this world who had not, at the time, received the privilege of partaking of mortality" (Smith, 2:97). While the presence of a flaming sword was evidence of divine protection of the tree of life after the Fall, the scriptures are silent regarding its nature and appearance.

The Bible states that God placed cherubim and a flaming sword "to keep the way of the tree of life," but it does not explain why this was done (Gen. 3:24). The Book of Mormon provides this explanation and teaches how this act was essential to the plan of salvation. If Adam and Eve had been permitted to eat from the tree of life after their transgression, there would have been no death, contrary to God's word. In addition, "our first parents" would have been "forever miserable, having no preparatory state," or "time to prepare to meet God" (Alma 12:22–26)—"to repent and serve God" (Alma 42:2–5)—and "thus the plan of redemption would have been frustrated" (Alma 12:26).

See also Fall of Adam and Eve, the; Tree of knowledge of good and evil.

BIBLIOGRAPHY

McConkie, Bruce R. *Mormon Doctrine*. 2d ed. Salt Lake City: Bookcraft, 1966.

Smith, Joseph Fielding. *Answers to Gospel Questions*. Compiled by Joseph Fielding Smith Jr. 5 vols. Salt Lake City: Deseret Book, 1957–66.

ROC

Chiasmus The literary technique of presenting a set of words or ideas in a certain order and then retracing them in the opposite order. The word *chiasmus* comes from the Greek *chiazein*, meaning to mark with an *x*, or a *chi*. The device is useful for several purposes, especially for concentrating attention on the main point of a passage by placing it at the central turning point of the text rather than in a topic sentence at the beginning of a paragraph, as is the common practice of modern Western writers. Chiasmus has often been pointed out in recent years by literary analysts in studying the texts of the Bible, the Book of Mormon, and other literature. It can aid memorization, teach by means of calculated repetition, and confer a sense of completeness or closure to a lengthy textual development.

Among the main Nephite writers, king Benjamin was particularly effective in creating chiastic structures. Most of his chiasms feature a centerpiece of two or more parallel lines (Mosiah 3:18–19; 5:10–12). An excellent example is Mosiah 5:10–12 (emphasis added).

a whosoever shall not take upon him the **name** of Christ
  b must be **called** by some other name;
    c therefore, he findeth himself on the **left hand of God**. . . .
      d ye should **remember** also, that this is the name that I said I should give unto you
        e that never should be **blotted out**,
          f except it be through **transgression**;
          f therefore, take heed that ye do not **transgress**,
        e that the name be not **blotted out** of your hearts. . . .
      d ye should **remember** to retain the name written always in your hearts,
    c that ye are not found on the **left hand of God**,
  b but that ye hear and know the voice by which ye shall be **called**,
a and also, the **name** by which he shall call you.

In most cases the use of chiasmus appears to be a conscious choice, but it need not always be intentional. Poets, authors, composers, musicians, and other artists create their works without being aware of every facet of their compositions. Yet, a high degree of precision in chiastic repetition indicates that the author was likely using this literary tool consciously. For example, Leviticus 24:13–23 reports the case of the blasphemer in the form of an extended chiasm so precise that it seems unlikely to be accidental (Welch, "Biblical Law," 5–22). Similarly, in the Odyssey, it appears probable that Homer and the Homeric bards were aware that when Odysseus in the underworld asks the shade of his mother, Anticleia, seven questions, she responds by addressing the questions in exactly the reverse order (*Odyssey* 11:170; Welch, *Antiquity*, 253–54).

Passages can manifest varying degrees of "chiasticity." Some passages are short, and their inverted order is obvious. For example, Genesis 1:27 reads: "[a] God created man [b] in his own image, [b] in the image of God [a] created he him." The a–b–b–a order here is objectively verifiable. Longer structures often become more tenuous, however, and analysis must be conducted cautiously to avoid overstatement and misunderstanding. For other biblical examples, see Genesis 7:21–23; Psalms 3:7–8; 58; Isaiah 55:8; 60:1–3; Amos 5:4–6; Matthew 10:39; 13:13–18.

Several conditions should be satisfied before one can speak meaningfully of chiasmus in a given passage (Welch, "Criteria," 1–14). The more fully a particular text fulfills these criteria, the higher its degree of chiasticity. Chiasms are stronger when they consist of elements that are objectively observable in the text, that is, when they are apparently placed in a passage intentionally for stylistic purposes and are the dominant forms that operate across a literary unit as a whole. The inverted parallel orders should be relatively self-evident in the passage. Several chiasms in the Book of Mormon are composed of objectively observable elements. In addition to the examples detailed here, see 2 Nephi 6:16–17; 9:20; 29:13; Jacob 4:9; Enos 1:8–12; Mosiah 2:5–6, 7–8, 31–41; 4:6–7, 21; Alma 18:34–39; 34:9; and Helaman 16:2–3.

Strong, extended chiasmus featuring precise word repetition is found in several Book of Mormon texts, such as Helaman 6:7–13. These chiasms exhibit balance—elements on both sides of the proposed focal point are nearly equal in numbers of words, lines, or elements—and create a convincing sense of return and completion from the beginning to the end. Similarly, the more compact the chiasm—or the fewer irrelevancies between its elements—and the longer the chiasm, the higher its degree of chiasticity. For instance, the structure of Helaman 6:10 is a–b–c–d–e–e–d–c–b–a (emphasis added):

a Now the land **south**
  b was called **Lehi**, and
    c the land **north**
      d was called **Mulek**,
        e which was after the son of Zedek**iah**;
        e for the **Lord**
      d did bring **Mulek**
    c into the land **north**,
  b and **Lehi**
a into the land **south**.

This chiasm would be stronger in Hebrew, because the theophoric suffix *-iah* and the word *Lord (YHWH)* are etymologically related.

Chiasmus qualifies as a dominant feature in a text when it is the only structuring device used, as appears to be the case in several passages in king Benjamin's speech (e.g., Mosiah 2:26; 3:18–19; 5:10–12). A powerful structural design revolves around major concepts, unique phrases, or focal words. In some instances, the only occurrences of a word or phrase in the Book of Mormon are found in two chiastically matched occurrences (e.g., "natural man" twice in Mosiah 3:19; and "left hand" in Mosiah 5:10, 12). Moreover, because the crux of chiasmus falls generally at its central turning point (Lund, 40–41), it is significant that Book of Mormon writers often placed a well-defined centerpiece at the heart of their chiastic structures. Many factors like these give evidence of a high degree of chiasticity in several Book of Mormon texts. Their use of this form was fluid, consistent, and well balanced, yet it did not draw undue attention to itself.

Chiasmus was not used equally by all writers in the Book of Mormon. Benjamin and Alma[2] appear to have used it the most. They lived in a golden era of Nephite civilization, when great creative forces in literature, politics, theology, law, calendar, weights and measures, and military technology were at work among the people. It would follow that chiastic writing would also flower among Nephite authors at this time. Alma used this form most expansively and creatively. The overall structure of Alma 36 contains seventeen key elements, each repeated twice (verse numbers are in parentheses; italics added; *see* fig. 1).

Especially impressive is the repetition of the name "Jesus, thou Son of God" at the very center of the chapter. Alma's cry for mercy was clearly the turning point of his life, making this chapter one of the best examples of any author placing the most important concept at the central turning point of his passage (Welch, "Masterpiece," 114–31).

Another important example of chiasmus is found in Alma 41:13–14 (*see* fig. 2). The twist here is creatively elegant: After listing four pairs of terms, Alma then pairs two lists of four terms and reverses their order at the same time (Welch,

a My son, give ear to my **words** (1)
  b **Keep the commandments** and ye shall **prosper in the land** (1)
    c Do **as** I have done (2)
      d **Remember the captivity** of our fathers (2)
        e They were in **bondage** (2)
          f He surely did **deliver** them (2)
            g **Trust** in God (3)
              h Supported in **trials, troubles, and afflictions** (3)
                i lifted up at the **last day** (3)
                  j I **know** this not of myself but **of God** (4)
                    k **Born of God** (5)
                      l I sought to destroy the church (6–9)
                        m My **limbs** were paralyzed (10)
                          n Fear of being in the **presence of God** (14–15)
                            o **Pains** of a damned soul (16)
                              p **Harrowed up by the memory of sins** (17)
                                q I remembered **Jesus** Christ, a **son of God** (17)
                                q I cried, **Jesus, son of God** (17)
                              p **Harrowed up by the memory of sins** no more (19)
                            o Joy as exceeding as was the **pain** (20)
                          n Long to be in the **presence of God** (22)
                        m My **limbs** received strength again (23)
                      l I labored to bring souls to repentance (24)
                    k **Born of God** (26)
                  j Therefore **my knowledge** is **of God** (26)
                h Supported under **trials, troubles, and afflictions** (27)
              g **Trust** in him (27)
            f He will **deliver** me (27)
              i and raise me up at the **last day** (28)
        e As God brought our fathers out of **bondage** and captivity (28–29)
      d Retain in **remembrance their captivity** (28–29)
    c Know **as I** do know (30)
  b **Keep the commandments** and ye shall **prosper in the land** (30)
a This according to his **word** (30)

Fig. 1. Alma 36; verse numbers are in parentheses; emphasis added.

a_1a_2 **good** for that which is **good**;
b_1b_2 **righteous** for that which is **righteous**;
c_1c_2 **just** for that which is **just**;
d_1d_2 **merciful** for that which is **merciful**.
Therefore, my son, see that you are
d_1 **merciful** unto your brethren;
c_1 deal **justly**,
b_1 judge **righteously**,
a_1 and do **good** continually;
and if ye do all these things then shall ye receive your reward; yea,
d_2 ye shall have **mercy** restored unto you again;
c_2 ye shall have **justice** restored unto you again;
b_2 ye shall have a **righteous** judgment restored unto you again; and
a_2 ye shall have **good** rewarded unto you again.

Fig. 2. Alma 41:13–14; emphasis added.

"Book of Mormon," 69–84). But even prophets like Benjamin and Alma did not write chiastically all the time; chiasm was only one of several literary devices at their disposal.

Chiasmus is not exclusive to ancient Hebrew texts but has also been found in Akkadian, Ugaritic, Egyptian, Aramaic, Greek, Latin, and Mayan texts. Although it occurs in many ancient works of literature and also to an extent in modern authors, chiasmus has been used more extensively and purposefully in the Hebrew Bible and in the Book of Mormon than anywhere else.

Some chiasms are lost in any translation process, but larger chiastic patterns and conceptual parallelisms are usually preserved. The Book of Mormon is no exception to this rule. Of all poetical devices, extended chiasms and parallelisms are among the most likely to survive translation. Although knowledge is necessarily somewhat limited in this regard, it appears that several Book of Mormon structures were faithfully preserved through Joseph Smith's translation process.

Not much was known about chiasmus in Joseph Smith's day. In England, two authors published books in the 1820s about sacred Hebrew literature, exploring the presence of chiasmus in the Bible. Some early reviewers and Horne's popular commentary endorsed the idea of chiasmus, but there is no known evidence that Joseph Smith was aware of it while translating the Book of Mormon. The chance that Joseph Smith unconsciously assimilated chiasmus through his familiarity with the Bible assumes a great deal about literary osmosis.

Discovered in 1967 by an LDS missionary serving in Regensburg, Germany, the presence of chiasmus in the Book of Mormon is strong evidence that these writings are orderly, complex, artistic, purposeful, and consistent with ancient literary conventions.

See also Book of Mormon, as literature; Parallelism.

BIBLIOGRAPHY

Lund, Nils W. *Chiasmus in the New Testament*. Boston: Hendrickson, 1992.

Homer. *The Odyssey.*

Pinnock, Hugh W. *Finding Biblical Hebrew and Other Ancient Literary Forms in the Book of Mormon*. Provo, Utah: FARMS, 1999.

Welch, John W. "Chiasmus in Biblical Law: An Approach to the Structure of Legal Texts in the Hebrew Bible." *Jewish Law Association Studies* 4 (1990).

———. "Chiasmus in the Book of Mormon." *BYU Studies* 10:1 (1969): 69–84.

———. "Criteria for Identifying the Presence of Chiasmus." *Journal of Book of Mormon Studies* 4:2 (1995).

———. "A Masterpiece: Alma 36." *Rediscovering the Book of Mormon*. Edited by John L. Sorenson and Melvin J. Thorne. Salt Lake City: Deseret Book, 1991.

———. "What Does Chiasmus in the Book of Mormon Prove?" *Book of Mormon Authorship Revisited: The*

CHILDREN, BAPTISM OF LITTLE

Evidences for Ancient Origins. Edited by Noel B. Reynolds. Provo, Utah: FARMS, 1997.

———, ed. *Chiasmus in Antiquity: Structures, Analyses, Exegesis*. Hildesheim: Gerstenberg, 1981; reprint, Provo, Utah: FARMS, 1999.

JWW

Children, baptism of little Mormon described the baptism of little children who have not yet reached the age of accountability as a "gross error" and "solemn mockery before God" that denies the atonement of Christ (Moro. 8:6, 9). In writing to his son Moroni, he shared a revelation he had received on the matter: "Little children are whole, for they are not capable of committing sin; wherefore the curse of Adam is taken from them in me" (Moro. 8:7–8). Baptism is efficacious only after one has obtained faith in

Suffer Little Children to Come unto Me; *painting by Carl Heinrich Bloch; courtesy DNMF.*

Christ and repented of one's sins. The infant child can do neither. To suppose that baptism is essential to the salvation of little children who have no power to determine whether they are baptized is to make God "a partial God, and also a changeable God, and a respecter to persons; for how many little children have died without baptism! Wherefore, if little children could not be saved without baptism, these must have gone to an endless hell. Behold I say unto you, that he that supposeth that little children need baptism is in the gall of bitterness and in the bonds of iniquity; for he hath neither faith, hope, nor charity; wherefore, should he be cut off while in the thought, he must go down to hell" (Moro. 8:8–14). Speaking to father Abraham the Lord said, "Children are not accountable before me until they are eight years old" (JST Gen. 17:11). This same principle was also revealed to Joseph Smith (D&C 68:27).

See also Alive in Christ; Children, salvation of little; Curse of Adam, the; Dead works; Law of circumcision.

JFM

Children, salvation of little Book of Mormon prophets emphatically declared that little children who die before reaching the age of accountability are redeemed through Christ. These children are "alive in Christ," they are not capable of sinning (Moro. 8:8–12), and their destiny is eternal life (Mosiah 15:25). King Benjamin explained that even though children are not capable of sin, they can only be saved through the blood of Christ, as they are still subject to the consequences of the fall of Adam (Mosiah 3:15–18). Christ affirmed, "The curse of Adam is taken from them in me" (Moro. 8:8).

See also Alive in Christ; Children, baptism of little; Curse of Adam, the.

JFM

Children of Christ Those who are BORN AGAIN through the Atonement become sons and daughters of the Lord Jesus Christ. King Benjamin told his people, "And now, because of the covenant which ye have made ye shall be called the children of Christ, his sons, and his daughters; for behold, this day he hath spiritually begotten you; for ye say that your hearts are changed through faith on his name; therefore, ye are born of him and have become his sons and his daughters" (Mosiah 5:7).

Because of the Fall, all people are alienated from righteousness and from the family of God (Alma 34:9). Through the Atonement people are not only forgiven of sin but also reconciled to the Father and reinstated in the royal family. The children of Christ are those who have entered into the covenant of baptism (Mosiah 5:7–8; Moro. 6:3), hearkened to the words of the prophets (Mosiah 15:11–12), put off the natural man (Mosiah 3:19), and become "new creatures" through the Holy Ghost. Fathers give life. Jesus' redemptive act affords both rebirth in this life (Mosiah 27:23–26) and the opportunity for eternal life in the world to come (Ether 3:14).

RLM

Choice seer Joseph Smith was identified by Joseph[1] of Egypt as a "choice seer" in an important prophecy he uttered concerning the restoration of his posterity in the latter days (2 Ne. 3:6–7; JST Gen. 50:26–27; cf. D&C 21:1). In a blessing given by Lehi[1] to his son Joseph[2], Lehi retold or quoted this prophecy, which contains at least thirteen points pertaining to the foreordained mission of Joseph Smith. The following descriptive phrases are taken from Joseph's prophecy:

"Choice seer unto the fruit of my loins" (2 Ne. 3:6). Clearly Joseph Smith was to do a "marvelous work" for the posterity of Joseph of Egypt (1 Ne. 22:8–9). That work centered in bringing "unto" them the gospel message of salvation and the Book of Mormon, the record of their ancestors (2 Ne. 3:21; cf. 1 Ne. 15:13–16; 2 Ne. 30:3–6). The words Joseph Smith would translate were "as if the fruit" of the loins of Joseph "had cried unto [their posterity] from the dust" (2 Ne. 3:19).

"A choice seer will I raise up out of the fruit of thy loins" (2 Ne. 3:7). Joseph Smith was from the loins of Abraham, Isaac, Jacob, and Joseph. The Lord told Joseph Smith, "Abraham received promises concerning his seed, and of the fruit of his loins—from whose loins ye are" (D&C 132:30).

CHOICE SEER

Joseph Smith (1805–1844); courtesy CCA.

"He shall be esteemed highly among the fruit of thy loins" (2 Ne. 3:7). Joseph Smith was esteemed highly by believers and unbelievers. Believer John Taylor wrote of him, "Joseph Smith, the Prophet and Seer of the Lord, has done more, save Jesus only, for the salvation of men in this world, than any other man that ever lived in it" (D&C 135:3). Unbeliever Josiah Quincy, a former mayor of Boston, wrote after only a brief acquaintance: "It is by no means improbable that some future textbook . . . will contain a question something like this: What historical American of the nineteenth century has exerted the most powerful influence upon the destinies of his countrymen? And it is by no means impossible that the answer to the interrogatory may be thus written: Joseph Smith, the Mormon Prophet" (Roberts, 2:349–50).

"I give commandment that he shall do a work for the fruit of thy loins . . . even to the bringing of them to the knowledge of the covenants" (2 Ne. 3:7). The work of the choice SEER was to be of "great worth" in bringing Joseph of Egypt's descendants to a knowledge of the covenants God made with Joseph's fathers (i.e., Abraham, Isaac, and Jacob).

"I will give unto him a commandment that he shall do none other work, save the work which I shall command him" (2 Ne. 3:8). True to the Lord's directive, Joseph Smith dedicated his life to building up the Lord's kingdom on earth. He translated the Book of Mormon and portions of the Pearl of Great Price. He compiled revelations in the Doctrine and Covenants and prepared an inspired revision of the Bible. As he magnified the Lord's command "that he shall do none other work," he fulfilled his seeric ministry (2 Ne. 3:8; cf. D&C 24:9).

"I will make him great in mine eyes" (2 Ne. 3:8). Because of the greatness of Joseph Smith in the sight of God, his followers were told by the Lord, "His word ye shall receive, as if from mine own mouth, in all patience and faith" (D&C 21:5). Joseph had been given the keys of God's "kingdom, and a dispensation of the gospel for the last times; and for the fulness of times" (D&C 27:13; cf. 81:2–3).

"He shall be great like unto Moses" (2 Ne. 3:9). The phrase "be great like unto Moses" epitomized the confidence the Lord had in his servant Joseph Smith before his earthly ministry. Both Moses and Joseph would stand at the head of their respective dispensations. Both were foreordained to redemptive missions: Moses was to be the great deliverer; Joseph Smith, the great restorer. Both brought forth scripture, performed great miracles, and were instruments in the Lord's hands in gathering the house of Israel. In modern revelation the Lord assured his Saints that "no one shall be appointed to receive commandments and revelations in this church excepting my servant Joseph Smith, Jun., for he receiveth them even as Moses" (D&C 28:2).

"Unto him will I give power to bring forth my word unto the seed of thy loins—and not to the bringing forth my word only, saith the Lord, but to the convincing them of my word, which shall have already gone forth among them" (2 Ne. 3:11). Joseph Smith was given a revelatory instrument—the URIM AND THUMMIM, or interpreters—to translate the word of God that had been written by ancient American prophets (Mosiah 8:15–19;

CHOICE SEER

D&C 5:10). The Book of Mormon: Another Testament of Jesus Christ, is a confirming witness of the truths of salvation and the testimony of Jesus Christ written by ancient biblical prophets. The book fulfills the prophecy, "That which shall be written by the fruit of thy loins, and also that which shall be written by the fruit of the loins of Judah, shall grow together, unto the confounding of false doctrines and laying down of contentions" (2 Ne. 3:12).

In addition Joseph Smith was given the power to bring forth the Doctrine and Covenants, Pearl of Great Price, and the Inspired Version of the Bible.

"Out of weakness he shall be made strong" (2 Ne. 3:13). Despite humble circumstances and natural weakness, Joseph Smith became a strong and mighty prophet (JS–H 1:28–29, 55, 61; D&C 135:3). As a seer he was blessed to know "of things which are past, and also of things which are to come" (Mosiah 8:17). After faithfully fulfilling his seeric ministry, the Lord declared to Joseph, "I am well pleased with your offering and acknowledgments, which you have made; for unto this end have I raised you up, that I might show forth my wisdom through the weak things of the earth" (D&C 124:1).

"They that seek to destroy him shall be confounded" (2 Ne. 3:14). Those who sought to destroy Joseph and thwart the Lord's work were confounded but not until Joseph had passed through much tribulation. "God is my friend in him I shall find comfort," the imprisoned seer wrote to his wife (Smith, *Personal Writings,* 239). The Lord comforted his servant in Liberty Jail: "My son, peace be unto thy soul; thine adversity and thine afflictions shall be but a small moment. . . . Fear not what man can do, for God shall be with you forever and ever" (D&C 121:7; 122:9).

"His name shall be called after me; and it shall be after the name of his father" (2 Ne. 3:15). "In the meantime we had a son whom we called Joseph after the name of his father," are words attributed to Lucy Smith about the birth of her third son (Smith, *Joseph,* 46). They convey much more than the simple naming of a child. Joseph was known by name millennia before his birth and had been foreordained to a great work in the latter days. His father was likewise known and foreordained. Father Smith declared, "I have never denied the Lord. . . . The Lord has often visited me in visions and dreams, and has brought me, with my family, through many afflictions, and I this day thank his holy name" (Book of Patriarchal Blessings Index, 1:1).

"He shall be like unto me" (2 Ne. 3:15). Joseph Smith was also to be like Joseph of old, who was also responsible for a work that would bring salvation to the house of Israel. As Joseph of Egypt was the Lord's instrument in saving Israel temporally from starvation (Gen. 45:4–8), Joseph Smith was to be the Lord's instrument in saving them spiritually—bringing them out of "darkness unto light" (2 Ne. 3:5). Joseph of old was blessed with the spirit of revelation and the interpretation of dreams (Gen. 37:5–9; 40; 41:1–39). Joseph Smith received visions, angelic visitations, revelations, and the "keys of the mystery of those things which have been sealed, even things which were from the foundation of the world" (D&C 35:18; cf. 28:7; 64:5). And like his predecessor (Gen. 37:18–24; 39:20), Joseph Smith was persecuted, hated, and imprisoned (D&C 121; 122).

"I will make for him a spokesman" (2 Ne. 3:18). Sidney Rigdon was appointed as a SPOKESMAN for Joseph Smith. The Lord told Joseph, "It is expedient in me that . . . my servant Sidney [Rigdon] . . . be a spokesman unto my servant Joseph" (D&C 100:9; cf. 124:104).

See also Smith, Joseph, Jr.; Smith, Joseph, Jr., Book of Mormon prophecies of.

BIBLIOGRAPHY

Book of Patriarchal Blessings Index 1:1. Church Archives, The Church of Jesus Christ of Latter-day Saints, Salt Lake City, Utah.

Smith, Joseph. *Personal Writings of Joseph Smith.* Compiled and edited by Dean C. Jessee. Salt Lake City: Deseret Book, 1984, 2002.

Smith, Lucy Mack. *History of Joseph Smith by His Mother.* Edited by Preston Nibley. Salt Lake City: Bookcraft, 1958.

Roberts, B. H. *A Comprehensive History of The Church of Jesus Christ of Latter-day Saints.* 6 vols. Provo, Utah: Brigham Young University Press, 1965. 2:349–50.

SB

Chosen To be called of God while yet in the councils of heaven for a particular labor or purpose. Those receiving such premortal appointments are often spoken of as having been "chosen," "elected," or "foreordained." The concept of the spirit children of God being called before their mortal birth to perform a particular labor on the earth finds expression throughout the Book of Mormon.

As would be expected, the most notable illustration of premortal choosing in the Book of Mormon is Christ. Detailed messianic prophecies foretell the place and manner of his birth, the nature of his ministry, his death, his resurrection, and his subsequent appearance on the American continent (1 Ne. 11; 12; Mosiah 3; Alma 7). Elsewhere in scripture the Father referred to Christ as "my Beloved Son, which was my Beloved and Chosen from the beginning" (Moses 4:2). Prophecies about Mary, honored to be the earthly mother of the Son of God, make it obvious that she too was a "precious and chosen vessel," appointed to her role in the councils of heaven (Alma 7:10; 1 Ne. 11:12–21; Mosiah 3:8). Nephi[1], in vision, saw the Holy Ghost fall upon the "the twelve disciples of the Lamb" who were "ordained of God, and chosen" to "minister unto [his] seed" (1 Ne. 12:7–8). Foreshadowing the ministry of John the Baptist, Lehi[1] rehearsed some of the very words John would speak (1 Ne. 10:7–10; cf. Matt. 3:3; Mark 1:7; Luke 3:16; John 1:26–29). Nephi wrote certain parts of his marvelous vision, but he was told not to write all of it, for that responsibility had already been given to one of the apostles of the Lamb who would be known by the name of John (1 Ne. 14:18–28). In a prophecy given by Joseph of Egypt and repeated by Lehi in blessing his son Joseph[2], the labor and ministry of the Prophet Joseph Smith was foretold (2 Ne. 3). This prophecy identified Joseph Smith as a CHOICE SEER who would do a great labor among the posterity of Joseph[1], son of Jacob[1]. An early central focus of that labor was to bring forth the Book of Mormon. It was prophesied that he would bear the same name as Joseph of old, which would also be the name of his father (2 Ne. 3:15).

The labors of many other unnamed faithful servants of the Lord are foreshadowed, including those spoken of by Alma[2] who were "called and prepared from the foundation of the world according to the foreknowledge of God, on account of their exceeding faith and good works; in the first place," or what Abraham called the "first estate" (Alma 13:3–5; Abr. 3:22–26). Such were "called" and "ordained unto the high priesthood of the holy order of God" to teach the commandments of God "unto the children of men" (Alma 13:6). Among these high priests are "chosen vessels of the Lord" to whom angels declare "the word of Christ . . . that they may bear testimony of him . . . that the residue of men may have faith in Christ" (Moro. 7:29–32). Those covenant spokesmen for the Lord, acting in the office and calling of a prophet, were foreordained to their mission, inasmuch as "every man who has a calling to minister to the inhabitants of the world was ordained to that very purpose in the Grand Council of heaven before this world was" (Smith, 365).

Other scriptural texts extend the doctrine of a chosen, or elect, people in a broader sense to the whole house of Israel (Deut. 7:6; 32:7–9; 1 Ne. 17:40). Those so chosen are called out of the world to be a people of purity and faith who represent the Lord in blessing "all the kindreds of the earth" (1 Ne. 15:18) with "the blessings of the Gospel, which are the blessings of salvation" (Abr. 2:9–11; 1 Ne. 22:9; 3 Ne. 20:25–27). The special place covenant Israel holds with the Lord does not preclude the possibility that they may fall from their chosen state if they fail to live up to the birthright that is theirs (1 Ne. 17:23–44). Neither does it preclude the reality that others not of the earthly lineage of Abraham, Isaac, and Jacob were also "chosen," "elected," "foreordained" to receive the gospel, thereby *becoming* "Abraham's seed, and heirs according to the promise" (Gal. 3:26–29; Abr. 2:9–11).

The apostate Zoramites[2] falsely applied the principle of an "elect," or "chosen," people. They prayed, "Holy, holy God . . . we believe that thou hast elected us to be thy holy children . . . and thou hast elected us that we shall be saved, whilst all around us are elected to be cast by thy wrath down to hell" (Alma 31:15–17). In contrast, the Book of Mormon teaches the correct doctrine of individuals and groups being "chosen," "elected," "foreordained," while yet in the premortal life, to certain blessings and responsibilities on earth, the fulfillment of which depends upon their faithfulness.

See also Premortal existence.

BIBLIOGRAPHY

Smith, Joseph. *Teachings of the Prophet Joseph Smith.* Selected by Joseph Fielding Smith. Salt Lake City: Deseret Book, 1976.

JFM

Christ, alive in *See* Alive in Christ.

Christ, doctrine of *See* Gospel, the.

Christ, in the name of Everything redemptive is accomplished in the name of Christ, who mediates all transactions between God and man. Concerning the name of Christ, the Book of Mormon teaches the following truths:

1. God moved initially to "call on men, in the name of his Son, (this being the plan of redemption . . .) saying: If ye will repent, and harden not your hearts, then will I have mercy upon you, through mine Only Begotten Son" (Alma 12:33; cf. D&C 18:23).

2. Christ calls upon men in his own name. "The good shepherd doth call you . . . in his own name . . . which is the name of Christ; and if ye will not hearken . . . to the name by which ye are called . . . ye are not the sheep of the good shepherd" (Alma 5:38; cf. 3 Ne. 20:39; D&C 59:5; 136:40).

3. Saints are to act in the name of Christ. Christ instructed his disciples, "Whatsoever ye shall do, ye shall do it in my name" (3 Ne. 27:7). Accordingly, baptisms (3 Ne. 11:25–27), ordinations to the priesthood (Moro. 3), blessing of the sacrament (Moro. 4; 5) and personal prayers are all done in the name of Christ (3 Ne. 18:19–21). "Ye must not perform any thing unto the Lord," taught Nephi[1], "save in the first place ye shall pray unto the Father in the name of Christ, that he will consecrate thy performance unto thee" (2 Ne. 32:9; cf. Hel. 3:27–28; 3 Ne. 4:30; D&C 133:6, 37–40; Moses 5:8).

4. No other name brings salvation to anyone. "There shall be no other name given nor any other way nor means whereby salvation can come unto the children of men, only in and through the name of Christ" (Mosiah 3:17; cf. 2 Ne. 31:20–21; Alma 11:40; Moro. 7:38; D&C 18:23; 109:4). "The Lord will be merciful unto all who call on his name," and "he has all power to save every man that believeth on his name" (Alma 9:17; 12:15).

5. Men take Christ's name upon them through the ordinance of baptism. "And none were received unto baptism save they took upon them the name of Christ" (Moro. 6:3; cf. 2 Ne. 31:13, 17; cf. 9:23–24; 31:14; Mosiah 5:8, 12; 18:10; 26:18; Alma 34:38; 46:15, 21; 3 Ne. 27:4–6; Morm. 8:38; D&C 18:21–25; 20:37). Partaking of the sacrament is a witness to the Father of one's continued willingness to bear the name of his Son (Moro. 4; 5; D&C 20:77, 79).

6. The name of Christ is removed from any person's heart by unrepented sin. "This is the name . . . that never should be blotted out, except it be through transgression; therefore, take heed . . . that the name [of Christ] be not blotted out of your hearts" (Mosiah 5:11; cf. 1:11–12; 5:10). Not only will the name of Christ be blotted out of the hearts of transgressors, but the very name of the transgressor "shall be blotted out" and "shall not be mingled with the names of my people," for only "the names of the righteous shall be written in the book of life, and unto them"—to them alone—"will I grant an inheritance at my right hand" (Alma 5:57–58; cf. 6:3; 46:18; Moro. 6:3–4, 7). Benjamin counseled his people "to retain the name [of Christ] written always in your hearts, that ye are not found on the left hand of God, but that ye hear and know the voice by which ye shall be called, and also, the name by which he shall call you" (Mosiah 5:12).

7. The third commandment given to Moses on Sinai condemns all misuses of Christ's name (Ex. 20:7; 2 Ne. 26:32; Mosiah 13:15). A person's character is clearly revealed in the way he speaks the name of the Lord, for "that which cometh from above is sacred, and must be spoken with care, and by constraint of the Spirit" and "in this there is no condemnation" (D&C 63:64). Taking the name of the Lord in vain is condemned (D&C 136:21). One aspect of

taking the Lord's name in vain is to use it without authority (D&C 63:62–63). "I will not suffer my name to be polluted," said the Lord (1 Ne. 20:11 // Isa. 48:11). Using the name of Christ thus involves a warning and a promise: "Wherefore, let all men beware how they take my name in their lips" (D&C 63:61), for "I will raise up unto myself a pure people, that will serve me in righteousness; and all that call upon the name of the Lord . . . shall be saved" (D&C 100:16–17).

HCW

Christ, merits of *See* Merits of Christ.

Christ, reconciled unto *See* Reconciled unto Christ.

Chronology, Bible Many biblical events and persons are mentioned in the Book of Mormon. Biblical chronology is useful to Book of Mormon readers to provide a frame of reference for these events and persons, but biblical chronology is difficult for several reasons. First, virtually all chronological information in the Bible is given in terms of relative dates—without a fixed reference point. Most of the data appears in the form of birth dates and death dates or the dates of kings, their age at accession, length of reign, and age at death. So while it is possible to reconstruct relative chronology, there is no fixed point from which to calculate the dates to locate them precisely in the B.C./A.D. system. Second, there is considerable variation in the dates found in the three major biblical texts: the Samaritan Pentateuch and the Septuagint contain dates different from the Masoretic Text from which the King James Version was translated. Third, the dates of the kings in the Old Testament must be used with caution as some of the reigns of the kings overlap due to a system of coregencies. Most of the dates should be considered about (ca.).

In the last century much work was done that increased the precision of biblical chronology. For example, today it is possible to correlate the dates of biblical events and people with other contemporary sources from the ancient Near East. Many ancient Near Eastern records from Mesopotamia and from Egypt contain information about astronomical events, such as eclipses of the sun and the moon, that can be assigned with great precision to absolute dates. But though much progress has been made in the study of biblical chronology, several significant issues of chronology have not been completely resolved, such as the dates of the events of the universal history in Genesis 1–11, the dates of the Patriarchs, and the exact dates of the Exodus and the conquest of Canaan.

The standard handbook discussing the problems of biblical chronology is Finegan's *Handbook of Biblical Chronology* (rev. ed.). There are also comprehensive articles on Old Testament (Cogan) and New Testament (Donfried) chronology in the *Anchor Bible Dictionary.* Robert Smith, an LDS scholar, has created a meticulously detailed study documenting the evidence for the ancient Near Eastern and Old Testament dates relevant to the Book of Mormon from the year 793 B.C., the reign of Jeroboam II, to 445 B.C., the return of Nehemiah from Babylon and the rebuilding of the walls of Jerusalem ("Structure").

The accompanying chronology reflects some of the most recent scholarship on these dates. The dates of the kings of Israel and Judah are given in a simplified form, apart from coregencies.

Events of universal history (Gen. 1–11)

The dates of the events of universal history in Genesis 1–11 are very difficult to determine accurately. The famous Bishop Ussher (1581–1656) combined the biblical data with extrabiblical sources, including Jewish and Christian traditions, and created a dating system for the Old and the New Testaments that has been widely used by Christian readers of the Bible. Calculating that Jesus was born in 4 B.C., Ussher came up with the dates of 4004 for the Creation, 2349 for the Flood, and 2200 for the Tower of Babel (Finegan, 403–5). Ussher's dates were inserted and published in various editions of the King James Bible and were thus used by many biblical scholars and commentators. It must be remembered that dates for this period differ significantly between the various

A CHRONOLOGY OF THE BIBLICAL PERIOD

Events of Universal History (Gen. 1–11)	
	Adam and Eve
	Great Flood
	Tower of Babel

Patriarchs (Gen. 12–50) (approximate dates B.C.)	
2000	Abraham
1900	Isaac
1800	Jacob
1750	Joseph

Exodus/Conquest/Judges (B.C.)	
1260	Exodus
1220	Crossing the Jordan
1220–1045	Judges

United Monarchy (1045–931 B.C.) (dates of reigns)	
1045–1011	Saul
1011– 971	David
971– 931	Solomon

Divided Monarchy (931–722; 931–586 B.C.)	
931	Division of the Kingdom

Israel, or Northern Kingdom (931–722 B.C.)

SELECTED KINGS		PROPHETS	
931–909	Jeroboam		
885–873	Omri		
873–853	Ahab		
			Elijah
841–813	Jehu		
			Elisha
		ca. 760	*Hosea*
		ca. 755	*Amos*
740–732	Pekah		
732–722	Hoshea		
722	Fall of Samaria and Israel		

Judah, or Southern Kingdom (931–586 B.C.)

SELECTED KINGS		PROPHETS	
931–913	Rehoboam		
767–740	Uzziah		
		ca. 740–687	*Micah*
		ca. 740–701	*Isaiah*
740–735	Jotham		
735–715	Ahaz		
715–687	Hezekiah		
701	Assyrian siege of Jerusalem		
687–642	Manasseh		
642–640	Amon		
640–609	Josiah		
		ca. 627–585	*Jeremiah*
			Zephaniah
			Nahum
609	Jehoahaz		
609–598	Jehoiakim		
605 (?)	Daniel and his friends taken to Babylon		
			Habakkuk
597	Jehoiachin		
597	Many exiled to Babylon, including Jehoiachin and Ezekiel		

continued

continued

Judah, or Southern Kingdom (931–586 B.C.)		
SELECTED KINGS		PROPHETS
597–586	Zedekiah	ca. 593–563 *Ezekiel*
586	Destruction of Jerusalem by the Babylonians; exile of Judah to Babylon	

Exile and Return		
	LEADERS & EVENTS	PROPHETS
539	Cyrus conquers Babylon	
538	Some Jews return from Babylon	
520–515	Temple rebuilt and dedicated	*Haggai, Zechariah*
458	Ezra	
445	Nehemiah	
		ca. 400 *Malachi*

Intertestamental Period	
331	Alexander the Great conquers the Persian empire, including Judah
320	Judea under Ptolemaic rule
198	Judea shifts to Seleucid rule
175	Antiochus Epiphanes IV, Seleucid king, comes to throne and eventually outlaws Judaism
167–165	Maccabean Revolt against Seleucid rule resulted in cleansing and rededication of the temple
63	Pompey, Roman general, conquers Jerusalem

New Testament Period	
6–1 B.C.	Birth of Jesus Christ
A.D. 33	Death of Jesus, if born in 1 B.C.
ca. 67–68	Death of Peter and Paul
66–70	First Jewish revolt against Rome
70	Destruction of Jerusalem by the Romans
ca. 95	John the Revelator writes Revelation
135	End of the Bar Kochba Revolt (second Jewish revolt)

biblical textual traditions and versions, so these dates must be viewed with caution.

Patriarchs (Gen. 12–50)

The age of the Patriarchs can best be dated to the Middle Bronze Age, between 2200 and 1550 B.C. Thus, a reasonable date for Abraham can be located between 2200 and 1800. By dating Abraham to 2000 B.C., approximate dates are derived for the Patriarchs (Finegan, 197–224).

Israel in Egypt, the Exodus, the conquest of Canaan, judges

The dating of the sojourn of Jacob and his family in Egypt and the Exodus is open to some discussion. A note in 1 Kings 6:1 says that Solomon began to build the temple in the fourth year of his reign, in the 480th year after the Israelites came out of Egypt. Exodus 12:40 states that the Israelites dwelt in Egypt 430 years. Counting backwards from the reign of Solomon puts the date of the Exodus at 1446 B.C., a date still maintained by some as probable. But many scholars believe that the figure of 480 years is not to be taken as a literal number but rather as a symbolic number derived from twelve times forty years—the period of a generation. The mention of the Israelites building the city of Ramses in Exodus 1:11 makes it likely that the Exodus occurred under Ramses II or his successors. This evidence, as well as the archaeological evidence in the land of Canaan for the conquest and settlement in the thirteenth century B.C., at the end of the Late Bronze Age (1200 B.C.) and the beginning of the Iron Age (1200–1000 B.C.), leads most scholars to postulate a date of ca. 1260 for the Exodus (Finegan, 224–45).

United monarchy (1045–931); divided monarchy (931–722; 931–586)

The dates of the united monarchy (Saul, David, and Solomon) can be derived with relative precision within a decade or two. Likewise, based on the extensive chronological information in the accounts of the kings in the divided monarchy, it is possible to date the reigns of all of the kings of Israel and Judah to within several years. Because the ministries of the prophets are tied to the reigns of the kings of Israel and Judah, it is also possible to date their ministries with relative precision.

The exact date of the destruction and exile of the northern kingdom is somewhat problematic, however. The Babylonian Chronicle and the biblical data (2 Kgs. 17:3–6) put the destruction at 722 B.C., during the last year of the reign of the Assyrian king Shalmaneser V. The annals of his successor, Sargon II, claim the fall of Samaria for Sargon's accession year, 722–721 B.C. Yet, the evidence is in favor of 722 as the correct date. Sargon's claim was likely propaganda referring to his mopping-up operation after Shalmaneser's victory. Thus scholars often give the date of the destruction of the north as 722/1. Likewise, the date of the destruction of Jerusalem by the Babylonians is disputed. According to the Babylonian Chronicle, Zedekiah was appointed king in 597 B.C., in Nebuchadnezzar's seventh year; according to the Bible, Jerusalem was captured in Zedekiah's eleventh year (2 Kgs. 25:2), which would be 587 B.C. But 2 Kings 24:12 says that Zedekiah came to the throne in Nebuchadnezzar's eighth year (rather than the seventh year, as the Babylonian Chronicles would indicate), and therefore the destruction of Jerusalem occurred in 586 B.C. (Finegan, 255–60). Because the portion of the Babylonian Chronicle that deals with the actual years of the siege and destruction of Jerusalem is lost, this discrepancy cannot be satisfactorily resolved. Thus, scholars often give the date of the destruction of Jerusalem as 587/6.

Scholars disagree about whether there were two or three exiles of Jews. The Bible, supported by extrabiblical historical sources, records that on at least two occasions, King Nebuchadnezzar besieged and conquered Jerusalem and took the ruling king of Judah and many citizens into exile to Babylon. The first of these exiles was in 597 B.C. (2 Kgs. 24:10–16), and the second in 586 B.C. (2 Kgs. 25:1–17). The chronological note introducing the book of Daniel, however, mentions another capture of Jerusalem and exile "in the third year of the reign of Jehoiakim" (606–605 B.C.) when Daniel was taken to Babylon (Dan. 1:1–2). This exile is not mentioned in any of the extrabiblical historical sources, and for many scholars it seems to be in conflict with known historical evidence that Nebuchadnezzar did not actually become king until 605 and did not arrive at Jerusalem until the conquest in 597 B.C. Thus, many scholars believe that the date mentioned in Daniel is inaccurate, perhaps due to a misunderstanding of 2 Kings 24:1 and 2 Chronicles 36:5–7, and that the exile referred to in Daniel 1:1–2 is actually the exile of 597 B.C.—meaning that Daniel and Ezekiel went into exile at the same time.

Other scholars maintain that the date in Daniel should be taken seriously, postulating that soon after his victory at Carchemish in 605 B.C., Nebuchadnezzar made a lightning strike, capturing Jerusalem and taking Daniel and his friends into exile. Although this exile is not known from sources other than Daniel, scholars who hold this view argue that it would fit in with evidence in the Babylonian records that Nebuchadnezzar successfully campaigned in the west before his conquest of Jerusalem in 597 B.C. (Finegan, 254).

The Exile, the Return, and the intertestamental period

Because there are many historical sources from this period, the dates of the Exile, the Return, and the intertestamental period are relatively secure.

New Testament period

The date of the birth of Jesus is much discussed and debated. Because the death of Herod the Great, who played a prominent role in the story of the nativity in Matthew 2, is thought to have occurred in 4 B.C., biblical scholars argue that Jesus was born between 6 B.C. and 4 B.C. and provide evidence that the calendar now in use in the western world, the Gregorian calendar, incorrectly calculates the birth of the Savior. Some LDS scholars argue that Doctrine and Covenants 20:1 is a statement that Christ was born in 1 B.C. A few scholars have argued that Herod died in 1 B.C. and thus Jesus may have been born later than 4 B.C. (Finegan, 298–301). Peter and Paul are generally thought to have been killed at the end of the reign of Nero in A.D. 67 or 68, and John the Revelator, whose writings are mentioned in the Book of Mormon (1 Ne. 14:19–27; Ether 4:16), is thought to have written the book of Revelation during the persecutions that occurred in the reign of Domitian (A.D. 81–96).

See also Chronology, Book of Mormon; Israel, historical background of.

BIBLIOGRAPHY

Cogan, Mordechai. "Chronology: Hebrew Bible." *Anchor Bible Dictionary.* Edited by David Noel Freedman. New York: Doubleday, 1992. 1:1003–11.

Donfried, Karl P. "Chronology: Hebrew Bible." *Anchor Bible Dictionary.* Edited by David Noel Freedman. New York: Doubleday, 1992. 1:1011–22.

Finegan, Jack. *Handbook of Biblical Chronology.* Rev. ed. Peabody, Mass.: Hendrickson, 1998.

Smith, Robert F. "Book of Mormon Event Structure: The Ancient Near East." *Journal of Book of Mormon Studies* 5:2 (1996): 98–147.

DRS

Chronology, Book of Mormon The aim of Book of Mormon chronology is twofold: (1) to identify and correlate all phrases dealing with chronology in the text in order to determine the correct dates of the people and events in the Book of Mormon (internal chronology), and (2) to correlate the chronology of the Book of Mormon with the dates in the modern Gregorian B.C./A.D. calendar (external chronology). Knowledge of Book of Mormon chronology can greatly enhance a reader's understanding of the interrelationships of the significant events, personalities, and lessons found in the Book of Mormon narrative.

Mormon's abridgment of the Nephite record preserves the Nephite chronology of the events of their history covering more than one thousand years—from Lehi's departure from Jerusalem, dated six hundred years before the coming of the Messiah (1 Ne. 10:4), to the final battle at Cumorah, 385 years after the coming of Christ (Morm. 6:5). Moroni[2] completed and closed the record more than 420 years after Christ (Moro. 10:1). The chronology of the Jaredite civilization is not so clear. The record of the Jaredites preserved in the book of Ether does not contain enough specific dates to reconstruct the internal chronology of the Jaredites with any degree of certainty. The chronological record of the Jaredites (the book of Ether) is linked primarily to the kingship genealogy, which began with the sons of Jared[1] and ended with king Coriantumr[2], who "was discovered by the people of Zarahemla; and [who] dwelt with them for the space of nine moons" (Omni 1:21). Jared "came forth with his brother and their families, with some others and their families, from the great tower, at the time the Lord confounded the language of the people, and swore in his wrath that they should be scattered upon all the face of the earth; and according to the word of the Lord the people were scattered" (Ether 1:33). Although some references to time are noted, especially in reference to the reigns of the kings, no consistent calendaring system is referred to in the book of Ether. It is generally believed, however, that Jaredite history occurred sometime between 2200 and 130 B.C. (Sorenson, 4–5).

Attempts to correlate the events in Nephite history with the modern calendar can be done with some amount of precision, but exactness is difficult due to uncertainties in biblical chronology and the lack of specific information about the Nephite calendar. The correlation of the events in Jaredite history with the modern calendar is even more difficult.

The Nephite calendar

The Book of Mormon records that the Nephites reckoned their time with days, weeks, months, and years, but it does not include enough information to reconstruct their calendar. In particular, the text does not define how many days were in a Nephite year or whether they used more than one calendar. Lehi and his family were certainly familiar with the calendar used in ancient Israel, which is partially described in the Old Testament. Because the

CHRONOLOGY, BOOK OF MORMON

Nephites lived the law of Moses, it is likely that they continued to use some form of the calendar that was so central to the determination of the various festivals of the law. Unfortunately, the Old Testament does not describe the Israelite calendar with enough detail for it to be reconstructed, either, and it appears from the biblical record that the calendar employed by the Israelites was significantly altered during the course of their history. The calendar described in the Old Testament was a lunar calendar of twelve months that used a new year in the spring (Ex. 12:2; 13:3–4) and one in the fall (Ex. 23:16; 34:22). It was almost certainly calibrated by intercalation (the periodic addition of days, weeks, or months) to maintain the regularity of the seasons, though it is not known how this was done. In addition, Lehi may have been familiar with the calendars used in ancient Egypt (one solar calendar and two lunar) and the calendars used in Mesopotamia (Spackman, "Calendar," 51–53). The Nephite calendar could have been a continuation of any one or more of these several calendars with which they might have been familiar in Jerusalem, or it may have been a variation or combination of any or all of them. Whatever calendar they used may also have developed and been modified throughout the thousand years of their history. It has been suggested that the Nephite calendar could also have been influenced by indigenous peoples with whom the Nephites came into contact in the New World (Spackman, "Introduction," 20–26; "Calendar," 52–56).

Nephite internal chronology

The Nephites carefully kept records of the internal chronology of their history, which they measured by three different systems:

1. Initially the Nephite record keepers calculated their history by counting the years from the time that Lehi[1] and his family left Jerusalem (e.g., Jacob 1:1; Enos 1:25; Mosiah 6:4; 29:46) sometime during the first year of the reign of Zedekiah, king of Judah (3 Ne. heading), six hundred years before the coming of the Messiah (1 Ne. 10:4; 19:8). The Nephites continued to use this system of counting the years from Lehi's departure from Jerusalem to record more than five hundred years of Nephite kingship, from 1 Nephi through the book of Mosiah, up to the time that Mosiah[2] instituted the reign of the judges (1 Ne. 1:4; Jacob 1:9–11; Mosiah 29:46; Alma 1:1).

2. When Mosiah replaced the government by kings with judges, the record keepers dated events in their narrative by the years of the reigns of the judges. This practice began in Mosiah 29 and was used for one hundred years, in the books of Alma and Helaman and in the beginning of 3 Nephi (Mosiah 29:44; Alma 1:1; 3 Ne. 1:1, 26; 2:5–8).

3. In the ninety-second year of the reign of the judges (3 Ne. 1:1), the signs of the birth of Christ were given (3 Ne. 1:15) and the Nephites began to calculate their time from that event (3 Ne. 2:8). This system was used from 3 Nephi through the book of Moroni. It was in the 385th year after the birth of Jesus that Mormon led his people in battle at Cumorah (Morm. 6:5) and after the 420th year that Moroni closed the Book of Mormon (Moroni 10:1).

Nephite external chronology

Three dates in the Book of Mormon can be correlated with biblical events: the commencement of the reign of Zedekiah; the birth of Christ (3 Ne. 1:15; cf. Hel. 14:2–5); and the death of Christ. Each of these events is precisely located in one or more of the Book of Mormon systems of internal chronology. The beginning of the reign of Zedekiah is identified as the year that Lehi left Jerusalem, six hundred years before the coming of Christ. The birth of Christ was calculated as occurring in the ninety-second year of the reign of the judges after six hundred years had passed from the time Lehi had left Jerusalem. The death of Christ is identified as the beginning of the thirty-fourth year after the signs were given of the birth of Christ. Because these dates are held in common with external biblical events, they offer the possibility of correlating Book of Mormon chronology with the modern calendar.

At present, however, it is not possible to correlate these dates precisely with the results of biblical scholarship. Although there is general agreement among biblical scholars as to the exact date of the first year of the reign of Zedekiah in 597 B.C. (Finegan, 257–59), scholars continue to debate the exact year of the birth and hence the death of Jesus Christ, with most putting the birth between 6 and 4 B.C.

The discrepancy can be illustrated by the accompanying table. The issues can be explained as follows:

1. First year of the reign of Zedekiah. The Book of Mormon dates the first year of the reign of Zedekiah to six hundred years before the birth of Christ, the same year Lehi departed from Jerusalem (1 Ne. 1:4; 10:4; 19:8; 2 Ne. 25:19; superscription of 3 Nephi). Based on a series of correlations between the biblical text, ancient Near Eastern texts, and scientifically verifiable astronomical events, scholars date the beginning of the reign of king Zedekiah to 597 B.C. (Finegan, 257–59).

2. Birth of Christ. The Book of Mormon dates the birth of Christ to the ninety-second year of the judges, six hundred years after Lehi's departure from Jerusalem (3 Ne. 1:1, 15, 21, 26). The B.C./A.D. calendar now in use in the Western world, called the Gregorian calendar, places the birth of Jesus in 1 B.C.—the year A.D. 1 being the year after the birth of Jesus. But it is not certain if this calendar accurately identifies the year of the birth of Christ. Because extrabiblical evidence strongly suggests that Herod the Great, an important figure in the nativity narrative (Matt. 2:1; Luke 1:5), died in 4 B.C., most scholars date the birth of Jesus between 6 and 4 B.C. (Finegan, 292–98). Recently, a few scholars have argued that the death of Herod may have occurred in 1 B.C., giving a date between 2 and 3 B.C. for the birth of Jesus (Finegan, 298–301). Many LDS scholars have pointed to Doctrine and Covenants 20:1 as an indication that Jesus was born in 1 B.C. (Lefgren, *April Sixth;* Pratt, "Prophecy," "Passover"). Others have argued that the phrase "being one thousand eight hundred and thirty years since the coming of our Lord" (D&C 20:1) was not meant to be an argument for an exact date for the birth of Jesus but simply to indicate the date A.D. 1830 in the current calendar (see McConkie, 1:349–50 n. 2; Brown et al.).

3. Death of Christ. The Book of Mormon clearly puts the death of Jesus in the beginning of the thirty-fourth year after his birth (3 Ne. 8:5). Thus, the precise date for the death of Jesus depends on the date of his birth. This date closely matches chronological data in the New Testament. The Gospel of Luke says that Jesus began his ministry at "about" age thirty (Luke 3:23), and John records three Passovers in his ministry (John 2:13; 6:4; 11:55), with the possibility of a fourth between the Passovers of John 2:13 and 6:4. If Jesus was born in 1 B.C., then the date of his death would be A.D. 33. From an alternative point of view, a birthdate between 6 and 2 B.C. would give a death date between A.D. 28–32.

Six Hundred Years

Nephi taught that the Messiah would come six hundred years after Lehi left Jerusalem (1 Ne. 10:4; cf. 19:8; 2 Ne. 25:19). That would have been in the first year of the reign of Zedekiah (1 Ne. 1:4; superscription to 3 Nephi). Scholars have placed the beginning of the reign of Zedekiah in 597 B.C. (Finegan, 257–59). Assuming that Christ was born in 1 B.C. gives a discrepancy of three years between the Book of Mormon and the scholarly calculations of the beginning of the reign of Zedekiah. So six hundred years from 597 B.C. would be A.D. 3. If Jesus was born between 6 and 4 B.C., the discrepancy gets larger—seven to nine years—because the date of 1 B.C. allows for only a 591- to 594-year time span instead of six hundred years.

Several explanations for this discrepancy have

EVENT	BOOK OF MORMON	BIBLICAL SCHOLARSHIP
first year of the reign of Zedekiah	600 years before Christ	597 B.C.
birth of Christ	92nd year of judges	
	600 years after Lehi left Jerusalem	6–1 B.C.
death of Christ	34 years after signs of birth	A.D. 28–34

been suggested. Some LDS scholars have simply assumed the Book of Mormon dating is more correct than the dates arrived at by biblical scholars who have not taken into account the data in the Book of Mormon. LDS scholar John Pratt has reasoned that the Book of Mormon dates are compatible with the scholarly biblical dates. Pratt argues that Lehi departed Jerusalem in 601 B.C., exactly six hundred years before the birth of Christ, and that Lehi began to preach in 608 B.C. in the first year of Jehoiakim, whom Nephi called Zedekiah (Pratt, "Prophecy").

Several LDS scholars accept the dating of the birth of Jesus before 4 B.C. and seek to explain the discrepancy in other ways. One has argued that the Nephites used a 360-day calendar without intercalation and that 600 such 360-day years account for the 593 years between 597 B.C. and 4 B.C. (Huber). Another scholar has similarly argued that the Nephites used a 354-day calendar, that Lehi and his family did not leave Jerusalem in the first year of the reign of Zedekiah but later in 587 B.C., just before the destruction (1 Ne. 7:14; 2 Ne. 25:10), and that this gives enough time for 600, 354-day lunar years between 587 and the birth of Jesus in 5 B.C. (Spackman, "Calendar"; "Introduction").

Jaredite chronology

The Jaredite record, as abridged by Moroni[2] from the twenty-four gold plates, contains insufficient chronological information to confidently reconstruct Jaredite chronology. Nevertheless, based on the textual evidence in the Book of Mormon and the Bible, the origin and migration of the Jaredites to the New World is generally supposed to have occurred sometime in the range of dates between approximately 2200 and 1750 and the collapse of Jaredite civilization between 586 and 130 B.C.

The Jaredites claimed their origin "from the tower, at the time the Lord confounded the language of the people" (Omni 1:22; Ether 1:33), usually understood to be a reference to the Tower of Babel (Gen. 11:1–9). Unfortunately, the date of the great tower in Genesis cannot be pinpointed with certainty. The biblical evidence indicates that Peleg was the last of the Shemites to have lived before the age of the great tower (Gen. 10:25) and that Abraham lived five generations (191 years) after Peleg (Gen. 11:17–26). Therefore, it can be deduced from the dates of the generations from Peleg to Abraham, assuming this information is correct in the Bible, that the events surrounding the great tower occurred about 200 years before Abraham. Because Abraham is generally thought to have lived during the Middle Bronze Age (2200–1550 B.C.), the date of the great tower—and thus the origin of the Jaredites—according to biblical reckoning would fall within the range of 2400 to 1750 B.C.

The date of the end of Jaredite civilization can also be calculated, based on evidence in the Book of Mormon, to be between 586 and 130 B.C. The book of Omni records that the last Jaredite king, Coriantumr[2], who survived the destruction of the Jaredite people, appeared among the people of Zarahemla, the Mulekites, and "dwelt with them for the space of nine moons" (Omni 1:20–21). The discovery of Coriantumr by the people of Zarahemla is not dated in Omni, but it had to have occurred after the people of Zarahemla arrived in the land and before the reign of Mosiah[1]. The people of Zarahemla had left Jerusalem at the time of its destruction in 586 B.C. (Omni 1:15–16; Hel. 8:21), and the reign of Mosiah must be dated before ca. 130 B.C. (cf. Mosiah 6:4).

John Sorenson, an anthropologist specializing in Mesoamerica, believes that the data from the Old World, including the contradictory evidence in the biblical tradition, is not reliable. He assigns the tower to an earlier date than traditional biblical scholarship and has thus attempted to synchronize the origin of Jaredite civilization with the beginning of the Mesoamerican Long Count calendar. Based on data from the New World, Sorenson has argued that the Jaredite migration to the New World occurred as early as 3114 B.C., a significant date in the Long Count calendar (4). He further argues that the fall of the Jaredite civilization should be identified with the dramatic fall of the Olmec civilization in ca. 550 B.C. (11). Sorenson thus proposes a date of ca. 550 B.C. for the end of Jaredite civilization and Coriantumr's sojourn among the people of Zarahemla. Sorenson points out that the Lord's promise to Ether (Ether

A CHRONOLOGY OF THE BOOKS OF THE BOOK OF MORMON

This chronology shows the relationship between events, characters, and dates from one book to another according to the B.C./A.D. calendar familiar to modern readers. Approximate B.C./A.D. dates can be deduced from internal Book of Mormon chronology, which is based on three events: Lehi's leaving Jerusalem, the inception of the reign of judges, and the giving of the signs of the birth of Jesus Christ; however, the text of the Book of Mormon does not always supply enough data to make these dates more than approximate. For example, the Book of Mormon does not give the exact dates for the end of the books of 2 Nephi, Jacob, or Mormon or the date of the beginning of the book of Enos. Nor is it possible to assign exact dates in the B.C./A.D. system according to the Gregorian calendar because of the uncertainty of the accuracy of the system itself, because of the uncertainty of the absolute dates of the events from which the internal dating systems of the Book of Mormon derive, and because of a lack of specific information about the Book of Mormon calendar system. Because it is unlikely that any book of the Book of Mormon ended on December 31 and the next book began on January 1, ending dates and beginning dates are overlapped.

1 NEPHI–2 NEPHI	**600–544 B.C.**		
	No specific date is given for the end of 1 Nephi or 2 Nephi		
	600–592 B.C.	**592–559 B.C.**	**559–544 B.C.**
1 Ne. 1–17:4	Lehi leads his family from Jerusalem into the wilderness—*Lehi, Sariah, Laman, Lemuel, Sam, Nephi, Zoram, Ishmael*		
1 Ne. 17:5–2 Ne. 5:33		Lehi and his family build a ship and arrive in the promised land. Lehi's family separates into Nephites and Lamanites	
2 Ne. 5:34–33:15			Ministry of Nephi[1]; Jacob[2] and Joseph[2] ordained priests

JACOB	**544–420 B.C.**
Jacob 1–7	Jacob's ministry—*Jacob, Sherem*
	Neither the date of the end of Jacob's book nor his death date is given in the Book of Mormon. Jacob almost certainly had died long before 420 B.C.

ENOS	**544–420 B.C.**
Enos 1	Record of Enos
	The date of the beginning of Enos' record is not given in the Book of Mormon

JAROM	420–361 B.C.
Jarom 1	Record of Jarom

OMNI	361–130 B.C.
Omni 1	Record of Omni, Amaron, Chemish, Abinadom, Amaleki; king Mosiah[1] discovers people of Zarahemla; people of Zarahemla report having discovered Coriantumr, the last of the Jaredites; Benjamin becomes king

WORDS OF MORMON	about A.D. 385
W of M 1	Mormon delivers the plates to his son and explains his addition of the small plates to the abridged record from the large plates

MOSIAH	200–91 B.C.				
	200–121 B.C.	145–120 B.C.	130–121 B.C.	121 B.C.	120–91 B.C.
Mosiah 1–6			King Benjamin gives his speech and appoints his son Mosiah[2] to be king		
Mosiah 7–8				Ammon[1] goes to the land of Lehi-Nephi and finds the people of Limhi (descendants of the people of Zeniff) in bondage	
Mosiah 9–22	Record of Zeniff: his people leave Zarahemla to go to the land of Lehi-Nephi, are taken into bondage and are finally delivered back to Zarahemla—*Zeniff, king Noah, Gideon, Abinadi, Alma[1], Limhi, Amulon*				
Mosiah 23–24		Alma leads his people out of bondage to Zarahemla			
Mosiah 25–29					Conversion of Alma[2] and the sons of Mosiah[2]; king Mosiah[2] institutes system of judges

continued

continued

ALMA 91–52 B.C.

	91–77 B.C.	77–74 B.C.	74–52 B.C.
Alma 1–16	Ministry of Alma[2]—*Alma, Nehor, Amlici, Nephihah, Amulek, Zeezrom, Zoram[2]*		
Alma 17–27	Ministry of the sons of Mosiah; Alma[2] and the sons of Mosiah return to Zarahemla—*Ammon[2], king Lamoni, king Lamoni's father, Aaron[3], Omner, Himni, Anti-Nephi-Lehies*		
Alma 28–44		Record of Alma[2]—*Korihor, Helaman[2], Shiblon, Corianton*	
Alma 45–63			Record of Helaman: Alma departs; wars between the Nephites and the Lamanites; Nephite migrations—*Captain Moroni, Moronihah, Pahoran[1]*

HELAMAN 52–1 B.C.

	52–24 B.C.	24–7 B.C.	7–6 B.C.	6–1 B.C.
Hel. 1–6	Nephite and Lamanite wars; Gadianton robbers flourish—*Pahoran[1], Pahoran[2], Kishkumen, Pacumeni, Moronihah, Helaman[3], Nephi[2], Lehi[4], Cezoram*			
Hel. 7–12		Prophecy of Nephi[2]—*Seantum, Seezoram*		
Hel. 13–15			Prophecy of Samuel the Lamanite	
Hel. 16				Signs and wonders given: some of the people believe, and some do not

3 NEPHI 1 B.C.–A.D. 34

	1 B.C.–A.D. 34	A.D. 34
3 Ne. 1–7	Signs of Christ's birth given—*Lachoneus[1], Nephi[2], Nephi[3], Giddianhi, Lachoneus[2]*	
3 Ne. 8–30		Christ in America

4 NEPHI	**A.D. 34–321**	
	A.D. 34–201	**A.D. 201–321**
4 Ne. 1:1–22	Church built, peace in the land—*Nephi[4], Amos[1], Amos[2]*	
4 Ne. 1:23–48		Pride, many churches, wickedness, and Gadianton robbers fill the land—*Ammaron*

MORMON	**A.D. 321–401**	
	A.D. 321–385	**A.D. 401**
Morm. 1–7	Mormon's ministry; Nephite and Lamanite wars; destruction of Nephites at the hill Cumorah	
Morm. 8–9		Moroni[2] finishes the record of Mormon

ETHER	**ca. 2200 (?)–130 B.C.**		
	See the discussion of the date 2200 B.C. in Chronology, Book of Mormon		
	ca. 2200 B.C.	**between 2200–130 B.C.**	**between 586–130 B.C.**
Ether 1–6	Jaredites leave Old World and travel to the promised land—*Jared[1], brother of Jared*		
Ether 7–11		History of the Jaredite civilization in the promised land—*Orihah, Shule, Cohor, Akish, Emer, etc.*	
Ether 12–15			*Ether, Coriantumr[2], Shiz*

MORONI	**A.D. 401–421**
Moro. 1–10	Record of Moroni

DRS

11:20–21) to bring "another people to possess the land" implies that the later migrants to the promised land of America (Nephites and Mulekites) had not yet arrived in the day of Ether, the last Jaredite prophet. In that case, Sorenson deduces, the end of Jaredite civilization occurred early in the period 586 to 130 B.C. rather than later (4–5). Based on these assumptions, he has created a plausible chronology distributing the reigns of the kings and events of Jaredite civilization between approximately 3100 and 550 B.C. (9–11).

Another prominent LDS anthropologist specializing in Mesoamerica, Bruce W. Warren, also attempts to correlate Jaredite chronology with the Olmec Long Count calendar and the rise and fall of Olmec civilization ("Timechart"). He dates the Flood at 3127 B.C. (*New Evidences,* 14) and the great tower and the Jaredite migration from the Old World (Ether 1:1–6:21) to the period of 2650 to 2600 B.C. Warren identifies the rise of Jaredite civilization, from Orihah to Heth (Ether 6:22–9:35), with the Early Formative I period (2600–1850 B.C.); the period of the Jaredites from Shez to Riplakish (Ether 10:1–8) as the Olmec Early Formative II and III periods (1850–1350 B.C.); the period from Morianton to Ahah (Ether 10:9–11:10) as the Middle Formative I and II periods (1350–400 B.C.); and the decline and end of Jaredite civilization from Ethem to Ether (Ether 11:11–15:34) with the Middle Formative III period (400–236 B.C.). He argues that the final Jaredite destruction at the hill Ramah occurred in 301 B.C. (Warren, *New Evidences,* 322–23).

Warren argues that names such as Aha, Gilgal, Heshlon, Ramah, Seth, and Shurr in the Jaredite narratives are reminiscent of Hebrew names common in Syro-Palestine at the time of the Mulekites. He argues that they may be best explained by the Jaredites' contact with the Mulekites and thus argues that the fall of Jaredite civilization must have come some time after the arrival of the Mulekites in the New World.

See also Chronology, Bible; Jaredite civilization.

BIBLIOGRAPHY

Brown, S. Kent, C. Wilfred Griggs, and H. Kimball Hansen. "Review of April Sixth by John C. Lefgren." *Brigham Young University Studies* 22 (Summer 1982): 375–83.

Finegan, Jack. *Handbook of Biblical Chronology.* Rev. ed. Peabody, Mass.: Hendrickson, 1998.

Huber, Jay H. "Lehi's 600-Year Prophecy and the Birth of Christ." FARMS Preliminary Report, 1982.

Lefgren, John C. *April Sixth.* Salt Lake City: Deseret Book, 1980.

McConkie, Bruce R. *The Mortal Messiah: From Bethlehem to Calvary.* 4 vols. Salt Lake City: Deseret Book, 1979–81.

Pratt, John. "Book of Mormon Chronology." *Encyclopedia of Mormonism.* Edited by Daniel H. Ludlow et al. 4 vols. New York: Macmillan, 1992. 1:169–71.

———. "Lehi's 600-Year Prophecy of the Birth of Christ." Unpublished manuscript.

———. "Passover: Was It Symbolic of His Coming?" *Ensign* (January 1994): 38–45.

———. "The Restoration of Priesthood Keys on Easter 1836. Part 1: Dating the First Easter." *Ensign* 15 (June 1985): 59–68.

———. "Yet Another Eclipse for Herod." *Planetarium* 19 (December 1990): 8–14.

Smith, Robert F. "Book of Mormon Event Structure: The Ancient Near East." *Journal of Book of Mormon Studies* 5:2 (1996): 98–147.

Sorenson, John. "The Years of the Jaredites." FARMS Preliminary Report, 1969.

Spackman, Randall P. "Introduction to Book of Mormon Chronology: The Principal Prophecies, Calendars, and Dates." Provo, Utah: FARMS, 1993.

———. "The Jaredite/Nephite Lunar Calendar." *Journal of Book of Mormon Studies* 7:1 (1998): 48–59, 71.

Warren, Bruce W., with Blaine M. Yorgason and Harold Brown. *New Evidences of Christ in Ancient America.* Provo, Utah: Stratford Books, 1999.

———. "Timechart of Jaredite Kingdoms." Unpublished manuscript.

DRS

Church, great and abominable *See* Great and abominable church.

Church discipline The formal process used by ecclesiastical leaders to help church members resolve grievous sins and to insure "that there should be no iniquity" in the Church (Moro. 6:7). After Alma[1] "poured out his whole soul to God" (Mosiah 26:14) concerning how to judge church members who had fallen into iniquity, the Lord instructed him that "whosoever transgresseth against me, him shall ye judge according to the sins which he has committed; and if he confess his sins before thee and me, and repenteth in the sincerity of his heart, him shall ye forgive, and I will forgive him also. Yea, and as often as my people repent will I forgive them their trespasses against me. . . . And whosoever will not repent of his sins the same shall not be numbered among my people; and this shall be observed from this time forward" (Mosiah 26:29–30, 32). The Lord taught Alma that this pattern of judgment in the Church was parallel to what would occur at the Final Judgment (Mosiah 26:20–28).

Church discipline is sometimes necessary in the repentance process (Alma 42:16). Mormon wrote, "It became expedient that those who committed sin . . . should be admonished by the church" (Mosiah 26:6). "The gospel is to save men, not to condemn them," President Harold B. Lee taught, "but to save, it is sometimes necessary to confront and to discipline as the Lord has directed" (118).

In addition to helping transgressors repent, formal church discipline serves to cleanse the Church. When sin goes unchecked in the Church, the Spirit of the Lord withdraws, and the entire institution is adversely affected (Cannon, 26:139). The Lord's authorized leaders have a solemn obligation to protect the Church from such danger (Alma 5:59–60; 4:10; D&C 20:83; 107:72; Taylor, 78). Christ taught his disciples that those who will not repent "shall not be numbered among my people, that [they] may not *destroy* my people, for behold I know my sheep, and they are numbered" (3 Ne. 18:31; italics added; Smith, 66–67). "Nevertheless," Jesus continued, "ye shall not cast [them] out of your synagogues . . . for unto such shall ye continue to minister; for ye know not but what they will return and repent . . . and I shall heal them" (3 Ne. 18:32). Jesus' instructions, which teach intolerance of sin and yet compassion for the transgressor, echo his words to the Prophet Joseph Smith: "For I the Lord cannot look upon sin with the least degree of allowance; nevertheless, he that repents and does the commandments of the Lord shall be forgiven" (D&C 1:31–32; cf. Alma 45:16).

Alma's implementation of the Lord's instructions was a blessing to individuals and to the Church, for "they began again to have peace and to prosper exceedingly in the affairs of the church, walking circumspectly before God, receiving many, and baptizing many" (Mosiah 26:37).

Moroni[2], writing on various aspects of the Nephite Church (Moro. 2–6), noted the use of witnesses in the Church discipline process: "They were strict to observe that there should be no iniquity among them; and whoso was found to commit iniquity, and three witnesses of the church did condemn them before the elders, and if they repented not, and confessed not, their names were blotted out" (Moro. 6:7). This pattern for the perfection of the Saints taught in the Book of Mormon also guides the modern Church (D&C 20:83; 42:80–83; 102; 134:10).

See also Blotted out; Justice, law of; Mercy; Repentance.

BIBLIOGRAPHY

Cannon, George Q. *Journal of Discourses*. 26 vols. London: Latter-day Saints' Book Depot, 1854–86.

Lee, Harold B. *The Teachings of Harold B. Lee*. Edited by Clyde J. Williams. Salt Lake City: Bookcraft, 1996.

Smith, Joseph. *Teachings of the Prophet Joseph Smith*. Selected by Joseph Fielding Smith. Salt Lake City: Deseret Book, 1976.

Taylor, John. Conference Report, April 1880.

BLT

Church of God (Christ) in ancient America

Three priesthood-directed organizations, or churches, of varying structure were established among the Nephites over a period of six hundred years. Although there is no specific mention of the first of these churches in the days of Nephi[1], its existence is clearly implied. A Christ-centered theocracy was established before 570 B.C., with Nephi functioning as both spiritual leader and nominal king (2 Ne. 5:18; 6:2). He consecrated his younger brothers, Jacob[2] and Joseph[2], "priests and teachers" in God's "holy order," the Melchizedek Priesthood (2 Ne. 5:26; 6:2; Jacob 1:18). Nephi and his brethren "labor[ed] diligently" in testifying of Christ, the gospel, and its relationship to the LAW OF MOSES (2 Ne. 25:23–30; 31:1–33:1). After the deaths of Nephi and Jacob, other PRIESTS and TEACHERS are mentioned, together with "exceedingly many prophets" (Enos 1:22; cf. Jarom 1:11).

CHURCH OF GOD (CHRIST)

The plates of brass containing the writings of Moses and the ancient prophets down to Jeremiah[1] constituted the basic Nephite scripture (1 Ne. 5:10–13). Although Nephi wrote, "The law [of Moses] hath become dead unto us," the law and its rituals were strictly observed (2 Ne. 25:25; 1 Ne. 4:15–16; 2 Ne. 5:10; Jarom 1:5), and a temple patterned after that of Solomon's was built (2 Ne. 5:16).

Nevertheless, some time late in the third century this original Nephite society came to an end. The seeds of its destruction were planted during the reign of Nephi's successor (Jacob 1:15–16). Jacob prophesied that if the Nephites did not repent, the Lamanites would conquer the land of Nephi "and the Lord God will lead away the righteous out from among you" (Jacob 3:4). Later prophets also warned that transgression would result in these Nephites being "destroyed from off the face of the land" (Jarom 1:10).

The generations came and went as unnamed prophets and priests labored to persuade the Nephites to honor their covenants with God. In the end, prophetic warnings were to no avail. According to Amaron, by ca. 280 B.C. "the more wicked part of the Nephites were destroyed" (Omni 1:5). Thereafter, in fulfillment of the prophecy of Jacob, Mosiah[1] led an exodus of "as many as would hearken unto the voice of the Lord" from the land of Nephi toward the north where they united with the people of Zarahemla (Omni 1:12–14). Some years later, when Zeniff's colony returned to the land of Nephi, they became subject to the Lamanites who, as prophesied, had overrun the land (Omni 1:27–30; W of M 1:13; Mosiah 9). The former Nephite inhabitants had either been destroyed or assimilated into the Lamanite culture (Alma 3:9–10, 15).

The people of Zarahemla—descendants of exiles from Jerusalem at the time of Zedekiah[1]—spoke a corrupted language, had no scriptures, and no belief in God (Omni 1:15–17; Hel. 8:21). Consequently, they had to be schooled in the preparatory law of Moses before they could receive the higher law of Christ. The preparatory law "is the gospel of repentance and of baptism, and the remission of sins, and the law of carnal commandments" (D&C 84:26–27). Thus, although the prophets knew of and were committed to Christ (Omni 1:26), the learning and the living of the preparatory law appears to have been the dominant religious concern of the people during the reigns of Mosiah and his son Benjamin.

In king Benjamin's day false Christs, false prophets, and false teachers came among the people. Benjamin "with the assistance of the holy prophets" labored with his might to teach the people and establish peace in the land (W of M 1:16–18). Eventually, in 124 B.C. king Benjamin, quoting the words of an angel, taught of Christ as "the Lord Omnipotent," the Savior and Redeemer of mankind (Mosiah 3). Wrought upon by the Spirit of the Lord and entering into a covenant with Christ, the people became the "children of Christ, his sons, and his daughters" (Mosiah 4:3; 5:7). They had taken his name upon them at last. Benjamin appointed priests among his people to teach the gospel and remind the people of the oath they had made (Mosiah 6:3).

Alma[1], a priest of king Noah[3] and the sole convert of the martyred prophet Abinadi (Mosiah 17:1–4), restored the gospel and the Church among his converts twenty years before he and his followers arrived in Zarahemla. Alma and his followers "were called the church of God, or the church of Christ, from that time forward" (Mosiah 18:17; cf. Alma 5:3; ca. 147 B.C.). This is the first specific reference in the Book of Mormon to a church of God among the Nephites.

Upon Alma's arrival in Zarahemla in ca. 121 B.C., he was authorized by king Mosiah[2] to form branches or "churches" of the one "church of God" throughout "all the land of Zarahemla" and to ordain priests to declare Alma's doctrines (Mosiah 25:19–24; 26:8–12). Having "power and authority from God" (Alma 5:3) to restore the Church in his day, Alma was acknowledged by the Nephites in the land of Zarahemla as "the founder of their church" and the first presiding HIGH PRIEST (Mosiah 29:42, 47). According to Mormon, this was "the first church which was established among them after their transgression" (3 Ne. 5:12; cf. Omni 1:12–13).

CHURCH OF GOD (CHRIST)

In 91 B.C., Alma[1] died, and his son Alma[2] assumed leadership of the Church (Mosiah 29:42–45). The office of ELDER is mentioned for the first time in his administration (Alma 4:7; 6:1). During this period the first Lamanite conversions, numbering in the thousands, took place (Alma 23:4–18). In time, in an astonishing reversal of roles, Lamanites, such as the prophet Samuel[2], became missionaries to the Nephites (Hel. 6:4–6; 13–16). But, as before, the conversions of many were shallow. They accepted God's blessings but not his commandments (Hel. 12:1–2). Consequently, apostasy was more the rule than the exception. So the Church in general see-sawed between fervent repentance and rampant apostasy (Hel. 12:1–7). This vacillation continued down to the time of Christ's glorious appearance in A.D. 34.

Whereas there had been a pronounced break between Nephi[1]'s original priestly organization in the land of Nephi and the multibranched organization established by Alma[1] throughout the land of Zarahemla, the third church described in 3 Nephi 11–26 emerged out of Alma's church, which still existed at the time of the great destructions accompanying Jesus' crucifixion (3 Ne. 7:15–26). One dispensation ended, and a new dispensation began. The law of Moses was fulfilled with Jesus' death (3 Ne. 15:4–5). For the first time, twelve disciples were appointed to preside over the Church (3 Ne. 11:18–22; 12:1; 18:36–37). Blood sacrifice was replaced with a new ordinance, one that Jesus personally introduced to commemorate his atonement: the SACRAMENT of the Lord's Supper (3 Ne. 18:1–11). And every person baptized with water was baptized "with fire and with the Holy Ghost" (3 Ne. 12:1–2; 26:17).

In testifying of himself, in recounting his teachings to the Jews, in making plain the principles and ordinances of life and salvation, and in explaining the relationship of latter-day Israel to the Gentiles, Jesus bound together the eastern and western churches in the common bonds of the gospel. Fully established, the Church was formally named the Church of Jesus Christ (3 Ne. 27:3–10).

Within two years "the people were all converted" (4 Ne. 1:2). Having "all things common among them" (4 Ne. 1:3), the Church enjoyed unblemished prosperity, equality, and happiness for more than a century and a half, experiencing a spiritual and temporal oneness never before or since attained in Israel (4 Ne. 1:1–18). Christ personally expounded all things from the beginning of time to the Final Judgment (3 Ne. 26:1–4). These Saints are the only people to whom the visions of the brother of Jared[1] have as yet been revealed (Ether 3:21–22; 4:1–2).

Tragically, the Church of Jesus Christ, which reached its spiritual zenith through the Redeemer's personal ministry, experienced its nadir four centuries later (3 Ne. 27:30–32). Indeed, for sheer barbarity and unmitigated cruelty, nothing that had previously occurred even began to equal that which was to come in the closing moments of Book of Mormon history (Moro. 9:7–21). The unity of the Church was broken in A.D. 194 when a "small part" of the people assumed the name Lamanites (4 Ne. 1:20). From then on the gulf between the people steadily grew wider as many false churches sprang up (4 Ne. 1:26, 29, 34, 41). By A.D. 301, both Nephites and Lamanites had become "exceedingly wicked one like unto another" (4 Ne. 1:45).

In A.D. 322, the first of the final series of wars between the two peoples began (Morm. 1:8). Soon thereafter, the three translated disciples were taken away, miracles ceased, spiritual gifts were lost, "and the Holy Ghost did not come upon any" (Morm. 1:13–16; cf. 8:10). The gifts of God were replaced with the counterfeits of Satan. It was a time of SORCERY, witchcraft, and magic: "The power of the evil one was wrought upon all the face of the land" (Morm. 1:19; cf. 2:10).

In A.D. 360 Mormon made one last attempt to redeem the Church, but his efforts failed (Morm. 3:2–3). This once-enlightened people had succumbed to the grossest darkness. Mormon wrote: "And there never had been so great wickedness among all the children of Lehi, nor even among all the house of Israel, according to the words of the Lord, as was among this people" (Morm. 4:12).

A heavenlike season of perfect righteousness and peace had blessed the lives of three generations of Nephites and Lamanites (1 Ne. 12:11;

3 Ne. 27:32). Now that season was over, and a long night of spiritual darkness spread across the western hemisphere. Dawn would not break again for fourteen hundred years. It would await the coming of another visitation from on high, another prophet, another Church of Jesus Christ.

See also Church discipline; Holy order of God; Nephite civilization; Priesthood among the Nephites; Temples.

RT

Church of the devil *See* Great and abominable church.

Church of the Lamb of God The Church of Jesus Christ, authorized and directed by Jesus Christ, who is the Lamb of God, the Messiah (1 Ne. 12:18; D&C 76:85). The phrase "church of the Lamb of God" appears three times in the Book of Mormon, twice in 1 Nephi 14:10, and once in 1 Nephi 14:12. A similar phrase, "church of the Lamb," is used twice (1 Ne. 14:12, 14).

The Savior organized his church in the meridian of time in Galilee and Judea, authorizing chosen leaders to direct the Church and administer the ordinances of salvation (Matt. 10:1–4; Eph. 4:11–16). Similarly, he organized his Church among the Nephites (3 Ne. 11:21–22; 12:1–2). In both cases the Church was driven "into the wilderness" through apostasy (D&C 86:1–3), ceasing to be the true Church of Jesus Christ administering the fulness of the gospel. In the dispensation of the fulness of times, the Church of the Lamb of God was restored to the earth and designated by revelation "The Church of Jesus Christ of Latter-day Saints" (D&C 115:4; 1:17–30; 20:1–16; JS–H 1:11–19; Smith, 166).

Nephi[1] was shown the church of the Lamb of God in the latter days, made up of the "saints of God," the covenant people of the Lord. "Its numbers were few . . . and their dominions upon the face of the earth were small" (1 Ne. 14:12). Nephi also saw "multitudes upon the face of all the earth, among all the nations of the Gentiles" gathered together "to fight against the Lamb of God" (1 Ne. 14:13). In the midst of this opposition Nephi beheld that "the power of the Lamb of God . . . descended upon the saints of the church of the Lamb . . . and they were armed with righteousness and with the power of God in great glory" (1 Ne. 14:11–14). Nephi assured the righteous that they "need not fear; for thus saith the prophet, they shall be saved, even if it so be as by fire" (1 Ne. 22:17). He further explained that when the Lord would return to the earth to "reign in dominion, and might, and power, and great glory," those who "fight against Zion shall be cut off," Satan shall have "no power over the hearts" of the children of men, and the Lord's people, gathered from all nations of the earth, will dwell in righteousness and peace under the direction of the "Holy One of Israel" (1 Ne. 22:19–28).

As the Lord's second coming draws near, there will be "a great division among the people" (2 Ne. 30:10), for "the devil shall have power over his own dominion. And also the Lord shall have power over his saints, and shall reign in their midst, and shall come down in judgment upon Idumea, or the world" (D&C 1:35–36). An 1845 proclamation of the Twelve Apostles addressed to the rulers and people of all nations declares, "As this work progresses in its onward course, and becomes more and more an object of political and religious interest and excitement, no king, ruler, or subject, no community or individual, will stand *neutral.* All will at length be influenced by one spirit or the other; and will take sides either for or against the kingdom of God, and the fulfilment of the prophets, in the great restoration and return of his long dispersed covenant people" (*Messages,* 1:257). Perhaps such a statement lends meaning to the words of the angel to Nephi: "Behold there are save two churches only; the one is the church of the Lamb of God, and the other is the church of the devil; wherefore, whoso belongeth not to the church of the Lamb of God belongeth to that great church, which is the mother of abominations" (1 Ne. 14:10). Similarly, the Savior declared, "He that is not with me is against me; and he that gathereth not with me scattereth abroad" (Matt. 12:30; cf. 2 Ne. 10:16). To be "with" or "against" the Lord is not simply a matter of where one claims membership but

CHURCHES, FALSE

how one behaves or does not behave. The degree to which one withholds support from, or fights against, the cause of Christ, the Church, or the people of the Lamb of God, to that degree he promotes the cause of the church of the devil. And the degree to which one sustains and promotes the cause of Christ, to that degree he identifies himself with the Church of the Lamb of God.

Ultimately, to qualify for all the blessings promised faithful members of the Church of the Lamb of God, one must have faith in Christ, repent of one's sins, receive the saving ordinances, and obey the law of the celestial kingdom (2 Ne. 31; 3 Ne. 11:31–41; 27:13–21; D&C 76:50–70; 88:22–28).

See also Churches, false; Great and abominable church.

BIBLIOGRAPHY

Smith, George Albert. Conference Report, April 1947.

Messages of the First Presidency of The Church of Jesus Christ of Latter-day Saints. 6 vols. Compiled by James R. Clark. Salt Lake City: Bookcraft, 1965–75.

LED

Churches, false Nephi[1] and Moroni[2] prophesied concerning the characteristics and teachings of false churches among the Gentiles in the latter days (2 Ne. 26:20–21, 28; Morm. 8:26–41). They foresaw that there would be very few people not associated with false churches (1 Ne. 14:12; 2 Ne. 28:14; Morm. 8:36). In part, this "stumbling block, that [the Gentiles] have built up many churches" (2 Ne. 26:20) would be created because of the loss of "plain and precious" gospel truths (1 Ne. 13:25–29, 32). Some members would be full of pride, deny the power and miracles of God, preach their own wisdom and learning for gain, mistreat the poor, and cause envy, strife, and malice (2 Ne. 26:20–21). Their pride would be exhibited in various ways. For example, many of these churches would contend with one another that theirs was the Lord's church and teach false doctrines that justified committing sin without serious consequences (2 Ne. 28:3, 7–12). Leaders and teachers would even envy the members of their own churches (Morm. 8:28). Pride would further reveal itself through persecutions and ill will toward one another, as well as through the love of money and material possessions at the expense of helping the needy and afflicted (2 Ne. 28:12–14; Morm. 8:32–40).

Other teachers of false doctrine would deny the guiding voice of the Holy Ghost and plead for allegiance to human authority with claims that either God did not exist or that God was no longer a God of miracles because he had given all his power unto men (2 Ne. 28:4–6). Some would also be guilty of offering forgiveness of sins in exchange for money; that is priestcraft, which is preaching for the purpose of getting gain (2 Ne. 26:29–31; Morm. 8:32–33). Still others would deny the existence of hell and the devil, as well as deny the need for more of the word of God (2 Ne. 28:21–30). Nephi and Moroni both warned that all who continued to teach and practice these things would not escape the judgments of God (2 Ne. 28:9–10, 15–16, 23; Morm. 8:33, 41). Yet, Nephi further testified, the Lord, who is always eager to forgive, would be merciful to those who repent of these sins and come unto him (2 Ne. 28:17, 32).

Additionally, the Book of Mormon chronicles the apostasy that caused a proliferation of false churches and teachings beginning approximately 165 years after the appearance of Christ in America. The characteristics of these churches somewhat mirror the churches Nephi and Moroni foresaw in the latter days (4 Ne. 1:26–29, 34, 41).

The term "church" may sometimes be taken in a nonspecific sense of an "assembly . . . or association of people" (Robinson, 34). An angel of the Lord declared to Nephi that false churches are any churches that are not the true church of Christ (1 Ne. 14:10). Viewed in this light, collectively "false churches" may also refer to any religious, political, educational, business, or social group that practices or teaches that which is contrary to the true Church of Christ. Individually, membership in these false churches is "based more on who has your heart than on who has your records" (Robinson, 37).

See also Book of Mormon, selected purposes of, to confound false doctrine; Church of the Lamb of God; Great and abominable church; Priestcraft; Prophecy in the Book of Mormon.

BIBLIOGRAPHY

Robinson, Stephen E. "Warring against the Saints of God." *Ensign* 18 (January 1988): 34–39.

FJ

Cimeter *See* Weapons.

Circumcision, law of *See* Law of circumcision.

Circumspectly *See* Appendix C.

Cite *See* Appendix C.

Clapped *See* Appendix C.

Cohor[1] *See* Jared[1], posterity of.

Cohor[2] *See* Jared[1], posterity of.

Cohor[3] Jaredite who lived in the days of Ether and Coriantumr[2]. All the record indicates about Cohor is that his children did not repent (Ether 13:17).

Colophons Brief introductions or outlines of what will follow, or brief summaries of what preceded in the book. Colophons are a typical feature of ancient Near Eastern literature. Nephi[1] set the pattern for the writing of colophons. At the book heading before chapter 1 of 1 Nephi, he indicates that this book is an "account of Lehi and his wife Sariah, and his four sons." In 1 Nephi 1:1–4, following the final words of the heading, "This is according to the account of Nephi; or in other words, I, Nephi, wrote this record," he continues his colophon by introducing himself again ("I, Nephi"), indicating his parentage ("having been born of goodly parents" and "my father, Lehi"), stating the period of time in which he is writing ("in the commencement of the first year of the reign of Zedekiah, king of Judah"), discussing the language in which he is writing ("I make a record in the language of my father, which consists of the learning of the Jews and the language of the Egyptians"), and describing his own circumstances as background and justification for writing this book ("I was taught somewhat in all the learning of my father," "having been highly favored of the Lord"). Several other books of the Book of Mormon contain colophons: the headings of 2 Nephi and Jacob; Words of Mormon 1:1–5; the headings to chapters 23 and 24 of Mosiah; a heading at the beginning and a summary at the end of the book of Alma, with headings before chapters 5, 7, 9, 17, 21, 36, and 45; an extended heading in Helaman with headings before chapters 7 and 13; and headings at the beginning of 3 Nephi and 4 Nephi. The title page of the Book of Mormon is itself a lengthy colophon, describing the background, content, and authorship of the book.

See also Book of Mormon, ancient Near Eastern roots of.

SDR & JAT

Columbus, Christopher Latter-day Saint apostles and prophets have taught that Christopher Columbus was the man Nephi[1] saw in his prophetic vision when, among other events, he saw the discovery and colonization of the PROMISED LAND (1 Ne. 13:12). In this passage Nephi recorded, "And I looked and beheld a man among the Gentiles, who was separated from the seed of my brethren by the many waters; and I beheld the Spirit of God, that it came down and wrought upon the man; and he went forth upon the many waters, even unto the seed of my brethren, who were in the promised land."

Elder Orson Pratt identified Columbus as the subject of 1 Nephi 13:12 in a footnote in the 1879 edition of the Book of Mormon. Indeed, Columbus himself proclaimed that he was guided by the Spirit in his voyage of discovery: "With a hand that could be felt, the Lord opened my mind to the fact that it would be possible to sail. . . . This was a fire that burned within me. . . . Who can doubt that this fire was not merely mine, but also of the Holy Spirit . . . urging me to press forward?" (West and Kling, 105). On another occasion Columbus wrote, "Our Lord with provident hand unlocked my mind, sent me upon the sea, and gave me fire for the deed. Those who heard of my emprise called it foolish, mocked me, and laughed. But who can doubt but that the Holy Ghost inspired me?" (Wassermann, 19–20). President Spencer W.

Kimball testified, "I'm sure that [God] inspired a little boy, Christopher Columbus, to stand on the quays in Genoa, Italy, and yearn for the sea. He was filled with the desire to sail the seas, and he fulfilled a great prophecy made long, long ago, that this land, chosen above all other lands, should be discovered. And so when he was mature, opportunity was granted to him to brave the unknown seas, to find this land . . . and to open the door, as it were" (427).

Several modern-day apostles and prophets have also taught that Columbus and the founding fathers of the United States of America were inspired by God to help prepare America to become the seat of the restoration of the gospel of Jesus Christ in this last dispensation. For example, George Q. Cannon taught, "Columbus was inspired to penetrate the ocean and discover this Western continent, for the set time for its discovery had come; and the consequences which God desired to follow its discovery have taken place—a free government has been established on it. The men who established that Government were inspired of God. . . . We believe it was a preparatory work for the establishment of the kingdom of God" (Cannon, 14:55).

Without question, Columbus' first voyage to America is one of the most significant events of the history of humanity. His expedition brought two worlds into permanent contact with each other, the Old World of Europe and Asia, and the New World of the Americas, and it set in motion a chain of events that would transform both worlds forever. Among other things, Columbus' encounter with the Americas opened the door to a flood of exploration, colonization, missionary work, and fortune-seeking. Latter-day Saints honor Columbus for being a forerunner to the restoration of the gospel of Jesus Christ in these latter days. He laid the foundation for the establishment of a nation that would "be set up as a free people by the power of the Father, that [the Book of Mormon and the fulness of the gospel] might come forth" (3 Ne. 21:4).

See also Nephi[1]'s vision.

BIBLIOGRAPHY

Cannon, George Q. *Journal of Discourses*. 26 vols. London: Latter-day Saints' Book Depot, 1854–86.

Jensen, DeLamar. "Columbus and the Hand of God." *Ensign* 22 (October 1992): 7–13.

Kimball, Spencer W. *Teachings of Spencer W. Kimball*. Edited by Edward L. Kimball. Salt Lake City: Bookcraft, 1982.

Wassermann, Jacob. *Columbus: Don Quixote of the Seas*. Translated by Eric Sutton. Boston: Little, Brown, and Company, 1930.

West, Delno C., and August Kling. *The* Libro de las profecias *of Christopher Columbus*. Gainesville: University of Florida Press, 1991.

AKG

Com[1] *See* Jared[1], posterity of.

Com[2] *See* Jared[1], posterity of.

Combinations, secret *See* Secret combinations.

Commandment(s) Directions from the Lord as to how to live and act. OBEDIENCE to the commandments brings happiness, temporal blessings, and eternal salvation (1 Ne. 22:30–31; Mosiah 2:24, 41; 12:33; Alma 7:16; 12:31–32; 3 Ne. 12:19–20; 18:14). By keeping the commandments one also demonstrates love for the Savior and a willingness to follow him (2 Ne. 31:10; cf. John 14:15).

Commandments often have both a blessing (for obedience) and a curse (for disobedience) attached to them. For example, one of the most frequently repeated themes of the Book of Mormon is that "inasmuch as ye shall keep my commandments ye shall prosper in the land; but inasmuch as ye will not keep my commandments ye shall be cut off from my presence" (2 Ne. 1:20 see also v. 9; 1 Ne. 2:20; 2 Ne. 4:4; Jarom 1:9; Mosiah 1:7; Alma 36:30; 3 Ne. 5:22). Additionally, the reader is taught that the Lord prepares a way for his commandments to be kept (1 Ne. 3:7; 17:3), that one covenants to keep the commandments at baptism (Mosiah 18:10; cf. 2 Ne. 31:7; Alma 7:15), that a primary purpose of scripture is to preserve the commandments (1 Ne. 4:14–16; 5:21; Mosiah 1:3–5), that those who have the commandments are held to a higher degree of accountability (2 Ne. 9:27; Alma 5:18), and that knowing and obeying the commandments is a prerequisite for receiving revelation (1 Ne. 15:11; Alma 12:9).

Jesus Christ set the supreme example of

obedience by fulfilling the will and commandments of the Father (3 Ne. 11:11; cf. 15:13–15; 16:3; 20:10).

Some specific commands include to believe in Christ, repent, be baptized, and receive the Holy Ghost (e.g., 2 Ne. 2:21; 9:23; 31:14–18; Mosiah 16:12; Alma 9:12; 3 Ne. 11:32; 12:19; 27:20; Morm. 7:10), to have charity (2 Ne. 26:30), to avoid priestcraft (2 Ne. 26:29; 3 Ne. 30:2), to pray (Mosiah 26:39; 3 Ne. 20:1; Ether 3:2), and to keep the TEN COMMANDMENTS (Mosiah 13).

Alma[2] taught that God gave Adam and Eve commandments "*after* having made known unto them the plan of redemption" (Alma 12:31–32; italics added). This order of teaching indicates that commandments are best understood in light of God's whole plan of salvation. Such understanding of the commandments inspires obedience.

Most important is the Savior's commandment to "come unto me" (3 Ne. 12:19–20; 18:25; 27:20; Moro. 7:34; Ether 4:13–18). The point and purpose behind every commandment is to bring one to Christ, for it is only by coming to him that one may be saved (Moro. 10:32–33; cf. Mosiah 5:8).

KMM

Common, all things *See* All things common.

Comnor, hill Hill near the valley of Shurr on which Coriantumr[2] gathered his Jaredite armies and sounded a trumpet inviting Shiz's armies to battle. In the last of the three ensuing conflicts, Coriantumr received so many "deep wounds" that he "was carried away as though he were dead" (Ether 14:28–30).

Conceive by the power of the Holy Ghost Alma[2] prophesied that Mary would "be overshadowed and conceive by the power of the Holy Ghost" (Alma 7:10). Abinadi testified that the Son of God would be "conceived by the power of God" (Mosiah 15:3). The angel Gabriel explained to Mary that "the Holy Ghost shall come upon thee, and the power of the Highest shall overshadow thee: therefore also that holy thing which shall be born of thee shall be called the Son of God" (Luke 1:35). Clearly, if the power of God were to attend Mary, the power of the Holy Ghost would of necessity be present also, "for no [mortal] man has seen God at any time in the flesh, except quickened by the Spirit of God" (D&C 67:11; cf. Moses 1:11). President Ezra Taft Benson has stated the position of the Church regarding this matter: "The Church of Jesus Christ of Latter-day Saints proclaims that Jesus Christ is the Son of God in the most literal sense. The body in which He performed His mission in the flesh was sired by that same Holy Being we worship as God, our Eternal Father. Jesus was not the son of Joseph, nor was He begotten by the Holy Ghost. He is the Son of the Eternal Father" (4).

See also After the manner of the flesh; Condescension of God.

BIBLIOGRAPHY

Benson, Ezra Taft. *Come unto Christ.* Salt Lake City: Deseret Book, 1983.

LED

Concubines The Book of Mormon does not define *concubine,* but in the biblical world it meant a wife of inferior legal status, such as war captive or a domestic servant. Her situation might be limited because of her legal standing, but in general her relationship with her husband differed little from that of a regular wife.

In the Book of Mormon, the word is found exclusively in the plural, in nine instances. It is used in only three contexts, each with the phrase "many wives and concubines": (1) the teaching of Jacob[2] regarding the wicked desires of some Nephites (Jacob 1:15; 2:24, 27; 3:5), (2) the sinful behavior of king Noah[3] and his priests (Mosiah 11:2, 4 [twice], 14), and (3) the wicked rule of the Jaredite king Riplakish (Ether 10:5).

KPJ

Condemnation A divine censure or penalty invoked upon those who violate God's laws and commandments. For one to receive condemnation, a law must first exist, one must be subject to that law, and one must of his own volition trespass that law. All little children and those who are "without the law" (Moro. 8:22) are saved through the redemptive power of the Atonement and thus are exempt from condemnation (2 Ne. 9:25; Mosiah 3:16, 21; 15:24–25). In such cases there is no need for repentance. Mormon explained, "Repentance is unto them that are under condemnation and under the curse of a broken law" (Moro. 8:22–24; cf. Alma 42:17–24). One may incur condemnation through either sins of commission (3 Ne. 18:33) or sins of omission (e.g., Mosiah 26:31; Moro. 9:6). The degree of condemnation one receives is related to the light and knowledge one possesses (D&C 82:3). Thus, the willful rejection of a known commandment invites "great condemnation" (Jacob 2:34; cf. 2 Ne. 9:27; Hel. 14:19) and leads to a loss of light and knowledge (2 Ne. 28:30; Alma 12:9–11). Mormon testified, "And if it so be that they [the Gentiles] will not believe these things, then shall the greater things be withheld from them, unto their condemnation" (3 Ne. 26:8–10). Ultimately, the rebellious and the unfaithful bring condemnation upon themselves (Alma 3:19; Hel. 14:29).

RCF

Condescension of God The word *condescension* means "to descend" (from the Latin *com,* an intensive, and *descendere* "to descend"). In English the word means that an entity of superior status does something beneath its rank for the benefit of someone else. The phrase "condescension of God" occurs twice in the Book of Mormon, both in NEPHI[1]'S VISION of the TREE OF LIFE: one has reference to God the Father (1 Ne. 11:16), and the other refers to Jesus Christ (1 Ne. 11:26). The condescension of God is a manifestation of love. Nephi[1] learned from his vision that the meaning of the tree was "the love of God, which sheddeth itself abroad in the hearts of the children of men" (1 Ne. 11:22). Three references are made to the Lord's "condescension[s] unto the children of men" describing God's grace and mercy (2 Ne. 4:26; 9:53; Jacob 4:7).

Applied to the Father

Nephi saw in a vision the tree of life. When he asked the Spirit of the Lord for an interpretation of the tree, the Spirit replied, "Knowest thou the condescension of God?" (1 Ne. 11:16). Nephi then beheld "the mother of the Son of God, after the manner of the flesh" and the birth of Jesus Christ who was the "Son of God," even "the Son of the Eternal Father" (1 Ne. 11:18–21). Elder Bruce R. McConkie interpreted this passage as a reference to the condescension of the Father: "Thus the condescension of God (meaning the Father) consists in the fact that though he is an exalted, perfected, glorified Personage, he became the personal and literal Father of a mortal Offspring born of mortal woman" (155).

Applied to the Son

Nephi also saw a rod of iron that led to the tree of life. Again the Spirit said, "Look and behold the condescension of God!" (1 Ne. 11:25–26). This time Nephi saw a vision of the Savior: his baptism, his ministry, the calling of the Twelve Apostles, Jesus healing the sick and casting out devils, his crucifixion for the sins of the world, and the multitudes of the earth gathered up to fight against the Lamb of God. Elder McConkie interpreted this as the condescension of the Son: "And the condescension of God (meaning the Son) consists in the fact that though he himself is the Lord Omnipotent, the very Being who created the earth and all things that in it are, yet being born of mortal woman, he submitted to all the trials of mortality" (155). Other Book of Mormon prophets described the ministry of Jesus Christ in similar terms. King Benjamin taught that "the Lord Omnipotent who reigneth, who was, and is from all eternity to all eternity, shall come down from heaven among the children of men" (Mosiah 3:5), and Abinadi prophesied: "God himself shall come down among the children of men, and shall redeem his people" (Mosiah 15:1).

Thus the Father and the Son came down to earth to provide a Savior who "descended below all things that He might rise above all things" (First Presidency). Their condescension ensured that their children could "be lifted up at the last day" (3 Ne. 27:22).

See also Atonement, the; Fruit; Love of God.

BIBLIOGRAPHY

First Presidency. "Christmas Greeting." *Deseret News,* December 17, 1904.

McConkie, Bruce R. *Mormon Doctrine.* 2d ed. Salt Lake City: Bookcraft, 1966.

DRS

Confession of sin *See* Repentance.

Confounded *See* Appendix C.

Consecrate To do something "with sacredness," to dedicate, devote, and focus oneself toward the realization of a sacred end. In addition, it is to set apart and designate for sacred purposes, as when priests and teachers are called and put in place in the Church (2 Ne. 5:26). The Saints of the Most High consecrate their resources to God when they enter into the law of consecration and stewardship (3 Ne. 26:19; 4 Ne. 1:3; D&C 42:30). If they are submissive, the people of the Lord may have their desires and their works consecrated by God to their eternal gain (2 Ne. 32:9; 33:4).

HDG

Consecration, law of *See* All things common.

Consign *See* Appendix C.

Constrain *See* Appendix C.

Constrained *See* Appendix C.

Contention Throughout the Book of Mormon, "contentions" occurred among the people, always with negative consequences. The term is synonymous to or used in conjunction with such words and expressions as "wars" (1 Ne. 12:3; Jacob 7:26), "dissensions" (Jarom 1:13), "hatred" (Jacob 7:26), "fight[ing] and quarrel[ing]" (Mosiah 4:14), stirring hearts to anger (Alma 51:9; 3 Ne. 11:29), "disputations" (4 Ne. 1:2), and "great doubtings" (3 Ne. 8:4). The prophet Mormon was grieved by contention among the people (Moro. 8:4), and the Savior clearly taught the Nephites that "the devil . . . is the father of contention," and anyone "that hath the spirit of contention is not of me." He proclaimed, "This is not my doctrine, to stir up the hearts of men with anger, one against another; but this is my doctrine, that such things should be done away" (3 Ne. 11:29–30).

Contention arose throughout the Book of Mormon as the product of greed, pride, and ambition; it was the disrupter of peace, the forerunner of war. For example, Alma 50:25–26 details the contentions that arose over claims to certain Nephite lands, while Alma 51:2–9 describes the beginning of contentions over the Nephite form of government. Those who wanted "kings were those of high birth" who themselves "sought to be kings; and they were supported by those" ambitious for "power and authority" (Alma 51:8). These internal contentions diverted and enervated the Nephite nation, very nearly delivering it into the hands of its external enemies. Only the valor of men like Moroni[1], Helaman[2], and Pahoran[1], fighting in the strength of the Lord, preserved it. In the end, contention contributed to the destruction of both the Nephite and the Jaredite nations.

The record verifies that contention accompanies wickedness. When the people are righteous and loving, peace prevails and the Church and its people flourish. When they are not righteous and loving, wars and contentions abound. The nearly two hundred years of peace and happiness that followed the Savior's ministry in the New World were a direct result of the absence of "envyings," "strifes," "tumults," and all other forms of wickedness (4 Ne. 1:16). The antidote to contention is said to be the "love of God" (4 Ne. 1:15). Mormon declared the marvelous results of a contention-free society: "Surely there could not be a happier people among all the people who had been created by the hand of God" (4 Ne. 1:16).

BRM

Conversion *See* Born again.

Corianton A younger son of Alma[2], Corianton (ca. 74 B.C.) accompanied his father and others on a mission to the Zoramites[2]. But on that mission, much to his father's consternation, he was distracted by the harlot Isabel and he forsook the ministry. His actions damaged the missionary effort, for as Alma told him, "when they saw your conduct they would not believe in my words" (Alma 39:11). Chapters 39 through 42 of Alma record the prophet's teachings in his effort to bring his son to repentance. One senses in these chapters not only Alma's great knowledge and spiritual power but also his tender concern for a son who had fallen into error. Through inspiration, Alma taught Corianton basic gospel doctrine, tailoring his instruction to specific concerns raised by Corianton. In so doing, Alma used the word of God to nullify any of the rationalizations Corianton might have employed in an effort to excuse his behavior (Alma 39:3–6; 40:1; 41:1; 42:1, 30). That Corianton responded repentantly to his father's words is suggested by Alma's sending him forth again to "declare the word" and bring those who had fallen into error "unto repentance" (Alma 42:31). The record confirms that Corianton did return to his ministry (Alma 43:1–2; 49:30). After the reestablishment of peace and the passing of Helaman[2] and Moroni[1], Corianton is said to have left to carry provisions to the Nephites who emigrated north by sea (Alma 63:10).

The inclusion of these chapters by Mormon fulfills important Book of Mormon purposes. Alma's words to Corianton confirm and amplify biblical teachings on vital gospel subjects. They also contain truths that have special application to the latter days. For example, Alma taught the seriousness of immorality (Alma 39:5–6), condemning fornication and showing its place in the hierarchy of grievous sins. By analyzing the narrative, the reader living in a time of rampant immorality can gain insight about how to remain morally pure. Moreover, Alma's words to Corianton teach those who succumb to this sin the necessary steps to true REPENTANCE, the doctrines that make repentance possible, and the eternal consequences that await the wicked as well as the righteous.

Alma's teachings to his son clarify other doctrines as well. In compelling prose, he affirmed the antiquity of the gospel (Alma 39:15–19) and presented priceless truths regarding the resurrection and the spirit world (Alma 40), the law of restoration (Alma 41), the plan of salvation and God's placing cherubim and the flaming sword in Eden to prevent Adam and Eve from partaking of the tree of life after their fall (Alma 42:2–6), the effects of the Fall and the need for redemption (Alma 42:6–14), and the relationship between justice and mercy (Alma 42:15–25).

Not to be overlooked is the contribution the Corianton story makes to parents and teachers seeking help in bringing a wayward child or sin-bound adult back to the fold. Alma sought to change his son's behavior by teaching him gospel doctrine, an effective antidote for sin. In Alma's view, the word of God had a "powerful effect upon the minds" of human beings, more powerful "than the sword, or anything else" (Alma 31:5).

See also Chastity.

MA

Coriantor *See* Jared[1], posterity of.

Coriantum[1] *See* Jared[1], posterity of.

Coriantum[2] *See* Jared[1], posterity of.

Coriantumr[1] *See* Jared[1], posterity of.

Coriantumr[2] The last Jaredite king and sole survivor of his people. More a warrior than a diplomat, Coriantumr[2] was "studied . . . in all the arts of war and all the cunning of the world" (Ether 13:16). He reigned during a time of intense crime, secret combinations, political upheaval, and constant civil war. A contemporary of the prophet Ether, he and his people were warned on several occasions to repent. The Lord had said specifically that unless Coriantumr and his household repented, Coriantumr alone would survive to witness the destruction of the entire Jaredite nation (Ether 13:20–22). The prophecy was ignored, and it was fulfilled.

The account of Coriantumr chronicles a series of battles over a number of years, battles in which Coriantumr was wounded several times by those who sought his throne. Only after "nearly two millions of his people" were slain did Coriantumr begin "to repent of the evil which he had done" and "remember the words" of the prophets (Ether 15:2–3). But it was too late. His efforts to negotiate peace with his arch enemy Shiz failed (Ether 15:4–6, 18). Shiz's relentless pursuit of Coriantumr was fueled by the loss of his brother in battle and by his desire to prove untrue a prophecy recorded by Ether (Ether 14:24).

After four years of building their armies—consisting of Jaredite men, women, and children, all of whom had lost the Spirit of God and were filled with vengeance and anger (Ether 15:9–22)—the armies of Coriantumr and Shiz engaged in a final battle that lasted a matter of days. By the last hour, only Coriantumr and Shiz were alive. In a dramatic episode, Coriantumr beheaded Shiz (Ether 15:30–31).

Ether had prophesied that Coriantumr would witness "another people receiving the land for their inheritance" (Ether 13:21). This prophecy was fulfilled when Coriantumr "was discovered by the people of Zarahemla; and he dwelt with them for the space of nine moons" (Omni 1:21) until his death (Ether 13:21).

MOR

Coriantumr[3] A Nephite defector esteemed for his "strength and . . . great wisdom" by the Lamanite king Tubaloth, who led Lamanite armies against the Nephites (Hel. 1:16). Coriantumr boldly captured the Nephite capital city of Zarahemla but was subsequently slain in battle as the Nephites reclaimed their cities (Hel. 1:15–33). The story of Coriantumr adds yet another name to the list of hardened dissenters whose defection to the Lamanites proved deadly for the Nephites.

KJW

Corihor[1] *See* Jared[1], posterity of.

Corihor[2] Jaredite who lived in the days of Ether and Coriantumr[2]. All the record indicates about Corihor is that his children did not repent (Ether 13:17).

Corihor, land of and valley of Jaredite regions to which Shiz and his armies fled after being defeated by the troops of Coriantumr[2]. Sweeping off all in their path who would not join them (Ether 14:26–27), the armies of Shiz camped in the valley of Corihor. From there they answered Coriantumr's challenge to a fierce and deadly battle on the hill Comnor (Ether 14:28–29).

Corom *See* Jared[1], posterity of.

Corruption, incorruption Words used in the Book of Mormon to contrast the nature of mortal things and immortal things, of TEMPORAL things and spiritual things. In all cases, except for Lehi[1]'s more general use of the terms in his discussion of the need for opposition in all things (2 Ne. 2:11), "corruption" refers to the mortal body, which is subject to death and dissolution, and "incorruption" refers to the immortal body, which is resurrected, SPIRITUAL, and will abide forever (2 Ne. 9:7; Mosiah 16:10; Alma 5:15; 11:45; 12:18; 40:2; 41:4; Morm. 6:21).

See also Mortal, mortality; Resurrection, the.

LED

Costly apparel Jacob[2], Alma[2], and Mormon warned against the wearing of costly apparel, or expensive attire and costly ornaments, as indicative of excessive pride and hearts set upon worldly riches. Wearing costly apparel, they implied, is too costly for the soul, obtained as it is at too great a sacrifice: the loss of eternal life. Jacob chastened his people, whose pride was manifest in "the costliness of [their] apparel" (Jacob 2:13). The wicked Nehor's pride was evidenced, Mormon wrote, in his own "very costly apparel" (Alma 1:6). Mormon included the wearing of costly apparel in a long list of sins that characterized those who did not belong to the Nephite Church in Alma[2]'s day (Alma 1:32; ca. 90 B.C.). Later Alma rebuked the Church for the same prideful display (Alma 5:53; cf. 4:6).

Mormon described the effects of pride and prosperity on his people, who, only one hundred sixty-seven years after Christ's ministry, "had become exceedingly rich" (4 Ne. 1:23), rejected "the true church of Christ" (4 Ne. 1:26), and began to be "lifted up in pride, such as the wearing of costly apparel, and all manner of fine pearls, and of the fine things of the world" (4 Ne. 1:24). Alma the Younger rebuked the Zoramites[2], whose worldliness he called on God to witness: "Behold, O my God, their costly apparel . . . and all their precious things" (Alma

31:28). He warned them of the eternal consequences of preferring materialism to the designs of God. From the example of one prosperous group of Nephites, it appears that avoiding costly apparel is one key to avoiding the negative effects of prosperity (Alma 1:25–31).

RHC

Countenance The radiance of one's appearance or demeanor, reflecting one's spiritual state. Alma[2] linked spiritual rebirth to having God's image engraved upon one's countenance (Alma 5:14, 19). The LIGHT that emanates from a Christlike life is discernible in the countenances of individuals who have been purified through the Atonement (3 Ne. 19:25; cf. 13:22–23). The apostle Paul said of his own rebirth, "Christ liveth in me" (Gal. 2:20). Conversely, the absence of this light in the countenance of the wicked is a witness against them (2 Ne. 13:9).

ACS

Covenant people of the Lord Although the phrase "covenant people of the Lord" occurs only six times in the Book of Mormon (1 Ne. 14:14; 15:14; 2 Ne. 30:2; Morm. 3:21; 8:15, 21), the concept of a "covenant people" belonging to the Lord is a major theme of that sacred record. On one level, the terminology points to inheritors of the Lord's covenant with Abraham (1 Ne. 15:14–18; 2 Ne. 29:14). On another, it refers to recipients of the covenant made with the Israelites at Sinai (1 Ne. 17:40; Ether 4:15). Such covenant people include Jews (2 Ne. 25:15–19; Morm. 3:21), the house of Israel, including all the descendants of Israel, or Jacob (1 Ne. 22:3–12), and the "children of men" (Moro. 7:31–32).

As with all covenant relationships initiated by the Lord, blessings come for obedience (Mosiah 4:3; 5:2–9) as well as penalties or curses for disobedience (2 Ne. 9:1, 27–38). The Lord calls his covenant people "my people" (2 Ne. 29:14), and such persons who faithfully keep their covenants are allowed to dwell "with God in a state of never-ending happiness" (Mosiah 2:41; cf. Alma 34:36).

SKB

Covenant(s) A solemn agreement between two or more parties. God makes covenants with individuals and peoples promising certain blessings for obedience to his will. One important purpose of the Book of Mormon is "to show unto the remnant of the House of Israel what great things the Lord hath done for their fathers; and that they may know the covenants of the Lord" (Title Page). Accordingly, God's covenants are an essential element of the Book of Mormon. The term "covenant" and its variants appear 154 times in the Book of Mormon.

Two major types of covenant relationships are found in the scriptures, which may be referred to as vertical covenants and horizontal covenants. Vertical covenants are agreements and vows made between God and man; horizontal covenants are promises and oaths between man and man. Approximately three-fourths of the covenant citations in the Book of Mormon refer to sacred relationships between God and mortals in the vertical dimension, either collectively (such as with the house of Israel or the posterity of Lehi[1]), or individually, through special covenant ordinances such as baptism or in private vows and promises (e.g., Mosiah 18:10–13; 21:31–32; Alma 7:15). Those with whom God makes covenants are referred to as a "covenant people" (e.g., 1 Ne. 14:14; 2 Ne. 6:13, 17). The Jews are referred to as an ancient covenant people (2 Ne. 29:4–5), but God makes it clear that being part of a covenant people is more dependent upon righteousness than genealogy (e.g., 2 Ne. 30:2). Examples of peoples with whom God has made covenants include members of the house of Israel, who were promised that they would ultimately be gathered and redeemed both spiritually and temporally (e.g., 1 Ne. 22:6–12; 2 Ne. 10:7; 29:1, 14; 3 Ne. 5:24–26; 16:5–12; 20:21–31), and Lehi's posterity, a remnant of Israel who were promised that as a people they would "not utterly be destroyed . . . but that [God] would preserve them; and in future generations they shall become a righteous branch unto the house of Israel" (2 Ne. 9:53). Examples of covenants God has made with individuals include the covenant God made with Abraham, which promised Abraham that through his posterity "all the kindreds of the earth" would be blessed (1 Ne.

15:18; 3 Ne. 20:25), God's covenant to Lehi that the promised land of America would "be a land for the inheritance of [his] seed" (2 Ne. 1:5; cf. 1 Ne. 13:30; 3 Ne. 15:12–13), the covenant to Enos that the Book of Mormon would eventually be brought forth to the Lamanites (Enos 1:16), the promise to Alma[2] that he would have eternal life (Mosiah 26:20), and the promise to Joseph[1] that a righteous branch of Israel would be raised up from him, that the Messiah would be "made manifest unto them in the latter days," and a "CHOICE SEER" descended from him would play a vital role in restoring God's covenants (2 Ne. 3:3–7). At the end of the Book of Mormon, Moroni[2] summarized one of God's greatest covenants with his children: "And again, if ye by the grace of God are perfect in Christ, and deny not his power, then are ye sanctified in Christ by the grace of God, through the shedding of the blood of Christ, which is in the covenant of the Father unto the remission of your sins, that ye become holy, without spot" (Moro. 10:33). The Book of Mormon bears witness that God has, does, and will remember and keep his covenants (e.g., 1 Ne. 17:40; 19:15; 22:11; 2 Ne. 10:15; Enos 1:17; 3 Ne. 5:25; 16:11; 29:3, 8; Morm. 8:23).

Nephi[1] was told by an angel that the book he beheld in vision among the Gentiles (the Bible) was "a record of the Jews, which contain[ed] the covenants of the Lord" (1 Ne. 13:23). Unfortunately, the great and abominable church subsequently took away many of those gospel covenants (1 Ne. 13:26, 28). Nephi received the promise, however, that in the last days those covenants would be restored and fulfilled, especially by the coming forth of the Book of Mormon and the restoration and spreading of the gospel through the work of faithful Gentiles who would be "numbered among" (1 Ne. 14:2) the covenant people (1 Ne. 13:23–14:17; cf. 15:12–19; 22:3–27; 3 Ne. 20:21–31; 21:1–7, 12–29).

Less often in the Book of Mormon, agreements or covenants, also called OATHS, were made (horizontal dimension) between individuals or groups of people (e.g., Mosiah 9:6; Alma 44:14–20; 46:20, 35; 51:6; 53:17; 62:16). Sometimes covenants were entered into to facilitate evil, such as covenants and oaths associated with SECRET COMBINATIONS (e.g., Alma 37:27, 29; Hel. 1:11–12; 2:3; 6:21–30; 3 Ne. 6:28–30).

See also Abrahamic covenant; Israel, covenants unto; Joseph[1], covenants unto.

VLL

Cowdery, Oliver *See* Witnesses of the Book of Mormon.

Creation, the God's act of bringing into existence the heavens, earth, and all things therein. Many of the greatest prophet-teachers in the Book of Mormon, as well as God himself, taught the doctrine of the Creation. Their statements place the Creation at the heart of the Father's grand, eternal plan of salvation, along with the Fall and the ATONEMENT of Jesus Christ. The Creation, the Fall, and the Atonement are, according to Elder Bruce R. McConkie, "the three pillars of eternity" and are inextricably linked to one another. The close association between "these three divine events . . . inseparably woven together into one grand tapestry" (McConkie, *Witness,* 81) is summarized by Moroni[2]: "Behold he [God] created Adam, and by Adam came the fall of man. And because of the fall of man came Jesus Christ, even the Father and the Son; and because of Jesus Christ came the redemption of man" (Morm. 9:12). The teachings of Ammon[2] and Aaron[3] to Lamoni and his father also reflect this seminal relationship (Alma 18:36, 39; 22:12–13).

At least nine other important aspects concerning the Creation are presented in the Book of Mormon. Many of these truths were likely understood from the brass plates, which contained the five books of Moses with its account of the Creation (1 Ne. 5:10–12; Alma 22:12). What is said of the Creation in the Book of Mormon is consistent with the accounts of the Creation in the King James Version of the Bible as well as scripture of the Restoration (e.g., Alma 22:12; Gen. 1:26; Moses 2:26):

1. The Creation is the direct result of God's all-encompassing power, will, wisdom, and purposes (2 Ne. 2:13–15; Jacob 4:9; Mosiah 4:9; 5:15; cf. D&C 29:30–31; Moses 1:31, 33). If there were no God, "there could have been no creation" (2 Ne. 2:13).

2. God created the heavens, the earth, and all

things therein (2 Ne. 2:14; Mosiah 4:9; 5:15; Alma 22:10–11; Morm. 9:11).

3. Because God created all things, he is above all his creations; he speaks, and his creations obey (Jacob 4:9; Mosiah 5:15; cf. D&C 88:41; Abr. 3:16–19).

4. The God who created the heavens, the earth, and all things that in them are is the Lord Jesus Christ, the Redeemer (Mosiah 5:15; 3 Ne. 9:15; Morm. 9:11), who is also JEHOVAH of the Old Testament (3 Ne. 15:5). When the prophets, as well as Jehovah himself, say that he (Jehovah) created all things, they were speaking in broad terms and referring to the principle of divine investiture of authority: "Jehovah was, under the direction and by appointment of the Father, the executive in the creation. He created all things on earth, except man. 'When it came to placing man on earth, there was a change in Creators. That is, the Father himself became personally involved. All things were created by the Son, using the power delegated by the Father, except man. In the spirit and again in the flesh, man was created by the Father'" (McConkie, *Promised*, 62; qtd. in McConkie et al., 4:278).

5. God created all things for a specific purpose: "The earth that it should be inhabited . . . his children that they should possess it" (1 Ne. 17:36; cf. Moses 1:39). Joseph Smith learned that marriage and family life lie at the core of God's reason for creating the earth and its inhabitants: "For marriage is ordained of God unto man . . . that he should have one wife, and they twain shall be one flesh, and all this that the earth might answer the end of its creation; and that it might be filled with the measure of man, according to his creation before the world was made" (D&C 49:15–17).

6. God created the heavens, the earth, and man by the power of his word in a seemingly miraculous way to the understanding of mortal beings (Morm. 9:17). Although humankind does not and cannot now know all the particulars about the Creation, the Lord has promised that such knowledge will be revealed in a future day (D&C 101:32–34).

7. God created man after his own image, indicating, as the Lord himself said, that there is a profound similarity between man and God as well as between the physical bodies and spirits of mankind (Ether 3:15–16; cf. Alma 18:34; 22:12; Moses 1:6; 3:5; Gen. 1:26).

8. God created Adam, who was the first man and the first parent (1 Ne. 5:11; Alma 22:12; Morm. 9:12). This truth was taught to the ancient patriarchs from the very beginning (Moses 3:7).

9. God created all things in a paradisiacal, immortal state before the fall of Adam, after which the earth entered a lower, fallen condition (2 Ne. 2:22). Of four distinct phases through which God's created things have passed or will pass before their final, eternal state, the Book of Mormon provides information on three. No reference can be found in the Book of Mormon regarding the first phase, or spirit creation, of "all things," which is known from Moses 3:5 and Doctrine and Covenants 29:31–34, but the Book of Mormon does teach of a premortal existence of mankind (Alma 13:3–5). The second phase of created things is the paradisiacal or physical-spiritual state, when there was no death and Adam was not subject to the vicissitudes of mortality before his fall (2 Ne. 2:15–22). The third phase of creation is the mortal, temporal, or natural state that was introduced by the Fall, in which all things became subject to death and humans began to experience pain, suffering, and a sinful nature (2 Ne. 2:19, 23–26; Mosiah 3:11, 19; Alma 42:7–14; Ether 3:2). The fourth phase is the paradisiacal, millennial condition, when Satan will have no power over the hearts of the people and "cannot be loosed for the space of many years," when Jesus Christ will reign (1 Ne. 22:26), and people and animals will live together in peace (2 Ne. 21:6–9).

See also Fall of Adam and Eve, the; Heaven; Man, creation of; Plan.

BIBLIOGRAPHY

McConkie, Joseph Fielding, Robert L. Millet, and Brent L. Top. *Doctrinal Commentary on the Book of Mormon.* 4 vols. Salt Lake City: Bookcraft, 1987–92.

McConkie, Bruce R. *A New Witness for the Articles of Faith.* Salt Lake City: Deseret Book, 1985.

———. *The Promised Messiah.* Salt Lake City: Deseret Book, 1978.

ACS

Cross *See* Appendix C.

Cross, suffer his *See* Suffer his cross.

Cross yourself To cross is to erase, cancel, preclude, or stop (Webster). Corianton, errant son of Alma[2], was counseled to "go no more after the lusts of your eyes, but cross yourself in all these things" (Alma 39:9). Thus Alma seemed to be calling his son to "take up his cross" and deny himself of ungodliness and worldly lusts (JST Matt. 16:25, 26), to put off the natural man (Mosiah 3:19), and repent—literally, to "turn away from" (2 Ne. 9:45) or to work at cross purposes to deeds and attitudes that reflect a fallen or unredeemed nature.

BIBLIOGRAPHY

Webster, Noah. *An American Dictionary of the English Language.* 1828.

RLM

Crosses *See* Appendix C.

Crucify, crucified A form of punishment practiced by such peoples as the Assyrians, Persians, and Romans that brought about death by prolonged suspension from a cross. Nephi[1] knew of crucifixion, having seen the Savior "lifted up upon the cross and slain for the sins of the world" (1 Ne. 11:33). Christ attributed symbolic significance to being "lifted up." He taught his disciples, "I had been lifted up upon the cross, that I might draw all men unto me, that as I have been lifted up by men even so should men be lifted up by the Father, to stand before me, to be judged of their works" (3 Ne. 27:14). Jacob[2] learned that "because of priestcrafts and iniquities" those at Jerusalem would "stiffen their necks against [Christ], that he be crucified" (2 Ne. 10:3–5). Additionally, the family of Lehi[1] knew of Christ's crucifixion from Neum's prophecy recorded on the brass plates (1 Ne. 19:10). After Christ's resurrection, 2,500 people testified of his crucifixion, having seen with their eyes and felt with their hands "the prints of the nails in his hands and in his feet," adding their witness that he was the promised Messiah of whom all the prophets had foretold (3 Ne. 11:15).

CF

Crying from the dust A phrase, or variations of it, used in two ways by Book of Mormon prophet-writers.

First, "crying from the dust" refers to their individual messages, testimonies, and records that would be read and taught long after they had died and their physical bodies returned to the dust, or were buried in their graves. Thus, they would seem to "speak as if it were from the dead" (2 Ne. 27:13; 3:19–20; Morm. 9:30; Moro. 10:27). Isaiah's prophetic metaphor of the dead speaking or whispering "out of the dust" (Isa. 29:4) was clearly understood by Nephite prophets to be their words or records, which would come forth at a future time. For example, Nephi[1] prophesied, "Those who shall be destroyed [the Nephites] shall speak [cry] unto them [their descendants living in the last days] out of the ground, and their speech shall be low out of the dust" (2 Ne. 26:16). Nephi consciously wrote his record with this in mind: "I speak unto you as the voice of one crying from the dust" (2 Ne. 33:13).

Second, the concept is used by Moroni[2] to refer to the pleas of departed Saints, which cry out for fulfillment of the Lord's promises or for "vengeance" (justice) (Ether 8:24) upon the wicked (Morm. 8:21–24; Ether 8:23–25; cf. 2 Ne. 28:10; 3 Ne. 9:11).

The concept of truth coming forth from the earth also applies to the Book of Mormon itself, a record sealed up and hid in the ground but brought forth from the earth by the Lord in modern times (Morm. 8:16, 26; cf. Moses 7:62).

See also Familiar spirit.

ACS

Cubit A measurement of length used commonly in the ancient Near East, referred to in the Book of Mormon only in Jesus' sermon at the temple (3 Ne. 13:27). Although the standard size of the cubit seems to have varied somewhat through time and among cultures, it was roughly equivalent to the distance from the elbow to the tip of the fingers, or about 18 inches. In teaching the "twelve whom he had chosen" in the Americas about their dependence on God, Jesus asked, "Which of you by taking thought can add

The Crucifixion of Christ; *courtesy VRL.*

one cubit unto his stature?" (3 Ne. 13:25, 27; cf. Matt. 6:27; Luke 12:25).

TBB

Cumber *See* Appendix C.

Cumeni, city of Nephite city captured by the Lamanites (Alma 56:13–14) and then retaken when Helaman[2] and his army surrounded the city and cut off supplies to the Lamanite army within (Alma 57:7–12; ca. 63 B.C.). Soon another Lamanite army arrived with reinforcements and provisions for the troops at Cumeni, but Helaman and his forces defeated them. Helaman attributed the victory to the return of a group of soldiers who had been sent to escort Lamanite prisoners to Zarahemla and to the faith and fortitude of the 2,060 STRIPLING WARRIORS (Alma 57:17–23).

Cumenihah Nephite military leader killed with his ten thousand troops in the last battle between the Nephites and Lamanites (Morm. 6:14; A.D. 385).

See also Cumorah, battle of.

Cumoms *See* Animals.

Cumorah, battle of The final conflict between the Nephites and Lamanites took place approximately A.D. 385 in "the land of Cumorah, by a hill which was called Cumorah" (Morm. 6:2). It was the culmination of continual wars waged between two wicked peoples. The leader of the Nephite armies was the prophet Mormon. Nephite men, women, and children gathered under his direction at Cumorah and fearfully waited for the superior Lamanite armies to fall upon them. At least 230,000 Nephite soldiers were killed. From the top of the hill Cumorah, the wounded Mormon lamented over the loss of his people while he and twenty-four survivors beheld the bodies of the dead strewn upon the battlefield (Morm. 6:10–11, 17–22). Among the survivors was Mormon's son Moroni to whom, just prior to the time of the battle, Mormon entrusted the plates upon which he had made his inspired abridgment of the Nephite records. A few other surviving Nephites escaped to the land southward following the battle at Cumorah, but they were later hunted down by the Lamanites and destroyed (Morm. 6:15; 8:2).

The battle of Cumorah fulfilled prophecy. Approximately one thousand years earlier Nephi[1] saw in vision that "because of the pride of [his] seed, and the temptations of the devil," the seed of his brethren (Lamanites) would overpower the Nephites (1 Ne. 12:19–20; 2 Ne. 26:10, 18; cf. Jacob 5:40). Further, Alma the Younger confided to his son Helaman[2] that "in four hundred years from the time that Jesus Christ shall manifest himself unto them . . . the people of Nephi shall become extinct" (Alma 45:9–11). The reason for such great consequences is "they shall sin against so great light and knowledge" (Alma 45:12; cf. 9:18–23; Hel. 15:17). The destruction of the Nephite nation at Cumorah confirms the principle that "whatsoever nation shall possess [the promised land] shall serve God, or they shall be swept off . . . when they are ripened in iniquity" (Ether 2:9).

CJO

Cumorah, hill The modern-day hill Cumorah is a glacial deposit called a drumlin, one of hundreds in upstate New York, and is located in the township of Manchester about three miles southeast of the Joseph Smith Sr. farm. In September 1823 the angel Moroni showed Joseph Smith the hill and told him that buried there was a book written on GOLD PLATES containing an account of the former inhabitants of this land and the fulness of the gospel as delivered by the Savior (JS–H 1:34). Joseph wrote, "I knew the place the instant that I arrived there. . . . On the west side of this hill, not far from the top, under a stone of considerable size, lay the plates, deposited in a stone box" (JS–H 1:50–51). In addition to being the place of safekeeping for the gold plates, the hill Cumorah was the place where each autumn for four years young Joseph received further instruction concerning "what the Lord was going to do, and how and in what manner his kingdom was to be conducted in the last days" (JS–H 1:54). Brigham Young reported that when Joseph returned the plates, "the hill opened, and they walked into a . . . large and spacious room . . .

CUMORAH, HILL

[containing] more plates than probably many wagon loads" (Young, 19:38).

The prophets Mormon and Moroni[2] are the only Book of Mormon writers to use the name Cumorah and all references are associated with the hiding of Nephite records and the destruction of the Nephite and Jaredite nations. The Nephites gathered to the land Cumorah near the hill Cumorah for their final battle with the Lamanites (Morm. 6:2–6; 8:2). The Jaredites were destroyed as a nation at the hill Ramah, which was the same as the Nephite hill Cumorah where Mormon hid up the sacred records (Ether 15:11; Morm. 6:6).

Some modern scholars believe there are two Cumorahs, one in Central America where the final battle between the Nephites and Lamanites took place and where Mormon hid all the records, and a second hill in New York State where the gold plates were deposited by Moroni and where Joseph Smith received them from the angel Moroni (Palmer, 346–47).

Hill Cumorah as it appeared in 1907; photograph by George Edward Anderson, August 1907; courtesy LDS Family and Church History Archives.

Hill Cumorah as it appeared in 1981; photograph by Jed A. Clark; courtesy VRL.

Just when this New York hill was first called Cumorah is difficult to determine, but by 1835 the name Cumorah seemed to be well-known, at least among Church members. Joseph Smith referred to the hill but only used the name Cumorah once in his personal writings: "Glad tidings from Cumorah!" (D&C 128:20). The U.S. Geological Survey of 1898 called the hill "Mormon Hill." In 1952, however, the name was officially changed to Hill Cumorah. Between 1914 and 1928 the Church acquired a portion of the hill by purchasing a ninety-seven-acre farm owned by James Inglis. In 1928 the heirs of Pliny T. Sexton finally agreed to sell their portion of the hill to the Church (about 482 acres). On 2 February 1928, Willard W. Bean wrote to the First Presidency, setting forth the terms of the purchase. Bean received a letter from the First Presidency, also dated 2 February 1928, instructing him to purchase the hill if at all possible. Bean said, "Rather a peculiar coincidence that they should be writing me the same day and possibly the same hour to do something which I was telling them I had already carried into effect to the very last detail" (Bean, 686).

In July 1935 a forty-foot shaft of Vermont granite topped by a nine-foot bronze statue of Moroni was placed at the highest point of the hill Cumorah, near the north end. The monument symbolizes a "pillar of light" and contains four bronze sculptured panels on the base depicting (1) Joseph Smith receiving the plates, (2) the Three Witnesses to the plates' authenticity, (3) the Eight Witnesses to the plates' authenticity, and (4) Moroni's challenge to Book of Mormon readers as recorded in Moroni 10:4.

Speaking at the dedication of the monument, David O. McKay of the First Presidency said: "We are not erecting [the monument] to perpetuate the deeds of Moroni, nor are we erecting it to honor his father Mormon, nor indeed to perpetuate the life and deeds of Joseph Smith. . . . This monument is built as an expression of gratitude for the restoration of the gospel of Jesus Christ and as a manifestation to all the world of our faith in the personality and divine fatherhood of God" (qtd. by Porter, 79).

See also The Coming Forth of the Book of Mormon, 9; Cumorah, battle of; Moroni[2], visits of, to Joseph Smith.

BIBLIOGRAPHY

Bean, Willard W. "Change of Sentiment." *Improvement Era* 31 (June 1928): 682–87.

Palmer, David. "Hill Cumorah." *Encyclopedia of Mormonism.* Edited by Daniel H. Ludlow et al. 4 vols. New York: Macmillan, 1992.

Porter, Larry C., Milton V. Backman, and Susan Easton Black. *Regional Studies in Latter-day Saint Church History: New York.* Provo, Utah: Brigham Young University, 1992.

Young, Brigham. *Journal of Discourses.* 26 vols. London: Latter-day Saints' Book Depot, 1854–86.

RCR

Cunning *See* Appendix C.

Cureloms *See* Animals.

Curious *See* Appendix C.

Curse, cursing(s) Most frequently, God's censure of wickedness (e.g., 1 Ne. 2:23); less often, a person's censure of God or another individual (e.g., Alma 49:27). Curses from God took the forms of destruction of life, of forced social differentiation, and of loss of personal property. Concerning destruction of life, the Book of Mormon specifies that wars and civil conflicts, which resulted in widespread death, stemmed from transgression of God's laws (e.g., 2 Ne. 5:25; Ether 11:6). Social differences between Nephites and Lamanites came about because of willful sinning by Lamanite ancestors (e.g., 2 Ne. 5:21–23; Alma 3:6–10). The loss of property, particularly that hidden in the earth, affected Nephites and Lamanites as well as Jaredites before them. For example, Samuel the Lamanite had prophesied that when the Lord cursed the earth and the people's riches, their treasures and tools would "become slippery." These same people would "weep and howl," lamenting, "O that we had remembered the Lord our God . . . for behold, our riches are gone from us" (Hel. 13:30–36; cf. Morm. 1:17–18; Ether 14:1).

Curses and blessings often have to do with a people inhabiting a promised land. The book of Deuteronomy focuses much attention on the Lord's "blessings" that will come to the land and its people because of righteous living and, in contrast, the "curses" resulting from iniquity (Deut. 27:11–28:68; cf. Abr. 2:6). Similarly, the Book of Mormon speaks repeatedly of blessings and curses that awaited descendants of Lehi[1] and Sariah, depending on their attention to the commandments. For example, when Lehi addressed his children shortly before his death, he declared the following principle: "This land is consecrated unto him whom [God] shall bring. . . . If iniquity shall abound cursed shall be the land for their sakes, but unto the righteous it shall be blessed forever" (2 Ne. 1:7). Thus, the Lord established the pattern for those who inherited the land, including consequences—"curses"—for disobedience (cf. Enos 1:10; Alma 45:16; Hel. 13:17). Importantly, the earlier Jaredite people had lived under the same obligations, illustrating the Lord's consistency in dealing with peoples in lands of promise (e.g., Ether 7:23).

After writing of the wicked Amlicites who had brought a cursing upon themselves because of their "open rebellion against God," Mormon taught, "And even so doth every man that is cursed bring upon himself his own condemnation" (Alma 3:18–19; cf. 30:53). As a remedy, only appropriate repentance can remove curses imposed by God (e.g., Ether 9:16–35).

See also Curse of Adam, the.

SKB

Curse of Adam, the An expression unique to Christ in a revelation to Mormon (Moro. 8:8). The curse of Adam is the state of SPIRITUAL DEATH, or alienation from God, that befell Adam and Eve after their transgression (Alma 42:7). This curse was imposed upon their posterity: "All mankind became a lost and fallen people" (Alma 12:22). Yet, "the Son of God hath atoned for original guilt, wherein the sins of the parents cannot be answered upon the heads of the children, for they are whole from the foundation of the world" (Moses 6:54; cf. Moro. 8:8). Consequently, all souls are born innocent and spiritually alive (D&C 93:38). They remain in this saved state until they themselves commit sin upon attaining the age of accountability (Mosiah 3:16; D&C 20:71). Though the "curse of Adam" (Moro. 8:8), the first spiritual death, has long since been lifted through the Atonement, those who fail to repent of their sins will be subject to a "second" (Alma 12:32) spiritual death following the last judgment (Alma 12:31–36; Hel. 14:15–19; D&C 19:3; 29:41).

See also Children, salvation of little; Fall of Adam and Eve, the.

RT

Cut off To be severed from someone or something. Because of the Fall, mankind was "cut off both temporally and spiritually from the presence of the Lord" (Alma 42:7). To be cut off temporally generally means to die physically, i.e., to be "cut off out of the land of the living" (Mosiah 14:8), "cut off from the face of the earth" (Alma 9:11; 42:6; Morm. 3:10; cf. Moro. 8:14). Several references point to that specific time period of earth's history when Christ will come to "execute judgment in righteousness," and the wicked, as a group, will be destroyed from the earth, or "cut off from among the people" (1 Ne. 22:20–21; 3 Ne. 20:23; 21:11–21; cf. D&C 133:63–64). To be "cut off [spiritually] from the presence of the Lord" is to lose the power and blessings of God's Spirit, to be "without God in the world" (1 Ne. 2:21; Alma 41:11), left "to depend upon their own strength and upon their own wisdom" (Hel. 16:15). This is the condition the hard of heart, the disobedient, and the rebellious bring upon themselves (2 Ne. 1:20; Alma 36:30; 37:13). Those who persist in their rebellion, even until the final judgment, will be "cut off and destroyed forever," suffering a permanent "spiritual death" or "second death" (2 Ne. 1:17; Hel. 14:16–18; cf. Alma 40:26; D&C 88:35).

"Cut off" is also used in reference to one group of people intercepting the movements of another group (Alma 46:30–31; 50:11–12; 3 Ne. 4:24–26; Morm. 5:4), or severing a group from its "support" or supply source (Alma 57:10–12; 58:15–20).

See also Cast off; Judgment, the; Spiritual death.

LED

For behold he judgeth, and his judgment is just; and the infant perisheth not that dieth in his infancy; but men drink **damnation** to their own souls except they humble themselves and become as little children, and believe that salvation was, and is, and is to come, in and through the atoning blood of Christ, the Lord Omnipotent.

MOSIAH 3:18

Damnation The Book of Mormon speaks of damnation in two contexts: (1) being denied SALVATION, meaning a fulness of salvation, or eternal life (Alma 9:28; 3 Ne. 26:5); and (2) being "delivered up to the devil" (Mosiah 16:11).

Persons denied salvation include those who refuse to believe, repent, and receive the ordinance of baptism (2 Ne. 9:24; 3 Ne. 11:34; Morm. 9:23; Ether 4:18); those who fail to become as little children (Mosiah 3:18); those who partake of the sacrament of the Lord's Supper unworthily (3 Ne. 18:29); and those who build up churches unto themselves "to get gain" (Morm. 8:33).

Being delivered up to the devil, in an ultimate sense, is the fate of sons of perdition. It is for those who willfully choose to follow "the evil spirit" to the end (Mosiah 2:32–33). At the Judgment "they are consigned to an awful view of their own guilt and abominations, which doth cause them to shrink from the presence of the Lord into a state of misery and endless torment, from whence they can no more return; . . . mercy could have claim on them no more forever" (Mosiah 3:25–26). For sons of perdition, then, this damnation is permanent (Alma 12:16–18; D&C 76:37–39, 43–48). Others suffer the buffetings of Satan temporarily, suffering as do the permanently damned, but not forever. Some of these persons will experience the pains of hell in the postmortal spirit world (D&C 76:84–85, 106; 138:30–37, 58–59); others experience the pains of damnation for a time here on earth. Alma[2], for example, testified that "for three days and for three nights" he was "racked, even with the pains of a damned soul." Those hellish pains turned to peace and joy as he "cried within [his] heart: O Jesus, thou Son of God, have mercy on me, who am in the gall of bitterness, and am encircled about by the everlasting chains of death" (Alma 36:12–21).

Book of Mormon prophets describe the suffering of the damned as "misery and endless torment," which "torment is as a lake of fire and brimstone, whose flames are unquenchable," (Mosiah 3:25–27) and which "has no end" (2 Ne. 9:16). Abinadi said the wicked who are unredeemed "shall have cause to howl, and weep, and wail, and gnash their teeth" (Mosiah 16:1–3). As miserable as they are, under "a consciousness of [their] filthiness before [God]," Moroni[2] concluded that they would be "more miserable to dwell with a holy and just God" than with "the damned souls in hell" (Morm. 9:3–5).

At the Judgment, all those who suffer damnation in either context—being denied the fulness of salvation or being permanently delivered up to the devil—"shall confess before God that his judgments are just" (Mosiah 16:1). Each will be "constrained to exclaim: Holy, holy are thy judgments, O Lord God Almighty—but I know my guilt; I transgressed thy law, and my transgressions are mine" (2 Ne. 9:46).

See also Hell; Lake of fire and brimstone; Spiritual death.

LED

Darkness, night of *See* Night of darkness.

Dash *See* Appendix C.

Daunted *See* Appendix C.

David A king of Israel, father of Solomon. Jacob[2] referred to him as "David of old" (Jacob 1:15). During the days of Jacob, Nephite men were committing whoredoms by practicing unauthorized PLURAL MARRIAGE and using the scriptural accounts of David and Solomon to justify, or "excuse," their behavior (Jacob 2:23–24; cf. D&C 132:38–39).

David, land of One area from which the young Mormon's troops were driven (ca. A.D. 327). His frightened army retreated north to the city of Angola and then to the lands of David and Joshua. This marked his initial experience in combat (Morm. 2:3–6).

Day of the Lord According to Isaiah and Malachi, the time when the Lord would return to the earth to cleanse it of iniquity and usher in his millennial reign (2 Ne. 12:12–13; 23:6, 9; 3 Ne. 25:5). The Zoramites[2] also used this phrase to signify the one day of the week when they worshipped God (Alma 31:12).

See also Jesus Christ, second coming of.

BRM

Dead works Religious works without the life or confirmation of the Spirit and thus the life of salvation. These are works without saving merit because they are performed contrary to true doctrine or divinely given procedures, as in the case of the baptism of little children (Moro. 8:7–10, 23), Mosaic ordinances after Christ had fulfilled the law (Heb. 9:13–14), or sacred ordinances performed by those not having authority (D&C 22:2). The baptism of little children is a dead work because the purposes of baptism do not apply to them; they are saved by the "pure mercies of God" through the Atonement, without baptism. They cannot sin and thus have no need for repentance (Moro. 8:19–22; cf. D&C 29:46–48; 74:7).

See also Children, baptism of little.

JFM

Deadness of the law Phrase used by Nephi[1] to teach that salvation is through Christ, not through obedience to the LAW OF MOSES. For when the ultimate objective of the law of Moses is fulfilled—to lead people to Christ—the law becomes dead, meaning it has achieved its intended purpose (2 Ne. 25:24–27; cf. 11:4). When Israel sinned in the wilderness, God took away the fulness of the gospel and the Melchizedek Priesthood and gave Israel instead the lesser law of Moses (D&C 84:24–25; JST Ex. 34:1–2; Gal. 3:19). This law was to continue until Christ's coming, when the fulness of the gospel would be restored (3 Ne. 1:24–25; 15:3–5; D&C 84:26–27; JST John 1:20–28). The apostle Paul repeatedly taught concerning the "deadness" of this lesser law after Christ had replaced it. As a remedial program for sinful Israel (Gal. 3:24–25), it could not "justify" those who violated its precepts nor grant them eternal life (Rom. 3:20–28; Gal. 3:10–13; cf. 2 Ne. 2:5–8; JST John 1:17–18). The prophet Abinadi bore similar witness when he explained that "salvation doth not come by the law alone," for without the atonement of Christ, people "must unavoidably perish, notwithstanding the law of Moses" (Mosiah 13:27–31). Although the Nephites had both the gospel and the Melchizedek Priesthood and were "made alive in Christ because of [their] faith," they continued to obey the law of Moses for obedience' sake, even though they understood that the law itself would be "done away" when Christ would come to fulfill it (2 Ne. 25:24–27).

See also Justification.

SER

Dearth *See* Appendix C.

Death and hell The eternal state of suffering which would befall all humankind had there been no atonement. Jacob[2] referred to the two with the singular epithet "that awful monster" (2 Ne. 9:26). In this way he linked them as one single power, defining SPIRITUAL DEATH as HELL (2 Ne. 9:10, 12; cf. Rev. 6:8; 20:13–14).

Jacob spoke of two deaths: "temporal" death, meaning the separation of the body and the spirit, and "spiritual death," meaning the separation of the individual from God (2 Ne. 9:10–12). TEMPORAL DEATH will be fully overcome for all through the power of the resurrection; all graves will be forever empty (2 Ne. 9:11; Alma 11:41, 45; 12:18). Spiritual death denotes that condition which befalls the wicked in the SPIRIT WORLD. There they suffer under the power of the devil (2 Ne. 9:19). For most, this state is only temporary, because the power of Satan, along with that of death and hell, will be destroyed through the power of the Atonement and the resurrection of the Lord (2 Ne. 9:12); however, some, the filthy still, will suffer the effects of the second death eternally, CUT OFF from God, consigned to a place where "their torment is as a lake of fire and brimstone" (2 Ne. 9:16; 28:22–23).

See also Awful monster; Lake of fire and brimstone.

RDD

Death, bands of *See* Bands of death.

Death, spiritual *See* Spiritual death.

Death, taste of *See* Taste of death.

Death, temporal *See* Temporal death.

Death, view his *See* View his death.

Decrees of God The laws, or eternal proclamations, of God. The Book of Mormon makes two points concerning the decrees of God. First, they are unalterable (Alma 29:4; 41:8). God has decreed, for example, that mankind will receive either "life or death," salvation or destruction in the eternities according to their desires for good or for evil (Alma 29:5). Second, God has decreed that the land of the Book of Mormon "is a land of promise; and whatsoever nation shall possess it shall serve God, or they shall be swept off when . . . they are ripened in iniquity" (Ether 2:9). If the inhabitants of this land will worship Jesus Christ, the God of this land, they "shall be free from bondage, and from captivity, and from all other nations under heaven" (Ether 2:12).

PYH

Deliverance *See* Book of Mormon, selected themes of, bondage and deliverance.

Demands of justice Rewards or punishments strictly applied in response to obedience or disobedience to irrevocable laws of God (2 Ne. 2:10; 9:17; Alma 7:20; 42:16; D&C 130:20–21). Inasmuch as all mankind are "fallen" and to some degree or another disobedient, they are in the "grasp of justice" (Alma 42:14), which exacts payment for every broken law. MERCY, through the atonement of Jesus Christ, satisfies the "demands of justice" for those who are ignorant of the law and for those who knowingly disobey but repent, "while he that exercises no faith unto repentance is exposed to the whole law of the demands of justice" (Alma 34:16; cf. 2 Ne. 9:26; Mosiah 2:38; 15:8–9, 24; Alma 42:15; Moro. 8:22).

See also Appease; Justice, law of; Satisfy.

RCF

Descendants of the Jews Citizens of the kingdom of Judah regardless of their blood line (2 Ne. 30:4). When Lehi[1] led his people out of the land of Jerusalem[1] around 600 B.C., the only kingdom remaining of the original two Israelite kingdoms was the southern kingdom of JUDAH. All of the northern Israelite kingdom and parts of the kingdom of Judah had been destroyed more than 110 years earlier. Thus, while Lehi and his posterity were blood descendants of the tribe of Joseph[1] (1 Ne. 5:14), they were also political and cultural descendants of the kingdom of Judah (2 Ne. 30:4; 1 Ne. 1:4), the only Israelite kingdom remaining. Individuals who can trace their heritage back to the southern kingdom of Judah may likewise be classified as "descendants of the Jews."

See also Jew(s).

PYH

Deseret Jaredite name for honeybee (Ether 2:3). When Jared[1], his brother, their relatives, and their friends left the tower at the time the Lord confounded the language of the people and departed for the promised land, they took with them animals, fish, seeds, and "deseret."

PYH

Desire(s) The longings of the heart, that for which one truly hopes. Desire plays a critical role in the plan of salvation. Alma[2] testified, "I know that [God] granteth unto men according to their desire, whether it be unto death or unto life; yea, I know that he allotteth unto men, yea, decreeth unto them decrees which are unalterable, according to their wills, whether they be unto salvation or unto destruction. Yea, and I know that good and evil have come before all men; he that knoweth not good from evil is blameless; but he that knoweth good and evil, to him it is given according to his desires, whether he desireth good or evil, life or death, joy or remorse of conscience" (Alma 29:4–5).

One of God's unalterable decrees is that those who inherit the kingdom of God must have experienced a change of heart, a change from desiring the things of the world to desiring the things of God. This was the case with the people of king Benjamin, who testified of the "Spirit of the Lord Omnipotent, which has wrought a mighty change in us, or in our hearts, that we have no more disposition to do evil, but to do good continually" (Mosiah 5:2). After a similar experience, king Lamoni and his servants all declared that "their hearts had been changed; that they had no more desire to do evil" (Alma 19:33). Alma[2] experienced such a change of heart at the time an angel appeared to him and he was "born of the Spirit." The Lord explained to Alma "that all mankind, yea, men and women, all nations, kindreds, tongues and people, must be born again; yea, born of God, changed from their carnal and fallen state, to a state of righteousness, being redeemed of God, becoming his sons and daughters; and thus they become new creatures; and unless they do this, they can in nowise inherit the kingdom of God" (Mosiah 27:24–26). Alma had been an unbeliever who went about seeking to destroy the church of God. Now, as he contemplated the heavens with "numberless concourses of angels . . . singing and praising their God," he said, "my soul did long to be there" (Alma 36:22). This longing, this consuming desire for the things of God, comes through the sanctifying power of the Holy Ghost to those who yield their hearts to God. Those so blessed become like the ancient Saints who "could not look upon sin save it were with abhorrence" (Alma 13:12; Hel. 3:35). Proclaiming his testimony of this principle, Joseph Smith taught "that the nearer man approaches perfection, the clearer are his views, and the greater his enjoyments, till he has overcome the evils of his life and lost every desire for sin" (Smith, 51). Thus, rather than desiring to walk in the paths of sin, these individuals seek to partake of the FRUIT of the TREE OF LIFE, or the LOVE OF GOD, which Nephi[1] described as "most desirable above all things" and "the greatest of all the gifts of God" (1 Ne. 11:22; 15:36; cf. 8:10, 12, 15; Alma 32:40–42).

The Lord delights to grant the desires of the righteous, knowing they will not ask amiss (Hel. 10:1–10; cf. D&C 38:39; 41:1; 50:26–29; 59:20; 76:5). Thus, he granted the desires of his twelve disciples, three who wanted to continue their ministry on the earth until the end of time and nine who requested that when they reached the "age of man" they could speedily come to the Savior and "find rest" in his kingdom (3 Ne. 28:1–10). Likewise, because of his "great desires to know of the mysteries of God," Nephi[1] was visited by the Lord and thereby obtained a testimony of his father's words (1 Ne. 2:16; cf. 11:1–5). The brother of Jared[1] testified that the Lord commanded them to "call upon" him so that they "may receive according to [their] desires" (Ether 3:2).

The righteous not only desire the things of God for themselves but desire that all others enjoy the blessings of the gospel and salvation as well. For example, Lehi[1] (1 Ne. 8:12), Jacob[2] (2 Ne. 6:3), Enos (Enos 1:9, 13), the sons of Mosiah[2] (Mosiah 28:3), and Alma[2] (Alma 29:1–2; 36:24), after they had tasted of the goodness of God, longed for those same blessings for others. In addition to the desire to be part of God's fold and stand as a witness of God, Alma[1] listed the desire to care for and help others as requisite for baptism (Mosiah 18:8–10).

In contrast to the desire for righteousness, the wicked "love darkness rather than light" (D&C 10:21). In the premortal life Lucifer became the devil, a fallen angel, "having sought that which was evil before God." After he "had become miserable forever, he sought also the misery of all mankind." Indeed, "he seeketh that all men might be miserable like unto himself" (2 Ne. 2:17–18, 27). His followers, like Sherem, endeavor to shake others from their faith in God (Jacob 7:1–5).

Truly, God grants unto men according to their desires, "one raised to happiness according to his desires of happiness, or good according to his desires of good; and the other to evil according to his desires of evil; for as he has desired to do evil all the day long even so shall he have his reward of evil when the night cometh. And so it is on the other hand. If he hath repented of his sins, and desired righteousness until the end of his days, even so he shall be rewarded unto righteousness" (Alma 41:5–6).

See also Judgment, the; Restoration, plan of.

BIBLIOGRAPHY

Smith, Joseph. *Teachings of the Prophet Joseph Smith.* Selected by Joseph Fielding Smith. Salt Lake City: Deseret Book, 1976.

LED

Desolation, land of and city of A Nephite land in the far north. The land of Desolation was the place where the people of Jared first landed (Alma 22:30; Ether 6:12; 7:6). It was in this region that Limhi's people discovered the Jaredite ruins, describing the land as being "covered with bones of men" and "ruins of buildings" (Mosiah 8:8; cf. Ether 11:6; ca. 121 B.C.).

The city Desolation was built on the borders of the land Desolation, "by the narrow pass which led into the land southward" (Morm. 3:5–7). Desolation repeatedly changed hands during battles between Lamanites and Nephites near the end of the Nephite civilization (Morm. 3:7; 4:2–3, 8, 13, 19; ca. A.D. 361–375). Mormon lamented the barbarity and carnage of the period, declaring that "there never had been so great wickedness among all the children of Lehi, nor even among all the house of Israel" (Morm. 4:10–12).

Desolation of Nehors The state of things in the land of Ammonihah after the utter destruction of its inhabitants by Lamanite armies (ca. 81 B.C.). The dead apostates "of the profession of Nehor" were "covered with a shallow covering," and "the scent thereof" was so offensive that people avoided the area "for many years" (Alma 16:3, 9–11).

Despair A state of hopelessness: "If ye have no hope ye must needs be in despair" (Moro. 10:22). "And what is it that ye shall hope for? . . . that ye shall have hope through the atonement of Christ . . . to be raised unto life eternal" (Moro. 7:41; cf. Alma 26:19). Despair for eternal life comes through sin: "despair cometh because of iniquity" (Moro. 10:22) and is taken away through faith in Christ, for "if a man have faith he must needs have hope" (Moro. 7:42).

DKJ

Devil, captivity of the *See* Captivity of the devil.

Diligence Portrayed in the Book of Mormon as a trait of righteousness which brings blessings (Alma 49:30), *diligence* implies persistent or steady effort and is used in context with keeping the commandments (1 Ne. 15:11; Enos 1:10; Mosiah 1:11; 4:27; Alma 7:23; 3 Ne. 6:14), laboring to preach the word of God (1 Ne. 17:15; Jacob 1:19; Jarom 1:11; Hel. 15:6), serving God (Mosiah 7:33; 3 Ne. 5:3), giving heed to God and his word (Alma 7:26; 12:9–11), nourishing the growth of the word of God (Alma 32:41–43), and laboring in ecclesiastical callings (Jacob 2:3). Those who exhibit this careful and constant effort in spiritual activities are blessed. The sons of Mosiah[2] obtained the spirit of prophecy and revelation and the ability to teach with power because of their diligence in scripture study, fasting, and prayer (Alma 17:2–3; cf. Mosiah 1:7).

BLT

Dim *See* Appendix C.

Disannul *See* Appendix C.

Disciple, discipleship A disciple is a pupil and follower of a master teacher or leader. Disciples of Christ, therefore, seek to know Christ's teachings and follow them (2 Ne. 31:10; Jacob 4:6; Alma 14:1; 17:2; 3 Ne. 23:1; D&C 41:5; Matt. 11:29; John 8:31; 13:35).

Thirteen men are specifically identified as Christ's disciples in the Book of Mormon: the Twelve to whom Christ gave "power and authority to baptize," with a particular commission to testify that they had seen the resurrected Lord (3 Ne. 12:1–2; cf. 1 Ne. 12:8), and Mormon, who declared that he was "a disciple of Jesus Christ, the Son of God" and, as such, had "been called of him to declare his word among his people, that they might have everlasting life" (3 Ne. 5:13).

The Book of Mormon contains many examples of individuals whose lives reflect faith, commitment, sacrifice, and a conscious decision to be followers of Jesus Christ. They are people who are examples of committed, rather than convenient, discipleship (Holland, 68–73). Lehi[1] and Nephi[1] were obedient to the Lord's commandment to leave Jerusalem and retrieve the brass plates from Laban (1 Ne. 1–4); Abinadi submitted to the Lord's will to preach to wicked Nephites which eventually led to his martyrdom (Mosiah 11–17); Amulek responded to the Lord's call to serve even though it meant the loss of wealth and family (Alma 8:19–15:18); and the ANTI-NEPHI-LEHIES manifested their commitment to follow Christ at all costs, being willing to die rather than commit sin by taking up their swords again to kill others (Alma 24; 27:27–29).

In addition to examining the lives of Book of Mormon prophets, one can learn much about discipleship from their words. Disciples are those who look to "the rock from whence [they] are hewn" (2 Ne. 8:1), bring "forth good works" (Alma 5:41), separate themselves from the wicked (Alma 5:57; cf. Moro. 7:11), are brought down "into the depths of humility" (Hel. 6:5), have "a sufficient hope by which [they] can enter into the rest of the Lord" (Moro. 7:3), are "filled with [Christ's] love" (Moro. 7:48), and are "born again; yea, born of God, changed from their carnal and fallen state, to a state of righteousness, being redeemed of God, becoming his sons and daughters; and thus . . . become new creatures" (Mosiah 27:25–26; cf. Alma 5).

Two important sermons, one by Nephi[1] and one by king Benjamin, contain valuable insights on discipleship. Nephi recorded Christ's commandment to "follow me, and do the things which ye have seen me do" (2 Ne. 31:12; cf. Matt. 16:24; JST Matt. 16:26). He then listed things Christ did, which include "humbl[ing] himself before the Father" (cf. Mosiah 15:7) and "keeping his commandments" (2 Ne. 31:7).

Nephi asked whether individuals can "follow Jesus save [they] shall be willing to keep the commandments of the Father" (2 Ne. 31:10; cf. 2 Ne. 31:6–7; John 5:19; 8:28). The commandments of the Father for his children include repentance, baptism, and receiving the Holy Ghost. Nephi taught that disciples must obey these commandments "with full purpose of heart, acting no hypocrisy and no deception before God, but with real intent" (2 Ne. 31:11–13). Thus Christ's disciples must "reconcile [them]selves to the will of God" (2 Ne. 10:24). As Elder Neal A. Maxwell stated, "The submission of one's will is really the only uniquely personal thing we have to place on God's altar" ("Swallowed Up," 24). After being baptized by water and receiving the Holy Ghost, "then are ye in [the] strait and narrow path which leads to eternal life" (2 Ne. 31:18). Nephi listed five imperatives for disciples after they have entered the path, each of which Christ exemplified in perfection as he sought to do his Father's will on earth: (1) "press forward with a steadfastness in Christ," (2) have "a perfect brightness of hope," (3) have a "love of God and of all men," (4) feast "upon the word of Christ," and (5) "endure to the end" (2 Ne. 31:20).

King Benjamin's lifelong service models true discipleship. He "had taught [his people] to keep the commandments of God, that they might rejoice and be filled with love towards God and all men" (Mosiah 2:4). He taught them that they were "eternally indebted to . . . [God], to render to him all that [they] have and are" (Mosiah 2:34), and to serve God by serving one another (Mosiah 2:17–18; cf. 18:8–10, indicating that such service is part of the baptismal covenant). King Benjamin noted that no man "knoweth . . . the master whom he has not served, and who is a stranger unto him, and is far from the thoughts and intents of his heart" (Mosiah 5:13).

He also identified important characteristics of sincere disciples who have experienced "great joy," having received a remission of their sins (Mosiah 4:11). For example, they "shall always rejoice, and be filled with the love of God." They "will not have a mind to injure one another, but to live peaceably, and to render to every man according to that which is his due" (Mosiah 4:12–13). These disciples teach their children to walk in the gospel path, "to love one another, and to serve one another," and they will succor "those that stand in need" (Mosiah 4:14–16). In essence, they will seek to emulate the very things Christ did during his ministries in both the eastern and western hemispheres.

Discipleship in the Book of Mormon focuses on following the master teacher, Jesus Christ. Those who "come unto Christ" can be "perfected in him" (Moro. 10:32), fulfilling Christ's own commission: "What manner of men ought ye to be? Verily I say unto you, even as I am" (3 Ne. 27:27).

See also Book of Mormon, selected themes of, come unto Christ; Born again; Disciples, twelve Nephite.

BIBLIOGRAPHY

Holland, Jeffrey R. "The Inconvenient Messiah." *Ensign* 14 (February 1984): 68–73.

Maxwell, Neal A. "Swallowed Up in the Will of the Father." *Ensign* 25 (November 1995): 22–24.

———. "King Benjamin's Speech: A Manual for Discipleship." *King Benjamin's Speech: "That Ye May Learn Wisdom."* Edited by John W. Welch and Stephen D. Ricks. Provo, Utah: FARMS, 1998.

GS

Disciples, twelve Nephite The twelve individuals chosen by Christ to preside over and administer the affairs of the Church in the New World. When Christ appeared at the temple in Bountiful[2] he conferred upon the Twelve the authority to baptize (3 Ne. 11:18–22; 12:1) and commissioned them to minister to the people, which included baptizing, preaching the gospel (3 Ne. 12:1; 19:6; Morm. 9:22), testifying of Christ (3 Ne. 12:2), and administering the sacrament (3 Ne. 18:1–10). Later Christ also "gave them power to give the Holy Ghost" (3 Ne. 18:36–37). Throughout the Book of Mormon, the Nephite Twelve are designated as "disciples" rather than "apostles," possibly to distinguish them from the Twelve Apostles of the New Testament. Although the roles of the two groups are similar, the Nephite disciples have particular stewardship over Nephi's seed; the New Testament apostles are to judge the twelve tribes of Israel (1 Ne. 12:8–10). It seems clear, however, that the Nephite disciples functioned as apostles (Moro. 2:1–2; Smith, 4:538).

Although the Twelve are identified by name in 3 Nephi 19:4, little is known about the individual disciples, with the exception of Nephi[3], who played a prominent role in 3 Nephi. Collectively, it was the Twelve who received Christ's instruction concerning his Church (3 Ne. 27:1–12) and his gospel (3 Ne. 27:13–28), and to whom Christ asked, "What is it that ye desire of me, after that I am gone to the Father?" (3 Ne. 28:1). In response to their answers, he promised nine of the Twelve that they would come to him and "find rest" in his kingdom after they had fulfilled their mortal ministry (3 Ne. 28:3). He promised the remaining three that they would be translated and allowed to continue their missionary activities among mortals (3 Ne. 28:7–9).

Six centuries before their call, Nephi[1] was shown the Nephite Twelve in vision. An angel told Nephi that "they are righteous forever; for because of their faith in the Lamb of God their garments are made white in his blood" (1 Ne. 12:7–8, 10). The fulfillment of this prophecy was described, in part, when the Twelve prayed "without ceasing" (3 Ne. 19:24) and in the process were gloriously transformed to be "as white as the countenance and also the garments of Jesus" (3 Ne. 19:24–25, 30). It was an indescribably sacred moment as the Nephite disciples prayed, and Christ prayed, and the multitude was blessed to hear and understand the words Christ uttered. Thus Jesus declared, "So great faith have I never seen among all the Jews" (3 Ne. 19:35).

See also Apostles, the Twelve; Nephites, the Three.

BIBLIOGRAPHY

Smith, Joseph. *History of The Church of Jesus Christ of Latter-day Saints.* Edited by B. H. Roberts. 7 vols. 2d ed. rev. Salt Lake City: The Church of Jesus Christ of Latter-day Saints, 1932–51.

GS

Discipline, Church *See* Church discipline.

Disposition One's nature, desires, inclinations, or feelings (Alma 43:6). A disposition not to sin "but to do good continually" (Mosiah 5:2) is a consequence of the spiritual rebirth that occurs through the application of the atonement of Jesus Christ and through the power of the Holy Ghost (Mosiah 4:1–3). When the Holy Ghost effects a mighty change in the heart, one's life enters a new state of existence, the inclination to commit sin disappears, and the person is redeemed from a worldly and fallen condition (Mosiah 27:24–26).

ACS

Dissenters Individuals and groups within Nephite society who openly opposed and fought the prophets and the legally constituted civil authorities. They are identified as "dissenters" in the Book of Mormon. Numerous individuals and groups dissented for a variety of reasons over the course of their history. Laman[1], Lemuel, and the sons of Ishmael[1] were the first to openly oppose Nephi[1] and his followers, on the grounds that he had "wronged" them at various stages in their flight from Jerusalem, had "taken the ruling of the people out of their hands," and had "robbed them" in taking "the records which were engraven on the plates of brass" (Mosiah 10:12–16). Later, such individuals as Sherem, king Noah[3], Alma the Younger, the sons of Mosiah[2], Nehor, and Korihor appeared. All of them prideful men, they spoke persuasively against fundamental doctrines and principles of the gospel and caused serious dissension within the Church (Jacob 7:1–5; Mosiah 11:2–15; 27:8–10; Alma 1:2–6, 16; 30). Although some, such as Alma and the sons of Mosiah, repented and became stalwarts in the faith, such others as the Zoramites[2], Amalekites, and Amulonites actually institutionalized their new "doctrines" by creating their own churches. They took their dissent from the gospel so far as to join forces with the Lamanites (Alma 31:1–23; 35:10–11; 43:4; 21:2–8).

The desire for personal gain manifested itself in other forms of dissension as well. After the reign of the judges had commenced, several ambitious individuals, including Amlici, Amalickiah (who was supported by "lower judges of the land" who were also "seeking for power"; Alma 46:4), and assorted "king-men" (men "of high birth . . . [who] were supported by those who sought power and authority over the people"; Alma 51:8), stirred up dissension among the Nephites by seeking to have themselves established as kings (Alma 2; 46:1–10; 51:2–8). Similarly, people dissented when men they did not support were appointed as chief judge (Hel. 1:1–9; 2:1–5), or, as in the case of Morianton[2], when there were disputes over land (Alma 50:25–35).

Individuals who dissented from the Nephites, for whatever reason, generally destroyed themselves spiritually. Mormon, commenting on the fate of various dissenters over the years, noted that even though they had "been instructed in the same knowledge of the Lord" as other Nephites, "not long after their dissensions they became more hardened and impenitent, and more wild, wicked and ferocious than the Lamanites" (Alma 47:36). Some went so far as to "cause the Lamanites that they should harden their hearts" even further, "that they should wax strong in wickedness and their abominations" (Alma 21:3). The evil transformation of such persons seems to have been complete and almost permanent. For example, when "thousands" of Lamanites converted to the gospel, "only one" of the dissident Amalekites converted with them (Alma 23:5, 14).

With the possible exception of the "contention and . . . dissensions" that resulted in the departure of many Nephites to settle the land northward in 46 B.C. (Hel. 3:3–11), dissension, for a number of reasons, weakened the Nephites collectively and invariably led to war with the Lamanites. Many Nephite dissenters joined the Lamanites or formed alliances with them, adding to their strength numerically (Alma 24:1–2; 61:3–8) and stirring them up to war against the Nephites (e.g., Alma 35:10–11; Hel. 4:4). Lamanite leaders, moreover, were quick to take advantage of the dissenters' "more wicked and murderous disposition" and their familiarity with Nephite defense capabilities by appointing them leaders over Lamanite armies (Alma 43:6; 48:5; Hel. 1:15).

Dealing with dissension also served to distract the Nephites and channel their energies away from the performance of important tasks such as defense, which gave the Lamanites further advantage (Alma 53:8–9). The first time Zarahemla fell to the Lamanites, for example, it was because there was "so much contention and so much difficulty in the government, that they [the Nephites] had not kept sufficient guards" in the area (Hel. 1:18). Captain Moroni, fully aware of the disastrous effects of dissent among his people, made it "his first care to put an end to such contentions and dissensions among the people; for behold, this had been hitherto a cause of all their destruction" (Alma 51:16; cf. 60:23–36).

See also Apostasy.

AHH

Divers *See* Appendix C.

Divorce *See* Writing of divorcement.

Doctrine A teaching, tenet, principle, or precept that either comes from God (true) or from Satan (false). The gospel or "doctrine of Christ" (2 Ne. 31:2, 21) is the rock upon which people

D & C, WHAT IT SAYS ABOUT THE B OF M

should build their lives (3 Ne. 11:39–40). Saints are commanded to learn and teach the doctrine of the kingdom (D&C 88:77). The Book of Mormon is designed to help confound false doctrine (2 Ne. 3:12; 27:35). There is power in the declaration of true doctrine. "True doctrine, understood, changes attitudes and behavior," Elder Boyd K. Packer testified. "The study of the doctrines of the gospel will improve behavior quicker than a study of behavior will improve behavior. . . . That is why we stress so forcefully the study of the doctrines of the gospel" (Packer, 20).

See also Points of doctrine.

BIBLIOGRAPHY

Packer, Boyd K. Conference Report, October 1986.

RLM

Doctrine and Covenants, what it says about the Book of Mormon A number of the revelations in the Doctrine and Covenants refer to the Book of Mormon. Generally these passages speak of events and instructions surrounding the coming forth of the Book of Mormon, the role the book is to play in God's plan, and the Lord's admonitions concerning the book.

The coming forth of the Book of Mormon

The Doctrine and Covenants teaches that Moroni[2], to whom was "committed the keys of the record of the stick of Ephraim," was sent to Joseph Smith to reveal the Book of Mormon (D&C 27:5; cf. 128:20). Joseph Smith, by the mercy and power of God, was given the ability to translate the Book of Mormon (D&C 1:29; cf. 5:4; 24:1; 135:3) "by the means" of the Urim and Thummim which God had prepared in advance (D&C 20:8).

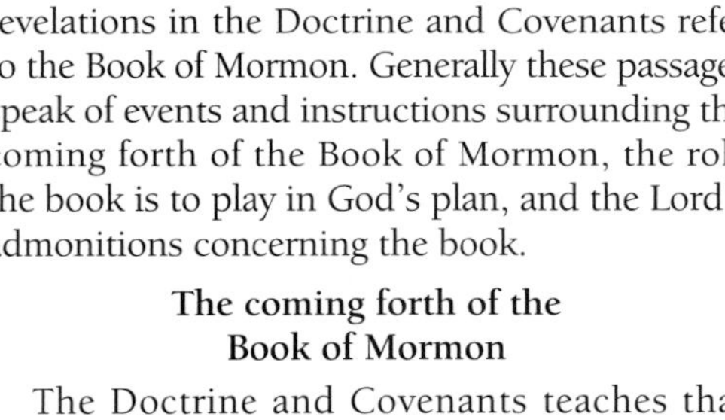
8 And [a]gave him power from on high, by the [b]means which were before prepared, to translate the Book of Mormon;
9 Which contains a [a]record of a fallen people, and the [b]fulness of the [c]gospel of Jesus Christ to the Gentiles and to the Jews also;

Doctrine and Covenants 20:8–9

The Doctrine and Covenants rehearses the story of Joseph Smith's loss of the first portion of the translation of the plates because he gave them to a "wicked man," Martin Harris (D&C 3:12–13; 10:1, 6–9). He was commanded not to retranslate the lost portion but rather to substitute for it the account on the plates of Nephi that basically parallels (but "throw[s] greater views upon [the] gospel"; D&C 10:45) the record contained in the lost manuscript. God would thus confound those evil men who had stolen and altered the first translation (D&C 10:1, 30, 38–46).

Several men were called to support and assist with the work of translating and publishing the Book of Mormon, including Oliver Cowdery (D&C 6:17; 9:4), Hyrum Smith (D&C 11:19), and Martin Harris (D&C 19:26). The Three Witnesses (Oliver Cowdery, Martin Harris, and David Whitmer) were called especially to view the plates and other sacred relics so that they could add to Joseph Smith's their own testimony of their reality (D&C 5:11–15; 17:1–6). The Lord's wise purpose in preserving these things is to be made known to future generations (D&C 5:9; cf. Alma 37:14–16).

Thus, the Doctrine and Covenants testifies that the Book of Mormon was "given by inspiration," confirmed by "the ministering of angels," and "declared unto the world" by its witnesses (D&C 20:10).

The role of the Book of Mormon

The Doctrine and Covenants teaches that the Book of Mormon, "the record of the Nephites" (D&C 1:29), "a fallen people" (D&C 20:9), contains the "fulness of the gospel" (D&C 20:9; 27:5; 42:12; cf. 14:10; 35:12, 17; 39:11) and "the truth and the word of God" (D&C 19:26). It was preserved and brought forth in the latter days through Joseph Smith (D&C 5:4–10) to go first to the Gentiles and then to the "Jew, of whom the Lamanites are a remnant" (D&C 19:26–27; cf. 20:9) to be another testimony of the Savior (D&C 3:16–19). By the Book of Mormon the Jews would be persuaded to "believe the gospel, and look not for a Messiah to come who has already come" (D&C 19:27; cf. 2 Ne.

DOCTRINES TAUGHT IN THE BOOK OF MORMON ACCORDING TO D&C 20:17–36

DOCTRINE TAUGHT	VV.	BOOK OF MORMON EXAMPLE
"there is a God"	v. 17	2 Ne. 2:14; 11:7; Alma 11:24, 27; 22:8; 30:43–44; Morm. 9:2–6
"[God] is infinite and eternal"	v. 17	1 Ne. 12:18; 2 Ne. 2:12; 9:8; 26:12; Mosiah 15:4; Alma 11:44; 34:9; Moro. 10:4, 34
"[God is] the framer of heaven and earth"	v. 17	Jacob 2:5; Mosiah 3:8; 4:2, 9; 5:15; 15:4; Alma 18:28; Hel. 14:12
"[God] created man, male and female"	v. 18	1 Ne. 17:36; 2 Ne. 2:14–15; Jacob 2:21
"And [the Lord] gave unto them [Adam and Eve] commandments"	v. 19	2 Ne. 2:21; Alma 12:31–32; 22:12
"By the transgression . . . man became sensual and devilish, and . . . fallen"	v. 20	2 Ne. 9:6; Mosiah 16:3; Alma 28:13; 42:6–12
"the Almighty God gave his Only Begotten Son"	v. 21	Jacob 4:5; Alma 5:48; 9:26; 12:33–34
"[Christ] suffered temptations but gave no heed unto them"	v. 22	Mosiah 15:5; Alma 7:11
"[The Savior] was crucified, died, and rose again the third day"	v. 23	1 Ne. 19:10; 2 Ne. 6:9; 10:3, 5; 25:13; Mosiah 3:9–10; 15:7; Alma 33:22; Hel. 14:20
"[The resurrected Savior] ascended into heaven"	v. 24	Mosiah 18:2; Alma 40:20; 3 Ne. 10:18; 11:12, 21; 18:39; 26:15; Moro. 7:27
"as many as would believe and be baptized . . . endure in faith to the end, should be saved"	v. 25	2 Ne. 9:24; 2 Ne. 31:13–21; 3 Ne. 11:33; 12:1; 27:16–21; Ether 4:18
"Not only those who believed after he came . . . but all those from the beginning . . . should have eternal life"	v. 26	2 Ne. 9:26; Mosiah 15:24; Ether 12:16
"the holy prophets . . . truly testified of him in all things"	v. 26	Jacob 7:11; Alma 34:6–8; Hel. 8:19–20; 3 Ne. 23:5
"men must repent and believe on . . . Jesus Christ, and worship the Father . . . and endure in faith"	v. 29	2 Ne. 33:4; Jacob 4:5; Morm. 7:5
"justification through the grace of . . . Jesus Christ is just and true"	v. 30	1 Ne. 16:2; 2 Ne. 2:7; Mosiah 14:11
"sanctification through the grace of . . . Jesus Christ is just and true"	v. 31	Mosiah 3:19; Hel. 3:35; Moro. 10:33
"there is a possibility that man may fall from grace"	v. 32	2 Ne. 9:27; Alma 24:30; 29:5; 47:36
"let the church take heed and pray always, lest they fall into temptation"	v. 33	2 Ne. 32:9; 3 Ne. 18:15, 18; Moro. 6:4–5
"those who are sanctified take heed also"	v. 34	Mosiah 4:30; Alma 13:28
"these things are true and according to the revelation of John, neither adding to, nor diminishing from the prophecy of his book"	v. 35	1 Ne. 1:3; 14:18–30; 22:30; 2 Ne. 25:20; 3 Ne. 5:17–18; Ether 4:11; Moro. 10:4

25:17–20). The plates containing the Nephite records, preserved "that the promises of the Lord might be fulfilled, which he made to his people" (D&C 3:19; cf. Enos 1:13–18), were also intended to help the Lamanites come to the knowledge of their fathers, know the promises of the Lord, believe the gospel, rely on and be glorified through faith in Christ, and be saved through repentance (D&C 3:20).

Moreover, the Book of Mormon proves "to the world that the holy scriptures are true, and that God does inspire men and call them to his holy work in this age and generation, as well as in generations of old; thereby showing that he is the same God yesterday, today, and forever" (D&C 20:11–12). Mormon's abridgment contains truths of the gospel that the Book of Mormon prophets and disciples most desired future generations to have (D&C 10:38–50).

The Lord's admonition concerning the Book of Mormon

The Doctrine and Covenants contains God's own witness that the Book of Mormon is true (D&C 6:17; 17:6; 18:2). He warned that those who "come to a knowledge of this work" shall be judged thereby. Those "who receive it in faith, and work righteousness, shall receive a crown of eternal life," but those who reject it will be condemned (D&C 20:13–15; 5:15–19; 84:54–58; cf. 2 Ne. 25:22).

Doctrines taught in the Book of Mormon according to Doctrine and Covenants 20:17–36 are outlined in the accompanying table.

See also The Coming Forth of the Book of Mormon, 9; Book of Mormon, condemnation for treating lightly the; Book of Mormon, lost manuscript of (116 pages); Witnesses of the Book of Mormon.

MSN

Doctrine of Christ *See* Gospel, the.

Doctrine, points of *See* Points of doctrine.

Doctrines, false *See* Book of Mormon, selected purposes of, to confound false doctrine.

Dog *See* Animals.

Dove, form of a *See* Form of a dove.

Dreams *See* Revelation.

Dregs *See* Appendix C.

Dross *See* Appendix C.

Durst *See* Appendix C.

Dust, crying from the *See* Crying from the dust.

Dust of the earth, less than *See* Less than the dust of the earth.

Dwindle *See* Appendix C.

And in that day there shall be a root of Jesse, which shall stand for an **ensign** of the people; to it shall the Gentiles seek; and his rest shall be glorious.

2 NEPHI 21:10

Earth, cleansing of *See* Earth, the.

Earth, new heaven and a new *See* Heaven.

Earth, the Term that has at least three meanings in the Book of Mormon.

1. One of many worlds created by Jesus Christ, the God of the earth, under the direction and according to the will of God the Father (1 Ne. 17:36; Jacob 4:9; Mosiah 3:8; 3 Ne. 9:15; Moses 1:31–33). Christ created the earth to be a place for man to experience mortality (1 Ne. 17:36), be tested, and "prepare to meet God" (Alma 12:24–25; 34:32; Abr. 3:24–25). The earth and its elements are subject and obedient to God, who often controls those elements to reprove, direct, or bless man (e.g., Hel. 12:8–18; 13:18, 30–31; 3 Ne. 9:1–12; Gen. 3:17–19). God cleansed the earth of wickedness by flood during the days of Noah[1] (Gen. 6–9). He will cleanse it again at the beginning of his millennial reign (1 Ne. 22:16–19, 25–26; D&C 29:10–11), and he will cleanse it a final time after the MILLENNIUM, at which point the earth will pass away and become a new, sanctified earth (3 Ne. 26:3; Morm. 9:2; D&C 29:22–23). The new earth will become a habitation for those receiving a celestial glory (D&C 88:17–20, 25–26).

2. Collective term referring to all the inhabitants of this world (e.g., 1 Ne. 19:17; 2 Ne. 21:9).

3. The soil or ground (e.g., 1 Ne. 18:24; 21:23; Mosiah 6:7; Alma 48:8).

See also Creation, the; Heaven; Life, purpose of; World, the.

TBB

East wind In the biblical world, the east wind (the hot desert winds that bring death to vegetation) represents destruction from God (Gen. 41:23; Ezek. 19:12; Hosea 13:15; Jonah 4:8). The phrase is used twice in the Book of Mormon, both times in Mosiah: "If my people shall sow filthiness they shall reap the east wind, which bringeth immediate destruction" (Mosiah 7:31) and "they shall also be smitten with the east wind" (Mosiah 12:6).

DKO

Eden, the garden of The place where Adam and Eve lived prior to their fall. The Book of Mormon confirms biblical teachings concerning Eden and what occurred there, such as the existence of the garden (2 Ne. 2:19), the FORBIDDEN FRUIT and the TREE OF LIFE (2 Ne. 2:15; Alma 12:21), the placing of the CHERUBIM AND A FLAMING SWORD to guard the tree of life (Alma 12:21; 42:2), the presence of the serpent (2 Ne. 2:17–18), and the fall of Adam and Eve (2 Ne. 2:19). In addition, the Book of Mormon enhances understanding of the Genesis account regarding Eden's role in the plan of salvation. For example, Adam and Eve could not have children in the garden of Eden (2 Ne. 2:23, 25; cf. Moses 5:11); therefore, "if Adam had not transgressed he would not have fallen, but he would have remained in the garden of Eden. And all things which were created must have remained in the same state in which they were after they were created; and they must have remained forever, and had no end" (2 Ne. 2:22); there, cherubim and a flaming sword guarded the tree of life to ensure both the decreed punishment of death and a mortal probationary state for God's children (Alma 12:23–24, 26; 42:2–10; cf. 2 Ne. 2:21); and there, the serpent was indeed Satan (2 Ne. 2:18). Moreover, from the Eden story readers learn that "opposition in all things" (2 Ne. 2:11) is a necessary part of God's plan, "the forbidden fruit in opposition to the tree of life; the one being sweet and the other bitter" (2 Ne. 2:15).

See also Fall of Adam and Eve, the.

Effectual *See* Appendix C.

Egypt The land of ancient Israel's captivity, located in northeastern Africa (*see* map, page 412; Bible Maps 2, 9). It is mentioned by various prophets who commented on the Lord's power and mercy in delivering the children of Israel out of bondage (1 Ne. 5:15; 17:40; 19:10; 2 Ne. 3:10; 25:20; Mosiah 7:19; 12:34; Alma 36:28). Egypt also figures in references to the ancestry of Lehi[1] through Joseph who was sold into Egypt (1 Ne. 5:14; 2 Ne. 3:4; 4:1).

Egyptian, reformed *See* Reformed Egyptian.

Egyptians The people from whom the Israelites under Moses escaped bondage. Nephite prophets used the EXODUS narrative to engender faith and trust in God by extolling his power to assist his people and deliver them from their enemies (1 Ne. 4:3; 17:23–27; Alma 29:12; 36:28; Hel. 8:11).

Lehi[1] was taught in the language of the Egyptians, the language of the engraving on the brass plates (1 Ne. 1:2; Mosiah 1:4).

Elder(s) A priesthood office in the Nephite Church both before and after the coming of Christ, with presumably similar duties as in the Church today. Alma[2] consecrated elders, among other priesthood officers, "by laying on his hands according to the order of God" (Alma 4:7; 6:1). When Alma gave up the chief judgeship, he selected Nephihah, "a wise man who was among the elders of the church," to replace him (Alma 4:16–17). The duties of elders explicitly mentioned in the Book of Mormon include presiding and watching over the Church (Alma 6:1), ordaining other priesthood officers (Moro. 3:1), "administering the flesh and blood of Christ unto the church" (Moro. 4:1), and sitting in judgment concerning members of the Church accused of committing sin (Moro. 6:7). Moroni[2] indicated that the "disciples," probably meaning the presiding officers of the Church, were called elders (Moro. 3:1). This terminology accords with the latter-day practice of designating apostles and other general authorities as elders.

The Book of Mormon also mentions "the elders of the Jews" (1 Ne. 4:22, 27). Perhaps this term applies to those entrusted with governmental affairs among the Jews rather than to a priesthood office (cf. Matt. 15:2; Acts 4:5; 25:15).

See also Church of God (Christ) in ancient America; Elders of the Jews; High priest(s); Priest(s); Teacher(s).

MDR

Elders of the Jews A group of Jewish men with whom Laban associated. The phrase "elders of the Jews" appears only twice in the Book of Mormon (1 Ne. 4:22, 27). Apparently in this context the term "elders" does not refer to holders of the office of elder in the Melchizedek Priesthood but rather to a group of community leaders. Among ancient Israelites, the elders (Hebrew, literally "bearded ones," that is, old men, or elders, as officials; *Dictionary,* 4:122–31) were heads of families, clans, and tribes who provided counsel, judgment, and leadership.

As an institution, "the elders" were well established by the time of Moses. To them Aaron[1] announced God's intention to take the Israelites out of Egypt, and they accompanied Moses when he went to see Pharaoh (Ex. 3:16–18; 4:29; cf. 17:5; 19:7). With Moses "seventy of the elders of Israel" (Ex. 24:1, 9) were privileged to see God, and seventy elders, or "officers over" (Num. 11:16) the people, met the Lord in the Tabernacle, where they received a portion of the Spirit, and thus they could share Moses' burden in leading the people (Num. 11:11–30). Centuries later, Israelite elders requested Samuel[1] to give them a king (1 Sam. 8:4–6), asked Abner to make David king (2 Sam. 3:17), installed David as king over all Israel (2 Sam. 5:3), and participated in the dedication of Solomon's Temple (1 Kgs. 8:1, 3). On a local level, elders handled certain kinds of judicial matters at the city gate, or place of judgment (Deut. 21:18–21; 22:15, 18–19; 19:12; 21:3, 6; Ruth 4:1–12; 1 Kgs. 21:11–13).

There were elders "of Israel" (Ex. 3:18), "of my people" (1 Sam. 15:30), "of the congregation" (Judg. 21:16), "of Judah" (2 Sam. 19:11), "of the town" (1 Sam. 16:4), "of the land" (1 Kgs. 20:7), "of [the city of] Jabesh" (1 Sam. 11:3), "of Moab" (Num. 22:7), "of [the king's] house" (2 Sam. 12:17), "of the priests" (2 Kgs. 19:2; Isa. 37:2; cf. Jer. 19:1), and of "all the people . . . carried away captive from Jerusalem to Babylon" (Jer. 29:1).

See also Elder(s).

BIBLIOGRAPHY

Theological Dictionary of the Old Testament. Edited by G. Johannes Botterweck and Helmer Ringgren. Translated by David E. Green. Grand Rapids, Mich.: Eerdmans, 1980.

KHM

Election, doctrine of *See* Chosen.

Elephant *See* Animals.

Elijah A prophet who ministered in the kingdom of Israel during the ninth century B.C. Elijah is especially remembered for his Old Testament prophecies to the wicked monarchs Ahab and Jezebel, his sealing of the heavens causing a drought before bringing rain again, his miracles during his stay with the widow of Zarephath, his confrontation with the priests of Baal on Mt. Carmel, and his visitation by the Lord on Mt. Horeb (1 Kgs. 17–22).

Elijah departed dramatically from the earth in "a chariot of fire" (2 Kgs. 2:11), becoming a translated being reserved to fulfill a future mission (Smith, 191). Part of that mission was an appearance with Moses, another translated being, on the Mount of Transfiguration to bestow the keys of the SEALING POWER on the apostles Peter, James, and John (Matt. 17:3; *Elias* in this verse is the Greek form of *Elijah*). These keys are the power to bind or loose on earth and in heaven (Matt. 16:19). They make all gospel ordinances valid for eternity as well as mortality.

The only specific reference to Elijah in the Book of Mormon is the Savior's quotation of the final two verses of the prophecy of Malachi, which promises a future return of Elijah before the "great and dreadful day of the Lord," or the second coming of Christ (3 Ne. 25:5–6; cf. Mal. 4:5–6). This prophecy was fulfilled on 3 April 1836 in Kirtland, Ohio, in the temple of The Church of Jesus Christ of Latter-day Saints when Elijah returned to commit the keys of the sealing power to Joseph Smith (D&C 110:13–16).

See also Translation.

BIBLIOGRAPHY

Smith, Joseph. *Teachings of the Prophet Joseph Smith.* Selected by Joseph Fielding Smith. Salt Lake City: Deseret Book, 1976.

BRM

Emer *See* Jared[1], posterity of.

Emron *See* Archeantus.

Endless torment, eternal torment, never-ending torment The suffering of the wicked, described as "guilt, and pain, and anguish, which is like an unquenchable fire" (Mosiah 2:38). The term "endless torment" is used by Jacob[2] (2 Ne. 9:19, 26; Jacob 6:10), Nephi[1] (2 Ne. 28:23), and Mormon (Mosiah 28:3; Moro. 8:21). "Eternal torment" is the term used by Alma[2] (Mosiah 27:29; Alma 36:12). "Never-ending torment" is used by an angel and king Benjamin (Mosiah 2:39; 5:5).

For the devil and his angels, those who are sons of perdition, this torment is truly endless, eternal, and never-ending in the usual sense of those terms. Through accepting the atonement of Jesus Christ, all others will be released from such suffering in time (2 Ne. 9:12; D&C 76:37–39, 85, 106; 138:58–59). Alma[2], for example, suffered "eternal torment" he described as "bitter" and "exquisite," filling his soul with "inexpressible horror" (Alma 36:12–21). When he accepted Christ, repented, and pleaded for mercy, he was delivered from his suffering and experienced "joy," which he said was "as exceeding as was [his] pain" (Alma 36:20–21). How something "endless," "eternal," and "never-ending" can come to an end is explained in latter-day revelation (D&C 19:6–12). Truly, while the torment is being experienced it is constant, without even momentary relief, and in that sense is endless. But when the demands of justice are met in harmony with the plan of redemption, "endless punishment" and "eternal punishment," meaning "God's punishment," ends—for "Endless" and "Eternal" are names of God.

See also Hell.

LED

Endurance to the end A principal component of the GOSPEL of Jesus Christ (3 Ne. 27:13–21); a condition of SALVATION requiring followers of Christ to be obedient to their gospel covenants (e.g., baptismal covenants) until the end of their mortal lives. Nephi[1] taught that "unless a man shall endure to the end, in following the example of the Son of the living God, he cannot be saved" (2 Ne. 31:16; cf. 1 Ne. 22:31; 2 Ne. 9:24; 33:4; Omni 1:26; Morm. 9:29; Moro. 8:3). To follow Christ's example requires baptism, reception of the Holy Ghost, and then endurance to the end—one must "continue" (2 Ne. 33:9) to walk on the gospel path (2 Ne. 31:10–20). King Benjamin taught that salvation will come to those who "trust in the Lord," are "diligent in keeping his commandments," and who "continue in the faith even unto the end of [their lives], I mean the life of the mortal body" (Mosiah 4:6–7; cf. 5:5). Christ declared that if a man "endureth to the end, behold, him will I hold guiltless . . . when I shall stand to judge the world. . . . And no unclean thing can enter into his kingdom; therefore nothing entereth into his rest save it be those who have washed their garments in my blood, because of their faith, and the repentance of all their sins, and their faithfulness unto the end" (3 Ne. 27:16, 19; cf. 1 Ne. 13:37; 3 Ne. 15:9). Having the determination to retain one's faith unto the end of mortal life is essential for those wishing to be baptized. In recounting the requirements for baptism, Moroni[2] wrote that "none were received unto baptism save they took upon them the name of Christ, having a determination to serve him to the end" (Moro. 6:3; cf. Mosiah 18:9). The concept of endurance was part of the set prayer for ordaining priests and teachers. The elders of the Church would lay their hands upon the one to be ordained and say, "In the name of Jesus Christ . . . I ordain you to be a teacher, to preach repentance and remission of sins through Jesus Christ, by the endurance of faith on his name to the end" (Moro. 3:3).

The Doctrine and Covenants also includes enduring to the end as a gospel requirement (D&C 14:7; 18:22; 20:25, 29) and provides additional insight concerning the possibility of growth and development beyond the grave (D&C 138:30–37, 58–59).

In addition to emphasizing the necessity of enduring to the end in righteousness to gain eternal life, the Book of Mormon is instructive on *how* to endure to the end. Nephi testified that the "words of Christ" and the Holy Ghost reveal "all things what ye should do" (2 Ne. 32:3, 5). Specific principles and practices that will strengthen a disciple's quest to remain faithful include praying (2 Ne. 32:8–9; Ether 2:14–15), holding to the iron rod (1 Ne. 8:30; 15:23–24), "feasting" on the word of God (2 Ne. 31:20; 32:3), remembering the Lord (Mosiah 4:11; 3 Ne. 18:7, 11), building a foundation upon Christ (Hel. 5:12; 3 Ne. 14:24–27), being on guard against the devil, anti-Christs, and false doctrines (3 Ne. 18:15, 18; Alma 30; Jacob 7; 2 Ne. 28), meeting together often (3 Ne. 18:22; Moro. 6:5–6), having a personal testimony of the truth (Jacob 7:5; Alma 5:45–46; 30:39), seeking first the kingdom of God (Jacob 2:18), having faith in Christ (Alma 14:26; 32; 58:10–12; Ether 12), having hope in Christ (Ether 12:4; Moro. 7:41), having charity, the "pure love of Christ" (Moro. 7:47), trusting in the Lord (Mosiah 4:6; 7:33; Alma 36:2, 27), putting on the armor of righteousness (1 Ne. 14:14), partaking of the sacrament (3 Ne. 18:1–13), hearkening to the words of the prophets (Mosiah 15:11; 3 Ne. 10:12), repenting (Mosiah 26:30; Alma 36:16–21), fasting (Hel. 3:35), and serving God (Mosiah 2:17; 7:33; Alma 37:34).

DLL

Enos Nephite prophet and record keeper, son of Jacob[2], and father of Jarom (544 to 420 B.C.). Enos' reflections about his life just before his death provide all that is known about him. In consequence of "having been wrought upon by the power of God," Enos wrote, "I must preach and prophesy unto this people, and declare the word according to the truth which is in Christ" (Enos 1:26). The compulsion to preach and prophesy of Christ characterized his life and was the source of his greatest joy. Akin to the apostle Paul, Enos knew he had "fought a good fight"; thus, his last words reflect the confidence of a life well spent: "I soon go to the place of my rest, which is with my Redeemer; for I know that in him I shall rest" (2 Tim. 4:7; Enos 1:27).

Although Enos descended from prophets and was therefore the recipient of a noble spiritual heritage, his achievement of a higher level of spirituality required a significant price in effort and attitude. Enos would be forever blessed by a hunting trip that provided circumstances that allowed the teachings of his father to sink deeply into his heart. In the seclusion of the forest Enos' spiritual renewal was effected through a mighty prayer that brought the personal revelation: "Enos, thy sins are forgiven thee, and thou shalt be blessed" (Enos 1:5). Characteristic of a soul touched by the atonement of Jesus Christ, Enos then turned his attention outward, praying both for his people and for the Lamanites, his enemies (Enos 1:9, 11). This personal experience with Christ's redemptive power was the catalyst for Enos' lifelong service.

Enos lived in a day of apostasy among both the Nephites and the Lamanites. Presumably, he was an integral part of the struggle to restore to the true faith the Lamanites who had sworn the destruction of Nephite records, traditions and people (Enos 1:14) and also to stir up the Nephites "continually to keep them in the fear of the Lord" (Enos 1:23). Efforts among the Lamanites were in vain, for "their hatred was fixed" (Enos 1:20). Among the stiffnecked Nephites only harsh threats and "great plainness of speech, would keep them from going down speedily to destruction" (Enos 1:23). In addition to this spiritual decay, Enos noted that during his lifetime he had seen "wars between the Nephites and Lamanites" (Enos 1:24). Likely Enos' plea that God preserve the Nephite records to bless future Lamanites was motivated by these current events as well as his knowledge of the prophecies recorded on the small plates of Nephi, prophecies concerning the eventual destruction of the Nephites and the subsequent dwindling in unbelief of the Lamanites (Enos 1:13–18; 1 Ne. 12:14–23; 2 Ne. 26:15–17; D&C 3:19–20).

Enos became the steward of the small plates of Nephi after the death of his father Jacob. When Jacob transferred the plates to Enos, he also communicated the commandment Nephi[1] had given concerning the nature of their contents (1 Ne. 6:4, 6; Jacob 1:1–4)—a commandment that Enos obeyed (Jacob 7:27). Consistent, then, with the central purpose of the small plates, to "persuade men to come unto the God of Abraham, and the God of Isaac, and the God of Jacob, and be saved" (1 Ne. 6:4), Enos chose to tell of how he came unto Christ and received a remission of his sins (Enos 1:1–8). This account adds yet another voice to the Book of Mormon list of prophets "crying from the dust" (2 Ne. 33:13), testifying that Jesus is the Christ, the Son of God.

See also Enos, book of.

DLL

Enos, book of Fourth book recorded on the small PLATES OF NEPHI, written by the prophet Enos between 544 and 420 B.C.

Content and message

The suggested dating for the events recorded in the book of Enos is between 544 and 420 B.C. Within this 124-year period, Nephi[1] died (Jacob 1:12), Jacob[2] completed his writings and died (Jacob 7:27), and Enos grew old (Enos 1:25–27).

The contents of the book of Enos reflect Nephi's wishes concerning the small plates. Enos knew his writing must be of worth to the children of men and persuade them to come to Christ (1 Ne. 6:4–6). He was to give an account of the ministry of his people and touch only lightly on Nephite history (1 Ne. 9:3; Jacob 1:2; 7:27). Although only twenty-seven verses long, Enos' brief but vital testament reflects these purposes and constraints. The unity, flow, and reflective tone of the book of Enos suggest the possibility that he wrote the entire book in a brief period, perhaps just before his death (Enos 1:25–27).

OUTLINE OF ENOS

I. Introduction: Credit given by Enos to his father Jacob[2] for teaching him his language and about the Lord (1:1; cf. 1 Ne. 1:1; Mosiah 1:2)

II. Enos receives a forgiveness of his sins through his FAITH in Jesus Christ (1:2–8)

III. Prayer of Enos for both the Nephites and Lamanites, asking the Lord to preserve the Nephite records (1:9–18)

IV. Description of the apostate Lamanites and stiffnecked Nephites, and the efforts of righteous Nephites to reclaim them (1:19–24)

V. Conclusion (1:25–27)

The book of Enos is replete with gospel precepts: first and preeminent, Jesus is the Christ. Enos' story provides yet another testimony of redemption through Christ (Enos 1:2–8). It also teaches that FORGIVENESS of sin is not easy but sometimes requires a "wrestle" before God (Enos 1:2) and that it comes through faith in Jesus Christ (Enos 1:8; cf. Mark 2:1–5; Luke 8:43–48). Enos' receiving forgiveness and subsequent concern for the welfare of his people, the Nephites, and even for that of his enemies, the Lamanites, illustrates a fundamental sequence—CHARITY and the desire to do good follow individual, personal reconciliation with God (Enos 1:9, 11, 19, 26; cf. Moro. 8:25–26).

The story of Enos also testifies to the powerful influence parents can have on their children. Enos credited his father with instruction in language as well as teaching him in the way of the Lord (Enos 1:1). When Enos went into the forest to pray, he reflected on his father's teachings "concerning eternal life, and the joy of the saints" (Enos 1:3). Gospel teaching in the home can strengthen children during critical times as it did Enos (Alma 36:17; 56:47–48).

Furthermore, from the narrative of the book of Enos, readers learn the manner by which revelation may be received (Enos 1:10; cf. D&C 8:2–3). They also are reminded that the Lord visits his children according to their diligence in keeping the commandments (Enos 1:10) and that he honors his covenants, a truth that brings peace (Enos 1:16–17).

Enos requested of the Lord that in the event that the Lamanites were to destroy the Nephites, He would preserve the Nephite records to bring the Lamanites to salvation. The Lord answered Enos' prayer and "covenanted . . . that he would bring [the records] forth unto the Lamanites in his own due time" (Enos 1:16). The fulfillment of this promise was confirmed by the Lord in modern times: "And for this very purpose are these plates preserved, which contain these records—that the promises of the Lord might be fulfilled, which he made to his people; and that the Lamanites . . . may believe the gospel and rely upon the merits of Jesus Christ" (D&C 3:19–20; cf. 2 Ne. 26:15–16).

DLL

Ensign Term (Hebrew *nes*) meaning banner (2 Ne. 23:2) or "standard" (1 Ne. 21:22; cf. Num. 2:2); employed by Isaiah to represent a rallying or gathering point. Specific references to an ensign or a standard refer to the Book of Mormon (2 Ne. 29:2); others point to the restored gospel or church (2 Ne. 21:10, 12; 6:6; cf. 1 Ne. 22:8).

The Lord promised Nephi[1] and his father Lehi[1] that their words and those of their seed (the Book of Mormon) would "proceed forth" out of his mouth to their descendants and that his words would "hiss forth" to the ends of the earth for a standard or an ensign to his people, which were of the house of Israel (2 Ne. 29:2). He also identified the time period for the raising of this standard as "that day" when he would remember the covenants he had "made unto the children of men, that I may set my hand again the second time to recover my people, which are of the house of Israel" (2 Ne. 29:1). These promises are being fulfilled in the latter days as the ensign (the Book of Mormon) has been raised to the nations to bring people to Christ and his church.

Organized in 1830 through the Prophet Joseph Smith, the restored Church also acts as an ensign as individuals gather to it through conversion. The Gentiles and the house of Israel were to seek this ensign (2 Ne. 21:10, 12), which is identified in the Doctrine and Covenants as the Lord's "everlasting covenant" that he sent into the world (D&C 45:9), later identified as the "fulness of [the] gospel" (D&C 133:57). Joseph Smith brought forth the Book of Mormon and organized the Church, both being ensigns to the nations (2 Ne. 15:26; 21:10; 29:2).

See also Second time.

MSN

Entreated *See* Appendix C.

Ephraim, hill A Jaredite hill from which Shule smelted ore to make steel swords to arm those who supported his quest to regain the kingdom for his father Kib (Ether 7:9).

EPHRAIM, STICK OF/JOSEPH, STICK OF

Ephraim, stick of/Joseph, stick of Name for the writings of the descendants of Joseph[1], including the Book of Mormon (D&C 27:5). The Lord referred to the "stick of Ephraim" (synonymous with the "stick of Joseph") when he charged Ezekiel to write on two sticks, one for Judah and the other "for Joseph, the stick of Ephraim," and to "join them one to another into one stick," making them "one in thine hand" (Ezek. 37:15–17). Ezekiel was further instructed that when the people asked him what the joining of the two sticks meant, he was to prophesy of a time when the divided kingdoms of Israel would be gathered and reunited under one messianic king and would dwell in righteousness (Ezek. 37:18–28). Latter-day Saints see a fulfillment of this prophecy in the coming forth of the Book of Mormon, "the stick of Joseph," to unite with the Bible, "the stick of Judah," as a witness for Jesus Christ.

As prophesied by Joseph and recorded in the Book of Mormon, the two sticks are to be used as a tool to gather scattered Israel back to the covenants of the Lord (2 Ne. 3:12; cf. 1 Ne. 13:32–41). Thus, Bible and Book of Mormon prophecies both show that these two books were prepared by the Lord to do his marvelous work. Christ told the Nephites that the future coming forth of their records (the Book of Mormon) would be a "sign" that the gathering of Israel was

Joseph Smith and Ezekiel; *painting by Robert Barrett; courtesy VRL. Ezekiel's ancient prophecy of the two "sticks," or books, does more than foresee the unification of the Bible and the Book of Mormon. It also marks the coming forth of the Book of Mormon as the beginning of the great latter-day gathering.*

"about to take place" (3 Ne. 21:1–7; cf. 29:1). Accordingly, after the Book of Mormon was published, missionaries with both scriptures joined in hand began to gather the Lord's people back to him.

Speculation over how a "stick" could be thought of as scripture has led some to think the term refers to scrolls or tally sticks (e.g., Nibley, 279–81). Others note that in ancient Babylonia, where Ezekiel prophesied, scribes typically wrote not only on clay tablets and parchments but also on boards covered with wax, such as Greeks and Romans used.

Wax writing boards were so easy to make and so practical to use that scribes used them for many different kinds of records, including business, religious, literary, military, and so forth (e.g., Meservy, 4–13; Mallown, "Excavations," 98–107; *Remains*, 149–63; Nicolo, 59–70). Scholars further note that the "stick" upon which Ezekiel wrote is translated from the Hebrew word *ets*, which means literally a tree, wood, or something wooden and could therefore be referring to a wax writing board (Meservy, 4–13).

Other actions by Ezekiel seem to parallel what Babylonian scribes did when they wrote on writing boards. For example, he followed the Babylonian practice of writing the owner's name on each board: "For Judah, and for the children of Israel his companions: then . . . for Joseph, the stick [board] of Ephraim, and for all the house of Israel his companions" (Ezek. 37:16). Moreover, he joined both boards to make one board set (Ezek. 37:17), just as the Mesopotamian writing boards were joined by hinges or thongs. In fact, one wax-board set found in Assyria contained 7,500 lines of text on sixteen boards, making it the equivalent in length of a modern book.

See also Bible, what it says about the Book of Mormon.

BIBLIOGRAPHY

Mallown, M. E. L. "Excavations at Nimrud:1953." *IRAQ* XVI (1956): 98–107.

———. *Nimrud and Its Remains.* Vol. 1. London: Collins, 1966.

Meservy, Keith H. "Ezekiel's Sticks and the Gathering of Israel." *Ensign* 17 (February 1987): 4–13.

Roman wax tablets; courtesy Keith Meservy. It now seems clear that the prophet Ezekiel was referring to wax writing boards in his prophecy about the "sticks" of Judah and Joseph. Wooden or ivory boards were filled with wax, inscribed with a stylus, and then bound together to protect the writing surfaces, making them "one in the hand" of the scribe.

Nibley, Hugh. *An Approach to the Book of Mormon.* Salt Lake City: Deseret News Press, 1957.

Nicolo, San. "Haben die Babylonier Wachstafeln als Shrifttraeger gekannt?" *Orientalia* 17 (1948): 59–70.

KHM

Epistles Epistles are thought of today, often facetiously, as long letters, but in the Book of Mormon, as in the New Testament, the word *epistle* designates simply a letter or message. There are eight epistles written in the first person in the Book of Mormon. These letters are from Moroni[1] to Ammoron (Alma 54:5–14), Ammoron to Moroni (Alma 54:16–24), Helaman[2] to Moroni (Alma 56:2–58:41), Moroni to Pahoran[1] (Alma 60:1–36), Pahoran to Moroni (Alma 61:2–21), Giddianhi to Lachoneus[1] (3 Ne. 3:2–10), and two letters of Mormon to his son, Moroni[2] (Moro. 8:2–30; 9:1–26). In addition, there are references to ten other epistles: Ammoron asked Moroni[1] for an exchange of prisoners (Alma 54:1); Helaman[2] received an epistle from Ammoron promising to deliver the city of Antiparah to Helaman in exchange for prisoners of war (Alma 57:1); Helaman declined Ammoron's proposal (Alma 57:2); Moroni wrote his first epistle to Pahoran (Alma 59:3); the Lamanite king sent an epistle

EPISTLES

to Mormon (Morm. 3:4); Mormon wrote to the Lamanite king and received a response (Morm. 6:2–3); Coriantumr[2] sent an epistle to Shiz and received one in return (Ether 15:4–5); and Coriantumr sent another epistle to Shiz (Ether 15:18).

Taking an expanded view of the epistle form, Sidney B. Sperry found a ninth epistle in Ether 5, the instructions of Moroni[2] to the future translator of the Book of Mormon (106). Here, Moroni said, "I have told you the things which I have sealed up; therefore touch them not in order that ye may translate" (Ether 5:1). Building on Sperry's insight, one could think of Moroni elsewhere as writing epistles to the Gentiles and the Lamanites. Indeed, the Book of Mormon as a whole might be considered as an epistle to a latter-day audience.

Looking closely at the epistles in the Book of Mormon, one can see how striking differences in personalities and purposes emerge from the ways the letters are presented.

Moroni[1] to Ammoron (Alma 54:5–14)

Moroni had received a letter from Ammoron "desiring that he would exchange prisoners" (Alma 54:1). Ammoron had earlier proposed a prisoner exchange with Helaman. The latter declined the proposal, saying he was confident his forces could take the city of Antiparah and thereby reclaim the Nephite prisoners, which they did (Alma 57:1–5).

There are several ways to read Moroni's letter to Ammoron. While Moroni initially "felt to rejoice exceedingly" at Ammoron's request, he then thought about the many Nephite women and children who had been taken prisoner and determined to get Ammoron to "deliver up a man and his wife and his children, for one prisoner" (Alma 54:2–3, 11). Moroni had "a stratagem to obtain as many prisoners of the Nephites from the Lamanites as it were possible" (Alma 54:3). While it is not clear what that stratagem was, it may have been to use the force of language rather than the force of arms to threaten Ammoron. It appears, however, that Moroni became genuinely angry and exaggerated his threatening, which, as Ammoron's subsequent letter to Moroni indicated, did not intimidate Ammoron. On the other hand, Ammoron agreed to Moroni's counteroffer, but he did so in such an offending manner that Moroni refused the exchange.

Moroni enlisted God on his side, whose "sword of his almighty wrath . . . doth hang over you except ye repent" and retreat (Alma 54:6). He evoked an "awful hell" and said Ammoron would "pull down the wrath of that God whom you have rejected upon you, even to your utter destruction" (Alma 54:7, 9). Moroni also called Ammoron "a child of hell" and said that Moroni's people, including his women and children, would fight Ammoron "until you are destroyed from off the face of the earth" (Alma 54:11–12). One can see the intensification of anger in this letter, from the somewhat formulaic "sword of his almighty wrath" to Moroni's affirming "we will maintain our religion and the cause of our God" to "I am in my anger, and also my people; ye have sought to murder us, and we have only sought to defend ourselves" (Alma 54:6–13). That concluding statement, coming after Moroni had made his main proposal, penetrated to the quick.

Ammoron to Moroni (Alma 54:16–24)

Ammoron responded angrily. He picked up the charge of murder in Moroni's letter and reciprocated: "I am the brother of Amalickiah whom ye have murdered. . . . And if it so be that there is a devil and a hell, behold will he not send you there to dwell with my brother whom ye have murdered, whom ye have hinted that he hath gone to such a place?" (Alma 54:16, 22). Further, he claimed, "We fear not your threatenings" (Alma 54:19). His letter responded nearly item by item to Moroni's, including a rather rational agreement to Moroni's proposal regarding the exchange of prisoners: "I will grant to exchange prisoners according to your request" (Alma 54:20). His response, however, was intended to be as offensive as possible, so in his attempt to bring about the exchange, he was as ineffectual in his writing as was Moroni. Upon reading this letter, the even "more angry" Moroni determined not to exchange prisoners unless Ammoron rescinded his malign purposes (Alma 55:1–2).

While both Moroni and Ammoron failed in their written communications, Moroni tried a stratagem that did work: He enticed the Lamanite guards to become drunk and then armed the Nephite prisoners. As a consequence, he took more Lamanite prisoners at the same time he freed the Nephite men, women, and children who had been imprisoned in the city (Alma 55:3–24).

Helaman[2] to Moroni (Alma 56:2–58:41)

Helaman's letter to his "dearly beloved brother, Moroni, as well in the Lord as in the tribulations of our warfare" (Alma 56:2) intertwines the two themes found in his salutation: warfare and being "in the Lord." While recounting various stratagems and battles, Helaman emphasized the devotion and courage of his two thousand stripling warriors—his "sons" (Alma 56:46)—who not only fought valiantly but were totally faithful to what their mothers had taught them. "Never were men known to have fought with such miraculous strength," Helaman said, affirming both physical strength in battle and heaven-sent aid (Alma 56:56). His youthful soldiers obeyed "with exactness" and "according to their faith it was done unto them" (Alma 57:21). Preserved against great odds, Helaman's "sons" exercised "exceeding faith" and were spared through "the miraculous power of God" (Alma 57:26). Helaman said his young soldiers "stand fast in that liberty wherewith God has made them free" (Alma 58:40).

In addition to these main themes, Helaman cited the repeated deliverance of the Nephites, their remarkable successes in reclaiming cities taken by the Lamanites, and his consternation that "the government does not grant us more strength" (Alma 58:34).

Moroni's second epistle to Pahoran[1] (Alma 60:1–36)

Responding immediately to Helaman's concern about lack of support from the government, Moroni wrote his first epistle to Pahoran, the chief governor, asking for reinforcements for Helaman's armies (Alma 59:3). Subsequently, the great city of Nephihah fell because there was not a large enough defense force (Alma 59:5–11). Not receiving a response (and it is possible the first letter was never delivered), Moroni became angry with the government because of "their indifference concerning the freedom of their country" (Alma 59:13). It may also be that Moroni felt frustrated at not having helped defend Nephihah himself, having "supposed" the government would do it (Alma 59:9).

Actually, the second letter to Pahoran was not just to Pahoran alone but "also to all those who have been chosen by this people to govern and manage the affairs of this war" (Alma 60:1). In it Moroni recounted his armies' sufferings, decrying the great neglect of the government in not sending reinforcements and in withholding provisions, and his great sorrow at the loss of the city of Nephihah. Reflecting the real problem, Moroni recalled the wickedness of the KING-MEN and the consequent murder of women and children (Alma 60:15–17).

Moroni initially qualified his accusations: "We know not but what ye are also traitors to your country" (Alma 60:18). "Or is it," he surmised, "that ye have neglected us because ye are in the heart of our country and ye are surrounded by security" (Alma 60:19). With this forthright man whose strong feelings, as in his letter to Ammoron, soon turned to anger, suppositions seem to have become actualities in his mind. "Except ye do repent of that which ye have done," he said, he would have to cleanse "our inward vessel, yea, even the great head of our government" (Alma 60:24). He called for defense of the country, showing the style and rhetoric he undoubtedly had used earlier to rally people behind him (Alma 60:29). And in his last element of appeal, he said he had been directed by God, who declared, "If those whom ye have appointed your governors do not repent of their sins and iniquities, ye shall go up to battle against them" (Alma 60:33). His concluding statements are forcefully balanced: Send provisions and men "speedily," or I will "come unto you speedily. . . . I seek not for power, but to pull it down. I seek not for honor of the world, but for the glory of my God, and the freedom and welfare of my country" (Alma 60:34–36).

Pahoran to Moroni (Alma 61:2–21)

Whether or not Moroni's first letter miscarried, his second one brought a quick response from Pahoran. The king-men "have daunted our freemen that they have not come unto you,"

EPISTLES

Pahoran wrote (Alma 61:4). Implicitly, Pahoran had been daunted, too. In contrast to Moroni's impassioned rhetoric and incorrect suppositions, Pahoran responded mildly, "I am not angry, but do rejoice in the greatness of your heart" (Alma 61:9). His is the rhetoric of a politician or a diplomat, not a warrior: "We would not shed the blood of the Lamanites if they would stay in their own land. . . . We would subject ourselves to the yoke of bondage if it were requisite with the justice of God, or if he should command us so to do" (Alma 61:10, 12). His first approach was to "resist evil . . . with our words," and, failing that, to resist rebellions "with our swords" (Alma 61:14). In contrast with Moroni, the man of action, Pahoran expressed worry about "whether it should be just in us to go against our brethren" (Alma 61:19). And this was from a leader who had been expelled from the capital city and whose people in the outlying areas were being slaughtered because of the king-men. Further, the king-men were treasonous, having entered into a covenant with the Lamanite king to control Zarahemla and thus assist the Lamanites in conquering the rest of the land. Pahoran was encouraged, however, by Moroni's affirmation: "But ye have said, except they repent the Lord hath commanded you that ye should go against them" (Alma 61:20). He ended his letter by advising Moroni to "strengthen Lehi and Teancum in the Lord" and come help him (Alma 61:15, 17–18, 21). Moroni obeyed with great success, defeating the king-men and "immediately" arranging for provisions and men to be sent to Helaman (Alma 62:12).

Giddianhi to Lachoneus[1] (3 Ne. 3:2–10)

The epistle from Giddianhi to Lachoneus began with flattering words dripping with hypocrisy as well as an undercutting snideness: "Lachoneus, most noble and chief governor of the land, behold, I . . . do give unto you exceedingly great praise because of your firmness . . . in maintaining *that which ye suppose* to be your right and liberty; yea, ye do stand well, *as if ye were* supported by the hand of a god, in the defence of your liberty, and your property, and your country, *or that which ye do call so*" (3 Ne. 3:2; italics added). I am "feeling for your welfare," he said (3 Ne. 3:5). It may have been a velvet paw, but the lion's claws were revealed soon enough in Giddianhi's saying he desired Lachoneus' people to "yield up unto this my people, your cities, your lands, and your possessions" (3 Ne. 3:6), claiming that the works of the Gadianton secret society were good and that the Nephites had taken their rights of government from them. Giddianhi then swore "with an oath" that if Lachoneus would not yield to his demands, he and his robbers would "let fall the sword upon you even until ye shall become extinct" (3 Ne. 3:8).

Astonished by Giddianhi's boldness, Lachoneus saw through his demands and threatenings "and could not be frightened" by them (3 Ne. 3:12). Subsequently, he gathered all his people and their substance unto one place to withstand a long siege and eventually defeated the Gadianton robbers.

Two letters: Mormon to his son Moroni[2] (Moro. 8:2–30; 9:1–26)

In his first epistle to his son, Mormon provided an extensive answer, given by revelation, to disputations concerning child baptism. Besides being the fullest treatment in the scriptures of this topic, the letter is a poignant testimony of Mormon's love for his son Moroni and for children, whom he loved "with a perfect love" (Moro. 8:17). The motivation for this type of love, he revealed later, comes by following right principles, which brings "the Holy Ghost, which Comforter filleth with hope and perfect love, which love endureth by diligence unto prayer" (Moro. 8:26). The spirit of this letter is similar to that in Mormon's sermon recorded in Moroni 7 with its instructions on faith, hope, and charity. It is an important letter which would have helped Moroni respond to the disputations. Further, it was one which Moroni was impelled to preserve for a future generation, doing so with little space left and under extreme difficulties.

Mormon's second epistle paralleled Moroni's own situation in writing to future readers, after finding himself still alive longer than he had anticipated. Mormon wrote so his son "may know that I am yet alive" (Moro. 9:1) but related something he found grievous—the wickedness of a people "whose delight is in so much abomination" and concerning whom Mormon cried to

God that he "come out in judgment" against them (Moro. 9:13–15). After including some horrific details of the Nephites' depravity, Mormon appealed to his son to continue his righteous labor, "that we may conquer the enemy of all righteousness, and rest our souls in the kingdom of God" (Moro. 9:6). Moroni confirmed his acceptance of that commission in the closing words of his record.

From its position in the book of Moroni, this letter has the effect of being Mormon's farewell to his son. In the earlier letter he had said farewell until he wrote or met his son again; here he gave his last injunction to his son to be faithful in Christ and bestowed his benediction: "May the grace of God the Father . . . and our Lord Jesus Christ . . . be, and abide with you forever. Amen" (Moro. 9:26). Of course Mormon did see Moroni again and delivered up to him the plates (Moro. 9:24), but this epistle remains the last known written communication of Mormon to Moroni, one which undoubtedly gave Moroni sustenance as he continued to be a lone witness of the "utter destruction" of the Nephites (Moro. 9:22).

General epistles in the Book of Mormon

When in his last words Moroni[2] said, "I write unto my brethren, the Lamanites" (Moro. 10:1), the effect is that of a general epistle to the Lamanites. The phrase "write unto" in the New Testament is associated with writing an epistle, for example, Luke to Theophilus (Luke 1:3), Paul to Timothy (1 Tim. 3:14), and Peter's second epistle (2 Pet. 3:1). Perhaps, however, Moroni thought of his written word as not limited to those who would read it: "And when ye shall receive these things," he said (Moro. 10:4), rather than "read these things." His words would be declared "like as one crying from the dead, yea, even as one speaking out of the dust" (Moro. 10:27). The implication is that those who were not able to read Moroni's instructions and testimony themselves, would somehow be made aware of them.

Nephi[1] said, "I write unto my people" (2 Ne. 25:3), with the effect of his writing being a general epistle to his people, both in the near future and in the last days (2 Ne. 25:21). And just as Mormon said to his "beloved son, I write unto you again" (Moro. 9:1), so he said to his latter-day audience, "I write unto you, Gentiles, and also unto you, house of Israel. . . . Yea, behold, I write unto all the ends of the earth" (Morm. 3:17–18). This could also be considered a general epistle; Mormon did not simply write *for* these people, he wrote *unto* them.

There are many different literary genres in the Book of Mormon, but the effect of the overall work is that of a lengthy letter delivered to a latter-day audience. Mormon and Moroni were not just writing a history. Rather, they had specific audiences in mind. "I speak unto you, ye remnant of the house of Israel," Mormon wrote (Morm. 7:1). "Jesus Christ hath shown you unto me, and I know your doing," Moroni said to a latter-day audience (Morm. 8:35). Again, "And now I, Moroni, bid farewell unto the Gentiles, yea, and also unto my brethren whom I love, until we shall meet before the judgment-seat of Christ" (Ether 12:38). Moroni's writings are directed to a specific audience and contain personal appeals; they are, in effect, epistles.

BIBLIOGRAPHY

Sperry, Sidney B. *Our Book of Mormon.* Salt Lake City: Stevens & Wallace, 1948.

RDR

Errand from the Lord To be on the Lord's errand is to be called and sent under his direction. The phrase "errand from the Lord" appears only once in the Book of Mormon (Jacob 1:17). In the case of Jacob[2], his errand began when he and his brother Joseph[2] "had been consecrated priests and teachers of [the Nephites], by the hand of Nephi" (Jacob 1:18; 2 Ne. 5:26). When Jacob said that he taught his people in the temple, "having first obtained [his] errand from the Lord" (Jacob 1:17), he was likely referring to his immediate "errand" to rebuke, warn, and teach the Nephites concerning pride and immorality (Jacob 2–3), a responsibility given him through revelation (Jacob 2:11).

CJW

Esrom *See* Jared[1], posterity of.

Esteem *See* Appendix C.

Eternal life *See* Salvation.

Eternal torment *See* Endless torment, eternal torment, never-ending torment.

Ethem *See* Jared[1], posterity of.

Ether Son of Coriantor and last prophet among the Jaredites. Ether wrote the final Jaredite record, consisting of twenty-four plates (Ether 1:1–6). Moroni[2] indicated that the record was called the book of Ether (Ether 1:2); his abridgment of the writings of Ether constitutes the present book of Ether. Ether was a direct descendant of Jared[1], who helped lead a small group of faithful people from the tower of Babel to the New World (Ether 1:6–33).

Highly praised by Moroni, Ether lived and prophesied boldly among the almost universally wicked Jaredites during the reign of Coriantumr[2], the last king before the Jaredite destruction. Ether, Moroni said, "could not be restrained because of the Spirit of the Lord which was in him" (Ether 12:2); "great and marvelous were the prophecies of Ether" (Ether 13:13). Unceasingly, Ether urged the people, from daylight till dark, to repent; otherwise, he warned, they would be destroyed (Ether 12:3). Not only did Ether serve as a warning voice but he taught the Jaredites about the power of faith and hope (Ether 12:3–4). He also rehearsed the sacred history of mankind, beginning with Adam (Ether 1:3–5); he "saw the days of Christ"; he prophesied concerning the biblical Jerusalem and the future New Jerusalem on the American continent (Ether 13:1–11).

The wicked Jaredites, however, "esteemed" their great prophet "as naught, and cast him out." By day, he hid in a cave and there completed the remainder of his large record. At night he ventured out to view the destruction of his people as they fought a lengthy and bloody civil war (Ether 13:13–15). It was Ether who spoke "the word of the Lord" to Coriantumr, prophesying that if he and his household would repent, he would retain his kingdom, and his people would be spared. "Otherwise they should be destroyed" and Coriantumr would be the only survivor, living long enough to witness the fulfilling of prophecy concerning "another people" inheriting the land (Ether 13:20–21). Coriantumr, his household, and his people failed to heed Ether's words and sought to kill him (Ether 13:22). Ether lived to witness the fulfillment of the inspired words he uttered. He observed the final battles, including the hand-to-hand combat between Coriantumr and Shiz, leaving Coriantumr as the sole survivor (Ether 15:13–32). Ether completed his writings and hid them away "in a manner that the people of Limhi did find them" a few centuries later (Ether 15:33; Mosiah 8:6–9). The last words of Ether contemplate whether he would be translated or die as other men, the option not mattering to him as long as he would be "saved in the kingdom of God" (Ether 15:34).

See also Ether, book of; Jared[1], posterity of; Plates of Ether.

BAV

Ether, book of An abridgment by Moroni[2] from a much longer record known as the PLATES OF ETHER (Ether 1:2; 15:33). The original unabridged narrative began at the creation of the world and continued through the story of Adam to the days of the tower of Babel. Aware that those accounts were available to his audience elsewhere, Moroni chose to concentrate on the record's unique material concerning the Jaredites (Ether 1:1–5; cf. Mosiah 28:17).

Content and message

The narrative in the book of Ether commences with the tower of Babel, when the people of Jared[1] and his brother were granted an exemption from the confusion of tongues and began their divinely led journey to the New World (Ether 1:33–43). During this journey, the premortal Jesus Christ appeared to the brother of Jared (Ether 3:1–16), revealing truths about the nature of God, the role of Christ, and the nature of the spirit body.

The longest portion of Jaredite history is covered in only a few chapters (Ether 7–11). It is, however, a highly instructive history, vividly illustrating the practical effects of both righteous and evil choices and showing that these alternatives have been available from the beginning. One noteworthy contribution of the book is its account of the rise of secret, satanic, oath-bound conspiracies among the Jaredites, based on ancient models found in the documents they had brought with them from the Old World (Ether 8:7–18; 9:1; cf. Moses 5:29–31, 49–55). Righteous kings, too, looked to the ancient past for direction. By contrast, though, they repeatedly remembered the mighty deeds of God on behalf of their ancestors, and, in effect, patterned their lives upon the sacred history of their people (e.g., Ether 6:30; 7:27; 10:2).

The fall of the Jaredite nation is chronicled in the last three chapters (Ether 13–15). From their earliest days, the Jaredites were cautioned that wickedness and apostasy would lead to their utter destruction (Ether 2:8; 9:20; 14:25; cf. 2:11). Somewhat later they were warned of their possible replacement by another people (Ether 11:20–21; 13:21). Toward the end of their history, these warnings became more and more intense and were conveyed by many prophets (Ether 11:1–20). Ether, who lived during the reign of Coriantumr[2], the last Jaredite king, was one of these inspired messengers. But the people rejected his message and cast him out. Obliged to watch the destruction of his nation from "the cavity of a rock," going out only at night to observe, he recorded what he saw and what it meant (Ether 12:1–3; 13:13–14, 20–22). At one point, before the end, Ether was sent to the king himself, warning Coriantumr that if he did not repent, the Jaredites would be annihilated while Coriantumr himself would survive to receive burial at the hands of a foreign nation. The king paid no attention. Later, however, Coriantumr recognized the magnitude of the evil that he and his peers had committed and sought to repent, but it was too late (Ether 13:20–22;

OUTLINE OF ETHER

I. The founding of the Jaredite nation (1–6)
- A. Introduction of the book and primary characters (1:1–32)
- B. Escape from Babel (1:33–4:1)
  1. God's blessings to the Jaredites (1:33–43)
  2. The journey to the seashore and the construction of barges (2:1–7, 13–25)
  3. God's everlasting decree concerning the PROMISED LAND (2:8–12)
  4. The appearance of Jesus Christ and a vision of earth's history (3:1–4:1)
- C. Moroni's editorial comments on faith and reception of additional revelation (4)
- D. Instructions to the Prophet Joseph Smith concerning the sealed portion of the records and future witnesses to the Book of Mormon (5)
- E. The ocean voyage and arrival in the New World (6)

II. The history of the Jaredites in the New World (7–11)
- A. The rise and fall of various kings and kingdoms (7:1–22; 7:26–8:6; 9:1–11:23)
- B. The ministry of prophets among them (7:23–25)
- C. SECRET COMBINATIONS (8:7–26)
  1. Formation of secret combinations among the Jaredites (8:7–19)
  2. Moroni's warning to the Gentiles about secret combinations (8:20–26)

III. The exhortation of the prophet Ether and Moroni's commentary on FAITH (12)

IV. The destruction of the Jaredites (13–15)
- A. The people's rejection of Ether (13:1–14)
  1. Ether's teachings about the NEW JERUSALEM (13:1–12)
  2. The casting out of Ether and his hiding in a cave to watch and record the destruction of the Jaredites (13:13–14)
- B. Coriantumr's wars with various rivals (13:15–14:31)
- C. The final battle and destruction of all Jaredites except Coriantumr[2] (15:1–32)
- D. The last words of Ether (15:33–34)

15:1–5, 18–19). "The Spirit of the Lord had ceased striving with them, and Satan had full power over the hearts of the people; for they were given up unto the hardness of their hearts, and the blindness of their minds that they might be destroyed" (Ether 15:19). The final destruction of the Jaredite nation occurred near the hill Ramah, in the same location where the Nephites, who knew the hill as Cumorah, would later meet their end (Ether 15:11). Divinely commanded to do so, Ether emerged from his hiding place to certify that the prophecies had been fulfilled and to finish and bury his record so that it might be found by the foreign people he knew would come (Ether 15:33).

The earliest of the Book of Mormon peoples to come across the wreckage of Jaredite civilization were the people of Zarahemla. They had made their first landing in an area rather far to the north that came to be known among the Nephites as Desolation. It earned this designation because of the bones and ruins that marked it (Alma 22:30). There they discovered Coriantumr, the sole Jaredite survivor named in the Book of Mormon narrative, other than the prophet Ether himself (Ether 15:29–32). They also recovered a large engraved stone, or stela, bearing Coriantumr's royal genealogy. When the Nephites and the people of Zarahemla united under the rule of Mosiah[1], he translated the stone's inscriptions (Omni 1:19–22).

The people of king Limhi found the original book of Ether on twenty-four gold plates late in the second century before the coming of Christ. When Limhi's people were reunited with the people of Zarahemla, Mosiah[2], grandson of Mosiah[1] and king of Zarahemla, received the plates and translated them (Mosiah 22:13–14; 28:11–17).

Nonetheless, and despite strong indications of popular interest in the contents of the plates (e.g., Mosiah 8:12, 19; 22:14; 28:12), there was considerable reluctance among subsequent Nephite record keepers to disclose fully what the Jaredite record contained. The Nephite authorities were especially troubled by the book's account of secret combinations. For instance, although Alma[2] encouraged his son Helaman[2] to share with his people the cautionary tale of the evil and destruction wrought by such combinations among the Jaredites, he also advised him to withhold anything specific relating to their actual oaths and covenants, lest these prove seductive (Alma 37:21, 27, 29, 32; 63:12; Hel. 6:25). It appears that the forbidden items were indeed kept secret. Later, when the Nephites themselves learned of such oaths and covenants, it was not from the Jaredite records but through direct satanic inspiration (Hel. 6:26). Moroni was forbidden to write all of the prophecies of Ether (Ether 13:13).

Despite its brief and summary nature, the book of Ether contributes richly to latter-day understanding of the gospel and the ways in which the Lord acts to teach, discipline, and save his earthly children. Its discussion of the Americas as a "land of promise" (Ether 2:8–12) remains deeply relevant to modern-day inhabitants of the New World. Its inspired words and dramatic history portray not only the rewards of righteousness and the penalties that follow sin, verifying the principles taught in the Nephite record, but confirm what happens to a society when it reaches a "fulness of iniquity" (Ether 2:10). Its prophetic description of the coming forth of additional scripture (Ether 4:1–17) eloquently testifies to one of the unique truths of the gospel—that true Saints of all ages can look forward to receiving more of the word of God. Most importantly, throughout its pages, but particularly in the account of the premortal Savior's appearance to the brother of Jared (Ether 3:1–16), the book of Ether is a powerful witness and another testament of Jesus Christ as the atoning, divine Redeemer of the world.

See also Babel, tower of; Fulness of iniquity; Jaredite civilization; Jesus Christ, premortal appearances of; Sealed portion of the gold plates.

DCP

Ether, plates of *See* Plates of Ether.

Eve The first mortal woman and the wife of Adam. Eve and Adam are the first parents of humankind (1 Ne. 5:11). The Book of Mormon confirms the biblical account of Eve being tempted by the serpent in the garden of Eden and the consequences that followed her transgression. The Book of Mormon clarifies that the serpent in the Genesis narrative was the devil, "the father of all lies" (2 Ne. 2:18–19; cf. Gen. 3:4–5, 23).

See also Eden, the garden of; Fall of Adam and Eve, the.

Everlasting fire *See* Lake of fire and brimstone.

Evil, concept of Evil is the antithesis of good. As Christ personifies all that is good, Satan personifies all that is evil. Good and evil coexist under opposition: there is good because there is evil, life because there is death, and so forth (2 Ne. 2:11–13). In mortality the distinction between true good and true evil is often blurred because fallen men and women, being a compound of both spiritual and carnal natures, frequently have difficulty comprehending the difference. But mankind is not left alone in discerning between good and evil: "For behold, the Spirit of Christ is given to every man, that he may know good from evil; wherefore, I show unto you the way to judge; for every thing which inviteth to do good, and to persuade to believe in Christ, is sent forth by the power and gift of Christ; wherefore ye may know with a perfect knowledge it is of God. But whatsoever thing persuadeth men to do evil, and believe not in Christ, and deny him, and serve not God, then ye may know with a perfect knowledge it is of the devil" (Moro. 7:16–17; cf. James 1:17). Hence Isaiah's warning: "Wo unto them that call evil good, and good evil, that put darkness for light, and light for darkness, that put bitter for sweet, and sweet for bitter" (2 Ne. 15:20 // Isa. 5:20). Moroni[2] counseled, "Lay hold upon every good gift, and touch not the evil gift, nor the unclean thing" (Moro. 10:30). In succumbing to evil, one's moral vision becomes increasingly distorted.

Whatever leads mankind away from Christ and his commandments is evil regardless of how good it may appear to be. Evil can be overcome. Through Christ's atonement and the sanctifying power of the Holy Ghost, all evil can be purged out of the human soul, rendering it "spotless, pure, fair, and white . . . at that great and last day" (Morm. 9:6; cf. Mosiah 5:2; Alma 19:33).

See also Good, concept of; Light of Christ.

RT

Evil one The "evil one" (2 Ne. 4:27) can refer to the devil himself as a spirit personage as well as to the influence, disposition, or ambience characteristic of him. Lehi[1] spoke of "an angel of God" who fell from heaven and became the devil, "the father of all lies," who seeks "the misery of all mankind" (2 Ne. 2:17–18). He is the "evil one" who seeks to captivate and destroy the souls of men (Hel. 8:28; 2 Ne. 2:27; Alma 34:35). His spirit, or influence, promotes PRIDE (2 Ne. 9:28), ANGER and CONTENTION (2 Ne. 28:20; Moro. 9:3; 3 Ne. 11:29), carnal security and hedonism (2 Ne. 9:30; 28:21; Hel. 12:1–6). It is the same spirit that attends SECRET COMBINATIONS of murder and darkness (2 Ne. 9:9). In short, his spirit is one of anti-Christ, anti-prayer, and anti-happiness, even despair (2 Ne. 32:8; Alma 41:10–11; Moro. 7:17; 10:22).

See also Satan.

LED

Exalt *See* Appendix C.

Excommunication *See* Blotted out.

Exhort *See* Appendix C.

Exhortation *See* Appendix C.

Exodus, the The story of God's gracious rescue of the ancient Israelites from bondage in Egypt, including the events in the Sinai wilderness (Ex.-Deut.; Bible Map 2). Drawing on the account preserved on the plates of brass, Book of Mormon prophets and teachers frequently appealed to the Exodus, both when expressing important doctrinal teachings, particularly the Atonement, and when proving that God, in his "tender mercies," offers to his people "the power of deliverance" (1 Ne. 1:20).

The Book of Mormon presents a broad recollection of incidents from the Exodus. In fact, the Book of Mormon starts earlier than the Bible by taking note of a prophecy about Moses' birth (2 Ne. 3:17). In addition, there is reference to Moses' call at the burning bush (1 Ne. 17:24; Ex. 3:1–4:23), Moses' rod (2 Ne. 3:17; Ex. 4:1–5), the Hebrews' inability to free themselves (1 Ne. 17:24–25; Ex. 3:7–8; 6:5–7), Israel's escape from PHARAOH by way of the RED SEA (1 Ne. 4:2; 17:27; Ex. 14), the manna that God miraculously provided to feed Israel (1 Ne. 17:28; Ex. 16), the rock that brought forth water to quench their thirst (1 Ne. 17:29; Ex. 17:6), the divine guidance that the Lord provided (1 Ne. 17:30; Ex. 13:21–22), and Israel's rebellion in the wilderness (1 Ne. 17:30, 41–42; Jacob 1:7; Ex. 16:2, 8; 32).

Doctrines taught and events occurring at Mt. Sinai, or Mt. Horeb, receive prominent notice in the Book of Mormon, including God's covenant with Israel and the TEN COMMANDMENTS (Mosiah 12:33–36; 13:11–24; 3 Ne. 15:5, 8; 25:4; Ex. 20:1–17), the law given to Moses (e.g., 2 Ne. 3:17; Alma 25:15; Ex. 31:18), the SACRIFICES and burnt offerings that Nephites continued to offer (1 Ne. 5:9; Mosiah 2:3–4; Lev. 1–7), and the later BRAZEN SERPENT, which Moses raised on a pole (2 Ne. 25:20; Hel. 8:14–15; Num. 21:4–9). At least one of Moses' prophecies, that about the prophet "like unto me," received attention from the resurrected Savior (3 Ne. 20:23; 1 Ne. 22:20–21; Deut. 18:15, 18–19). Moses' shining face is referred to (Mosiah 13:5; Ex. 34:29–35), as is his being "buried by the hand of the Lord" (Alma 45:19; Deut. 34:5–6).

For Nephi[1], the Exodus was proof that God could and would bless and deliver his people, even miraculously (1 Ne. 4:1–3; 17:23–42). He saw that the brazen serpent prophetically prefigured the Savior (2 Ne. 25:20). God's role as deliverer also embraces the teaching of God as redeemer and points directly to Jesus' atonement (Ex. 3:8; 12:12–13, 27). In a personal report of the power of the Atonement to rescue a sinful person, Alma[2] overtly linked his own deliverance from sin through the Atonement to the might of God manifested both in freeing the Hebrew slaves under Moses and in guiding his ancestors in their flight from Jerusalem (Alma 36:2, 18–21, 27–29; cf. 38:8–9). It is doctrinally significant that Alma saw spiritual deliverance from sin and temporal deliverance from afflictions as parts of a whole.

See also Book of Mormon, selected themes of, bondage and deliverance; Law of Moses; Fiery flying serpents; Sinai, mount; That prophet.

BIBLIOGRAPHY

Brown, S. Kent. *From Jerusalem to Zarahemla*. Provo, Utah: Religious Studies Center, Brigham Young University, 1998.

Daube, David. *Exodus Pattern in the Bible*. London: Faber and Faber, 1963.

Szink, Terry. "Nephi and the Exodus." *Rediscovering the Book of Mormon*. Edited by John L. Sorenson and Melvin J. Thorne. Salt Lake City: Deseret Book and FARMS, 1991.

SKB

Expedient *See* Appendix C.

Experiment upon my word To test or examine the truth of the gospel. The experiment first requires giving place for it in one's heart (Alma 32:27–28). Gospel knowledge is attained through obedience (John 7:17); thus, further, the experiment to determine truth entails living gospel principles. Using the metaphor of a planted SEED, Alma[2] compared good seeds that grow with one's coming to a knowledge of gospel truth (Alma 32:28–34).

CJW

Expounded all the scriptures in one The Savior demonstrated how the scriptures and the prophetic word bear harmonious witness, especially of him (2 Ne. 11:4; Jacob 4:4; 7:11; cf. Luke 24:27). The risen Lord "expounded all the scriptures in one" and then commanded the Nephites to teach what he had expounded (3 Ne. 23:14; cf. 26:1).

RLM

Extolled *See* Appendix C.

Eye of faith To see with the eyes of a believer and thus patiently anticipate the fulfillment of all that God has declared and promised (Alma 5:15; 32:40). For example, with an eye of faith Nephi[1] pressed forward toward the promised land with enthusiasm and gratitude for his blessings (1 Ne. 17:2). Devoid of such faith in future blessings, Laman[1] and Lemuel rebelliously desired to return to Jerusalem (1 Ne. 17:20–21). Abraham and Sarah were faithful, being "persuaded" of promises they had seen only "afar off" (Heb. 11:13). Similarly, Moses esteemed the blessings of being a disciple of Christ "greater riches than the treasures in Egypt" (Heb. 11:24–27). Enos' sins were forgiven because of his faith in Christ whom he had "never before heard nor seen" with his natural eyes (Enos 1:8). Elder Boyd K. Packer taught that to see with the eye of faith is "to see with the eyes [you] possessed before [you] had a mortal body; . . . to hear with ears [you] possessed before [you] were born; . . . to push back the curtains of mortality and see into the eternities" (Packer, 6). Moroni[2] recorded that the faith of many in mortality was "so exceedingly strong" that they were blessed to see with their physical eyes those things they had seen with an eye of faith (Ether 12:19).

BIBLIOGRAPHY

Packer, Boyd K. "The Great Plan of Happiness." *Doctrine and Covenants/Church History Symposium Speeches.* Salt Lake City: The Church of Jesus Christ of Latter-day Saints, 1993.

CF

Ezias Nonbiblical Old World prophet who lived before 600 B.C. Mentioned once in the record by Nephi[2] (Hel. 8:20), Ezias was listed with the prophets who taught faith in and redemption through Christ (Hel. 8:13–23).

Ezrom *See* Nephite weights and measures.

Wherefore, whoso believeth in God might with surety hope for a better world, yea, even a place at the right hand of God, which hope cometh of **faith**, maketh an anchor to the souls of men, which would make them sure and steadfast, always abounding in good works, being led to glorify God. ETHER 12:4

Faggots *See* Appendix C.

Fain *See* Appendix C.

Fair *See* Appendix C.

Faith Trust, confidence, and belief, based on evidence, in someone or something that motivates one to resolve and to act (Talmage, 96, 100, 102; Smith, *Lectures,* 1:1, 9, 10). From a gospel perspective, faith is the trust and confidence in and reliance upon the merits, mercy, and grace of Jesus Christ that leads to repentance and obedience to his commandments. Faith is the first principle of the GOSPEL of Jesus Christ (A of F 4; 3 Ne. 27:16–21; cf. 11:31–38; 2 Ne. 31:17–20). It is a gift of the Spirit (Moro. 10:11), a divine endowment. The Lord extends his arm of mercy toward those who trust in him rather than in the arm of flesh (2 Ne. 4:34; Mosiah 23:22; 29:20). Of the two thousand stripling warriors, Helaman[2] noted, "Now this was the faith of these of whom I have spoken; they are young, and their minds are firm, and they do put their trust in God continually" (Alma 57:27). Nephi[1] explained that the Saints of God were able to come unto Christ through "relying wholly upon the merits of him who is mighty to save" (2 Ne. 31:19). Moroni[2] likewise wrote that people are nourished by the good word of God, "to keep them in the right way . . . relying alone upon the merits of Christ, who was the author and the finisher of their faith" (Moro. 6:4). Jacob[2] added the sobering conclusion to the matter: only those who have "perfect faith in the Holy One of Israel"—meaning, presumably, a wholehearted belief in, a complete trust in, and a total reliance upon the cleansing power of Christ's redeeming blood—can be saved in the kingdom of God (2 Ne. 9:23).

Aaron[3] taught the father of king Lamoni that "since man had fallen he could not merit anything of himself" (Alma 22:14). Man's good works, though acceptable to God, will always be insufficient to save him (2 Ne. 25:23). Thus there is a need for an atonement, a means of reconciling finite man with an infinite Deity. Because "all have sinned, and come short of the glory of God" (Rom. 3:23), man cannot be justified—pronounced innocent or free from sin—by law or by works alone. Man's only option is to be justified by faith, to lean upon One who did in fact keep the law of God perfectly. In the words of Amulek, the atonement of Christ "bringeth about means unto men that they may have faith unto repentance" (Alma 34:15; cf. Rom. 5:2).

God the Father is the ultimate object of worship (2 Ne. 25:16; Jacob 4:5; D&C 18:40; 20:19; JST John 4:25–26). Faith is therefore exercised in God the Father, just as it is in the Son. To have faith in the Son of God is to have faith in God the Father. Thus "as Christ is the way to the Father, faith centers in him and in his redeeming sacrifice and goes thereby to the Father, who is the Creator" (McConkie, 185).

Saving faith is based in true evidence

The Lord does not leave honest seekers in the dark, void of divine assistance; he provides evidence upon which to build houses of faith. "All belief is founded on evidence," Elder Orson Pratt explained. "A true faith is founded on true evidence; a false faith on false evidence. And in no case can a man have faith, either true or false, unless it is the result of true or false evidence. The greater the evidence, the greater will be the faith resulting from that evidence" (Pratt, 48; cf. Heb. 11:1; McConkie, 166). Korihor had every reason to have faith in God; as Alma[2] pointed out, he had evidence from the prophets and the scriptures as well as the order of the cosmos (Alma 30:44; cf. D&C 88:45–47). But he rejected that evidence and thereby laid the foundation for his own destruction. Near the end of the Nephite saga, Mormon prayed with all his heart for the deliverance of his people, but his prayers were "without faith, because of the hardness of their hearts" (Morm. 3:12). Mormon was unable to exercise faith in their behalf because his people, who refused to accept divine evidence of the truth, offered no evidence that they intended to repent of their wickedness or change their ways.

Alma[2] explained that to have "faith is not to have a perfect knowledge of things" but to have a "hope for things which are not seen, which are *true*" (Alma 32:21 italics added; cf. Ether 12:6; Heb. 11:1). Sincerity and devotion to a cause are not sufficient; saving faith can only be exercised in that which is true. Thus no matter how committed the Zoramites[2] were to their liturgy atop the Rameumptom (Alma 31), their false beliefs concerning God could not result in faith unto life and salvation. Their refusal to believe in the coming condescension of God the Son precluded salvation, no matter how consistently they cried out to their deity in their weekly ritual.

In the scriptures, there is no distinction between true faith and true belief; belief is a synonym for faith. To have faith in Christ is to believe in Christ, to "believe that he is, and that he created all things, both in heaven and in earth; [to] believe that he has all wisdom, and all power, both in heaven and in earth" (Mosiah 4:9). The Nephite prophets labored diligently to invite their people "to believe in Christ, and to be reconciled to God" (2 Ne. 25:23), "for the Lord covenanteth with none save it be with them that repent and believe in his Son, who is the Holy One of Israel" (2 Ne. 30:2). The Nephites were called upon to "believe in Christ, and view his death, and suffer his cross and bear the shame of the world" (Jacob 1:8). Truly, "whosoever shall believe on the Son of God, the same shall have everlasting life" (Hel. 14:8; cf. Morm. 7:10).

Faith as a principle of power

The Prophet Joseph Smith taught that faith is a principle of power, the power by which gods and men bring to pass divine purposes (Smith, *Lectures,* 1:13–17; 7:2; cf. Heb. 11:3). Through faith the power of God is accessed or made manifest. When imprisoned, Alma and Amulek prayed, "O Lord, give us strength according to our faith which is in Christ, even unto deliverance. And they broke the cords with which they were bound . . . and the walls of the prison were rent in twain. . . . And Alma and Amulek came forth out of the prison" (Alma 14:26–28). When people operate by faith, they operate according to the mind and will of God (McConkie, 167, 191–92, 206). Faith is not merely the power of suggestion, the power of positive thinking. People do not exercise faith by wishing and willing something to be. Faith is centered in what the Lord wants, not what man wishes. Men and women operate by faith when they seek to know the mind of God on a matter and then proceed confidently; they first obtain their "errand from the Lord" (Jacob 1:17) and then move forward with a quiet but dynamic assurance that God will work his wonders through them. Nephi was "led by the Spirit, not knowing beforehand the things which [he] should do" (1 Ne. 4:6). He could move into difficult and even life-threatening situations, such as retrieving the brass plates, without knowing the details of his assignment, for his confidence was centered in God and in the knowledge that God had indeed commanded Lehi to have him return to Jerusalem to obtain the sacred records (1 Ne. 3:7). Abinadi evidenced his faith in the Savior when he sealed his messianic witness with his life's blood (Mosiah 11:20–17:20), just as Zenos (Hel. 8:19) and Zenock (Alma 33:15–17) had done many years before. Ammon[2], Aaron[3], Omner, and Himni exercised their faith in the redemption of Christ, volunteered for missionary service, and became instruments in the hands of God to lead many thousands of Lamanites to the gospel (Mosiah 28:1–9; Alma 17–23). Alma[2] and Amulek were delivered from captivity through their faith (Alma 14:26–28; Ether 12:13). Nephi[2] and Lehi[4], sons of Helaman[3], both men of profound faith and spiritual maturity (Hel. 3:21; 11:18–19), participated in the spiritual rebirth of a large number of Lamanites (Hel. 5; Ether 12:14). Because of the faith of the brother of Jared[1], he was able to remove a mountain (Ether 12:30). In addition, the brother of Jared "could not be kept from beholding within the veil." Indeed, "the Lord could not withhold anything from him, for he knew that the Lord could show him all things" (Ether 3:19, 26; 12:20).

Fruits of faith

There are numerous fruits of faith, attitudes and actions that derive from believing, trusting, and relying upon Christ. It is through faith, for example, that forgiveness comes, by which the soul is cleansed (1 Ne. 12:10) and by which people are made whole and alive in Christ (2 Ne. 25:25; Enos 1:8). Faith leads to joy and peace of conscience (Mosiah 4:3; Hel. 5:47). It is by faith that men and women undergo a mighty change of heart when they come into the gospel covenant (Mosiah 5:7; Alma 5:12).

Faith and patience often result in deliverance (1 Ne. 1:20; 7:17; Jacob 3:1; Mosiah 24:11–16; Alma 14:26–28). Helaman[2] wrote how "the Lord our God did visit us with assurances that he would deliver us; yea, insomuch that he did speak peace to our souls, and did grant unto us great faith, and did cause us that we should hope for our deliverance in him" (Alma 58:11). Through faith, deliverance comes not only from physical bondage or oppression but also from temptation and from Satan's grasp. Alma instructed his son Helaman to teach the people "to humble themselves and to be meek and lowly in heart; teach them to withstand every temptation of the devil, with their faith on the Lord Jesus Christ" (Alma 37:33).

Spiritual gifts, signs, and wonders are also fruits of faith in Christ (2 Ne. 26:13; 27:23). Jesus announced to the Nephites that signs "follow them that believe" (Morm. 9:22–24). Mormon explained that "it is by faith that miracles are wrought; and it is by faith that angels appear and minister unto men" (Moro. 7:37; cf. Mosiah 8:18; 3 Ne. 19:35). Before listing the various gifts of the Spirit, Moroni[2] exhorted his readers to "deny not the power of God; for he worketh by power, according to the faith of the children of men, the same today and tomorrow, and forever" (Moro. 10:7).

Faith and HOPE are inextricably connected: to have true faith in Christ is to have hope in Christ. Ether taught, "Whoso believeth in God might with surety hope for a better world, yea, even a place at the right hand of God, which hope cometh of faith" (Ether 12:4). Individuals like the Zoramites begin with the simple hope that there is a Savior (Alma 32:27). On the other end of the continuum are those who know their Lord, have treasured up his word, and have been valiant in their witness. Theirs is "a more excellent hope" (Ether 12:32), a hope for eternal life (Moro. 7:40–42). Disciples of Christ have hope, not in the worldly sense (wishing or yearning) but rather in the sense of anticipation, expectation, and assurance that through the Divine Redeemer they will enjoy peace in this world and eternal glory in the world to come. Thus, the final fruit of faith is eternal life (Alma 32:41).

Faith and knowledge

Faith and knowledge build upon one another. A certain degree of knowledge is necessary to exercise even "a particle of faith" (Alma 32:27). One must first have the knowledge, the idea that there is a God, for example, before one can begin to develop saving faith. Then, after one has begun to develop faith, new and added knowledge comes—new feelings and desires, new insights, new perspectives. There is a sense in which one might speak, as Alma[2] did to the Zoramites[2] (Alma 32:34; cf. Ether 3:19), of one's faith being replaced by knowledge whenever a testimony of a particular principle has been obtained. In this process faith does not disappear but instead is added upon and further strengthened. Though one's knowledge may be perfect and one's faith dormant "in that thing," or in the principle tested, one must continue to exercise faith in the future applications of the principle involved. For example, even after one receives a spiritual witness of tithing or the blessings associated with the payment of it, one must still exercise faith in the principle of tithing in the future. And each time a principle is applied and blessings are realized, turning faith into knowledge, faith in that principle increases. Faith can thus grow from one level to another—"a particle of faith" (Alma 32:27), "sufficient" faith (3 Ne. 17:8), "much faith" (Mosiah 27:14), "strong" faith (Alma 7:17), "exceeding faith" (Mosiah 4:3), "exceedingly great faith" (Moro. 10:11)—into "perfect faith" (2 Ne. 9:23), perfect faith being "the principle of power which existed in the bosom of God, by which the worlds were framed" (Smith, *Lectures*, 1:15; cf. Heb. 11:3). Perhaps at that level, faith and knowledge could be considered synonymous. God is the embodiment of faith and knowledge, just as he is the embodiment of truth and love and light and justice and judgment and mercy. And so mortals are working not toward that day when they will no longer live and act by faith but rather toward that day when they operate by perfect faith. "In the eternal sense," Elder Bruce R. McConkie wrote, "because faith is the power of God himself, it embraces within its fold a knowledge of all things. This measure of faith, the faith by which the worlds are and were created and which sustains and upholds all things, is found only among resurrected persons. It is the faith of saved beings" (209).

Further, Moroni[2] set forth the truth found also in the New Testament, the doctrine that one gains faith and comes to "know" as they "do" (John 7:16–17). He confirmed that "faith is things which are hoped for and not seen; wherefore, dispute not because ye see not, for ye receive no witness until after the trial of your faith" (Ether 12:6). President Harold B. Lee taught that one must be willing to "walk to the edge of the light, and perhaps a few steps into the darkness, and you will find that the light will appear and move ahead of you" (cited in Packer, 184). Thus one grows in faith through continued faithfulness, which in turn increases one's knowledge as one receives a deeper witness (evidence) from the Spirit. Confirming signs or evidence thereby follow one who believes (Morm. 9:24–25; D&C 63:9–11).

How to obtain faith

"Faith comes by hearing the word of God," Joseph Smith taught, "through the testimony of the servants of God; that testimony is always attended by the spirit of prophecy and revelation" (Smith, *Teachings,* 148). Nephi[1] read the words of Isaiah to his people that he "might more fully persuade them to believe in the Lord their Redeemer" (1 Ne. 19:23). The Zoramites were called upon to plant the word in their hearts, to ponder upon and pray over the idea that Christ should come to earth and offer salvation to all men (Alma 32:26–31; 33:14–23; 34:4–5). In his sermon on faith (Alma 32–33), Alma described the process by which the faithless can, in time, develop the saving faith in Christ that leads to life eternal. That process entails belief, action, and spiritual confirmation. One begins through demonstrating a willingness to experiment upon the idea of a Savior, to plant that idea in one's heart. One then performs the actions appropriate to spiritual investigation, such as prayer, scripture study, association with the people of God, and meaningful service to fellowmen. Then comes a confirmation, the peaceful but powerful assurance that the word is good, that in fact Jesus is the Christ, the Redeemer of the world, and that salvation comes through him. There also follows the corollary change of nature that flows from faith in the Lord. The believer begins over time to embody and exemplify Christlike attributes, for "every seed bringeth forth unto its own likeness" (Alma 32:31).

Faith is built upon and strengthened through submission and surrender to the Lord. Mormon spoke of a time when the Nephites "did fast and pray oft, and did wax stronger and stronger in their humility, and firmer and firmer in the faith of Christ, unto the filling their souls with joy and consolation, yea, even to the purifying and the sanctification of their hearts, which sanctification cometh because of their yielding their hearts unto God" (Hel. 3:35). Nephi[2], son of Helaman[3], taught that faith comes as people repent and cry unto God, so that "the cloud of darkness shall be removed from overshadowing you" (Hel. 5:41).

In the first estate mankind walked by sight and by faith. Those who were valiant in the premortal existence demonstrated "exceeding faith and good works" there and were foreordained to significant assignments here (Alma 13:1–6). In this life mankind walks by faith (2 Cor. 5:7). That is, he proceeds through life with the Spirit-given assurance that his actions are approved of God and will result in the salvation of his soul. Therefore, to see with an "eye of faith" (Alma 5:15; 32:40) is to act according to the witness of the Spirit, to act as though one has seen and thus has perfect knowledge. The Saints of God thus view things with an EYE OF FAITH in this life, until one day, because of their faithful endurance, they will see "with their eyes the things which they had beheld with an eye of faith" (Ether 12:19). Those who are true to their covenants in this life will eventually develop and acquire that level of faith that God enjoys, until faith dwells in them independently (McConkie, 169).

Faith, the pathway to eternal life

The Prophet Joseph Smith taught that "when men begin to live by faith they begin to draw near to God; and when faith is perfected they are like him; and because he is saved they are saved also; for they will be in the same situation he is in, because they have come to him; and when he appears they shall be like him, for they will see him as he is." In this sense, the plan of salvation is "a system of faith—it begins with faith, and continues by faith; and every blessing which is obtained in relation to it is the effect of faith, whether it pertains to this life or that which is to come. To this all the revelations of God bear witness" (Smith, *Lectures,* 7:8, 17).

Alma[2] taught that if people will nourish the word, especially the proposition concerning the redemptive reality of Jesus the Christ, the fruits of faith will be forthcoming in their lives, and the seed of faith in Christ "shall take root; and behold it shall be a tree springing up unto everlasting life. And because of your diligence and your faith and your patience with the word in nourishing it, that it may take root in you, behold, by and by ye shall pluck the fruit thereof, which is most precious, which is sweet above all that is sweet, and which is white above all that is white, yea, and pure above all that is pure; and ye shall feast upon this fruit even until ye are filled, that ye hunger not, neither shall ye thirst" (Alma 32:41–42).

See also Belief, believe; Trial of faith; Unbelief.

BIBLIOGRAPHY

McConkie, Bruce R. *A New Witness for the Articles of Faith.* Salt Lake City: Deseret Book, 1985.

Packer, Boyd K. *The Holy Temple.* Salt Lake City: Bookcraft, 1980.

Pratt, Orson. *Orson Pratt's Works.* Salt Lake City: Parker Pratt Robison, 1965.

Smith, Joseph. *Lectures on Faith.* Compiled by N. B. Lundwall. Salt Lake City: Deseret Book, 1985.

———. *Teachings of the Prophet Joseph Smith.* Selected by Joseph Fielding Smith. Salt Lake City: Deseret Book, 1976.

Talmage, James E. *Articles of Faith.* London: The Church of Jesus Christ of Latter-day Saints, 1924.

RLM

Faith, eye of *See* Eye of faith.

Faith, trial of *See* Trial of faith.

Faith unto repentance The motivating power that leads one to REPENTANCE and spiritual rebirth (Alma 34:15–17; Hel. 15:7). Thus, FAITH is "unto," not separate from, repentance. Faith unto repentance is possible because of the atonement of Christ and is required to gain the blessings of "the great and eternal plan of redemption" (Alma 34:15–16).

BLT

Fall of Adam and Eve, the The Fall occurred as a consequence of Adam and Eve's partaking of the FORBIDDEN FRUIT in the Garden of Eden. All things had been created in a paradisiacal, terrestrial, spiritual condition (not subject to death; 2 Ne. 2:22). When Adam and Eve fell, all things on earth fell with them; the nature of life on earth changed dramatically. All forms of life then existed in a telestial condition and were subject to disease, decay, death, and sin. Lehi[1] learned from the brass plates that had Adam and Eve not partaken of the fruit of the TREE OF KNOWLEDGE OF GOOD AND EVIL, "all things which were created must have remained in the same state in which they were after they were created; and they must have remained forever, and had no end" (2 Ne. 2:22). That is to say, if Adam and Eve had not taken the fruit, they would still be in the Garden some six thousand years later, in their same state, and the other sons and daughters of God would have remained in an unimproved, premortal condition. The great PLAN of happiness would have been frustrated. There would have been no children, no blood, no mortality and death, no probationary experience on earth, no atoning sacrifice, no forgiveness, no resurrection, and thus no hope for joy here or eternal glory hereafter. Thus, "Adam fell that men might be; and men are, that they might have joy" (2 Ne. 2:23–25; cf. Moses 3:9; 5:11; 6:48).

Compared with the teachings of many Christian churches, the Latter-day Saint concept of the fall of Adam and Eve is remarkably optimistic. Joseph Smith and modern prophets have taught that the Fall was as much a part of the foreordained plan of the Father as was the ATONEMENT, that Adam and Eve went into the Garden of Eden to fall (2 Ne. 2:25; Moses 6:48). The scriptures of the Restoration affirm

FALL OF ADAM AND EVE

that partaking of the forbidden fruit constituted a transgression and not a sin. Although the Book of Mormon does not differentiate between sin and transgression, in this case at least there is a technical distinction (2 Ne. 2:22; 9:6; Mosiah 3:11; Moses 5:10–11; 6:59; A of F 2; Smith, 63; Oaks, 98). Thus Latter-day Saints do not believe that Adam and Eve's transgression resulted in human depravity or in a type of "original sin" that entails upon their posterity that would necessitate infant baptism (Moro. 8:8–24). In the words of Elder Orson F. Whitney, "The fall had a twofold direction—downward, yet forward. It brought man into the world and set his feet upon progression's highway" (287).

The Book of Mormon testifies that the Fall is a companion doctrine with the Atonement. "Just as a man does not really desire food until he is hungry," President Ezra Taft Benson observed, "so he does not desire the salvation of Christ until he knows why he needs Christ. No one adequately and properly knows why he needs Christ until he understands and accepts the doctrine of the Fall and its effect upon all mankind. And no other book in the world explains this vital doctrine nearly as well as the Book of Mormon" (33). In other words, to teach the Atonement without understanding the Fall is to offer medication without knowing of the malady, to present a solution without pointing out the problem.

The Fall brought upon all mankind a physical death; every man and woman is born into this life, and every man and woman must die—their spirits will be separated from their bodies. The Fall also brought about SPIRITUAL DEATH, an alienation and estrangement from the presence and influence of Deity; all mankind were thus fallen and thereby "in the grasp of justice; yea, the justice of God" (Alma 42:9, 14). Lehi explained that all mankind would remain in a lost and fallen condition unless they learned to rely upon the merits and mercy of Christ the Redeemer (1 Ne. 10:6; 2 Ne. 2:8). God "gave commandment that all men must repent; for he showed unto all men that they were lost, because of the transgression of their parents" (2 Ne. 2:21). As Adam learned, men and women are "conceived in sin" (Moses 6:55), in that they come forth into a world of sin; and conception becomes the vehicle, the means whereby a fallen nature is transmitted to the posterity of Adam and Eve. Because the seeds of sin and death are present from the time of conception, as children "begin to grow up, sin conceiveth in their hearts, and they taste the bitter, that they may know to prize the good" (Moses 6:55). The brother of Jared[1] noted that "because of the fall our natures have become evil continually" (Ether 3:2).

To say that men are not responsible or accountable for their first parents' action is not to say that they are unaffected by it; to say that they do not inherit an original sin through the Fall is not to say that they do not inherit a fallen nature—mortality, what the scriptures call "the flesh"—and thus the capacity to sin. Fallenness and mortality are inherited, and they are a natural consequence of physical life. An angel thus explained to king Benjamin that all people, including little children, are in desperate need of the Atonement: "For behold, as in Adam, or by nature, they [children] fall, even so the blood of Christ atoneth for their sins" (Mosiah 3:16). The angel went on to explain that the NATURAL MAN, or the spiritually unregenerated man, is an enemy to God and will remain an enemy unless or until he or she is born of the Spirit and thus transformed in Christ (Mosiah 3:19). As Alma[2] later taught, "all men that are in a state of nature"—in an unrefined, unredeemed condition—are in a state contrary to the state of happiness and are thus working against their own best interest (Alma 41:10–11).

It is only through the recognition of one's mortal limitations that a person is in a position to come unto Christ and have weakness transformed into strength (Jacob 4:7; Ether 12:27; 2 Cor. 12:9). Truly, "since man had fallen he could not merit anything of himself; but the sufferings and death of Christ atone for their sins, through faith and repentance, and so forth" (Alma 22:14). In short, mortals cannot be saved by their own merits, for they would forevermore come short of the divine standard. It is only through reliance upon the merits and grace of the Holy Messiah that the effects of the Fall may be canceled and the goodness and mercy of Jesus imputed to a person's account (2 Ne. 2:8;

FALL OF ADAM AND EVE

31:19; Moro. 6:4). President Brigham Young taught, "Do not suppose that we shall ever in the flesh be free from temptations to sin. . . . I think we shall more or less feel the effects of sin so long as we live, and finally have to pass the ordeals of death" (Young, 10:173). Nephi[1], surely one of the most faithful men who ever lived, grieved over his susceptibility to sin. "O wretched man that I am!" he cried out. "I am encompassed about, because of the temptations and the sins which do so easily beset me" (2 Ne. 4:17–18). Nevertheless, Nephi knew in whom he had trusted: "My God hath been my support" (2 Ne. 4:19–20). Nephi knew his Lord and trusted in Christ's infinite power to sanctify and save him.

It is not an overstatement to say that Latter-day Saints glory in the fall of Adam and Eve. Because of the Fall, mortality and all its blessings and challenges came to be. Because of the Fall, all are able to come to earth, take a physical body, learn to bridle their passions and yield their wills to the will of God, and know the sweet peace that accompanies righteous living. Because of the Fall, these corruptible bodies will die "to fulfil the merciful plan of the great Creator" (2 Ne. 9:6). To answer the effects of the Fall, Jesus the Christ came to earth as a sinless offering, an infinite and eternal atoning sacrifice. In short, had there been no fall, there would have been no atonement and thus no hope for joy in this world and eternal glory in the world to come.

See also Awful monster; Curse of Adam, the; Eden, the garden of; First judgment; Innocence, state of; Sin, transgression.

Expulsion from the Garden of Eden; *painting by Thomas Cole; courtesy MFAB. "And after Adam and Eve had partaken of the forbidden fruit they were driven out of the garden of Eden, to till the earth"* (2 Ne. 2:19).

BIBLIOGRAPHY

Benson, Ezra Taft. *A Witness and a Warning*. Salt Lake City: Deseret Book, 1988.

Oaks, Dallin H. Conference Report, October 1993.

Smith, Joseph. *The Words of Joseph Smith*. Compiled by Andrew F. Ehat and Lyndon W. Cook. Provo, Utah: Religious Studies Center, Brigham Young University, 1980.

Whitney, Orson F. *Cowley and Whitney on Doctrine*. Compiled by Forace Green. Salt Lake City: Bookcraft, 1963.

Young, Brigham. *Journal of Discourses*. 26 vols. London: Latter-day Saints' Book Depot, 1854–86.

RLM

Fallen people, record of The Book of Mormon is "a record of a fallen people" (D&C 20:9). It chronicles the rise and fall of two major civilizations in America: the Nephites-Lamanites and the Jaredites. In addition, it testifies solemnly that if men and women do not repent and apply the atoning blood of Christ, they will remain forevermore in their lost and fallen state (1 Ne. 10:6; Mosiah 3:18–19; 16:1–8; Alma 42:6–15).

RLM

False churches *See* Churches, false.

False prophets *See* Prophets, false.

Familiar spirit An English translation of the Hebrew word *owb* that refers to (1) a spiritual medium or necromancer who communicates with the dead or (2) a ghost or spirit who speaks through a necromancer. Isaiah used the term to warn Ariel (another name for Jerusalem) that its inhabitants would be besieged, destroyed, and left to "speak out of the ground" like "one that hath a familiar spirit" (Isa. 29:1–4). Isaiah's prophecy also refers to the Nephite nation, whose progenitors came out from Jerusalem. Nephi[1] knew his people would likewise be destroyed, but through the preservation of their words in the Book of Mormon "those who shall be destroyed shall speak . . . out of the ground, and their speech shall be low out of the dust, and their voice shall be as one that hath a familiar spirit" (2 Ne. 26:15–17). Book of Mormon authors understood that their words would indeed speak from the grave to future generations (2 Ne. 3:19–20; 33:13; 27:6–14; Morm. 8:23–27; 9:30; Moro. 10:27).

See also Bible, what it says about the Book of Mormon; Crying from the dust.

KHM

Family The Book of Mormon can be seen as the journal and saga of a family over a millennium. The opening line of the sacred volume is written by an appreciative son: "I, Nephi, having been born of goodly parents, therefore I was taught somewhat in all the learning of my father" (1 Ne. 1:1). Moreover, the record keepers of the Book of Mormon were often fathers and sons.

In the record many important truths about the family and family relations are taught and illustrated. For example, the importance of families in the divine plan can be seen in the Lord's commandment to Lehi[1] to have his sons return to Jerusalem to obtain wives, for "it was not meet . . . [that Lehi] should take his family into the wilderness alone; but that his sons should take daughters to wife, that they might raise up seed unto the Lord in the land of promise" (1 Ne. 7:1).

Further, Lehi taught the importance of families as he testified to Jacob[2] that one of the reasons the fall of Adam and Eve was necessary was so that they could have children and bring forth "the family of all the earth" (2 Ne. 2:19–25; cf. 9:21). Jacob later severely chastised wicked husbands among the Nephites (Jacob 2:7–9) who had committed "whoredoms" and been unfaithful to their wives and children. He explained how their moral misconduct had "broken the hearts of [their] tender wives," "lost the confidence of [their] children," and made them more wicked than the Lamanites who were, in spite of their other sins, faithful to their families (Jacob 2:23–35; 3:1–8). Moroni[1] spoke of the "sacred support" that fathers owe to their families (Alma 44:5), a belief that led them to establish the "title of liberty" (Alma 46:12–13) and fight valiantly to preserve their families (e.g., Mosiah 20:11; Alma 35:14; 43:9, 45; 48:10, 24; Morm. 2:23).

The record also illustrates that marrying and having children is part of being a righteous society (4 Ne. 1:10–11). Furthermore, faithful parents deeply desire that their families will accept the gospel and reap the rewards of righteousness (e.g., 1 Ne. 8:12; 2 Ne. 1:13–19; 4:15; 25:26; Jacob 4:2–3). They teach their children true doctrine and strive to instill faith (e.g., 1 Ne. 2:8–10; 2 Ne. 1–3; Mosiah 1:2–8; 4:14–15; Hel. 5:5–12; Alma 36–42; Moro. 8–9). Children are blessed when they remember these teachings, live faithful to them, and look to them in times of need (e.g., 1 Ne. 1:1; Enos 1:1, 3; Alma 36:17–18; 56:47–48).

Nephite history shows the tragedy of sibling rivalry. Sadly, centuries of war between the wayward posterity of Laman[1] and Lemuel and the descendants of Nephi[1] resulted primarily over the issue of family leadership (e.g., 1 Ne. 16:37–38; 18:10; 2 Ne. 5:3; Mosiah 10:12–17; Alma 18:38; 54:17).

See also Marriage; Parenting.

DEB

Fasting Abstinence from food and drink for specified periods of time. As it is among Latter-day Saints, fasting was a significant aspect of the religious life in ancient Israel and among the Nephites. Fasts—private and public, periodic and spontaneous—were important observances.

Periodic fasts

Day of Atonement: The only fast prescribed for the ancient Israelites in the five books of Moses took place on the Day of Atonement, "the tenth day of [the] seventh month" of the ancient Israelite calendar (the first month of the current Jewish calendar; e.g. Lev. 23:27; cf. 16:29, 31; Num. 29:7–10). The observance of the Day of Atonement is never mentioned outright in the Book of Mormon but may be connected with Alma 44:24 and 45:1, where fasting, rejoicing, and prayer are mentioned as taking place at the beginning of the year, or the first month, perhaps the very time when the Day of Atonement was celebrated among the Nephites.

Spontaneous fasts

Fasting following a death: Both the Book of Mormon and the Bible provide examples of fasting as a sign of mourning following a death. Public fasting along with prayer and mourning occurred in the Book of Mormon after the murder of the chief judge Seezoram (Hel. 9:10). No reason is given in Helaman for these fasts, but they may have been to obtain solace for the living rather than mercy for the dead. Similarly, after Israel was defeated by the Philistines, the corpses of Saul and his sons were hung upon the walls of Beth-shan. The men of Jabesh-gilead retrieved their bodies and fasted for seven days (1 Sam. 31:11–13; 1 Chr. 10:12), as did David and his companions (2 Sam. 1:12).

Petitionary fasting: Examples of spontaneous petitionary fasts may be found several times in the Book of Mormon and the Old Testament. In the Book of Mormon, when Alma the Younger lay speechless and paralyzed, his father gathered the priests "to fast, and to pray to the Lord their God that he would open the mouth of Alma, that he might speak" (Mosiah 27:22–23; cf. Alma 10:7). So, too, David "fasted, and went in, and lay all night upon the earth" as he prayed to the Lord to spare the life of his first son with Bathsheba (2 Sam. 12:16–23; cf. Neh. 1:4; Ps. 69:10; 109:24; Dan. 6:18; 9:3).

Preparatory fasting: Fasting in preparation to obtain the gifts of the Spirit can be seen in the Book of Mormon in the account of the sons of Mosiah[2], who gave themselves "to much prayer, and fasting; therefore they had the spirit of prophecy, and the spirit of revelation" (Alma 17:3, 9; cf. 5:46; 8:26). Similarly, Moses fasted on the mountain for forty days before receiving the Ten Commandments (Ex. 34:28; Deut. 9:9).

Fasting as a religious exercise: Although there are three passages in the Book of Mormon that may refer to fasting as a religious exercise before the resurrected Christ appeared to the Nephites (Omni 1:26; Alma 6:6; Hel. 3:35), following His appearance, fasting is mentioned in the Book of Mormon only as a devotional practice in the worship of the Christian community (3 Ne. 27:1; 4 Ne. 1:12; Moro. 6:5). Fasting as a devotional exercise, though not found in the Old Testament before the Babylonian exile, burst into full bloom during the early pre-Christian centuries and is also frequently mentioned in the New Testament (*Testament of Joseph* 3:4; 9:2; Judith 8:6; Luke 2:36–38).

Examples of fasting in the Old Testament and

in passages of the Book of Mormon from before the visit of the resurrected Lord show numerous sources of motivation, but communal fasting as a devotional act plays a relatively minor role. By the time of Christ, however, religious devotion had become an important motive for fasting and remained so both in the ancient Church in the Holy Land and in the Christian community in the New World.

SDR

Fatherhood *See* Parenting.

Fatness *See* Appendix C.

Favored Term used to describe those individuals and nations who are blessed, protected, and prospered of the Lord on account of their faithfulness and obedience to the commandments of God (e.g., 1 Ne. 1:1; 3:6; 17:35; 2 Ne. 1:19; Mosiah 1:13; 10:13; Alma 48:20; cf. D&C 130:20–21). A person or nation once favored of the Lord may lose those blessings and fall from such a state through rebellion and wickedness (e.g., Alma 9:18–23).

See also Respecter of persons.

BLT

Fear The word *fear* appears in several contexts throughout the Book of Mormon.

1. Fear of the Lord. Reverence, honor, deference, or worship of God (e.g., 2 Ne. 21:2, 3; 27:34; cf. Deut. 6:2; 10:20; Ps. 25:14; Prov. 10:27; Jer. 32:40). "In good men, the *fear* of God is a holy awe or reverence of God and his laws, which springs from a just view and real love of the divine character, leading the subjects of it to hate and shun every thing that can offend such a holy being, and inclining them to aim at perfect obedience" (Webster). Fear of the Lord in this context, a central concept throughout the Old Testament, is brought into the Book of Mormon through material quoted from Isaiah and Malachi and is found in many other passages as well. Those who fear God are those whom God declares his "jewels" (3 Ne. 24:17), and they shall be protected, healed, and cared for (3 Ne. 24:16–25:2). The Book of Mormon gives examples of men who feared God rather than man (Alma 60:28; 3 Ne. 4:10), and contains the admonition to "work out [one's] salvation with fear before God" (Alma 34:37; Morm. 9:27).

2. Fear of God's judgment. Being afraid of divine punishment (2 Ne. 12:10, 19, 21; Enos 1:23; Mosiah 4:1–2; Alma 36:7). Nephi[1] feared or worried concerning the fate of his wicked brothers (1 Ne. 17:47; 18:10; cf. 8:4, 36). The ANTI-NEPHI-LEHIES refused further armed conflict for fear that even one additional slaying might bring them condemnation despite their repentance for past killings (Alma 27:23; Hel. 15:9). Some individuals' recognition of their sins brought fear, for example, Sherem (Jacob 7:19), Lamoni (Alma 18:5), and Alma[2] (Alma 36:11). Similarly, many felt fear during divine manifestations of God's power (e.g., Alma 14:26–27, 29; 19:24; 22:21, 23; Hel. 5:23, 28, 34). Fear of mortal judgment is likewise described (e.g., Alma 1:17–18; 17:29; Hel. 2:11). This type of fear helped expose Seantum as the killer of the chief judge (Hel. 9:30, 34–35).

3. Fear or absence of fear of mortals (e.g., Mosiah 20:3; Alma 20:11, 23; 47:2; 49:17; Hel. 8:4, 10; Ether 14:18; 3 Ne. 4:10), particularly towards an enemy during battle (e.g., Alma 2:23; 44:15; 58:29; Hel. 11:32). Related to this absence of fear towards others is the lack of fear (terror) some felt towards death during battle. On the righteous side, the stripling warriors did not fear death because of their faith (Alma 56:47; cf. 27:28); on the wicked side, the last Nephites were so vengeful it seemed to Mormon they had no fear of death (Moro. 9:5).

4. Fear or being concerned about something (e.g., Mosiah 21:19; 26:13; 29:7; Alma 26:10; 31:4; 50:32). Often it appears in the phrase, "I fear lest," and this fear might be best interpreted "worry" (e.g., Ether 12:25; Alma 22:22; 56:55).

5. The challenge to "fear . . . not." Appears in exhortations (e.g., 2 Ne. 8:7; 9:46) and in words of comfort—"the righteous need not fear" (1 Ne. 22:17, 22; 2 Ne. 9:40). One of the blessings of the millennial day will be rest from fear (2 Ne. 24:3).

6. False teachings about fear. Nehor taught that one "need not fear nor tremble" because all mankind would be saved (Alma 1:4). And the

Lord proclaimed that he would do a "marvelous work and a wonder" among latter-day people, because their fear towards him was taught by the "precepts of men" (2 Ne. 27:25–26). One of the false philosophies exposed by the Book of Mormon was the notion that one could fear God, yet still "eat, drink, and be merry" because the future judgment would be light (2 Ne. 28:8).

BIBLIOGRAPHY

Webster, Noah. *An American Dictionary of the English Language.* 1828.

JWL

Fiery flying serpents Associated with the Egyptian Sinai (Isa. 30:6), these serpents were considered extremely poisonous and came to represent agents of divine chastisement (2 Ne. 24:29). In recounting the proofs of God's power manifested in the EXODUS (1 Ne. 17:23–42), Nephi[1] observed that because of the "iniquity" of the Israelites God had "sent fiery flying serpents among them." But in his mercy God had also "prepared a way that they might be healed" (1 Ne. 17:41). The means of healing consisted of a brass representation of a serpent twisted on a pole upon which the Israelites could gaze (Num. 21:4–9). This brass serpent was interpreted by later Book of Mormon prophets to typify the Savior (Hel. 8:14–15; cf. John 3:14–15).

See also Brazen serpent.

BIBLIOGRAPHY

Handy, Lowell K. "Serpent (Religious Symbol)." *The Anchor Bible Dictionary.* Edited by David Noel Freedman et al. 6 vols. New York: Doubleday, 1992. 5:1113–15.

SKB

Filthy, filthiness A condition of being polluted, defiled, or unclean. All who have sinned are filthy, and only those who have been washed through the blood of the Savior will be found clean (Alma 5:21–22). The term "filthy" is also used to describe hell and its inhabitants. In Lehi[1]'s vision of the tree of life, a river of filthy water constituted an "awful gulf" which separated the wicked from the tree (1 Ne. 15:26–29; 8:13). This river represented "the depths of hell" (1 Ne. 12:16), which is a place prepared for those who are found filthy at the judgment bar (2 Ne. 9:16; Morm. 9:14), for "the kingdom of God is not filthy" and no unclean thing can enter therein (1 Ne. 15:33–34; Alma 7:21). The term "filthy" is also used to describe the polluting effect of sin upon an entire people (1 Ne. 12:23; Jacob 3:5, 9–10; Morm 5:15). The Book of Mormon illustrates that such filthiness is a condition which can afflict successive generations (Jacob 3:9–10).

RCF

Fine *See* Appendix C.

Fire, baptism of *See* Baptism of fire.

Fire, lake of *See* Lake of fire and brimstone.

Firebrands *See* Appendix C.

Firm and steadfast and immovable Being firm and immovable is arriving at that state of faith and conviction which enables the saints of God to undergo tribulation, temptation, and persecution while remaining resolute and unwavering in their spiritual convictions. This attribute is mentioned several times in the Book of Mormon. King Benjamin concluded his great sermon with these words: "I would that ye should be steadfast and immovable . . . that Christ . . . may seal you his" (Mosiah 5:15). Father Lehi, fearful for the future of his son Lemuel, said, "O that thou mightest be like unto this valley, firm and steadfast, and immovable in keeping the commandments of the Lord!" (1 Ne. 2:10). Alma[2] pointed out that despite considerable contention, many of his people "did stand fast in the faith," and "were steadfast and immovable in keeping the commandments of God, and they bore with patience the persecution which was heaped upon them" (Alma 1:25). Mormon recounted how, in times of "great persecutions," the "more humble part of the people" were strengthened in their trial, "and did wax . . . firmer and firmer in the faith of Christ" (Hel. 3:34–35). Samuel the Lamanite lauded those Lamanite converts to the Church who remained "firm and steadfast in the faith"

(Hel. 15:8, 10), and the record kept by Nephi[3], grandson of Helaman[3], similarly praises the Lamanite converts for being "firm, and steadfast, and immovable, willing with all diligence to keep the commandments of the Lord" (3 Ne. 6:14).

RHC

First judgment Physical and SPIRITUAL DEATH, the decreed consequence of Adam and Eve's transgression in partaking of the FORBIDDEN FRUIT (Alma 12:23–24; Hel. 14:16; Gen. 2:17; Moses 3:17). Jacob[2] testified that without the infinite atonement of Jesus Christ the "first judgment" would be "endless"—"this flesh must have laid down to rot and to crumble to its mother earth, to rise no more. . . . And our spirits must have become like unto [the devil] . . . to be shut out from the presence of our God" (2 Ne. 9:7–10).

See also Awful monster; Fall of Adam and Eve, the.

DLL

First place Alma[2] explained that "in the first place"—in the premortal existence—men were "left to choose good or evil." Being endowed with moral agency in that first estate (Abr. 3:22–26), many exercised "exceeding faith and good works" and were therefore foreordained to receive the priesthood in mortality (Alma 13:3).

See also Premortal existence.

RLM

Firstfruits, first-fruits, first fruits Term used at least three ways in the Book of Mormon.

1. Jesus Christ himself, as "the first that should rise" from the dead, or be resurrected, and also "the firstfruits unto God, inasmuch as he shall make intercession for all the children of men" (2 Ne. 2:8–9; 1 Cor. 15:20, 23; Col. 1:15–18). In addition, the term "firstfruits" in reference to Jesus Christ is appropriate because he is the "Firstborn" spirit child of Elohim (D&C 93:21). As a foreshadowing of Jesus Christ as "firstfruits" the ancient Israelites were commanded to "give," or dedicate to God, the "firstborn of [their] sons" (Ex. 22:29), to sacrifice to God the "firstling males" of their flocks and herds (Deut. 15:19–21), and to bring "the first of the firstfruits" of their land "into the house of the Lord" (Ex. 23:19). Book of Mormon peoples followed this same practice, "according to the law of Moses," specifically noting the sacrifice of the "firstlings of their flocks" (Mosiah 2:3).

2. Followers of Christ who are worthy to come forth in the first resurrection and be "presented as the first-fruits of Christ unto God" (Jacob 4:11), the first harvest of souls redeemed through the atonement of Christ.

3. The first action as a consequence of another action or principle. For example, "the first fruits of repentance is baptism" (Moro. 8:25).

See also Fruit.

KJW

Flatter, flattery "To coax; to attempt to win by . . . praise or enticements," also "false praise; commendation . . . for the purpose of gaining favor and influence" (Webster). Flattery appears in context with deception (Mosiah 26:6), idolatry (Mosiah 11:7), apostasy (Alma 46:7), cunning words (Ether 8:2), vain words (Mosiah 11:7), leading hearts to do wickedly (Alma 46:10; Mosiah 27:8), bringing souls to destruction (Alma 30:47), false prophets (Hel. 13:27–28), false doctrine (Jacob 7:2), powerful speech attributed to the power of the devil (Jacob 7:4), and making promises for personal gain (Alma 46:5; Hel. 2:5; Ether 8:17). Only once is flattery used in a positive sense—Ammon[2] "flattered," (persuaded or encouraged) his fellow servants at the waters of Sebus to retrieve the scattered flocks (Alma 17:31).

Flattery is one of Satan's most effective tools. "And behold," Nephi[1] taught, "others he flattereth away, and telleth them there is no hell; and . . . I am no devil, for there is none—and thus he whispereth in their ears, until he grasps them with his awful chains, from whence there is no deliverance" (2 Ne. 28:22).

President Joseph F. Smith identified flattery as one of the three great temptations facing the Latter-day Saints (Smith, 312–13).

BIBLIOGRAPHY

Smith, Joseph F. *Gospel Doctrine.* Salt Lake City: Deseret Book, 1986.

Webster, Noah. *An American Dictionary of the English Languaage.* 1828.

RLB

Flaxen cord A single lightweight linen strand. This type of cordage is not durable and with some effort it can be broken. The phrase "flaxen cord" symbolizes Satan's effort to use a sin or spiritual weakness to lead an individual from one degree of sin to another. If one does not sever himself from these weaker "cords" (i.e., sins) but "justify . . . a little sin" (2 Ne. 28:8), SATAN will eventually bind him permanently with his "strong cords" (2 Ne. 26:22; Alma 34:35).

CJW

Flesh A word used with three principle meanings: (1) the physical body (e.g., 1 Ne. 17:48; 2 Ne. 9:4–8; Mosiah 12:2); (2) mankind in mortality (e.g., 1 Ne. 19:14; 21:26; 22:22; 2 Ne. 2:5, 8, 21; 4:34; Alma 31:26); and (3) tendencies and temptations associated with the physical, fallen body (e.g., 1 Ne. 19:6; 22:23; 2 Ne. 2:28–29; 4:17, 27; 10:24).

Were it not for the Savior's atonement, "this flesh must have laid down to rot and to crumble to its mother earth, to rise no more" (2 Ne. 9:7–8). The broken bread of the sacrament represents the broken flesh of the Savior (3 Ne. 18:5–7) who took upon himself flesh and blood (Mosiah 7:27), and having laid down his life, took it up again to bring to pass the resurrection (2 Ne. 2:8) of all mankind in which spirit and flesh will be reunited to stand before God and be judged according to the works performed in the flesh, or in the mortal body (Alma 5:15; 11:43–44).

God "created all flesh . . . the one being . . . as precious in his sight as the other," his purpose being that "they should keep his commandments and glorify him forever" (Jacob 2:21). But, as all men are lost and fallen (1 Ne. 10:6), no flesh (no fallen person) can be justified before God, nor can any flesh dwell in his presence except through the regenerating power of the Atonement (2 Ne. 2:5, 8). Man's task is to repent while in the flesh, a period of probation for that purpose (2 Ne. 2:21).

The devil seeks to subject mankind through the appetites of the flesh, while God works with man's spirit through the enticing of the Holy Spirit (2 Ne. 2:28–29; Mosiah 3:19; cf. 1 Ne. 22:23). Jacob[2] pled with his brethren to "reconcile yourselves to the will of God, and not to the will of the devil and the flesh" (2 Ne. 10:24), earlier reminding them that "to be carnally-minded is death, and to be spiritually-minded is life eternal" (2 Ne. 9:39).

MCT

Flesh, according to the *See* According to the flesh.

Flesh, after the manner of the *See* After the manner of the flesh.

Flowers Plant reproductive structures. Parts or types of flowers are referred to three times in the Book of Mormon in the context of metaphors and similes used to warn and teach the people. Isaiah warned the wicked that in the day the Lord punishes them, "their blossoms shall go up as dust," suggesting that they will not be allowed posterity (2 Ne. 15:24 // Isa. 5:24). Abinadi apparently warned wicked king Noah[3] that he would soon be driven from his throne just like the wind drives away the blossoms or down of a thistle flower (Mosiah 12:12). The Savior instructed the Nephite Twelve disciples that while they ministered to the people they should rely on the Lord for sustenance, as do the beautiful "lilies of the field" (3 Ne. 13:28; cf. Matt. 6:28; Luke 12:27).

See also Trees.

Foods *See* Agriculture in the Book of Mormon.

Forbidden fruit The fruit of the TREE OF KNOWLEDGE OF GOOD AND EVIL was forbidden to Adam and Eve upon penalty of death (2 Ne. 2:15–19; Mosiah 3:26; Alma 12:22–23; Moses 3:9, 16–17). The nature of the forbidden fruit has not been revealed. Elder Bruce R. McConkie suggested that when Adam and Eve partook of this fruit they "complied with whatever the law was that brought mortality into being"

(McConkie, 86). Thus God's prohibition against partaking of the "forbidden fruit" may have been essentially a statement of consequences, what would come about if and when they did partake: The Lord said that if Adam "wished to remain as he was in the garden, then he was not to eat the fruit, but if he desired to eat it and partake of death he was at liberty to do so" (Smith, 231).

See also Cherubim and a flaming sword; Fall of Adam and Eve, the.

BIBLIOGRAPHY

McConkie, Bruce R. *A New Witness for the Articles of Faith.* Salt Lake City: Deseret Book, 1985.

Smith, Joseph Fielding. "Was the Fall of Adam Necessary?" *Improvement Era* 65 (April 1962): 230–31.

RLM

Foreknowledge of God The ability of God to see and know the future. The Book of Mormon affirms unequivocally the foreknowledge of God—"For he knoweth all things, and there is not anything save he knows it" (2 Ne. 9:20). This knowledge includes the history of the earth and of individuals from their beginning to their end (Ether 3:25–27; cf. 1 Ne. 11–15; 14:26; 2 Ne. 27:7, 10; Moses 1:8). God's foreknowledge permits his followers to have absolute trust in him. They can trust him because "he prepareth a way to accomplish all his works among the children of men; for behold, he hath all power unto the fulfilling of all his words" (1 Ne. 9:6; cf. Smith, 4:5, 11). Additionally, God's foreknowledge testifies to the "obstinate" that the true source of this knowledge is God, not an idol (1 Ne. 20:3–8).

Centuries before particular events took place, God revealed to his prophets important details pertaining to the history and salvation of mankind on this earth. Some of these events included the birth and ministry of the Savior (1 Ne. 11:12–21; Mosiah 3:5–10), the great apostasy (1 Ne. 13:2–9, 20–29), the scattering and gathering of Israel (Jacob 5; 1 Ne. 22:3–12), the history of the Nephites and Lamanites (1 Ne. 12; 2 Ne. 26:1–10), the discovery and colonization of America (1 Ne. 13:12–19; 3 Ne. 21:4), the coming forth of the Book of Mormon (1 Ne. 13:34–36; 2 Ne. 27), the restoration of the gospel (1 Ne. 15:13–15; 22:8–11; 2 Ne. 3), the last days (Morm. 8:26–35), the second coming of Christ (3 Ne. 24), and the Millennium (1 Ne. 22:24–28; 2 Ne. 30:12–18).

Furthermore, the Book of Mormon teaches that in the premortal existence, God foreordained those whom he foreknew to hold his priesthood and become leaders in his kingdom on the earth (Alma 13:3, 7; cf. Abr. 3:23; Jer. 1:5; JS–H 1:33).

BIBLIOGRAPHY

Smith, Joseph. *Lectures on Faith.* Compiled by N. B. Lundwall. Salt Lake City: Deseret Book, 1985.

RDD

Foreordination *See* Chosen.

Forgiveness Two related meanings of this word may be found in the Book of Mormon.

1. The MERCY that one extends to a fellow being who has injured, offended, or trespassed against him. The Lord expects those who profess to be his disciples to "forgive one another [their] trespasses." One who fails to forgive others "hath brought himself under condemnation" (Mosiah 26:31; cf. D&C 64:9–11). Christ taught his disciples that forgiveness of personal sin is directly linked to their forgiveness of others (3 Ne. 13:11, 14–15; cf. Matt. 6:14–15; 18:21–35).

2. A remission of sins. Through FAITH in the Lord Jesus Christ, REPENTANCE, and BAPTISM, a sinner applies the ATONEMENT of Jesus Christ to sins for which he is accountable, and he is forgiven, being made pure and clean before the Lord (Mosiah 4:2,10; 3 Ne. 27:19–20). There is one sin for which forgiveness is unavailable: denying the Holy Ghost (Alma 39:6; D&C 76:30–38; 132:27). Though "all manner of sin and blasphemy shall be forgiven unto men," except "blasphemy against the Holy Ghost" (Matt. 12:31–32; cf. Smith, 356–57), one can sin seriously enough that forgiveness cannot be granted on the same basis it is granted for less serious sins. Murderers, for instance, must traverse a different path than others to obtain forgiveness. Faith, repentance, ordinances, and grace by virtue of the atonement of Christ are not enough in their case. These things are

necessary but not sufficient; they must also suffer "through hell" (Smith, 339) even "until they have paid the last farthing" (Smith, 189; cf. 359; Alma 39:6). President Boyd K. Packer taught that "forgiveness does not, however, necessarily assure exaltation, as is the case with David (see D&C 132:38–39; see also Ps. 16:10; Acts 2:25–27)" (21 n. 15).

The Book of Mormon teaches how to know that one has obtained a forgiveness of sins. There are numerous examples of people, such as Enos, king Benjamin's people, and Alma the Younger, who received and recognized forgiveness. Among the indicators or "fruits of forgiveness" is a peace of conscience. To Enos, the Lord declared, "Thy sins are forgiven thee, and thou shalt be blessed" (Enos 1:5). Enos wrote, "My guilt was swept away" (Enos 1:6). King Benjamin's people knew they had been forgiven of their sins by "having [a] peace of conscience" (Mosiah 4:3; cf. 27:29). Forgiveness of sins also brings increased feelings of divine joy and love for and from God (Mosiah 4:2–3; Alma 5:26; Moro. 8:26). King Benjamin's people further attested that as they gained a remission of their sins, the Lord "wrought a mighty change in us, or in our hearts, that we have no more disposition to do evil, but to do good continually" (Mosiah 5:2; cf. Alma 13:11–12; 19:33). Obtaining forgiveness of sin also brings increased love for our fellowmen and a desire to serve and save them (1 Ne. 8:12; Mosiah 4:11, 13, 16; Alma 36:24). As evidenced by the sons of Mosiah[2] and others, receiving forgiveness through the Atonement not only cleanses one of sins but inspires devotion to others and thus enables greater service in the

Form of a Dove; *painting by Liz Lemon Swindle; courtesy Liz Lemon Swindle. "After he was baptized with water the Holy Ghost descended upon him in the form of a dove"* (2 Ne. 31:8).

kingdom of God (Mosiah 27:35–36; 28:2–4; cf. Enos 1:9, 11).

King Benjamin taught that after obtaining forgiveness, one must strive to "retain a remission of . . . sins" through remembering "the greatness of God," humbling oneself, praying, and "standing steadfastly in the faith" (Mosiah 4:11–12).

See also Born again; Murder; Unpardonable sin.

BIBLIOGRAPHY

Packer, Boyd K. "The Brilliant Morning of Forgiveness." *Ensign* 25 (November 1995): 18–21.

Smith, Joseph. *Teachings of the Prophet Joseph Smith*. Selected by Joseph Fielding Smith. Salt Lake City: Deseret Book, 1976.

BLT

Form of a dove Nephi[1] testified that after Jesus' baptism, the Holy Ghost would descend "upon him in the form of a dove" (1 Ne. 11:27; 2 Ne. 31:8). Joseph Smith explained that John "led the Son of God into the waters of baptism, and had the privilege of beholding the Holy Ghost descend in the form of a dove, or rather in the *sign* of the dove, in witness of that administration[.] The sign of the dove was instituted before the creation of the world, a witness for the Holy Ghost, and the devil cannot come in the sign of a dove. The Holy Ghost is a personage, and is in the form of a personage. It does not confine itself to the *form* of the dove but in *sign* of the dove. The Holy Ghost cannot be transformed into a dove; but the sign of a dove was given to John to signify the truth of the deed, as the dove is an emblem or token of truth and innocence" (Smith, 275–76).

BIBLIOGRAPHY

Smith, Joseph. *Teachings of the Prophet Joseph Smith*. Selected by Joseph Fielding Smith. Salt Lake City: Deseret Book, 1976.

CF

Fornication *See* Chastity.

Forswear *See* Appendix C.

Fortifications Man-made structures designed to limit the mobility of attackers and protect defenders from attack. The Book of Mormon describes the use of a number of types of fortifications including walled cites, ditches, wooden palisades, breastworks of timber and earth, fortified gates, pickets, towers, and strongholds.

The most detailed description of fortifications in the Book of Mormon comes from the great wars in the early first century B.C. (Alma 49:2–22; 50:1–11; 53:3–7). The fortifications described in these examples seem to have been typical of Book of Mormon fortifications in general (Alma 50:6). The foundation of the fortification was an earthen wall created by digging a "ditch" (Alma 49:18; 53:3) and "cast[ing] up" (Alma 53:4) a "ridge of earth round about" (Alma 49:4, 50:1). The ditch faced outward, toward the enemy, thus in effect doubling the height of the earthen wall (Alma 49:18), since an enemy would have to both climb out of the ditch and over the wall. This basic fortification could be strengthened by adding a timber palisade on top of the earthen wall (Alma 50:1–2), or a timber structure to support the earthen wall (Alma 53:4). They could be further strengthened by wooden towers (Alma 50:2–4).

This description corresponds quite closely to archaeological evidence of Mesoamerican fortifications such as those found at Becan. It has only been in the past few decades that strong archaeological evidence concerning the extensive use of fortifications in pre-Columbian Mesoamerica has been properly evaluated. Recent archaeological studies have demonstrated that fortifications were widespread in Mesoamerica from at least the first millennium B.C. Pre-Columbian fortifications identified by archaeologists include walls of earth, mud brick, or stone; wooden palisades; spike and thorn barriers; moats and trenches; fortified bridges and gates; special fortifications for missile troops (archers, slingers, and javelin men); and towers and other elevated structures, broadly paralleling the types of fortifications described in the Book of Mormon.

In contrast to ancient Near Eastern siegecraft but in parallel with pre-Columbian siegecraft, no types of pre-gunpowder artillery, siege engines, or siege towers are mentioned in the Book of Mormon.

See also Armor; Warfare in the Book of Mormon; Weapons.

BIBLIOGRAPHY

Sorenson, John L. "Fortifications in the Book of Mormon Account Compared with Mesoamerican Fortifications." *Warfare in the Book of Mormon.* Edited by Stephen D. Ricks and William J. Hamblin. Salt Lake City: Deseret Book, 1990.

WJH

Foundation Two meanings for this term may be found in the Book of Mormon.

1. That period in the premortal existence when preparations were made to carry out God's great and eternal purposes, the plan of redemption. Hence, Book of Mormon prophets employed the phrase "from the foundation of the world" in referring to the time during which God prepared the plan of redemption (1 Ne. 10:18; Mosiah 15:19; Alma 12:25, 30; 18:39; 22:13; 42:26), provided for a Savior (Mosiah 18:13; Hel. 5:47; Ether 3:14), foreordained priesthood bearers (Alma 13:3, 5), and prepared his kingdom for the righteous (2 Ne. 9:18).

2. A direct reference to Jesus Christ. Jacob[2] and Helaman[3] taught that as the "stone" or "rock" upon which faith must be built, Christ is the "only sure foundation" of everyone's hope for redemption, even for the Jews, though they would reject him during his mortal ministry (Jacob 4:15–17; Hel. 5:12).

ACS

Fountain A body or source of water, such as a spring, well, pool, reservoir, or sea. Used literally, the word is consistent with ancient Near Eastern language patterns, as in the phrases "the fountain of the Red Sea" (1 Ne. 2:9) or "a fountain of pure water" (Mosiah 18:5).

Often "fountain" is used metaphorically to refer to a concentrated source of righteousness or wickedness. Lehi[1], for example, exhorted Lemuel to be like the river they had seen emptying into the Red Sea, "continually running into the fountain of all righteousness" (1 Ne. 2:9). Nephi[1] saw in vision that the rod of iron, or word of God, "led to the fountain of living waters" which was "a representation of the love of God" (1 Ne. 11:25). On the other hand, he learned that "the fountain of filthy water . . . and the depths thereof are the depths of hell" (1 Ne. 12:16). Mormon taught that an evil man cannot do that which is good (Moro. 7:10). He illustrated his point by using the analogy of a fountain: "For behold, a bitter fountain cannot bring forth good water; neither can a good fountain bring forth bitter water; wherefore, a man being a servant of the devil cannot follow Christ; and if he follow Christ he cannot be a servant of the devil" (Moro. 7:11).

Ultimately, "fountain" is used as a symbol for Jesus Christ, as Mormon implied. Moroni was commanded to write in order that the children of men might "come unto the fountain of all righteousness and be saved" (Ether 8:26). He was further taught by the Lord that the "fountain of all righteousness" is the Lord himself (Ether 12:28). Indeed, Jesus Christ is the source and reservoir of all truth and goodness. The Savior taught this concept in the eastern hemisphere to the Samaritan woman at the well during his mortal ministry. He referred to himself as the source or well of "living water. . . . springing up into everlasting life" (John 4:10, 14; cf. Alma 32:41).

ACS

Fowl *See* Animals.

Freedom A condition or state that allows self-determination to act or carry out choices resulting from the exercise of AGENCY. In the Book of Mormon, *freedom* refers primarily to the absence of bondage or enslavement to others, although the book's central message is the acquisition of freedom from the bondage of sin and death through Christ (Mosiah 5:8; cf. 2 Ne. 2:26–27; Alma 58:41). From the days of Nephi[1] (2 Ne. 5:14; Jacob 1:10), the righteous sought to preserve their "freedom from bondage" by defending themselves against their enemies when commanded by the Lord (Alma 51:21; 43:45–49; 3 Ne. 2:12; cf. D&C 98:23–33). Mormon described captain Moroni as a great preserver of freedom (Alma 48:11–13) who fought against the Lamanites and Nephite dissenters by inspiring his troops with thoughts of liberty (Alma 43:48). He established the standard known as the TITLE OF LIBERTY, which stated, "In memory of our God, our religion, and freedom, and our peace, our wives, and our children" (Alma 46:12). Pahoran[1] equated this "spirit of freedom" with having the "Spirit of God" (Alma 61:15).

To remind the Nephites of the blessings of freedom, Alma the Younger admonished them to remember both the captivity of their fathers (Alma 5:6; 29:11–12; 36:28–29) and the source of their deliverance from bondage (Alma 5:4; 36:2), a message he had personally received from an angel (Mosiah 27:16).

Additionally, the Book of Mormon teaches concerning the necessity of establishing governments and electing political leaders that will preserve freedom (Mosiah 29:18, 25; Alma 50:39; 59:13; cf. Ether 6:22–23); it warns against establishing secret combinations, which will "overthrow" freedom (Ether 8:25; cf. 3 Ne. 9:9); it proclaims the "decrees of God" to those who live on the promised land who desire to maintain freedom (Ether 2:9–12); and it contains prophecies pertaining to God's involvement in the establishment of America as a free land to accomplish his divine purposes (1 Ne. 13:17–19; 3 Ne. 21:4).

See also Book of Mormon, selected themes of, bondage and deliverance.

BRM

Freemen Nephite citizens who "covenanted to maintain their rights and the privileges of their religion by a free government" and who favored the retention of Pahoran[1] as chief judge (Alma 51:6; 67 B.C.). The freemen, also called the "people of liberty" (Alma 51:7, 13) opposed the KING-MEN, a Nephite faction who desired that the laws of the land be altered to establish a king. When Pahoran refused the petitions of the king-men to change the law, they were angry and sought his removal (Alma 51:3–4). To settle the contention between the two divisions (king-men and freemen), an appeal was made to the VOICE OF THE PEOPLE, resulting in favor of Pahoran and the freemen. Although the king-men were defeated, they persisted in their efforts to establish a king, even to the extent of driving Pahoran and the freemen from Zarahemla (Alma 61:3–5). Upon being informed of this internal rebellion through an epistle from Pahoran, captain Moroni hastened to Pahoran's assistance with "a small number of men." Rallying troops en route, they arrived in the land of Gideon, united forces with Pahoran and the freemen, and retook Zarahemla (Alma 62:1–9; ca. 62 B.C.).

The freemen are also mentioned as troops under Moroni's command in the wars with the Lamanites (Alma 60:25).

CKM

Fro *See* Appendix C.

Fruit The word *fruit* has four different meanings in the Book of Mormon.

1. The LOVE OF GOD. Partaking of the fruit of the TREE OF LIFE is the focus of LEHI[1]'S DREAM. Eating the fruit represents partaking of the love of God—the greatest manifestation being the CONDESCENSION OF GOD—Christ's birth, life, and atonement (1 Ne. 11:2–33). God's love is evidenced by his children in such ways as forgiveness, joy, resurrection, spiritual gifts, and the ultimate gift of eternal life (Enos 1:2–8; Mosiah 4:1–3; Alma 36:16–21; 2 Ne. 2:8; Mosiah 15:9; Moro. 10:8–18; 1 Ne. 15:36; D&C 14:7). The fruit tasted sweeter, appeared more white, and produced greater joy and desire for righteousness than anything Lehi had ever experienced. All who "press . . . forward, continually holding fast to the rod of iron" will likewise be able to experience this glorious fruit (1 Ne. 8:30, 10–12).

In his sermon to the outcast Zoramites[2] (Alma 32–33), Alma[2] identified fruit as the reward of a process, begun by planting a seed of desire to believe in Christ, and nurtured by faith, diligence, and patience. Descriptive of the bounteous blessings of Christ's atonement, the fruit is most precious, sweet, white, and filling, leaving a disciple to no more hunger or thirst (Alma 32:42).

2. The product of a person's endeavors, whether righteous or evil, and the basis for Christ's judgment. The Savior taught that people are known by their fruits or works (3 Ne. 14:15–20; cf. Moro. 7:5–11). Qualification for baptism requires a candidate to bring "forth

fruit . . . worthy of it" (Moro. 6:1). Worthy fruit includes sincere repentance, a broken heart and contrite spirit, and a determination to serve Christ to the end (Moro. 6:2–3; D&C 20:37). All are invited to bring "forth fruit meet for repentance" to receive the Lord's greatest blessings (Alma 12:15; 13:13; 34:30).

In Zenos' allegory (Jacob 5), preserving the fruit of the olive trees is the sole concern of the Lord. This effort represents the Lord's purpose, his work and glory (Jacob 5:54; Moses 1:39). The fruit itself, good or bad, represents people's response to Christ's labors on their behalf. He grieves when the fruit becomes bitter despite his constant care and efforts. He rejoices with his laborers when much good fruit (righteous, covenant-keeping people) is produced and becomes "like unto one body" and "equal" (Jacob 5:74), descriptive of a Zion-like people (Moses 7:18).

3. Progeny. Described as "the fruit of my loins" (2 Ne. 3:4, 14; Jacob 2:25).

4. The edible part of a plant (1 Ne. 17:5–6; 18:6; Mosiah 9:9; 3 Ne. 24:11).

See also Firstfruits, first-fruits, first fruits; Forbidden fruit; Fruit meet for repentance.

CF

Fruit meet for repentance Deeds or "fruit" that are "meet for," meaning appropriate to repentance or indicative of it. Alma[2] declared that to be saved and enter into the "rest of the Lord," one must bring forth "fruit meet for repentance" (Alma 12:15; 13:12–13). This "fruit" includes works of righteousness, humility, faith, obedience, and baptism for the remission of sins (Alma 5:33–36, 54; Moro. 8:25).

BLT

Fulfill all righteousness Nephi[1] explained that the Savior "fulfill[ed] all righteousness" by being baptized in that he showed the "straitness of the path, and the narrowness of the gate," demonstrating humility and obedience to the will of the Father and setting an example for all mankind (2 Ne. 31:5–21; cf. Matt. 3:15). The Prophet Joseph Smith observed that no accountable person, not even the sinless Son of Man, can enter the kingdom of God without baptism (Smith, 266).

BIBLIOGRAPHY

Smith, Joseph. *Teachings of the Prophet Joseph Smith.* Selected by Joseph Fielding Smith. Salt Lake City: Deseret Book, 1976.

RLB

Fulness of his own time *See* Fulness of time.

Fulness of iniquity The stage of sin and evil that inevitably leads to destruction. "It is the everlasting decree of God" that the people who inhabit the Americas "shall serve God or shall be swept off" when they have reached the "fulness of iniquity" (Ether 2:10). This stage is reached when the people, by rejecting "every word of God" (1 Ne. 17:35), have "ripened in iniquity" (Ether 2:9).

The Book of Mormon mentions conditions that lead to a fulness of iniquity. For example, when the great destructions among the Nephites and Lamanites occurred immediately before the appearance of Christ in the Americas, the survivors were told why the wicked had been destroyed. They had killed the prophets and cast out the righteous from among them (3 Ne. 9:10–11; cf. Alma 10:23; Hel. 13:13–14).

The Book of Mormon also mentions other specific types of wickedness that characterize societies that are approaching the fulness of iniquity: delight in violence (Morm. 4:11), support of secret combinations (3 Ne. 9:9; Ether 8:20–22), indulgence in the occult (Morm. 1:19; 2:10), and gross debauchery (Moro. 9:8–11). When people seek "for happiness in doing iniquity" all the days of their lives, the days of their "probation are past . . . [and] it is everlastingly too late, and [their] destruction is made sure" (Hel. 13:38). They reach the fulness of iniquity.

Near the end of Nephite society, the military leader and prophet Mormon, writing to his son Moroni, explained why he felt that his people would be destroyed. He lamented, "How can we expect that God will stay his hand in judgment against us? . . . O the depravity of my people! They are without order and without mercy. . . . Behold, thou knowest the wickedness of this people; thou knowest that they are without principle, and past feeling. . . . Behold, my son, I cannot recommend them unto God lest he should smite me" (Moro. 9:14, 18–21).

PYH

Fulness of the Gentiles That period of time, beginning with the restoration of the gospel through Joseph Smith, in which the fulness of the gospel is taken primarily to Gentile nations. The fulness of the Gentiles culminates or is "fulfilled" at or near the second coming of Christ, after the Gentiles have had a full opportunity to receive the gospel. Gospel preaching will then be directed principally to the Jews and all the house of Israel.

The term "fulness of the Gentiles" is used twice in the Book of Mormon, once by Nephi[1] and once by Christ. Nephi prophesied that "through the fulness of the Gentiles . . . in the latter days . . . shall the fulness of the gospel of the Messiah come unto the Gentiles, and from the Gentiles unto the remnant of our seed" (1 Ne. 15:13). To his twelve disciples in America the Savior explained that "through the fulness of the Gentiles" the scattered descendants of the Jews, "my people at Jerusalem," would be brought to a knowledge of their Redeemer. He clarified that such would happen "in the latter day" when the "fulness of these things [would] be made known" to the Gentiles (3 Ne. 16:4–7).

Although Book of Mormon prophets clearly taught that the Gentiles would take the gospel to all the house of Israel and to all nations, they did not always use the phrase "fulness of the Gentiles" in discussing this concept (Title Page; 1 Ne. 21–22; 2 Ne. 27, 29–30; Jacob 5–6; 3 Ne. 21). In one instance, Nephi employed the phrase "days of the Gentiles" to refer to this concept and the designated time period, "the last days" (2 Ne. 27:1).

In 1823 Moroni[2] told Joseph Smith "that the fulness of the Gentiles was soon to come in" (JS–H 1:41). The Doctrine and Covenants contains the phrase "times of the Gentiles" instead of "fulness of the Gentiles," but "times of the Gentiles" refers to the same period and specifies what marks the beginning and ending of that era: "When the times of the Gentiles is come in, a light shall break forth among them that sit in darkness, and it shall be the fulness of my gospel" (D&C 45:28), a clear reference to the Restoration. In one sense, the times of the Gentiles "began" in the days of Paul, when he turned from preaching to the Jews and offered the gospel to the Gentiles (Acts 13:46–47). In Paul's day the gospel was preached first to the Jews and then to the Gentiles. In the latter days the gospel goes first to the Gentiles and then to the Jews (1 Ne. 13:42). The restoration of the gospel through the Prophet Joseph Smith marks the beginning, or the coming in, of the "times of the Gentiles" in the latter days. The fulfilling of the times, or fulness of the Gentiles, will take place in a generation that rejects the light "because of the precepts of men," a generation that will "see an overflowing scourge . . . a desolating sickness" covering the land, as well as war, natural calamities, and "many desolations" (D&C 45:29–33). Moreover, Luke stated that "the generation when the times of the Gentiles be fulfilled, shall not pass away, till all be fulfilled" (JST Luke 21:32; cf. D&C 45:35–44).

An important promise the Lord made to the Jews will be realized when the times (fulness) of the Gentiles is fulfilled: Although they have been trodden down and "led away captive into all nations," they will be gathered again to Jerusalem and taught of the Lord (Luke 21:24; Rom. 11:25; D&C 45:24–25, 48–53). Nephi prophesied that even before the full realization of this promise, the Jews would "begin to believe in Christ; and they shall begin to gather in upon the face of the land" (2 Ne. 30:7).

See also Gentiles, Book of Mormon message concerning; Israel, gathering of; Jews, Book of Mormon message concerning; Last shall be first, and the first shall be last.

LED

Fulness of the gospel The Book of Mormon contains the fulness of the GOSPEL, as defined by the Savior (D&C 20:9; 27:5; 42:12). As a second witness, this record declares the good news or glad tidings that Jesus Christ came into the world to ransom and redeem fallen men and women from sin and death, and that through faith in the Lord Jesus Christ, repentance, baptism, the reception of the Holy Ghost, and enduring faithfully to the end (3 Ne. 27:13–22; A of F 3; 4) mankind may partake of the blessings of the Atonement and thereby be saved (D&C 39:6; 76:40–42). This "does not mean it contains every teaching, every doctrine ever revealed. Rather, it means that in the Book of Mormon we will find the fulness of those doctrines required for our salvation" (Benson, 18).

BIBLIOGRAPHY

Benson, Ezra Taft. *A Witness and a Warning*. Salt Lake City: Deseret Book, 1988.

RLM

Fulness of time A phrase referring to the time when the Savior would come to the earth to perform his mortal ministry, including the Atonement. It is used twice by Lehi[1] in instructing his son Jacob[2] (2 Ne. 2:3, 26) and once by Nephi[1] (2 Ne. 11:7), though Nephi used an expanded form of the phrase—"the fulness of his own time." Paul used "the fulness of the time" (Gal. 4:4), with the same meaning as in the Book of Mormon. A similar phrase, "fulness of times" (plural) is used many times in the Doctrine and Covenants, usually referring to the "dispensation of the fulness of times," the dispensation beginning at the restoration of the gospel through the Prophet Joseph Smith (D&C 27:13; 112:30; 121:31; 124:41; 128:18–20; 138:53). Doctrine and Covenants 76:106 employs the phrase "fulness of times" to refer to the end of the Millennium.

LED

Wherefore, how great the importance to make these things known unto the inhabitants of the earth, that they may know that there is no flesh that can dwell in the presence of God, save it be through the merits, and mercy, and **grace** of the Holy Messiah, who layeth down his life according to the flesh, and taketh it again by the power of the Spirit, that he may bring to pass the resurrection of the dead, being the first that should rise. 2 NEPHI 2:8

Gad, city of An otherwise unknown city that Christ, during the calamities that attended his crucifixion, "caused to be burned with fire, and the inhabitants thereof, because of their wickedness in casting out the prophets" (3 Ne. 9:10–11).

Gadiandi, city of After Christ's crucifixion, the city of Gadiandi and others sank in the earth, burying their inhabitants. Hills and valleys replaced cities, literally hiding their wickedness (3 Ne. 9:8).

Gadianton Leader of the band of robbers organized by Kishkumen during the judgeship of Helaman[3] (50 B.C.). Gadianton was known for his prowess in speaking and his secret murders and robbery. He promised his followers that if they succeeded in helping him obtain the judgment-seat, he would place them in power (Hel. 2:4–5). Following Kishkumen's death in the failed assassination attempt on chief judge Helaman, Gadianton fled to escape execution (Hel. 2:10–11). From the time he took control of the group until the end of Nephite history, this band was called the GADIANTON ROBBERS (Hel. 6:18; 4 Ne. 1:42; Morm. 2:28). According to Mormon, Gadianton did not get his secret oaths and covenants from the Jaredite records in Helaman's care but rather from Satan himself (Hel. 6:26, 29). Mormon noted that "this Gadianton did prove the overthrow, yea, almost the entire destruction of the people of Nephi" (Hel. 2:13).

MDR

Gadianton robbers A wicked band originally led by a man named Kishkumen, united to murder, rob, and gain power (Hel. 2:8; ca. 52 B.C.). This band began with a group of Nephites who supported Paanchi in his desire to be the new Nephite chief judge. When the people selected his brother Pahoran[2] to rule, Paanchi rebelled and was arrested, tried, and condemned to death (Hel. 1:5–8). His angry supporters sent Kishkumen to murder Pahoran (Hel. 1:9–11). Afterwards, Kishkumen and those who sent him entered into a covenant never to reveal who murdered the chief judge. Gadianton, a man noted for his oratorical ability and skill in killing and robbery, soon rose to be the leader of this group (Hel. 2:4). From then until the end of Nephite history, the band was named after Gadianton (Hel. 6:18; 4 Ne. 1:42; Morm. 2:28).

Gadianton promised power to his group if they would successfully help him achieve the chief judgeship. Accordingly, Kishkumen again sought to murder the chief judge, but this time he failed and was killed. Fearing for his life, Gadianton escaped into the wilderness (Hel. 2:11). During the next few years he continued his work, establishing SECRET COMBINATIONS "in the more settled parts of the land" (Hel. 3:23; 50 B.C.).

In 25 B.C., "Gadianton's robbers and murderers" flourished among both Nephites and Lamanites but particularly "among the more wicked part of the Lamanites" (Hel. 6:18). Righteous Lamanites were successful the following year in eliminating the robbers by preaching "the word of God" to them (Hel. 6:37). But the Nephites took a different course and chose to "build them up and support them," and thus the Gadianton robbers were able to gain "sole management" of the Nephite government (Hel. 6:38–39). Their work of assassinating Nephite chief judges continued with the killing of both Cezoram and his son (Hel. 6:19) and later Seezoram (Hel. 8:27–28; 9:27; between 23 and 20 B.C.). To carry out their crimes and to hide their deeds, the Gadianton robbers made wicked covenants inspired by Satan (2 Ne. 26:22; Hel. 6:26–30).

For a brief period the Gadianton robbers were "swept away" by repentant Nephites who "were about to perish by famine" (18 B.C.), but they returned "in the space of not many years" to again cause "havoc" and destruction among Nephites and Lamanites (Hel. 11:7, 10, 26–27; 12 B.C.). By around 11 B.C. the Gadianton robbers had become so powerful that they were able to defy the combined armies of both the Nephites and the Lamanites (Hel. 11:32).

Several years after the birth of Christ, because of the size and immense destruction caused by the robbers, "it became expedient that all the people, both the Nephites and the Lamanites, should take up arms against them," and a series of devastating wars followed (3 Ne. 2:11–19; A.D. 13–15). The chief robber Giddianhi wrote the Nephite chief judge Lachoneus[1] a letter demanding that the Nephites surrender and join them (3 Ne. 3; A.D. 16). Lachoneus did not respond to the letter but instead enacted a plan wherein all his people gathered with their belongings and food to the center of their land (3 Ne. 3:21–25; A.D. 17). The robbers, who could no longer survive on plundering, were forced to come out in open battle and were then defeated (3 Ne. 4:1–7, 12–13, 26–27; A.D. 19–21).

Only a few years later (A.D. 29) the secret practices of the Gadianton robbers resurfaced, which resulted in the complete breakdown of the Nephite government (3 Ne. 6:28–30; 7:1–3). The destruction of the wicked at the time of Christ's crucifixion eliminated the Gadianton robbers from among the Nephites and Lamanites, but by about A.D. 260 "the wicked part of the people began again to build up the secret oaths and combinations of Gadianton" (4 Ne. 1:42), and it was not long before they again spread over the entire land (4 Ne. 1:46).

After introducing the man Gadianton in his abridgment of the plates of Nephi, Mormon's knowledge of the destructive role the Gadianton robbers played in Nephite history caused him to note for his readers, "Ye shall see that this Gadianton did prove the overthrow, yea, almost the entire destruction of the people of Nephi" (Hel. 2:13; cf. Ether 8:19–21).

MDR

Gadiomnah, city of Wicked city mentioned only in connection with its destruction at the time of Jesus' death. The Lord caused the city and its inhabitants to be buried "in the depths of the earth," and he "made hills and valleys in the places thereof" (3 Ne. 9:8).

Gainsaying *See* Appendix C.

Garment(s) Literally, article(s) of clothing (1 Ne. 4:19; Mosiah 12:3). Metaphorically, a term used to represent a person's soul, which can be soiled or sanctified (2 Ne. 9:44; Alma 46:21–23; Morm. 9:35; Ether 12:38; 1 Ne. 12:11; Alma 13:12; Ether 13:10; Mosiah 2:28).

For example, dereliction of duty or sin has a staining effect on one's garments (Jacob 1:19; Alma 5:22–24). Jacob[2] reported that they labored "with all diligence," "answering the sins of the people upon our own heads if we did not teach them the word of God . . . wherefore, by laboring with our might their blood might not come upon our garments; otherwise their blood would come upon our garments, and we would not be found spotless at the last day" (Jacob 1:19; 2:2).

Because "no unclean thing can enter into his kingdom," all must have their garments cleansed through the Atonement. The Savior taught how to wash one's garments clean: "Nothing entereth into his rest save it be those who have washed their garments in my blood, because of their faith, and the repentance of all their sins, and their faithfulness unto the end" (3 Ne. 27:19; cf. Alma 5:27).

In Isaiah's writings "garment" is used in describing the fate that will come upon those who condemn the Lord's servant: "They shall wax old as a garment, and the moth shall eat them up" (2 Ne. 7:9). Additionally, "the earth shall wax old like a garment" (2 Ne. 8:6) and "Jerusalem, the holy city" is invited by the Lord to "put on thy beautiful garments"; perhaps a reference to Jerusalem's restoration to righteousness when "henceforth there shall no more come into thee the uncircumcised and the unclean" (2 Ne. 8:24 // Isa. 52:1; D&C 113:7–8; cf. 1 Ne. 21:18 // Isa. 49:18; Zeph. 1:7–8; Rev. 19:7–8).

RLB

Garners *See* Appendix C.

Gate(s) A point of access into a place or state, often used figuratively by the Savior and his prophets. Jacob[2] taught that the path leading to eternal life can only be accessed through a gate of which Christ alone is the keeper (2 Ne. 9:41; Jacob 6:11). Christ described this gate as "strait," meaning narrow or strict (3 Ne. 14:14), yet it is open to all who have true faith (Hel. 3:28). Nephi[1] explained that a person enters this gate through repentance and baptism followed by the reception of the Holy Ghost (2 Ne.

31:17–18; 33:9). He further taught that the gate is only the beginning of the path and that one must continue in righteousness to achieve eternal life (2 Ne. 31:19–20). In contrast, the Savior taught that the gates to destruction or hell are wide and well used (3 Ne. 14:13) and that "the gates of hell stand open to receive" those who alter his doctrine (3 Ne. 11:39–40; 18:13).

Literal gates are also mentioned in the Book of Mormon (Mosiah 7:10; 21:23; Hel. 7:10). For protection, the Nephites constructed high walls around many of their cities, obliging their enemies to attempt entrance through the gates. Being constricted and well guarded, the gates made access possible only at great cost of human lives (Alma 49:18–21).

See also Strait, straight.

RLB

Gathering of Israel *See* Israel, gathering of.

Gazelem Name or title given to a servant of God who would use a "stone," or the Urim and Thummim, in order to translate the twenty-four plates of the Jaredites from which came the book of Ether (Alma 37:21–24). The name-title likely refers to Joseph Smith, since he used the Urim and Thummim to translate the Book of Mormon, including the book of Ether. Moreover, in revelations recorded in the Doctrine and Covenants, Joseph Smith is called "Gazelam," which is perhaps a variant of Gazelem (pre-1981 editions only—D&C 78:9; 82:11; 104:26, 43, 45, 46; McConkie, 307–8; Smith, 2:56–57).

BIBLIOGRAPHY

McConkie, Bruce R. "Gazelam." *Mormon Doctrine.* 2d ed. Salt Lake City: Bookcraft, 1979.

Smith, Joseph. *History of The Church of Jesus Christ of Latter-day Saints.* Edited by B. H. Roberts. 7 vols. 2d ed. rev. Salt Lake City: The Church of Jesus Christ of Latter-day Saints, 1932–51.

RH

Gems, stones, and rocks The Book of Mormon contains no references to gems and precious stones, except for one reference to pearls (4 Ne. 1:24) and a quotation from the prophet Isaiah in which the Lord pledged to build up his once-afflicted people: "I will lay thy stones with fair colors, and lay thy foundations with sapphires. And I will make thy windows of agates, and thy gates of carbuncles, and all thy borders of pleasant stones" (3 Ne. 22:11–12). Ancient gem names commonly identified minerals entirely different from the minerals known by those same names today. For example, "sapphire" is said to be Hebrew and is used repeatedly in the Old Testament for the gem known today as lapis lazuli (Moore, 166–67). Bible translators sometimes supplied gem names common in their culture without regard for biblical intent (*Interpreter's,* 2:899). For example, "carbuncle" is a term from the Middle Ages referring to any cabochon-cut red stone, usually garnet.

Although the Nephite records are largely silent on the subject, the Americas are not devoid of precious gems. Southwest Brazil is one of the most prolific gem regions on earth. Central Mexico is the leading source of fire opal, and the early Spanish conquerors returned with abundant jade from the Aztecs of Mesoamerica and emeralds from the Incas of Peru.

The one gem acknowledged by the Nephites in the context of their own lifestyle is the pearl (4 Ne. 1:24), probably taken from the coastal waters of the southern Caribbean, west coast Central America, or the Gulf of California, judging from modern sources of supply. Any large river of the temperate zones may have provided freshwater pearls.

Stones

Stones are cited in the Book of Mormon as a medium for use by a seer in the translation of earlier writings (Mosiah 7:13; 28:13–16; Ether 3:23).

One engraved stone (stela) is cited in the Book of Mormon record (Omni 1:20). It was translated by Mosiah[1], and its engravings "gave an account of one Coriantumr, and the slain of his people" (Omni 1:21). Similar engraved marker stones, or stelae, were common in ancient Canaan, Syria, and Mesopotamia, revealing the deeds of mighty leaders. They were commonly made of granite or some dense fine-grained rock such as basalt or limestone.

The brother of Jared[1] "did molten out of a rock sixteen small stones," subsequently to be touched by the finger of God to "shine forth in darkness" (Ether 3:1–4) and provide light for the enclosed seagoing Jaredite vessels. They were described as "white and clear, even as transparent glass" (Ether 3:1). If these stones derived from molten rock, as the text seems to suggest, they may indeed have been glass, in contrast to crystalline solids. Glassy materials containing impurities are often fluorescent, providing a very low intensity light for a brief period after exposure to visible or ultraviolet light. The Ether narrative makes it clear, however, that the light that emanated from the stones was provided by God (Ether 3:4–6).

Stone is also used as a metaphor for Christ. Jacob[2] prophesied that "by the stumbling of the Jews they will reject [Christ,] the stone upon which they might build and have safe foundation" (Jacob 4:15–17).

Brimstone

BRIMSTONE is a common name for sulfur or sometimes pitch. It is cited often in the Book of Mormon, always in association with "fire," as a metaphor for the torment of the unrighteous (e.g., 2 Ne. 9:16, 19, 26; Jacob 3:11; 6:10).

Cement

The Nephites are said to have become "exceedingly expert in the working of cement" and to have built houses of cement "in the which they did dwell" (Hel. 3:7) because "timber was exceedingly scarce in the land northward" (Hel. 3:10). Cement is mixed with sand, gravel, and water to become a building aggregate called "concrete." The physical and chemical nature of concrete changes with changing technology. Likely the Book of Mormon writer intended to convey a building material similar to what is now called concrete.

Rock

The word ROCK appears in the Book of Mormon largely as a metaphor for a firm foundation (Hel. 5:12; 3 Ne. 11:39) and salvation (2 Ne. 4:30). Nephi[1] and his brothers hid in the "cavity of a rock" (1 Ne. 3:27) and Ether "dwelt in the cavity of a rock" (Ether 13:18). Rock cavities, caves, or caverns are formed almost exclusively in limestone and similar "carbonate" rocks. Limestone is impure calcium carbonate ($CaCO_3$) deposited most commonly in shallow ocean waters, ancient and modern. It is a very common type of rock on all continents and is the dominant rock type of the Holy Land.

BIBLIOGRAPHY

The Interpreter's Dictionary of the Bible. 4 vols. Edited by George A. Buttrick. Nashville: Abingdon, 1962.

Jeweler's Dictionary. Edited by Donald S. McNeil. 3d ed. Radnor, Pa.: Jeweler's Circular-Keystone, 1976.

Moore, N. F. *Ancient Mineralogy.* New York: Amo Press, 1978.

Wright, R. V., and L. Chadbourne. *Gems and Minerals of the Bible.* New Canaan, Conn.: Keats Publishing, 1970.

WRP

Generation, generations Terms referring to a group of people living during the same period of time and, by extension, the period of time itself. The terms "generation" and "generations" are common in the Book of Mormon and the Bible. In the Old Testament these words are usually translations of the Hebrew root *dor,* meaning a "circle," as in a "cycle of life" or "lifetime," or meaning "assembly," as a "circle of contemporary people." The terms are used in several different senses in the Old Testament and the Book of Mormon.

1. The period between the birth of parents and the birth of their children. Adult contemporaries of the parents are considered part of the parents' generation; their children belong to the next generation. The common Book of Mormon phrase "from generation to generation" (2 Ne. 8:8; 25:16; Moro. 10:28) simply means "from parents to children," without any specific chronological implication. The phrase "unto the third and fourth generation" (Ex. 20:5; Mosiah 13:13) indicates that the actions of parents can have a serious effect on their descendants.

2. The period of time during which all of the contemporaries live and die. This use seems to be the sense of the term in 4 Nephi 1:14, 18–22, where most of the first generation after Christ had died by the year A.D. 110 (v. 14), and most of the second had died by A.D. 200 (v. 22). Book of Mormon prophets and the Savior prophesied that the fourth generation from the coming of Christ (that is, within four hundred years) would

turn from righteousness and would be destroyed (1 Ne. 12:11–12; 2 Ne. 26:9; Alma 45:10–12; Hel. 13:5–10; 3 Ne. 27:32).

3. A designation or characterization of a specific group of people at a given time, such as "blessed are this people in this generation" (Alma 27:12), a "wicked and perverse generation" (Alma 9:8; 10:17, 25; Hel. 13:29), and "unto future generations" (Alma 24:14; 37:18–19; 3 Ne. 26:2).

BIBLIOGRAPHY

Freedman, D. N., J. Lundbom, and G. J. Botterweck. *Theological Dictionary of the Old Testament.* Edited by G. Johannes Botterweck. Grand Rapids, Mich.: Eerdmans, 1978. 3:169–81. S.v. "Dor."

WJH

Gentile(s) A word used to translate the Hebrew *goyim,* literally meaning "the nations." The use of the term has varied with time and among people. In the Book of Mormon, the Gentiles are generally all those who are not JEWS or who did not come from the Jewish people. Thus, by this definition, the Gentiles may include those who are of the blood of Israel but who have lost their identity and been assimilated into non-Jewish nations.

Early in the Old Testament record, the word *Gentile* appears to have been used by the descendants of Jacob[1] to refer to anyone not of the nation or house of Israel (e.g., Gen. 10:5). By the end of the seventh century B.C., the location and identity of many of the tribes of Israel were lost, due largely to the Assyrian conquest and deportation of the kingdom of Israel (1 Ne. 22:4; 2 Kgs. 17:5–23; 722 B.C.). The remnant of the house of Israel who remained in the Holy Land began to refer to themselves simply as the "Jews," either because they were literal descendants of Judah or because they had been assimilated into the kingdom of Judah. Thus Lehi[1] and his posterity considered themselves to be "descendants of the Jews." They were cultural or political Jews, although they knew their actual forefather was Joseph[1] rather than Judah (2 Ne. 30:4; 33:8; 1 Ne. 5:14).

From the perspective of Nephi, who identified his people as Jews (2 Ne. 30:4; 33:8), there were only two groups of people—Jews and Gentiles. This view of Jew and Gentile is maintained today by those who consider themselves Jews (e.g., 3 Ne. 15:21–22).

The Book of Mormon refers to Gentiles during Christ's time (e.g., 3 Ne. 15:21–22), before the restoration of the gospel (e.g., 1 Ne. 13:12–19, 29–30), and after the restoration of the gospel (e.g., 1 Ne. 14:1–2; 2 Ne. 29:3; 3 Ne. 30). It is not always easy to discern whether the word *Gentiles* refers to non-Israelites or Israelites in a Gentile culture (cf. D&C 109:60).

The Book of Mormon makes clear that the gospel was to be restored in the last days in a great Gentile nation, the United States of America, and go forth to all people who inhabit the nations of the earth (1 Ne. 13:38–40; 15:13–14; 22:7–12). Those through whom the gospel was restored were cultural or political Gentiles but of the blood of Israel: "Thus Joseph Smith, of the tribe of Ephraim, the chief and foremost tribe of Israel itself, was the Gentile by whose hand the Book of Mormon came forth, and the members of The Church of Jesus Christ of Latter-day Saints, who have the gospel and who are of Israel by blood descent, are the Gentiles who carry salvation to the Lamanites and to the Jews" (McConkie, 233; cf. Title Page; D&C 109:60).

See also Descendants of the Jews; Fulness of the Gentiles; Gentiles, Book of Mormon message concerning; Gentiles, mother; Gentiles, nations of the; Israel, numbered among.

BIBLIOGRAPHY

McConkie, Bruce R. *The Millennial Messiah: The Second Coming of the Son of Man.* Salt Lake City: Deseret Book, 1982.

MSN

Gentiles, Book of Mormon message concerning The GENTILES, as the term is used in the Book of Mormon, are all those who are not JEWS, including those who may be of the blood of Israel but have lost their identity and been assimilated into non-Jewish nations. The Book of Mormon speaks to the Gentiles as it describes the blessings and responsibilities the Lord offers them and warns of the consequences that would follow if they fall into sin and apostasy.

Blessings

The latter days were designated by Christ as the "times of the Gentiles" and by Nephi[1] as the "days of the Gentiles" (D&C 45:28; 2 Ne. 27:1). The Book of Mormon explains why this designation is fitting. In a vision of the future of the PROMISED LAND, Nephi learned that in the latter days the Spirit of God would come upon a man (Columbus) who was among the Gentiles (in Europe) and lead him to the promised land (the Americas). Other Gentiles would also be "wrought" upon by the Spirit to bring them out of captivity to the promised land (1 Ne. 13:12–14). These Gentiles would be blessed and prosper in the land (1 Ne. 13:15–16; 2 Ne. 10:10–11). Their mother Gentiles (England) would gather to battle against them (the Revolutionary War), but the Lord would come to the aid of the Gentiles in his choice land, and they would be delivered out of their enemies' hands (1 Ne. 13:17–19). These events that brought the Gentiles to the land of promise and "set [them] up as a free people" were all part of God's plan to restore his gospel and bring forth the Book of Mormon (3 Ne. 21:4).

The latter-day Gentiles would have the Bible, from which many "plain and precious" truths had been removed by the "great and abominable church," causing them to stumble and giving Satan power over them (1 Ne. 13:20–29, 34). But through the Book of Mormon and other latter-day scriptures, the Lord in his mercy would bring forth his gospel among the Gentiles and restore the precious truths that were lost (1 Ne. 13:32–42; cf. 2 Ne. 26:14–17; 27:6–35; 3 Ne. 16:6–7). Christ taught that this restoration would be a sign to scattered Israel that he was about to gather them in from their "long dispersion" (3 Ne. 21:1–7). If the Gentiles would then hearken unto Christ and accept the gospel they would be "numbered among the house of Israel" (1 Ne. 14:1–2; cf. 2 Ne. 10:18; 30:1–2; 3 Ne. 16:13; 30:1–2), help build the NEW JERUSALEM (3 Ne. 21:22–24), and eventually have all the revelations of God unfolded unto them (Ether 4:6–13). Thus "the times of the Gentiles," also known as the "fulness of the Gentiles" (1 Ne. 15:13; 3 Ne. 16:4), is that time in the latter days when they shall have access to the fulness of the gospel.

Responsibilities

Although Gentiles would initially scatter the house of Israel, including the descendants of Lehi (1 Ne. 13:14, 30–31; 15:17; 22:7; 2 Ne. 26:15; 3 Ne. 16:8; 20:27–28; Morm. 5:9, 20), after they receive the gospel and the Book of Mormon, they are expected to share it with the world, especially to the remnant of Lehi's descendants and others of the scattered house of Israel (1 Ne. 15:13–17; 22:8–9; 2 Ne. 30:3–8; 3 Ne. 21:2–5; Morm. 5:10; cf. 1 Ne. 10:11–14). As they do so, the Gentiles will be like "nursing fathers, and . . . nursing mothers" carrying the lost and scattered people back to the Lord and his covenants (1 Ne. 21:22–23; 22:8; 2 Ne. 10:8–9, 18).

Warnings

The Book of Mormon warns of the sin and apostasy that will be prevalent among the Gentiles. Nephi[1] saw the great and abominable church among the Gentile nations and that it would persecute and slay the Saints of God (1 Ne. 13:4–9). He further warned of the PRIDE, FALSE CHURCHES, false doctrines, PRIESTCRAFT, and SECRET COMBINATIONS that would plague the latter-day Gentiles and cause them to reject the Book of Mormon (2 Ne. 26:20–22, 29; 27:1–5; 28; 29; cf. Morm. 8:26–41; Ether 8:23–26). He promised that through the "marvelous work" of the restoration of the gospel and the coming forth of the Book of Mormon, God would establish truth, correct wrong thinking, and expose the wicked (2 Ne. 27:26–35).

Christ explained that the opportunity to have the gospel would be extended to the latter-day Gentiles because of their belief in Christ and the unbelief of the house of Israel (3 Ne. 16:7; cf. Morm. 5:19). He then warned the Gentiles that if they did not accept the gospel and persisted in sin, then he would allow the house of Israel to "tread them down" (3 Ne. 16:8–15; cf. 20:15–21, 28; 21:11–12; Morm. 5:22–24). Nephi foresaw that such apostasy on the part of the Gentiles would result in their being destroyed both spiritually and temporally (1 Ne. 14:5–7; cf. 2 Ne. 30:1–2; 3 Ne. 21:14–21; Ether

12:35), and Moroni[2] explained that the Gentiles could only continue in the promised land upon conditions of righteousness (Ether 2:9–12).

See also Ensign; Fulness of the Gentiles; Israel, gathering of; Israel, numbered among.

MSN

Gentiles, fulness of the *See* Fulness of the Gentiles.

Gentiles, mother Those European countries from which colonists immigrated to the Americas, and which subsequently, and unsuccessfully, "gathered together upon the waters, and upon the land also, to battle against" those colonists (1 Ne. 13:17). England, France, Spain, and Portugal all waged unsuccessful wars against colonists in the New World.

AHH

Gentiles, nations of the All non-Israelite nations (e.g., nations other than the kingdom of Judah and the Nephite/Lamanite nations) of the world. Nephi[1] saw in vision the "nations and kingdoms of the Gentiles" (1 Ne. 13:1–3). He beheld COLUMBUS and other Gentiles from the Gentile nations of Europe cross the ocean to the Americas discovering the descendants of Lehi[1] whom Nephi termed "the seed of my brethren" (1 Ne. 13:12–14). After arriving in their New World promised land, Nephi prophesied that the Lord would "raise up a mighty nation among the Gentiles, yea, even upon the face of this land" (1 Ne. 22:7). This mighty GENTILE nation, the United States of America, would be the place for the restoration of the gospel of Jesus Christ (1 Ne. 22:8; cf. 3 Ne. 21:4). Nephi taught that it would be the Gentiles who would gather scattered Israel (including their own posterity) in the latter days through the preaching of the gospel (1 Ne. 15:13–19; cf. 1 Ne. 10:14; 2 Ne. 21:22). Moreover, the Lord proclaimed that Gentile nations would be instrumental in "carrying [the JEWS] forth to the lands of their inheritance" (2 Ne. 10:8).

Nephi also saw in his vision the formation of the "great and abominable church" (1 Ne. 13:6) "among the nations of the Gentiles" (1 Ne. 13:4). This church would take away plain and precious parts of the Bible, after which the Bible would go "unto all the nations of the Gentiles" including across the ocean to the New World (1 Ne. 13:29).

Furthermore, the Book of Mormon contains prophecies concerning the wickedness that would exist among the nations of the Gentiles and warns of impending judgments "except they repent" (3 Ne. 20:20; 1 Ne. 14:13; 2 Ne. 27:1).

See also Nephi[1]'s vision.

RCR

Gentiles, times of the *See* Fulness of the Gentiles.

Geography The specific locations of the ancient Book of Mormon civilizations are unknown. And the Church of Jesus Christ of Latter-day Saints does not sponsor research with the intention of ultimately designating an exact geography. Instead Church leaders emphasize the spiritual messages of the record and its cardinal purpose as "Another Testament of Jesus Christ" (e.g., Hinckley, 52; Nelson, 69). Still, students of the Book of Mormon have sought to more fully understand the book and its message through studying what Book of Mormon record keepers did say about their lands and cities. Such understanding of the physical settings gives insight into the dynamics of the narrative, as well as providing readers with mental images of the stage upon which the Nephite, Lamanite, and Jaredite stories took place. From geographical cues within the Book of Mormon text it can be assumed that the region in which Book of Mormon peoples lived was both topographically and ecologically diverse. The text speaks of mountains (e.g., Alma 47:7; 3 Ne. 8:10) and valleys (e.g., Mosiah 24:20; Alma 2:20), rivers (e.g., Alma 2:15; Hel. 3:4) and "waters" (e.g., Mosiah 18:8; Morm. 6:4), wildernesses (e.g., Mosiah 7:4; Alma 22:27–28) and seashores (e.g., Alma 51:32; Morm. 4:3). It speaks of journeys "up" and journeys "down" between major population centers (e.g., Mosiah 7:1–2, 4; Alma 27:5). Moreover, the record mentions a "sea east," "sea west," "sea south," and a "sea north" (Alma 22:27; Hel. 3:8). The territory was apparently longer going north to south than east to west and had two major divisions, the "land southward" and the "land northward" (e.g., Alma 22:32; 3 Ne. 3:24). These lands were divided by a "narrow neck of land" (e.g., Alma 63:5; Ether 10:20). Such descriptions have led many to the assumption that Book of Mormon lands are roughly shaped like an hour glass.

Since the coming forth of the Book of Mormon, researchers have sought to place Book of Mormon cities and geographical features in a modern setting. Efforts to impose geographical clues within the text upon a modern map have produced many proposals. Historically, these proposals range from geographic models that identify South America as the land southward, North America as the land northward, and Central America as the narrow neck of land, to models that place all of the Book of Mormon cities and geographical features in the northeastern part of the United States.

The most widely accepted models today locate all of the Book of Mormon cities and geographical features in Mesoamerica (i.e., Middle or Central America). Proponents of these and other models have attempted to identify existing cities (ruins), lands, and geographical features that are consistent with the Book of Mormon text.

When considering the validity of various geographical models important questions should be considered. For example, is the proposed model compatible with current archaeological and cultural evidence? Is there evidence that the area proposed was populated with sufficient cities and people during Book of Mormon times? Did these people have the writing and technological skills described in the narrative? Does the model adequately match geographical features mentioned in the record such as bodies of water, wilderness areas, and the narrow neck of land with real world features? Does the model adequately account for distances between lands with proper consideration given to travel time, direction, speed, and terrain? These and other issues have given rise to much study and discussion. The fact that careful, honest scholars examine the same available data and propose somewhat different models is evidence that all the information needed to establish an exact model is not yet known. In the words of Elder John A. Widtsoe, "All such studies are legitimate, but the conclusions drawn from them, though they may be correct, must at best be held as intelligent conjectures" (3:93).

See also Archaeology.

BIBLIOGRAPHY

Hinckley, Gordon B. "The Cornerstone of Our Faith." *Ensign* 14 (November 1984): 50–53.

Nelson, Russell M. "A Testimony of the Book of Mormon." *Ensign* 29 (November 1999): 69–71.

Widtsoe, John A. *Evidences and Reconciliations.* 3 vols. Salt Lake City, Utah: Bookcraft, 1943.

The following sources provide in-depth discussion of issues dealing with Book of Mormon geography:

Allen, Joseph L. *Exploring the Lands of the Book of Mormon.* Orem, Utah: S. A. Publishers, 1989. Treatise exploring Mesoamerica as a geographical setting for the Book of Mormon. Discusses dates and languages relative to the topic. Reviews archaeological, historical, cultural, and geographical connections between the region and the Book of Mormon. Surveys current models for a Mesoamerican setting for the text and then systematically proposes locations for lands, journeys, cities, and various geographical features mentioned in the Book of Mormon. Contains a brief history of the geography question from 1830 to 1989. Includes numerous photographs and drawings. (437 pages)

Clark, John. Review of F. Richard Hauck, *Deciphering the Geography of the Book of Mormon: Review of Books on the Book of Mormon.* Vol. 1. Provo, Utah: FARMS, 1989. Briefly reviews Hauck's model for a Mesoamerican setting for the Book of Mormon, followed by a suggested internal model for Book of Mormon geography based on a study of geography passages from the text itself. Includes several maps of proposed internal geography. (51 pages)

———. "Book of Mormon Geography." *Encyclopedia of Mormonism.* Edited by Daniel H. Ludlow et al. 4 vols. New York: Macmillan, 1992. 1:176–79. Discusses considerations and challenges in reconstructing Book of Mormon geography. Provides a general overview of Book of Mormon geography extracted from the text itself. Notes that while many researchers currently conclude that Mesoamerica is the likely setting for the Book of Mormon, no official Church endorsement has been given to any internal or external geography. Includes a review of statements regarding Book of Mormon geography by various Church leaders. (4 pages)

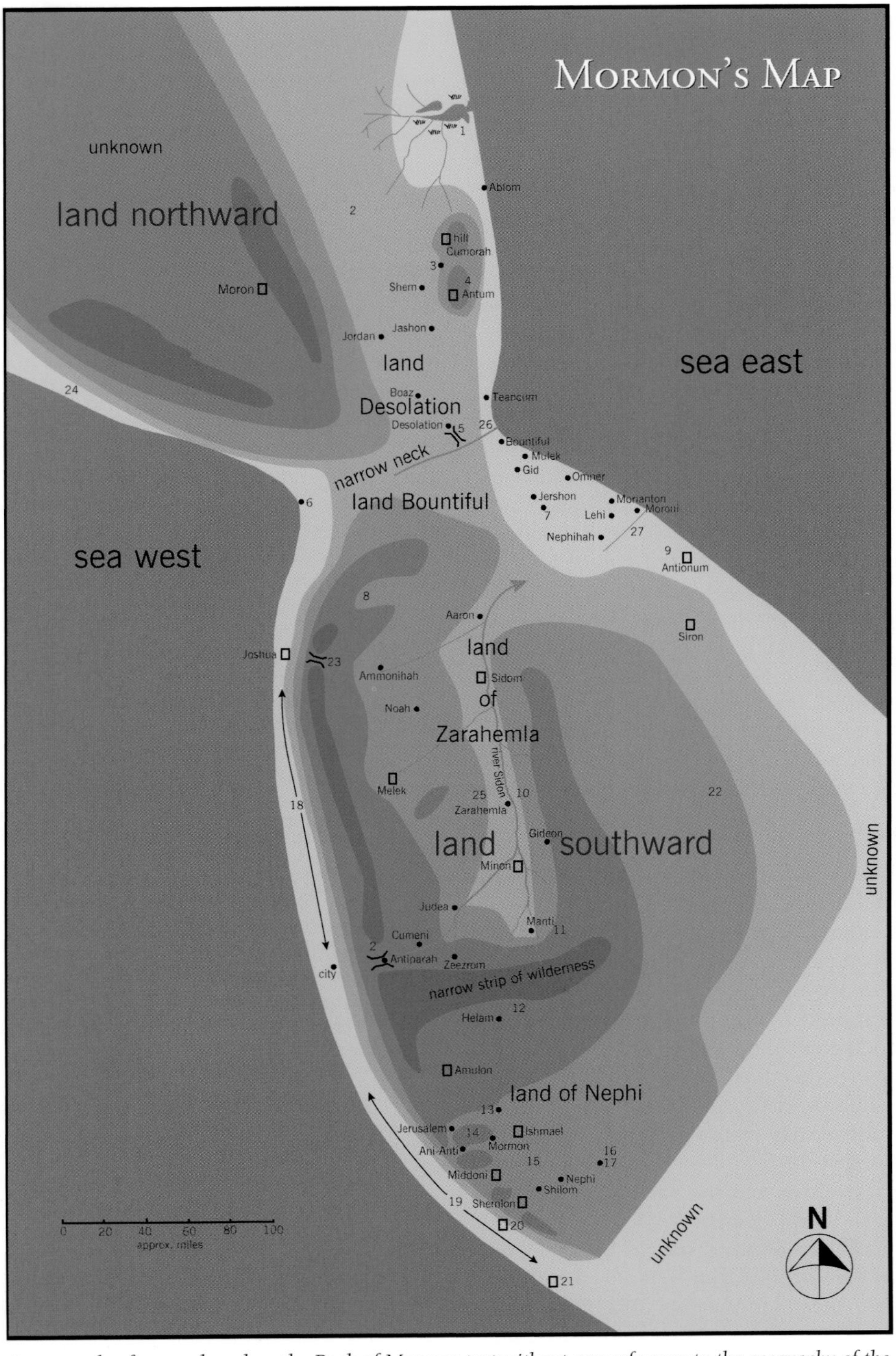

An example of a map based on the Book of Mormon text without any reference to the geography of the Americas; courtesy John L. Sorenson from Mormon's Map *(Provo: FARMS, 2000).*

"Mormon's Map" shows a plausible arrangement of Nephite and Lamanite geographical features based on all the information in the record of Mormon and his son Moroni[2]. (Capitalization of names follows the practice of the published text of the Book of Mormon.)

LEGEND

1. waters of Ripliancum
2. limit of Nephite retreat
3. Shiz's death; plates left
4. hill Shim
5. narrow pass or passage
6. Hagoth's shipbuilding site
7. Camp of Moroni[1]
8. Nephites' refuge between the land Bountiful and the land of Zarahemla (see 3 Nephi 3:23, 25)
9. hill Onidah
10. hill Amnihu
11. hill Riplah
12. valley of Alma
13. dispersal point of the sons of Mosiah[2]
14. waters of Mormon
15. hill north of Shilom
16. mount Antipas
17. place Onidah
18. wilderness on the west of the land Zarahemla
19. wilderness on the west in the land of Nephi
20. Lamanite king's land
21. land of first inheritance
22. wilderness (see Alma 43:22)
23. mountain pass
24. Hagoth's likely destination
25. wilderness of Hermounts
26. "line" between Desolation and Bountiful
27. defense "line"

• settlement

□ land, no city mentioned

)(mountain pass

swamp

River tributaries illustrative only.
Darker color indicates higher elevation.

Hauck, F. Richard. *Deciphering the Geography of the Book of Mormon.* Salt Lake City: Deseret Book, 1988. Proposes a Mesoamerican setting for the Book of Mormon. Develops internal spatial maps of Book of Mormon geography based on routes, settlements, history, topography, and other geographical features mentioned in the text. The maps are then laid over modern maps to evaluate possible correlations. Includes many maps and charts. (239 pages)

Palmer, David A. *In Search of Cumorah: New Evidences for the Book of Mormon from Ancient Mexico.* Bountiful, Utah: Horizon Publishers, 1981. A treatise supporting the "two Cumorah" theory. Distinguishes between "Moroni's Cumorah" in New York where the plates were deposited and "Mormon's Cumorah" where the final battle occurred and which it identifies as Cerro Vigia in Mexico. Considers historical, cultural and textual evidence to propose locations for many other Book of Mormon sites as well. Includes numerous photographs, illustrations and maps. (254 pages)

Sorenson, John L. *An Ancient American Setting for the Book of Mormon.* Salt Lake City and Provo: Deseret Book and FARMS, 1985. An in-depth study of a plausible setting for Book of Mormon geography in Mesoamerica. Reviews both the culture, history, and geography of the region as understood by current scholars, and the culture, history, and geography of the Book of Mormon as described in the text. Throughout, the volume offers suggestions of how the Book of Mormon people, lands, and culture fit into the proposed Mesoamerican setting. Includes many photographs and detailed graphical depictions of possible Book of Mormon locations. (415 pages)

———. *The Geography of Book of Mormon Events: A Source Guide.* Provo, Utah: FARMS, 1992. Reviews the history of the problem of Book of Mormon geography. Provides a summary of many of the models proposed for Book of Mormon geography by various researchers. Gives a list of all passages related to geography in the text and offers suggestions for evaluating geography models. Includes many maps. (428 pages)

———. *Mormon's Map.* Provo, Utah: FARMS, 2000. Primarily focuses on developing an internal map ("Mormon's Map") for Book of Mormon lands. Uses the text to consider the overall configuration, geographical features, distances, directions, and the environment of the lands. Also discusses Book of Mormon cultural and historical issues relative to the geography. Includes an extensive scripture reference for geographical sites. (154 pages)

EDS.

Gid Nephite chief military officer (ca. 63 B.C.) who, with his men, quelled a rebellion of prisoners of war, helped defend the city Cumeni (Alma 57:22, 28–35), and later helped

Helaman[2] and Teomner take the city Manti by stratagem (Alma 58:13–23). Gid was a man of faith who attributed their deliverance in battle to God.

CDT

Gid, city of Nephite city captured by Amalickiah and the Lamanites (Alma 51:26), fortified as a prisoner compound, and then cleverly retaken by Moroni[1] without bloodshed. Moroni used a descendant of Laman[1] from among his ranks, whose name was also Laman[4], to take strong wine to the Lamanite guards in Gid. When the guards were drunken and asleep, Moroni's men, in the silence of the night, "cast" weapons in to the Nephite prisoners within the city and surrounded the Lamanite army. In the morning, when the Lamanites saw their plight both within and without the city, they surrendered and pleaded for mercy (Alma 55:4–24).

Giddianhi Governor of the GADIANTON ROBBERS (A.D. 15) whose band emerged as a major threat to both Nephites and Lamanites after the birth of Christ. Because the Nephites had gathered their substance into one place and Giddianhi's people could no longer subsist without robbing and plundering, Giddianhi led his fearful armies in an assault against the Nephites. In this campaign he was eventually slain by the armies of Gidgiddoni (3 Ne. 4:5–14).

Knowledge of the character of Giddianhi stems principally from the threatening epistle he wrote the Nephite chief judge Lachoneus[1]. In the epistle he demanded the surrender of Nephite lands and possessions, and he threatened destruction if Lachoneus failed to comply (3 Ne. 3:2–10). Elements of Giddianhi's letter echo the character, strategy, and designs of SATAN.

To influence the chief judge, Giddianhi used insincere flattery, or "exceedingly great praise" (3 Ne. 3:2; cf. 2 Ne. 28:22), and then sought to shake Lachoneus' faith by challenging his belief that the Nephites were supported by God (3 Ne. 3:2; cf. Matt. 4:6; 27:40). Giddianhi was mocking ("it seemeth a pity unto me"), intimidating ("that ye should be so foolish and vain as to suppose that ye can stand against so many brave men"), and arrogant ("who are at my command") (3 Ne. 3:3; cf. Moses 1:19–20). His bold assertions were fueled by "everlasting hatred" and a perverted view of right and wrong (3 Ne. 3:4; cf. 2 Ne. 15:20). Although Giddianhi pretended otherwise, he had no concern for the welfare of others (3 Ne. 3:5). Finally, Giddianhi proposed, "I write unto you, desiring that ye would yield up unto this my people, your cities, your lands, and your possessions . . . and unite with us . . . that ye may be like unto us . . . [and] ye shall not be destroyed" (3 Ne. 3:6–8). Similarly, Satan's ultimate destructive design is for humankind to "yield up" unto him their souls and to "unite" with him. What Satan does not reveal is the ultimate consequence of such a course—eternal misery (2 Ne. 2:27; 9:9; 28:21–22).

See also Book of Mormon, selected purposes of, to reveal the enemies of Christ.

DLL

Giddonah[1] Father of Amulek, son of Ishmael[2], and descendant of Aminadi who interpreted writing on the wall of the temple, "which was written by the finger of God" (Alma 10:2).

Giddonah[2] High priest in the land of Gideon who questioned Korihor (ca. 74 B.C.), asking why he taught against Christ and "the prophecies of the holy prophets." When Korihor replied with a series of false and blasphemous accusations, Giddonah and the chief judge refused to respond to them. Instead, they sent Korihor bound to the high priest Alma[2] and to the chief judge Nephihah at Zarahemla (Alma 30:21–29).

Gideon A Nephite military leader and patriot (ca. 145–91 B.C.) who fought against the evils of king Noah[3] (Mosiah 19:4). As a captain to king Limhi, he counseled with the king and helped avoid war with the Lamanites over their kidnapped daughters (Mosiah 20:17–22). Later he devised an inspired escape plan to deliver the Nephites out of bondage (Mosiah 22:3–9; 25:16; Alma 1:8). As an old man, Gideon was a teacher in the Church. He withstood the false teachings of Nehor with the "words of God," and Nehor slew him in anger (Alma 1:7–9). The

Nephites named a land, a valley, and a city after the righteous Gideon (Alma 2:20; 6:7), who represents the ideal of faithful courage.

CDT

Gideon, land of, valley of, and city of Land, valley, and city on the eastern side of the River Sidon, named after Gideon, a Nephite patriot during the reigns of kings Noah[3] and Limhi. The valley of Gideon is first mentioned as an encampment during the battle of Alma[2] with the Amlicites (Alma 2:20). Later, after Alma had relinquished the judgment-seat to Nephihah, he traveled to the valley of Gideon where the city of Gideon was located and there commended the people for their righteousness and preached the coming of Jesus Christ (Alma 6:7–8:10; ca. 83 B.C.). Nine years later the anti-Christ Korihor attempted to preach in the land of Gideon but with little success. He was bound and brought before Gideon's chief judge, and also the high priest Giddonah[2] (Alma 30:21, 23). More than a decade after that event, the king-men took over Zarahemla and the chief judge Pahoran[1] fled to Gideon. There he awaited the assistance of captain Moroni[1] in regaining Zarahemla from the dissenters (Alma 61:5, 15; 62:3–7).

Ironically, many years later, Samuel the Lamanite specifically named Gideon as a city that would experience "wo" because of the wickedness of her inhabitants (Hel. 13:15; ca. 6 B.C.).

Gidgiddonah Nephite military leader killed with his ten thousand troops in the last battle between the Nephites and Lamanites (Morm. 6:13; A.D. 385).

See also Cumorah, battle of.

Gidgiddoni A Nephite prophet and chief commander of the Nephite armies (ca. A.D. 16). Gidgiddoni's military appointment was according to Nephite custom, which mandated that chief captains be individuals with "the spirit of revelation and also prophecy" (3 Ne. 3:19). It was Gidgiddoni who warned the Nephites about staging an offensive against the Gadianton robbers, advising them instead to maintain a defensive posture by gathering to the center of their land and forcing the robbers to come against them (3 Ne. 3:21; cf. Alma 43:46–47). He led the righteous Nephites and Lamanites (3 Ne. 2:11–16) in their successful defense against the fearsome robbers (ca. A.D. 18–19), but the slaughter in that battle exceeded any known "among all the people of Lehi since he left Jerusalem" (3 Ne. 4:11–13). Under the leadership of Gidgiddoni and Lachoneus[1] the Nephites prospered, the Gadianton robbers were eliminated, and peace was established in the land until ca. A.D. 28 (3 Ne. 5:4–6; 6:4–9).

CJW

Gifts of the Spirit *See* Spiritual gifts.

Gilbert, John Hulburd The compositor for the first printing of the Book of Mormon, published by E. B. Grandin's printing shop in Palmyra, New York, in 1830. Gilbert (1802–1895), who lived and worked in Palmyra for more than seventy years, set the type and created the pages for that first edition.

Most available information about Gilbert's role in the printing of the Book of Mormon comes from two letters written to James Cobb (10 February and 16 March 1879), and an 8 September 1892 memorandum. In these documents Gilbert stated that after Grandin agreed to publish the Book of Mormon, Hyrum Smith and Martin Harris brought him each morning the pages he was to set in type that day. Each

John Hulburd Gilbert (1802–1895); courtesy VRL.

GILBERT, JOHN HULBURD

night they retrieved the pages to guard against possible theft. Gilbert also noted that the Prophet Joseph Smith entered the print shop only once, for a few minutes, during the entire course of the work.

The pages Hyrum and Martin brought Gilbert were nearly always pages from a second copy of the manuscript, called the printer's copy, which Joseph had asked Oliver Cowdery to prepare. The original dictated manuscript was to remain in their keeping. In producing the printer's copy, Oliver was to correct grammar and spelling errors found in the original manuscript, apparently because it had been written very rapidly. Gilbert could not merely replicate the printer's copy but divided it into sentences and paragraphs because "every Chapter, if I remember correctly, was one solid paragraph, without a punctuation mark, from beginning to end" (Wood, xxix). Both the original and printer's copies show each chapter to be a solid paragraph with a period only at the end. When Gilbert asked Hyrum and Martin about sentences and paragraphs, they instructed him to make them as needed but not to change any words.

It was no easy task to set the type, punctuate, and make the paragraphs for a five-hundred-page manuscript that Gilbert was permitted to see only in segments (the first segment was twenty-four pages long and included the title page). The whole procedure was ripe for error. But the most significant challenge Gilbert faced was his total ignorance of the book he had to set in type. Nearly all the people, places, and circumstances were totally unfamiliar to him. He had never heard of Moroni, or the Lamanites, or the Jaredites; he did not know who they were or what relationship any might have had to any other. Examination of the title page, which was reproduced from the printer's copy, illustrates the difficulty. The entire page was written with indiscriminate capital letters and no periods. Slash marks indicated the ends of lines. Gilbert had to decide what words to place in the title, which in the subtitle, and what sizes of type he should set them in. When modern readers look at the printed page, it all seems so simple, but creating the printed page from a handwritten account without punctuation was no easy matter. In his attempt "to make it read as I supposed the Author intended" (Wood, xxix), Gilbert made a major error on the title page. Because he had not yet been able to read the book of Ether, he did not know that it was the record of the Jaredites, so he placed the statements about those people in two different paragraphs, as if they referred to two different records. This error was printed on the title page of the first edition of the Book of Mormon but was changed in the second edition printing in 1837. Finally, Gilbert requested and received permission to take the manuscript home and punctuate it at night so he could "get along faster in the day time," for, as he explained, "now I have frequently to stop [setting type] and read half a page to find how to punctuate it" ("Memorandum," 2). Gilbert promised to protect the pages and not leave them at the shop overnight.

Gilbert said he worked from August 1829 until early March 1830 before he had the Book of Mormon all set and printed. It went then to the bindery, and some bound copies became available for sale 26 March 1830.

John H. Gilbert performed an extremely valuable service to the Church in setting the type, punctuating the sentences, and building the paragraphs for the first edition of the Book of Mormon. All his obituaries note that Gilbert was most widely known as the typesetter for the first Book of Mormon.

See also Book of Mormon, printing and publication of; Book of Mormon, title page of; Grandin, Egbert Bratt.

BIBLIOGRAPHY

Gilbert, John H. Letters to James Cobb, 10 February and 16 March 1879. New York Public Library, New York City.

———. "Memorandum, made by John H. Gilbert Esq., Sept. 8th 1892." King's Daughters Library, Palmyra, New York.

Tate, Charles D., Jr. "John H. Gilbert's Work on the Book of Mormon." *Regional Studies in Latter-day Saint Church History: New York.* Edited by Larry C. Porter, Milton V. Backman Jr., and Susan Easton Black. Provo: Department of Church History and Doctrine, Brigham Young University, 1992.

Wood, Wilford C. *Joseph Smith Begins His Work.* Salt Lake City: Deseret News Press, 1963.

CDT

Gilead Jaredite who fought Coriantumr[2] two years after Coriantumr had defeated and killed his brother Shared. Gilead was beaten by Coriantumr and driven into the wilderness of Akish, after which an intense and costly battle took place. Coriantumr's SIEGE in the wilderness failed when Gilead and his men escaped in the night and "slew" part of Coriantumr's drunken army. Gilead went to Moron and "placed himself upon the throne of Coriantumr" but was later murdered by his high priest (Ether 14:3–9).

Gilgah *See* Jared[1], posterity of.

Gilgal Nephite military leader killed with his ten thousand troops in the last battle between the Nephites and Lamanites (Morm. 6:14; A.D. 385).

See also Cumorah, battle of.

Gilgal, city of The city of Gilgal was sunk and buried in the earth because of its wickedness during the calamities that attended the death of Jesus Christ (3 Ne. 9:6).

Gilgal, valley of Scene of two fierce Jaredite battles between the armies of Coriantumr[2] and Shared. In the first, which lasted three days, Coriantumr was victorious and continued to pursue Shared to the plains of Heshlon. There Shared prevailed, forcing Coriantumr back to the valley of Gilgal. But the tide turned again, and Coriantumr killed Shared in battle (Ether 13:28–31).

Gimgimno, city of Wicked city mentioned only in connection with its destruction at the time of Jesus' death. The Lord caused the city and its inhabitants to be buried "in the depths of the earth," and he "made hills and valleys in the places thereof" (3 Ne. 9:8).

Gird *See* Appendix C.

Glory Term used three ways in the Book of Mormon.

1. Noun denoting respect, fame, or honor. "For none can have power to bring it [the Book of Mormon record] to light save it be given him of God; for God wills that it shall be done with an eye single to his glory" (Morm. 8:15; cf. 1 Ne. 20:10–11).

2. Noun referring to the splendor and radiance associated with the power of God. "Yea, thus saith the Spirit: Repent, all ye ends of the earth, for the kingdom of heaven is soon at hand; yea, the Son of God cometh in his glory, in his might, majesty, power, and dominion" (Alma 5:50; cf. 2 Ne. 12:21; 3 Ne. 26:3).

3. Verb expressing delight or pleasure. "I glory in plainness; I glory in truth; I glory in my Jesus" (2 Ne. 33:6; cf. Alma 26:16; 29:9).

RDD

Glut *See* Appendix C.

Gnashing *See* Appendix C.

God, nature of The God testified of in the Book of Mormon is the God of Abraham, Isaac, and Jacob (1 Ne. 6:4); Jehovah; JESUS CHRIST. He is the same God known to Latter-day Saints as they read the Bible and the revelations of the Restoration. The Book of Mormon establishes and confirms many important truths about the nature of God.

God is omnipotent, omniscient, and omnibenevolent

The God of the Book of Mormon prophets has all attributes of godliness in their perfection. He is omnipotent (all powerful), omniscient (all knowing), and omnibenevolent (all good). Challenging his people to have faith, king Benjamin said, "Believe in God; believe that he is, and that he created all things, both in heaven and in earth; believe that he has all wisdom, and all power, both in heaven and in earth; believe that man doth not comprehend all the things which the Lord can comprehend" (Mosiah 4:9). Moroni[2] testified that God knows "all things, being from everlasting to everlasting, behold, he sent angels to minister unto the children of men, to make manifest concerning the coming of Christ; and in Christ there should come every good thing" (Moro. 7:22; cf. 2 Ne. 2:24; 9:20; W of M 1:7; Alma 26:35; 40:5, 10). Jacob[2] spoke of God's MERCY, wisdom, GRACE, goodness, justice, holiness, and power (2 Ne. 9:6, 8, 10, 17, 20; Jacob 2:5; cf. Mosiah 4:9; Alma 26:35;

Ether 3:4; cf. Smith, 4). Similarly, Alma[2] taught that the "plan of redemption" requires God to maintain a perfect balance between mercy and justice. If he were to fail to do so, he "would cease to be God" (Alma 42:13, 15).

The premortal Jesus (Jehovah), a spirit Man

The first chapter of Genesis announces that man was created in the image and likeness of God (Gen. 1:26–27). Many, holding to the notion that God is spirit, without bodily form, view this declaration figuratively and suggest it means there is something in the intellect, mind, or soul of man that in some vague way represents the mind of God. The Book of Mormon makes it clear that the premortal Jehovah was a spirit man and that mankind was literally created in his image and likeness. In the account of the brother of Jared[1], he asked the Lord to touch the stones he had prepared to give light in the barges in which his people would travel from the Old World to the New. When the Lord did so, the veil was taken from the eyes of the brother of Jared, and he saw that the finger of the Lord "was as the finger of a man, like unto flesh and blood" (Ether 3:6). The Lord told the brother of Jared, "Because of thy faith thou hast seen that I shall take upon me flesh and blood" (Ether 3:9). Then, because of the faith of the brother of Jared, the Lord fully manifested himself unto him and said, "I am he who was prepared from the foundation of the world to redeem my people. Behold, I am Jesus Christ. I am the Father and the Son" (Ether 3:14). "Seest thou that ye are created after mine own image?" the brother of Jared was asked. Christ then explained, "Yea, even all men were created in the beginning after mine own image. Behold, this body, which ye now behold, is the body of my spirit; and man have I created after the body of my spirit; and even as I appear unto thee to be in the spirit will I appear unto my people in the flesh" (Ether 3:15–16). This explanation to the brother of Jared is a clear indication that the physical mortal body the Savior would take upon himself on this earth would be in the same form as his premortal spirit body (cf. D&C 77:2).

The corporeality of God

Abinadi testified that "God himself shall come down among the children of men," take upon himself flesh, suffer death, and be resurrected (Mosiah 15:1–9). Amulek described resurrection as the union of body and spirit "never to be divided" (Alma 11:45), and Alma[2] noted that "even a hair of the head shall not be lost; but all things shall be restored to their proper and perfect frame" (Alma 40:23; 41:2). Thus the physical body created by God for man, that body which he described as being in his image and likeness, is as eternal in its resurrected state as the spirit that inhabits it. Such, also, is the nature of the God who created it. Christ retained the body of flesh he regained at resurrection, the body that would "never . . . be divided" from his spirit after resurrection. And that body is forever a glorified resurrected body of flesh and bones "as tangible as man's" (D&C 130:22).

The corporeality of the resurrected Christ is confirmed in the Book of Mormon when Christ appeared in the New World and commanded the people to place their hands in his side and feel the prints of the nails in his hands and feet, that they might know that he is "the God of Israel, and the God of the whole earth," who had been slain for the sins of the world (3 Ne. 11:14).

God is unchanging

Moroni[2] testified that God is the "same yesterday, today, and forever, and in him there is no variableness neither shadow of changing" (Morm. 9:9). Alma[2] bore similar witness and promised that God will not "vary from that which he hath said" nor turn from "that which is right to that which is wrong," and "therefore, his course is one eternal round" (Alma 7:20).

A God of revelation and miracles

The God of the Book of Mormon is a God of REVELATION and a God of MIRACLES. To suppose that revelation has ceased, that miracles are a thing of the past, or that gifts, healings, or other spiritual manifestations have been done away is to suppose that God has changed. But Nephi[1] declared that because God is unchanging he has and will continue to unfold his "mysteries" to those that diligently seek him (1 Ne. 10:18–19).

Similarly, Moroni[2] wrote, "If ye have imagined up unto yourselves a god who doth vary, and in whom there is shadow of changing, then have ye imagined up unto yourselves a god who is not a God of miracles. But behold, I will show unto you [that is, the Book of Mormon will teach and testify of] a God of miracles, even the God of Abraham, and the God of Isaac, and the God of Jacob; and it is that same God who created the heavens and the earth, and all things that in them are" (Morm. 9:9–11).

See also Body of my spirit; God is the same yesterday, today, and forever; God the Father; Jesus Christ, role of, as Father and Son; Justice, law of; One eternal round; One God.

BIBLIOGRAPHY

Smith, Joseph. *Lectures on Faith.* Compiled by N. B. Lundwall. Salt Lake City: Deseret Book, 1985.

JFM

God is the same yesterday, today, and forever God's absolute integrity and constancy in being willing to reveal his will, effect miracles, and dispense the gifts of the Spirit to mankind in all ages of the world according to their faith. With God, "there is no variableness neither shadow of changing" (Morm. 9:9; Alma 7:20). He is "unchangeable from all eternity to all eternity" (Moro. 8:18); "the course of the Lord is one eternal round" (1 Ne. 10:18–19). If this were not so, "doubt would take the place of faith" (Smith, 3:21). Not only does the Book of Mormon proclaim God's unchanging nature in this regard but is tangible evidence of it (2 Ne. 29:9; cf. D&C 20:8–12).

God's nature does not change, but he works among men according to their faith or their unbelief (2 Ne. 27:23). Moroni[2] testified that God "is the same yesterday, today, and forever, and that all these gifts of which I have spoken, which are spiritual, never will be done away, even as long as the world shall stand, only according to the unbelief of the children of men" (Moro. 10:19). Mormon affirmed that if God were a changeable being "he would cease to be God," adding, "he changeth not . . . and he ceaseth not to be God, and is a God of miracles. And the reason why he ceaseth to do miracles among the children of men is because that they dwindle in unbelief" (Morm. 9:19–20). Not only are miracles wrought by faith but "it is by faith that angels appear and minister unto men; wherefore, if these things have ceased wo be unto the children of men, for it is because of unbelief, and all is vain" (Moro. 7:37).

With all of man's variableness, God remains unchangeable, responding to mankind's needs and faith "according to that which is just and true" (Alma 29:8; 12:10–11; Hel. 12:1–6). Elder Bruce R. McConkie taught, "We are saved today by obedience to the same eternal laws that have saved men in all ages past and that will save them in all ages future. The Author and Finisher of our faith is the same yesterday, today, and forever" (1:51).

See also God, nature of; One eternal round.

BIBLIOGRAPHY

McConkie, Bruce R. *The Mortal Messiah: From Bethlehem to Calvary.* 4 vols. Salt Lake City: Deseret Book, 1979–81.

Smith, Joseph. *Lectures on Faith.* Compiled by N. B. Lundwall. Salt Lake City: Deseret Book, 1985.

CJW

God of Abraham, and Isaac, and Jacob Phrase referring to Jehovah (*Yahweh*), the premortal name for Jesus Christ, the God with whom the prophet-patriarchs Abraham, Isaac, and Jacob made covenants (1 Ne. 17:40; Abr. 2:6–11; Gen. 17; 26:1–4, 24; 28). Referring to the Lord in this manner would remind the Nephites, who were descendants of Abraham, of their covenant relationship with God. Nephi[1] recorded that the purpose of his writing was to "persuade men to come unto the God of Abraham, and the God of Isaac, and the God of Jacob, and be saved" (1 Ne. 6:4). The phrase was also used when reminding the people of God's power in connection with the miraculous Exodus from Egypt (1 Ne. 19:10; Mosiah 7:19; 23:23), and Alma[2] used it in reference to the deliverance of his people (Alma 29:11; 36:2). The use of this phrase evidently endured to the end of Nephite history, because Moroni[2] used it in his testimony of the great God of miracles (Morm. 9:11).

VLL

God the Father That God who is the literal father of Jesus Christ (1 Ne. 11:16–21; Alma 7:10). Although the scriptures teach little about the Father directly, one learns much about him through Christ.

Christ is separate from and obedient to the Father

The Book of Mormon teaches that Christ is separate and distinct from the Father and that the Son is subservient to his Father. Explaining why it was necessary for Christ to be baptized, Nephi[1] said: "Notwithstanding he being holy, he showeth unto the children of men that, according to the flesh he humbleth himself before the Father, and witnesseth unto the Father that he would be obedient unto him in keeping his commandments" (2 Ne. 31:7). Christ came to glorify the Father, which could be done only by his suffering "the will of the Father in all things" (3 Ne. 11:11). When the resurrected Christ ministered among the Nephites, he demonstrated his distinctness from the Father and his deference to him as he prayed to the Father on their behalf (e.g., 3 Ne. 17:15–18; 19:19–34).

Christ taught the doctrine of the Father

As to that which he taught, Christ said, "It is the doctrine which the Father hath given unto me" (3 Ne. 11:32). Thus Christ said, "He that will not believe me will not believe the Father who sent me" (Ether 4:12). As the Atonement is to reconcile men to the Father, so all that Christ did and taught centered the attention of those he taught upon the Father. When Christ gave the Nephites the words of Malachi, he said, "These scriptures, which ye had not with you, the Father commanded that I should give unto you" (3 Ne. 26:2). Speaking of the latter-day gathering of Israel, Christ said, "Then shall the work of the Father commence at that day, even when this gospel shall be preached among the remnant of this people. Verily I say unto you, at that day shall the work of the Father commence among all the dispersed of my people . . . to prepare the way whereby they may come unto me, that they may call on the Father in my name" (3 Ne. 21:26–27).

Worshipping the Father in the name of Christ

The true Saint worships the Father in the name of the Son (2 Ne. 25:16; Jacob 4:5). Accordingly, one is to pray to the Father in the name of Christ (2 Ne. 32:9; 3 Ne. 17:3; 18:20; 19:6; 21:27) and keep the Father's commandments by following Christ (2 Ne. 31:10–11). As Christ prayed for the Nephites, he taught that as they believe in him they become "one" with him and the Father (3 Ne. 19:23, 29; cf. John 17:20–23). Thus, when the voice of the Father is heard, he directs listeners to "hear" his Beloved Son (e.g., 3 Ne. 11:1–7; JS–H 1:17).

See also God, nature of; Godhead; Jesus Christ, role of, as Father and Son.

JFM

Godhead GOD THE FATHER, his Son JESUS CHRIST, and the HOLY GHOST, three separate and distinct personages, constitute the Godhead. Because they enjoyed the blessings of the fulness of the gospel, the Book of Mormon prophets knew by revelation and scripture (the brass plates) that there was a Heavenly Father, a Beloved Son, and a Holy Ghost. Evidence in the Book of Mormon of a three-member Godhead includes the following:

God and his prophets have declared from the beginning that Christ should come as a Savior and Messiah (1 Ne. 10:4; Jacob 7:11; Moro. 7:23). Zenos and Zenock, two of the major prophets of the brass plates, clearly taught that the mercies of the Father come through the mediation of the Son (Alma 33:11, 15–16).

Prayer is to the Father in the name of the Son (2 Ne. 32:9; 3 Ne. 18:19–20; Morm. 9:27; Ether 4:15; Moro. 4:3; 5:2; 8:3; 10:4).

Worship is of the Father in the name of the Son (2 Ne. 25:16; Jacob 4:4–5).

The Father, Son, and Holy Ghost constitute ONE GOD or, in other words, one Godhead (2 Ne. 31:21; Alma 11:44; 3 Ne. 11:27, 36; Morm. 7:7; Ether 12:41; The Testimony of the Three Witnesses).

It is through the condescension of the Son of the Most High God that redemption comes (1 Ne. 11:6, 24; Mosiah 3:5–9).

Christ received power from his Father to reconcile the repentant to the Father (Mosiah 15:2–3; Alma 12:33–34; Hel. 5:10–11; Morm. 7:5; Moro. 7:22–27).

Christ received direction from his Father and worked in harmony with him (2 Ne. 31:10–12; 3 Ne. 11:32; 26:2).

See also Jesus Christ, role of, as Father and Son.

RLM

Gold plates Metal plates containing ancient records delivered to Joseph Smith by the angel Moroni from which the Book of Mormon was translated. Historical sources indicate that at least thirteen individuals were privileged to see the gold plates: Joseph Smith (the translator); Oliver Cowdery, David Whitmer, and Martin Harris (the Three Witnesses); Joseph Smith, Sr., Hyrum Smith, Samuel Smith, Christian Whitmer, Jacob Whitmer, Peter Whitmer Jr., John Whitmer, and Hiram Page (the Eight Witnesses); and Mary Musselman Whitmer, wife of Peter Whitmer Sr. (Cook, 13, 28, 33, 50–51,182, 214, 216, 217–18). Of these thirteen persons who saw the gold plates, only Martin Harris, David Whitmer, and Joseph Smith left known published descriptions. Harris estimated the size of the plates to be 8 x 7 x 4 inches (length-width-height) and the weight in the vicinity of 40 to 50 pounds. He also said that the three rings that bound the volume together were made of silver (Harris, 165). Whitmer gave several varying descriptions of the sacred record, indicating the length and width of the plates to be 8 x 7 (Cook, 172, 254), and 8 x 4 (Cook, 248). In two accounts he indicated that the plates were "wider than long," 6–7 x 8 (Cook, 21), and 6 x 9 (Cook, 64). Furthermore, Whitmer stated the sealed portion appeared "as solid to my view as wood" and composed about half of the entire volume (Cook, 20–21), while on another occasion he indicated "one-third . . . appeared to be loose" (Cook, 75). Emma Smith, the prophet's wife, was never permitted to view the plates while they were uncovered, but she had some firsthand knowledge of the general size and feel of the plates. She stated that the plates "often lay on the table . . . wrapped in a small linen table cloth. . . . I once felt of the plates, as they thus lay on the table, tracing their outline and shape. They seemed to be pliable like thick paper, and would rustle with a metalic [*sic*] sound when the edges were moved by the thumb, as one does sometimes thumb the edges of a book." While she indicated that she never uncovered or looked at the plates, she frequently lifted them. "I moved them from place to place," she said, "as it was neccessary [*sic*] in doing my work" (Bidamon, 290).

The most accurate and reliable description of the gold plates was given by Joseph Smith in 1842: "These records were engraven on plates which had the appearance of gold, each plate was six inches wide and eight inches long and not quite so thick as common tin. They were filled with engravings, in Egyptian characters and bound together in a volume, as the leaves of a book with three rings running through the whole. The volume was something near six inches in thickness, a part of which was sealed. The characters on the unsealed part were small, and beautifully engraved. The whole book exhibited many marks of antiquity in its construction and much skill in the art of engraving" (Smith, 1:431). Joseph Smith said that the record had the "appearance of gold." Based upon descriptions by eyewitnesses and considering known factors and principles associated with metallurgy, it seems the plates would not have been made from pure 24-carat gold, for that would have made them too heavy and too pliable. They were likely fashioned from an alloy of gold mixed with copper and silver to make approximately 8-carat gold material (Putnam, 788–89, 828–30).

Joseph Smith had the plates in his possession from 22 September 1827 until approximately 1 July 1829, or a period of just over twenty-one months. The only exception was during the summer of 1828 when the plates were taken from him for a short period in consequence of Martin Harris's losing the 116 pages of translated Book of Mormon manuscript. Upon completion of the translation, the Prophet delivered the plates back to the angel Moroni, who "has them in his charge until this day" (JS–H 1:60).

See also The Coming Forth of the Book of Mormon, 9; The Structure of the Book of Mormon, 17; Book of Mormon, translation of; Metals, ancient writing on; Metals of the Book of Mormon; Moroni[2], visits of, to Joseph Smith; Plates of Mormon; Sealed portion of the gold plates; Stone boxes, burial of documents in; Witnesses of the Book of Mormon.

BIBLIOGRAPHY

Bidamon, Emma Hale Smith. "Last Testimony of Sister Emma." *Saints' Herald* 26 (1 October 1879).

Cook, Lyndon W., ed. *David Whitmer Interviews: A Restoration Witness.* Orem, Utah: Grandin Book, 1991.

Harris, Martin. "Statement," in "Mormonism—No. II." *Tiffany's Monthly* 5 (1859).

Putnam, Reed H. "Were the Golden Plates Made of Tumbaga?" *Improvement Era* 69 (September 1966): 788–89.

Smith, Joseph. *Papers of Joseph Smith.* Vol. 1, *Autobiographical and Historical Writings.* Edited by Dean C. Jessee. Salt Lake City: Deseret Book, 1989.

ALB

Good, concept of Jesus Christ is the touchstone of all that is genuinely and lastingly good: "And whatsoever thing is good is just and true; wherefore, nothing that is good denieth the Christ, but acknowledgeth that he is" (Moro. 10:6). He declared, "Good cometh of none save it be of me. I am the same that leadeth men to all good" (Ether 4:12; cf. Omni 1:25; Alma 5:40; Moro. 7:12, 24; 10:6). Mormon taught, "For every thing which inviteth to do good, and to persuade to believe in Christ, is sent forth by the power and gift of Christ; wherefore ye may know with a perfect knowledge it is of God" (Moro. 7:16). Sadly, too many having a knowledge of this principle fail to apply it when confronted with evil and temptation. They sin against light, against goodness (Alma 10:6; 45:12). Those who lack knowledge to distinguish between good and evil are "blameless" (Alma 29:5; cf. 2 Ne. 9:25–26), but for those who willfully sin against light, their darkness deepens (Alma 12:9–11; 2 Ne. 9:27). One's true motives and feelings determine whether a supposedly righteous act is good or evil: "For behold, God hath said a man being evil cannot do that which is good" (Moro. 7:6). That is, for the doer, an act is evil if the spirit behind it is corrupt, even though the act itself may have the appearance of being good and may even result in good for another. The act takes on the nature of the actor. Joseph Smith defined the word "Mormon" as meaning "more good" (Smith, 300). The Book of Mormon reflects this definition in its powerful declaration of Christ as the source and epitome of all that is eternally good.

See also Evil, concept of.

BIBLIOGRAPHY

Smith, Joseph. *Teachings of the Prophet Joseph Smith.* Selected by Joseph Fielding Smith. Salt Lake City: Deseret Book, 1976.

RT

Goodly *See* Appendix C.

Goodly parents This phrase appears once in the Book of Mormon, at the opening of Nephi[1]'s record on the small plates: "I, Nephi, having been born of goodly parents" (1 Ne. 1:1). According to the 1828 edition of Webster's *American Dictionary of the English Language,* the word *goodly* meant graceful or pleasant in Joseph Smith's day. Nephi repeated the word "parents" only one other time, when referring to Adam and Eve (1 Ne. 5:11).

Nephi partially explained the meaning of the expression "goodly parents" when he noted, "Therefore I was taught somewhat in all the learning of my father . . . having had a great knowledge of the goodness and the mysteries of God" (1 Ne. 1:1). In Nephi's words, his parents' teaching was an important element when he described them as "goodly." This teaching had both a practical side—"I make a record in the language of my father" (1 Ne. 1:2)—and spiritual dimension. It was this combination in his parents' instruction, a feature of "goodly parents," that prepared Nephi to "make a record" which "is true" (1 Ne. 1:1, 3).

SKB

Gospel, fulness of the *See* Fulness of the gospel.

Gospel, the The "good news" concerning Christ's ATONEMENT, RESURRECTION, and JUDGMENT by which all mankind may be saved in the kingdom of God through FAITH, REPENTANCE, BAPTISM, receiving the HOLY GHOST, and enduring in faithfulness unto the end (3 Ne. 11:32–39; 27:13–21; D&C 76:40–43, 51–53). The Book of Mormon equates the gospel with the "doctrine of Christ," both consisting of the same principles (Jacob 7:6; 1 Ne. 15:14; 2 Ne. 31:2–21; 3 Ne. 11:31–40). It also confirms the antiquity of the gospel (Moses 5:59); it was taught to the Book of Mormon peoples long before Christ's mortal ministry (e.g., 2 Ne. 31).

Christ taught that "the gates of hell shall not prevail against" those who build upon his gospel (3 Ne. 11:39). Building upon the gospel includes obedience to the first principles and ordinances —faith, repentance, baptism, receiving the Holy Ghost—becoming as a little child, pressing forward with a "steadfastness in Christ, having a perfect brightness of hope, and a love of God and of all men . . . feasting upon the word of Christ," and enduring in righteousness unto the end (2 Ne. 31:20; 3 Ne. 11:32–36; cf. A of F 3, 4). Nephi[1] taught that "this is the way; and there is none other way nor name given under heaven whereby man can be saved in the kingdom of God" (2 Ne. 31:21). By following this path one washes one's garments in Christ's blood and will stand "spotless" before him at the last day (3 Ne. 27:16–20), inheriting eternal life (2 Ne. 31:20). Nephi learned that even the Lamb of God submitted to the gospel ordinance of baptism to "fulfill all righteousness" and show that "he would be obedient unto [the Father] in keeping his commandments" (2 Ne. 31:6–7). Christ is thus the great exemplar inviting all people to come "follow me, and do the things which ye have seen me do" (2 Ne. 31:12; 3 Ne. 27:21).

In contrast, Christ also taught that those who "declare more or less than this, and establish it for my doctrine" are built upon a sandy foundation and "the gates of hell stand open to receive" them (3 Ne. 11:40; cf. D&C 20:35; Deut. 4:2; Rev. 22:18). Declaring "more or less" would include denying that Christ is the source of salvation and perverting the "true points of . . . doctrine" (3 Ne. 21:6), as did Sherem, Nehor, and Korihor (Jacob 7; Alma 1; 30). It would also include the deliberate excising of "plain and most precious" parts of the gospel and "many covenants of the Lord," which were "taken away out of the gospel of the Lamb" by the "great and abominable church" during the early part of the Christian era. This loss would cause "an exceedingly great many [to] stumble" (1 Ne. 13:24–29), enabling Satan to have "great power over them" (1 Ne. 13:29). Churches built upon false doctrine, or upon only parts of the gospel of Jesus Christ, whether in Book of Mormon times or in the latter days, will not endure, though they may have "joy in their works for a season" (3 Ne. 27:11; 1 Ne. 22:23; 2 Ne. 26:20; 28:3–4; 4 Ne. 1:26–30; Morm. 8:28–32). The Savior taught the Nephites that the distinguishing features of his church are that it bears his name and that it is built upon his gospel: "And if it so be that the church is built upon my gospel then will the Father show forth his own works in it" (3 Ne. 27:8–10).

One powerful contribution of the Book of Mormon in today's world, therefore, is the knowledge that it brings that the Lord has remembered his covenant with Israel and restored the fulness of the gospel so that they may "come to the knowledge of their Redeemer and the very points of his doctrine, that they may know how to come unto him and be saved" (1 Ne. 15:14; 3 Ne. 16:11–12). The role of the Book of Mormon in clarifying the doctrines of the gospel was enunciated by the Lord himself millennia ago. He told Joseph who was sold into Egypt that in the latter days the record written by the descendants of Judah (the Bible) and the record written by Joseph's descendants (the Book of Mormon) would "grow together, unto the confounding of false doctrines and laying down of contentions" (2 Ne. 3:12).

As Book of Mormon prophets taught "the gospel," they did not attempt to include all the principles contained therein. They would often emphasize a particular point of doctrine or discuss a few specific elements of the gospel, depending upon the needs of their listeners. In so doing, however, all the other principles and ordinances that make up the gospel of Jesus

Christ remain implicit. This is in accord with a recognized rhetorical device known as *merismus,* wherein explicitly highlighting one aspect of a topic invokes implicitly the complete definition of that topic in the mind of the reader or listener (Reynolds, 43–47). Two clear examples are the teachings of king Benjamin and Amulek. Both explicitly discussed the attainment of salvation "through faith on [Christ's] name" (Mosiah 3:9), or "faith unto repentance" (Alma 34:15–16), without mentioning the other necessary remaining principles and ordinances of the gospel. Similarly, Jacob[2] (2 Ne. 9), Abinadi (Mosiah 15), and Alma[2] (Alma 33:22; 36:12–21) all proclaimed the central doctrine of the gospel, the atonement of Christ, without delineating the other necessary principles and ordinances that must follow faith in Jesus Christ. Indeed, "none of the prophets have written, nor prophesied, save they have spoken concerning this Christ" (Jacob 7:11). And whenever they so spoke or wrote, the necessity of accepting the fulness of the gospel was clearly implied.

The Book of Mormon not only contains explications of the gospel but also illustrates the effects of obedience to or rejection of the gospel in people's lives. Early in the record is a sharp contrast between the Lamanites, who rejected the gospel and who "did become an idle people, full of mischief and subtlety" (2 Ne. 5:24), and the Nephites, who "did observe to keep the judgments, and the statutes, and the commandments of the Lord" (2 Ne. 5:10). The gospel brought to king Benjamin's people, to Alma[2] and the four sons of Mosiah[2], and to many others peace of conscience and great joy because of forgiveness of their sins, a change of heart or disposition, an honest concern for others, and a commitment to serve God to the end of their days (Mosiah 4:3; 5:1–5; 27; 28:1–8; Alma 5:11–14; 13; 19). "Thousands" of previously warlike Lamanites (Anti-Nephi-Lehies) were converted to the gospel by the sons of Mosiah and "never did fall away" (Alma 23:5–6). They laid down their swords and were prepared to suffer death rather than take them up again (Alma 24:18). In contrast, the Ammulonites and Amalekites, Nephite dissenters who had rejected the gospel, became "more hardened, and thus their state [became] worse than though they had never known these things" (Alma 24:30). These same patterns of behavior and outcomes associated with accepting or rejecting the gospel of Jesus Christ are illustrated again and again throughout the Book of Mormon.

Through latter-day revelation, the Lord affirmed that the Book of Mormon contains the fulness of the gospel (D&C 20:9; 27:5; 42:12; 135:3; JS–H 1:34). It teaches and expounds "those laws, doctrines, ordinances, powers, and authorities needed to enable men to gain the fulness of salvation" (McConkie, 333).

See also Book of Mormon, selected purposes of, to confound false doctrine; Endurance to the end; Fulness of the gospel; More or less; Plain and precious things, loss of and restoration of.

BIBLIOGRAPHY

McConkie, Bruce R. *Mormon Doctrine.* 2d ed. Salt Lake City: Bookcraft, 1966.

Reynolds, Noel B. "The Gospel of Jesus Christ as Taught by the Nephite Prophets." *Brigham Young University Studies* 31 (Summer 1991): 31–50.

GS & LED

Go to *See* Appendix C.

Government, principles of The establishment of a system of government is an act of moral agency and thus is something for which men are held accountable by God. Latter-day revelation affirms "that governments were instituted of God for the benefit of man; and that he holds men accountable for their acts in relation to them, both in making laws and administering them, for the good and safety of society. . . . that no government can exist in peace, except such laws are framed and held inviolate as will secure to each individual the free exercise of conscience, the right and control of property, and the protection of life. . . . that all men are bound to sustain and uphold the respective governments in which they reside, while protected in their inherent and inalienable rights by the laws of such governments" (D&C 134:1–2, 5).

All varieties of civil governance perform several necessary functions, including the creation of rules or norms that govern and justify social action, resolution of conflict within society, punishment of lawbreakers through governmental use of instruments of coercion,

GOVERNMENT, PRINCIPLES OF

and the construction of mechanisms of social cooperation to achieve valued ends. Book of Mormon governments all provided such functions for their peoples through systems of law, armed force, incarceration and punishment, adjudication, and taxation.

There is a critical relationship between the civil government and the spiritual growth of its constituents—the possibilities fostered or hampered by a civil government for its people to establish Zion.

The ideal form of government is a theocracy with God as the head, a kingdom with Christ as king. On earth such a government would be best represented by the Lord's Zion, a righteous people led by revelation from God to prophet-leaders and confirmed to the people themselves by the Spirit of God. Thus a standard of comparison is provided by which the merits of all government systems, and peoples' response to them, can be judged. Elements of Zion-like civil governance would include (1) the equality of persons, that no man is esteemed above another (Mosiah 23:7; 27:3–5; 29:38; cf. D&C 78:5–6); (2) the erasure of privileges based upon race, lineage, wealth, learning, and so forth (4 Ne. 1:17; cf. 3 Ne. 6:12); (3) the elimination of temporal poverty (4 Ne. 1:3; cf. Moses 7:18); (4) the establishment of laws that are consistent with God's commandments (Mosiah 2:13; 29:25); and (5) the preservation of the moral agency of the individual, especially in reference to religious belief (Alma 30:7–11; cf. D&C 98:5; 101:77–78; 134:2, 4).

The establishment of Zion is one of God's foremost desires for all of his children. To the extent that governments hinder God's children from their destiny, they bring about misery, evil, and death, both spiritual and temporal. Hence, to understand the saga of the Book of Mormon peoples, it is important to examine their choices in government. These choices were fraught with spiritual significance and either brought them closer to their God or severed them from him.

There are several ways in which civil governments may circumscribe the ability of a people to establish Zion and cause them to stumble: (1) the actual form of government; (2) the manner in which the governing of a people is carried out by their leaders, regardless of the form of government; (3) the beliefs or ideology upon which the government is built; and (4) the degree to which the people who are governed acquiesce or collude in governmental departure from the ideals of Zion.

As illustrated in Jaredite, Nephite, and Lamanite history, the Book of Mormon provides a wonderful treatise on these four aspects of spiritual danger in human governance.

The form of government

The Book of Mormon teaches that some forms of government provide greater possibility of spiritual progress and lesser threat of spiritual regress than others. Perhaps the riskiest form of government, from a spiritual perspective, is mortal autocracy, or supreme rule by one man over all others. Despite the righteous rule of KINGS such as Benjamin and Mosiah[2], the prophet leaders of the Book of Mormon all counseled against an autocratic system of government because of the spiritual risk involved. The people of Nephi[1], after living for a time in the promised land, desired that he should become their king, but he resisted and "was desirous that they should have no king" (2 Ne. 5:18). When Alma[1] fled from king Noah[3] with those who had converted to the gospel, his people requested that he become their king. Alma refused, explaining, "Behold, it is not expedient that we should have a king; for thus saith the Lord: Ye shall not esteem one flesh above another, or one man shall not think himself above another" (Mosiah 23:7). In the minds of some, autocracy itself appears to legitimize social inequality, which is anti-Zion (D&C 78:5–6). At what is arguably one of the pinnacles of Nephite society, king Mosiah transformed the system of government from a monarchy to a system of judges because of the danger of unjust kings (Mosiah 29:16). At one point, Nephite civilization was threatened with utter destruction by their enemies because of the rebellion of the KING-MEN, who wished to establish autocratic privilege for themselves in society. Only the destruction of the king-men by Nephite armies (Alma 51) and later executions of those who would not "take up arms in the defense of their country" prevented the worst from occurring (Alma 62:9–11). Though the Book of Mormon does not explain the precise form of government the Nephites had before their total destruction approximately four hundred years after Christ's appearance, most other societal destructions in the Book of Mormon were of autocratically ruled societies, such as the Jaredites, the people of king Noah, the tribal leagues, and robber bands.

Behavior of leaders, regardless of the form of government

The reason that Nephi, Alma, Mosiah, and others spoke against autocracy had to do with the manner in which the governors of society rule, regardless of the form of government. Alma and Mosiah both plainly taught that "if it were possible that ye could always have just men to be your kings it would be well for you to have a king" (Mosiah 23:8; 29:13). Nevertheless, because of the dire consequences of an unjust king being in power, both also strongly opposed government by kings for their people. After reminding his hearers of the "iniquity of king Noah and his priests," Alma warned, "trust no man to be a king over you" (Mosiah 23:9, 13). Mosiah explained that "because all men are not just it is not expedient that ye should have a king or kings to rule over you. For behold, how much iniquity doth one wicked king cause to be committed, yea, and what great destruction!" (Mosiah 29:16–17). Alma decried how the abominations favored by a king are forced upon or adopted by the people, creating a "snare" wherein the people become "bound with the bands of iniquity" (Mosiah 23:9, 12). Mosiah testified, "Ye cannot dethrone an iniquitous king save it be through much contention, and the shedding of much blood. For behold, he has his friends in iniquity, and he keepeth his guards about him; and he teareth up the laws of those who have reigned in righteousness before him; and he trampleth under his feet the commandments of God; and he enacteth laws, and sendeth them forth among his people, yea, laws after the manner of his own wickedness; and whosoever doth not obey his laws he causeth to be destroyed; and whosoever doth rebel against him he will send his armies against them to war, and if he can he will destroy them; and thus an unrighteous king doth pervert the ways of all righteousness" (Mosiah 29:21–23). There is also the problem of the crushing tax burden a wicked king places upon his people so that he might live in leisure and high consumption (Mosiah 11:1–6).

The Book of Mormon contains an account in which personal behavior on the part of the leader, the Jaredite king Morianton[1], caused him to be "cut off from the presence of the Lord," although his behavior in regards to his kingship was by and large just (Ether 10:10–11). Morianton's ability to compartmentalize his wicked behavior is highly unusual, especially in autocracy, and should probably be regarded an exception rather than the rule.

Although iniquity may be more likely in an autocracy because of the concentration of so much power in the hands of one person, or just a few, it can also pervade other forms of government. The Book of Mormon shows that even the system of judges set up by the Nephites after the reign of king Mosiah could be rendered ineffective by unrighteous leaders. Despite an elaborate system of checks and balances whereby lower judges could be overruled by higher judges, and a combination of lower judges could remove a higher judge from office (Mosiah 29:28–29), eventually wicked judges and those who sought to restore a system of nobility and privilege from which they themselves would benefit ruined the government and brought destruction upon their society (Alma 10:27; 3 Ne. 6; A.D. 29–34).

Beliefs or ideology upon which a government is based

The Book of Mormon teaches that the "incorrectness of the traditions of their fathers" may warp a society and cause its members to pursue evil goals (Alma 9:16–17; Hel. 15:4). False ideology in the Book of Mormon is most often connected with the evil traditions of Lamanite fathers, which traditions caused their descendants to forget great spiritual knowledge, to hate their brethren, and to seek "by the power of their arms to destroy [the Nephites] continually" (Jacob 7:24; cf. Mosiah 10:12–17). Elements of Nephite society also demonstrated the wickedness and conflict that can be created by governments established by wicked individuals for self-serving purposes, as in the case of wicked king Noah (Mosiah 11) and the king-men (Alma 51, 61, 62), where the traditions of nobility passed onto them by their fathers was corrupted and misapplied.

Acquiescence and collusion of the governed in departure from the ideals of Zion

In a nonautocratic society, accountability for the manner and actions of the government ultimately rests upon the people. Mosiah, in arguing for the benefits of the new system of judges he proposed, stated that the election of judges by the VOICE OF THE PEOPLE would permit them to have the government they wanted. Of course, this is a double-edged sword. If the people are generally good, then a nonautocratic system of government should yield a generally benign and responsive government. On the other hand, if the people are generally evil, then the government would reflect their corruption. Mosiah noted: "Now it is not common that the voice of the people desireth anything contrary to that which is right; but it is common for the lesser part of the people to desire that which is not right; therefore this shall ye observe and make it your law—to do your business by the voice of the people. And if the time comes that the voice of the people doth choose iniquity, then is the time that the judgments of God will come upon you; yea, then is the time he will visit you with great destruction even as he has hitherto visited this land" (Mosiah 29:26–27). Because all of the people—not just one wicked ruler who has caught his people in a "snare"—are at fault, societal destruction is the inevitable and just consequence.

In summary, the system of government established in any society has an integral relationship to the spiritual progress and regress therein. In a sense, the government and its workings are a symbol of the spiritual state of a society. Given the benchmark of Zion, the Lord will hold man accountable for his actions in establishing and enacting government. The history of the peoples of the Book of Mormon is an eloquent treatise in this regard.

See also Judges, reign of.

VMH

Grace Favor or goodwill extended by God to his children. Grace is part of God's eternal, unchanging nature, perfectly expressed through the plan of salvation and the ATONEMENT of Jesus Christ (Moro. 10:32–33).

The Book of Mormon affirms that grace is an attribute of God the Father, of Jesus Christ, and of the Holy Ghost (Ether 12:41). At times the record refers simply to "the grace of God," without delineating any one member of the Godhead (2 Ne. 10:24; Jacob 4:7; Mosiah 18:16, 26; 27:5). At other times the record specifically points to either the grace of the Father (Moro. 8:3), the grace of both Jesus and the Father (Moro. 7:2; 9:26), or the grace of Jesus Christ (2 Ne. 2:6, 8; Alma 5:48; 9:26–27; 13:9; Ether 12:26, 27, 36).

Inasmuch as the Father, Son, and Holy Ghost compose one Godhead, or "one God" (2 Ne. 31:21), the term "God" includes any and all of them, and the grace that flows from them is the same.

God's attitude towards human beings is positive; he is neither neutral nor disinterested. He is predisposed to act in their behalf; he wants them to succeed. The blessings that God showers upon mankind to help them succeed constitute expressions of his grace or favor.

In human relationships, "to find grace in someone's eyes" (e.g., Gen. 39:4) is to be viewed favorably by another person, to be accepted, liked, or approved of. To receive of God's grace is similarly a token of his approval and support; however, expressions of grace differ from other kinds of blessings in that they are gifts. They are given not as rewards but simply because it is God's nature to help others when they are unable to help themselves (Moses 1:39; 1 Jn. 4:7–8).

Like any loving parent, God is predisposed to act in his children's behalf, and he freely blesses them with many things, through his grace, that they do not earn or deserve (e.g., Mosiah 2:21, 24; cf. Rom. 11:6). Otherwise, grace becomes a wage or reward, and wages are not gifts but are justly owed to those who earn them. Yet long before mortals could obey or disobey God, before they could earn or deserve either reward or punishment, before they were even born, God already loved them and was already acting in their behalf—through his grace.

Most expressions of God's grace, his predisposition to act in his children's favor, are given to all human beings unconditionally. Just as human parents normally love and bless their children even before their children can respond in kind, so God loves and blesses his children with gracious gifts motivated by his love for them. Among these gifts are a divine parentage, agency, and the atonement of Jesus Christ. Though offered to all, not everyone will accept the opportunities offered through God's grace. Divine grace can be resisted and rejected, for God will force no one into his kingdom. Thus, it is possible to "grow in grace" through faithfulness (2 Pet. 3:18) or "fall from grace" through unfaithfulness (D&C 20:32; cf. Gal. 1:6; 5:4). Happily, for those who truly desire God's kingdom, the grace of God is sufficient to overcome any obstacle but an unwilling or disloyal heart (2 Ne. 2:6–7; Ether 12:26–27; Moro. 10:32; D&C 17:8; 18:31; 2 Cor. 12:9). God has, through his grace, already done more for human beings than he is generally given credit for, and he will, through grace, overcome all obstacles for those who continue to seek him. Truly, mankind is saved by grace. Lehi[1] testified "there is no flesh that can dwell in the presence of God, save it be through the merits, and mercy, and grace of the Holy Messiah" (2 Ne. 2:8). The Book of Mormon makes clear however, that salvation does not come by grace alone. Nephi[1] and Jacob[2] explained that salvation comes by the grace of God, "after all we can do" "after ye are reconciled unto God" (2 Ne. 25:23; 10:24). What mankind can do to be reconciled to God is to come unto Christ through faith, repentance, and baptism by water and Spirit (2 Ne. 31:17–21; Alma 24:10–11; A of F 3; 4). These works of themselves save no one. They do, however, provide "access" to God's grace (Rom. 5:1–2).

In sum, then, grace refers to all those loving gifts that God has bestowed upon his children that enable them, but never force them, to return to his presence.

See also Mercy; Merits of Christ.

SER

Grafting Grafting is a common horticultural process whereby a branch or bud of one plant is attached to and allowed to grow from the root stock of a compatible plant variety (*see* photograph of grafting, page 619). This process allows the desired qualities (usually the fruit) of the top of one plant to grow from a plant with desirable root qualities. The allegory of the olive tree in Jacob 5 uses this common practice of grafting in a metaphorical way to explain (1) how and why the house of Israel will be scattered throughout the world and why non-Israelites will be brought into the house of Israel during this scattering period, and (2) how, in the latter days, the scattered house of Israel will be brought back to its roots. The first process began some time before and continued long after Lehi[1]. In this period God had tame olive branches (members of the house of Israel) scattered around the world and branches of the wild olive tree (non-Israel) grafted into the tame olive tree (Israel). In the latter days God began grafting back into the root stock of Israel the tame branches he had earlier grafted into wild olive trees. The later grafting represents a return to the covenants associated with the house of Israel. This return, or gathering of the house of Israel, continues today as the scattered descendants of Israel begin, through the Prophet Joseph Smith and the Restoration, to understand their relationship to the house of Israel and begin to accept "the knowledge of the true Messiah" (1 Ne. 10:14) and "the very points of his doctrine" (1 Ne. 15:14).

See also Adoption; Israel, gathering of; Israel, scattering of; Olive trees; Zenos, allegory of.

PYH

Grain *See* Agriculture in the Book of Mormon.

Grandin, Egbert Bratt A Palmyra, New York, publisher who printed the first edition of the Book of Mormon.

Grandin was born in Freehold, Monmouth County, New Jersey, on 30 March 1806 to William and Ame (Amy) Lewis Grandin. At age four (in 1810) he moved with his family to northern Ontario County, New York (later Wayne County). The Grandins located at Pultneyville,

GRANDIN, EGBERT BRATT

town of Williamson, on the shore of Lake Ontario. At about age sixteen or seventeen (ca. 1822–1823), E. B. Grandin entered into an apprenticeship with Pomeroy Tucker in the village of Palmyra, New York (Maxson; *Guide,* 83).

Tucker, who had purchased the *Palmyra Herald and Canal Advertiser* from Timothy C. Strong in 1823 and changed the name to *Wayne Sentinel,* later published the newspaper jointly with John H. Gilbert (1824–27). Grandin received training as an apprentice in the shop of these two qualified printers, a shop initially located on the southeast corner of Main Street and what would become Fayette Street in 1829. Tucker next relocated his printing establishment two blocks east of the present Grandin building at the "first door" of the "James Jenner Block" (erected in 1825) on the northwest corner of the intersection of East Main and Clinton Streets. The *Wayne Sentinel* for 17 January 1826 places the paper at the new location. In April 1827, at age twenty-one, Grandin himself purchased the *Wayne Sentinel* and became its editor and publisher until 1832. He later sold half of the *Sentinel* to Theron R. Strong, 30 January 1832 (Hamilton, 275, 302–4; Grandin, 30 January 1832; Lowe).

Grandin printed his first issue of the *Wayne Sentinel* on 13 April 1827. John Gilbert announced in that number that "a sale and transfer of this paper, and of the Printing and Bookselling establishment connected with it, has been made to Mr. EGBERT B. GRANDIN, who will now assume the management of the paper and other affairs of the concern." It was later stated in the 14 November 1828 *Sentinel,* "The next number of this paper will be issued from the new office, in the third story of the west apartment of Thayer and Grandin's Block, where all kinds of Job and Book PRINTING will continue to be executed with accuracy and despatch." The three-story space in the west bay of the newly constructed "Thayer & Grandin's Row" was located on the north side of East Main Street between William and Market Streets. One of the earliest references to the building later being called the more familiar "No. 5, Exchange Row" appeared in the *Wayne Sentinel,* 1 July 1831.

E. B. Grandin (1806–1845); painting by Alonzo Parks; courtesy VRL.

Today the building is designated as 219 East Main, "Book of Mormon Historic Publication Site." The Church of Jesus Christ of Latter-day Saints owns the first two bays on the west side (Enders; Lowe). E. B. Grandin rented the west bay of the newly constructed Federal-style commercial building (built 1827–28) from his brother Philip Grandin and business partners Joel and Levi Thayer, twin brothers. In addition to maintaining his printing shop on the third story, he entered into a partnership with Luther Howard during the fall and winter of 1829–30 while the publication of the Book of Mormon was in progress. Grandin and Howard jointly operated the Palmyra Bookstore on the first story, and Howard supervised the book bindery on the second level (*Wayne Sentinel,* 12 June 1829; Enders; Lowe).

Grandin had married Harriet Rogers, 23 December 1828. Harriet was born 27 October 1810 in Williamson, New York, the daughter of William and Hannah Selby Rogers. Pomeroy Tucker had previously married Harriet's sister, Lucy Rogers, in 1824. Thus Grandin's former printing mentor also became his brother-in-law (Enders; Maxson; Hamilton, 303–4).

The Prophet Joseph Smith said that as the translation of the golden plates was nearing completion at the Peter Whitmer Sr. farm in Fayette, New York, "we went to Palmyra, Wayne county, N.Y: Secured the copyright; and agreed with Mr. Egbert Grand[i]n to print five thousand copies, for the sum of three thousand dollars" (*Times and Seasons,* 3:943). Pomeroy Tucker remembered that it was in June 1829 that the Prophet, Hyrum Smith, Oliver Cowdery, and Martin Harris applied to Grandin to print the Book of Mormon (Tucker, 50). John H. Gilbert recalled that "in the forepart of June, 1829, Mr. E. B. Grandin, the printer of the 'Wayne Sentinel,' came to me and said he wanted I should assist him in estimating the cost of printing 5000 copies of a book that Martin Harris wanted to get printed. . . . It was the second application of Harris to Grandin to do the job" ("Memorandum").

Joseph Smith filed for coverage under the 1790 U.S. copyright act which required that an author or proprietor "before publication deposit a printed copy of the title of such . . . book or books, in the clerk's office of the district court where the author or proprietor shall reside: And the clerk of such court is hereby directed and required to record the same forthwith, in a book to be kept by him for that purpose, in the words following, (giving a copy thereof to the said author or proprietor, under the seal of the court, if he shall require the same)." Then follows a sample of the required document (Peters, 1:125). Grandin was the printer who prepared the required copy of the title page of the Book of Mormon, which was submitted to R. [Richard] R. [Ray] Lansing, clerk of the Northern District Court, who had his home and office at Utica, New York (Bagg, 332–34; Spafford, copyright page, 535). Lansing then entered the title application in a formatted record book under date of 11 June 1829. It is not certain whether Joseph Smith simply submitted his title entry by mail to Lansing at Utica, New York, or whether it was delivered by hand. Lansing filed the copyright entry with the title page in Washington, D.C. (Lansing), and Joseph Smith was given an author's copy of Lansing's record. This copy is handwritten and not an exact duplicate as to line spacing and the like (copy in Church Archives). Only a portion of the copyright application issued by Lansing was subsequently copied into the "Printer's Manuscript" of the Book of Mormon prepared by Oliver Cowdery. When type was set for the copyright page in the first edition, the entire document was included as required by law (Printer's manuscript; Lansing; Smith; compare Skousen, 48–49).

Grandin also printed a copy of the title page of the Book of Mormon in the *Wayne Sentinel* on 26 June 1829 with the introductory comment, "We have been furnished with the following, which is represented to us as intended for the title page of the work—we give it as a curiosity." Then follows the title page, with minor punctuation changes, as it was eventually printed in the 1830 edition. Grandin later accurately printed, save for some punctuation changes, copies of the title page in issues of the *Wayne Sentinel* for 26 March 1830 (the day the Book of Mormon was first made available to the public at Grandin's Palmyra Bookstore), for 2, 9, and 16 April, and for 7 May 1830. This notice was accompanied by the following comment, "The above work, containing about 600 pages, large Duodecimo, is now for sale, wholesale and retail, at the Palmyra Bookstore." The purpose appears to be that of providing an advertisement for the book, but, as suggested by Richard L. Anderson, it may also have been an attempt at "curing," or satisfying the legal requirement of the copyright law which specified that "such author or proprietor shall, within two months from the date thereof, cause a copy of the said record [the clerk's copyright entry] to be published in one or more of the newspapers printed in the United States, for the space of four weeks." Anderson further suggests that the printers "may have thought they were complying with the intent of the law by printing just what they had originally submitted to the clerk of the court—the title page" (interview; Peters, 1:125; 2:171). The comparative length of the title page alone may have been a factor. It is important to note, however, that the U.S. copyright act called for the newspaper to print the complete copyright entry as prepared by the clerk of the district court and not just the content of the title page itself. The 1790 act provided a definite outline to follow (Peters, 1:125). Grandin knew the law and the proper format as evidenced by his printing of Lansing's copyright entry for himself when he, Grandin, filed a title submission to print "*Notes*

GRANDIN, EGBERT BRATT

on Title IV. Chapter II. of part III. of the Revised Statutes of the State of New York" in May of that same year (*Wayne Sentinel,* May 7, 14, 21, 28, and 4 June 1830). Interestingly, both Grandin's personal legal notice and the Book of Mormon title page appear on the same page in the 7 May 1830 issue of the *Sentinel.*

The original printing of the title page of the Book of Mormon on 26 June 1829 would further suggest the general time period in which ongoing negotiations with Grandin for the printing of the Book of Mormon were taking place. Finding that Martin Harris was to provide the financial security for the project, Grandin initially expressed his reluctance to publish the Book of Mormon as requested, "believing the whole affair to be a wicked imposture and a scheme to defraud Mr. Harris, who was his friend" (Tucker, 51). Joseph Smith and his friends were under the necessity of going to Rochester, New York, where they next applied to Thurlow Weed, former printer of the *Rochester Daily Telegraph* with Robert Martin in 1826, and current editor of the Rochester *Anti-Masonic Enquirer* (1828–1830) to act as publisher. Weed, operating out of the office of the *Rochester Daily Telegraph,* twice rejected their request (Weed, 1:358–59; Hamilton, 306–7). The Prophet then visited the Rochester office of book publisher Elihu F. Marshall, who "gave his terms for the printing and binding of the book, with his acceptance of the proffered mode of security for the payment" (Tucker, 52).

Even with Marshall's affirmation, the Prophet made yet another attempt to enlist Grandin. Grandin was informed that the job would be done with or without him and that because of the convenience and money-saving aspects of working with a Palmyra publisher close to their residence he was still their preference. Tucker observed, "It was upon this statement of the facts, and in this view of the case, that Mr. Grandin, on taking the advice of several discreet, fair-minded neighbors, finally reconsidered his course of policy, and entered into contract for the printing and binding of five thousand copies of the Book of Mormon" (Tucker, 52–53). Grandin's grandson Henry Allen stated that "after consulting friends who felt that it was merely a business matter and that he would be in no way related to the religion, he consented" (qtd. in Porter, 52).

Agreement was reached on the terms of the publication between the parties and the requisite number of copies to be printed between mid-August 1829 and 26 March 1830. Milton W. Hamilton put this accomplishment in an interesting perspective when he stated, "Two outstanding publishing events occurred in western New York in this period (1785–1830). The first was the printing of William Morgan's revelation of Masonry in the office of David C. Miller, in Batavia (1826), which, with attendant events, profoundly influenced the development of the press within the state. The second was the publication of the *Book of Mormon* or 'Golden Bible' of Joseph Smith by E. B. Grandin, of Palmyra (1830)" (Hamilton, 78–79).

Through the *Wayne Sentinel,* Grandin became an influential spokesman for the Wayne County Democratic Party and was a strong Jacksonian. He also served the Palmyra community in such civic functions as a village trustee (Grandin, 7 February 1831), collector of taxes, clerk of the board of inspectors of elections, and constable (*Guide,* 84). In 1831 and 1832 Grandin experienced a series of unfortunate financial reverses that necessitated his divesting himself of his printing establishment, which was accomplished by April 1833 (*Guide,* 85). Theron R. Strong is listed as publisher with the 2 January 1833 issue of the *Wayne Sentinel.* Over a period of years, Grandin was occupied in a succession of businesses, i.e., "butcher, tanner, public servant, superintendent of an Erie Canal cargo boat, farmer, and commissioning and forwarding merchant." He was periodically drawn back to the *Wayne Sentinel* office to work for later owners (*Guide,* 85–86; Hamilton, 303–4).

A virtually unexplored opportunity to extract valuable information from Grandin on the circumstances surrounding the publication of the Book of Mormon ended abruptly when he died at age thirty-nine. While recovering from a protracted illness, he suffered a relapse due to complications of pneumonia and passed away on 16 April 1845 (*Wayne Sentinel,* 23 April 1845, 3). Grandin is buried in the Palmyra City

Cemetery, Section R, Lot 111. His epitaph reads, "An honest man, the noblest work of God."

See also Book of Mormon, printing and publication of; Gilbert, John Hulburd.

BIBLIOGRAPHY

Allen, Henry M. "Letter to the Librarian of the Palmyra Library." March 1964. E. B. Grandin file, King's Daughters' Free Library. Palmyra, New York.

Anderson, Richard L. Personal interview. 2 June 1998. Provo, Utah.

Bagg, M. M. *The Pioneers of Utica.* Curtiss and Childs, 1877.

Enders, Donald L. Personal interview. 28 January 1998. Salt Lake City, Utah.

Gilbert, John H. "Memorandum, made by John H. Gilbert Esq, Sept 8th. 1892," King's Daughters' Free Library, Palmyra, New York.

Grandin, Egbert B. *Diary.* 1 January 1831 to 2 February 1841. Church Archives, The Church of Jesus Christ of Latter-day Saints, Salt Lake City, Utah.

Guide to Exhibits at the Book of Mormon Historic Publication Site at Palmyra, New York. Salt Lake City: The Church of Jesus Christ of Latter-day Saints, 1998. Courtesy of Donald L. Enders, Church Archives.

Hamilton, Milton W. *The Country Printer: New York State, 1785–1830.* Port Washington, L. I., New York: Ira J. Friedman, 1964.

Lansing, R. R. See Joseph Smith, copyright entry in Court of the United States for the Northern District of New York, September 1826 to May 1831; 116:107. Copyright Office, Library of Congress, Washington, D.C.

Lowe, Robert O. Personal interview. 18 July 1998. Palmyra, New York, village and town historian.

Maxson, Anna L., great-great-granddaughter of E. B. Grandin. Personal correspondence. Toledo, Ohio, 3 June 1998.

Peters, Richard, Esq., ed. *The Public Statutes at Large of the United States of America from the Organization of the Government in 1789, to March 3, 1845.* 2 vols. Boston: Charles C. Little and James Brown, 1845.

Porter, Larry C. "The Book of Mormon: Historical Setting for Its Translation and Publication." *Joseph Smith: The Prophet, the Man.* Edited by Susan Easton Black and Charles D. Tate Jr. Provo, Utah: Religious Studies Center, Brigham Young University, 1993.

Printer's manuscript of the Book of Mormon. Community of Christ Library-Archives, Independence, Missouri.

Skousen, Royal. *The Printer's Manuscript of the Book of Mormon: Typographical Facsimile of the Entire Text in Two Parts.* Provo, Utah: FARMS, 2001.

Smith, Joseph. The Book of Mormon. Palmyra, N.Y.: E. B. Grandin, 1830.

Spafford, Horatio Gates. *A Gazetteer of the State of New York.* Albany: B. D. Packard, 1824.

Times and Seasons. 3 (15 October 1842): 943.

Tucker, Pomeroy. *Origin, Rise, and Progress of Mormonism.* New York: D. Appleton and Company, 1867.

Wayne Sentinel. 12 June 1829.

Weed, Thurlow. *Autobiography of Thurlow Weed.* Edited by Harriet A. Weed. Vol. 1. Boston: Houghton, Mifflin and Company, 1884.

LCP

Great and abominable church A great evil Nephi[1] saw in an important vision he experienced while en route to the promised land. In chapters 13 and 14 of 1 Nephi, the prophet Nephi described the vision in which he saw the future of the world and its kingdoms. NEPHI[1]'S VISION is the type of revelation known in biblical literature as apocalyptic, and it is represented in the New Testament most fully by the Revelation of John. The revelations of Nephi and of John have more in common, however, than merely the apocalyptic form, for Nephi's vision (1 Ne. 14:19–28) anticipates that of John. The two are complementary, centering in part on the same characters and themes: the Lamb and his church, the Apostasy, the great and abominable church of the devil, and the restoration of the gospel in the latter days. When added to the information found in John's revelation and other pertinent scriptures, Nephi's descriptions point to some historical conclusions about the nature of the Apostasy and the identity of the great and abominable church.

In an attempt to understand the message of Nephi and John, terms must be defined. The Greek word *apostasia* (apostasy) means "rebellion" or "revolution." It conveys the sense of an internal takeover within an organization or institution by factions hostile to the intentions of its previous leaders. The translation "mutiny" for *apostasia*, calls up the image of a ship being commandeered by those who are not authorized to do so and being taken in a direction the ship was not intended to go. Because early Christians often thought of the Church as a ship, it seems "mutiny" conveys exactly the right sense of what Paul and others meant by the term "apostasy."

It is also important to analyze and define the component parts of the phrase "great and abominable church." In this context, "great" is an adjective of size rather than of quality and (like the Hebrew *gadol* or the Greek *megas*) informs of the great size of the abominable entity. Secondary meanings might refer to great wealth or power. The term "abominable" is used in the Old Testament to describe that which God hates, which cannot fail to arouse his wrath. In the book of Daniel, the abomination of desolation is that thing which is so hateful to God that its presence in the temple causes the divine presence to depart, leaving the sanctuary desolate (Dan. 11:31; 12:11; Matt. 24:15; JS–M 1:12–20). In the Old Testament, the terms translated into English as "abominable" or "abomination" (Hebrew roots *shiqqutz, ta'ab, piggul;* Greek Septuagint and New Testament *bdelugma)* are usually associated with one of two practices: idolatrous worship or gross sexual immorality (e.g., Lev. 18:22; 20:13; Deut. 27:15; 2 Chr. 15:8; Jer. 44:3–5; Ezek. 22:11).

The term "church" (Hebrew *qahal* or *edah;* Greek *ekklesia)* had a slightly broader meaning anciently than it does now and referred to an assembly, congregation, or association of people that bonded them together and commanded their loyalties. Thus the term was not necessarily restricted to religious associations and, in fact, at Athens was used to denote the legislative assembly of government. When all this is put together, it appears that the phrase "great and abominable church" means an immense assembly or association of people bound together by their loyalty to that which God hates. Most likely this will be a religious association involved specifically in sexual immorality and/or idolatry (that is, false worship—abandoning the God of Israel and worshipping anything else).

While the revelation of John does not use the exact term "great and abominable church," the entity so described by Nephi is clearly the harlot described by John in Revelation 17–18, because identical and similar terms "mother of abominations," "mother of harlots," and "the great whore that sitteth upon many waters" are used by both prophets (1 Ne. 14:10–12, 16; Rev. 17:1, 5).

Characteristics of the great and abominable church in 1 Nephi may be listed as follows:

1. It persecutes, tortures, and slays the Saints of God (13:5).
2. It seeks wealth and luxury (13:7).
3. It is characterized by sexual immorality (13:7).
4. It has excised plain and precious things from the scriptures (13:26–29).
5. It has dominion over all the earth, among all nations, kindreds, tongues, and people (14:11).
6. Its fate is to be consumed by a world war, in which the nations it incited against the Saints turn to war among themselves until they destroy the great and abominable church itself (22:13–14).

These same characteristics are also attributed to the whore (Babylon) in the Revelation of John:

1. She is drunk with the blood of the Saints and with the blood of the martyrs of Jesus and of the prophets (17:6; 18:24).
2. She is characterized by the enjoyment of great wealth and luxury (17:4; 18:3, 11–16).
3. She is characterized by sexual immorality (17:1, 2, 5).
4. She has dominion over all nations (17:15, 18; 18:3, 23–24).
5. Her fate is to be consumed by the very kings who have made war on the Lamb under the influence of her deceptions (17:14–16; 18:23).

It should be noted that one characteristic not common to both prophetic descriptions is Nephi's statement that the great and abominable church held back important parts of the canon of scripture. But because John's record is one of the very scriptures to which Nephi refers (14:20–23), this omission in John's account is not surprising.

It must also be noted that in John's revelation the whore cannot be equated with the two beasts; they do not represent the same things. The one beast supports the whore (Rev. 17:3), but the beast and the whore are separate entities with separate functions in the evil empire, both motivated by the same evil genius, Satan. The whore of Revelation 17–18 is specifically the satanic counterpart of the woman in chapter 12

GREAT AND ABOMINABLE CHURCH

who symbolizes the church of Jesus Christ which was forced into the wilderness (that is, became inaccessible to human beings). Symbolizing the great and abominable church (the counterfeit) as a whore underscores the nature of her evil: she is physically and spiritually unfaithful; that is, she represents both sexual immorality and idolatry, the twin abominations of the Old Testament. Thus she is the "mother of abominations."

Since the great and abominable church from 1 Nephi is identified in every aspect with the whore, while the beast is never even mentioned in Nephi's vision, it follows that when discussing *the* great and abominable church, one must not confuse the whore which Nephi saw and described with the beast which he did not. There are no references to the beasts of Revelation in Nephi's vision of the great and abominable church. As both John and Nephi make clear, the nations outlast the whore, and they eventually destroy her. Both beast and whore are component parts of the kingdom of the devil, but they are *separate* parts even though they sometimes work together.

Perhaps the greatest difficulty in Nephi's description of the great and abominable church is an apparent contradiction between chapters 13 and 14. In 1 Nephi 13 the great and abominable church is one specific church among many. Indeed, Nephi's description of it as "most abominable above all other churches" (13:5, 26) makes no sense otherwise. Moreover, it has a specific historical description: it would be formed among the Gentiles *after* the Bible has been transmitted in its purity to the Gentiles by the Jews (13:25–26), and it is the specific historical agent responsible for excising plain and precious truths from the scriptural record. It would appear that in chapter 13 Nephi described a specific historical institution as the great and abominable church. To this one must add the information given in Doctrine and Covenants 86:1–4, which states that the great and abominable church did its work after the apostles had fallen asleep, that is, around the end of the first century. Similarly, in the Revelation of John, the role of the whore has a historical frame. She comes into the picture after the beasts, upon which she rides and which give her support, and she is eliminated from the picture while they yet continue. Again, the great and abominable church (Babylon) is not a term identical with "the kingdom of the devil," for the whore is only one of the component parts of a larger empire, together with the beasts, the image, the horns, and the false prophet—and also with other false churches. This last idea is clearly brought out in 1 Nephi 22:22–23: "But it is *the kingdom of the devil,* which shall be built up among the children of men, which kingdom is established among them which are in the flesh—for the time speedily shall come that *all churches* which are built up to get gain, and all those who are built up to get power over the flesh, and those who are built up to become popular in the eyes of the world, and those who seek the lusts of the flesh and the things of the world, and to do all manner of iniquity; yea, in fine, *all those who belong to the kingdom of the devil* are they who need fear, and tremble" (italics added).

Indisputably, the full kingdom of the devil is made up of many churches (or denominations) and will be until the end of the world. Taking 1 Nephi 13 and 22 as starting points, one might be justified in asking which of all those false denominations is the *actual* great and abominable church of the devil. The apparent contradiction comes in 1 Nephi 14:10, in which it is said that there are only *two* churches: "And he said unto me: Behold there are save two churches only; the one is the church of the Lamb of God, and the other is the church of the devil."

How can this be? How can the devil's church or churches be one and many at the same time? The apparent contradiction actually gives the solution to the larger puzzle and ultimately the identification of the great and abominable church.

The answer is that the term is used in two different ways in these two chapters. In chapter 13 it is used historically, and in chapter 14 it is used typologically, or apocalyptically. In apocalyptic literature (both Revelation and 1 Nephi 13–14 are apocalyptic in nature) the seer is caught up in vision and sees things from God's perspective. Time ceases to be an important element. This is why the chronology of John's revelation at times seems to be scrambled. Apocalyptic visions are highly symbolic, usually requiring an angelic interpreter for the seer to understand what he sees. But the symbols are inclusive; that is, they stand for archetypical categories into which all specific instances of something can be placed. This is why the whore can be called Nineveh (some of John's language comes from Nahum's description of Nineveh), or Babylon, Sodom, Egypt, Jerusalem[1], or Rome. It doesn't matter; the names change, but the character "that great city" remains the same in every dispensation. To illustrate, consider the name of the whore, or great and abominable church: Babylon. A literal reading would lead one to believe that some particular city is being described, and one would want to know which city it was. But in reading carefully, it can be seen that Babylon in John's revelation is not one city but many cities, all of which fall into the larger category of "that great city," which is the antithesis of the city of God, the heavenly Jerusalem or Zion. Just as Zion is wherever the pure in heart dwell (D&C 97:21), so Babylon is where the whore lives. Because Latter-day Saints understand that Zion is a spiritual category, which may in different contexts mean Salt Lake City, Far West, Jerusalem, or the City of Enoch, they should also understand Zion's opposite, Babylon, in the same way. It is precisely this variable identity that Jacob[2] taught when he said, "Wherefore, he that fighteth against Zion, both Jew and Gentile, both bond and free, both male and female, shall perish; *for they are they who are the whore of all the earth; for they who are not for me are against me, saith our God*" (2 Ne. 10:16; italics added). In other words Babylon, "the whore of all the earth," is in this context anyone who fights against Zion.

In apocalyptic literature the cast of characters is constant in every dispensation; they are these same archetypical categories into which all things can be placed. From the apocalyptic point of view there is one script, one plot, from the foundation of the world until its end. The characters in the play and the lines they deliver are always the same from dispensation to dispensation, although the individual actors who play the roles and speak the lines may change with time. Therefore, there is always the role of "that great city," though the part might be played at different times in history by Sodom, Egypt, Nineveh, Babylon, Rome, Berlin, Moscow, or Washington, D.C. The important thing is to know what the archetypical patterns are and their identifying characteristics. Then one can orient oneself in any time or place and know who functions *now* in the role of Babylon and where Zion is located.

Once it is understood that the term "great and abominable church" has two extensions, the one open, inclusive, and archetypical, and the other limited and historical, the rest is easy. In chapter 14, Nephi described the archetypical roles themselves: "There are save two churches only" (that is, Zion and Babylon). But in chapter 13 he referred to the specific institution (the actor, if you will) who played the role of Babylon in the Roman Empire in the second century A.D. Nevertheless, it will not do much good in the twenty-first century to know who played Babylon in the second. One needs to recognize Babylon now, in this era, although the actors have been changed.

Apocalyptic literature is also dualistic. Because it deals with archetypes, it boils everything down to opposing principles: love and hate, good and evil, light and dark. There are no gray areas in apocalyptic scripture. At the very least, everything can be reduced to the opposing categories of A and not-A ("They who are not for me are against me, saith our God"; 2 Ne. 10:16). In the realm of religion, there are only two categories: religion that will save and religion that will not. The former is the church of the Lamb, and the latter—no matter how well intentioned—is a counterfeit. Thus, even a "good" church must still be part of the devil's kingdom in the sense used in 1 Nephi 14 ("there are save two churches only"), for it cannot do what it pretends to do. Nevertheless, such a church cannot be called the "great and abominable church" in the sense used in 1 Nephi 13, for its intentions are good and honorable, and quite often such churches teach people enough truth that they can then recognize the true church when they meet

GREAT AND ABOMINABLE CHURCH

it. These churches do not slay the saints of God, they do not seek to control civil governments, nor do they pursue wealth, luxury, and sexual immorality. Such churches may belong to the kingdom of the devil in the apocalyptic sense, where there are only two categories, A and not-A, but they cannot be called the great and abominable church in the historical sense—the description is just not accurate. Furthermore, individual orientation to the Church of the Lamb or to the great and abominable church is not only by membership but by loyalty. Just as there are those on the records of The Church of Jesus Christ of Latter-day Saints who belong to the great and abominable church by virtue of their loyalty to Satan and his lifestyle (2 Ne. 10:16), so there are members of other churches who will eventually belong to the Lamb by virtue of their loyalty to him and to his lifestyle, which will lead to their accepting the saving ordinances. The distinction is based on who has your heart, not on who has your records. Hence, it is unwise and inaccurate to point to any particular church or political system as *the* great and abominable church. No single organization meets all the requirements:

1. It must have been formed among the Gentiles and must have controlled the distribution of the New Testament scriptures, which it edited and from which it deleted plain and precious things.

2. It must have slain the Saints of God and killed the apostles and prophets.

3. It must be in league with civil governments and use their police power to enforce its religious views.

4. It must have dominion over all the earth.

5. It must pursue wealth, luxury, and sexual immorality, and must last until essentially the end of the world.

The conclusion is inescapable: no *single* entity can be *the* great and abominable church from the beginning of the world to the end. Rather, the role has been played by many different actors in many different times, and the great and abominable church that Nephi described in 1 Nephi 13 is not the same one that crucified Christ or that martyred Joseph and Hyrum.

Can the historical agency that acted as the great and abominable church in earliest Christianity and which Nephi and others describe be identified? It seems clear that the great and abominable church Nephi described in chapter 13 had its origins in the second half of the first century and had essentially done its work by the middle of the second century. This period might be called the blind spot of ecclesiastical history, for it is here that the fewest primary historical sources have been preserved. Essentially, what happened is that there are good sources for New Testament Christianity (the New Testament documents themselves). Then the lights go out (that is, there are very few historical sources), and in the dark one hears the muffled sounds of a great struggle. When the lights come on again a hundred years or so later, one finds that someone has rearranged all the furniture and that Christianity is something very different from what it was in the beginning. That different entity can be accurately described by the term "hellenized Christianity." The hellenization of Christianity is a phenomenon that has long been recognized by scholars of Christian history, but it is one which Latter-day Saints know better as the Great Apostasy. Hellenization means imposing Greek culture on the native cultures of the East. The result was a synthesis of East and West, with elements of the Greek West predominating, creating a melting-pot, popular culture that was virtually worldwide.

But in the realm of religion, synthesis means compromise, and when one speaks of the gospel, compromise with the popular culture of the world means apostasy from the truth. When Jewish Christianity and Greek culture met head-on in the Gentile mission field in the middle of the first century, the Greeks eventually won, and Jewish Christianity was ultimately "revised" to make it more attractive and appealing to a Greek audience. Primary prejudices of the Hellenistic world were the "absolute" nature of God (that is, he cannot be bound or limited by anything) and the impossibility of anything material or physical being eternal. To accommodate these ideas and thus appeal to a broader Gentile audience, Christianity had to discard the doctrines of an anthropomorphic God and the resurrection of the dead or else "reinterpret" them in a manner that had the same effect. That is precisely what some Greek Christians at Corinth had already done and against which Paul responded with such force in 1 Corinthians 15:12: "Now if Christ be preached that he rose from the dead, how say some among you that there is no resurrection of the dead?"

Clearly, whatever denominational name is given to it, the great and abominable church described by Nephi and John and the earliest apostate church are identical. The fact is no one knows really what name to give it. "Hellenized Christianity" is more a description than a name. Babylon in the first and second centuries may even have been a collection of different movements. Some Jewish Christians could not let go of the law of Moses and so eventually gave up Christ instead. The "orthodox" adopted Greek philosophy. The Gnostics wallowed in the mysteries and in unspeakable permissiveness on the one hand, or in the mysteries and a neurotic asceticism on the other. Tatian and Marcion rewrote the scriptures, the latter boldly chopping out anything he did not like, and all of them together forced the virtuous woman, the true church of Jesus Christ, into the wilderness.

See also Church of the Lamb of God; Mother of abominations; Mother of harlots; Plain and precious things, loss of and restoration of; Whore of all the earth.

BIBLIOGRAPHY

Robinson, Stephen E. "Early Christianity and 1 Nephi 13–14." *The Book of Mormon: First Nephi, the Doctrinal Foundation*. Edited by Monte S. Nyman and Charles D. Tate Jr. Provo, Utah: Religious Studies Center, Brigham Young University, 1988. 177–91.

———. "Warring against the Saints of God." *Ensign* 18 (January 1988): 34–39.

SER

Great and last sacrifice Jesus Christ was the great and last sacrifice (Alma 34:14). From the time of Adam's expulsion from the Garden of Eden, prophets have taught that the Lamb of God, his Only Begotten Son, would one day be sacrificed to answer the demands of a higher law (Moses 5:5–9; 2 Ne. 2:5–7). That sacrifice would make God's plan of redemption operative in bringing about the salvation of all people. The sacrificial offerings that were part of the law of Moses foreshadowed the atoning sacrifice of Jesus Christ and ended when it was accomplished (Alma 34:13; 3 Ne. 9:19). Thus his atoning sacrifice fulfilled the law of Moses and was the great and the last sacrifice.

See also Atonement, the.

AKP

Great and spacious building *See* Lehi[1]'s dream.

Guile *See* Appendix C.

Guilt A consequence of transgressing the law. In a legal sense, guilt is a judgment pronounced from having broken civil or religious law (Alma 1:12), but the more frequent use of the word *guilt* in the Book of Mormon centers on the emotional and spiritual anguish experienced by mankind because of having "set at defiance the commandments of God" (Alma 5:18). King Benjamin taught, "The demands of divine justice do awaken [man's] immortal soul to a lively sense of his own guilt, which doth cause him to shrink from the presence of the Lord, and doth fill his breast with guilt, and pain, and anguish, which is like an unquenchable fire, whose flame ascendeth up forever and ever" (Mosiah 2:38). Alma[2] described his experience with guilt by writing, "For three days and for three nights was I racked, even with the pains of a damned soul" (Alma 36:16). While God would have guilt be genuine and lead to REPENTANCE and FORGIVENESS (Alma 24:10; 39:7; 42:29), Satan would have mankind experience a counterfeit sorrow. The prophet Mormon taught the following concerning the sorrowful but unrepentant Nephites: "Their sorrowing was not unto repentance, because of the goodness of God; but it was rather the sorrowing of the damned, because the Lord would not always suffer them to take happiness in sin" (Morm. 2:13).

At the Judgment Bar the unrepentant have a perfect recollection of all their guilt (2 Ne. 9:14; Alma 5:18; 11:43). Guilt is to the spirit as physical pain is to the body. Elder Boyd K. Packer counseled, "While neither pain nor guilt is pleasant, and an excess of either can be destructive, both are a protection" (54, 59). President Ezra Taft Benson taught, "Godly sorrow is a gift of the Spirit. It is a deep realization that our actions have offended our Father and our God" (72). The Lord taught Enos that his "guilt was swept away. . . . Because of [his] faith in Christ" (Enos 1:6–8; cf. Alma 24:10).

BIBLIOGRAPHY

Benson, Ezra Taft. *Teachings of Ezra Taft Benson.* Salt Lake City: Bookcraft, 1988.

Packer, Boyd K. "To Young Women and Men." *Ensign* 19 (May 1989): 53–59.

DKJ

Gulf An abyss or chasm separating "the wicked from the tree of life, and also from the saints of God" (1 Ne. 15:28). This separation is required by the justice of God and is symbolized by the river of filthiness in Lehi's dream (1 Ne. 12:18; 15:26–30). The gulf is "a representation of that awful hell . . . prepared for the wicked" (1 Ne. 15:28–29). The torment of the wicked who create this gulf for themselves can be experienced in mortal life (1 Ne. 15:31–32), in the postmortal SPIRIT WORLD (Alma 40:13; Luke 16:19–31), and for some, eternally (1 Ne. 15:34–35). The only way to overcome this "gulf of misery and woe" (2 Ne. 1:13) is through Jesus Christ and his mercy (Alma 26:20; Hel. 5:12). "Yea, we see that whosoever will may lay hold upon the word of God, which is quick and powerful, which shall divide asunder all the cunning and the snares and the wiles of the devil, and lead the man of Christ in a strait and narrow course across that everlasting gulf of misery which is prepared to engulf the wicked" (Hel. 3:29–30).

See also Hell; Outer darkness; Paradise.

LED

And when they had all gone forth and had witnessed for themselves, they did cry out with one accord, saying: Hosanna! Blessed be the name of the Most High God! And they did fall down at the feet of Jesus, and did worship him.

3 NEPHI 11:16–17

Hagoth Described as "an exceedingly curious man," Hagoth was a shipbuilder who facilitated the Nephite migrations northward at about 55 B.C. (Alma 63:5–7). The maiden voyage of his first ship, which he launched "into the west sea, by the narrow neck," was successful, but the second trip was presumed fatal, as the emigrants "were never heard of more" (Alma 63:5, 7–8). Hagoth "built other ships" that sailed northward, presumably including the supply ship that carried Alma[2]'s son Corianton into that land, and "one other ship," whose whereabouts remained a mystery (Alma 63:7–10).

DLL

Halt *See* Appendix C.

Hands, laying on of A procedure used when conferring divine authority and performing priesthood ordinances. The Lord has established "the laying on of hands" as part of the process whereby his servants are to be empowered in all ages (A of F 5). Alma[2] ordained priests and elders in Zarahemla by the laying on of hands (Alma 6:1; cf. Moro. 3:2; Num. 27:23). Later he "clapped his hands" upon his fellow missionaries among the Zoramites[2] (Alma 31:36)—presumably meaning that he "thrust" (*see* Appendix C, s.v. "clapped") or placed his hands upon the heads of his co-workers and set them apart for their missionary labor. Christ laid his hands upon the Nephite Twelve to give them authority to bestow the Holy Ghost (3 Ne. 18:36–38; Moro. 2:2). The Twelve thereafter conferred the Holy Ghost by the laying on of hands upon those who had been baptized (Moro. 2:3). The laying on of hands was also used among the Nephites to administer to the sick (Morm. 9:24; cf. James 5:14–15; D&C 42:43–44).

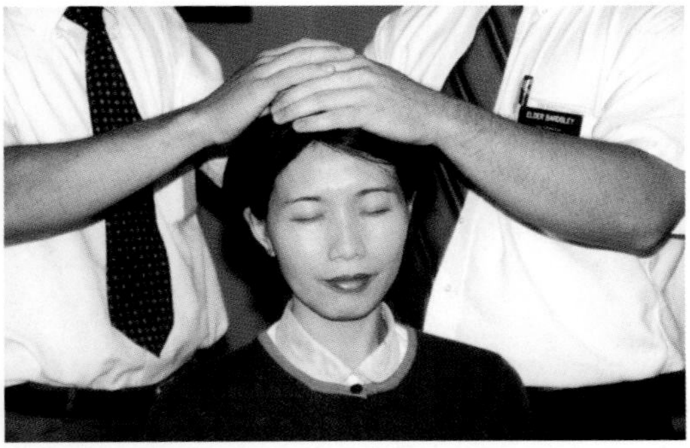

Laying on of hands; courtesy Deila Taylor.

TBB

Happiness A state of JOY, contentment, and felicity—the very reason for man's existence (2 Ne. 2:25; Smith, 255–56). Happiness and misery are eternal opposites and exist according to eternal law. Whereas righteousness brings happiness, wickedness brings punishment and misery—"for it must needs be, that there is an opposition in all things." Accordingly, Lehi[1] taught, "If there be no righteousness there be no happiness. And if there be no righteousness nor happiness there be no punishment nor misery" (2 Ne. 2:10–13, 23; Alma 3:26; 42:16; Morm. 8:38).

Although men may find a kind of "joy" in wickedness "for a season," such pleasure is short-lived (3 Ne. 27:11). Mormon observed that the "lamentation" and "mourning" of the decadent Nephites of his day was not unto repentance but was the "sorrowing of the damned, because the Lord would not always suffer them to take happiness in sin" (Morm. 2:12–13). Samuel the Lamanite, some three hundred years earlier, said of another wicked generation of Nephites, "But behold, your days of probation are past . . . and your destruction is made sure; yea, for ye have sought all the days of your lives for that which ye could not obtain; and ye have sought for happiness in doing iniquity, which thing is contrary to the nature of that righteousness which is in our great and Eternal Head" (Hel. 13:38; Alma 41:10–11).

God's "great plan of happiness" (Alma 42:8) affords happiness to the righteous in mortality (2 Ne. 5:27; Alma 50:23), in the spirit world (Alma 40:12), and eternally after the resurrection (Mosiah 16:11; Alma 3:26; 28:12; Morm. 7:7; 8:38). King Benjamin taught that those who "keep the commandments of God . . . are blessed in all things, both temporal and spiritual," and "if they hold out faithful to the end they are received into heaven, that thereby they may dwell with God in a state of never-ending happiness" (Mosiah 2:41). Of the days of captain

Moroni, Mormon wrote, "there never was a happier time among the people of Nephi, since the days of Nephi" (Alma 50:23). Moroni attributed Nephite happiness to "the maintenance of the sacred word of God" (Alma 44:5). The most enduring period of happiness in the Book of Mormon narrative came after the Savior's visit, when all were converted to the Lord and righteousness prevailed for nearly 200 years—"and surely there could not be a happier people among all the people who had been created by the hand of God" (4 Ne. 1:16, 2–3, 15).

BIBLIOGRAPHY

Smith, Joseph. *Teachings of the Prophet Joseph Smith.* Selected by Joseph Fielding Smith. Salt Lake City: Deseret Book, 1976.

LED

Hard-heartedness Willful closing of one's heart against the Holy Spirit, in rebellion against God, in order to accomplish one's own will (Alma 10:6). Hard-heartedness can result in the Spirit's ceasing to strive with a person (Moro. 9:4) and in spiritual death (Jacob 6:6). Hard-heartedness can lead progressively from indulging oneself somewhat in wrongdoing (Jacob 1:15) to gross wickedness (Hel. 6:2). Hard-heartedness is associated with complaining or murmuring (1 Ne. 2:12; 16:20–22), UNBELIEF (Alma 33:21), blindness of mind (1 Ne. 7:8), anger (Alma 9:31; cf. Mosiah 13:4), impenitence (Hel. 6:2), STIFFNECKEDNESS (Hel. 13:29), PRIDE and sexual sin (Jacob 1:15), desire for vengeance (Moro. 9:4–5), abominations, cruelty, and murder (Moro. 9:9–10). Hard-heartedness restricts spiritual understanding and can eventually lead to "know[ing] nothing" concerning the mysteries of God, and then being "taken captive by the devil" (Alma 12:10–11; 10:25; cf. 1 Ne. 7:8; Mosiah 13:32). It resists the softening action of the Holy Spirit and its attendant virtues, like MEEKNESS, compassion, and HUMILITY (Alma 13:28). Hard-heartedness is a state of unrest and prevents one's entry into the Lord's rest (Alma 12:36). It renders one vulnerable to lies, and blind to divine signs and wonders (Hel. 13:29; 3 Ne. 1:22; Ether 8:25). Hard-heartedness "against the Holy One of Israel" brings the judgments of God, "even blood, and fire, and vapor of smoke" (1 Ne. 22:18). It flourishes in conditions of ease and prosperity (Hel. 12:2). For those who repent and harden not their hearts, the great plan of redemption immediately begins to function (Alma 34:31). God promises them mercy, remission of sins, rest, and salvation through his Only Begotten Son (Alma 12:33–34; 34:31; Jacob 6:4–5).

See also Blindness, spiritual; Stiffnecked, stiffneckedness.

MCT

Harlots, mother of *See* Mother of harlots.

Harris, Martin *See* Witnesses of the Book of Mormon.

Harrow *See* Appendix C.

Haughty *See* Appendix C.

Hearken *See* Appendix C.

Heart The center of both physical and spiritual well-being. The Book of Mormon contains many references to the heart, only a few of which refer to it as a physical organ—and most of those have to do with the slaying of individuals by the piercing of their hearts with weapons (e.g., Alma 47:24; 51:34; 62:36; Hel. 2:9). In the Book of Mormon, the heart is most often spoken of as both the seat of emotion, the inner core of being, and the receptor for spiritual infusions. Jacob[2], for instance, chastised the Nephite men for breaking "the hearts of [their] tender wives" (Jacob 2:35), and Abinadi condemned the priests of king Noah[3] for failing to apply their "hearts to understanding" (Mosiah 12:27). The term "heart" is used figuratively and frequently to suggest qualities of character, either negative or positive.

Negative attributes of heart, called HARD-HEARTEDNESS in the Book of Mormon, are typified by a man like Nehor, who, Alma[2] said, launched into apostasy when he "began to be lifted up in the pride of his heart" (Alma 1:6). Samuel the Lamanite condemned the Nephites because they were willing to listen to anyone who encouraged them to "walk after the pride of [their] own hearts" and "do whatsoever [their] heart[s] desireth" (Hel. 13:27). Moroni[2] prophetically saw the same propensities manifested in the latter days, even among churches and their professing members (Morm. 8:28–38).

The record's use of the term "heart" to signify positive qualities of character and an individual's desire to be open to spiritual promptings is perhaps even more prevalent. Lehi[1], for example, received his vision of the judgment on Jerusalem specifically because he "prayed . . . with all his heart, in behalf of his people" (1 Ne. 1:5). The spiritual rebirth of Alma[2] began when he "cried within [his] heart" for Christ to have mercy on him (Alma 36:18). The heart of a despairing Zeezrom "began to take courage" when he heard that Alma and Amulek had come to Sidom (Alma 15:4). The Zoramite[2] poor sought out Alma and his teachings precisely because they were "poor in heart" (Alma 32:3–4). And it was while Nephi[2] was "pondering in his heart" that God promised him that he would be blessed forever (Hel. 10:3–5).

To achieve harmony and a spiritual connection with things divine requires a level of humility described by terms like "lowliness of heart" (Alma 32:8, 12; 37:33), or a "broken heart and a contrite spirit" (2 Ne. 2:7; 3 Ne. 9:20; 12:19). For those struggling between positive and negative feelings and traits of character, or "heart," the Book of Mormon offers hope that faith, repentance, and humility can facilitate a "change of heart," a spiritual rebirth (Alma 5:11–14, 26; Hel. 15:7; Mosiah 5:2–7). It is in coming to Christ "with full purpose of heart" (2 Ne. 31:13; 3 Ne. 18:32) that a true change of heart occurs—and it is to these disciples Christ promised, "Blessed are all the pure in heart, for they shall see God" (3 Ne. 12:8).

See also Broken heart and contrite spirit; Lowliness of heart.

GS

Heart, lowliness of *See* Lowliness of heart.

Heart, uncircumcised of *See* Uncircumcised of heart.

Hearthom *See* Jared[1], posterity of.

Heaven The term "heaven" has various meanings in the Book of Mormon.

1. The abode of Deity, where God and his angels dwell (Alma 18:30; cf. Dan. 2:28; Matt. 6:9). Christ descends from heaven to dwell on earth and ascends to heaven after performing his labors here (1 Ne. 11:7; Mosiah 3:5; 15:8–9; 18:2; cf. Acts 1:11). The Holy Ghost comes from heaven to manifest himself to the sons and daughters of men (Hel. 5:45; cf. Acts 2:2–4), and the heavenly New Jerusalem will descend from heaven in future times (Ether 13:3; cf. Rev. 21:10). Furthermore, Lucifer fell from heaven in premortality (2 Ne. 2:17; 24:12 // Isa. 14:12; cf. Rev. 12:8–9).

2. The expanse or firmament containing the sun, moon, and stars (2 Ne. 23:10; Mosiah 4:9; cf. Gen. 1:1, 16–17). The Book of Mormon identifies Jesus Christ as the "Creator," or "Father" of both heaven and earth (Mosiah 3:8; 4:2; 2 Ne. 25:12; Alma 11:39; Hel. 14:12).

3. The eternal residence of the righteous (Mosiah 5:15; Alma 7:25). King Benjamin taught that those who "keep the commandments of God. . . . and . . . hold out faithful to the end . . . are received into heaven, that thereby they may dwell with God in a state of never-ending happiness" (Mosiah 2:41).

4. "Heaven" is also used in the phrase "kingdom of heaven" with the Lord referred to as the "king of heaven" (2 Ne. 10:14). Alma[2] used the phrase "kingdom of heaven" to refer to Christ's coming "upon the face of the earth" (Alma 7:9–10). He also asserted that "the kingdom of heaven is soon at hand" to encourage the Nephites to repent, to prepare for the impending judgments which would attend Christ's visit to the Americas, and perhaps his second coming (Alma 5:28, 50; 9:25; 10:20). Alma, Mormon, and the Lord himself all used "kingdom of heaven" to refer to the final reward of the righteous, as discussed in number three above (Alma 5:25, 51; 7:14, 25; 11:37; Hel. 3:30; 3 Ne. 12:3, 10; 14:21).

5. The phrase "new heaven" is used in the scriptures to describe millennial conditions, as well as the celestial kingdom (McConkie, 531).

The time period spoken of by the prophets is not always easy to discern (D&C 29:22–25; 77:1; 88:16–32; 101:23–31; Isa. 65:17–25; 66:22–24; Rev. 21). Moroni, in writing of the time when the "earth shall pass away," proclaimed that "there shall be a new heaven and a new earth; and they shall be like unto the old save the old have passed away, and all things have become new" (Ether 13:8–9).

See also Earth, the.

BIBLIOGRAPHY

McConkie, Bruce R. *Mormon Doctrine.* 2d ed. Salt Lake City: Bookcraft, 1966.

CF

Heavenly Father *See* God the Father.

Hebraisms Hebrew-like words, phrases, or sentence structure in a text translated from Hebrew, which are unusual in English but normal in Hebrew. This definition would also apply to the translation of a document not written in Hebrew but influenced by the Hebrew of a native speaker. Many hebraisms occur, for example, in the King James Version of the Old Testament, reflecting its translation from Hebrew. Since the Book of Mormon was translated from records kept by a people who originally spoke Hebrew, one might expect to find hebraisms in it as well. Hebraisms in the Book of Mormon are mainly of three types: syntactical, lexical, and frequency. Some of the more commonly cited examples of each type are outlined in the accompanying table.

HEBRAISMS

I. Syntactical hebraisms

Syntactical hebraisms exhibit unusual English sentence structure which would be normal for Hebrew.

A. The construct state

1. Where typical English would use an adjective and a noun, Hebrew uses two nouns together with an implied "of." For example, in Isaiah 45:19 the original Hebrew phrase "land [of] darkness" has been translated "a dark place" in English. The Book of Mormon often maintains the phrasing as in Hebrew.

Book of Mormon	Typical English
(1 Ne. 8:23) "mist of darkness"	dark mist
(Jacob 4:14) "words of plainness"	plain words

For additional examples, see 2 Ne. 25:2; 30:17; Jacob 6:5; Mosiah 12:10; Hel. 5:28; Ether 13:15.

2. Hebrew also uses two nouns in the construct state to describe the material from which something is made. Thus a stone pillar is a "*pillar* [of] *stone*" in Hebrew (compare Gen. 35:14, where the King James Version has retained the Hebrew pattern).

Book of Mormon	Typical English
(1 Ne. 3:3) "plates of brass"	brass plates
(1 Ne. 8:19) "rod of iron"	iron rod
(Alma 31:28) "ornaments of gold"	gold ornaments

For additional examples, see Mosiah 11:8; 21:27; Hel. 3:7.

3. The construct state is also used to describe possession—"Nahor's son" (Gen. 24:47) reads "[the] *son* [of] *Nahor*" in Hebrew.

continued

continued

Book of Mormon	Typical English
(1 Ne. 7:4) "the house of Ishmael"	Ishmael's house
(2 Ne. 5:14) "the sword of Laban"	Laban's sword

For additional examples, see Words of Mormon 1:3, 13; Mosiah 3:11; Alma 5:16; Hel. 7:10.

4. An interesting example in which the Book of Mormon follows the Hebrew construct pattern even more closely than the King James Version is in the expression the "mount of Sinai" (Mosiah 12:33). This pattern accounts for almost all of the possessive relationships indicated in the Book of Mormon.

B. The suffixed possessive pronoun

When the possessor is expressed by a pronoun (his, her, etc.), the pronoun is suffixed to the thing possessed. Thus, "his sack" (Gen. 42:27) is "the sack [of] him" in Hebrew.

Book of Mormon	Typical English
(2 Ne. 10:8) "the eyes of me"	my eyes
(Jacob 5:2) "the words of me"	my words

For additional examples, see 1 Ne. 22:14; 2 Ne. 9:25; Jacob 4:8; Moro. 8:20.

C. Repetition of the possessive pronoun

In Hebrew the possessive pronoun is usually suffixed to each item possessed if more than one is specified.

Examples

(1 Ne. 2:4) "his house, and . . . his inheritance, and his gold, and his silver, and his precious things"

(3 Ne. 2:12) "their lives and their women and their children . . . their rights . . . and their freedom and their liberty"

For additional examples, see 1 Ne. 2:11; 3:22; 16:15; Mosiah 4:6; Alma 2:25; 3:5. This feature is not consistently carried out in Hebrew, and, as can be seen by reading the complete verses cited, is not rigidly applied in the Book of Mormon, either.

D. Repetition of the preposition

When several words are governed by the same preposition it is common to repeat the preposition with each word—thus, "played . . . on harps, and on psalteries, and on timbrels, and on cornets, and on cymbals" (2 Sam. 6:5).

Examples

(1 Ne. 14:1) "in word, and also in power, in very deed"

(1 Ne. 19:11) "by tempest, by fire, and by smoke . . . and by the opening of the earth, and by mountains"

For additional examples, see 2 Ne. 6:15; Jarom 1:8; Alma 31:24; 44:5; Hel. 10:5; 3 Ne. 10:14; 29:6; Ether 8:14.

E. Cognate accusative

1. Hebrew verbs and related nouns are often built from the same root letters. Consequently, a verb and its object may sound alike, as in "wept a weeping" (Ezra 10:1); "vow a vow . . . or swear a swearing" (Num. 30:2 [30:3 in Hebrew]). These are rephrased in the English Bible to "wept very sore" and "swear an oath." This type of pairing occurring in English may not sound unusual, like "dreamed a dream" (1 Ne.

3:2) or "build buildings" (2 Ne. 5:15), but other combinations such as "work a . . . work" (1 Ne. 14:7), "written . . . a new writing" (1 Ne. 16:29), and "desire which I desired" (Enos 1:13) do sound strange. For additional examples, see 2 Nephi 3:18; Alma 1:1.

2. Similarly, the noun of a prepositional phrase following a verb may be of the same root, as in Mosiah 7:15, "taxed with a tax." For additional examples, see 1 Ne. 2:23; Mosiah 8:8; Alma 2:18; Ether 10:5.

F. Enumeration

It is common practice in Hebrew to place an "and" before each element when expressing numbers, as in Genesis 5:15, "sixty and five years."

EXAMPLES

(Jacob 1:1) "fifty and five"
(3 Ne. 28:3) "seventy and two"

For additional examples, see Mosiah 20:5; Alma 2:19; 4 Ne. 1:20; Ether 7:2; 10:15.

G. Subordinate conjunctions

In English one uses words such as "because," "before," and "after" singly as subordinate conjunctions. In Hebrew such words are combined with the conjunction "that" as in Ezekiel 40:1, "after *that* the city was smitten."

EXAMPLES

(3 Ne. 12:2) "because *that* ye shall testify"
(3 Ne. 20:27) "after *that* ye were blessed"
(3 Ne. 28:6) "before *that* I was lifted up"

For additional examples, see 2 Ne. 2:26; Jacob 5:37, 60; Enos 1:8 (1830 ed.); 3 Ne. 27:14; Moro. 7:26.

H. Formation of adverbs

Hebrew has few words which are adverbs as such. It compensates by using "in" or "with" in conjunction with a noun, as in "lifting up the voice with joy" (1 Chr. 15:16).

BOOK OF MORMON	TYPICAL ENGLISH
(2 Ne. 28:28) "with gladness"	gladly
(Mosiah 11:15) "in abundance"	abundantly

For additional examples, see 1 Ne. 15:11; 18:11; Mosiah 22:14; 29:22; Alma 26:27.

I. Compound subject

In Hebrew the order of presentation when there is a compound subject is first person, second, then third, as in 1 Samuel 14:40, "I and Jonathan my son." The proper English pattern would be "my son and I," or, colloquially, "me and my son."

EXAMPLES

(1 Ne. 3:10) "I and my brethren"
(1 Ne. 5:20) "I and my father"

For additional examples, see 1 Ne. 7:22; 22:31; Mosiah 9:7, 16, 17; Alma 27:15.

J. Compound prepositions

Hebrew forms many prepositions by combining two prepositions or a preposition with a noun, as "upon the face of" (Gen. 1:2) or "from before" (Judg. 11:23).

continued

continued

EXAMPLES

(1 Ne. 4:28) "they fled *from before* my presence"
(2 Ne. 1:9) "*upon the face of* this land"
(Alma 10:4) "*by the hand of* my industry"

For additional examples, see 2 Ne. 5:12; 28:6; 3 Ne. 9:8; Morm. 2:24; Hel. 10:12; Ether 1:1.

K. Varied meanings of "and"

Hebrew avoids long, complex sentences with subordinating conjunctions. It is an *and*-loving language—beginning one clause after another with "and." Consequently, "and" (Heb. w^e) replaces other conjunctions such as "for," "but" (contrastive), and "while" (circumstantial), leaving the reader to infer these meanings from the context. Additional examples: and = *when* (Mosiah 19:22); and = *which was* (Mosiah 21:27); and = *so that* (Mosiah 29:32); and = *who* (Alma 21:5); and = *nor* (4 Ne. 1:2); and = *whose* (Morm. 2:9); and =*so* (Ether 6:27).

EXAMPLES

(Alma 8:11) "thou art high priest over the church . . . and [*but*] we are not of thy church"
(Alma 17:33) "Encircle the flocks . . . and [*while*] I go and contend"
(3 Ne. 2:2) "that it was wrought by men and [*or*] by the power of the devil"

II. Lexical hebraisms

Lexical hebraisms are single words used with a meaning which does not fit the context or correspond to proper or normal English usage but could represent a literal translation of a Hebrew word which would be appropriate. For example, the word "seed" (zera') is used in reference to seeds of plants but also to the offspring or descendants of a person. In normal English, one does not refer to someone's "seed." In a verse such as Gen. 12:7, "Unto thy seed will I give this land," the King James translators translated the Hebrew literally, resulting in a hebraism.

The various meanings of the conjunction "and" given above are examples of lexical hebraisms.

Alma 14:18 contains a good example of a lexical hebraism. The verse reads, "They questioned them about many words." The proper word in this context in English would be "things" or "matters." In Hebrew, however, the same word is used for "word" or "thing." Here it appears that the meaning "word" was used where the translation "things" would have been better.

Usually the divergence from normal English is not so great. All of the following italicized words or phrases are not typical English but represent exactly what a Hebrew speaker would have written.

BOOK OF MORMON	TYPICAL ENGLISH
(1 Ne. 5:14) "a genealogy of *his fathers*"	forefathers, ancestors
(1 Ne. 5:19) "he prophesied many things concerning his *seed*"	descendants
(1 Ne. 14:11) "she sat *upon* many waters"	beside, near
(1 Ne. 17:14 [1830 ed.]) "arrived *to* the promised land"	at, in
(Jarom 1:8) "*upon the face of* the land"	throughout
(Mosiah 21:28) "on learning *from the mouth of* Ammon"	from
(Mosiah 25:21) "delivered to him *by the mouth of* Alma"	by
(Alma 8:22) "he blessed Amulek and his *house*"	household, family

(Alma 17:24) "Ammon should *take* one . . . *to wife*"	marry
(Alma 20:28) "Lamoni *found favor in the eyes of* the king"	pleased
(3 Ne. 5:8) "things transpired which, *in the eyes of* some"	opinion
(Ether 2:10) "the *children* of the land"	inhabitants

III. Frequency hebraisms

Frequency hebraisms are words used with a frequency that is abnormally high for English but is typical for Hebrew.

1. *And:* the word "and" occurs with great frequency in both the Old Testament and the Book of Mormon due to the abundance of coordinate clauses and the frequency of the expression "and it came to pass."
2. *Behold:* this attention-getting particle occurs about 1,000 times in the Old Testament and some 1,400 times in the Book of Mormon. Its usage is generally foreign to English.
3. *Word(s):* "word(s)" occurs nearly 900 times in the Old Testament and over 800 times in the Book of Mormon. Its frequency in the Old Testament is due to its broad range of connotations in Hebrew, including "thing," "advice," "command," "remark," etc. Similarly, in the Book of Mormon, "word" has many connotations.
4. *Heart(s):* Due to its frequent use in metaphors in Hebrew, "heart(s)" occurs approximately once in every 700 words in the Old Testament. It occurs more than once in every 600 words in the Book of Mormon, frequently in metaphors uncommon to English.

The English of the Book of Mormon contains many expressions and stylistic features which seem to reflect an underlying influence of a foreign language. Many of these features resemble characteristics of the Hebrew language. These hebraic features or hebraisms may be considered one more piece of evidence that the Book of Mormon is what it claims to be, a record of a group who left Jerusalem in antiquity.

BIBLIOGRAPHY

Bramwell, E. Craig. "Hebrew Idioms in the Small Plates of Nephi." Unpublished master's thesis. Provo, Utah: Brigham Young University, 1960.

Pack, M. Deloy. "Possible Lexical Hebraisms in the Book of Mormon (Words of Mormon–Moroni)." Unpublished master's thesis. Provo, Utah: Brigham Young University, 1973.

Tvedtnes, John A. "Hebraisms in the Book of Mormon: A Preliminary Survey." *Brigham Young University Studies* 11 (Autumn 1970): 50–60.

———. "The Hebrew Background of the Book of Mormon." *Rediscovering the Book of Mormon*. Edited by John L. Sorenson and Melvin J. Thorne. Salt Lake City: Deseret Book, 1991.

MDP

Hebrew language The language of the Book of Mormon exhibits early nineteenth-century English known to its translator Joseph Smith, religious language that is characteristic of the King James Version of the Bible, and expressions that evidently belong to non-English languages, such as REFORMED EGYPTIAN or Hebrew.

Nephi[1] stated that his record (the small plates) was made using the "learning of the Jews and the language of the Egyptians" (1 Ne. 1:2). Moroni[2] explained that the record was written "in the characters which are called . . . reformed Egyptian" (Morm. 9:32). Joseph Smith noted that "the language of the whole" ran "the same as all Hebrew writing in general" (Smith, 1:71) which is usually interpreted to mean that the characters were read from right to left.

Some scholars have proposed that "the Nephite scribes used Egyptian script to write Hebrew text" (Tvedtnes and Ricks, 156–57). Many recent textual discoveries tend to confirm this statement (Tvedtnes and Ricks, 158–63). Additionally, there are many Hebrew-like traits in the Book of Mormon, called HEBRAISMS, which have survived both the alterations of the language through centuries of Nephite record keeping as well as its translation into English.

Moroni[2] explained that "we have written this record [in] . . . reformed Egyptian. . . . And if our plates had been sufficiently large we should have written in Hebrew; . . . and if we could have written in Hebrew, behold, ye would have had no imperfection in our record" (Morm. 9:32–33). These comments suggest that although Hebrew would have taken more room on the plates, it would have produced a more precise and accurate record; however, reformed Egyptian was used by the Nephite scribes because it took less room on the precious plates. Hebrew is a considerably more compact language than English. For example, the first three verses of Genesis use fifty words and 195 characters in the KJV English Bible but only twenty-seven words and 104 characters in the Hebrew text. If reformed Egyptian took less space to write than Hebrew, then it must have been an exceptionally compact text.

See also Book of Mormon, language of the translated text of.

BIBLIOGRAPHY

Smith, Joseph. *History of The Church of Jesus Christ of Latter-day Saints.* Edited by B. H. Roberts. 7 vols. 2d ed. rev. Salt Lake City: The Church of Jesus Christ of Latter-day Saints, 1932–51.

Tvedtnes, John A., and Stephen D. Ricks. "Jewish and Other Semitic Texts Written in Egyptian Characters." *Journal of Book of Mormon Studies* 5:2 (1996).

DWP

Hedge *See* Appendix C.

Heed *See* Appendix C.

Helam A Nephite who lived in the land of Nephi during the reign of king Noah[3] (ca. 147 B.C.). One of the initial converts of Alma[1], Helam was "one of the first" to be baptized among the people of king Noah (Mosiah 18:12). Helam's baptism was unique in that when Alma baptized him he also immersed himself, perhaps to demonstrate humility and recommit himself to God (Mosiah 18:14). Although the record offers no further information about Helam, it is assumed that he served as an example of devotion and faith. Presumably, the place to which Alma and his followers fled from Noah's pursuing army was named after him (Mosiah 23:19–20).

CJW

Helam, land of and city of Land in the borders of the land of Nephi settled by Alma[1] and his people after their eight-day flight into the wilderness to escape the pursuing armies of king Noah[3] (Mosiah 23:3–4, 19–20; between 145 and 121 B.C.). Presumably named after one of Alma's first converts (Mosiah 18:12–14), Helam was described as "a very beautiful and pleasant land, a land of pure water" (Mosiah 23:4).

Here Alma's people built a city by the same name (Mosiah 23:19–20). The city of Helam was eventually seized by the Lamanites in alliance with the wicked priests of king Noah (Mosiah 23:25–39). After suffering greatly at the hands of their oppressors, Alma's people sought the Lord's help, and he blessed them with two miracles. First, he "strengthened" them that they could bear with ease the Lamanite bondage and oppression they were under, and second, he caused a deep sleep to come upon their captors, allowing them to escape from Helam to Zarahemla (Mosiah 24:8–20). This bondage and deliverance was not without divine purpose (Mosiah 23:21–24; 24:13–14). Alma's people had covenanted at the waters of Mormon to be witnesses for God "at all times and in all things, and in all places" (Mosiah 18:9). The test of this covenant came in Helam—the time and place of their bondage.

Helaman[1] A son of king Benjamin (ca. 130 B.C.). King Benjamin "caused" that his three sons (Mosiah[2], Helorum, and Helaman) "should be taught in all the language of his fathers," and personally taught them the importance of the writings contained in the brass plates and the plates of Nephi (Mosiah 1:2–8).

Helaman[2] Eldest son of Alma[2]; keeper of sacred records, the interpreters, and the Liahona; high priest and military leader (Alma 31:7; 37:1–3, 21, 24, 38–41; 46:6; 53:19; 56:9). Helaman lived during a period of Nephite history characterized by the building up of the Church on the one hand and severe conflict and war on the other. Yet, Alma had prepared Helaman well for the challenges inherent in his record keeping responsibilities, his ministry to the Church, and his military leadership (e.g., Alma 36; 37; 45:2–15). Alma taught Helaman that deliverance, both temporal and spiritual, comes through Jesus Christ (Alma 36) and that "whosoever shall put their trust in God shall be supported in their trials, and their troubles, and their afflictions, and shall be lifted up at the last day" (Alma 36:3). Having received authority, presumably from his father Alma, Helaman built up the Church through ordaining other priests and teachers (Alma 45:22–23) and preaching the word of God (Alma 48:19). While captain Moroni was instrumental in maintaining peace among the Nephites (Alma 46:36–37), "Helaman and the high priests did also maintain order in the church; yea, even for the space of four years did they have much peace and rejoicing in the church" (Alma 46:38; cf. 48:19–20; 49:30).

Eventually war commenced between the Nephites and the Lamanites. The ANTI-NEPHI-LEHIES, converted Lamanites who were under Nephite protection after having made an oath as part of their repentance to never kill again, were "moved with compassion" seeing the "many afflictions and tribulations which the Nephites bore for them" and desired to break their oath to defend their country (Alma 53:13). Thinking more of their eternal welfare than the added strength their assistance would afford, Helaman persuaded them to keep their oath (Alma 53:10–15; 56:7–8). This incident in Nephite history gave rise to the formation of a band of 2060 young sons of the ANTI-NEPHI-LEHIES who, not being bound with the oath of their fathers, took up the sword in defense of the Nephites. Notwithstanding many other admirable characteristics, Helaman is perhaps best known for his tender command of these young warriors. Helaman noted that they had been taught by their mothers, that "if they did not doubt, God would deliver them" (Alma 56:47). With the aid of these STRIPLING WARRIORS, Helaman joined forces with the army of Antipus and defeated the Lamanites. Not one of the young men perished (Alma 56:55–56).

Helaman is shown to be an adept spiritual and military leader. Like Moroni, Helaman boldly declared his faith, led a large army, fought for the liberties of the people, and used strategy to reclaim Nephite lands and cities—preferably without the shedding of blood (e.g., Alma 48:19; 49:30; 56:20–23, 28; 57:7–12; 58:1–28; 62:44–46).

Helaman exercised great courage when dealing with the Lamanite king Ammoron. In a letter Ammoron proposed that the Lamanites would return the city of Antiparah for the release of Lamanite prisoners, but Helaman rejected the offer and stated that his own forces were sufficient to retake the city. He would only agree to exchange prisoners. Ammoron rejected this offer, but shortly thereafter the Lamanites abandoned Antiparah (Alma 57:1–4).

Following the war, Helaman returned to Zarahemla and taught the word of God "with much power unto the convincing of many people of their wickedness, which did cause them to repent of their sins and to be baptized unto the Lord their God" (Alma 62:45). The Church and people prospered as a result of Helaman's last missionary efforts (Alma 62:42–51). After Helaman's death (57 B.C.), Shiblon "took possession of [the] sacred things" that had been entrusted to Helaman (Alma 62:52; 63:1–2). Before his death Shiblon conferred the "sacred things" upon the son of Helaman, who was named Helaman[3] "after the name of his father" (Alma 63:11).

Mormon's abridgment of Helaman[2]'s record (Alma 45–62) underscores the blessings of obedience to the Lord and the serious consequences of disobedience. One poignant message that emerges is the dramatic account of the rise of Amalickiah from Nephite dissenter to king of the Lamanites (Alma 46–48). In these chapters, one can readily see the contrast between the two main leaders of this period: Amalickiah, who was deceptive and wicked; and captain Moroni, who was a man of faith and righteousness.

Mormon described Helaman and his brethren as "men of God. . . . no less serviceable unto the people than was [captain] Moroni; for they did preach the word of God, and they did baptize unto repentance all men whosoever would hearken unto their words" (Alma 48:18–19).

BMH

Helaman³ The son of Helaman² and the grandson of Alma², Helaman³ was made keeper of the sacred records by Shiblon, his father's brother (Alma 63:11; 53 B.C.). He wrote the first part of the book of Helaman. And in 50 B.C. he was chosen as chief judge by the voice of the Nephites. He ruled at a dangerous and critical time, for both judges before him had been slain in office and a plot to kill him resulted in the death of his would-be assassin Kishkumen.

Helaman is remembered for the great instruction he gave his two sons, Nephi² and Lehi⁴ (Hel. 5:6–13). He gave them ancestral names so they would remember the good Lehi and Nephi had done and would want to do the same. He also taught them that man can be saved "only through the atoning blood of Jesus Christ," who would come "to redeem [his people] from their sins," and that they must anchor their lives upon "Christ, the son of God" (Hel. 5:9–12). Helaman "did fill the judgment-seat with justice and equity; yea, he did observe to keep the statutes, and the judgments, and the commandments of God; and he did do that which was right in the sight of God continually" (Hel. 3:20). Helaman died in 39 B.C., in the fifty-third year of the reign of judges (Hel. 3:37).

See also Helaman, book of.

CDT

Helaman, book of An abridgment by Mormon from the record of Helaman³ and his sons on the large PLATES OF NEPHI. The book of Helaman summarizes a tumultuous fifty-year period between the death of Helaman² and the birth of Christ (52 B.C.–1 B.C.). Its key figures are sons and grandsons of leaders in the book of Alma, as well as the Lamanite prophet Samuel. The book is named after Helaman³, the son of Helaman² and grandson of Alma the Younger. Helaman³ received the records from his uncle Shiblon and eventually assumed the judgment-seat as well (Hel. 1–4). He was succeeded by his son Nephi², who ultimately relinquished the judgment-seat to devote all his energies to preaching the gospel in company with his brother Lehi⁴ (Hel. 5–12). They enjoyed notable success in converting the Lamanites. From the Lamanites arose a mighty prophet, Samuel², who called the Nephites to repentance and foretold the signs of Christ's birth and death (Hel. 13–16).

Content and message

The book of Helaman describes a people who were awaiting the coming of Christ. Their society was infiltrated by SECRET COMBINATIONS established by the Gadianton robbers (Hel. 3:23) and was characterized by great prosperity. Prosperity led to great PRIDE among the people and their pride resulted in the persecution of the humble, the oppression of the poor, the mocking of sacred things, and to all manner of iniquity (Hel. 3:34; 4:11–12). Because of their wickedness the Lamanites gained ascendancy in the land, the Church began to dwindle (Hel. 4:13), and Helaman noted that "they who chose evil were more numerous than they who chose good, therefore they were ripening for destruction" (Hel. 5:2). The prophets Nephi, Lehi, and Samuel the Lamanite were called to preach repentance to the people and to prepare them for the coming of Christ.

The book of Helaman contains numerous editorial passages by Mormon, typically beginning "thus we see." Through his commentary Mormon shaped and directed his abridgment of Helaman to its latter-day readers who find themselves in a world with challenges similar to those faced by the ancient Nephites. Mormon interrupted his narrative for an entire chapter (Hel. 12) to comment on the "unsteadiness" of mankind who, in prosperity, "forget the Lord their God" and "will not remember him" unless chastened by "many afflictions"—which leads to repentance, prosperity, and the resurgence of pride and iniquity (Hel. 12:1–3). This is Mormon's fullest articulation of the cyclical pattern evident in Book of Mormon history. Mormon also frequently editorialized on the sinister influence of the Gadianton robbers who emerged during this era, lamenting the destructive role they would play in Nephite history (Hel. 2:13–14).

HELAMAN, BOOK OF

Mormon acknowledged that his redaction could not contain "a hundredth part" of the historical records from this complex time period (Hel. 3:14). Consequently, the book of Helaman focuses on the ministry of two prophets: Nephi and Samuel. Wearied by wickedness and emboldened by their father's teachings, Nephi and Lehi determined, like the sons of Mosiah[2], to forgo politics in order to preach the gospel, especially to the Lamanites. They converted 8,000 Lamanites in the land of Zarahemla but were subsequently imprisoned in the land of Nephi. As they were about to be slain, Nephi and Lehi were "encircled about as if by fire," yet not burned (Hel. 5:23). This miracle was accompanied by earthquakes, darkness, a voice from heaven, and the ministry of angels. Those who witnessed these marvels were converted and subsequently helped convert the "more part of the Lamanites" (Hel. 5:50). Thus the ministry of Nephi and Lehi resulted in a righteous epoch for the Lamanites.

OUTLINE OF HELAMAN

I. Tumultuous rule of judges from Pahoran[2] to Nephi[2] (1–4)
   A. Pahoran elected chief judge, murdered by Kishkumen (1:1–12)
   B. Pacumeni slain by Coriantumr[3], who captured Nephite heartland but is defeated by Moronihah[1] (1:13–34)
   C. Helaman[3] named chief judge; foiled assassination attempt by Kishkumen; Gadianton flees (2)
   D. Rule of Helaman: period of prosperity, migration, and church growth (3)
   E. Rule of Nephi: period of internal and external strife (4)

II. Mission of Nephi and Lehi (5–6)
   A. Nephi surrenders judgment-seat to Cezoram; Nephi and Lehi devote lives to the ministry (5:1–20)
   B. Nephi and Lehi miraculously saved from prison; Lamanites converted (5:21–52)
   C. Lamanites more righteous than Nephites; season of peace, prosperity, and free trade (6:1–14)
   D. Cezoram and son murdered; period of political intrigue and murder; GADIANTON ROBBERS gain control of government (6:15–41)

III. Preaching and prophesying of Nephi (7–11)
   A. Nephi prays on garden tower, tells Nephites they must repent or perish (7)
   B. Nephi cites prophecies of Christ, contends with corrupt leaders, reveals that chief judge Seezoram has been murdered (8)
   C. Nephi arrested, accused as accomplice in murder of judge, reveals that Seantum is murderer (9)
   D. God confers sealing power on Nephi, commands him to preach, and conveys him by the Spirit to safety (10)
   E. Nephi invokes famine; people repent; Nephi asks God to revoke famine (11:1–19)
   F. Period of peace and prosperity, followed by dissensions and rise of Gadianton robbers among both Nephites and Lamanites (11:20–38)

IV. Commentary by Mormon on the cyclical pattern of Nephite history (12)

V. Preaching and prophecies of Samuel the Lamanite upon Zarahemla's wall (13–15)
   A. Samuel predicts ultimate destruction of Nephite civilization (13)
   B. Samuel prophesies signs of Jesus' birth and death (14)
   C. Samuel contrasts destinies of Lamanites with Nephites (15)

VI. Reaction to Samuel's message and events prior to Savior's coming (16)
   A. Samuel flees; some believe him and are baptized by Nephi; more do not (16:1–8)
   B. Signs and wonders appear, but many harden their hearts (16:9–25)

Ironically, at the same time the Nephites became "hardened and impenitent" (Hel. 6:2) and were ultimately dominated by Gadianton robbers (Hel. 6:39). Discouraged by this predicament, Nephi prayed from his garden tower while a crowd of onlookers gathered around him (Hel. 7). He rebuked the people for their iniquities and announced the murder of the chief judge. Arrested as an accomplice in the murder, Nephi was released when Seantum confessed to the crime and declared that Nephi was innocent (Hel. 8–9).

As a result of Nephi's "unwearyingness" in declaring the word (Hel. 10:4), and the Lord's confidence that he would "not ask that which is contrary to [God's] will" (Hel. 10:5), Nephi was given power to effect God's will on earth. Like Elijah (1 Kgs. 17:1), Nephi invoked a famine upon the people to "stir them up in remembrance of the Lord" (Hel. 11:4). When their hearts finally softened, after about four years, Nephi asked God to revoke the famine. The famine had a humbling effect upon the people, and a season of peace and prosperity followed (Hel. 11). Yet, with increased prosperity came pride, dissension, and the rise again of the Gadianton robbers. This cycle prompted Mormon's commentary in chapter 12.

The book ends with several chapters recounting the prophecies of Samuel (Hel. 13–15). Like John the Baptist, Samuel was commanded to "cry unto this people, repent and prepare the way of the Lord" (Hel. 14:9). He predicted the utter destruction of Nephite civilization unless the people repented (Hel. 13). He also prophesied signs to occur at the Savior's birth and death, taught the power of the Atonement to redeem all humankind from spiritual and temporal death (Hel. 14), and foretold that the Lord would extend his mercy to the Lamanites in the latter days (Hel. 15). Samuel was rejected by the majority of the Nephites—physically with stones and arrows, and spiritually with hardened hearts. As the time of Christ's birth drew nearer, the predicted signs began to appear (Hel. 16). The book of Helaman ends, tragically, with most of the people hardening their hearts and trying to explain the signs away as merely coincidental (Hel. 16:16–21).

See also Book of Mormon, selected themes of, cycles of prosperity and destruction.

JST

Helaman[2], sons of *See* Stripling warriors.

Helem *See* Ammon[1].

Hell An English translation of the Hebrew word *Sheol* and the Greek word *Hades*, broadly meaning the world of departed spirits but most commonly used in reference to the abode or the suffering of the wicked. Although the reformed Egyptian term which Joseph Smith translated as "hell" is not known, the meaning of *hell* as used in the Book of Mormon is consistent with that expressed in the other standard works.

The ultimate and final place called hell is that kingdom without glory to which the devil and his followers will be consigned at the Final Judgment. There the devil will "reign" over those who have suffered a second death, a permanent SPIRITUAL DEATH, "into a state of misery and endless torment," which "torment is as a lake of fire and brimstone" (Mosiah 3:25–27; 2 Ne. 2:27–29; 9:16; Alma 12:16–18; cf. D&C 76:25–48; 88:24, 34–35). Hell is also used to identify that place in the postmortal spirit world where the wicked suffer before the Final Judgment. Those assigned there include the devil and his angels, as well as the spirits of departed mortals who died unrepentant. By the power of the atonement of Christ, all except sons of perdition will be brought out of this hell—after they have suffered for their sins according to the justice of God, and after they have complied with at least a telestial level of eternal law—and will be resurrected to some degree of glory in the "kingdom of God" (Alma 40:11–14, 23–26; 2 Ne. 9:10–17; cf. D&C 76:81–89, 98–112; 138:30–37, 58–59).

As a state of mind or spiritual condition, hell is not limited to any particular place or time. Anyone who knowingly violates the laws of God will suffer some degree of hell, the intensity of which will be commensurate with the seriousness of the sin. Such suffering is described as "guilt, and pain, and anguish, which is like an unquenchable fire" (Mosiah 2:38), or as fearful anxiety, anticipating the judgments of God (Alma 40:14). Alma[2] explained that his soul was racked with "inexpressible horror" as he suffered "the pains of a damned soul" (Alma 36:14–16). Through faith in Christ, repentance, and spiritual rebirth, one can be released from hell (2 Ne. 1:13; 9:45). Guilt can be "swept away" (Enos 1:6), replaced by "joy, . . . having peace of conscience" (Mosiah 4:3). No longer, then, need a person be "harrowed up by the memory of [his] sins" (Alma 36:19). The word hell appears sixty-two times in the text of the Book of Mormon. Thirty-three times it stands alone, without modifiers or explanation of what it means, as in, "And thus we see the end of him who perverteth the ways of the Lord; and thus we see that the devil will not support his children at the last day, but doth speedily drag them down to hell" (Alma 30:60). Twenty-nine times the word hell is used with descriptive modifiers, for example, "depths of hell" (1 Ne. 12:16), "hell which hath no end" (1 Ne. 14:3–4), "awful hell" (1 Ne. 15:29, 35; Alma 19:29; 54:7), "sleep of hell" (2 Ne. 1:13), "gates of hell" (2 Ne. 4:32; 3 Ne. 11:39–40; 18:13), "pains of hell" (Jacob 3:11; Alma 14:6; 26:13; 36:13), "chains of hell" (Alma 5:7, 9, 10; 12:11; 13:30; 26:14), "child of hell" (Alma 11:23; 54:11), "powers of hell" (Alma 48:17), "everlasting hell" (Hel. 6:28), "hell fire" (3 Ne. 12:22; Morm. 8:17), and "endless hell" (Moro. 8:13).

Numerous times in the Book of Mormon other terms or phrases are used to mean hell. These include "fountain of filthy water" or "awful gulf" in Lehi[1]'s dream, which separated the wicked from the tree of life and from the Saints of God (1 Ne. 12:16–18; 15:26–29), "eternal gulf of misery and woe" (2 Ne. 1:13), "kingdom of the devil" (2 Ne. 28:19; 2:29; Alma 41:4), "spiritual death" (2 Ne. 9:12), "awful monster" (2 Ne. 9:10), "lake of fire and brimstone" (2 Ne. 9:19, 26; 28:23), "misery and endless torment" (Mosiah 3:25; Moro. 8:21), "awful chains" (2 Ne. 28:22), "everlasting chains of death" (Alma 36:18), "slumber of death" (Jacob 3:11), "deep sleep" (Alma 5:7), "second death" (Alma 13:30), "place of filthiness" (1 Ne. 15:34), "endless night of darkness" (Alma 41:7), "misery which never dies" (Morm. 8:38), and "dregs of a bitter cup" (Alma 40:26).

The Savior warned the Nephites that the gates of hell "stand open to receive" those who "declare more or less" than his doctrine, and "establish it for [his] doctrine," and at the same time promised them that the gates of hell shall not prevail against those who build upon his true doctrine of faith, repentance, baptism, receiving the gift of the Holy Ghost, and enduring to the end (3 Ne. 11:28–41; 2 Ne. 31:1–21; cf. 3 Ne. 27:13–21).

See also Captivity of the devil; Damnation; Endless torment, eternal torment, never-ending torment; Judgment, the; Lake of fire and brimstone; Night of darkness; Spirit world.

LED

Helorum A son of king Benjamin (ca. 130 B.C.). Benjamin taught his three sons (Mosiah[2], Helorum, and Helaman[1]) to search the scriptures and to keep the commandments of God (Mosiah 1:2–8).

Hem *See* Ammon[1].

Hermounts Wilderness infested by ravenous beasts on the west and north, "away beyond the borders" of the land (i.e., Zarahemla). The combined Lamanite and Amlicite army was driven there by the troops of Alma[2], where many of them died of wounds and were "devoured" by beasts and vultures (Alma 2:36–38; ca. 87 B.C.).

Heshlon, plains of Jaredite region to which the armies of Coriantumr[2] drove Shared after defeating him in the valley of Gilgal. In the plains of Heshlon, however, the tables turned and Shared defeated his adversary, driving him back to Gilgal (Ether 13:27–29).

Heth[1] *See* Jared[1], posterity of.

Heth[2] *See* Jared[1], posterity of.

Heth, land of Jaredite region in which Jared[2] dwelt after rebelling against his father, king Omer (Ether 8:2).

High priest(s) Usually an ecclesiastical office. The Book of Mormon uses the title in several different contexts.

The priests of King Noah[3] are in one place called high priests (Mosiah 11:11). Whether they ever had true priesthood, despite their wickedness, is uncertain from the record.

High priest is the normal term for the leader of the Nephite Church of Jesus Christ, the equivalent of today's president of the Church. The term is never used in reference to the earliest church established by Lehi[1] and Nephi[1]. It first appears with reference to Alma[1], both before and after his people's reunion with the Nephites in Zarahemla (Mosiah 23:16; 26:7–8). In most instances the term is used for Alma[2], who succeeded his father in the position (Mosiah 29:42; Alma 4 heading; 4:4, 18, 20; Alma 5 heading; 5:3; 8:11, 23; 16:5). For eight years (91–83 B.C.), Alma was concurrently the chief judge, or head of the Nephite government. He remained high priest over the whole Church for a total of seventeen years, until about 74 B.C.

The presiding authority over smaller areas of the Church was also called the high priest. Ammon[2] was a high priest over the people of Ammon (his Lamanite converts) in Jershon (Alma 30:20). Giddonah[2] was the high priest over the Church in Gideon (Alma 30:21–23, 29).

In the days of Helaman[2] and Helaman[3], the term was used with regard to general church leaders but only in the plural—"high priests" (Alma 46:6, 38; Hel. 3:25). During the chaotic years that preceded Christ's coming, when the Nephite Church was wracked with turmoil, some parts of it were under the control of dissenters. Persons called high priests (or perhaps former high priests) are listed among the apostates who opposed the Lord's prophets (3 Ne. 6:21–22, 27). The title high priest does not appear in the Nephite record after the coming of Christ. The Jaredite record in the book of Ether uses it only once, for a man in an apostate religion in the days of Coriantumr[2] (Ether 14:9).

In his great discourse at Ammonihah, Alma[2] used the term with reference to those who hold the high priesthood. They were foreordained and received it through faith, repentance, and righteousness, thereby becoming "high priests forever, after the order of the Son" (Alma 13:8–10). Melchizedek was one such high priest (Alma 13:14–19; cf. 13:1–20).

See also Church of God (Christ) in ancient America; Priesthood among the Nephites; Priest(s).

KPJ

Himni Nephite missionary, a son of king Mosiah[2] (ca. 100–74 B.C.). Himni was "numbered among the unbelievers," but after an angelic appearance he attempted to amend the harm he had caused striving to destroy the Church (Mosiah 27:8–10, 32–36). Like his brothers, he chose not to succeed his father as king but rather set out with them on what proved to be a successful but challenging fourteen-year Lamanite mission in the land of Nephi (Mosiah 28:1–10; Alma 17:2–18; 23:1–3; 25:17; 26:29–30). Along with his brothers, Himni was described as a man of God (Alma 48:18). He was a man who had a "sound understanding" of the gospel, who had the "spirit of prophecy, and the spirit of revelation," and who taught with power. These characteristics were attributed to his diligent scripture study, and to his "much prayer, and fasting" (Alma 17:2–3). From the wording in Alma 31:6 it appears that Alma[2] left Himni in Zarahemla specifically to attend to the affairs of the Church while he, Shiblon, Corianton, Zeezrom, and the other sons of Mosiah went on a mission to the Zoramites[2] (Alma 31:6–7).

See also Mosiah[2], sons of.

Hiss *See* Appendix C.

Hiss and a byword A derogatory idiom. In Joseph Smith's day, *hiss* meant an expression of contempt, and *byword* had to do with a common, proverbial saying. Thus, the combination of these terms is intended to portray something or someone who is commonly or proverbially held in low regard.

The expression first appears in a quotation from the prophet Zenos and points to the low esteem in which Jews were to be held after the death of Jesus (1 Ne. 19:14), a situation that would be reversed (3 Ne. 29:8). The only other use of the phrase arises in Jesus' prophecy about the Gentile people of "this land" (3 Ne. 16:8) and refers to descendants of the Nephites and Lamanites who will "be smitten, and . . . afflicted, and . . . slain" (3 Ne. 16:9).

SKB

Holy Ghost, the A personage of spirit and the third member of the GODHEAD. The Book of Mormon testifies of the unity of the Godhead in doctrine, purpose, and witness (2 Ne. 31:21; 3 Ne. 11:25, 27, 36; Ether 5:4), as well as clearly teaching that the Holy Ghost is a separate and distinct being from the Father and the Son. When Nephi[1] described the baptism of Jesus he spoke of each member of the Godhead—the Father, the Son, and the Holy Ghost—as separate and distinct personages (1 Ne. 11:27; 2 Ne. 31:8, 11–12; cf. Matt. 3:16, 17; Mark 1:9–11; Luke 3:21–22; D&C 130:22–23).

The Book of Mormon also verifies that the Holy Ghost functioned in Old Testament times. It contains more than 85 direct references to the Holy Ghost, beginning as early as 592 B.C., when Nephi taught that the Holy Ghost was "the gift of God unto all those who diligently seek him, as well in times of old as in the time that he should manifest himself unto the children of men" (1 Ne. 10:17–19; 12:18). The Book of Mormon restores the knowledge that the gospel of Jesus Christ, including the gift of the Holy Ghost, was received and enjoyed anciently, before the advent of Jesus Christ (e.g., 2 Ne. 31; Jacob 7:12–13; Alma 9:21; cf. Moses 5:9, 14, 58).

The Book of Mormon identifies various roles of the Holy Ghost. These include bearing witness of the Father and the Son and of all truth, revealing the things of God, bringing spiritual rebirth and sanctification, and administering the gifts of the Spirit.

The Holy Ghost is a witness

The Holy Ghost testifies of the Father and the Son (2 Ne. 31:18; 3 Ne. 11:32; 16:6; 28:11; Ether 5:4; cf. 2 Cor. 13:1). Book of Mormon prophets taught that the Holy Ghost would play a significant role in bearing witness of Jesus Christ to the Gentiles in the last days (1 Ne. 10:11; 2 Ne. 26:12–13; 3 Ne. 15:23; 16:6). Moroni[2] promised that each person who will read the Book of Mormon, ponder the goodness of God, and pray with a sincere heart, real intent, and faith in Christ, can receive a witness of the truth of the Book of Mormon and even the "truth of all things" by the power of the Holy Ghost (Moro. 10:4–5).

The Holy Ghost is a teacher and revelator of truth

Nephi[1] sought to know the things his father Lehi[1] had learned through REVELATION, and he was taught concerning the tree of life and the goodness of God. He wanted to "see, and hear, and know of these things, by the power of the Holy Ghost" (1 Ne. 10:17–18). Nephi later declared that those who would "enter in by the way, and receive the Holy Ghost" would be shown "all things what [they] should do" (2 Ne. 32:5). Jacob[2] testified that "great and marvelous are the works of the Lord. . . . And no man knoweth of his ways save it be revealed unto him" (Jacob 4:8, 13; Alma 26:21–22; cf. D&C 50:17–22; 1 Cor. 2:14).

The Holy Ghost not only teaches individuals but authorizes them to teach and testify to others. Nephi related that the Holy Ghost gave him authority to teach (1 Ne. 10:22), and affirmed that "when a man speaketh by the power of the Holy Ghost the power of the Holy Ghost carrieth it unto the hearts of the children of men" (2 Ne. 33:1). The Savior promised that those who hunger and thirst after righteousness shall be filled with the Holy Ghost (3 Ne. 12:6), and Nephi taught that those who received the Holy Ghost could speak with the TONGUE OF ANGELS, for "angels speak by the power of the Holy Ghost" (2 Ne. 32:2–3).

King Benjamin and Alma[2] taught that the Holy Ghost can bring comfort, peace, and joy (Mosiah 4:3; Alma 36:24). Such comfort comes through forgiveness, removing the burdens of sin. The hope and love that follows is a result of true repentance (Moro. 8:25–26).

The Holy Ghost is a sanctifier

When the children of men come unto Christ through covenants, "yielding their hearts unto God" (Hel. 3:35), they are sanctified (made whole, or holy, without spot) by the GRACE of God and the power of the Holy Ghost. In the process of SANCTIFICATION they are spiritually born of God, or born of the Spirit, becoming new creatures with changed hearts. Through the continued influence of the Holy Ghost they come to deny themselves "all ungodliness" and to "love God with all [their] might, mind and strength" (Moro. 10:32–33; for the principle being taught, see 2 Ne. 31:13–21; Alma 5:54; 13:11–12; 3 Ne. 9:20; 11:33–35; 12:2; 27:20; 30:2; Ether 4:7; for examples in the Book of Mormon, see Mosiah 4:2–3; 5:1–11; 27:24–26; Alma 18–19; Moro. 6:4).

The Holy Ghost administers spiritual gifts

Appropriately, and "according to the faith of the children of men," the Holy Ghost administers "the gifts of God," or "manifestations of the Spirit of God unto men, to profit them" (Moro. 10:7–8). These SPIRITUAL GIFTS include faith, healing, miracles, prophecy, tongues, hope, charity, teaching wisdom and knowledge, and beholding angels and ministering spirits (Moro. 10:9–20; cf. 1 Cor. 12:4–11; D&C 46:8–25). Moroni[2] testified that "all these gifts of which I have spoken, which are spiritual, never will be done away, even as long as the world shall stand, only according to the unbelief of the children of men" (Moro. 10:19).

Denying the Holy Ghost

Mormon warned latter-day readers that the sword of God's justice would one day overtake those who deny the revelations and spiritual gifts that come by the power of the Holy Ghost (3 Ne. 29:5–6). Jacob[2] equated denying the power and word of Christ and the gift of the Holy Ghost with making a mockery of the great plan of redemption (Jacob 6:8). It is serious enough to deny the Holy Ghost by refusing to respond to his promptings or refusing to believe in the things of God, but it is infinitely more serious to "deny the Holy Ghost when it once has had place in you." Such denial "is a sin which is unpardonable" (Alma 39:6). Nephi[1] taught that it would be better not to have known the Savior than to deny him after one has received "the baptism of fire and of the Holy Ghost" (2 Ne. 31:14). To Joseph Smith the Lord revealed, "Thus saith the Lord concerning all those who know my power, and have been made partakers thereof, and suffered themselves through the power of the devil to be overcome, and to deny the truth and defy my power—They are they who are the sons of perdition, of whom I say that it had been better for them never to have been born" (D&C 76:31–35).

See also Conceive by the power of the Holy Ghost; Gospel, the; Spirit of the Lord; Unpardonable sin.

BLS

Holy Ghost, conceive by the power of the *See* Conceive by the power of the Holy Ghost.

Holy order of God The Book of Mormon term for the Melchizedek Priesthood, known to the ancients as the "Holy Priesthood, after the Order of the Son of God" (D&C 107:2–4). This, "the holiest order," is the authority by which the gospel is administered in all dispensations (D&C 84:18–20). Accordingly, those called into the holy order of God had both the authority and responsibility to preach the word of God and perform ordinances (2 Ne. 6:2; Mosiah 18:13; Alma 4:20; 5:44; 6:8; 7:22; 13:6–11; 43:2; 49:30; Hel. 8:18; Ether 12:10; Moro. 3–5).

In speaking to the people of Ammonihah, Alma[2] drew upon his knowledge of the ancient Saints. He taught that those who had entered into the holy order of God were first "called and prepared," or foreordained to the order, "from the foundation of the world . . . on account of their exceeding faith and good works" while "in the first place," or premortal existence (Alma 13:3–4). He further explained how their foreordination was fulfilled when, through faith, repentance, and righteousness, the ancient Saints were ordained to the holy order and entered into God's rest, being sanctified, having their garments "washed white through the blood of the Lamb" (Alma 13:6, 10–12). Alma then invited the Nephites to follow the example of those forefathers, particularly Melchizedek (Alma 13:14–21). The Book of Mormon witnesses that Nephites before and after Alma did indeed follow Melchizedek's example. Many held the Melchizedek Priesthood, enjoyed the fulness of the everlasting gospel, and officiated in Melchizedek Priesthood ordinances (McConkie, 412, 421, 427; e.g., 2 Ne. 6:2; Alma 6:8; 7:22; 43:2; Hel. 10:4–8).

President Ezra Taft Benson explained that to receive the highest blessings of the holy order is "the equivalent today of entering into the fulness of the Melchizedek Priesthood, which is only received in the house of the Lord" (Benson, 8; cf. Moses 6:64–67).

See also Priesthood among the Nephites.

BIBLIOGRAPHY

Benson, Ezra Taft. "What I Hope You Will Teach Your Children about the Temple." *Ensign* 15 (August 1985): 6–10.

McConkie, Bruce R. *The Promised Messiah.* Salt Lake City: Deseret Book, 1978.

RLM

Hope A gift of the Spirit (Moro. 8:26), through faith in the redeeming power of Christ, by which one steadfastly desires and anticipates being raised to life eternal (Moro. 7:41). This hope becomes an anchor for the soul during the trials of mortal probation (Ether 12:4; Heb. 6:19). Specific hopes mentioned include the ideas of being like Christ and being with Christ: (1) hope of being filled with the pure love of Christ, that is, charity, that "we may be purified even as he is pure" (Moro. 7:47–48); and (2) "a hope of his glory" (Jacob 4:4; Moro. 9:25) or "a good hope of glory in him" (Jacob 4:11), which might be understood to mean a hope of partaking of the same glory as Christ's (cf. 2 Ne. 1:15 and 2 Ne. 2:4 where one might hope to behold his glory in this life). And similarly, a "hope through the atonement of Christ and the power of his resurrection, to be raised unto life eternal" (Moro. 7:41; cf. Jacob 4:4; Moro. 9:25).

The Fall left man without visible means of hope for personal renewal or for a better world, but hope for a place with Christ in the highest glory comes by faith in his regenerating power. In contrast, despair, the opposite of hope, "cometh because of iniquity" or a lack of faith in the Lord (Moro. 10:22–23). Hope is kindled by searching the scriptures (Jacob 4:6) and through repentance and faith in Christ (Moro. 7:40–42; Hel. 15:7). One may be patient in present affliction through the hope that someday one will rest from all affliction (Alma 34:41). The Lord gives hope with assurances of deliverance (Alma 58:11).

Hope is often associated with FAITH and CHARITY because the three represent a progression. As a person's faith in Christ begins his own personal renovation, his hope in Christ is awakened and strengthened. His heart expands with greater love, even "perfect love," for others (Moro. 8:26). Thus personal hope springs from faith in Christ and leads to charity through the power of the Comforter (Moro. 7:42–44; 8:26). Nephi[1] connected these three principles when he taught that man must press forward with a steadfastness in Christ (faith), with a perfect brightness of hope, and a love of God and man (charity) in order to inherit eternal life (2 Ne. 31:20). A person must obtain hope in Christ or he cannot receive an inheritance in the kingdom of God (Ether 12:26–32; Moro. 10:21).

MCT

Horeb *See* Sinai, mount.

Horses *See* Animals.

Hosanna Hebrew translation for "save now, we pray thee (or we beseech thee)." Both an expression of exultation for God's goodness and a plea for salvation. "Hosanna" was proclaimed by the Spirit of the Lord when Nephi[1] declared his faith (1 Ne. 11:6); by Nephites, with "hearts . . . swollen with joy" after God delivered them in war (3 Ne. 4:32–33); and by witnesses of the resurrected Savior (3 Ne. 11:17).

CF

Humility Realization of one's dependence upon God (Mosiah 4:1–3), and a willingness to seek and follow his will (2 Ne. 31:7).

Humility is spoken of in association with SANCTIFICATION (Hel. 3:35; 3 Ne. 12:2), MEEKNESS, submissiveness, LOWLINESS OF HEART (Mosiah

HYPOCRISY

3:19; Alma 13:28; 32:8–12; Hel. 6:39), abasing oneself (Alma 4:13), becoming like a little child (Mosiah 3:19; Moro. 8:10), and believing in the word of God without compulsion (Alma 32:16). It is the opposite of PRIDE (Alma 1:20; 6:3), loftiness, haughtiness, and stubbornness of heart (2 Ne. 12:11; 15:15; 20:33; Alma 32:16), and is necessary if one is to "learn wisdom" concerning spiritual truths (Alma 32:12). Humility is one of the attributes of those who have put off the natural man by yielding to the "enticings of the Holy Spirit" and have, "through the atonement of Christ the Lord," become true Saints (Mosiah 3:19; cf. Alma 13:28; 34:38; 42:30). The humble who come unto Christ are promised joy (Mosiah 4:11–12; Hel. 3:35) and answers to their prayers (2 Ne. 9:42). It is better, taught Alma[2], that people "humble themselves without being compelled to be humble" (Alma 32:16).

The Book of Mormon identifies several factors which can motivate humility, including hearing the word of the Lord (1 Ne. 15:20; 16:5, 24; Hel 6:5), experiencing afflictions, wars, famines, pestilences (Alma 32:6; 62:41; Hel. 11:8–9), recognizing the justice, mercy, and long-suffering of God (Alma 42:30), and realizing a state of weakness (Ether 12:27).

Christ set a perfect example of humility in that he "humbleth himself before the Father, and witnesseth unto the Father that he would be obedient unto him in keeping his commandments" (2 Ne. 31:7). All who inherit eternal life must demonstrate their own humility by following the Son "with full purpose of heart" (2 Ne. 31:13, 20).

See also Broken heart and contrite spirit.

RDA

Hypocrisy In a gospel sense, hypocrisy is the pretense of religious conviction in the absence of true conviction; it is the claim to religious commitment without the practice of religious principles. A hypocrite feigns belief, while the heart is really serving personal pride and vain ambition. The Greek word translated as "hypocrite" in the New Testament is the word for an actor in a play, one who portrays someone different from the person he or she really is. President N. Eldon Tanner taught that a hypocrite is "one who pretends to have beliefs or principles which he does not have, or to be what he is not, especially a false assumption of an appearance of virtue or religion" (31). Hypocrisy is therefore a manifestation of the carnal or "natural man" and not of the truly converted "saint" (Mosiah 3:19).

Teaching the Nephites as he had taught in the Sermon on the Mount, Jesus described hypocrites as those who love to pray publicly, "that they may be seen of men." Being so seen, he said, was "their reward," and he clearly implied that it was their only reward (3 Ne. 13:5 // Matt. 6:5). Nephi[1] defined hypocrisy by telling what it is not, urging all to "follow the Son, with full purpose of heart, acting no hypocrisy and no deception before God, but with real intent" (2 Ne. 31:13).

Other writers of the Book of Mormon boldly emphasized the evils of hypocrisy and warned of severe consequences that await those who lead hypocritical lives. Amulek, for example, after perceiving the thoughts of the lawyers in Ammonihah who had been engaged to "catch [Alma[2] and Amulek] in their words" (Alma 10:13), denounced them as "wicked and perverse . . . hypocrites" who were "laying the foundations of the devil" by "laying traps and snares to catch the holy ones of God." This, he warned, would "bring down the wrath of God" on them (Alma 10:17–18). They, after all, were supposedly the guardians of justice and truth. Amulek similarly denounced as hypocrites those who pray for God's blessings and yet turn away the poor (Alma 34:28). Moroni[2] used the same designation for those within the Church who love their possessions more than they love the people who need their help (Morm. 8:37–40).

BIBLIOGRAPHY

Tanner, N. Eldon. "Woe unto You . . . Hypocrites." *Improvement Era* 73 (December 1970): 31–35.

BRM

And behold, this is the whole meaning of the law, every whit pointing to that great and last sacrifice; and that great and last sacrifice will be the Son of God, yea, **infinite** and eternal. ALMA 34:14

I never knew them A phrase used by Jesus directed to unrepentant people who never developed or continued in a covenant relationship with him and who will be CAST OFF at the Judgment Day (Mosiah 26:22–27; cf. Mosiah 5:5–13; 3 Ne. 14:21–23; JST Matt. 7:31–33). Because Christ is an omniscient being, and there is not anything he does not know (2 Ne. 9:20), his words "I never knew them" (Mosiah 26:27) refers not to information or facts about people but rather their relationship or lack of one with him. These are they who "never knew [Christ]" (Mosiah 26:25) and who "would not be redeemed" (Mosiah 26:26).

See also Judgment, the; Second trump.

TBP

Idolatry The sinful practice of making and worshipping graven images, or idols made of wood, stone, or metal. Idolatry was expressly forbidden and condemned by the Lord (Mosiah 13:12–13). In a broader sense idolatry is idolizing, worshipping, or making more important anything other than God. Hence, the love or worship of such things as money, COSTLY APPAREL, power, or worldly pleasures, is also a form of idolatry. For example, the idolatry of the Zoramites[2] included setting their hearts upon their riches, and being "puffed up . . . with the vain things of the world" (Alma 31:24–28). Even idleness is considered a form of idolatrous behavior (Alma 1:32).

Idolatry was one of the sins afflicting the peoples of the Book of Mormon. For example, Enos described the Lamanites as "full of idolatry" (Enos 1:20), while Mormon listed the idolatry of the Nephites as one of the reasons for "their wars and their destructions" (Alma 50:21). Mormon also prophesied that the remnant of the seed of Lehi[1] would become a "scattered . . . and a loathsome people . . . because of their unbelief and idolatry" (Morm. 5:15). The Jaredites during the reign of Shule were also guilty of idolatry, which sin "was bringing a curse" upon their lands (Ether 7:23).

RH

Ignominious *See* Appendix C.

Ignorance, died in To have died without a knowledge of the laws of God as revealed through his prophets. The atonement of Jesus Christ satisfied the demands of the law of justice for all those who "have not the law given to them" (2 Ne. 9:26) and who "died not knowing the will of God concerning them, or who have ignorantly sinned" (Mosiah 3:11; cf. Moro. 8:22). Those who "died before Christ came, in their ignorance, not having salvation declared unto them" will come forth in the first resurrection (Mosiah 15:24). A revelation to the Prophet Joseph Smith indicated that "all who have died [or will die] without a knowledge of this gospel, who would have received it if they had been permitted to tarry, shall be heirs of the celestial kingdom of God" (D&C 137:7–8). They will have the opportunity to be taught and accept the gospel in the spirit world (D&C 138).

See also Law, without the.

HDG

Immanuel One of many name-titles for the Messiah in the writings of Isaiah (2 Ne. 17:14; 18:8). The Hebrew appellation literally means "with us [is] God," clearly foreshadowing the coming of God himself into the world (Matt. 1:21–23).

See also Isaiah chapter reviews (2 Ne. 17 // Isa. 7).

DKO

Immersion *See* Baptism.

Incorruption *See* Corruption, incorruption.

Indolence *See* Appendix C.

Infant baptism *See* Children, baptism of little.

Infinite Boundless, limitless, immeasurable, or endless. The term "infinite" is used in the Book of Mormon as an adjective describing God's goodness, mercy, and grace in blessing his people (2 Ne. 1:10; Mosiah 5:3; 28:4; Hel. 12:1; Moro. 8:3). It is also used to describe Christ as the "great and last sacrifice," and with reference to the universal, all encompassing (not limited in scope or time) effects of the ATONEMENT. Amulek taught that only an "infinite atonement [would] suffice for the sins of the world," an act that could only be accomplished by a being who was also "infinite and eternal" (Alma 34:10–14; cf. 2 Ne. 9:7; 25:16).

DLL

Iniquity *See* Sin, transgression.

Iniquity, fulness of *See* Fulness of iniquity.

Innocence, state of Before the Fall, Adam and Eve were in a state of innocence for they had not yet been exposed to the conditions, challenges, and opportunities of this mortal state. Thus they knew neither its joys nor sorrows, neither good nor evil (2 Ne. 2:23; Moses 4:11).

JFM

Innocent blood Term used in the Book of Mormon in reference to Abinadi (Mosiah 17:10), king Lamoni (Alma 20:18–19), and the believing women and children of Ammonihah (Alma 14:11), and "might be thought of as the blood of those persons without guile, or of little ones who have not sinned" (Kimball, 119). The Doctrine and Covenants refers to the "innocent blood" of Joseph and Hyrum Smith with the same meaning (D&C 135:4, 7; 136:36). Additionally, modern revelation teaches that "innocent blood" can refer to the Savior's blood. To shed his innocent blood is to "assent unto [his] death" and is "blasphemy against the Holy Ghost" (D&C 132:27). In some scriptural contexts to shed innocent blood simply means to take life unjustly or against God's will (e.g., Deut. 19:10–13; 1 Kgs. 2:31; Jer. 22:3).

See also Murder; Unpardonable sin.

BIBLIOGRAPHY

Kimball, Spencer W. *The Miracle of Forgiveness.* Salt Lake City: Bookcraft, 1990.

DKJ

Insurrections *See* Appendix C.

Intercession Mediation; intervention to resolve a predicament. The term is used four times in the Book of Mormon, twice by Lehi[1] (2 Ne. 2:9–10), and twice by Abinadi (Mosiah 14:12 // Isa. 53:12; Mosiah 15:8), all referring to Christ's infinite ATONEMENT by virtue of which he obtained the right and power to save mankind from the awful plight of death and sin which resulted from the Fall (2 Ne. 9:6–13; Alma 42:1–26).

An important aspect of Christ's intercession is his advocacy for all mankind, his pleading unto the Father in their behalf, that all who believe in him will be saved (D&C 38:4; 45:1–5). Mormon explained, "Christ hath ascended into heaven, and hath sat down on the right hand of God, to claim of the Father his rights of mercy which he hath upon the children of men[.] For he hath answered the ends of the law, and he claimeth all those who have faith in him; . . . wherefore he advocateth the cause of the children of men" (Moro. 7:27–28).

The New Testament also speaks of Christ's intercession for mankind (e.g., Rom. 8:27; Heb. 7:25). And Paul wrote that not only Christ, "but the Spirit itself maketh intercession for us," at least in helping one to know what to pray for (Rom. 8:26).

See also Mediator.

LED

Intercourse *See* Appendix C.

Interposition *See* Appendix C.

Interpreters *See* Urim and Thummim.

Intrigue *See* Appendix C.

Irreantum After eight years in the wilderness, Lehi[1] and those traveling with him came to the sea (apparently the Arabian Sea) which they called Irreantum, "which, being interpreted, is many waters" (1 Ne. 17:4–5). While camped in the place they called "Bountiful," Nephi[1] and his brothers built a ship (1 Ne. 17:6–18:5).

Isaac The son of Abraham, most often referenced in the expression "the God of Abraham, and the God of Isaac, and the God of Jacob," as in 1 Nephi 6:4. Jacob[2] taught that the near sacrifice of Isaac by his father Abraham was "a similitude of God and his Only Begotten Son" (Jacob 4:5).

Isabel A harlot in the land of Siron who "did steal away the hearts of many," including Corianton, the son of Alma[2]. He forsook the ministry to pursue her (Alma 39:3–4; ca. 73 B.C.).

Isaiah[2] *See* Disciples, twelve Nephite.

Isaiah, life and ministry Isaiah was an Old Testament prophet who ministered in the kingdom of Judah from around 740 B.C. to at least 701 B.C. during the reigns of Uzziah, Jotham, Ahaz, and Hezekiah (Isa. 1:1). His was an era of political unrest, war, and apostasy. The house of Israel was divided into the two warring kingdoms, Israel in the north, and Judah in the south, and the threat of attack from the brutal Assyrian empire was ever present for both. In Israel the monarchy was in turmoil with kings, all wicked, being regularly assassinated or overthrown. Meanwhile in Judah, the Davidic kings alternated between righteous and wicked. In both kingdoms apostasy was rampant with idolatry generally more practiced than devotion to Jehovah. Isaiah labored to turn the people back to Jehovah. His message to the apostates is reflected in his name, which means "Jehovah is salvation." Sadly his message was largely rejected. Eventually Isaiah would witness the fall and removal of Israel to Assyria (ca. 722 B.C.), as well as the Assyrian conquest of much of Judah, and the unsuccessful Assyrian siege on Jerusalem (2 Kgs. 15–21).

The complexity and beauty of Isaiah's writings, complete with elegant poetic elements of metaphor, parallelism, and elevated language, suggest he was a well-educated man. He was married and had at least two children, both given names reflective of his prophecies (Isa. 7:3; 8:1–4, 18). He seems to have been a man of relatively high social station who could find audience with kings and aristocracy (e.g., Isa. 7:3; 37:1–36; 38:1). Jewish legend suggests that king Hezekiah was actually Isaiah's son-in-law (Ginsberg, 4:277, 279), which perhaps explains why Isaiah's counsel was often sought and followed by king Hezekiah (Isa. 37–40; cf. 2 Kgs. 19–20). And yet Isaiah's counsel was not popular with all the kings he advised (e.g., Isa. 7; cf. 2 Kgs. 16). A pseudepigraphic work records that Isaiah's life ended when he was sawed in half by king Hezekiah's wicked son Manasseh ("Martyrdom," 163; cf. Ginsberg, 4:279; Heb. 11:37).

Although he was a prophet primarily to the kingdoms of Judah and Israel, Isaiah also spoke many prophecies concerning nations that neighbored or interacted with them, such as Philistia, Moab, Phoenicia, Assyria, Babylon, and Egypt (e.g., Isa. 10; 13–16; 19–21; 23). Moreover, he prophesied not only about his contemporary time period and issues but also about subsequent dispensations as well. As Christ declared, "He spake as touching all things concerning my people which are of the house of Israel; therefore it must needs be that he must speak also to the Gentiles. And all things that he spake have been and shall be, even according to the words which he spake" (3 Ne. 23:2–3).

Isaiah's prophecies have been quoted and revered by men of God in every dispensation since his ministry. He is the most quoted prophet in the Book of Mormon, having approximately 35 percent of his Old Testament writings either quoted directly or paraphrased by Nephite prophets (e.g., 1 Ne. 20–21; 2 Ne. 7–8; 12–24; 26–27; Mosiah 14). Moreover, Isaiah is the prophet most quoted by Jesus Christ in the New Testament (e.g., Matt. 13:14–15; 15:7–9; Luke 4:18–19; 22:37). When Christ appeared as the resurrected Lord to the Nephites, he affirmed the importance of studying Isaiah, "And now, behold, I say unto you, that ye ought to search these things [the writings of Isaiah]. Yea, a commandment I give unto you that ye search these things diligently; for great are the words of Isaiah" (3 Ne. 23:1).

Perhaps Isaiah's prophecies were so regularly used and highly recommended by Christ and the Book of Mormon prophets because of two themes which pervade his writings: (1) the status and future of God's covenant people, and (2) the ministry and mission of the Messiah. For example, Nephi[1] and Jacob[2] cited Isaiah to teach about such events as the apostasy, scattering, and oppression of the house of Israel; the latter-day gathering of their descendants and their restoration to the gospel of Christ; and the

The Prophet Isaiah; *painting by Raphael, Church of St. Agostino, Rome.*

establishment of Zion—themes that concerned the Nephites because of their own Israelite ancestry (2 Ne. 6:6–18; 8; 10; 25:14–17; 26:14–30:18). Nephi also quoted Isaiah to teach about the coming forth of the Book of Mormon and the vital role it would play in the latter days (2 Ne. 27:6–35), and about the destruction of the wicked before the coming of the millennial Messiah and the era of peace that would follow the Savior's return (2 Ne. 12; 21:1–24:3). Abinadi quoted Isaiah's prophecies to teach about the mortal Messiah's ministry (Mosiah 14).

With his prophecies preserved not only in the Old Testament but also in the New Testament, the Book of Mormon, and the Doctrine and Covenants, Isaiah's ministry continues to bless and instruct students of the scriptures.

See also Isaiah, purposes for quoting; Isaiah, understanding of; Isaiah chapter reviews; Isaiah in the Book of Mormon.

BIBLIOGRAPHY

Ginsberg, Louis, trans. *Legends of the Jews.* Philadelphia: Jewish Publication Society of America, 1941.

"Martyrdom and Ascension of Isaiah." *The Old Testament Pseudepigrapha.* Edited by James H. Charlesworth. Garden City, N.Y.: Doubleday, 1985.

TBB

Isaiah, purposes for quoting The Book of Mormon prophets Nephi[1], Jacob[2], and Abinadi, as well as the resurrected Savior, all quoted extensively from Isaiah in their teachings. From their own statements of why they quoted Isaiah, and from the Isaiah texts themselves, it seems their purpose in quoting Isaiah was to highlight four major themes: (1) repentance and the judgments of God, (2) God's covenants and promises to the house of Israel, (3) messianic prophecies, and (4) key events relating to the latter days.

Repentance and the judgments of God

One primary function of all prophets is to call people to repentance and to declare the judgments of God. Nephi explained that one of the reasons for including the Isaiah passages in 2 Nephi 12–24 was so that his people and "all those that shall receive hereafter these things . . . may know the judgments of God" (2 Ne. 25:3). Throughout his book Isaiah called covenant Israel and all nations to repent of their sins and to come to the Lord. Nephi included many of these passages as a warning to his own people, the Nephites, and also to future readers, including the Jews, the Lamanites, and the Gentiles. For example, Isaiah included prophecies of repentance and impending judgment to JUDAH and Jerusalem[1] (Isa. 2:1–5:30 // 2 Ne. 12:1–15:30), to SYRIA and Ephraim (Isa. 7 // 2 Ne. 17), to ASSYRIA (Isa. 10 // 2 Ne. 20), and to BABYLON (Isa. 13–14 // 2 Ne. 23–24). During the ministry of Isaiah the prophecies of destruction against Syria, Ephraim, and Assyria were fulfilled. Jerusalem was destroyed during Nephi's lifetime. Nephi likely used the prophecies of Isaiah to demonstrate to his people and future readers of the Book of Mormon that Isaiah's prophecies of the future would all come to pass.

God's covenants and promises to the house of Israel

A major purpose of the Book of Mormon is to teach Israel about the Lord's covenants (Title Page, para. 2). Isaiah's writings especially fulfill this purpose. Nephi exhorted his people to "hear ye the words of the prophet [Isaiah], . . . which were written unto all the house of Israel, and liken them unto yourselves, that ye may have hope as well as your brethren from whom ye have been broken off" (1 Ne. 19:24). Jacob prefaced his Isaiah quotations similarly: "And now, the words which I shall read are they which Isaiah spake concerning all the house of Israel; wherefore, they may be likened unto you, for ye are of the house of Israel" (2 Ne. 6:5). Nephi quoted Isaiah 48 (1 Ne. 20), which contains the Lord's promise to apostate Judah that he would "defer" his anger "that I cut thee not off," and also the promise that "I will not give my glory unto another" (1 Ne. 20:9, 11 // Isa. 48:9, 11). He also quoted Isaiah 49 (1 Ne. 21), which highlights some significant covenant promises concerning the gathering of Israel. Nephi cited these chapters just after his family crossed the ocean as he taught his people about their destiny in a new land (1 Ne. 22:7–12). Years later, after Jacob[2] read Isaiah 50 and 51 (2 Ne. 7–8), he stated that he had read these things that they "might know concerning the covenants of the Lord that he has covenanted with all the house of Israel" (2 Ne. 9:1; *see* Israel, covenants unto). Centuries later, the resurrected Savior used Isaiah 52 and 54 as he delivered two sermons containing major teachings about his covenants (3 Ne. 15:1–17:3; 20:10–23:5). Jesus promised that as the words of Isaiah would be fulfilled, "then is the fulfilling of the covenant" (3 Ne. 20:12, 46).

Messianic prophecies

Nephi and Abinadi both quoted Isaiah as they delivered their important witnesses of Christ and his atonement. Nephi wrote that he quoted Isaiah to "more fully persuade [his people] to believe in the Lord their Redeemer" (1 Ne. 19:23). Nephi testified that he, his brother Jacob, and Isaiah had all seen the Lord (2 Ne. 11:2–3; cf. Isa. 6 // 2 Ne. 16). He desired to quote the words of both Isaiah and Jacob to "prove" the truth of his own words concerning Christ. This, he taught, accorded with the principle that "by the words of three, God hath said, I will establish my word" (2 Ne. 11:2–3; cf. Isa. 6 // 2 Ne. 16). In connection with this testimony, and speaking of the words of Isaiah, Nephi exulted, "My soul delighteth in his words. For I will liken his words unto my people . . . my soul delighteth in proving unto my people the truth of the coming of Christ" (2 Ne. 11:2, 4). Therefore, he explained, "I write some of the words of Isaiah, that whoso of my people shall see these words may lift up their hearts and rejoice for all men" (2 Ne. 11:8). The prophet Abinadi cited the powerful messianic passage found in Isaiah 53, the "suffering servant song," as he taught king Noah[3] and his priests (Mosiah 14). Abinadi's inspired commentary helps Book of Mormon readers understand how Christ can make intercession for his followers, as promised by Isaiah (Mosiah 15). Nephi quoted additional messianic prophecies of Isaiah 6–9 and 11 in 2 Nephi 16–19 and 21 as a prelude to his great testimony of Christ (2 Ne. 25; 31–33).

Key events relating to the latter days

Another reason Book of Mormon prophets quoted Isaiah is that his writings spoke "concerning things which are, and which are to come" (2 Ne. 6:4). Isaiah's words have particular relevance for latter-day people: "Wherefore," Nephi said, "for their good have I written them" (2 Ne. 25:7–8). Isaiah's prophecies about the significance of temples, the second coming of Jesus Christ, the Millennium (Isa. 2 // 2 Ne. 12), an invasion of armies from the north towards Jerusalem (Isa. 10 // 2 Ne. 20), the effect of key servants (Isa. 11 // 2 Ne. 21), the downfall of spiritual Babylon (Isa. 13–14 // 2 Ne. 23–24), the setting up of a "standard" to gather Israel (Isa. 49 // 1 Ne. 21), and the coming forth of the Book of Mormon (Isa. 29 // 2 Ne. 27) were all quoted by Nephi. He then provided additional inspired commentary in 2 Nephi 25–30. These prophecies highlight a variety of significant events in different parts of the world. Combined with Nephi's commentary, these Isaiah passages help students of the Book of Mormon better understand the marvelous fulfillment of God's work in the latter days. Christ testified, "And all things that [Isaiah] spake have been and shall be, even according to the words which he spake" (3 Ne. 23:3).

Conclusion

Regarding Isaiah's writings, the resurrected Lord admonished the descendants of Lehi[1], "Ye have them before you, therefore search them" (3 Ne. 20:11) and "Yea, a commandment I give unto you that ye search these things diligently; for great are the words of Isaiah" (3 Ne. 23:1). Accordingly, Moroni[2], the last writer on the plates of Mormon, exhorted future readers of the Book of Mormon to "search the prophecies of Isaiah" (Morm. 8:23). Understanding why and how the Isaiah passages are quoted in the Book of Mormon helps readers of Isaiah find clarity and meaning as they search all of his writings.

See also Isaiah, life and ministry; Isaiah, understanding of; Isaiah chapter reviews.

VLL

Isaiah, understanding of Immediately after Nephi[1] recorded Isaiah chapters 2–14 (2 Ne. 12–24) on the plates, he authored eight verses that are directed to future readers with keys to understanding Isaiah's words (2 Ne. 25:1–8). As Nephi explained, "Isaiah spake many things which were hard for many of my people to understand" (2 Ne. 25:1). Nephi's keys include the following:

1. Understand "the manner of the Jews" (2 Ne. 25:2). This concept was of sufficient importance to Nephi that he seems to use it as a theme throughout the eight verses. His phraseology includes the expressions " the manner of prophesying among the Jews" (v. 1), "the manner of the Jews" (v. 2), "the things of the prophets" (v. 5), "the things which were spoken unto the Jews" (v. 5), "the manner of the things of the Jews" (v. 5), and "the manner of the Jews" (v. 6). Exactly what Nephi had in mind with these statements is unclear, but they may refer to literary devices (e.g., prophetic speech forms, poetic parallelisms, symbolic language), and historical, cultural, and theological elements which composed the prophetic style of Isaiah.

2. Be "filled with the spirit of prophecy" (2 Ne. 25:4; cf. Rev. 19:10). Earlier Nephi explained to his brethren that the prophecies of Isaiah "were manifest unto the prophet [Isaiah] by the voice of the Spirit; for by the Spirit are all things made known unto the prophets" (1 Ne. 22:2). The spirit of prophecy provided the words of revelation to Isaiah in the first place, and subsequently provides those who diligently search Isaiah's prophecies with the interpretation of Isaiah's words (if the searchers follow the correct prescriptions in receiving the spirit of prophecy). A formula for receiving the spirit of prophecy is presented in Alma 17:2–3, where the key elements of diligently searching the scriptures and much prayer and fasting are set forth.

3. Be familiar with the regions round about Jerusalem (2 Ne. 25:6). Isaiah's prophecies include frequent mention of geographical place names and physical features connected with the ancient Near East. There are 106 different geographical place names in the book of Isaiah, including, for example, cities (Jerusalem, Sodom, Bozrah), nations (Egypt, Israel), regions (Bashan, Galilee, Naphtali), valleys (Achor, Rephaim), mountains (Carmel, Lebanon), and oases (Nimrim, Tema). Many place names appear more than once. For example, Jerusalem is mentioned forty-eight times, Egypt forty-one, Moab twenty-one, Samaria eight, Damascus seven, and Ethiopia six.

4. Live during the days that the prophecies of Isaiah are fulfilled (2 Ne. 25:7–8). This statement is set forth first in verse 7 and then again in verse 8. Note that Nephi specifically identified the "last days" as the time that many of Isaiah's prophecies would be fulfilled. Examples of Isaiah's prophecies fulfilled in the last days include the coming forth of the Book of Mormon (Isa. 29 // 2 Ne. 27) and the establishment of temples (Isa. 2:1–3 // 2 Ne. 12:1–3).

In addition to these four keys, Jesus set forth another essential key during his visit to the Nephites. He used the word search instead of read: "Behold they [the words of Isaiah] are written, ye have them before you, therefore search them" (3 Ne. 20:11). Later, Jesus commanded, "Yea, a commandment I give unto you that ye search these things diligently; for great are the words of Isaiah" (3 Ne. 23:1; cf. Morm. 8:23).

There are many other keys to understanding Isaiah beyond those set forth explicitly in the Book of Mormon. For example, one can benefit greatly by examining the quotations of Isaiah that are found in the Book of Mormon, New Testament, and Doctrine and Covenants, with the intent of learning why and how Isaiah's writings are used in these texts. The Joseph Smith Translation of Isaiah provides a multitude of new, inspired readings that are also beneficial. Doctrine and Covenants 113, revealed to Joseph Smith, includes a number of questions and answers that pertain to Isaiah 11 and 52:1–2. Elder Bruce R. McConkie suggested that as one gains a greater understanding of the various doctrines of the gospel and the plan of salvation one will more readily understand and appreciate the writings of Isaiah (78–83).

See also Isaiah, life and ministry; Isaiah, purposes for quoting; Isaiah chapter reviews; Isaiah in the Book of Mormon.

BIBLIOGRAPHY

McConkie, Bruce R. "Ten Keys to Understanding Isaiah." *Ensign* 3 (October 1973): 78–83.

DWP

Isaiah in the Book of Mormon Of all the prophetic writings available on the PLATES OF BRASS, Isaiah is the major resource used throughout the Book of Mormon. About one-third of Isaiah's sixty-six chapters are found in the Book of Mormon. Two large blocks of Isaiah chapters (2–14 and 48–54) are scattered among four books (1 Nephi, 2 Nephi, Mosiah, and 3 Nephi). In addition, Isaiah 29 is quoted in 2 Nephi. Twenty-one chapters of Isaiah are found in the Book of Mormon, as follows:

Isaiah 2–14 in 2 Nephi 12–24 for 13 chapters
Isaiah 29 in 2 Nephi 27 for 1 chapter

ISAIAH PASSAGES IN THE BOOK OF MORMON
(except whole chapters)

Isa. 5:26* in 2 Ne. 29:2	Isa. 49:23a* in 1 Ne. 22:8b; 2 Ne. 10:9a
Isa. 9:12–13 in 2 Ne. 28:32	Isa. 49:23 in 2 Ne. 6:7
Isa. 11:4 in 2 Ne. 30:9	Isa. 49:24–26 in 2 Ne. 6:16–18
Isa. 11:5–9 in 2 Ne. 30:11–15	Isa. 52:1a* in Moro.10:31a
Isa. 11:11a* in 2 Ne. 25:17a; 29:1b; cf. 25:11	Isa. 52:1–2 in 2 Ne. 8:24–25
Isa. 22:13* in 2 Ne. 28:7–8	Isa. 52:7* in 1 Ne. 13:37; Mosiah 15:14–18
Isa. 25:12* in 2 Ne. 26:15	Isa. 52:7–10 in Mosiah 12:21–24
Isa. 28:10, 13* in 2 Ne. 28:30	Isa. 52:8–10 in Mosiah 15:29–31; 3 Ne. 16:18–20; 20:32–35
Isa. 29:3–4* in 2 Ne. 26:15–16	Isa. 52:10* in 1 Ne. 22:10–11
Isa. 29:5* in 2 Ne. 26:18	Isa. 52:12* in 3 Ne. 21:29
Isa. 29:6 in 2 Ne. 6:15	Isa. 29:6–10 in 2 Ne. 27:2–5
Isa. 29:13 in 2 Ne. 28:9	Isa. 52:13–15* in 3 Ne. 21:8–10
Isa. 29:14a* in 1 Ne. 14:7a; 22:8a; 2 Ne. 25:17b; 29:1a	Isa. 49:22 in 1 Ne. 22:6
Isa. 29:15a* in 2 Ne. 28:9b	Isa. 53:8,10* in Mosiah 15:10–11
Isa. 29:21b* in 2 Ne. 28:16a	Isa. 54:2b* in Moro. 10:31a
Isa. 40:3* in 1 Ne. 10:8	Isa. 55:1* in 2 Ne. 26:25
Isa. 45:18* in 1 Ne. 17:36	Isa. 55:1–2 in 2 Ne. 9:50–51
Isa. 49:22* in 1 Ne. 22:8; 2 Ne. 6:6	

* Denotes a passage from Isaiah paraphrased in the Book of Mormon.

ISA. CHAP. REVIEW: 1 NE. 20 // ISA. 48

Isaiah 48–49 in 1 Nephi 20–21 for 2 chapters
Isaiah 50–51 in 2 Nephi 7–8 for 2 chapters
Isaiah 52 in 3 Nephi 20 for 1 chapter
Isaiah 53 in Mosiah 14 for 1 chapter
Isaiah 54 in 3 Nephi 22 for 1 chapter

Additional verses from Isaiah, mostly from these same chapters, are scattered throughout the Book of Mormon, as shown on the accompanying table. Many of the Isaiah passages have important differences from the corresponding verses in the King James Version of the Bible—that is, word changes or additions that significantly alter or enlarge the meaning of the verse. Many others of the Isaiah verses in the Book of Mormon have minor wording or punctuation changes that do not alter the verse's meaning, and about one-third are exactly the same as the corresponding biblical passages.

See also Isaiah, life and ministry; Isaiah, purposes for quoting; Isaiah chapter reviews.

BIBLIOGRAPHY

Isaiah in the Book of Mormon. Edited by Donald W. Parry and John W. Welch. Provo, Utah: FARMS, 1998.

VLL

Isaiah chapter reviews Each Isaiah chapter in the Book of Mormon has its own entry in this volume. Other articles include Isaiah, life and ministry of; Isaiah, purposes for quoting; Isaiah, understanding of; Isaiah in the Book of Mormon. All place names in the Isaiah chapters in the Book of Mormon can be found on Map A or Map B, pages 398–99. Articles on significant nations mentioned in the Isaiah chapters in the Book of Mormon—Assyria, Babylon, Israel, Judah, and Syria—also have accompanying maps.

Isaiah chap. review: 1 Nephi 20 // Isaiah 48

Background and synopsis

First Nephi 20 is the first place in the Book of Mormon in which an entire chapter from Isaiah (Isa. 48) is quoted. As a prelude Nephi[1] testified that the Lord had shown unto "the prophets of old all things concerning ['those who are at Jerusalem']; and also he did show unto many concerning us" (1 Ne. 19:20–21). It appears that Nephi quoted Isaiah 48–49 (1 Ne. 20–21) to illustrate this truth: chapter 20 pertaining to the "house of Jacob," or the Jews living in or about Jerusalem (1 Ne. 20:1), and chapter 21 pertaining to "us," or the descendants of Lehi[1], who were part of the house of Israel that had been "broken off" and "scattered abroad" (1 Ne. 21:1). Nephi explicitly quoted Isaiah to "more fully persuade [his brethren] to believe in the Lord their Redeemer" (1 Ne. 19:23). Like some of Nephi's brethren, many of Isaiah's contemporaries had difficulty maintaining faith in Jehovah, their Lord and Redeemer. Many in Israel at the time of Isaiah became worldly and proud, even worshipping other gods in the form of idols, in addition to Jehovah. Isaiah gave this prophecy (Isa. 48) to warn the people and to convince them to believe in the Lord. Isaiah's prophecy contains the words spoken by the Lord. First the Lord witnessed of his own omniscience and explained that he had revealed to Israel "from the beginning" those things which were to come to pass and lest they credit their false gods, or "idols," with his operations because he knew that Israel was "obstinate" (1 Ne. 20:1–8). Then the Lord expressed his love and patience in his efforts to purify and refine his people. The Lord's motive, his work and glory, that for which his very name stands, is to save mankind (1 Ne. 20:9–11). The Lord summoned Jacob to listen to his word, and testified of his omnipotence, declaring that he created the heavens, that he raised up a servant to lead and bless the people, that he guided them in the way they should go. He enumerated the blessings that they could have had, if they had hearkened to his commandments: peace like a river, "righteousness as the waves of the sea," seed as the sand, and offspring like gravel (1 Ne. 20:12–19). He called Israel to go out of Babylon and to proclaim the message that "the Lord hath redeemed his servant Jacob" (1 Ne. 20:20–21). The Lord closed his words with a solemn warning that "there is no peace . . . unto the wicked" (1 Ne. 20:22).

Definitions

20:1 *waters of Judah.* Referring to those who have taken upon themselves the covenant of

ISA. CHAP. REVIEW: 1 NE. 20 // ISA. 48

baptism. The phrase "or out of the waters of baptism" first appeared in the text of the third edition of the Book of Mormon (1840). This phrase was presumably added by the Prophet Joseph Smith. A phrase on the title page of the 1840 edition reads, "Third Edition, Carefully Revised by the Translator."

20:2 *holy city.* Jerusalem. Ironically the children of Israel who are called to be holy like their God (Lev. 19:2) "call themselves of the holy city" and "swear by the name of the Lord," yet "not in truth nor in righteousness" (1 Ne. 20:1–2).

20:2 *do not stay themselves upon the God of Israel.* Do not lean upon or put their trust in God.

20:4 *neck is an iron sinew, and thy brow brass.* Metaphors for pride and stubbornness.

20:8 *deal very treacherously.* To act deceitfully.

20:8 *transgressor from the womb.* The iniquity of Israel is so pervasive it is described here as if they had been rebellious from their birth (cf. Ps. 58:3).

20:10 *I have refined thee, I have chosen thee in the furnace of affliction.* Just as gold is smelted in the fire to remove impurities, so God tries his covenant people with fire to remove their impurities.

20:13 *spanned the heavens.* In this context meaning to stretch across or measure. Elsewhere the creation of the heavens is described as the Lord stretching out the heaven like a tent (Isa. 40:22).

20:14 *The Lord hath loved him; yea, and he will fulfill his word which he hath declared by them.* The person whom "the Lord hath loved" is called by the Lord to deliver Israel from Babylon. In the historical context of the Exile this is likely a reference to Cyrus, who conquered Babylon and freed Judah to return to the holy land (Ezra 1). Cyrus is referred to by name in Isaiah and

OUTLINE OF 1 NEPHI 20

I. The baptized members of the house of Jacob have apostatized (20:1–2)
   A. They swear by the name of the Lord, but not in truth or righteousness (20:1)
   B. They claim to be of the holy city, but do not rely on the Lord (20:2)
II. The omniscience of the Lord (20:3–8)
   A. House of Jacob has and will be shown things to come (20:3, 6)
   B. The Lord revealed things to come to convince obstinate people that he is God, and they should rely on him rather than upon their idols or their own wisdom (20:4–7)
   C. Israel has seen prophecy fulfilled and has been told of the future, and yet they would not hear; this the Lord also knew (20:8)
III. The Lord's love for his covenant people (20:9–11)
   A. House of Jacob will be spared and refined in the furnace of affliction (20:9–10)
   B. The Lord will not allow his name or people to be polluted (20:11)
IV. The omnipotence of the Lord (20:12–21)
   A. He created the earth and the heavens, and they obey him (20:12–13)
   B. He raised up a servant to declare his word (20:14–17)
      1. By the beloved servant the Lord will fulfill his words against Babylon (20:14)
      2. The servant will declare God's word and will be prospered by God (20:15)
      3. The servant was sent by the Lord (20:16–17)
   C. The Lord teaches the people the way they should go (20:17)
   D. Blessings are enumerated that Israel might have had if they had hearkened to the Lord (20:18–19)
   E. An admonition to flee wickedness and testify of the Lord's redemption of his people (20:20–21)
V. The warning of the Lord: "There is no peace . . . unto the wicked" (20:22)

ISA. CHAP. REVIEW: 1 NE. 20 // ISA. 48

designated a "shepherd" and the "anointed one" (Hebrew "messiah"; Isa. 44:28; 45:1). Thus, Cyrus can also be seen as a type of the servant or servants called by the Lord to deliver Israel from spiritual Babylon. Examples of servants who fit this type, besides the Deliverer himself (Mosiah 14 // Isa. 53) include Isaiah, Joseph Smith, and Israel as a whole (*see* Isaiah chapter reviews, 2 Ne. 21 // Isa. 49, background and synopsis). The phrase "he will fulfil his word which he hath declared by them" is found in 2 Nephi 20:14 but not in KJV Isaiah. This is probably a reference

SELECTED DIFFERENCES BETWEEN B OF M ISA. (1 NE. 20) AND KJV ISA. (ISA. 48)

	BOOK OF MORMON		KJV ISAIAH	COMMENTARY
20:1	. . . and are come forth out of the waters of Judah, **or out of the waters of baptism** . . . (phrase added to the text in the 1840 edition of the Book of Mormon).	48:1	. . . and are come forth out of the waters of Judah	Clarifies that waters of Judah means the waters of baptism, suggesting that this message is intended for those who had entered the covenant.
20:2	. . . they call themselves of the holy city, **but they do not** stay themselves upon the God of Israel . . .	48:2	. . . they call themselves of the holy city, and stay themselves upon the God of Israel . . .	Identifies apostate condition.
20:3	. . . and they went forth out of my mouth, and I showed them. I did **show** them suddenly.	48:3	. . . they went forth out of my mouth, and I shewed them; I did them suddenly, and they came to pass.	Clarifies that the Lord revealed rather than did things suddenly.
20:6	Thou hast **seen and heard** all this; and will ye not declare **them**?	48:6	Thou hast heard, see all this; and will not ye declare it?	Shows a more positive knowledge. Isaiah not only heard but saw.
20:11	. . . for mine own sake will I do **this**, for **I will not suffer** my name to be polluted . . .	48:11	. . . for mine own sake, will I do it: for how should my name be polluted? . . .	Clarifies why God intervenes.
20:14	All ye, assemble yourselves, and hear; **who** among them hath declared these things **unto them**? The Lord hath loved him; **yea, and he will fulfil his word which he hath declared by them;** and he will do his pleasure on Babylon . . .	48:14	All ye, assemble yourselves, and hear; which among them hath declared these things? The Lord hath loved him: he will do his pleasure on Babylon . . .	Apparently adds references to the prophets who do have the power to deliver the word of the Lord and prophesy of the future as opposed to the idols, who do not have this power.
20:17	**And** thus saith the Lord, thy Redeemer, the Holy One of Israel; **I have sent him,** the Lord thy God **who** teacheth thee to profit, **who** leadeth thee by the way thou shouldst go, **hath done it.**	48:17	Thus saith the Lord, thy Redeemer, the Holy One of Israel; I am the Lord thy God which teacheth thee to profit, which leadeth thee by the way that thou shouldest go.	Clarifies that the Lord sent the servant referred to in 20:14.
20:22	**And notwithstanding he hath done all this, and greater also,** there is no peace, saith the Lord, unto the wicked.	48:22	There is no peace, saith the Lord, unto the wicked.	Gives transition wording and clarifies the context.

to the other servants or prophets by whom the Lord has delivered his people from spiritual Babylon.

20:14 *he will do his pleasure on Babylon.* Do his will. This servant is likely Cyrus as a type of Christ.

20:14, 20 *Babylon.* Babylon would take Judah into exile in 586 B.C. but would be conquered by Cyrus the Persian in 539 B.C. Metaphorically, Babylon in the scriptures is a type of the world with its pride and wickedness (D&C 1:16; 133:14; Rev. 14:8). *See* Babylon, Babylonia.

20:14 *his arm shall come upon.* Referring to God's power; in this case manifested in wrath and judgment.

20:14, 20 *Chaldeans.* Inhabitants of Chaldea, or Babylonia.

20:15 *called him to declare, I have brought him, and he shall make his way prosperous.* The Lord called the servant(s)/prophet(s) mentioned in verse 14, and will make sure of his (their) success.

20:16 *Come ye near unto me; I have not spoken in secret; from the beginning, from the time that it was declared have I spoken; and the Lord, God, and his Spirit, hath sent me.* Throughout this chapter (1 Ne. 20:1–15) the Lord has been speaking. In this verse the speaker changes to another voice: "And the Lord, God, and his Spirit, hath sent me." This may be a reference to the prophet Isaiah, who is speaking on behalf of the Lord throughout the chapter, or it may be a reference to the other servants: the servant Cyrus, or the future Messiah.

20:17 *I have sent him.* The Lord speaking again as "I." The pronoun "him" is likely a reference to either Isaiah or the servant mentioned in verse 14.

20:19 *thy seed also had been as the sand; the offspring of thy bowels like the gravel thereof.* A promise of posterity, associated with the ABRAHAMIC COVENANT (e.g., Gen. 13:16; D&C 132:30). These promises (cf. 20:18) are those that Israel could have had if she had hearkened to the commandments of the Lord.

20:21 *they thirsted not; he led them through the deserts; he caused the waters to flow out of the rock for them; he clave the rock also and the waters gushed out.* A reference to blessings the Lord bestowed upon Israel during the EXODUS (cf. Ex. 17:6; Num. 20:11).

Selected differences between Book of Mormon Isaiah (1 Ne. 20) and KJV Isaiah (Isa. 48) are shown in the accompanying table.

Latter-day applicability

A latter-day covenant people, like Israel of old, likewise needs to recognize the omniscience and omnipotence of the Lord and the love he has for his people. The Lord has the power to accurately foretell the future. Just as ancient Israel could, so Latter-day Saints can recognize the fulfillment of many of the prophecies of Isaiah in the past and in the present and be assured that his prophecies for the future will also be fulfilled. In particular, just as the Lord delivered ancient Israel from Babylon and commanded them, "Go ye forth of Babylon, flee ye from the Chaldeans" (1 Ne. 20:20), so the Lord has commanded the Saints in the latter days, "Go ye out from Babylon. Be ye clean that bear the vessels of the Lord," and "Go ye out from among the nations, even from Babylon, from the midst of wickedness, which is spiritual Babylon" (D&C 133:5, 14). The chapter also bears witness that God calls servants to do his work and explains why he punishes or refines his covenant people. It further speaks of the blessings that can be attained by hearkening to God's commandments.

EDS.

Isaiah chap. review: 1 Nephi 21 // Isaiah 49

Background and synopsis

First Nephi 21 is addressed to the members of the house of Israel who have been "broken off," "driven out," and "scattered abroad" upon the "isles" (1 Ne. 21:1). Accordingly, Nephi[1] felt it had special application to his people (cf. 2 Ne. 10:21).

Throughout Isaiah's writings are a series of passages that are collectively called the "servant songs" (e.g., Isa. 42:1–4; 49:1–6; 50:4–11; 52:13–15; 53:1–12). These passages all speak of a servant or servants who, though they may suffer or appear insignificant, will yet do a great

ISA. CHAP. REVIEW: 1 NE. 21 // ISA. 49

work for the Lord. The preeminent servant is Jesus Christ, described as "a light to lighten the Gentiles, and the glory of . . . Israel" (Luke 2:32), who would deliver the world from sin, death, and hell and direct the work of all other servants. Many individuals from the house of Israel are in some way TYPES of Christ in their lives and in their efforts to bless those they serve. These individuals include Isaiah and other Old Testament prophets; Cyrus (a non-Israelite), called a "shepherd" and an "anointed one" (Isa. 43:28; 44:1), who would deliver ancient Judah from Babylon; and the Prophet Joseph Smith, whom the Lord used to restore the gospel and initiate the gathering of Israel in the latter days. The servant in 1 Nephi 21 who would gather the Lord's covenant people and be a light to the Gentiles is specifically identified as Israel (1 Ne. 21:2–3). This particular assignment is consistent with the teaching that through the "seed of Abraham," represented here by his grandson Jacob[1] (Israel), all nations of the earth will be blessed with the blessings of the gospel and the priesthood (1 Ne. 22:9; Abr. 2:9–11). These blessings would come to all nations through the restoration of the gospel of Jesus Christ. It would be the mission of *latter-day Israel*—the restored Church—to extend gospel blessings to both scattered Israel and the Gentiles (1 Ne. 22:6–12; D&C 45:9; 86:11).

This servant song tells of the servant's foreordination, power, preparation, and preservation for the future to glorify God (1 Ne. 21:1–3). The servant will do the Lord's work by gathering, restoring, and saving both scattered Israel and the Gentiles (1 Ne. 21:4–12). It then describes the joy that will result from this redeeming work (1 Ne. 21:13). The chapter continues with a figurative dialogue between ZION and the Lord, wherein he assures Zion he has not forgotten her (1 Ne. 21:14–17). It follows with a description of the magnitude of the latter-day gathering of Israel and an explanation to Zion of the significant role the Gentiles would play in both facilitating and joining in the gathering (1 Ne. 21:18–23; 22:9; cf. 2 Ne. 6:6–18). The chapter ends with the promise to Zion that the Lord would defend his people from their enemies (1 Ne. 21:24–26). Nephi provided inspired commentary and interpretation of this and the preceding chapter (1 Ne. 20 // Isa. 48) in 1 Nephi 22.

Definitions

21:1 *called me from the womb; from the bowels of my mother hath he made mention of my name.* Foreordained (cf. Jer. 1:5). A reference to the servant Israel.

21:1 *Listen, O isles.* Nephi explained that this expression referred to scattered Israel, including

OUTLINE OF 1 NEPHI 21

I. The servant (21:1–13)
   A. The servant was foreordained, prepared, and preserved to glorify God (21:1–3)
   B. The servant's mission will be to gather scattered Israel and be a light to the Gentiles. As a result of the Lord's work through his servant, kings shall be brought to see and princes shall worship; the heavens are invited to sing, and the earth invited to rejoice (21:4–13)

II. The Lord's dialogue with Zion confirming his support (21:14–26)
   A. Zion feels forsaken and forgotten (21:14)
   B. The Lord assures Zion he has not forgotten her (21:14–17)
   C. The Lord comforts Zion with a promise of a great gathering and restoration (21:18–20)
   D. Knowing her desolate and lost state, and seeing the multitude who is gathered to them, Zion will wonder from whence and how they came (21:21)
   E. The Lord explains that Gentiles will facilitate the gathering (21:22–23)
   F. The Lord promises to defend his people at that day (21:24–26)
      1. The Lord will contend with those who fight against his people (21:24–25)
      2. The wicked will fight among themselves (21:26)

ISA. CHAP. REVIEW: 1 NE. 21 // ISA. 49

Lehi's descendants, who were "scattered to and fro upon the isles of the sea" (1 Ne. 22:4; cf. 2 Ne. 10:20–22).

21:2 *made my mouth like a sharp sword.* A metaphor for the penetrating power of the word of God (cf. Rev. 1:16; 2:16; D&C 6:2).

21:2 *polished shaft.* A smooth arrow. A metaphor of being well prepared. Joseph Smith described himself and his mission in these terms: "Thus I will become a smooth and polished shaft in the quiver of the Almighty" (304).

21:4 *I have labored in vain, I have spent my strength for naught and in vain; surely my judgment is with the Lord, and my work with my God.* A modern translation of Isaiah renders

SELECTED DIFFERENCES BETWEEN B OF M ISA. (1 NE. 21) AND KJV ISA. (ISA. 49)

	BOOK OF MORMON		KJV ISAIAH	COMMENTARY
21:1	**And again: Hearken, O ye house of Israel, all ye that are broken off and are driven out because of the wickedness of the pastors of my people; yea, all ye that are broken off, that are scattered abroad, who are of my people, O house of Israel.** Listen, O isles, unto me . . .	49:1	Listen, O isles, unto me . . .	Clarifies that Isaiah is speaking to the scattered remnant of the house of Israel, and tells why they were scattered. Clarifies further that they were scattered abroad or to the isles of the sea (cf. 2 Ne. 10:20–22).
21:8	Thus saith the Lord: In an acceptable time have I heard thee, **O isles of the sea,** and in a day of salvation have I helped thee; and I will preserve thee, and give thee **my servant** for a covenant of the people . . .	49:8	Thus saith the Lord, In an acceptable time have I heard thee, and in a day of salvation have I helped thee: and I will preserve thee, and give thee for a covenant of the people . . .	Clarifies that the Lord is speaking to scattered Israel and that through his servant(s) the Lord will establish his covenant. Traditionally this servant song is thought to end at verse 6 but this addition extends the song through verse 12.
21:13	Sing, O heavens; and be joyful, O earth; **for the feet of those who are in the east shall be established;** and break forth into singing, O mountains; **for they shall be smitten no more;** for the Lord hath comforted his people, and will have mercy upon his afflicted.	49:13	Sing, O heavens; and be joyful, O earth; and break forth into singing, O mountains: for the Lord hath comforted his people, and will have mercy upon his afflicted.	Indicates an end to persecution and suffering for the Lord's people.
21:14	But, behold, Zion hath said: The Lord hath forsaken me, and my Lord hath forgotten me—**but he will show that he hath not.**	49:14	But Zion said, The Lord hath forsaken me, and my Lord hath forgotten me.	Indicates the Lord will demonstrate that Zion's thinking is faulty.
21:15	. . . they may forget, yet will I not forget thee, **O house of Israel.**	49:15	. . . they may forget, yet will I not forget thee.	Reiterates whom the Lord has not forgotten.
21:17	Thy children shall make haste **against** thy destroyers; and they that made thee waste shall go forth of thee.	49:17	Thy children shall make haste; thy destroyers and they that made thee waste shall go forth of thee.	Clarifies that Israel's posterity will gather against her enemies.

ISA. CHAP. REVIEW: 1 NE. 21 // ISA. 49

this verse "I have spent my strength in vain and for nothing. Yet what is due me is in the Lord's hand, and my reward is with my God" (NIV).

21:6 *light thing.* Meaning a comparatively small task. The servant's mission will not be limited to Israel (a relatively small task) but will represent the Lord to all the Gentiles to "the ends of the earth" (1 Ne. 21:6).

21:6 *raise up the tribes of Jacob, and to restore the preserved of Israel.* The servant(s) will gather scattered Israel.

21:6 *light to the Gentiles.* The gospel given to the Gentiles (D&C 45:28). As Israel is gathered through the work of the servant(s), the Gentiles will be given the opportunity to come unto Christ and be numbered with Israel, thus fulfilling the covenant made to Abraham (1 Ne. 22:9; Abr. 2:10).

21:8–9 *cause to inherit the desolate heritages.* Restore to former lands and covenants.

21:9 *prisoners.* Perhaps referring to those in spiritual bondage, whether on the earth or in the spirit world (cf. D&C 138:29–35).

21:9 *shall feed in the ways, and their pastures shall be in all high places.* A metaphor for the Lord's care and nurturing.

21:11 *make all my mountains a way, and my highways shall be exalted.* The Lord will prepare paths or means for the return of scattered Israel.

21:12 *these shall come from far; and lo, these from the north and from the west; and these from the land of Sinim.* Scattered Israelites will be gathered from all over the world. The location of Sinim is uncertain.

21:13 *feet of those who are in the east.* Perhaps referring to the covenant people in and around Jerusalem.

21:13 *Sing, O heavens; and be joyful, O earth; for the feet of those who are in the east shall be established; and break forth into singing, O mountains.* Nature is being called upon to witness the protection, comfort, and mercy of the Lord for his people.

21:14 *Zion.* Personification of the place where the covenant people will gather.

21:16 *graven thee upon the palms of my hands.* The image that the Lord has engraved his people on his hands signifies that the Lord has not forgotten his people. This may be an allusion to the marks of crucifixion in the palms of the hands of the Messiah—a graphic symbol of this truth.

21:16 *thy walls are continually before me.* Indicates that the Lord is ever mindful of his people.

21:17 *make haste against thy destroyers; and they that made thee waste shall go forth of thee.* The posterity of Israel will quickly turn upon their enemies (cf. Micah 5; 3 Ne. 21:12–20). Subsequently their enemies will depart.

21:18 *clothe thee with them all, as with an ornament, and bind them on even as a bride.* Suggests those who gather become like a wedding gown for the bride (the covenant people), who is awaiting the coming of the bridegroom (Christ) (e.g., Ezek. 16:6–14).

21:20 *The children whom thou shalt have, after thou hast lost the first.* Those to be gathered, brought into the covenant, and redeemed after the ancient covenant people reject the Lord and his covenants.

21:20 *The place is too strait.* Narrow, limited, or restrictive.

21:22 *standard.* A banner or flag to which people gather; used metaphorically for the restored gospel of Christ that would come forth among the Gentiles (cf. 1 Ne. 22:6). *See* Ensign.

21:22 *bring thy sons in their arms, and thy daughters shall be carried upon their shoulders.* A figurative expression indicating that the Gentiles, through whom the gospel is restored, will gather the Lord's covenant people (cf. 1 Ne. 22:6–10). In this context these latter-day Gentiles constitute the Lord's servant Israel mentioned earlier in the chapter (21:3). They are Gentiles by nationality and culture but Israelite by genealogical descent (cf. D&C 109:60). *See* Gentiles; Israel, gathering of.

21:23 *kings shall be thy nursing fathers, and their queens thy nursing mothers.* A metaphor suggesting that governing powers will also assist with the gathering and restoration of the covenant people (cf. 2 Ne. 10:7–9).

21:23 *lick up the dust of thy feet.* A figurative expression meaning to be humble and subservient. An explanation of this phrase was offered by Jacob[2], who quoted the same Isaiah passage. He identified those who "lick up the dust" of Israel's feet not as the kings and queens who would be nursing fathers and mothers aiding Israel's return but as those who fight against Zion and the covenant people of the Lord (2 Ne. 6:13). Hence, God does fulfill his covenants, and his people need not be ashamed (2 Ne. 6:12–13). Those who oppose his plans and purposes will in the end be humbled (cf. D&C 49:10).

21:24–25 *For shall the prey be taken from the mighty, or the lawful captives delivered? But thus saith the Lord, even the captives of the mighty shall be taken away, and the prey of the terrible shall be delivered.* Normally no one takes away from the mighty beasts their helpless prey, nor from the mighty political powers the captives that they have taken. But in this case the Lord will miraculously deliver Israel from her oppressors. JST Isaiah 49:25 reads, "But thus saith the Lord; even the captives of the mighty shall be taken away, and the prey of the terrible shall be delivered; for the mighty God shall deliver his covenant people."

21:26 *drunken with their own blood.* Internal warfare (cf. 1 Ne. 22:13–14).

Selected differences between Book of Mormon Isaiah (1 Ne. 21) and KJV Isaiah (Isa. 49) are shown in the accompanying table.

Latter-day applicability

The prophecies in 1 Nephi 21 are being fulfilled. The standard Isaiah wrote of has been erected, and the gathering of Israel is in progress. Nephi's commentary in 1 Nephi 22 explains how this prophecy would be fulfilled in the United States, the mighty Gentile nation in the latter days (22:7–9). Nephi understood that Isaiah's prophecy spoke of the mission of the Latter-day Saints and the role of the land of the Americas in connection with the redemption of the house of Israel.

See also Promised land, land of promise.

BIBLIOGRAPHY

Smith, Joseph. *Teachings of the Prophet Joseph Smith.* Selected by Joseph Fielding Smith. Salt Lake City: Deseret Book, 1976.

EDS.

Isaiah chap. review: 2 Nephi 7 // Isaiah 50

Background and synopsis

At the beginning of his stirring sermon to his people (2 Ne. 6–10), Jacob[2] quoted from Isaiah's prophecy in chapter 49 concerning the Gentiles' assistance in the gathering of Israel (2 Ne. 6:6–7 // Isa. 49:22–23). Jacob described the Babylonian captivity of Judah and the return to Jerusalem. He went on to prophesy of the future coming of the "Holy One of Israel" and his rejection and crucifixion. In consequence of this rejection, Israel would be scattered and smitten but would be gathered again "when they shall come to the knowledge of their Redeemer." Jacob then spoke of the second coming of the Messiah (2 Ne. 6:8–18). In 2 Nephi 7, Jacob quoted all of Isaiah 50, which begins with the Lord's clarification to Israel that he had not "put [his people] away" but rather that they had estranged themselves through their transgressions, leaving none to hearken to the Lord's call (2 Ne. 7:1–2). The Lord assured Israel that he had not lost his

OUTLINE OF 2 NEPHI 7

I. In spite of Israel's transgression the Lord has not abandoned the covenant people (7:1–3)
   A. The Lord has not divorced his covenant people; rather, they have left him (7:1)
   B. Israel has rejected the Lord in spite of his mighty acts (7:2–3)
II. The mission of Christ, the promised servant (7: 4–11)
   A. The servant brings comfort to Israel and performs the will of God but is rejected and persecuted (7:4–6)
   B. The servant will be delivered and vindicated (7:7–9)
   C. Those who reject the Lord and the "voice" of the servant will be left to walk by their own light and reap sorrow (7:10–11)

ISA. CHAP. REVIEW: 2 NE. 7 // ISA. 50

power to redeem them (2 Ne. 7:2–3). This introduction leads into a passage (2 Ne. 7:4–11) known as one of the Isaianic servant songs (cf. Isa. 42:1–4; 49:1–6; 50:4–11; 52:13–15; 53:1–12), which describe how a servant labors to bring salvation to others (*see* Isaiah chapter reviews, 1 Ne. 21 // Isa. 49, background and synopsis). The context and content of this servant song especially point to the Messiah, who during his mortal ministry fulfilled the will of God, though he was rejected and persecuted by his people (2 Ne. 7:4–6), and who ultimately, with the help of God, was triumphant (2 Ne. 7:7–9). All those who choose to trust in themselves rather than the servant are warned that they will eventually "lie down in sorrow" (2 Ne. 7:10–11).

Definitions

7:1 *bill of your mother's divorcement.* Under Mosaic law, a man could put away his wife but had to give her a bill of divorcement (Deut. 24:1–4). The Lord asks Israel to produce a "bill of divorcement" of her mother, which of course she cannot. In spite of her unfaithfulness, the Lord has not divorced Israel; rather, she has abandoned the Lord through her own transgressions.

7:1 *To whom have I put thee away, or to which of my creditors have I sold you? Yea, to whom have I sold you?* Rhetorical questions expecting a negative answer. The Lord has not put Israel away nor sold them.

7:2 *when I came, there was no man.* A metaphor describing the people's rejection of the Lord at his first coming (cf. 2 Ne. 7:2–3 with D&C 133:66–69).

7:2 *is my hand shortened.* The hand and arm of the Lord are symbols of his power. An extended hand is a symbol of the Lord manifesting his power. A pulled back, retracted, or "shortened hand" would then signify the opposite.

7:4 *The Lord hath given me the tongue of the learned.* The Lord gives the servant power to speak.

7:4 *in season.* When timely.

7:6 *I gave my back to the smiter, and my cheeks to them that plucked off the hair. I hid not my face*

SELECTED DIFFERENCES BETWEEN B OF M ISA. (2 NE. 7) AND KJV ISA. (ISA. 50)

	BOOK OF MORMON		KJV ISAIAH	COMMENTARY
7:1	**Yea for thus saith the Lord: Have I put thee away, or have I cast thee off forever? For** thus saith the Lord: Where is the bill of your mother's divorcement? . . .	50:1	Thus saith the Lord, Where is the bill of your mother's divorcement . . .	Clarifies that the following questions are rhetorical.
7:8	**And the Lord** is near, **and he** justifieth me . . . . . . Let him come near me, **and I will smite him with the strength of my mouth.**	50:8	He is near that justifieth me . . . . . . let him come near to me.	Emphasizes that it is the Lord who is justifying his servant. Identifies the word of God as the instrument used to defend his servants.
7:10	. . . and hath no light?	50:10	. . . and hath no light? let him trust in the name of the Lord, and stay upon his God.	Variant might indicate this phrase was a later addition to the text of Isaiah. Without it, verse 11 becomes more sharply a warning to those not obeying the Lord's voice as clarified in D&C 133:71.

ISA. CHAP. REVIEW: 2 NE. 8 // ISA. 51:1–52:2

from shame and spitting. The servant bears suffering for the salvation of Israel without retaliation, such as Christ did during his arrest, trial, and crucifixion (cf. Isa. 53:4–9 // Mosiah 14:4–9).

7:11 *walk in the light of your fire.* Those who reject the light of the gospel must live by the light of their own fire, which is tantamount to walking in darkness (2 Ne. 7:10; cf. D&C 1:16).

Selected differences between Book of Mormon Isaiah (2 Ne. 7) and KJV Isaiah (Isa. 50) are shown in the accompanying table.

Latter-day applicability

This chapter reminds latter-day people that God is constant, faithful, and dependable. He will always abide by the covenants he has made, and such covenants are broken only by the sin and rebellion of the people. Moreover, it reminds them that God does indeed have the power to redeem his children. It further indicates how redemption would be accomplished, even through the mortal ministry of Jesus Christ, who humbly and obediently accomplished God's work in spite of the rejection and persecution he faced. It finally invites all to hearken to the Lord, rather than trusting in themselves, which can only lead to sorrow.

A latter-day revelation in the Doctrine and Covenants quotes and paraphrases parts of 2 Nephi 7:2–3 regarding those who do not accept the Lord at his second coming (D&C 133:67–70) and records a solemn warning to those who reject the Lord and his servants. The Lord describes those who will be sent to outer darkness: "When I called to you out of the heavens; ye believed not my servants, and when they were sent unto you ye received them not" (D&C 133:71; cf. D&C 1:14).

EDS.

Isaiah chap. review: 2 Nephi 8 // Isaiah 51:1–52:2

Background and synopsis

In his address to the people of Nephi in 2 Nephi 6–10, Jacob[2] explained that he read from the writings of Isaiah (2 Ne. 6:6–7, 16–18; 7:1–8:25 // Isa. 49:22–26; 50:1–52:1–2) so that they "might know concerning the covenants of the Lord that he has covenanted with all the house of Israel" (2 Ne. 9:1). In 2 Nephi 7 Jacob quoted Isaiah 50. In 2 Nephi 8 he quoted a passage from Isaiah 51–52:1–2 concerning latter-day ZION that speaks of some of those covenants.

Second Nephi 8 begins with a call to those who "follow after righteousness" (2 Ne. 8:1), further identified as "my people," "O my nation," "ye that know righteousness," and "the redeemed of the Lord" (2 Ne. 8:4, 7, 11). The Lord reminded his people that he would "comfort Zion," "make her wilderness like Eden," and that "joy," "gladness," "thanksgiving," and "the voice of melody," as well as "righteousness" and "salvation" would be found in her (2 Ne. 8:3, 5, 8). Those who inhabit Zion would receive "everlasting joy . . . upon their heads." Also, "sorrow and mourning shall flee away" from these inhabitants, who are referred to as "the redeemed" (2 Ne. 8:11). Perhaps this is one reason why, in the following chapter (2 Ne. 9), Jacob gave a marvelous discourse on the Atonement in which he explained how ransom, or redemption, comes about.

The Lord called on the inhabitants of Jerusalem to wake from their spiritual slumber and turn from the sins that invoked the Lord's fierce anger (2 Ne. 8:17). Because of her wickedness, there would be "none to guide her among all [her] sons," but the Lord would send two sons to help her, two prophets raised up unto the Jews at the last day to act in great power and deliver them from destruction (2 Ne. 8:18–20). Again the Lord called Jerusalem to awaken, to return to strength and beauty and become an abode for the righteous (2 Ne. 8:24). She is further invited to arise from the dust and to sit down in a position of glory (2 Ne. 8:25).

Definitions

8:1 *rock from whence ye are hewn.* A metaphor for one's ancestry. Here it is used to invite Israel to remember her noble heritage.

8:2 *I called him alone, and blessed him.* A reference to the ABRAHAMIC COVENANT, through which Israel claims blessings (cf. Gen. 12:1–5; 17:1–22).

8:3 *Lord shall comfort Zion, he will comfort all her waste places.* Refers to the millennial restoration.

 ISA. CHAP. REVIEW: 2 NE. 8 // ISA. 51:1–52:2

8:3 *wilderness like Eden, and her desert like the garden of the Lord.* A metaphor for the healing and transforming power of the Lord, who can make a barren and desolate land (wilderness and desert) blossom and thrive like the garden of Eden.

8:4 *law shall proceed from me.* The Lord "our lawgiver" (Isa. 33:22) would reveal the gospel law.

8:4 *my judgment to rest for a light.* Not only is the Lord's judgment, or law, a light but the Lord himself is a light for the people (cf. Luke 2:30–32; D&C 45:9).

8:5 *mine arm shall judge the people.* The isles shall wait upon me, and on mine arm shall they trust: Here "arm" appears to refer to the power or will of the Lord. Thus, the Lord's arm of judgment (or justice) in this verse is the same as the arm on which the people may trust (the arm of mercy).

8:5 *isles.* Likely a reference to the scattered house of Israel (cf. 1 Ne. 21:1; 22:4). *See* Isles of the sea.

8:6 *heavens shall vanish.* The heavens as currently known will vanish, or "pass away," when the Lord comes again in glory; they will be replaced by new heavens (cf. Isa. 65:17; 66:22; 2 Pet. 3:10; 3 Ne. 26:3; Ether 13:9; D&C 45:22).

8:8 *moth shall eat them up like a garment.* All of temporal creation is transitory and subject to corruption and decay, just like a garment, but the Lord's righteousness never ends.

8:9 *Put on strength.* The Hebrew reads "clothe yourself with strength." Abraham Facsimile 2, Fig. 3, states that the Lord is "clothed with power and authority."

8:9 *cut Rahab, and wounded the dragon.* Rahab is an ancient Near Eastern name for a monster of chaos closely related to Leviathan (Isa. 27:1). In the Old Testament the power of God is explained in the imagery of Jehovah conquering Rahab, or chaos, through creation (Job 26:12; cf. 9:13; 38:8–11). The imagery of God's power in conquering chaos through creation is also applied in the Old Testament to the Lord's mastery over the sea and to the destruction of Rahab as a personification of the host of Pharaoh in the Exodus story (Ps. 89:9–10; Isa. 51:9; cf. Ps. 74:12–17). Thus Rahab is a poetic synonym for Egypt (Ps. 87:4). In a more general way, Rahab may be interpreted as a representation of Satan. In any case the point of the imagery is that the Lord has power over all of the elements and all of his enemies.

8:10 *dried the sea, the waters of the great deep; that hath made the depths of the sea a way.* In the review of God's power, the speaker remembers that God made the sea—and also dried it so the children of Israel who exited Egypt could cross.

8:10 *ransomed.* A reference to those who were delivered from bondage in Egypt, which is a type for the bondage of sin from which Christ

OUTLINE OF 2 NEPHI 8

I. A call to salvation (8:1–8)
   A. A commandment to the righteous to look to Abraham and Sarah (8:1–2)
   B. The Lord will comfort Zion (8:3)
   C. The Lord will bring salvation, judgment, and righteousness (8:4–8)
II. Israel appeals to the Lord: A plea for the Lord to "awake" as in days of old (8:9–10)
III. The reward for Israel's appeal: The redeemed of the Lord will return to Zion (8:11)
IV. The Lord reminds Israel of his great deeds of old (8:12–16)
V. The cup of God's wrath on Jerusalem (8:17–25)
   A. Jerusalem, who has drunk of the Lord's cup of fury, is told to "awake" (8:17)
   B. Two prophets minister in Jerusalem (8:18–20)
   C. The Lord removes the cup of his fury from Jerusalem (8:21–22)
   D. Jerusalem is again commanded to awake, repent, and be glorified (8:23–25)

ransoms humankind (cf. Isa. 35:10; Rom. 7:14; 1 Cor. 6:20; 7:23).

8:11 *Therefore, the redeemed of the Lord shall return, and come with singing unto Zion.* A reference to the building of Zion: "They that remain, and are pure in heart, shall return, and come to their inheritances . . . with songs of everlasting joy, to build up the waste places of Zion—And all these things that the prophets might be fulfilled" (D&C 101:18–19).

8:12 *man, who shall be made like unto grass.* Grass withers quickly and dies easily—as do humans (cf. Isa. 40:6–8).

8:14 *pit.* A place of captivity, such as a dungeon. This can also refer to Sheol, the place of the dead (cf. Isa. 42:22; Ps. 74:7; 89:40).

8:16 *I have put my words in thy mouth.* The Lord has given instruction to his people (cf. Isa. 49:2; 59:21; Jer. 1:9).

8:16 *shadow of mine hand.* The Lord protects and shelters his people (cf. Isa. 49:2).

8:16 *plant the heavens and lay the foundations of the earth.* As the Lord created heaven and earth originally, so shall he create a new heaven and a new earth in the millennial day (cf. Isa. 65:17; 66:22).

8:17 *hand of the Lord.* The Lord's hand represents the Lord himself, who has given Jerusalem the judgments she has received.

ISA. CHAP. REVIEW: 2 NE. 8 // ISA. 51:1–52:2

8:17 *the cup of his fury.* The judgments of the Lord.

8:17 *dregs.* The last vestiges, including the sediment in the bottom of the cup.

8:17 *wrung out.* The last drops of the cup of wrath will be drained out for Israel to drink.

8:18 *none to guide her.* Israel has lost prophetic leadership. This state of apostasy is described in Isaiah 50:1–2.

8:18 *sons she hath brought forth.* None of the natural sons of Israel have sufficient light to guide her.

8:19–20 *two sons are come unto thee, who shall be sorry for thee—thy desolation and destruction, and the famine and the sword—and by whom shall I comfort thee? Thy sons have fainted, save these two; they lie at the head of all the streets.* Because Israel has lost the gospel of Jesus Christ and its power to guide, direct, and save, God has sent two priesthood holders to assist and bless them. These two are the same "two witnesses" spoken of in Revelation 11:3. They will testify in Jerusalem for three and a half years, will be killed and left dead in the streets, and then will be resurrected and lifted up to meet Jesus Christ as he returns to make his appearance to the Jews.

8:20 *wild bull in a net.* A wild bull caught in a net is captive but still extremely dangerous. So it

SELECTED DIFFERENCES BETWEEN B OF M ISA. (2 NE. 8) AND KJV ISA. (ISA. 51:1–52:2)

	BOOK OF MORMON		KJV ISAIAH	COMMENTARY
8:2	. . . and blessed him.	51:2	. . . and blessed him, and increased him.	The phrase in the KJV is perhaps a later addition to the text intended to explain the blessings given to Abraham.
8:11	. . . and everlasting joy **and holiness** shall be upon their heads . . .	51:11	. . . and everlasting joy shall be upon their head . . .	Gives more detail and balances the poetic structure.
8:19	These two **sons** are come unto thee . . .	51:19	These two things are come unto thee . . .	Points more clearly to the two prophets mentioned in Rev. 11:3–12.
8:20	Thy sons have fainted, **save these two** . . .	51:20	Thy sons have fainted . . .	Clarifies that the two prophets alone will not faint.

must be with these two prophets, who are "full of the fury of the Lord."

8:21 *drunken, and not with wine.* Drunken rather with the cup of the Lord's fury (cf. Jer. 25:15–17; Ezek. 23:32–34).

8:23 *Bow down, that we may go over—and thou hast laid thy body as the ground and as the street to them that went over.* Imagery suggesting the humiliation put upon Israel by her enemies who are soon to experience God's wrath.

8:24 *put on thy strength.* Refers to putting on the authority of the priesthood (D&C 113:8).

8:24 *uncircumcised and the unclean.* Disobedient, sinners, or disbelieving Gentiles. Zion will be free of all such (cf. Joel 3:17).

8:25 *arise, sit down.* Get up from the dust, where slaves must sit (cf. 2 Ne. 8:22), and sit in a place of honor, as on a throne. In contrast, Babylon has been cast from a throne into the dust (cf. Isa. 47:1).

8:25 *bands of thy neck.* That which holds one captive. Here referring to the curses of God placed upon scattered Israel. These curses are removed as members of the house of Israel return to the Lord and repent of their sins (D&C 113:9–10).

Selected differences between Book of Mormon Isaiah (2 Ne. 8) and KJV Isaiah (Isa. 51:1–52:2) are shown in the accompanying table.

Jacob included the first two verses of Isaiah 52 with his quotation of Isaiah 51. Isaiah 52:1–2 is quoted in two other places in the Book of Mormon: by the Savior, in 3 Nephi 20:36–37; and by Moroni[2], in Moroni 10:31.

Latter-day applicability

Just as Jacob hoped his people would rejoice in the covenants of the Lord of which Isaiah spoke in this chapter, latter-day people should find hope and happiness in the promises that, in the last days, the Lord will bring an end to the fallen condition of the earth. He will renew the earth and will dwell among his people. Jerusalem will be called to put on her beautiful garments; Zion will be called to awaken, and they are to remove the bonds of captivity that have held them bound. Latter-day Saints, too, must awaken from spiritual slumbering, put on the garments of the priesthood, and take off the chains of sin. To be worthy to participate in Zion, they must leave Babylon and no longer have contact with that which is unclean.

As the events of the last days unfold, the Lord assures his covenant people that if they are righteous, they need not fear the works of mortals. The Lord is greater than any human, and he will help his covenant people. He reminds them of his works of power in times past and indicates that by that same power he will bring Zion and fulfill all his promises to her.

In the last days the Lord will reach forth to bring again Zion among the righteous. His followers will lift up their voices with the good news of the gospel and go forth to all nations. Saints today can participate in that work by seeking to establish Zion in their own homes and by joining their voices to others' who bear testimony of Christ and his gospel.

BIBLIOGRAPHY

Parry, Donald W., Jay A. Parry, and Tina M. Peterson. *Understanding Isaiah.* Salt Lake City: Deseret Book, 1998. 447–61.

DWP

Isaiah chap. review: 2 Nephi 12 // Isaiah 2

Background and synopsis

Chapters 12–14 of 2 Nephi (cf. Isa. 2–4) were directed to the southern kingdom of JUDAH. Isaiah was a citizen of this nation, which had been in existence for about two hundred years (since 931 B.C.). With dualistic insight, Isaiah connected major problems in Judah during his day with important prophecies of conditions and events in the latter days. Isaiah dramatically invited all of the house of Jacob, Judah in his day as well as future Israel, "Come ye and let us walk in the light of the Lord" (2 Ne. 12:5). In 2 Nephi 12, Isaiah first prophesied of a time in the latter days when a temple would be built and valued, when the Messiah would reign, and when humankind would live in peace (2 Ne. 12:2–4; cf. Isa. 2:2–4; Micah 4:1–3). Although this temple can be identified as the temple to be built in Jerusalem, Latter-day Saints see it as a type of other latter-day temples as well. Isaiah then contrasted the future millennial era with the pride and idolatry of Judah in his day. He described

ISA. CHAP. REVIEW: 2 NE. 12 // ISA. 2

how such apostate people will be humbled in the "day of the Lord," which for ancient Israel occurred when they were conquered by their enemies. This event was a type for the "day of the Lord" for future Israel that will occur at the Second Coming (2 Ne. 12:5–21). Isaiah closed with a command to the wicked to cease relying upon mere mortals (2 Ne. 12:22).

Definitions

12:1 *Amoz*. The father of Isaiah; anglicized as Amoz in the KJV. This is not the same name as that of the prophet Amos, who was Isaiah's contemporary.

12:2 *the mountain of the Lord's house shall be established in the top of the mountains, and shall be exalted above the hills*. The "mountain of the Lord's house" is a phrase used to describe a temple (cf. Isa. 27:13; 56:7; 65:25; 66:20). The image of the temple being exalted "above the hills" may be a description of a time when the temple and the instruction therein are valued more than other edifices or values.

12:3 *he will teach us of his ways*. Referring to people who gain spiritual insight in the temples of the Lord. President Gordon B. Hinckley related this prophecy to receiving instruction from Church leaders at general conference (89).

12:3 *Zion*. A title often used to describe both Old and NEW JERUSALEM. Modern prophets have interpreted ZION in this verse to be a reference to the New Jerusalem (Smith, 362), one of the two world capitals during the MILLENNIUM (D&C 84:2–4; 133:12–13; Ether 13:3–12; cf. A of F 10).

12:4 *and they shall beat their swords into plowshares, and their spears into pruning-hooks*. Weapons of destruction are turned into tools of production, symbolizing millennial peace. This verse is often quoted when modern peace treaties are signed.

12:5 *light of the Lord*. Light often symbolizes the presence of God and his truth, knowledge, and intelligence.

12:6 *replenished from the east*. Influenced by the philosophies and religions of the east, a reference especially to Israel's pagan neighbors Assyria and Babylon.

12:6 *soothsayers*. One who claims to be able to foresee the future, often from various signs in nature.

12:6 *please themselves in the children of strangers*. Consorting with people outside of the covenant.

12:12 *day of the Lord*. A great and dreadful day when the Lord pours out punishments upon the wicked. The Second Coming is a DAY OF THE LORD.

12:13 *cedars of Lebanon, for they are high and lifted up; and upon all the oaks of Bashan*. Prized TREES, valued for their durable, strong wood; symbolic of pride and the upper classes of society.

12:16 *ships of the sea, and upon all the ships of Tarshish*. The location of Tarshish is uncertain. In

OUTLINE OF 2 NEPHI 12

I. Introduction to Isaiah's prophecies for Judah and Jerusalem (12:1)
II. Isaiah's vision of "the mountain of the Lord's house" (12:2–4)
  A. In the last days, the Lord's house will be in the mountains (12:2)
  B. People will receive instruction from the Lord (12:3)
  C. The Lord will judge the nations and they will turn from war to peace (12:4)
III. The Lord invites all of the house of Jacob to walk in the light of the Lord (12:5)
IV. The day of the Lord: the Lord's judgment of the proud, worldly idolaters (12:6–21)
  A. The house of Jacob has gone astray with materialism and idolatry (12:6–8)
  B. The proud and mighty will be humbled (12:9–17)
  C. Fear of the Lord and the earth shaking will terrorize the wicked (12:18–21)
V. Judah is commanded to stop relying on man instead of God (12:22)

ISA. CHAP. REVIEW: 2 NE. 12 // ISA. 2

the Old Testament it is connected with shipping and wealth (1 Kgs. 10:22; 22:48; Jer. 10:9; Ezek. 27:12).

12:16 *pleasant pictures.* Commonly thought to be a parallel description of the ships of Tarshish.

12:20) *cast his idols of silver, and his idols of gold, which he hath made for himself to worship, to the moles and to the bats.* In panic and embarrassment the wicked will try to hide their idols, or sins, from the Lord.

12:22 *Cease ye from man, whose breath is in his nostrils.* An imperative not to rely on human ingenuity.

Selected differences between Book of Mormon Isaiah (2 Ne. 12) and KJV Isaiah (Isa. 2) are shown in the accompanying table.

Latter-day applicability

The first part of this chapter speaks of the latter-day gathering of Israel and the establishment of two world capitals, Zion and Jerusalem (McConkie, 1:95). This prophecy invites all the

SELECTED DIFFERENCES BETWEEN B OF M ISA. (2 NE. 12) AND KJV ISA. (ISA. 2)

	BOOK OF MORMON		KJV ISAIAH	COMMENTARY
12:2	. . . in the last days, **when** the mountain of the Lord's house . . .	2:2	. . . in the last days, that the mountain of the Lord's house . . .	Suggesting that the establishment of a temple is a sign that the millennial reign of the Messiah is near.
12:5	. . . let us walk in the light of the Lord; **yea, come, for ye have all gone astray, every one to his wicked ways.**	2:5	. . . let us walk in the light of the Lord.	Explains the need for Jacob to leave his sins and return to the Lord.
12:6	Therefore, **O Lord,** thou hast forsaken thy people . . . replenished from the east, and **hearken unto** soothsayers . . .	2:6	Therefore thou hast forsaken thy people . . . replenished from the east, and are soothsayers . . .	Clarifies that Judah is looking to soothsayers, rather than being soothsayers.
12:9	And the mean man boweth **not** down, and the great man humbleth himself **not . . .**	2:9	And the mean man boweth down, and the great man humbleth himself . . .	Suggests that the men of all classes are refusing to worship the Lord.
12:10	**O ye wicked ones,** enter into the rock . . . the glory of his majesty **shall smite thee.**	2:10	Enter into the rock . . . the glory of his majesty.	Emphasizes that it is the glorious power of the Lord that will destroy the wicked when he comes.
12:12	For the day of the Lord of Hosts **soon cometh upon all nations, yea,** upon every one; **yea, upon the** proud and lofty, . . .	2:12	For the day of the Lord of hosts shall be upon every one that is proud and lofty . . .	Gives warning of when these events will occur.
12:14	. . . and upon all the hills, **and upon all the nations which** are lifted up, **and upon every people;**	2:14	. . . and upon all the hills that are lifted up,	Clarifies that hills, trees, etc. are metaphors for proud peoples and nations.
12:16	**And upon all the ships of the sea,** and upon all the ships of Tarshish . . .	2:16	And upon all the ships of Tarshish . . .	Restores text retained in the Septuagint, an ancient Greek translation of the Old Testament.

world to come to temples in Zion and Jerusalem to worship the Lord. Latter-day Saints recognize that one of the two world capitals will be built on the American continent. Isaiah described the peace of the Millennium in the memorable image of beating swords into plowshares. The second half of the chapter describes the day of the Lord when all of the earth will be judged. It describes the proud and the wicked and their destruction at the Second Coming.

The whole chapter effectively contrasts key behaviors of the righteous and the wicked. The righteous go to the temples to worship the Lord, walk in the light of the Lord, and dwell with him in peace. The proud and the wicked, on the other hand, hearken to soothsayers, fill their lands with temporal wealth, and worship idols. They are embarrassed, panic, and flee into hiding places at his coming. Thus, the house of Jacob is warned against materialism and idolatry and undue trust in mortals instead of the Lord. At the Second Coming the proud will be humbled and destroyed. Thereby, Isaiah's words invite latter-day people to so live that the Second Coming will be a day of rejoicing rather than a day of shame and sorrow.

See also Jesus Christ, second coming of.

BIBLIOGRAPHY

Hinckley, Gordon B. Conference Report, October 2000.

Smith, Joseph. *Teachings of the Prophet Joseph Smith*. Selected by Joseph Fielding Smith. Salt Lake City: Deseret Book, 1976.

McConkie, Bruce R. *The Promised Messiah*. Salt Lake City: Deseret Book, 1978.

VLL

Isaiah chap. review: 2 Nephi 13 // Isaiah 3

Background and synopsis

Continuing the set of prophecies of destruction directed to the southern kingdom of JUDAH (2 Ne. 12–14 // Isa. 2–4), Isaiah prophesied that Judah would fall and Jerusalem would be ruined as all their leaders, soldiers, prophets, craftsmen, and teachers would be removed, leaving children and base types as rulers in the land. Famine, poverty, and anarchy would follow (2 Ne. 13:1–7). This prophecy was fulfilled anciently in 586 B.C. when Nebuchadnezzar conquered and carried away many of the inhabitants of Judah to Babylon (2 Kgs. 24:10–16). The chapter continues with an explanation of why such a catastrophe awaited the apostate people of Judah (2 Ne. 13:8–26). The men were particularly condemned for provoking the Lord with their sins and oppressing one another (2 Ne. 13:8–15). In an extended metaphor, the women are referred to as "the daughters of Zion." Like all good daughters of the covenant, they should have been keeping themselves pure and virtuous, preparing for the day when the bridegroom (a type for the Lord), to whom they are espoused, would arrive. Instead, this worldly people were doing just the contrary. Rather than virtuously preparing for the bridegroom and honoring their covenants, they were prostituting themselves.

OUTLINE OF 2 NEPHI 13

- I. The fall of Judah (13:1–8)
  - A. Men of power, wealth, intellect, and skill will be taken away (13:1–3)
  - B. The young, inexperienced, and base are left to rule and prey upon one another (13:4–8)
- II. The Lord cites the reasons for Judah's punishment (13:9–15)
  - A. They have provoked the Lord with sin (13:9–11)
  - B. They have oppressed one another (13:12–15)
- III. The metaphor of the immoral daughters of Zion (13:16–26)
  - A. Their seductive behavior is described and punished (13:16–17)
  - B. Their fashions and finery will perish (13:18–23)
  - C. They will be humbled like slaves, and their men will die in war (13:24–26)

ISA. CHAP. REVIEW: 2 NE. 13 // ISA. 3

They had decked themselves in all manner of worldly adornments to attract adulterous (idolatrous) lovers and were wantonly seeking for pleasure in promiscuity and indulgence (2 Ne. 13:16–23). Isaiah warned that because of their sins, all the temporal, vain, and worldly adornments with which the proud "daughters of Zion" had hoped to beautify themselves would be taken away, leaving them disgusting and repulsive, rather than tempting and alluring. In their humbled and contemptible state, they would sit at the gates of the city and wail but to no avail, for the lovers they sought would have fallen "by the sword" (2 Ne. 13:24–26), and those remaining would not take these foul and filthy daughters, regardless of what they offered (2 Ne. 14:1). Thus the people are taught that any alternative to the Lord's plan of happiness would ultimately fail and leave them in sorrow. From another perspective, this chapter could be viewed as a rebuke against the wicked men of Judah for their weak, selfish, and sinful leadership (2 Ne. 13:1–15), followed by a rebuke of the immoral women of Zion (2 Ne. 13:16–26).

Definitions

13:1 *staff of bread, and the whole stay of water.* The prophecy that the Lord would take away bread and water is probably a reference to physical famine but could also allude to loss of spiritual blessings.

13:6 *thou hast clothing, be thou our ruler.* A reference to a time when Judah is so poor and devoid of leaders that even the possession of clothing would qualify someone to be a leader.

13:8 *to provoke the eyes of his glory.* To defy or anger the Lord.

13:9 *the show of their countenance doth witness against them.* Their outward appearance bespeaks their inward guilt.

13:9 *sin to be even as Sodom.* Sodom was a city destroyed by the Lord because of its sexual iniquity and pride (Gen. 19; Ezek. 16:48–50). Consequently, Sodom became a type for wickedness.

13:15 *grind the faces of the poor.* To oppress the poor. According to the law of Moses oppressing the poor was a grievous offense (e.g., Ex. 22:21–24; Deut. 15:7–11).

13:16 *daughters of Zion.* A metaphor for the people of Judah who are espoused, or under covenant, to Jehovah. The daughter of Zion is also used as a personification of the city of Jerusalem (e.g., Isa. 1:8).

13:16 *walk with stretched-forth necks and wanton eyes, walking and mincing as they go, and making a tinkling with their feet.* Referring to the actions of proud and vain women who are obsessed with their appearance.

13:17 *discover their secret parts.* A metaphor for humiliation.

13:18–23 *their tinkling ornaments [to] and the veils.* Items of jewelry and clothing. A modern translation of Isaiah helps clarify the items: "In that day the Lord will snatch away their finery: the bangles and headbands and crescent necklaces, the earrings and bracelets and veils, the headdresses and ankle chains and sashes, the perfume bottles and charms, the signet rings and nose rings, the fine robes and the capes and cloaks, the purses and mirrors, and the linen garments and tiaras and shawls" (NIV). These items

SELECTED DIFFERENCES BETWEEN B OF M ISA. (2 NE. 13) AND KJV ISA. (ISA. 3)

	BOOK OF MORMON		KJV ISAIAH	COMMENTARY
13:6	. . . Thou hast clothing, be thou our ruler, and let **not** this ruin **come** under thy hand—	3:6	. . . Thou hast clothing, be thou our ruler, and let this ruin be under thy hand:	Clarifies that the plea is for the brother to repair the ruin, rather than simply assume kingship over it.
13:11	Wo unto the wicked, **for they shall perish;** for the reward . . .	3:11	Woe unto the wicked! it shall be ill with him: for the reward . . .	Specifies that the punishment of the wicked is destruction.

ISA. CHAP. REVIEW: 2 NE. 14 // ISA. 4

are a symbol of the vanity and iniquity of the people.

13:25 *Thy men.* Men in Judah will be killed in the destruction or war.

13:26 *her gates.* A reference to Jerusalem personified (cf. 13:1; Lam. 1).

Selected differences between Book of Mormon Isaiah (2 Ne. 13) and KJV Isaiah (Isa. 3) are shown in the accompanying table.

Latter-day applicability

This chapter warns latter-day covenant people that the Lord will not allow them to prosper in wickedness. It particularly warns that they must avoid pride, vanity, selfishness, worldliness, and oppression of the needy. It should remind them that true joy is found in trusting in the Lord's plan of happiness and in the Lord's covenants, for the worldly selfish avenues one might pursue will pass away, leaving only sorrow.

VLL

Isaiah chap. review: 2 Nephi 14 // Isaiah 4

Background and synopsis

Earlier, Isaiah prophesied the judgments that would come upon the apostate daughters of Zion because of their pride (2 Ne. 13:16–14:1). This destruction occurred anciently with the Babylonian devastation of Jerusalem in 586 B.C. But the pride of the daughters of Zion and their humiliation is a type that can be applied to the house of Israel in many periods of time. Nephi[1], in his interpretation of Isaiah 2–14, identified pride as an important element in the Jews' rejection of the Messiah and their eventual destruction (2 Ne. 25:12–15) as well as the downfall of the Nephites (2 Ne. 26:9–11). He also prophesied that pride would be one of the characteristics of the latter-day Gentiles (2 Ne. 26:20; 28:12) that would lead to their destruction unless they repent (2 Ne. 28:15–17).

This destruction of Israel would be followed by a restoration. Isaiah prophesied of the Restoration and blessings that would be poured out upon a righteous remnant of Israel, called the "branch of the Lord" (2 Ne. 14:2). The Lord will cleanse and purify his people in the millennial day (2 Ne. 14:4), and he will manifest his presence among them as he did in the days of the Exodus with a cloud of smoke by day and a flaming fire by night (2 Ne. 14:5; cf. Ex. 13:21).

Definitions

14:1 *And in that day.* A point of reference in a narrative. This verse is the final verse of the previous chapter in the Hebrew text and in Joseph Smith's translation of the biblical text of Isaiah. Here, the phrase probably refers to 2 Nephi 13:25–26, indicating the time when the men are killed. May also be a reference to the latter days (e.g., 2 Ne. 21:11; 24:3).

14:1 *seven women shall take hold of one man, saying: We will eat our own bread, and wear our own apparel; only let us be called by thy name to take away our reproach.* Suggests a scarcity of men because they were killed, as described in 2 Nephi 13:25, or a lack of willing, able men to be fathers. Widowhood, singleness, and childlessness were often desperate situations for a woman in ancient Israel (e.g., Gen. 30:1; Ruth; 1 Sam. 1:1–18). Women needed a husband not only to provide for the family but also to father a son so that the family inheritance could be passed on and to ensure that there would be someone to care for them in their old age. Hence singleness and childlessness were viewed as a "reproach." Here the situation may serve as a warning to the "daughters of Zion" of what awaits them for their worldliness and sin

OUTLINE OF 2 NEPHI 14

I. Seven women seek one man (14:1)
II. A holy people to be established in Zion (14:2–6)
    A. The righteous remnant of the people will be purified and made holy (14:2–4)
    B. The city of Jerusalem will be glorified as a place of holiness and refuge (14:5–6)

ISA. CHAP. REVIEW: 2 NE. 15 // ISA. 5

described in the previous chapter (2 Ne. 13:16–26).

14:2 *the branch of the Lord.* In this context the branch of the Lord appears to be a righteous remnant of Israel, who will be blessed, in contrast to the apostate daughters of Zion, who will be destroyed (cf. 2 Ne. 13:16–26). In some passages the term "branch" refers to the Messiah or his servants (e.g., Isa. 11:1; Jer. 23:5–6; 33:15–17; Zech. 3:8–10).

14:4 *washed away the filth of the daughters of Zion, and shall have purged the blood of Jerusalem from the midst thereof.* Metaphors of cleansing and purifying.

14:3 *holy.* A person (or place/object) which is consecrated for a sacred purpose.

14:5 *cloud and smoke by day and the shining of a flaming fire by night.* Symbols for the protection and presence of the Lord (cf. Ex. 13:21–22).

Latter-day applicability

The Lord promises in this chapter that he will cleanse the repentant and will favor them with his presence and protection. Ultimately the glory of Zion will be realized when a purified covenant people is redeemed and cleansed during the Millennium and when the Saints will, like Israel in the wilderness, enjoy the presence and protection of the Lord, day and night, as symbolized by a cloud and flaming fire.

VLL

Isaiah chap. review: 2 Nephi 15 // Isaiah 5

Background and synopsis

One of the most prevalent images found in Isaiah is the metaphor of Jehovah as a nurturing husbandman, caring for his crop Israel (Isa. 27:2–6; 28:23–29; 41:18–19; 44:2–4). Such a metaphor serves to illustrate the efforts the Lord has made to raise a covenant people and the way those people have responded and will respond to his care. Second Nephi 15 begins with an impressive example of this kind of imagery (2 Ne. 15:1–7). It commences as a song, possibly similar to those sung by the men of Judah during the grape harvest. The owner and husbandman of the vineyard is referred to as the "well-beloved" (2 Ne. 15:1) and identified as Jehovah, the Lord of Hosts (2 Ne. 15:7); the vineyard itself is clearly identified as the house of Israel (2 Ne. 15:7). The metaphor details how the well-beloved invested all the care requisite for an abundant harvest from this vineyard, yet instead of bringing forth sweet grapes it produced worthless, wild grapes (2 Ne. 15:2). In frustration, the husbandman determined to lay waste to the vineyard by ceasing to take care of it and withdrawing his protection from it. Consequently the vines would be trampled and ravaged, and eventually they would be displaced from their choice location by noxious vegetation, even briers and thorns (2 Ne. 15:3–7). Thus, the lesson of the vineyard gave a powerful warning to ancient Israel. If they would not respond to the nurturing direction and loving kindness of Jehovah, he would abandon them, allow them to be destroyed, and permit another people to possess their choice land.

Following this opening metaphor Isaiah specifically chronicled the "wild grapes" or evil works the people were bringing forth and the woe, desolation, captivity, and judgment that would come upon them as a consequence of their rebellion (2 Ne. 15:8–25).

The chapter finishes with a prophecy of destruction (2 Ne. 15:26–30), which may apply to two different time periods: Isaiah's own time and the latter days. The interpretation of the prophecy depends upon the time period in which it is to be fulfilled. As it pertains to Isaiah's time, the prophecy contains imagery which seems to be describing an attack upon the rebellious covenant people by a terrifying army whose invasion would be so swift that none would escape, and that would leave darkness and sorrow in its wake (2 Ne. 15:26–30). This prophecy was fulfilled several times in antiquity. The Assyrians conquered and deported the ten tribes of the northern kingdom of Israel in 722 B.C. and destroyed many of the cities in Judah in 701 B.C. In 586 B.C. the Babylonians conquered the southern kingdom of Judah, destroyed Jerusalem and the temple, and exiled many of the inhabitants. Again in A.D. 70 the Romans destroyed the temple and scattered the Jews.

The prophecy in 2 Nephi 15:26–30 has been applied by modern prophets to the latter days as

ISA. CHAP. REVIEW: 2 NE. 15 // ISA. 5

a prophecy of the gathering of Israel (Pratt, 16:84; Smith, 1:146; Richards, 229). They have interpreted the "ensign" to be the restoration of the gospel that signals to the nations to gather from the "end of the earth." Those that heed its message will "come with speed swiftly; none shall be weary nor stumble among them" (2 Ne. 15:26). This interpretation makes 2 Nephi 15 an account of apostasy, judgment, and restoration, a pattern that is found throughout Isaiah.

Definitions

15:1 *my well-beloved.* A reference to the Lord.

15:1 *a very fruitful hill.* The Hebrew literally means "a horn, a child of fatness," likely referring to a horn-like mountain peak with exceptionally fertile soil.

15:2 *choicest vine.* Not just ordinary vines (Hebrew *gephen*) but rather the superior vines (Hebrew *soreq*), which produce the choicest of bluish-red grapes.

15:2, 4 *wild grapes.* From a Hebrew word meaning stinking, sour, worthless things.

15:5 *take away the hedge thereof, and it shall be eaten up; and I will break down the wall.* Symbolizes that the Lord will withdraw his divine protection and allow his people to be destroyed by their enemies.

15:6 *briers and thorns.* Noxious weeds. In this instance likely a metaphor referring to another people displacing the covenant people. For example, following 722 B.C. pagan peoples were introduced into the northern kingdom (2 Kgs. 17:24), and after the destruction of the temple by the Romans in A.D. 70 foreign peoples inhabited the lands of the southern kingdom.

15:7 *behold, a cry.* The cry of the oppressed, which the Lord promised Israel he would hear (cf. Ex. 22:23; Gen. 18:20–21).

15:8 *join house to house, till there can be no place.* A reference to the practice of purchasing and hoarding land in violation of the law in Israel that hereditary land should be inalienable, reverting to the original family owners every fiftieth year (cf. Lev. 25:23–28).

OUTLINE OF 2 NEPHI 15

I. The song of the vineyard (15:1–7)
   A. Jehovah plants his vineyard (Israel and Judah) and cares for it (15:1–2)
   B. The vineyard brings forth worthless fruit (15:2)
   C. Jehovah forsakes the vineyard (15:3–7)
      1. He laments the vineyard's failure (15:3–4)
      2. He removes his protection from the vineyard (15:5)
      3. He ceases to cultivate and water the vineyard (15:6)
      4. Noxious weeds take over the vineyard (15:6)
      5. He laments the lack of justice and righteousness in the vineyard (15:7)

II. Description of the sins and punishments of the people (15:8–25)
   A. People become land mongers, therefore the land will be left desolate and unproductive (15:8–10)
   B. People are drunkards, gluttons, and unthankful, therefore they will be taken captive, humbled, and relegated to hell while the Lord is exalted and strangers occupy their lands (15:11–17)
   C. People seek sin, challenge righteous values, become proud, and take bribes; therefore the Lord will destroy them (15:18–25)

III. Two interpretations of a prophecy: destruction and gathering (15:26–30)
   A. In Isaiah's day an invading army will swiftly destroy the rebellious covenant people (15:26–30)
   B. In the latter days the righteous will swiftly gather to the restored gospel ensign (15:26–30)

ISA. CHAP. REVIEW: 2 NE. 15 // ISA. 5

15:10 *ten acres of vineyard shall yield one bath.* Literally "ten yokes," or the amount of land ten yoke of oxen could plow in a day, estimated to be about five acres, which would produce one bath or about six gallons. These values suggest crop failure and famine.

15:10 *seed of a homer shall yield an ephah.* One homer equals about fifty-eight gallons; an ephah equals about six gallons. These values suggest crop failure and famine.

15:13 *because they have no knowledge.* Perhaps better translated as "for lack of knowledge." Perhaps an allusion to the fact that Israel did not know the Lord nor his teachings (Isa. 1:3; cf. Amos 8:11–12; Hosea 4:6).

15:14 *hell hath enlarged herself.* The Hebrew word *Sheol* represents both death and hell. Here the destruction and captivity of the wicked Israelites is described with the image of *Sheol* personified as a monster that swallows up the Israelites with all of their pomp and pride (cf. 2 Ne. 9:10).

15:15 *mean man shall be brought down, and the mighty man.* The average or ordinary man and the "mighty man" will both be brought down, indicating a universal humbling of the men of Israel.

15:17 *lambs feed after their manner.* Perhaps better translated as "lambs feed in their pastures," where "their pastures" refers to those of the displaced covenant people and the lambs belong to the strangers who replace them in the land.

15:17 *waste places of the fat ones shall strangers eat.* Suggests that land once held by prosperous but wicked covenant people will be inhabited by another people.

15:18 *draw iniquity with cords of vanity, and sin as it were with a cart rope.* The image is of humans yoked to a cart full of their own iniquity that they drag behind them, suggesting that rather than fleeing temptation, they were anxiously looking for opportunity to sin. A modern translation reads, "Woe to those who draw sin along with cords of deceit, and wickedness as with cart ropes" (NIV).

15:22 *mighty to drink wine, and men of strength to mingle strong drink.* A modern translation reads, "Those who are heroes at drinking wine and champions at mixing drinks" (NIV).

15:23 *justify the wicked for reward.* To acquit criminals for a bribe.

15:23 *take away the righteousness of the righteous from him.* To deprive the innocent of their rights or justice.

15:24 *fire devoureth the stubble, and the flame consumeth the chaff.* A fire that burns fast and furious, consuming all.

15:24 *root shall be rottenness, and their blossoms shall go up as dust.* The root and the flower probably represent the whole plant. The root is the foundation of the plant and the flower may represent its posterity. Those who reject the teachings of the Lord are without foundation and will be completely destroyed.

15:26 *ensign to the nations.* A standard, banner, flag, or signal to which nations are to rally (2 Ne. 21:12). Here it calls all of the nations of the world to gather to punish Israel. It has also been interpreted to represent the restoration of the gospel and the ensuing gathering of Israel. *See* Ensign.

15:26 *hiss.* To whistle for or call.

15:27 *None shall slumber nor sleep; neither shall the girdle of their loins be loosed, nor the latchet of their shoes be broken.* Suggesting such speedy travel that there will be no time to sleep or change clothing.

15:28–30 *Whose arrows shall [to] the heavens thereof.* Imagery perhaps describing the weapons and attack of an invading army during Isaiah's time. As applied to the latter-day Restoration and gathering, these are images of the gathering of Israel who come in haste.

Latter-day applicability

The song of the vineyard reminds Latter-day Saints how the Lord nurtures and cares for them. He will provide for them all that is necessary to do his will and accomplish his designs. In return he expects his people to respond to his loving kindness by remaining faithful to gospel covenants. If they fail to do so they can expect the Lord's judgments. He will withdraw his Spirit, leaving them without protection—either spiritual or physical. They are left to themselves to suffer the consequences of their own disobedience, which can result in desolation, captivity, and destruction. Nephi[1] explained that unless

ISA. CHAP. REVIEW: 2 NE. 16 // ISA. 6

the wicked repent, "the devil will grasp them with his everlasting chains, and they be stirred up to anger, and perish" (2 Ne. 28:19). This warning should cause Latter-day Saints to seek the blessings promised in a similar vineyard song, wherein they are promised that if the vineyard responds, they will blossom, bud, and finally "fill the face of the world with fruit" (Isa. 27:2–6). This chapter also warns Saints against worldliness, drunkenness, gluttony, pride, arrogance, ungratefulness, and calling "evil good, and good evil." Modern prophets have interpreted this chapter as a wonderful promise of a latter-day restoration of the gospel as the Lord lifts his "ensign to the nations" to which all are invited to come (e.g., Pratt, 16:84).

BIBLIOGRAPHY

Pratt, Orson. *Journal of Discourses*. 26 vols. London: Latter-day Saints' Book Depot, 1854–86.

Richards, LeGrand. *A Marvelous Work and a Wonder.* Salt Lake City: Deseret Book, 1976.

Smith, Joseph Fielding. *Doctrines of Salvation*. Compiled by Bruce R. McConkie. 3 vols. Salt Lake City: Bookcraft, 1954–56.

TBB

Isaiah chap. review: 2 Nephi 16 // Isaiah 6

Background and synopsis

Second Nephi 16 contains an account of the prophetic call of Isaiah, who received a vision of the Lord on his throne in which he was told to cry repentance in the land of Israel. Isaiah was warned that because the people would not respond to his teachings a scattering would occur, but a future remnant would eventually return to the Lord (2 Ne. 16:9–13). The call came in the year of Uzziah's death (740 B.C.). Nephi[1]'s inclusion of Isaiah's vision of the Lord on his throne fulfills Nephi's purpose statement in 2 Nephi 11:2–3 where he identified three witnesses who had seen the Redeemer: himself, his brother Jacob, and Isaiah.

Definitions

16:1 *Uzziah*. King in Judah, also known as Azariah (2 Kgs. 14:21), who reigned from 767 to 740 B.C.

16:1 *train*. Hem of the Lord's royal garment.

16:1 *temple*. The house of the Lord. It is not clear whether Isaiah is seeing a vision of the Lord in his heavenly temple, or if the Lord is appearing to Isaiah in the temple in Jerusalem.

16:2, 6 *seraphim*. Angelic beings represented with wings. The Hebrew word literally means "burning ones."

16:2 *wings*. A symbol of power to move or to act (D&C 77:4).

16:4 *smoke*. A symbol of the glory of God (Ex. 19:18).

16:5 *Wo is unto me! for I am undone; because I*

OUTLINE OF 2 NEPHI 16

I. Isaiah's vision of the Lord and his attendants (2 Ne. 16:1–4)
   A. Isaiah beholds the glorified Lord upon an exalted throne in the temple (16:1)
   B. Isaiah sees seraphim praising the Lord; such praise causes the temple to quake and fill with smoke (16:2–4)

II. Isaiah's qualifications and call to the ministry (16:5–8)
   A. Isaiah feels unworthy in Jehovah's presence (16:5)
   B. Isaiah's tongue is cleansed by a live coal taken from the altar by one of the seraphim (16:6–7)
   C. Isaiah's willingness to serve the Lord (16:8)

III. Isaiah's ministerial rejection foretold, yet he is promised that a remnant (a tenth) shall return, or repent (16:9–13)
   A. Isaiah is warned that the people will harden their hearts against his message (16:9–10)
   B. Isaiah asks the Lord how long he must cry repentance and is told until the inhabitants are scattered and there are none left to warn (16:11–12; cf. 2 Ne. 25:9)
   C. Isaiah is told that a remnant shall return (16:13)

ISA. CHAP. REVIEW: 2 NE. 16 // ISA. 6

am a man of unclean lips. Expresses Isaiah's feelings of unworthiness to be in the presence of the Lord.

16:6 *live coal.* The seraph takes a coal from the altar. This could be a charred portion of the burnt offering from the great altar as a symbol of the Atonement (Lev. 16:14–19; 17:11), or it could be a coal from the incense altar as a symbol of purification (Lev. 16:12; Num. 16:46–47).

16:6 *altar.* A place where sacrifices are offered in similitude of the Atonement. If the vision is of the Jerusalem temple, this altar could be the great altar for burnt offerings in front of the temple or the incense altar in the holy place before the veil.

16:7 *laid it upon my mouth, and said: Lo, this has touched thy lips.* An act symbolizing the power of the Atonement to cleanse Isaiah of his sins preparatory to his prophetic calling.

16:8 *Here am I; send me.* Isaiah's expression of his willingness to serve. The Savior used this same phrase to express his willingness to fulfill the Father's plan in the premortal council (Abr. 3:27). Similar expressions are found in Genesis 22:1; Exodus 3:4; 1 Samuel 3:4–8.

16:10 *Make the heart of this people fat, and make their ears heavy, and shut their eyes.* The heart, ears, and eyes are the physical senses and represent the spiritual capacity to see, hear, and understand the word of the Lord. On the surface it appears as if the Lord is telling Isaiah to cause the people to reject his words. The Lord knows the hearts of the children of Israel. This statement is a prophecy to Isaiah that the children of Israel will exercise their own agency and reject his message of repentance. This is not the Lord's desire, but it is what will happen. It should be read as the prophesied result of Isaiah's mission and not the divine purpose (Dummelow, 417). Isaiah's words would cause the people to confront the truth with their heart, ears, and eyes, but they would not receive it. Zechariah described this process of rejection: "They refused to hearken . . . and stopped their ears, that they should not hear. Yea, they made their hearts as an adamant stone, lest they should hear the law" (Zech. 7:11–12). The heart is an organ of understanding. The people were made blind because they hardened their hearts: "For this people's heart is waxed gross" (Matt. 13:13–15), and thus they received a "lesser portion of the word" (Alma 12:9–10).

16:12 *And the Lord have removed men far away.* An allusion to the scattering of Israel that occurred in 722 B.C., 586 B.C., and A.D. 70.

16:13 *tenth, and they shall return, and shall be eaten, as a teil-tree, and as an oak whose substance is in them when they cast their leaves; so the holy seed shall be the substance thereof.* A part of Israel would return, and like the oak and terebinth, which though they are eaten or consumed right to their substance or stumps, yet they possess a seed in them that can regenerate.

16:13 *holy seed.* A reference to the covenant people (Ezra 9:2; Mosiah 15:10–12) or Jesus Christ (Gal. 3:16) or both.

SELECTED DIFFERENCES BETWEEN B OF M ISA. (2 NE. 16) AND KJV ISA. (ISA. 6)

	BOOK OF MORMON		KJV ISAIAH	COMMENTARY
16:2 16:6	Above it stood the **seraphim** . . . Then flew one of the **seraphim** unto me . . .	6:2 6:6	Above it stood the seraphims . . . Then flew one of the seraphims unto me . . .	A grammatical correction, seraphim is already a plural form in Hebrew, so seraphims is a double plural, such as using "mice" rather than "mices."
16:9	. . . Hear ye indeed, but **they understood** not; and see ye indeed, but **they perceived** not.	6:9	. . . Hear ye indeed, but understand not; and see ye indeed, but perceive not.	Clarifies that the people will reject Isaiah's message, but not at the Lord's command.

Selected differences between Book of Mormon Isaiah (2 Ne. 16) and KJV Isaiah (Isa. 6) are shown in the accompanying table.

Latter-day applicability

This revelation beautifully illustrates the divine manifestations that may attend the call of a prophet (e.g., 1 Ne. 1; Ezek. 1; Rev. 1, 4). Latter-day Saints can liken Isaiah's call to themselves and remember their covenant responsibility to invite all to come unto Christ (Mosiah 18:8–9). Furthermore, although Saints may feel inadequate with their callings, like Isaiah, they may become qualified and sanctified by the cleansing fire of the Holy Ghost at the altar of faith as they partake of the atonement of Jesus Christ. As they do so, they are led to continually proclaim, "Here am I; send me" (2 Ne. 16:8) and to "speak with the tongue of angels, and shout praises unto the Holy One of Israel" (2 Ne. 31:13).

BIBLIOGRAPHY

Dummelow, J. R. *The One-Volume Bible Commentary*. New York: Macmillan, 1936.

FEW

Isaiah chap. review: 2 Nephi 17 // Isaiah 7

Background and synopsis

During the later half of the eighth century B.C. ASSYRIA, in northern Mesopotamia, was establishing an empire throughout most of the ancient Near East. By 738 B.C. the Assyrian king Tiglath-pileser III had subjugated among others, the smaller states of SYRIA and Israel and forced them to pay tribute to the Assyrian empire or face military reprisal. In an effort to free themselves from vassalage, Rezin, the king of Syria, and Pekah, the king of Israel (also called Ephraim), formed a military alliance to fight Assyria. They invited the king of Judah to join their rebellious confederacy, but neither Jotham nor his successor on the throne, Ahaz, would ally himself with the rebellion. Feeling that JUDAH was vital to the success of the revolt, Rezin and Pekah threatened to besiege Jerusalem in an attempt to remove its uncooperative king Ahaz and place a more supportive ruler on the throne, a man known only as the son of Tabeal (2 Ne. 17:1–2, 6; cf. 2 Kgs. 15:37–16:6). About 734 B.C. the Lord sent the prophet Isaiah to Ahaz, the king of Judah, to assure him that the

OUTLINE OF 2 NEPHI 17

- I. Syro-Ephraimite coalition threatens war against Judah (17:1–2)
  - A. To date, the coalition could not prevail against Judah (17:1)
  - B. Judah is deeply distressed by the threat (17:2)
- II. Isaiah prophesies to Ahaz king of Judah (17:3–25)
  - A. Prophecy that the Syro-Ephraimite coalition will fail (17:3–9)
    1. Ahaz told not to fear the coalition (17:3–4)
    2. Coalition's plan to put a new king on the throne of Judah will fail (17:5–7)
    3. Within 65 years Ephraim and Damascus will both be destroyed (17:8–9)
  - B. Immanuel prophecy (17:10–16)
    1. Ahaz refuses invitation to ask for a sign from the Lord (17:10–12)
    2. Isaiah chastises Ahaz (17:13)
    3. Lord gives Ahaz a sign anyway (17:14–16)
       - a. Immanuel will be born of a virgin (17:14)
       - b. Before Immanuel reaches age of understanding, perhaps eight years old, the kings of Syria and Ephraim will be removed (17:15–16)
  - C. Prophecy against Judah (17:17–25)
    1. Judah will be invaded and besieged by Assyria and Egypt (17:17–19)
    2. People will be captured, humiliated, and enslaved (17:20)
    3. Once-cultivated land will be forsaken and overrun by briers and thorns, leaving it suitable only for hunters and grazing animals (17:21–25)

ISA. CHAP. REVIEW: 2 NE. 17 // ISA. 7

Syro-Ephraimite alliance would not succeed in its plans and that within sixty-five years the kingdom of Israel would cease to exist (2 Ne. 17:3–8). The prophecy was fulfilled in 722 B.C. when Assyria conquered the kingdom of Israel and carried away some of its inhabitants, now known as the ten lost tribes. Isaiah further promised Ahaz that if he did "not believe," he would "not be established" (2 Ne. 17:9). Isaiah then invited Ahaz to ask for a sign from the Lord to verify that the message he delivered was indeed from God (2 Ne. 17:11). Ahaz was a wicked man who served false gods, even practicing child sacrifice (2 Kgs. 16:1–2; 2 Chr. 28:1–4). He had no interest in trusting the Lord and so refused Isaiah's invitation by pretending he did not want to offend the Lord in asking for a sign. Isaiah subsequently chastised Ahaz for his hypocrisy and then declared that God would give him a sign anyway. He proclaimed that a virgin would conceive and bear a son, even IMMANUEL. He further prophesied that before the child reached the age of understanding good and evil, both the king of Syria and the king of Israel would be removed (2 Ne. 17:12–16). Moreover, he prophesied that Judah would also be attacked by Assyria and Egypt and left desolate. Consequently once-productive agricultural land would be overrun by briers and thorns, leaving it suitable only for hunters and grazing animals (2 Ne. 17:17–25).

Despite these prophecies, Ahaz, noted for his wickedness (2 Kgs. 16:2–4), did not trust the Lord to protect Judah from the Syro-Ephraimite threat but rather plundered the temple in Jerusalem to buy protection from the king of Assyria (2 Kgs. 16:5–9).

Definitions

17:1, 3, 10, 12 *Ahaz.* A wicked and idolatrous king of Judah who reigned 735–715 B.C. (2 Kgs. 16; 2 Chr. 28).

17:1 *Jotham.* A righteous king of Judah who reigned 740–735 B.C. (2 Kgs. 15:32–38).

17:1 *Uzziah.* A righteous and prosperous king of Judah who reigned 767–740 B.C. Also known as Azariah (2 Kgs. 15).

The Prophet Isaiah Foretells Christ's Birth; *painting by Harry Anderson; courtesy VRL. "Behold, a virgin shall conceive, and shall bear a son, and shall call his name Immanuel" (2 Ne. 17:14).*

ISA. CHAP. REVIEW: 2 NE. 17 // ISA. 7

17:1, 6, 17 *Judah.* Refers to the southern kingdom formed as a result of the political division of the twelve tribes of Israel after the death of Solomon 931 B.C. (1 Kgs. 12).

17:1, 4, 8 *Rezin.* A king who ruled southern Syria from his capital in Damascus. In this text he is referred to as the king of Syria. He led the anti-Assyrian coalition and reigned until Syria was incorporated into Assyria (732 B.C.).

17:1, 2, 4, 5, 8 *Syria.* Area northeast of Israel.

17:1 *Pekah.* Wicked king of Israel who reigned 740–732 B.C. He occupied the throne after assassinating his predecessor Pekahiah (2 Kgs. 15:23, 25–31).

17:1, 4, 5, 9 *Remaliah.* Father of Pekah. Little is known about him.

17:1 *Israel.* Refers to the northern kingdom formed as a result of the division of the twelve tribes of Israel after the death of Solomon (1 Kgs. 12; 931 B.C.). Also called Ephraim. *See* Israel, kingdom of.

17:2, 13 *house of David.* Refers to the kings of the Davidic dynasty in Judah.

17:2, 5, 8, 9 *Ephraim.* In this context, another name for the northern kingdom of Israel.

17:3 *Shearjashub.* Son of Isaiah whose name means "a remnant will return." This symbolic name constituted a prophecy to the covenant people.

17:3 *conduit of the upper pool.* Likely refers to an aqueduct that carried water from a pool formed by the Gihon spring in the Kidron valley that borders the eastern side of ancient Jerusalem. Ahaz was possibly inspecting the aqueduct to be certain it would provide water during a siege by the Syro-Ephraimite coalition.

17:3 *fuller's field.* Field used as a washing site. It is thought to be located at the confluence of the Hinnom and Kidron valleys to the south of Jerusalem.

17:4 *two tails of these smoking firebrands.* The smoldering ends of two sticks, Syria and Israel, soon to be extinguished and possessing no real heat or danger.

17:6 *son of Tabeal.* A person whose name is otherwise unknown, whom the Syro-Ephraimite coalition wanted to put on the throne of Judah apparently because he, unlike Ahaz, would join and support the anti-Assyrian rebellion.

17:8 *Damascus.* Rezin's capital in southern Syria.

17:9 *Samaria.* Capital of the northern kingdom of Israel.

17:12 *tempt the Lord.* To put God to the test, an act prohibited by Deuteronomy 6:16. There is hypocrisy in Ahaz's hiding behind the prohibition, for he was not a servant of Jehovah and cared little about offending him.

17:13 *weary.* To wear out. Used to indicate that someone has had enough of an opponent's argument.

17:14 *virgin.* The Hebrew term translated here as "virgin" can refer not only to a woman who has "never known a man" but also more generally to any young maiden of child-bearing age. *See* Virgin.

17:14 *Immanuel.* A name or title meaning "God is with us." Here the name appears to foreshadow the birth of two individuals: (1) Jesus of Nazareth, the Messiah, who would be born to the virgin Mary (cf. Matt. 1:18–25; 1 Ne. 11:13–20). The title "Immanuel" precisely describes the mortal ministry of Jesus Christ—the God who came in the flesh to deliver all (cf. 1 Ne. 11). (2) A child to be born in Isaiah's day. Some scholars see this as a reference to the birth of Hezekiah, son of Ahaz, who would become a righteous king of Judah; others suggest that perhaps it is a reference to any son soon to be born to a young woman. The language of 2 Nephi 18:1–4 // Isaiah 8:1–4 indicates that the prophecy of the son to be born in Isaiah's day is referring to Maher-shalal-hash-baz, a son of Isaiah himself. In the context of this prophecy the message to Ahaz is that by the time the child is old enough to make decisions, the Syro-Ephraimite coalition will no longer be a threat (17:15–16). The fulfillment of this prophecy was to be a type of Christ—the God who would be "with" Judah and deliver her from her enemies.

17:17 *day that Ephraim departed from Judah.* Refers to the division of the united kingdom of Israel into the southern kingdom of Judah and the northern kingdom of Israel (1 Kgs. 12; 931 B.C.).

17:17, 18 *Assyria.* Nation located in upper

Mesopotamia. A world power at the time of Isaiah.

17:18 *hiss.* To whistle for or call.

17:18 *the fly that is in the uttermost part of Egypt.* Perhaps referring to the swarming nature of invading Egyptian armies.

17:18 *Egypt.* North African kingdom, an ancient world power seeking resurgence during Isaiah's time.

17:18 *bee that is in the land of Assyria.* Perhaps referring to the stinging nature of invading Assyrian armies. Bee-keeping was prominent in Assyria.

17:20 *shave with a razor that is hired.* Likely refers to shaving the heads of a conquered people by victorious soldiers. A common practice by victors to mark, humiliate, and sanitize captured people. The razor is probably a reference to Assyria whom Ahaz has "hired" through his alliance with them.

17:20 *the head, and the hair of the feet; and it shall also consume the beard.* Refers to the complete conquest of the people and land.

17:21 *man shall nourish a young cow and two sheep.* After invasion flocks will be significantly reduced.

17:22 *abundance of milk.* Despite small flocks (*see* commentary on 2 Ne. 17:21) there will be plenty of milk for the survivors of the invasion due to reduced population.

17:23 *thousand silverlings.* Literally this means "a thousand pieces of silver." It is likely that this is a hyperbole indicating that the crops were very valuable.

17:24 *briers and thorns.* Vegetation indigenous to untended land (cf. 2 Ne. 15:5–6). A metaphor for desolation.

Latter-day applicability

In addition to a beautiful prophecy of the birth of Christ (17:14), this chapter illustrates how the Lord responds to a rebellious covenant people—then and now. A prophet was sent to reveal the will of God, to call them to repentance, and to encourage them to trust in the Lord. The promise was given that they would prosper or be established (17:9) if they would believe, but if not, the Lord could not bless and protect them. This message holds true for a covenant people as a whole and as individuals.

TBB

Isaiah chap. review: 2 Nephi 18 // Isaiah 8

Background and synopsis

The historical background to 2 Nephi 17 and 18 can be found in 2 Kings 16. Chapter 18 continues Isaiah's response to Ahaz in chapter 17. The Lord had sent Isaiah to warn Ahaz against joining the Syro-Ephraimite alliance because in a short time ASSYRIA would destroy both SYRIA and Ephraim, and he gave Ahaz the sign of IMMANUEL (2 Ne. 17:14–16). In chapter 18 Isaiah gave another sign of the imminent destruction of the alliance when he gave his newborn son the symbolic name Maher-shalal-hash-baz. Through a series of images the Lord promised JUDAH deliverance if she would trust in the Lord and destruction if she did not. Finally, the prophet bound up the words of his prophecies, sealed them in a scroll, gave them to his disciples, and warned the people against seeking the word of the Lord through spiritualism and necromancy. Ahaz did not join the Syro-Ephraimite alliance, but rather than trusting the Lord, he made an alliance with Assyria and eventually had to empty the temple treasury to send the required tribute to Assyria (2 Kgs. 16:8, 17–18). The prophesied destructions occurred when Syria and Ephraim were conquered in 732 B.C. Syria never recovered, while Ephraim was conquered again in 722 B.C. and many of its inhabitants were taken into exile to Assyria. Ahaz's son Hezekiah, a righteous king of Judah, later revolted against Assyria by refusing to send tribute. Assyria retaliated in 701 B.C. and destroyed many of the cities of Judah. Jerusalem, however, was miraculously preserved at that time (Isa. 36–37).

Definitions

18:1 *great roll.* The Hebrew word refers to either a scroll, roll, or tablet, perhaps a wooden writing tablet with a wax writing surface.

18:1 *Maher-shalal-hash-baz.* Name of Isaiah's son literally meaning in Hebrew "the spoil speeds, the prey hastens." An allusion to the impending Assyrian destruction of the Syro-Ephraimite confederacy.

18:2 *Uriah the priest, and Zechariah the son of Jeberechiah.* Legal witnesses of the symbolic act. Uriah may be the priest mentioned in 2 Kings

ISA. CHAP. REVIEW: 2 NE. 18 // ISA. 8

16:10–16, and Zechariah may be Ahaz's father-in-law (2 Kgs. 18:2).

18:3 *prophetess.* Isaiah's wife; the title may suggest that she, like her husband, enjoys the spiritual gift of prophecy. The same title is given to Miriam (Ex. 15:20), Deborah (Judg. 4:4), and Huldah (2 Kgs. 22:14).

18:4 *Samaria.* A title of the northern kingdom, also called Ephraim. Samaria was the capital city used to represent the whole of the kingdom.

18:6 *waters of Shiloah.* Shiloah was a conduit that was part of the elaborate water system of Jerusalem. It is not certain where it was. Here it is a metaphor of peace and serenity representing trust in the Lord. If the people reject the Lord, then come the mighty waters of the Assyrians (18:7). Because Isaiah met Ahaz near Jerusalem's water system (17:3), this conduit may have been visible as they spoke.

18:6 *Rezin.* King in southern Syria who led the Syro-Ephraimite coalition against Assyria to its destruction in 732 B.C.

18:6 *Remaliah's son.* Refers to Pekah, wicked king of Israel, who reigned from 740 to 732 B.C. and who joined the Syro-Ephraimite coalition that ended in disaster in 732 B.C. *See* Israel, kingdom of.

18:7 *waters of the river.* An allusion to the Euphrates, mightiest of the rivers in the Near East, compared to the Assyrian empire that will overflow and destroy those who stand against it.

18:8 *reach even to the neck.* An image of almost drowning, possibly an allusion to the Assyrian invasion in 701 B.C. in which they destroyed many of the cities of Judah but not Jerusalem.

18:8 *Immanuel.* Title meaning "God is with us" and signifying the protection of the Lord. Immanuel is a title of the Messiah that was fulfilled with the coming of Christ, when God came to earth. Here the name is used in the context of protection against enemies (*see* Isaiah chapter reviews, 2 Ne. 17 // Isa. 7, definitions, v. 14).

18:9 *gird yourselves.* Prepare for battle.

18:9–10 *Associate yourselves, O ye people, and ye shall be broken in pieces; and give ear all ye of far countries; gird yourselves, and ye shall be broken in pieces; gird yourselves, and ye shall be broken in pieces. Take counsel together.* These are references to human alliances.

18:10 *for God is with us.* In Hebrew "Immanuel," the same as in 2 Nephi 18:8; perhaps a reference to the sign promised in 2 Nephi 17:14.

18:12 *confederacy.* The Lord is warning

OUTLINE OF 2 NEPHI 18

I. The sign of Maher-shalal-hash-baz (18:1–4)
  - A. Isaiah, before witnesses, records the sign of Maher-shalal-hash-baz (18:1–2)
  - B. Birth of a son whose name signifies that Syria and Israel would soon be destroyed (18:3–4)

II. Prophecy of Shiloah and the waters of the river (18:5–8)
  - A. People do not trust in the Lord, symbolized by Shiloah, but desire to enter an alliance (18:5–6)
  - B. Assyria, symbolized by a great river, will almost destroy Judah (18:7–8)

III. Human alliances are vain for "God is with us" (18:9–10)

IV. Israel to trust in the Lord (18:11–15)
  - A. Israel warned against joining foreign alliances (18:11–12)
  - B. The Lord will be a sanctuary for those who trust him and a stumbling block to those who reject him (18:13–15)

V. The prophet seals up his testimony and leaves it with his disciples as a witness (18:16–18)

VI. Those who seek the word of the Lord through mediums will find darkness instead of light (18:19–22) not to look to such confederacies as the Syro-Ephraimite alliance for deliverance. The implication is that men should put their trust in God, not the arm of flesh (18:13–14).

18:14 *stone of stumbling, and for a rock of offense.* The Lord will be an obstacle to those who reject him. Peter and Paul interpreted this passage as an allusion to the Messiah, who would come and be rejected by the house of Israel (1 Pet. 2:8; cf. Rom. 9:33; 1 Cor. 1:23).

18:14 *gin.* A trap or snare.

18:16 *Bind up the testimony, seal the law among my disciples.* This phrase may be interpreted literally that Isaiah took the scroll upon which he had written these prophecies, rolled it up and tied it shut with a strip of leather or a cord, and then sealed it with a clay seal as a symbol that the prophecies were complete. Isaiah then gave the prophecies to his disciples for future reference. When his prophecies were fulfilled in the future, this would be a testimony that he was a true prophet (cf. Deut. 18:21–22). The phrase may also be simply a figurative way of saying that Isaiah solemnly affirmed the truthfulness of the words he had just uttered.

18:19 *Seek unto them that have familiar spirits, and unto wizards that peep and mutter.* Seeking the will of God from the spirits of the dead through mediums and witchcraft. *See* Familiar spirit.

18:20 *to the law and to the testimony.* Seek the scriptures and living prophets to find the word of God.

Latter-day applicability

This chapter reminds the covenant people to seek and to follow the word of the Lord as revealed through the prophets and to trust in the Lord rather than in alliances with foreign nations. Isaiah's prophecies of destruction were fulfilled against Syria, Israel, and Judah. The sign of "Immanuel" and the imagery of the "stone of stumbling" and "rock of offense" allude to the future coming and rejection of the Messiah, which was fulfilled in the life of Jesus Christ. The fulfillment of these prophecies testifies that Isaiah's other prophecies would come to pass as well.

DRS

Isaiah chap. review: 2 Nephi 19 // Isaiah 9

Background and synopsis

Second Nephi 19 consists of a messianic prophecy that speaks of Jesus' mortal ministry and kingship (2 Ne. 19:1–7) and a prophecy of judgment against the northern kingdom of Israel (2 Ne. 19:8–21). Second Nephi 19:1 begins with "nevertheless," linking it with the prophecies in chapter 18. The darkness brought about by those who relied on mediums instead of on prophets (2 Ne. 18:18–22) was dispelled with the coming of a light that would shine upon the people who hitherto had walked in darkness. Christ was the "great light" (2 Ne.19:2) that would shine upon the inhabitants of the lands of Zebulun and Naphtali, or Galilee, during his mortal mission (2 Ne. 19:2). He was the new king who would overthrow oppressive kingdoms, become God's son in the flesh, receive the government and the throne and the kingdom, and rule forever with judgment, peace, and justice (2 Ne. 19:4–7; cf. 2 Sam. 7:11–16; Ps. 2).

The final verses (2 Ne. 19:8–21) consist of a judgment against the northern kingdom of Israel. The Lord's word had gone forth unto the house of Israel through his prophets, and Israel would soon suffer destruction (2 Ne. 19:8–12). Because the covenant people did not seek the Lord, were hypocrites, spoke follies, and worked evil, the Lord would destroy all levels of their society, including leaders, followers, false prophets, young men, and even those who were usually oppressed, such as the fatherless and widows (2 Ne. 19:13, 15–21). This judgment was fulfilled by the Assyrian conquest and exile in 722 B.C.

Definitions

19:1 *land of Zebulun, and the land of Naphtali.* These two tribal lands were in the region of Galilee where Jesus spent most of his mortal ministry. Matthew noted that during this time Jesus dwelt in Capernaum, a city that was located "in the borders of Zabulon and Nephthalim," as a fulfillment of this prophecy (Matt. 4:13–16). Jesus was the "great light" seen by the inhabitants of this area (2 Ne. 19:2).

19:1 *her vexation, when at first he lightly*

ISA. CHAP. REVIEW: 2 NE. 19 // ISA. 9

afflicted the land of Zebulun, and the land of Naphtali, and afterwards did more grievously afflict by the way of the Red Sea. Recalls numerous occasions when this land was conquered. The land was a prime military target due to its strategic location at the junction of several major highways.

19:2 *walked in darkness.* Refers to people and nations who walk in darkness because they do not know Jesus Christ, the "great light" (cf. John 1:5).

19:2 *great light.* Jesus Christ. Matthew 4:13–16 presents the fulfillment of the prophecy found in Isaiah 9:1–2.

19:2 *land of the shadow of death.* Symbolizes the mortal world where there is darkness, and death.

19:3 *multiplied the nation.* A reference to the ABRAHAMIC COVENANT (Abr. 3:14; cf. Isa. 26:15; Neh. 9:23).

19:3 *increased the joy.* There is an increase of joy because Messiah has broken the rod of the oppressor (19:4) and because a child is born who will establish his righteous government and bring everlasting peace (cf. Luke 2:10–11).

19:3 *divide the spoil.* The joy that the Messiah brings is like the joy of those who receive spoils and booty after winning a battle.

19:4 *yoke of his burden, and the staff of his shoulder, the rod of his oppressor.* The yoke, staff, and rod signify forms of oppression. Similar to the manner that Moses delivered ancient Israel from Egypt's yoke and physical bondage, Jesus Christ delivers from the yoke of spiritual bondage.

19:5 *burning and fuel of fire.* Burning is a symbol of judgment and destruction.

19:6 *unto us a child is born, unto us a son is given.* Jesus Christ is the "son" and the "Holy Child" (Moro. 8:3).

19:6 *government shall be upon his shoulder; and his name shall be called, Wonderful, Counselor, The Mighty God, The Everlasting Father, The Prince of Peace.* These phrases and titles describe the various aspects of the power and authority of the Messiah.

19:7 *throne of David.* The throne is a metaphor for kingship and dominion (Gen. 41:40; 2 Sam. 7:16; 1 Kgs. 1:47). Jehovah, seated upon the throne of David as king of kings, rules with great glory and justice for eternity.

19:7 *zeal of the Lord of Hosts will perform this.* This phrase, also found in 2 Kings 19:31 and Isaiah 37:32, is a promise that the Lord will use his strength to fulfill his word.

19:9 *Ephraim and the inhabitants of Samaria.* Names that represent the northern kingdom of Israel (cf. 2 Ne. 17:2, 5, 8–9; Hos. 5:3, 11:8). *See* Israel, kingdom of.

OUTLINE OF 2 NEPHI 19

- I. The MESSIAH is the light that shines in the lands of Zebulun and Naphtali (19:1–2)
  - A. The Messiah ministers in the lands of Zebulun and Naphtali (19:1)
  - B. The Messiah is the "great light" who shines in the land of darkness (19:2)
- II. The Messiah—the Son becomes the new future King (19:3–7)
  - A. Joy increases because of the coming of the new King (19:3–4)
  - B. The wicked are destroyed with fire (19:5)
  - C. Description, birth, and throne names of the Messiah (19:6)
  - D. The Messiah possesses the government and rules with justice forever (19:7)
- III. Judgment against the northern kingdom of Israel (19:8–21)
  - A. Israel will be destroyed because of pride (19:8–12)
  - B. Israel condemned to destruction for following her wicked leaders (19:13–17)
  - C. The wicked inhabitants of Israel will be burned (19:18–21)
    - 1. Moral decay leads to anarchy in society (19:18–20)
    - 2. The tribes of Ephraim and Manasseh will fight against Judah (19:21)

19:9 *stoutness of heart.* A symbol of pride.

19:11 *adversaries of Rezin.* Rezin was the king in southern Syria. His chief adversary was Assyria.

19:12 *Syrians before and the Philistines behind.* Countries bordering Israel to the northeast and to the west. The Syrians, not allied with Rezin, and the Philistines will join together to fight the anti-Assyrian alliance of Rezin and Israel (*see* Isaiah chapter reviews, 2 Ne. 17 // Isa. 7 and 2 Ne. 18 // Isa. 8, background and synopsis).

19:12 *his hand is stretched out still.* A phrase that usually refers to the Lord stretching out his hand in anger and destruction, repeated again in 2 Nephi 19:17, 21; 10:4. In some contexts in the Book of Mormon his hand is stretched out in mercy as well (e.g., Jacob 6:4–5; cf. 2 Ne. 28:32).

19:14 *in one day.* Quickly.

19:18 *devour the briers and thorns, and shall kindle in the thickets of the forests.* "Briers," "thorns," and "thickets" are metaphors for the wicked (cf. Isa. 10:17, 34). All of these will be destroyed by fire.

19:19 *land darkened.* Metaphor for apostasy and the darkness that accompanies destruction.

19:20 *he shall snatch on the right hand and be hungry.* During these times of trouble and destruction, there will be a great shortage of food so that people will scavenge here and there for food but will not find enough to satisfy their hunger.

19:21 *Manasseh, Ephraim; and Ephraim, Manasseh; they together shall be against Judah.* Implies that tribes, families, and even brothers will contend against one another during these times of trouble. Earlier, Isaiah had stated that "no man shall spare his brother" (19:19) and "they shall eat every man the flesh of his own arm" (19:20).

Selected differences between Book of Mormon Isaiah (2 Ne. 19) and KJV Isaiah (Isa. 9) are shown in the accompanying table.

Latter-day applicability

This chapter invites latter-day people to cease walking in darkness by receiving Jesus Christ, who is the "great light" (2 Ne. 19:1–2). Those who do so will rejoice with him as he breaks the yoke, staff, and rod of the oppressor, even sin, death, and hell, through the Atonement (19:3–7).

Moreover, the destruction of the northern kingdom of Israel during Isaiah's time, which came about on account of the pride, lack of love, social injustices, and general wickedness of its people (19:9–21) is a type of the devastation that awaits the wicked at the Second Coming.

BIBLIOGRAPHY

Parry, Donald W., Jay A. Parry, and Tina M. Peterson. *Understanding Isaiah.* Salt Lake City: Deseret Book, 1998. 91–102.

DWP

Isaiah chap. review: 2 Nephi 20 // Isaiah 10

Background and synopsis

Second Nephi 20 contains a prophecy of the destruction of ASSYRIA, which is also a type of the "destruction of [the] wicked at the second coming" (2 Ne. 20 chapter heading; 2 Ne. 20:1–19, 28–34), and contains a promise that a remnant of Jacob would be preserved (2 Ne. 20:20–27).

Because of the sins of Israel (2 Ne. 20:1–4) the Lord permitted the Assyrian army, the Lord's "rod" (2 Ne. 20:5–11), to war against the

SELECTED DIFFERENCES BETWEEN B OF M ISA. (2 NE. 19) AND KJV ISA. (ISA. 9)

	BOOK OF MORMON		KJV ISAIAH	COMMENTARY
19:1	. . . by the way of the **Red** Sea beyond Jordan . . .	9:1	. . . by the way of the sea, beyond Jordan . . .	It is not known why the Book of Mormon text reads Red Sea.
19:3	Thou hast multiplied the nation, and increased the joy . . .	9:3	Thou hast multiplied the nation, and not increased the joy . . .	Eliminating the "not" clarifies that the light does increase joy.

ISA. CHAP. REVIEW: 2 NE. 20 // ISA. 10

apostate Israelites. Because of its pride and overzealousness (2 Ne. 20:7–15), Assyria would then be destroyed by her enemies. The fire that would destroy Assyria foreshadows the fire that will destroy the wicked at the Second Coming (2 Ne. 20:12–19).

Second Nephi 20:20–27 speaks of a time when the remnant of Israel will return to their lands of promise and "unto the mighty God" (2 Ne. 20:21). The expression "the remnant shall return" (20:21) recalls the prophetic name of Isaiah's son Shearjashub, which literally means "a remnant shall return" (2 Ne. 17:3; 18:18).

Second Nephi 20:28–34 describes the march of the great Assyrian army southward towards Jerusalem. As the army traveled it sacked and destroyed all towns and villages in its path. Some scholars believe Isaiah's prophecy was fulfilled either by the invasion of Sargon II in 713–712 B.C. or by king Sennacherib's invasion of Judah in 701 B.C. (Isa. 37:36–37). The Lord's destruction of Assyria (2 Ne. 20:33–34) may be a type of the eventual victory that Israel will achieve over her enemies as prophesied in 2 Nephi 21:14–15 // Isaiah 11:14–15. According to Moroni[2], Isaiah 11 is one of the chapters of Isaiah to be fulfilled in the last days (JS–H 1:40).

Isaiah's prophecy takes a positive turn in the final two verses when Jehovah, as the great forester, uses his mighty iron ax to chop down Assyria's armies as they approach Zion (Isaiah employed similar imagery elsewhere; 2 Ne. 12:12–18; 20:18–19).

Definitions

20:1 *Wo.* Severe anguish resulting from God's judgments.

20:1 *decree unrighteous decrees.* To create unjust laws that serve the rich and powerful but prey upon the weak, such as the fatherless and the widows (20:2).

20:1 *write grievousness.* To write oppressive laws.

20:2 *To turn away the needy from judgment, and to take away the right from the poor of my people, that widows may be their prey, and that they may rob the fatherless!* Those who create unjust laws (20:1) prey upon the socially deprived, including the needy, poor, widows, and fatherless.

20:3 *day of visitation.* A time of the Lord's judgment and indignation (Hosea 9:7; Micah 7:4; D&C 56:1, 16). It is also the time of the Second Coming, when Christ will visit the earth in power and glory (D&C 124:8, 10).

20:3 *desolation which shall come from far.* This may be a dual prophecy referring to the Assyrian army that will come from a far country to conquer, and to the Lord, who resides far off and will come to judge the world in the latter days.

20:3 *to whom will ye flee for help?* This is a rhetorical question, showing that during the day of visitation the wicked will have no one to turn to for help, for they have rejected God.

20:3 *where will ye leave your glory?* This may be translated, "Where will ye leave your riches?" At the Day of Judgment, one's riches will be meaningless and will not assist in saving one's soul.

20:4 *bow down under the prisoners, and they shall fall under the slain.* A modern translation of Isaiah renders this phrase, "so as not to crouch among the prisoners or fall among the slain" (NRSV). During the day of visitation the wicked

OUTLINE OF 2 NEPHI 20

I. Social injustices exist in Israel (20:1–4)
II. Assyria is an instrument in God's hand to punish Israel (20:5–11)
III. God destroys Assyria, which is a type of the destruction at the Second Coming (20:12–19)
IV. A remnant of Israel will return in the last days (20:20–27)
V. Assyria marches toward Jerusalem causing terror (20:28–34)

ISA. CHAP. REVIEW: 2 NE. 20 // ISA . 10

will fall in the destruction or become prisoners with other captives.

20:4 *his hand is stretched out still.* A phrase which usually refers to the Lord stretching out his hand in anger and destruction (e.g., 2 Ne. 15:25; Ex. 3:20). In the Book of Mormon the Lord stretches out his hand in mercy as well (e.g., Jacob 6:4–5; c.f. 2 Ne. 28:32).

20:5 *Assyrian.* Refers to the king of Assyria as well as his nation. "Assyria" also represents the wicked nations of the last days that will worship idols and false gods, war against Israel, and eventually be consumed by the Lord's glory and majesty during the Second Coming.

20:5 *rod of mine anger, and the staff.* Assyria is the rod and staff that will smite and chasten the people of Israel because they are an apostate nation (20:6). Assyria will smite Israel with the staff as a taskmaster smites a slave, and then Assyria will rule over Israel with the rod or scepter.

20:6 *hypocritical nation.* The Lord's people who do not keep their covenants.

20:6 *people of my wrath.* The children of Israel who are to be punished for their hypocrisy.

20:6 *to take the spoil, and to take the prey.* The Lord will permit Assyria to capture and plunder. "Spoil" and "prey" come from the prophetic name Maher-shalal-hash-baz, suggesting that Isaiah's earlier prophecy (2 Ne. 18:1–4) finds at least partial fulfillment in Assyria's captivity and plundering of Israel.

20:7 *in his heart it is to destroy.* Assyria's king does not know that he is being used as the Lord's instrument to punish his rebellious people. Instead, he intends to conquer the world's nations and to gain glory and riches for himself.

20:9 *Calno as Carchemish? Is not Hamath as Arpad? Is not Samaria as Damascus?* A boast of the proud Assyrians. As the king of Assyria and his armies moved westward and southward they destroyed many cities, including these listed. The question, "Is not Calno as Carchemish?" may be paraphrased as, "Has not Calno been destroyed even as Carchemish was destroyed?"

20:10 *my hand hath founded the kingdoms of the idols.* The proud king glorifies himself by stating that he conquered and ruled kingdoms of people who worship idols that are superior to those found in Israel (Samaria) and Judah (Jerusalem).

20:11 *so do to Jerusalem.* Assyria had destroyed kingdoms and was preparing to destroy Judah, represented here by the capital city Jerusalem.

20:12 *performed his whole work upon Mount Zion and upon Jerusalem, I will punish the fruit of the stout heart of the king of Assyria.* After the Lord has used Assyria to punish Jerusalem, he will then destroy Assyria. "Fruit" represents works. The Lord will punish the king of Assyria because of his evil works (cf. Jer. 21:14). Partial fulfillment of this promise of punishment came when an "angel of the Lord went out, and smote in the camp of the Assyrians," destroying 185,000 people while besieging Jerusalem in 701 B.C. (2 Kgs. 19:35). The king's "stout heart," denoting pride and haughtiness, is shown in 2 Kings 19:23.

20:12 *Mount Zion.* Refers to Jerusalem and the hill upon which it is built. By extension it may also be a reference to the temple at Jerusalem.

20:13 *I have moved the borders.* As the king conquered nations and kingdoms, he removed their political borders and annexed their lands into his own kingdom.

20:14 *nest the riches of the people; and as one gathereth eggs that are left have I gathered all the earth; and there was none that moved the wing, or opened the mouth, or peeped.* Israel is compared to a bird's nest, eggs, and wings. The eggs in the nest represent Israel's riches (20:13). That Israel was not able to move its wing or to make a peep signifies that it, like a little chick, was helpless before Assyria's ravenous armies.

20:15 *ax boast itself against him that heweth therewith? Shall the saw magnify itself against him that shaketh it?* These are tools used to cut down trees of the forest, which are mentioned in 2 Nephi 20:18–19. Here the "ax" or "saw" represents Assyria in the Lord's hand. Assyria and her king are proud enough to believe that they are greater than God, who holds the tools in his hands and uses them for his divine purposes.

20:16 *fat ones, leanness.* The Lord will then turn fatness (prosperity and blessings) of Assyria

ISA. CHAP. REVIEW: 2 NE. 20 // ISA. 10

(type for the wicked) into leanness (lack of temporal and spiritual blessings).

20:17 *burn and shall devour his thorns and his briers.* The Lord will destroy Assyria. Compare 20:33–34 where God, as the forester, cuts down the forest of Assyria with his mighty axe. The destruction of Assyria is a type of the destruction of the wicked (thorns and briers) at the Second Coming.

20:18 *shall consume the glory of his forest, and of his fruitful field.* Continued description of the destruction of Assyria. Scripturally, the "forest" may represent people (Jer. 21:14; Ezek. 20:45–47; Zech. 11:1–2), and the "field" may symbolize the world (1 Ne. 8:20; D&C 86:1–2).

20:18 *standard-bearer fainteth.* The Hebrew text of this phrase may be translated "as a sick man wastes away."

20:19 *trees of his forest shall be few.* Trees represent individuals. After the destruction the number of people who will remain will be so few that even a little child will be able to count and list them.

20:20 *stay upon him that smote them.* The remnant of Israel will no longer stay (lean) upon the rod (Assyria) that smote them (2 Kgs. 16:7), but they will lean upon or trust the Lord.

20:22 *consumption decreed.* God, through his prophets, decreed destruction upon the wicked.

20:26 *stir up a scourge.* Or "lash them with a whip." After Assyria serves the Lord's purposes by smiting Israel, he will lash the Assyrians with a whip, meaning he will punish them for their pride and wickedness.

20:26 *slaughter of Midian at the rock of Oreb; and as his rod was upon the sea so shall he lift it up after the manner of Egypt.* Just as God delivered Moses and the Israelites from Pharaoh's armies (Ex. 14:30–31) and provided deliverance to Gideon and the children of Israel from the Midianites (Judg. 6–7), he will once more save Israel.

20:26 *rod was upon the sea.* Referring to the rod that Moses used to divide the Red Sea and enable Israel to flee from the armies of Egypt. The imagery suggest that God will once again intervene to deliver his people.

20:27 *burden shall be taken away from off thy shoulder, and his yoke from off thy neck, and the yoke shall be destroyed because of the anointing.* Through the anointing (literally "because of oil"), captives will be freed. The imagery points to deliverance from Assyria and perhaps is a type of deliverance through Jesus the MESSIAH or anointed one.

20:28 *Aiath, he is passed to Migron; at Michmash.* Describing the Assyrian army's capture of Aiath, Migron, and Michmash on their way to Jerusalem.

20:28 *laid up his carriages.* At Michmash, the Assyrian army stores its equipment and supplies, perhaps so it will not be burdened as it approaches Jerusalem.

20:29 *They are gone over the passage.* This phrase describes the advance of the Assyrian army as they cross over an unnamed mountain pass on their way to Jerusalem.

20:29 *they have taken up their lodging at Geba.* The Assyrian army temporarily halts their advancements to rest at Geba.

20:29 *Ramath is afraid; Gibeah of Saul is fled.* As the Assyrian army approaches, the fearful inhabitants of Ramah and Gibeah flee.

20:30 *daughter of Gallim; cause it to be heard unto Laish, O poor Anathoth.* The inhabitants of Gallim and Anathoth raise up their voices in fear because of the impending devastation by the Assyrians.

20:31 *Madmenah is removed; the inhabitants of Gebim gather themselves to flee.* The inhabitants

SELECTED DIFFERENCES BETWEEN B OF M ISA. (2 NE. 20) AND KJV ISA. (ISA. 10)

	BOOK OF MORMON		KJV ISAIAH	COMMENTARY
20:5	O Assyrian, the rod of mine anger, and the staff in their hand is **their** indignation.	10:5	O Assyrian, the rod of mine anger, and the staff in their hand is mine indignation.	Identifies the indignation as Assyria's rather than the Lord's.

of Madmenah and Gebim also flee from the imminent destruction by the Assyrian army.

20:32 *yet shall he remain at Nob that day.* The Assyrians will pause at the city of Nob, which is located near Jerusalem, perhaps to rest, devise plans, and prepare for their attack against Jerusalem.

20:32 *shake his hand.* Assyria threatens Jerusalem.

20:33 *lop the bough.* Jehovah, the mighty forester who wields a great axe, chops down the tree (Assyria; Ezek. 31:3), preventing Assyria from destroying all of his children.

20:33 *high ones of stature shall be hewn down.* the forester also cut down Assyria's proud and haughty people.

20:34 *cut down the thickets of the forests with iron.* "Iron" here represents an iron axe.

20:34 *Lebanon.* A place noted anciently for its spectacular forests of cedar trees, which are a type for pride (cf. 2 Ne. 12:13).

Selected differences between Book of Mormon Isaiah (2 Ne. 20) and KJV Isaiah (Isa. 10) are shown in the accompanying table.

Latter-day applicability

The ancient nation of Assyria, with its proud, cruel, and bloody leaders and well-disciplined, fierce armies, thrived on other conquered nations. This picture of Assyria and war anticipates the warring nations of the present day and of the future where people and armies contend for land, power, and riches. As Assyria, her leaders, and her armies were destroyed according to God's plan, so also will the warring nations of the last days experience annihilation at the Second Coming. Isaiah's language—"burning of a fire," "fire," "flame," "devour," and "consume"—refers to the destruction of both ancient Assyria and all nations except for Zion when Christ comes in the clouds of glory. Meanwhile, a righteous remnant of Israel will be saved from the destruction during this time.

See also Jesus Christ, second coming of.

BIBLIOGRAPHY

Parry, Donald W., Jay A. Parry, and Tina M. Peterson. *Understanding Isaiah.* Salt Lake City: Deseret Book, 1998. 103–14.

DWP

Isaiah chap. review: 2 Nephi 21 // Isaiah 11

Background and synopsis

Second Nephi 21 begins with a beautiful prophecy of the coming of the MESSIAH (2 Ne. 21:1–5), followed by a description of the MILLENNIUM (2 Ne. 21:6–9). It then speaks of the restoration of the gospel and the gathering of the covenant people that will usher in the Millennium (2 Ne. 21:10–16).

The prophecy first introduces a servant, "a rod," and then speaks of the Messiah, "the stem of Jesse," who will have the "Spirit of the Lord" and "the spirit of wisdom and understanding" (2 Ne. 21:1–2; cf. D&C 113:1–2). The Messiah will serve as the righteous judge (2 Ne. 21:3) and will be the advocate of the poor and the meek (2 Ne. 21:4). In the end, the Messiah will "smite the earth" and "slay the wicked" (2 Ne. 21:4) at the Second Coming, resulting in the glorious conditions of the Millennium. Consequently, there will be a dramatic change in the order of the world in that the enmity between all God's creatures will cease—symbolized by the peaceful coexistence between the wolf and the lamb, the leopard and the kid, the calf and the lion, and the child and the asp. Peace will prevail, and none will hurt or destroy as the earth is filled with the knowledge of the Lord (2 Ne. 21:6–9).

Preparatory to that day, a great servant, the "root of Jesse," would raise an ENSIGN to which the righteous would gather. The Lord has revealed that this great servant would be a descendant of both Jesse and Joseph of old (D&C 113:3–6). This servant is generally understood by Latter-day Saints to be the Prophet Joseph Smith, and the ensign that he would raise to be the restored gospel of Jesus Christ. Through the Restoration the Lord would "set his hand" to gather and unify his people from all the nations of the earth. In this process he would destroy the power of his enemies (2 Ne. 21:11–16). All of these divine activities constitute "a marvelous work and a wonder among the children of men" (2 Ne. 25:17).

Definitions

21:1 *rod.* In the Doctrine and Covenants the rod is defined as "a servant in the hands of

ISA. CHAP. REVIEW: 2 NE. 21 // ISA. 11

Christ, who is a descendant of Jesse as well as of Ephraim, or of the house of Joseph, on whom there is laid much power" (D&C 113:3–4). The "rod" is generally understood among Latter-day Saints to be a reference to the Prophet Joseph Smith (cf. 2 Ne. 21:10; D&C 113:5–6; McConkie, *Millennial*, 339–40; Sperry, 41).

21:1 *stem of Jesse.* Christ descended from Jesse (D&C 113:1–2). Jesse is the father of David (Ruth 4:22) and hence the progenitor of the kings of Judah and Jesus Christ.

21:1 *branch.* Christ (Jer. 23:3–6; Zech. 3:7–10; McConkie, *Promised*, 192–5).

21:3 *not judge after the sight of his eyes.* The Messiah will not judge by outward appearance because he is able to see into the very heart of an individual (1 Sam. 16:7).

21:4 *judge the poor.* With equity, the Messiah will repair all of the injustices experienced by the poor and the meek.

21:4 *rod of his mouth, and with the breath of his lips.* Jesus will destroy the wicked with his word by simply speaking the truth and by uttering judgments against evil (cf. Rev. 19:15, 21).

21:5 *girdle of his loins.* The Lord is covered with righteousness and faithfulness; these two qualities represent his very existence.

21:6–8 *The wolf also shall dwell with the lamb. . . . And the sucking child shall play on the hole of the asp, and the weaned child shall put his hand on the cockatrice's den.* A metaphor for the peace that will prevail during the Millennium.

21:8 *asp, and the weaned child shall put his hand on the cockatrice's den.* The asp and cockatrice, poisonous snakes that once harmed and destroyed, will be harmless.

21:9 *They shall not hurt nor destroy.* Enmity will be removed from the earth, and peace, love, and kindness will rule.

21:9 *my holy mountain.* The holy mountain may be a reference to the temple, but here it likely refers to the righteous millennial earth as a whole (cf. Isa. 56:7; 65:11, 25).

21:9 *earth shall be full of the knowledge of the Lord.* Nephi[1] cited this verse and explained that "all things shall be made known unto the children of men," including "things of all nations," "secret" things, "work[s] of darkness," and things that have been revealed (2 Ne. 30:15–18).

21:10 *root of Jesse.* In the Doctrine and Covenants the root is defined as "a descendant of Jesse, as well as of Joseph, unto whom rightly belongs the priesthood, and the keys of the kingdom, for an ensign, and for the gathering of my people in the last days" (D&C 113:5–6; cf. Rom. 15:12). The "root of Jesse" is generally understood as a reference to the Prophet Joseph Smith (McConkie, *Millennial*, 339–40; Sperry, 34–38).

21:10 *ensign of the people.* Modern revelation explains that the everlasting covenant and Zion (the Church) both function as an ensign to which the Gentiles will gather (D&C 45:9;

OUTLINE OF 2 NEPHI 21

- I. The stem of Jesse (Jesus Christ) prophecy (21:1–5)
  - A. The Messiah will have the Spirit of the Lord and possess great qualities (21:1–3)
  - B. The Messiah will destroy the wicked (21:4–5)
- II. Glorious conditions of the Millennium (21:6–9)
  - A. Peaceful conditions will replace hostile situations (21:6–8)
  - B. Knowledge of the Lord will cover the earth (21:9)
- III. The Lord will set up an ensign to the nations and Israel will gather to it (21:10–16)
  - A. Root of Jesse will raise an ensign for the people (21:10)
  - B. Lord will recover the remnant of his people (21:11–16)
    1. The remnant will come from all parts of the world (21:11)
    2. The remnant will include people from both Israel and Judah (21:12–15)
    3. A highway will exist for the returning remnant (21:16)

ISA. CHAP. REVIEW: 2 NE. 21 // ISA. 11

64:41–42). In a similar way Isaiah states that the "root of Jesse," the prophet of the Restoration, will "stand for an ensign," or banner, and "to it [or, to him] shall the Gentiles seek" (2 Ne. 21:10).

21:11 *Lord shall set his hand again the second time.* The first time the Lord set his hand to gather his people was when he led them out of Egypt (Ex. 3:19–20). The "second time" is the Restoration (Smith, 14; Jacob 6:2) described in terms of the Exodus (2 Ne. 21:15). Appropriately, Moses, who led the first gathering from Egypt, was entrusted with the keys of the gathering of Israel which he restored to the Prophet Joseph Smith in the Kirtland Temple in 1836 (D&C 110:11). *See* Second time.

21:11 *from Assyria, and from Egypt, and from Pathros, and from Cush, and from Elam, and from Shinar, and from Hamath, and from the islands.* Isaiah lists many of the nations that surrounded ancient Israel. The list symbolizes the "four corners of the earth" (2 Ne. 21:12), from which God will gather the covenant people.

21:12 *ensign.* An ensign is a flag or banner to which people gather. Here it refers to the restored gospel.

21:13 *envy of Ephraim also shall depart.* The entire verse recalls the tensions and hostilities between Ephraim (the northern kingdom) and Judah (the southern kingdom), beginning with Jeroboam's break with Rehoboam at the death of Solomon (1 Kgs. 11–12). God's gathering will result in the uniting of Judah and Israel, which will be made possible because the gospel teaches peace and love.

21:14 *Philistines towards the west; they shall spoil them of the east together; they shall lay their hand upon Edom and Moab; and the children of Ammon.* The pronoun "they" refers to Israel—probably Ephraim and Judah together—as they overcome their ancient enemies Philistia, Edom, Moab, and Ammon. The description of Israel's victory over their ancient enemies is a type of latter-day Israel's overcoming the world. Edom, or Idumea, is a type of the world (D&C 1:36).

21:15 *tongue of the Egyptian sea.* "Tongue" refers to a gulf. This phrase recalls the Israelites crossing the Red Sea (Ex. 14:21–22) and anticipates the gathering of Israel in the last days, when no powerful nation, army, or natural barrier will stop the promised events of the gathering.

21:15 *with his mighty wind he shall shake his hand over the river, and shall smite it in the seven streams, and make men go over dry shod.* Three elements in this passage—"mighty wind," "hand," and "go over dry shod"—recall the Israelites' miraculous crossing of the Red Sea (Ex. 14:21–22) and the Jordan River (Josh. 3:7–17). In this verse the "river" is probably an allusion to the Euphrates River in Mesopotamia that will be crossed in 2 Nephi 21:16. The same powers that guided the ancient Israelites out of Egypt will guide modern Israel out of Egypt and Assyria (both representing the world) to their gathering places.

21:16 *highway for the remnant of his people which shall be left, from Assyria.* Isaiah said, "An highway shall be there, and a way, and it shall be called The way of holiness" (Isa. 35:8–10; 51:10–11). Elder Bruce R. McConkie taught that the returning tribes "will tread the highway of righteousness" (*New Witness,* 521). This highway might be thought of as similar or identical to the straight and narrow path of the gospel (cf. Isa. 40:3; 42:16; 49:11; 57:14; 62:10; D&C 133:27).

Latter-day applicability

Second Nephi 21 // Isaiah 11 has direct application to the Latter-day Saints. Joseph Smith recalled the angel Moroni's visit on the night of 21 September 1823 and wrote that Moroni "quoted the eleventh chapter of Isaiah, saying that it was about to be fulfilled" (JS–H 1:40). The prophecies in this chapter pertain to the restoration of the gospel of Jesus Christ through the Prophet Joseph Smith, the establishment of an ensign to which Israel will gather, and the Second Coming, when the Messiah will smite the earth, slay the wicked, and usher in the Millennium when he will rule with justice and righteousness (cf. A of F 10).

The final seven verses of this chapter (2 Ne. 21:10–16) describe the Restoration that will usher in the Millennium. The events Isaiah prophesied are now being fulfilled. The gospel ensign has been erected and Israel's exiles are gathering around it, events that constitute "a marvelous work and a wonder" (2 Ne. 25:17).

See also Jesus Christ, second coming of.

BIBLIOGRAPHY

McConkie, Bruce R. *The Millennial Messiah: The Second Coming of the Son of Man.* Salt Lake City: Deseret Book, 1982.

———. *The Promised Messiah.* Salt Lake City: Deseret Book, 1978.

———. *A New Witness for the Articles of Faith.* Salt Lake City: Deseret Book, 1985.

Parry, Donald W., Jay A. Parry, and Tina M. Peterson. *Understanding Isaiah.* Salt Lake City: Deseret Book, 1998. 115–25.

Smith, Joseph. *Teachings of the Prophet Joseph Smith.* Selected by Joseph Fielding Smith. Salt Lake City: Deseret Book, 1976.

Sperry, Sidney B. *The Voice of Israel's Prophets: A Latter-day Saint Interpretation of the Major and Minor Prophets of the Old Testament.* Salt Lake City: Deseret Book, 1965.

DWP

Isaiah chap. review: 2 Nephi 22 // Isaiah 12

Background and synopsis

Second Nephi 22 records two psalms of praise and thanksgiving to God that will be offered up by those who live to see the glorious events foretold in the previous chapter (2 Ne. 21), including the restoration of the gospel, the gathering of Israel, and the millennial reign of the Savior. Such an outpouring of gratitude and devotion expressed in hymns or psalms is common in the scriptures (e.g., Ex. 15; Judg. 5; 2 Ne. 4:15–35).

In the first psalm (2 Ne. 22:1–2) the jubilant witnesses declare that although the Lord was once angry with them, they still look to him as their comfort, their salvation, their strength, and their song. In the second psalm they invite others to join them in praise of the Lord for the "excellent things" he has done for them (2 Ne. 22:4–6). Between the two hymns, Isaiah adds his testimony that latter-day peoples will rejoice as they "draw water out of the wells of salvation" (2 Ne. 22:3).

Definitions

22:1 *in that day.* The day in which the prophecies contained in the preceding chapter (2 Ne. 21:10–11) are fulfilled.

22:1 *though thou wast angry.* Refers to the time when rebellious people were disciplined or forsaken by God (cf. 3 Ne. 22:7–8).

22:2 *song.* A praise in music.

22:2 *Jehovah.* The divine name, usually translated "LORD" in the KJV but here translated JEHOVAH (cf. Ex. 6:3; Ps. 83:18).

22:3 *draw water out of the wells of salvation.* To partake of those things necessary for eternal life (cf. John 4:1–26; 7:37–39; Rev. 21:6).

22:6 *thou inhabitant of Zion.* One living in the millennial day. *See* Zion.

22:6 *Holy One of Israel.* The Messiah, Jesus Christ, who will reign during the Millennium.

Latter-day applicability

These hymns offer a great millennial promise, foretelling a time when mortals will accept the Lord, praise him, and partake of his blessings. They bear witness that all who do so will find joy and yearn to share their love, gratitude, and testimonies with others.

TBB

Isaiah chap. review: 2 Nephi 23 // Isaiah 13

Background and synopsis

The prophet Isaiah not only spoke to the ancient house of Israel about events in their time

OUTLINE OF 2 NEPHI 22

I. First psalm of praise and thanksgiving (22:1–2)
   A. God's anger has been turned away (22:1)
   B. God is the source of comfort, salvation, strength, and song (22:1–2)
II. Isaiah's testimony: "With joy shall ye draw water out of the wells of salvation" (22:3)
III. Second psalm: An invitation to join in praise (22:4–6)

ISA. CHAP. REVIEW: 2 NE. 23 // ISA. 13

but also prophesied concerning other nations and other periods. This truth is well illustrated in 2 Nephi 23, which consists of a prophecy against the kingdom of BABYLON foretelling the reasons for its future destruction and the means by which it would be accomplished. During Isaiah's lifetime Babylon was a center of culture, learning, and literature in the ancient Near East. It was also a center of apostate religion, corruption, and sin. By the end of the seventh century B.C. Babylon displaced ASSYRIA as the dominant empire in the Fertile Crescent and inflicted suffering and captivity on its neighboring nations. Consequently Babylon became a symbol, or type, for the world and its wickedness (cf. D&C 1:16). Accordingly, Isaiah's description of the fall of Babylon also provides a description of the destruction of the worldly and wicked at the Second Coming.

The prophecy begins with a call to arms as the Lord of Hosts assembles an awesome army to punish the wicked (2 Ne. 23:1–5). It further describes the extent of the anguish, fear, and destruction that would accompany the punishment to be meted out by the Lord and his hosts (2 Ne. 23:6–10, 12–22). The imagery used in this prophecy suggests that the wicked would suffer not only from acts of war (2 Ne. 23:15–18) but also from natural calamities and disasters (2 Ne. 23:10, 13–14), leaving Babylon utterly wasted and desolate (2 Ne. 23:19–22). In the middle of this graphic description, the prophet listed the iniquities of Babylon that so incurred the Lord's wrath, including arrogance, pride, haughtiness, and cruelty (2 Ne. 23:11). Remarkably, the prophet specifically identified the Medes as one of the Lord's agents of destruction of Babylon. This part of the prophecy was fulfilled in the sixth century B.C. when the Medes, part of the Persian empire and once an ally of Babylon against Assyria, invaded and conquered Babylon in 539 B.C. Thereafter Babylon dwindled, never again to be a world power.

Definitions

23:1 *burden.* An utterance, message, or revelation, usually with an ominous content (Isa. 15:1; 17:1; 19:1).

23:1, 19 *Babylon.* The capital of Babylonia, an empire based in central and southern Mesopotamia that ruled the ancient Near East during the first half of the sixth century B.C. It had a long history as a center for culture, literature, science, religion, and wealth. It became a symbol, or type, for the world and all its wickedness.

23:2 *lift ye up a banner.* To raise a flag, ensign, or standard to which armies are to rally.

23:2 *exalt the voice unto them.* Call them with a loud voice.

23:2 *shake the hand.* Wave the hand as a signal or urgent beckoning.

23:2 *go into the gates of the nobles.* To enter the abodes of the nobles (sometimes translated as "the proud"), perhaps as conquerors, or to invite them to the battle.

23:3 *sanctified ones.* Those set apart or chosen to do the Lord's work.

23:3 *mighty ones.* Heroes and men of valor.

23:3 *them that rejoice in my highness.* Those who accept the Lord's sovereignty.

OUTLINE OF 2 NEPHI 23

- I. Jehovah musters his forces (23:1–5)
  - A. A call to arms issued to the sanctified and mighty (23:1–3)
  - B. Multitudes respond to the call (23:4–5)
- II. The fate of Babylon (23:6–22)
  - A. Men will fear and suffer in the day of the Lord (23:6–8)
  - B. The Lord will punish the arrogant, proud, and cruel (23:9–16)
  - C. The Medes will destroy without pity (23:17–18)
  - D. Babylon will be left desolate and destroyed (23:19–22)

ISA. CHAP. REVIEW: 2 NE. 23// ISA. 13

23:6, 9 *day of the Lord.* A day in which the Lord metes out rewards or punishments. One such day will be the Second Coming.

23:7 *all hands be faint.* All their arms will hang down limp, likely in fear or despondency.

23:8 *shall be amazed one at another.* To stare at each other aghast.

23:8 *faces shall be as flames.* Perhaps indicating the destruction of sinners when "the day of the Lord cometh, cruel both with wrath and fierce anger" (23:9); also an apt description of the suffering of the wicked at the Second Coming (cf. 3 Ne. 25:1).

23:10 *stars of heaven and the constellations thereof shall not give their light; the sun shall be darkened in his going forth, and the moon shall not cause her light to shine.* A cosmic upheaval will accompany the day of the Lord's vengeance and the heavenly lights will be darkened. The prophet Amos prophesied that for the wicked "the day of the Lord is darkness, and not light" (Amos 5:18).

23:11 *terrible.* Those who cause fear.

23:12 *make a man more precious than fine gold; even a man than the golden wedge of Ophir.* Precious in this context means rare, suggesting the survivors of the Lord's wrath will be few. Ophir, a renowned source for gold (e.g., 1 Kgs. 9:28; 22:48), is variously thought to be a country in India, Africa, or Arabia.

23:13–14 *shake the heavens, and the earth shall remove out of her place, in the wrath of the Lord of Hosts, and in the day of his fierce anger. And it shall be as the chased roe, and as a sheep that no man taketh up.* Imagery suggesting earthquakes and cosmic disasters causing panic among people, who will scatter like a chased roe or fleeing gazelle and like sheep who have no shepherd.

23:17 *Medes.* Country bordering the southern end of the Caspian Sea that formed a confederacy with Babylon to fight against Assyria in the seventh century B.C. and was part of the Persian empire that conquered Babylon in the sixth century B.C.

23:17 *shall not regard silver and gold.* Cannot be bribed with wealth.

23:19 *beauty of the Chaldees' excellency, shall be as when God overthrew Sodom and Gomorrah.* The Chaldeans of the first millennium B.C. were a Semitic people related to the Arameans. They were a founding people of the Neo-Babylonian Empire, whose marvelous capital, Babylon, was a monument to their accomplishments. The destruction of Babylon would be similar to God's destruction of the ancient cities of Sodom and Gomorrah (Gen. 18–19).

23:20 *Arabian.* Refers to nomadic wanderers of the region. Apparently Babylon was to be so devastated that even these hardy people would not choose to camp there.

23:20 *make their fold.* Cause their sheep to rest.

23:21–22 *But wild beasts of the desert shall lie there; and their houses shall be full of doleful creatures; and owls shall dwell there, and satyrs shall dance there. And the wild beasts of the islands shall cry in their desolate houses, and dragons in their pleasant palaces.* Imagery suggesting that Babylon will be so devastated that only wild desert creatures will dwell there.

23:21 *doleful creatures.* Some type of howling animal, perhaps a jackal or horned owl.

SELECTED DIFFERENCES BETWEEN B OF M ISA. (2 NE. 23) AND KJV ISA. (ISA. 13)

	BOOK OF MORMON		KJV ISAIAH	COMMENTARY
23:3	. . . I have also called my mighty ones, for mine anger **is not upon** them that rejoice in my highness.	13:3	. . . I have also called my mighty ones for mine anger, even them that rejoice in my highness.	Suggests that the faithful will be excluded from the Lord's wrath.
23:15	Every one that is **proud** shall be thrust through . . .	13:15	Every one that is found shall be thrust through . . .	Indicates that God will punish the proud.

ISA. CHAP. REVIEW: 2 NE. 24 // ISA. 14

23:21 *satyrs.* The Hebrew word means "he-goats."

23:22 *dragons.* The Hebrew word means "wild dogs" or "jackals."

Selected differences between Book of Mormon Isaiah (2 Ne. 23) and KJV Isaiah (Isa. 13) are shown in the accompanying table.

Latter-day applicability

This is a remarkable dualistic passage. It contains not only a vivid and accurate description of the downfall of ancient Babylon but also a poignant prophecy of the destruction of the worldly and the wicked at the Second Coming. The Lord will use forces in heaven and earth to punish and destroy the proud, the arrogant, the cruel, and the wicked (2 Ne. 23:1–19). Those who are faithful will find mercy and deliverance (2 Ne. 23:3, 22), but those who have not repented by the appointed time of that destruction will find no escape from the Lord's vengeance (2 Ne. 23:17–19, 22). Those living in the latter days are warned that all those worldly things in which individuals delight will come to an end (2 Ne. 23:19–22).

See also Jesus Christ, second coming of.

TBB

Isaiah chap. review: 2 Nephi 24 // Isaiah 14

Background and synopsis

The first portion of 2 Nephi 24 (24:1–23) is a continuation of the "burden" or prophecy of doom concerning BABYLON introduced in the preceding chapter (2 Ne. 23). As such it continues Isaiah's dualistic prophecy of the destruction of Babylon as a type of the destruction of the world at the Second Coming. Accordingly, as the prophet described the fall of Babylon and her king in this passage, he also presented a type for the ultimate fall of Satan and those who follow him (2 Ne. 24:1–23; *see* Isaiah chapter reviews, 2 Ne. 23 // Isa. 13, background and synopsis). The chapter finishes with prophecies against two other traditional enemies of Israel, the Assyrians (24:24–27) and the Philistines (24:28–32).

Isaiah began the passage with a promise that, coincident with the fall of Babylon, there would be a gathering and restoration of the covenant people (2 Ne. 24:1–3). He promised that the Restoration would be assisted by "strangers" or foreigners. The prophecy found fulfillment in ancient times (539 B.C.) when the "stranger" Cyrus, king of the Persian empire, overthrew Babylon and then not only allowed but also assisted the return of the exiles from Judah to their lands (cf. Isa. 44:28; 45:1; Ezra 1). In the latter days the prophecy is being fulfilled in both a spiritual and physical sense as missionaries from "stranger" nations gather and restore scattered Israel to gospel covenants and as Gentile nations assist with the physical establishment of the children of Abraham in the Holy Land (2 Ne. 10:7–8).

Following the prophecy of restoration, Isaiah recited a "proverb" or song of derision that the restored peoples would chant or sing over the defeated king of Babylon, who is a type for Satan (2 Ne. 24:4–20). In the taunting song the people rejoice that the once-powerful king who had wreaked havoc among them is now weak and insignificant (2 Ne. 24:4–11). They mock him for his failed attempt to exalt himself at the expense of others (2 Ne. 24:12–17). They delight in the fact that rather than enjoying a kingly burial, he is cast aside and trodden under foot (2 Ne. 24:18–20). The song is followed by an assurance that the children or followers of the king will likewise be destroyed (2 Ne. 24:21–23).

Isaiah then turned his attention to ASSYRIA, declaring that the Lord would bring that oppressing empire to his mountains and destroy it (2 Ne. 24:24–27). This prophecy perhaps refers to the destruction of the Assyrian army as they attempted to besiege Jerusalem in 701 B.C. during the reign of Hezekiah. While the Assyrians were camped in the mountains surrounding Jerusalem, the "angel of the Lord" passed through their camp and destroyed the majority of the soldiers (Isa. 37; 2 Kgs. 19). It may also be prophesying of the defeat of Gog in the latter days (cf. 2 Ne. 24:26; Ezek. 38–39).

Isaiah closed with a prophecy against "Palestina," or the Philistines, who lived primarily along the southern half of the western coast of Canaan and were constant enemies of the descendants of Israel. He warned the

ISA. CHAP. REVIEW: 2 NE. 24 // ISA. 14

Philistines against prematurely celebrating the death "of him that smote thee," for a more severe enemy, even a "fiery flying serpent," would follow, leaving destruction in its wake (2 Ne. 24:28–31). Historically the first oppressor or "rod that smote thee" is usually identified with king Ahaz (735–715 B.C.) of Judah, or Shalmaneser V (727–722 B.C.) of Assyria, and the serpent that followed is identified with Sargon II (722–705 B.C.) or Sennacherib (705–681 B.C.) of Assyria or Nebuchadnezzar (605–562 B.C.) of Babylon—all who took turns victimizing Philistia.

Definitions

24:1 *Jacob.* Another name for the twelve tribes of Israel.

24:1 *strangers.* Those not of Jacob.

24:2 *people shall take them and bring them to their place.* The restoration of Jacob to their land will be assisted by other peoples. Perhaps refers to Persians who supported the return of Judah in ancient times and to latter-day Gentile nations in modern times.

24:4 *proverb.* A song or saying. In this case a song of derision against the king of Babylon.

24:4 *king of Babylon.* Literally the title of the ruler of Babylonia in ancient times, who in turn is a type for Satan in all dispensations.

24:4 *the golden city.* The Hebrew word translated here as "golden city" probably means proud or arrogant.

24:6 *none hindereth.* No one restrains.

24:7 *The whole earth is at rest.* A reference to the relative freedom that followed the fall of ancient Babylon, as well as the peace that will accompany the MILLENNIUM.

24:8 *fir-trees rejoice at thee, and also the cedars of Lebanon, saying. Since thou art laid down no feller is come up against us.* Imagery illustrating how those who once were persecuted by the king of Babylon will rejoice when he has become powerless. Fir trees, cypress, and Lebanon cedars may have been chosen for the imagery because Babylon harvested ancient forests of these species to support their extravagant building practices.

OUTLINE OF 2 NEPHI 24

I. The promise of restoration (24:1–3)
  A. Jacob to be restored to promised land (24:1)
  B. Strangers will join with Israel and assist in the restoration (24:1–2)
  C. Oppressors will be conquered (24:2)
  D. People will rest from sorrow and bondage (24:3)

II. Taunt over the fallen king of Babylon as a type of Satan (24:4–20)
  A. The king of Babylon (Lucifer) has become weak and helpless (24:4–12)
  B. The king of Babylon has failed to exalt himself (24:13–15)
  C. The king of Babylon is cast out in derision and disgust (24:16–20)

III. Fate of the followers of Lucifer (24:21–23)
  A. They will not possess the land (24:21)
  B. Their name and posterity will be cut off (24:22)
  C. Their land will be left desolate (24:23)

IV. The fall of Assyria (24:24–27)
  A. Assyria will be defeated in the mountains of Canaan (24:25)
  B. People will be free from Assyrian bondage (24:25)
  C. Jehovah will surely destroy Assyria (24:24, 26–27)

V. The fall of Philistia (24:28–32)
  A. Date that the burden was given: the year of Ahaz's death (24:28) [715 B.C.]
  B. A more terrifying enemy of the Philistines will replace the old one (24:29–31)
  C. In contrast, Zion will be established (24:32)

ISA. CHAP. REVIEW: 2 NE. 24 // ISA. 14

24:8 *feller.* One who fells or cuts down trees.

24:9, 11 *Hell.* Translation of the Hebrew *Sheol* meaning the underworld or the place of the dead. *Sheol* is translated as "grave" in verse 11.

24:11 *noise of thy viols.* Sound of your harps.

24:11 *worm is spread under thee, and the worms cover thee.* Literally, "your bed is maggots and your blanket is worms" describes a fallen and disgusting condition.

24:12 *Lucifer.* An epithet for the king of Babylon or Satan, literally meaning "light bearer" or "shining one." Combined with the phrase "son of the morning" (D&C 76:26), it suggests a position of prominence, perhaps a type referring to Satan's station in the premortal world.

24:13 *above the stars of God.* Imagery suggesting the high station Lucifer sought for himself. Stars are a symbol for spirits in the premortal world (cf. Rev. 12:4; Abr. 3:18).

24:13 *mount of the congregation, in the sides of the north.* The Hebrew text of this phrase can be rendered "the mount of meeting furthest north" and appears to refer to a place where the "gods" assemble, a type of "oriental Mount Olympus" (Brown et al., 417). Thus Lucifer is seeking to deify himself.

24:16 *narrowly look upon.* To stare or squint at.

24:17 *opened not the house of his prisoners.* Would not release prisoners to go home.

24:18 *every one of them in his own house.* This phrase likely refers to their tombs, or perhaps their mortal bodies, neither of which Lucifer will have.

24:19 *cast out of thy grave like an abominable branch, and the remnant of those that are slain, thrust through with a sword, that go down to the stones of the pit; as a carcass trodden under feet.* Imagery describing how the king of Babylon—a type of fallen Lucifer—will be treated. He will be thrown aside in disgust like a useless tree cutting, or like clothes taken from men who have been stabbed to death, or like a corpse that has been trampled.

24:23 *a possession for the bittern.* Imagery suggesting desolation. Only the bittern (the Hebrew word possibly means a hedgehog), will live where the splendid city used to be.

24:23 *pools of water.* Marshes.

24:23 *besom.* A broom.

24:25 *Assyrian.* The northern Mesopotamian empire that victimized Israel and Judah, primarily during the eighth and seventh centuries B.C.

24:25 *my mountains.* Likely refers to the mountainous country of Canaan.

24:25 *yoke depart from off them, and his*

SELECTED DIFFERENCES BETWEEN B OF M ISA. (2 NE. 24) AND KJV ISA. (ISA. 14)

	BOOK OF MORMON		KJV ISAIAH	COMMENTARY
24:2	And the people shall take them and bring them to their place; **yea, from far unto the ends of the earth; and they shall return to their lands of promise.**	14:2	And the people shall take them, and bring them to their place:	Emphasizes the extent of the gathering of the covenant people, and clarifies that there will be more than one promised land or gathering place.
24:2	And the house of Israel shall possess them, **and** the land of the Lord **shall be** for servants and handmaids . . .	14:2	and the house of Israel shall possess them in the land of the Lord for servants and handmaids . . .	Emphasizes that those living in a promised land are to serve the Lord rather than the "strangers" becoming Israel's servants and handmaidens.

burden depart from off their shoulders. People will be freed from Assyrian vassalage.

24:26–27 *hand that is stretched out upon all nations. For the Lord of Hosts hath purposed, and who shall disannul? And his hand is stretched out.* Imagery referring to God's hand that is working in peoples' lives, punishing the wicked and rewarding the righteous.

24:28 *year that king Ahaz died (715 B.C.).* Ahaz was an unrighteous king of Judah who refused to follow Isaiah's counsel (cf. 2 Ne. 17).

24:29 *Palestina.* Philistia. The Philistines were long-standing enemies of Judah and Israel who lived primarily in the southwestern coastal region of Canaan.

24:29 *rod of him that smote thee is broken; for out of the serpent's root shall come forth a cockatrice, and his fruit shall be a fiery flying serpent.* Imagery explaining that while an oppressor of the Philistines may perish, another, more severe, will follow.

24:29 *serpent's root shall come forth a cockatrice.* A metaphor suggesting that Philistia's next oppressor (the cockatrice or deadly viper) will be somehow related to its first (the serpent or snake), perhaps a descendant.

24:29 *fiery flying serpent.* The description "fiery" may refer to the venom of the serpent and the image of "flying" to the speed with which it is able to strike, thus suggesting that Philistia's next oppressor will be a formidable enemy.

24:30 *first-born of the poor shall feed, and the needy shall lie down in safety.* Imagery suggesting that the demise of the Philistines will lead to rest, peace, and sustenance for others.

24:30 *I will kill thy root with famine, and he shall slay thy remnant.* Philistia will be left without ancestry (root), or progeny (remnant). "I" in this passage likely refers to the Lord, while "he" is perhaps the enemy discussed in the preceding verse.

24:31 *smoke.* Here meaning a cloud of dust or smoke, perhaps created by a large invading force coming from the north out of Assyria.

24:31 *none shall be alone in his appointed times.* The Hebrew from which this phrase is translated in the King James Version suggests no stragglers in the invading force.

24:32 *messengers of the nations.* Ambassadors, likely inquiring about the fall of Philistia.

Selected differences between Book of Mormon Isaiah (2 Ne. 24) and KJV Isaiah (Isa. 14) are shown in the accompanying table.

Latter-day applicability

The promise in this passage of a latter-day restoration of the covenant people, coincident with the ultimate conquest and fall of the adversary and his agents, offers hope to the Saints of this dispensation. Moreover, Latter-day Saints identify themselves with the strangers of verses 1–2 who are to assist with both the spiritual and physical gathering and restoration of the children of Abraham in this dispensation. Fundamental to Latter-day Saint theology is the doctrine that Satan fell from heaven in the premortal world for seeking to exalt himself and take glory to himself alone, contrary to the will of God (cf. D&C 29:36–38; Abr. 3:27–28; Moses 4:1–4). This doctrine is well supported as Satan's primordial ambitions are rehearsed in the verses 13–14. Because Satan rebelled and was cast out, he seeks now that all might become miserable like unto himself (2 Ne. 2:18, 27). As peace prevailed after the destruction of Babylon and her kings, so likewise when Satan is bound during the Millennium (1 Ne. 22:26; cf. D&C 88:110) will the "whole earth [be] at rest" (2 Ne. 24:7).

BIBLIOGRAPHY

Brown, Francis, S. R. Driver, and Charles A. Briggs. *The New Brown-Driver-Briggs-Gesenius Hebrew and English Lexicon.* [S. I.]: Christian Copyrights, 1983.

TBB

Isaiah chap. review: 2 Nephi 26:6, 15–18; 27 // Isaiah 29

Background and synopsis

Second Nephi 26–27 contain Nephi[1]'s prophecies about the future of his people. In these chapters Nephi foretold the coming of Christ to the Nephites and their eventual apostasy and destruction (2 Ne. 26:1–11) and then gave a detailed description of the apostasy of the latter days and the coming forth of the Book of Mormon that would bring the Gentiles, Lamanites, and Jews to Christ (2 Ne.

ISA. CHAP. REVIEW: 2 NE. 26:6; 27 // ISA. 29

26:12–27:35; cf. 2 Ne. 25:17–19; 30:2–7). To describe the coming forth of the Book of Mormon in the last days, Nephi cited passages of Isaiah, apparently from the brass plates, that parallel the King James Version of Isaiah 29. In chapter 29, Isaiah warned the people of Ariel (Zion in 2 Ne. 27:3) that they would be besieged, destroyed, and left to speak only from the dust (Isa. 29:1–6). He then prophesied that the Lord would bring forth a book and do a "marvelous work and a wonder" that would confound the wicked and correct false doctrine (Isa. 29:9–24). Nephi likely cited this text from Isaiah because he knew that his people also would be destroyed (2 Ne. 26:15, 18), and that the book of which Isaiah prophesied would be the record of the Nephites that would be left to speak from the dust, even the Book of Mormon. The passages of Isaiah that Nephi cited from the brass plates are interspersed with his own

OUTLINE OF 2 NEPHI 26:6, 15–18; 2 NEPHI 27

- I. Nephi prophesies concerning the fate of his people (26:6, 15–18)
  - A. At the death of Jesus destruction will come upon the wicked of Nephi's people (26:6; cf. Isa. 29:6)
  - B. Nephi prophesies of the last days (26:5–18 // Isa. 29:1–5; cf. 2 Ne. 26:14)
    1. Nephi's people will apostatize, be besieged, destroyed (26:15)
    2. The words written by the righteous of the Nephites will come forth in a book (26:15–17)
    3. The destruction of the wicked will be accomplished speedily (26:18)
- II. Iniquity in the last days will result in destruction and apostasy (27:1–5)
  - A. The Lord will respond to worldwide iniquity with great signs (27:1–2)
  - B. Nations who fight against Zion will suffer spiritual famine (27:3–5)
- III. The Lord will bring forth the Book of Mormon (27:6–22)
  - A. The Lord to bring forth a book containing words of them that have slumbered (27:6)
  - B. Sealed portion of the book will contain a revelation from the beginning to the end of the world, but the sealed information will not be given to the wicked (27:7–8)
  - C. The book will be delivered to a man (Joseph Smith) who will then deliver the words of the book to another (Martin Harris) (27:9; cf. 27:15–20; JS–H 1:63–65)
  - D. The sealed portion of the book will eventually be revealed to all (27:10–11)
  - E. Three witnesses and a few others will view the book (27:12–14, 22)
  - F. The words of the book will be taken to one who is learned (Charles Anthon), but he will not be able to read them (27:15–18; cf. JS–H 1:63–65)
  - G. The words of the book will be given again to one who is not learned (Joseph Smith) who will be able to read them and bring them forth (27:19–21)
  - H. The book will be sealed and hidden again to be brought forth, the remainder translated in the due time of the Lord (27:22)
- IV. The Lord will bring about a marvelous work and a wonder (27:23–35)
  - A. The Lord is a God of miracles (27:23)
  - B. The marvelous work—especially the Book of Mormon—will come forth and the wisdom of the wise and learned will perish (27:24–27)
  - C. Lebanon will be turned into a fruitful field and a forest (27:28)
  - D. The deaf, blind, and meek will hear, see, and rejoice in the words of the book (27:29–30)
  - E. Those that reject the book will be cut off (27:31–33)
  - F. The house of Jacob will sanctify and fear God (27:34)
  - G. Those that erred will learn doctrine (27:35)

comments in a way that often makes it difficult to distinguish between the text of Isaiah and the commentary of Nephi. The fulfillment of the prophecy of the coming forth of the Book of Mormon is recorded in Joseph Smith–History 1:27–75.

Definitions

26:6 *be as stubble.* Stubble left after a harvest is dry and explosively flammable. Hence when the Lord destroys the wicked it will be like a fire burning stubble—fast and furious.

26:15 *camped against them round about, and shall have laid siege against them with a mount, and raised forts against them; and after they shall have been brought down low in the dust.* Besieged them with the intent to destroy. Here Nephi directly applies the prophecy of Isaiah to the destruction of his own people (cf. Isa. 29:3).

26:16 *speak unto them out of the ground, and their speech shall be low out of the dust, and their voice shall be as one that hath a familiar spirit; . . . and their speech shall whisper out of the dust.* Imagery indicating that the written record of the Nephites will speak to later generations as one speaking from the grave. *See* Familiar spirit.

26:18 *as chaff that passeth away.* Imagery suggesting sudden annihilation. Chaff left after winnowing of a harvest passes away quickly and completely, either by burning in a fire or by a gust of wind.

27:1 *drunken with iniquity.* A metaphor for the senselessness and recklessness of those who are wicked.

27:3 *And all the nations that fight against Zion, and that distress her, shall be as a dream of a night vision; yea, it shall be unto them, even as unto a hungry man which dreameth, and behold he eateth but he awaketh and his soul is empty; or like unto a thirsty man which dreameth, and behold he drinketh but he awaketh and behold he is faint.* The nations who fight against Zion will be denied their expected victory (cf. 1 Ne. 22:14, 19; 2 Ne. 6:12–13; 10:16).

27:5 *Lord hath poured out upon you the spirit of deep sleep.* Referring to the spiritual blindness that is a consequence of apostasy (cf. Alma 12:9–11).

27:6 *slumbered.* Metaphor indicating the writers of the record have died.

27:7 *book shall be sealed.* A reference to the record on the gold plates. Part of this record was sealed and is to remain sealed and untranslated until the Lord sees fit to reveal it (27:8, 11, 22), while the part that was not sealed (27:15) was translated and published as the Book of Mormon.

27:9 *a man.* Joseph Smith.

27:9, 15 *another.* A reference to Martin Harris, to whom Joseph Smith entrusted a transcript and translation of some of the characters from the gold plates.

27:10 *words which are sealed.* Part of the gold plates, including the revelation given to the brother of Jared[1], that were sealed and will not be revealed until the Gentiles repent (Ether 3:22; 4:4–7).

27:12 *three witnesses.* Fulfilled by Oliver Cowdery, David Whitmer, and Martin Harris (D&C 5:11–15; 17:1; cf. Ether 5:2–4), the Three Witnesses to the divinity of the Book of Mormon. An angel of the Lord showed them the plates and the voice of the Lord declared that it was translated by the gift and power of God (The Testimony of Three Witnesses).

27:13 *save it be a few.* Fulfilled mainly by the Eight Witnesses who saw and handled the plates (The Testimony of Eight Witnesses).

27:15 *learned.* Professor Charles Anthon of Columbia University, an educated linguist of the day to whom Martin Harris took the characters copied from the plates and Joseph's translation of them (JS–H 1:64–65).

27:19 *not learned.* Joseph Smith, who had little formal education.

27:22 *seal up the book again.* Joseph Smith gave the gold plates back to Moroni.

27:25 *draw near unto me with their mouth, and with their lips do honor me, but have removed their hearts far from me.* Imagery for hypocrisy.

27:26 *marvelous work and a wonder.* The restoration of the gospel including the coming forth of the Book of Mormon.

27:26 *wisdom of their wise and learned shall perish, and the understanding of their prudent shall be hid.* Refers to the false teachings that will be exposed by the marvelous work and a wonder.

27:27 *seek deep to hide their counsel.* Refers to

ISA. CHAP. REVIEW: 2 NE. 26:6; 27 // ISA. 29

those who attempt to hide their wicked plans and desires from God.

27:27 *potter's clay.* Those who attempt to hide their counsel from the Lord are compared to clay and the Lord to a potter. The metaphor shows the foolishness of mortals who pretend to be mightier than their Creator (cf. D&C *10:5–34*).

27:28 *Lebanon shall be turned into a fruitful field; and the fruitful field shall be esteemed as a forest.* Imagery suggesting a change of values and perceptions among humankind. As a result of the marvelous work and a wonder (*see* discussion of 2 Ne. 27:26, above) the forests of Lebanon (a type for the pride and worldliness of people; cf. 2 Ne. 2:12–13; 19:9–10) will be replaced by fruitful fields (a type for productive covenant people of the Lord; e.g., Isa. 27:6; 37:31; cf. 2 Ne. 15:1–7). At that day these fruitful fields will be valued and esteemed just as much as the forests once were (cf. Isa. 32:15).

27:31 *terrible one is brought to naught, and the scorner is consumed.* As a result of the marvelous work and a wonder (*see* discussion of 2 Ne. 27:26, above), Satan and those who follow him

SELECTED DIFFERENCES BETWEEN B OF M ISA. (2 NE. 26:6, 15–18; 27) AND KJV ISA. (ISA. 29)

	BOOK OF MORMON		KJV ISAIAH	COMMENTARY
27:3	And all the nations that fight against **Zion,** and that distress her, shall be as a dream of a night vision . . .	29:7	And the multitude of all the nations that fight against Ariel, even all that fight against her and her munition, and that distress her, shall be as a dream of a night vision.	Changes Ariel, Jerusalem (Isa. 29:1) to Zion. Broadens the identification of the covenant people. *See* Zion.
27:4	**For behold, all ye that doeth iniquity,** stay yourselves and wonder, **for ye shall cry out,** and cry; **yea, ye shall be** drunken but not with wine, **ye shall** stagger but not with strong drink.	29:9	Stay yourselves, and wonder; cry ye out, and cry: they are drunken, but not with wine; they stagger, but not with strong drink.	Personalizes the message by identifying the drunken as second person rather than third.
27:5	For **behold,** the Lord hath poured out upon you the spirit of deep sleep. **For behold, ye have** closed your eyes, and **ye have rejected** the prophets; and your rulers, and the seers hath he covered **because of your iniquity.**	29:10	For the Lord hath poured out upon you the spirit of deep sleep, and hath closed your eyes: the prophets and your rulers, the seers hath he covered.	Clarifies that the people, not the Lord, have closed their eyes, that the people have rejected the prophets, and that the seers are covered because of the people's iniquity.
27: 6–23	Most of the material in these 18 verses is not found in KJV Isaiah but is found in JST Isaiah 29, leading some to believe that they were once part of the original text of Isaiah. Others consider the possibility that these verses include commentary by Nephi. The verses contain remarkable detail about events associated with the coming forth of and witnesses to the Book of Mormon (see outline).			
27: 24–25	**And again it shall come to pass that the Lord shall say unto him that shall read the words that shall be delivered him:** Forasmuch as this people draw near unto me with their mouth, and with their lips do honor me . . .	29:13	Wherefore the Lord said, Forasmuch as this people draw near me with their mouth, and with their lips do honour me . . .	Clarifies that verse 25 is addressed to Joseph Smith, the one to whom the record is delivered. The Lord quoted 2 Nephi 27:25 // Isaiah 29:13 to Joseph in the First Vision (see JS–H 1:19).

in rejecting and fighting against the Lord and his covenants will be silenced and destroyed.

27:32 *offender for a word.* Those who slander or condemn others because of, or with, their words.

27:32 *turn aside the just for a thing of naught.* Refers to those who reject truth and justice for some vain and temporal reward (i.e., those who reject the Book of Mormon) (cf. 2 Ne. 28:16; 29:3).

27:32 *lay a snare for him that reproveth in the gate.* To seek to undermine those who carry out justice. The area near the gate of a city was used anciently to conduct judgment and other types of business (cf. Deut. 21:19; Ruth 4).

27:33 *face now wax pale.* To grow white due to shame or embarrassment.

Selected differences between Book of Mormon Isaiah (2 Ne. 26:6, 15–18; 27) and KJV Isaiah (Isa. 29) are shown in the accompanying table.

Because Nephi's comments are interspersed in these chapters, it is difficult to separate the original Isaiah text from Nephi's commentary. Clearly Nephi knew that Isaiah's prophecies of apostasy and destruction applied to his people, and that the book about which Isaiah prophesied would be the Book of Mormon, the record of the Nephites. Only apparent significant Book of Mormon modifications to the Isaiah text are shown in this table.

Latter-day applicability

The value of the Book of Mormon to all people is well illustrated in this discourse by Nephi. Beginning in 2 Nephi 25 and continuing through 2 Nephi 29, Nephi addressed three groups of latter-day people: the Jews (e.g., 2 Ne. 25:9–20), the Lamanites (e.g., 2 Ne. 25:21–26:11), and the Gentiles (e.g., 2 Ne. 26:12–29:14). As he spoke of each group, he described the weaknesses, challenges, and problems they would face and then identified the Book of Mormon as a major part of the solution to their problems.

These chapters vividly describe the coming forth of the Book of Mormon and a sealed portion, containing the words of prophets long since passed away. These prophets prophesied that the book would be given to one who was unlearned, who would then give part to another, who in turn would take them to a "learned" person, who would declare that he could not read a sealed book. This prophecy was dramatically fulfilled when Moroni gave the gold plates, containing a sealed portion, to Joseph Smith, who gave a transcript of a portion of his work to Martin Harris, who then took it to Professor Charles Anthon, who declared, "I cannot read a sealed book" (JS–H 1:59–65).

The lesson is that the Lord is a "God of miracles" (2 Ne. 27:23). He will proceed with a "marvelous work and a wonder" in bringing forth the Book of Mormon (2 Ne. 27:26). The humble and meek will understand and accept the Book of Mormon while the proud will not. The deaf shall "hear the words of the book, and the eyes of the blind shall see out of obscurity and out of darkness" (2 Ne. 27:29). The "wisdom of [the] wise and learned shall perish" (2 Ne. 27:26) while the meek "shall increase, and their joy shall be in the Lord" (2 Ne. 27:30). Throughout this chapter, those who receive a portion of the book, the Book of Mormon, are promised the contents of the rest of the book, the sealed portion, in the due time of the Lord (2 Ne. 27:22; Ether 3:22; 4:4–7).

See also Anthon transcript; Marvelous work, marvelous work and a wonder; Sealed portion of the gold plates; Witnesses of the Book of Mormon.

MSN

Isaiah chap. review: Mosiah 14 // Isaiah 53

Background and synopsis

Isaiah 53 is the most explicit prophetic description of the mortal mission and ministry of the MESSIAH, the suffering servant, in the Old Testament. Abinadi recited this entire chapter in his discourse before king Noah[3] and his court in defense of his teaching "that God himself shall come down among the children of men, and . . . redeem his people" (Mosiah 15:1). The Isaiah quotation exemplified all past prophets' testimonies concerning "the coming of the Messiah," revealing that he would "take upon him the form of man" and that he would be "oppressed and afflicted" (Mosiah 13:33–35).

The opening verses describe the humble and

ISA. CHAP. REVIEW: MOSIAH 14 // ISA. 53

obscure beginnings of the Messiah (Mosiah 14:1–3); the following verses describe his sufferings and rejection as he fulfilled his mortal mission, took upon himself the sins and sufferings of the world, and healed humankind through his ATONEMENT (Mosiah 14:4–6). Isaiah then prophesied about events surrounding the Messiah's suffering and death in remarkable detail (Mosiah 14:7–9) and spoke of the necessity and results of the Atonement (Mosiah 14:10–12). Ultimately those who "make his soul an offering" for their sins become his "seed" or the children of Christ (Mosiah 14:10; cf. 5:7; 15:12).

Definitions

(14:1) *Who hath believed our report, and to whom is the arm of the Lord revealed?* The likely sense of the phrase "who hath believed our report" is that few have believed or understood the prophecies of the prophets that the Messiah would come into mortality in the form of a man. This belief and understanding comes only to those to whom the "arm of the Lord," or the power of God (Deut. 7:18–19), is revealed, for the things of God can only be understood by the Spirit of God (1 Cor. 2:11). Many do not respond to the Spirit because of hard-heartedness (John 12:39–41). Thus, the apostle John reported, "But though he had done so many miracles before them, yet they believed not on him; That the saying of Esaias the prophet might be fulfilled, which he spake, Lord, who hath believed our report? and to whom hath the arm of the Lord been revealed?" (John 12:37–38). In the case of Abinadi and the priests of Noah, Abinadi testified that God would come in the "form of a man, and go forth in mighty power upon the face of the earth" (Mosiah 13:34), and the priests of Noah "believed [not his] report" (Mosiah 14:1).

Abinadi quoted Isaiah 52:8–10 // Mosiah 15:29–31 concerning the arm of the Lord being ultimately and unmistakenly revealed to all:

OUTLINE OF MOSIAH 14

- I. Appraisal of the mortal Messiah (14:1–3)
  - A. He shall grow up as a tender plant (14:1–2)
  - B. He shall come forth as a root out of dry ground (14:2)
  - C. He shall have no form or comeliness (14:2)
  - D. He will be despised and rejected (14:3)
- II. Mission of the Messiah (14:4–6)
  - A. He will bear our griefs and carry our sorrows (14:4)
  - B. He will be wounded for our transgressions, bruised for our iniquities (14:5)
  - C. The chastisement of our peace will be upon him (14:5)
  - D. With his stripes we are healed (14:5)
  - E. He will bear the iniquities of all (14:6)
- III. Suffering and death of the Messiah (14:7–9)
  - A. He will be oppressed and afflicted (14:7)
  - B. He will not open his mouth (in the face of provocation) (14:7)
  - C. He will be brought forth from prison to be judged (14:8)
  - D. He will be cut off out of the land of the living (14:8)
  - E. He will experience death and burial with the wicked and rich (14:9)
- IV. Results of the Messiah's sacrificial mission (14:10–12)
  - A. The Father and Son will be pleased (14:10)
  - B. The Messiah shall see his seed (14:10)
  - C. He shall prolong his days (14:10)
  - D. His travail will result in glory (14:11)
  - E. He shall justify many (14:11)
  - F. He shall divide the spoil with the strong (14:12)

ISA. CHAP. REVIEW: MOSIAH 14 // ISA. 53

"The Lord hath made bare his holy arm in the eyes of all the nations; and all the ends of the earth shall see the salvation of our God" (Mosiah 15:31; cf. 16:1).

14:2 *tender plant.* A metaphor for Jesus' humble mortal beginning.

14:2 *a root out of dry ground.* The general spiritual condition of the children of Israel when Jesus entered the world was dry, hard, and impenetrable.

14:2 *he hath no form nor comeliness; and when we shall see him there is no beauty that we should desire him.* A description of Christ's physical appearance when he comes in the meridian of time as the mortal Messiah. Due to their years under political captivity and oppressors, many Jews were hoping for the appearance of the millennial Messiah who would come in supernatural power to overthrow their oppressors. His purposes, they supposed, would be well-known and publicized, and there would be no question about who he was. Everyone would recognize him at a glance. With this passage Isaiah made it clear that the Messiah of whom he was prophesying, the mortal Messiah, would not come as the bigger-than-life political deliverer that many expected.

14:3 *despised and rejected.* Isaiah clearly foretold the attitude of many in Israel regarding their Savior. Ironically, in rejecting these very words as a prophecy of the Messiah, his people were fulfilling them by despising and rejecting him. Many of his own family members failed to accept Jesus as Messiah at first (John 7:5); people in his hometown tried to kill him (Luke 4:16–30); his own countrymen rejected him (John 1:11); one of his closest associates betrayed him (Luke 22:48); in the end "all the disciples forsook him, and fled" (Matt. 26:56), and his enemies demanded his execution (Matt. 27:22–23). The people of Israel would hide their eyes from their God and not esteem his salvation (cf. 1 Ne. 19:7–9).

14:4 *Surely he has borne our griefs, and carried our sorrows.* In his vicarious sacrifice the Savior took upon himself not only all of mankind's sins but also their pains and sufferings—in this way he knows how to succor his followers in their hour of emotional need (cf. Alma 7:11–12; Heb. 2:18).

14:4 *stricken, smitten of God.* Some would think that he was afflicted by God because of his personal sins, but Isaiah taught otherwise—"he was wounded for *our* transgressions, he was bruised for *our* iniquities" (14:5; italics added).

14:5 *wounded for our transgressions, he was bruised for our iniquities; the chastisement of our peace was upon him; and with his stripes we are healed.* Descriptions of Christ's sufferings at Gethsemane and Golgotha wherein he took upon himself the sufferings and sins of the world to "heal" and redeem mankind.

14:5 *the chastisement of our peace was upon him.* "Peace" in Hebrew is *shalom,* which carries the connotation of wholeness. The Savior suffered chastisement so that all could be made whole.

14:6 *All we, like sheep, have gone astray.* Symbolizes the need for all to be saved by the atonement of Christ.

14:7 *he opened not his mouth.* While being accused and interrogated by the chief priests and Pilate, Jesus gave no answer (Mark 15:3; John 19:9), and while standing before Herod Antipas, Jesus answered him nothing (Luke 23:9). When the time came to be brought as a lamb to the slaughter, "the Lamb slain from the foundation of the world" (Rev. 13:8) opened not his mouth—just as a sheep is dumb, or mute, in the hands of the shearers.

14:8 *He was taken from prison and from judgment.* The Hebrew text implies that he was taken away from prison to be judged.

14:8 *who shall declare his generation? For he was cut off out of the land of the living.* In the Old Testament the value of one's life was often measured by his posterity, who would perpetuate his name, works, and merits. Inasmuch as Christ would be killed, "cut off out of the land of the living," who would be his posterity to carry on his work and glory? Who would declare the life and atoning mission of Jesus the Messiah? Abinadi seemed to be thinking in these terms when, in answer to the question "Who shall declare his generation?" he testified "that when [Christ's] soul has been made an offering for sin he shall see his seed" or posterity (Mosiah

15:10). Abinadi then taught that Christ's seed are those who believe in Christ and are redeemed through him—the prophets and those that believe on their words (Mosiah 15:10–12). They become his children, to perpetuate his name, works, and merits.

14:9 *he made his grave with the wicked, and with the rich in his death.* Perhaps referring to Christ's crucifixion between two thieves (Matt. 27:38) and his burial in the grave of a rich man, Joseph of Arimathea (Matt. 27:57–60).

14:10 *Yet it pleased the Lord to bruise him.* This phrase has at least two possible interpretations: (1) "Lord" is likely a reference to Elohim, the Father, thus teaching that this was a willing offering by the Father and the Son; or (2) Isaiah may be differentiating between the two roles of the Savior: it pleased Jehovah, the God of the Old Testament, to bruise Jesus, pointing to the fact that the great Jehovah would come in the person of Jesus, and that they are, indeed, one God (cf. Mosiah 15:2–4).

14:10 *when thou shalt make his soul an offering for sin he shall see his seed.* "His" and "he" in this passage are usually taken to mean Christ, while the pronoun "thou" is thought to refer to either God the Father or to those receiving the prophecy. In either case the message is the same for all—when one is forgiven of sins through the Atonement, one is spiritually begotten of Christ and becomes "his seed," or children (cf. Mosiah 15:10–12; D&C 84:36–38).

14:10 *he shall prolong his days.* Christ will be resurrected and become immortal.

14:11 *He shall see the travail of his soul.* Luke asked, "Ought not Christ to have suffered these things, and to enter into his glory?" (Luke 24:25–26). Jesus' crown of thorns came before his crown of glory. Having shown the way, he later taught that after much tribulation come the blessings (D&C 58:4). The grand purpose of all his suffering was for humankind to become his seed and declare his generation.

14:11 *justify many.* To make righteous and reconcile many. The use of "many" rather than "all" suggests that some, the unrepentant, will not be justified (cf. D&C 19:16–19).

14:12 *he shall divide the spoil with the strong.* The strong or faithful will become joint-heirs with the Savior to "the spoil," meaning the fulness of the Father (Rom. 8:17; D&C 50:26–28; 76:50–60; 88:107; 93:15–30; 132:20).

Latter-day applicability

Isaiah's poetic description of the Messiah teaches much about who Jesus was and about the purpose of his mortal ministry. Contrary to what was expected by many of the Jews in the meridian of time, who were looking for an invincible millennial Messiah to come in power and glory, the mortal Messiah Isaiah described would come from humble and obscure beginnings, would look like an ordinary man, and would suffer and die. In his first coming to earth he came as a suffering servant; in his second coming he will come as a reigning King. In his first coming he would not overthrow earthly kingdoms and governments but rather conquer something far greater, even sin and death. This chapter teaches how, through the Atonement, or the vicarious suffering of Jesus, individuals can be forgiven of sins and become the sons and daughters of Christ. Thus they become joint heirs with Christ to all the blessings of the Father (cf. Rom. 8:17; D&C 76:54–56, 59, 95).

DKO

Isaiah chap. review: 3 Nephi 20:32–45 // Isaiah 52:1–3, 6–15

Background and synopsis

After a miraculous administration of the sacrament to the righteous descendants of Lehi[1] who were gathered at the temple in Bountiful[2], the resurrected Savior informed them that he was about to "finish the commandment" or the teachings started the day before which he had received from the Father concerning them (3 Ne. 20:1–10). He then admonished those ancient Saints to search the words of Isaiah and promised that when Isaiah's words were fulfilled, they would know the Father was fulfilling the covenants he had made with the house of Israel, of which they were a part (3 Ne. 20:11–12; cf. 16:17–20). Jesus then explained that the Father's covenant included the future gathering of Israel, their restoration to a "knowledge of the

ISA. CHAP. REVIEW: 3 NE. 20 // ISA. 52

Lord their God," and the establishment of Lehi's descendants in the Americas (3 Ne. 20:13–14, 22). Christ quoted and paraphrased excerpts from Isaiah (Isa. 52) which describe the Restoration and subsequent joy that would accompany the fulfilling of the covenant (3 Ne. 20:32–42 // Isa. 52:1–3, 6–15), and which tell how in that day, he, who was afflicted "more than any man," would finally be acknowledged and revered (3 Ne. 20:43–45 // Isa. 52:13–15). Jacob[2], Abinadi, and Moroni[2] also quoted from Isaiah 52, making it the most quoted chapter of Isaiah in the Book of Mormon (2 Ne. 8:24–25; Mosiah 12:20–24; 15:13–18; Moro. 10:31; cf. 1 Ne. 13:37).

Definitions

20:32 *watchmen.* Servants of the Lord assigned to teach, warn, and nurture the people (cf. Ezek. 33:1–16).

20:32 *together shall they sing.* An act of rejoicing. The Lord through Joseph Smith revealed the words to this grand song in Doctrine and Covenants 84:99–102.

20:35 *The Father hath made bare his holy arm.* Describes the Lord when he comes forth in power and judgment (cf. D&C 133:1–3; Isa. 63:5–6).

20:36 *put on thy strength, O Zion.* Refers to the authority of the priesthood received by the people of Zion in the last days (D&C 113:7–8).

20:36 *put on thy beautiful garments.* A metaphor for the gathering of the righteous. The faithful gathering is like a bride putting on her wedding garments in preparation for the coming of the bridegroom, or Christ (Isa. 49:18). In the latter days, the metaphor represents the covenant Latter-day Saints as organized in stakes of Zion (D&C 82:14–15).

20:36 *uncircumcised.* Metaphor for those who refuse the Lord's covenants.

20:37 *arise, sit down, O Jerusalem.* God's people are to get up from the dust and seat themselves in his company.

20:37 *loose thyself from the bands of thy neck.* As scattered Israel returns to the Lord, God's curses, especially the curse of being scattered among the Gentiles, will be taken away (D&C 113:9–10).

20:38 *sold yourselves for naught.* Invested their faith, time, or assets in things of no value.

20:38 *redeemed without money.* Imagery that serves to remind all that eternal redemption is wrought not with worldly treasures but rather made available through the atonement of Christ.

20:40 *How beautiful upon the mountains are the feet of him.* Refers to Christ and his messengers who bring the gospel to the world. Note the prophet Abinadi's fourfold use of this phrase as he speaks of past, present, and future messengers and especially the Lord himself (Mosiah 15:15–18).

20:41 *vessels of the Lord.* Likely a reference to the holy vessels of the temple. Thus those that bear them are priesthood holders. *See* vessels of the Lord.

20:42 *ye shall not go out with haste nor go by flight.* Ancient Israel left Egypt with haste and flight (Ex. 12:39; Deut. 16:3), but latter-day Israel is to assemble in order (D&C 133:12–15).

20:42 *rearward.* A rearguard, or that which protects one's most vulnerable places.

OUTLINE OF 3 NEPHI 20:32–45

I. The covenant is fulfilled (20:32–42)
   - A. The people will rejoice as the Lord establishes Zion (20:32–35)
   - B. Zion and Jerusalem will be restored and freed from oppression (20:36–38)
   - C. The Lord and his messengers will be known and loved (20:39–40)
   - D. The people are gathered and cleansed as the God of Israel leads and protects them (20:41–42)

II. A marred servant will eventually be acknowledged and revered (20:43–45)

ISA. CHAP. REVIEW: 3 NE. 22 // ISA. 54

20:43 *my servant.* probably Jesus Christ. Some have also identified this servant with the Prophet Joseph Smith, citing 2 Nephi 21:7–11 as evidence that it must also apply to a servant who will come forth after Christ. *See* Smith, Joseph, Jr., Book of Mormon prophecies of.

20:44 *his visage was so marred.* Refers to the suffering of the servant, such as Jesus Christ or Joseph Smith.

20:45 *sprinkle.* Meaning to purify or make clean. Changed to "gather" in Joseph Smith's translation of Isaiah 52:15.

Latter-day applicability

The importance of these verses from Isaiah 52 is apparent as they are quoted so frequently in the Book of Mormon. They are also a subject of at least two sections of the Doctrine and Covenants (113; 133). As the Lord's messengers share the gospel throughout the earth and his purified people come together out of the wicked world, they can know that heavenly powers and protection will assist them. The Lord himself and his mighty servants help in this marvelous redemption.

VLL

Isaiah chap. review: 3 Nephi 22 // Isaiah 54

Background and synopsis

This significant chapter of Isaiah, quoted by the resurrected Savior to the descendants of Lehi[1], prophesies of a time when the children of the Gentile nations and returning Israelites will flood into the "tent" or covenant of Israel (3 Ne. 22:1–3). This prophecy is to be fulfilled as the Gentiles receive the gospel, take it to the Lamanites and the rest of scattered Israel, and together build the New Jerusalem (3 Ne. 21:1–22:1). The Lord promised that the "power of heaven [will] come down among them" and that he would be in their midst (3 Ne. 21:25; cf. 20:22). As the people repent in that day, the Lord makes a covenant that he will forgive and redeem them like a husband who reconciles with a once rebellious and wicked wife (3 Ne. 22:4–10). Consequently a time of prosperity, peace, and protection will follow (3 Ne. 22:11–17).

Definitions

22:1 *Sing, O barren, thou that didst not bear; break forth into singing, and cry aloud, thou that didst not travail with child; for more are the children of the desolate than the children of the married wife.* Imagery suggesting a great time of rejoicing when the Lord gathers and redeems his people. Apparently a large number will come from an overlooked, forgotten, or unexpected source (the desolate), likely the Gentile nations, including lost and scattered children of Israel (cf. Isa. 49:18–22; 56:3–8).

22:1 *barren.* Israel in her scattered, spiritually unproductive state.

22:1 *children of the married wife.* Latter-day covenant people of the Lord.

22:2 *Enlarge the place of thy tent, and let them stretch forth the curtains of thy habitations; spare not, lengthen thy cords and strengthen thy stakes.*

OUTLINE OF 3 NEPHI 22

I. Covenant people will be gathered after Israel has been scattered (22:1–8)
   A. People will rejoice at the multitude that gathers (22:1)
   B. So many will be gathered that more room will be required and desolate cities will be inhabited (22:2–3)
   C. Though once estranged, the Lord will forgive, restore, and redeem his people (22:4–8)

II. The Lord gives a promise of kindness and peace as a covenant (22:9–10)

III. The blessings of the redeemed (22:11–17)
   A. The redeemed will enjoy prosperity and peace (22:11–14)
   B. The redeemed will enjoy divine protection (22:15–17)

MAP A. NEAR EASTERN PLACE NAMES IN THE ISAIAH CHAPTERS IN THE BOOK OF MORMON

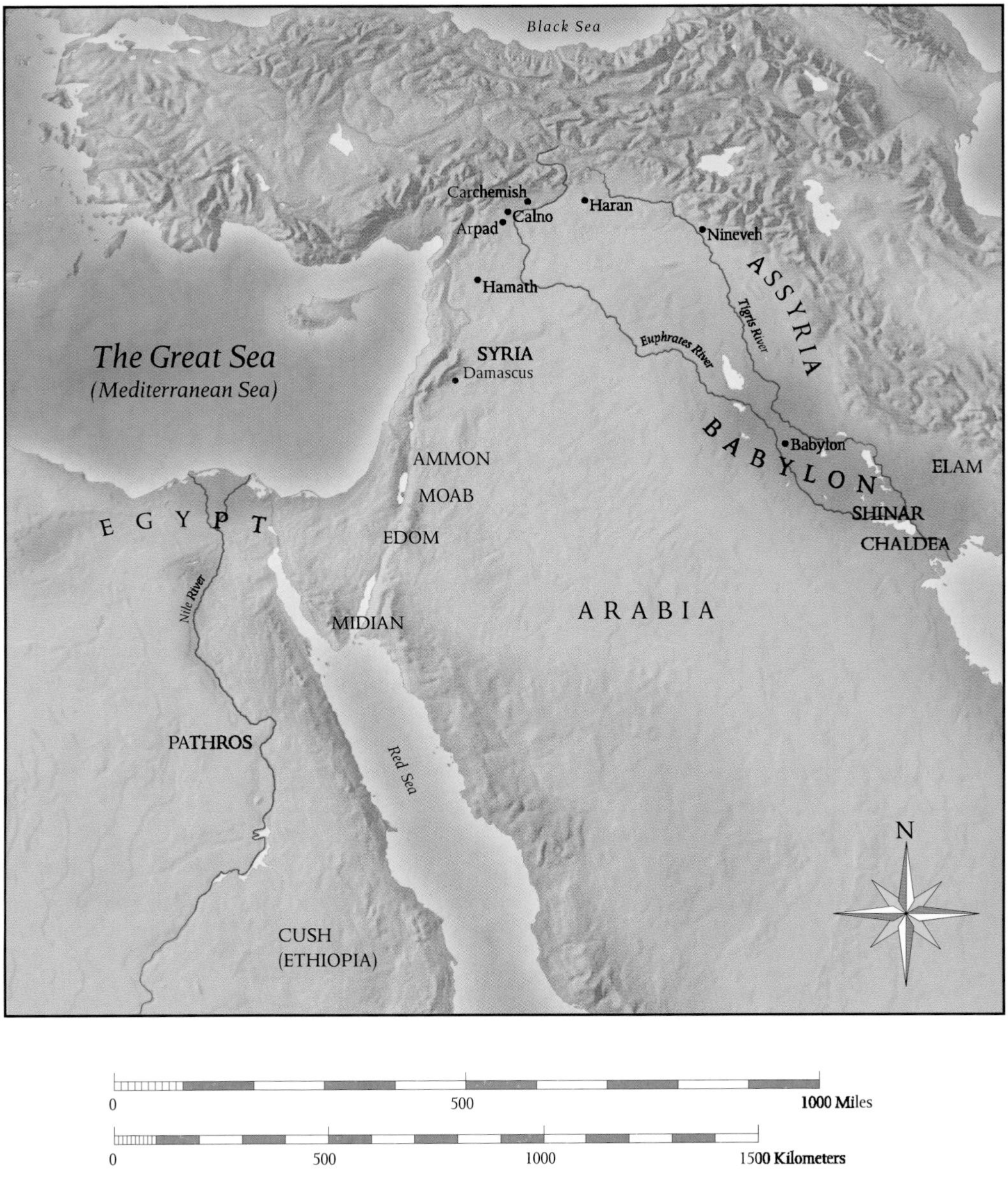

MAP B. HOLY LAND PLACE NAMES IN THE ISAIAH CHAPTERS IN THE BOOK OF MORMON

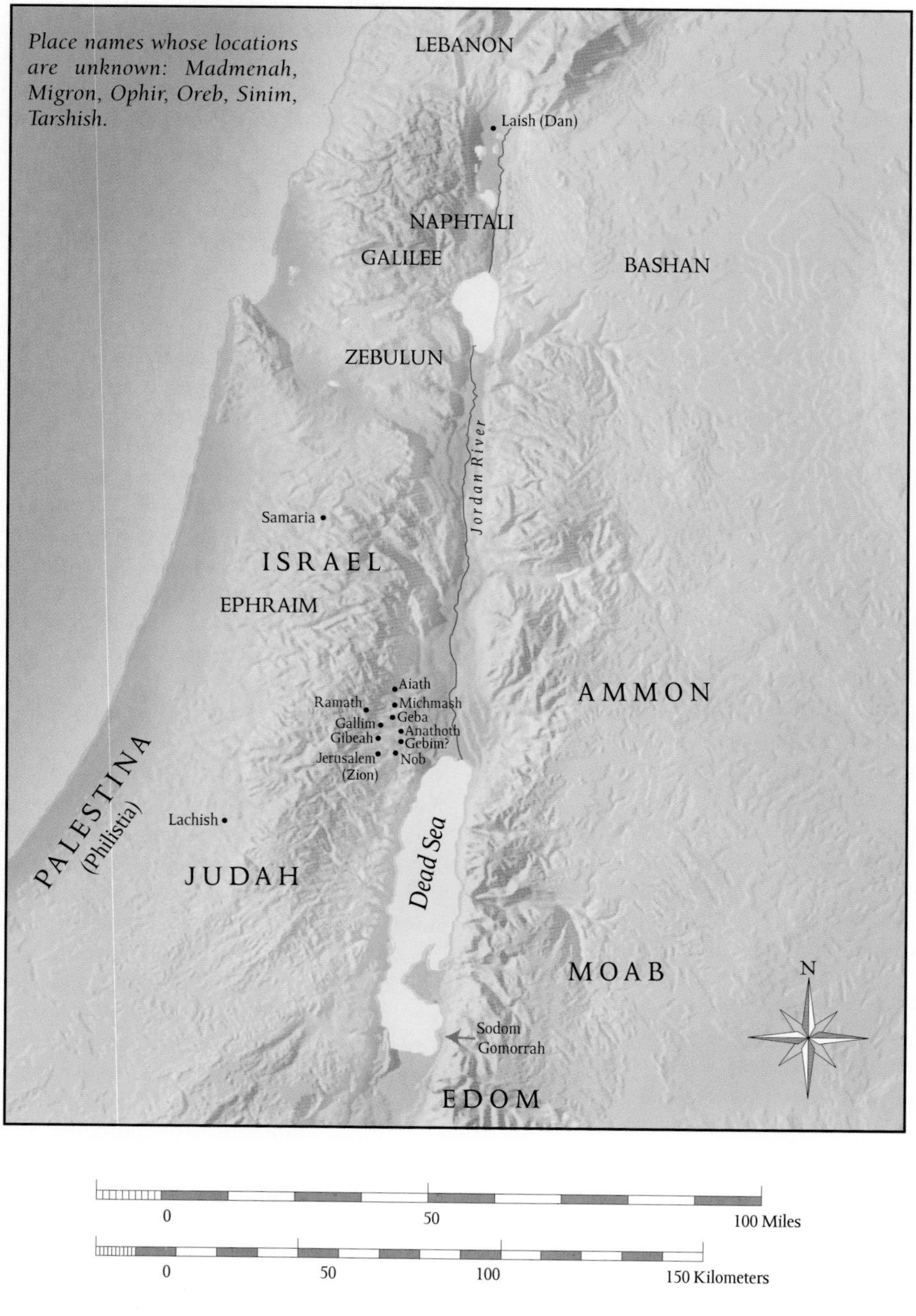

The tent is made larger to make room for those being gathered, especially as Zion is being expanded with new stakes (cf. D&C 82:14).

22:3 *thy seed shall inherit the Gentiles.* The Lord's people and the expanding families of Israelites, such as the Lamanites, will occupy desolate Gentile cities and even "adopt" the Gentiles, likely by converting them to the covenant and making them part of Israel (cf. Abr. 2:9–10; Isa. 56:3–8).

22:4 *Thou shalt forget the shame of thy youth, and shalt not remember the reproach of thy youth, and shalt not remember the reproach of thy widowhood.* Referring to that time when the people estranged themselves from God (cf. Isa. 50:1–2).

22:5–8 *thy husband, the Lord of Hosts . . . hath called thee as a woman forsaken and grieved in spirit, and a wife of youth. . . . For a small moment have I forsaken thee, but with great mercies will I gather thee. In a little wrath I hid my face from thee . . . , but with everlasting kindness will I have mercy on thee.* Imagery suggesting God will accept the gathered people back into the covenant just as a husband forgives, reconciles with, and cares for an estranged wife.

22:9 *waters of Noah unto me.* Suggesting that God will keep his covenants to fulfill the promises of this prophecy, just as he has kept his covenant with Noah[1] to never destroy the earth by flood again (cf. Gen. 9:11–13).

22:11–12 *lay thy stones with fair colors, and lay thy foundations with sapphires. And I will make thy windows of agates, and thy gates of carbuncles, and all thy borders of pleasant stones.* Various precious stones used as building materials in the dwelling place of the redeemed covenant people. These likely symbolize the prosperity and choice blessings of the Lord (cf. Rev. 21:18–21).

22:16 *created the smith that bloweth the coals in the fire, and that bringeth forth an instrument for his work; and I have created the waster to destroy.* Imagery bespeaking God's omnipotence, for he creates both those who makes things (the smith) and those who destroy (the waster). This imagery thus assures the people that God can keep his promises of redemption and protection.

Latter-day applicability

Third Nephi 22 and the surrounding material (3 Ne. 20:10–23:5) present a great discourse of the Savior that offers hope and motivation to latter-day covenant people. It assures them that as the millennial day approaches, Zion will be established, the gospel will go forth, Israel will be gathered, the city of the New Jerusalem will be built, and Christ will reign in the midst of his people. The Lord's people are promised forgiveness, redemption, prosperity, peace, and protection. Just as he promised that there would never be another great flood on the earth, God covenants to keep these promises with his covenant people.

VLL

Ishmael[1] Resident of Jerusalem (600 B.C.) and father of at least five daughters and two sons (1 Ne. 7:2, 6). Ishmael consented to take his family and join with Lehi[1] and his family in the wilderness when Nephi[1] spoke "unto him the words of the Lord" (1 Ne. 7:4). Even though he may have known Lehi beforehand, Nephi recorded that "the Lord did soften the heart of Ishmael" (1 Ne. 7:5). Nothing is recorded about Ishmael thereafter until his death at Nahom, which event was the catalyst for sorrow, rebellion, and a renewed desire by those opposed to Lehi and Nephi to return to Jerusalem (1 Ne. 16:34–37).

The significance of Ishmael in the Book of Mormon is substantial. It was the Lord who selected Ishmael and his family to marry Lehi's children and have posterity in the promised land (1 Ne. 7:1–2). In addition, the Prophet Joseph Smith reportedly taught that Ishmael was of the lineage of Ephraim, a son of Joseph[1] who was sold into Egypt (Snow, 23:184). Because Lehi was of Manasseh (Alma 10:3), another son of Joseph, the intermarriage of both families conjoined these two branches of Joseph's family. The Prophet Joseph Smith further taught that this union "thus fulfill[ed] the words of Jacob[1] upon Ephraim and Manasseh in the 48th chapter of Genesis, which says: 'And let my name be named on them, and the name of my fathers Abraham and Isaac; and let them grow into a multitude in the midst of the earth' [Gen. 48:16]" (Snow, 23:184–85).

The descendants of Ishmael, although mentioned several times in the Book of Mormon text as a separate people, like other groups, are identified as either Nephites or Lamanites (Jacob 1:13; Alma 47:35; 4 Ne. 1:38; Morm. 1:9).

BIBLIOGRAPHY

Snow, Erastus. *Journal of Discourses.* 26 vols. London: Latter-day Saints' Book Depot, 1854–86.

KJW

Ishmael[2] Grandfather of Amulek, a descendant of the Aminadi who interpreted writing on the wall of the temple "which was written by the finger of God" (Alma 10:2).

Ishmael, land of Portion of original land of Nephi over which the Lamanite Lamoni, a descendant of Ishmael, was king (Alma 17:21; ca. 90 B.C.). Ammon[2] served here while on his mission and helped convert Lamoni and his people (Alma 17:19, 21; 18:40; 19:33–36; 22:4). After Lamoni's conversion, he had synagogues built in the land (Alma 21:20). Later, under the threat of a Lamanite attack, Ammon and his brethren held a council in Ishmael with Lamoni and his brother, Anti-Nephi-Lehi, to plan the defense of the converted Lamanites who had made a covenant as part of their repentance not to fight (Alma 24:5–6). After the ensuing wars and slaughter of unarmed converts, many Lamanites gathered to the land of Ishmael and united with "the people of God" (Alma 25:13).

The land of Ishmael is also mentioned in the account of the altercation between Lamoni and his father, mainly over Lamoni's friendship with Ammon (a Nephite) and his intention to free Ammon's brothers from prison in Middoni. Lamoni's father commanded his son to return with him to the land of Ishmael (Alma 20:14–15).

Ishmaelites The descendants of Ishmael[1]. Just as the sons of Ishmael joined with Laman[1] and Lemuel in rebellion (1 Ne. 7:6; 18:9), so their descendants remained united with the Lamanites until they were rarely distinguished from them even in name (Jacob 1:13–14; Alma 43:13; 47:35; Morm. 1:8–9). They were subject to the same judgments that fell upon the Lamanites (Alma 3:7), but they would also eventually partake of the restoration of the gospel of Jesus Christ with them (D&C 3:18–19).

Isles of the sea A phrase that refers to the locations of scattered covenant people, "isles of the sea" appears initially in the prophecies of Isaiah (1 Ne. 21:8; cf. Isa. 49:8) and Zenos (1 Ne. 19:10, 12, 16). One finds prophecies about people on the isles of the sea only in the writings and sermons of Nephi[1] (1 Ne. 22:4; 2 Ne. 29:7) and his brother Jacob[2] (2 Ne. 10:8, 21).

God's scattering of his people onto "the isles of the sea" and elsewhere (1 Ne. 22:4; cf. 21:1) held interest for Nephi and Jacob because they understood their people to be among those whom the Lord had preserved by leading them from their homeland to "an isle of the sea" (2 Ne. 10:20). Because they felt uprooted themselves (Jacob 7:26), they looked forward to the day when the Lord would restore their people to their rightful place (1 Ne. 19:16; 2 Ne. 10:7–8).

SKB

Israel, concept of Israel was the new name given Jacob[1], the son of Isaac and the grandson of Abraham (Gen. 32:28). Pronounced *Yisrael* in Hebrew, the name combines two roots *sara* (persevere, persist) and *el* (god), and it literally means "let God prevail." Ideally, a true Israelite is one who both recognizes the "prevailing of God" and also "prevails with God" through earnest prayer and covenant righteousness. The term *Israel* (or *Israelite*) as found in the scriptures has three main contexts and can refer to a descendant of the man Israel, the land where the ISRAELITES lived, or a covenant people whose obedience empowers them to prevail together with God in righteousness. Lineage Israel are the descendants of Israel/Jacob. As the blood of Israel, they are often identified as a member of one of the tribes of Israel (Num. 2). The Jews are the most identifiable remnant of Israel's lineage on the earth today. The Book of Mormon title page states that the Nephites and Lamanites were also remnants of Israel and many divine promises were recorded for them by the Book of Mormon prophets. Most references to Israel in the Book of Mormon relate to the lineage or house of Israel.

ISRAEL, COVENANTS UNTO

Land Israel is the territory in biblical times variously called the land of Canaan, Israel, Judah/Judea, or the Holy Land. It is now mostly encompassed in the modern State of Israel. Many special promises are recorded in the scriptures concerning the land of Israel and its inhabitants (e.g., Gen. 17:7–8; 3 Ne. 20:29–38; Ether 13:11). Similar promises concerning a new land of promise (America) are recorded for the Book of Mormon peoples (e.g., 2 Ne. 1:3–11; 3 Ne. 20:14, 21–22).

Covenant Israel includes those who are true believers of the Lord Jesus Christ, regardless of lineage or geographical location. Nephi[1] was taught that those who would not harden their hearts against Jesus Christ would eventually be numbered among the covenant people of Israel (1 Ne. 14:2). GENTILES who come unto Christ are also a part of covenant Israel (3 Ne. 21:6); however, those of the lineage of Israel who do not repent, follow the Lord, and honor their covenants will be cut off from the house of Israel (2 Ne. 30:1–2; 3 Ne. 20:23–25; cf. 21:20; Rom. 2:25–29). Covenant Israelites are the true heirs to the great promises given to Abraham, Isaac, and Jacob. Thus, the blessings promised to the patriarch Israel may be passed on to his descendants and to the inhabitants of the land of Israel, but the ultimate fulfillment of Israel's blessings will be enjoyed by all of covenant Israel.

See also Abrahamic covenant; Adoption; Israel, covenants unto; Israel, gathering of; Israel, numbered among; Israel, scattering of; Joseph[1], covenants unto.

VLL

Israel, covenants unto The Lord's covenants with Israel are founded upon four promises given to Abraham: (1) that Abraham's seed would grow and continue forever (Gen. 17:4–9), (2) that his posterity would inherit lands of promise (Gen. 13:14–15), (3) that his descendants would hold the priesthood and enjoy its blessings (Abr. 1:18; 2:11), and (4) that through his seed "shall all families of the earth be blessed" (Gen. 12:3; cf. 1 Ne. 15:18; Gal. 3:8). As a part of blessing the families of the earth, the Lord promised Abraham that his seed would eventually carry the gospel to all nations (Abr. 2:9, 11).

Later prophets confirmed these Abrahamic blessings to the house of Israel and prophesied how they would be fulfilled. Moses and Joshua taught the Israelites the conditions upon which these blessings are predicated (Deut. 5–6; 28–30; Josh. 23–24). Isaiah prophesied concerning the covenant blessings of Israel and stressed that they must live worthily to receive them (Isa. 48–52; 1 Ne. 20–21; 2 Ne. 7–8; 3 Ne. 20). As recorded in the Book of Mormon, the Lord promised that in the last days all the promises to Israel would be fulfilled (3 Ne. 20:12; 23:1–3). The Book of Mormon not only provides additional prophetic teachings about the Lord's covenants with Israel but also indicates its own key role in presenting the covenant concepts of the gospel to the world in the latter days.

The Book of Mormon, as its title page proclaims, plays a special role in recording the Lord's covenants with Israel. First, this work of scripture shows unto the house of Israel "what great things the Lord hath done for their fathers" as it demonstrates the Lord's promises which have already been fulfilled. It also reaffirms to Israel those covenants which are yet to be fulfilled, "that they may know the covenants of the Lord, that they are not cast off forever" (cf. 3 Ne. 15:4–8).

The resurrected Savior taught about God's covenants with Israel in three major public sermons recorded in the Book of Mormon. The first sermon, similar to the Sermon on the Mount (Matt. 5–7), began with a covenant, or contract, between Christ and his New World followers wherein the Lord promised particular blessings, and rewards for those who develop and demonstrate certain Christlike behaviors and attitudes (3 Ne. 12:1–12 // Matt. 5:1–12). The Savior's second sermon, found in 3 Nephi 15–16, could be referred to as "The Law and Covenant Discourse." In it, Jesus declared that he was the one who gave the law to Moses and that he also was the one who covenanted with his people of the house of Israel (3 Ne. 15:5). Further, he clarified that "the covenant which I have made with my people is not all fulfilled; but the law

ISRAEL, GATHERING OF

which was given unto Moses hath an end in me" (3 Ne. 15:8). He then spoke of some important elements of the covenant remaining to be fulfilled. Continuing his teachings the next day, the Savior delivered his third sermon, which could be called "The Covenant People Discourse" (3 Ne. 20:10–23:5). Christ devoted much of this sermon to enumerating to Israel those blessings which would be restored to them in the last days. He promised that as Israel proved faithful, the remnants of Israel would be gathered from the world to their various lands of inheritance. In fact, additional lands of inheritance were promised the house of Israel in the Americas (3 Ne. 20:22). As the Book of Mormon itself would come forth from the Gentiles to the Lamanites in the latter days, it would be the Lord's special sign to Israel that these covenant promises have already begun to be fulfilled (3 Ne. 21:1–7).

This sacred record, with its covenant teachings, signs, and promises, is one reason why various Book of Mormon prophets sought and obtained the promise that their writings would be preserved (e.g., Enos 1:13–18; cf. D&C 3:19–20). The Book of Mormon is God's instrument not just in instructing Israel and testifying to the world but also in fulfilling the prophecy to the house of Israel that through their seed "all the kindreds of the earth [shall] be blessed," as this scripture helps bring souls to salvation through a covenant relationship with the Lord Jesus Christ (1 Ne. 15:18; 5:17–19; 6:4; 22:8–12; 2 Ne. 3:12, 23; 25:17, 18, 23; 30:3–8; Alma 37:1–20).

See also Abrahamic covenant; Book of Mormon, selected purposes of, to show unto the remnant of the House of Israel what great things the Lord hath done for their fathers; Covenant(s); Israel, historical background of; Israel, house of; Joseph[1], covenants unto.

VLL

Israel, gathering of Anciently God made a covenant with Abraham, promising him the blessings of the gospel and the priesthood, a numerous posterity, and specific lands for inheritance. The covenant also included the responsibility to bear the gospel message to all nations so that all of God's children could be blessed (Abr. 2:6–11). The ABRAHAMIC COVENANT was passed on through Abraham's son Isaac and grandson Jacob (Gen. 26:3–4; 28:3–4). Thus Jacob's posterity, known as the house of Jacob, house of Israel, or simply Israel, were partakers of these covenant blessings and responsibilities. After Joshua led the children of Israel into the promised land, he divided the land and gave portions to each of Jacob's sons. Throughout Israel's history in the promised land, prophets warned the Israelites that if they turned away from Jehovah, they would be removed from the land and lose their covenant blessings. Israel ultimately rejected the words of the prophets and hardened their hearts against the "Holy One of Israel." This brought the Lord's condemnation and Israel's scattering among all nations (1 Ne. 19:13–14; 22:4–5; 2 Ne. 6:8–11; 10:5–6; Hel. 7:17–19). They were scattered not only from their lands but also from their Lord and those associations, covenants, and ordinances that lead to salvation.

In addition to prophecies of scattering, destruction, captivity, and lost promises, prophets foretold of a day of restoration—a day when scattered Israel would come back to their God, and the covenant would be reestablished (1 Ne. 22:7–12; 2 Ne. 10:6–7; 3 Ne. 5:24–26; Isa. 11:10–16; Ezek. 36–37). They would be blessed, prospered, and eventually gathered back to the land of their inheritance.

The beginning of the gathering of the house of Israel in the latter days

The restoration of the fulness of the gospel through the Prophet Joseph Smith is in fact the restoration of the Abrahamic covenant. Through this restoration Deity renewed for the Latter-day Saints all he promised to the former-day Saints (D&C 132:29–32; Abr. 2:8–11). Nephi[1] prophesied that in a "mighty nation among the Gentiles" God would restore "his covenants and his gospel" and thus renew the promises made to his ancient covenant people. The dispensation of the fulness of times is therefore designated as that day in which the Father will "make bear his arm in the eyes of the nations," that is, he will demonstrate his infinite power to gather his children throughout the earth (1 Ne. 22:7–12).

ISRAEL, GATHERING OF

Jacob[2] testified that "the Messiah will set himself again the second time to recover" his chosen people (2 Ne. 6:14; cf. 21:11 // Isa. 11:11). Indeed, the work of restoration in the last days would be that "marvelous work and a wonder" foreseen by Isaiah whereby the Lord Jehovah would "set his hand again the second time to restore his people from their lost and fallen state" (2 Ne. 25:17; cf. 29:1; Isa. 29:14).

The work of gathering thus began at the time the Church was organized in April of 1830. That work was formalized on 3 April 1836 in the Kirtland Temple through the bestowal by Moses of priesthood keys associated with the gathering of Israel (D&C 110:11). The Lord had explained earlier that "Israel shall be saved in mine own due time; and by the keys which I have given shall they be led, and no more be confounded at all" (D&C 35:25).

How Israel is gathered

The gathering of Israel consists of coming unto Christ, joining the true church, and gathering or congregating with the people of the covenant. Whenever the people of God "no more turn aside their hearts against the Holy One of Israel" (1 Ne. 19:15), when they "come to the knowledge of . . . their Redeemer" and his gospel, they are gathered (1 Ne. 10:14; 15:14–15).

The Book of Mormon teaches that the gathering of Israel is a two-fold process: spiritual and temporal, in that order. Israel is gathered, first, to Jesus Christ through gospel covenants and, second, to a place (2 Ne. 6:8–11; 10:3–8; 3 Ne. 5:23–26). In this regard, Mormon testified, "And as surely as the Lord liveth, will he gather in from the four quarters of the earth all the remnant of the seed of Jacob, who are scattered abroad upon all the face of the earth. . . . And then shall they know their Redeemer, who is Jesus Christ, the Son of God; and then shall they be gathered in from the four quarters of the earth unto their own lands, from whence they have been dispersed" (3 Ne. 5:24, 26; cf. 2 Ne. 10:7). Although some branches of Israel will physically move to lands promised them anciently (e.g., 3 Ne. 20:29; Ether 13:11), generally, baptized converts gather to meet and worship in the stakes and wards where they reside. President Spencer W. Kimball taught that "any person . . . who has accepted the restored gospel, and who now seeks to worship the Lord in his own tongue and with the Saints in the nations where he lives, has complied with the law of the gathering of Israel and is heir to all of the blessings promised the Saints in these last days" (439; cf. McConkie, *Millennial,* 193–205).

Thus, in principle, the gathering of the house of Israel is not just the gathering of the Jews, Lehi's descendants, or some other specific tribe, branch, or remnant of Israel. It is the gathering of all people to Christ and to the covenants and ordinances which bring salvation. The Lord admonished latter-day GENTILES to "come unto me, and be baptized in my name, that ye may receive a remission of your sins, and be filled with the Holy Ghost, that ye may be numbered with my people who are of the house of Israel" (3 Ne. 30:2; cf. 21:22; Gal. 3:27–29). Therefore, regardless of genealogical descent, people are gathered (numbered with Israel) through missionary work, as they accept the first principles and ordinances of the gospel and thereafter the ordinances of the temple (Smith, 307–8; Kimball, 438–39; McConkie, *Millennial,* 193–205).

The Gentiles and the gathering of Israel

The Book of Mormon teaches that it would be through the "fulness of the Gentiles" that Israel would be gathered. This means that the fulness of the gospel would be restored to the Gentiles and the Gentiles would take the gospel to Israel scattered throughout the world (1 Ne. 15:13–18; cf. 10:14; 21:22; 22:8–12; 2 Ne. 10:8; Morm. 5:10). The Lord promised, "Behold, I will lift up mine hand to the Gentiles, and set up my standard to the people; and they shall bring thy sons in their arms, and thy daughters shall be carried upon their shoulders" (1 Ne. 21:22). The standard God would establish among the Gentiles is the restored gospel of Jesus Christ, the "marvelous work." And carrying Israel in Gentile arms and upon Gentile shoulders is a metaphor for the tender and loving work Gentiles would perform in gathering Israel (1 Ne. 22:8). These latter-day Gentiles who would receive the restored gospel are really Israelites by lineal descent but Gentiles by culture. For example, Joseph Smith was a descendant of Joseph of Egypt (2 Ne. 3:7, 14–15), but he was a Gentile by culture and nationality. This truth, that the gospel was restored to literal descendants of the house of Israel, accords with the Lord's proclamation that it would be through the seed of Abraham that all the world would be blessed, "even with the blessings of the Gospel, which are the blessings of salvation" (Abr. 2:11).

Because Israel was scattered among the nations of the Gentiles, and because for centuries these scattered remnants of Israel intermarried with Gentiles, the blood of Israel can be found in all nations of the earth. Most of the gathering of Israel since the Restoration has been from Gentile nations. These converts, primarily Gentiles by culture but Israelites by descent, are brought to the knowledge of their Israelite heritage through restored gospel teachings and patriarchal blessings.

A remnant of the lost tribes of Israel—the tribe of Joseph (Ephraim and Manasseh)—has been the predominant tribe gathered since the beginning of the Restoration. Modern revelation teaches that eventually the remainder of the returning tribes of Israel will "fall down and be crowned with glory, even in Zion, by the hands of the servants of the Lord, even the children of Ephraim" (D&C 133:32).

The gathering of Lehi's descendants

Lehi's descendants have begun to gather to the gospel standard in great numbers. Nephi prophesied, "And the gospel of Jesus Christ shall be declared among them . . . and their scales of darkness shall begin to fall from their eyes; and many generations shall not pass away among them, save they shall be a pure and a delightsome people" (2 Ne. 30:4–6). Moreover, "they shall come to the knowledge of their Redeemer and the very points of his doctrine, that they may know how to come unto him and be saved. And then at that day [Nephi asked] will they not rejoice and give praise unto their everlasting God, their rock and their salvation? . . . Behold, I say unto you, Yea; they shall be remembered again among the house of Israel; they shall be grafted in, being a natural branch of the olive-tree, into the true olive-tree" (1 Ne. 15:14–18).

The gathering of the Jews

Nephi spoke of a time when the "the Jews which are scattered also shall begin to believe in Christ; and they shall begin to gather in upon the face of the land; and as many as shall believe in Christ shall also become a delightsome people" (2 Ne. 30:7). That is, one of a house and two of a city from among the Jews shall be converted before the Lord's coming, but the great day of Jewish conversion will not come until the second coming of Christ, after Christ appears on the Mount of Olives (D&C 45:48–53; Zech. 12:9–10; 13:6; McConkie, *Millennial,* 228–29). And as it is with all other branches of Israel, their gathering will be first to Christ and his gospel, and then to the lands of their inheritance (2 Ne. 6:8–11; 10:3–8; 20:29–33). Concerning the Jews, the Lord said that "when the day cometh that they shall believe in me, that I am Christ, then have I covenanted with their fathers that they shall be restored in the flesh, upon the earth, unto the lands of their inheritance" (2 Ne. 10:7; cf. 6:11; 25:16–17; 3 Ne. 20:29–39). In this process they will receive the testimony of the restored gospel (Morm. 3:21), be "restored to the true church and fold of God" (2 Ne. 9:2; cf. McConkie, *New Witness,* 511, 519–20, 564–65), and be washed in the blood of the Lamb (Ether 13:11). Thus the physical gathering of Jews to the Holy Land during the last century, although a part of the overall plan for God's covenant people, is preparatory to the complete gathering.

The millennial gathering of the scattered tribes of Israel

The great work of gathering Israel began with the restoration of the gospel through the Prophet Joseph Smith (1 Ne. 22:3–12). This gathering will continue to the time of the second coming of Christ and reach its zenith during his millennial reign. Concerning the millennial gathering, Jesus taught that after his coming (3 Ne. 21:25) the work of the Father—the work of the gathering of Israel—will commence (2 Ne. 30:7–15; 3 Ne. 21:26). It will "commence" in the sense that the gathering and conversions during the millennial day of peace and righteousness will eclipse all previous gathering. Inasmuch as the tribe of Joseph is one of the ten northern tribes, having been scattered among the nations for generations (1 Ne. 22:3–5; Morm. 3:17–18), missionaries have, in a sense, been gathering the lost tribes since the beginning of this dispensation. It is during the Millennium, however, that a large part of the lost tribes will be gathered: "And then," said Jesus, "shall the work of the Father commence at that day . . . among all the dispersed of my people, yea, even the tribes which have been lost, which the Father hath led away out of Jerusalem" (3 Ne. 21:25–26; cf. D&C 133:20–34; McConkie, *Millennial,* 322–26).

The Book of Mormon and the gathering of the house of Israel

The Book of Mormon is a vital element in the gathering of Israel. First, it defines the gathering and sets forth unmistakably what the chosen and scattered remnants of Jacob must do to return to their God. Second, the Book of Mormon, a vital key to conversion, is the vehicle, the means whereby people are gathered (Benson, 35). Individuals and congregations will be led to Christ and his restored gospel through the Book of Mormon (Morm. 3:17–21). This singular volume is the fulfillment of the ancient prophecy that righteousness would be sent down from heaven and truth would spring forth "out of the earth" to bear witness of the Redeemer, of his resurrection and atonement (Ps. 85:11; Moses 7:62). As Latter-day Saints share the Book of Mormon, Israel will be redeemed and gathered home. Other than the central message that Jesus is the Christ, the Eternal God, who manifests himself to all nations (2 Ne. 26:12; Title Page), no doctrinal thread weaves itself more consistently through the tapestry of the Book of Mormon than God's tender regard for the house of Israel. The mission and destiny of the Lord's chosen people are inextricably tied to the destiny of the earth and its inhabitants (3 Ne. 23:1–2; Morm. 5:10; Deut. 32:8). Just as the scattering of Israel symbolizes the Fall and the effects of alienation from things of righteousness, so also does the gathering of Israel typify and thus testify of the power of the Atonement, the power of the Almighty to gather and restore and reconcile and embrace his chosen people, the family of God (2 Ne. 9:1–4). The prophets of the Book of Mormon thus remind "the remnant of the House of Israel" of "what great things the Lord hath done for their fathers," and of "the covenants of the Lord" that Jehovah made with Abraham, Isaac, and Jacob. This unusual volume of scripture extends the comforting assurance to latter-day Israel that "they are not cast off forever" (Title Page).

See also Book of Mormon, selected purposes of, to be a sign of the Father's work; Fulness of the Gentiles; Gentiles, Book of Mormon message concerning; Israel, concept of; Israel, historical background of; Israel, lost tribes of; Israel, numbered among; Israel, scattering of; Jews, Book of Mormon message concerning; Jews, history of; Lamanites, Book of Mormon message concerning.

BIBLIOGRAPHY

Benson, Ezra Taft. *A Witness and a Warning.* Salt Lake City: Deseret Book, 1988.

Kimball, Spencer W. *The Teachings of Spencer W. Kimball.* Edited by Edward L. Kimball. Salt Lake City: Bookcraft, 1982.

McConkie, Bruce R. *The Millennial Messiah: The Second Coming of the Son of Man.* Salt Lake City: Deseret Book, 1982.

———. *A New Witness for the Articles of Faith.* Salt Lake City: Deseret Book, 1985.

Smith, Joseph. *Teachings of the Prophet Joseph Smith.* Compiled by Joseph Fielding Smith. Salt Lake City: Deseret Book, 1976.

RLM

Israel, historical background of Familiarity with the historical background of ancient Israel is beneficial, even essential for students of the Book of Mormon for many reasons, including the following: (1) so readers can appreciate the historical context in which the Lehites and Mulekites originated; (2) because the Book of Mormon prophets presupposed that their people (and latter-day readers of their records) were familiar with the Hebrew scriptures (the Christian Old Testament) and Israelite history as they refer to the Israelite EXODUS from Egypt, the

ISRAEL, HISTORICAL BACKGROUND OF

existence of ten "lost tribes" of Israel, and so on (e.g., 1 Ne. 17); (3) because the writings of Isaiah, employed extensively by Nephi[1], make regular reference to ancient Israel and its neighbors in the ancient Near Eastern world (the modern Middle East); (4) so readers can appreciate the conditions of "the Jews," the branch of the house of Israel which remained in the Near East and Mediterranean area, of whom Nephi, in particular, had much to say; (5) because Jesus experienced his mortal ministry in the land of Israel and then, as the resurrected Lord, visited Lehite-Mulekite descendants in the Americas and made reference to past Israelite prophets and contemporary Jews in the land of Israel; and (6) because understanding the dispersion or scattering of Israel is prerequisite for appreciating the magnitude of the gathering occurring in the latter days.

The following historical overview of the Israelite people begins with Abraham and Sarah (the grandparents of Jacob/Israel; ca. 2000 B.C.), and extends into the early Christian and rabbinic Jewish periods (ca. A.D. 200). It is divided into the time periods identified on the accompanying table.

Although the events narrated in the Bible are presented in a historical framework, there are many challenges to studying the history of Israel. These include (1) the authors and editors of the biblical books were not interested in history per se but in relating the unfolding of the Lord's work in the course of history (similar to Mormon's efforts), so their emphasis on events with a positive or negative religious component often results in the omission of other information that would be valuable in reconstructing the history of Israel with greater precision; (2) no person in the Hebrew Bible is mentioned in known, contemporary nonbiblical texts until the mid-800s B.C., more than a century after king David's death, meaning that readers are entirely dependent on the Bible and the "mute evidence" of archaeology for their evidence of all people and events prior to that time; and (3) there are certain discrepancies among the chronological data contained in the Hebrew Bible, between data in the Hebrew Bible and various ancient translations of the Bible, and between biblical data and nonbiblical documentary sources from the ancient Near East. None of these challenges, however, thwarts one's ability to understand the general picture and much of the detail of Israelite history. Furthermore, archaeological discoveries, both inscriptions and artifacts, generally validate Israelite history as depicted in the Bible.

Ca. 2000–1500 B.C.

The time of the Patriarchs—Abraham, Isaac, Jacob, and their families—covers most of the first half of the second millennium B.C. Abraham and Sarah were descendants of Noah[1]'s son Shem and natives of Mesopotamia (modern Iraq and northern SYRIA). JEHOVAH initiated a covenant relationship with Abraham while he lived in Ur, before his marriage to Sarah (Abr. 1:17–19; 2:1; Abraham's Ur was probably located in northern Mesopotamia, distinct from the Ur in southern Mesopotamia; Bible Map 9). At Jehovah's command their journey of faith began as they departed Ur for Haran, in northern Syria, sometime after 2000 B.C. (Gen. 11:27–32; Abr. 2:1–5). During their stay in Haran, Jehovah renewed and expanded his covenant with Abraham and Sarah and directed them to relocate southward to the land of Canaan (Gen. 12:1–6;

Ca. 2000–1500 B.C.	Patriarchal period; Joseph[1] and eventually all the Israelites in Egypt
Ca. 1500–1000 B.C.	Egyptian bondage; Exodus; conquest of Canaan; period of the judges
Ca. 1000–500 B.C.	Israelite monarchy; division into and destruction of the kingdoms of Israel and Judah; major dispersion of Israelites; first stage of the Judahite return from Babylon and building of the second temple
500–6/1 B.C.	Persian, Hellenistic, and Roman periods in the ancient Near East
6/1 B.C.–A.D. 200	Advent of Christianity and rabbinic Judaism in the Roman period

ISRAEL, HISTORICAL BACKGROUND OF

Abr. 2:6–16; e.g., 1 Ne. 15:18; 22:9). Their movement along the Fertile Crescent was part of a larger migration of Semites known as Amorites during this time period. Politically, Canaan consisted of a number of small city-states rather than a unified nation. Here Abraham and Sarah interacted with many of the peoples of the land but lived mainly on the outskirts of the cities. They built altars and worshipped at various locales, including Bethel and Mamre (near Hebron), in effect laying religious claim to the land for future generations of descendants to whom the Lord had promised it as part of the ABRAHAMIC COVENANT (Gen. 12–23). All the while, Jehovah continued to interact with Abraham and his family (Gen. 15; 17; 22).

Isaac, the son of Sarah and Abraham through whom the primary covenant line was established, was born and raised in Canaan. Rebekah, a relative, was brought from Haran to be his wife (Gen. 24). Of Isaac and Rebekah's twin sons, Jacob[1] ultimately received the birthright over Esau. Jehovah appeared to Jacob several times, designating him as the one through whom the family covenant of salvation he had established with Abraham and Sarah would continue (Gen. 25–28). To escape his brother's subsequent anger and to find an appropriate bride, Jacob journeyed to his ancestral homeland, Haran. He married Leah, then Rachel (his first love), and then their two handmaids, Bilhah and Zilpah (Gen. 29–30). When Jacob returned to Canaan some years later, his family included his wives, twelve sons, and at least one daughter (Dinah). Jacob renewed his covenant with the Lord, his name was changed to Israel, and he and Esau reconciled their differences (Gen. 31–35). Jehovah became known as the God of Abraham, Isaac, and Jacob, because of this covenant relationship with these families (e.g., Ex. 3:6; 1 Ne. 6:4; Mosiah 23:23). As a result of family tensions produced when Jacob and Rachel's son Joseph[1] shared his prophetic dreams with his family, Joseph was sold into slavery in Egypt by his older brothers (Gen. 37). The domination of northern Egypt by the Hyksos, non-Egyptians (mainly Amorites) who had migrated into the Nile delta area and who exercised control from ca. 1700–1550 B.C., is probably the historical context in which Jehovah arranged Joseph's rise to power in Egypt. Through his position Joseph was able to preserve his family from the effects of a famine in Canaan as they relocated to northeastern Egypt. The family's move to Egypt was permanent: Jacob and eventually all his children died there (Gen. 39–50). As noted above, the Bible is presently the sole source for knowledge about these people and their experiences.

Ca. 1500–1000 B.C.

The Egyptians reclaimed control over all Egypt ca. 1550, depriving the Hyksos of power. This resurgence of native Egyptian power culminated in the creation of an empire that included the land of Canaan through the 1300s B.C. (Bible Map 9). This was most likely the time of the Egyptian oppression of the Israelites in Egypt (Ex. 1). As this oppression became more severe, the Lord prepared a deliverer for his covenant people. Born to an Israelite mother but reared in the household of an Egyptian king, Moses had to flee to Midian to preserve his life. There he married and received his divine call to help deliver Israel from Egypt (Ex. 2–4). Many years earlier Jacob's son Joseph had prophesied of Moses and his mission (JST Gen. 50; 2 Ne. 3).

Certain biblical chronological data place the Israelite exodus from Egypt in the mid-1400s B.C., although various historical evidence has led scholars to prefer a date in the early to mid-1200s. The Bible relates how Moses and Aaron confronted an unnamed Egyptian pharaoh who pursued the Israelites into the parted Red Sea as they left Egypt and journeyed to meet Jehovah at Mt. Sinai (Ex. 5–14; 1 Ne. 4:2; 17:26–30; Bible Map 2). Having manifested his power over the Egyptians and over nature, Jehovah manifested his power at Sinai—"mount Sinai was altogether on a smoke, because the LORD descended upon it in fire . . . and the whole mount quaked greatly" (Ex. 19:18)—pronouncing the TEN COMMANDMENTS to all the Israelites (Ex. 19–20; Deut. 5; cf. Mosiah 12:33–37; 13:15–24). After the golden calf incident signaled the Israelites' unwillingness and unpreparedness to receive the higher laws and ordinances of the GOSPEL, Jehovah gave the Israelites the LAW OF MOSES, including the

ISRAEL, HISTORICAL BACKGROUND OF

preparatory gospel (Ex. 32–34; cf. JST Ex. 34:1–2; D&C 84:23–27; 1 Ne. 4:15; 5:11). It was also at Sinai that the tabernacle was constructed and that the Levites were chosen, organized and trained in their priesthood duties, with Moses' brother Aaron[1] as their high priest, all according to the Lord's will as revealed to Moses (Ex. 25–31; 35–40).

The powerful combination of Jehovah's redemption of the Israelites from the bondage of Egypt (celebrated in the holiday of Passover) and his initiation of a renewed covenant relationship with them at Sinai provided the basis for the Israelites' relationship with the Lord as they entered their promised land to claim at least some of the blessings of the Abrahamic covenant. Later Israelite prophets in the Bible and in the Book of Mormon drew on the saving symbolism of this pivotal episode in the history of Israel (e.g., Hosea 11:1; Amos 2:10; 3:1–2; Ezek. 20:5–12; 1 Ne. 17:40–42). Following the Israelites' faithless response to the report of twelve spies that Moses sent to reconnoiter the land of Canaan, Jehovah condemned that generation of Israelites to wander and die in the wilderness (Num. 13–14). Sometime later, "the LORD sent fiery [or poisonous] serpents among the people," because of their continuing resistance to the Lord and Moses (Num. 21:5–9). Several Book of Mormon prophets taught that the bronze serpent that Moses made and raised as an antidote to the snake bites was a type of Christ (e.g., 1 Ne. 17:41; Hel. 8:14–15). About forty years after Jehovah gave Israel his law at Mt. Sinai, Moses was translated near Mt. Nebo but not before warning the Israelites that the Lord, who was shortly going to bring them in to the land of Canaan/Israel, would not allow their posterity to remain in the promised land if they violated their covenant relationship (Deut. 29; 34; Bible Map 2; cf. 2 Ne. 1:5–10).

Jehovah chose Joshua to lead the new generation of Israelites across the Jordan River into the land of Canaan (Josh. 1–4; cf. 1 Ne. 17:32). The conquest and displacement of Canaanites under Joshua's leadership gave the Israelites control of the north-south ridge of hill country in the land of Canaan but left the Canaanites in control of the major valleys and the coastal plain. The book of Joshua and Judges chapter one report the Israelite conquest of Canaan and the allotment of territories to the various tribes. Although there is disagreement over the date of the Exodus and Conquest (ca. 1440/1400 or ca. 1270/1230 B.C.), by the end of the thirteenth century B.C. Canaan had slipped from Egyptian control and the Israelites were established in the land. Israel's neighbors were also establishing themselves during this general time period: the Semitic Edomites, Moabites, and Ammonites (in what is modern Jordan; ca. 1300 B.C.), and the non-Semitic Philistines, with origins in the Aegean area, settling along the southeastern Mediterranean coastal plain (Bible Maps 3, 10; ca. 1200 B.C). The earliest nonbiblical reference to the Israelites occurs in a victory hymn from the Egyptian king Merneptah, dating ca. 1210 B.C., which includes the baseless boast that he had destroyed the Israelites in the land of Canaan (Pritchard, 376–78).

The two centuries following the Israelite settlement in Canaan (ca. 1220–1020 B.C.) are designated the period of the judges, as outlined in the biblical book of the same name. These "judges," including Ehud, Deborah, Gideon, and Samson, are mainly depicted as military leaders for different Israelite tribes or combinations of tribes, not as judicial or political officials as in the Book of Mormon. The Bible indicates that these judges were chosen by the Lord to lead Israelites in military action to deliver them from subjection to various neighboring peoples. This subjection, attributed to Israelite unfaithfulness, produced repentance and appeals for deliverance, inducing Jehovah to provide judges to assist in freeing Israel. Generally, a period of peace was followed by another slide into apostasy and the pattern would repeat itself (e.g., Judg. 3). While the Israelites were connected through genealogy and religion, the book of Judges mentions no national political organization in Israel during this time. Kinship provided a major means of organization in this patriarchal society: tribes, clans, extended families. Although annual holidays were celebrated at the tabernacle, legitimate prophets and priests receive little mention in the book of

ISRAEL, HISTORICAL BACKGROUND OF

Judges. The main religious challenge for the Israelites of this era was the lure of Canaanite deities, especially Baal and Asherah. Most Israelites did not totally abandon the worship of Jehovah, but many corrupted it with concepts and practices borrowed from the Canaanites and by worshipping other deities in addition to Jehovah. Although some Israelites were involved in military, religious, or mercantile occupations, the vast majority of Israelites were engaged in the subsistence occupations of agriculture and animal husbandry, a situation that continued through the biblical era.

By the eleventh century B.C. pressures from neighboring peoples, especially the Philistines, encouraged some Israelites to press for the creation of an Israelite monarchy, rather than recognizing Jehovah as their only king. The Lord instructed Samuel[1], the last judge and the leading prophet of this period, to warn Israel about the consequences of kingship but then allowed him to institute monarchic rule (1 Sam. 8; cf. Mosiah 29:16–23). Israelite kingship ideally was to function as an extension of Jehovah's rule of his people. The king himself was subject to, not above, Israelite law, which had its basis in the law Jehovah revealed at Sinai. Unfortunately, this ideal was rarely approached. Samuel anointed Saul, a Benjamite, as the first king of Israel in the latter part of the eleventh century. His capital was his home town, Gibeah (Bible Map 4). Although initially successful, Saul fell out of favor with the Lord, and a young Bethlehemite named David, who had been anointed by Samuel to become king some time before he faced the Philistine Goliath, rose to prominence in the army of king Saul (1 Sam. 9–19).

Ca. 1000–500 B.C.

Several years after David was anointed by Samuel to become king, Saul and three of his sons were killed fighting the Philistines (1 Sam. 31; ca. 1011 B.C.). The tribe of Judah chose David as its ruler. Saul's general and cousin, Abner, supported Saul's remaining son Ish-bosheth as a puppet ruler of the northern tribes of Israel, but seven years later David became king of all Israel and captured the city of Jerusalem from the Jebusites, making it his new capital (2 Sam. 1–5). A relative power vacuum in the ancient Near East, coupled with David's energy and ability and the Lord's favor, allowed David to expand Israelite control over most of Israel's neighbors and collect tribute that greatly enriched the kingdom (Bible Map 4). Jehovah covenanted with David to establish David's descendants as rulers of Israel forever (2 Sam. 7). David's posterity did indeed rule in Jerusalem for almost four centuries, but ultimately this promise will be fulfilled in the millennial reign of the Lord (e.g., Isa. 9:7 // 2 Ne. 19:7; Ezek. 37:22–26). The Bible depicts David as a king who was always loyal to Jehovah, whose heart was never swayed to worship other gods; however, there were episodes which tarnished this golden age of Israel, including David's infidelity with Bathsheba and subsequent complicity in the death of Uriah and the family problems that plagued the latter years of his rule, including the rebellion of his son Absalom (2 Sam. 6–24). Just before David's death (ca. 971), the prophet Nathan anointed Solomon as David's successor (1 Kgs. 1). Solomon, loved of the Lord and noted for his wisdom, built the first Israelite temple to Jehovah in Jerusalem (1 Kgs. 6–8; cf. 2 Ne. 5:16). (This temple stood for more than three and a half centuries until it was destroyed by the Babylonians in 586 B.C.). By the end of his forty-year reign, Solomon had encountered political, economic, and personal spiritual challenges that he failed to successfully resolve (1 Kgs. 11).

At Solomon's death (931 B.C.) his son Rehoboam was unable to maintain the unity of the kingdom, and the Israelites divided into two political entities: the northern kingdom of Israel and the southern kingdom of JUDAH (Bible Map 10). Jeroboam I, the new ruler in the north, made his first capital in Shechem and introduced a number of innovations in his kingdom, including a new religious calendar, a non-Levitical priesthood, and new national religious shrines in Dan and Bethel, complete with a golden calf in each (1 Kgs. 12). These calves may have originally been intended as pedestals over which Jehovah could be expected to appear, but the redactors of 1 and 2 Kings criticized Jeroboam for abandoning Jehovah by introducing illegitimate forms of worship. During the next two hundred years (931–722 B.C.) these

ISRAEL, HISTORICAL BACKGROUND OF

two Israelite nations, Israel and Judah, coexisted, sometimes cooperatively and sometimes antagonistically. The nation of Israel was larger, richer, and more cosmopolitan than was Judah. The dominant tribes in the northern kingdom were Ephraim and MANASSEH; Judah was the principal tribe in the south.

About 880 B.C. king Omri made Samaria the capital of the northern kingdom, and it remained such until the end of the kingdom. Most of Elijah's prophetic activity occurred in the northern kingdom during the reign of Omri's son Ahab and his queen Jezebel (1 Kgs. 17–2 Kgs. 2; 873–853 B.C.). Elisha, Elijah's prophetic successor, also lived and ministered in the northern kingdom (2 Kgs. 2–13). Both of these prophets spent much of their ministry countering the influence of Ahab's and Jezebel's state-sponsored worship of Baal. The Bible provides less information about Judah during the ninth century B.C.; no prophets of the stature of Elijah and Elisha are mentioned.

During the mid-800s B.C., ASSYRIA (in northern Mesopotamia) began to exert its power in the Near East, and for a short time Israel became a vassal kingdom to Assyria. A lull in Assyria's empire-building efforts in the first half of the eighth century B.C., combined with stable and long-lived rulers in the kingdoms of Israel and Judah, produced a period of prosperity and expansion for both kingdoms. The prophets Hosea and Amos were active during the eighth century B.C., decrying the pride, social sins, and apostasy from Jehovah among the northern Israelites. This was also the time of Jonah's prophetic activity.

By 745 B.C. the Assyrians again began to exert military pressure in all directions and soon made the Syrian/Aramean states and the kingdom of Israel vassals to the Neo-Assyrian Empire (2 Kgs. 15:17–20; Pritchard, 281; Bible Map 5). An anti-Assyrian coalition, including the vassal kings in Damascus and Israel, rebelled ca. 735 B.C., resulting in the final conquest of Damascus and the deportation of thousands of Israelites from the Galilee area of the kingdom of Israel in 732 B.C. (2 Kgs. 15:29–30; Pritchard, 281; this is the context for events in Judah recounted in 2 Kgs. 16; Isa. 7–8 // 2 Ne. 17–18). Another Israelite rebellion brought the Assyrian army back to Israel (ca. 724 B.C.). They besieged Samaria and eventually conquered the northern kingdom of Israel in 722 B.C. (2 Kgs. 17:1–6). The Assyrians claimed to have deported 27,290 Israelites into northern Assyria (Pritchard, 284–85; no number of deportees is given in the Bible), attributing their success to their own might and the power of their gods. Nonetheless, the redactors of 2 Kings attributed Israel's conquest to apostasy and sinfulness (2 Kgs. 17:7–18). The Israelite deportees, mainly from the upper and middle classes, became known as the "lost ten tribes of Israel." Although these people became lost to history, some of them were apparently further dispersed into Europe and Asia. At least a part of the descendants of these Israelite deportees were a cohesive group visited by Jesus following his resurrection (1 Ne. 22:4; 2 Ne. 29:12–13; 3 Ne. 17:4; cf. the apocryphal account in 2 Esdras 13:41–46).

After deporting many Israelites, the Assyrians moved other conquered peoples into northern Israel (2 Kgs. 17:24–41). The integration of these new peoples with the remaining Israelite population produced the mixed group known as the Samaritans, whom their Judahite neighbors considered religiously as well as genealogically impure.

Archaeological evidence indicates a significant increase in the population of Judah about this time, suggesting that many northern Israelites fled south to escape the Assyrian conquest of Israel. Judah had been a vassal to Assyria since ca. 732. The Assyrians invaded Judah in 701 B.C., apparently for vassal treaty violations. Hezekiah, commended in the Bible for his faithfulness to Jehovah, was king at the time; Isaiah was his prophetic counselor. Jerusalem was miraculously spared from Assyrian conquest, although many Judahite cities were destroyed and thousands of Judahites were deported (according to an Assyrian claim); Judah remained a vassal kingdom to the Assyrians (2 Kgs. 18–19; Pritchard, 287–88). Judah continued as a vassal to Assyria in the first half of the seventh century B.C. during the long reign of Manasseh, son of Hezekiah (2 Kgs. 21; Pritchard, 291).

Josiah, designated the king most faithful to

THE NEAR EAST AT THE TIME OF ISAIAH AND LEHI

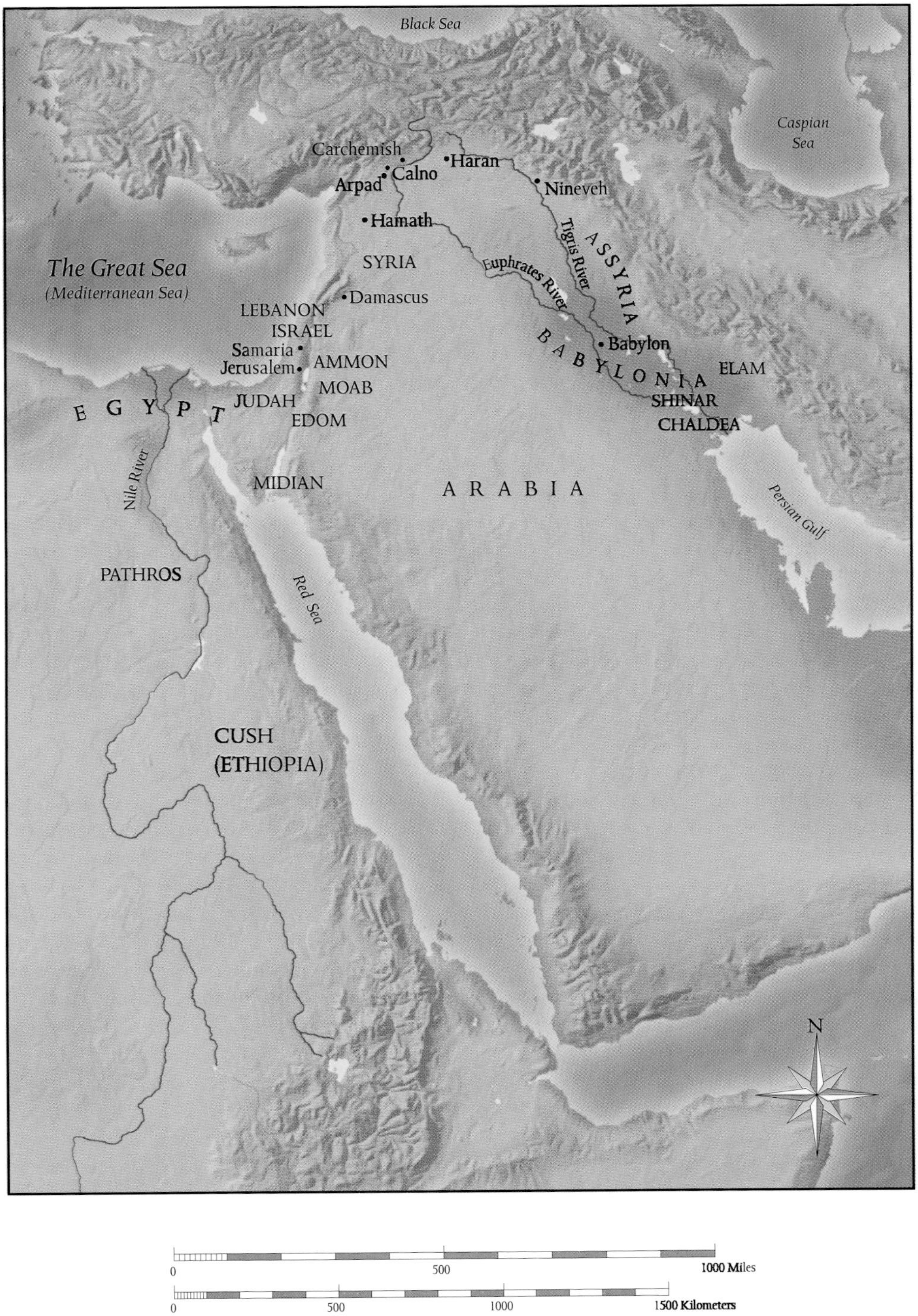

ISRAEL, HISTORICAL BACKGROUND OF

Jehovah since David, ruled Judah during the latter half of the seventh century B.C. (2 Kgs. 22–23). The lengthy prophetic ministry of Jeremiah[1] (ca. 627–585 B.C.) began in Jerusalem during Josiah's reign (Jer. 1:1–2; 640–609 B.C.). By the end of the seventh century, the Assyrian Empire had declined and was replaced by the Neo-Babylonian Empire as the dominant power in the ancient Near East (Bible Map 6). Judah became a vassal to the Babylonians ca. 600 B.C. but quickly rebelled. In response, the Babylonians besieged Jerusalem (597 B.C.) and deported thousands of upper-class Judahites to Babylonia (southern Mesopotamia), including Ezekiel, who became a prophet during the Babylonian exile (2 Kgs. 24; Ezek. 1:1–3; Dan. 1:1, if accurate, indicates that Daniel was taken to Babylon a few years before 597). Babylonian king Nebuchadnezzar II placed Zedekiah, the third son of Josiah, on the throne in Jerusalem, giving Judah one last chance to be a loyal vassal. Likewise, Jehovah was giving Judah one last chance to be loyal to him.

Lehi[1] received his prophetic call in Jerusalem in the first year of Zedekiah's reign (1 Ne. 1:4–18). Jeremiah, Lehi, and other prophets warned the Judahites of the imminent consequences of their apostasy and sinfulness (e.g., Jer. 7; 1 Ne. 1:4, 19). Zedekiah rebelled in 588, and the Babylonians responded by destroying much of the country and besieging Jerusalem for one and a half years. They then destroyed most of the city, including "Solomon's temple," and exiled Zedekiah and thousands more Judahites to Babylonia in 586 B.C. (2 Kgs. 24–25; Jer. 38–39; 2 Ne. 1:4; 25:10). The kingdom of Judah thus ceased to exist, becoming a province of the Babylonian Empire. Differing from Assyrian policy, the Babylonians did not relocate non-Israelites into the land of Judah. A few Judahites assassinated the governor of Judah in 582, inducing a group of them to flee to Egypt, kidnapping and taking Jeremiah with them (2 Kgs. 25:22–26; Jer. 41–43). This assassination caused a third, but smaller, deportation of Judahites to Babylonia (Jer. 52:30).

Lehi, Ishmael, and their families must have departed southward into the Arabian peninsula a short time after Lehi's call, for Nephi indicated that these families spent eight years in the wilderness before arriving at Bountiful[1] and then built a ship and sailed to the Americas prior to the Babylonian destruction of Jerusalem in 586 B.C. (1 Ne. 17:4–8; 18:5–6, 23; 2 Ne. 1:4). Mulek, a son of king Zedekiah, was "brought by the hand of the Lord" (Omni 1:16), along with an unidentified group of people, to the Americas at "the time that Zedekiah, king of Judah, was carried away captive into Babylon" (Omni 1:15–16; Mosiah 25:2; Hel. 6:10; 8:21).

The pre-Exilic period of Israelite history was over. Tens of thousands of Israelites from Israel and Judah had been exiled or scattered, and thousands more had been killed as a result of sinfulness and disloyalty to Jehovah, their divine ruler. Two of the three main "branches" or groups of Israelites were now permanently separated from their original homeland: the lost ten tribes had been deported to northern Assyria by the Assyrians in the late eighth century B.C., and the Lehites and Mulekites had recently left for the Americas under the Lord's direction (early sixth century B.C.). Those Israelites remaining in the land of Israel and those dispersed throughout the Near East and around the eastern Mediterranean Sea together constitute the third branch of the house of Israel. The dispersion of many in this group would continue over the course of several centuries, sometimes forced, as by the Babylonians, and sometimes voluntarily. This third branch of Israelites became known collectively, regardless of their original tribal affiliation, as "Jews" (e.g., Jer. 16:11–13; 1 Ne. 22:3–5; Jacob 5). The books of 1 and 2 Kings were completed in the Babylonian exile as part of a retrospective overview of the tragedy the Lord's covenant people had brought on themselves (similar to the efforts of Ether and Mormon).

The Neo-Babylonian Empire was short-lived, succumbing to the assault of Cyrus and the Persians in 539 B.C. (Bible Map 7). Cyrus, who proceeded to incorporate most of the Near East into his growing empire, allowed various peoples whom the Babylonians had deported to return to their homelands (Pritchard, 316; cf. Isa. 45:1–4), including the Jews. Some of the Jews did return from exile (Ezra 1–2; 1 Ne. 10:3; 2 Ne. 25:11). Under the direction of Zerubbabel the provincial

ISRAEL, HISTORICAL BACKGROUND OF

governor, Jeshua the Aaronic high priest, and the prophets Haggai and Zechariah, the Jews rebuilt the Lord's temple in Jerusalem, dedicating it in 515 B.C. (Ezra 3–6). This event, near the beginning of the post-exilic period, inaugurated the Second Temple period.

500–6/1 B.C.

Judah was now a small, insignificant province in the Persian Empire. The Bible relates that Ezra, a priest and scribe born and raised in Babylonia, led a group of Jews from Babylonia to Judah in the 450s B.C. (Ezra 7–10), about the time that Esther lived in Persia (modern Iran). A short time later, Nehemiah moved from Persia to Jerusalem, where he became governor (Neh. 1–2; 440s B.C.). Malachi, the last prophet mentioned in the Old Testament, also lived in Jerusalem about this time (3 Ne. 24–25).

During the two centuries that the Persians dominated the Near East (530s–330s), sizeable groups of Jews were living in Babylonia, Persia, Egypt, and elsewhere in the Near East and eastern Mediterranean region. Those Jews living outside the land of Israel lived in the Diaspora, a term designating a "dispersion."

Taking advantage of a weakening Persian Empire, Alexander the Great of Macedonia (northern Greece) conquered the Near East beginning in 332 B.C. and brought Hellenistic (Greek-like) culture to the region. Although he did not live long, Alexander's conquests had a dramatic effect on cultural developments in the Near East for centuries to come. Ptolemy, one of Alexander's generals, established a kingdom in Egypt which controlled the land of Israel during the third century B.C. Seleucus, another of Alexander's generals, established a kingdom in Syria which later controlled the land of Israel from 201 to 167 B.C. Rebelling against a religiously oppressive edict from the Seleucids, the Hasmoneans, a Jewish priestly family, led a two-decades-long resistance effort that culminated in Jewish independence from Seleucia in 145 B.C. Members of this family, nicknamed the Maccabees, ruled Judah until 63 B.C. Although their original motives were admirable, the Maccabees quickly became corrupt like previous foreign rulers had been. Their corruption extended beyond politics to religion, as the buying of the office of Aaronic high priest attests. The Jewish sects of the Pharisees, Sadducees, and Essenes originated during this period. Some of the Jews associated with the latter group were responsible for collecting and composing the cache of documents known as the Dead Sea Scrolls found near Qumran on the northwest shore of the Dead Sea. Most of these documents date from ca. 150 B.C. to A.D. 50. The main religious challenge for Jews of this era was no longer the influence of Canaanite deities, as in the pre-Exilic period, but the influence of Greek philosophies and cultural practices which were seemingly more sophisticated and attractive than the Lord's teachings and Jewish traditions.

The Romans, who had been expanding their control over the countries around the Mediterranean Sea for over a century, gained control of Syria and Israel in 63 B.C. (Judaea, the Greek form of the name Judah, and the rest of the land of Israel remained under Roman and then Byzantine [eastern Roman empire] control until the Arabs arrived in A.D. 638). Herod the Great, building on opportunities created by his father, was appointed king over Israel by the Romans in 40 B.C. Three years later he acquired his throne and ruled from 37–4/1 B.C. (Bible Map 8). Discrepancies in chronological data have resulted in the dates 4 or 1 B.C. for the death date of king Herod. This uncertainty has led to suggestions that Jesus was born sometime between 6 and 1 B.C. because he was born near the end of Herod's reign (long-term chronologies were not systematically calculated nor were chronologies reckoned by the B.C./A.D. system in the Mediterranean world until several centuries after Jesus' birth; contrast the development recounted among the descendants of Lehi in 3 Ne. 2:7–8). Herod is usually remembered for his bursts of brutality, such as ordering the deaths of his favorite wife and her sons and the male infants in Bethlehem (Matt. 2). He did, however, bring a large measure of stability and prosperity to Judaea and was renowned for his building activity, including the rebuilding of the Jerusalem temple and the surrounding courtyards on a grand scale (Bible Map 12). The second temple had not been destroyed but was five hundred years old by then and was deemed

ISRAEL, HISTORICAL BACKGROUND OF

by Herod to be neither large enough nor sufficiently elaborate. When John the Baptist and Jesus were born near the end of the reign of Herod the Great (Luke 2), Caesar Augustus, the first Roman emperor, was still ruling the empire.

6/1 B.C.–A.D. 200

Jesus was born into a Jewish family in a Jewish society that emphasized devotion to God through observance of the Mosaic law and the traditional practices that had developed in connection with the law. Yet, Jews in the land of Israel were under Roman political control and were affected by the influence, especially in the cities, of Greek culture and philosophies. Furthermore, Jewish religion was not a seamless whole at this time but consisted of several sects, the Pharisees and Sadducees being most influential. After the death of Herod the Great, his kingdom was divided among three of his sons, but the Romans soon replaced the king of Judaea with a string of Roman governors, including Pontius Pilate, whose term (A.D. 26–36) coincided with the ministries and executions of John the Baptist and Jesus. Jesus, whose three-year mortal ministry was almost exclusively restricted to the relatively small land of Israel, was charged with blasphemy by some Jewish religious authorities who then persuaded Pilate to condemn him for sedition (Matt. 26:59–66; 27:1–2, 11–38; Bible Maps 11, 12).

Sometime following his death and resurrection, Jesus visited the Lehites in the Americas, where he proclaimed his gospel and organized his Church (3 Ne. 8:5; 10:18–19; 11:1–28:12). Peter, the chief apostle and president of the Church in the land of Israel, was instructed by the Lord that Christians must take the gospel to Gentiles as well as to the Jews (Acts 1; 10). Although missionaries no doubt went out in all directions to fulfill the Lord's directive to take the gospel to "all nations" (Matt. 28:19), the canon of the New Testament rather narrowly focuses on the areas now denominated Israel/Palestine, Syria, Turkey, Greece, and Rome, primarily relating the ministries of Peter and Paul. Paul, originally named Saul, was a Benjamite Jew who was born in the Diaspora. He converted from Pharisaic Judaism to Christianity within a year or so of Jesus' resurrection and went on to direct a major missionary force to Jews and Gentiles in the northeastern Mediterranean region (Bible Map 13). Both Paul and Peter were martyred in Rome in the mid-60s A.D. There is no biblical indication of any apostolic activity after this, except for that of John the Revelator (into the 90s A.D.). The Church of that dispensation did not wholly survive the effects of the extensive, rapidly spreading apostasy that was well underway only decades after Jesus' ministry and resurrection. Nevertheless, Christianity continued on, despite external persecution and internal disputes regarding authority and doctrine, eventually becoming the official religion of the Roman empire in the late fourth century A.D.

Meanwhile, Jews in Judaea during the mid-first century A.D. struggled against antagonistic Roman governors, growing economic and social strain, and religious corruption among some Jewish leaders. Many Jews cultivated messianic expectations, while others increasingly favored a militant nationalism. The first Jewish revolt against the Romans began in A.D. 66. By A.D. 70 the revolt had been crushed, except for a few bands of revolutionaries, including those who endured on Masada until A.D. 73. Tens of thousands of Jews were killed, many were exiled, and the temple in Jerusalem was completely destroyed, as prophesied by Jesus (Matt. 24:1–2; cf. 2 Ne. 25:14–15). About six decades later (A.D. 132–135), the Jews in Judaea unsuccessfully revolted again against the Romans. This time they were banned from the city of Jerusalem. The center of Jewish religious life in Israel shifted to the Galilee region, where the Mishnah, the first great collection of postbiblical rabbinic thought, was compiled ca. A.D. 200.

There were more Jews living in the Diaspora than in the land of Israel during the centuries that the Greeks and Romans controlled the Near East, a condition that has continued to the present. The Bible and the Book of Mormon contain extensive prophecies concerning the physical and spiritual gathering of the scattered branches of the house of Israel, many of which are being fulfilled.

See also Babylon, Babylonia; Babylonian captivity; Chronology, Bible; Israel, concept of; Israel, covenants unto; Israel, gathering of; Israel, house of; Israel, kingdom of; Israel, lost tribes of; Israel, numbered among; Israel, scattering of; Jeremiah[1], prophecies of; Jerusalem[1], city of; Jerusalem[1], destruction of, at 586 B.C.; Jerusalem[1], destruction of, at A.D. 70; Jews, history of; Joseph[1], covenants unto; Remnant.

BIBLIOGRAPHY

Pritchard, James B. *Ancient Near Eastern Texts*. 3d ed. Princeton: Princeton University Press, 1969.

DMP

Israel, house of Covenant people of the Lord who descend from Jacob[1], son of Isaac (e.g., 1 Ne. 13:23; 15:14; 19:11, 16; 3 Ne. 10:4; 21:22–23). They enjoy the blessings and responsibilities of the ABRAHAMIC COVENANT (1 Ne. 15:18; 22:9; 2 Ne. 29:14; 3 Ne. 20:25). Occasionally, the Lord speaks of them as "my people," or one reads of "his people," terms that also point to their covenant status (e.g., 2 Ne. 29:1–2; 3 Ne. 16:8–9, 11, 15; 20:46; 21:4). In some passages the expression "house of Jacob" is synonymous with house of Israel (e.g., 1 Ne. 20:1; 4 Ne. 1:49; Morm. 5:12). Gentiles who accept the gospel are "numbered with" the house of Israel (3 Ne. 30:2; 1 Ne. 14:2; 2 Ne. 10:18).

See also Israel, historical background of; Israel, numbered among; Remnant.

SKB

Israel, kingdom of The northern kingdom of Israelites that existed from 931 to 722 B.C. The Lord changed the name of Jacob[1], son of Isaac, to Israel (Gen. 32:28). Before their division into two kingdoms, the descendants of Jacob's twelve sons were variously referred to as "Israel," "the house of Israel," "the people of Israel," "the [twelve] tribes of Israel," "the Israelites," and the "remnant of the house of Israel." Upon the death of Solomon, the northern tribes refused to follow Solomon's son Rehoboam, and chose the Ephraimite, Jeroboam, to be their king (1 Kgs. 12; 931 B.C.). This division began the period known as the Divided Monarchy (931–722 B.C.) with ten tribes forming the kingdom in the north and, predominantly, two tribes—JUDAH and

KINGDOM OF ISRAEL AT THE TIME OF ISAIAH AND LEHI

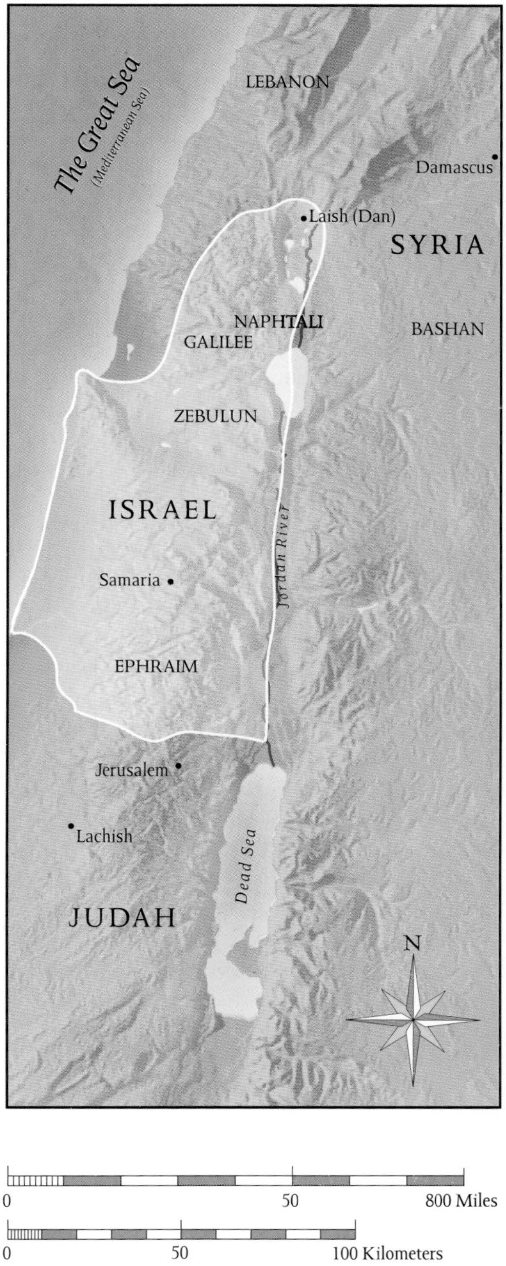

Benjamin—in the south. In the Bible the northern kingdom retained the name Israel. In addition it is often called Ephraim, after the leading northern tribe, or Samaria, the capital city. The southern kingdom was called Judah after the ruling tribe Judah, or Jerusalem, after its capital city. Throughout the Old Testament the northern kingdom was considered apostate, following the idolatrous practices of their first king Jeroboam (1 Kgs. 12:25–33). Lehi[1] was a descendant of the tribe of Manasseh whose inheritance was in the lands of the northern kingdom. At some undetermined time his ancestors moved to Jerusalem.

The history of the northern kingdom of Israel is recounted in 1 Kings 12–2 Kings 17. Prophets including Elijah, Elisha, Hosea, Amos, and Isaiah were sent to warn the northern kingdom to repent or be destroyed. Several passages of Isaiah found in the Book of Mormon refer to the history of the northern kingdom and prophesy its destruction by the Assyrians (2 Ne. 17–18 // Isa. 7–8; 2 Ne. 19:8–20:4 // Isa. 9:8–10:4).

Pekah, king of Israel (740–732 B.C.), entered into an alliance with Rezin the king of Syria (735 B.C.) that led to the Assyrian conquest in 732 B.C. Judah was preserved during this period by making an alliance with ASSYRIA. Eventually the northern kingdom revolted again and Assyria conquered them with a vengeance and took many of the northerners into captivity (722 B.C.). The scriptures record little of what happened to these peoples, hence they are often referred to as the lost ten tribes. The Book of Mormon teaches that these tribes eventually were scattered throughout the earth and that in the latter days the work of gathering them back to the Lord and his covenants would begin (1 Ne. 22:4–12; 2 Ne. 21:10–16 // Isa. 11:10–16; 3 Ne. 5:24–26; 15:13–15; 16:1–5; cf. Jer. 3:18; 16:14–21; D&C 133:26–35). Those that remained in their land intermarried with the pagan peoples introduced by the Assyrians and became the Samaritans (2 Kgs. 17:24–41).

In the Book of Mormon "Israel" is most often used in reference to all of the descendants of Jacob, especially in the phrase "house of Israel," and the titles of Deity as "God of Israel" and "Holy One of Israel." Only in the Isaiah passages is the term "Israel" used referring to the descendants of Jacob in the northern kingdom as opposed to those in the southern kingdom of Judah (2 Ne. 17:1; 19:8, 12, 14; 21:12).

See also Isaiah chapter reviews (2 Ne. 17 // Isa. 7; 2 Ne. 18 // Isa. 8; 2 Ne. 19 // Isa. 9); Israel, gathering of; Israel, historical background of; Israel, house of; Israel, lost tribes of; Israel, scattering of.

DRS

Israel, lost tribes of Descendants of Israelites who were removed from the land of Israel, whose history was unknown to those who remained, including to the writers of the Bible and the Book of Mormon.

The expression "lost tribes" is found in only two verses of scripture (2 Ne. 29:13; 3 Ne. 17:4), both referring to members of the house of Israel outside their ancestral homeland. Nephi[1] indicated that the word "lost" shows the perspective of the Israelites in the Holy Land: the tribes were "lost from the knowledge of those who are at Jerusalem" (1 Ne. 22:4).

In the eighth century B.C., the kingdom of Israel, consisting of the northern ten tribes, was destroyed because of the wickedness of its people. Many of its inhabitants were removed from their land by Assyrian conquerors and relocated in other places (2 Kgs. 15:29; 17:3–6, 23), where they became lost from the view of the rest of Israel. The family of Lehi[1] became lost from the knowledge of their countrymen when the Lord led them away to a new land. Their descendants remain lost except to believers in the Book of Mormon, who recognize their Israelite heritage. The Jews were taken into exile and eventually scattered into many parts of the world. Yet they are not lost, because they have retained a knowledge of who they are.

Thus, the lost tribes are Israelites whose identity is not known to the world and in some cases not even to themselves. When the term is used for the descendants of the deported northern tribes, it is synonymous with "ten tribes" (found only in D&C 110:11 and A of F 10). These are likely the "other sheep," unknown to the Jews and the people of the Book of Mormon, whom

Jesus visited after his resurrection (3 Ne. 16:1–3; 15:15, 20; 17:4).

Although there is much about the history of the lost tribes of Israel that is not known, they are not really lost. The scriptures teach where they went, where they are today, and how they will return. Moses foretold the fate of the Israelites if they became wicked: "The Lord shall scatter thee among all people, from the one end of the earth even unto the other" (Deut. 28:64; cf. 4:27). Nephi wrote, "The house of Israel, sooner or later, will be scattered upon all the face of the earth, and also among all nations. . . . Yea, the more part of all the tribes have been led away; and they are scattered to and fro" (1 Ne. 22:3–4). Scattered throughout all the world, the lost tribes have forgotten their identity and have assimilated into the nations in which they live (Amos 9:9; Ezek. 20:23). Their descendants remain scattered now, generally ignorant of their heritage in the house of Israel. Some scriptures describe their scattered exile as being in "the north," using metaphorical language from the perspective of the rest of Israel, who last saw them being taken away in that direction (Jer. 16:15; Zech. 2:6; D&C 110:11; 133:26).

The restoration of the gospel has brought back the keys of the gathering of the lost tribes (D&C 110:11), and scriptures teach that they will be gathered in from their dispersion: "And then shall the remnants, which shall be scattered abroad upon the face of the earth, be gathered in from the east and from the west, and from the south and from the north" (3 Ne. 20:13; cf. Isa. 43:5–6). As they gather, they will forsake the old enmities that once separated the branches of Israel (2 Ne. 21:12–13), and each will possess the sacred records of the other (2 Ne. 29:11–14). Many are gathering now, as they embrace the message of the gospel, join The Church of Jesus Christ of Latter-day Saints, accept the covenants and ordinances, receive patriarchal blessings, and thus regain their identity as members of the house of Israel. The Book of Mormon is a key to their conversion (Title Page; 3 Ne. 16:4–5). Most members of the Church today are gathered descendants of the lost tribes. Ephraim, the chief of the ten tribes and the one by which all are sometimes identified (Isa. 7:2–17; 11:13; Hosea 5:3–14), is already gathering in large numbers. But a greater gathering, and the final return and restoration of all who were once lost, will be in the Millennium (3 Ne. 20:11–13, 29–37; 16:17–20; 21:25–29).

See also Assyria; Israel, gathering of; Israel, historical background of; Israel, kingdom of; Israel, scattering of.

KPJ

Israel, numbered among To be recognized as a member of the family of Abraham, Isaac, and Jacob. God promised Abraham that "as many as receive this Gospel shall be called after thy name, and shall be accounted thy seed" (Abr. 2:10). Those who are not lineal descendants of Abraham may, through hearkening to the Lamb of God (1 Ne. 14:1–2), repenting, and being baptized into the true Church (3 Ne. 21:6, 22; 30:1–2) be numbered with Israel. Both Nephi[1] and the apostle Paul taught that only those who come unto Christ are truly Israel—they become "covenant people of the Lord" (2 Ne. 30:2; Rom. 9:6).

See also Abrahamic covenant; Adoption; Gentile(s); Israel, concept of; Israel, gathering of.

MSN

Israel, remnant(s) of *See* Remnant.

Israel, scattering of The prophesied dispersion of the house of Israel among the nations of the world. Because the promised land was one of the blessings of God's covenant with his chosen people (Gen. 13:14–15, 17; 17:8), their possession of it was conditioned on their obedience to his commandments. Moses prophesied what would happen if the Israelites rebelled against God: "The Lord shall scatter you among the nations, and ye shall be left few in number among the heathen, whither the Lord shall lead you" (Deut. 4:27). "The Lord shall scatter thee among all people, from the one end of the earth even unto the other" (Deut. 28:64).

The kingdom of David and Solomon was divided in 931 B.C. into two kingdoms: Israel and Judah. Israel, consisting of the northern ten tribes and usually dominated by Ephraim, had an inglorious history of almost uninterrupted apostasy. Beginning in 732 B.C., prophecy was fulfilled when Assyrian kings began conquering Israel and deporting much of its population to other locations in their empire (2 Kgs. 15:29). In 722 B.C. the kingdom of Israel was destroyed as Samaria, its capital city, fell. Thousands of its people were taken away and settled in various places in Mesopotamia and elsewhere (2 Kgs. 17:3–6, 23). From these beginnings, descendants of the tribes of Israel, including Ephraim, eventually assimilated into other societies, lost their identity, and became scattered throughout the world (1 Ne. 22:3–5). These are what are often called the lost ten tribes. They will be gathered again as they accept the covenants of the gospel (1 Ne. 22:6–9).

The scattering of the tribe of Judah followed a different pattern, because its people have generally retained their identity to the present time. In the early sixth century B.C., king Nebuchadnezzar of Babylon conquered Judah and exiled much of its population to Babylonia. Many Jews had already left to different locations. By the time of Jesus, probably two-thirds of all Jews lived outside the Holy Land, with Jewish communities scattered throughout the Mediterranean region and the Near East, where many persisted into the twentieth century A.D. As a result of the destruction of Jerusalem by the Romans in A.D. 70 and the Second Jewish Revolt in A.D. 132–135, Jews fled or were deported from their homeland in huge numbers. Eventually large populations grew in scattered locations in Europe as well. The Book of Mormon teaches that the Jews' ancient scatterings were punishment for unrighteousness and that their descendants would be gathered when they accepted the gospel of Jesus Christ (2 Ne. 6:8–11; 10:3–7; 25:14–17).

Lehi's[1] family represents a different kind of scattering, because their departure from the land of Israel was not punishment for their wickedness; rather, they were led away by the Lord to preserve a righteous branch of Israel in a new promised land (3 Ne. 15:19). Lehi's descendants became scattered as they spread throughout the Americas and the Pacific islands and eventually fell into apostasy, lost their Israelite identity, and were later dispersed, oppressed, and partially assimilated or exterminated by immigrants from other lands (1 Ne. 13:14; 22:7; 2 Ne. 1:9–12).

The Book of Mormon gives glimpses into other scatterings for which there is no scriptural record. Jacob[2] taught of other places "inhabited also by our brethren. For behold, the Lord God has led away from time to time from the house of Israel, according to his will and pleasure" (2 Ne. 10:21–22). Among these are perhaps the Mulekites (Omni 1:16). Jesus spoke of "other sheep" (3 Ne. 16:1–3)—"the lost tribes of Israel" (3 Ne. 17:4)—whom he would visit after his appearance among Lehi's descendants, but he did not identify them specifically.

Today, patriarchal blessings identify Latter-day Saints throughout the world as scattered Israelites who have been gathered again through the covenants of the gospel.

See also Babylonian captivity; Israel, gathering of; Israel, historical background of; Israel, house of; Israel, lost tribes of; Jerusalem[1], destruction of, at 586 B.C.; Jerusalem[1], destruction of, at A.D. 70; Other sheep.

KPJ

Israelites Descendants of Jacob[1] and his twelve sons, from which the family of Lehi[1] traced their descent. The textual reference is to the parting of the Red Sea that allowed the Israelites to pass through (Hel. 8:11).

And it came to pass that he stretched forth his hand and spake unto the people, saying: Behold, I am Jesus Christ, whom the prophets testified shall come into the world. And behold, I am the light and the life of the world; and I have drunk out of that bitter cup which the Father hath given me, and have glorified the Father in taking upon me the sins of the world, in the which I have suffered the will of the Father in all things from the beginning. 3 NEPHI 11:9–11

Jacob[1] The younger twin son of Isaac and Rebecca (Gen. 25:24–26). His name was later changed to Israel (Gen. 32:24–28). Jacob was the father of twelve sons and at least one daughter. The posterity of his sons became the twelve tribes of Israel (Gen. 29:31–30:24; 35:16–18). Although a younger son, he obtained the birthright and covenant status (Gen. 25:23, 28–34; 27:37; 28:10–15).

In the Book of Mormon, little is said of Jacob's life. The text preserves only one quotation, a prophecy not found in the Bible that concerns the eventual fate of his son Joseph's posterity (Alma 46:24–25). But Jacob's name appears frequently in covenantal contexts. Perhaps his memory was carried on by naming children after him (e.g., 1 Ne. 18:7; Alma 52:20).

The covenantal title "house of Jacob," which apparently came into Nephite usage from the writings of Isaiah, often means "the house of Israel," the covenant people of God (e.g., 2 Ne. 24:1–2 // Isa. 14:1–2) or refers to the southern Israelite kingdom of JUDAH (e.g., 1 Ne. 20:1 // Isa. 48:1). Moreover, with slight variations, the Lord of the covenant is called "the God of Abraham, and Isaac, and Jacob" (e.g., Mosiah 7:19), or simply "the God of Jacob" who delivers (Alma 29:11), "the Holy One of Jacob" who redeems (2 Ne. 27:33–34 // Isa. 29:22–23), or "the Mighty One of Jacob" (1 Ne. 21:26 // Isa. 49:26). Additionally, Isaiah labeled those separated from the covenant people, whom God will gather back, as the "the remnant of Jacob" (2 Ne. 20:21 // Isa. 10:21).

Jacob's name appears in connection with events of the last days (e.g., the gathering of his posterity; 3 Ne. 5:24–26). The future promise holds that those who are faithful will be able to "sit down with Abraham, and Isaac, and with Jacob" in the heavenly kingdom where Jacob already resides (e.g., Hel. 3:30).

See also Israel, historical background of; Israel, house of; Israelites.

SKB

Jacob[2] The fifth son of Lehi[1] and Sariah, Jacob was the elder of two sons (Jacob and Joseph[2]) born in the wilderness, apparently not long after his family left Jerusalem about 599 B.C. (1 Ne. 18:7). Jacob grew up amid intensifying family strife caused by the rebellion of Laman[1] and Lemuel, his two oldest brothers—rebellion against the Lord, his prophet-father, and his obedient brothers, Nephi[1] and Sam. The shipboard mutiny of these eldest sons almost cost the lives of the grieving Sariah and her distraught husband, Lehi (1 Ne. 18:17–18), and, recalled Nephi, the very young "Jacob and Joseph . . . were grieved because of the afflictions of their mother" (1 Ne. 18:19).

The family schism and its consequences greatly influenced Jacob's life. By the time Jacob was approaching forty, recorded Nephi, "We had already had wars and contentions with our brethren" (2 Ne. 5:34). Father Lehi, in pronouncing his patriarchal blessing upon Jacob, acknowledged the impact of the terrible conflict upon his son: "Thou art my first-born in the days of my tribulation in the wilderness. And behold, in thy childhood thou hast suffered afflictions and much sorrow, because of the rudeness of thy brethren" (2 Ne. 2:1).

Even at the end of his life, saddened by his failure to "reclaim and restore the Lamanites" (Jacob 7:24), fearful for the future of his people, and feeling personally responsible for the shortfall, Jacob summarized in profoundly melancholic and poignant words the trying conditions of their lives: "Our lives passed away like as it were unto us a dream, we being a lonesome and a solemn people, wanderers, cast out from Jerusalem, born in tribulation, in a wilderness, and hated of our brethren, which caused wars and contentions; wherefore, we did mourn out our days" (Jacob 7:26).

These afflictions played a key role, however, in spiritually attuning Jacob for his early appointment as a dynamic teacher, minister, and prophet to his people, and as one of the great theologians of ancient America. In fact, Lehi not only promised Jacob that God "shall consecrate thine afflictions for thy gain" and foresaw that Jacob's "days shall be spent in the service of thy God" (2 Ne. 2:2–3) but taught Jacob the principle of opposition, so vital to his grasp of the plan of redemption: "For it must needs be, that there is an opposition in all things" (2 Ne.

2:11). Spiritually sensitive, the obedient and faithful Jacob learned early "the greatness of God" (2 Ne. 2:2). In blessing Jacob, Lehi reminded his son that "thou hast beheld in thy youth his [the Redeemer's] glory" (2 Ne. 2:4), an event which Nephi affirmed by testifying that "Jacob, also has seen him [the premortal Christ] as I have seen him" (2 Ne. 11:3).

Therefore, while his brother Nephi became the political king or "protector" of the fledgling Nephite nation, as well as its spiritual leader (Jacob 1:10), Jacob, in his turn, also became an important spiritual leader, "called of God, and ordained after the manner of his holy order," and "consecrated" by Nephi to minister spiritually unto their people (2 Ne. 6:2; 5:26; Jacob 1:18). But he did not succeed Nephi as monarch. Having "first obtained [his] errand from the Lord" (Jacob 1:17), Jacob spent the rest of his life laboring "diligently" among the Nephites, "that we might persuade them to come unto Christ," and to "believe in Christ, and view his death, and suffer his cross and bear the shame of the world" (Jacob 1:7–8).

Nephi's inclusion of part of Jacob's two-day sermon (2 Ne. 6–10) provides insight not only into Jacob's teachings (2 Ne. 6:3) and his gifted and inspired oratory but reveals his deep pastoral concern for the spiritual welfare of his people, for whom he felt great "anxiety" (2 Ne. 6:3; Jacob 4:18) and keen personal responsibility (Jacob 1:19). Jacob included in his address extensive passages from Isaiah chapters 50–52 that support his emphasis on God's covenants with the house of Israel (2 Ne. 9:1) and the mission of the Messiah, the Lord Jesus Christ, whose name Jacob was the first to make known to the Nephite nation, having been told the name by an angel of God (2 Ne. 10:3). In the section of his sermon recorded in 2 Nephi 9, Jacob taught that deliverance from death and hell, "the death of the body" and "the death of the spirit," comes only through the "infinite atonement" of Jesus Christ, the "great Creator" (2 Ne. 9:5–16, 19–22, 25–26; cf. 10:24–25). He also spoke concerning what one must do to be saved in the kingdom of God (2 Ne. 9:18, 23–24), issued stern warnings (2 Ne. 9:27–38), admonished his people to remember a variety of spiritually critical matters (2 Ne. 9:39–41, 44, 51–52), and invited them to "come unto the Holy One of Israel" (2 Ne. 9:50–51).

When Jacob was nearly fifty-five years old, the aging Nephi commissioned him to record on the small plates the religious (not the political) history of their people—"things which [he] considered to be most precious" (Jacob 1:1–4). True to Nephi's charge, Jacob left for a future age testimony that the early Nephites enjoyed "many revelations, and the spirit of much prophecy; wherefore, [they] knew of Christ and his kingdom, which should come" (Jacob 1:6).

In fact, Jacob's principal calling was to testify of Jesus Christ, whom he beheld (2 Ne. 11:3; 2:4), whose voice "I had heard . . . speaking unto me in very word, from time to time," and whose angels had ministered to him (Jacob 7:5). Such certitude speaks from every page of the book of Jacob and enabled his dramatic triumph in behalf of the Lord Jesus Christ in his confrontation with the charismatic Sherem. Sherem, wrote Jacob, "had hope to shake me from the faith, notwithstanding the many revelations and the many things which I had seen" (Jacob 7:5). To Sherem's demand for a sign as proof that Christ would come, Jacob proclaimed that he would leave that for God to decide (Jacob 7:14). Immediately and dramatically, Sherem was struck helpless by the power of God, but shortly before his death, he mustered strength to recant publicly his false teachings (Jacob 7:17–20).

Ever anxious about the materialistic, proud, and unchaste predilections of his people, Jacob shouldered the responsibility of calling them to repentance. In one memorable recorded sermon, he rebuked wealthy Nephites who, because of their RICHES, were "lifted up in the pride of [their] hearts" supposing they were better than others (Jacob 2:13). He then taught them concerning the proper attitude and use of their wealth (Jacob 2:17–21). Jacob chastised the Nephite men in particular for their infidelity (Jacob 2:23–35). He regretted wounding again the already wounded feelings of the wives and children of these men. This moving sermon demonstrates Jacob's strengths, but also his tenderness and compassion. Jacob also took his people to task for their prejudice against the Lamanites. The Lamanites, he said, bore a curse, but they "are not filthy like unto you" (Jacob 3:3).

In his unique style, Jacob, a powerful and persuasive writer, employed a vivid, dramatic, and "intimate vocabulary either unique to him or disproportionately present." Thus two-thirds of the use of the words "grieve" and "tender" in the Book of Mormon are attributed to Jacob, as are his solitary use of such intimately expressive words as "delicate," "contempt," "lonesome," "sobbings," "dread," and "wound," the latter used only in reference to emotions and not bodily injury (Tanner, 714). A gifted orator, Jacob achieved similar dramatic effects in his recorded sermons. Near the end of the sermon included in 2 Nephi, for example, he suddenly removed his outer garments and shook them in the faces of his audience, in "witness that I shook your iniquities from my soul" (2 Ne. 9:44). He dramatized his teachings about the scattering and gathering of the house of Israel by including in his book the prophet Zenos' lengthy allegory of the tame and wild olive trees, which dramatically and tellingly presents, as Elder Joseph Fielding Smith asserted, "one of the greatest parables ever recorded" (4:141). The parable of the olive tree symbolizes God's remembrance of the scattered branches of Israel, "both roots and branches" (Jacob 6:4), which he would patiently prune, regraft, and cultivate until the tree yielded pure fruit (Jacob 5–6).

The portrait of Jacob that emerges from the Book of Mormon shows a prophet who, like his Savior, was "a man of sorrows, and acquainted with grief" (Isa. 53:3), a prophet who nevertheless tirelessly pressed on in teaching his people the plan of redemption and testifying of the coming Christ. Spiritually sensitive, a profound theologian, a powerful and poetic writer and preacher, Jacob successfully labored all his days among his people as an exemplary and personal witness for the Lord Jesus Christ.

Summary of major teachings

1. Prophecies. The return of the Jews to Jerusalem after the Babylonian captivity; the coming of the Messiah, his rejection and death; the judgments of God upon those who harden their hearts against the "Holy One of Israel" (2 Ne. 6:10); the gathering of the Jews after they "shall come to the knowledge of their Redeemer" (2 Ne. 6:8–11; 10:3–5; Jacob 4:14–15); the apostasy and restoration of Lehi's descendants (2 Ne. 10:2; Jacob 3:6); the role of Gentile nations in the gathering of the Jews (2 Ne. 10:7–9, 18); the blessings of God upon the Gentiles (2 Ne. 6:12; 10:10–11, 18); and the Nephite loss of the land of Nephi to the Lamanites, except they repent (Jacob 3:4; cf. Omni 1:12).

2. Quotations from Isaiah (2 Ne. 6:6–7 // Isa. 49:22–23; 2 Ne. 7 // Isa. 50; 2 Ne. 8 // Isa. 51; 52:1–2; 2 Ne. 10:9 // Isa. 49:23). For the purpose of teaching the Nephites "concerning the covenants of the Lord that he has covenanted with all the house of Israel" (2 Ne. 9:1; cf. 6:12; 10:15, 17). *See also* 2 Nephi 6:4–5 for additional reasons Jacob quoted Isaiah. *See* Isaiah, purposes for quoting.

3. The omniscience of God. "O how great the holiness of our God! For he knoweth all things, and there is not anything save he knows it" (2 Ne. 9:20).

4. Salvation through the INFINITE atonement of Jesus Christ. The ATONEMENT provides deliverance from physical and spiritual death, the consequences of the fall of Adam and Eve, and restores all mankind to God's presence for JUDGMENT (2 Ne. 9:7–16, 19, 22); Jesus suffered "the pains of all men, yea, the pains of every living creature . . . who belong to the family of Adam" (2 Ne. 9:21); the Atonement satisfies the DEMANDS OF JUSTICE by extending MERCY to those who "have not the law given to them" (2 Ne. 9:25–26). *See* Awful monster; First judgment; Law, without the; Resurrection, the.

5. Specific instructions on what one must do to inherit the kingdom of God (2 Ne. 9:18, 23–24).

6. Warnings (2 Ne. 9:27–38), admonitions (2 Ne. 9:39–41, 44, 46, 51–52; 10:20, 23–24; Jacob 3:11–12; 4:8–11), and invitations to "come unto the Holy One of Israel" (2 Ne. 9:50–51, 45).

7. Consequences of PRIDE; warnings (Jacob 2:13–17, 20–21).

8. Wealth, proper priorities concerning its

acquisition and use. "But before ye seek for riches, seek ye for the kingdom of God. And after ye have obtained a hope in Christ ye shall obtain riches, if ye seek them; and ye will seek them for the intent to do good" (Jacob 2:17–19).

9. Consequences of immorality (Jacob 2:29, 31–35); authorized (Jacob 2:30) and unauthorized PLURAL MARRIAGE (Jacob 2:23–28). *See* Chastity.

10. Quotation of Zenos' allegory to teach how the Jews can return to Christ, "the only sure foundation," after having rejected him (Jacob 4:15–18; 5–6). *See* Zenos, allegory of.

11. The antiquity of the gospel. All the holy prophets believed in Christ and worshipped the Father in his name, as did the Nephites (Jacob 4:4–5).

See also Jacob, book of.

BIBLIOGRAPHY

Arnold, Marilyn. *Sweet Is the Word: Reflections on the Book of Mormon, Its Narrative, Teachings, and People.* American Fork, Utah: Covenant Communications, 1996.

Matthews, Robert J. "Jacob: Prophet, Theologian, Historian." *The Book of Mormon: Jacob through Words of Mormon—To Learn with Joy.* Edited by Monte Nyman and Charles Tate Jr. Provo, Utah: Religious Studies Center, Brigham Young University, 1990.

Smith, Joseph Fielding. *Answers to Gospel Questions.* Compiled by Joseph Fielding Smith Jr. 5 vols. Salt Lake City: Deseret Book, 1957–66.

Tanner, John S. "Jacob, Son of Lehi." *Encyclopedia of Mormonism.* Edited by Daniel H. Ludlow et al. 4 vols. New York: Macmillan, 1992.

RHC

Jacob[3] A Zoramite[2] who became a leader of a Lamanite army (Alma 52:20; 64 B.C.). During a battle over the city of Mulek, Jacob and his army were the victims of a clever Nephite decoy strategy devised by Moroni[1] and Teancum (Alma 52:21–32). Credited with "having an unconquerable spirit" and leading his troops "with exceeding fury," Jacob was killed in battle (Alma 52:33–35).

Jacob[4] The apostate Nephite chosen as king over a secret combination (3 Ne. 7:9) that was established in the wake of the collapse of the central Nephite government (ca. 29–30 B.C.). Jacob had been one of the leaders who spoke against the prophets who testified of Christ (3 Ne. 7:10). Outnumbered by the Nephite TRIBES that united against him, Jacob commanded his people to flee north and there build themselves a kingdom (3 Ne. 7:11–13). His city, Jacobugath, was destroyed by fire at the time of Christ's death as a result of wickedness (3 Ne. 9:9).

Jacob, book of The book of Jacob comprises seven chapters translated from Jacob[2]'s own inscriptions on the small PLATES OF NEPHI. The record begins with the death of Nephi[1], 55 years after Lehi[1] left Jerusalem[1] (544 B.C.), and ends just before Jacob's death an undetermined number of years later.

The book may be divided into four parts: an introductory chapter, a sermon at the temple, a discourse on God's relationship with Israel, and an account of Jacob's encounter with an anti-Christ.

Content and message

Jacob's purpose was to persuade people to repent and "come unto Christ" (Jacob 1:7; cf. 4:11–12; 6:5–12), whom he had seen (2 Ne. 2:3; 11:2–3) and of whom he delighted to speak: "For why not speak of the atonement of Christ, and attain to a perfect knowledge of him . . . ?" (Jacob 4:12). Obedient to Nephi's charge, Jacob touched but "lightly" on history, while touching "as much as it were possible, for Christ's sake," on "preaching," "revelation," and "prophesying" (Jacob 1:2–4). Narrative links are thus minimal and little space is given to either social or personal detail.

Nonetheless, the record provides significant glimpses into the lives of its author and his people. For example, Jacob revealed that before he died, Nephi divided and distributed his combined duties as king, priest, and scribe: anointing as king an unnamed successor who assumed the name "Nephi" as a royal title (Jacob 1:9–14), consecrating his brothers Jacob and Joseph[2] as "priests and teachers" (Jacob 1:18), and appointing Jacob as scribe and conservator of the small plates (Jacob 1:1–3). Similarly, Jacob indicated that his people quickly prospered in the new land and that prosperity engendered PRIDE, invidious social distinctions, and other sins (Jacob 2:12–21). He also disclosed that the Nephites kept the law of Moses with knowledge of and hope in Christ's atonement (Jacob 4:4–6), and that Christ-centered observance of the law was not uniformly accepted but was attacked as blasphemous by the likes of Sherem and his followers (Jacob 7:7). Finally Jacob reported rumblings from a tragic history marked by the Nephites' vain efforts to reclaim their Lamanite cousins, implacable hatred dividing Lehi's posterity, and bloody internecine warfare (Jacob 7:24).

Jacob's focus, however, was fixed not on history but on preaching, especially of Christ. Three sermons compose the bulk of Jacob's writing, one in 2 Nephi 6–10 and two in Jacob 2–6. These discourses share doctrinal and stylistic similarities. Typically, Jacob acknowledged "anxiety" for the welfare of his people, quoted Old Testament prophecy (especially pertaining to scattered Israel), testified of Christ and of the Atonement, and admonished his audience to repent. And he did all this employing a distinctive vocabulary.

The first sermon in the book of Jacob was delivered at the temple. It reprises the themes of pride and unchastity against which Jacob had preached previously (cf. 2 Ne. 9:30, 36). "Having first obtained [his] errand from the Lord" (Jacob 1:17), Jacob inveighed against the pride of those whose RICHES prompted them to "suppose that [they were] better than" others, forgetting that "one being is as precious in [God's] sight as the other" (Jacob 2:13, 21). Jacob then turned to a "grosser crime," which may or may not be linked to pride and riches (as in many societies multiple wives are associated with wealth and social standing). Jacob excoriated his hearers for "whoredoms," specifically condemning Nephite men for engaging in the unauthorized practice of PLURAL MARRIAGE and concubinage. He roundly rebuked husbands for breaking "the hearts of your tender wives, and [losing] the confidence of your children" (Jacob

OUTLINE OF JACOB

- I. Transmittal of the small plates and death of Nephi (1)
  - A. Nephi's charge and Jacob's statement of purpose (1:1–8)
  - B. Social conditions following Nephi's death (1:9–19)
- II. Sermon against Nephite pride and whoredoms (2–3)
  - A. Preamble explaining Jacob's determination to speak plainly against sin (2:1–11)
  - B. Rebuke of Nephites for pride induced by riches (2:12–22)
  - C. Rebuke of Nephites for whoredoms (2:23–35)
  - D. Consolation for the pure and condemnation for the impure (3:1–11)
  - E. Conclusion (3:12–14)
- III. Discourse on God's relationship with Israel (4–6)
  - A. Jacob's testimony that his people knew of Christ and kept the law of Moses with hope in Christ's atonement (4)
  - B. Zenos' prophetic allegory of the olive trees, figuring God's care for Israel throughout history (5)
  - C. Jacob's prophetic exhortations based on Zenos' allegory (6)
- IV. Encounter with Sherem and Jacob's farewell (7)
  - A. Description of Sherem, an anti-Christ (7:1–5)
  - B. Dialogue with Sherem in which Sherem demands a sign and is cursed (7:6–15)
  - C. Sherem's confession and death (7:16–23)
  - D. Description of Lamanite hatred for their Nephite cousins and Jacob's poignant farewell (7:24–27)

2:35). Implicit in Jacob's condemnation is criticism of Nephite prejudice toward the Lamanites (cf. Jacob 2:35; 3:3–9).

No context is given for Jacob's next discourse, recorded in chapters 4–6, which clearly forms a single discursive unit. Broadly stated, the subject of these chapters is God's loving relationship with Israel. Jacob first focused on how believers before Christ, including "all the holy prophets," worshipped God through Christ (Jacob 4:4; cf. 7:11). Jacob testified that his people also "knew of Christ," kept the law of Moses in anticipation of Christ, and performed miracles in Christ's name. He admonished his brethren to be reconciled to God "through the atonement of Christ" (Jacob 4:4–12). The Jews, by contrast, would not hear such "words of plainness" from prophets but were blinded by "looking beyond the mark" (Jacob 4:14). Hence, Jacob prophesied, they would reject Jesus. God, however, would not utterly reject his people, despite their constant backsliding, but would nurture them and become for them a stone on which to build. To illustrate this point, Jacob quoted an extended allegory of wild and tame olive trees by an otherwise unknown Old Testament prophet, Zenos. This allegory is remarkable both as prophecy of Israel's many scatterings and gatherings and as parable of God's loving care. Jacob then concluded his discourse by urging his readers to remember God's mercies to them as "he remembereth the house of Israel," and to "cleave unto God as he cleaveth unto you" (Jacob 6:4–5).

The final chapter recounts Jacob's confrontation with Sherem, a powerful speaker who had convinced many that the doctrine of Christ was blasphemy, that it perverted the "right way of God" as embodied in the law of Moses, and that no man could know the future, including the predicted birth of Christ (Jacob 7:7). But Jacob could not be shaken, for he had "seen angels," "heard the voice of the Lord," and felt prophecies of Christ confirmed "by the power of the Holy Ghost" (Jacob 7:5, 12). He so testified to Sherem, who was smitten by God and died, after first publicly recanting his lies. The people then repented and turned again to God and the scriptures.

The book ends with Jacob's entrusting the record to Enos, his son. After this, Jacob composed a melancholy and poignant farewell, which eloquently encapsulates the lonely existence of a man who had witnessed his father's family split into warring civilizations, who had spent his early days as a wanderer between two worlds, each infected by corruption, and who ultimately died perched on the edge of a wilderness amidst enmity and contention. Amid such tribulations, Jacob inscribed the remarkable book that bears his name.

See also Zenos, allegory of.

JST

Jacob, city of Wicked city mentioned only in connection with its destruction at the time of Jesus' death. The Lord caused the city and its inhabitants to be buried "in the depths of the earth," and he "made hills and valleys in the places thereof" to hide their wickedness, so that the blood of the martyred prophets and Saints might cease to testify against them (3 Ne. 9:8).

Jacob, house of *See* Israel, house of.

Jacobites Descendants of Jacob[2]. From the time of Jacob, Jacobites were usually not distinguished from the larger group called Nephites, made up primarily of Nephites, Jacobites, Josephites, and Zoramites[1] (Jacob 1:13–14; 4 Ne. 1:36–37; Morm. 1:8; D&C 3:17).

Jacobugath, city of Iniquitous city inhabited by Nephite dissenters and followers of the apostate king Jacob[4] after the splintering of the Nephite nation into TRIBES (A.D. 29–30). Led north by Jacob to establish a kingdom, they became the most wicked people on earth because of their secret murders and combinations. After his crucifixion, Jesus Christ caused Jacobugath to be burned because they had "destroy[ed] the peace of my people and the government of the land" (3 Ne. 7:6–13; 9:9).

Jacom *See* Jared[1], posterity of.

Jared[1] Brother of the prophet Mahonri Moriancumer, or "brother of Jared," one of the patriarchs of the Jaredite nation, and ancestor of the prophet Ether. Jared came forth with his family and friends from the Tower of Babel to the promised land. Through revelation to the brother of Jared, the Lord granted Jared's inspired desire that their pure language not be confounded and that they be led to a choice land (Ether 1:6–42). The Lord commanded them to gather animals and seeds, and he directed their journey into pristine wilderness. They built a first set of barges in which they crossed many waters (Ether 2:6), eventually arriving on the seashore at a place they called Moriancumer (Ether 2:13). Four years later they built another set of barges (Ether 2:16) and sailed for the promised land (Ether 6:4–12). Jared had twelve children, eight daughters and four sons (Ether 6:20). He may have contributed to the subsequent fall of his people by ignoring his brother's warning that anointing a king would lead the people into captivity. Jared's son Orihah was anointed to be the first Jaredite king (Ether 6:22–27).

MCT

Jared[2] Son of the Jaredite king Omer. "Jared rebelled against his father," defeated him, and consigned him to captivity. Omer begat children in his long captivity, and two of his sons eventually defeated Jared, though they spared his life, and restored Omer to the throne (Ether 8:1–6). Jared's daughter, seeing her father's distress, reminded him of accounts in the Jaredite records about ancient conspiracies and secret schemes to acquire kingdoms and glory. She conceived a plan in which, by her dancing, she would lure a traitorous man named Akish to Jared's service. Jared would give her hand in marriage in exchange for Omer's head (Ether 8:8–12). The pact was made, and Akish formed a secret society of "all his kinsfolk" (Ether 8:13). In Jared's house they swore to support Akish in his wicked deeds (Ether 8:13–18), thus launching the Satan-inspired SECRET COMBINATIONS among the Jaredites. But before Akish could slay the king, the Lord warned Omer, who took his family and escaped (Ether 9:2–3). With Omer gone, Jared became king again and, as agreed, gave his daughter to Akish in marriage (Ether 9:4). Soon, however, Akish lusted after the kingdom for himself. Using the same secret society, Akish arranged for the murder of his father-in-law and succeeded him on the throne (Ether 9:5–6).

See also Jared[1], posterity of.

MDR

Jared[1], brother of A Jaredite prophet who led his people from the tower of Babel to the promised land (Ether 1–3; 6). He was the brother of a man named Jared[1] who helped lead the group and whose sons became the kings among the Jaredites. The brother of Jared's name is not given in the Book of Mormon, but it was revealed through the Prophet Joseph Smith as Mahonri Moriancumer (or possibly just Moriancumer; Reynolds, 282). He is described as "a large and mighty man, and a man highly favored of the Lord" (Ether 1:34) and is known for his great faith. The Lord said to him, "Never has man come before me with such exceeding faith as thou hast" (Ether 3:9). The scriptures record that because of his faith he was privileged to be the first man to see the premortal Christ in such a manner (Ether 3:6–20; 12:19–21; cf. Holland, 18–19; McConkie, 599–600).

The story of the Jaredites began at "the great tower, at the time the Lord confounded the language of the people" and scattered them "upon all the face of the earth" (Ether 1:33; Gen. 11:1–9). The brother of Jared cried unto the Lord to have compassion on his people. Because of his prayers the Lord did not confound the language of his family and friends, and promised to lead them to a land choice above all others and to raise up a great nation of their seed (Ether 1:33–43). The Lord directed them as they went forth from the valley of Nimrod into the wilderness, across "many waters" to the "great sea [that] divideth the lands," where they pitched their tents upon the seashore at a place they called Moriancumer (Ether 2:1, 5–6, 13).

At the end of four years the Lord came in a cloud and spoke to the brother of Jared: "And for the space of three hours did the Lord talk with the brother of Jared, and chastened him because he remembered not to call upon the name of the Lord" (Ether 2:14). After obtaining forgiveness, the Lord instructed the brother of Jared and his people to build BARGES like the ones they had previously built (Ether 2:15–17).

Petitioning the Lord concerning darkness inside the barges, the brother of Jared was taught a powerful lesson on faith. The Lord asked, "What will ye that I should do that ye may have light in your vessels?" (Ether 2:23). The brother of Jared exercised his own initiative and went to mount Shelem and "did molten out of a rock sixteen small stones; and they were white and clear, even as transparent glass." He then carried the stones to the top of the mount and cried to the Lord, "Touch these stones, O Lord, with thy finger, and prepare them that they may shine forth in darkness . . . that we may have light while we shall cross the sea" (Ether 3:1, 4).

The Lord touched each stone, "and the veil was taken from off the eyes of the brother of Jared, and he saw the finger of the Lord" (Ether 3:6). He was frightened, but he learned much from this encounter. The Lord explained, "Because of thy faith thou hast seen that I shall take upon me flesh and blood." The Lord then inquired, "Sawest thou more than this?" The brother of Jared replied, "Nay; Lord, show thyself unto me," to which the Lord answered, "Because thou knowest these things ye are redeemed from the fall; therefore ye are brought back into my presence; therefore I show myself unto you" (Ether 3:9–10, 13).

The brother of Jared learned that the Lord was Jesus Christ, and he would come into the world to redeem his people. He also learned that Christ appeared to him in his spirit body, which was in the likeness of the body that he would take upon himself in his mortal ministry, and that man was created in his image (Ether 3:14–16). He was shown all the inhabitants of the earth throughout time and was told to record his vision and seal it up with the two stones that would "magnify to the eyes of men these things which ye shall write" (Ether 3:24). This sealed record was not to come forth until after the ministry of the Lord in the flesh, in the "due time" of the Lord (Ether 3:21–28; 4:1–2).

After 344 days on the water, the brother of Jared and his company established themselves in the promised land. Eventually the people came to Jared and his brother and asked them to anoint one of their sons to be a king over them (Ether 6:22). The brother of Jared warned them against having a king and prophesied, "Surely this thing leadeth into captivity" (Ether 6:23). Nevertheless, the people first offered the kingship to each of the sons of the brother of Jared, but they refused. Eventually Orihah, one of Jared's sons, accepted and was anointed king over the people. One of Orihah's descendants, Corihor[1], rebelled against his father, king Kib, and usurped the throne and took Kib captive, thus fulfilling the prophecy of the brother of Jared (Ether 7:5). The brother of Jared was the father of twenty-two children (Ether 6:20). His death is recorded in Ether 6:29.

Moroni[2] extolled the great faith of the brother of Jared, and he recorded that because of his faith "the Lord could not withhold anything from his sight; wherefore he showed him all things" (Ether 12:19–21). The brother of Jared commanded the mountain Zerin to "remove—and it was removed" (Ether 12:30). Moroni also revealed that the brother of Jared was a powerful writer. Addressing the Lord, Moroni compared the writing of the Nephites with that of the brother of Jared: "Thou hast not made us mighty in writing like unto the brother of Jared, for thou madest him that the things which he wrote were mighty even as thou art, unto the overpowering of man to read them" (Ether 12:24).

Moroni sealed up the writings of the brother of Jared with the "interpreters" to go forth unto the Gentiles when the Lord would "manifest unto them the things which the brother of Jared saw, even to the unfolding unto them all my revelations" (Ether 4:4–7; cf. 3:25–28). Joseph Smith was given the URIM AND THUMMIM, the interpreters originally given to the brother of Jared, and he used them to translate the Book of Mormon and to receive numerous revelations (D&C 17:1).

See also Ether, book of; Jaredite civilization; Jesus Christ, premortal appearances of; Moriancumer, Mahonri; Sealed portion of the gold plates.

BIBLIOGRAPHY

Holland, Jeffrey R. "I Have a Question." *Ensign* 4 (April 1974): 18–19.

McConkie, Bruce R. *The Promised Messiah.* Salt Lake City: Deseret Book, 1978.

Reynolds, George R. "The Jaredites." *Juvenile Instructor* 27 (May 1, 1892): 282–85.

JHS

Jared[1], posterity of The narrative in the book of Ether chronicling the reign of the many Jaredite kings adds confirmatory witness to cardinal teachings already rehearsed repetitively in the Nephite saga: the evils of secret combinations, kingdoms and peoples prospering when they keep the commandments of God, and the eventual destruction and misery that accompany the rejection of God and his prophets.

The following listing represents Jared's progeny as written by Ether in Ether 1:6–32 and expanded in the subsequent narrative. The term "begat" assumes a father-son relationship. Names of wives, dates, and localities (place names) are not given in the book of Ether. There are ambiguities within the book of Ether regarding personal names and relationships. Shiblon in Ether 1:12 is spelled Shiblom in Ether 11:4, but it is assumed that the two names refer to the same person. In Ether 1:6, Ether is shown as a "descendant of Coriantor," but in Ether 11:23 he is designated as a son of Coriantor. For purposes of this chart it is assumed that Ether was Coriantor's son. The numbers in the following list correspond with the numbers in the accompanying genealogical chart.

1. *Jared[1]—see* Jared[1].

2. *Jacom*—son of Jared[1], probably his firstborn. Jacom refused the kingship offered him at the inception of the Jaredite monarchy (Ether 6:14, 27).

3. *Gilgah*—son of Jared[1]. Gilgah refused the offer to be crowned the first Jaredite king (Ether 6:14, 27).

4. *Mahah*—one of the four sons of Jared[1]. Like two of his brothers, Mahah refused to be the first king of the Jaredites, a position that was afterwards bestowed upon his brother Orihah (Ether 6:14, 27).

5. *Orihah*—son of Jared[1]. Orihah was appointed the first king of the Jaredites and executed judgment in righteousness. Orihah had thirty-one children, twenty-three of which were sons (Ether 1:32; 6:14, 27–30; 7:1–3).

6. *Kib*—reigned in his father Orihah's stead. Kib lost his throne to his rebellious son Corihor, after which he dwelt in captivity. Kib's son Shule restored him to his throne (Ether 1:32; 7:3–5, 7–10).

7. *Corihor[1]*—overthrew his father Kib and reigned as king until his brother Shule deposed him and reenthroned Kib. Corihor repented and was granted power when Shule became Kib's successor (Ether 7:3–5, 8–9, 13–14).

8. *Shule—see* Shule.

9. *Noah[2]*—rebelled against his father, Corihor[1], and uncle Shule, drawing many people away from Shule, the king. Noah fought Shule and gained a part of the kingdom, after which they fought again, and Noah obtained the kingdom and imprisoned Shule. At a time when Shule's execution was imminent, Shule's sons assassinated Noah in his house, rescued their father, and restored him to his kingdom. "The son of Noah did build up his kingdom in his stead," and the country was divided into two kingdoms: the kingdom of Shule and the kingdom of Cohor[2], the son of Noah (Ether 7:14–20).

10. *Cohor[1]*—son of Corihor[1] and brother of Noah[2] who joined in Noah's rebellion against their father Corihor and uncle Shule (Ether 7:15).

11. *Cohor[2]*—son of Noah[2] who succeeded him and ruled over part of the kingdom during the time of king Shule. Cohor waged a war against Shule, was defeated, and lost his life (Ether 7:19–22).

12. *Nimrod[2]*—son of Cohor[2] who, following the defeat and death of his father, relinquished the kingdom of Cohor to Shule. Nimrod pleased Shule and was granted "great favors" (Ether 7:22).

13. *Omer*—son of Shule who reigned in Shule's stead in the kingdom. Omer was deposed by his son Jared[2] and lived in captivity until his (Omer's) sons, Esrom and Coriantumr[1], overthrew Jared and restored him to his throne. Afterwards Jared plotted Omer's assassination but Omer was warned in a dream to depart from the land to be saved. Eventually Omer was again

THE POSTERITY OF JARED[1]

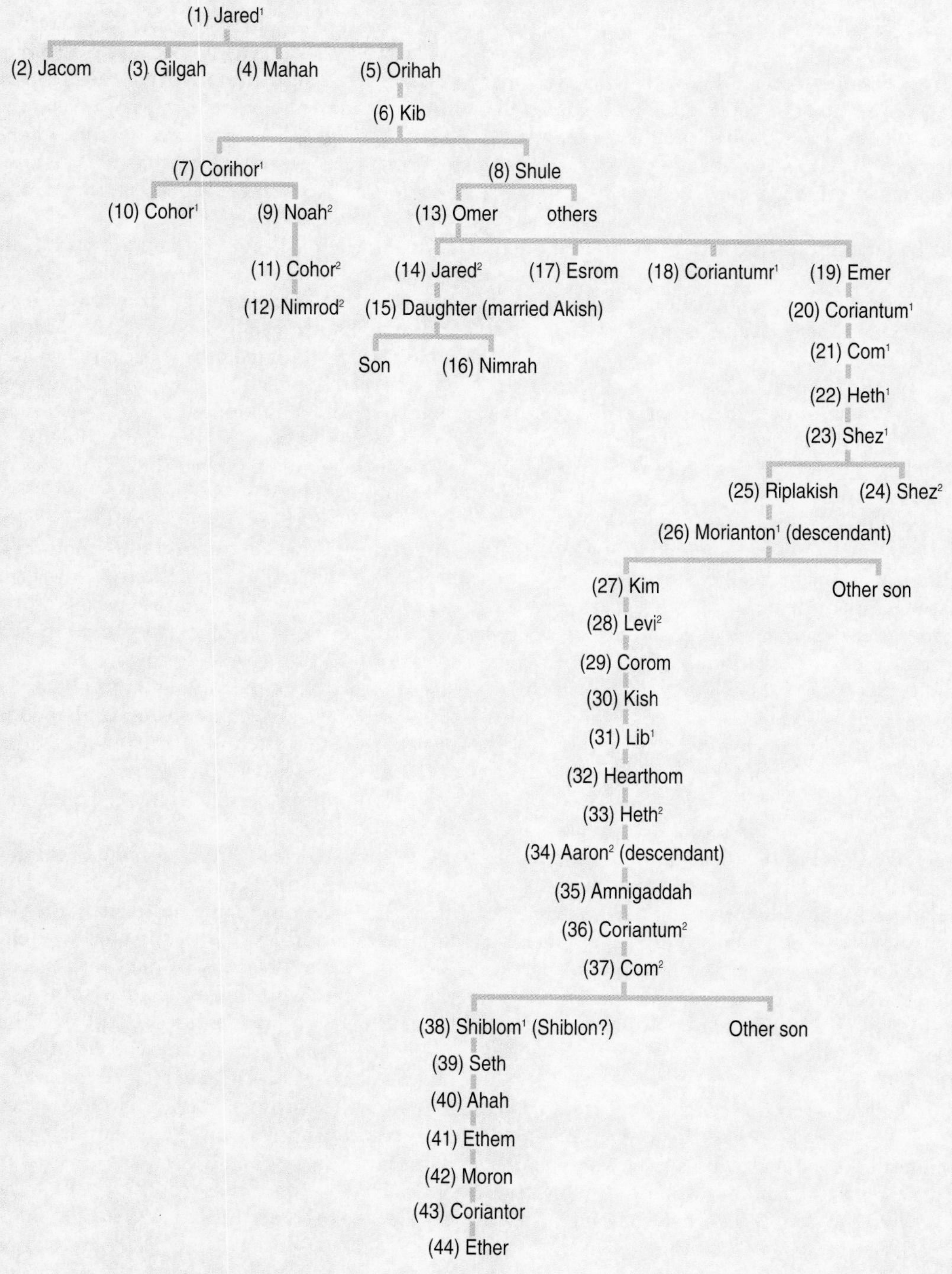

JARED[1], POSTERITY OF

established as king (Ether 1:29–30; 8:1–17; 9:1–15).

14. *Jared²*—*see* Jared².

15. *Jared²*, daughter of—*see* Jared², daughter of.

16. *Nimrah*—son of Akish who became angered at Akish for causing his brother's death. Nimrah gathered "a small number of men, and fled out of the land, and came over and dwelt with Omer" (Ether 9:7–9). *See* Akish.

17. *Esrom*—son of Omer who helped restore his father's throne usurped by his brother Jared² (Ether 8:3–6).

18. *Coriantumr¹*—son of Omer who helped restore his father's throne usurped by his brother Jared² (Ether 8:3–6).

19. *Emer*—begat by Omer and anointed to be king and reign in Omer's stead. Emer executed judgment in righteousness and the house of Emer prospered. Emer saw the Son of Righteousness and was reported to have died in peace (Ether 1:29; 9:14–22).

20. *Coriantum¹*—appointed king by his father, Emer. Coriantum walked in the steps of his father and built many mighty cities and did administer that which was good unto his people in all his days. Coriantum lived to be 142 years old (Ether 1:28; 9:21–25).

21. *Com¹*—son of Coriantum¹. Reigned in his father's stead for forty-nine years and then was slain by the sword of his son Heth (Ether 1:27; 9:25–27).

22. *Heth¹*—son of Com¹. Heth embraced secret combinations and gained the throne through murdering his father, Com. During his reign he commanded his people to cast out the prophets who were sent to cry repentance; in some cases they were cast into pits to perish. Consequently a great dearth came upon the land, as well as a plague of poisonous serpents. Heth perished by famine (Ether 1:26; 9:26–10:1).

23. *Shez¹*—son (descendant?) of Heth (Ether 1:25; 10:1). Shez was the only one of the "household" of Heth who survived the famine. He was a righteous king who built many cities and lived to "an exceedingly old age" (Ether 10:1–4).

24. *Shez²*—eldest son of Shez¹. Shez² rebelled against his father, the king. A robber killed him "because of his exceeding riches," bringing peace again to his father (Ether 10:3).

25. *Riplakish*—son of Shez¹. Riplakish reigned in his father's stead. He did not find favor in the Lord's eyes—he had many wives and concubines, burdened the people with taxes, and afflicted the people with whoredoms and abominations. After reigning for forty-two years the people rose up against Riplakish and he was killed (Ether 1:24; 10:4–8).

26. *Morianton¹*—descendant of Riplakish. Morianton gathered "an army of outcasts" and won a lengthy war enabling him to gain power and establish himself as king. Afterwards he gained "favor" with the people because he eased their burdens. For this they anointed Morianton their king. Although Morianton was a just leader he was a wicked man (Ether 1:23; 10:9–13).

27. *Kim*—son of Morianton. Kim was an unrighteous king who reigned after his father. Kim's brother rebelled against him and placed him in captivity where he spent the remainder of his life. His son Levi² was born in captivity (Ether 1:22; 10:13–14).

28. *Levi²*—son of Kim. Levi served in captivity for forty-two years, after which he fought against the king of the land and did obtain the kingdom. Levi was righteous, and his people prospered (Ether 1:21; 10:15–16).

29. *Corom*—son of Levi². Corom was a righteous king who reigned after his father Levi (Ether 1:20; 10:16–17).

30. *Kish*—son of Corom, appointed to reign in his father's stead (Ether 1:19; 10:17).

31. *Lib¹*—son of Kish who reigned after his father. He found favor with the Lord by doing good all his days and his people were exceedingly blessed while he reigned as king. Lib became a great hunter (Ether 1:18; 10:18–29).

32. *Hearthom*—son of Lib¹ who ruled in his father's stead. When he had reigned for twenty-four years the kingdom was taken from him, and he served in captivity for the remainder of his days (Ether 1:17; 10:30).

33. *Heth²*—son of Hearthom. Heth lived in captivity all his days (Ether 1:16; 10:31).

34. *Aaron²*—descendant of Heth². Aaron lived all his days in captivity (Ether 1:16; 10:31).

35. *Amnigaddah*—son of Aaron[2]. Amnigaddah lived all his days in captivity (Ether 1:15; 10:31).

36. *Coriantum*[2]—son of Amnigaddah. Coriantum lived all his days in captivity (Ether 1:14; 10:31).

37. *Com*[2]—begat by Coriantum[2]. Com drew away half of the kingdom and reigned for forty-two years. He went to battle against king Amgid and eventually gained the entire kingdom. During Com's reign it was reported that he did not prevail against the "robbers in the land" although he fought "much" against them. Prophets came in the days of Com to call the people to repentance. After being rejected they fled to Com for protection and "prophesied unto Com many things; and he was blessed in all the remainder of his days" (Ether 1:13; 10:31–11:3).

38. *Shiblom*[1]—son of Com[2], who reigned in his father's stead. Shiblom's brother rose up against him and war followed. He also had all the prophets who had prophesied of his people's impending destruction killed. Wars, famine, pestilence, and "great destruction" did come in the days of Shiblom, "such an one as never had been known upon the face of the earth," and Shiblom was eventually slain (Ether 1:12; 11:4–7).

39. *Seth*—Shiblom's son who lived in captivity all his days (Ether 1:11; 11:9).

40. *Ahah*—wicked son of Seth, whose reign as king caused much bloodshed. Ahah's days were "few" (Ether 1:10; 11:10–11).

41. *Ethem*—wicked son of Ahah, who obtained Ahah's kingdom and executed "judgment in wickedness all his days." Ethem's people rejected the many prophets who came among them (Ether 1:9; 11:11–14).

42. *Moron*—wicked son of Ethem who obtained his father's kingdom. Because of a rebellion among the people attributed to secret combinations, Moron lost one-half of his kingdom, but after many years he regained it. Subsequently Moron was again overthrown, after which he spent the remainder of his days in captivity (Ether 1:8; 11:14–18).

43. *Coriantor*—begat of Moron, Coriantor dwelt all his days in captivity and died there. During Coriantor's day prophets again came and foretold destruction and again were rejected. This rejection occurred "because of their secret society and wicked abominations." Coriantor begat Ether (Ether 1:7; 11:18–23).

44. *Ether*—*see* Ether.

See also Chronology, Book of Mormon; Ether, book of; Jaredite civilization.

KS

Jared[2], daughter of A wicked Jaredite woman who schemed to bring her father Jared[2] back to power after he had lost his throne to his father Omer, whom he had deposed years earlier. She persuaded him to follow the evil methods employed by secret combinations in the past, methods described in the records brought to the New World by the Jaredite fathers (Ether 8:8–10). Her plan was to please a man named Akish by dancing before him. Akish would then desire her as his wife and therefore accept her father's evil proposition to deliver Omer's head in exchange for permission to marry his daughter (Ether 8:11–12). Omer, however, was warned by God and escaped. But he was deposed, and Jared became king, only to be slain by Akish and his fellow conspirators (Ether 9:2–5). The text is silent concerning the role of Jared's daughter after her father's assassination.

See also Jared[1], posterity of.

MDR

Jaredite civilization The Jaredites were a pre-Israelite, pre-Nephite civilization that migrated from Mesopotamia and flourished in the New World between approximately the third millennium and the second century B.C. The history of the Jaredites is found largely in the book of Ether, as abridged by Moroni[2]. Although a number of prophets preached to the Jaredites, for the most part their society was described as idolatrous and wicked. Throughout their history the Jaredites were plagued by political instability, criminal conspiracy, royal coups, and wars, culminating in their collapse in the midst of a catastrophic civil war between rival factions for the throne.

It is clear that the book of Ether is a heavily edited abridgment of the original twenty-four gold PLATES OF ETHER that were found by Limhi's people (Mosiah 8:9; 28:17; Ether 1:2, 4; 15:33). Moroni[2], the principal editor, seems to have written substantial sections of the text which may include Ether 1:1–6a; 2:9–13a; 3:17–20; 4:1b–6:1; 8:18–26; 9:1a; 9:20; 12:6–13:1 (Welch, 7). Some portions of the rest of the text may have been paraphrased, edited, or abridged by Moroni; others are undoubtedly full translations of the original records. Thus, the book of Ether is a composite document, a selective narrative history edited to emphasize one of Moroni's fundamental prophetic lessons: that failure to follow the teachings of the Lord and allowing the establishment of SECRET COMBINATIONS leads to the destruction of a civilization (Ether 8:18–26).

Basic history of the Jaredites

The book of Ether begins with an editor's introduction by Moroni (Ether 1:1–5), followed by a genealogy of the royal descendants of Jared[1] (Ether 1:6–32). At the time of the "great tower," the brother of Jared cried to the Lord that his clan might be spared from the confounding of their language. The Lord showed compassion on this people and revealed a plan for them to migrate to a promised land, "choice above all the lands of the earth" (Ether 1:33–43). The Lord promised the brother of Jared that his descendants would be a "great nation," that there would be "none greater" (Ether 1:43). This status, however, was dependent upon their obedience—they would have to serve God or be swept off the land "when . . . ripened in iniquity" (Ether 2:9–10).

The Jaredites migrated across the Old World and settled for four years on the shores of the ocean (Ether 2:1–13). There the Lord gave instructions to the brother of Jared to build BARGES to take them across the ocean to the promised land (Ether 2:14–25). It was during the preparation of these barges that the brother of Jared, through his faith, received a unique vision of Jesus Christ (Ether 3). The Jaredites traveled across the ocean (Ether 6:1–12) and founded colonies in the promised land (Ether 6:12–18). Upon their arrival, they chose to be governed by kings (Ether 6:19–30). This institution of kingship lasted throughout their history and followed a clear pattern: righteous kings brought peace, stability and prosperity, while wicked kings brought war, contention, and destruction.

The reigns of the early Jaredite kings are described in Ether 7–8. Some are given only brief notice, while others are described in more depth. Early in their history, struggles over succession to the throne arose (Ether 7). Eventually the Jaredites discovered secret combinations, and Akish and Jared[2] used them to overthrow king Omer (Ether 8:1–17; cf. 8:22–23; 9:11; 11:15). These secret combinations among the Jaredites led to murder and warfare and eventually the final violent collapse of their civilization (Ether 10:33–34; 11:4, 6, 15–18; 13:20–15:34). Moroni strongly warned the readers of the Book of Mormon against such secret combinations. He observed that secret combinations led to the destruction of the Jaredites and the Nephites, and he warned the future Gentiles that "whatsoever nation shall uphold such secret combinations, to get power and gain, until they shall spread over the nation, behold, they shall be destroyed" (Ether 8:18–26).

Omer's loss of the throne was only temporary (Ether 9:1–14). His return from exile precipitated the first golden age under his son, the prophet-king Emer, and his grandson Coriantum[1] (Ether 9:15–24). Civil strife and secret combinations were renewed after the death of Coriantum (Ether 9:25–35), followed by increasingly wicked, tyrannical kings such as Riplakish and his descendant Morianton[1] (Ether 10:1–13). The wicked king Riplakish took many concubines, taxed the people heavily, built "many spacious buildings," a "beautiful throne," and "many prisons" (Ether 10:5–6). Following a period of political chaos after the death of Morianton (Ether 10:14–17), the righteous king Lib established a second golden age and built a great and prosperous city (Ether 10:18–29). Lib's descendants were not able to retain the throne, however, which passed into the hands of an unknown dynasty who were not necessarily descended from Jared[1], and about whom almost nothing is known (Ether 10:30–31). Power was restored to the house of Jared by Com[2] (Ether 10:31–34), and his descendants ruled in wickedness; secret combinations prevailed, despite repeated warnings by unnamed prophets (Ether 11).

The final acts of Jaredite history commenced "in the days of Coriantumr . . . [who] was king over all the land." His people rejected the teachings and prophecies of the prophet Ether, and they "cast him out" (Ether 12:1–5; 13:2–13). A "great war," which brought death to many, ensued between Coriantumr[2] and those who sought his kingdom (Ether 13:15–18). Ether went to Coriantumr and prophesied "that, if he would repent, and all his household, the Lord would give unto him his kingdom and spare the people—Otherwise they should be destroyed, and all his household save it were himself." Ether further told Coriantumr that he would live long enough to see another people inherit the promised land (Ether 13:20–21). Coriantumr and his family and people refused to repent, the wars continued, and they sought to kill Ether. Finally Ether, hiding in a cave, concluded his record with a detailed description of the final suicidal wars between Coriantumr and Shiz and the prophesied destruction of Jaredite civilization (Ether 13:18–15:34).

Although the book of Ether describes the destruction of Jaredite civilization, that may not necessarily imply the complete annihilation of all Jaredite peoples. When the social and political structures collapsed, it is likely that many individuals fled and thus survived the massacres during the last great war. For example, Jaredite names are found in Nephite portions of the Book of Mormon (e.g., Moron compared to Moroni; Corihor/Coriantor/Coriantumr compared to Corianton/Korihor), indicating some type of cultural continuity, perhaps through Mulekite intermediaries (Sorenson, *Setting*, 119–20; Nibley, 242–46).

Origin of the name Jaredite

The word *Jaredite* does not seem to be the original ethnonym used by the peoples of the book of Ether to describe themselves. The name occurs only once in the Book of Mormon, when Moroni[2], the editor of the book of Ether, compared the collapse of his own Nephite civilization with that of the "Jaredites" (Moro. 9:23). "Jaredites" is not found in the book of Ether and seems thus to be late Nephite nomenclature for their little-known predecessors in the New World. This name is misleading because the book of Ether is a history not just of the descendants of Jared[1] but of all of the descendants of Jared's unnamed father. Nonetheless, the main royal lineage described in the book of Ether is that of Jared, and the use of *Jaredite* to refer to all peoples of the book of Ether has become normative in LDS culture.

Geography

The broad outlines of Jaredite geography are relatively clear, although the exact details are open to a range of interpretation. Based on the correlation of place names such as the "great tower" in Shinar/Sumer (Gen. 11:2, 4), and the "valley of Nimrod" (Ether 2:4), the name of a person who is associated with Mesopotamian cities (Gen. 10:8–12), it is generally assumed that Jared and his brother originally lived in Mesopotamia. From there they migrated northward (Ether 2:1), and probably eastward (though this is ambiguous), crossing uninhabited territory (Ether 2:5) and "many waters" (Ether 2:6). All of this is consistent with migration through Central Asia, broadly following what is now called the Silk Road. From a temporary resting place (Ether 2:13–14), presumably on the east coast of Asia, the Jaredites crossed the Pacific Ocean, landing on the west coast of the New World. A combination of archaeological and chronological information makes it plausible that the core lands of the Jaredites in the New World could well be equated with Mesoamerica.

Chronology

The book of Ether does not provide sufficient calendrical information to develop a precise chronology for the Jaredites. All attempted chronologies are founded upon one or more unverifiable assumptions. Nonetheless, a broad outline can be determined, limiting the range of chronological options.

The beginning of Jaredite history is said to be at the time of the "great tower" described in the Bible (Ether 1:33; Omni 1:22; Gen. 11:1–9). Unfortunately, this great tower cannot be dated with certainty. By synchronizing the origin of Jaredite civilization with the beginning of the

JAREDITE CIVILIZATION

Mesoamerican Long Count calendar, it has been suggested that the Jaredite migration to the New World occurred around 3114 B.C. (Sorenson, "Years," 4). Alternatively, if Peleg were the last of the Shemites to have lived before the age of the great tower (Gen. 10:25), and because Abraham lived five generations (191 years) after Peleg (Gen. 11:17–26), it can be speculated that the events surrounding the great tower occurred around two hundred years before Abraham. Because Abraham is generally thought to have lived during the Middle Bronze Age (2200–1550 B.C.), the date of the great tower—and the origin of the Jaredites—would be somewhere within the range of about 2400 to 1750 B.C. The possible range of dates for the end of Jaredite civilization can be more precisely defined. The Jaredite state system had clearly collapsed by the time of Mosiah (ca. 130 B.C.), yet was still in existence after the arrival of the Mulekites sometime following the destruction of Jerusalem in 586 B.C. (Omni 1:15–16, 20–21). Thus, the origin and migration of the Jaredites to the New World can be dated some time between roughly 3100 and 1750 B.C. and their collapse some time between approximately 586 and 130 B.C. As noted below, this time frame broadly corresponds with the rise and fall of the Olmecs in Mesoamerica. *See* Chronology, Book of Mormon.

Ethnicity and language of the Jaredites

Both the language and the ethnicity of the Jaredites remain uncertain. Because a few Semitic names are found in the book of Ether (e.g., Jared, Levi, Aaron, Seth), it is possible that the ancestors of the Jaredites spoke a Semitic language. On the other hand, these names may represent borrowings from Semitic neighbors of Jared in the Old World, or translations by Moroni, who extensively edited the record. Furthermore, most Jaredite names do not appear to be obviously Semitic.

Archaeology and the Jaredites

Since the 1950s archaeologists have uncovered progressively more remains of the oldest known civilization of the New World. Called "Olmecs" by archaeologists (their original ancient name is unknown), this ancient civilization flourished in Mesoamerica from roughly 1500 to 500 B.C. (Clark, 16–17; Rosenbaum, 11). Based on the geographical setting, the cultural patterns, and the agreement in chronology, some LDS scholars have attempted to correlate the Jaredites with the broader range of artifacts associated with the age of the Olmecs (Sorenson, *Setting,* 119). In the past few decades archaeologists of the Olmecs have discovered many artifacts and characteristics of culture and civilization which can be seen as parallel to those described in the book of Ether. These include location around an isthmus with a large body of water (Ether 10:20; 15:8); a chronological range of at least a thousand years from the second millennium to the mid first millennium B.C.; the existence of cities (Ether 7:9; 9:23; 10:4, 9, 12, 20; 14:17) and monumental buildings (Ether 10:5–6); writing and inscriptions on stone (Ether 15:5; Omni 1:20); the essential role of religion and the practice of idol worship (Ether 7:23, 26); iron working (Ether 7:9; 10:23); extensive trade networks (Ether 10:22); the centrality of kingship (Ether 6:22–27); and warfare and the final violent collapse of the civilization (Ether 10:33–34; 11:4, 6; 11:15–18; 13:20–15:34). Mesoamerica is the only region in the New World to exhibit all of these characteristics during this period.

Jaredite civilization as a model

The story of the Jaredite civilization gives perspective to the history and destiny of the Americas as "a choice land above all other lands, a chosen land of the Lord; wherefore the Lord would have that all men should serve him who dwell upon the face thereof" (Ether 13:2). The establishment of the Jaredites in the promised land is alluded to in the allegory of the olive tree as the branch that was planted in the spot of ground choice above all other parts of the vineyard that "withered away" to be replaced by the Nephites (Jacob 5:43–44). The rise and fall of the Jaredite civilization is another witness to the principles taught in the Book of Mormon that the righteous prosper and the wicked will eventually be destroyed. Moroni, it appears, shaped his abridgment of the record of the Jaredites to highlight the similarities between the Jaredites and his people the Nephites. The Lord delivered both peoples and led them to a land of promise, where their prosperity and survival was dependent on their righteousness. Both the Jaredites and the Nephites became prosperous, proud, and wicked, and both civilizations fostered secret combinations that eventually contributed to their destruction (Ether 8:20–21). Moroni directed his message to the Gentiles of the latter days who would inhabit the same promised land. If they would repent and serve the God of the land, Jesus Christ, they would be free from bondage and captivity. Otherwise they, like the Jaredites and Nephites before them, would suffer the wrath of God (Ether 2:9–12).

See also Agriculture in the Book of Mormon; Animals; Babel, tower of; Book of Mormon, selected themes of, cycles of prosperity and destruction; Ether, book of; Jared[1], posterity of; Linen; Metals of the Book of Mormon; Names in the Book of Mormon; Silk.

BIBLIOGRAPHY

Clark, John E. *Los Olmecas en Mesoamerica*. Mexico: El Equilibrista, 1994.

Hamblin, William J. "The Genealogies and Chronology of the Jaredites." Unpublished manuscript, 1998.

Honey, D. "Ecological Nomadism Versus Epic Heroism in Ether." *Review of Books on the Book of Mormon*. Vol. 2. Provo, Utah: FARMS, 1990. 143–63.

Nibley, Hugh. *Lehi in the Desert; The World of the Jaredites; There Were Jaredites*. Vol. 5 of *The Collected Works of Hugh Nibley*. Edited by John W. Welch, Darrell L. Matthews, and Stephen R. Callister. Salt Lake City: Deseret Book and FARMS, 1988.

Rosenbaum, Allen, ed. *The Olmec World: Ritual and Rulership*. Princeton: Art Museum, 1996.

Sorenson, John L. *An Ancient American Setting for the Book of Mormon*. Salt Lake City: Deseret Book and FARMS, 1985.

———. *Images of Ancient America: Visualizing Book of Mormon Life*. Provo, Utah: Research Press, FARMS, 1998.

———. "The Years of the Jaredites." FARMS Preliminary Report, 1969.

Welch, John W. "Preliminary Comments for Discussion on the Sources behind the Book of Ether." Unpublished manuscript, 1985.

WJH

Jarom Keeper of the small plates of Nephi for 59 years (ca. 420–361 B.C.), Jarom received the records from his father Enos. He wrote only fifteen verses himself, contending that the revelations he and others had received could add nothing significant to the record. He wrote that the Nephites were led by "mighty men in the faith of the Lord" and that the continuation of the Nephite civilization verified the Lord's promise that he would prosper those who keep his commandments (Jarom 1:7, 9). Jarom also noted that Nephite prophets, priests, and teachers taught that the intent of the law of Moses was to bring the people to the Messiah (Jarom 1:11). He gave the plates to his son Omni (Jarom 1:15).

See also Jarom, book of.

CDT

Jarom, book of Written by Jarom, the son of Enos, on the small PLATES OF NEPHI, the book

OUTLINE OF JAROM

- I. Jarom's introduction (1:1–2)
  - A. The commandment of Enos to Jarom concerning the record (1:1)
  - B. The purpose of the record: to benefit the Lamanites (1:2)
- II. Jarom's testimony of God's mercy and the blessings of righteousness (1:3–12)
  - A. Nephite transgressions and God's mercy in not yet destroying them (1:3)
  - B. Faithful Nephites received many revelations and manifestations of the Holy Spirit (1:4)
  - C. Nephite obedience to the law of Moses (1:5; 399 B.C.)
  - D. Apostate condition of the contemporary Lamanites (1:6)
  - E. Verification of the blessings of hearkening to righteous leadership: faith, prosperity, and victory (1:7–12)
- III. Jarom's final remarks and passing of the plates to Omni (1:13–15; 361 B.C.)

of Jarom sketches Nephite history from ca. 420 to 361 B.C. For the Nephites this was a period in which there were "wars, and contentions, and dissensions" (Jarom 1:13). Jarom wrote that it was "expedient that much should be done among this people, because of the hardness of their hearts" (Jarom 1:3). Nevertheless, God was "exceedingly merciful unto them," blessing the faithful with "many revelations," and providing prophets and righteous leaders to teach the people and call them to repentance (Jarom 1:3–13).

Content and message

Claiming that the writings of his "fathers" had already sufficiently revealed the plan of salvation, Jarom chose not to write about his own prophesying or revelations on the limited space remaining on the small plates of Nephi (Jarom 1:2). Rather, his intent in writing a "little" seems to have been to illustrate and verify, through a brief sketch of Nephite history, the truth of the Lord's words that "inasmuch as ye will keep my commandments ye shall prosper in the land" (Jarom 1:9). Jarom began by using vivid imagery to describe the spiritual condition of his people, depicting them as hard of heart, deaf of ear, blind of mind, and stiff of neck (Jarom 1:3). He then spoke of God's mercy in forestalling their destruction and of God's blessing the faithful among them with many revelations and manifestations of the Holy Spirit (Jarom 1:3–4). He further described how, through the diligent teaching and warning of their righteous leaders, the Nephites "observed to keep the law of Moses," which was given to persuade them to "look forward unto the Messiah" (Jarom 1:5, 7, 10–11). Jarom reported that as the Nephites hearkened to the teachings of their righteous leaders, they prospered and were preserved in their many wars against the Lamanites (Jarom 1:5–12).

Jarom's words verify to covenant people of any age that God keeps his promises: He will bless those who keep his commandments (Jarom 1:9; cf. 1 Ne. 2:20; 2 Ne. 1:20; Omni 1:6).

CDT

Jashon, land of and city of Nephite region south of the land Shem and near the land Antum where Ammaron deposited all the sacred Nephite records (Morm. 1:3; 2:17, 20). The Nephites passed through here during a great retreat before the Lamanites. During this period Mormon retrieved the plates of Nephi according to Ammaron's instructions (Morm. 1:4; 2:16–20; A.D. 346).

Jehovah An anglicized form of the Hebrew *YHWH* (meaning "eternal one" or "self-existent one"). Found twice in the Book of Mormon (2 Ne. 22:2; Moro. 10:34), *Jehovah* is related to the name-title *I AM* in Hebrew (Ex. 3:14–15). As Moroni[2] indicated by using language similar to that of the New Testament (Acts 10:42; 2 Tim. 4:1; 1 Pet. 4:5), Jehovah is one of the name-titles of Jesus Christ, the God and Judge of this world.

ACS

Jeneum Nephite military leader killed with his ten thousand troops in the last battle between the Nephites and Lamanites (Morm. 6:14; A.D. 385).

See also Cumorah, battle of.

Jeremiah[1] A prophet descended from a priestly family in Anathoth, a village about three miles northeast of Jerusalem[1]. Jeremiah was a contemporary of the prophets Lehi[1], Zephaniah, Habakkuk, Obadiah, Daniel, and Ezekiel. The Lord called Jeremiah to be a prophet in ca. 627 B.C. (Jer. 1:1–2). Just like Lehi, he was called to cry repentance to his people in Jerusalem (Jer. 1:7; 1 Ne. 1:4; 7:14). His prophecies were preserved on the brass plates (1 Ne. 5:13) and are referred to in Helaman 8:20. For forty years he warned of the impending destruction of Jerusalem that was finally accomplished in 586 B.C. His writings reflect a lifetime of the same kind of rejection recorded by Lehi in his short ministry in 1 Nephi 1. Jeremiah's prophecies are collected in the biblical books of Jeremiah and Lamentations, which contain many details about his prophetic call and his ministry.

Jeremiah's lifetime spans many dramatic events that shaped the world of Lehi and Nephi[1]:

the reign of king Josiah, who cleansed the temple and led his people in a ceremony of covenant renewal (2 Kgs. 23), the destruction of the Assyrian empire, the rise of Babylon, the destruction of Jerusalem, and the exile of his people to Babylon in 597 and 586 B.C. Jeremiah prophesied during the reigns of five kings of Judah, from Josiah to Zedekiah. He remembered Josiah as a righteous king and lamented his death (Jer. 22:15–16; 2 Chr. 35:25), but the rest of the kings rejected his message. King Jehoiakim had Jeremiah's prophecies read aloud and then burned the scroll (Jer. 36). Likewise, Zedekiah sought out Jeremiah on several occasions to ascertain the word of the Lord but ultimately rejected it (Jer. 37–38). Because the word of the Lord commanded the kings to submit to the Babylonians, Jeremiah was arrested during the reign of Zedekiah on suspicion of desertion to the Babylonians and of subverting the war effort. Consequently, he was thrown into a cistern. He was saved by his friends in the royal court, but he remained under arrest throughout the Babylonian siege (Jer. 37–38). Jeremiah was a witness to the fulfillment of the prophecies of destruction he had delivered to his people (Jer. 39). He was like Mormon, who also spent his life crying repentance to an unrepentant people, only to witness and lament their destruction (Jer. 8:18–9:1; cf. Morm. 6:16–18). When given a choice by the Babylonians to go to Babylon or remain with his people, Jeremiah chose to stay with his people. At the end of his life a group of Jews, fearful of Babylonian reprisals for renewed Judean revolts, forced Jeremiah to accompany them to Egypt, where presumably he died (Jer. 42:1–43:7).

Jeremiah faithfully delivered the word of the Lord throughout his lifetime but was constantly met with rejection, ridicule, and persecution. A series of his personal laments attests to the suffering he endured in fulfilling his prophetic ministry and reveals him to be a type of Christ. He rejoiced in the word of the Lord: "Thy word was unto me the joy and rejoicing of mine heart" (Jer. 15:16), and he described the overpowering need to proclaim the word of God: "His word was in mine heart as a burning fire shut up in my bones" (Jer. 20:9). At the same time he lamented his life of persecution, rejection, and loneliness: "I am in derision daily, every one mocketh me" (Jer. 20:7); "I sat alone because of thy hand" (Jer. 15:17). On one occasion he lamented, "Cursed be the day wherein I was born" (Jer. 20:14), and he described himself "like a lamb or an ox that is brought to the slaughter" (Jer. 11:19).

See also Jeremiah[1], prophecies of.

DRS

Jeremiah[2] *See* Disciples, twelve Nephite.

Jeremiah[1], prophecies of Jeremiah's prophecies up to the commencement of the reign of Zedekiah were included on the PLATES OF BRASS (1 Ne. 5:13) and were thus known to the Nephites. Nephi[2] noted the fulfillment of Jeremiah's prophecies concerning the destruction of Jerusalem and listed him among the prophets who foretold the first coming of the Son of God (Hel. 8:13–20; cf. Jer. 31:31–33). A collection of Jeremiah's prophecies has also been preserved in the Old Testament book of Jeremiah. Jeremiah's prophecies in the Bible include prophecies of the destruction of Jerusalem (Jer. 1–25), much like those of Lehi[1] (1 Ne. 1), and of the coming of a Davidic Messiah that seem to better fit the Second Coming (Jer. 23:5; 33:15). Prophecies of the first coming of the Messiah may have been preserved only on the plates of brass, or perhaps they were lost through the transmission of the biblical book. Jeremiah foretold the latter-day restoration, gathering, and reunification of Israel and Judah (Jer. 26–35). In particular, Jeremiah prophesied of a day when the Lord would make "a new covenant with the house of Israel, and with the house of Judah" (Jer. 31:31–34), a prophecy that was fulfilled first by the coming of the Savior (Matt. 26:28) and then by the restoration of the gospel in the fulness of times (Smith, 14–15). There is much biographical information about Jeremiah throughout his book but especially in chapters 36–45. Jeremiah closed with a collection of prophecies against foreign nations in chapters 42–51, and a description of the destruction of Jerusalem and exile (Jer. 52). According to Oliver Cowdery (108–12), Moroni[2] quoted several of Jeremiah's prophecies to Joseph Smith in connection with the Restoration, especially from chapters 30–31.

See also Jerusalem[1], city of; Jerusalem[1], destruction of, at 586 B.C.

BIBLIOGRAPHY

Cowdery, Oliver. *Messenger and Advocate* 1.7 (April 1835).

Jackson, Kent P. "The Appearance of Moroni to Joseph Smith." *The Pearl of Great Price*. Vol. 2 of *Studies in Scripture* series. Edited by Kent P. Jackson and Robert L. Millet. Salt Lake City: Randall Book, 1985. 339–66.

Smith, Joseph. *Teachings of the Prophet Joseph Smith*. Selected by Joseph Fielding Smith. Salt Lake City: Deseret Book, 1976.

DRS

Jershon Nephite land "on the east by the sea, . . . south of the land Bountiful" (Alma 27:22), perhaps most noted for the magnanimous Christian act of the Nephites in relinquishing it to converted Lamanite refugees, the ANTI-NEPHI-LEHIES or the people of Ammon. As part of the Nephite commitment to help the Anti-Nephi-Lehies, who had fled the land of Nephi to escape the continued murdering of believers by Lamanites, Amulonites, and Amalekites, they positioned their armies between Jershon and the land of Nephi to protect them from a possible attack (Alma 27:22–26). The Lamanite armies had pursued the people of Ammon into the wilderness and when they met the armies of the Nephites a war commenced that eclipsed all battles among the people to that point. "Tens of thousands of the Lamanites were slain," and although the Nephites prevailed, "there was a tremendous slaughter among the people of Nephi" (Alma 28:1–3; 30:2).

A church was established in Jershon (Alma 28:1), and Ammon[2] was the high priest (Alma 30:20). Korihor, the anti-Christ (ca. 74 B.C.), tried to preach his doctrines among the people in Jershon, but they arrested him and brought him before Ammon who then "caused that he should be carried out of the land" (Alma 30:21).

Jershon also became a place of refuge for another group of converts. The poor Zoramites[2] who believed the preaching of Alma[2]'s missionary group (Alma 31:5–7) were expelled from the land of Antionum "and they came over . . . into the land of Jershon" (Alma 35:3–6). Angered over the shelter the converts had received in Jershon, the Zoramite "chief ruler" requested that they be "cast out" (Alma 35:8), but instead they were cared for and given "lands for their inheritance" (Alma 35:9). In retaliation against the people of Ammon in Jershon, the Zoramites mixed with the Lamanites and incited them to anger and eventually to war. Facing the prospect of another war, the people of Ammon left Jershon and went to Melek, and the Nephite armies prepared in Jershon to fight the Lamanites and Zoramites (Alma 35:10–13). When the armies of the Lamanites met the Nephite armies "in the borders of Jershon" they feared the Nephites because of their armor, and they withdrew into the wilderness (Alma 43:18–22). Captain Moroni left part of his army to guard Jershon and then marched in pursuit of the Lamanites (Alma 43:25).

See also Names in the Book of Mormon.

DLL

Jerusalem[1], city of The chief city of the kingdom of JUDAH and site of Jehovah's temple, it was also the home of Lehi[1] and his family before they migrated to the New World (*see* map, page 412). An appreciation for Jerusalem's place in the minds and hearts of its inhabitants, including Lehi's family, may be gained by reviewing its history.

Jerusalem is first mentioned in historical hieroglyphic documents from Egypt. These execration texts (written curses against people or places) dating to the nineteenth century B.C. refer to it as "rushalimum." Jerusalem is also discussed in fourteenth-century B.C. Egyptian diplomatic correspondence written in cuneiform, the Tell el-Amarna letters, where it is called "urusalim" (which is very close to its present-day English name). Jerusalem appears to have been a town under Canaanite control during much of this time. Archeological remains from this earliest historical period of Jerusalem's existence reveal a well-fortified town surrounded by a wall as much as ten feet thick (Shanks, 2).

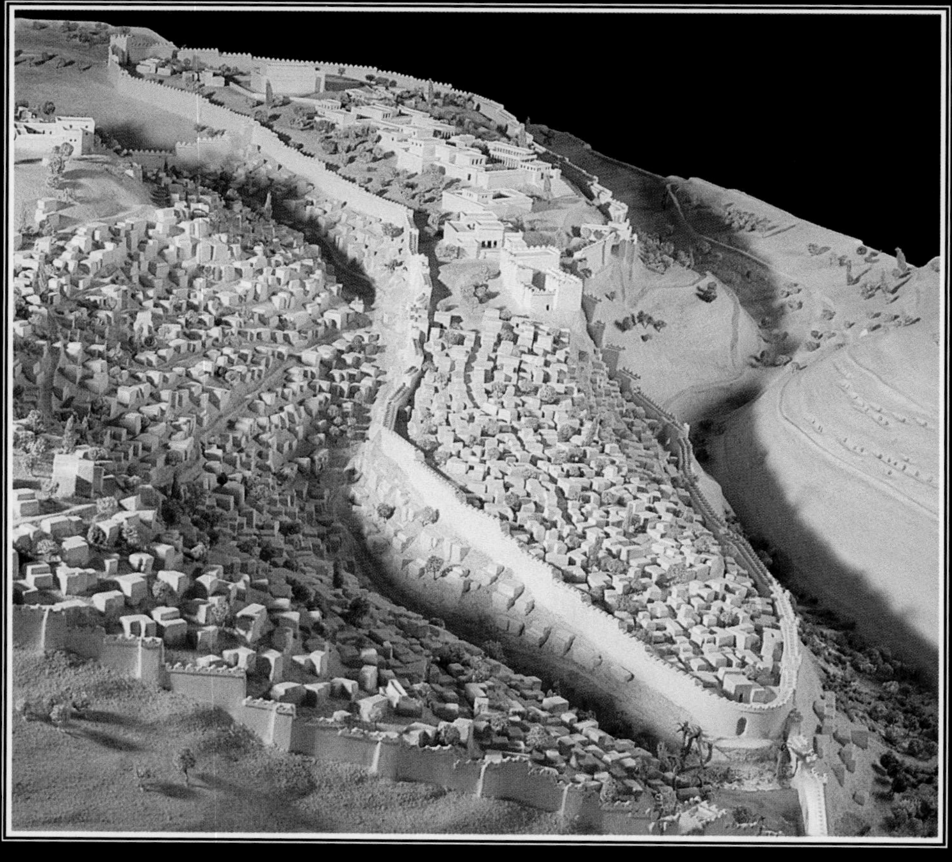

Jerusalem at the Time of the First Temple; *courtesy Bible Lands Museum.*

Two issues critical to Jerusalem's location from the start were water and geographical security. An adequate water supply for Jerusalem's inhabitants came from the Gihon spring, which seems to have been reached via an elaborate tunnel system that prevented the inhabitants from having to exit the city in order to obtain water. In this early period, Jerusalem was situated on a rocky spur (outside and to the south of the present-day Old City), and was surrounded on three sides by ravines (referred to as valleys) and neighboring ridges beyond the ravines, high enough to be called mountains by the inhabitants. The names of the valleys are the Tyropoeon ("Cheesemakers Valley"), which was much deeper and more precipitous in very ancient times because it had not yet been filled in with debris; the Hinnom, referred to as "Gehenna" by New Testament times because it symbolized hell (the city's refuse was continually burned there); and the Kidron, containing a stream bed which separated the rocky spur of Jerusalem from the Mount of Olives.

Surrounded on three sides by deep valleys and high hills, ancient Jerusalem was regarded by its inhabitants as a natural fortress, or "castle" in seventeenth century English parlance (1 Chr. 11:7).

With this picture in mind, one can better appreciate the Psalmist's later use of geographical imagery to teach the lesson of Jehovah's watchful care over his covenant people: "As the mountains are round about Jerusalem, so the Lord is round about his people from henceforth even for ever" (Ps. 125:2). All of this undoubtedly promoted a false sense of security among the city's apostate inhabitants and helps to explain, in part, why the Jews of Lehi's day immediately mocked him when he began to prophesy of Jerusalem's destruction (1 Ne. 1:18–19). As early as the reign of king David, Jerusalem began to be known as the "strong hold of Zion" (2 Sam. 5:7). The first scriptural mention of the name "Jerusalem" is found in Judges 1:8 as part of the discussion of the Israelite conquest of the land of Canaan. It is often argued that the patriarch Melchizedek was the first biblical figure to have lived at Jerusalem when it was known by its earlier name of Salem. Genesis 14:18–19 indicates that Melchizedek was king of Salem and priest of the Most High when Abram went there to pay tithes (cf. Alma 13:5–18; JST Gen. 14:32–34; Josephus, 6:10:1; "Location of Zion," 474).

The Bible indicates that during the Israelite conquest of the Holy Land, the tribe of Judah was able to conquer Jerusalem early on (Judg. 1:8), but it also infers that neither they nor the tribe of Benjamin were able to retain control of it: "And the children of Benjamin did not drive out the Jebusites that inhabited Jerusalem; but the Jebusites dwell with the children of Benjamin in Jerusalem unto this day" (Judg. 1:21). Therefore, when king David sought to establish a new capital for the united monarchy, he had to take Jerusalem away from the Jebusites (2 Sam. 5:4–10).

Under both David and Solomon, Jerusalem flourished and became an important, internationally recognized city. It began to take on the physical appearance and religious atmosphere it would display during Lehi's day. David brought to Jerusalem the Ark of the Covenant (2 Sam. 6:1–17), which was regarded by Israel as the very dwelling place of God's presence on earth (Ex. 25:21–22). Though David wanted to build a temple, he was not allowed to do so (1 Chr. 22:1–11). Nevertheless, he purchased the threshing floor of Araunah (Ornan) on Mt. Moriah, where he erected an altar and offered sacrifices to the Lord (2 Sam. 24:16–25). This bedrock threshing floor became the foundation of the temple built later by Solomon (2 Chr. 3:1).

Jerusalem was also the seat of the royal residence or palace, built for David by a foreign king, Hiram of Tyre (2 Sam. 5:11), as well as the location of something named the "house of the mighty" (Neh. 3:16), which may have been a hall of honor, museum, or military barracks. At this time Jerusalem came to be called the City of David (2 Sam. 5:7). Jerusalem also became another kind of royal residence from David's time onward—the royal necropolis, or city of the dead. According to the Bible, all of the kings of Jerusalem from David through Hezekiah were buried in the city.

Under Solomon (died 931 B.C.), the united kingdom of Israel reached its apex geographically and culturally, with Jerusalem as the center. During Solomon's reign both the atmosphere and physical features of Jerusalem changed appreciably. No person except for Herod the Great nine centuries later had a greater influence on the physical character of the city in ancient times. The Gihon spring, the city's main water supply, acquired an aura of regal importance and divine sanctity when Solomon was anointed king there by Zadok the priest and Nathan the prophet (1 Kgs. 1:33–34). Solomon extended the Gihon's usefulness by building an aqueduct (Siloam Channel) to carry water into a collection pool at the southern end of the city. The Siloam Channel is mentioned by Isaiah as "the conduit" (Isa. 7:3 // 2 Ne. 17:3; Isa. 36:2).

In Solomon's day, Jerusalem became a bustling international center of commodities (1 Kgs. 10:10–11, 14, 22, 26–27), and construction projects abounded. The Millo, a terraced structure created to shore up and expand the spur on which the city was situated, was reinforced and the city walls repaired (1 Kgs. 11:27). The king also expanded the city to the north by building an extensive and expansive complex that included the new royal palace; a structure called the "house of the forest of Lebanon," a hypostyle hall which was the largest of the palatial buildings, furnished with forty-five cedarwood columns; a porch or hall of pillars; the throne hall of judgment; the main ceremonial hall, furnished with a great ivory throne overlaid with gold and surrounded by lions; and a house for Pharaoh's daughter, Solomon's principal wife. All of this took thirteen years to build and was constructed of costly hewn stones and cedarwood (1 Kgs. 7:1–11). It was probably located in the large area where the Muslim fountain, El Kas, and the Al-Aqsa Mosque presently stand (Galbraith et al., 55).

Just to the north of his palace complex, on the crest of the slope called Mt. Moriah, Solomon built the House of the Lord. Jerusalem then became Jehovah's temple city. Solomon levied heavy taxes on his kingdom to finance the building projects and raised a "corvee" (unpaid mandatory labor force) of tens of thousands of Israelite men to help with the construction. He required male citizens to devote part of their time to cut cedars in Lebanon, float them by raft to Jerusalem's port at Jaffa, and haul them by wagon up to the capital. The temple was built according to the Lord's specifications but with the expertise of Phoenician craftsmen, especially the artisans, carpenters, and masons of king Hiram of Tyre, and thus is sometimes described as bearing the imprint of Phoenician design. The temple was double the size of the wilderness tabernacle, but still not large by modern standards (approximately 90 feet long by 30 feet wide by 45 feet high, compared to the Salt Lake Temple, which measures 186 feet long by 118 feet wide by 210 feet high; *see* illustration of Solomon's temple, page 753).

The temple faced east and was a tripartite structure, built in three progressive segments consisting of the porch, or entrance hall; the sanctuary, or Holy Place; and the inner sanctuary called the Holy of Holies, or the Most Holy Place. At the east entrance stood two ornately decorated thirty-seven-foot-high bronze columns of symbolic significance. One column was named *Yachin* (Hebrew, perhaps from "He [God] shall establish" as in Ps. 89:4) and the other *Boaz* (Hebrew, perhaps from "In him [God] is strength," as in Ps. 21:1). Inside the Holy of Holies sat the Ark of the Covenant with its Mercy Seat, both overlaid with gold, which the appointed priests and Levites brought to the temple once it was completed after seven years of work. At the dedication of the temple, which included Solomon's dedicatory prayer as well as thousands of sacrifices, fire came down from heaven (2 Chr. 7:1), a holy cloud filled the House of the Lord, and the glory of Jehovah was manifest in the temple and, thus, in Jerusalem (1 Kgs. 8:10–11).

For nearly four hundred years the temple on Mt. Moriah was the heart and soul and showpiece of Jerusalem, as well as the spiritual focal point and center of worship for God's chosen people. Jerusalem became known as "the holy city" (Isa. 52:1; Neh. 11:1), and its inhabitants always pretended to rely upon the Lord, but in reality they increasingly lived a lie (Isa. 48:1–2). The royal palace complex, together with the house of the Lord, presented an awesome image to the citizens of Jerusalem in Lehi's day. Even a foreign visitor to the capital city in Solomon's time was left breathless after a tour of the place (1 Kgs. 10:1–5). Nevertheless, in stark reminder of the fulfillment of God's promises to destroy the wicked if they do not repent, not one of Solomon's buildings is left in Jerusalem today (Galbraith et al., 55).

After the northern tribes revolted from the southern tribes and two kingdoms were created, Jerusalem became the capital of the southern kingdom of Judah. Jerusalem was strengthened and its population increased as people fled from the northern kingdom to the capital of the south (2 Chr. 11:13–17). It is possible that Lehi's forefathers (of the tribe of Manasseh) came to reside in Jerusalem during this migration. Not long after this, pharaoh Shishak came up against Jerusalem and took away the treasures of the House of the Lord as well as some of the city's other wealth (2 Chr. 12:2, 9). From this point on there is no mention of the Ark of the Covenant. Though this calamity occurred because the people transgressed the commandments of God, the people of Lehi's day seem to have forgotten their vulnerability.

The wickedness of Ahab and Jezebel in the northern kingdom of Israel further afflicted Jerusalem in the ninth century B.C. as their daughter, queen Athaliah (841–835 B.C.), ruled in Jerusalem and introduced Baal worship into the holy city. At length, however, she was executed near the royal palace and the pagan shrines destroyed. The temple priests, the new king Joash, and the people of Jerusalem joined in a solemn covenant to obey Jehovah. All the people of the land rejoiced and Jerusalem found peace for a time (2 Kgs. 11:1–20).

While the menace of the Assyrian empire was held in abeyance for a period during the eighth century B.C., Jerusalem experienced its greatest expansion in the history of the divided kingdoms. King Uzziah (767–740 B.C.) built new fortifications, prepared new weaponry for the walls of Jerusalem, and fostered extensive agricultural projects. Jerusalem also expanded to the northwest, encompassing many more acres, and making it by far the largest city or town in the kingdom of Judah. New commercial and residential districts of the city were developed during this period: The *Makhtesh* (Hebrew, "hollow") was a business section of the city in the Tyropoeon Valley; the *Mishneh* (Hebrew, "second, additional") or Second Quarter of the city (Zeph. 1:10), also called the "college" (2 Kgs. 22:14), was a residential area encompassing the entire western hill overlooking the rest of the city (Galbraith et al., 83).

When king Hezekiah came to power (715–687 B.C.) he cleansed the temple, reestablished a righteous priesthood to officiate in the ordinances of the House of the Lord, and tried to set Israel on a righteous course by reestablishing proper holy days, removing idolatrous images, and breaking down pagan altars. With the Assyrian threat looming large (they had destroyed the northern kingdom in 722 B.C.), Hezekiah began preparing Jerusalem for an invasion by fortifying the city walls with material provided by dismantled houses (one section of wall unearthed by archaeologists is twenty-five feet thick and appropriately named the "broad wall"). He also cut a new underground tunnel to ensure a constant water supply from the Gihon spring into the Siloam pool (John 9:7) inside the city (Isa. 22:9–10; 2 Chr. 32:30). Hezekiah's famous water tunnel, which still exists today, was 1748 feet long and chiseled out of solid rock. Jerusalem was miraculously delivered from the Assyrian onslaught in fulfillment of the prophecy made by one of Israel's greatest prophets, Isaiah of Jerusalem (2 Kgs. 19: 6–7, 32–37). Hezekiah kept the commandments and trusted in the Lord to a greater degree than any other king during Jerusalem's three centuries as a political and spiritual capital.

Ironically, king Hezekiah's son Manasseh (687–642 B.C.) and grandson Amon (642–640 B.C.) were the two worst kings Jerusalem ever had. They desecrated the temple and promoted wickedness, sacrilege, and profane practices from which the holy city never quite recovered. Such evils brought upon Jerusalem the Lord's prophetic pronouncement recorded in 2 Kings 21:12–13: "Thus saith the Lord God of Israel, Behold, I am bringing such evil upon Jerusalem and Judah, that whosoever heareth of it, both his ears shall tingle. . . . and I will wipe Jerusalem as a man wipeth a dish, wiping it, and turning it

JERUSALEM[1], CITY OF

upside down." This prophecy was fulfilled in a devastating way after Lehi and his family left the once-mighty city (2 Ne. 1:4), but not before it enjoyed a short reprieve under righteous king Josiah (640–609 B.C.).

Josiah witnessed and helped bring about Jerusalem's last period of greatness before the Babylonian empire finally destroyed the city in at least two tremendous waves of invasion. The young king instituted religious reforms, repaired the temple, discovered a copy of the book of the Law (perhaps Deuteronomy) during the temple renovation, held a solemn assembly and read to the city's inhabitants from the sacred book, and put everyone under covenant to keep the Lord's commandments (2 Kgs. 22:4–23:15). Tragically, the king died in a battle at Megiddo fighting against pharaoh Necho of Egypt, and with him went Jerusalem's hopes for renewal and survival. By 604 B.C. the entire Levant was the domain of king Nebuchadnezzar of Babylon (2 Kgs. 24:7), who was poised to lay waste to Judah and Jerusalem.

Jerusalem in Lehi's day was an amalgam of all the construction and expansion that had taken place the previous four centuries. It truly had become a great city just as Lehi and his family so regarded it (1 Ne. 2:13). It is estimated that its walled area covered at least 125 acres with the population being at least 25,000 persons inside the walls. (King David's Jerusalem was only 12 acres in size with a population of 2,000; Broshi, 12). Archaeological excavations from the time of the Babylonian conquest (586 B.C.) have revealed well-made houses, some quite large for that historical period, with such impressive amenities as private lavatory facilities. The most complete housing structure dating from Lehi's time is the so-called "house of Ahiel," named from potsherds found inside the building and inscribed with the personal name Ahiel. The house of Ahiel was a typical four-room stone domicile of the late Judean period in Jerusalem. It had two stories, a roof made of wooden beams, and a small toilet (the seat was found intact over an 8-foot-deep cesspit) connected to the north side of the house (Ogden and Chadwick, 204). A layer of ash over the remains of the structures in the area of Ahiel's house testify of the Babylonian destruction just as the Bible reports: "And he burnt . . . all the houses of Jerusalem, and every great man's house burnt he with fire" (2 Kgs. 25:9). It is important to note here that the city was the site of houses of "great men"—the rich and famous.

Jerusalem's external features in Lehi's day bespoke security: Jehovah's temple, the massive palace complex, Hezekiah's broad wall, and the like. The city had withstood the siege of the mighty and terrifying Assyrian Empire. Jerusalem was an island of continuity in a sea of upheaval; empires rose and fell during the four hundred years of Israel's occupation of Jerusalem, but the holy city endured. Even the northern kingdom of Israel had been humiliated and a significant portion of the population enslaved and deported while Jerusalem and her inhabitants remained intact. All of this must have reinforced in the minds of Jerusalem's citizens the city's preeminent position with God himself, and made any notion of its conquest unthinkable, even heretical. Such pride, however, was at the very heart of the problem. Prophet after prophet warned the people to return to God, but such messages went unheeded (2 Kgs. 17:13–14). In fact, prophets who spoke against Jerusalem's inhabitants or their king were in grave danger of losing their lives. For example, the book of Jeremiah reports that a man named Urijah, son of Shemaiah, prophesied against Jerusalem just like Jeremiah. He incurred the wrath of king Jehoiakim (609–598 B.C.), fled to Egypt, and was hunted down by the king's men who put him to death, brought his body back to Jerusalem, and flung it into the graves of the common people (Jer. 26:20–23). Such an episode indicates just how much danger Lehi (and Jeremiah) faced and how spiritually recalcitrant the upper echelons of society had become ("the king, with all his mighty men, and all the princes"; Jer. 26:21).

Thus, though Jerusalem presented an external veneer of strength and stability, internally it was falling apart. Politically, socially, and spiritually Jerusalem in Lehi's day was at an all-time low, filled with instability, arrogance, hypocrisy, and gross iniquity of every kind, especially idolatry and immorality. The year Lehi fled the doomed city, the first year of Zedekiah's eleven-year reign, three different kings occupied the throne. Jehoiakim, who had also ruled for eleven years, died shortly after he rebelled against king Nebuchadnezzar of Babylon (a foolish act of overconfidence). His son Jehoiachin reigned for three months before Nebuchadnezzar arrived to quash the rebellion his father had started. Jehoiachin quickly submitted to Babylon, thus saving the city, but he, his mother, wives, children, officials, mighty men, artisans, and craftsmen (in short, ten thousand of society's best and strongest) were carried away captive to Babylon (2 Kgs. 24:11–16; Jer. 29:1–2). This deportation included Ezekiel and Daniel. In addition, the treasures of the temple and king's palace were all cut up and taken away. Zedekiah was installed on the throne by Nebuchadnezzar because he swore an oath of allegiance to the Babylonian king (2 Kgs. 24:17–18; 2 Chr. 36:11–13).

Jeremiah is a great source of information regarding Jerusalem's moral bankruptcy during this period: "They [people of Jerusalem] are wise to do evil, but to do good they have no knowledge" (Jer. 4:22). The city was filled with fornication and adultery, and Jeremiah wished he could have escaped such vile behavior: "Oh that I had in the wilderness a lodging place [for] wayfaring men; that I might leave my people, and go from them! for they be all adulterers, an assembly of treacherous men" (Jer. 9:2). Jeremiah employed some striking images to describe conditions in the city: The people "assembled themselves by troops in the harlots' houses," and like well-fed stallions, "every one neighed after his neighbour's wife" (Jer. 5:7–8). The prophet also lamented over the pervasive covetousness and dishonesty of Jerusalem's citizens: "From the least of them even unto the greatest of them every one is given to covetousness; and from the [false] prophet even unto the priest every one dealeth falsely" (Jer. 6:13). Jeremiah testified of the people's hypocrisy when he said, "One speaketh peaceably to his neighbour with his mouth, but in heart he layeth his wait" (Jer. 9:8).

Worse was that the people were so steeped in wickedness that they did not even recognize their evil ways: "No man repented him of his wickedness, saying, What have I done?" (Jer. 8:6). The Lord told Jeremiah that such would be the attitude he would encounter: "And it shall come to pass, when thou shalt shew this people all these words, and they shall say unto thee, Wherefore hath the Lord pronounced all this great evil against us? or what is our iniquity? or what is our sin that we have committed against the Lord our God?" (Jer. 16:10). Thus, students of the Book of Mormon can more fully understand why this same attitude afflicted the brothers of Nephi[1] and where it originated. Laman[1] and Lemuel were products of that same wicked society about to be destroyed and they harbored the same spiritual blindness: "And we know that the people who were in the land of Jerusalem were a righteous people . . . and our father hath judged them, and hath led us away because we would hearken unto his words; yea, and our brother is like unto him. And after this manner of language did my brethren murmur and complain against us" (1 Ne. 17:22).

The sacred records testify that there were many true prophets in Jerusalem during Lehi's day who warned of impending destruction (1 Ne. 1:4; 2 Chr. 36:15). But there were also many false prophets in Jerusalem society who pandered to the evil ways of the people and played on and supported their arrogance and false sense of security. These false prophets flatly contradicted the word of the Lord. For example, as Jeremiah was writing to the already captive exiles in BABYLON and telling them to plan for a long stay in the foreign land (he told them to build houses, plant gardens, and raise families; Jer. 29:1, 4–7), the false prophet Hananiah was going around promising in the name of the Lord that within two years the yoke of Babylon would be broken and the exiles would be brought back to Jerusalem—which never happened, of course, but such talk pacified the population (Jer. 28:1–4). When Jeremiah prophesied of tumult, war, and SIEGE against Jerusalem (Jer. 6:3–6, 22–23), false prophets cried, "Peace, peace," to placate the people (Jer. 6:14).

Ultimately all that had been prophesied by true prophets concerning Jerusalem and its inhabitants came to pass. While the Lord's anointed continued to cry destruction and desolation if no repentance was forthcoming, the king and people of Jerusalem became hardened and emboldened in their false security and arrogance. Zedekiah was pressed to break his oath of allegiance to Nebuchadnezzar, which brought down upon Jerusalem the full weight of Babylonian wrath and might. The city was besieged for a year and a half and thoroughly destroyed: its walls broken down, the temple destroyed by fire, and the once-proud king captured, blinded, bound with fetters of brass and carried away to Babylon, but not before he was made to watch the execution of his sons (2 Kgs. 24:20–25:1–9). As predicted, thousands of Jerusalem's citizens died by famine and the sword, all because they would not listen to the Lord through his chosen messengers. Even in the final days of the siege of Jerusalem, when Zedekiah desperately sought advice, Jeremiah promised that the city would be saved if the king would immediately surrender to the Babylonians, but Zedekiah refused to listen for fear of offending the leading citizens (the "princes") of the city (Jer. 38:17–27). And so, as Lehi had both prophesied and witnessed vicariously through vision, the great city of Jerusalem was destroyed (2 Ne. 1:4).

See also Babylonian captivity; Chronology, Bible; Israel, historical background of; Jeremiah[1], prophecies of; Jerusalem[1], destruction of, at 586 B.C.; Jerusalem[1], destruction of, at A.D. 70.

BIBLIOGRAPHY

Broshi, Magen. "Estimating the Population of Ancient Jerusalem." *Biblical Archaeology Review* 4:2 (June 1978): 10–15.

Galbraith, David B., D. Kelly Ogden, and Andrew C. Skinner. *Jerusalem, the Eternal City.* Salt Lake City: Deseret Book, 1996.

Josephus. *Wars of the Jews,* in *The Complete Works of Josephus.* Translated and edited by William Whiston. Grand Rapids, Mich.: Kregel, 1960.

Meservy, Keith H. "Jerusalem at the Time of Lehi and Jeremiah." *Ensign* 18 (January 1988): 22–25.

Ogden, D. Kelly, and Jeffrey R. Chadwick. *The Holy Land.* Jerusalem: Barry Segal International Ltd., 1990.

Shanks, Hershel. *Jerusalem: An Archaeological Biography.* New York: Random House, 1995.

"The Location of Zion, or the New Jerusalem." *Times and Seasons* 2, no. 18 (15 July 1841).

ACS

Jerusalem[1], destruction of, at 586 B.C. The destruction of Jerusalem is a landmark event in Book of Mormon history. Just as the Lord had delivered ancient Israel from destruction and bondage in Egypt so he delivered Lehi[1] and his family from certain death or exile in the Babylonian destruction of Jerusalem (1 Ne. 17:23; Alma 36:28–29). Thus, the Book of Mormon contains many references to this destruction and the fate of those who stayed behind in Jerusalem. The Mosaic covenant made at Sinai was conditional: blessings of prosperity and protection for obedience, or destruction and scattering for disobedience (Deut. 27–29). Biblical prophets warned the people of impending destruction unless they repented. Because of wickedness the northern kingdom fell in 722 B.C. and was taken into captivity to ASSYRIA. Isaiah, Jeremiah[1], and Ezekiel warned JUDAH that if she did not repent she would suffer the same fate. Lehi was called to prophesy repentance to Jerusalem, but his message was rejected (1 Ne. 1:18–20). Finally, the Lord warned Lehi to take his family out of Jerusalem before it was destroyed. Biblical accounts of the destruction can be found in 2 Kings 24–25; Jeremiah 37–39; 52; Lamentations; and 2 Chronicles 36.

A series of significant events led up to the destruction of Jerusalem. For many years Judah was ruled by Manasseh (687–642 B.C.), the most wicked king in the history of Judah. He led his people to idolatry and much wickedness. He built up high places and altars where he sacrificed to pagan gods in the temple and throughout the land. He promoted the occult, sacrificed his son, and shed much innocent blood (2 Kgs. 21). Eventually he was succeeded by his righteous grandson Josiah (640–609 B.C.), who cleansed the temple and led his people in a ceremony of covenant renewal (2 Kgs. 22–23). In a stunning sermon at the temple, Jeremiah warned the people that Josiah's cleansing of the temple and the renewal of the covenant had only been superficial. He accused the people of hypocrisy in worshipping at the temple but continuing to break the commandments and worship other gods. He prophesied that unless they repented they would be destroyed (Jer. 7). In 605 B.C. the Babylonians destroyed the

Assyrian empire at Carchemish and eventually took control of Judah. Nebuchadnezzar took Ezekiel, Daniel, the crown prince Jehoiachin, and many other Judahites into captivity in BABYLON, and he put Zedekiah on the throne of Judah. The Book of Mormon opens in the first year of Zedekiah's reign. Zedekiah was expected to be a loyal vassal of Babylon, but he constantly vacillated between his loyalty to Babylon and nationalistic fervor from advisors who urged him to revolt against Babylon and revive the Davidic empire. On numerous occasions Jeremiah told him that it was the will of the Lord that he remain a vassal to Babylon (e.g., Jer. 21:4–10; 27:1–11; 38:1–2, 17–18).

Finally, in 588 B.C. Zedekiah rebelled against Babylon by stopping the payment of tribute. Nebuchadnezzar advanced on Jerusalem and besieged the city, building SIEGE walls and siege engines. The city held out for eighteen months and was ravaged by famine and pestilence. In the course of the siege, famine became so intense that some resorted to eating their own children (Lam. 4:10), as had been prophesied by Moses (Deut. 28:57). Finally a breach was made in the walls, and the city fell. Zedekiah was captured, all of his sons except Mulek were killed (Hel. 8:21), and he was taken in chains to Babylon. About a month after Jerusalem fell, Nebuchadnezzar ordered the complete destruction of the city. The temple, the king's palace, and the houses in the city were burned. The walls of Jerusalem were broken down, and many of the prominent surviving Jews were taken to Babylon, where they joined their fellows in the Exile. Some of the poor people were left in Judah to tend to the land. Many of the large bronze objects of the temple were broken up and melted down and the bronze taken to Babylon. Other vessels from the temple were taken whole to Babylon and were brought back with the people in 539 B.C. when Cyrus allowed the Jews to return to their land (Ezra 1:7–11).

See also Babylonian captivity; Israel, historical background of; Israel, scattering of; Jeremiah[1], prophecies of; Jerusalem[1], city of; Jerusalem[1], destruction of, at A.D. 70; Jews, history of; Vessels of the Lord.

BIBLIOGRAPHY

Meservy, Keith H. "Jerusalem at the Time of Lehi and Jeremiah." *Ensign* 18 (January 1988): 22–25.

Nibley, Hugh W. "Dark Days in Jerusalem: The Lachish Letters and the Book of Mormon." *Book of Mormon Authorship.* Edited by Noel B. Reynolds. Provo, Utah: Religious Studies Center, Brigham Young University, 1982. 103–20.

DRS

Jerusalem[1], destruction of, at A.D. 70 Book of Mormon prophets foretold two destructions of Jerusalem: the first by the Babylonians soon after Lehi[1], Ishmael, and their families fled Jerusalem (1 Ne. 1:13, 18; 2 Ne. 6:8; 25:10; 586 B.C.), and the second by the Romans in A.D. 70, one generation after Jesus was crucified and resurrected. Nephi[1]'s prophecy of the second destruction is quite specific: "And behold it shall come to pass that after the Messiah hath risen from the dead, and hath manifested himself unto his people, unto as many as will believe on his name, behold, Jerusalem shall be destroyed again" (2 Ne. 25:14).

During his mortal ministry Jesus also foretold the destruction of Jerusalem which would occur due to the great iniquities of many of his generation (Matt. 23:29–24:2). He described the manner in which the city would be destroyed (Luke 19:41–44; 21:20–24) and provided his disciples with signs to prepare them for this and other great events (JS–M 1:1–21).

Jerusalem was indeed destroyed according to prophecy when in A.D. 70 the Roman general Titus led his forces against the city. As a result of the Roman SIEGE, many of Jerusalem's inhabitants were slaughtered; others were "scattered among all nations," as Nephi had prophesied would happen (2 Ne. 25:15). Survivors were sold as slaves, sent to fight in arenas, shipped to work the Egyptian quarries, and were otherwise deported from their homeland. The temple itself was destroyed so that no one today knows exactly where it stood, and many of Jerusalem's buildings were burned or razed. Elder Bruce R. McConkie wrote, "Hunger exceeded human endurance; blood flowed in the streets; destruction made desolate the temple; 1,100,000 Jews were slaughtered; Jerusalem was ploughed as a field; and a remnant of a once mighty nation was scattered to the ends of the earth. The Jewish nation died, impaled on Roman spears, at the hands of Gentile overlords" (1:644).

See also Israel, historical background of; Israel, scattering of; Jerusalem[1], city of; Jerusalem[1], destruction of, at 586 B.C.; Jews, history of.

BIBLIOGRAPHY

Josephus, Flavius. *The Complete Works of Josephus.* Translated by William Whiston. Grand Rapids, Mich.: Kregel, 1981. 522–88.

McConkie, Bruce R. *Doctrinal New Testament Commentary.* 3 vols. Salt Lake City: Bookcraft, 1965–73.

KHM

Jerusalem[1], land of Region surrounding the city of Jerusalem. Towns and villages that surrounded larger cities were regarded in ancient times as belonging to the land of those larger cities. Accordingly, not only Bethlehem but also Hebron (Aharoni, 214–15), fifteen miles south of Bethlehem, was considered part of the "land of Jerusalem." For example, El Amarna letter 287 mentions the "land of Jerusalem" several times.

Several other scriptural cities are also labeled as lands. For example, Ammonihah was a city and also a land (Alma 8:6; 14:23). The area surrounding the city of Ur was likewise known as the land of Ur (Abr. 1:20). The Damascus Rule, from the Dead Sea Scrolls, twice refers to the region surrounding the Syrian capital of Damascus as the "land of Damascus."

Alma said that the Messiah "shall be born of Mary, at Jerusalem which is the land of our forefathers" (Alma 7:10). Herein Jerusalem is referred to as the land rather than the city where Jesus' birth would occur. Although Joseph Smith obviously knew that Jesus was born at Bethlehem, his translation of Alma's geographical note is compatible with similar biblical and extrabiblical figures of speech and is evidence of the passage's authentic ancient origin.

BIBLIOGRAPHY

Aharoni, Yohanan. *The Land of the Bible—A Historical Geography.* London: Burns & Oates, 1979.

DKO

Jerusalem[2], land of and city of Lamanite area in the land of Nephi, adjoining the borders of Mormon, named "after the land of their fathers' nativity" (Alma 21:1). Here, the Lamanites, Amalekites, and Amulonites jointly built the city of Jerusalem (Alma 21:2). It was in the city of Jerusalem that Aaron[3] began his missionary labors among the Lamanites (ca. 90 B.C.). He first preached in the synagogues of the Amalekites, but only one Amalekite was ever converted (Alma 21:4–11; 23:14). After the conversion of the ANTI-NEPHI-LEHIES, the Amalekites and Amulonites stirred up the unconverted in Jerusalem and "in all the land round about" to wage war against them (Alma 24:1–2).

This iniquitous city sank into the earth in the cataclysms that accompanied the Savior's crucifixion (3 Ne. 9:7).

Jerusalem, New *See* New Jerusalem.

Jesus Christ Second member of the GODHEAD and the only name by which salvation is administered to the human family.

Jesus is the most significant person who lived or ever will live on this earth and along with his Father is man's greatest benefactor. Jesus' atoning sacrifice and resurrection exceed in importance all earthly events because they are his divine response to man's greatest need: He conquered death for all mankind and provided the only relief from the consequences of sin. Jesus is both God and Son of God. He was God before he came to earth, was God while on earth, is God now in the heavens, and will return as God of the whole world. In each of these spheres Jesus actively fills an essential dimension of his eternal mission.

Sources of knowledge

By divine design the scriptures are written to testify of Jesus Christ, with the Bible and the Book of Mormon being companion sources. These ancient records—one written by prophets in the eastern hemisphere and the other by prophets in the western hemisphere—are treasures of divine testimony about Jesus. Although not complete and sometimes ambiguous, the Bible is wonderfully informative about Jesus Christ, particularly his doings on earth during his mortal life. The Book of Mormon confirms the fundamentals of Jesus' mission as taught in the Bible and does so with greater clarity. Whereas the Bible tells many "who" and "what" things about Jesus, the Book of Mormon often goes further, showing "why" those things are doctrinally important. This is particularly evident regarding the ATONEMENT. The Book of Mormon also testifies of many truths about Jesus not available from the Bible.

The Doctrine and Covenants and the Pearl of Great Price are also witnesses of Jesus Christ, and contain many points of his doctrine. From these major written sources one learns that Jesus' ministry is more comprehensive, and of greater depth than is at first apparent from his short mortal life. His active ministry extends throughout eternity from the distant premortal past through all time to come. Furthermore, his personal appearances on earth are far more numerous than the Bible records.

Jesus Christ in the premortal life

Brief scriptural evidences refer to an ancient heavenly council that greatly influenced this earth (Abr. 3:22–28). In that council, Jehovah (Jesus) was submissive to the Father's will and was chosen to be the future Redeemer; Lucifer rebelled and became Satan, the devil. Important truths pertaining to Jesus Christ's appointment in the premortal council include (1) the selection of Jehovah (Jesus) to be the Redeemer was made before the need actually occurred, but was done according to the foreknowledge and plan of the Father who knew the need would arise, and (2) Jehovah's responsibilities and activities as the one to be sent to the earth to redeem it began at

A detail from Christ and the Rich Young Ruler; *painting by Heinrich Hofman; courtesy VRL.*

JESUS CHRIST

least as early as his appointment, and will continue always. This doctrinal and historical background provides perspective to the many statements by Jesus that he did not come to earth on his own authority but was "sent" by his Father. For example, Jesus told the Jews, "I have not spoken of myself; but the Father which sent me, he gave me a commandment, what I should say" (John 12:49). The book of John alone asserts in at least forty instances, mostly by Jesus himself, that he was "sent" by the Father. To the Nephites Jesus said, "I came into the world to do the will of my Father, because my Father sent me. And my Father sent me that I might be lifted up upon the cross . . . that I might draw all men unto me, . . . to stand before me, to be judged of their works" (3 Ne. 27:13–14; cf. D&C 49:5).

In accord with his foreordination, Jesus created the earth. After the fall of Adam upon the earth, Jesus revealed the plan of redemption to man, by angels and by personal manifestations of himself to the prophets. "All the prophets" knew of and testified of Christ (Mosiah 13:33–35). They knew that the Lord Jehovah, the Creator, the "very Eternal Father of heaven and of earth," was also Jesus, the Messiah to be born in the flesh on the earth (Alma 11:39–40), and that "from the foundation of the world," Christ, the priesthood, the plan of salvation, the "great and eternal purposes" of God were all in place (Alma 42:26; Mosiah 18:13; Alma 12:30; 13:3, 5; 18:39; Ether 3:14; 4:19).

Understanding the fall of Adam

It is impossible to understand why there is a need for Christ unless the power and purposes of the fall of Adam are known. The fall of Adam, which caused the need for a Redeemer, was known and contemplated by the Father long before it occurred. When viewed in this context, the Fall is recognized as an essential part of the redeeming process, giving well-deserved dignity to Adam's contribution to man's eternal journey.

The Fall was necessary because without it Adam and Eve "would have had no children" (2 Ne. 2:23; Moses 5:11; 6:48), and humanity would never have been on this earth and would never have had physical bodies. Salvation cannot be complete without a physical body (D&C 93:33–34; Smith, 181). Furthermore, mortality is an essential preparatory condition because it enables mankind to gain experience and provide for progress in ways not possible in the premortal spirit world. Speaking of the necessity and value of the Fall, Lehi[1] declared, "Behold, all things have been done in the wisdom of him who knoweth all things. Adam fell that man might be; and men are, that they might have joy. And the Messiah cometh . . . that he may redeem the children of men from the fall" (2 Ne. 2:24–26).

The Fall brought upon all mankind a spiritual death (separation from God and from righteousness) and also a temporal death (death of the physical body). The power of the Fall is harsh and exacting. Every human inherits these two deaths from Adam and Eve. If left unchecked the Fall causes the following: (1) the physical body dies, decays, and returns to earth, without the ability to resurrect itself; (2) the spirit becomes subject to the devil, is miserable, and becomes a devil (2 Ne. 9:6–11). Without the redemption of Christ, these conditions would be permanent.

Effects of the Fall are far-reaching and severe. Because of the Fall man's nature has an evil texture (Ether 3:2), and "the natural man is an enemy to God" (Mosiah 3:19; 16:3–6). The effects (but not the responsibility or guilt) of the Fall are passed to each child biologically (Mosiah 3:11; Moro. 8:8; Moses 6:55), so that even little children (who have no personal sin) could not be saved without the atonement of Christ (Mosiah 3:16). Furthermore, each person's situation is worsened by individual sins, which need personal repentance. The Fall extends beyond the human family. All life, and the earth itself, has partaken of its effects, and thus everything natural to this mortal world is in need of Christ (2 Ne. 2:22; D&C 29:24–25; 88:25–26; A of F 10).

Mortal ministry of Jesus Christ

When Jesus was born on earth, he was significantly different from all other humans in two ways essential to enable him to fulfill his redemptive mission: (1) his physical body was the biological son of the mortal Mary and of God the Father (1 Ne. 11:16–21), giving Jesus power over death, and (2) the spirit inhabiting that specially prepared body was the Omnipotent Jehovah, the foreordained Redeemer, the God of Israel (3 Ne. 15:5).

Jesus showed perfect obedience to the Father's commandments. He was baptized in water according to the requirement for righteousness (2 Ne. 31:4–9) and received the Holy Ghost. He proclaimed the gospel of faith, preached repentance, performed baptisms, ordained apostles, worked miracles, instituted the ordinance of bread and wine and other essential ordinances, and lived without sin. He shed his blood and died on the cross, to pay for the fall of Adam, and also man's personal sins on condition of repentance.

Jesus is the model of personal restraint, humility, self-sacrifice, meekness, and love. Mistreated and unappreciated by his countrymen, he did not revile nor seek revenge. Nephi[1] said that Jesus "doeth not anything save it be for the benefit of the world; for he loveth the world, even that he layeth down his own life" (2 Ne. 26:24, 33; Acts 10:38). "Wherefore they scourge him . . . and they smite him. . . . Yea, they spit upon him, and he suffereth it, because of his loving kindness and his long-suffering towards the children of men" (1 Ne. 19:9; 1 Pet. 2:22–23).

The sacrifice required of Jesus was painful and strenuous, requiring extreme physical and spiritual suffering (Mosiah 3:6–8). After his death his body was buried in a stone sepulcher.

Ministry in the spirit world

While his body lay in the tomb, Jesus went as a spirit among departed spirits. He taught redemption from the Fall and the doctrine of the RESURRECTION, and commissioned righteous spirits to preach repentance to those who had not obeyed the gospel as mortals. This phase of Jesus' ministry is mentioned briefly in the Bible (1 Pet. 3:18–20; 4:6), more extensively in the Doctrine and Covenants (76:73; 138:1–60), but is not discussed in the Book of Mormon.

Postresurrection ministry

On the third day after his burial, Jesus' spirit reentered his body and he rose from the dead with an immortal body. This ultimate miracle brings resurrection and judgment to the entire human family. After Jesus' resurrection he showed his glorified body to more than 500 persons (Matt. 28:7, 16, 17; 1 Cor. 15:5–6). Having completed all requirements, he ascended into heaven. Soon after his ascension in the Holy Land, Jesus personally visited the Nephites in the land Bountiful in America, showing his glorious body to 2500 persons and commanding them to touch it with their own hands, one by one, giving them perfect knowledge that he was resurrected: "And they did fall down at the feet of Jesus, and did worship him" (3 Ne. 11:12–17; 17:25). Jesus told this group that he would also visit the lost tribes and show them his body (3 Ne. 16:1–3; 17:4).

Jesus explained to the Nephites that he would personally visit only the house of Israel and not the Gentiles. He said that the Gentiles would receive the gospel through the preaching of Israelite prophets and Christ would be manifested to them by the Holy Ghost. This distinct visiting schedule is explained only in the Book of Mormon (1 Ne. 10:11; 3 Ne. 15:16–24), although the Bible hints at it (Matt. 15:22–24). This experience recorded in the Book of Mormon gives a proper understanding of the "other sheep" in John 10:16.

Jesus' ongoing ministry to the earth

Jesus' work with the earth and its people is not finished. The Lord said to Nephi, "My work is not yet finished; neither shall it be until the end of man, neither from that time henceforth and forever" (2 Ne. 29:9). Through prophets and apostles of his choosing, Jesus still works with man to teach the gospel of Jesus Christ throughout the earth, gather and restore the house of Israel, build holy cities such as Jerusalem and New Jerusalem, establish Zion, and prepare a people for his second coming. This will be followed by a millennium of intense spiritual activity and eventual celestialization of the earth. In all this, Jesus is the central figure.

The foregoing describes a long view of Jesus' ministry, and it is especially evident that Nephi had this extended understanding. Nephi said he often read many scriptures to his people, "but that I might more fully persuade them to believe in the Lord their Redeemer I did read unto them that which was written by the prophet Isaiah"

(1 Ne. 19:22–23). Nephi provided several examples of his use of Isaiah passages, all dealing more with the Abrahamic covenant, restoration of Israel, the defeat of evil, and other world-wide events than with the circumstances of Jesus' short mortal ministry on earth (1 Ne. 20–21; 2 Ne. 12–24). These are long-term accomplishments of the Redeemer. Jacob[2] also cited chapters of Isaiah about the restoration of Israel as being the work of Jesus Christ (2 Ne. 6–8). Jesus himself, when he visited the Nephites, cited passages of Isaiah, Malachi, Moses, and Micah pertaining to the Abrahamic covenant and the redemption of Israel, the establishment of New Jerusalem, and the end of wickedness on the earth, rather than passages limited to his mortal life. Book of Mormon prophets regarded Jesus' mortal mission of the greatest importance (Alma 7:7), but they saw his ministry in its wider context.

Special considerations

The preceding paragraphs discuss fundamental doctrinal dimensions of Jesus' eternal ministry. Additional matters of testimony about Jesus are given below. Most of the following are unique to the Book of Mormon, but others, though not unique, are included because of the distinct clarity and emphasis the Book of Mormon gives them.

Jesus is God

Book of Mormon prophets had no doubt that Jesus is God. They did not confuse him with the person of the Father but knew that he is both God and Son of God. The following attest to Christ's Godhood:

1. "JESUS is the CHRIST, the ETERNAL GOD, manifesting himself unto all nations" (Title Page; 2 Ne. 26:12).

2. The very God of Israel, the God of Abraham, Isaac, and Jacob will be crucified and buried (1 Ne. 19:7, 10, 13).

3. God is the Holy One of Israel, and he is Christ (2 Ne. 9:11, 19, 24; 25:29).

4. "There is a God, and he is Christ" (2 Ne. 11:7).

5. "The Lord Omnipotent . . . shall come down from heaven . . . [and] dwell in a tabernacle of clay. . . . He shall be called Jesus Christ, . . . the Creator . . . and his mother shall be called Mary," yet many shall consider him only a man (Mosiah 3:5–9).

6. Christ is God, who will come from heaven, and "take upon him the image of man" with flesh and blood (Mosiah 7:27).

7. God himself will make the Atonement; will come down in the form of man, and bring to pass the resurrection (Mosiah 13:28, 34).

8. "God himself shall come down . . . and shall redeem his people" (Mosiah 15:1).

9. The atoning sacrifice cannot be a human sacrifice, nor an animal sacrifice, but must be an "infinite and eternal sacrifice" (Alma 34:9–12).

10. "God himself atoneth for the sins of the world" (Alma 42:15).

11. Christ is God (Hel. 8:22–23).

12. Jesus: "I am the God of Israel, and the God of the whole earth" (3 Ne. 11:14).

13. Jesus: "Behold, I am he that gave the law [of Moses], and I am he who covenanted with my people Israel" (3 Ne. 15:4–5).

14. Nephite disciples called Jesus "their Lord and their God," and he did not deny it nor correct them (3 Ne. 19:18).

15. Jesus is "the very Christ and the very God" (Morm. 3:20–21).

Although the Book of Mormon testifies of Jesus' Godhood, it does not discuss Jesus being the first of the Father's spirit children and man's elder brother in the premortal world, a truth made known in other scripture (Rom. 8:29; Heb. 1:6; D&C 93:21).

No other name, no other way but Jesus

Book of Mormon prophets stated positively that Jesus Christ, and he alone, is the Savior. There is no ambiguity, no room for misunderstanding, no other interpretation.

1. Nephi[1]: There is only one true Messiah—the one who will be rejected by the Jews. He will be named Jesus Christ, and "there is none other name given under heaven," nor any other way, by which salvation can be obtained (2 Ne. 25:18–20; 31:21).

2. King Benjamin: There is "no other name given nor any other way nor means" for salvation (Mosiah 3:17; 5:8). There is not any other

JESUS CHRIST

salvation nor any other condition for salvation besides the doctrine of Christ (Mosiah 4:8).

3. Abinadi: "Only in and through Christ" can men be saved (Mosiah 16:13).

4. Alma[2]: "There is no other way or means whereby man can be saved, only in and through Christ" (Alma 38:9).

5. Helaman[3], quoting king Benjamin: Salvation is possible only through Christ's blood; there is no other way nor means (Hel. 5:9).

Special significance attaches to the fact that all of the foregoing passages occur before the Lord came in the flesh, and therefore before the Atonement was accomplished. A statement by Peter in the New Testament is similar in content (Acts 4:12) but was written after the Atonement was made. The added strength of the Book of Mormon passages, in addition to being more specific and detailed than Peter's, is that having been spoken before the fact, they show that Jesus always was the only Redeemer. No consideration was ever given for another; there never was an alternate plan or alternate redeemer (D&C 18:23; 109:4; Moses 6:52).

Precise time of Jesus' birth known beforehand

Early Book of Mormon prophets knew that Jesus would be born precisely 600 years from the time Lehi left Jerusalem (1 Ne. 10:4; 19:8; 2 Ne. 25:19), but Alma[2] did not seem to be as specific on this matter in 82 B.C. (Alma 13:25–26). About 77 years later, Samuel the Lamanite prophesied that Christ would be born in five years, accompanied by a day, a night, and a day with no darkness, as a sign of his birth (Hel. 14:1–9). At the appointed time, which was 600 years from Lehi's departure from Jerusalem, the sign was given (3 Ne. 1:1, 5–21). Nothing in the Bible suggests that the Jews had such precise prophetic knowledge of when Jesus would be born.

Ancient prophets, mentioned only in the Book of Mormon, testified of signs to be given at Christ's death, which were literally fulfilled (1 Ne. 19:10–12; Hel. 14:4, 20–29; 3 Ne. 8:1–23).

Mary, the mother of Jesus

Nephite prophets knew centuries in advance that Jesus would be born of Mary, a virgin from Nazareth (1 Ne. 11:13–20; Mosiah 3:8; Alma 7:10). This is more specific than the present Old Testament (Isa. 7:14).

Abraham and Isaac

Abraham and his son Isaac are "a similitude of God and his Only Begotten Son" (Jacob 4:5).

Holy One of Israel

"Holy One of Israel" occurs at least thirty-one times in the Old Testament, chiefly in Isaiah's words. Perceptive readers probably discern that it means Christ; however, the Bible does not so designate. Second Nephi 25:29 forthrightly states, "Christ is the Holy One of Israel."

The Book of Mormon includes more than one hundred other name-titles for Jesus.

The power of God

As Jesus ministered to the people in America the power of God was manifested in many ways, exceeding the miracles Jesus performed in the Holy Land. Following is a partial review of events, some of which happened more than once. On Jesus' first visit he healed many sick, blind, dumb, and crippled. He blessed little children one by one. He also prayed for the people with such wonderful words that "no tongue can speak, neither can there be written . . . so great and marvelous things" as Jesus spoke. "And no one can conceive of the joy which filled our souls at the time." Angels came down, and fire from heaven encircled the people (3 Ne. 17:7–24). Jesus afterward returned to heaven.

The next day, after a baptismal service, the Holy Ghost descended, fire again encircled the people, and angels attended. Jesus also appeared. As Jesus prayed the countenances and clothing of both Jesus and the disciples became extremely white and brilliant (3 Ne. 19:11–15, 25). Again the words of Jesus were too great to be written or uttered by man yet were understood by those present (3 Ne. 19:32–34). Jesus blessed more children, who then uttered such

JESUS CHRIST

marvelous things that no one was able to write or repeat them. These children spoke "even greater [things] than [Jesus] had revealed." Jesus did all manner of cures, raised a man from the dead (3 Ne. 26:14–16), and miraculously provided bread and wine (3 Ne. 20:3–9). He expounded all things "great and small"—everything from the beginning of the earth to the Judgment Day (3 Ne. 26:1–5). Third Nephi contains less than "a hundredth part" of what Jesus said and did in America (3 Ne. 26:6–8).

Also, Jesus said, "So great faith have I never seen among all the Jews; wherefore . . . there are none of them that have seen . . . neither have they heard so great things" (3 Ne. 19:35–36).

Jesus with a smiling countenance

Never in the Bible is it stated that Jesus smiled, but two such instances occur in 3 Nephi 19:25, 30.

Nature and purpose of Jesus' suffering

The Book of Mormon makes clear that Jesus not only suffered for the sins of all mankind, but that he suffered "pains and afflictions . . . of every kind," including the "pains and the sicknesses of his people" (Alma 7:11). Such suffering brought to the Savior understanding and empathy, "according to the flesh," or through personal, actual experience, "that he may know . . . how to succor his people according to their infirmities" (Alma 7:12). Concerning these realities, Elder Neal A. Maxwell taught: "Imagine, Jehovah, the Creator of this and other worlds, 'astonished'! Jesus knew cognitively what He must do, but not experientially. He had never personally known the exquisite and exacting process of an atonement before. Thus, when the agony came in its fulness, it was so much, much worse than even He with his unique intellect had ever imagined! No wonder an angel appeared to strengthen him! (See Luke 22:43.) The cumulative weight of all mortal sins—past, present, and future—pressed upon that perfect, sinless, and sensitive Soul! All our infirmities and sicknesses were somehow, too, a part of the awful arithmetic of the Atonement" (72–73).

Christ in the New World; *painting by C. C. A. Christensen; courtesy Robert Skabelund. "I would that ye should behold that the Lord truly did teach the people, for the space of three days; and after that he did show himself unto them oft" (3 Ne. 26:13).*

Jesus' concern for the individual; his love and tenderness for the faithful and little children

Not only did Jesus show himself to a multitude but he had "about two thousand and five hundred souls" (3 Ne. 17:25) come forward "one by one" (3 Ne. 11:15) to see and to feel his body. He healed their sick, commended them for their faith, and prayed for them. He wept. And "he took their little children, one by one, and blessed them, and prayed unto the Father for them. And when he had done this he wept again" (3 Ne. 17:5–22; cf. Matt. 19:14).

Jesus' interest in written records

The Book of Mormon shows that Jesus has great interest in written records.

1. Prophecy of Samuel the Lamanite. The resurrected Jesus questioned the Nephite leaders asking why they had not written certain elements of Samuel's prophecy about the resurrection of the dead. Jesus was specific in stating that a written record would verify the truth of the prophecy. He commanded them to supply the missing part to validate Samuel's testimony (3 Ne. 23:7–13).

2. Writings of Malachi. Because Malachi lived in the Holy Land after Lehi's departure, the Nephites did not have his words. Jesus therefore gave them what is today identified as Malachi chapters 3 and 4 (3 Ne. 24, 25), which he said would be of value to "future generations" (3 Ne. 26:2).

3. Commandment to search Isaiah's words. Jesus commanded the people to search diligently the prophecies of Isaiah, and he testified of the great truth and value of Isaiah's writings (3 Ne. 23:1–3).

4. Commandment to write Jesus' words. Jesus commanded the Nephites to write his words (3 Ne. 23:4), not only for their current use, but for future generations. This is especially noteworthy in 3 Nephi 15 with reference to the Jews' lack of understanding of his "other sheep" prophecy (John 10:16). Jesus wanted the Nephites to record the event (in case the Jewish Church did not ever gain an understanding), so that the knowledge would be available in the last days through the Book of Mormon (3 Ne. 15:11–24).

Pray in the name of Jesus Christ

Jesus taught the Nephite disciples to pray to the Father, in the name of Christ (3 Ne. 18:19–23). The disciples taught this to the people (3 Ne. 19:6–8). It is clear from many passages that Jesus said that prayers should be to the Father in his name (3 Ne. 27:2, 7); however, when Jesus appeared to the disciples, they prayed directly to him, prompting him to note that they did so only because he was with them (3 Ne. 19:18–25, 30).

Name of the Church

In response to an inquiry as to what the name of the Church should be, Jesus said, "Ye must take upon you the name of Christ, which is my name . . . therefore ye shall call the church in my name . . . if it be called in the name of a man then it be the church of a man; but if it be called in my name then it is my church, if it so be that they are built upon my gospel" (3 Ne. 27:1–8).

The New Jerusalem

Jesus spoke extensively to the Nephites about the gathering of Israel, the New Jerusalem, and the fulfillment of the prophets (3 Ne. 20–25).

Conclusion

Nephi[1] captured the central message of all Book of Mormon prophets when he wrote: "For we labor diligently to write, to persuade our children, and also our brethren, to believe in Christ, and to be reconciled to God; for we know that it is by grace that we are saved, after all we can do. . . . And we talk of Christ, we rejoice in Christ, we preach of Christ, we prophesy of Christ, and we write according to our prophecies, that our children may know to what source they may look for a remission of their sins" (2 Ne. 25:23, 26). Such is the testimony of the Book of Mormon concerning Jesus Christ, the Son of God, the Redeemer and Savior of the world.

See also Book of Mormon: Another Testament of Jesus Christ; Condescension of God; Fall of Adam and Eve, the; Fulfill all righteousness; Jesus Christ, names of; Jesus Christ, Nephite anticipation of; Jesus Christ, premortal appearances of;

Jesus Christ, role of, as Father and Son; Jesus Christ, second coming of.

BIBLIOGRAPHY

Maxwell, Neal A. "Willing to Submit." *Ensign* 15 (May 1985): 70–73.

Smith, Joseph. *Teachings of the Prophet Joseph Smith.* Selected by Joseph Fielding Smith. Salt Lake City: Deseret Book, 1976.

RJM

Jesus Christ, baptism of *See* Fulfill all righteousness.

Jesus Christ, condescension of *See* Condescension of God.

Jesus Christ, names of The writings of Book of Mormon prophets, including scripture quoted from Old World prophets, refer to Jesus Christ by more than a hundred different names. From the first reference to him as "Lord" in 1 Nephi 1:1 to the final name in the Book of Mormon given him as "Eternal Judge" in Moroni 10:34, there are many distinctive name variations designating Jesus Christ, including the following:

Almighty (2 Ne. 23:6)
Almighty God (Jacob 2:10)
Alpha and Omega (3 Ne. 9:18)
Being (Mosiah 4:19)
Beloved (2 Ne. 31:15)
Beloved Son (2 Ne. 31:11)
Christ (2 Ne. 10:3)
Christ Jesus (Alma 5:44)
Christ the Lord (Mosiah 16:15)
Christ the Son (Alma 11:44)
Counselor (2 Ne. 19:6)
Creator (2 Ne. 9:5)
Creator of all things from the beginning (Mosiah 3:8)
Eternal Father (Mosiah 15:4)
Eternal God (1 Ne. 12:18)
Eternal Head (Hel. 13:38)
Eternal Judge (Moro. 10:34)
Everlasting God (1 Ne. 15:15)
Father (Jacob 7:22)
Father of heaven (1 Ne. 22:9)
Father of heaven and earth (Mosiah 3:8)
Father of heaven and of earth (Hel. 14:12)
First (1 Ne. 20:12)
Founder of peace (Mosiah 15:18)
Fountain of all righteousness (Ether 8:26)
God (2 Ne. 1:22)
God of Abraham (1 Ne. 19:10)
God of Abraham, and Isaac, and Jacob (Mosiah 7:19)
God of Abraham, and of Isaac, and the God of Jacob (1 Ne. 19:10)
God of Isaac (Alma 29:11)
God of Israel (1 Ne. 19:7)
God of Jacob (2 Ne. 12:3)
God of miracles (2 Ne. 27:23)
God of nature (1 Ne. 19:12)
God of the whole earth (3 Ne. 11:14)
God, the Father of all things (Mosiah 7:27)
Good shepherd (Alma 5:38)
Great and true shepherd (Hel. 15:13)
Great Creator (2 Ne. 9:5)
Great Spirit (Alma 18:2)
Holy Child (Moro. 8:3)
Holy God (2 Ne. 9:39)
Holy Messiah (2 Ne. 2:6)
Holy One (2 Ne. 2:10)
Holy One of Israel (1 Ne. 19:14)
Holy One of Jacob (2 Ne. 27:34)
Husband (3 Ne. 22:5)
Immanuel (2 Ne. 18:8)
Jehovah (Moro. 10:34)
Jesus (2 Ne. 31:10)
Jesus Christ (2 Ne. 25:19)
Keeper of the gate (2 Ne. 9:41)
King (2 Ne. 16:5)
King of all the earth (Alma 5:50)
King of heaven (2 Ne. 10:14)
Lamb (1 Ne. 13:35)
Lamb of God (1 Ne. 10:10)
Last (1 Ne. 20:12)
Life and the light of the world (Alma 38:9)
Lord (1 Ne. 10:14)
Lord God (2 Ne. 1:5)
Lord God Almighty (2 Ne. 9:46)
Lord God Omnipotent (Mosiah 3:21)
Lord God of Hosts (2 Ne. 13:15)
Lord Jehovah (2 Ne. 22:2)
Lord Jesus (Moro. 6:6)
Lord Jesus Christ (Mosiah 3:12)
Lord my God (2 Ne. 5:1)
Lord of Hosts (1 Ne. 20:2)
Lord of the vineyard (Jacob 5:8)

Lord Omnipotent (Mosiah 3:5)
Lord our God (Mosiah 9:3)
Lord their God (Mosiah 11:22)
Lord thy God (Mosiah 13:13)
Lord thy maker (2 Ne. 8:13)
Maker (2 Ne. 9:40)
Man (3 Ne. 11:8)
Master of the vineyard (Jacob 5:4)
Mediator (2 Ne. 2:28)
Messiah (1 Ne. 1:19)
Mighty God (2 Ne. 6:17)
Mighty One of Israel (1 Ne. 22:12)
Mighty One of Jacob (1 Ne. 21:26)
Most High (2 Ne. 24:14)
Most High God (Alma 26:14)
One (1 Ne. 1:9)
Only Begotten of the Father (2 Ne. 25:12)
Only Begotten Son (Jacob 4:5)
Prophet (1 Ne. 22:20)
Redeemer (1 Ne. 10:6)
Redeemer of all men (Alma 28:8)
Redeemer of Israel (1 Ne. 21:7)
Redeemer of the world (1 Ne. 10:5)
Rock (1 Ne. 15:15)
Savior (2 Ne. 31:13)
Savior Jesus Christ (3 Ne. 5:20)
Savior of the world (1 Ne. 10:4)
Shepherd (1 Ne. 13:41)
Son (2 Ne. 31:13)
Son of God (1 Ne. 10:17)
Son of Righteousness (Ether 9:22)
Son of the Eternal Father (1 Ne. 11:21)
Son of the everlasting God (1 Ne. 11:32)
Son of the living God (2 Ne. 31:16)
Son of the most high God (1 Ne. 11:6)
Stone (Jacob 4:16)
Supreme Being (Alma 11:22)
Supreme Creator (Alma 30:44)
The Everlasting Father (2 Ne. 19:6)
The Mighty God (2 Ne. 19:6)
The Prince of Peace (2 Ne. 19:6)
True and living God (1 Ne. 17:30)
True Messiah (2 Ne. 1:10)
True shepherd (Hel. 15:13)
True vine (1 Ne. 15:15)
Well Beloved (Hel. 5:47)
Wonderful (2 Ne. 19:6)

Each of the names given to Jesus Christ signifies an attribute or characteristic of Christ and reveals something unique, essential, and deeply inspirational about him. Each name is used to convey recognition of who he is and important truths concerning his mission. For example, "Lord Omnipotent" means that Christ is the Lord of all, possessing all power. "Holy One" signifies that he is holy and without sin, being perfect in all things. "God of the whole earth" reflects his universal interest in all people and in their individual redemption. "Only Begotten Son" connotes that he is the only Son of the Father in the flesh. "Savior" means that Jesus came to save his people from their sins. "Rock" reminds followers of the firmness of his ways and teachings. "Good Shepherd" suggests his loving and tender care of his people. "Keeper of the gate" reflects his role as judge, and the title "Father" indicates his role in granting eternal life to the "children of Christ," those who have been "spiritually begotten," through the Atonement (Mosiah 5:7; Ether 3:14).

Jesus Christ is truly the central character of the Book of Mormon. The prophet scribes had a conviction of his divinity, for they knew him and loved him (e.g., 2 Ne. 11:2–6; Morm. 1:15; Ether 12:39).

SB

Jesus Christ, Nephite anticipation of The Nephites' anticipation of the advent of Christ is a theme that runs throughout the Book of Mormon, starting in 1 Nephi and culminating in the story of Christ's birth in 3 Nephi 1. Abinadi taught that all the prophets who ever prophesied, from the beginning of the world onward, testified of the coming of the MESSIAH (Mosiah 13:33). They included the prophet Lehi[1] and his posterity, as confirmed by Jacob[2] when he said that his family possessed a deep and abiding messianic expectation "many hundred years before his coming" (Jacob 4:4).

The very beginning of Nephi[1]'s personal record mentions his father's vision, in which Lehi was shown the coming of a Messiah and the redemption of the world (1 Ne. 1:19; ca. 600 B.C.). In later chapters Nephi further expounded on the messianic prophecies of his father. Lehi not only described a special forerunner who would baptize the Messiah but also pinpointed the time

JESUS CHRIST, NEPHITE ANTICIPATION OF

when Christ would appear in mortality (1 Ne. 10:4–9).

Nephi reported in detail his own vision of the future Messiah's birth, unique parentage, baptism, mortal ministry, association with the Twelve Apostles, crucifixion, and subsequent appearance to Lehi's seed after they had lived for many generations upon the promised land (1 Ne. 11:18–21, 27–29, 31–33; 12:6). Nephi understood all of this to be part of the incomparable CONDESCENSION OF GOD (1 Ne. 11:16, 26). He quoted Isaiah (one of the greatest of the ancient prophets to foretell the coming of the Messiah) in order to persuade his brethren to believe in the coming of Christ (1 Ne. 19:23). Nephi's efforts to teach his family about Christ were constant throughout his life: "For we labor diligently to write, to persuade our children, and also our brethren, to believe in Christ, and to be reconciled to God; for we know that it is by grace that we are saved, after all we can do. . . . And we talk of Christ, we rejoice in Christ, we preach of Christ, we prophesy of Christ, and we write according to our prophecies, that our children may know to what source they may look for a remission of their sins" (2 Ne. 25:23, 26).

Just before his death, Lehi testified to his son Jacob[2] that he knew he (Jacob) had been redeemed through the coming Messiah: "I know that thou art redeemed, because of the righteousness of thy Redeemer; for thou hast beheld that in the fulness of time he cometh to bring salvation unto men" (2 Ne. 2:3; between 588 and 570 B.C.). Jacob learned from his own experience with an angel that the name of the Messiah would be Christ (2 Ne. 10:1–5). In turn, and through personal revelation, Jacob's son Enos came to know of Christ's redeeming mission as he sought forgiveness of his sins (Enos 1:5–8; between 544 and 421 B.C.). Enos' son, Jarom, reaffirmed that the prophets, priests, and teachers of his people diligently taught the Mosaic law as well as "the intent for which it was given; persuading them to look forward unto the Messiah, and believe in him to come as though he already was" (Jarom 1:11; 399–361 B.C.).

Anticipation of a future Messiah continued to be an important theme in Nephite society long after the passing of Lehi's immediate family. One of the most stunning summary statements of messianic expectation in the entire Book of Mormon was delivered to king Benjamin by an angel. The life of Christ—his ministry, miracles, sufferings, and atonement were described with significant detail (Mosiah 3:5–21; ca. 124 B.C.).

Abinadi, Alma the Younger, Aaron[3], and Amulek repeatedly proclaimed their confidence in the coming of Christ and his redemption. Abinadi not only quoted Isaiah's messianic prophecies but also taught the true perspective on the ways in which the future Messiah was to be regarded as both the Father and Son. In addition, he described how Christ's redemption and anticipated resurrection would affect all humankind (Mosiah 14; 15:1–12, 19–25; 16; ca. 148 B.C.).

Several decades later, as a missionary, Aaron taught powerfully about the Messiah and supported his belief in the coming of Christ by an appeal to the scriptures (Alma 21:9; ca. 90 B.C.). After the destruction of Ammonihah, Alma[2], Amulek, and other righteous priests endeavored to prepare the hearts of the people for the "coming of the Son of God" (Alma 16:15–20; ca. 78 B.C.). Alma effectively combated the challenge of the anti-Christ, Korihor, who argued that there would be no Christ because no one could know the future (Alma 30:12–13). Such beliefs were foolish traditions of the fathers, according to Korihor's rationalist views (Alma 30:14–27). But Alma testified powerfully of the correctness of the fathers' traditions regarding Christ's advent (Alma 30:39) and through priesthood power exposed Korihor's lies (Alma 30:48–53; ca. 74 B.C.). Amulek testified that he knew that Christ would come to earth to atone for the sins of the world, and gave a significant theological discourse on the nature of Christ's infinite and eternal sacrifice (Alma 34:8–15; ca. 74 B.C.). When Alma reproved his son Corianton, he spoke plainly of sin and also of the source of redemption from sin, who is Christ. Alma reminded Corianton that he had been called to preach the coming of Christ. Alma told his son why it was so important that a knowledge of Christ be made known so far in advance of his advent in mortality, for "a soul at this time [is] as precious unto God as a soul will be at the time of his coming" (Alma 39:15–19; ca. 73 B.C.). In a powerful response to some of the wicked judges of his day, Nephi[2] proclaimed that Moses, Abraham, Zenos, Zenock, Ezias, Isaiah, and Jeremiah[1] all prophesied of the coming of the Son of God in the flesh (Hel. 8:13–20). These prophetic writings would have all been found on the brass plates.

The capstone of messianic anticipation in the Book of Mormon is found in the prophecies of Samuel the Lamanite to the Nephites. Samuel predicted the time of the Savior's birth in an exact number of years (Hel. 14:2), foretold the atmospheric signs attendant on his birth (Hel. 14:3–7), and prophesied the signs and wonders that would accompany his death (Hel. 14:21–28; ca. 6 B.C.). Nephi[3], son of Nephi[2], whose faith in the traditions of the fathers concerning the coming of Christ became sure knowledge, reported the fulfillment of Samuel's prophecies as well as the expectations of all other true prophets (3 Ne. 1:4–25; A.D. 1).

See also Law of Moses; Prophecy in the Book of Mormon; Sacrifices.

ACS

Jesus Christ, premortal appearances of

Christ was clearly the focus of the religion of faithful Nephites and Lamanites before his resurrection, but the Book of Mormon only rarely mentions Jesus appearing to his servants among them.

In the first chapter of the Book of Mormon, Lehi[1] was carried away in a vision. Among other things that he witnessed, he saw "One descending out of the midst of heaven," whose "luster was above that of the sun at noon-day" (1 Ne. 1:9). That the One was Christ is suggested in the following verse, where twelve others of lesser luster followed (1 Ne. 1:10). It seems that a distinction should be made between this visionary experience and an actual appearance.

Nephi[1] (2 Ne. 11:3) and Jacob[2] (2 Ne. 2:4; 11:3) saw Christ, as did king Lamoni (Alma 19:13). While the sacred events (whether visions or appearances) are only mentioned in passing, in each of these Christ is called the "Redeemer," and his atonement is attested (2 Ne. 2:3–9; 11:2–7; Alma 19:13). The faithful Jaredite king Emer saw "the Son of Righteousness," and he "did rejoice and glory in [Christ's] day" (Ether 9:22).

The Book of Mormon preserves from the plates of brass an account of Jehovah, the God of Israel, appearing to the biblical prophet Isaiah (2 Ne. 16 // Isa. 6). Nephi noted, perhaps with that appearance in mind, that Isaiah had seen his Redeemer (2 Ne. 11:2).

The only actual account of (as opposed to reference to) the premortal Christ appearing to a Book of Mormon prophet is that of his appearance to the brother of Jared[1] in Ether 3. Comprising twenty-three verses (Ether 3:6–28), it is one of the fullest accounts of a divine manifestation anywhere in scripture. Jesus said to the brother of Jared, "Never have I showed myself unto man whom I have created" (Ether 3:15). This statement has been interpreted in different ways, most commonly with the suggestion that Christ had never appeared as plainly or distinctly before (Smith, 1:37). One interpretation based on Ether 3:14 emphasizes that the Lord does not reveal himself to unbelieving men but only to those who believe and trust in him (Sperry, 467–68). Still another possibility is that while the premortal Jehovah had appeared previously to other prophets, he had done so in his role as Father, Sovereign, and Creator. The appearance to the brother of Jared is perhaps scripture's earliest account of him appearing and specifically identifying himself as Jesus Christ, the Son. Moroni[2] punctuated the account by summarizing, "Jesus showed himself unto this man in the spirit, even after the manner and in the likeness of the same body even as he showed himself [many centuries later and after his resurrection] unto the Nephites" (Ether 3:17).

BIBLIOGRAPHY

Jackson, Kent P. "'Never Have I Showed Myself unto Man': A Suggestion for Understanding Ether 3:15a." *Brigham Young University Studies*, no. 3 (Summer 1990): 71–76.

Smith, Joseph Fielding. *Doctrines of Salvation.* Compiled by Bruce R. McConkie. 3 vols. Salt Lake City: Bookcraft, 1954–56.

Sperry, Sidney B. *Book of Mormon Compendium.* Salt Lake City: Bookcraft, 1970.

KPJ

Jesus Christ, reconciled unto *See* Reconciled unto Christ.

Jesus Christ, role of, as Father and Son Jesus Christ is designated in scripture as both the Father and the Son (Ether 3:14). Elohim is the Father of the spirits of all men and women, including Jesus Christ, who is the firstborn spirit child of God (Num. 16:22; Rom. 8:29; Col. 1:15; Heb. 12:9; D&C 93:21). Jesus is the literal physical Son of God and the Only Begotten in the flesh (2 Ne. 25:12; Jacob 4:5, 11; Alma 5:48; 9:26; 12:33–34; 13:5, 9).

Jesus Christ or Jehovah is also known by the title of Father (First Presidency, 466–73). First, Christ is known as Father by virtue of his role as the Creator. Acting under the injunction of his Father, he became the Creator of worlds without number (Moses 1:31–33; 7:30) and was thereby known as the Lord Omnipotent (Mosiah 3:5) long before he entered mortality. Thus the Savior is appropriately known in the Book of Mormon as "the Father of heaven and earth, the Creator of all things from the beginning" (Mosiah 3:8; cf. 2 Ne. 25:12; Alma 11:39; 3 Ne. 9:15).

Second, Christ is Father through spiritual rebirth. As the atoning Savior and foreordained Messiah, Jesus Christ became "the author of eternal salvation unto all them that obey him" (Heb. 5:9). Thus the gospel of God the Father (Rom. 1:1) became known as the gospel of Jesus Christ. Those on earth who accept his gospel and comply with its requirements become the sons and daughters of Jesus Christ and therefore take upon them the Lord's name; they become Christians. The Book of Mormon prophets taught the necessity of spiritual rebirth (Mosiah 5:1–15; 15:11–12; 27:23–27; Alma 5:14; 7:14; Ether 3:14; cf. Moses 6:59–60).

Third, Christ is known as Father by divine investiture of authority. President Joseph Fielding Smith explained that "all revelation since the fall has come through Jesus Christ, who is the Jehovah of the Old Testament. In all of the scriptures, where God is mentioned and where he has appeared, it was Jehovah who talked with Abraham, with Noah, Enoch, Moses and all the prophets. . . . The Father has never dealt with man directly and personally since the fall, and he has never appeared except to introduce and bear record of the Son" (1:27). The Master explained to a group in the meridian of time, "I am come in my Father's name" (John 5:43). He acted and spoke on behalf of the almighty Elohim. Thus, "the Father-Elohim has placed his name upon the Son, has given him his own power and authority, and has authorized him to speak in the first person as though he were the original or primal Father" (McConkie, 63). This principle whereby the words of the Father are spoken by the Son is evident in the Pearl of Great Price (Moses 1:4–6, 32–33; 6:51–52), as well as in the Doctrine and Covenants. In fact, in the Doctrine and Covenants there are occasions wherein the Lord chooses to speak as both Christ and Elohim in the same revelation (D&C 29:1, 42; 49:5, 28). Truly the words of Jehovah are the words of Elohim; these two beings are of one mind.

In addition, one of the significant teachings of the Book of Mormon is that Jesus Christ is Father because he received through conception the attributes and capacities of God: "This is a matter of his Eternal Parent investing him with power from on high so that he becomes the Father because he exercises the power of that Eternal Being" (McConkie, 371; Mosiah 15:2–3).

Thus Abinadi's testimony of the Fatherhood and Sonship of Christ in Mosiah 15 is a discussion of the dual nature of Jesus Christ as the Only Begotten of the Father in the flesh. Because of that dual nature—possessing the powers of both mortality and immortality—the Redeemer was able to do for man what no other person could do: bear their griefs, carry their sorrows, be wounded for their transgressions and bruised for their iniquities, transform their nature, and raise them from the dead (2 Ne. 2:8; Mosiah 14:3–5; Hel. 5:11; 3 Ne. 27:15; Morm. 7:5; John 10:17–18).

Summary of Abinadi's teachings (Mosiah 15:1–4)

1. God himself—Jehovah, the God of ancient Israel—will come to earth, take a physical body, and make redemption available for all (Mosiah 15:1).

2. The will of the Son will be swallowed up in

JESUS CHRIST, SECOND COMING OF

the will of the Father. That is, the flesh will become subject to the spirit, the mortal subject to the immortal. In short, Jesus will do what the Father would have him do (Mosiah 15:2).

3. Because Jesus will have a physical body and dwell in the flesh—like every other son and daughter of God—he will be known as the Son of God. On the other hand, because he will be conceived by the power of God and have within him the powers of the Spirit, he will be known as the Father (Mosiah 15:2–3; cf. D&C 93:4, 12–14).

4. Christ will be both Father and Son. He will be called the Father because he was conceived by the power of the Father and inherited all of the divine attributes, including immortality, from his exalted Sire. He will be called the Son because of the flesh—his inheritance from his mortal mother Mary. Therefore Christ will be both flesh and spirit, both man and God, both Son and Father. And these titles, roles, and attributes—the Son and the Father, the man and the God, the flesh and the spirit—will be blended wondrously in one being, Jesus Christ (Mosiah 15:3–4).

BIBLIOGRAPHY

First Presidency and the Twelve. "The Father and the Son: A Doctrinal Exposition by the First Presidency and the Twelve." *The Articles of Faith*, by James E. Talmage. London: The Church of Jesus Christ of Latter-day Saints, 1924.

McConkie, Bruce R. *The Promised Messiah*. Salt Lake City: Deseret Book, 1978.

Smith, Joseph Fielding. *Doctrines of Salvation*. Compiled by Bruce R. McConkie. 3 vols. Salt Lake City: Bookcraft, 1954–56.

RLM

Jesus Christ, second coming of The Savior's return to the earth in power and glory as the prelude to his millennial reign.

The day of the Second Coming is described as a great and dreadful day (3 Ne. 25:5 // Mal. 4:5). It will be a dreadful day for the wicked when in shame and sorrow they seek to hide from the judgments of the Lord (2 Ne. 12:10–21 // Isa. 2:10–21), but will find no escape from the "fulness of the wrath of God" that will destroy them (1 Ne. 22:15–18; 2 Ne. 23:6–16 // Isa. 13:6–16; 2 Ne. 30:10; 3 Ne. 25:1 // Mal. 4:1). The return of Jesus Christ to the earth will be a great day. In that day "the Son of Righteousness [will] arise with healing in his wings" (3 Ne. 25:2–3 // Mal. 4:2–3; 2 Ne. 8:3 // Isa. 51:3) to begin his millennial reign in might, power, and glory (1 Ne. 22:24; Alma 5:50). At that time Satan will be bound by the righteousness of the people and the power of God (1 Ne. 22:26; 2 Ne. 30:18; D&C 45:55; 101:28; Cannon, 86), the faithful will be gathered (1 Ne. 22:25; 3 Ne. 21:25–28), there will be an outpouring of truth and knowledge (2 Ne. 30:18), and the millennial era of righteousness and peace will begin (2 Ne. 12:4 // Isa. 2:4; 2 Ne. 21:6–9 // Isa. 11:6–9; 30:12–15).

The Book of Mormon contains prophecies of events that signal the approach of the second coming of the Lord. One of the most prominent signs is the coming forth of the Book of Mormon itself. The Savior told the Nephites that "when these things [the bringing of the Book of Mormon to the descendants of Lehi by way of the Gentiles] come to pass that thy seed shall begin to know these things—it shall be a sign unto them, that they may know that the work of the Father hath already commenced unto the fulfilling of the covenant which he hath made unto the people who are of the house of Israel" (3 Ne. 21:7). Mormon explained that the intent of this sign is that "ye may know that the words of the Lord, which have been spoken by the holy prophets, shall all be fulfilled; and ye need not say that the Lord delays his coming unto the children of Israel" (3 Ne. 29:1–2). Other preparatory events to the Second Coming include the discovery of America and the establishment of the United States as a free land (1 Ne. 22:7; 3 Ne. 21:4), the restoration of the gospel through the instrumentality of a "choice seer" (2 Ne. 3:6–15; 1 Ne. 15:13–14; 22:8–11; 3 Ne. 16:7; 21:9–11; D&C 45:9), the commencement of the gathering of Israel (1 Ne. 22:11–12; 2 Ne. 21:10–12; Jacob 6:2–3; 3 Ne. 5:23–26), the establishment and acceptance of temples (2 Ne. 12:1–3 // Isa. 2:1–3), the coming of the Lord to his temple (3 Ne. 24:1 // Mal. 3:1), the appearance of Elijah to "turn the heart of the fathers to the children, and the heart of the children to their fathers" (3 Ne. 25:5–6 // Mal. 4:5–6), and the Gentiles' acceptance of the gospel and their helping to build the New Jerusalem (3 Ne. 21:22–24).

President Ezra Taft Benson noted, "The record of the Nephite history just prior to the Savior's visit reveals many parallels to our own day as we anticipate the Savior's second coming" (37). Some parallels between Book of Mormon people awaiting the coming of Christ in the meridian of time and latter-day people awaiting his return include the proliferation of secret combinations (Hel. 6:38; 3 Ne. 7:6–9; cf. Morm. 8:27; Ether 8:20, 22–24; D&C 42:64), wars, wickedness (3 Ne. 2–7; cf. D&C 45:26–27), and pride (Hel. 13:22; 3 Ne. 6:10–14; cf. Morm. 8:36; D&C 1:16; 38:39). Additional parallels can be seen in materialistic attitudes (Hel. 13:21–23; cf. 2 Ne. 12:19–21), efforts of the people to find "happiness in doing iniquity" (Hel. 13:38; cf. 2 Ne. 28:7–8), and the presence and acceptance of false prophets, teachers, and doctrines (Hel. 13:27–29; cf. 2 Ne. 28:9–12; Morm. 8:31–33). Also common to both time periods is the warning voice of the Lord and his prophets, seeking to help prepare the people for both Christ's coming (Alma 5:28–29; Hel. 14:11–12; cf. D&C 1:11–16; 39:20–22; 64:23–25) and the impending destruction of the wicked (3 Ne. 8–10; cf. 25:1; D&C 29:9; 133:41, 51, 63–64).

Recognizing the importance Christ placed upon being prepared for his second coming (e.g., Matt. 24–25), latter-day people can learn much by studying Nephite society during this critical period prior to Christ's appearance. By so doing, taught President Benson, "we can determine why some were destroyed in the terrible judgments that preceded His coming and what brought others to stand at the temple in the land of Bountiful and thrust their hands into the wounds of His hands and feet" (20–21).

See also Malachi chapter review (3 Ne. 24–25 // Mal. 3–4); Types.

BIBLIOGRAPHY

Benson, Ezra Taft. *A Witness and a Warning*. Salt Lake City: Deseret Book, 1988.

Cannon, George Q. *Gospel Truth*. Selected by Jerreld L. Newquist. Salt Lake City: Deseret Book, 1987.

RDD

Jesus Christ, types of *See* Types.

Jew(s) The meaning of the term "Jew" varies in biblical and Book of Mormon passages depending upon the time period and context of the passage. The modern English word *Jews* is used to translate the Hebrew *Yehudim,* or "Judahites," originally meaning the descendants of Judah, the son of Jacob/Israel. Later the term Judahites applied specifically to the inhabitants of the southern kingdom of Judah, founded after Solomon's death. Although named after the dominant tribe of Judah, the kingdom of Judah included the tribe of Simeon, half the tribe of Benjamin, many Levites, and some of the tribe of Dan. The rest of the Israelite tribes were in the northern kingdom of Israel. By the time of Lehi[1], however, many people from the northern Israelite tribes had migrated south to Judah during times of religious persecution (such as during the days of Ahab and Jezebel in the ninth century B.C.) and military invasion (such as during the Assyrian wars of the eighth century B.C.). Thus, segments of most, if not all, of the Israelite tribes living in Judah in 600 B.C. considered themselves Judahites, or citizens of the southern kingdom. In a similar pattern, citizens of the United States of America, originating from many nations, call themselves Americans, even though they are not descendants of the Italian-born navigator Amerigo Vespucci for whom America was named.

In the Book of Mormon, "Jew" can refer to any Israelite, an inhabitant or descendant of the kingdom of Judah during different historical periods, or someone influenced by Jewish culture. "Jew" (or "Jews") appears ninety times in the Book of Mormon, with sixty-nine of these references appearing in 1 and 2 Nephi as cited by Nephi[1]. The other 21 citations are by Jacob[2], Amaleki[1], the resurrected Savior, Mormon, and Moroni[2]. These references to the Jews appear in five different contexts:

1. The records, language, or learning of the Jews (a cultural entity: 29 references). Nephi's

JEWS, B OF M MESSAGE CONCERNING

people came from a Jewish culture which provided the intellectual and religious framework of their society. Nephi often referred to this Jewish background (e.g., 1 Ne. 1:2; 3:3; 13:23–24; 2 Ne. 25:1–2; Omni 1:14).

2. Jews living in Judah during the middle Old Testament period (a political entity: 24 references). Early Book of Mormon writers referred to the Jews in Judah especially as they described events surrounding the departure of Lehi's family from Jerusalem and the scattering of the Jews by the Babylonians (e.g., 1 Ne. 1:19–20; 2 Ne. 25:5–6, 15; Jacob 4:14).

3. Jews as a representation of the house of Israel (a symbolic, covenant entity: 17 references). Any Israelite or the whole house of Israel as a contrast to the Gentiles, as in the phrase "Jew and Gentile" (e.g., Title Page; 1 Ne. 13:42; 15:17, 20; 2 Ne. 10:16; 3 Ne. 28:27–28).

4. Jews living in Judea during the Savior's lifetime (a sociopolitical entity: 11 references). In Book of Mormon prophecies and accounts of the earthly ministry of Jesus, Christ is placed in the historical context of his Jewish roots (e.g., 1 Ne. 10:4, 11; 2 Ne. 10:3; Jacob 4:15–16; 3 Ne. 19:35).

5. Prophecies about the Jews in the last days (a communal, eschatological entity: 9 references). Important Book of Mormon prophecies are recorded concerning the gathering and restoration of the Jews in the latter days (e.g., 1 Ne. 15:19–20; 2 Ne. 29:13; 30:7; Morm. 5:14).

Also note the following significant passages where the Jews are not specifically identified by name but are accurately described in their biblical and medieval historical context and where important premillennial promises are given: 1 Nephi 19:13–16; 2 Nephi 6:8–11; 10:5–8.

See also Descendants of the Jews; Gentile(s); Jews, Book of Mormon message concerning.

VLL

Jews, Book of Mormon message concerning
The declaration of the Book of Mormon to the Jews is that they must return to the faith of their fathers to lay claim to the promises given their fathers—that is, they must believe in Christ, the Son of God, and his atonement, and "worship the Father in his name, with pure hearts and clean hands, and look not forward any more for another Messiah . . . for there should not any come, save it should be a false Messiah which should deceive the people; for there is save one Messiah spoken of by the prophets, and that Messiah is he who should be rejected of the Jews" (2 Ne. 25:16, 18). Critics of the Book of Mormon regard such declarations as anachronistic, claiming that acceptance of Christ and the idea of worshipping the Father in his name are doctrines unknown to those of the Old Testament. The Book of Mormon consistently declares otherwise. Its story begins six hundred years before the birth of Christ in Jerusalem where Lehi[1] testified of the coming of Christ and was rejected by the Jews (1 Ne. 1:19–20). The testimony of the Book of Mormon is that the southern kingdom of Judah was destroyed, with its survivors taken captive into Babylon, because they rejected Christ, "the Holy One of Israel," and the covenants they made with him (1 Ne. 22:5; 2 Ne. 25:9–10; 3 Ne. 5:25). Nevertheless, the faithful among the house of Israel from the days of Moses understood that the law given him on Sinai, with all its ritual and symbolism, pointed to Christ (2 Ne. 11:4; 25:24–30; Alma 25:15–16; 34:14). The prophet Jacob[2] affirmed that one of the purposes for their writing was to inform future readers that they knew of Christ: "For, for this intent have we written these things, that they may know that we knew of Christ, and we had a hope of his glory many hundred years before his coming; and not only we ourselves had a hope of his glory, but also all the holy prophets which were before us." Jacob explained that not only did "all the holy prophets" believe in Christ but they "worshiped the Father in his name." Using Abraham as an illustration, Jacob said that he offered his son Isaac as a sacrifice in "similitude of God and his Only Begotten Son" (Jacob 4:4–5; cf. Hel. 8:16–20). The brazen serpent that Moses raised upon a pole they understood to be a prophecy of the Son of God being lifted up on the cross so that as many as would look to him might live, while those who refused to do so would perish (2 Ne. 25:20; Alma 33:19; Hel. 8:14–15).

JEWS, B OF M MESSAGE CONCERNING

"The Jews were a stiffnecked people," Jacob explained, "and they despised the words of plainness, and killed the prophets, and sought for things that they could not understand." Thus they became blind to the things of the Spirit and began to look "beyond the mark." Then God, who blesses men according to the desires of their hearts, gave them "many things" which they could not understand "because they desired it God hath done it, that they may stumble" (Jacob 4:14–15).

Jacob prophesied that after their Babylonian captivity the Jews would again return to the land of their inheritance where "the Lord God, the Holy One of Israel," would manifest himself unto them "in the flesh." Nevertheless, prophecy held that they would "scourge him and crucify him," that once again his judgments would come upon them, and they would be "scattered, and smitten" (2 Ne. 6:9–11; 10:3–5; 25:12–16; 1 Ne. 19:13–14). The promise was that "when they shall come to the knowledge of their Redeemer, they shall be gathered together again to the lands of their inheritance" (2 Ne. 6:11; 10:6–9).

When Christ visited the Nephites he assured them that he had not forgotten the covenants he made with his ancient covenant people and that he would gather them in his own due time to the land of their fathers, meaning the land of Jerusalem. It is not to be supposed that this prophecy is being fulfilled in the creation of the modern state of Israel and in the subsequent gathering of Jews to the Holy Land. This gathering is more a cultural/political gathering, and is not the spiritual gathering spoken of in the Book of Mormon. The promise of Christ was that when they again chose to believe in him as the Son of God and to pray to the Father in his name, these blessings would be given them (3 Ne. 20:29–31; cf. 1 Ne. 19:15–16; 2 Ne. 9:2; 3 Ne. 5:25–26). This prophecy will not see completion in full measure until the Millennium. Until that time, as Nephi[1] wrote, the Jews "shall begin to believe in Christ; and they shall begin to gather" (2 Ne. 30:7). It is in a millennial context that the Book of Mormon speaks of both a New Jerusalem and the Jerusalem of old. The inhabitants of the Jerusalem of old are described as having been "washed in the blood of the Lamb; and they are they who were scattered and gathered in from the four quarters of the earth," thus constituting the "fulfilling of the covenant which God made with their father, Abraham." Thus shall be fulfilled the prophecy that says the last shall be first and the first shall be last (Ether 13:11–12).

As with Isaiah and Jeremiah[1], the prophets of the Book of Mormon wrote by way of consolation to scattered Israel, foreshadowing a future day when they would be returned to the blessings and glories of their fathers. "I spake unto them concerning the restoration of the Jews in the latter days," said Nephi[1]. "And I did rehearse unto them the words of Isaiah, who spake concerning the restoration of the Jews, or of the house of Israel; and after they were restored they should no more be confounded, neither should they be scattered again" (1 Ne. 15:19–20). Nephi further taught how this restoration of the Jews would commence: "The Lord will set his hand again the second time to restore his people from their lost and fallen state. Wherefore, he will proceed to do a marvelous work and a wonder among the children of men. Wherefore, he shall bring forth his words [the Book of Mormon] unto them, which words shall judge them at the last day, for they shall be given them for the purpose of convincing them of the true Messiah, who was rejected by them" (2 Ne. 25:17–18; Title Page; Jacob 4:15–18; 5; 6:2). Mormon similarly wrote, "And behold, they [the Nephite records] shall go unto the unbelieving of the Jews; and for this intent shall they go—that they may be persuaded that Jesus is the Christ, the Son of the living God; that the Father may bring about, through his most Beloved, his great and eternal purpose, in restoring the Jews, or all the house of Israel, to the land of their inheritance, which the Lord their God hath given them, unto the fulfilling of his covenant" (Morm. 5:14). This prophesied restoration of the Jews to a knowledge of their Redeemer and the covenants made with their fathers was to come "by way of the Gentile[s]," through whom the Book of Mormon was brought forth and the gospel was to be restored in the latter days (Title Page; 1 Ne. 21:22; 22:6–12; 15:13–20).

There is but one gospel plan. It is the same for Jew and Gentile. Teaching this to Nephi, the Lord said, "I say unto you that as many of the Gentiles as will repent are the covenant people of the Lord; and as many of the Jews as will not repent shall be cast off; for the Lord covenanteth with none save it be with them that repent and believe in his Son, who is the Holy One of Israel" (2 Ne. 30:2).

See also Israel, covenants unto; Israel, gathering of; Israel, historical background of; Israel, scattering of; Jew(s); Jews, history of.

JFM

Jews, descendants of the *See* Descendants of the Jews.

Jews, history of Book of Mormon prophets understood well the history of their people up to the year 600 B.C., when they left Jerusalem[1]. The brass plates contained the history of the Jews down to Zedekiah (1 Ne. 5:12). The twelve sons of Jacob[1] became tribes, who entered into a covenant with the Lord at Sinai following their captivity in Egypt (Ex. 20–24). The Lord promised them great blessings of prosperity and protection if they obeyed the covenant, or destruction and scattering if they disobeyed (Deut. 27–29). Eventually they settled in the promised land and were molded into a united kingdom under the direction of David and Solomon (ca. 1000 B.C.). The twelve tribes divided into the northern and the southern kingdoms after the death of Solomon (931 B.C.). The northern kingdom consisted of ten of the tribes and was called Israel, Samaria, or Ephraim, after the leading tribe. The southern kingdom was called after the leading tribe, JUDAH, or after Jerusalem, the capital. Prophets were sent to both kingdoms to call the people to repentance. The northern kingdom was destroyed in 722 B.C. by the Assyrians and many were taken into exile in Assyria where they became the lost tribes of Israel. Judah remained alone in the promised land, and her descendants became the Jews. Lehi[1] and his family were descendants of Joseph[1] and probably lived in the north originally, but at some time they had moved to the southern kingdom of Judah, perhaps to escape the destruction in 722 B.C. Nephi[1] identified himself closely with the Jews because he had come from Jerusalem (2 Ne. 33:8). Prophets continued to warn Judah to repent or face the same destruction and scattering that had befallen the northern kingdom. Finally, Lehi and his family were told to leave Jerusalem in 600 B.C.

Several prophets saw in vision the history of the Jews from 600 B.C. to the end of time. For example, Jacob[2] saw the destruction of Jerusalem and the Exile, their eventual return, the coming of Christ, the scattering of the Jews, and their eventual gathering and return (2 Ne. 6). Nephi and others saw similar visions that the Jews would be destroyed, taken captive, return again, witness the coming of the Messiah, be destroyed again, scattered, and in the fulness of times gathered and come to a knowledge of Jesus Christ (2 Ne. 25:10–18). In 597 B.C. the Babylonians attacked Jerusalem and took captives into exile to Babylon. Jeremiah[1] warned the Jews to submit to the Babylonians, but they revolted, and in 586 B.C. Nebuchadnezzar attacked and conquered Judah and Jerusalem again, burned the temple, and took many more of the Jews into exile to Babylon. The Babylonian empire fell in 539 B.C. to the Persians, and Cyrus allowed the Jews to return to Jerusalem, where they rebuilt and rededicated the temple (515 B.C.) under the direction of Zerubbabel. Alexander the Great conquered the Persian Empire in 331 B.C., and upon his death in 323 B.C. his empire was divided among his generals. For approximately the next two hundred years, Judah was subject to Greek kingdoms set up by those generals, the Ptolemies first and then the Seleucids. Eventually the Jews declared their own independent state under the Maccabees (165 B.C.) which was later conquered by the Romans in 63 B.C. Because of disobedience to their covenants with God and their rebellion against Rome, Jerusalem was destroyed again in A.D. 70, and the Jews were scattered throughout the world.

Many Book of Mormon prophets saw the eventual gathering of the Jews in the latter days (e.g., 1 Ne. 22:25; 2 Ne. 10:8; 29:14; 3 Ne. 21:1). Jacob prophesied, "When they shall come to the knowledge of their Redeemer, they shall be gathered together again to the lands of their inheritance" (2 Ne. 6:11; 30:7).

See also Babylonian captivity; Israel, gathering of; Israel, historical background of; Israel, scattering of; Jerusalem[1], destruction of, at 586 B.C.; Jerusalem[1], destruction of, at A.D. 70; Jew(s); Jews, Book of Mormon message concerning.

DRS

Jews, manner of the *See* Isaiah, understanding of.

Jews, record of the *See* Record of the Jews.

John the Baptist A prophet and contemporary of Jesus Christ. Born of priestly lineage to Zacharias and Elisabeth (Luke 1:5), John baptized the Savior and prepared a people to receive him (Matt. 3:13–17; Mark 1:2–8; Luke 3:3–18). Christ called him "a burning and a shining light" (John 5:35) and proclaimed, "Among those that are born of women there is not a greater prophet than John the Baptist" (Luke 7:28; Matt. 11:11). Like Isaiah (Isa. 40:1–3) and Malachi (Mal. 3:1), both Lehi[1] and Nephi[1] wrote prophetically concerning John's mission. The Nephites knew that John would be the forerunner for Christ, baptize in the Jordan River near Bethabara, teach that Jesus was superior to himself, and bear record that Jesus "should take away the sins of the world" (1 Ne. 10:7–10; 11:27; 2 Ne. 31:4).

See also Fulfill all righteousness.

CF

John the Beloved/Revelator One of Jesus' twelve original apostles (Matt. 10:2) and one of the three "pillars" of the early Christian Church (Gal. 2:9). John was foreordained to view and record the same panoramic vision of the world that Nephi[1] saw but could only partially report (1 Ne. 14:18–28)—a vision that the brother of Jared[1] and others were permitted to record but commanded to seal up "to come forth in their purity . . . in the own due time of the Lord" (1 Ne. 14:26; Ether 4:16).

In his vision of the tree of life, Nephi learned that John's writings would be recorded in the book he had seen earlier that would come forth "out of the mouth of the Jew." Originally this book would be "plain and pure" and "easy to the understanding of all men" (1 Ne. 14:23), but alterations to it by the great and abominable church would cause many to stumble (1 Ne. 13:25–29).

The Nephite record verifies the biblical account that John did not taste of death (John 21:20–23). Like the Three Nephites, John desired a continued ministry on earth until Christ returns (3 Ne. 28:6; cf. D&C 7).

CF

Jonas[1] *See* Disciples, twelve Nephite.

Jonas[2] *See* Disciples, twelve Nephite.

Jordan, city of The Nephite city to which Mormon and the Nephite armies fled when pursued by the Lamanites. For a time the Nephite armies withstood the Lamanites and defended the city, only to be forced again to flee (Morm. 5:3–7; ca. A.D. 375–380).

Jordan, river Major river in the Holy Land. It flows into and out of the sea of Galilee and terminates in the Dead Sea. The "river Jordan" is mentioned in reference to Israelites crossing into the promised land (1 Ne. 17:32) and the baptism of the Messiah in the river at BETHABARA, which is "beyond Jordan," apparently meaning at the east side of the river opposite Jericho (1 Ne. 10:9; *see* map, page 93).

DKO

Joseph[1] Son of the patriarch Jacob[1] and his wife Rachel. He was born ca. 1750 B.C. and lived 110 years (Gen. 50:22). Joseph was hated by his brothers for his visions, which indicated he would one day rule over them, and for being especially favored by his father (Gen. 37). Through his brothers' treachery, he was sold into slavery in Egypt, where he endured many trials and temptations (Gen. 37; 39–40). Because he remained faithful through his adversities, the Lord directed and blessed Joseph's life so that eventually he rose to become the most powerful and influential man of his era, second only to the king of Egypt. Later, because of his position, he was able to bring his family to Egypt and rescue them from famine (Gen. 40–50). Joseph recognized that his troubles were a prelude to the rescue of his family from famine, and he acknowledged God's hand in his life. He explained to his brothers, "But as for you, ye thought evil against me; but God meant it unto good" (Gen. 50:20). His descendants figure prominently in both Bible and Book of Mormon lands. For example, Lehi[1] and his family were descendants of Joseph through Manasseh; such great biblical leaders as Joshua and Samuel[1] were descendants of Joseph through Ephraim (Num. 13:8; Deut. 34:9; 1 Sam. 1:1). In Isaiah's day, the kingdom of Israel was sometimes simply referred to as "Ephraim" (e.g., Isa. 7:2, 5, 8; 9:9; 11:13).

Joseph of Egypt is frequently mentioned in the Book of Mormon. From reading his genealogy written on the plates of brass, Lehi "knew that he was a descendant of Joseph . . . who was the son of Jacob, who was sold into Egypt, and who was preserved by the hand of the Lord, that he might preserve his father, Jacob, and all his household from perishing with famine" (1 Ne. 5:14; 2 Ne. 3:4; 4:1–2; Ether 13:7). Joseph is also mentioned in reference to his prophecies (2 Ne. 3:5, 14, 16). Nephi[1] said that Joseph "prophesied concerning all his seed. And the prophecies which he wrote, there are not many greater" (2 Ne. 4:2).

The blessing given through Jacob[1] to Joseph that he would be "a fruitful bough, even a fruitful bough by a well; whose branches run over the wall" (Gen. 49:22) referred to Lehi's descendants, who are called "a branch who have been broken off" (1 Ne. 19:24) and a "branch from the fruit of the loins of Joseph" (Jacob 2:25). Joseph Fielding Smith taught: "According to the word of the Lord to Joseph Smith the continent of America was given to Joseph and his posterity as an everlasting inheritance. That is what is meant by the branches [i.e., Joseph's posterity] running over the wall [i.e., migrating to the Americas]" (93). Thus various individuals and groups in the Book of Mormon are referred to as a "descendant of Joseph" (1 Ne. 5:14, 16; 6:2; 2 Ne. 3:4), "of the loins of Joseph" (Jacob 2:25), a "remnant of Joseph" (Alma 46:24), the "house of Joseph" (3 Ne. 15:12; Ether 13:8), or of the "seed of Joseph" (Alma 46:23, 24, 27; 3 Ne. 5:21, 23; 10:17; Ether 13:6, 7, 10).

Joseph Smith is also alluded to in the Book of Mormon in a prophecy of Joseph of Egypt. In speaking to his youngest son Joseph[2], father Lehi mentioned a prophecy of Joseph of Egypt concerning the stature of Joseph Smith as a prophet and restorer, and that out of the fruit of his loins (i.e., of Joseph of Egypt) a seer (i.e., Joseph Smith) would be raised up who would be given power to bring forth God's word to his descendants (2 Ne. 3:11). Further, Joseph of Egypt prophesied concerning Joseph Smith that "his name shall be called after me; and it shall be after the name of his father. And . . . the thing, which the Lord shall bring forth by his hand, . . . shall bring my people unto salvation" (2 Ne. 3:15).

See also Choice seer; Joseph[1], coat of; Joseph[1], covenants unto.

BIBLIOGRAPHY

Smith, Joseph Fielding. *The Restoration of All Things.* Salt Lake City: Deseret Book, 1973.

SDR

Joseph[2] Last child of Lehi[1], "born," his father said, "in the wilderness of mine afflictions; yea, in the days of my greatest sorrow" (2 Ne. 3:1; ca. 595 B.C.). Joseph, unlike his brothers Laman[1] and Lemuel, was a faithful son and was consecrated a priest and teacher over the people (2 Ne. 5:26). Lehi learned from reading the brass plates that he was descended from Joseph, son of Israel, which likely led to his son's naming. In blessing Joseph, Lehi recounted the covenants given Joseph of old and informed his son that those covenants extended to him (2 Ne. 3). Included was the promise of a great latter-day seer who would also be named Joseph (2 Ne. 3:15).

AKP

Joseph[1], coat of In Genesis, Jacob[1] gave his son Joseph[1] a coat of "many colors" as a symbol of love and perhaps as a sign of the birthright. This gift fostered jealousy in his brothers who conspired against him (Gen. 37:3–4). After selling Joseph into Egypt, the brothers deceived their father into believing Joseph had been killed by a wild animal by dipping his coat in blood and presenting it to Jacob. The Book of Mormon notes that the "coat was rent by his brethren into many pieces" (Alma 46:23). The Hebrew term translated "many colors" is obscure. The Septuagint rendered it with a word meaning "a long sleeved coat."

Captain Moroni referred to an episode lost from the Bible (but probably in the brass plates) in which Jacob, before he died, "saw that a part of the remnant of the coat of Joseph was preserved and had not decayed" (Alma 46:23–27). Jacob then prophesied that Joseph's seed was like Joseph's coat: a remnant would be preserved while the remainder would perish. This passage occurs in the episode in which Moroni invited his people to enter into a covenant to maintain liberty in the land. The people signified their willingness to enter into this covenant by two dramatic gestures: rending their garments and then trampling upon them, symbolizing what would happen to them if they did not fulfill their covenant (Alma 46:21–22). Moroni applied Jacob's prophecy to his own situation and suggested that the lost remnants of Joseph's coat could be likened to the Nephites who had dissented.

See also Joseph[1], covenants unto.

DRS

Joseph[1], covenants unto As descendants of Joseph[1], son of Jacob[1], Lehi[1] and his posterity had a keen interest in the covenants God made unto their forefather. While the Bible tells of some promises God made to Joseph (Gen. 48; 49:22–26; Deut. 33:13–17), the Book of Mormon sets forth more clearly and in greater detail the many promises and covenants God made to him and his descendants. These covenants include the following:

1. God would be merciful to Joseph's descendants so that they would not perish, but be preserved forever (2 Ne. 3:4–5, 16, 23; 9:53; 25:21; Alma 46:24; Ether 13:7).

2. He would raise up a righteous branch from Joseph's posterity that would be broken off from the rest of the house of Israel (2 Ne. 3:5). This refers to the descendants of Lehi.

3. The Messiah would be manifest to Joseph's posterity in the latter days to bring them out of darkness to light, and from captivity to freedom (2 Ne. 3:5).

4. He would raise up a CHOICE SEER of Joseph's lineage (2 Ne. 3:6). This seer would be like Joseph and would also be named Joseph, as would his father (2 Ne. 3:15). This prophet would bring God's word to Joseph's posterity and bring them to a knowledge of the covenants God made with their fathers (2 Ne. 3:7, 11, 23; 3 Ne. 5:23), convince them also of the truth of God's word which had already gone forth among them (2 Ne. 3:11), and bring them to salvation (2 Ne. 3:15). This prophecy clearly speaks of the Prophet Joseph Smith.

5. He would give the western hemisphere to be a land of inheritance for the descendants of Joseph, and there they would build a holy city, even the New Jerusalem (2 Ne. 1:5; 3 Ne. 15:12–13; Ether 13:6, 8). The Lord revealed through the Prophet Joseph Smith that this New Jerusalem would be built in Independence, Missouri (D&C 84:2–4; 57:2–3).

6. Prophets of both Joseph's and Judah's posterity would write, and in the latter days the writings of these two would come together to combat false doctrine and bring the posterity of Joseph to a knowledge of their forefathers and God's covenants (2 Ne. 3:12; Ezek. 37:15–19). The writings of Joseph's posterity include the Book of Mormon ("the stick of Ephraim"; D&C 27:5), as well as other scriptures that were revealed through Joseph Smith (1 Ne. 13:39).

See also Covenant(s); Ephraim, stick of/Joseph, stick of; Israel, covenants unto.

MDR

Joseph, stick of *See* Ephraim, stick of/Joseph, stick of.

Joseph Smith Translation and the Book of Mormon Nephi[1] saw in vision that many plain and precious truths as well as many covenants of the Lord would be kept back or taken away from the Bible by a great and abominable church, causing many in the religious world to stumble (1 Ne. 13:26–29). Nephi also beheld a time of restitution, a day when the Lord would restore many of those truths and covenants to the earth. That restoration would come first through the divine delivery of "other books" that would bear witness of Christ and thereby confirm the essential message of the Bible (1 Ne. 13:20–40). In addition to modern, ongoing revelation through the Lord's anointed servants, the other books would presumably be the Book of Mormon, Doctrine and Covenants, the Pearl of Great Price, and Joseph Smith's Translation of the Bible (JST).

The Book of Mormon came off the press in late March 1830. By June 1830 Joseph Smith began an inspired translation of the King James Version of the Bible. Although the Church does not possess the exact revelation commanding the Prophet to begin this work, it is certain that it was a labor God had appointed to him (D&C 42:56; 76:15), a labor the Prophet Joseph Smith considered to be an important branch of his calling as prophet, seer, revelator, and translator (D&C 21:1; 107:92; Smith, 1:238). Under inspiration the "choice seer" (2 Ne. 3:6–7) altered more than 3,410 verses in the King James Bible through additions and occasional deletions to the scriptural text. This revelatory work—one of the greatest evidences of his prophetic calling—is known today as Joseph Smith's Translation of the Bible.

The translation of the Book of Mormon proved to be an excellent preparation for Joseph Smith's work with the Bible. The Prophet thereby became intimately acquainted with the spirit of revelation and, more especially, the spirit of translation, the means whereby the knowledge of ancient doctrines and ancient events was brought forward in time. The Prophet's acquaintance with the workings of the Holy Ghost, as well as his intense study of the Book of Mormon and how it should be rendered, must have expanded his mind and provided a marvelous spiritual and doctrinal background for the work with the Bible. Further, the clarification of some matters of doctrine in the Book of Mormon—such as the reality of Adam and Eve, the importance of the Fall and the plight of fallen humanity, the absolute necessity for redemption in Christ, the proper balance of grace and works, the need for ordinances, and so forth—was foundational for this later work of translation. In addition, it may be that, other than those parts found in the Book of Mormon, the JST is the closest approximation to the spirit and content of the PLATES OF BRASS, the fundamental scriptural record of the Nephites.

Careful study will show similarities in content between the JST and the Book of Mormon: the fall of Lucifer (2 Ne. 2:17–18; cf. Moses 4:1–4; note: the book of Moses in the Pearl of Great Price is Joseph Smith's Translation of the early chapters of Genesis), the Creation, Fall, and Atonement (2 Ne. 2:22–25; 9:6; Alma 18:36, 39; 22:10–14; cf. Moses 3:9; 5:5–11; 6:48), the salvation of little children (Moro. 8:8, 11; cf. Moses 6:54), the origin of secret combinations (Hel. 6:26–27; cf. Moses 5:16–55), the prophecies of Joseph[1] of old (2 Ne. 3; 4:1–2; cf. JST Gen. 50), Abraham's knowledge of the Messiah (Hel. 8:16–17; cf. JST Gen. 15:9–12), and the ministry of Melchizedek (Alma 13:14–19; cf. JST Gen. 14:26–34).

There are places in the text of the Book of Mormon where the language parallels the King James Version, whereas the JST provides a variant reading (e.g. 3 Ne. 13:12; 14:23). Elder Bruce R. McConkie observed that "the Sermon on the Mount in the Book of Mormon preserves, with a few improvements, the language of the King James Version [of the Bible]. But, later, the Joseph Smith Translation renders much of this sermon in a way that excels even the Book of Mormon" (McConkie, 291). The Prophet's increased spiritual maturity as well as the readiness of the Saints may have made it possible for additional insights to come through the Joseph Smith Translation that may not have come through in the translation of the golden plates. Robert J. Matthews, a noted authority on the Joseph Smith Translation of the Bible, wrote: "It isn't a matter of 'correct' or 'incorrect' as much as it is a matter of purpose. The nature of human language is such that there can be no 'literal' translation of any extensive or intricate document. Every translation is, in effect, an interpretation. The language is not the revelation; it is the awkward vehicle by which a revelation or a concept is expressed. Thus, texts might often be enlarged or paraphrased by a prophet in order to give a certain emphasis or perspective beneficial to his hearers" ("Question," 17).

The Lord explained to Sidney Rigdon, an important scribe of the JST, "Thou shalt write for him [Joseph Smith]; and the scriptures shall be given, even as they are in mine own bosom, to the salvation of mine own elect" (D&C 35:20). Through the work of restoration of biblical passages and events, the prophet was making known "many important points touching the salvation of man [that] had been taken from the Bible, or lost before it was compiled" (Smith, 1:245). The Lord began to unfold through his latter-day seer the ancient order of things, things that had once been recorded by former-day Saints, such as those who had kept the record known as the brass plates. As one searches and studies the JST, he or she recognizes a familiar spirit, a quiet but pervasive and instructive spirit that is to be found also in the Book of Mormon. It is the Spirit of God, testifying both to the gospel's antiquity and, more important, the record's truthfulness.

BIBLIOGRAPHY

Matthews, Robert J. *A Plainer Translation: Joseph Smith's Translation of the Bible, a History and Commentary.* Provo, Utah: Brigham Young University Press, 1975.

———. "I Have a Question." *Ensign* 11 (September 1981): 16–17.

McConkie, Bruce R. *Doctrines of the Restoration.* Edited by Mark L. McConkie. Salt Lake City, Utah: Bookcraft, 1989.

Millet, Robert L., and Robert J. Matthews, eds. *Plain and Precious Truths Restored: The Doctrinal and Historical Significance of the Joseph Smith Translation.* Salt Lake City: Bookcraft, 1995.

Smith, Joseph. *History of The Church of Jesus Christ of Latter-day Saints.* Edited by B. H. Roberts. 7 vols. 2d ed. rev. Salt Lake City: The Church of Jesus Christ of Latter-day Saints, 1932–51.

RLM

Joseph Smith Jr. *See* Smith, Joseph, Jr.

Josephites Descendants of Joseph[2]. From the time of Jacob[2], Josephites were normally included among and called Nephites (Jacob 1:13–14; 4 Ne. 1:36–37; Morm. 1:8; D&C 3:17).

Josh Nephite military leader killed with his ten thousand troops in the last battle between the Nephites and Lamanites (Morm. 6:14; A.D. 385). *See also* Cumorah, battle of.

Josh, city of Christ caused the city of Josh and its inhabitants to be burned to hide their wickedness at the time of his crucifixion, that the blood of the martyred prophets and Saints who had been sent among them might cease to testify against them (3 Ne. 9:10–11).

Joshua, land of The area "in the borders west by the seashore" where Mormon gathered the Nephites together to battle against the Lamanites. It was here that Mormon had his first victory as a young military commander (Morm. 2:6–9; A.D. 331).

Jot, tittle A figure of speech referring to something very small, or the least part of something. Literally, "jot" refers to the tenth letter of the Hebrew alphabet, or "yod" (cf. Greek letter "iota"). In Hebrew script it is the smallest letter, similar to the English apostrophe in shape and size. "Tittle" literally means something "hornlike" and refers to the small flourish of a Hebrew letter. Thus when Christ taught that "one jot nor one tittle hath not passed away from the law, but in me it hath all been fulfilled" he was assuring that even the smallest parts of the Mosaic law found their fulfillment in him (3 Ne. 12:18; cf. 3 Ne. 1:25; Matt. 5:18). About 74 B.C. Amulek likewise used the terms to describe how thoroughly Christ would fulfill the Mosaic law (Alma 34:13), suggesting that this figure of speech was in use even before the Savior's mortal ministry.

TBB

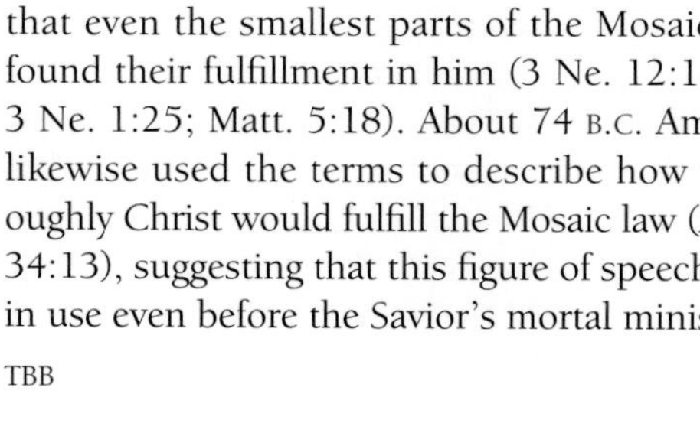

The name Ya'akov (Jacob)

Joy A strong feeling of contentment or HAPPINESS; the ultimate purpose of existence.

Lehi[1] declared, "Adam fell that men might be; and men are, that they might have joy" (2 Ne. 2:25). The prophet Jacob[2] testified that righteous Saints who had faith in Christ and "endured the crosses of the world" would receive joy that would be "full forever" (2 Ne. 9:18; cf. 2 Ne. 22:3; Alma 28:12; 41:4; 3 Ne. 12:12; 28:10). This is what Alma[2] called God's "great plan of happiness" for his children, which plan is "as eternal . . . as the life of the soul" (Alma 42:8, 16).

While eternal joy in the life to come is the ultimate reward for the righteous, joy can be obtained during mortality as one comes to a knowledge of God's goodness, tastes of his love, and receives a remission of his or her sins (Mosiah 4:11; cf. 1 Ne. 11:22–23; Mosiah 3:13; Alma 4:14; 31:38; Hel. 3:35; 3 Ne. 17:17–18). King Benjamin's people cried to have Christ's atoning blood applied to them and were "filled with joy" (Mosiah 4:3, 20; 5:4); upon conversion the Lamanite king Lamoni received such joy in his soul that he was completely overcome by it (Alma 19:6, 13); and Alma[2] told of being "racked with torment . . . by the memory of [his] many sins," and then, after calling upon Christ for mercy, he testified that his "joy [was] as exceeding as was [his] pain" (Alma 36:17–20).

Joy also comes to those who assist Christ in his redeeming work through teaching others the gospel, the "tidings of great joy" (1 Ne. 13:37). In the allegory of Zenos, joy is promised to those who labor with Christ in his vineyard (Jacob 5:71, 75; cf. Alma 28:14). One such laborer, Alma[2], declared, "And this is my glory, that perhaps I may be an instrument in the hands of God to bring some soul to repentance; and this is my joy" (Alma 29:9–10, 13–16). Ammon[2], "seeing the Spirit of the Lord poured out according to his prayers upon the Lamanites," began to offer thanks to God and was "overpowered with joy" (Alma 19:14; cf. 26:10–11, 16, 30, 35–37; 27:17–19; cf. D&C 18:10–16).

The resurrected Christ, upon seeing the faith and joy of his people in the New World, declared, "Behold, my joy is full" (3 Ne. 17:20; cf. Jacob 5:60). Similarly, Christlike people rejoice in the blessings and righteousness of others (Mosiah 22:14; 24:25; 25:8; Alma 7:4–5, 17; 17:2; 30:34; 32:6; 62:1; Hel. 6:3; 3 Ne. 27:30–31), and parents find joy in the righteousness of their children (2 Ne. 1:21; Alma 38:2–3).

"Joy" is also used to describe happiness resulting from desirable circumstances or events, such as the preservation of the stripling warriors (Alma 56:56; 57:25, 36; cf. 45:1); the safe return of the sons of Lehi[1] with the brass plates (1 Ne. 5:1, 7); the "liberty and the freedom" of the Nephites (Alma 48:11); and the enjoyment of faith, righteousness, and peace in society (Hel. 3:32, 35).

While the wicked may experience temporary happiness or "joy" in their evil works, including rejoicing in the afflictions and trials of others, their ultimate end is misery (3 Ne. 1:6; 4:9; 27:11; Morm. 2:13–14).

CBM

Judah Name with various meanings:

1. The fourth son of Jacob[1] and Leah (Gen. 29:35).

2. The tribe of Israelites who descended from Judah, son of Jacob[1].

3. The southern kingdom of Israelites (931–586 B.C.).

Judah, son of Jacob, was promised the blessing of kingship (Gen. 49:10), fulfilled anciently in part by the reigns of David and his descendants who prefigured Jesus' messianic kingship. As Israelites settled Canaan, the tribe of Judah was allotted most of the territory south of Jerusalem and Jericho, bounded on the east by the Dead Sea and on the west by the Mediterranean coastal plain that was inhabited by the Philistines. Following the division of the united Israelite kingdom at the death of Solomon (1 Kgs. 12; 931 B.C.), the southern kingdom was called Judah due to the size and significance of the tribe of Judah (Bible Map 10). Jerusalem, the capital of united Israel, remained the political and religious capital of Judah after the division of the kingdom. According to the Bible, Hezekiah (715–687 B.C.; contemporary with Isaiah) and Josiah (640–609 B.C.) were the two most righteous kings of Judah (2 Kgs.

18:1–5; 2 Chr. 34:1–7; 35:24–26). Judah was a vassal to ASSYRIA and then to BABYLON during most of the time between 732 and 586 B.C. The last Davidic king to rule in Jerusalem was Zedekiah[1], a contemporary of Jeremiah[1] and Lehi[1] (2 Kgs. 24:17; 1 Ne. 1:4). He was placed on the throne by the Babylonians (597 B.C.) when they deported thousands of Israelites from Judah to Babylonia, including king Jehoiachin and the future prophets Daniel and Ezekiel (2 Kgs. 25). The kingdom of Judah ceased to exist in 586 B.C. when the Babylonians destroyed the temple and much of Jerusalem, and deported many more Israelites (2 Kgs. 25; 1 Ne. 10:3; 2 Ne. 1:4). The remnants of this kingdom became known as the JEWS.

Later Greek forms of *Judah* are *Judaea* (geographic name) and *Judas* (personal name).

The twenty-two occurrences of the name "Judah" in the Book of Mormon, mainly in biblical quotations, fall into four categories: (1) "Judah," the southern kingdom or political nation, used in passages with a historical focus, such as 2 Nephi 17:5–6; 18:8, and several times in conjunction with a king's name, such as "Zedekiah, king of Judah" (1 Ne. 1:4; 5:12; Omni 1:15), and "Ahaz . . . king of Judah" (2 Ne. 17:1); (2) "Judah," designating the Lord's covenant people, born into any of the tribes, but living in the kingdom of Judah, used in combination with the name "Jerusalem" in Nephi[1]'s quotations of passages from Isaiah (2 Ne. 12:1; 13:1; 15:3). "Judah and Jerusalem" in 3 Nephi 24:4, where Jesus quoted Malachi 3:4, has the same sense, but in relation to the last days when conditions like "the days of old" will exist; (3) "Judah," the "fruit of the loins" or descendants "of Judah," referred to in Joseph[1]'s prophecy (2 Ne. 3:12), and Isaiah's latter-day prophecy that the "outcasts of Israel" and the "dispersed of Judah" will be gathered and dwell together in peace as one faithful people (2 Ne. 21:12–13); and (4) the singular expression "out of the waters of Judah" (1 Ne. 20:1; cf. Isa. 48:1) is explained by a modern prophetic interpretation first appearing in the 1840 edition of the Book of Mormon as "out of the waters of baptism."

KINGDOM OF JUDAH AT THE TIME OF ISAIAH AND LEHI

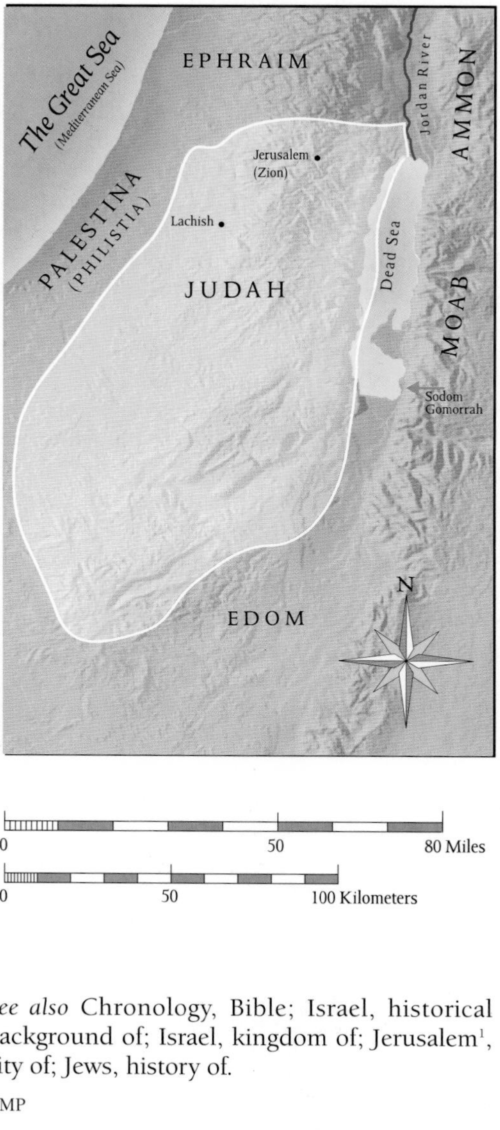

See also Chronology, Bible; Israel, historical background of; Israel, kingdom of; Jerusalem[1], city of; Jews, history of.

DMP

Judea, city of Nephite city fortified and defended by Antipus' army and strengthened by the arrival of the stripling warriors of Helaman[2] (Alma 56:9–10; ca. 66 B.C.). Upon seeing these reinforcements, the Lamanites suspended their battle plans against the city, which gave the Nephite army time to strengthen itself (Alma 56:18–19, 27–29). From Judea, the Nephites "kept spies out round about" to watch Lamanite troop movements and carry out strategic maneuvers to regain Nephite cities (Alma 56:22, 30, 57).

Judges, reign of Between 91 B.C. and A.D. 30, the Nephites were ruled by a series of judges. King Mosiah[2], fearful that a wicked king could arise in the future and lead the people astray, established this system of government with the support of the people at the end of his reign. Under this government, the judges were chosen by the "voice" of the people. Those so chosen were then to judge the people according to the laws "given them by the hand of the Lord" (Mosiah 29:25; cf. Hel. 1:2–5). These judges were paid "according to the time which they labored to judge those who were brought before them to be judged" (Alma 11:1). King Mosiah provided for a hierarchy of lower and higher judges, none of whom were above the law themselves; a lower judge who ceased to judge righteously was to be tried by a higher judge, and a small number of lower judges could pass judgment on an unrighteous higher judge (Mosiah 29:28–29). All ultimately answered to a single chief judge, who was accountable to the voice of the people and, presumably, lower judges as well.

Though the chief judge and other judges were sustained by the VOICE OF THE PEOPLE, it appears that at least sometimes a chief judge who was retiring had a role in appointing his successor (e.g., Alma 4:16). It is further apparent that the people generally chose one of the sons of the chief judge to rule following his death (Alma 50:39; Hel. 1:2–4; 3:37; 6:15), although others, like Helaman[3], could be appointed (Hel. 1:1–2; 2:1–2). The chief judge could also hold prominent office in the Church (Mosiah 29:42; Alma 4:16–17) and was frequently described as the people's governor (Alma 2:16; 50:39; 61:1; 3 Ne. 1:1).

As happens with many of the Lord's efforts to improve the condition of mankind, the Nephite system of judges met many challenges over the course of its history. Within five years of its institution, one Amlici unsuccessfully attempted to overthrow the system by force after failing in his attempt to be appointed a king by the voice of the people (Alma 2). Some four years later, Alma[2] and Amulek had only partial success in correcting the errors introduced into the system by a number of unrighteous lawyers at Ammonihah, whose desires for gain were undermining the liberty of the people (Alma 8:17; 10:27). In ca. 73 B.C., a number of lower judges, "seeking for power," sought to establish another man, Amalickiah, as king when he influenced them through flattery to rebel against the government (Alma 46:1–7). Four years later, still another group, calling themselves king-men, agitated for

REIGN OF THE JUDGES

91 B.C.	Alma[2] (91–83 B.C.) retires to preach the gospel
83 B.C.	Nephihah (83–68 B.C.)
68 B.C.	Pahoran[1] (68–52 B.C.)
52 B.C.	Pahoran[2] (52 B.C.) murdered
52 B.C.	Pacumeni (52–51 B.C.) killed by Lamanites
51 B.C.	Judgment-seat vacant due to war with Lamanites (51–50 B.C.)
50 B.C.	Helaman[3] (50–39 B.C.)
39 B.C.	Nephi[2] (39–30 B.C.) retires to preach the gospel
30 B.C.	Cezoram (30–26 B.C.) murdered
26 B.C.	Son of Cezoram (26 B.C.) murdered
26 B.C.	Seezoram (26–23 B.C.) murdered
23 B.C.	Unknown (23 B.C.–A.D. 1)
A.D. 1	Lachoneus[1] (A.D. 1–30)
A.D. 30	Lachoneus[2] (A.D. 30) murdered, government collapses

the establishment of a king (Alma 51:1–5). Though unsuccessful, these efforts weakened the Nephites and contributed to a longer period of warfare. Later, the Gadianton robbers, a secret society whose object was "to murder, and to rob, and to gain power" (Hel. 2:8) infiltrated the system after Nephi[2] relinquished his position as chief judge in ca. 30 B.C. War and famine purged the government of this society's influence for a time; however, wicked judges, desertion to the Lamanites, increased desires for a king, and the resurgence of the Gadianton robbers combined to weaken and finally destroy the government shortly before the resurrected Lord visited the people (3 Ne. 7:1–2). There is no mention of judges in the Book of Mormon following Christ's appearance to the Nephites.

See also Government, principles of; Kings.

AHH

Judgment, first *See* First judgment.

Judgment, the A principal component of the GOSPEL of Jesus Christ (3 Ne. 27:13–15; cf. Alma 33:22–23). Rewards or punishments are assigned to individuals based upon an assessment of their righteousness or wickedness. Important questions about the Judgment can be answered from the Book of Mormon.

Why is the Judgment necessary?

The "great and eternal plan of redemption" (Alma 34:16) includes some eternal laws which can only be maintained if there is a judgment. Those laws include AGENCY, ACCOUNTABILITY, justice, MERCY, and the commandments with their associated rewards and punishments (2 Ne. 2:22–27; 9:6–29; Alma 34:8–17, 31–36; 42:1–26). Moreover, inasmuch as no unclean thing can dwell in the kingdom of God (1 Ne. 10:21; 15:33–34; Alma 7:21; 11:37; 40:26; Hel. 8:25; 3 Ne. 27:19), only those who are judged worthy, those who have been "cleansed from all stain," whose "garments were washed white through the blood of the Lamb" (Alma 5:21; 13:11; cf. 7:25; 3 Ne. 27:19), may enter therein. Accordingly, the "whole human family of Adam . . . must stand to be judged of [their] works, whether they be good or evil" (Morm. 3:20), where the "plan of restoration," which is "requisite with the justice of God," will restore to every person a reward "according to their works" (Alma 41:1–15; 2 Ne. 29:11).

Who is to be the judge?

Alma[2] taught that everyone shall be "arraigned before the bar of Christ the Son, and God the Father, and the Holy Spirit, which is one Eternal God, to be judged according to their works" (Alma 11:44). Other scriptural verses make it clear that Jesus Christ, by virtue of the Atonement and assignment from the Father, will represent that "one Eternal God" (Alma 11:44) in rendering judgment (3 Ne. 27:19; Morm. 3:20; D&C 19:1–3; John 5:22). Although others will be there and may assist in some way—for example, Nephi[1] (2 Ne. 33:11), Jacob[2] (Jacob 6:13), and Moroni[2] (Moro. 10:27)—"the twelve whom Jesus chose to be his disciples in the land of Jerusalem" and "the twelve whom Jesus chose in this land" (Morm. 3:18–19; cf. 1 Ne. 12:9–10), Jacob assured his readers that "the keeper of the gate is the Holy One of Israel; and he employeth no servant there; and there is none other way save it be by the gate; for he cannot be deceived, for the Lord God is his name" (2 Ne. 9:41). Whatever role any others may play, it is certain that all decisions at the Final Judgment bar will be in total harmony with those of "Jehovah, the Eternal Judge of both quick and dead" (Moro. 10:34).

Book of Mormon prophets further taught that in at least two ways every man is, in a sense, his own judge. First, because men are free to act for themselves, and to be "judges, whether to do good or do evil," and the daily choices they make ultimately determine final outcomes (Alma 41:7; 2 Ne. 2:26–27; Alma 41). Second, because at the judgment bar all will have a "perfect knowledge" of both their guilt and righteousness, they will recognize what the rewards or punishments should be, and acknowledge them as just (2 Ne. 9:14, 46; Mosiah 16:1; Morm. 9:1–5).

When does the Judgment come?

There are several preliminary judgments and a final judgment. Jacob[2] spoke of the judgment of physical and spiritual death passed upon man at the fall of Adam, indicating that it would have been a final judgment were it not for the atonement of Christ (2 Ne. 9:7–12). Throughout mortality "the judgments of God" come to mankind based upon their wickedness or righteousness (1 Ne. 18:15; Mosiah 29:27; Alma 37:28–31; Hel. 4:22–26; Ether 11:20–21). Alma[2] taught of another preliminary judgment, one that takes place at the time of mortal death, when spirits go to the postmortal SPIRIT WORLD and are received into a "state" of "happiness or misery," depending upon their works while in the flesh (Alma 40:11–15).

In a very real sense, the Final Judgment comes for an individual at the time of resurrection (2 Ne. 9:15, 22; Alma 40:21; 42:23; 3 Ne. 26:4–5; Morm. 9:13), for as the Lord revealed to Joseph Smith, "your glory shall be that glory by which your bodies are quickened" (D&C 88:28). Inasmuch as there are different times of resurrection (Mosiah 15:21–26; Alma 40:16–23), there will be different times of final judgment. Many Saints were resurrected, and therefore judged, at the time of Christ's resurrection (Hel. 14:25; 3 Ne. 23:8–13). Latter-day revelation speaks of a general resurrection and judgment at the beginning of the Millennium, and another at the end of the Millennium (D&C 88:92–101), with people passing from mortality to a resurrected state "in the twinkling of an eye" throughout the Millennium, when they reach the "age of a tree," specified as "an hundred years old" by Isaiah (D&C 63:50–51; 101:30–31; Isa. 65:20). It may also be appropriate to speak of the "final judgment" as that time at the end of the Millennium "when all men shall have passed from this first death unto life, insomuch as they have become immortal" (2 Ne. 9:15), when "the heavens and the earth [shall] pass away . . . and . . . all people . . . shall stand before God, to be judged of their works" (3 Ne. 26:3–5), when "there shall be a new heaven and a new earth," and all will receive a formal assignment to an eternal reward (D&C 29:22–24; 88:110–16).

What are the criteria for the Judgment?

The Savior and his prophets testify that mankind will be judged "according to their works, whether they be good or whether they be evil" (Alma 11:44; cf. 1 Ne. 15:33; 2 Ne. 9:44; Mosiah 3:24; Alma 5:15; 41:3; 3 Ne. 27:15). Those works, which are all recorded in the "book of life," or the "record which is kept in heaven," where "all things are written by the Father" (D&C 128:7; 3 Ne. 27:26), will be measured against the truths found in the scriptures and the light and knowledge given to an individual from heaven (2 Ne. 9:23–27; 29:11; W of M 1:9–11; Mosiah 15:24–26; 3 Ne. 27:25–26; Moro. 8:22). Some of the works specifically mentioned include accepting the gospel (Hel. 8:25), receiving such saving ordinances as baptism (3 Ne. 27:16; Morm. 7:10), forgiving others (Mosiah 26:31), judging righteously between good and evil (Moro. 7:15–18), judging others righteously (Alma 41:14; 3 Ne. 14:1; Morm. 8:19), and teaching others the gospel (Jacob 1:19).

In addition to works, mankind will be judged individually by their thoughts, feelings, and DESIRES (Mosiah 4:30; Alma 12:14; 29:3–4; 41:3–5).

What rewards and punishments are given at the Judgment?

Book of Mormon prophets emphasized the extremes in regards to the rewards and punishments assigned to mankind at judgment. Punishments of the wicked include being CAST OFF forever from the kingdom of God (1 Ne. 10:21; 15:33), remaining eternally in a FILTHY or unclean state (1 Ne. 15:33; Morm. 9:14), suffering endless misery and unhappiness (Alma 41:4–5; Morm. 9:14), being dead as to things pertaining unto righteousness (1 Ne. 15:33; Alma 12:16), suffering torment as a LAKE OF FIRE AND BRIMSTONE (2 Ne. 28:23; Mosiah 3:27; Alma 12:17; Moro. 8:21), and being captive to the devil (Alma 12:17). In contrast, the righteous will dwell eternally in the kingdom of heaven with God and Christ (Mosiah 26:24; 3 Ne. 28:40) in a state of righteousness and happiness (Mosiah 2:41; Alma 41:4; Morm. 7:7).

The Book of Mormon does not discuss what rewards or punishments are to be given to those who are worthy of something in between the extremes of HEAVEN and HELL. It is that very question which led Joseph Smith to receive the revelation known as Doctrine and Covenants 76.

When should we prepare for the Judgment?

Amulek declared that "this life is the time for men to prepare to meet God; yea, behold the day of this life is the day for men to perform their labors" (Alma 34:32). This life is frequently referred to as a probationary state granted for the very purpose of preparing for the Judgment (1 Ne. 10:21; 15:32; 2 Ne. 2:21; 9:27; Alma 12:24; 42:4, 10, 13; Hel. 13:38; Morm. 9:28). Amulek warned that those who procrastinate the day of their repentance until "the end" will come to a "night of darkness wherein there can be no labor performed," a time of "awful crisis," when the devil "doth seal you his . . . and . . . hath all power over you" (Alma 34:33–35). For some, the sons of perdition, this constitutes a final judgment, or "the final state of the wicked" (Alma 34:35). Implied but not clearly explained in the Book of Mormon is the doctrine of post-mortal opportunity for receiving the blessings of the gospel for those who lived on earth in ignorance of its truths (Mosiah 15:24; Moro. 8:22). Latter-day revelation makes clear that, except for sons of perdition, mankind's probationary state, to some degree at least, extends into the post-mortal spirit world (Moses 7:36–39; D&C 138:29–37, 58–59). But, as President Spencer W. Kimball stated, procrastination can have serious consequences: "It is true that the great principle of repentance is always available, but for the wicked and rebellious there are serious reservations to this statement. For instance, sin is intensely habit-forming and sometimes moves men to the tragic point of no return. Without repentance there can be no forgiveness, and without forgiveness all the blessings of eternity hang in jeopardy. As the transgressor moves deeper and deeper in his sin, and the error is entrenched more deeply and the will to change is weakened, it becomes increasingly near-hopeless, and he skids down and down until either he does not want to climb back or he has lost the power to do so" (Kimball, 117).

See also Justice, law of; Night of darkness; Paradise; Restoration, plan of.

BIBLIOGRAPHY

Kimball, Spencer W. *The Miracle of Forgiveness*. Salt Lake City: Bookcraft, 1969.

TBB

Judgment bar *See* Judgment, the.

Judgment-seat Nephi[1] (1 Ne. 10:21; 2 Ne. 33:7), Jacob[2] (2 Ne. 9:15), Mormon (3 Ne. 28:31; Morm. 3:22; Moro. 8:21), and Moroni[2] (Title Page; Ether 12:38) used this term in reference to the throne of the Lord from which he will judge all men (cf. 2 Cor. 5:10).

During the reign of the judges (ca. 91 B.C.–A.D. 29), "judgment-seat" was used to describe the seat of Nephite government occupied by the chief judge (Alma 1:2; cf. Acts 25:10).

BRM

Judgments of God God's role as judge is often represented in the Book of Mormon. His justice divides the good from the evil (1 Ne. 15:30), and his judgments are always just and holy (Mosiah 29:12), punishing the unrighteous and vindicating the worthy (1 Ne. 18:15; 2 Ne. 9:15; 25:3; Mosiah 17:11; Alma 4:3; 60:14; Hel. 14:11; 3 Ne. 12:21; Morm. 4:5; 9:14).

The judgment of God is often proclaimed by a prophet who identifies the reason for the punishment by referring to the sins the people have committed. Hebrew prophets who delivered judgment speeches usually spoke alone and sometimes called on heaven and earth as their witnesses. In this context they typically gave a warning or accusation similar to a legal indictment (Micah 6:1–8; Hosea 4:1–3).

Several Book of Mormon judgment speeches given by Jacob[2], Abinadi, king Benjamin, and Samuel the Lamanite are uttered in the form of prophetic lawsuits in which God symbolically took legal action against his people who had violated their covenants (Jacob 2–3; Mosiah 11:20–12:30; 1–6; Hel. 13:2–39; 15:3–8). Such prophetic lawsuits involve the calling of witnesses, the lodging of an accusation, the consideration of a defense, and the issuance of a judgment (Welch, *Law,* 156–80).

Woe oracles are another form in which the judgments of God are articulated. Abinadi pronounced woes against Noah[3] and his people, proclaiming that the Lord would visit them in his anger, that they would be brought into bondage, and that vultures and dogs would eat their flesh (Mosiah 12:2). Jacob likewise pronounced woes on many forms of wickedness (2 Ne. 9:27–38).

The Book of Mormon frequently declares that all men and women will be resurrected so that they may stand, resurrected, to be judged by God as to whether their works, thoughts, and deeds be good or evil (Mosiah 3:10, 24; 15:22–27; Alma 12:12–15). The judgments will result in misery and destruction for the wicked but happiness and blessings for the righteous (Mosiah 2:38–41).

BIBLIOGRAPHY

Welch, John W. *Law in the Book of Mormon*. Provo, Utah: J. Reuben Clark Law School, 1996.

———. "Benjamin's Speech as a Prophetic Lawsuit." *King Benjamin's Speech: "That Ye May Learn Wisdom."* Edited by John W. Welch and Stephen D. Ricks. Provo, Utah: FARMS, 1998.

JWW

Justice, demands of *See* Demands of justice.

Justice, law of Justice is one of the necessary attributes of God (Smith, 4:13–17). Without justice, "God would cease to be God" (Alma 42:13, 22–25) because he is a God of law, and justice and law are inseparable principles. In the execution of eternal law God is both impartial and consistent (Moro. 8:12; D&C 1:35; Alma 7:20).

Justice may be equated with cause and effect, the law of the harvest: "For whatsoever ye sow, that shall ye also reap" (D&C 6:33). Alma[2] called this "the plan of restoration" (Alma 41:2). It applies in both the physical and moral realms (Alma 41:2–6, 15).

Because of the Fall, if God were restricted to justice alone, no one could escape endless physical death and bondage to Satan (2 Ne. 9:6–9). Yet, God is also merciful. MERCY was introduced into the divine equation of salvation through the ATONEMENT of his Son Jesus Christ. In doing so, Jesus "satisfied the demands of justice," standing between the sinner and justice, taking the sinner's punishment upon himself (Mosiah 15:9). In this way mercy "overpowereth justice" (Alma 34:15; 42:15).

For Christ's sacrifice to be efficacious, however, justice demands that the sinner truly repent (2 Ne. 2:7; Alma 34:15–16) and accept by covenant the sacrifice made in his behalf (Mosiah 18:10; 3 Ne. 27:16–20): "For behold, justice exerciseth all his demands, and also mercy claimeth all which is her own; and thus, none but the truly penitent are saved. What, do ye suppose that mercy can rob justice? I say unto you, Nay; not one whit. If so, God would cease to be God" (Alma 42:24–25). Thus, the genius of the plan of salvation preserves God's justice while at the same time enabling him to temper it with mercy.

All mankind must return to God in a resurrected state for judgment (1 Ne. 15:33; Mosiah 16:10; Alma 42:23; Hel. 14:17–19). Those who have totally rejected Christ will stand naked before the justice of God (2 Ne. 9:14–17; Alma 11:40–41; 34:16). They, together with Satan and his fallen host, will be banished to hell, the second death (Alma 12:16–18; 40:26).

God rarely interferes in a pervasive way, such as the Flood, in man's misuse of moral agency lest He compromise that agency. But justice delayed will not be justice denied. It is as wrong for the innocent to be punished as it is for the guilty to go unpunished. Christ himself spoke of his Second Coming as "the day of vengeance which was in my heart" (D&C 133:51). In the end, justice will have the final word when the righteous are vindicated and the unregenerate wicked confront the wrath of God (2 Ne. 9:46). "For the Lord suffereth the righteous to be slain that his justice and judgment may come upon the wicked; therefore ye need not suppose that the righteous are lost because they are slain; but behold, they do enter into the rest of the Lord their God" (Alma 60:13; cf. 14:11).

All mankind will eventually be divided by justice and mercy. Those who have accepted Christ will stand at his right hand because of mercy. Those who have totally rejected Christ will stand at his left hand because of justice (Mosiah 5:8–10). All will acknowledge that "all his judgments are just; that he is just in all his works" (Alma 12:15).

See also Judgment, the; Justification; Law, answer the ends of; Restoration, plan of.

BIBLIOGRAPHY

Smith, Joseph. *Lectures on Faith.* Compiled by N. B. Lundwall. Salt Lake City: Deseret Book, 1985.

RT

Justification God's declaring an individual righteous, guiltless, and therefore worthy of salvation. Inasmuch as no one who is unclean, or unjustified, can be saved in the kingdom of God (1 Ne. 15:34; 3 Ne. 27:19), and inasmuch as all mankind fall short of keeping the laws of God, "by the law no flesh is justified; or, by the law men are cut off" (2 Ne. 2:5). There is no way for mankind to reclaim themselves from this unjustified state, but God can reclaim the repentant soul, imputing righteousness to him because of the ATONEMENT—"mercy can satisfy the demands of justice, and encircles them in the arms of safety" (Alma 34:16; cf. 2 Ne. 2:7; Mosiah 14:11; Alma 42:12–23). Thus God justifies righteous, covenant persons through the merits of the atonement of Jesus Christ (2 Ne. 2:7–11; Alma 34:9), while the wicked are not justified, standing condemned before the law (Alma 11:40–41; 34:16; 41:15; 42:22).

See also Justice, law of; Mercy; Merits of Christ; Sanctification.

RDD

Justified *See* Justification.

And it came to pass that those who were desirous that Pahoran should be dethroned from the judgment-seat were called **king-men**, for they were desirous that the law should be altered in a manner to overthrow the free government and to establish a king over the land.

ALMA 51:5

Kib *See* Jared[1], posterity of.

Kim *See* Jared[1], posterity of.

Kimnor Father of Akish, the Jaredite who initiated secret combinations to assassinate king Omer in exchange for permission to marry the daughter of Jared[2] (Ether 8:10).

King-men Nephite faction in the land of Zarahemla, comprising those who wanted to change the form of government from a chief judge to a king during the administration of Pahoran[1] (Alma 51:1–8; 67 B.C.). The king-men were a prideful stubborn people who professed to be of nobility (Alma 51:21). At first the king-men peacefully petitioned to alter the law in order to lawfully remove the chief judge Pahoran; however, Pahoran refused to alter the law, which resulted in a dispute among the king-men and other Nephites known as FREEMEN (Alma 51:3–6). The dispute was settled by the VOICE OF THE PEOPLE in favor of the freemen, and the king-men were compelled to maintain the cause of freedom (Alma 51:7). On at least two occasions over the next five years the king-men committed treason against their country. When Amalickiah and the Lamanites came to war against the Nephites, the king-men were "glad in their hearts" and refused to "take up arms to defend their country" (Alma 51:13). An angered captain Moroni successfully sought for authority from the government to "compel" the king-men "to defend their country or to put them to death" (Alma 51:14–16). Moroni's army killed 4,000 king-men, surviving leaders were imprisoned for later trials, and others made a commitment to defend their country: "Thus Moroni put an end to those king-men" (Alma 51:17–21).

The king-men resurfaced a few years later orchestrating a successful revolt driving Pahoran and the freemen out of Zarahemla. As was their original intent, they crowned a king, after which they sought a Lamanite alliance to strengthen their hold on Zarahemla (Alma 61:3–8). Again Moroni dealt forcefully with these DISSENTERS, joining with Pahoran, retaking Zarahemla, and then executing the king-men and their leader, "according to the law" (Alma 62:3–10; ca. 62 B.C.).

CKM

Kingdom of heaven *See* Heaven.

Kings Nephite, Lamanite, and Jaredite societies were all ruled by kings at various times. First appearing among the Nephites shortly after the division of Lehi[1]'s family into Lamanites and Nephites (2 Ne. 5:14, 18; cf. Jacob 1:9–11, 14–15), kings were an integral part of Nephite government until king Mosiah[2], with popular support, replaced them with judges in 91 B.C. (Mosiah 29). No mention is made of Lamanite kings until the book of Mosiah (Mosiah 7:15), after which they figure prominently in missionary accounts and recorded wars between the Nephites and Lamanites prior to large-scale Lamanite conversions to the gospel (Hel. 5). Along with a "king over all the land" (Alma 20:8), the Lamanites also had, at least for a time, a number of vassal kings and were occasionally ruled by kings of Nephite descent (e.g., Alma 47:35). Beginning with Jared[1]'s son Orihah (Ether 6:27), kings also ruled various factions of the Jaredites for centuries, until apostasy and civil war destroyed their civilization.

Kings came to power in a number of ways. Nephi[1] "anointed" his own successor (Jacob 1:9). Orihah, the first Jaredite king, was selected by the people and anointed king after all his brothers rejected the opportunity (Ether 6:22–27). For both peoples, the right to rule apparently passed from father to son (Mosiah 1:10; 29:1–9; Alma 24:3; Ether 7:3, 10). The same seems to have generally held for the Lamanites (Alma 24:3), although usurpers, especially among the Lamanites and Jaredites, were common (Alma 47:35; Ether 7:5, 15–17; 9:4).

The Book of Mormon recounts the reigns of both wicked and righteous kings. Wicked kings fought against the gospel and promoted iniquity (e.g., Mosiah 11:1–15), and waged unjust and devastating wars (Alma 48–62). Righteous kings among all three peoples promoted the gospel among their subjects and enacted laws against persecuting members of the Church and gospel teachers (Mosiah 25:19; 27:2; Alma 21:20, 22; 23:1–4; Ether 7:24–25). Righteous kings like

Benjamin were also influential teachers of the gospel (Mosiah 2–5). King Benjamin's son Mosiah[2] was identified as a prophet, seer, and revelator (Mosiah 8:14–16).

Nephite and Jaredite prophets generally spoke against the need for kings. When told that his people wanted to anoint a king before his death, the brother of Jared prophetically responded that such a move would lead the people into captivity (Ether 6:22–23). Conceding that "it would be well . . . to have a king" if just men could always be found for the position (Mosiah 23:8), Alma the Elder nevertheless taught that the inequality engendered through the institution of kingship was contrary to the Lord's commands (Mosiah 23:7), and that, given a wicked king's ability to lead his people astray (Mosiah 23:9, 12), free persons should "trust no man to be a king over" them (Mosiah 23:13). Mosiah[2] reiterated these ideas (Mosiah 29:13, 16–17, 35–36) and pointed out the difficulties attending the removal of an unrighteous king from the throne (Mosiah 29:21–23), and the fact that the iniquities of a people who were led by an unrighteous king were answered upon the head of the king (Mosiah 29:31). He also discussed "the trials and troubles" inflicted upon righteous kings by their subjects, and concluded that "these things ought not to be; but that the burden should come upon all the people, that every man might bear his part" (Mosiah 29:33–34). In spite of these pleas, various groups continued to agitate for a king after the establishment of the judges (Alma 2:2; 51:5; 61; 3 Ne. 7:9–10).

See also Anoint; Government, principles of; Judges, reign of.

AHH

Kish *See* Jared[1], posterity of.

Kishkumen A founder of secret combinations among the Nephites. Kishkumen murdered the chief judge Pahoran[2] in retaliation for the decision by "the voice of the people" to execute Pahoran's ambitious and rebellious brother Paanchi (Hel. 1:8–12). The robber Gadianton later assumed leadership of Kishkumen's secret band, and together they plotted to assassinate chief judge Helaman[3]. The plot was discovered by a servant of Helaman, and Kishkumen was killed in a failed attempt to carry it out (Hel. 2:3–9).

TBB

Kishkumen, city of One of the wicked cities burned in the destruction that accompanied the crucifixion of Jesus Christ. The inhabitants had cast out and stoned the prophets and Saints (3 Ne. 9:10–11).

Korihor An ANTI-CHRIST who preached "against the prophecies which had been spoken by the prophets, concerning the coming of Christ" (Alma 30:6; ca. 74 B.C.). Capitalizing on the right to exercise freedom of conscience under Nephite law (Alma 30:11), Korihor attacked the heart of Nephite religious tradition, calling the anticipation of Christ's coming "a foolish and a vain hope" (Alma 30:13). His teachings, which led to whoredoms and other wickedness among the Nephites, resulted in his arrest. Although variant beliefs were protected and tolerated, disobedience to the laws of the land, which were based on the commandments of God, was not (Alma 30:10, 18; Mosiah 27:2–4; 29:11, 25). Although he enjoyed some success in Zarahemla, Korihor's preaching was ended abruptly in the land of Jershon when the people of Ammon, stalwart Lamanite converts, promptly arrested him and expelled him from their borders at the command of their high priest. Korihor met a similar reception in Gideon, but he pridefully and stubbornly continued to orate his views before Gideon's high priest (Giddonah[2]) and chief judge. Rather than responding to his wranglings when observing Korihor's obstinacy, they sent him to Zarahemla to appear before Alma[2], the high priest of the church, and Nephihah, the chief judge over all the land (Alma 30:19–29). Korihor again persisted with his blasphemous charges against Nephite religious leaders, accusing them of PRIESTCRAFT—"leading away the people . . . for the sake of glutting on the labors of the people"; Alma's retort, "Thou knowest that we do not," disclosed Korihor's deliberate deceitfulness (Alma 30:31–32). In the dialogue that followed, Alma bore personal witness of

God's existence and the coming of Christ and challenged Korihor's own lack of evidence, "[his] word only." Alma ascribed Korihor's behavior to his being "possessed with a lying spirit," and being overpowered by the devil (Alma 30:39–42). Lacking a substantive argument, Korihor asked for a sign "that I may be convinced that there is a God." Alma responded, "Thou hast had signs enough," citing as evidence the testimony of "all these thy brethren, and also all the holy prophets . . . the scriptures . . . yea, and all things denote there is a God; yea, even the earth, and all things that are upon the face of it" (Alma 30:43–44). In the face of Korihor's stubbornness, Alma affirmed, "It is better that thy soul should be lost than that thou shouldst be the means of bringing many souls down to destruction" (Alma 30:45–47; cf. 1 Ne. 4:13). Alma's warning, "If thou shalt deny again, behold God shall smite thee, that thou shalt become dumb," seemed to give Korihor a moment's pause. "I do not deny the existence of a God," he said, then quickly added, "but I do not believe that there is a God" (Alma 30:47–48), perhaps a clever appeal to Nephite law that one could not be punished for his personal belief (Alma 30:11). Korihor asked again for a sign; Alma granted his request. "In the name of God," Alma pronounced, "ye shall be struck dumb" (Alma 30:49–50). Forced to acknowledge the power of God, but now being unable to speak, Korihor confessed in writing, "I always knew that there was a God," attributing his deception to SATAN, whom he claimed had appeared to him and taught him what to say, and to the success he had among the people, his teachings being "pleasing unto the carnal mind" (Alma 30:52–53; Matt. 12:39; 16:4). Korihor pleaded for a reversal of his predicament, but Alma prophetically revealed that if his speech were restored he would return to his former efforts to lead the people astray. Korihor's fate, Alma said, would be left up to the Lord. The once proud Korihor was "cast out." He became a beggar, and in the end, he was trampled to death by the Zoramites[2]. From Korihor's experience, Mormon drew a pointed moral: "Thus we see the end of him who perverteth the ways of the Lord." Furthermore, "at the last day," the devil will not stand by or support his followers, "but doth speedily drag them down to hell" (Alma 30:54–60).

The inclusion of the Korihor narrative fulfills an important Book of Mormon purpose: to expose the "enemies of Christ" (Benson, 3). Korihor's teachings echo many latter-day debates and challenges to religious faith on such matters as the existence and divinity of Christ (Alma 30:12, 39), whether religion frees or binds its followers (Alma 30:24), and whether there is religious truth that can be known apart from belief that is simply a product of social tradition (Alma 30:13–14, 39–40, 44). Korihor's arguments, inspired by Satan, pose challenging questions to believers in any age: Can one know the truth of something unseen? (Alma 30:15). Can one really know of future events? (Alma 30:13; cf. Jacob 7:7). Is guilt a tool to keep believers in bondage to commandments invented by designing priests? (Alma 30:23, 27–28). Is it the motive of religious leaders to get rich from offerings of naive followers? (Alma 30:27).

Korihor's teachings reflect philosophies that are anti-Christ and anti-gospel, and thus their inclusion in the text of the Book of Mormon constitutes a warning voice for readers. Korihor's arguments attempt to reduce religion to fanciful myths which bind followers so they "durst not enjoy their rights and privileges . . . [and] durst not make use of that which is their own" (Alma 30:27–28). Korihor intended to liberate his unsophisticated Christian audience from these myths by proclaiming that the people should "lift up their heads," "look up with boldness," and avoid being "brought down." In essence, he urged them to sin confidently, without fear (Alma 30:18, 27, 23). By contrast, true prophets teach the opposite—sin is sin, and all mankind stands accountable to God. If they do not repent, their sins "will stand as a testimony against [them] at the last day" (Alma 39:7–8; 2 Ne. 2:26–27; Alma 5:15–21; Hel. 13:26–29; 3 Ne. 27:13–21).

For Korihor, it was not rational to believe in something he could not see, or to believe in a being who was to come at some unknowable future time. Such beliefs he considered "the effect of a frenzied mind" (Alma 30:16). Characteristically, an individual like Korihor needs proof to create belief. His "seeing is believing" philosophy is the opposite of the "believing is seeing" formula Alma later taught the Zoramites (Alma 32:27–35). Korihor's reasoning that "no man can know of anything which is to come" (Alma 30:13) spawns a series of false assumptions that tumble like dominoes, spiraling downward to conclusions that eliminate Christ. If the future cannot be known, then prophets are pretenders, unable to prophesy truthfully that a Savior would come and atone for the sins of mankind. If "whatsoever a man did was no crime" (Alma 30:17), there is no such thing as sin, no need for Christ and an atonement, no need for guilt, nor repentance and forgiveness. If "when a man was dead, that was the end thereof" (Alma 30:18), there need be no fear of giving an account of oneself before the judgment bar of God. Such teachings can foster license for any and all manner of wickedness. What naturally follows is a "survival of the fittest" environment wherein "every man fared in this life according to the management of the creature . . . prospered according to his genius, and . . . conquered according to his strength" (Alma 30:17). Such a humanistic emphasis on one's own genius and strength is counter to the repeated Book of Mormon teaching which links prospering and conquering to reliance upon God (2 Ne. 4:34; 28:31; Alma 39:2; Morm. 3:8–16) through obedience to his commandments (1 Ne. 2:20; 17:13; 2 Ne. 1:20; Jarom 1:9; Omni 1:6; Alma 9:13–14).

The Book of Mormon provides guidelines for anyone who encounters anti-Christs. At times, rather then "reviling" with "revilers" (D&C 19:30), no response is appropriate (Alma 30:29). Personal testimony is essential for personal strength and fortification—Alma's witness of the truth through revelation from God was his first line of defense (Alma 30:39; cf. 5:45–47). In addition, believers can be nourished and strengthened through the witness of other believers (Moro. 6:4–6), the testimony and teachings of living prophets (2 Ne. 26:8; 3 Ne. 12:1), the written word of God in the scriptures (Alma 33:2; 3 Ne. 23:1–5), and the witness that comes from observing God's creations (Alma 30:44).

See also Book of Mormon, selected purposes of, to latter-day people, that we might learn to be more wise; Book of Mormon, selected purposes of, to reveal the enemies of Christ.

BIBLIOGRAPHY

Benson, Ezra Taft. *A Witness and a Warning*. Salt Lake City: Deseret Book, 1988.

DLL

Kumen *See* Disciples, twelve Nephite.

Kumenonhi *See* Disciples, twelve Nephite.

And now, my son, I have somewhat to say concerning the thing which our fathers call a ball, or director—or our fathers called it **Liahona**, which is, being interpreted, a compass; and the Lord prepared it. ALMA 37:38

Laban Laban (ca. 600 B.C.) was a prominent inhabitant of Jerusalem, a descendant of Joseph[1] (1 Ne. 5:16); a custodian of the PLATES OF BRASS (1 Ne. 3:3, 12); a military leader—a commander of fifty (1 Ne. 3:31); and master of a servant named Zoram[1] (1 Ne. 4:20, 35). He possessed a sword of "exceedingly fine" workmanship (1 Ne. 4:9), met at night in full armor with the "elders of the Jews" (1 Ne. 4:19, 22), and had charge of his own treasury (1 Ne. 4:20).

After Lehi[1] had led his family out of Jerusalem into the wilderness, the Lord commanded Lehi to send his sons back to Jerusalem to obtain the plates of brass (1 Ne. 3:2–4). Laban opposed Nephi[1] and his brothers Laman[1] and Lemuel when they tried to fulfill the Lord's command. In the first attempt, Laban became angry and had Laman thrown out of his house under the pretext that Laman was a robber (1 Ne. 3:11–13). In a second attempt, Laban "lust[ed] after" Lehi's property and sought to kill Nephi and his brothers to obtain their possessions (1 Ne. 3:22–26). In a third attempt, Nephi left his brothers hidden "without the walls" and set out alone at night towards Laban's house in Jerusalem. Being led by the Spirit, Nephi came upon Laban lying unconscious in the street "drunken with wine" (1 Ne. 4:5–7). Finally, Nephi obtained the plates of brass, but only after fulfilling the Lord's commandment to slay Laban (1 Ne. 4:5–38). Laban was killed with his own sword (1 Ne. 4:9, 18–19), and Nephi took this sword with him to the New World, where it was used as a model for making Nephite swords (2 Ne. 5:14) and was passed on throughout the succession of Book of Mormon record keepers (Mosiah 1:16). Laban's sword was eventually shown to the three witnesses of the golden plates (D&C 17:1).

See also Laban, slaying of; Sword of Laban.

BMH

Laban, slaying of When necessary "the Lord slayeth the wicked to bring forth his righteous purposes" under the guiding principle that "it is better that one man should perish than that a nation should dwindle and perish in unbelief" (1 Ne. 4:13; 17:32–35; D&C 98:28–32; Ex. 23:20–28). This was the principle when Nephi[1] slew Laban.

Lehi[1] had a dream wherein the Lord instructed him to send his sons back to Jerusalem to obtain the PLATES OF BRASS from Laban (1 Ne. 3:2–4). After two unsuccessful attempts to obtain them (1 Ne. 3:11–14, 22–27), Nephi and his brethren knew that Laban would continue to resist their efforts. Nephi, in a third attempt, left his brothers hidden "without the walls" and set out alone at night towards Laban's house in Jerusalem. He was "led by the Spirit, not knowing beforehand the things which [he] should do" (1 Ne. 4:5–6). Near Laban's house, Nephi found Laban lying unconscious,"drunken with wine" (1 Ne. 4:7). Nephi drew Laban's sword from the sheath and was "constrained by the Spirit" to kill him (1 Ne. 4:10). After an intense moral struggle, Nephi followed the Lord's command by taking "Laban by the hair of the head, and . . . [smiting] off his head with his own sword" (1 Ne. 4:11–18).

Responding to a question about how one might explain Nephi's slaying of Laban, Brother Jeffrey R. Holland mentioned seven points to reflect upon:

1. Consider how Nephi took such pains to preserve for future readers an action so difficult for him to perform, one which has been so widely misunderstood. Despite the limited space on the small plates which were to contain only things "pleasing unto God" and "of worth unto the children of men" Nephi chose to include the account of his slaying of Laban (1 Ne. 6:5, 6): "Maybe there's a clue in all of that" (Holland, 83).

2. It is clear from the story that Nephi did not wish to take the life of Laban. Nephi stated that he had never before "shed the blood of man," and he initially resisted the prompting of the Spirit: "And I shrunk and would that I might not slay him" (1 Ne. 4:10).

3. Other prophets have been commanded to take the lives of the disobedient. For example, Moses at Mount Sinai caused that 3,000 idolatrous Israelites be slain (Ex. 32:15–28), and David was revered for taking the life of Goliath (1 Sam. 17:51).

4. Laban was not "guiltless in his dealings

Nephi and Laban; *painting by Herman H. Haag; courtesy MCHA. "It is better that one man should perish than that a nation should dwindle and perish in unbelief"* (1 Ne. 4:13).

with Lehi[1]'s family" (Holland, 83). In the story it is clear that Laban (1) had not hearkened to the Lord's commandments (1 Ne. 4:11); (2) accused Laman[1] falsely of robbery (1 Ne. 3:13); (3) coveted the property of Lehi and his family (1 Ne. 3:25); (4) had stolen their property (1 Ne. 3:26–27); and (5) sought to kill Lehi's sons twice (1 Ne. 3:13, 25). The "Spirit" described Laban as a "wicked" man delivered into Nephi's hands by the Lord (1 Ne. 4:11–13).

5. In modern revelation the Lord revealed, "And him that repenteth not of his sins, and confesseth them not, ye shall . . . do with him as the scriptures saith unto you, *either by commandment or by revelation*. And this ye shall do that God may be glorified—not because ye forgive not, having not compassion, but that ye may be justified in the eyes of the law, *that ye may not offend him who is your lawgiver*" (D&C 64:12–13; italics added). Brother Holland asserted, "The judgment against Laban *is* being received 'by revelation,' and Nephi ultimately must slay Laban for the very reason which initially led him to shrink from it—so that he will not offend the divine 'lawgiver' (see D&C 98:23–32)" (83).

6. Application of laws may change according to the commands of God. Joseph Smith taught: "God said, 'Thou shalt not kill;' at another time He said, 'Thou shalt utterly destroy.' This is the principle on which the government of heaven is conducted—by revelation adapted to the circumstances in which the children of the kingdom are placed. Whatever God requires is right, no matter what it is, although we may not see the reason thereof till long after the events transpire" (256).

7. Nephi's obedience to revelation seems to be the central message in the slaying of Laban. The taking of a life is secondary in this instance: "God can restore life in time and eternity; he can do almost nothing with willful disobedience. The quality of our obedience to God's commandments is still the clearest expression of the quality of our faith in him" (Holland, 84).

Nephi's inclusion of this event also "underscores the monumental—yes, even life-and-death—importance of sacred scripture" (Holland, 84). So that ancient and modern descendants would not "dwindle and perish in unbelief" (1 Ne. 4:13), Nephi was determined to obtain the plates of brass "no matter what the cost to his own life or others" (Holland, 84).

BIBLIOGRAPHY

Holland, Jeffrey R. "How Can I Explain Nephi's Killing Laban to My Nonmember Friends? Some Really Reject It As Scriptural." *Ensign* 6 (September 1976): 83–84.

Smith, Joseph. *Teachings of the Prophet Joseph Smith*. Selected by Joseph Fielding Smith. Salt Lake City: Deseret Book, 1976.

BMH

Lachoneus[1] Nephite chief judge, governor, prophet (3 Ne. 1:1; 3:19; ca. A.D. 1), and contemporary of Nephi[3], the son of Nephi[2]. Lachoneus, described as a just and courageous man (3 Ne. 3:12), occupied the judgment-seat for twenty-nine or thirty years (3 Ne. 1:1; 6:17, 19). The period of his rule was punctuated by momentous events, both positive and negative. For example, Christian persecution (3 Ne. 1:5–9) was followed by fulfillment of the signs foretold by Samuel the Lamanite concerning the birth of Christ (3 Ne. 1:15–21), and peace and gospel conversions (3 Ne. 1:23, 26) were accompanied by major growth of the GADIANTON ROBBERS (3 Ne. 1:26–30; 2:11). Contentions led to war (3 Ne. 2–4), which cycled into a short period of righteousness and peace, which in turn was interrupted by an escalation of pride, dissension, and wickedness (3 Ne. 5–6).

Lachoneus' strength and wisdom were demonstrated by his response to the threats of Giddianhi, the leader of the Gadianton robbers, by his strategy to defeat the robbers, and by his appointment of Gidgiddoni, "a great prophet" (3 Ne. 3:19), as chief captain of the Nephite armies. Giddianhi wrote Lachoneus an epistle wherein he threatened destruction of the Nephites if they did not yield to his demands. He also offered a partnership in which the Gadiantons would share Nephite properties if the Nephites were willing to join them (3 Ne. 3:6–7). Although "astonished, because of the boldness of Giddianhi," Lachoneus "could not be frightened by the demands and the threatenings of a robber; therefore he did not hearken to the epistle of Giddianhi" (3 Ne. 3:11–12). The instructions Lachoneus gave his people to pray, to gather themselves and their belongings to the land of Zarahemla, to make fortifications and post guards, and to repent, saved them from their enemies (3 Ne. 3:13–16, 22–25; 4:33). Lachoneus, with a sacred oath, prophesied that deliverance from the robbers would be conditional upon prayers and repentance (3 Ne. 3:15). The inspired leadership of Lachoneus is attested to in this statement: "And so great and marvelous were the words and prophecies of Lachoneus that they did cause fear to come upon all the people; and they did exert themselves in their might to do according to the words of Lachoneus" (3 Ne. 3:16). Lachoneus is yet another example of a strong and righteous leader who saved his people from destruction in an era of instability and vacillation.

Lachoneus' son, whose name was also Lachoneus[2], assumed the judgment-seat after his father (3 Ne. 6:19; ca. A.D. 29–30).

DLL

Lachoneus[2] The last Nephite chief judge prior to the coming of Christ to America; son and successor of Lachoneus[1] (ca. A.D. 29–30). During his brief administration iniquity and pride were rampant. The people were in a "state of awful wickedness," brought on by their willful rebellion against God (3 Ne. 6:17–19). Inspired messengers sent to testify of their iniquity were put to death by Nephite judges without Lachoneus' knowledge. When these judges' deeds were discovered and they were arrested, a secret combination was formed to protect them, murder Lachoneus, and establish a king. The wicked conspirators successfully carried out their assassination of Lachoneus but failed to establish a king. Instead their act served as the catalyst which caused the collapse of the central government and the division of the people into TRIBES (3 Ne. 6:20–7:1).

Lake of fire and brimstone Figurative description of the final state of Satan, his devils, and those who become like them. The imagery comes from volcanism focusing on the intense heat of magma beds and sulfurous gases (BRIMSTONE) associated therewith. The awful yet poetic metaphor describes the condition of those who suffer the full and eternal wrath of a just God. By their deeds and disposition, they have kindled his hot displeasure and, as a result, he will consign them to this eternal state of mental torment. This, however, does not take place until after the Final Judgment (2 Ne. 28:23).

This imagery in the Book of Mormon does not refer to the HELL in the SPIRIT WORLD, which will eventually be emptied (2 Ne. 9:12; D&C 76:105–6), but to the final state of those whom the scriptures call the "filthy still" (2 Ne. 9:16; Morm. 9:14; D&C 88:35, 102). The primary inhabitants of the lake will be the devil and his angels. Nephi[1] testified that these "shall go away into everlasting fire, prepared for them; and their torment is *as* a lake of fire and brimstone, whose flame ascendeth up forever and ever and has no end" (2 Ne. 9:16; italics added). But they are not alone. All who suffer the second death are also filthy and they, too, are consigned to the same fate—"they shall be as though there had been no redemption made" (Alma 12:16–18). Because of the awful possibility, Jacob[2] warned his people to "loose yourselves from the pains of hell that ye may not become angels to the devil, to be cast into that lake of fire and brimstone which is the second death" (Jacob 3:11).

The pain which tortures these souls arises not from fire or brimstone but from a searing conscience as God assigns them "to an awful view of their own guilt and abominations, which doth cause them to shrink from the presence of the Lord into a state of misery and endless torment, from whence they can no more return" (Mosiah 3:25).

The tragedy of this suffering is that no mortal has to endure it. Through the Atonement, the Savior can save not only the repentant from this awful fate (2 Ne. 9:19), but also "those who have not the law given to them" (2 Ne. 9:26). Therefore, those who experience the eternal fire do so because they would rather suffer that torture than accept the willing hand of the Master.

While references in the New Testament imply a literal torment of the wicked with fire and brimstone (Rev. 14:10; 19:20; 20:10; 21:8), the Book of Mormon clarifies that this torment "is as a lake of fire and brimstone" (2 Ne. 9:16; Mosiah 3:27; Alma 12:17).

See also Endless torment, eternal torment, never-ending torment; Spiritual death.

RDD

Lamah Nephite military leader killed with his ten thousand troops in the last battle between the Nephites and Lamanites (Morm. 6:14; A.D. 385).

See also Cumorah, battle of.

Laman[1] Eldest son of Lehi[1] and Sariah; brother of Lemuel, Sam, Nephi[1], Jacob[2], Joseph[2], and unnamed sisters (2 Ne. 5:6); husband to one of the daughters of Ishmael[1] (1 Ne. 16:7); and progenitor of the Lamanite people and tradition.

From the beginning of the scriptural record Laman is described as stiffnecked and continually guilty of murmuring and inciting others to "stir up their hearts to anger" (1 Ne. 16:38; 2:11) against those in authority, principally Lehi and Nephi. Laman was resentful of his father for having led the family into the wilderness from their comfortable circumstances in the land of Jerusalem (1 Ne. 17:21). Bitterness towards Nephi was based upon his belief that his younger brother had wrongly sought "to make himself a king and a ruler" (1 Ne. 16:38) over his elder brothers (1 Ne. 16:37; 18:10; 2 Ne. 5:3; Mosiah 10:11–17; cf. 1 Ne. 2:22). Under ancient Israelite law Laman would have had the BIRTHRIGHT privilege and leadership associated with being the firstborn son, but he disqualified himself because of unrighteousness (1 Ne. 2:21–22). The issue of whose right it was to rule was a matter of serious contention throughout the Book of Mormon (Mosiah 10:11–17; Alma 54:17).

Many of the hardships experienced by Lehi and his family during their travels became further justification in Laman's mind for his animosity toward Lehi, Nephi, and even God. Nephi recorded that the underlying reason for the murmuring of Laman and his co-conspirator Lemuel was "because they knew not the dealings of that God who had created them" (1 Ne. 2:12). Lehi's prophetic vision of Laman and Lemuel's refusal to "partake of the fruit" of the tree of life (1 Ne. 8:18) taught of the hardness of their hearts and the blindness of their minds (e.g., 1 Ne. 7:8; 17:44–45). Lehi feared for Laman and Lemuel that "they should be cast off from the presence of the Lord" (1 Ne. 8:36).

Laman can be viewed as a prototype of the "natural man . . . an enemy to God," who ultimately failed to "[yield] to the enticings of the Holy Spirit" (Mosiah 3:19) and to the power of God manifested in various ways. Laman's body shook at the powerful preaching of his father Lehi in the valley of Lemuel (1 Ne. 2:14), he saw and was rebuked by an angel (1 Ne. 3:29), he witnessed the miraculous loosing of the cords with which he and others had bound Nephi (1 Ne. 7:18–18), he was "chastened by the voice of the Lord" (1 Ne. 16:39), he was wrought upon by the Spirit in consequence of Nephi's powerful preaching (1 Ne. 17:52), he was shaken by the Lord when Nephi "stretched forth" his hand (1 Ne. 17:53–54), he was humbled by the "exceedingly fine" quality of the ship he had not believed Nephi could build (1 Ne. 18:4; 17:17–19), and he witnessed the failure of the divine "compass" and the "great storm" and "terrible tempest" that arose after he and others tied Nephi up on the ship (1 Ne. 18:11–13). Laman also witnessed the reversal of these conditions when they let Nephi go (1 Ne. 18:15, 21). These multiple efforts by the Lord to save Laman and convince him of the truth affirms God's long-suffering, love, and mercy towards his children. Laman's life also illustrates that although God is merciful in his efforts to convince, persuade, and redeem, he is also just, and his Spirit "will not always strive with man" (2 Ne. 26:11; 1 Ne. 7:14; Morm. 5:16; Ether 2:15). While the scriptural account includes incidents of Laman's repentance (1 Ne. 3:29–31; 16:5; 18:20), the evidence suggests it was episodic, self-serving, and insincere. Being "swift to do iniquity but slow to remember the Lord," having rejected God's Spirit and power, Laman eventually became "past feeling" as pertaining to the things of God (1 Ne. 17:45).

Not long after Lehi's death the issue of leadership in the family resurfaced, and Laman and others sought again to kill Nephi (1 Ne. 5:2–3). The Lord commanded Nephi that he should "depart from them and flee into the wilderness" (2 Ne. 5:5).

Many of Laman's descendants became known as "Lamanites," consisting of "a compound of Laman and Lemuel, and the sons of Ishmael, and all those who had dissented from the Nephites, who were Amalekites and Zoramites, and the descendants of the priests of Noah" (Alma 43:13).

Although Laman "did not look unto the Lord as [he] ought" (1 Ne. 15:3) and initiated a wicked tradition, Lehi, acknowledging the power of tradition, promised Laman's descendants that "if ye are cursed, behold, I leave my blessing upon you, that the cursing may be taken from you and be answered upon the heads of your parents. Wherefore, because of my blessing the Lord God will not suffer that ye shall perish; wherefore, he will be merciful unto you and unto your seed forever" (2 Ne. 4:6–7, 9).

See also Lamanite civilization; Lamanites, Book of Mormon message concerning.

DKJ

Laman² Lamanite king who made a covenant that Zeniff could occupy the cities and lands of Lehi-Nephi and Shilom (Mosiah 7:21; 9:6; ca. 200 B.C.). Laman's ulterior motive was to bring Zeniff's people into bondage that the Lamanites might "glut themselves with the labors of [their] hands" (Mosiah 9:12). After twelve years Laman feared the settlers were growing too strong, and thus he began "to stir up his people" against them. Zeniff's people went forth to battle "in the strength of the Lord" and defeated Laman's forces (Mosiah 9:11–19). Peace ensued until Laman died and his son succeeded him to the throne (Mosiah 10:6).

Laman³ King of the Lamanites, son of Laman² (178 B.C.). When Laman became king following the death of his father, he waged an unsuccessful war against Zeniff's people (Mosiah 10:6). His armies were slaughtered by the people of Zeniff and driven out of the land (Mosiah 10:20).

Laman⁴ One of captain Moroni's men and a former servant of the Lamanite king who was slain by Amalickiah. Laman and a few others were appointed by Moroni to carry out a strategy designed to recapture the city of Gid from the Lamanites and free the Nephite prisoners held there. Because his Lamanite ancestry would win the trust of the Lamanite guards, Laman was chosen to carry wine to them. When the guards were drunken and asleep, Moroni, with "profound silence," "cast in weapons of war" to the Nephite prisoners within the city (Alma 55:16–17), and then surrounded the Lamanite army. The next morning, seeing their plight both within and without the city, the Lamanites surrendered and pleaded for mercy (Alma 55:4–24).

Laman, city of Wicked city burned in the catastrophic events that accompanied Christ's crucifixion in the Old World. The inhabitants who had martyred the prophets and Saints were destroyed to hide their wickedness (3 Ne. 9:10–11).

Laman, river A river emptying into the RED SEA. Lehi¹ camped nearby and named it after his son, urging Laman¹ to make his life resemble the river, "continually running into the fountain of all righteousness!" (1 Ne. 2:5–9).

Lamanite civilization Most of the Book of Mormon narrative centers on peoples identified as either Nephites or Lamanites. These groups can often be distinguished on genealogical grounds, as descendants of, respectively, either Nephi¹ or his brothers, Laman¹ and Lemuel. But close examination reveals a much more complex story (e.g., Jacob 1:13–14; Alma 43:13; 47:35; Morm. 1:8–9), and the general rule in the text is to "call them Lamanites that seek to destroy the people of Nephi," while "those who are friendly to Nephi" and the tradition he established were termed "Nephites, or the people of Nephi" (Jacob 1:14; cf. Alma 3:11). Some of the Lamanites, for example, were actually descendants of the sons of Ishmael (Alma 17:19, 21). Moreover, dissenting Nephites often adopted the title of Lamanite (Alma 43:4; 45:13–14; 54:24; Hel. 3:16; 11:24), and Lamanite converts to the gospel sometimes became Nephites (Alma 23:17; 27:27; 53:10; 3 Ne. 2:12, 14–16). Indeed, after the coming of Christ the distinction between Lamanites and Nephites temporarily disappeared (4 Ne. 1:17) and then reappeared as a matter of ideological choice (4 Ne. 1:20, 35–39; 4 Ne. 1:38 may suggest a continuing ethnic factor). But the conflict between the Nephites and the Lamanites had always been primarily ideological. Mormon reported that "whosoever should worship God in spirit and in truth, the true and the living God, the Lamanites would destroy" (Alma 43:10; cf. 44:2).

The conflict began with the founders of the Lamanite tradition, Lehi[1]'s two eldest sons, Laman[1] and Lemuel (1 Ne. heading; 1 Ne. 2:5, 12). Lehi and Nephi were deeply concerned about the spiritual state of these brothers (1 Ne. 2:18; 8:4, 36–37; 17:47; 2 Ne. 1:12–24). They were hard-hearted (1 Ne. 7:8; 17:19, 46; 18:10–20), and their wickedness made them incapable of understanding the things of God (1 Ne. 2:12; 15:7–11; 16:1–3; 2 Ne. 1:26)—including the direct ministration of an angel (1 Ne. 3:28–31)—because they were "past feeling" (1 Ne. 17:45). Light-minded, irreverent, and often cruel, they caused their family deep pain (1 Ne. 18:9–22; 2 Ne. 2:1). They regarded Lehi's prophecies as fanciful inventions and resented that in leaving Jerusalem they had been obliged to abandon their wealth (1 Ne. 2:11–12; 3:5). Like the people of Jerusalem, they thought the city indestructible, and they sought the life of their father (1 Ne. 2:13; 17:44). Indeed, they wanted to return to Jerusalem (1 Ne. 7:7, 15; 16:36), whose residents they considered a righteous people (1 Ne. 17:22). (Not surprisingly, a later Lamanite land and city would be called Jerusalem; Alma 21:1–2.) Often discontented during the journey to the New World, Laman and Lemuel did little to relieve their own unhappiness or to help in the family's assigned mission. Instead, their very murmuring revealed the extent of their dependence upon their father and, more especially, upon their younger brother Nephi (1 Ne. 16:18, 20, 22–24, 27, 31, 35–39; 17:7–22).

The Lord had promised Nephi early that if Laman and Lemuel persisted in rebellion, they would be cut off from the divine presence and Nephi would inherit the right to rule, which typically belonged to the eldest son (1 Ne. 2:21–24; cf. 7:8). Although Lehi confirmed Nephi as his heir (2 Ne. 1:25–29; 3:25) and subsequent events fulfilled the promise (2 Ne. 5:19–20; Alma 9:14), his elder brothers ever after complained that Nephi had usurped their legitimate rights (1 Ne. 16:37–38; 18:10; 2 Ne. 5:3).

When Lehi died, they refused to accept their brother's authority (2 Ne. 4:13–14). Their evaluation of Nephi had always been harsh. Whereas they ascribed Lehi's prophetic utterances to "the foolish imaginations of his heart" (1 Ne. 2:11), they attributed Nephi's obvious prophetic gifts to deliberate deception, and sought to kill him (1 Ne. 16:37–38; 17:20, 48; 2 Ne. 5:2–4). Eventually, he was forced to flee with his followers into the wilderness (2 Ne. 5:1–6).

Because of wickedness, the Lamanites were "cut off from the presence of the Lord" (2 Ne. 5:20–23), and the Lord "set a mark upon them . . . that their seed might be distinguished from the seed of their brethren [the Nephites], that thereby the Lord God might preserve his people, that they might not mix and believe in incorrect traditions which would prove their destruction" (Alma 3:7–8).

Violence soon erupted between the two groups (2 Ne. 5:14, 34; Jacob 7:24; Enos 1:14, 20; Alma 17:14). "Their hatred was fixed," reported the Nephite prophet Enos (Enos 1:20; cf. Alma 20:10, 13; 25:1–2; 26:9). Indeed, the Lamanites tended to dehumanize the Nephites, and, projecting their own hostility onto their enemies, they held exaggerated notions of what the Nephites could and would do to them (e.g., Alma 19:26; 20:13). Accordingly, the Lamanites could be remarkably cruel (e.g., Alma 56:12; 60:17; Hel. 1:27; Moro. 9:7–8; cf. Morm. 7:4). At the end of Book of Mormon history, they engaged in human sacrifice (Morm. 4:14, 21). But their hostility to the Nephites was not uniformly intense (Alma 20:30). Commonly, only dissenting Nephites could incite the Lamanites to go to war against their brethren (Alma 21:3; 24:1–2, 28–30; 27:2, 12; 43:6–8, 43–44; 46–51; 52:33; 60:32; 62:35; 63:14; Hel. 1:15; 4:2–4, 8; 11:24), and the dissenters, unlike ethnic Lamanites, virtually never converted to the gospel (Alma 23:13–14).

Nephi recorded that as a result of the curse

LAMANITE CIVILIZATION

placed upon the Lamanites they "did become an idle people, full of mischief and subtlety, and did seek in the wilderness for beasts of prey" (2 Ne. 5:24; cf. Alma 17:14–15; contrast 23:18; 24:18). Somewhat later, Enos reported that "they were led by their evil nature that they became wild, and ferocious, and a blood-thirsty people, full of idolatry and filthiness; feeding upon beasts of prey; dwelling in tents, and wandering about in the wilderness with a short skin girdle about their loins and their heads shaven; and their skill was in the bow, and in the cimeter, and the ax. And many of them did eat nothing save it was raw meat" (Enos 1:20; cf. Mosiah 10:8, 11–12; Alma 3:4–5; 43:20–21, 37).

"They loved murder and would drink the blood of beasts," says Jarom 1:6, referring to a practice condemned in the law of Moses. Even as late as the century before Christ, Nephite sources describe the Lamanites as "a lazy and an idolatrous people" (Mosiah 9:12; Alma 17:14).

Ideological "Lamanitism" remembered little of Hebrew-Nephite religious tradition (Mosiah 10:11; 24:5; Alma 17:16, 35). For example, at the time of Alma[2], the Lamanite kings apparently did not understand the Nephite term "God," although they knew of a "Great Spirit." And, although Lamoni knew this "Great Spirit" had created the earth, he was unsure concerning the heavens (Alma 18:2–5, 11, 18–32; 19:25, 27; 22:7, 9–11, 18; 54:21). Some Lamanites thought it possible—in perhaps a distorted echo of Lehi's messianic teachings—that this Great Spirit could come down among them as a man (Alma 18:4) or send a human representative to them (Alma 19:25, 27). King Lamoni and his father's belief in a Great Spirit seems to have had little impact upon their behavior (Alma 18:5). When the Nephite missionaries came among these kings and their people, they taught them the gospel and convinced many of them of their sins (Alma 24:9–13, 15, 25; 27:6, 8). As the Nephite missionaries ministered to the Lamanites, they taught them about "the records and the holy scriptures of the people" since Adam, as well as the basic doctrines of the Creation, Fall, and redemption of mankind (Alma 18:36, 39; 22:12–13; 19:31, 33).

Lamanite ideology included important political and historical elements. Lamanites believed that Lehi had been driven from Jerusalem because of his sins, and that Nephi had repeatedly wronged their ancestors in the wilderness, while crossing the sea, in the land of their first inheritance, and, most particularly, in seeking to rule over them and, as they saw it, in robbing them of their patrimony. Lamanite children were accordingly taught to hate, injure, and where possible, kill Nephites (Mosiah 10:12–17; Alma 54:17–18, 20, 23–24; 55:1). Thus, Lamanites seized any Nephite who came into their territory (Alma 17:20), and their hostility toward the Nephites was so severe that it could even override kinship and political loyalties (e.g., Alma 20:15–16; 24:2). By contrast, Nephites who hoped to reclaim the fallen Lamanites first had to convince them of the wickedness of their fathers (Mosiah 28:2; Alma 9:17; 17:9; 18:37–38; 21:17; 23:3; 24:7; 25:6; 26:24; 37:9; Hel. 5:19, 51), whom the prophets held responsible for their spiritual state (2 Ne. 4:3–9; Jacob 3:7–9; Mosiah 1:5; Alma 9:15–17, 23; 17:15; 19:14; 60:32; Hel. 7:23–24; 15:4, 14–15), and to persuade them to accept the Nephite account of their history (Alma 18:41; 23:5; Morm. 7:5, 9–10). The Lamanites therefore sought to destroy the records containing that history (Enos 1:14; Morm. 6:6). Without records themselves, they evidently lost the ability to understand "the language of Nephi," and lapsed into widespread illiteracy (Mosiah 24:1–7). At the end of the Book of Mormon narrative, the Lamanites sought to physically exterminate the Nephites—although the ideological nature of the conflict appears again, in the fact that they would spare any Nephite who renounced the gospel of Christ (Morm. 8:2, 7; Moro. 1:1–2).

Not everything Lamanite was evil, as several Nephite accounts concede (e.g., Mosiah 9:1; Alma 19:10). Although the Nephites tended to view the Lamanites as "cunning" and crafty (Mosiah 10:18; 24:7) and not to be trusted (Mosiah 23:36–37), several stories illustrate their scrupulous, if rather legalistic, keeping of oaths (Mosiah 19:25; 20:15, 24; 21:3; cf. Alma 44:8; 53:16). Indeed, it is clear from Nephite behavior, even in times of warfare, that the Nephites expected them to keep their oaths (see Alma 44:15, 20; 62:16–17; 3 Ne. 6:3), an expectation probably rooted in experience. Despite their fierce reputation, some Lamanites were compassionate (Mosiah 19:13–14; 20:26; 21:15; 23:28–29, 33–34; Alma 24:23–25). They generally treated women well (Jacob 2:34–35; 3:3, 5–9; Mosiah 19:13–14; 20:1, 6, 15; 23:33–34; cf. Alma 19:12–13). Among Book of Mormon peoples, only the Lamanites are identified as having "queens," and it is clear that those queens had real authority (Alma 19:2–18, 29–30; 22:19–21, 24; 47:32–35), yet there were arranged royal marriages (Alma 17:24). They are said to have been "friendly one with another" and to have limited their bloodthirstiness and thievery to those beyond their kinship group (Mosiah 24:5, 7). Naturally, there were some exceptions (Alma 17:35; 18:7; Morm. 8:8; Moro. 1:2). When converted, they were extraordinarily faithful (Alma 23:6; 24:6, 18; 27:27; Hel. 15:7, 9). For a substantial period of Nephite history, the Lamanites exceeded the Nephites in righteousness (Hel. 5:50; 6:1–5, 34, 36–37; 13–15).

At least by the period just preceding the coming of Christ, the Lamanites had developed a sedentary lifestyle resembling that of the Nephites, although some, predominantly in the west, continued to be "idle" and to live a presumably nomadic life in tents (Alma 22:28). They had sepulchers (Alma 19:1, 5), prisons (Alma 20:2–5, 7, 22, 27–30; 22:2; 26:29), synagogues, temples, sanctuaries, and religious assemblies (Alma 21:16; 23:2, 4; 26:29). They may have had their own system of time-keeping (Alma 18:14) and traditional mourning practices (Alma 18:43). By the second century before Christ, they had created a system in which subordinate kings reigned under an overall Lamanite monarch (Mosiah 9:5; 24:2; Alma 18:9; 20:1, 4, 7–8, 14, 24, 26; 21:21–22; 22:1). These kings had servants over whom they exercised power of life and death (Alma 17:25–28; 18:6–12, 43; 19:20; 20:6; 22:3, 19–23), as well as palaces (Alma 22:2) and court protocol (Alma 47:22–23).

See also Jaredite civilization; Lamanites, Book of Mormon message concerning; Nephite civilization.

DCP

Lamanites *See* Lamanite civilization.

Lamanites, Book of Mormon message concerning The Book of Mormon was "written to the Lamanites, who are a remnant of the house of Israel; and also to Jew and Gentile" (Title Page). The central message to the Lamanites is that they would not perish as a people, they would be restored in the latter days to a knowledge of their Israelite heritage, and the covenants God made with their fathers, they would come unto Christ, rejoice, and become a blessed people.

The original Lamanites were the wicked sons of Lehi[1]—Laman[1] and Lemuel—and their posterity who broke away from the people of Nephi[1], or the Nephites (2 Ne. 5:1–14). They were "cut off from the presence of the Lord" because they did not keep God's commandments (2 Ne. 5:20–24; Jacob 3:3–5). Yet, a generation after the Lamanites and Nephites had separated, Jacob[2] proclaimed that the Lamanites were a "more righteous" people than the backsliding Nephites and that Lamanite "filthiness came because of their fathers" (Jacob 3:5, 7–9). Alma[2] delivered a similar message to wicked Nephites: "There are many promises which are extended to the Lamanites; for it is because of the traditions of their fathers that caused them to remain in their state of ignorance; therefore the Lord will be merciful unto them and prolong their existence in the land" (Alma 9:16; ca. 82 B.C.). Alma prophesied that "at some period of time [the Lamanites] will be brought to believe in his [Christ's] word, and to know of the incorrectness of the traditions of their fathers" (Alma 9:17). This prophecy was partially fulfilled through the efforts of the sons of Mosiah[2] (Alma 26:3–9, 24, 31–34; between 90 and 77 B.C.) and later through the preaching of Nephi[2] and Lehi[4] (Hel. 5:39–52; 6:1; ca. 30 B.C.). Samuel the Lamanite added, "Behold my brethren, the Lamanites hath [the Lord] hated because their deeds have been evil continually, and this because of the iniquity of the tradition of their fathers. But behold, salvation hath come unto them through the preaching of the Nephites; and for this intent hath the Lord prolonged their days" (Hel. 15:4; cf. 15:10).

The ultimate fulfillment of Book of Mormon prophecies and promises to the Lamanites, however, were to occur in the latter days. Present-day Lamanites, to whom the promises pertain, are not necessarily descendants of Laman, but actually are a mixture of Book of Mormon peoples—the "children of Lehi." In 4 Nephi the term "Lamanites" seems to be more a theological-political designation than a blood relationship (4 Ne. 1:20, 36–39).

In a blessing he gave to his grandchildren, the sons and daughters of Laman[1], Lehi[1] promised that "the Lord God will not suffer that ye shall perish; wherefore, he will be merciful unto you and unto your seed forever" (2 Ne. 4:7; cf. 4:8–9). Jacob[2] likewise prophesied that "the Lord God will not destroy [the Lamanites], but will be merciful unto them; and one day they shall become a blessed people" (Jacob 3:6). Samuel the Lamanite declared that even though the Lamanites would be scattered and smitten, "having no place for refuge, the Lord shall be merciful unto them" (Hel. 15:12). The Doctrine and Covenants adds that the Lamanites "shall blossom as the rose" (D&C 49:24; cf. Isa. 27:6; 35:1).

This blossoming would occur both temporally and spiritually. For example, temporally, the Lamanites are promised that they will be preserved upon the earth (2 Ne. 9:53; Hel. 15:16). Spiritually, "the gospel of Jesus Christ shall be declared among them; wherefore, they shall be restored unto the knowledge of their fathers, and also to the knowledge of Jesus Christ, which was had among their fathers. And then shall they rejoice . . . and their scales of darkness shall begin to fall from their eyes . . . [and] they shall be a pure and a delightsome people" (2 Ne. 30:5–6). Samuel the Lamanite prophesied, "[The Lamanites] shall again be brought to the true knowledge . . . of their Redeemer, and their great and true shepherd, and be numbered among his sheep" (Hel. 15:13; cf. 1 Ne. 15:12–16). This spiritual restoration of the Lamanite people was to come in the latter days through the Gentiles. Nephi[1] prophesied that the "Lord God will proceed to do a marvelous work among the Gentiles [the restoration of the gospel of Jesus Christ through

President George Albert Smith reading from the Book of Mormon with two Native Americans; courtesy LDS Family and Church History Archives.

the Prophet Joseph Smith], which shall be of great worth unto our seed [descendants of Lehi]." Further, Nephi applied a prophecy of Isaiah, likening the benefits of this "marvelous work," to the Gentiles nourishing his posterity and carrying them "in their arms and upon their shoulders" (1 Ne. 22:8; cf. 21:22–23). In addition to partaking of gospel blessings, the Lamanites will share in the gospel work. Christ taught that this "remnant of Jacob" would be included among those who will "build a city, which shall be called the New Jerusalem" (3 Ne. 21:22–23).

The Nephite prophets knew that their writings would be instrumental in a future day in assisting the Lamanites to come back to the gospel of Jesus Christ (2 Ne. 25:21; 3:5–6, 23; 26:14–16; Enos 1:13–18; W of M 1:6–8; D&C 3:16–20). Moroni[2] dedicated his own book of Moroni to "my brethren, the Lamanites" that they "in some future day" will find the record to be of worth to them (Moro. 1:4). Mormon's closing message was dedicated to the Lamanites—"the remnant of this people who are spared" (Morm. 7:1). Above all he wanted them to know that they were of the house of Israel. He called them to repentance, to lay down their weapons of war and to delight no longer in bloodshed, to believe in Christ, especially in his victory over the grave, and to lay hold of the gospel of Jesus Christ which "shall be set before you," in both the Book of Mormon and the Holy Bible (Morm. 7:2–8). He assured them, "Ye are numbered among the people of the first covenant; and if it so be that ye believe in Christ, and are baptized, first with water, then with fire and with the Holy Ghost, following the example of our Savior, according to that which he hath commanded us, it shall be well with you in the day of judgment" (Morm. 7:10).

See also Lamanite civilization.

BAV

Lamanites, twenty-four daughters of Twenty-four young Lamanite women who were kidnapped by a group of renegade Nephite priests who afterwards forced them to become their wives (Mosiah 20:1–5; 23:33–34). The illegal capture of these twenty-four Lamanite daughters led to the breaking of a covenant between two peoples and later to an extended manhunt for the abductors (Mosiah 19:15–20:16).

There must have been witnesses to the abduction because the Lamanite king knew how they had disappeared (Mosiah 20:15). Even so, the priests escaped; they were found years later by a Lamanite army lost in the wilderness (Mosiah 23:30–31). These women, along with their husbands and children, were subsequently integrated into Lamanite society (Mosiah 23:34–24:6; Alma 21:2). Family members suffered horribly in a rebellion (Alma 24:1–2; 25:1–9) and in military conflicts with Nephite armies (Alma 25:3–4; 43:13).

The closest parallel in other scripture appears in the forced marriages of women of Shiloh to men of the tribe of Benjamin, as recorded in Judges 21 (Goff, 67–74). In addition, the account of the abducted Lamanite daughters brims with legal and social dimensions that offer glimpses inside Nephite and Lamanite societies between 150 and 121 B.C. (Brown, 99–112).

BIBLIOGRAPHY

Brown, S. Kent. *From Jerusalem to Zarahemla.* Provo, Utah: Religious Studies Center, Brigham Young University, 1998.

Goff, Alan. "The Stealing of the Daughters of the Lamanites." *Rediscovering the Book of Mormon.* Edited by John L. Sorenson and Melvin J. Thorne. Salt Lake City: Deseret Book, 1991.

SKB

Lamoni Lamanite king over the land of Ishmael, a descendant of Ishmael (Alma 17:21), and the first Lamanite convert of Ammon[2]. Although an enemy of the Nephites and a king of an apostate people, Lamoni was still a man of reason and conscience. He eventually became a man of great faith and an example of the joy and dedication that accompanies spiritual rebirth, as well as a tremendous tool in the hand of the Lord that led to thousands of Lamanites coming to a knowledge of the truth (Alma 17–21).

When the Nephite missionary Ammon was first captured and brought before Lamoni, rather than having him slain, imprisoned, or thrown out of the land, Lamoni listened to the young man and was moved by his sincere desire to "dwell among" the Lamanites (Alma 17:20–23). He was so impressed that he offered Ammon his daughter to wife, but Ammon chose rather to be a servant to the king (Alma 17:24–25). His first assignment was to join other servants in watching over the king's flocks, a task which had brought punishment by death to former servants because they failed to fend off Lamanite marauders who had scattered the flocks (Alma 17:25, 28; 18:5–6). After Ammon demonstrated his faithfulness and the power of God by protecting the king's flocks (Alma 17:26–18:7), fulfilling the king's commandments (Alma 18:8–10), and discerning the king's thoughts (Alma 18:12–18), Lamoni was anxious and willing to be taught by Ammon, even wondering if the Nephite was the Great Spirit (Alma 18:18–23). As Ammon taught Lamoni about the creation of the world, Adam, the Fall, the plan of redemption, and the coming of Christ, the humbled king believed all the missionary's words and pleaded with the Lord to have mercy upon him and his people (Alma 18:24–41). Subsequently he came "under the power of God" (Alma 19:6) and sank to the earth "as if he were dead" (Alma 18:42). He remained in that state for two days and two nights while "the dark veil of unbelief was being cast away from his mind" and the light of God "infused . . . joy into his soul" (Alma 19:6). When he finally arose he blessed God, declared that he had seen his Redeemer, and bore testimony that Christ would "redeem all mankind" (Alma 19:12–13). So powerful was his witness that he was once again overcome with joy and "sunk down" to the earth along with his wife, his servants, and Ammon (Alma 19:13–16). Afterwards, at the invitation of a woman named Abish, the Lamanites gathered to observe and wonder concerning those who were lying "prostrate upon the earth" (Alma 19:16–28). Eventually Lamoni, his servants, and the queen all arose. The queen bore witness of Jesus and the king taught the people the words of Ammon, as did his servants who testified that "their hearts had been changed; that they had no more desire to do evil" (Alma 19:29–33). As this group of converts taught of the "things of God, and of his righteousness" many of the Lamanites "did believe in their words," were baptized, and they established a church among them (Alma 19:34–36). Thus king Lamoni's willingness to listen, and his ability to recognize truth led to the conversion of many of his people.

Later Lamoni and Ammon set out for Middoni to free Ammon's brothers who were imprisoned there (Alma 20:1–8). As they journeyed they met the father of Lamoni, who was furious that his son had missed an important feast and was traveling with a Nephite (Alma 20:8–13). In his rage, Lamoni's father, who was the supreme king over all the land, commanded Lamoni to slay Ammon, but true to his faith and loyal to his friend, Lamoni refused (Alma 20:14–15). The old king then sought to slay Lamoni for what he perceived as insolence on the part of his son, but Ammon defended Lamoni with the sword (Alma 20:16–25). When Lamoni's father recognized the bond of love between his son and Ammon, he was "astonished exceedingly" and not only granted Ammon's request that Lamoni be allowed to retain his kingdom and that his brethren in Middoni be set free, but also desired that Ammon and his brethren would come to teach him (Alma 20:26–28). Later, in an experience very much like his son's, Lamoni's father was converted and worked to convert his people (Alma 22–23).

After returning to Ishmael from Middoni, Lamoni built synagogues, taught his people the gospel, and granted them religious liberty (Alma 21:18–23). Later, Lamoni held council with Ammon and his brethren to determine how to defend the Lamanite converts, the ANTI-NEPHI-LEHIES, from their unconverted brethren who were determined to slay them (Alma 24:1–5). As a further manifestation of the depth of their conversion, Lamoni and his people refused to take up arms, for they all feared that if they did so they could not again find forgiveness from God for the murders they had previously committed (Alma 24:6–17).

JRC

Lamoni, father of Unnamed in the Book of Mormon but a man of great political power—king over all the Lamanites (ca. 90–77 B.C.)—who had a tremendous impact on the spiritual history of the Lamanite nation. His conversion illustrates how teaching the word can touch individuals and thereby change the hearts of entire societies. The king's story was told in two parts. In the first, he was influenced by the missionary Ammon[2], one of the sons of Mosiah[2]. In the second, he was taught by Ammon's brother Aaron[3] and converted to Jesus Christ. The king's coincidental encounter with Ammon began on a threatening note. Traveling to Middoni to effect the release of other Nephite missionaries from prison, Ammon was with the king's son, a lesser king named Lamoni who was already converted. While journeying Lamoni and Ammon met Lamoni's father, who was angered because his son had failed to attend an important feast and because he was in company with a Nephite, whom the king regarded as a child "of a liar" (Alma 20:6–13). Lamoni refused to kill Ammon when his father, the king, commanded it. Furious, the king drew his sword to slay his son, but Ammon stopped the contention by reasoning with the king that his son was an "innocent man" (Alma 20:18). The king then turned to slay

Ammon but was soon bested. Fearing for his life, he promised whatever Ammon required, even half his kingdom. Ammon asked only that his brethren be released and that Lamoni be allowed to retain his kingdom, to be restored to his father's good graces, and to "do according to his own desires in whatsoever thing he thinketh" (Alma 20:24). Astonished, the king granted what Ammon asked (Alma 20:14–27).

The second part of the king's story is told in Alma 22, when, after his release from prison in Middoni, Aaron was "led by the Spirit to the land of Nephi, even to the house of the king," who "was the father of Lamoni" (Alma 22:1). The king had been "troubled in mind" over Ammon's "generosity" and words, and he was ready to be taught (Alma 22:3). The ensuing dialogue between Aaron and the king contributes to major Book of Mormon purposes. Readers are presented with yet another model of what is required to "come unto Christ," and how one can know God. Aaron taught the king, reading from scriptures, about the Creation, the Fall, and the plan of redemption through Jesus Christ (Alma 22:12–14). Then, in response to the king's questions concerning what to do to receive eternal life and what to do to be born of God, Aaron taught that if the king would repent and pray in faith, he would be granted his desires. It is significant that earlier the king had offered half his kingdom in exchange for his physical life, but now he would gladly sacrifice all he possessed to save his spiritual life (Alma 22:15–16; cf. Matt. 13:44–46). Following a humble prayer to God promising to "give away all my sins to know thee," the king was blessed with a dramatic spiritual experience parallel to the conversion of his son Lamoni (Alma 22:17–18; cf. 18:41–43).

The king then ministered to his household, and they were all converted (Alma 22:23). He sent a proclamation throughout the land granting the Nephite missionaries freedom to preach anywhere (Alma 22:27; 23:1–4). As a result, "thousands were brought to the knowledge of the Lord" (Alma 23:5) and were greatly blessed. They laid down their weapons of war and refused to take them up again (Alma 24:6, 17). Lamoni's father died in the same year that the unconverted Lamanites took up arms against their converted brethren (Alma 24:2–4). True to their vows, the converted Lamanites chose to suffer death rather than to defend themselves (Alma 24:21–23). The unwavering faith of these ANTI-NEPHI-LEHIES and the valor of their faithful sons (the STRIPLING WARRIORS) can be traced to the conversion of Lamoni's father.

WJM

Language *See* Book of Mormon, language of the translated text of.

Large plates of Nephi *See* Plates of Nephi.

Lasciviousness *See* Appendix C.

Last days, latter days Phrase used in the prophetic discourses of Lehi[1] (2 Ne. 3), and especially Nephi[1] (1 Ne. 15; 2 Ne. 25; 26; 27), to describe that future period of earth's history when the Lord would restore the fulness of the gospel to the Gentiles, and they, in turn, would take it to the remnant of Lehi's posterity (1 Ne. 15:13). As a period of tremendous restoration, the last or latter days would be a time when the Book of Mormon would "grow together" with the Bible to confound false doctrine (2 Ne. 3:5, 12; cf. 26:14–17), Israel would be gathered (1 Ne. 15:19–20), and a remnant of the seed of Joseph[1] would once again be brought to a knowledge of the Lord and his covenant with them (3 Ne. 5:23–25).

Nephi called the last days "the days of the Gentiles," a time when all nations (Jews and Gentiles) would be drunken with iniquity (2 Ne. 27:1). He prophesied that the Lord would raise up a mighty nation among the Gentiles where the gospel would be restored (1 Ne. 22:7–9; 3 Ne. 21:1–4). Further, in the last days the prophecies of Isaiah would "be of great worth unto [the Gentiles] . . . for in that day shall they understand them" (2 Ne. 25:7–8).

Nephi taught that the last days would commence "many generations after the Messiah shall be manifested in body unto the children of men" (1 Ne. 15:13). He declared that during this period the promises made to Abraham anciently would be fulfilled as all the families of the earth were blessed through Abraham's posterity (1 Ne.

15:18). Nephi also reiterated Isaiah's prophecy that a temple would be established in the tops of the mountains during the last days in preparation for a great period of peace (2 Ne. 12:2–4).

Elder Bruce R. McConkie wrote that the last days constitute "that period of time just preceding the millennium . . . the specified time, period, or age in which the necessary prerequisites to the Second Coming will occur. The last days are the days of the dispensation of the fulness of times, the days when the signs of the Second Coming are shown forth, the days of 'restitution of all things, which God hath spoken by the mouth of all his holy prophets since the world began' (Acts 3:21)" (431).

BIBLIOGRAPHY

McConkie, Bruce R. *Mormon Doctrine*. 2d ed. Salt Lake City: Bookcraft, 1966.

ACS

Last records An angel explained to Nephi[1] that "these last records . . . shall establish the truth of the first" (1 Ne. 13:40). These last records include the Book of Mormon, the Doctrine and Covenants, the Pearl of Great Price, and the Joseph Smith Translation of the Bible—the scriptures of the Restoration (Maxwell, 1). These last records would establish the essential truthfulness of the first, the Bible.

BIBLIOGRAPHY

Maxwell, Neal A. *Plain and Precious Things*. Salt Lake City: Deseret Book, 1983.

SAJ

Last shall be first, and the first shall be last Phrase indicating the order and timing in which the gospel was and will be preached to the JEWS (Israel) and the GENTILES (1 Ne. 13:42; cf. Jacob 5:62–64). At the Lord's first coming, he ministered strictly to the Jews, commanding his apostles to do the same (Matt. 10:5–6; 15:24). Thus these Israelites received the gospel first. Only after his rejection by the Jews did he send his apostles out to the world—consequently the Gentiles received the gospel last, or after the Jews (see Acts 10). The Restoration began where the New Testament work ended, bringing the gospel to the Gentiles. Accordingly, the last to hear the gospel in the days of Jesus and the apostles became the first to hear it in the latter days. But, "when the Gentiles shall sin against my gospel," Jesus taught, "I will bring the fulness of my gospel from among them. And then will I remember my covenant which I have made unto my people, O house of Israel, and I will bring my gospel unto them" (3 Ne. 16:10–11). Thus, those who first received the gospel in Jesus' day, shall in the latter days receive it last, or after the Gentiles.

Moroni[2] envisioned one aspect of the fulfillment of these words in the establishment of two holy cities. The Old Jerusalem in the Holy Land, which was first built up anciently, will be established last or after the building of the NEW JERUSALEM (Ether 13:9–12; cf. 3 Ne. 21:22–23). From these two millennial cities shall blessings flow, "for out of Zion shall go forth the law, and the word of the Lord from Jerusalem" (2 Ne. 12:3).

RDD

Law, answer the ends of The principle that the demands of the law must be appeased or satisfied (2 Ne. 2:7; cf. Alma 34:16; 42:15). In consequence of the Fall, both a spiritual and temporal death were imposed upon mankind. These deaths were overcome through the ATONEMENT of Christ (Alma 42:23; Hel. 14:17), leaving mankind accountable for their own sins. Inasmuch as no one keeps the whole law perfectly, "no flesh is justified" or innocent before God, and "men are cut off" (2 Ne. 2:5). Lehi[1] taught that through the merciful and expiatory sacrifice of Christ, the demands of the law were answered for all who have faith in Christ (Moro. 7:28) and who repent (2 Ne. 2:7). For the unrepentant, justice "executeth the law, and the law inflicteth the punishment" (Alma 42:22).

See also Appease; Demands of justice; Justice, law of; Mercy; Satisfy.

RCF

Law, civil A discussion of Nephite law emerges from the outlines of Nephite political history. Soon after their separation from the Lamanites, the Nephites established Nephi[1] as their first king (2 Ne. 5:17–19; cf. Jacob 1:9–15). During this time, the Nephites "did observe to keep the judgments, and the statutes, and the commandments of the Lord in all things, according to the law of Moses" (2 Ne. 5:10). King Benjamin reaffirmed this practice when he united his people by a "covenant with . . . God to do his will, and to be obedient to his commandments in all things" (Mosiah 5:5).

Before his death, Nephi anointed a successor (Jacob 1:9–12) and a series of KINGS ruled the NEPHITE CIVILIZATION for approximately four hundred fifty years. Mosiah[2] was the last of the Nephite kings (Mosiah 29:46–47), and before his death he established laws that "were acknowledged by the people" (Alma 1:1) and legal administration based on judges. Thus began a new legal system referred to as the "reign of the judges." So momentous was the change that the Nephites began to reckon time according to this event.

The record of the reign of the judges is rich with information concerning the Nephite system of laws and legal procedure. Although there is no formal statement of particulars concerning any Nephite code, several legal proceedings reveal some specifics of the Nephite legal system. Some of these legal proceedings involve anti-Christs or political dissenters: Nehor (Alma 1:2–15), Korihor (Alma 30), Paanchi (Hel. 1:7–8). Nephi[2], Seantum, and five others were tried for the murder of Seantum's brother (Hel. 9: 1–38). The Book of Mormon also records legal proceedings that involve accusations against Nephite prophets: Abinadi (Mosiah 17:5–20), Alma[2] and Amulek (Alma 14), and Nephi[2] (Hel. 8). In the earlier era, Jacob[2] prevailed in a contest involving legal and religious accusations brought against him by Sherem (Jacob 7:1–23).

The LAW OF MOSES was observed by the Nephites until the coming of Jesus Christ (2 Ne. 25:24; 3 Ne. 1:24–25) and greatly influenced the Nephite system of laws and penalties. For example, Abinadi was put to death for allegedly "reviling" against king Noah[3] (Mosiah 17:11–12); such a cause of action is grounded in the Mosaic code (Ex. 22:28). The Nephite concept of "freedom of belief" was apparently based on Joshua's ancient injunction to "choose ye this day, whom ye will serve" (Alma 30:7–8; Josh. 24:15). This concept was tested during the trial of Korihor. Under the reforms of Mosiah, "there was no law against a man's belief" and no law to punish those that did not believe in God (Alma 30:11). As a result, Nephite law had no claim on Korihor when he preached against Christ, but only when he became blasphemous and reviled against God and the priests and teachers (Alma 30:29–31). The trial of Paanchi affirmed the Nephites' commitment to the concept of "liberty" (Hel. 1:7–8). The Nephite system of civil liberty was based on a fundamental belief in equality (Mosiah 29:32; Alma 30:7–11).

The Book of Mormon contains specific information about Nephite judges and lawyers during the first century before Christ. Judges were established by the "voice of the people" with provision being made for a form of judicial review (Mosiah 29:25–29). Judges were paid according to their time (Alma 11:1–3). Lawyers were hired or appointed by the people "to administer the law at their times of trials," often in a type of prosecutorial function (Alma 10:14–16, 24). Zeezrom received prominent notice as the lawyer that examined Alma and Amulek (Alma 11:20–46). Amulek spoke against the corrupt practices of judges and lawyers and prophesied that their unrighteousness would lay the foundation for the destruction of the Nephite civilization (Alma 10:25–27). This prophecy was fulfilled (3 Ne. 6:21–30; 7:1–3). There is no mention of trial by jury in the Book of Mormon; however the "voice of the people" had great influence on political affairs, legal proceedings, and judicial appointments (Mosiah 29:25–27; Alma 2:2–7).

The record of the Jaredite society provides less information about civil law. Jared reluctantly anointed one of his sons as king, concerned that kingship could lead to captivity (Ether 6:19–30). Thereafter Jaredite life was largely dominated by a cycle of righteous and wicked kings, dissension, warfare, and destruction.

See also Government, principles of; Judges, reign of.

EEV

Law, spiritual The divinely ordained conditions by which salvation comes. It is only by obedience to the laws of heaven that the blessings of heaven are obtained (D&C 130:20). As there is but one Christ so there is but one plan of salvation or system by which salvation comes. It is not for man to add to or take away from the laws of God (3 Ne. 11:40). Though obedience to law is essential to salvation it cannot be found independent of the grace of Christ. Thus Lehi[1] explained that "no flesh is justified" by the law alone, for all have fallen short of the law, be it temporal or spiritual. Redemption, he said, comes "in and through the Holy Messiah" (2 Ne. 2:5–7). Capturing this idea, Joseph Smith said, "We believe that through the Atonement of Christ, all mankind may be saved, by obedience to the laws and ordinances of the Gospel" (A of F 3).

See also Law, temporal.

JFM

Law, temporal A law limited in duration is temporal. The law of Moses was a temporal or carnal law. Though there is no salvation in temporal laws, God's children are duty bound to obey them until the higher law is given. Lehi[1] explained to Jacob[2] that "by the law no flesh is justified" (2 Ne. 2:5), meaning that because all have fallen short of the full measure of the law all stand condemned by the law. Thus he taught "that there is no flesh that can dwell in the presence of God, save it be through the merits, and mercy, and grace of the Holy Messiah" (2 Ne. 2:8).

See also Law, spiritual.

JFM

Law, without the Without the principles and ordinances of the gospel. A just God does not hold people accountable for laws they have not been given (Moro. 8:22). Where there is no law there is no sin (2 Ne. 2:13; 9:25–27). Abinadi testified that "they that have died before Christ came, in their ignorance, not having salvation declared unto them" will come forth in the first resurrection (Mosiah 15:24). Joseph Smith learned through modern revelation that this is conditioned upon their reception of the gospel in the postmortal spirit world (D&C 137:7–10; 138).

See also Accountability; Ignorance, died in.

JFM

Law and the prophets An expression for the scriptural word of God, especially as it bears witness of Jesus Christ. Law refers to the LAW OF MOSES. Nephi[1]'s understanding of the scriptures on the brass plates is expressed in sections, among which are the five books of Moses and the prophecies of the holy prophets (1 Ne. 5:10–14). The law pointed to Christ as did the testimony of the prophets (Mosiah 3:13–15; 13:13–34; Hel. 8:16–20; cf. Luke 24:44; John 1:45). To deny Christ was to deny the prophets and the law (2 Ne. 25:28). When Christ came, he fulfilled the law. The prophets, at least insofar as their word pertained to the future, remained (3 Ne. 15:4–8). The Savior also used the expression "the law and the prophets" to refer to the ideal of behavior, the golden rule (3 Ne. 14:12).

RAC

Law of circumcision The only reference to circumcision in the Book of Mormon is found in an epistle written by Mormon to his son Moroni[2]. In the fourth century A.D., a time of rampant apostasy among the Nephites, disputations arose concerning the baptism or washing of little children (Moro. 8:4–5). After Moroni reported these disputations, a grieved Mormon inquired of God concerning the issue and received "the word of the Lord" through the power of the Holy Ghost: "Little children are whole, . . . they are not capable of committing sin; . . . the curse of Adam is taken from them . . . and the law of circumcision is done away in me" (Moro. 8:7–8).

The law of circumcision was instituted with Abraham some six hundred years before the time of Moses as a token of the covenant between God and his chosen people, and also to signify "that children are not accountable before [the Lord] until they are eight years old" (JST Gen. 17:11). Newborn males were to be circumcised when eight days old (Gen. 17:9–14).

This practice was incorporated into the Mosaic code, the law of carnal commandments (Ex. 12:48–49).

It was presumably observed by those Book of Mormon peoples subject to the LAW OF MOSES until the risen Christ declared, "The law in me is fulfilled, for I have come to fulfill the law; therefore it hath an end" (3 Ne. 15:5). Thereafter, the people "did not walk any more after the performances and ordinances of the law of Moses" (4 Ne. 1:12).

To the Nephites Christ denounced the need for little children to be baptized. He further taught that circumcision, which had served as a reminder that little children were "not capable of committing sin," was no longer required in the new and everlasting covenant of the gospel (Moro. 8:8).

See also Children, baptism of little; Curse of Adam, the.

RT

Law of Moses The divinely revealed law that governed the house of Israel from the time of Moses until the atonement of Jesus Christ. While the Old Testament contains the law's requirements, the functions of its priests, and the procedures used in its ordinances, the Book of Mormon is unsurpassed in explaining the law's meaning and intent.

The gospel of Jesus Christ was revealed in the beginning to Adam (Moses 5:7–9; 6:51–62) and was known and taught by prophets long before Christ's coming (Hel. 8:13–20; cf. John 8:56; JST Gen. 15:11–12). It has always been the only means of salvation for all humankind (2 Ne. 31:21; Mosiah 5:8). When Moses brought the Israelites out of Egypt, he sought to establish the gospel among them. But because of rebellion, its blessings were withdrawn from them, including the Melchizedek Priesthood and its ordinances. The Israelites were given the law of Moses—a lesser law with lesser knowledge, governed by the lesser priesthood (JST Ex. 34:1–2; D&C 84:19–27).

The priesthood given to administer the lesser law was the Aaronic Priesthood, with its three hereditary offices. The *high priest* held the keys of the priesthood and presided over its functions, including the temple and its sacrifices. He was to be the first-born son of the lineage of Aaron[1]. Aaron's other male descendants were the *priests,* who performed the sacrifices at the temple. The *Levites* were the rest of the men of the tribe of Levi. They assisted the priests in their duties.

The law of Moses was the system of government, commandments, and rituals by which the Israelites were to live. It was revealed to them because "they were a stiffnecked people, quick to do iniquity, and slow to remember the Lord their God; Therefore there was a law given them, yea, a law of performances and of ordinances, a law which they were to observe strictly from day to day, to keep them in remembrance of God and their duty towards him" (Mosiah 13:29–30). The law of Moses can be divided into three parts: (1) the *Ten Commandments,* fundamental laws necessary to preserve a tranquil society; (2) a collection of *civil and religious laws* that taught holiness, purity, justice, and obedience; and (3) *sacrifices* and related *ordinances of purification.* The sacrifices included *burnt offerings*—acts of worship revealed first to Adam and performed by faithful Saints since the beginning; *peace offerings*—acts of thanks and celebration performed in conjunction with vows and commemorations; and *sin and trespass offerings,* performed for the purpose of atonement—making reconciliation with God following a violation of a law.

Because the Israelites were unable or unwilling to receive all that the Lord could reveal to them, in his mercy he gave them "the lesser portion of the word" (Alma 12:9–10; 29:8) to be their standard. But the Old Testament shows that many or most among them fell short of even the lesser law's expectations. In the early pages of the Book of Mormon, knowledge of Christ and the fulness of the gospel was revealed to Lehi[1] and his sons—knowledge that their fellow Judahites apparently did not have. The Nephites, beginning with Lehi and his family, were blessed with the higher priesthood and, while they lived the law of Moses, they administered the gospel through the Melchizedek Priesthood (2 Ne. 6:2; Alma 6:1, 8; cf. 13). Because they knew the gospel and looked forward to Jesus' coming, they viewed their adherence to the law of Moses as a temporary legal requirement until it would be fulfilled: "It was expedient that they should keep the law of Moses as yet, for it was not all fulfilled. But notwithstanding the law of Moses, they did look forward to the coming of Christ, considering that the law of Moses was a type of his coming, and believing that they must keep those outward performances until the time that he should be revealed unto them" (Alma 25:15; cf. 2 Ne. 25:24–25, 27, 30; Alma 30:3).

The law of Moses was a "type" of Jesus' coming because it taught justice and mercy, the twin pillars on which the Atonement rests. Its strict laws, rituals, and penalties taught justice. For every violation there must be accountability and punishment.

But the sacrifices taught mercy. Mercy came by means of vicarious redemption, when an unblemished, innocent creature was sacrificed to receive the punishment that the worshipper deserved, dying in his or her behalf. Thus the law's sacrificial ordinances prefigured the sacrifice of Jesus Christ, who suffered and died in place of others to remove their sins. When the ordinance of animal sacrifice was revealed at the beginning of human history, Adam was taught, "This thing is a similitude of the sacrifice of the Only Begotten of the Father, which is full of grace and truth. Wherefore, thou shalt do all that thou doest in the name of the Son" (Moses 5:7–8).

Because of continuing apostasy, the Israelites in the Holy Land generally lost whatever knowledge they had of the real intent of the law of Moses. But Lehi and his righteous descendants were taught the true meaning of the law (2 Ne. 2:5–8)—that it had been given to point them to Christ, with its precepts and sacrifices typifying his atonement: "Behold, my soul delighteth in proving unto my people the truth of the coming of Christ; for, for this end hath the law of Moses been given" (2 Ne. 11:4). We "look forward with steadfastness unto Christ, until the law shall be fulfilled. For, for this end was the law given" (2 Ne. 25:24–25). "By knowing the deadness of the law, [our children] may look forward unto that life which is in Christ, and know for what end the law was given" (2 Ne. 25:27). "We worship the Father in his name. And for this intent we keep the law of Moses, it pointing our souls to him" (Jacob 4:5). "They did look forward to the coming of Christ, considering that the law of Moses was a type of his coming. . . . The law of Moses did serve to strengthen their faith in Christ; and thus they did retain a hope through faith, unto eternal salvation" (Alma 25:15–16).

But the sacrifices of the law of Moses could not remove sin and could not save anyone. In reality, the law could only teach. In ancient Israel, "many signs, and wonders, and types, and shadows showed he unto them, concerning his coming; . . . and yet they hardened their hearts, and understood not that the law of Moses availeth nothing except it were through the atonement of his blood" (Mosiah 3:15). "Salvation doth not come by the law alone; and were it not for the atonement, which God himself shall make for the sins and iniquities of his people, that they must unavoidably perish, notwithstanding the law of Moses. . . . But behold, I say unto you, that all these things were types of things to come. And now, did they understand the law? I say unto you, Nay, they did not all understand the law; and this because of the hardness of their hearts; for they understood not that there could not any man be saved except it were through the redemption of God" (Mosiah 13:28, 31–32). Perhaps humble persons in ancient Israel who lived in obedience to the law were prepared to receive the fulness in the spirit world, just as some of their descendants later received it in life through the ministry of Christ and his apostles.

The Book of Mormon speaks of the law of Moses in doctrinal terms but reveals very little about how Lehi's descendants practiced it. However it is clear that "they were strict in observing the ordinances of God, according to the law of Moses" (Alma 30:3; cf. 2 Ne. 5:10; Hel. 13:1; 15:5). They had the TEN COMMANDMENTS (see Mosiah 12:33–36; 13:12–24), but it is not certain that they had the same collection of Mosaic laws and rituals that is in the Bible today, including all the Aaronic temple ordinances of Exodus and Leviticus. Temples are mentioned briefly (e.g., 2 Ne. 5:16; Mosiah 1:18; 11:10; 3 Ne. 11:1), but their function is not given. There were sacrifices. But without priests of Aaronic lineage, they must have been done by holders of the Melchizedek Priesthood and perhaps not according to the Aaronic rules of the Bible. The only sacrifices mentioned by name are burnt offerings (Mosiah 2:3; 3 Ne. 9:19), which had been performed by Melchizedek Priesthood holders since Adam. None of the annual feasts of the law of Moses are mentioned specifically.

In short, the Book of Mormon leaves many questions unanswered concerning how Book of Mormon people lived the law of Moses. With their knowledge of the gospel and with the higher priesthood, it may be that the Lord required a different observance from Nephite and Lamanite Christians than was required in the society from which Lehi came. Mormon, the book's author/compiler, never lived under the law of Moses himself, but he knew that his latter-day readers would not live under it either, and perhaps felt it unnecessary to discuss it in his record.

The Book of Mormon teaches that the law would be fulfilled when Christ's final sacrifice, to which it pointed, would take place. The prophet Amulek taught, "For it is expedient that there should be a great and last sacrifice; yea, not a sacrifice of man, neither of beast, neither of any manner of fowl; for it shall not be a human sacrifice; but it must be an infinite and eternal sacrifice. . . . There can be nothing which is short of an infinite atonement which will suffice for the sins of the world. Therefore, it is expedient that there should be a great and last sacrifice, and then shall there be, or it is expedient there should be, a stop to the shedding of blood; then shall the law of Moses be fulfilled; yea, it shall be all fulfilled, every jot and tittle, and none shall have passed away. And behold, this is the whole meaning of the law, every whit pointing to that great and last sacrifice; and that great and last sacrifice will be the Son of God, yea, infinite and eternal. And thus he shall bring salvation to all those who shall believe on his name; this being the intent of this last sacrifice, to bring about the bowels of mercy, which overpowereth justice, and bringeth about means unto men that they may have faith unto repentance" (Alma 34:10, 12–15).

When Jesus came to Lehi's descendants in America, he announced that in him the law of Moses was fulfilled. It had served its purpose as a "schoolmaster until Christ" (JST Gal. 3:24), but now worshippers would be privileged to live a higher law: "Behold, by me redemption cometh, and in me is the law of Moses fulfilled. . . . And ye shall offer up unto me no more the shedding of blood; yea, your sacrifices and your burnt offerings shall be done away, for I will accept none of your sacrifices and your burnt offerings. And ye shall offer for a sacrifice unto me a broken heart and a contrite spirit. And whoso cometh unto me with a broken heart and a contrite spirit, him will I baptize with fire and with the Holy Ghost. . . . Behold, I have come unto the world to bring redemption unto the world, to save the world from sin" (3 Ne. 9:17, 19–21). "Behold, I am he that gave the law, and I am he who covenanted with my people Israel; therefore, the law in me is fulfilled" (3 Ne. 15:5).

See also Deadness of the law; Great and last sacrifice; Jot, Tittle; Law, civil; Law and the prophets; Performances and ordinances; Sacrifices.

KPJ

Leah *See* Nephite weights and measures.

Lehi[1] Prophet-leader (ca. 600 B.C.); descendant of Joseph who was sold into Egypt; father of Laman[1], Lemuel, Sam, Nephi[1], Jacob[2], and Joseph[2], and at least two daughters (2 Ne. 5:6). The father of both the Nephite and Lamanite nations, Lehi led his family and those associated with them out of Jerusalem[1] to the PROMISED LAND (the Americas) before the great BABYLONIAN CAPTIVITY.

Lehi was an example to his family of courage, righteousness, and willingness to trust in the Lord. Upon hearing other prophets in Jerusalem predicting the city's destruction, Lehi believed and prayed "with all his heart, in behalf of his people" (1 Ne. 1:4–5). In answer, he received a resplendent vision of the glory of God and his Son, and confirmation of the impending destruction of Jerusalem (1 Ne. 1:6–9, 13, 18). Lehi was

LEHI[1]

filled with thanksgiving that the Lord would "not suffer those who come unto [him] that they shall perish" (1 Ne. 1:14), and he joined in preaching repentance to the people of Jerusalem (1 Ne. 1:18).

Lehi exemplified other important gospel principles as well, notably obedience and repentance. At the Lord's command, and despite the opposition of his eldest sons, he obediently took his family into the wilderness, leaving behind his home and all his possessions (1 Ne. 2:2–14). At the Lord's command and in spite of potential danger, Lehi sent his sons back to Jerusalem to acquire the brass plates from Laban

Lehi Preaching to the Jews; *painting by C. C. A. Christensen; courtesy MCHA. "After the Lord had shown so many marvelous things unto my father, Lehi, yea . . . behold he went forth among the people, and began to prophesy and to declare unto them concerning the things which he had both seen and heard" (1 Ne. 1:18).*

LEHI[1]

(1 Ne. 3:2–9). He later sent them again to persuade Ishmael[1] and his family to join with them in the wilderness, thereby providing wives for his sons (1 Ne. 7:1–5). Lehi was also obedient in moving onward in the wilderness at the Lord's command (1 Ne. 16:9–12), heeding the directions of the LIAHONA, an instrument the Lord provided to aid him in guiding his family through the wilderness and across the sea to the promised land (1 Ne. 16:9–16, 26–33; 18:8, 21–23).

Lehi further exemplified obedience in his observance of the law of Moses by making offerings unto the Lord. Shortly after arriving in the wilderness from Jerusalem, he "built an altar of stones, and made an offering" on it, giving thanks to God (1 Ne. 2:7). He also offered "sacrifice and burnt offerings" when his sons returned safely with the brass plates (1 Ne. 5:9), with Ishmael's family (1 Ne. 7:22), and possibly again when food was obtained after Nephi broke his bow (1 Ne. 16:32).

Not only was Lehi obedient but, like such other prophets of the Lord as Peter and Joseph Smith, Lehi served as an example of repentance. When Nephi broke his bow, Lehi joined Laman and Lemuel and the sons of Ishmael in murmuring against the Lord (1 Ne. 16:20). Refusing to join their complaint, Nephi spoke to them "in the energy of [his] soul," humbling them all. On this occasion, Lehi was "truly chastened" by the Lord, caused to "fear and tremble exceedingly" because of what was written on the Liahona, and was "brought down into the depths of sorrow" over his lapse of faith (1 Ne. 16:24–27). But Lehi also apparently received what Nephi had asked him to seek—indications about where to look for game, which Nephi then followed to obtain food for the family (1 Ne. 16:23, 30–31). Lehi's sin and repentance clearly demonstrated to his sons the Lord's response to sin: first, chastening, but, upon true repentance, continued guidance and revelation (1 Ne. 18:5).

Again and again, even in advanced age, Lehi demonstrated his calling as a prophet through his testimony of Christ, his visions and prophecies of the future, and his teachings and admonitions. Lehi worked especially hard to keep his own family in the path of righteousness, even naming a river and a valley in the wilderness after his two eldest sons, as symbolic lessons for them. He used the constancy of the river and the steadfastness of the valley to exhort them to righteousness (1 Ne. 2:9–10). Lehi's exhortations were so powerful that his sons "durst not utter against him" (1 Ne. 2:14).

One of Lehi's most familiar teachings came in the context of a remarkable dream, a vision of the tree of life (1 Ne. 8:2–35). In LEHI'S DREAM, he had wandered for a long time in "a dark and dreary wilderness" (1 Ne. 8:4, 8). Upon praying for relief, he beheld a tree from which he partook of fruit that was white and "desirable to make one happy" (1 Ne. 8:10–11). In the dream he urged his family to come and also partake, but only his wife Sariah and sons Sam and Nephi would do so (1 Ne. 8:12–16); Laman and Lemuel refused (1 Ne. 8:17–18, 35). Lehi used this dream to exhort his sons to righteousness. A more expansive explanation of the dream and its symbols was given by Nephi (1 Ne. 11–12; 15) who was blessed to see in vision the things his father had spoken of (1 Ne. 14:29).

Lehi also prophesied the pending destruction of Jerusalem and Babylonian captivity, the Jews' return after the captivity, and most importantly, the coming of Christ six hundred years after his departure from Jerusalem. He spoke, too, of other prophets' testimonies of Christ and prophesied about John the Baptist's work. Additionally, he prophesied of the Savior's death and resurrection, and the scattering and subsequent gathering of Israel to the Savior (1 Ne. 10:2–14).

Furthermore, Lehi taught that his family's journey to "the land of promise" was fulfilling the Lord's word regarding the scattering of Israel throughout the earth (1 Ne. 10:13).

Because the book of Lehi was lost through the carelessness of Martin Harris, it is fortunate indeed that Nephi recorded some of his father's teachings on the small plates of Nephi. Lehi's prophetic pronouncements concerning the promised land are powerful (2 Ne. 1:5–11). The patriarchal blessings Lehi delivered prior to his death are also significant, particularly those for his younger sons, Jacob and Joseph. Exhorting Laman and Lemuel to "put on the armor of righteousness" and to "come forth out of obscurity, and arise from the dust" (2 Ne. 1:23), he promised these rebellious sons, along with Ishmael's children, blessings if they would heed Nephi's counsel and do what is right (2 Ne. 1:28–29). He also promised Zoram[1] and Sam blessings for their faithfulness (2 Ne. 1:30–32; 4:11), and he blessed Laman and Lemuel's children that any curse brought on them by their fathers' actions would not remain (2 Ne. 4:3–9). Nephi's blessing does not appear in the record. To his son Joseph[2] who, like Jacob, was born in the wilderness, Lehi recounted prophecies made earlier by Joseph of Egypt, a prophecy of the coming of Moses, and of another great seer to be named Joseph (Joseph Smith) whom the Lord would raise up in the latter days to do a great work for the posterity of Joseph of old (2 Ne. 3:5–25).

Lehi's words to Jacob contain some of the most profound doctrine in all scripture about the plan of salvation and the necessity of "opposition in all things" (2 Ne. 2:11), in order that agency be operative. If there were no sin or punishment in opposition to righteousness and happiness, Lehi explained, then "there is no God" (2 Ne. 2:13), and creation would be nullified and purposeless (2 Ne. 2:12). Mortals must have a choice between good and evil; if there were no choice—no opposition—then there would be no purpose to mortal existence. It is in this context, in the assertion that joy is meaningless and good is nonexistent unless their opposites—misery and sin—also exist, that Lehi proclaimed God's ultimate design for his children: "Adam fell that men might be; and men are, that they might have joy" (2 Ne. 2:25). At the center of Lehi's teachings concerning Adam's fall, agency, and mortality as a probationary state, is his testimony that redemption is only through Jesus Christ, the "Holy Messiah" (2 Ne. 2:6–8; 1 Ne. 10:6). Plainly, this discourse is the product of an inspired, enlightened, and active intellect. The aged Lehi was hardly the foolish visionary Laman and Lemuel pretended he was. Lehi was, instead, a powerful testifier of Christ and his gospel until the end.

The sins of Lehi's wayward sons caused him and his wife much sorrow and grief: "They were brought down, yea, even upon their sickbeds" to the point of death during the ocean crossing to the promised land (1 Ne. 18:17–18). Nephi recorded that after Lehi had spoken to all his family, "according to the feelings of his heart and the Spirit of the Lord which was in him, he waxed old. And it came to pass that he died, and was buried" (2 Ne. 4:12).

Summary of major teachings

1. Dream of the tree of life. Depiction through symbolic representation of humankind's response to the word of God (1 Ne. 8; cf. 11–12; 15).

2. Prophecies. The destruction of Jerusalem; Babylonian captivity; return of the Jews to Jerusalem; the ministry of John the Baptist; the coming of Jesus Christ, his rejection, death, and resurrection; Christ's ministry through the Holy Ghost to the Gentiles; the scattering of Israel and their gathering through the instrumentality of the Gentiles (1 Ne. 10:3–14). *See* Jews, history of.

3. "All mankind [are] in a lost and in a fallen state, and ever would be save they should rely" upon Christ (1 Ne. 10:6).

4. Prophetic pronouncements concerning the promised land (2 Ne. 1:5–11).

5. God has provided a way (plan) for his children; salvation is only for the repentant through the "merits, and mercy, and grace" of Christ who made intercession for all men. All men will stand before God to be judged (2 Ne. 2:4–10).

6. The necessity of OPPOSITION IN ALL THINGS (2 Ne. 2:11–13, 15).

7. The purpose of the FALL OF ADAM AND EVE; conditions before and after the Fall; mortality as a probation for God's children (2 Ne. 2:15–25).

8. The role of the devil in the fall of man; the devil's intent to make men miserable (2 Ne. 2:17–18, 27).

9. Mankind is "free to choose liberty and eternal life" through Christ, or "captivity and death, according to the captivity and power of the devil" (2 Ne. 2:27).

10. Prophecies of Joseph of Egypt concerning a "choice seer" God would raise up to do a work for his seed. The Lord covenanted with Joseph of

Egypt that his seed would never perish (2 Ne. 3). *See* Choice seer.

See also Book of Mormon, lost manuscript of (116 pages); Lehi, book of; Lehi[1], journey to the promised land.

CBM

Lehi[2] *See* Zoram[2].

Lehi[3] A great Nephite military leader (ca. 74 B.C.). Lehi played a significant role in the long war described in Alma 43–62. During the Lamanite attempt under Zerahemnah to capture the land Manti, Lehi commanded the army that encircled the Lamanites from behind and caused them to flee over the river Sidon where the army of Moroni[1] was waiting for them (Alma 43:35–41). Expecting the Lamanites to attack the city of Noah, Moroni appointed Lehi to be chief captain over the forces there. The Lamanites did attack and lost more than one thousand men while Lehi's forces did not lose one man (Alma 49:15–24). Lehi and his troops were also instrumental in carrying out the successful strategy to recapture the city of Mulek. Lehi's men engaged the Lamanites that had been pursuing Teancum's forces. This caused the Lamanites to retreat to Mulek, only to meet Moroni's men who, unknown to them, had been pursuing them from the rear. Thus, Moroni's men blocked the Lamanite retreat to Mulek, and Lehi's army attacked from the rear. It was the "fury" of Lehi's attack that led to the Lamanite defeat (Alma 52:27–36). Captain Moroni then gave Lehi command of the recaptured city (Alma 53:2).

Lehi and Teancum were left in charge of most of the armies of the Nephites while Moroni went to the aid of Pahoran[1] to restore the government in the land of Zarahemla (Alma 62:3). Lehi participated in driving the Lamanites from the land of Moroni which ended the long wars (Alma 62:34–38). He was later called on to stop a Lamanite army led by Coriantumr[3] from getting to the land Bountiful[2] (Hel. 1:28–29).

Lehi, who had much success in battle, made a mark as a military leader. His enemies "feared Lehi exceedingly" (Alma 49:17), but he was more than a successful military leader. Lehi was described as "a man like unto Moroni" who was "beloved by all the people of Nephi" (Alma 53:2).

PVJ

Lehi[4] The valiant younger son of Helaman[3] (ca. 45 B.C.), whose chief accomplishments centered around his missionary labors with his brother Nephi[2]. Lehi's recorded ministry stretches from ca. 30 B.C. to 13 B.C. Lehi and his brother were named after their early progenitors (Hel. 3:21; 5:6). "Not a whit behind [Nephi] as to things pertaining to righteousness" (Hel. 11:19), Lehi received abundantly of the Spirit and taught with great knowledge and authority (Hel. 11:18–19, 23). When Nephi delivered up the judgment-seat, he and Lehi dedicated the rest of their lives to preaching the gospel (Hel. 5:4), commencing their labors among the Nephites at Bountiful[2]. In the land of Zarahemla they taught the Lamanites with such power that 8000 of them, and many Nephite dissenters who had joined the Lamanites, repented and were converted (Hel. 5:14–19). The brothers met with a very different reception in the land of Nephi, however, where they were taken captive "by an army of the Lamanites and cast into prison" (Hel. 5:20–21).

The events that transpired in that prison when their captors came to slay them are among the most glorious in all scripture. They include the surrounding of Lehi and Nephi by a pillar of fire; the trembling of the earth; the Lord's voice speaking above a dense cloud; the sight of Lehi and Nephi through the cloud, conversing with heavenly beings; the descent of "the Holy Spirit of God" (Hel. 5:45) into the hearts of Lehi and Nephi; the voice of the Father speaking to them; the opening of the heavens; and the ministering of angels to the two brothers. The 300 persons who witnessed these miraculous events, events in which Lehi played a major role, were instrumental in the subsequent conversion of many of their people (Hel. 5:22–52) and the repentance of many Nephites (Hel. 6:4–5). Of such marvelous happenings Moroni[2] wrote that "it was the faith of Nephi and Lehi that wrought the change upon the Lamanites" (Ether 12:14). Subsequently, Nephi and Lehi went to preach in the land northward (Hel. 6:6). Nephi is the focus of the narrative that follows (Hel. 7–11), but Lehi is mentioned again in Helaman 11 as one who, like his brother, was able to quell strife because he knew and preached "the true points of doctrine, having many revelations daily" (Hel. 11:23).

RCF

Lehi, book of Lost among the 116 manuscript pages translated by Joseph Smith and lent to Martin Harris, the book of Lehi[1] can be recovered only in part from quotations and summaries that appear in the writings of Lehi's two sons Nephi[1] and Jacob[2].

That Nephi depended heavily on his father's work can be seen in his list of the contents of Lehi's record, an account that Nephi had copied onto his large plates (1 Ne. heading). Significantly, this list also generally describes the subject matter of the books of 1 Nephi and 2 Nephi 1–3: "Upon the [large] plates . . . I did engraven the record of my father, and also our journeyings in the wilderness, and the prophecies of my father" (1 Ne. 19:1). In this document, Lehi had "written many things which he saw in visions and in dreams; and he also hath written many things which he prophesied and spake unto his children" (1 Ne. 1:16). Hence, based on Nephi's list, it seems clear that Lehi had kept an extensive journal not only of the travels of his family from Jerusalem to the promised land, but particularly of his spiritual and family-centered experiences.

The sections of Nephi's record that evidently depend on his father's account are rather extensive. Even though Nephi began the record on the small plates as if it were entirely his own—"I make a record of my proceedings in my days" (1 Ne. 1:1)—it becomes evident very quickly that he is retelling the story of his father, beginning with Lehi's first two visions, followed by his preaching in the city of Jerusalem (1 Ne. 1:5–20). Further, it was Lehi who detailed receiving instructions from the Lord to take his family into the desert, whither they fled (1 Ne. 2). In this light, the chapters that go back to Lehi's narrative in one form or another are the following: calling, preaching, and flight of Lehi and his family (1 Ne. 1–2); events in Lehi's camp, inventory of the plates of brass (1 Ne. 5); command of the Lord to Lehi that his sons return to bring Ishmael's family (1 Ne. 7:1–2); vision of Lehi (1 Ne. 8); prophecy of Lehi (1 Ne. 10); the wilderness journey (most comes from Lehi, as the "we" passages indicate) (1 Ne. 16); construction of the boat, voyage to and arrival in the promised land (much comes from Lehi) (1 Ne. 18); Lehi's last will and testament (2 Ne. 1–3).

Thus these chapters, which evidently depend on Lehi's record completely or in part, form the frame of the record of 1 Nephi through 2 Nephi, chapter three.

Jacob preserved less. Even so, in an important sermon delivered at the first Nephite temple, Jacob referred to a revelation about fidelity in marriage and the sacred character of marriage vows which, he noted, had been received by his father Lehi (Jacob 2:23–33). Speaking specifically to men in the congregation, Jacob summarized, "My brethren, ye know that these commandments [about faithfulness in marriage] were given to our father, Lehi; wherefore, ye have known them before" (Jacob 2:34).

Some of Lehi's teachings that may have been selected from his record to be incorporated in the small plates, concern the fall of Adam and Eve (2 Ne. 2:15–25), the doctrine of opposition in all things (2 Ne. 2:11–14), and the restoration of the gospel through a "choice seer" descended from Joseph of Egypt (2 Ne. 3:5–15). But it is important to see these teachings of Lehi particularly in light of his concern with the Redeemer (2 Ne. 2:5–10), noting his early preaching about the coming Messiah (1 Ne. 1:19; 10:4–6, 11) and the Messiah's role in the plan of salvation (2 Ne. 2:26–27).

See also Book of Mormon, lost manuscript of (116 pages).

BIBLIOGRAPHY

Brown, S. Kent. "Recovering the Missing Record of Lehi." *From Jerusalem to Zarahemla.* Provo, Utah: Religious Studies Center, Brigham Young University, 1998.

SKB

Lehi[1], journey of, to the promised land The journey of Lehi[1], his family, and others to "the promised land" (1 Ne. 2–18) took them from Jerusalem[1] to the southeast coast of the Arabian peninsula, a distance of about 2,100

LEHI[1], JOURNEY OF, TO THE PROMISED LAND

miles. On the seacoast, the party built and launched a ship that bore them to the New World, ending a saga that later generations remembered for a thousand years but was not known to the wider world until the publication of the Book of Mormon.

In this journey, three geographic locales are known: Jerusalem, the RED SEA, and the Indian Ocean. Nephi[1] called the ocean "the sea, which we called Irreantum, which, being interpreted, is many waters" (1 Ne. 17:5). Joseph Smith, in turn, called it "the great Southern Ocean" (267). Tenable locations for the first camp, NAHOM, and Bountiful[1] have also been established.

More than half of the space in Nephi's first book ties to events associated with the first camp (1 Ne. 2:2–16:12), which was in the area known anciently as Midian. Nephi mentioned leaving Jerusalem, reaching the Red Sea, continuing another three days (presumably between forty-five and seventy-five miles depending on the speed of the travelers) and finally making camp by a river they named Laman, in a valley they called Lemuel (1 Ne. 2:5–10; 10:16). Explorers have suggested two plausible locations for the camp, both north of the Straits of Tirān (Hilton; Potter). Nephi's narrative does not tell readers the exact route of this segment of the trip, a distance of about two hundred fifty miles. The party could have traveled south, turning eastward into the Jordan Valley and then journeying south until reaching the Red Sea. Party members could also have gone east through the Jordan Valley into the hills of Moab before turning south and generally following the King's Highway (Ogden, 22–23; Brown, "New Light from Arabia").

Nephi recalled that when the party left the first camp the general direction was "south-southeast" (1 Ne. 16:13), the proper direction for traveling along the west coast of Arabia. After traveling four days they camped again at a place they called "Shazer" (1 Ne. 16:13). From there they continued to travel "in the most fertile parts of the wilderness . . . in the borders near the Red Sea" as they were led by the LIAHONA (1 Ne. 16:14–16).

Eventually they came to "the place which was called Nahom" (1 Ne. 16:34). The wording suggests that party members learned the name "Nahom" from others. The locale likely lies in the area of Wadi Jawf in northwest Yemen. The keys to this identification are three inscribed altars from the seventh century B.C.—the time of Lehi and Sariah—recently discovered at the Bar'ān temple in Marib, the ancient capital of the Sabaean kingdom. According to the inscriptions on the altars, they were dedicated by a man named Biʿathar of the Nihm tribe, a tribe which has resided near Wadi Jawf for at least three millennia. The consonants NHM of both Nahom and Nihm connect these names and make the identification of Nahom with the ancient tribal area of the Nihmites a reasonable conclusion (Brown, "Place"; "New Light from Arabia"; Aston, "Newly Found"). At some point, party members had to cross the Al-Sarāt mountain chain that divides the coastal lowlands from the interior highlands in order to reach Nahom whence they turned eastward (1 Ne. 17:1). Otherwise, the mountains would have formed a formidable barrier to eastward travel because there are few passes. Although Nephi preserved hints of a mountain crossing—for example, the unusual success at hunting implies ample cover for the hunters (1 Ne. 16:14–15)—he did not include information as to where the crossing may have occurred.

From Nahom Lehi's group traveled "nearly eastward"—the direction of travel along the incense trail from the area of Nahom/Nihm (Brown, "New Light from Arabia")—finally arriving at a land they "called Bountiful, because of its much fruit and also wild honey" (1 Ne. 17:1–5). Bountiful most probably lay in the Dhofar region on the southern coast of the Sultanate of Oman. It is the only area on the seashore of Arabia that matches Nephi's description of fruit, honey, and timbers (1 Ne. 17:5; 18:1). Moreover, a number of lagoons or inlet bays lie along that coast where a group of persons could build and launch a ship. There, the monsoon rains of summer sustain a rich, diverse vegetation which supports human and animal life (Ball et al.).

The party spent "eight years in the wilderness" (1 Ne. 17:4). Although the distance from the first camp to Nahom is approximately 1,150 miles and represents the longest leg of the

Lehi's Family Departing Jerusalem; *painting by Kelly Hale; courtesy Kelly Hale. "And it came to pass that the Lord commanded my father, even in a dream, that he should take his family and depart into the wilderness"* (1 Ne. 2:2).

LEHI'S JOURNEY: POSSIBLE ROUTE

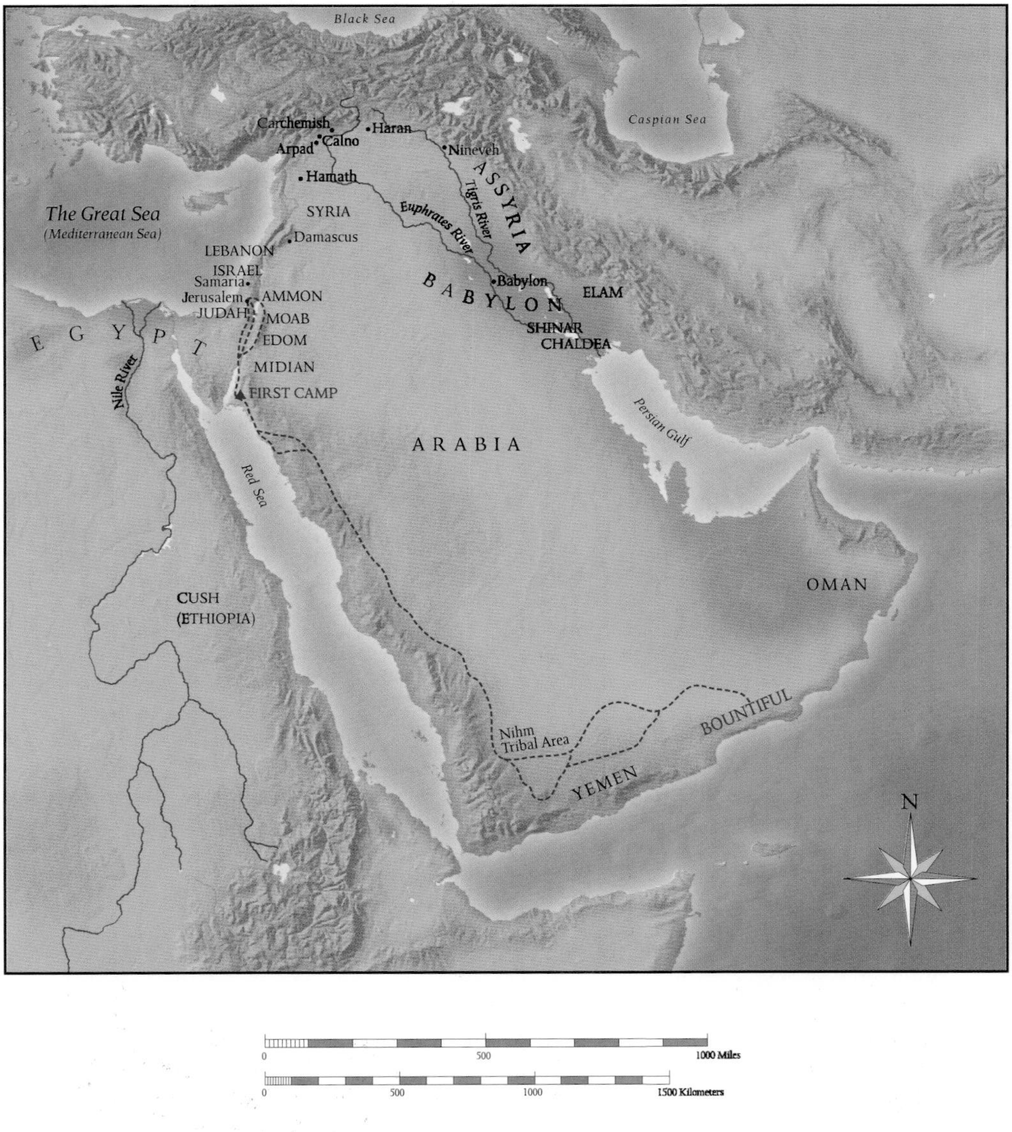

journey, the party may have covered the distance in less than one year. This conclusion is suggested from Nephi's placement of his notes about marriages of the sons of Lehi and Sariah to the daughters of Ishmael[1] (1 Ne. 16:7) and about the births of the first children (1 Ne. 17:1). The marriages occurred before party members left the camp and Nephi noted the births only after the arrival at Nahom. As a comparison, the ancient geographer Strabo wrote of a Roman military expedition that traveled basically the same route in six months and returned under forced march in two months (*Geography*, 16.4.23–24). These observations mean that the party probably spent the bulk of the eight years between Nahom and Bountiful (Brown, "Case").

Other Book of Mormon authors showed familiarity with a fuller account of this journey. Their brief recollections evidently point to the eastward segment of the trip because they added details about troubles that differ from Nephi's rather complete report of the first segment of the journey from Jerusalem to Nahom. Alma[2] explained to his son Helaman[2] that the reason "they tarried in the wilderness, or did not travel a direct course, and were afflicted with hunger and thirst, [was] because of their transgressions." As a result divine guidance through the Liahona ceased and "they did not progress in their journey" (Alma 37:41–42). Similarly, king Benjamin recalled that because of unfaithfulness party members "did not prosper nor progress in their journey, but were driven back, and incurred the displeasure of God upon them; and therefore they were smitten with famine and sore afflictions, to stir them up in remembrance of their duty" (Mosiah 1:17).

Interestingly, the visions of Lehi and Nephi (revelations enjoyed while the travelers were encamped in the valley of Lemuel) seem to correspond with many scenes that Lehi's family would encounter en route to the promised land. Such scenes connect readers with ancient Arabia, a very different world from Joseph Smith's upstate New York. Consider the following examples (Brown, "New Light from Arabia"):

"A terrible gulf" (1 Ne. 12:18; 15:28)—deep canyons known as wadis were almost impossible to traverse.

"Filthy water" (1 Ne. 12:16; 15:27)—after rains, the seasonal streams in the wadis fill with muddy water and debris.

"Forbidden paths" and "strange roads" (1 Ne. 8:23, 28, 32)—desert areas where the unwary would become "lost."

"Travel[ing] for the space of many hours in darkness" (1 Nephi 8:4–8)—night travel was the preferred time for traveling in the desert.

People whose "manner of dress was exceedingly fine" (1 Ne. 8:27)—the wealth of south Arabia was widely known in antiquity.

"A mist of darkness" (1 Ne. 8:23)—heavy mists and fog at times blanket the coasts of Arabia during the monsoon season.

A "spacious building . . . in the air, high above the earth (1 Ne. 8:26)—skyscraper buildings have been an architectural feature in Yemen from the eighth century B.C. to the present.

See also Bountiful[1], land of; Lemuel, valley of; Shazer; Transoceanic crossings, pre-Columbian.

BIBLIOGRAPHY

Aston, Warren P. "Newly Found Altars from Nahom." *Journal of Book of Mormon Studies* 10:2 (2001): 56–61.

Aston, Warren P., and Michaela Knoth. *In the Footsteps of Lehi.* Salt Lake City: Deseret Book, 1994.

Ball, Terry B., S. Kent Brown, Arnold H. Green, David J. Johnson, and W. Revell Phillips. "Planning Research on Oman: The End of Lehi's Trail." In *Journal of Book of Mormon Studies* 7:1 (1998): 12–21.

Brown, S. Kent. *From Jerusalem to Zarahemla.* Provo, Utah: Religious Studies Center, Brigham Young University, 1998.

———. "A Case for Lehi's Bondage in Arabia." *Journal of Book of Mormon Studies* 6:2 (1997): 205–17.

———. "New Light from Arabia on Lehi's Trail." *Echoes and Evidences of the Book of Mormon.* Edited by Donald W. Parry, Daniel C. Peterson, and John W. Welch. Provo, Utah: FARMS (2002): 55–126.

———. "'The Place That Was Called Nahom': New Light from Ancient Yemen." *Journal of Book of Mormon Studies* 8:1 (1999): 66–68.

Groom, Nigel. *Frankincense and Myrrh: A Study of the Arabian Incense Trade.* London: Longman Group Ltd., 1981.

Hilton, Lynn M., and Hope A. Hilton. *In Search of Lehi's Trail.* Salt Lake City: Deseret Book, 1976.

Nibley, Hugh W. *Lehi in the Desert; The World of the Jaredites; There Were Jaredites.* Vol. 5 of *The Collected Works of Hugh Nibley.* Edited by John W. Welch, Darrell L. Matthews, and Stephen R. Callister. Salt Lake City: Deseret Book and FARMS, 1988.

Ogden, D. Kelly. "Answering the Lord's Call." *1 Nephi to Alma 29*. Vol. 7 of *Studies in Scripture* series. Edited by Kent P. Jackson. Salt Lake City: Deseret Book, 1987.

Phillips, W. Revell. "Metals of the Book of Mormon." *Journal of Book of Mormon Studies* 9:2 (2000): 36–43.

Potter, George D. "A New Candidate in Arabia for the Valley of Lemuel." *Journal of Book of Mormon Studies* 8:1 (1999): 54–63.

Smith, Joseph. *Teachings of the Prophet Joseph Smith*. Selected by Joseph Fielding Smith. Salt Lake City: Deseret Book, 1976.

Strabo. *Geography*.

SKB

Lehi[1], land of and city of Nephite land which was the location of a border dispute between people living in the land of Lehi and the neighboring land of Morianton (Alma 50:25–36).

The city of Lehi, located "in the north by the borders of the [east] seashore," was built in an unspecified "particular manner" during a time of Nephite prosperity (Alma 50:15–18; 51:26; 72 B.C.). Four years later, the city was seized by Amalickiah and his armies during a Lamanite offensive (Alma 51:24–27). The recapturing of the city of Lehi by the Nephites is not mentioned, but presumably it was recovered with other coastal cities (Alma 62:30–31).

Lehi[2], land of The name given the land south because Lehi[1] originally landed there (Hel. 6:10). Mentioned in connection with the prosperity that accompanied a period of peace between the Nephites and Lamanites, the land was said to be full of gold, silver, and other precious metals, and was suitable for raising crops and herds (Hel. 6:9, 11–12).

Lehi[1]'s dream A prophetic dream given to Lehi in the valley of Lemuel en route to the promised land (1 Ne. 8). The account is an abridgment by Nephi[1] of his father's words (1 Ne. 8:29–30). The dream, like Jesus' parable of the sower (Matt. 13:3–8, 18–23), depicts through symbolism humankind's varying responses to the gospel of Jesus Christ. While some interpretations of the symbols are given in Lehi's dream, a more complete identification of the symbols and their meaning is given in NEPHI[1]'S VISION, and in Nephi's later explanations to his brothers Laman[1] and Lemuel (1 Ne. 11–15). The central focus of Lehi's dream was a tree that had FRUIT "desirable to make one happy" (1 Ne. 8:10). Lehi also saw a "spacious field," a "strait and narrow path" that led to the tree, a "rod of iron" that extended parallel to the path, a "river of water" located between the tree and a "great and spacious building," and a "mist of darkness" that stretched across the path to the tree (1 Ne. 8:9–26). The accompanying table summarizes the symbols and their meanings.

SYMBOLISM IN LEHI[1]'S DREAM

SYMBOL	MEANING
The tree of life	The love of God (1 Ne. 11:21–22).
Large and spacious field	The world (1 Ne. 8:9, 20).
The strait and narrow path	The road all must travel to reach the tree of life (1 Ne. 8:20).
The rod of iron	The word of God (1 Ne. 11:25; 15:23–24).
The river of water	HELL; GULF separating "the wicked from the tree of life, and also from the saints of God" (1 Ne. 15:26–29; 12:16).
The great and spacious building	The pride and wisdom of the world; the "vain imaginations and the pride of the children of men" (1 Ne. 12:18; 11:35–36).
The mists of darkness	The temptations of the devil (1 Ne. 12:17).

LEHI'S DREAM

In addition to these symbols, Lehi saw four groups of people which responded differently to the dream's setting. The first group commenced on the path to the tree but strayed because they were blinded by the mists of darkness and consequently thrown off course (1 Ne. 8:21–23; cf. Matt. 13:7, 22). The second group made it through the mists of darkness to the tree by "clinging to the rod of iron." As they were partaking of the fruit of the tree, however, they became ashamed because of the mockery from finely dressed people across the river in a "great and spacious building." They "fell away into forbidden paths and were lost" (1 Ne. 8:24–28; cf. Matt. 13:5–6, 20–21). The third group also achieved their goal of arriving at the tree, but this group remained, not giving "heed" to those who mocked them (1 Ne. 8:30, 33; cf. Matt. 13:8, 23). The fourth group of people never sought the tree, desiring the great and spacious building as their destination. Lehi saw that many were drowned or lost in their quest, and that those who did reach the building joined in mocking those partaking of the fruit of the tree (1 Ne. 8:31–33; cf. Matt. 13:4, 19).

Lehi viewed his dream's setting and symbols in the context of his own family. He saw his wife Sariah and sons Nephi and Sam at the head of the river, standing "as if they knew not whither they should go" (1 Ne. 8:14). He called unto them to come to the tree and partake of its desirable fruit, which they did. He then called for Laman and Lemuel to come and partake, but they refused (1 Ne. 8:15–18). Because of his dream Lehi said, "I have reason to rejoice in the Lord because of Nephi and also of Sam; for I have reason to suppose that they, and also many of their seed, will be saved" (1 Ne. 8:3). But concerning Laman and Lemuel, Lehi "exceedingly feared . . . lest they should be cast off from the presence of the Lord" (1 Ne. 8:36).

Nephi saw the same symbols in his vision, but he described them in the context of the coming of Christ and the future of Lehi's descendants (1 Ne. 11–12, 15). He beheld that the tree of life, a representation of "the love of God" (1 Ne. 11:21–22), was manifested to mankind through the condescension of God—the birth, life, and atoning sacrifice of Jesus Christ (1 Ne. 11:4–33). This love, Nephi testified, was "most desirable above all things" and "most joyous to the soul" (1 Ne. 11:22–23; cf. 8:12, 15). After witnessing Christ's death in vision, Nephi saw the subsequent persecution of the "apostles of the Lamb" by the "multitudes of the earth" (1 Ne. 11:34). These multitudes were gathered together "in a large and spacious building" which Nephi described as being "like unto the building which [his] father saw." The angel instructing Nephi in his vision then said: "Behold the world and the wisdom thereof; yea, behold the house of Israel hath gathered together to fight against the twelve apostles of the Lamb" (1 Ne. 11:34–35). Nephi saw the fall of the large building (the pride of the world) and heard the angel testify, "Thus shall be the destruction of all nations, kindreds, tongues, and people, that shall fight against the twelve apostles of the Lamb" (1 Ne. 11:36).

Nephi also saw that his own people would be destroyed centuries later because of pride and the temptations of the devil (mists of darkness) (1 Ne. 12:16–19).

Lehi's dream offers many lessons central to the plan of salvation. For example, the dream can be viewed as a TYPE depicting the journey all people must make in order to "come unto Christ." Lehi was invited by a man "dressed in a white robe" to follow him. As he followed he found himself in a "dark and dreary waste." After traveling in darkness for "many hours" Lehi prayed to the Lord for MERCY, after which he was shown a beautiful tree with white fruit. After partaking of the fruit of the tree Lehi experienced great JOY and then desired to share his joy with his family (1 Ne. 8:5–12). Similarly, Christ invites all people to come follow him. As one follows Christ and learns of him and his plan, one becomes increasingly aware of his or her own mortal and fallen condition. Understanding the need to be saved from this darkness, the necessary cry is for mercy, for every person sins and needs redemption from the Fall. After the cry for mercy the Lord manifests the source of his mercy: a tree which is "a representation of the love of God" (1 Ne. 11:25). The greatest manifestation of this love is Jesus Christ and his atonement (John 3:16; 1 Ne. 19:9). After partaking of the Atonement, as represented by partaking of the fruit of the tree, one experiences great joy and feels a desire to share that joy with others. Elements of this conversion pattern—darkness, a cry for mercy, forgiveness, joy, then the ensuing desire to share this joy—are reflected in the stories of Enos (Enos 1:1–11), king Benjamin's people (Mosiah 4:1–3), Zeezrom (Alma 15:3, 9–12), king Lamoni (Alma 18:41; 19:6), king Lamoni's father (Alma 22:15–18, 23), Alma[2] (Alma 36:12–21, 24), and the sons of king Mosiah[2] (Mosiah 28:3).

Further, Lehi's dream portrays the opposition people face as they seek to partake of the tree of life. Mists of darkness, or the temptations of Satan, are intended to blind the eyes. Without sight travelers wander in strange roads and can drown in unseen rivers of filthiness. The "great and spacious building" also poses a challenge to those on the straight and narrow path. Its appearance, large and spacious, and its residents, all finely dressed, create a distraction to those susceptible to materialistic desires and embarrassment because of the mocking of proud and worldly people. Lehi beheld that the building "stood as it were in the air, high above the earth" and Nephi saw its eventual fall (1 Ne. 8:26; 11:36). While the building, evidently without foundation, was destined to be destroyed, conversely, one who builds a foundation upon Christ "cannot fall" (Hel. 5:12).

Lehi saw in his dream the solution to the opposition posed by the mists of darkness and the great and spacious building. First, those who made it through the mists of darkness held continually to the "rod of iron," or the word of God (1 Ne. 8:30; 15:23–24). Nephi declared that "whoso would hearken unto the word of God, and would hold fast unto it, they would never perish; neither could the temptations and the fiery darts of the adversary overpower them unto blindness, to lead them away to destruction" (1 Ne. 15:24–25; cf. 1 Tim. 3:1–7, 12–15). Second, those who successfully remained at the tree were those who "heeded" not those in the spacious building (1 Ne. 8:33–34). To give heed means to notice, observe, regard, or give attention to; "a steady look" (Webster). To withstand temptation and ridicule, one's devotion must not be divided (2 Ne. 31:20; James 1:8), and one's "heed" must be to God's word (1 Ne. 15:25; cf. Hel. 3:29–30).

BIBLIOGRAPHY

Webster, Noah. *An American Dictionary of the English Language.* 1828.

DLL

Lehi-Nephi, land of and city of *See* Nephi, land of and city of.

Lehonti Leader of a dissident group of Lamanites who refused to obey the king's command to go to war against the Nephites (72 B.C.). The king of the Lamanites sent the Nephite traitor Amalickiah with the remainder of his troops to compel the deserters to return and fight. In a secret meeting with a reluctant Lehonti, Amalickiah proposed that he deliver his troops to Lehonti on the condition that Lehonti appoint him second in command. Amalickiah arranged for Lehonti to be poisoned and thus became commander of the entire Lamanite force (Alma 47:1–19).

Lemuel Son of Lehi[1] and Sariah, brother of Laman[1], Sam, Nephi[1], Jacob[2], Joseph[2], and unnamed sisters (1 Ne. Heading; 18:7; 2 Ne. 5:6), and husband of one of the daughters of Ishmael[1] (1 Ne. 16:7). The Book of Mormon story of Lemuel is inextricably connected to the story of his older brother, Laman. Almost all of the references to Lemuel in the text are in connection with the attitudes and actions of Laman. Consequently, it was the brothers "Laman and Lemuel" who murmured (1 Ne. 2:11–12; 3:31), rebelled (1 Ne. 3:28; 7:6; Alma 18:38), sought to kill Nephi (1 Ne. 7:16; 16:37; 2 Ne. 5:1–2), and refused to partake of the tree of life in Lehi's dream (1 Ne. 8:17–18, 35–36). When Lehi blessed his family, the two rebellious brothers received the same promises in their blessings, as did their children (2 Ne. 1:28–29; 4:3–9). En route to the promised land, Lehi's family stopped in a valley by the Red Sea. Because of Lemuel's "stiffneckedness," Lehi said to Lemuel: "O that thou mightest be like unto this valley, firm and steadfast, and immovable in keeping the commandments of the Lord!" (1 Ne.

2:10). Nephi related this incident, and thereafter referred to this valley as the "valley of Lemuel" (e.g., 1 Ne. 2:14; 9:1). Although Lemuel and his descendants (Lemuelites) maintained their distinct identity, they were called "Lamanites" because they followed Laman in opposing Nephite leadership and religious teachings (2 Ne. 5:1–14; Jacob 1:13–14; Alma 47:35; Morm. 1:8–9).

Lemuel, city of One of the seven Lamanite cities and lands that were "converted unto the Lord," whose people "laid down . . . all their weapons of war" and called themselves ANTI-NEPHI-LEHIES (Alma 23:12–13, 17; between 90 and 77 B.C.).

Lemuel, valley of Valley near the RED SEA where Lehi[1] and his family dwelt after fleeing Jerusalem[1] (1 Ne. 2:6). From this valley Lehi's sons were sent back to Jerusalem twice: first to retrieve the brass plates, and second to enlist Ishmael's family to accompany them. Here Lehi and Nephi[1] received marvelous visions (1 Ne. 8; 11–14) and the family acquired the Liahona (1 Ne. 16). Lehi counseled his son Lemuel to be like the valley named after him—"firm and steadfast, and immovable" in obedience (1 Ne. 2:10).

See also Lehi[1], journey to the promised land.

Lemuelites Descendants of Lemuel. From the time of Jacob[2], Lemuelites were normally included among the larger group called Lamanites, made up primarily of Lamanites, Lemuelites, and Ishmaelites (Jacob 1:13–14; Alma 43:13; 47:35; 4 Ne. 1:38; Morm. 1:8–9; D&C 3:18). Some descendants of Lemuel joined the Church during the great Lamanite conversion (Alma 24:29).

Less than the dust of the earth Being dependent upon God and the earth for its very existence, the mortal body is described in the Book of Mormon as being "less than the dust of the earth" (Mosiah 4:2; 2:25). Further, whereas the earth is ever obedient to God's will, mankind in its fallen, carnal state is "quick to do iniquity, and how slow to do good" (Hel. 12:4).

This view of man's moral nature should not be confused with the doctrine of the utter depravity of man. Being "less than the dust of the earth" is simply a metaphor to dramatize man's fallen nature. The nature of Christ's atonement affirms mankind's true worth and potential (Mosiah 4:2–3; 5:1–7).

RT

Letters *See* Epistles.

Levi[1] Third son of Jacob[1] (Israel), born of Leah, forefather of Moses and Aaron[1] (3 Ne. 24:3 // Mal. 3:3; D&C 13:1; 128:24; Gen. 29:34; Ex. 2:1–10; 4:14). Under Mosaic law, descendants of Levi had stewardship over the Tabernacle and ministered in the ordinances thereof (Num. 3:5–13).

See also Malachi chapter review (3 Ne. 24–25 // Mal. 3–4).

Levi[2] *See* Jared[1], posterity of.

Liahona A device miraculously provided by the Lord to Lehi and his family which gave divine directions and instructions to them for their travels to the land of promise. It was "a round ball of curious workmanship" which contained "two spindles; and the one pointed the way whither [they] should go into the wilderness" (1 Ne. 16:10). The Liahona also contained writing "which was plain to be read" and which was "changed from time to time" (1 Ne. 16:29). This "ball, or director" (Alma 37:38) functioned only "according to the faith and diligence and heed" which the people gave to it (1 Ne. 16:28).

While there is no record of its being used after the time of Lehi[1] and Nephi[1], the Liahona remained an object sacred to the faithful Nephites. It was passed down from generation to generation with the plates and the sword of Laban, and, in this dispensation, it was among the items seen by the three witnesses when they viewed the Book of Mormon plates (D&C 17:1). Alma[2] explained the Liahona's continuing symbolic significance: "And now I say, is there not a type in this thing? For just as surely as this director did bring our fathers, by following its course, to the promised land, shall the words of Christ, if we follow their course, carry us beyond this vale of sorrow into a far better land of promise" (Alma 37:45). Along with other symbols derived from the Book of Mormon (e.g., the angel Moroni, the rod of iron, the tree of life), "Liahona" has become an important element of LDS culture. The term still represents the means by which the Lord can give guidance to his people. For instance, the counsel of the modern prophets, inspiration of the Holy Ghost, and teachings of the scriptures can all be viewed as modern-day Liahonas. For the faithful, the Book of Mormon itself is a type of Liahona for it contains "the word of Christ, which will point to you a straight course to eternal bliss" (Alma 37:44). Like the Liahona, the Book of Mormon was in fact "prepared for [all people], that if they would look they might live" (Alma 37:44–46). "Liahona" has been used as the title for several Church publications and for the Church's high school in Tonga.

NEL

Lib[1] *See* Jared[1], posterity of.

Lib[2] Late Jaredite king who obtained his throne through the use of SECRET COMBINATIONS. Coriantumr[2], strengthened after a two-year period following his conflicts with Gilead, came to battle against Lib and after three separate conflicts eventually (when he arrived at the plains of Agosh) defeated him. Lib's brother Shiz continued the conflict (Ether 14:10–17).

Life, purpose of Lehi[1] stated, "men are, that they might have joy" (2 Ne. 2:25). To achieve joy God prepared a PLAN variously known as the "plan of the great Creator" (2 Ne. 9:6), the "plan of our God" (2 Ne. 9:13), the "plan of redemption" (Jacob 6:8; Alma 12:25, 30–33; 34:16; 42:11), the "plan of salvation" (Jarom 1:2; Alma 42:5), the "plan of the Eternal God" (Alma 34:9), and the "great plan of happiness" (Alma 42:8, 16). This plan provides a way for God's children to experience joy by guiding them through a mortal curriculum leading to "immortality and eternal life" (Moses 1:39). Thus they may become "even as" their Father in Heaven (3 Ne. 12:48).

Mortality affords God's children the opportunity to experience joy by obtaining a physical body and proving themselves worthy of eternal life.

Obtaining a physical body

God the Father and Jesus Christ have glorified and perfected bodies of flesh and bone (D&C 130:22). To become like them and experience their joy, God's spirit children too must obtain a body of "element" as a counterpart to the spirit body (D&C 93:33–34). Both the physical body and the spirit body are created in the image of God (Mosiah 7:27; Ether 3:16–17). Though at death the spirit separates from the mortal body, at the time of RESURRECTION the two bodies will be permanently reunited in a state of immortality (Alma 11:42–45; 40:23).

Proving worthy of eternal life

God's mortal family lives in an environment where good and evil exist side by side thus allowing the exercise of AGENCY (2 Ne. 2:11, 16, 26–27; Alma 12:31). God's children are tried and tested in their mortal environment to see if they will obey the divine commandments (Abr. 3:25–26). Divine judgment is suspended temporarily in order for the principle of repentance to operate (Alma 42:13, 16, 18). Mortality thus becomes a "probationary state" wherein God's children learn lessons essential to exaltation and are "to prepare to meet" him (Alma 12:24; 34:32; 42:10). As part of mankind's preparation, they are to come unto Christ through exercising faith, repenting of their sins, being baptized, receiving the Holy Ghost, serving God, and enduring to the end (2 Ne. 31:11–21; Alma 42:4; 3 Ne. 11:31–40; 27:16–20; cf. 2 Ne. 2:21; Alma 34:33–35). By so doing they can be redeemed through the ATONEMENT and be brought into the presence of God to enjoy eternal life (2 Ne. 2:6–9; Mosiah 26:24; Alma 41:5–8; 42:23–24; Morm. 7:7; 9:13; A of F 3). Those who fail to do so "remain as though there had been no redemption made, except it be the loosing of the bands of death" (Alma 11:41). "Exposed to the whole law of the demands of justice" (Alma 34:16), unrepentant souls suffer for their sins and are denied salvation in the kingdom of God

(1 Ne. 10:21; 15:32–36; 2 Ne. 2:10; Alma 11:41; 12:12–18; 42:24–27).

See also Gospel, the; Happiness; Joy; Opposition in all things; Salvation.

DEB

Light That which stimulates and allows vision. In the Book of Mormon the word *light* is used symbolically and literally as follows:

1. A metaphor for an example or guide. The restored gospel is a light to the latter-day Gentiles (2 Ne. 8:4), and the Savior is a light for those who hear his word (2 Ne. 10:14). Priestcraft consists in men setting themselves up as the light (2 Ne. 26:29). The Savior taught that his people are to be a light for others (3 Ne. 12:14–16; 15:12), and that he is the light they are to hold up (3 Ne. 18:16, 24), for "He is the light and the life of the world; yea, a light that is endless, that can never be darkened" (Mosiah 16:9; cf. D&C 10:70; 11:28). This light stands in contrast to darkness, or that which leads to evil. Choosing darkness kindles God's wrath (Hel. 13:29–30). Therefore, people must be brought from darkness into light (2 Ne. 3:5).

2. A metaphor for understanding and knowledge which comes via the Spirit to the soul. The Lord condemns those who will not seek to gain such light (2 Ne. 32:4). Alma[2] warned that those who murdered against this light would have a hard time finding forgiveness (Alma 39:6) and that the Nephites would perish if they rebelled against the greater light (Alma 9:19). Rejecting the sure light carries heavy consequences (D&C 82:3; 93:31–32).

3. A metaphor for the agent or power by which God gives understanding and knowledge of the great things of his kingdom, and discernment between good and evil. Nephi[1] testified that "the Lord God giveth light unto the understanding" of his word (2 Ne. 31:3; cf. D&C 50:24; 84:45–46; 88:66–67; John 1:6–12). This "light of Christ," or "Spirit of Christ," "fill[s] the immensity of space" (Moro. 7:16–19; D&C 88:6–13).

4. A metaphor for that period when one can come to God, when "his arm of mercy is extended towards you in the light of the day" (Jacob 6:5).

5. Literal light that allows physical vision (e.g., Alma 56:41; 3 Ne. 8:22).

See also Light of Christ.

RDD

Light of Christ Also called the "Spirit of Christ," the light of Christ is a source of REVELATION given of God "to every man, that he may know good from evil" (Moro. 7:16; John 1:9). Mormon urged Church members, "the peaceable followers of Christ" (Moro. 7:3), to "search diligently in the light of Christ that ye may know good from evil," and he warned against judging "wrongfully" between the two, "for with that same judgment which ye judge ye shall also be judged" (Moro. 7:18–19). This light will lead those who live by it to the gospel of Jesus Christ (Alma 16:16–17; D&C 84:45–48). While those who follow the light of Christ receive more and more spiritual truths, those who "harden their hearts, to them is given the lesser portion of the word until they know nothing concerning his mysteries" (Alma 12:10–11; 1 Ne. 17:45; 2 Ne. 28:30).

In addition to being a source of revelation, the light of Christ is defined as the power of God which "proceedeth forth from [his] presence to fill the immensity of space," a creative and governing force that gives life and light to all things (D&C 88:5–13).

The light of Christ is the means by which members of the Godhead are omnipresent, and also the means through which the Holy Ghost communicates gifts and blessings to all mankind (Smith, 1:40, 54).

BIBLIOGRAPHY

Smith, Joseph Fielding. *Doctrines of Salvation.* Compiled by Bruce R. McConkie. 3 vols. Salt Lake City: Bookcraft, 1954–56.

ALW

Liken A literary device used as a teaching tool by Nephi[1], Zenos, and Jesus to help increase the understanding of their listeners in two ways: (1) by comparison and (2) by application.

Liken is sometimes used as a synonym for compare: "I will liken thee, O house of Israel, like unto a tame olive-tree" (Jacob 5:3; cf. 1 Ne.

10:12). Through the use of this imagery, Zenos compared things familiar to the Israelites, such as olive trees, pruning a vineyard, or transplanting and grafting branches, to gospel principles such as a chosen people, the judgments of God, the scattering of Israel, or the gathering of Israel.

Jesus taught "whoso heareth these sayings of mine and doeth them, I will liken him unto a wise man, who built his house upon a rock" (3 Ne. 14:24). In this comparison, the house represents a disciple's life and the ROCK represents Christ's teachings. As a rock foundation protects a house against physical elements, so also is a life founded on Jesus' teachings fortified against the temptations of the world.

Furthermore, Nephi used the term "liken" in connection with how he wanted his people to consider the principles and messages of the scriptures. To "liken" the scriptures to one's life is to see the contemporary relevance and application of their teachings. For example, Isaiah's teachings, which were directed to the house of Israel, would also apply to Nephi's people, who were of that same lineage and subject to the same commandments and covenants. Understanding the importance of personalizing the scriptures in this way, Nephi wrote, "I did liken all scriptures unto us . . . for our profit and learning" (1 Ne. 19:23–24; cf. 2 Ne. 11:8).

See also Book of Mormon, figures of speech in.

TBP

Limhah Nephite military leader killed with his ten thousand troops in the last battle between the Nephites and Lamanites (Morm. 6:14; A.D. 385).

See also Cumorah, battle of.

Limher *See* Amnor.

Limhi Third in a line of kings (ca. 121 B.C.) that ruled over a group of Nephites who had left from Zarahemla around 200 B.C. Their goal was to inherit the land of their fathers, the land of Nephi, a land then occupied by the Lamanites. Limhi was the son of king Noah[3] (the wicked king responsible for Abinadi's death) and the grandson of Zeniff, who led the expedition. Some of the events surrounding Limhi are told twice, first in Mormon's summary account (Mosiah 7–8), and second in the more chronological record of Zeniff (Mosiah 9–22).

Limhi became king of the Nephite colony when the Lamanites overran the land and his wicked father Noah was killed by some of his own men. When Ammon[1], head of a search party from Zarahemla, arrived at Limhi's court, he found Limhi and his people under painful subjection to the Lamanite monarch. The Lamanite king required of them half of everything they produced. Limhi, a just man, rejoiced to learn Ammon's identity, and took hope that his people might be delivered from bondage. Calling them together, Limhi delivered an important address (Mosiah 7:17ff.) in which he declared that by their wickedness, his people had earned their afflictions. Nonetheless, he spoke hopefully, urging his people to "lift up [their] heads and be comforted," and to "rejoice, and put [their] trust in God" (Mosiah 7:18–19).

Before Ammon's arrival, an expedition sent by Limhi in search of Zarahemla had come upon the remains of the Jaredite civilization. The group returned to Limhi carrying twenty-four inscribed gold plates. He rejoiced to learn from Ammon that the Nephite king had special interpretive instruments and a gift for interpreting languages (Mosiah 8:19; 21:28). Fired with a longing to escape and rejoin the Nephites in Zarahemla, Limhi and many of his people "covenant[ed] with God . . . to serve him and keep his commandments" (Mosiah 21:32). Moreover, "they were desirous to be baptized as a witness and a testimony that they were willing to serve God with all their hearts" (Mosiah 21:35). Through a stratagem devised by the faithful Gideon, Limhi and his people took flight and arrived safely in Zarahemla. After being taught by Alma[1], they were all baptized (Mosiah 25:17–18).

BRM

Limnah *See* Nephite weights and measures.

Linen A fabric made from plant fibers. In the Book of Mormon linen is always described as either "fine" or "fine-twined," and is often cited as a sign of prosperity and pride among the

Nephites (2 Ne. 13:23; Mosiah 10:5; Alma 1:29; 4:6; Hel. 6:13). It was characteristic of the great and abominable church as described by Nephi[1] (1 Ne. 13:7, 8). The Jaredites had linen as well (Ether 9:17; 10:24).

Usually "linen" is a term used to describe a cloth made from the pounded fibers of the cultivated flax plant *Linum usitatissimum*. This flax was grown throughout the ancient world, especially in Egypt. There is currently no evidence that cultivated flax was grown in the Americas in Book of Mormon times, though several wild species are native. It is possible that the Jaredites and/or Nephites could have brought domestic flax with them, or perhaps the word linen in the Book of Mormon is describing cloths made from the fibers of native plants. For example, a fiber called henequen, from the leaf of the agave plant, and a cloth made from the bark of the fig tree were common in Mesoamerica.

See also Silk.

BIBLIOGRAPHY

Sorenson, John L. "Possible 'Silk' and 'Linen' in the Book of Mormon." *Reexploring the Book of Mormon*. Edited by John W. Welch. Salt Lake City and Provo: Deseret Book and FARMS, 1992.

DRS

Lion *See* Animals; Micah.

List *See* Appendix C.

Loathsome *See* Appendix C.

Loins 1. The waist or midsection of the body, considered by Old Testament cultures to be the seat of vigor or strength. To "gird" one's loins means to cover or protect this area of the body (e.g., Alma 43:20; 46:13), or to attach some piece of equipment about the waist (e.g., 1 Ne. 4:21). Isaiah prophesied that when the millennial Messiah reigns "righteousness shall be the girdle of his loins" (2 Ne. 21:5; 30:11) suggesting that he will be clothed with and govern in righteousness.

2. That which generates posterity—for example, "out of the fruit of his loins" (2 Ne. 3:5), or, "a righteous branch from the fruit of the loins of Joseph" (Jacob 2:25).

DLL

Long-suffering Bearing long with some adversity (i.e., offense, hardship, provocation) in performing a task or in working with people. Not merely an alternative phrase for PATIENCE, but patient perseverance over an extended period with a certain degree of difficulty. Prior to their missionary labors among the Lamanites, the Lord told the sons of Mosiah[2], "Yet ye shall be patient in long-suffering and afflictions" (Alma 17:11; cf. 38:3–4).

Long-suffering is an attribute of God (Mosiah 4:6, 11; Alma 5:6; 9:11, 26; 26:16; 42:30). Christ's merciful restraint while in the hands of his persecutors, and his subsequent atoning sacrifice epitomized this element of his nature. Nephi[1] wrote, "They scourge him, and he suffereth it; and they smite him, and he suffereth it. Yea, they spit upon him, and he suffereth it, because of his loving kindness and his long-suffering towards the children of men" (1 Ne. 19:9; cf. Moro. 9:25). Mormon identified long-suffering as a characteristic of one who has charity: "Charity suffereth long, and is kind . . . is not easily provoked . . . beareth all things, believeth all things, hopeth all things, endureth all things" (Moro. 7:44–45; cf. 1 Cor. 13:4). The allegory of Zenos illustrates well the long-suffering of God, showing his merciful forbearance throughout history: the Lord spared the vineyard despite wickedness and apostasy, and he made continual efforts to encourage his people to be righteous (Jacob 5; 6:4).

The Book of Mormon also speaks of long-suffering in context with gaining spiritual knowledge (Alma 32:41–43) and with exhorting people to diligence and obedience (Jarom 1:11; Mosiah 27:33). Alma[2] taught that the Holy Spirit, obtained through humility and prayer, can lead one to become "full of love and all long-suffering" (Alma 13:28; cf. Mosiah 3:19).

MMM

Looking beyond the mark To look beyond Christ, for "the mark is Christ" (Maxwell, 26). The English word *mark* means "target" or "goal." Thus the image is of one who misses the target because he looks beyond it. The prophet Jacob[2] was using this idiomatic expression to identify the cause of the spiritual blindness of the Jews that caused them in Old Testament times to look beyond the plain truths of the gospel of Jesus Christ: "But behold, the Jews were a stiffnecked people; and they despised the words of plainness, and killed the prophets, and sought for things that they could not understand. Wherefore, because of their blindness, which blindness came by looking beyond the mark, they must needs fall; for God hath taken away his plainness from them, and delivered unto them many things which they cannot understand, because they desired it" (Jacob 4:14). Jacob continued to prophesy that such blindness would cause the Jews to reject Christ, "the stone upon which they might build and have safe foundation," when he came in the flesh (Jacob 4:15).

Elder Gene R. Cook used the metaphor "looking beyond the mark" to warn against "exotic extremes in any principle, like excessively lengthy prayers, false doctrines about the Savior or about Adam, or extremes in diet, or politics, or investments" (26).

See also Blindness, spiritual; Plainness.

BIBLIOGRAPHY

Cook, Gene R. "Spiritual Guides for Teachers of Righteousness." *Ensign* 12 (May 1982): 25–27.

Maxwell, Neal A. "Jesus of Nazareth, Savior and King." *Ensign* 6 (May 1976): 26–27.

DKJ

Lost manuscript of the Book of Mormon (116 pages) *See* Book of Mormon, lost manuscript of (116 pages).

Lost tribes *See* Israel, lost tribes of.

Love *See* Charity.

Love of God The mercy, tender regard, and condescension of God toward his children. A supreme evidence of God's love is the gift of his Son Jesus Christ (1 Ne. 11:4–8, 21–22, 25; John 3:16; D&C 34:3), the fruits flowing from the Atonement being "most desirable above all things" (1 Ne. 11:22). As people are forgiven and born of the Spirit, they "sing the song of redeeming love" (Alma 5:26) and are enabled to love others as God loves them (1 Ne. 8:12; 2 Ne. 31:19–20; Enos 1: 2–11; Moro. 7:48; 8:26).

RCR

Lowliness of heart A spiritual state ascribed to the Lord (Zech. 9:9; Matt. 11:29), often coupled with MEEKNESS and closely akin to HUMILITY. It is characterized by a readiness to hear the word of God and by true penitence (Alma 32:6–8, 12). The Lord commended the faith of Nephi[1] for seeking Him with lowliness of heart (1 Ne. 2:19). Alma[2] taught that the meek and lowly in heart "find rest to their souls" (Alma 37:33–34). Mormon connected lowliness of heart with other spiritual gifts—it precedes the gifts of faith, hope, and charity; that is, one "cannot have faith and hope, save he shall be meek, and lowly of heart. If so, his faith and hope is vain, for none is acceptable before God, save the meek and lowly in heart" (Moro. 7:43–44). He further taught that "the remission of sins bringeth meekness, and lowliness of heart; and because of meekness and lowliness of heart cometh the visitation of the Holy Ghost, which Comforter filleth with hope and perfect love" (Moro. 8:26).

MCT

Lucifer *See* Satan.

Lucre *See* Appendix C.

Luram *See* Archeantus.

Therefore, whosoever repenteth, and hardeneth not his heart, he shall have claim on **mercy** through mine Only Begotten Son, unto a remission of his sins; and these shall enter into my rest. ALMA 12:34

Mahah *See* Jared[1], posterity of.

Make his paths straight An idiom denoting preparation. John the Baptist used this phrase in parallel with his cry to "prepare . . . the way of the Lord" (1 Ne. 10:8; Matt. 3:3; cf. Isa. 40:3). Alma[2] taught the Gideonites that they were "making his paths straight" by walking in "paths of righteousness." It is this path "which leads to the kingdom of God" (Alma 7:19). Alma also taught them that the Lord "cannot walk in crooked paths" (Alma 7:20) and "his course is one eternal round" (Alma 37:12; D&C 3:2). When people walk in crooked paths they hinder not only their own progression but also the progression of those around them (e.g., Alma 36:14; 39:11). In order, therefore, to "make his paths straight," one must remove all obstacles that create detours. Alma identified repentance as the principal means of doing so (Alma 7:9; cf. Matt. 3:1–3). Christ, however, also participates in preparing the path (2 Ne. 4:33). He removes obstacles (2 Ne. 9:10), the ultimate ones being death (Alma 40:3) and the consequences of sin for those who come unto him (2 Ne. 9:21–23).

GS

Malachi chapter review: 3 Nephi 24–25 // Malachi 3–4

Background and synopsis

In Jewish tradition Malachi is the last of the Hebrew prophets, but the book of Malachi gives little information about when Malachi lived and prophesied. Sacrifices were being offered at the temple (Mal. 1:7–10; 3:8), and a reference is made to a Persian official (Mal. 1:8); therefore it must be dated after the rebuilding of the temple in 515 B.C. and before the Persian empire was conquered by Alexander the Great in 331 B.C. The book of Malachi is usually dated to the period between 450–400 B.C. Malachi addressed a community who had returned from Babylon in 539 B.C., had rebuilt the temple, had renewed their allegiance to the covenant under Ezra (Neh. 8–10), but were already in apostasy. He called them to repentance and promised them that the Lord would send messengers to prepare the way for the coming of the Lord. When Christ came in glory he would judge the earth, the righteous he would refine and purify, and the wicked he would destroy.

Jesus commanded the Nephites "that they should write the words which the Father had given unto Malachi, which he should tell unto them" (3 Ne. 24:1). The Lord then quoted Malachi 3 and 4 in their entirety in 3 Nephi 24–25. These two chapters of Malachi were important to the Book of Mormon peoples as a warning of future apostasy, and as a comfort that the Lord would one day send messengers to restore the covenant and prepare the way for his return in glory. The Savior emphasized the importance of these passages, explaining, "These scriptures, which ye had not with you, the Father commanded that I should give unto you; for it was wisdom in him that they should be given unto future generations" (3 Ne. 26:2). Therefore they are even more relevant to the Saints in the latter days who will witness and participate in their fulfillment.

Some of the language Malachi used was also familiar to Nephi[1], who lived two centuries before Malachi: "consumed as stubble," "led up as calves of the stall," and "the Son of righteousness shall appear unto them; and he shall heal them" (1 Ne. 22:23–24; 2 Ne. 26:9). It may be that this is because the Lord spoke to both prophets with similar language. It is also possible that this language was common and proverbial in biblical culture or that Nephi quoted from one of the prophets on the brass plates that may have been a source Malachi used.

Definitions

24:1 *Malachi.* Last Israelite prophet, probably 450–400 B.C. His name in Hebrew means "my messenger."

24:1 *my messenger, and he shall prepare the way before me.* It is not clear if a specific messenger is intended or if this is speaking collectively of the many messengers that the Lord would send. Many messengers were and are involved in the preparation for the coming of the Lord. Messengers preparing the way for the first coming included Malachi himself, whose name means "my messenger"; John the Baptist (Matt. 11:10); Elijah and Moses (Matt. 17:3); Samuel the Lamanite (Hel. 13–15); and Nephi[3]

MAL. CHAP. REVIEW: (3 NE. 24–25 // MAL. 3–4)

(3 Ne. 7). Messengers preparing the way for the Second Coming include Moroni[2] (JS–H 1:30–54); John the Baptist (D&C 13; JS–H 1:68–74); Peter, James, and John (JS–H 1:68–74); Moses, Elias, Elijah (D&C 110:11–16); Michael, Gabriel, Raphael (D&C 128:21); and Joseph Smith (D&C 1:17–30). In the Doctrine and Covenants the restored gospel is also referred to as a messenger: "I have sent mine everlasting covenant into the world . . . to be a messenger before my face to prepare the way before me" (D&C 45:9).

24:1 *the Lord whom ye seek shall suddenly come to his temple.* The Lord suddenly came to his temple in Kirtland on 3 April 1836 (D&C 110:1–10). It is likely this prophecy has multiple fulfillments and also refers to a future appearance in the temple to be built in Jackson County, Missouri.

24:1 *even the messenger of the covenant.* The Lord Jesus Christ.

24:2 *who may abide the day of his coming.* The righteous Saints and all those worthy of a terrestrial glory will be able to endure the glory of the coming of Christ (Smith, *Doctrines,* 1:86–87; 3:63–64).

24:2 *refiner's fire.* This is a simile of purifying metals by burning out impurities, symbolic of the purification of the repentant through the Atonement.

24:2 *fuller's soap.* A fuller was one who cleaned or whitened cloth. He used a strong alkaline salt or soap in cleaning fabrics. Like the refiner's fire, it is symbolic of the purification of the repentant.

24:3 *an offering in righteousness.* This offering may refer to more than one thing (D&C 13; 84:31). Joseph Smith taught that animal sacrifice will be restored as part of the restoration of all things and would be part of this offering by the sons of Levi (*Teachings*, 172–73). Malachi 3:2–3 is also quoted in D&C 128, and the Prophet Joseph Smith exhorted the members of the Church to "offer unto the Lord an offering in righteousness . . . a book containing the records of our dead" (D&C 128:24).

24:5 *And I will come near to you to judgment.* Here the Lord answers the question, "But who may abide the day of his coming" by listing

OUTLINE OF 3 NEPHI 24–25

I. Messengers to prepare for the coming of the Lord (24:1–5)
   A. A messenger to precede the coming of the Lord to his temple (24:1)
   B. Coming of the Lord to refine and purify (24:2)
   C. Lord to purify the sons of Levi[1] who will offer an offering to the Lord in righteousness (24:3–4)
   D. Wicked to be destroyed (24:5)

II. If the sons of Jacob will repent, the Lord will return to them (24:6–7)

III. The Lord will bless those who are faithful in tithes and offerings (24:8–12)

IV. Rewards for those who serve the Lord (24:13–25:3)
   A. Some say it is vain to serve the Lord (24:13–15)
   B. Those that fear the Lord are recorded in a book of remembrance and become the Lord's "jewels" (24:16–17)
   C. In the end the righteous and the wicked will be discerned and distinguished (24:18)
   D. Wicked to be burned as stubble and the Son of Righteousness will come with healing in his wings (25:1–3)

V. Restoration of all things (25:4–6)
   A. Remember the law of Moses (25:4)
   B. Elijah will return before the great and dreadful day of the Lord (25:5)
   C. Elijah will turn the heart of the fathers to the children and the children to the fathers (25:6)

MAL. CHAP. REVIEW: (3 NE. 24–25 // MAL. 3–4)

those who will *not* be able to endure the Second Coming (3 Ne. 24:2).

24:5 *against those that oppress the hireling in his wages, the widow and the fatherless, and that turn aside the stranger.* Jesus considered mercy among the "weightier matters of the law" (Matt. 23:23). In the eyes of the Lord the oppression of widows, orphans, and strangers is a serious offense (Ex. 22:21–24). The gravity of this matter is reaffirmed in D&C 136:8.

24:8 *tithes and offerings.* Because the Savior reiterated this commandment after the fulfillment of the Mosaic law it is clear that tithing and offerings had a place in the practice of the higher law before the law of Moses was institutionalized, just as it does in the restored gospel (D&C 119:3–4).

24:10 *windows of heaven.* A metaphor for rain (Gen. 7:11; 2 Kgs. 7:2). In ancient Israel rain was essential for the survival and prosperity of the people and was preeminent among the spiritual and temporal blessings promised for obedience to the covenant (Lev. 26; Deut. 11:13–17).

24:11 *devourer.* Perhaps a reference to the locust that would eat the crops. This was one of the curses pronounced upon the people if they did not keep the covenant (Deut. 28:38–42).

24:16 *they that feared the Lord.* The Hebrew verb meaning "to fear" can also be translated "to revere" or "to honor."

24:16 *book of remembrance.* Other passages in scripture teach that the names of the righteous will be recorded in the book of life (Alma 5:57–58; Ex. 32:33; Dan. 12:1; Rev. 3:5; 20:12, 15), the members of the church of the Firstborn will be written in heaven (D&C 76:68), and those who will inherit eternal life shall be written in the "Lamb's Book of Life" (D&C 132:19).

24:17 *jewels.* This is the same word used to express the covenant relationship between God and his people as "peculiar treasure" in Exodus 19:5 (cf. D&C 101:3).

25:1 *stubble.* Image of harvest when grasses and grains were cut close to the ground and removed and the remaining short stiff stalks were burned. This image is a symbol of the destruction of the wicked after the righteous have been "harvested."

25:1 *root nor branch.* Image of total destruction derived from the withering of an uprooted tree or plant (cf. Ezek. 17:8–9). Perhaps the root symbolizes one's ancestors and branches one's posterity. To be without "root or branch" in this sense would describe someone for whom the sealing blessings of the Melchizedek Priesthood had not been performed or someone who had not been worthy of these blessings. The keys to these priesthood blessings were restored by Elijah (D&C 110:13–16).

25:2 *Son of Righteousness arise.* Malachi reads, "Sun of righteousness." Both refer to the coming of Christ.

25:2 *healing in his wings.* The power of the Atonement to overcome sin and death and "to comfort all that mourn" (Isa. 61:2) and "wipe away tears from off all faces" (Isa. 25:8; Rev. 21:4).

25:2 *ye shall go forth and grow up as calves in the stall.* Calves that were fed and fattened in the stalls, as opposed to grazing on the range, were especially healthy and strong and produced the best breeding stock and meat. This may be a figurative expression for the children of the covenant, "hand-fed" and raised by the Lord. Similarly, the Doctrine & Covenants refers to the faithful inheriting the earth at the Second Coming and promises "their children shall grow up without sin unto salvation" (D&C 45:58).

25:4 *law of Moses.* Moses, the giver of the law and the mediator of the covenant was translated (Alma 45:19) and restored the keys of the gathering of Israel on the Mount of Transfiguration (Matt. 17:3) and in the Kirtland Temple (D&C 110:11).

25:5 *Elijah the prophet.* Israelite prophet (ca. 900–800 B.C.). Elijah was translated (2 Kgs. 2:10–12) and restored the keys of sealing power on the Mount of Transfiguration (Matt. 17:3) and in the Kirtland Temple (D&C 110:13–16).

25:6 *turn the heart of the fathers to the children, and the heart of the children to their fathers.* An image of the power of sealing keys to connect the fathers and the children. The Prophet Joseph Smith commented, "the word *turn* here should be translated *bind*, or seal" (*Teachings*, 330). Moroni[2] further clarified this phrase in D&C 2:2: "And he shall plant in the hearts of the children the promises made to the fathers, and the hearts of the children shall turn to their fathers." The "promises made to the fathers" refers to the promise of the everlasting covenant that the time would come when the dead would be redeemed (Smith, *Doctrines*, 2:154).

25:6 *lest I come and smite the earth with a curse.* Without the keys of the kingdom the earth would not be prepared to receive the Savior at his coming. Joseph Smith taught that this curse would come upon the earth "unless there is a welding link of some kind or other between the fathers and the children" through baptism and priesthood sealings for the dead (D&C 128:17–18).

Significant differences between Book of Mormon Malachi (3 Ne. 24–25) and KJV Malachi (Mal. 3–4)

Several passages differ slightly in wording with little difference in meaning. In verses 5, 13, and 16 of Malachi 3, words that are italicized in the KJV are eliminated in 3 Nephi. The most significant difference is the phrase "Sun of righteousness" (Mal. 4:2) that occurs in 3 Nephi 25:2 as "Son of Righteousness." When Moroni quoted Malachi 4:5–6 to Joseph Smith, he made some significant changes from the KJV and from 3 Nephi 25. Moroni quoted Malachi 4:5, "Behold, I will reveal unto you the Priesthood, by the hand of Elijah the prophet" (JS–H 1:38) instead of the KJV, "Behold, I will send you Elijah the prophet." He also cited Malachi 4:6, "And he shall plant in the hearts of the children the promises made to the fathers, and the hearts of the children shall turn to their fathers" (JS–H 1:39) rather than the KJV, "And he shall turn the heart of the fathers to the children, and the heart of the children to their fathers."

Latter-day applicability

Moroni quoted portions of Malachi 3 and all of Malachi 4 to Joseph Smith, together with other Old Testament prophecies, promising that they were about to be fulfilled (JS–H 1:36–40). Latter-day Saints live in a time similar to that of Malachi, when temples are built and functioning. Modern culture presents many of the challenges faced by ancient Israel at the time of Malachi: doubting that the Lord loves his covenant people (Mal. 1:2–6), offering the worst instead of the best to the Lord (Mal. 1:6–8, 12–14), divorce and marriage to those outside the covenant (Mal. 2:14–16), not being honest and faithful in financial obligations to the Lord (Mal. 3:8–12), complaining that the wicked prosper while the righteous do not (Mal. 2:17), and believing it is vain to serve the Lord—calling "the proud happy" (Mal. 3:13–15). Malachi reminded the Saints that the Lord has promised to send messengers to prepare the way for his coming. Many of these messengers have already come and have restored keys and prepared the way. Through Elijah the sealing keys of the priesthood are restored making it possible for all to partake of the sealing power to be found in the temples—to establish holy eternal bonds between fathers, mothers, and their children, and their children to their ancestors (D&C 110:13–15). Great promises are made to those who are faithful and who "fear the Lord": they will be able to endure his coming, they will be purified and their names recorded in the book of remembrance, they will become the Lord's jewels, and they will be healed by the Son of Righteousness. On the other hand, the wicked, the proud, and those who fear not the Lord will face destruction.

See also Jesus Christ, second coming of; Pride.

BIBLIOGRAPHY

Smith, Joseph. *Teachings of the Prophet Joseph Smith*. Selected by Joseph Fielding Smith. Salt Lake City: Deseret Book, 1976.

Smith, Joseph Fielding. *Doctrines of Salvation*. Compiled by Bruce R. McConkie. 3 vols. Salt Lake City: Deseret Book, 1954–56.

DRS

Mammon An Aramaic word designating wealth (Hauck, 4:388–90). The Book of Mormon repeatedly stresses the negative effects of wealth (e.g., Jacob 2:13; Alma 4:6–8) when it displaces God as the center of one's devotions (3 Ne. 13:24; Hel. 13:22).

See also Riches.

BIBLIOGRAPHY

Hauck, F. *Theological Dictionary of the New Testament.* 8 vols. Edited by Gerhard Kittel. Translated by Geoffrey W. Bromiley. Grand Rapids, Mich.: Eerdmans, 1964–76. S.v. μαμωνᾶς.

GS

Man, creation of It is clear that Book of Mormon peoples, both Jaredites and Nephites, possessed accounts of the creation of man (Ether 1:3; 1 Ne. 5:11), though the texts of those accounts are not repeated in the Book of Mormon. Likely the Nephite version, on the "plates of brass," was much the same as that found in the book of Moses in the Pearl of Great Price (Reynolds, 2:136–73). Ammon[2] and Aaron[3] both used one such scriptural account of the creation of man in introducing the gospel to king Lamoni and his father (Alma 18:36–39; 22:12–13).

An arresting detail about the creation of man found in the Book of Mormon concerns the words of the premortal Jesus to the brother of Jared[1]: "Seest thou that ye are created after mine own image? Yea, even all men were created in the beginning after mine own image. Behold, this body, which ye now behold, is the body of my spirit; and man have I created after the body of my spirit" (Ether 3:15–16). In light of what is taught elsewhere in scripture and prophetic commentary about the role of the Father and the Son in the creation of man, it is probable that Jesus, in this instance, was speaking as if he were the Father, according to the principle of "divine investiture of authority" (First Presidency, 470–71; cf. Moses 2:1; Abr. 4:26–27; Heb. 1:1–2; Gen. 1:26–27).

Other references to the creation of man in the Book of Mormon focus upon the purposes of his CREATION. Lehi[1] explained that after God created "all things," including "our first parents," in order "to bring about his eternal purposes" He gave "unto man that he should act for himself," which entailed enticement either toward "the forbidden fruit" of the tree of knowledge, or toward "the tree of life; the one being sweet and the other bitter" (2 Ne. 2:14–16). By extension, one purpose of creation was to tender an environment of opposition and AGENCY to all who would come after Adam and Eve. Explaining further as to God's purpose in creating man, Lehi specified that the creation of Adam and Eve was planned to lead to the Fall, and therefore to bringing children into the world "that they might have joy" (2 Ne. 2:22–25). Alma[2] added the insight that Adam and Eve were not permitted to partake of the tree of life after the Fall, because such a course would have frustrated the plan of redemption, resulting in their being "forever miserable" rather than happy (Alma 12:21–28).

Thus, the Book of Mormon contributes more to understanding the purposes of the creation of man than to how the creation took place, explaining that the crowning purpose was to bring about man's JOY or HAPPINESS, the fulness of which is found in obtaining immortality and eternal life (Mosiah 2:41; 16:11; cf. Moses 1:39; D&C 93:33–34).

See also Body of my spirit; Earth, the; Fall of Adam and Eve, the; Life, purpose of.

BIBLIOGRAPHY

First Presidency and the Quorum of the Twelve Apostles. "The Father and the Son: A Doctrinal Exposition by the First Presidency and the Twelve." *The Articles of Faith,* by James E. Talmage. London: The Church of Jesus Christ of Latter-day Saints, 1924.

Reynolds, Noel B. "The Brass Plates Version of Genesis." *By Study and Also by Faith,* 2 vols. Edited by John M. Lundquist and Stephen D. Ricks. Salt Lake City: Deseret Book, 1990.

SKB

Man, natural *See* Natural man.

Manasseh Eldest son of Joseph[1] and Asenath (Gen. 41:50–51; 46:20). His grandfather Jacob[1] blessed him and promised that his posterity would become a great people (Gen. 48:1–20). A tribe of Israel descended from Manasseh and was given an inheritance in the promised land west of the Jordan River, around the area of Samaria, and east of the Jordan River in the pasture lands of Bashan and Gilead (Num. 32:33, 39–41; Deut. 3:13; Josh. 17:1–12; 22:7). Lehi[1] and his family were descendants of Joseph through Manasseh (1 Ne. 5:14; Alma 10:3). Old

Testament prophets spoke of this particular branch of Joseph's family. For example, when Lehi's family came to the Americas from Jerusalem they fulfilled in part the prophetic promise Jacob pronounced upon his son Joseph that his descendants, as "a fruitful bough," would "run over the wall" of a "well," or cross the oceans (Gen. 49:22). The Nephites recognized their status as a branch of Israel broken off or separated from their homeland (1 Ne. 15:12; 19:24; Jacob 2:25; Alma 36:26). Moreover, the record that Lehi's family wrote is the "stick of Joseph" about which Ezekiel prophesied (Ezek. 37:15–19; 2 Ne. 3:12; D&C 27:5). Furthermore, as Moses blessed the tribes of Israel he promised that the descendants of Manasseh, along with Ephraim's, would "push" or gather "the people together to the ends of the earth" (Deut. 33:17). This prophecy finds fulfillment in the latter-day gathering of the covenant people initiated by these descendants of Joseph (D&C 58:44–45).

BIBLIOGRAPHY

Smith, Joseph Fielding. *Doctrines of Salvation*. Compiled by Bruce R. McConkie. 3 vols. Salt Lake City: Bookcraft, 1954–56. 3:209–12.

TBB

Manti *See* Amnor.

Manti, hill The apostate Nehor was carried to "the top of the hill Manti" after being pronounced guilty of killing the righteous Gideon (ca. 91 B.C.). There Nehor acknowledged his false teachings and suffered an "ignominious death" (Alma 1:2–15).

Manti, land of and city of One of the Nephite lands, located southward from the land of Gideon (Alma 17:1). The land of Manti is mentioned as one of the dividing borders between the Nephite and Lamanite territories (Alma 22:27). Alma[2] was journeying toward the land of Manti when he met the sons of Mosiah[2] (Alma 17:1; ca. 91 B.C.). The land of Manti was also the site of a strategic battle between the armies of Moroni[1] and the Lamanites (Alma 43:22–42; ca. 74 B.C.). It is also referenced in other confrontations (Alma 56:14; 58:1–28).

The city of Manti located in the land of Manti was conquered by the Lamanites (Alma 56:13–14) and later retaken through a cunning strategy by Helaman[2] (Alma 58:1–2, 13–28; ca. 63 B.C.). As instructed by Helaman, Gid and Teomner hid their small forces in the wilderness to the right and left of Helaman's army. When the numerically superior Lamanite forces came out of Manti to attack, Helaman led a mock retreat toward Zarahemla with the Lamanite army in hot pursuit. Manti was thus left virtually undefended, and Gid and Teomner retook it handily. Fearing a trap as they drew nearer to Zarahemla, the Lamanite army reversed its course and camped for the night. But while the Lamanites slept, Helaman doubled back to Manti. When the Lamanites arrived to find the Nephites in possession of the city—and prepared for war—they fled into the wilderness.

Manuscripts, original/printers *See* Book of Mormon, manuscripts of.

Mar *See* Appendix C.

Marriage Although the Book of Mormon makes little direct reference to marriage relationships, the place and importance of marriage in the plan of salvation is clearly evident.

At the outset, the Lord instructed Lehi[1] to send his sons back to Jerusalem for Ishmael[1] and his family, consisting of both sons and daughters, so the children of Lehi would have marriage partners to "raise up seed unto the Lord in the land of promise" (1 Ne. 7:1–6; 16:7; 2 Ne. 5:6). Also by command of the Lord to Lehi, Nephite marriages were to be monogamous, and faithfulness to a single marriage partner was enjoined. Jacob[2] severely chastised certain Nephite men of his day who sought "to excuse themselves in committing whoredoms, because of the things which were written concerning David, and Solomon his son"—events pertaining to a different people living in a different time and under different commandments pertaining to marriage (which commandments some did not observe appropriately) (Jacob 2:22–35; cf. D&C 132:38–39). During his personal ministry among the Nephites, the Lord affirmed the higher law of marriage, in which divorce is not appropriate "saving for the cause of fornication" (3 Ne. 12:31–32).

Indirectly, for the careful reader, the Book of Mormon yields a number of valuable insights related to marriage and family. For example, Lehi's tender, faith-filled response to the complaints of his wife, Sariah, provides a model for settling some marital difficulties (1 Ne. 5:1–9). A lesson can also be learned by comparing the response of wicked and righteous husbands in times of crisis. The wicked priests of king Noah[3] abandoned their marriage partners (Mosiah 19:11), while righteous husbands protected and defended their wives and children, even by war, when necessary (Alma 43:47; 48:10). Furthermore, maintaining spirituality through gospel living is essential to happiness in marriage. After the visit of the resurrected Lord in America, a blissful Nephite society was characterized for nearly two hundred years by righteous, happy marriages: "They were married, and given in marriage, and were blessed according to the multitude of the promises which the Lord had made unto them. . . . There was no contention in the land, because of the love of God which did dwell in the hearts of the people. . . . There were no envyings, nor strifes, nor tumults, nor whoredoms, nor lyings, . . . and surely there could not be a happier people among all the people who had been created by the hand of God" (4 Ne. 1:11, 15–16).

In addition to providing these direct and indirect messages pertaining to marriage, the Book of Mormon can strengthen marriage relationships by conveying doctrinal truths central to the plan of salvation. Concerning the influence doctrine can have in one's life, Elder Boyd K. Packer has taught, "True doctrine, understood, changes attitudes and behavior. The study of the doctrines of the gospel will improve behavior quicker than a study of behavior will improve behavior. Preoccupation with unworthy behavior can lead to unworthy behavior. That is why we stress so forcefully the study of the doctrines of the gospel" (20). Some examples of doctrinal truths having important application in marriage include personal accountability for one's behavior towards others, such as thoughts, words, and deeds (Mosiah 4:30; Alma 12:14); the Holy Ghost revealing "all things what ye should do" (2 Ne. 32:3, 5); and prayer as a critical link to spiritual blessings (2 Ne. 32:9; Alma 5:46; 17:3; 34:17–27). Through the exercise of self-discipline, based on a correct understanding of true doctrine, men and women can bring their behavior into conformity with eternal principles, resulting in happy, fulfilling marriages.

Consistent with Book of Mormon teachings about marriage, a proclamation published in 1995 by prophets, seers, and revelators confirmed "that marriage between a man and a woman is ordained of God" (First Presidency).

BIBLIOGRAPHY

First Presidency and the Quorum of the Twelve Apostles. "The Family: A Proclamation to the World." *Ensign* 25 (November 1995): 120.

Packer, Boyd K. Conference Report, October 1986.

DEB

Marvelous work, marvelous work and a wonder The restored gospel of Jesus Christ as revealed through the Prophet Joseph Smith (Smith, 1:35). Book of Mormon readers first encounter this expression in the first book of Nephi: "For the time cometh, saith the Lamb of God, that I will work a great and a marvelous work among the children of men" (1 Ne. 14:7). After citing extracts from the writings of Isaiah found on the brass plates (1 Ne. 21 // Isa. 49), Nephi[1] provided inspired commentary on passages which related specifically to the last days when the descendants of Lehi[1] would receive the true gospel again: "And after our seed is scattered the Lord God will proceed to do a marvelous work among the Gentiles, which shall be of great worth unto our seed" (1 Ne. 22:8). Nephi further stated that this work would also be of "worth unto the Gentiles" and "all the house of Israel," bringing the Lord's covenants and gospel to them (1 Ne. 22:9–11).

After another lengthy citation of Isaiah's prophecies, Nephi again provided commentary for those living in his day as well as for the modern reader. His explication provides an inspired view of Israel's future (2 Ne. 25). Nephi stated that after the rejection of the Messiah and the subsequent scattering of the Jews, "the Lord will set his hand again the second time to restore his people from their lost and fallen state. Wherefore, he will proceed to do a marvelous work and a wonder among the children of men" (2 Ne. 25:17). The verse immediately following refers directly to the coming forth of the Book of Mormon, a principal part of this marvelous work: "Wherefore, he shall bring forth his words unto them, which words shall judge them at the last day, for they shall be given them for the purpose of convincing them of the true Messiah, who was rejected by them" (2 Ne. 25:18). The Book of Mormon title page affirms that one of the purposes of its coming forth is to convince "the Jew and Gentile that JESUS is the CHRIST, the ETERNAL GOD, manifesting himself unto all nations."

Nephi continued his Isaiah quotations and commentary in 2 Nephi 27. As a solution to latter-day apostasy the Lord promised, "Therefore, I will proceed to do a marvelous work among this people, yea, a marvelous work and a wonder, for the wisdom of their wise and learned shall perish, and the understanding of their prudent shall be hid" (2 Ne. 27:6–26). Again, Nephi's Isaiah quotations emphasized the Book of Mormon as a key element of the marvelous work: "And it shall come to pass that the Lord God shall bring forth unto you the words of a book, and they shall be the words of them which have slumbered. . . . And in that day shall the deaf hear the words of the book, and the eyes of the blind shall see out of obscurity and out of darkness" (2 Ne. 27:6, 29).

Nephi quoted the Lord again in 2 Nephi 29, in which the Lord said he would "do a marvelous work," whereby he would remember his covenants "unto the children of men, . . . to recover [his] people, which are of the house of Israel." This marvelous work would include delivering the words of the Nephites to later generations (2 Ne. 29:1–2). When the risen Christ appeared to the children of Lehi[1], he also prophesied of this marvelous work, a work he would do among latter-day Gentiles: "For in that day, for my sake shall the Father work a work, which shall be a great and a marvelous work among them" (3 Ne. 21:9).

Modern scripture also speaks directly of the "marvelous work . . . about to come forth among the children of men" (D&C 4:1; 6:1; 11:1; 12:1; 14:1; 18:44). These prophecies were generally fulfilled when the Book of Mormon was published and The Church of Jesus Christ of Latter-day Saints was established in 1830.

BIBLIOGRAPHY

Smith, Joseph Fielding. *Church History and Modern Revelation.* 4 vols. Salt Lake City: Deseret Book, 1953.

RNH

Mary The mother of the Son of God "after the manner of the flesh" (1 Ne. 11:18; Mosiah 3:8; Alma 7:10; 19:13). The Book of Mormon account both confirms Isaiah's foreknowledge of a VIRGIN who would be the mother of the Messiah (Isa. 7:14) and records additional prophecy understood by the children of Lehi[1]. They knew that she would live in Nazareth (1 Ne. 11:13), would be called by the name "Mary" (the English equivalent of the Hebrew

Be It unto Me; *painting by Liz Lemon Swindle; courtesy Liz Lemon Swindle. "Behold, the virgin whom thou seest is the mother of the Son of God, after the manner of the flesh" (1 Ne. 11:18).*

Miriam) while on earth (Mosiah 3:8), and that she was a "precious and chosen vessel" (Alma 7:10). Nephi[1] saw Mary in vision and described her as "most beautiful and fair above all other virgins" (1 Ne. 11:15).

See also After the manner of the flesh; Conceive by the power of the Holy Ghost.

CF

Mathoni *See* Disciples, twelve Nephite.

Mathonihah *See* Disciples, twelve Nephite.

Mediator One who acts to reconcile an estranged relationship. Because of the Fall and because all people sin, all are estranged from God. Christ, "the great Mediator of all men," reconciles this relationship for those who seek forgiveness through the Atonement, and who are obedient to the laws and ordinances of the gospel (2 Ne. 2:27; A of F 3). Lehi[1] taught that no flesh can dwell in the presence of God if it were not for the INTERCESSION of Jesus Christ—his merits, MERCY, and GRACE (2 Ne. 2:8–10). Men and women are dependent upon Jesus Christ as their advocate to plead their cause before the Father (D&C 45:3–5; 1 Tim. 2:5).

See also Merits of Christ.

SAJ

Meekness Gentleness; submission to divine will. A quality that the Lord attributes to himself (Matt. 11:29); a childlike quality (Mosiah 3:19; Matt. 11:29), often coupled with LOWLINESS OF HEART (e.g., Alma 37:33; Moro. 7:43). Meekness characterizes those who have faith in Christ (Moro. 7:39), and is one of the fruits of the Spirit (Alma 13:28; D&C 19:23; Gal. 5:22–23). Though often persecuted by the proud and rich (2 Ne. 9:30; 28:13; Hel. 6:39), the meek are promised rest to their souls (Alma 37:34) and the earth as their eternal inheritance (3 Ne. 12:5). Meekness before God provides access to his GRACE (Ether 12:26–27). The remission of sins brings meekness "and because of meekness . . . cometh the visitation of the Holy Ghost, which Comforter filleth with hope and perfect love" (Moro. 8:26). Mormon taught that "none [are] acceptable before God, save the meek and lowly in heart" (Moro. 7:44).

See also Humility.

MCT

Meet *See* Appendix C.

Melchizedek Name-title (Hebrew, "King of Righteousness") given to the presiding patriarch of the covenant people around 2000 B.C. Melchizedek was king, high priest, and keeper of the storehouse of God in the land of Salem (JST Gen. 14:25–40; Alma 13:14–18). Also called the "Prince of peace," the "King of peace," and the "king of heaven," Melchizedek is considered a type of the Messiah (JST Gen. 14:33–36). His people had become extremely wicked, but by exercising faith and priesthood, he helped them repent and establish peace. Eventually his people were taken up to join Enoch's city of Zion (JST Gen. 14:34; cf. Moses 7:27). He conferred the priesthood on Abraham (D&C 84:14). To avoid too-frequent repetition of the Lord's name and to honor Melchizedek as a great high priest, Melchizedek was honored to have the higher priesthood named after him (D&C 107:2–4). Alma[2] testified, "There were many before him, and also there were many afterwards, but none were greater" (Alma 13:19).

See also Types.

DKO

Melchizedek Priesthood *See* Priesthood among the Nephites.

Melek, land of Nephite region west of the river Sidon, "on the west by the borders of the wilderness," three days' journey south of Ammonihah (Alma 8:3, 6). Alma[2] ministered here and through his efforts people "were baptized throughout all the land" (Alma 8:5; 82 B.C.). At the end of his life Alma departed from Zarahemla "as if to go into the land of Melek," but "the saying went abroad in the church that he was taken up by the Spirit" before reaching his destination (Alma 45:18–19; 73 B.C.). The land of Melek also became the home of those living in the land of Jershon who gave up their land to Nephite armies for the common defense (Alma 35:13; 74 B.C.).

Mercy Compassion, forbearance, withholding deserved punishment. Mercy is one of the necessary attributes of God (e.g., 1 Ne. 1:20; 2 Ne. 9:8, 19, 53; 11:5; Jacob 4:10; Alma 9:26; 26:37; 38:7; 3 Ne. 17:7). If people did not have the conviction that God is a merciful being, they "would faint in the midst of the tribulations, afflictions, and persecutions which they have to endure for righteousness' sake" (Smith, 4:15).

God is a God of mercy; he is also a God of justice. It is through the ATONEMENT of Jesus Christ that these two attributes of God are made compatible. Although mercy cannot rob justice —"Nay; not one whit" (Alma 42:25)—mercy "overpowereth justice" and "can satisfy the demands of justice" (Alma 34:15–16), because Jesus took upon himself the punishments demanded by justice for the sins of all men and women of all ages, an "atonement, which is infinite for all mankind" (2 Ne. 25:16). Further, he suffered "pains and afflictions and temptations of every kind . . . that his bowels may be filled with mercy, according to the flesh, that he may know according to the flesh how to succor his people according to their infirmities" (Alma 7:11–12; cf. Mosiah 3:7). Such suffering and such understanding, gained through agonizing personal experience, enables the Savior to be "a perfect, just God, and a merciful God also" (Alma 42:15–16; cf. 2 Ne. 2:8; Mosiah 15:9), permitting him to sit "down on the right hand of God, to claim of the Father his rights of mercy which he hath upon the children of men" (Moro. 7:27).

Because Jesus satisfied all the demands of justice, the debt all mankind once owed to justice now transfers to the Savior, and he determines the conditions for resolving the debt. He offers mercy, forgiving any debt, to all those who do not harden their hearts, but who repent, love him, and keep his commandments (Mosiah 13:14; Alma 12:33; 32:13; 34:15–16; 42:12–14, 21–25). To the more righteous of the Nephites and Lamanites who survived the destructions in connection with his death and resurrection, the Savior said, "O all ye that are spared because ye were more righteous than they, will ye not now return unto me, and repent of your sins, and be converted, that I may heal you? Yea, verily I say unto you, if ye will come unto me ye shall have eternal life. Behold, mine arm of mercy is extended towards you, and whosoever will come, him will I receive" (3 Ne. 9:13–14). But mercy "hath no claim" on the unrepentant (Mosiah 2:38–39). They are not forgiven and cleansed through the suffering of Christ; they must suffer for their own sins, the same penalties justice would impose (Alma 11:40–41; 34:16; D&C 19:15–18; 29:17). The Atonement does, however, make their suffering efficacious, in that they (except for the sons of perdition) will eventually be brought forth from death and hell and placed in a kingdom of glory (2 Ne. 9:5–12; cf. D&C 76:81–85, 99–106).

The Book of Mormon makes clear that God is anxious to respond to those who come unto him with full purpose of heart, pleading for mercy. Alma[2] (Alma 36:12–22), king Lamoni (Alma 18:41–43; 19:1–36), and the people of king Benjamin (Mosiah 4:2–3; 5:1–5), all pled for mercy and were granted spiritual rebirth. Moreover, the wicked lawyer Zeezrom (Alma 15:10–12) was made whole, and Lehi[1] was granted a marvelous vision of the tree of life (1 Ne. 8:8–12).

The Book of Mormon teaches that the eternal "plan of mercy" (Alma 42:15), made possible through the Atonement, extends to all of God's children (1 Ne. 1:14; 2 Ne. 9:21). Through the Lord's tender mercy those who repent are forgiven of their sins. God grants mercy also to the unrepentant in that he is patient and long-suffering with the wicked, withholding immediate punishment, diligently seeking their repentance and redemption (e.g., Jacob 6:4; Alma 38:7).

See also Appease; Arms of safety; Demands of justice; Grace; Justice, law of; Long-suffering; Satisfy.

BIBLIOGRAPHY

Smith, Joseph. *Lectures on Faith*. Compiled by N. B. Lundwall. Salt Lake City: Deseret Book, 1985.

LED

Merits of Christ The right and power of the Savior to forgive sins and grant SALVATION to those who believe on him, given to him by the Father because of Christ's perfect obedience and infinite ATONEMENT (Hel. 14:13; D&C 38:4; 45:4).

With the single exception of the Lord JESUS CHRIST, no human being has ever deserved the celestial kingdom of God (2 Ne. 31:5–7; 3 Ne. 12:48; Rom. 3:23). No one has ever earned salvation (Mosiah 2:21–24), and no mortal has ever merited God's full approval (Alma 22:14). Therefore, without the merits of Jesus Christ, no human being could ever be judged worthy to enter the presence of God (2 Ne. 2:8).

Because the Saints are told to keep the commandments and because they may not inherit eternal life unless they strive earnestly to obey the Lord's injunctions, they sometimes mistakenly assume that their efforts can somehow earn them salvation. As important as mortal efforts are, however, they are inevitably imperfect and flawed. They are always inadequate for salvation. All that mortals are capable of, or "all we can do" (2 Ne. 25:23), is to come to Christ through faith, repentance, and baptism (Alma 24:10–11). Humanity's work is to come to Christ; Christ's work is to save humanity. Only Jesus Christ lived a perfect life; only Christ was perfectly obedient. Therefore, only Christ has earned or deserves the celestial kingdom. Yet, if mortals come to him, enter into his covenant, and remain true to that covenant relationship, then through his love and GRACE he will share his merits with them. Nephi[1] testified, "There is no flesh that can dwell in the presence of God, save it be through the merits, and mercy, and grace of the Holy Messiah" (2 Ne. 2:8). Emphasizing this truth, Nephi and Moroni[2] enjoined their readers not merely to rely upon his merits but to rely "wholly," or rely "alone," upon them (2 Ne. 31:19; Moro. 6:4; cf. Rom. 3:24).

In the task of coming to Christ and remaining faithful to him, mankind's works, their best efforts, play an important role, but the task of redeeming mankind and saving them in God's kingdom is the work of the divine Savior alone.

SER

Messiah The English form of the Hebrew noun *mashiach,* meaning "anointed one." The Greek cognate, *christos,* is regularly rendered "Christ" in the New Testament.

Jesus is *the* Messiah, or Anointed One, because of his premortal appointment as the sole, legitimate Redeemer of the world. The Bible contains numerous messianic prophecies that foretell some aspect of the first and/or second coming of Jesus as the Messiah or Christ. In the preserved Hebrew Bible (Old Testament), however, the noun *mashiach* is never explicitly used as a title for Jehovah (the premortal Jesus) and occurs only once in a prophecy of the Messiah's coming (Isa. 61:1). This noun is primarily employed in reference to the Israelite kings Saul, David, and David's descendants, as "the LORD's anointed," "his anointed," or "mine anointed" (1 Sam. 24:6; 26:11; 2 Sam. 19:21; 22:51; Ps. 18:50; 132:17; sometimes, as in Ps. 2:2, the Davidic king serves as a "type" of Jesus the Messiah). Also, the Aaronic High Priest (Lev. 4:5) and even Cyrus, a Persian king (Isa. 45:1), were designated "anointed" ones. Ideally, Israelite priests and kings were supposed to symbolize the attributes and authority of Jesus, the heavenly Messiah. Daniel prophesied of a future "Messiah the Prince," considered by most Christians to be Jesus (Dan. 9:25–26). The prophecy in Isaiah 10:27 // 2 Nephi 20:27 that "the yoke [of Assyria] shall be destroyed because of the anointing" (Hebrew, literally "because of oil") may be an allusion to the power of the Anointed One or to the chosen status of Israel. The Hebrew verb *mashach,* "to anoint," occurs in the Bible in a secular context in reference to pouring or smearing ointment on a person (Amos 6:6), oil on cakes (Ex. 29:2) and on a shield (Isa. 21:5), and even red paint on a house (Jer. 22:14). Much more frequent and important is the use of this verb with the religious sense of anointing with oil to consecrate or set apart. People who were anointed include kings (1 Kgs. 1:39), prophets (1 Kgs. 19:16), and priests (Ex. 30:30). Consecrated objects, such as the sacrificial altar, the tabernacle, and objects used therein, were also anointed (Ex. 40:9–11). The verb *mashach* also occurs in a messianic prophecy in Isaiah 61:1: "the LORD hath anointed me to preach good tidings unto the meek . . . to proclaim liberty to the captives" (cf. Luke 4:16–21).

The oldest manuscripts of the New Testament are in Greek, so the title "Messiah" is generally expressed therein by the Greek cognate *christos*, "Christ" (with the exception of John 1:41 and 4:25, where the transliterated form *messias* occurs).

Latter-day Saint scripture indicates that prophets who lived before Jesus' birth understood and taught that Jehovah/Jesus was the Messiah who would come (Moses 7:50, 53; 1 Ne. 10:5; Mosiah 13:33; Hel. 8:13–20; Jacob[2] teaches the same thing, but uses the term "Christ" in Jacob 4:4–5). Even the lesser law of Moses was given to persuade Israelites "to look forward unto the Messiah, and believe in him to come as though he already was" (Jarom 1:11). Because the term *mashiach* is not clearly preserved as a title for Jehovah in the Hebrew Bible nor in the minimal corpus of Israelite inscriptions, it is not possible to determine how many Israelites in Jerusalem at the time of Jeremiah[1] and Lehi[1] (ca. 600 B.C.) knew or believed that Jehovah himself would come to earth as the anointed Son of God, the Messiah.

"Messiah" occurs thirty-two times in the Book of Mormon; all but three are in 1 and 2 Nephi. In contrast to the preserved biblical text, Nephi[1] indicated that when Lehi preached repentance in Jerusalem he taught "plainly of the coming of a Messiah, and also the redemption of the world" (1 Ne. 1:19). The Jews' angry response to Lehi's preaching could indicate their sense of guilt and/or an apostate notion that Lehi was in some way teaching false doctrine. Nephi did not relate that Lehi taught the identity of the future Messiah to the Jews, but does report that Lehi later taught his family many details concerning the (first) coming of the Messiah, including that this "Savior of the world" was the "Redeemer" who would be baptized, killed, and "should rise from the dead" (1 Ne. 10:4–11; cf. 2 Ne. 2:6, 8, 26). Similarly, Nephi observed that "the Son of God was the Messiah who should come" (1 Ne. 10:17), and an angel taught him that "the Messiah . . . is the Lamb of God" (1 Ne. 12:18). Lehi also prophesied that as part of the great latter-day gathering "remnants of the house of Israel" would "come to the knowledge of the true Messiah, their Lord and their Redeemer" (1 Ne. 10:14; cf. 1 Ne. 15:13–14). Furthermore, both Lehi and Jacob taught that the Messiah would gather the remnants of latter-day Israel (1 Ne. 10:14; 15:13; 2 Ne. 3:5; 6:13–14).

Jacob was the first to use the title "Christ" in the Book of Mormon (2 Ne. 10:3), indicating that an angel taught him this "name," presumably meaning the Greek equivalent of the Hebrew title Messiah by which Jesus would come to be commonly designated (cf. 2 Ne. 25:19). Subsequently, Nephi regularly used "Christ" instead of "Messiah" in his record, except in 2 Nephi 26:3 and 2 Nephi 25 (eight times), where he stated in his message to the Jews (2 Ne. 25:9–20) that Jesus Christ is the "name" of the Messiah (2 Ne. 25:19). In 2 Nephi 25:16, Nephi used "Messiah" and "Christ" interchangeably. "Christ" is regularly used in the translated text of the Book of Mormon from this point onwards (with the exception of Jarom 1:11; Mosiah 13:33; Hel. 8:13), apparently indicating the preference of the Nephite prophets for that revealed form over the Hebrew form "Messiah."

DMP

Metals, ancient writing on The Book of Mormon mentions five sets of metallic inscriptions: the plates of brass, the plates of Ether, the small plates of Nephi, the large plates of Nephi, and the plates of Mormon. Modern misconceptions about the nature of ancient writing make it difficult for some to believe that such records could actually be inscribed and preserved on metal plates. A review of archaeological evidence suggests such skepticism is not well founded.

Because metals are durable and, like most tangible surfaces, were used for protoliterate inscriptions the world over, thousands of metallic documents survive from antiquity (Anchor 6.1001–2). They were used for military diplomas, judicial ballots ("dikasts' pinakia"), foundation documents and other hidden writings (concealed in all sorts of buried containers),

METALS, ANCIENT WRITING ON

letters, political propaganda, economic texts, maps, dedications, enactments, prayers, historical records, mummy tickets, blessings, curses, and much else (Wright, 468–71). Examples include a bronze plate ("delton chalken") predicting Alexander's conquest of Persia, the earliest Greek letter (written on a leaden tablet), the Pyrgi tablets (three gold-leaf inscriptions), an inscribed bronze treaty terminating the first Peloponnesian war, more than four hundred leaden curse tablets taken from a Boeotian jar in 1860, many lead rolls (and a few bronze inscriptions) found in Cyprus, and more than one hundred Roman military diplomas discovered by 1924 (Wright, 457–62).

Ancient metallic documents were often lengthy and important. The copper scroll from Qumran is a good example, as is a lead book ("molybdon") containing the full text of Hesiod's *Works and Days*. The bronze tablets of Iguvium, seven brass plates discovered at Gubbio in 1844, vary from 12 to 16 inches wide and 22 to 33

Stone box with gold and silver plates of Darius (516–151 B.C.*) found at Persepolis (located in modern Iran); courtesy HBLL. Viewed at this angle, the trilingual inscription on the large gold plate is upside down.*

inches long and contain more than four thousand words. Treaties, like the Thirty Years' Peace and the accords of Khetasira with Ramses II of Egypt, were often metallic documents, the latter filling a large silver tablet and requiring two hundred lines for its English translation. Another bronze inscription on four sizable plates fills three lengthy pages in translation; it summarizes Roman laws that controlled provincial mining operations in order to govern a typical mining town by regulating its miners, cobblers, barbers, fullers, schoolmasters, and public baths (Wright, 464–65).

As products of sacral cultures, ancient metal documents were inevitably religious. The gold bible of Orphism, which resembles Egyptian Books of the Dead, consisted of nine golden plates for guiding departed souls into their afterlives; it was to ordinary Greeks what Plato's sophisticated myth of Er was to intellectuals. Incantations of chanted magic, inscribed on various metals by anyone invoking supernatural agents to bless or curse others, survive from most ancient cultures: blessings normally appear on gold or silver tablets, curses on strips of lead or tin (which were often rolled up, pierced with nails, and thrown into graves or cisterns). Golden books from ancient Burma provide additional examples: two gold plates inscribed with Buddhist scriptures were concealed in a false brick discovered at Maunggun in 1898. A golden book from Hmawza, which resembles India's palm-leaf manuscripts, contains twenty gold leaves of inscriptions between two gold covers: its leaves were "bound together by a thick gold wire . . . fastened to the covers by sealing wax and small glass beads"; there were "two holes in each leaf and cover, through which the gold wire was passed, to keep the whole in position," and "it was necessary to cut this wire in order to free the leaves" (Wright, 467–68). The existence of other metal books in ancient Burma is attested by still another discovery of sixteen small fragments of gold and silver plates covered with Pyu inscriptions. Thus, in the ancient world, inscribing important and sacred text on metal plates was not a practice unique to the Book of Mormon authors.

See also The Coming Forth of the Book of Mormon, 9; Gold plates; Stone boxes, burial of documents in.

BIBLIOGRAPHY

The Anchor Bible Dictionary. Edited by David Noel Freedman et al. 6 vols. New York: Doubleday, 1992.

Wright, H. Curtis. "Metallic Documents of Antiquity." *Brigham Young University Studies* 10:4 (1970): 457–77. Consult this publication for author's primary sources.

HCW

Metals of the Book of Mormon The ancient Near East knew six metals—gold, silver, copper, iron, lead, and tin—and only one fabricated alloy—bronze (*Interpreter's*, 3:366; Num. 31:22; Ezek. 22:20). Nephi[1] taught his people to work iron, copper, brass, gold, and silver, and apparently steel as well (2 Ne. 5:15).

Copper, bronze, and brass

Copper occurs in nature as a native metal; however, most copper in antiquity was smelted from secondary blue and green copper carbonates like malachite. Bronze, the copper-tin alloy, was known as early as 3000 B.C. and was the metal of choice for much of ancient Near East history. Brass, the copper-zinc alloy, was not introduced into the Holy Land as a deliberate alloy before the first century B.C. (Tylecote, 58).

The ancient Hebrew word *nechosheth* and the Greek *chalkos* may be translated either "copper" or "bronze" (Brown, 230–31). In the language of Tudor England, "brass" denoted any copper alloy and was derived from the Old English word *braes* (*Interpreter's,* 1:461; *New Standard,* 576). The word *bronze* did not come into use until the eighteenth century and does not appear in the Book of Mormon or the King James Version of the Bible, although it is common in other Bible translations. As Joseph Smith was very familiar with the King James Bible and Lehi[1] left Jerusalem before copper-zinc alloys were fabricated in the Near East, it appears likely that the "brass" objects in the Book of Mormon were either copper or bronze. The "brass" plates of Laban may have been copper, as copper is more malleable than bronze, and the Liahona, which was of supernatural origin, was made of some material that Nephi chose to call "fine brass."

Iron and steel

By Nephi's time, Canaan had entered the Iron Age (Tylecote, 40), and Nephi must have brought with him a few iron and steel objects (e.g., Laban's sword and Nephi's bow) as well as a knowledge of smelting. When commanded to make tools for ship building, Nephi asked help to find ore but seemed to know how to proceed from there (1 Ne. 17:8–11). A simple fire pit furnace, even with bellows, cannot melt iron, but yields iron "bloom" by the reduction of iron oxide ores. This spongy mass of tiny iron crystals is forged to "wrought iron" with hammer and anvil after the manner of the western pioneer blacksmiths. Wrought iron may become steel by "carburizing" in the same pit furnace (Phillips, 41). This technology was well known in Jerusalem by 600 B.C.

The earlier Jaredite record makes reference to "iron" (Ether 10:23) and "steel" (Ether 7:9), and Jared[1]'s great-grandson Shule was said to be a maker of steel swords (Ether 7:9). Because Jared and his brother departed the Near East at the time of the great tower and the confounding of languages (Ether 1:33), the record implies a date for iron and steel centuries before the Hittites of Asia Minor introduced iron in the second millennium B.C. As archaeologists have found no artifacts of smelted iron in the New World earlier than the Spanish conquest (Tylecote, ix) and the Spanish found Mesoamerica in a pre-bronze age (Tylecote, 12), it seems likely that (1) the knowledge of iron and steel smelting and working was known to the Book of Mormon peoples and subsequently lost; (2) the terms "iron" and "steel" in the Book of Mormon do not denote the same metals identified by those names today; (3) archaeological evidence is incomplete. All of these choices are probably true to some degree (Lechtman, 1).

Gold and silver

Nephi stated that the "promised land" yielded "all manner of ore, both of gold, and of silver, and of copper" (1 Ne. 18:23, 25), which is consistent with the New World wealth found by Spanish conquistadors and by modern miners of the American cordillera. The metals designated "gold" and "silver" should be unambiguous. Both may occur as native metals, which can be worked directly and, along with copper, are malleable, making them the metals of choice for the pages of ancient records because they could be pounded to very thin sheets (Tylecote, 37). Great intrinsic value make gold and silver the obvious choice for barter and, as the standard of wealth and prosperity, they repeatedly led to pride and apostasy in the narrative.

Ziff

The word *ziff* appears only twice in the Book of Mormon (Mosiah 11:3, 8), and as it occurs in a list of metals, it is usually assumed to be a metal. The only known metals not considered above are tin and lead. Ziff could be either or some other alloy, but lead is most likely as it is common and easily recovered from galena (PbS), which is also the principal source of silver.

See also Metals, ancient writing on.

BIBLIOGRAPHY

Brown, Roland W. *Composition of Scientific Words.* Baltimore: Brown, 1954.

Funk & Wagnalls New Standard Bible Dictionary. New York: Funk and Wagnalls Co., 1936.

The Interpreter's Dictionary of the Bible. Edited by George A. Buttrick. 4 vols. Nashville: Abingdon, 1962.

Lechtman, Heather. "Issues in Andean Metallurgy." In *Pre-Columbian Metallurgy of South America.* Edited by Elizabeth P. Benson. Washington, D.C.: Dumbarton Oaks Research Library and Collections, 1979.

Phillips, W. R. "Metals of the Book of Mormon." *Journal of Book of Mormon Studies* 9:2 (2000).

Tylecote, R. F. A *History of Metallurgy.* London: The Metals Society, 1976.

WRP

Mete *See* Appendix C.

Methought *See* Appendix C.

Micah A biblical prophet, contemporary with Isaiah, who prophesied in Judah between 742–687 B.C. Micah prophesied the destruction of Samaria and Judah, as well as hope for their eventual gathering and restoration. His teachings focus on social justice, condemning those who profit by taking advantage of others (Micah 3). Micah is best known for his familiar prophecies of the Lord's house being established in the top of the mountains (Micah 4:1–3; cf. Isa. 2:2–5) and that the Messiah would "come forth" from Bethlehem (Micah 5:2). Chapters 4–5 prophesy the future restoration of Israel and the destruction of her enemies. It is possible Micah's prophecies were recorded on the brass plates.

The resurrected Savior quoted several passages from Micah's writings (chapters 4–5) to the descendants of Lehi in 3 Nephi 16, 20, 21. In quoting Micah the Lord spoke in the first person "I" (e.g., 3 Ne. 20:18) where the prophet Micah referred to God as "he" or "the Lord" (e.g., Micah 4:12). The passages from Micah quoted by Christ share the common theme of Israel overcoming the wicked Gentiles. Therein the Gentiles are warned that if they do not repent "a remnant of the house of Jacob, [shall] go forth among them; and . . . shall be in the midst of them who shall be many; and . . . shall be among them as a lion among the beasts of the forest, and as a young lion among the flocks of sheep, who, if he goeth through both treadeth down and teareth in pieces, and none can deliver." Israel's "hand," the Lord continued, "shall be lifted up upon thine adversaries, and all thine enemies shall be cut off" (3 Ne. 20:16–17; cf. Micah 5:8–9; see also 3 Ne. 16:15; 21:12). Elder Bruce R. McConkie wrote: "These words of our Lord to the Nephites are quoted from Micah 5:8–9 and have reference to the desolations and ultimate burning that shall destroy the wicked at the Second Coming. . . . The righteous—here called the remnant of Jacob—shall abide the day. And then, in the prophetic imagery, it will be as though the remnant of Israel overthrew their enemies as a young lion among the flocks of sheep" (248).

Indeed, the Lord at his coming will gather his people together and make them mighty against their enemies (3 Ne. 20:18–19; cf. Micah 4:12–13; 3 Ne. 25:3). Still quoting from Micah, Christ warned of specific destructions that would occur as well as specific sins that would be "cut off," "in that day"—the DAY OF THE LORD (3 Ne. 21:14–18; cf. Micah 5:10–14). He then described the millennial conditions that will come in consequence of this cleansing: "All lyings, and deceivings, and envyings, and strifes, and priestcrafts, and whoredoms, shall be done away" (3 Ne. 21:19).

BIBLIOGRAPHY

McConkie, Bruce R. *The Millennial Messiah: The Second Coming of the Son of Man.* Salt Lake City: Deseret Book, 1982.

DRS

Middoni, land of Lamanite land where Aaron[3], Muloki, and Ammah were imprisoned for preaching the word of God (Alma 20:2; 21:11–13; between 90 and 70 B.C.). There, they suffered extremes of hunger, thirst, and physical abuse (Alma 20:29–30; 21:12–15). Their deliverance was accomplished by Ammon[2] and Lamoni as the converted Lamoni had some influence with the king in Middoni (Alma 20:1–7, 14–15, 27–28; 21:14). Subsequently, the missionaries were allowed to preach freely, and the people from Middoni and elsewhere were converted and became known as the ANTI-NEPHI-LEHIES (Alma 23:8, 10).

Midian, land of Lamanite land east of Lehi-Nephi where Ammon[2] met with his brethren after learning that the Lamanites were preparing to attack the ANTI-NEPHI-LEHIES. They then went to counsel with king Lamoni and his brother Anti-Nephi-Lehi concerning the threat (Alma 24:5).

Millennium, the The thousand-year period when Christ "the Holy One of Israel reigneth" on the EARTH following his second coming (1 Ne. 22:26, 24; 3 Ne. 21:25; D&C 43:29–30; A of F 10). Although the word *millennium* is not used in the Book of Mormon, much can be gleaned on the subject from its pages. For example, the Millennium will be a time of peace among men and in the animal kingdom: "Nation shall not lift up sword against nation, neither shall they learn war any more" (2 Ne. 12:4), "then shall the wolf dwell with the lamb; and the leopard shall lie down with the kid, . . . and a little child shall lead them" (2 Ne. 30:12–14). Isaiah taught that "the earth shall be full of the knowledge of the Lord" (2 Ne. 21:9), and Nephi[1] added, "all things shall be made known unto the children of men" (2 Ne. 30:16), and "all things which have been revealed unto the children of men shall at that day be revealed" (2 Ne. 30:18). Moroni[2], drawing upon the teachings of Ether, and Christ both spoke of the NEW JERUSALEM, a "holy city" that would be built upon "this land" (the American continent) (Ether 13:2–10; 3 Ne. 21:21–25), which city would serve as a governing center during the Millennium (2 Ne. 12:2–3; D&C 45:67). Moreover, it would be a millennial day when Jerusalem of old would once again be blessed and inhabited by those of Israel "who were scattered and gathered in from the four quarters of the earth" (Ether 13:11).

During the Millennium the earth will "be renewed and receive its paradisiacal glory"—"there [will] be a new heaven and a new earth" (A of F 10; Ether 13:9). A "new heavens and a new earth" is used in scripture to refer to the change that is to take place at the beginning of the Millennium (Isa. 65:17–25; 66:22–24; 2 Pet. 3:10–13; cf. D&C 101:23–31), as well as to the transformation that will occur at the end of the Millennium when the earth becomes a celestial kingdom (D&C 29:22–24; 88:25–26). In some of the verses it is not always clear which period is being spoken of or whether the designation could apply to both time periods (e.g., Ether 13:9; Rev. 21:1–4).

The Book of Mormon teaches that Satan will be bound during the Millennium. The initiation of this restraint would be through the destruction of the wicked at the coming of Christ (1 Ne. 22:15–17; 2 Ne. 30:10; 3 Ne. 24:2–3; 25:1). Further, Nephi taught that "because of the righteousness of his people, Satan has no power; wherefore, he cannot be loosed for the space of many years; for he hath no power over the hearts of the people" (1 Ne. 22:26). This "space of many years" was referred to in the allegory of Zenos as the "long time" when the "vineyard is no more corrupted" (Jacob 5:75–76; cf. 2 Ne. 30:18). Zenos also taught that following this long period of righteousness there will be wickedness once more, "the good and the bad [will] be gathered," the good will be preserved, the bad will be cast away; and the vineyard (the earth) will be burned with fire (Jacob 5:77). This teaching corresponds with latter-day revelation which indicates that Satan will be loosed but "he shall only reign for a little season, and then cometh the end of the earth" (D&C 43:31–32; 29:22).

Following the Savior's visit to America the righteous enjoyed peace and prosperity for nearly two hundred years (4 Ne. 1:2–18). This period of ZION among Book of Mormon people foreshadows the conditions that will exist during the Millennium.

See also Jesus Christ, second coming of.

PVJ

Minister To attend to someone's needs, to give aid or supply relief, to serve (Webster). In the Book of Mormon the word *minister* is usually found in the context of teaching and preaching—serving others through the spoken word (e.g., Jacob 4:1; Hel. 5:50; Alma 22:23). The word is used exclusively as a verb throughout the Book of Mormon with the exception of Alma[1]'s warning his people to "trust no one to be your teacher nor your minister [*noun*], except he be a man of God" (Mosiah 23:14). In this isolated instance, the term refers to the wicked priests of king Noah[3] and means those who had been authorized to conduct the religious affairs of his kingdom (Mosiah 11:5; 23:12–13). The word *minister* differs from *administer* in that the latter typically suggests a giving or dispensing of something tangible, such as food, clothes, land, or the like.

Jesus Christ is clearly the exemplar of one who ministers (e.g., 1 Ne. 11:28; 13:35; 15:14; 2 Ne. 2:4; 16:1; 19:15; 26:14; Ether 3:18, 20). All others who minister do so as emissaries of God. For example, angels frequently minister to mortals (1 Ne. 11:30; 16:38; 2 Ne. 4:24; Jacob 7:5, 17; Hel. 5:48; 3 Ne. 7:18; 17:24; 19:14; Moro. 7:22, 25, 29, 30, 37; 10:14), and the twelve disciples were chosen by the resurrected Lord to minister by way of teaching, baptizing, and bestowing the Holy Ghost among the descendants of Lehi[1] (1 Ne. 12:8; 3 Ne. 12:1; 13:25; 19:7–8; 26:19; 28:16, 18). Three of the twelve disciples, commonly referred to as the Three Nephites, continue to serve as special witnesses, ministering to the scattered tribes of Israel as well as all nations, kindreds, tongues, and people, bringing many souls to Christ (3 Ne.

28:26, 29; Morm. 8:11). All others who minister in the Book of Mormon can be identified as righteous followers of Jesus Christ. These include Jacob[2] (Jacob 4:1), king Lamoni's father (Alma 22:23), Alma[2], along with other faithful missionaries (Alma 35:7; Hel. 5:50), and Nephi[3] (3 Ne. 7:17).

The Savior taught the members of his Church that they have an obligation to minister to those who are unworthy to partake of the sacrament or who refuse to repent, in hopes that someday they may return to the Lord with full purpose of heart (3 Ne. 18:28–32). Mormon taught that angels appear and minister to mortals according to faith (Moro. 7:37), and Moroni[2] indicated that the beholding and ministering of angels is a gift given of God (Moro. 10:8, 14).

See also Angels, ministry of; Ministering spirits.

BIBLIOGRAPHY

Webster, Noah. *An American Dictionary of the English Language.* 1828.

DMW

Ministering spirits Spirits sent by God to minister to his children on earth. Moroni[2] taught that one of the gifts of the Spirit is the gift of "the beholding of angels and ministering spirits" (Moro. 10:14). The difference between angels and ministering spirits is not made known in the Book of Mormon. A revelation in the Doctrine and Covenants teaches that an angel is a resurrected being (or translated being) with a body of flesh and bones, while spirits who appear to individuals are the spirits of just men made perfect (D&C 129:1–3; 7). Throughout the scriptures this distinction is not always applicable, however, as "angels" and "spirits" are at times used interchangeably (Mosiah 27:11; D&C 76:88; JST Heb. 1:6–7; Heb. 1:14). Examples of ministering spirits in the Book of Mormon include the Lord appearing to the brother of Jared[1] (Ether 3), the angel appearing to Alma[2] and Amulek (Alma 8:14–15, 20), and the angel who came to king Benjamin (Mosiah 3:2).

See also Angels, ministry of.

HDG

Minon, land of Nephite land, just west of the river Sidon, "above the land of Zarahemla, in the course of the land of Nephi" (Alma 2:24). Here the spies of Alma[2] were "astonished" and fearful to see Nephites fleeing toward Zarahemla before a combined Lamanite-Amlicite army (Alma 2:21–25).

Miracles Events which mortals do not understand and of themselves cannot duplicate. The Book of Mormon teaches and illustrates that miracles are wrought through God's power (Alma 37:40; 4 Ne. 1:30; Morm. 7:9) in the name of Christ (Jacob 4:6; 3 Ne. 8:1) to benefit man (2 Ne. 26:24; Mosiah 8:18; Ether 3:4). The prophet Moroni[2] explained that faith is a requisite of miracles, for "if there be no faith among the children of men God can do no miracle among them" (Ether 12:12; cf. 2 Ne. 26:3; 27:23; Alma 37:40; 3 Ne. 19:35). Moroni further testified that in addition to faith, righteous living and a knowledge of God are required for miracles (Morm. 9:20; cf. 3 Ne. 8:1).

Although miracles, in combination with preaching and revelation, may help bring one to a knowledge of truth (Alma 23:6), they do not supplant the need for faith in acquiring a testimony of the divinity of God. Moroni emphasized that even the miracle of gaining a testimony is received only after faith is exercised (Ether 12:6).

Nephi[1] warned that in the last days false churches and evil men would teach that miracles have ceased (2 Ne. 28:3–6; cf. 3 Ne. 29:7). Book of Mormon prophets, however, testified that miracles always have and always will be part of God's handiwork, for he is the "same yesterday, today, and forever" (2 Ne. 27:23; Morm. 9:7–19). Accordingly, the Book of Mormon offers a second witness of past miracles detailed in the Old Testament, such as the creation of the earth (2 Ne. 2:14–15; Alma 22:10–12; Morm. 9:11–12), the flood in the days of Noah[1] (Alma 10:22), the parting of the Red Sea (1 Ne. 4:2; Mosiah 7:19; Hel. 8:11), and the providing of manna for Israel in the wilderness (1 Ne. 17:28–29). The text also chronicles miracles that were contemporary with the Book of Mormon peoples, such as the working of the Liahona (Alma 37:40), the numerous miraculous escapes of the righteous (1 Ne. 7:17–18; Mosiah 24:19; Alma 14:26–29; 4 Ne. 1:30), the raising of the dead (3 Ne. 7:19; 19:4), and the moving of a mountain (Ether 12:30). Furthermore, the Book of Mormon contains prophecies of New Testament miracles, such as the divine conception and mortal birth of Christ (1 Ne. 11:13–21; Alma 7:10; 3 Ne. 1:19), the miraculous healings by the Savior and his apostles (1 Ne. 11:31; Morm. 9:18), the infinite atonement (Mosiah 3:7–8, 11; Alma 7:11–13), and the resurrection (Mosiah 3:10; 3 Ne. 11). Moroni reasoned that God would certainly continue to be a "God of miracles" in the future as long as there are Saints to be redeemed through Christ, earthly tabernacles to be resurrected from the dead, and souls to be brought before the judgment bar (Morm. 9:11–15). Thus, Moroni's witness is that miracles are an essential part of God's work and glory (Moses 1:39).

MOR

Missionary service As the missionary's most important tool, the Book of Mormon lies at the heart of latter-day missionary service, where it plays a multi-faceted role. First, the book foretells a great latter-day gathering to Christ, his church, and gospel covenants (e.g., 1 Ne. 15:12–18; 22:7–12; 2 Ne. 30:2–7; 3 Ne. 5:24–26). This gathering would be effected by servants, called and sent out into the Lord's vineyard for the "last time," following a period of universal apostasy and before the end of the world (Jacob 5). Second, the book's coming forth was foretold as a sign that would mark the time when this gathering would begin (3 Ne. 21:1–7). Third, the Book of Mormon assists in the gathering to Christ and to the church of Christ (2 Ne. 30:3–4; 3 Ne. 16:4–5; Morm. 7:8–10) by providing "another testament of Jesus Christ" and a tangible witness of the truth of the Restoration through the Prophet Joseph Smith. Fourth, it provides those seeking religious truth with the "fulness of the gospel" (D&C 20:9), and it restores "plain and precious" gospel truths that were lost from the Bible (1 Ne. 13:26–29, 32–36, 40–41). Fifth, it equips missionaries with answers to questions that challenge the necessity for a second book of scripture (2 Ne. 29; Morm. 9:7–27). Sixth, the book includes a formula by which readers can come to know, personally, the truth of the gospel and gain a testimony of the Book of Mormon (Alma 32; Moro. 10:3–7). And seventh, it contains numerous principles pertaining to the accomplishment of effective missionary work.

Sharing the Book of Mormon; courtesy D. L. Largey.

The accompanying table summarizes important missionary attributes, attitudes, understandings, and practices gleaned from the Book of Mormon narrative.

DLL

Mist of darkness *See* Lehi[1]'s dream.

Mitchill, Dr. Samuel Latham *See* Anthon transcript.

Mocum, city of After his crucifixion, Christ caused waters to cover Mocum and its inhabitants to hide their wickedness, that the blood of martyred prophets and Saints would cease to testify against them (3 Ne. 9:7).

Molder *See* Appendix C.

Monetary system *See* Nephite weights and measures.

More *See* Appendix C.

More or less Adding to or taking away from the approved teachings of Jesus Christ (3 Ne. 11:39–40; 18:12–13; D&C 10:68; 93:25; Deut. 4:2; Rev. 22:19). Incomplete or embellished doctrines (the precepts of men) tarnish truth with error and thus have no power to save. They are

ASPECTS OF MISSIONARY SERVICE FROM BOOK OF MORMON NARRATIVES

Missionary Attributes

Faith in Jesus Christ (Ether 12:15).

Patience and long-suffering in afflictions (Alma 17:11; 38:3–4).

Courage (Alma 17:12).

Trust in the Lord (Alma 17:13).

Humility (Alma 38:11, 14).

Devotion to service (Alma 18:10).

"Great love" for investigators (Alma 20:26; cf. 38:12).

Spiritual discernment to understand people's needs and desires (Alma 18:16).

Gospel understanding to be able to explain basic gospel doctrines and how the doctrines are interrelated (e.g., Creation, Fall, Atonement [Alma 18:36–40; 22:10–14]).

"Boldness, but not overbearance" (Alma 38:12).

Spiritual purity to be able to "feel a desire for the welfare of [others]" (Enos 1:2–11).

Missionary Attitudes

Truly desiring to dwell among the people in one's assigned field of labor (Alma 17:23).

Aspiring to serve those one wishes to teach (Alma 17:25).

Being cheerful (Alma 17:31).

Intending "none other object save it be the everlasting welfare of [people's] souls" (2 Ne. 2:30; cf. Mosiah 28:3).

Missionary Understandings

Great is the missionary undertaking (Alma 17:13).

Success comes when one teaches with the "power and authority of God," "by the power of the Holy Ghost" (Alma 17:3; 2 Ne. 33:1; Hel. 5:18–19).

Success is defined by one's obedience to the call to preach the gospel, not in the number of converts (1 Ne. 1:18–19; 2:1; Alma 8:10–15; 21:12).

The missionary is "a disciple of Jesus Christ, the Son of God," and has "been called of him to declare his word among his people, that they might have everlasting life" (3 Ne. 5:13; cf. Alma 17:16).

Teaching truth enables the light of the gospel to dispel the "dark veil of unbelief" (Alma 19:6).

When investigators "experiment upon [the word]," the gospel seed will take root and grow into a testimony (Alma 32; e.g., 22:15–18).

Missionaries experience opposition to their mission labors, even persecution at times (e.g., Alma 8:13; 14:21–25; 20:29–30; Hel. 5:21).

Great joy comes to those who labor to bring souls to Christ (Alma 26:11–13; 29:10; 36:24–26; Jacob 5:71; cf. D&C 18:10–16).

Missionary Practices

Establishing honest friendships (Alma 18:3).

Seizing upon opportunities to win hearts (Alma 17:29).

Being "good examples" to the people (Alma 17:11). A good example can cause a stirring of conscience among friends, neighbors, or investigators (Alma 18:5). Bad examples of missionaries or members can devastate missionary work (Alma 4:10; 39:11).

Searching the scriptures diligently to know the word of God (Alma 17:2).

Fasting and praying to receive the spirit of prophecy and the spirit of revelation (Alma 17:3, 9).

Seeking the Spirit in order to be "an instrument in the hands of God" (Alma 17:9).

Assessing what the investigator believes before teaching (Alma 18:24–28).

Avoiding contention (Alma 14:14–19; 21:10–11; 30:29; 3 Ne. 11:29).

Using the scriptures (Alma 12:1; 18:36–38; 21:9; 22:12–13).

Receiving knowledge and power from the Spirit, according to faith and desire (Alma 18:34–35; cf. 17:3).

Proselyting by the Spirit (Alma 21:16).

Saying "I don't know" when questions are asked to which the answer has not been revealed, or the missionary may not know the answer (Alma 37:11; 40:19–21).

"Refrain[ing] from idleness" (Alma 38:12).

Relying upon "the mercies of God" (Alma 26:28).

as sand compared to the rock of the gospel. In the Old World, Christ did not hesitate to discredit what the Pharisees had added to the law of Moses (Matt. 15:13).

DLL

Moriancumer, land of Place by the sea where the Jaredites dwelt four years before embarking on their journey to the promised land (Ether 2:13). It was here that the Lord chastened the brother of Jared[1] for neglecting to call upon him (Ether 2:14). It was also here that they built barges to carry them across the ocean (Ether 2:16–17) and here, on mount Shelem, that the brother of Jared received a miraculous vision of the premortal Christ (Ether 3:6–16). The area was probably named after the brother of Jared, whose name, Mahonri Moriancumer, was revealed through the Prophet Joseph Smith.

See also Moriancumer, Mahonri.

Moriancumer, Mahonri In an unusual incident, the Prophet Joseph Smith revealed the name of the brother of Jared[1]. George Reynolds recorded, "While residing in Kirtland Elder Reynolds Cahoon had a son born to him. One day when President Joseph Smith was passing his door he called the Prophet in and asked him to bless and name the baby. Joseph did so and gave the boy the name of Mahonri Moriancumer. When he had finished the blessing he laid the child on the bed, and turning to Elder Cahoon he said, the name I have given your son is the name of the brother of Jared; the Lord has just shown [or revealed] it to me. Elder William F. Cahoon, who was standing near heard the Prophet make this statement to his father; and this was the first time the name of the brother of Jared was known in the Church in this dispensation" (282 n). The above incident took place sometime in 1834, because records indicate that on 25 July 1834, a son was born to Reynolds and Thirza Stiles Cahoon whom they named Mahonri Moriancumer Cahoon (Black, 8:217). Significantly, the name Moriancumer does appear in the scriptural text. After crossing many waters and a stretch of wilderness, the Jaredite colony pitched their tents in a place they called Moriancumer (Ether 2:13), which place-name possibly corroborates the modern revelation given to the Prophet Joseph Smith concerning the name of the brother of Jared.

BIBLIOGRAPHY

Reynolds, George. "The Jaredites." *Juvenile Instructor* 27 (1 May 1892); brackets in original.

Black, Susan Easton. *Membership of The Church of Jesus Christ of Latter-day Saints, 1830–1848.* 50 vols. Provo, Utah: Religious Studies Center, Brigham Young University, 1989.

ALB

Morianton[1] *See* Jared[1], posterity of.

Morianton[2] A hot-tempered and wicked man who led the people of the land of Morianton in a border dispute against Nephites in the neighboring land of Lehi (Alma 50:25–27; ca. 68 B.C.). Fearing retaliation from the army of Moroni[1], Morianton planned to lead his people to the land northward. His plan was foiled, however, when a maidservant whom he had beaten in a fit of anger defected to Moroni's camp. Learning of Morianton's intent and fearing that the people of Bountiful[2] would join forces with Morianton (Alma 50:29–31), Moroni sent Teancum's army to stop his flight. Teancum slew Morianton and returned to the camp of Moroni with prisoners (Alma 50:33–36).

Morianton, land of and city of Nephite coastal region bordering the land of Lehi (Alma 50:25), possibly named after a prominent leader, Morianton[2] (see Alma 50:28; ca. 68 B.C.). Under Morianton the people became involved in a land dispute with the inhabitants of Lehi, but before they could carry out their violent intentions, the people in the land of Lehi fled to captain Moroni for assistance. Fearing Moroni, Morianton attempted to lead his people northward. They were prevented by force of arms, and under a covenant of peace they were restored to their land (Alma 50:25–36). Within a year, however, they were driven out by the Lamanites and eventually joined forces with other refugees (Alma 51:26; 59:5). Moroni began preparations to retake Morianton in 63 B.C., but the city was heavily fortified. The record does not say when or if it was liberated (Alma 55:33).

Moriantum Nephite locale. In a letter to his son Moroni[2], written just prior to the final destruction of the Nephite nation, Mormon described in horrific detail the depravity of some Nephites in Moriantum. They captured many Lamanite women, sexually assaulted them, tortured them to death, and then devoured their flesh "for a token of bravery." Mormon denounced their acts and lamented the state of his people (Moro. 9:9–15).

Mormon[1] Father of Mormon[2] (the primary abridger of the Book of Mormon) and a descendant of Nephi[1] (Morm. 1:5). The only reference to him is the note that he carried his eleven-year-old son Mormon into the land of Zarahemla (Morm. 1:6; ca. A.D. 322).

Mormon[2] Late Nephite prophet, historian, general of armies, and abridger of the Nephite records (ca. A.D. 311–85).

Mormon was a descendant of Nephi[1] and was named after his father Mormon[1] and the land of Mormon, where Alma[1] established the Church after fleeing from the servants of the apostate king Noah[3] (3 Ne. 5:12; Morm. 1:5; Mosiah 18). As author-editor of the abridged sacred record of the Nephite peoples, Mormon is the ancient prophet to whom modern readers of the Book of Mormon are perhaps most indebted. Mormon's life spanned the final tragic era in Book of Mormon history, and Mormon grieved deeply as he watched his people ripen fully in iniquity. So steeped in wickedness was this society that the Lord "did take away his beloved disciples" (Morm. 1:13, 16), and spiritual gifts were withdrawn. Not only did Gadiantonism reappear, but Satan's influence was manifest in every conceivable evil, including the practices of idolatry, witchcraft, sorcery, whoredoms, murder, thievery, and cannibalism (Morm. 1:19; 2:10; 4:14; Moro. 9:8–11). Mormon wrote sorrowfully that he saw nothing among his people but wickedness and war "all my days" (Morm. 2:19). In the end, he witnessed total Nephite annihilation. It was nothing short of miraculous that a child born and reared in a society glutted with iniquity could remain spiritual, loving, and tenderhearted. The sweetness in Mormon's nature is evident in his anguish over the wickedness and suffering of his people, in his decision at the end to serve them again on the battlefield, and in his prayers for them even after they were beyond hope. It is also evident in his tender, fatherly words to his son Moroni[2], in the letters that constitute chapters eight and nine of the book of Moroni. Mormon was, indeed, an unusual child, "sober," Ammaron said, and "quick to observe" (Morm. 1:2). When Mormon was only ten years old, Ammaron, the current keeper of the sacred records, informed Mormon that he would one day have charge of them. He instructed Mormon about their care and told him that at age twenty-four Mormon was to recover the records from the hill where Ammaron had placed them for safekeeping. At age fifteen, in what may have been Mormon's first significant spiritual experience, he was "visited of the Lord" (Morm. 1:15), perhaps much as the boy Joseph Smith was many centuries later. Mormon was, however, "forbidden to preach" to the Nephites "because of the hardness of their hearts" (Morm. 1:17). Then, incredibly, in his "sixteenth year" (Morm. 2:2) Mormon was appointed to lead the Nephite armies. He modestly attributed this appointment to his imposing physical stature. His first recorded encounter in the field of battle proved disheartening as his frightened troops "would not fight." They fled from city to city until finally some four years later they beat the Lamanites, giving Mormon his first victory (Morm. 2:2–9).

At only one juncture over many years of warfare did Mormon take heart, when his people actually began to lament their plight. Mormon's hopes were soon dashed, however, for "their sorrowing was not unto repentance, because of the goodness of God; but it was rather the sorrowing of the damned" (Morm. 2:13). Nevertheless, when Mormon was in his middle thirties (A.D. 346), the Nephites rallied under his inspired leadership and met with success on the battlefield. A treaty was signed (A.D. 350), and ten years of relative peace ensued. The Lord, in an attempt to bless the Nephites, instructed Mormon to urge them to repent and promised they would be spared. This ten-year hiatus in

MORMON[2]

fighting may have given Mormon the opportunity he needed to study the Nephite records, perhaps even to begin the work of ABRIDGMENT. When warfare resumed and the Nephites emerged victorious, in their pride they desired vengeance on their enemies. Mormon would have no part of their aggression—the Lord forbade it as he had consistently forbidden it among the Nephites—and Mormon resigned as commander (Morm. 3:4–11).

At this point (see Morm. 3:16–22) Mormon assumed in earnest his spiritual role as record keeper, historian of his times, witness to future generations, and testifier of Christ "unto all the ends of the earth" (Morm. 3:18). What he wrote was intended not only for the twelve tribes of Israel, including and especially the Lehite remnant, but also for "every soul who belongs to the whole human family of Adam" (Morm. 3:20). Finally, knowing of the judgments of God that awaited his people because of their failure to repent, "without hope" Mormon consented to lead his fallen people in battle once again. This time they were fighting not for vengeance but for their lives.

Mormon knew they were lost, but they were his people and he loved them. One of only a few survivors of a mighty nation now fallen, Mormon was "rent with anguish" (Morm. 6:16) as he watched the demise of civilization in his part of the world. "O ye fair ones," he cried in a highly poetic and agonized lament over the needless destruction of a once faithful and blessed people (Morm. 6:17). In the end, even Mormon was a victim of the mindless slaughter, as his son Moroni recorded (Morm. 8:3).

Mormon's contribution

It would be impossible to overstate Mormon's achievements spiritually, physically, and intellectually. He established a relationship with God in his teenage years, and it sustained him throughout a life stamped by upheaval and grief. What Mormon achieved militarily—leading a hopelessly corrupt people to a number of major victories—would have won him lasting fame in any society. But to the modern reader, his military leadership is secondary to his spiritual and intellectual accomplishments. Mormon understood perfectly why a record had to be prepared; he knew that he and his predecessors wrote for future peoples. He knew the record was to contain the saving gospel of Jesus Christ. When he spoke editorially, throughout his abridgment of the large PLATES OF NEPHI, as well as when he wrote as historian and prophet of his era (abridging his own historical account; see Morm. 2:18; 5:9, 12–13), Mormon addressed latter-day peoples directly.

He spoke to Gentiles yet unborn (3 Ne. 29–30), but more particularly he addressed the remnant seed of Jacob, the descendants of the Lamanites who would outlast the wars of his day (Moro. 7).

An attentive reader of the Book of Mormon is ever aware of Mormon as a presence. He was more than an editor, more than an abridger. Clearly, he effectively assimilated the writings of his predecessors, including the prophets represented on the brass plates. He knew the scriptures and seemed to carry them in his mind; he was full of them and fed by them, and as such was fortified against the evils of his day, and strengthened in his work. Many of his phrases echo those of earlier Nephite prophets (e.g., Mosiah 23:22; cf. Morm. 2:19 / Enos 1:4; cf. Morm. 3:12 / Hel. 13:38; cf. Morm. 2:13 / Alma 43:45; cf. Morm. 2:23), and they especially echo the words of Christ recorded in 3 Nephi (e.g., 3 Ne. 16:8–9, 11; cf. Morm. 5:20 / 3 Ne. 26:3; cf. Morm. 5:23 / 3 Ne. 14:20; cf. Moro. 7:5). Mormon alluded specifically to Samuel[2] and Abinadi (Morm. 1:19).

The entire Book of Mormon was shaped by Mormon's sense of purpose. His was a divine commission. As he said in a late epistle to Moroni, "We have a labor to perform whilst in this tabernacle of clay" (Moro. 9:6). It was after he had abridged the writings of prophets from Lehi down to the time of Benjamin (large plates) that Mormon came upon the small plates of Nephi (W of M 1:3). Reading them, he was further strengthened concerning the divine purposes for his work with the plates. Nephi[1], who spoke repeatedly of the nature and purposes of the record, in a sense became his tutor, and what Mormon learned from the small plates would have informed and helped shape the

Mormon Abridging the Plates; *painting by Tom Lovell; courtesy VRL.*

remainder of his work (Packer, 276). Nephi testified with great power that he wrote the words of Christ and that those words would come forth in a later day (2 Ne. 26; 33). Mormon also read Nephi's prophecy of the destruction of the Nephite nation.

Thus, contemporary events, though heartbreaking, would not have come as a surprise. Mormon was able to conclude that because prophecies "concerning us down to this day have been fulfilled," prophecies that "go beyond this day must surely come to pass" also (W of M 1:4). It might be asked of any editor or abridger why he or she selected some materials for inclusion and bypassed others. Large amounts of material can be quite challenging, as reflected in Mormon's seeming lament, "I cannot write the hundredth part of the things of my people" (W of M 1:5). For many editors, the materials shape the purpose. Editors typically identify patterns and themes after they have completed their collecting and research. Guided by the Lord and by what he knew concerning the purposes of the record, Mormon worked the other way. He searched the records to find materials that suited his predetermined commission, which was to prepare a record that would bring latter-day peoples to Christ and ready them for his second coming. Of Mormon's selection process for inclusion of material in the Book of Mormon, President Ezra Taft Benson taught: "The Book of Mormon was written for us today. God is the author of the book. It is a record of a fallen people, compiled by inspired men for our blessing today. . . . Mormon, the ancient prophet after whom the book is named, abridged centuries of records. God, who knows the end from the beginning, told him what to include in his abridgment that we would need for our day" (Benson, 2).

Mormon knew that the record he was preparing was to come forth in a day of apostasy and confusion (1 Ne. 13; 2 Ne. 27–29). He also knew that the record was intended to be a solution to these problems by restoring "the plain and precious things" that would be removed from the Bible (1 Ne. 13), truths needed to dispel the spiritual darkness engulfing the latter-day world. That knowledge of his record's purpose assuredly guided Mormon's inspired editorial labors.

For example, Mormon chose to include a good number of battle strategies as well as the inspired answers of Alma[2] to one son's doctrinal questions. In a day when war is almost a way of life, modern people can profit from the example of captain Moroni's faith in Christ and his ability to win battles without bloodshed, or from the faith and courage of the ANTI-NEPHI-LEHIES, or from the valor of the youthful warriors of Helaman[2]. These stories all point to Christ in some way (e.g., Alma 27:27–28; 43:3; 48:13; 53:21; 56:47–48; 57:21, 26).

Alma's counsel to Corianton clarifies several important doctrines, such as those pertaining to resurrection, judgment, and justice (Alma 40–42). Mormon included none of his own sermons or formal discourses in the book he prepared. Helaman 12, however, which contrasts the "unsteadiness" and "nothingness" of prideful mortals with the greatness of God, seems to be Mormon's work (Hel. 12:1, 7). And Mormon's son Moroni elected to add one of Mormon's sermons (to Church members) and two letters (to Moroni) to the record. Mormon himself had not intended these discourses to be part of the abridgment, but they carry truths applicable for modern-day peoples nonetheless. Then, too, throughout the Book of Mormon, he added considerable commentary. He moralized on events, he counseled and warned latter-day readers in language that splendidly testifies of Christ and Christ's redemptive mission, and he spoke of the importance of the record and its purposes. In all Mormon's commentary and counsel, the abiding theme is that when mortals keep God's commandments in humility and faith, they prosper spiritually and materially. In Mormon's words, "the Lord in his great infinite goodness doth bless and prosper those who put their trust in him" (Hel. 12:1).

Mormon's sermon (Moro. 7), which treats the related subjects of faith, hope, and charity, affirms first that all good comes from God, and that the true followers of Christ perform good works and give good gifts. Conversely, the followers of Satan do nothing but evil. Mormon says further that all mortals receive the light of

Christ, enabling them to discern between good and evil. The key is the exercise of faith in Christ, and "it is by faith that miracles are wrought" (Moro. 7:37). Faith, Mormon said, leads to "hope through the atonement of Christ" (Moro. 7:41) and to charity. When Mormon spoke of charity, he echoed the words of Paul in 1 Corinthians 13, confirming that both men were inspired in their utterances. Mormon, however, added the insightful definition of charity as "the pure love of Christ" and explained how it may be attained (Moro. 7:47; 8:25–26). A theme that emerges from Mormon's second letter to his son (Moro. 9) is his sorrow over the deep-seated anger in his people, an anger that has destroyed love—charity—among them. They had, in fact, become dehumanized.

Summary of major teachings

1. To Jew and Gentile—Jesus is the Christ (e.g., 3 Ne. 29–30; Morm. 3:21).

2. The "children of men" are "quick to be lifted up in pride" and they are "slow . . . to remember the Lord their God" (Hel. 12:4–5).

3. God will bless and prosper the obedient (Hel. 6:34; 12:1; 3 Ne. 5:22).

4. Scattered Israel will be gathered to Christ, to the covenants, and to their lands (3 Ne. 5:24–26).

5. "Every soul who belongs to the whole human family of Adam . . . must stand to be judged of [their] works, whether they be good or evil" (Morm. 3:20, 22; 6:21–22).

6. Latter-day children of Lehi must come to a knowledge of their birthright as Israelites, repent, believe in Christ, be baptized, and lay hold upon the gospel in both the Bible and the Book of Mormon (Morm. 7; W of M 1:8).

7. Gifts must be given and prayers must be offered with proper intent to be acceptable to God (Moro. 7:5–11).

8. Through the "spirit of Christ" one can discern good from evil (Moro. 7:12–19).

9. Through faith mankind can lay hold on "every good thing" (Moro. 7:20–39).

10. The "ministry" of angels "is to call men unto repentance, and to fulfil and to do the work of the covenants" (Moro. 7:29–32).

11. There is an integral interrelationship between FAITH, HOPE, AND CHARITY (Moro. 7:2–48).

12. CHARITY, "the pure love of Christ," and the "greatest of all" gifts (Moro. 7:46–47), can be obtained through prayer and obedience (Moro. 7:48; 8:25–26).

13. Infant baptism is an abomination to God for "little children are alive in Christ" and "need no repentance, neither baptism" (Moro. 8:11–12).

See also And thus we see; Book of Mormon, selected purposes of; Book of Mormon, selected themes of; Children, baptism of little; Light of Christ; Mormon, book of; Words of Mormon.

BIBLIOGRAPHY

Benson, Ezra Taft. A *Witness and a Warning*. Salt Lake City: Deseret Book, 1988.

Hardy, Grant R. "Mormon as Editor." *Rediscovering the Book of Mormon*. Edited by John L. Sorenson and Melvin J. Thorne. Salt Lake City: Deseret Book, 1991.

Holland, Jeffrey R. "Mormon: The Man and The Book: Part I." *Ensign* 8 (March 1978): 15–18.

———. "Mormon: The Man and The Book: Part II." *Ensign* 8 (April 1978): 56–59.

Keller, Roger. "Mormon and Moroni as Authors and Abridgers." *Reexploring the Book of Mormon*. Edited by John W. Welch. Salt Lake City: Deseret Book, 1992.

Mackay, Thomas W. "Mormon and the Destruction of Nephite Civilization." *Alma 30 to Moroni*. Edited by Kent P. Jackson. Vol. 8 of *Studies in Scripture* series, edited by Robert L. Millet and Kent P. Jackson. Salt Lake City: Deseret Book, 1988.

Packer, Boyd K. *Let Not Your Heart Be Troubled*. Salt Lake City: Bookcraft, 1991.

Perry, David E. "Mormon—a Man for Our Time." *A Symposium on the Book of Mormon*. Salt Lake City: The Church of Jesus Christ of Latter-day Saints, 1979.

Peterson, Daniel C. "Their Own Worst Enemies." *Alma 30 to Moroni*. Edited by Kent P. Jackson. Vol. 8 of *Studies in Scripture* series, edited by Robert L. Millet and Kent P. Jackson. Salt Lake City: Deseret Book, 1988.

Tvedtnes, John A. "Mormon's Editorial Promises." *Rediscovering the Book of Mormon*. Edited by John L. Sorenson and Melvin J. Thorne. Salt Lake City: Deseret Book, 1991.

MA

Mormon, book of Book written by the prophet Mormon (Morm. 1–7) and Moroni[2] (Morm. 8–9), covering the history of the period

MORMON, BOOK OF

between A.D. 321 and 401. The chapters by Mormon are apparently his abridgment of his own more complete record, originally written on the large PLATES OF NEPHI (Morm. 2:18; 5:9). Mormon's part of the record covers the story of his life and the dramatic downfall of the Nephite civilization (Morm. 1:2, 6; 6:5; A.D. 321–385). Moroni's part, probably added in A.D. 401 (Morm. 8:6), consists principally of his discourse to people in the latter days.

Content and message

Mormon's short book reflects a profound understanding of the whole of the Nephite record contained in the larger Book of Mormon—a book that he spent a significant part of his life abridging. For example, the slippery treasures, sorceries, witchcraft, and the power of the evil one (Morm. 1:18–19; 2:10) that filled the land in Mormon's day fulfilled the prophecies of Abinadi and Samuel the Lamanite (Hel. 13:18–21); Mormon's observation that the Lord would not suffer his people "to take happiness in sin" (Morm. 2:13) is an echo of the teachings of Samuel the Lamanite (Hel. 13:38); and Mormon's exhortation to his people to "fight for their wives, and their children, and their houses, and their homes" (Morm. 2:23) is almost a direct quotation of the words of captain Moroni[1] on the title of liberty (Alma 46:12). Moreover, Mormon attributed Nephite military defeat in the year A.D. 363 to their choice to pursue offensive warfare without provocation (Morm. 4:4), contrary to the law of war described in the book of Alma (Alma 43:46–47; 48:14–15). Mormon named his own son Moroni, perhaps in hopes that he would be a man like Moroni[1] of old (Alma 48:17–18).

Book of Mormon prophets, including Christ (3 Ne. 27:32), foretold the destruction of the Nephites that Mormon later described in his book: specifically, Nephi[1] (1 Ne. 12:14–23; 2 Ne. 26:10–11, 15), Alma[2] (Alma 45:9–14), and Samuel the Lamanite (Hel. 13:8–10; 15:17). Thus Mormon's account verifies the fulfillment of these repeated prophecies that the Nephites would be destroyed for their wickedness and pride. Mormon's description of the spiritual and temporal downfall of his people serves as a powerful lesson to future readers, instructing them on how to avoid a similar destruction (cf. Morm. 6:16–22; 8:26–41; 9:31).

In chapters 1–6, Mormon included the story of his own life, a life that was inextricably connected with the events of the end of Nephite civilization. His record is a sorrowful one as he chronicled each step in the moral decline of his people and their eventual destruction.

Mormon lived in a time when the Nephite society had reached complete apostasy (Morm. 1:13–14). He, however, was a sober and observant child (Morm. 1:2), who at the age of fifteen was "visited of the Lord, and tasted and knew of the goodness of Jesus" (Morm. 1:15). Nevertheless, the Lord forbade him to preach to his people because they had "wilfully rebelled against their God" (Morm. 1:16–17). The land was cursed for their sake, their treasures "became slippery," and Gadianton robbers, sorceries, witchcrafts, magics, and the power of the evil one filled the land (Morm. 1:18–19).

Mormon was called to do manly things at a young age. When he was about ten years old, Ammaron commissioned him to be the future Nephite record keeper (Morm. 1:2–5). In his sixteenth year, Mormon became the leader of the Nephite armies (Morm. 2:2; A.D. 327). His army retreated for four years before he finally obtained his first victory in his twentieth year (Morm. 2:9). After leading his people to victory he rejoiced, thinking that the Nephites were beginning to repent of their iniquities, but he soon observed that "their sorrowing was not unto repentance, . . . but it was rather the sorrowing of the damned, because the Lord would not always suffer them to take happiness in sin" (Morm. 2:13). At "about twenty and four years" of age (Morm. 1:3), Mormon retrieved the plates and began to make a full account of the record of his people on the plates of Nephi (Morm. 2:17–18). At age thirty-five, he urged his people to stand boldly before the Lamanites and, echoing the words of general Moroni, "fight for their wives, and their children, and their houses, and their homes" (Morm. 2:23; cf. Alma 46:12; A.D. 346). The Nephites were victorious, but Mormon recorded, "the strength of the Lord was not with us; yea, we were left to ourselves, . . . we had become weak like unto our brethren"

(Morm. 2:26). Four years later, the Nephites and Lamanites made a treaty (A.D. 350).

The people then enjoyed ten years of peace in which the Lord commanded Mormon to preach repentance and to invite the people to be baptized, to build up the Church again, and thus be spared from destruction (Morm. 3:1–2; A.D. 350–360). Mormon's efforts were in vain, and war broke out again (Morm. 3:3–8). After a great victory Mormon recorded the mounting pride of the Nephites: "They began to boast in their own strength, and began to swear before the heavens that they would avenge themselves of the blood of their brethren" (Morm. 3:9). At age fifty-one, Mormon refused to lead his proud and wicked people (Morm. 3:11; A.D. 362), but he continued his ministry as an "idle witness to manifest unto the world the things which [he] saw and heard" (Morm. 3:16). After recording his revelation of the Lord's intent to "cut off [the

OUTLINE OF MORMON

- I. Writings of Mormon (1–7)
  - A. Record of Mormon from age ten to age fifteen (1)
    - 1. Call of Mormon to be record keeper (1:1–5)
    - 2. Nephite and Lamanite wars and iniquities (1:6–19)
  - B. Nephite battles under the command of Mormon (2)
  - C. Continuation of Nephite wars (3)
    - 1. Victory of the unrepentant Nephites (3:1–10)
    - 2. Mormon's refusal to lead the Nephites; he becomes an "idle witness"(3:11–16)
    - 3. Mormon's message to the Gentiles and tribes of Israel (3:17–22)
  - D. Nephite and Lamanite wars and atrocities (4)
    - 1. Nephite offensive (4:1–18)
    - 2. Nephite defeat and flight (4:19–23)
  - E. Command of Nephite armies resumed by Mormon (5)
    - 1. Further Nephite defeats (5:1–7)
    - 2. Mormon's prophecy of the coming forth of the Book of Mormon (5:8–14)
    - 3. Lamanites to receive the gospel in the future from the Gentiles (5:15–24)
  - F. Last battle at Cumorah (6)
    - 1. Final Nephite defeat and destruction in battle (6:1–15)
    - 2. Mormon's lament over his fallen people (6:16–22)
  - G. Mormon's admonition to the Lamanites to accept the gospel and believe in Christ (7)
- II. Writings of Moroni[2] (8–9)
  - A. Cumorah's aftermath—conditions in the land (8:1–11)
    - 1. Report of the death of Mormon and Moroni's kinfolk (8:1–5)
    - 2. The destruction of the surviving Nephites by the Lamanites (8:6–7)
    - 3. Lamanites continue in warfare against each other; none are righteous save the THREE NEPHITES, whom Mormon and Moroni have seen (8:8–11)
  - B. Prophecies of the coming forth of the Book of Mormon in days of pride (8:12–41)
    - 1. The Book of Mormon to come forth in the latter days (8:12–25)
    - 2. Conditions in the latter days when the book will come forth (8:26–34)
    - 3. Moroni's rebuke of those who "walk in the pride of [their] hearts" (8:35–41)
  - C. Moroni's message to the future readers of the Book of Mormon (9:1–29)
    - 1. Moroni's message to those who do not believe in Christ (9:1–6)
    - 2. Moroni's message to those who deny revelations and miracles (9:7–29)
  - D. Moroni's farewell (9:30–37)
    - 1. Language and purpose of the plates (9:30–35)
    - 2. Nephite desire for Lamanite salvation (9:36–37)

Nephites] from the face of the earth" for their failure to repent (Morm. 3:15), Mormon then addressed the Gentiles and the house of Israel. He invited them to repent of their sins, to believe in the gospel of Jesus Christ, and to prepare themselves to "stand before the judgment-seat of Christ" (Morm. 3:17–22).

Mormon indicated that the demise of the Nephites began in the year A.D. 363 (Morm. 4:1, 4, 18) and pointed out the specific reasons for their eventual destruction. First, the Nephites went on the offensive: "The Nephites went up unto the Lamanites that they began to be smitten; for were it not for that, the Lamanites could have had no power over them" (Morm. 4:4). Second, when the Nephites were victorious, they did "boast of their own strength" (Morm. 4:8). Third, the Nephites "repented not of the evil they had done, but persisted in their wickedness continually" (Morm. 4:10). Fourth and finally, "every heart was hardened, so that they delighted in the shedding of blood continually" (Morm. 4:11). Mormon recorded "there never had been so great wickedness among all the children of Lehi, nor even among all the house of Israel" (Morm. 4:12), and "from [that] time forth did the Nephites gain no power over the Lamanites, but began to be swept off by them" (Morm. 4:18).

At age sixty-four, Mormon, seeing that the Lamanites were about to conquer the land, collected all of the records of Ammaron from the hill Shim (Morm. 4:23; A.D. 375) and resumed his command of the Nephite armies (Morm. 5:1), a command that he would hold until their destruction at Cumorah (A.D. 385). But he led his people "without hope" because they would not repent of their sins (Morm. 5:2). At this point in the narrative Mormon departed from his people's history. He prophesied the future scattering of the Lamanites by the Gentiles, as well as the day when the Lord would "remember the covenant which he made unto Abraham and unto all the house of Israel" (Morm. 5:20–21). He foresaw that the Gentiles "who have care for the house of Israel" (Morm. 5:10) would be instrumental in bringing forth the Book of Mormon, which would bring the "remnant of the house of Jacob" (Morm. 5:12)—including the Lamanites and the Jews—to Christ (Morm. 5:8–24).

Mormon's last battle against the Lamanites was in the land of Cumorah (Morm. 6:2). At age seventy-four he prepared his people for war and buried his record in the hill Cumorah, except for a few plates that he gave to his son Moroni (Morm. 6:6; A.D. 385). Mormon was wounded in battle but was still able to witness the destruction of tens of thousands of his people (Morm. 6:8–15). A small group of twenty-four Nephites survived, including Mormon and Moroni; a few others escaped into the south countries; and a few deserted to the Lamanites (Morm. 6:15). Mormon finished the description of the destruction of the Nephites with a lament over his fallen people (Morm. 6:16–22).

In chapter 7, Mormon addressed the Lamanites as "the remnant of this people who are spared" (Morm. 7:1). He proclaimed their Israelite heritage and exhorted them to repent and believe in Jesus Christ (Morm. 7:2–5). He further invited them to "lay hold upon the gospel of Christ" which one day would be "set before" them in both the Bible and the Book of Mormon (Morm. 7:8–9), and then declared that if they would believe in Christ and be baptized, "it shall be well" for them in the Day of Judgment (Morm. 7:10).

Moroni finished his father's book (chapters 8–9), in which he wrote a "few things . . . which things I have been commanded by my father" (Morm. 8:1).

Most of Moroni's writings in chapters 8–9 are addressed directly to the future readers of the Book of Mormon. Moroni promised, "And whoso receiveth this record, and shall not condemn it because of the imperfections which are in it, the same shall know of greater things than these" (Morm. 8:12). He told how the Book of Mormon would come forth by the power of God and even described the conditions that would exist at the time the Book of Mormon would come forth (Morm. 8:12–34).

Moroni then addressed future readers: "Behold, I speak unto you as if ye were present, and yet ye are not. But behold, Jesus Christ hath shown you unto me, and I know your doing" (Morm. 8:35). He proceeded to chastize them for the same problems that caused the end of the Nephite civilization: pride, envy, strifes, malice, persecutions, the love of money and fine apparel, and all manner of iniquity. In particular Moroni rebuked religion devoid of charity for the needy (Morm. 8:36–41).

In the final chapter Moroni addressed two specific audiences: those who do not believe in Christ (Morm. 9:1–6), and those who deny revelation and miracles (Morm. 9:7–29). He pleaded for unbelievers to "turn . . . unto the Lord" and pray that they might be found worthy at the last day (Morm. 9:6). To those who deny revelation and miracles he reasoned that "God is the same yesterday, today, and forever" (Morm. 9:9). If there were miracles anciently, then "why has God ceased to be a God of miracles and yet be an unchangeable Being?" (Morm. 9:7–19).

Mormon is one of the great poets of the Book of Mormon. His writings in his short book contain vivid, dramatic, and memorable metaphors and images, especially of war and its terrible consequences, a topic with which he had much firsthand experience. He described the Nephite destruction in battle by the Lamanites as being "swept off by them even as a dew before the sun" (Morm. 4:18). He described the tragedy of his people in their final years: "They were once a delightsome people, and they had Christ for their shepherd; yea, they were led even by God the Father. But now, behold, they are led about by Satan, even as chaff is driven before the wind, or as a vessel is tossed about upon the waves, without sail or anchor, or without anything wherewith to steer her; and even as she is, so are they" (Morm. 5:17–18). He described the feeling among the Nephites while preparing for their final battle at Cumorah as "that awful fear of death which fills the breasts of all the wicked" (Morm. 6:7), and the thousands of resulting corpses as "being left by the hands of those who slew them to molder upon the land, and to crumble and to return to their mother earth" (Morm. 6:15). His final poignant lament over his people summarizes the message of his own book as well as his abridgment of the whole of the Book of Mormon: "O ye fair ones, how could ye have departed from the ways of the Lord! O ye fair ones, how could ye have rejected that Jesus, who stood with open arms to receive you! Behold, if ye had not done this, ye would not have fallen. But behold, ye are fallen, and I mourn your loss. O ye fair sons and daughters, ye fathers and mothers, ye husbands and wives, ye fair ones, how is it that ye could have fallen! But behold, ye are gone, and my sorrows cannot bring your return" (Morm. 6:17–20).

DRS

Mormon, forest of *See* Mormon, waters of.

Mormon, place of *See* Mormon, waters of.

Mormon, plates of *See* Plates of Mormon.

Mormon, waters of A fountain of pure water near a forest, located in a place called Mormon which bordered the land of Lehi-Nephi (Mosiah 18:4–5, 30). It was in this location that Alma[1] and 204 souls were baptized, and the "church of Christ" flourished (Mosiah 18:13–30). Because of the approach of the army of king Noah[3], which had been sent to destroy them for supposed rebellion, this group of new converts, which had grown to 450 souls, was forced to leave (Mosiah 18:34–35).

This beautiful area became a sacred place in Nephite religious history because of the spiritual resurgence that occurred there (ca. 147 B.C.). The prophet-historian Mormon was named after this land (3 Ne. 5:12), and Alma[2] spoke of the events there in his efforts to preach repentance to Nephites in Zarahemla (Alma 5:3–13).

CJW

Mormon, Words of *See* Words of Mormon.

Moron *See* Jared[1], posterity of.

Moron, land of Land where most Jaredite kings dwelt, "near the land which is called Desolation by the Nephites" (Ether 7:6). Because it was the political capital, it was also the site of considerable military activity and insurrection as various rivals sought the throne (Ether 7:5, 17; 14:6, 11). No specific city is mentioned in the land of Moron.

Moroni[1] Chief captain of Nephite armies during the period 74 B.C. to 57 B.C., an extraordinarily difficult period of Nephite history. Appointed when he was only twenty-five years old (Alma 43:16–17), Moroni stood as a striking example of righteous leadership in a challenging time of war and internal strife (Alma 43–63). Moroni's son Moronihah[1] succeeded him as chief captain shortly before his death (Alma 62:43; 63:3).

Moroni is notable for several reasons, including the following:

1. Moroni was an impressive military strategist. When he is first mentioned in the Book of Mormon, Moroni is leading a Nephite army against Zarahemna and a numerically superior invading force of Lamanites (Alma 43–44). Responding to this incursion, Moroni divided and deployed his forces with ingenious skill. Furthermore he provided his own men with thick clothing, breastplates, and protective devices for their arms and heads (Alma 43:18–19), all of which helped them prevail against the Lamanites. In a later battle, Moroni also won a significant victory by decoying the Lamanites out of the city of Mulek, "one of [their] strongest holds" (Alma 53:6), and trapping them between surrounding Nephite armies (Alma 52:19–40). In yet another strategic maneuver, he entered the city of Nephihah using cords and ladders to surprise a sleeping Lamanite army: "Thus had Moroni and Pahoran obtained the possession of the city of Nephihah without the loss of one soul" (Alma 62:18–26). On another occasion he recovered a large group of Nephite prisoners by surreptitiously giving wine to the Lamanite guards, making them drunken, and then arming the prisoners inside. When the Lamanites awakened, they surrendered without a fight (Alma 55:3–24). Moroni "did not delight in . . . bloodshed, but he delighted in the saving of his people from destruction; and . . . he would not fall upon the Lamanites and destroy them in their drunkenness" (Alma 55:19).

2. Moroni was a great patriot. He was one who loved, supported, and defended his country and his heritage. He rallied his troops again and again by "inspiring their hearts" and reminding them that they "were not fighting for monarchy nor power but they were fighting for their homes and their liberties, their wives and their children, . . . [for] their lands, their country, and their rights, and their religion" (Alma 43:45–48; cf. 46:11–12). His civic devotion is apparent in his angry letter to the Nephite government of Pahoran[1], as Moroni wrote regarding what he saw as "their indifference concerning the freedom of their country" (Alma 59:13) and their failure to provide needed supplies and reinforcements. Moroni's letter of censure dealt pointedly with the "wickedness which first commenced at our head" and also made clear his own willingness to follow the God-given course laid out regarding his country's leadership: "God has said that the inward vessel shall be cleansed first, and then shall the outer vessel be cleansed also. And now, except ye do repent . . . behold it will be expedient that we contend no more with the Lamanites until we have first cleansed our inward vessel, yea, even the great head of our government" (Alma 60:23–24). Moroni's response was clear and unequivocal, as he said in his letter, "I do not fear your power nor your authority, but it is my God whom I fear; and it is according to his commandments that I do take my sword to defend the cause of my country" (Alma 60:28). Upon learning that the Nephite government was not at fault, that dissenters had seized the government, Moroni marched to Zarahemla with his army and crushed those in revolt (Alma 61–62:1–11).

3. Perhaps most important of all, Moroni was a leader in righteousness. He was a man of mighty prayer (Alma 46:13–16); he knew the importance of scripture and the significance of righteous covenants. For instance, in rallying the Nephites with the TITLE OF LIBERTY, he reminded the people of the symbolic significance of Joseph[1]'s torn "coat of many colors" and its typological significance for them as a remnant of Joseph. Additionally, Moroni tore his own coat and wrote on a piece of it: "In memory of our God, our religion, and freedom, and our peace, our wives, and our children" and fastened the fragment on the end of a pole (Alma 46:12). Then he went forth "among the people, waving the rent part of his garment in the air, that all

might see the writing" (Alma 46:19), and by this symbol invited them to join in a covenant relationship with each other and with their God. "Behold," he proclaimed, "whosoever will maintain this title upon the land, let them come forth in the strength of the Lord, and enter into a covenant that they will maintain their rights, and their religion, that the Lord God may bless them" (Alma 46:20). In response, "the people came running together with their armor girded about their loins, rending their garments in token, or as a covenant, that they would not forsake the Lord their God" (Alma 46:21).

Moroni's faith was well illustrated on the battlefield. For example, after encircling the Lamanites and causing them to withdraw from fighting, Moroni proclaimed to their leader Zerahemnah, "I would that ye should understand that this is done unto us because of our religion and our faith in Christ" (Alma 44:3–4; cf. 60:25–27). Moroni had implicit faith that the powers of heaven would bless and protect his armies. As he told Pahoran, "Behold I will leave a part of my freemen to maintain this part of our land, and I will leave the strength and the blessings of God upon them, that none other power can operate against them . . . and I will come unto you" (Alma 60:25–27).

Moroni lived worthy of receiving direct revelation from the Lord. To chief judge Pahoran, Moroni wrote, "Behold, the Lord saith unto me: If those whom ye have appointed your governors do not repent of their sins and iniquities, ye shall go up to battle against them" (Alma 60:33; 61:19–20).

Mormon, who had much in common with captain Moroni, provided a memorable summary of the qualities for which this great chief captain is remembered: "Moroni was a strong and a mighty man; he was a man of a perfect understanding; yea, a man that did not delight in bloodshed; a man whose soul did joy in the liberty and the freedom of his country, and his brethren from bondage and slavery; yea, a man whose heart did swell with thanksgiving to his God, for the many privileges and blessings which he bestowed upon his people; a man who did labor exceedingly for the welfare and safety of his people. Yea, and he was a man who was firm in the faith of Christ, and he had sworn with an oath to defend his people, his rights, and his country, and his religion, even to the loss of his blood. . . . Yea, verily, verily I say unto you, if all men had been, and were, and ever would be, like unto Moroni, behold, the very powers of hell would have been shaken forever; yea, the devil would never have power over the hearts of the children of men" (Alma 48:11–13, 17).

See also Epistles; Joseph[1], coat of.

NEL

Moroni[2] The final writer in the Book of Mormon, the abridger of the book of Ether, and the son of the prophet and historian Mormon (ca. A.D. 421). Moroni was a military commander as well as a church leader over whom his father "rejoice[d] exceedingly" (Moro. 8:2). Like the other major writers and abridgers of the Book of Mormon, Nephi[1], Jacob[2], and his father, Mormon (2 Ne. 2:3; 11:2–3; Morm. 1:15), Moroni was blessed to see Jesus Christ. He testified, "I have seen Jesus, and . . . he hath talked with me face to face" (Ether 12:39). He was also privileged in his life to see and be ministered to by the Three Nephite disciples who had lived generations earlier but had been translated (Morm. 8:11).

The precise date of Moroni's birth is unknown, but his life spanned the end of the fourth and the beginning of the fifth centuries A.D. Very likely the namesake of captain Moroni[1], whom Mormon admired immensely (Alma 48:11–13, 17–19), Moroni[2] was reared in a faithful home, one where he was nurtured in the principles and practices of the gospel of Jesus Christ (Moro. 8:2–3). Yet, simultaneously, he lived in a civilization plagued with wickedness and violence.

Following the destruction of the Nephite nation at the battle of Cumorah, Moroni was left to wander alone for more than three decades in a hostile land. He had not only his own life to protect, but the records of two civilizations which were entrusted to his care. He watched the destruction of everything in his world—home, family, friends, and country. Despite all that Moroni saw and suffered, he kept the faith.

The introduction to Moroni's message

includes a heart-rending lament that reveals much about the extent of his suffering and the bleakness of his prospects: "My father hath been slain in battle, and all my kinsfolk, and I have not friends nor whither to go; and how long the Lord will suffer that I may live I know not" (Morm. 8:5). Moroni realized that he was left "alone to write the sad tale of the destruction of [his] people" (Morm. 8:3). Moreover, his message would need to include warnings and admonitions to future generations. Moroni's writings evidence his closeness to the Lord and the guidance he received in choosing what to record (e.g., Ether 4:6; 8:26). Moroni gave the initial impression that his comments would be brief, not knowing whether he would be captured and killed by the Lamanites (Morm. 8:3–7). In fact, he concluded the record twice before he finally sealed it and buried it with the other records and materials in his care, to come forth in a much later day (Morm. 8:12–14; Ether 12:38; Moro. 1:1, 4).

What Moroni did write was choice and important to Book of Mormon purposes. He prophesied concerning the coming forth of the Book of Mormon, and he foretold many of the circumstances that would attend this event and that would be prevalent in modern times—including the pervasiveness of secret combinations, apostate churches, priestcrafts, wars, fires, tempests, earthquakes, pollutions, and "all manner of abominations" (Morm. 8:26–32). Reflecting on all the Lord had shown him about those days, Moroni personalized his warning, saying that "Jesus Christ hath shown you unto me, and I know your doing" (Morm. 8:35). What Moroni was shown brought forth his stinging rebuke directed at latter-day people who "transfigured the holy word of God" for personal gain, and who neglected the poor. He called them "pollutions," "hypocrites," and teachers who had sold themselves for the "praise of the world" (Morm. 8:32–41). He foresaw that many in the latter days would "walk in the pride of [their] hearts" (Morm. 8:36). In Mormon 9, Moroni's writings first address "those who do not believe in Christ" (Morm. 9:1), and then he shifted and gave most attention to those "who deny the revelations of God, and say that they are done away" (Morm. 9:7). In his response to this particular latter-day audience Moroni defended the validity of miracles and revelations in any age, giving doctrinal reasons (Morm. 9:7–26) to counteract those who would reject the coming forth of the Nephite records because they would not believe in revelations and miracles in their modern age. Moroni cautioned that if miracles cease to occur, their absence is a result of unbelief and not because God has changed (Morm. 9:15–20).

The book of Ether is Moroni's abbreviated account of approximately two millennia of Jaredite history, intermingled with his personal commentary. Because of the account's brevity, it may be assumed that Moroni included only what he regarded as significant for latter-day people. Moroni indicated that he was the engraver of the sealed portion of the plates from which the Book of Mormon was translated (Ether 4:4–5; 5:1), that portion which contains "a revelation from God, from the beginning of the world to the ending thereof" (2 Ne. 27:7). Midway through his discussion of faith, hope, and charity in Ether 12, Moroni revealed a personal struggle with feelings of inadequacy, and his fear that "the Gentiles will mock at these things, because of our weakness in writing" (Ether 12:23). He also referred to this concern in Mormon 8:17 and in Mormon 9:31–33 where he asked that his readers not condemn him or the work itself because of his imperfections in writing. Commending all to seek Jesus, Moroni ended his personal commentary and returned to his historical abridgment of the Jaredite record (Ether 12:41–13:1), which concluded with some of Ether's prophecies and experiences as darkness settled over the Jaredite civilization. The last of the Nephites, Moroni was perfectly positioned to rehearse the account of Ether, another lonely survivor of a fallen civilization.

In addition to his own writings, Moroni recorded some important doctrinal truths his father had taught in the synagogue concerning how to discern good from evil, and the relationship between faith, hope, and charity (Moro. 7). He also included two letters his father had written to him. The first letter addressed why baptism of little children is unnecessary

(Moro. 8), and the second consisted of a description of the depravity the Nephites had reached prior to their destruction (Moro. 9).

In the year A.D. 421, Moroni wrote his farewell, a final exhortation and testimony to latter-day peoples found in Moroni 10. He enjoined all to "remember how merciful the Lord hath been . . . and ponder it in [their] hearts" (Moro. 10:3). Then he issued the sublime promise that one would know the truth of these things by praying and receiving the witness of the Holy Ghost (Moro. 10:4–5). Following his discussion of spiritual gifts, Moroni turned again to the three great virtues of faith, hope, and charity. His final invitation to readers of this era was to "come unto Christ, and be perfected in him" (Moro. 10:32).

Even though Moroni's written message was then finished, his ministry and responsibility for the sacred Nephite record was not. He was given

Moroni Burying the Plates; *painting by Tom Lovell; courtesy VRL.*

the special charge by the Lord "to reveal the Book of Mormon" and to hold "the keys of the record of the stick of Ephraim" (D&C 27:5). On 21 September 1823, in a small farmhouse in New York state, the resurrected Moroni appeared to young Joseph Smith. After recording the most complete description of a resurrected personage in the standard works, the Prophet Joseph wrote, "He called me by name, and said unto me that he was a messenger sent from the presence of God to me, and that his name was Moroni; that God had a work for me to do" (JS–H 1:33). Four years later, on 22 September 1827, Moroni delivered the record engraved on GOLD PLATES to Joseph Smith for translation by the gift and power of God. Thus, Moroni helped usher in a new era: the dispensation of the fulness of times. The sacred record which he had finished and buried so long before was to be brought forth to the very world for which it was written.

Summary of major teachings

1. The Book of Mormon. The record is of "great worth; and whoso shall bring it to light, him will the Lord bless" (Morm. 8:14). By the power of God the records would be "brought out of the earth" to "shine forth out of darkness" (Morm. 8:16). Those that condemn the text, "let him be aware lest he shall be in danger of hell fire" (Morm. 8:17–20). The truth of the Book of Mormon and "all things" can be known through the power of the Holy Ghost (Moro. 10:4–5). *See* Moroni[2]'s promise.

2. Prophecies concerning the latter days, the day the plates would come forth. "It [the plates] shall come in a day when it shall be said that miracles are done away . . . when the blood of saints shall cry unto the Lord, because of secret combinations . . . when the power of God shall be denied . . . when there shall be great pollutions upon the face of the earth; there shall be murders, and robbing, and lying, and deceivings, and whoredoms, and all manner of abominations" (Morm. 8:26–32).

3. Messages and admonitions to latter-day people. To those who persecute the latter-day work of the Lord: "The eternal purposes of the Lord shall roll on" (Morm. 8:22). To those who practice PRIESTCRAFT: "Ye hypocrites, ye teachers, who sell yourselves for that which will canker, . . . ye polluted the holy church of God" (Morm. 8:38). To "those who do not believe in Christ" (Morm. 9:1): "Ye unbelieving, turn ye unto the Lord; cry mightily unto the Father in the name of Jesus, that perhaps ye may be found spotless, pure, fair, and white, having been cleansed by the blood of the Lamb, at that great and last day" (Morm. 9:1, 6). To those who "deny the revelations of God" and spiritual gifts: "He that denieth these things knoweth not the gospel of Christ. . . . God is the same yesterday, today, and forever" (Morm. 9:7–27).

4. Instructions to Joseph Smith concerning the sealed portion of the plates and witnesses. "Touch them not [the sealed portion] in order that ye may translate; for that thing is forbidden you, except by and by it shall be wisdom in God. And behold, ye may be privileged that ye may show the plates unto those who shall assist to bring forth this work" (Ether 5:1–2).

5. SECRET COMBINATIONS. "The Lord worketh not in secret combinations" (Ether 8:19). And the warning that "whatsoever nation shall uphold such secret combinations, to get power and gain, until they shall spread over the nation, behold, they shall be destroyed" (Ether 8:22).

6. The TRIAL OF FAITH. "Ye receive no witness until after the trial of your faith" (Ether 12:6–22, 30–31).

7. FAITH, HOPE, and CHARITY. "Except ye have charity ye can in nowise be saved in the kingdom of God; neither can ye be saved . . . if ye have not faith; neither can ye if ye have no hope" (Moro. 10:21; Ether 12:29–34).

8. SPIRITUAL GIFTS. "Deny not the gifts of God, for they are many" (Moro. 10:8). Spiritual gifts are bestowed "by the Spirit of Christ . . . unto every man severally" (Moro. 10:17), "to profit them" (Moro. 10:8). "Every good gift cometh of Christ" (Moro. 10:18).

9. Come unto Christ. "I would exhort you that ye would come unto Christ. . . . Yea, come unto Christ, and be perfected in him" (Moro. 10:30–32; Ether 12:41). *See* Book of Mormon, selected themes of, come unto Christ.

See also The Structure of the Book of Mormon, 17; Ether, book of; Moroni, book of.

BRM

Moroni, book of The final book of the Book of Mormon, written by Moroni[2] at the end of Nephite history (between A.D. 401 and 421). The book of Moroni consists of a compilation of specific practices of the Nephite Church detailing gospel ordinances and church administration, a recorded discourse, two letters from Moroni's father Mormon, and Moroni's concluding words of exhortation.

Content and message

After his comments in Mormon 8 and 9 and his abridgment of the record of Ether, Moroni supposed that he was finished with the book that would one day bear his father's name. Contrary to his expectations, he later returned to the GOLD PLATES and thought it wise to record a few more things for the benefit of his "brethren, the Lamanites" (Moro. 1). He included significant information concerning doctrines and practices of the Nephite Church. He described the manner in which the Nephites bestowed the gift of the Holy Ghost, were ordained to the priesthood, blessed the sacrament (including the precise sacramental prayers), and participated in religious ordinances and observances (Moro. 2–6). Moroni 7 is an address Mormon gave to "the peaceable followers of Christ" (Moro. 7:3). It is a supernal discourse on giving gifts and praying with real intent of heart, of discerning good from evil, and on the interplay of faith, hope, and charity. Mormon explained that "charity is the pure love of Christ," and that all must "pray unto the Father with all the energy of heart, that [they] may be filled with this love" (Moro. 7:47–48). Chapter 7 also discusses the ministry of angels to "chosen vessels of the Lord, that they may bear testimony of him. And by so doing, the Lord God prepareth the way that the residue of men may have faith in Christ" (Moro. 7:31–32).

OUTLINE OF MORONI

- I. Practices of the ancient church of Christ (1–6)
  - A. Moroni's introduction of his record (1)
  - B. Bestowal of the gift of the Holy Ghost (2)
  - C. Priesthood ordinations (3)
  - D. Manner of administration of the sacrament (4–5)
  - E. Church administration (6)
    - 1. Repentance, baptism, and taking the name of Christ: the way to be numbered among the people of God (6:1–4)
    - 2. The purpose for and conducting of Church meetings under inspiration of the Holy Ghost (6:5–9)
- II. Moroni's record of the words of his father Mormon (7–9)
  - A. Mormon's sermon to Church members (7)
    - 1. Giving gifts and praying with real intent of heart (7:1–10)
    - 2. Discernment of good and evil (7:11–19)
    - 3. Laying hold on every good thing: FAITH (7:20–39), HOPE (7:40–43), and CHARITY (7:44–48)
  - B. Mormon's first epistle denouncing the baptism of little children (8)
  - C. Mormon's second epistle describing Nephite and Lamanite depravities (9)
- III. Moroni's farewell and invitation to come unto Christ (10)
  - A. The truth of the Book of Mormon and all things made known by the power of the Holy Ghost (10:1–7)
  - B. Gifts of the Spirit (10:8–19)
  - C. Faith, hope, and charity (10:20–23)
  - D. Moroni's words to stand as a witness (10:24–29)
  - E. Come unto Christ (10:30–34)

Moroni 8 and 9 are letters from Mormon to Moroni written long before Moroni recorded them on the gold plates. Moroni had kept them safe during more than three decades of wandering alone after the last battle at Cumorah. These letters contain the following comforting words from a father to a son: "My beloved son . . . I rejoice exceedingly that your Lord Jesus Christ hath been mindful of you. . . . I am mindful of you always in my prayers" (Moro. 8:2–3). The letter in chapter 8 addresses an important doctrinal issue that had not been treated in Mormon's abridged record, but which Moroni deemed important for latter-day peoples. It states forcefully that "little children need no repentance, neither baptism" (Moro. 8:11). They are saved through the atonement of Christ, and to baptize them "setteth at naught the atonement of him and the power of his redemption" (Moro. 8:20). Chapter 9 is a sad letter recounting the degenerate state of the Lamanite and Nephite peoples. It serves as a warning to those in the latter days to "be more wise" than Mormon and Moroni's people had been (Morm. 9:31), and it also illustrates the faith and sense of mission that enabled these prophets to continue to serve their fellow men with a sense of hope in such a discouraging world (Moro. 9:6, 22, 25–26).

Statue of the angel Moroni, Salt Lake Temple, Salt Lake City, Utah; photograph by Craig Dimond; courtesy VRL.

Moroni 10 contains Moroni's final farewell and testimony. In it he used the word "exhort" —meaning to strongly advise or recommend— and its derivative "exhortation" nine times. He exhorted his readers to "remember how merciful the Lord hath been . . . and ponder it in [their] hearts" (Moro. 10:3). He then issued the promise, "And when ye shall receive these things, I would exhort you that ye would ask God, the Eternal Father, in the name of Christ, if these things are not true; and if ye shall ask with a sincere heart, with real intent, having faith in Christ, he will manifest the truth of it unto you, by the power of the Holy Ghost. And by the power of the Holy Ghost ye may know the truth of all things" (Moro. 10:4–5). Moroni warned his readers not to deny the power of God evidenced by the SPIRITUAL GIFTS given by the spirit of Christ, and then reiterated the importance of the three great virtues—faith, hope, and charity. Moroni's words increase in intensity and power as he boldly professed to "speak unto all the ends of the earth" (Moro. 10:24), as he declared the truth of his prophetic calling (Moro. 10:27–29), and as he echoed the plea of the prophets before him, inviting all to "come unto Christ, and be perfected in him" (Moro. 10:32). He closed by bidding all farewell until he would meet them at "the pleasing bar of the great Jehovah" on the final Day of Judgment (Moro. 10:34).

See also The Structure of the Book of Mormon, 17; Angels, ministry of; Book of Mormon, selected themes of, come unto Christ; Children, baptism of little; Church of God (Christ) in ancient America; Epistles; Evil, concept of; Good, concept of; Moroni[2]'s promise; Sacrament prayers.

BRM

Moroni, land of and city of The land of Moroni is described as being "in the borders by the seashore" (Alma 62:25). It became a stronghold for the Lamanites during their conflict with Moroni[1] (Alma 62:25–33).

The city of Moroni was built during a time of

MORONI[2], VISITS OF, TO JOSEPH SMITH

Nephite prosperity; it was located "by the east sea . . . on the south by the line of the possessions of the Lamanites" (Alma 50:13, 17–18). Amalickiah and the Lamanite armies took possession of the city during a time when Moroni was resolving internal conflict with the kingmen. The Nephites who fled from the city of Moroni traveled to the city of Nephihah (Alma 51:22–24). The city of Moroni was sunk into the depths of the sea during the calamities that attended the death of Jesus Christ (3 Ne. 8:9; 9:4).

Moroni[2], visits of, to Joseph Smith Moroni was the principal heavenly messenger who directed Joseph Smith in finding and translating the Book of Mormon. Joseph received about 22 recorded angelic visits directly pertaining to that work. Most of these were appearances of Moroni, though the Prophet indicated other angels also came to him before he obtained the plates in 1827. Joseph Smith's dialogues with Moroni, which continued over the course of six years, offer an excellent example of effective spiritual teaching, employing explanations, scriptural prophecy, visual illustration, repetition, application, correction, and sustained encouragement.

Joseph Smith obtained the plates on 22 September 1827, "after having received many visits from the angels of God unfolding the majesty and glory of the events that should transpire in the last days" (Smith, *Church,* 4:537). But Joseph clearly identified the angel who commissioned him: "Moroni, the person who deposited the plates, from whence the book of Mormon was translated, in a hill in Manchester, Ontario County New York, being dead, and raised again therefrom, appeared unto me, and told me where they were; and gave me directions how to obtain them" (Smith, *Elders' Journal,* 42–43; also in *Church,* 3:28; cf. D&C 27:5). In the 1838–39 dictated portion of Joseph's history, Nephi was named as the angel who appeared to reveal the hidden record. Several early sources agree on a different personage, suggesting that "Nephi" may have been a scribal error. Soon after the history was first printed, the Prophet wrote to the Church about "glad tidings from Cumorah! Moroni . . . declaring the fulfilment of the prophets—the book to be revealed" (D&C 128:20). When Oliver Cowdery first described the angel's visits in an 1834–35 series in the church newspaper, the *Messenger and Advocate,* he stated that Joseph Smith "has offered to assist us" in order to ensure the accuracy of the account (Smith, *Papers,* 17). Oliver named "the angel Moroni, whose words I have been rehearsing, w[h]o communicated the knowledge of the record of the Nephites" (Smith, *Papers,* 70). Nephi's name may have come into the manuscript history because, as Brigham Young said, Moroni delivered the plates to Joseph, "but Nephi also visited him" (Smith, *Papers,* 277 n. 1).

The most complete account of Moroni's arrival is the Prophet's own account, dictated in 1838 and reproduced in the Pearl of Great Price. In the First Vision, in response to the question of which church he should join, Joseph Smith was told that the true church was not on earth, and that he should "continue as [he] was until further directed" (JS–H 1:26). Further direction came on a night three years later, as he approached God in "prayer and supplication" for forgiveness and a knowledge of his "standing before him" (JS–H 1:29). Moroni appeared with a "countenance . . . as lightning," clothed with "garments . . . pure and white above all other whiteness" (D&C 20:6; cf. JS–H 1:30–32). Oliver Cowdery offered details about this visit that he undoubtedly learned from Joseph Smith, writing of Moroni's "pleasing, in[n]ocent and glorious appearance, so much so, that every fear was banished from the heart, and nothing but calmness pervaded the soul" (Smith, *Papers,* 51). Moroni, calling Joseph by name, explained that he, Joseph, was called to a work so far-reaching that his fame would extend worldwide "for good and evil" (JS–H 1:33). In an 1832 summary of his early visions, Joseph also said the angel assured him "the Lord had forgiven me my sins" (Smith, *Papers,* 8). Moroni then told of a buried record that spoke of early American civilizations. He emphasized its great value because "the fulness of the everlasting Gospel was contained in it, as delivered by the Savior to the ancient inhabitants" (JS–H 1:34). Joseph was shown a vision of the location of the plates, and was informed that buried with the plates were "two

MORONI[2], VISITS OF, TO JOSEPH SMITH

stones" which "God had prepared . . . for the purpose of translating the book" (JS–H 1:35).

At this first visit Joseph Smith reported that Moroni reviewed Old and New Testament prophecies that would be fulfilled in God's latter-day work (Mal. 3–4; Isa. 11; Acts 3:22–23; Joel 2:28–32). In quoting Malachi to Joseph, Moroni expanded the traditional text, or restored its original form, stating that Elijah would "reveal . . . the Priesthood," and "plant in the hearts of the children the promises made to the fathers" (JS–H 1:36–39; cf. Mal. 4:5–6). Moroni "quoted the eleventh chapter of Isaiah, saying that it was about to be fulfilled." He quoted Acts 3:22–23, "precisely as they stand in our New Testament," explaining that the great prophet like Moses was Christ, whom all Israel would ultimately be required to hear (JS–H 1:40). Isaiah 11 and Acts 3 testify of Christ's millennial reign. Isaiah pictured a time of peace, wherein the earth would be "full of the knowledge of the Lord" (Isa. 11:9), and the Messiah, of the house of David, would rule in righteousness (Isa. 11:3–5). Isaiah wrote that in preparation for this period, God will set up "an ensign for the nations," and call to "the four corners of the earth" to gather the faithful descendants of all the tribes of Israel (Isa. 11:12–13).

Moroni affirmed that Joel's prophecies were soon to be fulfilled (JS–H 1:41)—that God would pour out judgments but would also call a "remnant" in a day when prophecy and visions would be renewed (Joel 2:28–32). Moroni further declared "that the fulness of the Gentiles was soon to come in" (JS–H 1:41). *See* Fulness of the Gentiles.

Joseph Smith said that in addition to the scriptural passages he specifically identified, the angel Moroni "quoted many other passages of scripture, and offered many explanations" (JS–H 1:41). In his articles on Moroni's coming, Oliver Cowdery evidently cited many of those "other passages of scripture," a number of which pertain to the latter-day gathering of Israel. And Oliver admitted to only giving a general view of Moroni's instruction. Oliver's paraphrasing of the angel's words to Joseph at the first interview include the following: "He has therefore chosen you . . . to . . . bring to pass a marvelous work and a wonder. . . . Those who draw near to God with their mouths, and honor him with their lips, while their hearts are far from him, will seek its overthrow. . . . The scripture must be fulfilled . . . which says that the words of a book, which were sealed, were presented to the learned; for thus has God determined to . . . show to the meek that his arm is (not) short[e]ned that it cannot save" (Smith, *Papers,* 53). Thus, Moroni must have cited Isaiah 29 and explained its relevance to the work of restoration to which Joseph Smith had been called.

Oliver implied that Moroni used another scripture when first addressing young Joseph Smith, stating that God was calling him as one of the weak things of the world to confound the wise (Smith, *Papers,* 52; cf. 1 Cor. 1:27–28). As shown by the dramatic prophecies quoted by Moroni, God would use Joseph Smith to change the world. In his "outline of the conversation of the angel," Oliver said the messenger announced an "ushering in of the fulness of the gospel, to prepare the way for the second advent of the Messiah, when he comes in the glory of the Father with the holy angels" (Smith, *Papers,* 73). In later repeating this language in his Wentworth letter, the Prophet verified these words as coming from Moroni, who added "that the time was at hand for the gospel, in all its fulness to be preached in power, unto all nations that a people might be prepared for the millennial reign" (Smith, *Papers,* 430; Smith, *History,* 4:537).

Twice more that night, and once the next morning, the angel reappeared and repeated his message, burning the basics of gospel restoration into the soul of the young prophet. In the morning Moroni instructed Joseph to tell his father of the visions. When he did so, his father immediately believed and told Joseph "to go and do as commanded by the messenger." Joseph proceeded to the hill, "to the place where the messenger had told me the plates were deposited" (JS–H 1:50). What first seemed so easy took on solemn dimensions, for Moroni met Joseph at the hill and denied him possession of the records, for "the time for bringing them forth had not yet arrived, neither would it, until four years from that time" (JS–H 1:53).

After uncovering the plates, Joseph tried three times to take them out of their repository, and three times he received a shock which "deprived him in a measure, of his natural strength" (Smith, *Papers,* 86). In thinking of fame and gain, Joseph had ignored the caution that God would release the record only for the purpose "of building his kingdom" (JS–H 1:46). This lesson was powerfully reinforced by a vision at the hill described by Oliver Cowdery. As Joseph received the angel's correction with humble repentance and prayer, "the heavens were opened and the glory of the Lord shone round about and rested upon him." At the same time he was shown Satan and his attendants. Moroni's words were pointed—Joseph was shown the powers of good and evil and told "that you may know hereafter the two powers and never be influenced or overcome by that wicked one" (Smith, *Papers,* 87). According to Oliver, Moroni's corrections to Joseph at the hill were concluded with expressions of confidence in Joseph and assurance that the restored kingdom of God would indeed succeed. Moroni promised that priesthood authority to baptize and confer the Holy Ghost would be given, and that though there would be enemies of the Church, "it will increase the more opposed, and spread farther and farther" to prepare the world for Christ's coming (Smith, *Papers,* 89).

Joseph was told to return to the hill each year until the plates could be given him. He did so, and of these interviews he said, "I found the same messenger there, and received instruction . . . respecting what the Lord was going to do, and how and in what manner his kingdom was to be conducted in the last days" (JS–H 1:54).

Joseph finally received the buried record with a charge of strict accountability. He compromised this charge to a degree when he insisted that the Lord allow him to loan the 116 pages of translation to Martin Harris to show to designated family members. After Martin's carelessness caused the loss of these 116 pages, the plates and Urim and Thummim were taken from Joseph for a time in the summer of 1828, and then returned by Moroni, again with encouragement. Not much translating was done from that time until April 1829, when Oliver Cowdery became the prophet's scribe. Then, within less than three months the translation was finished. When the translation was nearing completion, an "angel" showed the plates to Joseph and the Three Witnesses. Most likely that angel was Moroni, because the Lord had committed to him "the keys of the record of the stick of Ephraim" (D&C 27:5). A few days after the Three Witnesses had been shown the plates, Joseph was permitted to show them to the Eight Witnesses. Once Joseph had "accomplished . . . what was required at [his] hand" with the plates, Moroni, "according to arrangements . . . called for them," and Joseph reported 2 May 1838, "has them in his charge until this day" (JS–H 1:60)

Thus, Moroni protected the sacred record, repeatedly visiting Joseph Smith, instructing, warning, disciplining, and encouraging him concerning it. Awareness of Moroni's education of Joseph Smith immensely increases confidence in the Prophet. He emerged from this process at age twenty-three, seasoned in obedience and deeply aware of what was expected in organizing and directing Christ's restored church.

See also The Coming Forth of the Book of Mormon, 9.

BIBLIOGRAPHY

Smith, Joseph. *History of The Church of Jesus Christ of Latter-day Saints.* Edited by B. H. Roberts. 7 vols. 2d ed. rev. Salt Lake City: The Church of Jesus Christ of Latter-day Saints, 1932–51.

———. *The Papers of Joseph Smith.* Vol. 1. *Autobiographical and Historical Writings.* Edited by Dean C. Jessee. Salt Lake City: Deseret Book, 1989.

———. *Teachings of the Prophet Joseph Smith.* Selected by Joseph Fielding Smith. Salt Lake City: Deseret Book, 1976.

———, ed. *Elders' Journal.* 1 (July 1838).

RLA

Moronihah[1] A righteous Nephite general who accepted command of the Nephite armies when his father Moroni[1] retired (Alma 62:43; ca. 60 B.C.). Peace ensued for a number of years (ca. 60–53 B.C.), but dissension and conflicts with Lamanites, usually incited by Nephite dissenters, plagued Nephite society for the next two decades. Over those years, which were punctuated by periods of peace, Moronihah led the

Nephite armies in several battles to regain Nephite territory from the Lamanites. To retake Zarahemla, he and Lehi[3] defeated the army of Coriantumr[3] by attacking with their strength from the periphery of Nephite lands, while Coriantumr was caught in the middle (Hel. 1:22ff.). As the Nephites grew more wicked and were left without the Lord's fortifying strength, they lost more and more of their lands. Moronihah, who clearly saw the connection between obedience to God and prosperity—in war and peace alike, preached repentance to them, as did Helaman[3]'s sons Lehi[4] and Nephi[2]. When the Nephites repented, Moronihah was heartened and returned to war. His people were preserved, but the most Moronihah could do was retake and maintain half of their former lands and holdings (Hel. 4:14ff.).

DAW

Moronihah[2] Nephite military leader killed with his ten thousand troops in the last battle between the Nephites and Lamanites (Morm. 6:14; A.D. 385).

See also Cumorah, battle of.

Moronihah, city of Wicked Nephite city destroyed in the cataclysms attending the Savior's death. The record says "the earth was carried up upon the city of Moronihah," making in its place "a great mountain" (3 Ne. 8:10, 25; 9:5).

Moroni[2]'s promise An invitation and exhortation given by Moroni[2] to future Lamanites (Moro. 10:1), as well as Jews and Gentiles (Title Page), to read the Book of Mormon, PONDER its message in their hearts, and then "ask God, the Eternal Father, in the name of Christ" if the book is true. Those who ask in faith may gain a testimony of its truth and divinity by the power of the HOLY GHOST (Moro. 10:3–5). Moroni listed the steps that would enable a reader to receive a divine witness of the truthfulness of the Book of Mormon.

1. "Read these things" (Moro. 10:3). The Book of Mormon itself, rather than a commentary about the book, must be carefully studied and examined, a process that may cover a period of time and is not usually accomplished in a single sitting.

2. "Ponder it in your hearts" (Moro. 10:3). The English word *ponder* comes from the Latin *pondus* or *pound,* which refers to weight. Readers are to ponder or to "weigh" carefully "these things"—the mercies of God and the words or messages of the Book of Mormon.

3. "Ask God . . . in the name of Christ" (Moro. 10:4). Ultimately, the answer to the question, "Is the Book of Mormon true?" must come from God. Moroni stipulated that the asking for a knowledge of the truthfulness of the Book of Mormon must be done with a "sincere heart, with real intent" (Moro. 10:4). The prayer is not a token request, not a mere formality. It must be a wholehearted, unfeigned attempt to find truth. As noted by Elder Dallin H. Oaks: "'With real intent' means that if the Holy Ghost witnesses the truth of the book, the prayerful seeker is committed to act on that witness by being baptized into The Church of Jesus Christ of Latter-day Saints. Moroni did not promise a manifestation of the Holy Ghost to those who seek to know the truth of the Book of Mormon for hypothetical or academic reasons, even if they 'ask with a sincere heart.' The promise of Moroni is for those who are committed in their hearts to act upon the manifestation if it is received. Prayers based on any other reason have no promise because they are not made 'with real intent'" (19–20). Additionally, Moroni taught that the foundational premise upon which one asks must consist of "faith in Christ" (Moro. 10:4). One must exercise an active belief that through Jesus Christ an answer can and will come.

The blessing for reading, pondering, and praying about the Book of Mormon will be God "manifest[ing] the truth of it unto you, by the power of the Holy Ghost" (Moro. 10:4). The Holy Ghost is a revelator and a testifier providing the power of discernment and judgment. Just as "no man can say that Jesus is the Lord, but by the Holy Ghost" (1 Cor. 12:3), no man can know the Book of Mormon is true but by the Holy Ghost. The Lord told Joseph Smith that the spirit of revelation comes to the "mind and . . . heart, by the Holy Ghost" (D&C 8:2–3). The witness, therefore, comes both to a person's thoughts and feelings. One cannot determine the book's truthfulness through intellect alone. The witness of the Holy Ghost must also come to a person's heart through feelings. If people are reticent to trust their feelings they may be forfeiting the opportunity to receive a witness of the Book of Mormon through the Holy Ghost. Concerning the manner in which the answer or manifestation will come, Elder Spencer W. Kimball declared, "Remember in the book of Moroni 10:4–5 the promise is given that on certain conditions God 'will manifest the truth of it unto you, by the power of the Holy Ghost. And by the power of the Holy Ghost ye may know the truth of all things.' Such a testimony is not promised to anyone who reads the book with a critical attitude nor one who reads it to satisfy curiosity nor to one who resists it, but definitely it will come to everyone who has fully surrendered himself with an open mind and heart. And when this testimony comes to readers it is quite unlikely that it will come by flourish of trumpets or by handwriting on the wall or by audible voice, but by a burning of hearts in bosoms, and he that will receive it will know it and appreciate it, but if there is resistance it will not come" (Kimball, 134).

The remarkable thing about Moroni's promise is that it applies not only to the Book of Mormon, but to "all things" (Moroni 10:5). If one is willing to accept Moroni's challenge to find out if the Book of Mormon is true then other truths will follow. The last paragraph of the "introduction" page of every Book of Mormon contains this promise: "Those who gain this divine witness from the Holy Spirit will also come to know by the same power that Jesus Christ is the Savior of the world, that Joseph Smith is his revelator and prophet in these last days, and that The Church of Jesus Christ of Latter-day Saints is the Lord's kingdom once again established on the earth, preparatory to the second coming of the Messiah."

BIBLIOGRAPHY

Kimball, Spencer. *Teachings of Spencer W. Kimball.* Edited by Edward L. Kimball. Salt Lake City: Bookcraft, 1982.

Oaks, Dallin H. *Pure in Heart.* Salt Lake City: Bookcraft, 1988.

TBP

Mortal, mortality The period of time between birth and death (Enos 1:27; Mosiah 2:26; 18:13; Alma 40:11). Mortality is also referred to as the "second estate" (Abr. 3:26). Alma[2] emphasized that mortality was a "probationary state; a time to prepare to meet God" (Alma 12:24; 42:4, 10, 13; cf. 34:32). Amulek counseled the Nephites to not "procrastinate the day of [their] repentance," and further warned that, "if we do not improve our time" while in mortality, "then cometh the night of darkness wherein there can be no labor performed" (Alma 34:33). Mortality is temporary. In the resurrection, mankind will become immortal and live forever (Enos 1:27; Mosiah 16:10; Alma 5:15; 11:44–45; 12:12; 41:4; Morm. 6:21).

See also Life, purpose of.

ALB

Moses Noble prophet of ancient Israel and the most influential personage in the Old Testament. Moses enjoys high status in the Book of Mormon as well, chiefly because of the predominance of the LAW OF MOSES among Nephites and, at times, among Lamanites. Moreover, the Book of Mormon both clarifies biblical teachings and presents information about Moses not known from other sources.

Although Book of Mormon authors offer no details about Moses' birth and youth, they knew of a prophecy about his calling and ministry which was received many centuries before by Joseph of Egypt, a prophecy not contained in the present biblical text. In it, Joseph learned that Moses would receive "power . . . in a rod" and "judgment . . . in writing," though he would not be "mighty in speaking." Nonetheless, the Lord vowed to "write unto him [his] law by the finger of mine own hand." (In this connection, when referring to events at Sinai, the resurrected Jesus affirmed that he himself "gave the law, and I am he who covenanted with my people Israel" [3 Ne. 15:5], clarifying that he personally had given the law to Moses.) Moreover, the Lord promised, "I will make a spokesman for him" (2 Ne. 3:17), a reference to the role of his brother Aaron[1].

Of events that enmeshed Moses with the EXODUS of the Hebrew slaves, Nephi[1] referred indirectly to the call of Moses at the holy mount ("Moses was commanded of the Lord"; 1 Ne. 17:26) and then directly to his confrontation with Pharaoh's army at the RED SEA (1 Ne. 4:2; 17:27). Nephi also gave prominence to Moses' actions in the miraculous crossing of the sea (1 Ne. 4:2; 17:26; Ex. 14:13–22) and in the Lord's miracle of providing fresh water in the desert (1 Ne. 17:29; 2 Ne. 25:20; Ex. 17:6; Num. 20:11). Indirectly, Moses' second reception of the law was affirmed when Alma[1] referred to the face of Abinadi shining "as Moses' did while in the mount of Sinai" (Mosiah 13:5; Ex. 34:28–35).

The Book of Mormon records several other experiences of Moses in the desert. For example, the Israelite rebellions against Moses receive attention as examples of rebellion against the Lord and his servants (e.g., 1 Ne. 17:30, 42), including that which led the Lord to send "fiery flying serpents among them" whose deadly venom was counteracted by Moses' manufacture of the BRAZEN SERPENT (1 Ne. 17:41; Hel. 8:13–15; Num. 21:4–9). Further, Moses' prophecy of the coming of a "Prophet . . . like unto me" (Deut. 18:15, 18–19) found fulfillment in the risen Jesus (1 Ne. 22:20–21; 3 Ne. 20:23).

The Book of Mormon also corrects the Bible with regard to the death of Moses. According to the book of Deuteronomy, Moses died on Mount Nebo and was buried thereafter by the Lord (Deut. 34:1, 5–6). But the plates of brass must have recorded another version of his end because Helaman[2], son of Alma[2], was aware not only of the tradition that the Lord buried Moses, but also of an account in "the scriptures" that Moses "was taken up by the Spirit" (Alma 45:19).

The legacy of Moses' ministry lived on, of course, in the Mosaic law, which was carefully observed in most eras of Nephite civilization and among the converted ANTI-NEPHI-LEHIES before the coming of the risen Jesus (e.g., Jarom 1:5; 3 Ne. 12:18; Alma 25:15). Although the Book of Mormon does not mention explicitly the observance of individual celebrations tied to the work of Moses, such as Passover (Ex. 12:1–30) and the Feast of Tabernacles, also called Ingathering (e.g., Ex. 23:16; Lev. 23:33–36), it does suggest that such may have been observed. Nephi[1] mentioned that he and his followers "did observe to keep the judgments, and the statutes, and the commandments of the Lord in all things, according to the law of Moses" (2 Ne. 5:10). It is clear that temple sacrifice, as required in the law of Moses, formed an important part of religious life (e.g., Mosiah 2:3). Moreover, the Mosaic code served as the basis for civil law, as was hinted at in the trial of Abinadi (Mosiah 12:27–37; 13:11–26) and in the extensive civil reform of king Mosiah[2] (Mosiah 29:15, 25; Alma 1:1, 14).

It is not only in connection with the Mosaic law and certain historical events that Moses is mentioned in the Book of Mormon, however. Both Abinadi and Nephi[2] spoke of the prophecies Moses uttered "concerning the coming of the Messiah" (Mosiah 13:33; Hel. 8:13–16). Jesus himself confirmed that Moses "wrote of me" (John 5:45–46; cf. 3 Ne. 15:10).

See also Fiery flying serpents; Sinai, mount; Ten Commandments.

SKB

Moses, five books of Probably the books of Genesis, Exodus, Leviticus, Numbers, and Deuteronomy; also called the Torah, the Law, or the Pentateuch. After Nephi[1] and his brothers returned to their wilderness encampment with the PLATES OF BRASS, Lehi[1] diligently searched the sacred record from the beginning (1 Ne. 5:10). He found that the plates of brass included "the five books of Moses, which gave an account of the creation of the world, and also of Adam and Eve" (1 Ne. 5:11). The Book of Mormon further suggests that the plates of brass version of the five books of Moses contained additional information not found in the current text of the Old Testament (1 Ne. 13:23; cf. Moses 1:41).

Book of Mormon prophets used the plates of brass in their preaching and writing. The information Nephi used in his recounting of Israel's exodus from Egypt, as well as Lehi's discourses to his sons on the fall of Adam (2 Ne. 2) and the prophecies of Joseph[1] (2 Ne. 3) likely would have come from the five books of Moses (1 Ne. 17). Later prophets, such as Abinadi, Ammon[2],

Amulek, Alma[2], and Nephi[2] apparently used the five books of Moses as a source of inspiration for their teaching (Mosiah 12:33–37; 13:5–35; Alma 18:36; 33:19–20; 34:7; Hel. 8:13–20).

RH

Mosiah[1] King over the people of the land of Zarahemla. While still living in the land of Nephi, Mosiah had been warned by the Lord to take as many righteous people as would follow him and flee from the land of Nephi (Omni 1:12). Mosiah's departure fulfilled the prophecy of Jacob[2] (Jacob 3:4) and verified Nephi[1]'s words that the Lord "leadeth away the righteous into precious lands" (1 Ne. 17:38). The Book of Mormon is silent concerning the fate of the Nephites who remained behind in the land of Nephi. Mosiah and his people were directed by God through a wilderness to the city and to the people of Zarahemla (Omni 1:13–14). The people of Zarahemla rejoiced "because the Lord had sent the people of Mosiah with the plates of brass" (Omni 1:14). Mosiah had the Nephite language taught to the people of Zarahemla, and the two peoples united with Mosiah as their king (Omni 1:18–19). During his reign "there was a large stone brought unto him with engravings on it," which he was able to translate "by the gift and power of God" (Omni 1:20). The inscription gave a partial history of the Jaredites who had previously occupied the land. Mosiah[1] was succeeded as king by his son Benjamin and his grandson Mosiah[2].

See also Omni, book of; Zarahemla, people of (Mulekites).

PYH

Mosiah[2] Nephite king (154 to 91 B.C.), son of king Benjamin, grandson of king Mosiah[1], and SEER. Mosiah[2] ascended the throne (ca. 124 B.C.; Mosiah 6:3–4) when his father consecrated him to be king. Thereafter, Mosiah ruled in the city of Zarahemla as a righteous king over the people of Nephi (by this time a mixture of Nephites and Mulekites; Omni 1:19; Mosiah 25:13), following in his father's example of "walk[ing] in the ways of the Lord, and . . . observ[ing] his judgments and his statutes" (Mosiah 6:6; 29:14–15; cf. 2:13). Mosiah died in the thirty-third year of his reign at the approximate age of sixty-three. He was loved and revered by the people because they did not view him "as a tyrant who was seeking for gain"; rather, they "did esteem him more than any other man" and "did wax strong in love towards" him (Mosiah 29:40).

Mosiah is most noted for three events during his reign. First, Mosiah sent out a search party to find the people of Zeniff who had left Zarahemla during the reign of his father (or perhaps his grandfather) to return to the land of Nephi. During his reign the two remnants of the people of Zeniff, Alma[1] with his people and Limhi with his people, both originally from the land of Nephi, returned separately to Zarahemla. After Alma's return, Mosiah granted him permission to organize the Church throughout all the land of Zarahemla (Mosiah 25:19).

Second, Mosiah was a seer, as well as a prophet and revelator (Mosiah 8:13–18). With this "gift from God, whereby he could interpret" ancient languages (Mosiah 21:28), he translated the plates of gold found by Limhi's people in their search for Zarahemla (Mosiah 28:11–19; 8:8–9). These plates contained the record of the Jaredites who inhabited the land before the Nephites, but who were destroyed in a series of catastrophic wars about the time the people of Zarahemla entered the land.

Finally, Mosiah proposed a change in the Nephite governmental system. Up to the end of the reign of Mosiah, the Nephites had employed a hereditary monarchy to govern the people. Near the end of his reign, Mosiah proposed to the Nephite people that a system of judges be instituted to rule the people in the place of a king (Mosiah 29:11, 25). He proposed this change partly because none of his children wanted to be king (Mosiah 29:3–9) and partly because of the evil that one wicked, hereditary king could cause (Mosiah 29:16–24). The judges would be answerable to the people and therefore could be removed if they proved unfit to be a judge. The people accepted the change, and they appointed judges to rule over them. Alma[2], the head of the Church, was chosen to be the first chief judge; lesser judges were also appointed (Mosiah 29:42).

See also Government, principles of; Judges, reign of; Mosiah, book of; Mosiah[2], sons of.

PYH

Mosiah, book of Mormon's abridgment of a part of the large plates of Nephi, covering a period ca. 200–91 B.C. Sources for Mormon's abridgment include the records of Nephite kings during this period, inscribed on the large plates, as well as the records of Zeniff and Alma[1] (Headings, Mosiah 9; 23). Whether Zeniff's and Alma's records came to Mormon as separate sets of plates or whether these accounts were already incorporated into the large plates of Nephi before Mormon's day remains unknown.

The book bears the name of the last Nephite king, Mosiah[2]. It opens with the final discourse of king Benjamin, Mosiah's father, and the consecration of Mosiah to serve as king in his father's stead. The book closes with the report of Mosiah's death in the thirty-third year of his reign (Mosiah 29:46). The work chronicles events in two geographical areas, the land of Zarahemla and the land of Lehi-Nephi. On the narrative level, the book rehearses two stories, one of unity between peoples of different origins—Nephites and the people of Zarahemla (Mulekites), who were separate peoples yet whose origins went back to Jerusalem—and another of the absorption of colonists back into the parent society two generations after the colonists had left.

Content and message

The book of Mosiah is complex because it chronicles events in two geographical areas, the land of Zarahemla and the land of Lehi-Nephi. In addition, the book presents a series of flashbacks to different time periods. The opening section (Mosiah 1:1–8:21) recounts the period from ca. 130 to 121 B.C., the end of the reign of king Benjamin and the beginning of the reign of his son Mosiah[2]. Having selected Mosiah to succeed him, king Benjamin gathered his people and delivered his masterful final address in which he recounted his own stewardship as king, taught of the coming of Christ and his atonement, and called his people to repent of their sins and enter into a covenant to become sons and daughters of Christ (Mosiah 2–5). At the end of his sermon, king Benjamin recorded the names of the people who had entered into a covenant to keep the commandments of God, and he turned the kingship over to his son Mosiah (Mosiah 6:1–7:1). The section closes with the account of an expedition led by a man named Ammon[1] who went to the land of Lehi-Nephi to learn about the fate of colonists who had left perhaps fifty or more years before (Omni 1:29–30; Mosiah 7:2–8:21). There he met king Limhi, son of Noah[3], son of Zeniff. Zeniff had led a group many years earlier from the land of Zarahemla to explore and possess the land of their fathers, occupied by the Lamanites.

The next segment is a flashback that recounts the reigns of Zeniff, Noah, and Limhi in the period from ca. 170 to 121 B.C. (Mosiah 9–22). Zeniff was the first king of the colonists from Zarahemla who came to repossess their former lands. Surprisingly, the king of the Lamanites peacefully relinquished the land of Lehi-Nephi and the land of Shilom to Zeniff and the colonists. But the king's long-range plan was to conquer them in order to live off their labors and possessions. Later Zeniff and the colonists successfully defended themselves against king Laman[2] and the Lamanites, and afterwards against Laman's son also named Laman[3], thus foiling this plan (Mosiah 9–10). Zeniff was succeeded by his son Noah, who ruled in corruption and immorality (Mosiah 11–19). During Noah's reign the Lord chose the prophet Abinadi to call the king and his wicked priests to repentance and to teach them about the coming Messiah. King Noah's agents arrested Abinadi and, after allowing Abinadi to deliver his message, executed him (Mosiah 12–17). Abinadi's only known convert was a priest of Noah named Alma[1], who escaped after attempting to defend Abinadi. In the seclusion of a remote wooded area, Alma gained converts and established the Church of Christ. King Noah, charging Alma with rebellion, sent an army to destroy Alma's people, but they escaped into the wilderness (Mosiah 18:33–34). Ultimately king Noah's people were conquered by a Lamanite army. The king, who had escaped the initial attack, was burned to death by his own subjects who were angered when he directed them not to return to their wives and children whom they abandoned when fleeing the Lamanites. Noah's righteous son Limhi succeeded the king and became the last colonial ruler. Limhi began his reign in bondage to the Lamanites, paying one half of "all they possessed" as tribute to the Lamanite king (Mosiah 19). A Nephite named Ammon found the colonists in this unbearable situation and assisted them in escaping and returning to Zarahemla (Mosiah 21–22; 29:18–20).

OUTLINE OF MOSIAH

I. End of king Benjamin's reign and coronation of Mosiah[2] (1–8)
  A. Education of king Benjamin's sons (1:1–8)
  B. Installation of Mosiah as king (1:9–6:3)
    1. Benjamin's charge to Mosiah (1:9–17)
    2. Assembly at the temple (1:18–2:8)
    3. King Benjamin's address on service and Jesus' ATONEMENT (2:9–4:30)
    4. The people's covenant to follow Benjamin's instruction (5:1–6:3)
  C. Early years of Mosiah's reign (6:4–7:1)
  D. Ammon[1]'s expedition to find the colony of Zeniff (7:2–8:21)

II. The record of Zeniff (9–22)
  A. Establishment of Zeniff's colony (9:1–10)
  B. Zeniff's two wars (9:11–10:22)
  C. Enthronement and early years of king Noah[3] (11:1–19)
  D. First and second ministries of Abinadi (11:20–12:8)
  E. Abinadi's arrest and defense before Noah's court (12:9–16:15)
  F. Alma[1]'s escape after defending Abinadi (17:1–4)
  G. Death of Abinadi (17:5–20)
  H. Establishment of Alma's church among dissident colonists (18:1–31)
  I. Noah's unsuccessful pursuit of Alma (18:32–35)
  J. Noah's confrontation with Gideon; the Lamanite invasion; Noah's subsequent death by fire (19:1–25)
  K. Limhi's coronation and early military failures (19:26–21:22)
  L. Limhi's unexpected meeting with Ammon[1] and his soldiers; miraculous escape and return to Zarahemla (21:23–22:16)

III. The account of Alma and his people (23–24)
  A. The flight of Alma and followers from Noah's army and their settlement of the landof Helam (18:34–35; 23:1–20)
  B. Bondage and miraculous escape to Zarahemla (23:21–24:25)

IV. Major events of Mosiah's reign (25–29)
  A. Formal gathering of the people of Zarahemla (Mulekites) and the Nephites, including the recently returned colonists (25:1–18)
  B. Appointment of Alma to establish churches and ordain priests and teachers; Nephite prosperity (25:19–24)
  C. Alma's struggle with the issues of persecution and apostasy (26:1–27:7)
  D. Conversion of Alma's son Alma[2] and the sons of Mosiah (27:8–28:9)
  E. Mosiah's translation of the twenty-four gold plates and the transfer of the records to the custody of Alma the Younger (28:10–20)
  F. Mosiah's governmental reform and its system of elected judges; Alma[2]'s election as chief judge (29:1–47)

MOSIAH, BOOK OF

A third section is an account of the period from ca. 145 to 120 B.C. and concerns Alma's own colonizing efforts in the wilderness, the eventual bondage of his people, and their miraculous flight to Zarahemla (Mosiah 23–24).

The fourth and final segment returns to the original narrative of chapters 1–8, rehearsing the reabsorption of the former colonists (the people of Zeniff/Limhi and Alma) into the society of Zarahemla. King Mosiah appointed Alma to organize and preach to the Church. Alma's son Alma[2] and the four sons of Mosiah sought to destroy the Church but were miraculously converted and began to preach to the Nephites and later to the Lamanites. At the end of his ministry Mosiah changed the government from a monarchy to one of elected representation (Mosiah 25–29).

The basic theme of the book of Mosiah can be stated in one word: deliverance. This concept appears first as exhortation in king Benjamin's address on the atonement of Christ (Mosiah 2–6). It then receives emphasis in the narrative reports of the escape of the people of Limhi from their captors and the almost simultaneous escape of the people of Alma[1] from their captors. Both escapes succeeded because of the rescuing influence of the Lord (Mosiah 22:10–16; 24:16–25; 29:19–20). The deliverance theme is based on the observation that, as God delivered his people in the past, so he would deliver the Nephite people from bondage, whether it be spiritual bondage, as Benjamin's speech stressed, or whether it be physical bondage, as was the case with the two groups of colonists. The common prerequisite for divine aid, as Mormon noted in an editorial aside, is that one must be willing to put one's entire "trust" in the Lord (Mosiah 23:22; cf. 7:33): "the Lord in his great infinite goodness doth bless and prosper those who put their trust in him" (Hel. 12:1). Significantly, then, throughout the book the theme of deliverance is joined to that of TRUST or FAITH, thus underscoring the chief value of the work as an inspirational document.

The arrangement of the book of Mosiah shows Mormon making his historical interests serve his higher, religious purposes. For example, he clustered his important chronological notices near the beginning and ending of the book (Mosiah 6:4–5; 7:1, 4–5; 29:45–46). Further, he merely noted the passage of time among the Zeniffite colonists, with no apparent intent to connect events there with events at Zarahemla (Mosiah 9:11, 14; 10:3; 12:1; 17:6). As a result, Mormon eschewed chronological reporting in favor of the spiritually rich moments that he sought to accentuate. Such moments, of course, include (1) the notable address of king Benjamin on the atonement of Christ, which itself incorporated a message from an angel about the coming Messiah's ministry (Mosiah 2–6); (2) the spirited courtroom defense of the prophet Abinadi on the same subject (Mosiah 12–16); (3) the formal and spiritual adoption of the returning colonists into the society in the land of Zarahemla (Mosiah 25); (4) the landmark revelation received by Alma the Elder on dealing with apostasy within the Church (Mosiah 26); and (5) the miraculous conversion of Alma the Younger and his four friends, who were sons of king Mosiah (Mosiah 27).

The one chronological note that Mormon repeated twice concerns the third year of Mosiah's reign (Mosiah 6:7; 7:1). This year saw not only the departure of the expedition of sixteen "strong men" to make contact with the colonists (Mosiah 7:2–3) but, more significantly, their successful return with the colonists in tow (Mosiah 22:13–14). Otherwise, Mormon did not include much chronological information. For example, just before sketching the background to the story of Alma the Younger and his friends, Mormon illustrated the passing of time by mentioning "the rising generation that could not understand the words of king Benjamin, being little children at the time he spake unto his people" (Mosiah 26:1; 27). Thus, by recounting no other events in Zarahemla, the record does not report on the generation between the time Mosiah assumed the throne and the time at which his sons were old enough to cause serious trouble for the youthful Church.

Concerning civil matters, the early chapters of the book of Mosiah illuminate the procedures for succession in the Nephite monarchy (Mosiah 1; 6). Further, the book includes a view of a Nephite legal proceeding (although unrighteous) in the trial of Abinadi, and gives an account of an unusually peaceful change in government

(Mosiah 29). This change in government is painted in bright colors because of the stark contrasts between two righteous kings, Benjamin and Mosiah, and the self-indulgent, wicked king Noah. In fact, in urging his people to adopt a government of judges, king Mosiah pointed to this contrast as justification for abolishing the monarchy (Mosiah 29:13–23). In a long letter to his people he wrote, "If it were possible that you could have just men to be your kings, . . . then it would be expedient that ye should always have kings to rule over you." In contrast, "an unrighteous king doth pervert the ways of all righteousness" (Mosiah 29:13, 23). Therefore, "because all men are not just" (Mosiah 29:16), Mosiah urged his subjects to "choose you by the voice of this people, judges, that ye may be judged according to the laws which . . . were given them by the hand of the Lord" (Mosiah 29:25).

Concerning king Benjamin, one sees that his highly influential sermon rests on a prophecy about the coming ministry of Christ that can be summarized in a pair of expressions: Christ the king, Christ the servant. For Benjamin, the willingness of Christ the Eternal King to become Christ the humble servant served as an example that he and his people were to imitate (Mosiah 2:16–21). The purpose of Benjamin's prophetic sermon was to bring his people to Christ through a covenant that entailed receiving the name of Christ and promising to follow his example (Mosiah 5:6–9). At the heart of the sermon, and influencing its message, stood the words of an angel who had appeared to the king (Mosiah 3). The angel's words revealed in broad outline the mortal ministry of Jesus Christ, the Lord Omnipotent. According to the angel, Christ's future ministry would ensure "that a righteous judgment might come upon the children of men" (Mosiah 3:10). Moreover, the people's response to the king's words illustrates that the Messiah's atonement raises individuals from being less than "the dust of the earth" to the status of son or daughter of Christ (Mosiah 4:2; 5:7; cf. 2:25–26). This assurance that Christ would thus rescue people from their lowly state brings this sermon within Mormon's broad interest in deliverance.

Concerning the life of the prophet-martyr Abinadi, little is known. The Lord called him to prophesy against the evil excesses of king Noah and the colonists in the land of Lehi-Nephi. But when the king tried to arrest him, the prophet withdrew to an unknown destination (Mosiah 11:20–29). Two years later, Abinadi returned, only to be arrested and tried before a court made up of Noah's priests (Mosiah 12:1–18). Abinadi's appearance before the court is notable because he seized the occasion to preach to Noah and his wicked priests about the coming Christ. After quoting all of chapter 53 of Isaiah, Abinadi offered one of the most important statements about the atonement of Christ ever uttered (Mosiah 14–15). He said that Christ "breaketh the bands of death," thus assuring resurrection for all, and that he is "filled with compassion towards the children of men" and has "taken upon himself their iniquity . . . and satisfied the demands of justice." But, he declared, only "those that have kept the commandments of God, shall come forth in the first resurrection . . . to dwell with God who has redeemed them." In contrast, "the Lord redeemeth none such that rebel against him and die in their sins." In time, Abinadi promised, this message of "the salvation of the Lord shall be declared to every nation, kindred, tongue, and people" (Mosiah 15:8–9, 22–23, 26–28). Although Abinadi did not escape death at the hands of the court—his death was to stand as a witness against evil (Mosiah 17:13–20)—his message about Christ's redemption fits within the larger lesson of deliverance in the book of Mosiah.

See also Book of Mormon: Another Testament of Jesus Christ; Book of Mormon, selected themes of, bondage and deliverance; Government, principles of; Isaiah chapter reviews (Mosiah 14 // Isa. 53); Mosiah[2], sons of; Nephite civilization; Noah[3], priests of; Zarahemla, people of (Mulekites).

BIBLIOGRAPHY

Nyman, Monte S., and Charles D. Tate, eds. *The Book of Mormon: Mosiah—Salvation Only through Christ.* Provo, Utah: Religious Studies Center, 1991.

SKB

Mosiah², sons of Aaron³, Ammon², Omner, and Himni; rebellious sons of king Mosiah² who, along with Alma², sought to destroy the church of God, but were converted by the appearance of an angel (Mosiah 27). Following their conversions they zealously sought "to repair all the injuries which they had done to the church" (Mosiah 27:35) by teaching the gospel throughout the land (Mosiah 27:35–37; Alma 17–23). Despite persecution by unbelievers, the sons of Mosiah continued to report the visitation of the angel. Their acknowledgment of their sins, along with their preaching and exhortations, brought many people "to the knowledge of their Redeemer" and also served to console church members and confirm their faith (Mosiah 27:32–37). Although converted by miraculous means, with seemingly instantaneous transformations from sinners to Saints, the sons of Mosiah were not spared the pains of true repentance. Their earlier rebellion cost them "much anguish of soul" and fear for their own eternal welfare (Mosiah 28:4).

Driven by the desire to save "any human soul" from perishing and suffering "endless torment," the sons of Mosiah aspired to declare salvation to "every creature" (Mosiah 28:3). Thus, they approached their father and asked permission to "impart the word of God to their brethren, the Lamanites" (Mosiah 28:1). All of them declined the crown to serve missions, which led Mosiah to propose a system of elected judges among the Nephites (Mosiah 29:1–3; Alma 17:6). The sons' lofty mission goals included bringing the Lamanites "to the knowledge of the Lord," convincing "them of the iniquity of their fathers," and "cur[ing] them of their hatred towards the Nephites." Success would bring joy in the Lord, new friendships between former enemies, and peace in the land (Mosiah 28:2). The task would be formidable, as the Lamanites' hatred for the Nephites had been entrenched for some 500 years (2 Ne. 5:14; Jacob 7:24; Enos 1:20; Mosiah 1:14; 10:17; 11:17; Alma 20:10–14; 4 Ne. 1:39). After inquiring of the Lord, king Mosiah granted his sons permission to do as they had requested, and the Lord promised them protection (Mosiah 28:6–7).

Their fourteen-year Lamanite mission was a great success. The conversions of king Lamoni and his father through Ammon and Aaron opened opportunities to preach freely among the Lamanite people (Alma 21:20–23; 23:1–4), and "thousands were brought to the knowledge of the Lord" (Alma 23:5). In regard to those Lamanite converts who called themselves ANTI-NEPHI-LEHIES, the missionary goals of the sons of Mosiah had been accomplished (Alma 23:5–13; 25:17), through their faith (Ether 12:15) and through the power of the inspired records (scriptures) that testified of Jesus Christ (Alma 37:9).

The mission of the sons of Mosiah, however, was not without several intense challenges. Aaron and some of his companions were imprisoned and suffered "hunger, thirst, and all kinds of afflictions" (Alma 20:29; 21:13–14); Ammon single-handedly fought off a band of Lamanite marauders (Alma 17:33) and was later saved from a Lamanite sword by the power of God (Alma 19:22); and more than a thousand of their converts were martyred in consequence of conversion (Alma 24:22).

After securing the safety of their Lamanite converts by helping them settle in the Nephite land of Jershon (Alma 27:21–27), the sons of Mosiah continued their labors in the ministry (Alma 30:20; 31:5–6; 49:30).

The lives of Ammon, Aaron, Omner, and Himni exemplified the power of true conversion. They are described in the record as having become "men of a sound understanding" who "had searched the scriptures diligently, that they might know the word of God" (Alma 17:2). Furthermore, through "much prayer, and fasting" they enjoyed "the spirit of prophecy, and the spirit of revelation, and when they taught, they taught with power and authority of God" (Alma 17:3). In essence, the four sons of king Mosiah were staunch and courageous "men of God" (Alma 48:18).

DLL

Mote A small chip of wood or twig (Liddell, 402). Although the mote may seem inconsequential when compared to the BEAM, it still constitutes a risk to the eye, just as any sin poses a risk to the soul. Thus, when Christ condemned those with a beam in their eye who judge others with a mote in their eye, he still taught the importance of ultimately having the mote removed (3 Ne. 14:1–5 // Matt. 7:1–5).

BIBLIOGRAPHY

Liddell, H. G. *An Intermediate Greek-English Lexicon.* Oxford: Clarendon Press, 1992. S.v. κάρφος.

GS

Mother of abominations A designation for the great and abominable church (1 Ne. 14:9–16; D&C 88:94), emphasizing the role of that evil entity as the origin or source of all that the Lord hates (abominates). Five practices commonly designated in scripture as abominations are ritual pollution, occultism, idolatry, murder, and sexual sin (e.g., Lev. 7:18; Deut. 17:1; 18:9–12; 29:17–18; Alma 39:3–5; Jacob 2:28).

See also Great and abominable church; Mother of harlots; Whore of all the earth.

SER

Mother of harlots Another name for the great and abominable church or Babylon (1 Ne. 13:34; 14:16–17; D&C 133:14; Rev. 17:5) which emphasizes Babylon's willingness to sell what is sacred in order to make money. A harlot is a prostitute, and whoever accepts rewards for misusing or defiling that which is sacred, whether physically or spiritually, is a harlot and a daughter of Babylon.

See also Great and abominable church; Mother of abominations; Whore of all the earth.

SER

Motherhood *See* Parenting; Stripling warriors.

Mouth of a Jew, mouth of the Jew Expressions used by Nephi[1]'s angelic guide when referring to the Jewish writers of the biblical records (1 Ne. 13:23–24; 14:23). Nephi learned that these words of the Jews would originally contain pure gospel truths, many of which would later be taken away by those desiring to "pervert the right ways of the Lord" (1 Ne. 13:24–29). He also saw that the "book of the Lamb of God, which had proceeded forth from the mouth of the Jew" would eventually be brought by the Gentiles to the descendants of Lehi[1] (1 Ne. 13:38).

VLL

Mulek A son of the last king of Judah (Zedekiah[1]). Mulek escaped the destruction of Jerusalem though his father was blinded and carried "captive into Babylon" and his brothers were all slain (Omni 1:15; 2 Kgs. 25:7). That Zedekiah had a son who escaped is known only through the Book of Mormon. Independent of Lehi[1], Mulek and his party were led by the Lord to the promised land (Omni 1:16). The Lord brought "Mulek into the land north, and Lehi into the land south" (Hel. 6:10). The descendants of these people became known to the Nephites as the "people of Zarahemla," apparently named after their leader when the Nephites discovered them (Omni 1:13–19). Eventually, they were numbered with the Nephites (Mosiah 25:13). Readers of the Book of Mormon sometimes refer to the people of Zarahemla as Mulekites.

See also Zarahemla, people of (Mulekites).

KHM

Mulek, city of Nephite city, south of Bountiful[2], "on the east borders by the seashore." Mulek was conquered during Amalickiah's advance into Nephite lands (Alma 51:25–26; ca. 67 B.C.). Later, Nephite commander Teancum received orders to retake the city from Jacob[3] and his Lamanite forces. When the apostate Zoramites[2] refused to come out of Mulek to do battle, a stratagem was employed to draw them out. Teancum marched a small number of men "down near the seashore" as Moroni[1] hid his army in the wilderness west of the city (Alma 52:22). Discovering the movement of Teancum's army, the Lamanites pursued them, supposing an easy victory against fewer Nephites. As the Lamanites chased Teancum, Moroni sent part of his army to retake Mulek and the other part to follow the Lamanites. When the Lamanites reached Bountiful in pursuit of Teancum they met the army of Lehi[3], which had been stationed there to protect the city. Weary and fearful of meeting a fresh foe, the Lamanites turned and fled back to Mulek. Lehi pursued them until they were caught between his and Moroni's armies. Surrounded and confused, the Lamanites were defeated in a furious battle (Alma 52:15–38).

Mulek, descendants of *See* Zarahemla, people of (Mulekites).

Mulek, land of Land named after Mulek, the son of Zedekiah. The land of Mulek was located to the north of the land of Lehi, "for the Lord did bring Mulek into the land north, and Lehi into the land south" (Hel. 6:10).

Mulekites *See* Zarahemla, people of (Mulekites).

Muloki *See* Ammah.

Murder The selfish, unauthorized, intentional taking of human life (Hel. 7:21), second only to denying the Holy Ghost in order of seriousness. It is one of the "most abominable" of sins (Alma 39:5). Nephi[1] described the devil as being "the founder of murder" (2 Ne. 26:22).

The Lord God has "commanded that men should not murder" (2 Ne. 26:32), and Amulek explained that "the law requireth the life of him who hath murdered" (Alma 34:12; cf. 2 Ne. 9:35). It is clear that in some cases CAPITAL PUNISHMENT was indeed a penalty for those found guilty of murder among the Nephites (e.g., Alma 1:1–15).

A just and loving God has provided for every man to be judged according to the level of law he has been given, and "where there is no law given there is no punishment" (2 Ne. 9:25; 2:5; Alma 39:6; D&C 82:3). Thus, in some cases, repentance for murder may be available. For example, the ANTI-NEPHI-LEHIES were "convinced" of the "many murders" they had committed before being taught the gospel, but God "granted" them the opportunity to repent and be forgiven (Alma 24:9–10). Likewise, king Lamoni, who had his servants killed, subsequently was forgiven and enjoyed a marvelous spiritual manifestation (Alma 17:27–19:31). Moreover, the Savior invited the latter-day Gentiles to repent and be forgiven of the sin of murder: "Turn, all ye Gentiles, from your wicked ways; and repent of your . . . murders . . . and come unto me, and be baptized in my name, that ye may receive a remission of your sins, and be filled with the Holy Ghost, that ye may be numbered with my people who are of the house of Israel" (3 Ne. 30:2). President Boyd K. Packer taught, "Save for the exception of the very few who defect to perdition, there is no habit, no addiction, no rebellion, no transgression, no apostasy, no crime exempted from the promise of complete forgiveness" (20). He went on to state, "Forgiveness does not, however, necessarily assure exaltation, as is the case with David (see D&C 132:38–39; see also Ps. 16:10; Acts 2:25–27; *Teachings of the Prophet Joseph Smith,* p. 339)" (21 n. 15). Alma[2] warned those who "murdereth against the light and knowledge of God . . . that it is not easy for him to obtain a forgiveness" (Alma 39:6).

War with one's enemy does not provide indiscriminate justification for the taking of life. In the context of war, the only legitimate cause to take life is to preserve life (Alma 43:45–47; 48:23–24): "The Nephites were taught to defend themselves against their enemies, even to the shedding of blood if it were necessary . . . to preserve their lives" (Alma 48:14).

A person may be guilty of a type of murder by leading others astray. Alma the Younger recounted that he had "murdered many of [God's] children, *or rather led them away unto destruction*" (Alma 36:14; italics added).

See also Blood crying from the ground.

BIBLIOGRAPHY

Packer, Boyd K. "The Brilliant Morning of Forgiveness." *Ensign* 25 (November 1995): 18–21.

DKJ

Murmur The act of expressing discontent or ANGER; complaining. Fifteen of the thirty-three verses that contain the word *murmur,* or a form of it, refer to Laman[1] and Lemuel and their constant haggling against the revelations and the related activities of Lehi[1] and Nephi[1]. Murmuring in this context is shown as a precursor to rebellion. Because murmuring shows a lack of understanding or due reverence for spiritual truths, one antidote is the teaching of true DOCTRINE (1 Ne. 2:12).

AKP

Mysteries of God, the Truths known through revelation, such as doctrines of the gospel, and the "ways" or divine actions and attributes of God (Jacob 4:8; cf. Alma 26:22). For example, Nephi[1], "having great desires to know of the mysteries of God," sought the Lord in prayer to "see, and hear, and know" concerning the prophetic words of his father (1 Ne. 2:16; 10:17–19). Alma[2], in response to Zeezrom's questions concerning the doctrines of resurrection and judgment, taught how gospel truths (mysteries) are revealed (Alma 12:8–11), and Jacob[2] quoted the allegory of Zenos to reveal the "mystery" concerning the Lord's work in bringing the Jews back to Christ after they had rejected him (Jacob 4:18).

The mysteries of God are taught in the scriptures (Mosiah 1:3, 5), by inspired men (Alma 12:9; Mosiah 2:9; cf. Jacob 4:18), and through the power of the Holy Ghost (1 Ne. 10:19), according to the faithfulness of those who read or hear (1 Ne. 10:19; Jacob 4:8; Alma 12:9). One demonstrates the needed faithfulness or "heed and diligence" (Alma 12:9) by opening one's ears, heart, and mind (Mosiah 2:9), offering sincere and continual prayer (e.g., 1 Ne. 2:16; Alma 26:22), diligently seeking (1 Ne. 10:19), and practicing faith, repentance, and good works (Alma 26:22). Those who faithfully seek such knowledge are "favored" to know God's goodness (e.g., 1 Ne. 1:1), the Lord visits them and softens their hearts by the power of the Holy Ghost (e.g., 1 Ne. 2:16; 10:19), they no longer suffer "in ignorance" (e.g., Mosiah 1:3), and they become instruments in the hands of God to bring others to repentance (Alma 26:22). In contrast, the hard-hearted lose revealed knowledge "until they know nothing concerning his mysteries," are "taken captive by the devil," and stand condemned before God (Alma 12:10–11; cf. 2 Ne. 28:29–30).

JCT

And it came to pass that I looked and beheld the great city of Jerusalem, and also other cities. And I beheld the city of **Nazareth**; and in the city of Nazareth I beheld a virgin, and she was exceedingly fair and white. 1 NEPHI 11:13

Nahom Place in Lehi[1]'s journey through the Arabian peninsula where Ishmael was buried. The sojourn at Nahom was a low point in the journey through the wilderness. The death of Ishmael caused his daughters to "mourn exceedingly" and to murmur against Lehi because of their many afflictions (1 Ne. 16:34–36). Prompted by Laman[1], Lemuel and the sons of Ishmael rebelled against Lehi and Nephi[1] (1 Ne. 16:37–38). Only a chastening from the Lord brought them to repentance (1 Ne. 16:39). The name Nahom may be related to the Hebrew words *nāham,* to "groan," or *nāḥam,* to "be sorry, console oneself" (Brown et al., 625, 636). It has been suggested that Nahom may be identified with Nihm in Yemen (Brown, 66–68; *see* map, page 514).

See also Lehi[1], journey to the promised land.

BIBLIOGRAPHY

Brown, Driver, and Briggs Hebrew and English Lexicon of the Old Testament. Based on the lexicon of W. Gesenius as translated by E. Robinson. Edited by F. Brown, S. R. Driver, and C. A. Briggs. Oxford: Clarendon, 1980.

Brown, S. Kent. "The Place That Was Called 'Nahom': New Light from Ancient Yemen." *Journal of Book of Mormon Studies* (August 1999): 66–68.

TLS

Names in the Book of Mormon The proper names and appellations of the Book of Mormon exhibit what might be expected from a book that openly claims roots in another culture, but which at the same time also consciously proclaims that its culture and languages have departed from their roots. Even the Jaredite record, which claims a nexus with an as yet unidentifiable Old World origin, contains a mixture of original and perhaps retained names.

The personal and geographic names in the Book of Mormon provide a window to the language and people who produced that book. Of the 337 proper names in the Book of Mormon, 188 (about 56 percent) by current count are unique to the Book of Mormon. Ninety-six names (about 28 percent) occur in passages in which the Bible is being quoted or paraphrased. That leaves 53 names (about 16 percent) which occur in both the Book of Mormon and the Bible but in unrelated passages.

Though most of the names in the Book of Mormon are Lehite-Mulekite (i.e., those people descended from the original Lehi colony and from the people of Zarahemla, who trace themselves back to the colony of Mulek), a sizable number are Jaredite, the language group of the first inhabitants of Book of Mormon lands. Of the 188 names unique to the Book of Mormon, 142 are Lehite-Mulekite, 41 are Jaredite, and 5 are common to both groups.

Some appellations in the Book of Mormon were obviously influenced by a Hebrew background. For example, when the Lamanite servants of king Lamoni spoke to Ammon[2], they called him *rabbanah,* which the Book of Mormon interprets to mean "powerful or great king" (Alma 18:13). *Rabbanah* resembles Hebrew words that derive from a common Semitic root *rbb* meaning "to be big or many." Even more telling for Book of Mormon history is that the Lamanites, who seem to have strayed culturally from their Nephite cousins, still preserved their Hebrew/Semitic language background.

Other names in the Book of Mormon have not appeared to come from a Hebrew background at first glance but have proven in the meantime to reflect authentic Israelite origins. Perhaps the best example of this is the prominent Book of Mormon name Alma, which does not appear in any biblical text. For years the name lacked an ostensible Hebrew root and therefore could easily be explained as the feminine form from the Latin root meaning "nurture." Yet, the name Alma does appear in authentic Hebrew documents of the Bar Kochba period (ca. A.D. 130). There the name appears as a masculine name spelled exactly as might be expected, *'lm',* (*Alma*) and *'lmh,* (*Almah*) (Yadin, 176). This find unequivocally places the Book of Mormon name Alma within the Israelite tradition of names. Of the 53 names that the Bible and the Book of Mormon share in unrelated passages (16 percent of the total), two names appear to be Greek: the personal name Timothy and the geographic name Antipas. This should not be surprising, given that a Greek: presence in the Levant is known from at least the eighth

The Bar Kokhba document containing the name Alma; *photograph by David W. Hawkinson; courtesy Israel Antiquities Authority. This legal contract was written on papyrus in Hebrew and hidden away during the second Jewish revolt against the Romans,* A.D. *134–135. The name* Alma *occurs twice, each time artificially highlighted in this photograph, but with two different acceptable spellings:* אלמא *('alma') four lines from the top and* אלמה *('almah) four lines from the bottom (5/6Hev 44).*

century B.C. and contact between the Levant and the Aegean existed at least as early as the end of the Late Bronze Age, 1400 to 1200 B.C.

Plays on words, especially with names, are very common in the Hebrew Bible. That such plays on words found their way into the Book of Mormon seems evident from the name Jershon in Alma 27:22. *Jershon* appears to be derived from the Hebrew root meaning "to inherit," the root being *yrö*. Thus, Jershon could mean "inheritance." If this line of reasoning is correct, then a wonderful play on words in that verse is developed: "This land Jershon [namely, inheritance] is the land which we will give unto our brethren for an inheritance."

Jaredite names cannot at the present be linked to any known language. (This is not unusual: Kassite names of the Middle Babylonian Period in Mesopotamia cannot be linked to any known language.) A few Jaredite names might be related to Semitic roots, such as the name Jared. But most Jaredite names, such as Coriantumr, are most likely not related to Israelite origins. Interesting, though, are the Jaredite names that reappear in the Nephite record, as if there were some conscious continuity between the two cultures. For example, after the union of the people of Zarahemla and the fleeing Nephite remnant under king Mosiah[1], the two most infamous apostates both bear names with clear resemblances to Jaredite names, Corihor/Korihor and Nehor/Nehor, seemingly as though these apostate movements were inspired by Jaredite precedents.

BIBLIOGRAPHY

Yadin, Yigael. *Bar Kokhba*. New York: Random House, 1971.

PYH

Narrowly *See* Appendix C.

Natural branches Term used in the scriptures as a metaphor for the house of Israel. In the allegory of the olive tree in Jacob 5 this metaphor is used to describe the scattering of the house of Israel throughout the world. At the same time, non-Israelites, represented by "wild branches," are mixed with the house of Israel. The allegory continues by describing how in the latter days the natural branches, which had been scattered throughout the world, will be grafted back into the natural tree. This grafting represents the gathering of the house of Israel back to the gospel of Jesus Christ. The metaphor of the natural branches is mentioned in three other scriptural passages: 1 Nephi 10:14; 1 Nephi 15:7, 13; and Romans 11:16–24.

See also Zenos, allegory of.

PYH

Natural man The natural birth gives rise to the natural man (McConkie, 282), and, as an angel explained to king Benjamin, "the natural man is an enemy to God" (Mosiah 3:19; Ether 3:2). The natural man is the unregenerated person, the man or woman who has received neither the revealed witness of the Spirit nor the cleansing powers of the Atonement. He or she lives in what Alma called a "state of nature," or "a carnal state," being "without God in the world" and thus living "contrary to the nature of God" and, sadly, "contrary to the nature of happiness" (Alma 41:11). The things of the Spirit of God seem alien and foolish to such a person (1 Cor. 2:14; cf. Alma 26:17–21). Acting without the Holy Ghost, the natural man can be proud, obsessed with self, overly competitive, reactionary, fiercely independent, driven by desires, appetites, worldly acclaim, or one who yields himself to the harsh and the crude. In general, the natural man is an unredeemed creature, a being who walks in darkness or in the light of his own fire and in the sparks he has kindled (2 Ne. 7:10–11). Such a one is acclimated to the nature of things about him, taking his cues and bearings from a fallen world.

The natural man will remain forevermore an enemy to God unless he or she turns away from sin, comes unto Christ, and partakes of the cleansing and quickening powers of the Atonement. More specifically, one puts off the natural man through yielding to the enticings of the Holy Spirit and subscribing to the first principles of the gospel—faith, repentance, baptism, and the reception of the Holy Ghost (2 Ne. 31; 3 Ne. 27:16–20). Such a person will then begin to come alive to things of righteousness and thereby begin to acquire Christlike attributes. Whereas the "works of the flesh" characterize the natural man, the "fruit[s] of the Spirit" flow from the life of one changed and renewed in Christ (Gal. 5:19–25; Mosiah 3:19; Alma 7:23).

See also Born again; Carnal, sensual, and devilish; Fall of Adam and Eve, the.

BIBLIOGRAPHY

McConkie, Bruce R. *A New Witness for the Articles of Faith.* Salt Lake City: Deseret Book, 1985.

RLM

Nazareth City located in the hills of Galilee that form the northern side of the Jezreel Valley. In a vision, Nephi[1] saw in Nazareth a beautiful virgin, the future mother of the Son of God, along with her infant son, Jesus, the Lamb of God (1 Ne. 11:13, 18, 20–21). He possibly saw Nazareth again when he saw the Redeemer being cast out (1 Ne. 11:28; cf. Luke 4:16–30).

DKO

Neas *See* Agriculture in the Book of Mormon.

Nehor Apostate Nephite who first introduced PRIESTCRAFT into Zarahemla (Alma 1:12). Nehor appeared during the first year of the reign of the judges (ca. 91 B.C.) as one who powerfully enticed others to do evil and who established a church to promote his cause.

Nehor was a large and strong man, which gave him a natural appeal. But it was his doctrine that many found a desirable alternative to the strict teachings of the prophets of God. Pretending also to be a prophet, Nehor taught that the priests of their religion should be popular, or people-pleasers, and that "they ought not to labor with their hands, but that they ought to be supported by the people" (Alma 1:3). He taught also that God would redeem and give eternal life to all men; therefore, "they need not fear nor tremble" before God "but that they might lift up their heads and rejoice" (Alma 1:4).

This new religion of Nehor institutionalized priestcraft, which is "that men preach and set themselves up for a light unto the world," taking praise and gain for their efforts (2 Ne. 26:29). In the true Church, priests are called of God by the laying on of hands of those who are in authority, and the light which they hold up to the world is

Jesus Christ (3 Ne. 18:24). In Nehor's religion, pride was encouraged as well as the wearing of costly apparel (Alma 1:6). But in the true Church, humility is required of all (Alma 1:20, 26–27). Nehor assured his listeners that they need not be concerned about sinning, for all would be forgiven and everyone would enjoy eternal bliss (Alma 1:4). But the true Church strictly enjoined everyone to repent of all sinning, for every sin would be accounted for on the Day of Judgment.

Not only did Nehor teach priestcraft, that men should make a business out of selling religion, but he attempted "to enforce it by the sword" (Alma 1:12). He contended verbally with Gideon, an elderly teacher in the "church of God," but Gideon withstood him "with the words of God" (Alma 1:7, 9). Angered at Gideon for his ability to counter his teachings, Nehor slew him (Alma 1:5–9). For this murder Nehor was put to death in accordance with the laws of the land (Alma 1:10, 14–15).

Being pleasing to the carnal mind, the teachings of Nehor continued, as did his church. "The order of the Nehors" was evident among the Nephites and the Lamanites for some time, giving a pretext of justification to those who chose not to worship the true and living God (Alma 21:4; 1:6; 16:11; 24:28–29).

CCR

Nehor, land of and city of Jaredite territory. Corihor[1] rebelled against his father, Kib, and "went over and dwelt in the land of Nehor" (Ether 7:4). In the city of Nehor, Shule defeated his brother Corihor[1] and restored the kingdom to his father, Kib (Ether 7:9).

Nehor, order of Religious sect that followed the teachings of Nehor (Alma 1). Individuals and groups identified with this persuasion were wicked. Amlici, the Nephite dissenter who wanted to be king (Alma 2:1); the judge in Ammonihah who threatened Alma[2] and Amulek with death (Alma 14:16); and many of the Amulonites and Amalekites, hard-hearted Nephite dissenters who lived among the Lamanites, were "after the order of the Nehors" (Alma 21:4; 24:28–29). The Amulonites and Amalekites built synagogues in the city of Jerusalem[2] that accorded with these religious beliefs (Alma 21:4). Perhaps it was the Amlicites, another group of Nephite apostates defecting to the Lamanites (Alma 1–2), who first introduced the teachings of Nehor to the Amulonites and Amalekites in the land of Nephi.

After the Lamanite destruction of the wicked Nephite city of Ammonihah, the area became known as the "Desolation of Nehors," because those who possessed Ammonihah "were of the profession of Nehor" (Alma 14:18; 16:11).

DLL

Nehors, Desolation of *See* Desolation of Nehors.

Nephi[1] Son of Lehi[1] and Sariah (ca. 615–544 B.C.), who holds a special place among Book of Mormon prophets. He was an essential figure, having founded the civilization and commenced the records on which the book is based, and an exemplary one. His life was characterized by unfailing obedience to the will of God. Nephi's final words could well serve as his epitaph: "For thus hath the Lord commanded me, and I must obey" (2 Ne. 33:15).

Throughout his life, Nephi was determined to "go and do the things which the Lord hath commanded" (1 Ne. 3:7). Whether this meant following his father into the wilderness, returning to Jerusalem for the brass plates, slaying Laban, building a ship, crossing an ocean, establishing a new civilization, erecting a temple, ruling and protecting his people, or fashioning and engraving a sacred record on metal plates, Nephi proved both willing and able to faithfully perform the Lord's will, however formidable the obstacles. His was a heroic life, writ large in Book of Mormon history and in the hearts of his people.

Nephi was the fourth son of a wealthy, well-educated family living in Jerusalem shortly before the Babylonian captivity. As a young man, Nephi fled into the wilderness with his family after his father was warned by God of Jerusalem's impending doom (1 Ne. 1–2). Nephi twice returned to Jerusalem: once to retrieve scriptures recorded on brass plates and again to enlist the family of Ishmael[1], whose daughters Lehi's sons could marry (1 Ne. 3–4; 7:1–5). After eight hard years in the wilderness, this group came to a land by the sea, a land they named Bountiful[1]. There God commanded Nephi to build a ship to take them to a promised land. Despite periods of trying opposition from his older brothers, Nephi built the ship and sailed across the sea (1 Ne. 17–18).

Shortly after arriving in the promised land Lehi died, leaving Nephi to carry the lonely burden of leadership amid his enemies, a condition that seems reflected in his psalm (2 Ne. 4:15–35). To escape his fratricidal brothers, Nephi obeyed the Lord's warning and fled deeper into the wilderness with those who remained faithful (2 Ne. 5:5–6). There, in a land they named Nephi, Nephi became the ruler, teacher, protector, and priest for a people who called themselves "the people of Nephi" (2 Ne. 5:9), or simply "Nephites." Nephi led his people as prophet-king for the remainder of his life, thereby fulfilling the Lord's words that Nephi would "be made a ruler and a teacher over [his] brethren" (1 Ne. 2:22). When Nephi died, fifty-five years after leaving Jerusalem, his people honored him by designating all subsequent kings by the title "Nephi," so great was their love for their mighty founding prophet and protector (Jacob 1:11).

Teachings

Nephi engraved two sets of plates, the large and small PLATES OF NEPHI (1 Ne. 19:1–6). The Book of Mormon preserves intact Nephi's writings from the small plates, which Nephi reserved for the account of his ministry, prophecies (1 Ne. 19:3–4), and "the things of [his] soul" (2 Ne. 4:15). Consequently, 1 Nephi and 2 Nephi are rich in teaching, prophecy, and scriptural commentary, if somewhat sparse in biographical and historical detail, especially regarding events in the promised land. Among Nephi's most important prophecies and teachings are his vision of the tree of life (1 Ne. 11–14), his prophecies of the Messiah and last days (1 Ne. 22; 2 Ne. 25–30), and his distillation of the "doctrine of Christ" (2 Ne. 31–33).

Vision of the tree of life (1 Ne. 11–14)

Having heard his father recount a remarkable vision of the tree of life (1 Ne. 8), Nephi sought to experience the same vision (1 Ne. 10:17–19). Accordingly, Nephi was "caught away in the Spirit . . . into an exceedingly high mountain" (1 Ne. 11:1) where he "saw the things which [his] father saw" (1 Ne. 14:29). Nephi's account includes interpretations of key symbols—such as the tree of life, rod of iron, spacious building, fountain of filthy water, and mists of darkness—as well as prophecies of the Savior's ministry on two continents and the coming forth of the Book of Mormon in the latter days. These details are missing from Nephi's admittedly incomplete redaction of his father's vision (1 Ne. 8:29, 36). Whereas Lehi's account focuses on the salvation of his immediate family, Nephi's account focuses on the salvation of his seed throughout history. Thus Nephi foresaw Jesus' ministry not only among the Jews in the Holy Land (1 Ne. 11) but also among his own seed in the promised land (1 Ne. 12). He foresaw, too, the coming of the Gentiles to the promised land, the coming forth of the Book of Mormon among his seed in the latter days (1 Ne. 13), and the great conflict between the church of the Lamb and the church of the devil that would persist until the end of the world (1 Ne. 14). Nephi's vision burdened him with the painful foreknowledge of the Nephites' eventual destruction (1 Ne. 15:5; 2 Ne. 26:7, 10); but at the same time, it blessed him with the joyful assurance of God's grand designs for scattered Israel. The knowledge of futurity that Nephi gained in this vision, especially about the Messiah and the last days, informed both his understanding of Isaiah and his own prophecies.

Prophecies of the Messiah and the last days (1 Ne. 22; 2 Ne. 25–30)

Twice Nephi engraved onto the small plates extensive quotations from Isaiah (1 Ne. 20–21; 2 Ne. 12–24), which he knew applied to his people, a branch of scattered Israel (1 Ne. 19:23; 2 Ne. 11:8), as well as to latter-day peoples. After each quotation from Isaiah, Nephi supplied prophetic commentary. Because the Lord had shown him plainly the events that Isaiah also saw regarding the coming of the Messiah and the last days, and because Nephi delighted in plainness (2 Ne. 25:4; 33:6), he prophesied in "plainness . . . that no man can err" (2 Ne. 25:7).

At the end of 1 Nephi, Nephi expounded upon the Lord's "marvelous work among the Gentiles" in the last days, "which shall be of great worth unto our seed" as well as to the Gentiles themselves and the whole house of Israel (1 Ne. 22:8–9). His prophetic commentary repeated many elements in his vision of the tree of life, such as the scattering and gathering of Israel, the coming of the Messiah, the rise of a great and abominable church, and the reign of righteousness during the Millennium. Nephi cited the testimony of other prophets, including Moses, to supplement Isaiah's words and his own, so that his hard-hearted brothers "need not suppose that I and my father are the only ones that have testified" (1 Ne. 22:31).

Similarly, Nephi introduced Isaiah in 2 Nephi as a third witness of Christ to complement his own testimony and that of his brother Jacob[2] (2 Ne. 11:2–4). Likewise, Nephi's subsequent commentary again referred to events revealed not only to Isaiah but to Nephi himself in his vision of the tree of life: the birth, crucifixion, and resurrection of the Messiah (2 Ne. 25); the ministry of Christ to the Nephites and the condition of the Gentiles in the last days (2 Ne. 26); the coming forth of the Book of Mormon (2 Ne. 27); the workings of the devil and his abominable church in the last days (2 Ne. 28); the Gentiles' rejection of the Book of Mormon (2 Ne. 29); and the conversion of Gentiles, Jews, and Lehi's seed (2 Ne. 30:1–8) before the millennial day when "the earth shall be full of the knowledge of the Lord" and "Satan shall have power over the hearts of the children of men no more" (2 Ne. 30:15, 18). Thus Nephi's prophecies in 2 Nephi 25–30 correlate to both passages in Isaiah and to Nephi's vision of the tree of life.

Doctrine of Christ (2 Ne. 31–32)

Central to all Nephi's prophecies was his understanding of Christ. He knew that "there is none other name given under heaven save it be this Jesus Christ . . . whereby man can be saved" (2 Ne. 25:20). Consequently, "we labor diligently . . . to persuade our children, and also our brethren, to believe in Christ. . . . We talk of Christ, we rejoice in Christ, we preach of Christ, we prophesy of Christ . . . that our children may know to what source they may look for a remission of their sins" (2 Ne. 25:23, 26).

As Nephi closed his record, he determined to set forth plainly the "doctrine of Christ" (2 Ne. 31:2, 21; 32:6). His teachings in chapters 31–32 provide a trenchant summary of the first principles of the gospel. Nephi explained that all people must have faith, humble themselves, repent, and follow the example of Jesus "with full purpose of heart, acting no hypocrisy," by taking upon themselves the "name of Christ, by baptism," and subsequently receiving "the baptism of fire and of the Holy Ghost" (2 Ne. 31:13). After they have entered on the strait and narrow path by this gate, then they must "press forward with a steadfastness in Christ, having a perfect brightness of hope, and a love of God and of all men. Wherefore," Nephi added, "if ye shall press forward, feasting upon the word of Christ, and endure to the end, behold, thus saith the Father: Ye shall have eternal life" (2 Ne. 31:20). This is the "doctrine of Christ," or the gospel in brief.

Nephi concluded his record with a powerful valediction. In it, he expressed his love for his people, for whom he prayed by day and wept by night (2 Ne. 33:3). He bade farewell to "all ye ends of the earth" (2 Ne. 33:10). And, as "one crying from the dust" (2 Ne. 33:13), he called all people to repent and believe in Christ, solemnly testifying that God would hold the world accountable for how it would receive his testimony (2 Ne. 33:11, 14–15). Nephi's valedictory testimony is consistent with his initial statement of intent: "For the fulness of mine intent is that I may persuade men to come unto the God of Abraham, and the God of Isaac, and the God of Jacob, and be saved" (1 Ne. 6:4).

Summary of major teachings

1. Deliverance through faith in the Lord (1 Ne. 1:20; cf. 7:17–18).

2. Obedience. Exhortations (1 Ne. 4:1; 15:25; 17:23–55), blessings (1 Ne. 17:3), and

divine assistance (1 Ne. 3:7). *See* Book of Mormon, selected themes of, obedience.

3. Salvation. "The way is prepared for all men from the foundation of the world, if it so be that they repent and come unto [Christ]" (1 Ne. 10:18).

4. The eternal nature of God's work—the Lord's course is ONE ETERNAL ROUND; he reveals his mysteries by the power of the Holy Ghost to "[him] that diligently seeketh" in any era—"these times," "times of old," and "times to come" (1 Ne. 10:19; cf. 15:11).

5. The vision of the tree of life (1 Ne. 11–14), including additional interpretive commentary to his brothers on its symbols (1 Ne. 15). *See* Nephi[1]'s vision.

6. The rejection of the Messiah by "those who are at Jerusalem"; his crucifixion and burial according to the words of Zenock, Neum, and Zenos; the subsequent scattering of the Jews for this rejection; and their eventual gathering when they "no more turn aside their hearts against the Holy One of Israel" (1 Ne. 19:7–17; cf. 2 Ne. 25:9–20).

7. Prophecies of the Messiah and the last days, including the scattering and gathering of all the house of Israel, the restoration of the gospel, the coming forth of the Book of Mormon, conditions among the Gentiles, warnings against false teachings and the tactics of SATAN, the Second Coming, and the MILLENNIUM (1 Ne. 22; 2 Ne. 25–30). *See* Jesus Christ, second coming of; Israel, gathering of; Israel, scattering of.

8. The doctrine of Christ (2 Ne. 31–32). *See* Gospel, the.

9. The roles of the HOLY GHOST (2 Ne. 31–32; 33:1).

10. Principles of prayer: the Spirit teaches man to pray; "ye must pray always" (2 Ne. 32:8–9); the evil spirit teaches man "that he must not pray" (2 Ne. 32:8).

See also Gentiles, Book of Mormon message concerning; Jews, Book of Mormon message concerning; Laban, slaying of; Lamanites, Book of Mormon message concerning; Nephi, first book of; Nephi, second book of; Nephi[1]'s psalm.

JST

Nephi[2] The diligent and dutiful elder son of Helaman[3], whose public reign and sacred ministry spanned nearly forty years, ending just before Christ's birth (ca. 39 B.C.–A.D. 1). Though the Book of Mormon reveals nothing of Nephi's birth and little about his personal life, there is ample scriptural material attesting to the stellar quality of his character.

He filled the role of chief judge for nine years after his righteous father's death (Hel. 3:37). Because of the great pride and iniquity of his people, Nephi's judgeship constituted some of the bleakest years in Nephite history. During this time the Lamanites gained "possession of the land of Zarahemla . . . and also all the lands, even unto the land which was near the land Bountiful" (Hel. 4:5). The Nephites had become "weak" like the Lamanites, and the Spirit of the Lord ceased to "preserve them" (Hel. 4:24–25).

Weary of their transgressions and unrepentant behavior, Nephi relinquished his civil leadership to Cezoram, which enabled him to devote all his time to preaching the gospel "all the remainder of his days" (Hel. 5:1–4; 30 B.C.–A.D. 1). A man of enormous spiritual prowess and unforgettable personal courage and stamina, Nephi's intent was to testify of Christ and warn of imminent destruction if the people did not repent and forsake iniquity (e.g., Hel. 7:13–29). Therefore, the primary focus of Nephi's story is his activity as a missionary among the Nephites and Lamanites.

In association with his brother Lehi[4], Nephi began his ministry at the northern settlement of Bountiful[2], moving from city to city until he and his brother had "gone forth among all the people of Nephi who were in the land southward" (Hel. 5:16). Traveling next to the Lamanites in the land of Zarahemla, they preached with such "power and authority" that many Nephite dissenters, as well as 8,000 Lamanites, repented and were baptized (Hel. 5:17–19). Proceeding south to the land of Nephi, Nephi and Lehi were captured by Lamanite soldiers and imprisoned. Intent on slaying them, their captors and about 300 others (Hel. 5:49) experienced some of the most remarkable and wondrous happenings ever recorded: The prophet brothers were encompassed by fire but "not burned"; the earth and

NEPHI²

prison walls shook frequently; the Lord's piercing but mild voice cried repentance and spoke "marvelous words" three times above the darkness encircling the people; the apostate Nephite Aminadab explained that the two prisoners were communicating with heavenly beings; all present were eventually surrounded by fire as the "Holy Spirit of God" descended "and did enter into their hearts"; the "pleasant voice" of the Father declared "peace be unto [them], because of [their] faith in my Well Beloved"; and the heavens opened and angels ministered to the people (Hel. 5:21–48). The converted Lamanites became the influence that brought most of their people, as well as many Nephites, to repentance. The Lamanites manifested their sincerity by giving up their weapons, their hatred, and their traditions and by restoring to the Nephites their lands (Hel. 5:50–52; 6:4–5).

A short period of peace, stability, and prosperity resulted until pride again entered the hearts of the people, which permitted the secret band of Gadianton to flourish (Hel. 6:7–41). During this time Nephi and Lehi traveled northward to continue their ministry, but after prophesying "many things unto them" (Hel. 7:2), they were rejected (Hel. 6:6; 7:3). Nephi returned to his ancestral home in Zarahemla only to find that under the influence of Satan (Hel. 6:21–31), the Gadiantons had a corrupt grasp on the government throughout the land and were "doing no justice" (Hel. 7:4). Saddened, Nephi "pour[ed] out his soul unto God" from a tower in his garden (Hel. 7:10–14), eventually attracting a multitude whom he rebuked and cautioned that if they continued to sin against the "great knowledge which [they had] received" and did not repent, they would be "utterly destroyed" (Hel. 7:22–24).

Although the angry Gadianton judges attempted to incite public opposition, many regarded Nephi as a "good man," and they stood firm and supportive of his preaching (Hel. 8:7–9). Encouraged, Nephi added his witness of the coming of Christ to those of the prophets in the scriptures from the time of Abraham to Jeremiah[1], including Lehi[1] and Nephi[1] (Hel. 8:11–23). Boldly Nephi[2] enumerated the sins of the people and announced the murder of their chief judge Seezoram by his brother Seantum, who coveted his office (Hel. 8:24–27; 9:6). Nephi's seeric abilities were affirmed when Seezoram's slaying was discovered by five men sent to investigate the alleged crime. The five, however, were accused of the murder and imprisoned, only to be released when it was discovered that they were the same five sent to verify Nephi's claims (Hel. 9:1–18). Enraged, the judges persisted in their efforts to connect Nephi with the murder. Nephi responded by giving "another sign," challenging them to confront Seantum with the murder and telling them the details of his denial and subsequent confession (Hel. 9:25–37).

Despite the "great miracle which Nephi had done in telling them concerning the death of the chief judge," the people hardened their hearts (Hel. 10:13). As Nephi headed homeward, "cast down" and deep in thought, he was unexpectedly comforted and blessed by the Lord. The Lord acknowledged his courage, obedience, and "unwearyingness" in preaching the gospel, and in consequence, he promised Nephi, "I will bless thee forever; and I will make thee mighty in word and in deed, in faith and in works; yea, even that all things shall be done unto thee according to thy word, for thou shalt not ask that which is contrary to my will" (Hel. 10:2–5). Accordingly, Nephi was endowed with great power, including the SEALING POWER (Hel. 10:5–10). Nephi continued preaching but met rejection and abuse. When those who "revile[d] against him" sought to place him in prison, the Spirit "conveyed" him to safety (Hel. 10:14–16).

With the escalation of wickedness, Nephi pleaded with the Lord to send a famine that the people might "remember the Lord" (Hel. 11:7) rather than be "destroyed by the sword" (Hel. 11:4). Soon, famine filled the land, the people repented, the Church flourished, and the Gadianton bands were banished (Hel. 11:7–23). It was not long, however, until iniquity returned, and the people "ripen[ed] again for destruction" (Hel. 11:37).

At this point the Lord sent another witness to the Nephites, Samuel the Lamanite, to cry repentance and warn them of impending doom (Hel. 13–16). The Book of Mormon is silent about any contact between the two contemporary prophets other than to report that those who believed on the words of Samuel went to Nephi to be baptized: "For behold, Nephi was baptizing, and prophesying, and preaching, crying repentance unto the people, showing signs and wonders, working miracles among the people, that they might know that the Christ must shortly come" (Hel. 16:3–5). Just before the birth of the Savior, Nephi imparted the sacred records to his son Nephi[3] and then mysteriously left the land of Zarahemla, never to return—where he went "no man knoweth" (3 Ne. 1:2–3; 2:9).

Nephi's life encompassed experiences that ranged from the depths of sorrow and loneliness to some of the most extraordinary spiritual manifestations ever recorded. There were moments of great conversion as well as repeated rejection for this teacher and minister of "the true points of doctrine" (Hel. 11:23). A notable prophet, he exemplified faith, testimony, perseverance, and zeal. As with other prophets, he in many ways can be viewed as a type of Christ. He taught with power and authority (Hel. 5:17–19; cf. Mark 1:22); he knew the thoughts of the people's hearts (Hel. 9:41; cf. Mark 2:8); he was delivered from his enemies (Hel. 5:23; 10:16; cf. Luke 4:29–30); he was questioned, reviled, and falsely accused before wicked judges; and he was rejected by his own people (Hel. 9:16, 19; 10:15; cf. Matt. 26:57–68; 27:22–25). Nephi sacrificed the things of the world and personal interests, seeking only to do God's work (Hel. 10:4; cf. John 8:29), and as a result he was promised eternal blessings (Hel. 10:5).

MMM

Nephi[3] Eldest son of Nephi[2] and grandson of Helaman[3] (ca. A.D. 1), first of the Twelve called by Jesus Christ at the beginning of his ministry among the Nephites. Nephi wrote the record that Mormon abridged as 3 Nephi. He was the mortal leader of the true Church among the descendants of Lehi[1] in the years preceding the birth of the Savior in the flesh and throughout the years of his life and ministry in and around Jerusalem. Nephi presided during a lengthy period that spanned extremes of spiritual highs and lows. The lows were experienced in the terrible wickedness before the Savior's birth and again before his death. The highs were experienced in the righteousness and blessedness after the Savior's birth and especially in his ministry after the cataclysmic events that followed His death. Information is unusually scarce about a prophet and leader who served as long and faithfully as this man. Much can be deduced, however, from historical events themselves and from what Mormon mentions in his record.

Nephi was a man of immense spiritual power and extraordinary personal courage. He fearlessly taught the gospel of Jesus Christ through many years of great wickedness among his people, when prophets were hated and killed and the Church was sorely persecuted. The enemies of the Church "were angry with him," Mormon wrote, "even because he had greater power than they." They were angry, too, because his righteous power made it impossible for them to "disbelieve his words" (3 Ne. 7:18). It was this Nephi who prayed ceaselessly for an entire day, grieving over the persecutions suffered by those who watched faithfully for the prophesied signs of the Savior's birth. And it was he who received the glorious message that on that very "night shall the sign be given, and on the morrow come I into the world" (3 Ne. 1:13). It was this Nephi who guided the Church for the next three decades and more, this Nephi who survived the destruction and darkness following the crucifixion, this Nephi whom the Savior called to serve at his side and establish the Church in the fulness of the gospel, this Nephi who was chosen to take the Church from the law of Moses to the higher law.

The record contains no sermons or other discourses of this prophet, because, Mormon says, "all of them cannot be written, and a part of them would not suffice" (3 Ne. 7:17). Clearly, Nephi's main purpose in the record was to bear witness to the reality and divinity of Jesus Christ. Even his historical writing must have been powerful because Mormon's condensed rendering of it is magnificent. There are no more glorious scriptural passages anywhere than those describing Christ tenderly ministering in person to his stricken people and praying to the Father in their behalf (3 Ne. 17). Those passages are rivaled perhaps only by the account of the indescribable events that followed the baptisms of Christ's chosen twelve disciples (3 Ne. 19).

Nephi's life and ministry were sketched in broad strokes, for the most part. There are enough details, however, to provide some measure of the man. For example, in 3 Nephi 7, in the midst of chronicling deteriorating moral and political conditions, Mormon pauses to say something about Nephi. In just six verses, one learns a great deal: that he was "visited by angels and also the voice of the Lord"; that he foresaw "the ministry of Christ"; that he witnessed the people's "quick return" to "wickedness and abominations," but testified to them "boldly, repentance and remission of sins through faith on the Lord Jesus Christ"; that his ministrations were "many" and powerful, so much so that it "would not suffice" to tell only "a part of them"; that "angels did minister unto him daily"; that "in the name of Jesus did he cast out devils and unclean spirits"; that he raised his own brother "from the dead, after he had been stoned"; and that "he did also do many more miracles, in the sight of the people, in the name of Jesus" (3 Ne. 7:15–20).

Like several of his predecessors, Nephi was a type for Christ. For example, he raised his brother Timothy from the dead (3 Ne. 7:19; 19:4), as Christ had raised Lazarus (John 11:43–44). Like Jesus, too, he raised the ire of the people "because he had greater power than they," including the power to cast out devils and heal the sick (3 Ne. 7:18–20).

MA

Nephi[4] The son of Nephi[3], who was one of the twelve disciples of Jesus Christ. Nephi[4] inscribed the record of his people on the plates of Nephi (4 Ne. 1:19; ca. A.D. 34). He was blessed to live during the era of peace and unity that followed the ministry of Jesus Christ among the Nephites (4 Ne. 1:15–17). Following Nephi's death, Amos[1], his son, kept the record.

CJW

Nephi, first book of The first of two works written by Nephi[1] on the small PLATES OF NEPHI, this book recounts the heaven-led flight of the family of Lehi[1] and Sariah, along with others, from Jerusalem to "the land of promise" in the Americas (1 Ne. 18:25; ca. 600–589 B.C.). Nephi wrote this record on his "small [metal] plates" thirty years after his family left Jerusalem (2 Ne. 5:28–34), a record that covers the period from ca. 600 to 570 B.C.

Content and message

In Jerusalem at the end of the seventh century B.C., the four turbulent years preceding the initial visions of Lehi (1 Ne. 1) were characterized by high-handed interference by the Babylonians, which took the form of successive dethronements of kings of JUDAH (2 Kgs. 24:1–17). In this era, the kingdom of Judah had become a vassal state of Babylonia, and Nebuchadnezzar had placed Zedekiah on the throne of Judah as a puppet king not long before the departure of Lehi and his family (2 Kgs. 24:17–20; 1 Ne. 1:4; 2:1–4). It was also in this age that the prophets Jeremiah, Ezekiel, Nahum, Habakkuk, and Zephaniah were active. Moreover, Lehi's inventory of a record on PLATES OF BRASS indicates that Jeremiah's prophecies had gone through at least an initial compilation by ca. 600 B.C. (1 Ne. 5:13; Jer. 36).

After people of the city had rejected Lehi's preaching and begun to persecute him, the Lord commanded him to take his family south from Jerusalem into the desert (1 Ne. 2:1–4). The family made a base camp near the shore of the RED SEA (1 Ne. 2:5–6). It was from this spot that Lehi sent his sons back to the city to obtain the plates of brass and later to persuade a man named Ishmael and his family to join their trek. It was also here that an important vision came separately to Lehi and then Nephi (1 Ne. 8; 11–14). The entire group later began a journey "south-southeast" along the Red Sea coast, traveling approximately the route of the famous incense trail—in reverse. After taking eight years to cross the Arabian desert, the small party eventually found itself by the sea. They called this sea "Irreantum," meaning "many waters" (1 Ne. 17:4–5). Here, Nephi and his brothers, under the direction of the Lord, built a ship and set sail for the PROMISED LAND (1 Ne. 17–18). Although opinions differ, some believe that the most likely route took them across the Indian and Pacific Oceans, ultimately arriving in the New World (Hilton and Hilton, 77–116; Brown, "Case," 216).

Nephi ended his first book by drawing on prophecies that he found written on the brass plates (1 Ne. 19–21). In chapter 19 Nephi quoted from the prophets Zenock, Neum, and especially Zenos concerning the ministry, crucifixion, and death of the Messiah, as well as their predictions about the scattering and gathering of Israel. He then incorporated two chapters from Isaiah (48–49) that prophesy concerning the future of the house of Israel and the future of his own people (1 Ne. 20–21). Nephi devoted the last segment of his first book to a prophetic

OUTLINE OF 1 NEPHI

In general, Nephi's record accounts for seven main episodes. Most tie to geographical locales in the narrative. In terms of sources, the record rests on both the record of Nephi's father Lehi and on Nephi's own experiences (1 Ne. 1:16–17).

I. God's call of Lehi; his ministry in Jerusalem (1)

II. Journey of Lehi and his family to the first camp (2–16)
- A. Departure of family; the first signs of family discontent (2)
- B. Return of sons to Jerusalem to obtain the brass plates (3–4)
  1. Laban's refusal to surrender the plates; flight of Nephi and his brothers from Jerusalem (3)
  2. Nephi's acquisition of the plates (4)
- C. Lehi's inventory of the records on the brass plates; Nephi's summary of his record keeping (5–6)
- D. Return of the sons to Jerusalem to persuade Ishmael's family to join them in the wilderness; eruption of tensions (7)
- E. Account of Lehi's dream of the tree of life and his prophecy about the people of Israel and the coming of Christ (8–10)
- F. Account of Nephi's similar vision of future events (11–14)
- G. Nephi's interpretation of both visions (15)
- H. Marriage of children of Lehi and Ishmael; Lehi's discovery of the "round ball of curious workmanship" (16:1–11)

III. Journey of the party "south-southeast" from the first camp to Nahom (16:12–39)
- A. The breaking of Nephi's bow; scarcity of food; murmuring of family members; assistance of the Lord (16:12–32)
- B. Death of Ishmael at Nahom; eruption of family crisis; intervention of God (16:33–39)

IV. Journey of the party "nearly eastward" from Nahom to Bountiful on the sea (17:1–6)

V. Encampment at Bountiful (17:7–18:4)
- A. God's command to build a ship; resistance of brothers; Nephi's defense of his action (17:7–55)
- B. Construction and outfitting of ship for voyage to the promised land (18:1–4)

VI. Journey to the promised land (18:5–25)
- A. Crisis at sea; severe storm; control of the ship and the compass taken by Nephi (18:8–22)
- B. Arrival in the promised land; exploration and discovery (18:23–25)

VII. Nephi's quotations of prophecies from the brass plates (19–22)
- A. Prophecies of Zenock, Neum, and Zenos about the coming Messiah (19)
- B. Nephi's quotation of Isaiah (20–21 // Isa. 48–49)
- C. Nephi's explanation of Isaiah's prophecies; additional teachings (22)

commentary on his Isaiah quotes, the ultimate destruction of the wicked, and the Millennium (1 Ne. 22).

After arriving in the promised land, Nephi made two sets of metal plates for writing. The first set of plates, whose date of origin was ca. 588 B.C., became known as the large plates of Nephi. Upon them Nephi began recording a rather complete secular history of his people. This set of plates passed from one generation to another and provided the basic record that Mormon and Moroni would later abridge as the Book of Mormon (1 Ne. 19:4). Thirty years after the party had left Jerusalem (ca. 570 B.C.), the Lord commanded Nephi to make another record, this one to contain the spiritual dimensions of his people's history (1 Ne. 19:3; cf. 2 Ne. 5:28–33). This record became known as the small plates of Nephi. Its custodians continued this second record to the reign of king Benjamin (ca. 130 B.C.), at which time both the spiritual and secular accounts were kept together on the large plates, presumably by government scribes.

The chief theme of this book is deliverance, a term that Nephi placed prominently at the end of his extended introduction, pointedly informing readers of the purpose of his story: "Behold, I, Nephi, will show unto you that the tender mercies of the Lord are over all those whom he hath chosen, because of their faith, to make them mighty even unto the power of deliverance" (1 Ne. 1:20). Such a declaration suggests that Nephi wrote according to a predesigned outline that is discernible.

The theme of the Lord's deliverance appears throughout Nephi's records (e.g., 1 Ne. 1:14; 8:8; 21:10, 13; 2 Ne. 4:26; 11:5; 24:1). In practical terms, it occurs in the escape of Lehi's party from the destruction of Jerusalem (2 Ne. 1:3–4) and in Nephi's avoiding serious harm from his rebellious brothers during their journey in the wilderness (e.g., 1 Ne. 7:17–18; 17:48–52). It also appears in the Lord's rescue of the party from the dangers of storm at sea and his guidance of the ship to the promised land (1 Ne. 18:11–20).

Another important theme is the reality of continuing revelation and divine guidance. In the case of continuing revelation, the entire saga of the first book of Nephi rests on a series of revelations that Lehi received, revelations that informed him of the looming destruction of Jerusalem and of the coming Messiah (1 Ne. 1). These divine manifestations led to others, including the Lord's instructions to Lehi to send his sons to Jerusalem, first to obtain the plates of brass (1 Ne. 3–4) and then to persuade the family of Ishmael to join them in the desert (1 Ne. 7). Naturally, the continuing revelation found in the extended visions of Lehi (1 Ne. 8) and Nephi (1 Ne. 11–14) also fits into this category. In addition, Nephi wrote generously of the miraculous discovery and subsequent aid of the compass-like metallic ball known as the LIAHONA (1 Ne. 16:10, 16, 26–29) and of the Lord's revelation of the pattern for the ship that would carry the colonists to the New World (1 Ne. 17:8, 18, 51; 18:1–2).

Yet another theme of Nephi's book, that of obedience and associated blessings, mirrors the promises and warnings the Lord uttered before the Israelites reached their promised land under Moses and Joshua (Deut. 27–28). The connection between obedience and divine blessings in a promised land appears early in the record: "Inasmuch as ye shall keep [God's] commandments, ye shall prosper, and shall be led to a land of promise . . . which is choice above all other lands" (1 Ne. 2:20). The matter of obedience and prosperity, which is first featured here, continues throughout the entire Book of Mormon (e.g., Jarom 1:9; Omni 1:6; Mosiah 1:7; Alma 9:13).

Modern research has discovered that Nephi employed a variety of sophisticated literary structures, both to bring unusual unity to his work (Reynolds, "Outline") and to weave together a broad defense of his ascendancy in family government over his older brothers. He evidently undertook this latter task to answer criticism from his brothers and their descendants who claimed rights to govern the extended family (Reynolds, "Dimensions").

Besides the chief themes and structure of the record, Nephi plainly identified one of his main purposes for writing his account: "For the fulness of my intent is that I may persuade men to come unto the God of Abraham, and the God of Isaac, and the God of Jacob, and be saved" (1 Ne. 6:4). In part, Nephi accomplished his objective by rehearsing his father's vision of the coming of the Messiah (1 Ne. 10) and his own vision of Jesus Christ's dual ministry, one in the Old World and the other in the New World after his resurrection (1 Ne. 11–12). He thus emphasized that the coming of the Messiah was the most important news to which he could bear witness.

See also Babylonian captivity; Book of Mormon, selected themes of, obedience; Isaiah chapter reviews (1 Ne. 20 // Isa. 48; 1 Ne. 21 // Isa. 49); Jerusalem[1], city of; Jerusalem[1], destruction of, at 586 B.C.; Laban, slaying of; Lehi[1]'s dream; Lehi[1], journey of, to the promised land; Nephi[1]'s vision.

BIBLIOGRAPHY

Brown, S. Kent. *From Jerusalem to Zarahemla*. Provo, Utah: Religious Studies Center, Brigham Young University, 1998.

———."A Case for Lehi's Bondage in Arabia." *Journal of Book of Mormon Studies* 6 (Fall 1997): 205–17.

Brown, S. Kent, and David R. Seely. "Jeremiah's Imprisonment and the Date of Lehi's Departure." *Religious Educator* 2 (2001): 15–32.

Hilton, Lynn M., and Hope Hilton. *In Search of Lehi's Trail*. Salt Lake City: Deseret Book, 1976.

Reynolds, Noel B. "Nephi's Outline." *Book of Mormon Authorship*. Edited by Noel B. Reynolds. Provo, Utah: Religious Studies Center, Brigham Young University, 1982.

———. "The Political Dimensions of Nephi's Small Plates." *Brigham Young University Studies* 27 (Fall 1987): 15–37.

SKB

Nephi, fourth book of An abridgment by Mormon of the large PLATES OF NEPHI written by Nephi[4], son of Nephi[3] the disciple of Christ; Nephi's son and grandson, both named Amos; and a writer named Ammaron (4 Ne. heading; 1:19, 21, 47). It summarizes the rise and fall of the righteous civilization that developed after the visit of the resurrected Savior to the descendants of Lehi[1] (ca. A.D. 34–321).

Content and message

The book of 4 Nephi is important for at least four reasons. First, it is a testament of the profound effect of the Savior's visit on the lives of the people living in the western hemisphere. Second, it constitutes a classic study on the course and structure of righteousness and prosperity on the one hand versus wickedness and destruction on the other, showing human beings at their best and their worst. Third, the

OUTLINE OF 4 NEPHI

I. Setting: all people converted to the Church of Christ after his appearance (1:1–12)
   A. All things held in common (1:1–3)
   B. Peace and prosperity in all the land (1:4–11)
   C. Fasting, prayer, and meeting often (1:12)
II. Apex of society: complete unity (1:13–19)
   A. No wickedness (1:13–16)
   B. No "-ites" (1:17–19)
III. Decline of society: apostasy appears gradually (1:20–34)
   A. Small group revolts (1:20–22)
   B. Wealth produces pride (1:23–24)
   C. Social stratification—loss of unity (1:25–26)
   D. False churches arise, true disciples persecuted (1:27–34)
IV. Downfall of society: willful rebellion (1:35–46)
   A. Great division among the people, "-ites" proliferate, rebellion (1:35–38)
   B. Iniquity increases (1:39–41)
   C. Gadianton combinations develop, Nephites and Lamanites equally wicked (1:42–46)
V. Fate of the records (1:47–49)

NEPHI, LAND OF AND CITY OF

book succinctly demonstrates Mormon's inspired editorial ability and prophetic mantle. And fourth, the text is an instructive foreshadowing of the conditions to exist in the millennial future.

Mormon abridged the records of the actual eyewitnesses to the events recounted in 4 Nephi (Nephi[4], Amos[1], Amos[2], and Ammaron) and from them distilled the essential lessons of Nephite and Lamanite history, making those lessons more succinct, intense, and poignant by their brevity. In only forty-nine verses the record captures the heights and depths of a civilization's social, economic, spiritual, and moral condition, the practical workings of the law of the celestial kingdom—the true order of heaven on earth, the ideal pattern of welfare service, the circumstances and atmosphere that will exist during Christ's millennial reign, and the stark contrast of Satan's purposes, influence, and success in a temporarily fallen world. The insidious effects of pride, persecution of the Saints, and deliberate perversion of gospel truths are laid bare in unmistakable terms. Juxtaposed in stunning fashion are those elements that go together to create Zion (1:1–18) with those that destroy it (1:20–46).

Fourth Nephi spans almost one-third (approximately 300) of the years covered in the entire Book Mormon (approximately 1,000), excluding the Jaredite account. One may be tempted to lament that one of the greatest periods in Nephite, as well as human history, is given such relatively sparse historical treatment. Mormon's inspired purpose was not historical detail, however. Rather, he intended to set forth the important principles and truths that could be culled from sacred history to inform future generations. When originally published, 3 and 4 Nephi were together, one composition entitled "Nephi." In 1879 Orson Pratt separated them and added the titles 3 Nephi and 4 Nephi to distinguish them from each other.

See also Book of Mormon, selected themes of, cycles of prosperity and destruction.

ACS

Nephi, land of and city of Land located south of the land of Zarahemla and bordered on the east and west by two large bodies of water, the "sea east" and the "sea west" (Alma 22:1, 27). The land of Nephi and the land of Zarahemla were separated by a narrow strip of wilderness that ran from east to west and connected with both the east and the west seas (Alma 22:27). The Book of Mormon does not identify the southern boundaries of the land of Nephi. The land of Zarahemla must have been at a lower elevation than the land of Nephi because all movements from Zarahemla to Nephi are "up," although the direction is south, while all movements from Nephi to Zarahemla are "down," although the direction is north (e.g., Mosiah 7:2–4; 8:2; 9:3; Alma 17:8; Omni 1:13). "The place of their fathers' first inheritance" was located on the west of the land of Nephi by the seashore (Alma 22:28), indicating that Lehi[1] and his family must have landed on the west sea coast of the land. The climate of the land of Nephi was conducive to raising animals and cultivating such agricultural products as corn, wheat, and barley (2 Ne. 5:11; Mosiah 9:8, 9).

Control over the land and its cities alternated between the Nephites and the Lamanites. From the time that Nephi[1] and his people settled the land (2 Ne. 5:7–8; ca. 590–570 B.C.) until Mosiah[1] and his people left (ca. 200 B.C.), the Nephites ruled the land of Nephi. During the era of Zeniff, Noah[3], and Limhi (ca. 121 B.C.) and throughout the remainder of the Book of Mormon, the Lamanites maintained control over the land.

Many important events took place in the land of Nephi. In the early period, under Nephite rule of the land, there is record of Nephi[1] building a temple that was constructed "after the manner of the temple of Solomon" (2 Ne. 5:16), the preaching and prophesying of Jacob[2] and his encounter with the anti-Christ Sherem (2 Ne. 6–10; Jacob 1–7), and the conversion and prophecies of Enos (Enos 1). The Nephite period of rule concluded with Mosiah[1]'s leading his people out of the land of Nephi to the land of Zarahemla (Omni 1:12–13). The Book of Mormon history that follows also contains numerous references to occurrences in the land of Nephi, including the return of Zeniff (Mosiah 9), the preaching of the prophet Abinadi to king Noah and his wicked priests (Mosiah 11:20–17), the conversion of Alma[1] and the subsequent mass conversion of others at the waters of Mormon (Mosiah 17:2; 18:4–5, 16), the bondage of Limhi's people to the Lamanites and their escape (Mosiah 21, 22), the mission of the sons of Mosiah[2] to the Lamanites (Alma 17–26), and the imprisonment and miraculous deliverance of Nephi[2] and Lehi[4] (Hel. 5:20–50).

The city of Nephi, or Lehi-Nephi, was the chief city in the land of Nephi (Alma 47:20). It was first settled in the sixth century B.C. by Nephi[1] after he fled from his brethren (2 Ne. 5:5–8). Lehi-Nephi was the center of Nephite culture for approximately four hundred years from ca. 590 B.C. to 200 B.C. (2 Ne. 5:8; Omni 1:12–13). Later, following the Lamanite acquisition of the land of Nephi, Nephite colonists under the reigns of Zeniff, Noah, and Limhi occupied the city of Nephi for approximately eighty years (Mosiah 9:6; until ca. 121 B.C.).

The city of Nephi was likely located in a valley in a mountainous region, for when Ammon[1] and sixteen strong men from Zarahemla set out to inquire about the Nephites living there, they went *up* to the land of Nephi and then camped on a hill and went *down* into Shilom and Nephi, or Lehi-Nephi, as the region was then called (Mosiah 7:2–6; cf. 9:3).

With the exception of the city of Zarahemla, the city of Nephi is mentioned more often than any other city in the Book of Mormon. Many prominent people of the Book of Mormon lived all or a portion of their lives in the city of Nephi. Among them were Nephi[1], Jacob[2], Mosiah[1], Abinadi, Alma[1], Zeniff, Noah[3], Limhi, and Gideon.

JLA

Nephi, plates of *See* Plates of Nephi.

Nephi, second book of Written by Nephi[1] on the small PLATES OF NEPHI, the book of second Nephi is primarily a collection of prophetic discourses or treatises by Lehi[1] (2 Ne. 1:1–4:11), Jacob[2] (2 Ne. 6–10), and Nephi[1] (2 Ne. 4:15–35; 11–33) delivered some time between ca. 588 B.C. and 544 B.C. Both Jacob and Nephi cited substantial excerpts of the prophecies of Isaiah in their discourses (e.g., 2 Ne. 7–8; 12–24). Additionally, 2 Nephi records the death of father Lehi (2 Ne. 4:12) and the subsequent separation of his posterity into two peoples, the Lamanites and the Nephites (2 Ne. 5).

Content and message

Nephi testified that he had been commanded to record the "ministry and the prophecies" and the "more sacred things" of his people upon the small plates, of which 2 Nephi is a part (1 Ne. 19:3–5; cf. 2 Ne. 4:14–15; 5:29–33). The four discourses found in 2 Nephi appear to have been collected and recorded to fulfill that commandment. Lehi's discourse, delivered as he anticipated the end of his life, contains his final blessings and counsel to his family. Speaking first to his older sons Laman, Lemuel, and Sam, as well as to the sons of Ishmael, Lehi explained that he had seen in vision the destruction of Jerusalem and reminded them of the great mercy God had shown in bringing them to a "land of promise" (2 Ne. 1:1–4). He also explained the covenant of righteousness associated with the PROMISED LAND and urged his sons to repent and no longer rebel against Nephi, who had been an instrument of God in bringing them to the land (2 Ne. 1:5–27). He promised his first blessing to his older sons if they would hearken unto Nephi; otherwise, the blessing would rest upon Nephi (2 Ne. 1:28–29).

After admonishing his older sons, Lehi pronounced blessings and gave counsel to the rest of his posterity, either as individuals or as family groups (2 Ne. 1:30–4:11). His blessings contain prophecies and promises concerning the future of each individual or group in the covenant land and are followed by counsel "according to the workings of the Spirit" (2 Ne. 1:6). His teachings to his youngest sons, Jacob and Joseph, are especially significant. He taught Jacob such important doctrines as the plan of redemption through Jesus Christ, the necessity of opposition and agency, the role of Satan, and the importance of the fall of Adam and Eve (2 Ne. 2). In counseling his son Joseph, Lehi cited the prophecies of his ancestor Joseph of Egypt to teach his son about the preservation of his seed, the latter-day coming forth of the Book of Mormon, and the ministry of the CHOICE SEER Joseph Smith (2 Ne. 3).

The next section of 2 Nephi was written by

Nephi after he recorded the death of Lehi and the subsequent rebellion of Laman, Lemuel, and the sons of Ishmael (2 Ne. 4:12–13). Perhaps the highlight of the treatise is NEPHI'S PSALM (2 Ne. 4:15–35) in which, much like the biblical psalmist, Nephi used inspiring imagery and poetic parallelism to praise God for his goodness, to lament his own weaknesses, and to declare his devotion to the Lord.

Between Nephi's psalm and Jacob's discourse

OUTLINE OF 2 NEPHI

I. Lehi's discourse: his last admonitions and testament to his posterity (1–4)
   - A. Lehi's teachings concerning the promised land, and his counsel and warning to Laman[1], Lemuel, Sam, and Ishmael's sons: repent and prosper (1:1–29)
   - B. Lehi's blessing upon Zoram[1]: stay faithful and be blessed with Nephi's seed (1:30–32)
   - C. Lehi's teachings to Jacob[2]: the plan of redemption and the doctrine of opposition (2)
   - D. Lehi's teachings to Joseph[2]: the prophecies of Joseph[1] of Egypt (3)
   - E. Lehi's blessing upon his grandchildren: counsel to stay faithful and prosper (4:3–9)
   - F. Lehi's blessing upon Sam: to be numbered and blessed with Nephi's seed (4:11)

II. The death of Lehi and Nephi's admonition to his brethren (4:12–14)

III. Nephi's treatise: the psalm of Nephi (4:15–35)

IV. The separation of the Nephites and Lamanites (5)
   - A. The rebellion of Laman and Lemuel against Nephi and the Lord (5:1–4)
   - B. Nephi leads the righteous to the land of Nephi (5:5–19, 26–27)
   - C. Lamanites are "cut off from the presence of the Lord" (5:20–25)
   - D. Nephi commanded to make "other plates" (the small plates of Nephi) (5:29–33)
   - E. Wars and contentions between the Nephites and Lamanites (5:34)

V. Jacob's discourse: his teachings to the Nephites (6–10)
   - A. The scattering, gathering, and redemption of the covenant people (6)
   - B. A messianic prophecy of Isaiah (7; *see* Isaiah chapter reviews, 2 Ne. 7 // Isa. 50)
   - C. The latter-day gathering and redemption of the covenant people (8; *see* Isaiah chapter reviews, 2 Ne. 8 // Isa. 51–52:2)
   - D. The great plan of God: the Atonement, the resurrection, and the Judgment (9)
   - E. Prophecies concerning Lehi's descendants, the Jews, and the Gentiles (10)

VI. Nephi's final treatise (11–33)
   - A. Nephi's delight in Jesus Christ (11)
   - B. Isaiah's prophecies concerning the Messiah, the covenant people, and the destruction of the wicked (12–24; *see* Isaiah chapter reviews, 2 Ne. 12–24 // Isa. 2–24)
   - C. Nephi's commentary on the value of Isaiah's prophecies and how to understand them (25:1–8)
   - D. Nephi's message to the Jews, the descendants of Lehi, and the Gentiles (25–30)
     1. The message to the Jews: the scattering, the gathering, Christ, and the Restoration (25:9–20)
     2. The message to the descendants of Lehi: the record, the law of Moses, the coming of Christ, and the eventual destruction of the Nephites (25:21–26:11)
     3. The message to the Gentiles: Christ, the Book of Mormon, and latter-day apostasy (26:12–29:14)
     4. Conclusion: repentant Gentiles will be numbered among the covenant and will carry the gospel (via the Book of Mormon) to the Lamanites; Jews will "begin" to gather to Christ, and the Millennium will come (30:1–18)
   - E. The doctrine of Christ (the gospel) and the importance of prayer (31–32)
   - F. Nephi's farewell: his testimony of the importance of the Book of Mormon (33)

is a historical chapter that chronicles the separation of Lehi's posterity into two distinct peoples, the Nephites and the Lamanites (2 Ne. 5). In this chapter Nephi described the theological, cultural, and geographical divisions that developed between the brother nations and lamented that within forty years of separating they were at war one with another.

Jacob's discourse, as next recorded, is apparently two sermons delivered to the people of Nephi on two successive days. In the first sermon Jacob described what he had seen in vision and understood from the writings of Isaiah concerning Jerusalem and the Gentiles, including the Babylonian captivity and return, the coming of Christ and his crucifixion (2 Ne. 6:8–9), the subsequent scattering and oppression of the house of Israel, and with the help of the Gentiles, the latter-day gathering of Israel and their restoration by conversion to the GOSPEL of Christ (2 Ne. 6:6–18). Jacob then cited passages from Isaiah to teach of the Messiah and the redemption of his people (2 Ne. 7–8 // Isa. 50; 51–52:2). Concluding the first sermon with an enlightening explanation of how redemption is accomplished through "the plan of our God," Jacob taught of the ATONEMENT, the RESURRECTION, and the JUDGMENT (2 Ne. 9). In the second sermon delivered the following day, Jacob rehearsed the words spoken to him by an angel concerning Christ and his rejection by the Jews. He added commentary on Isaiah to summarize, reinforce, and augment the prophecies and teachings he had given in the first sermon concerning the scattering, gathering, and redemption of the covenant people (2 Ne. 10).

In his final treatise, Nephi, like Jacob, quoted extensively from the writings of Isaiah to teach the mission of the Messiah and the history and future of God's covenant people (2 Ne. 12–24 // Isa. 2–14). After quoting these chapters Nephi commented on them in chapters 25–30, incorporating portions of Isaiah 29 in his discussion. He specifically addressed the Jews (2 Ne. 25:9–20), the descendants of Lehi (2 Ne. 25:21– 26:11), and the Gentiles (2 Ne. 26:12–29:14). As Nephi spoke to each group, he tailored his comments to meet their needs, detailing problems and challenges they would face and the important role of the Book of Mormon in solving those problems. To the Jews he bore stirring witness of Jesus Christ, proclaiming the advent of Christ's mortal ministry, his rejection by the Jews, and the subsequent scattering of the Jewish people (2 Ne. 25:9–15). Nephi then prophesied of the marvelous work God would perform in the last days to gather the Jews and of the coming forth of the Book of Mormon "for the purpose of convincing them of the true Messiah" (2 Ne. 25:16–19). Nephi concluded his comments to the Jews with a sacred oath, "as the Lord God liveth, there is none other name given under heaven save it be this Jesus Christ . . . whereby man can be saved" (2 Ne. 25:20; cf. 31:21).

As Nephi shifted his attention from the Jews to his own people, he emphasized that his record, the Book of Mormon, would be preserved and handed down "that his seed should never perish" and that they be persuaded to believe in Christ (2 Ne. 25:21–23; cf. 3:3–5, 23; 9:53). He admonished them to keep the law of Moses until it would be fulfilled by Christ and testified that the "right way is to believe in Christ" and worship him (2 Ne. 25:24–30). He then foretold of the wars that would come between the Nephites and Lamanites, the signs that would accompany the birth and death of Jesus Christ, and the ministry of the resurrected Christ among Lehi's descendants (2 Ne. 26:1–9). Nephi also spoke of the three generations of peace that would follow Christ's ministry and warned that apostasy and speedy destruction would come after the fourth generation (2 Ne. 26:9–10). Later in the text, as Nephi spoke of the latter-day Gentiles, he taught that through the coming forth of the Book of Mormon and the restoration of the gospel, his own people would be restored to the truth and redeemed (2 Ne. 26:15–16; 27:6–26; 30:3–6).

Nephi's message to the Gentiles is no less clear: In the latter days, false churches, PRIESTCRAFT, and SECRET COMBINATIONS would abound (2 Ne. 26:20–22). SATAN would inspire men to teach false and seductive doctrines (2 Ne. 28), and many would refuse to accept additional revelation and scripture from God (2 Ne. 29). But, through the restoration of the gospel and the Book of Mormon, they would be brought to a knowledge of the truth, and the Gentiles would be numbered among and enjoy the blessings of the covenant people (2 Ne. 27:26, 29, 35; 30:1–3; *see* Isaiah chapter reviews, 2 Ne. 26:6, 15–18; 27 // Isa. 29).

Nephi closed his final treatise with a simple and beautiful explanation of the importance of faith, repentance, baptism, reception of the Holy Ghost, and endurance to the end—principles and ordinances he defined as the "doctrine of Christ" (2 Ne. 31). He then invited all to accept this doctrine and to pray and act in the name of Christ (2 Ne. 32). His final words are an admonition to all to believe in Christ and the Book of Mormon, for each testifies of the other (2 Ne. 33:10–15).

See also Churches, false; Gentiles, Book of Mormon message concerning; Isaiah chapter reviews (2 Ne. 12–24 // Isa. 2–14); Israel, gathering of; Israel, scattering of; Jews, Book of Mormon message concerning; Lamanites, Book of Mormon message concerning.

MSN

Nephi[1], sisters of Nephi mentioned his sisters when he listed those who went with him into the wilderness at the time the family of Lehi[1] divided into Nephites and Lamanites (2 Ne. 5:5–6). Presumably they were righteous, for "all those who would go with me," Nephi wrote, "were those who believed in the warnings and the revelations of God" (2 Ne. 5:6). There is no indication how many sisters Nephi had.

Nephi, third book of Mormon's abridgment of the record kept on the large plates by Nephi[3], "the son of Nephi, who was the son of Helaman" (3 Ne. heading). Third Nephi contains a description of events in the western hemisphere from ca. 1 B.C. to ca. A.D. 34, events focused primarily on Christ's ministry in ancient America. While 3 Nephi may not be at the physical center of the Book of Mormon, it clearly serves as its crowning jewel. Much of the record that precedes 3 Nephi, as well as that which follows, refers to Christ's ministry recorded in 3 Nephi. Some six hundred years previous, Nephi[1] prophesied that Christ would minister unto his seed (1 Ne. 12:6; 2 Ne. 26:9), and Jacob[2] wanted his readers to understand that "we knew of Christ, and we had a hope of his glory many hundred years before his coming" (Jacob 4:4). At the other end of the time line, Mormon looked back and lamented, "O ye fair ones, how could ye have rejected that Jesus, who stood with open arms to receive you!" (Morm. 6:17).

Third Nephi is sometimes referred to as the fifth Gospel (e.g., Roberts, 1:373–99) because it includes accounts of Christ's birth (cf. 3 Ne. 1:15–21; Matt. 2:2), death (cf. 3 Ne. 8:5–23; Matt. 27:50–54), and resurrection (3 Ne. 11:14–15; Luke 24:39); it also includes many of his teachings (cf. 3 Ne. 12–14; Matt. 5–7) and miracles (cf. 3 Ne. 17:7–9; 20:1–9; Mark 6:34–44; 8:1–9). The parallel accounts in 3 Nephi and the New Testament stand at the pinnacle of the role of the Book of Mormon as another testament of Jesus Christ. They reconfirm the reality of Christ's mortal ministry, atoning sacrifice, and position as God's "Beloved Son, in whom [He is] well pleased" (3 Ne. 11:7; cf. Matt. 17:5; Mark 1:11).

Content and message

Third Nephi illustrates the spiritual and temporal heights and depths of the ancient Book of Mormon society. The fulfillment of the prophecies of Samuel the Lamanite concerning Christ's birth created a spiritual revival among the Nephites: "The more part of the people did believe, and were converted unto the Lord" (3 Ne. 1:22). As a result, the Nephite society experienced a period of "peace in the land" when "there were no contentions," with the brief exception of a group who taught that the LAW OF MOSES was no longer required (3 Ne. 1:23–25). Third Nephi, however, identifies two major threats to the Nephites that attacked the very foundation of the peace that comes through living the gospel of Jesus Christ.

The major external threat to peace was the Gadianton robbers, who secreted themselves in the mountains, increasing in power with the addition of Nephite dissenters (3 Ne. 1:27–29) and frequent raids upon Nephite and Lamanite cities. This group became so powerful that the Nephites and Lamanites were forced to combine their resources to combat them. Even so, "the Nephites were threatened with utter destruction

OUTLINE OF 3 NEPHI

I. Western hemisphere events surrounding Christ's birth in fulfillment of Samuel[2]'s prophecy (1:1–27)
   A. The passing of the records from Nephi[2] to Nephi[3] (1:1–3)
   B. The plot of the wicked to put the righteous to death because the sign of Christ's birth had not occurred (1:4–9)
   C. Nephi[3]'s prayer on behalf of the righteous (1:10–11)
   D. The Lord's announcement to Nephi that "on this night shall the sign be given, and on the morrow come I into the world" (1:13–14)
   E. Signs of Christ's birth: no darkness for a day, night and a day (cf. Hel. 14:4), and the appearance of a new star (1:15–21)
   F. The conversion of the "more part of the people" after they see the signs (1:22–26)

II. Breakdown of Nephite and Lamanite society with the rise of the Gadianton robbers (1:27–7:26)
   A. The increase of the Gadianton robbers (1:27–30)
   B. The increase of wickedness and abominations among the people as they forget the signs and wonders they had seen (2:1–10)
   C. Wars between the Gadianton robbers and the faithful Nephites and Lamanites (2:11–4:33)
   D. Nephite repentance following victory over the robbers (5:1–7)
   E. Mormon introduces himself, comments on the records, teaches about the future gathering of Israel (5:8–26)
   F. Nephite prosperity and peace; return to wickedness (6)
   G. Breakdown of the government; formation of tribal units; ministry of Nephi[3] (7)

III. Events in the western hemisphere surrounding Christ's death in fulfillment of Samuel's prophecy (8–10; cf. Hel. 14:20–28)
   A. The cataclysmic events such as tempests, earthquakes, and whirlwinds that devastated the land for three hours, followed by three days of darkness (8)
   B. Christ's annunciation of the destruction throughout the land, the fulfillment of the law of Moses, and his desire to gather the house of Israel (9–10)

IV. Visitation of the resurrected Christ to the western hemisphere (11:1–28:12)
   A. Day 1 (11:1–19:3)
      1. Introduction of the Son by the Father (11:1–7)
      2. Jesus' self-introduction and encouragement for the multitude to come forth one by one and feel the physical signs of his crucifixion (11:8–17)
      3. Jesus' authorization to his disciples to baptize (11:18–28)
      4. Outline of Jesus' doctrine (11:29–41)
      5. Sermon at the temple (12–14; cf. Matt. 5–7)
      6. Further teachings: fulfillment of the Mosaic law (15:1–10), Jesus' other sheep (15:12–16:3; cf. John 10), and prophecy concerning the Jews and Gentiles (16:4–20)
      7. Jesus' administration to the sick and prayer for those assembled (17)
      8. Institution of the sacrament and conferral on disciples of authority to bestow the gift of the Holy Ghost (18)
      9. Gathering together throughout the night of others to hear the Savior "on the morrow" (19:1–3)
   B. Day 2 (19:4–26:15)
      1. Ministry of the disciples: multitude taught, prayers offered, baptisms performed, and the Holy Ghost manifested (19:1–14)

2. Jesus' return and prayer for his disciples and all those who believe on their words; the disciples are purified (19:15–36)
3. Miraculous provision of bread and wine for the sacrament (20:1–9; cf. Mark 6:34–44; 8:1–9)
4. Jesus' teachings on the gathering of Israel in the last days; Jesus quotes the prophets Micah and Isaiah (20:10–22:17)
5. Jesus' quotation of the prophets Samuel the Lamanite and Malachi (23:1–25:6)
6. Jesus' expounding of "all things" from the beginning to the end (26:1–14)
7. Jesus' ascension to the Father after he heals the sick and raises the dead (26:15)

C. Aftermath of Jesus' ministry (26:16–21)
1. The gathering of the multitude; babes speak marvelous things (26:16)
2. Continued ministry of the disciples: baptisms and subsequent manifestations of the Spirit (26:17–18)
3. The founding of the church of Christ (26:19–21)

V. Additional appearances and teachings of Jesus to his disciples (27:1–28:14)
A. Jesus' instructions to the disciples concerning the name of the Church (27:1–12) and the definition of the GOSPEL (27:13–22)
B. Jesus' granting his disciples their wishes: nine will come to Jesus in his kingdom at the conclusion of their earthly ministry, and three will be translated so they can continue their missionary efforts (28:1–11)
C. Jesus' departure; three disciples are "caught up into heaven" (28:12–14, 36)

VI. The nature of translated beings (28:15–40)
VII. The Book of Mormon as the sign for the gathering of Israel; warnings to latter-day people (29)
VIII. Mormon's admonition for the Gentiles to join with the house of Israel by coming to Christ (30)

because of this war" (3 Ne. 2:13). To protect their societies from the destabilizing force of Gadianton forays, the chief judge Lachoneus[1] and the commander of the Nephite forces, Gidgiddoni, caused that the people gather into one body and fortify themselves (3 Ne. 3:13–14, 21–26). Centralizing Nephite forces and provisions made the Gadianton SIEGE ineffective and led to the robbers' defeat (3 Ne. 4). The Nephites preached the "word of God" to all of their prisoners. Those who entered into a covenant were "set at liberty," while those who refused to do so were "punished according to the law" (3 Ne. 5:4–5; cf. Alma 4:19; 31:5). These actions "put an end," at least for a short time, to "all those wicked, and secret, and abominable combinations, in the which there was so much wickedness, and so many murders committed" (3 Ne. 5:6).

The other major threat to Nephite society came from within and was profoundly more destructive: PRIDE. Class distinctions developed on the basis of riches and the people's "chances for learning" (3 Ne. 6:12) and ultimately resulted in the breaking up of the Church (3 Ne. 6:14). The author specifically noted that these people "did not sin ignorantly, for they knew the will of God concerning them, for it had been taught unto them; therefore they did wilfully rebel against God" (3 Ne. 6:18). Although the Lord sent "men inspired from heaven" to testify "boldly of [their] sins and iniquities" and to testify "concerning the redemption which the Lord would make for his people" (3 Ne. 6:20; cf. Amos 3:7), by and large, the people rejected their testimonies and put them to death (3 Ne. 6:23; 9:5, 7–9, 11). In an effort to protect the wicked judges who had the prophets put to death secretly, a secret combination was formed, and the Nephite chief judge was assassinated

(3 Ne. 6:25–30; 7:1). After this murder the government collapsed, the people divided into tribal units (3 Ne. 7:2), SECRET COMBINATIONS flourished, and "the more righteous part of the people had nearly all become wicked; yea, there were but few righteous men among them" (3 Ne. 7:7). The most prominent of the righteous was Nephi[3], who during this time "had power given unto him that he might know concerning the ministry of Christ," had "angels . . . minister unto him daily," and raised his brother from the dead (3 Ne. 7:15–19).

It was in this state of spiritual apostasy that the Americas experienced the fulfillment of the prophecy of Samuel the Lamanite concerning the signs surrounding Christ's death. These signs included a great storm, "such an one as never had been known in all the land. . . . a great and terrible tempest . . . terrible thunder, insomuch that it did shake the whole earth as if it was about to divide asunder. . . . exceedingly sharp lightnings, such as never had been known in all the land," numerous cities destroyed, and a thick darkness that covered the land for three days (3 Ne. 8:3–25; cf. Hel. 14:20–28). Only the "more righteous" who had "received the prophets and stoned them not" survived these calamities (3 Ne. 10:12). These Nephites and Lamanites were qualified to participate in one of the seminal events in the earth's history—to come into the presence of the resurrected, glorified Son of God.

During his three-day ministry Christ invited the people to "come unto [him]" (e.g., 3 Ne. 12:3, 19–20, 23–24) in two important ways. The first was an immediate, tender, and personal effort on the Savior's part to be accessible to his people. He invited all those gathered together at the temple to come "forth one by one" to receive their own personal witness of the reality of his atoning sacrifice (3 Ne. 11:13–15). Then after

And He Healed Them Every One; *painting by Gary L. Kapp; courtesy Gary L. Kapp.*

teaching them for many hours, and when he was ready to conclude the first day's activities, he was still sensitive to the people's desire that he "tarry a little longer with them" (3 Ne. 17:4–5). Jesus surveyed the assembled crowd and said, "Behold, my bowels are filled with compassion towards you," and then he went about healing their sick, praying for the people, and blessing their children "one by one" (3 Ne. 17:6–25).

He was sensitive to the desires of his disciples, both in terms of their doctrinal questions about the name of the Church (3 Ne. 27) and in their personal requests about their status once they had completed their mortal ministries (3 Ne. 28:1–10).

The second way Christ invited his people to come unto him was through covenants (Ludlow, 22–35). The Savior specifically indicated that he came to the Americas to bless the people in turning them from their sins: "And this because ye are the children of the covenant" (3 Ne. 20:25–26). He then went into depth to expound for his audience their place in the covenantal scheme (3 Ne. 16–20). Christ quoted Malachi 3–4, at least in part because it contains a prophecy of his coming and a messenger that would prepare the way: "Behold, I will send my messenger, and he shall prepare the way before me, and the Lord whom ye seek shall suddenly come to his temple, even the messenger of the covenant" (3 Ne. 24:1). Although Christ's coming fulfilled the Mosaic law, the covenant was still in effect (3 Ne. 15:2–10). Christ invited the people to rise to a higher level of living that would more fully enable them to come unto him. His emphasis on the practical teachings of the Sermon on the Mount (3 Ne. 12–14) and his emphasis on the ordinances of BAPTISM (3 Ne. 11:19–39; 26:17–21), the sacrament (3 Ne. 18:1–11; 20:1–9; 26:13), and receiving the Holy Ghost (3 Ne. 11:35–36; 12:6; 18:36–38) are all ways for people, both then and now, to make covenants efficacious in their lives. Mormon summarized the message of 3 Nephi by imploring Gentiles to repent, come unto Christ, be baptized, and be filled with the Holy Ghost so "that ye may be numbered with my people who are of the house of Israel" (3 Ne. 30:1–2).

See also Book of Mormon: Another Testament of Jesus Christ; Israel, gathering of; Malachi chapter review (3 Ne. 24–25 // Mal. 3–4); Nephites, the Three; Prophets, rejection of; Sermon at Bountiful and Sermon on the Mount; Translation; Writing of divorcement.

BIBLIOGRAPHY

Benson, Ezra Taft. "The Book of Mormon—Keystone of Our Religion." *Ensign* 16 (November 1986): 4–7.

———. "The Savior's Visit to America." *Ensign* 17 (May 1987): 4–7.

Ludlow, Victor L. *Jesus' "Covenant People Discourse" in 3 Nephi* [pamphlet]. Religious Education Lecture Series. Provo, Utah, 1988.

Roberts, B. H. "The Fifth Gospel." *Defense of the Faith and the Saints*. 2 vols. Salt Lake City: Deseret News, 1907–12.

GS

Nephihah A wise man and an elder of the Church selected by Alma[2] and confirmed by the voice of the people as the second Nephite chief judge in Zarahemla (Alma 4:16–17; 50:37; ca. 83 B.C.). During his sixteen-year administration, Nephihah "filled the JUDGMENT-SEAT with perfect uprightness before God" (Alma 50:37). With the consent of his people, he admitted the converted ANTI-NEPHI-LEHIES into Nephite lands (Alma 27:20–22). Later he sat with Alma in judgment against the anti-Christ Korihor (Alma 30:29–30). He ruled during a period of severe crisis and conflict—first with Zerahemnah (Alma 43–44) and then with the traitor Amalickiah, who wished to overthrow the system of judges and establish himself as king (Alma 46–50). Nephihah died after the rebellion of Morianton[2] was quelled and was succeeded by his son, Pahoran[1] (Alma 50:39–40). Because Nephihah had declined to be custodian of the Nephite records, Alma passed them to his son Helaman[2] (Alma 50:38). Presumably the city of Nephihah mentioned in Alma 50:14 was named after him.

See also Judges, reign of.

Nephihah, land of, city of, and plains of Nephite land where Moroni[1] built the city of Nephihah, between the cities of Moroni and Aaron (Alma 50:14; ca. 72 B.C.). When the Lamanites seized Moroni, the dispossessed

Nephites fled to Nephihah, which itself fell about five years later (Alma 51:23–24; 59:5–11; 62 B.C.). Nephihah was the first city retaken during the final campaign of Moroni and Pahoran[1]. Although Moroni desired to fight the Lamanites upon the nearby plains of Nephihah, their refusal prompted a strategic night assault. Moroni's army recovered Nephihah by climbing the walls on the west side of the city while the Lamanite army slept on the east side and then attacking their startled and frightened enemy from within. Not one Nephite soldier was killed in this action, although Lamanite casualties were high. Many of the Lamanite captives chose to enter a covenant of peace rather than remain prisoners (Alma 62:14–30; ca. 61 B.C.).

The wording of Alma 51:25–26 suggests the possibility of a second city named Nephihah on the eastern coast.

Nephi[1]'s psalm Called both a psalm and a song, this poetic piece forms a most poignant depiction of Nephi[1]'s own struggles with sin and with feelings about rebellious members of his family (2 Ne. 4:17–35). Like some biblical psalms (e.g., Ps. 10; 78), Nephi's song may be "mixed" because it includes features of differing types, a personal lament coupled with a song of thanksgiving. The psalm offers a model of how Nephi sought to overcome discouragement. The opening lines picture him in personal pain (vv. 17–19), which he sought to reverse by counting his blessings (vv. 20–25). But his mind was still puzzled over why his soul was captured by sin and transgression (vv. 26–27). Even though he urged himself to more noble thoughts and deeds (vv. 28–30), in the end he acknowledged that only the Lord in His mercy could lift him (vv. 31–35).

As in the case of ancient Hebrew poetry, which Nephi knew from his own scriptures, his psalm exhibits poetic characteristics found in the Old Testament. Such features include parallelism of expression, often with the second and third thought repeating or intensifying the meaning of the first (Alter, 3–26). This sort of phrasing differs from western poetry, which rests on meter and often, in its modern forms, on rhyme.

The expected Hebrew parallelisms of expression appear in the following examples from Nephi's song (Rust, 71–75). In these words of lament, the second and third lines sharpen and deepen the initial sentiment, exposing sources of Nephi's frustration:

O wretched man that I am!
Yea, my heart sorroweth because of my
  flesh;
my soul grieveth because of mine
  iniquities. (4:17)

A similar intensification can be seen in Nephi's self-reassuring memories of the Lord's aid, in which Nephi passed from a general statement to specific examples of how the Lord had supported him:

My God hath been my support;
he hath led me through mine afflictions
  in the wilderness;
and he hath preserved me upon the
  waters of the great deep. (4:20)

Another feature of poetic parallelism lies in completing one thought with a succeeding one. Nephi achieved this end—the second line complementing the first, and the fourth line completing the third—when he spoke of the differing deeds of the Lord:

He hath filled me with his love,
  even unto the consuming of my flesh.
He hath confounded mine enemies,
  unto the causing of them to quake
  before me. (4:21–22)

The occasion for Nephi's poignant words seems partly to have grown out of his sorrow at losing his father in death, leaving Nephi, a younger sibling, to wrestle with difficulties that arose within the family. The other part evidently arose from the continuing series of conflicts with his older brothers: "Not many days after [Lehi's] death, Laman[1] and Lemuel . . . were angry with me because of the admonitions of the Lord" (2 Ne. 4:13). As is clear from Nephi's psalm, his response to the anger of his brothers had distressed him. In words that are poetically matched, he asked himself why he had allowed himself to become angry, and then he urged himself to better action: "Why am I angry because of mine enemy? . . . Do not anger again because of mine enemies" (2 Ne. 4:27, 29).

At the end, Nephi's final words brim with expressions of loyalty to the Lord who had delivered him both from his enemies and from his own worst self:

> I will cry unto thee, my God,
> the rock of my righteousness.
> Behold, my voice shall forever ascend up unto thee,
> my rock and mine everlasting God. (4:35)

See also Book of Mormon, as literature; Book of Mormon, poetry in; Parallelism.

BIBLIOGRAPHY

Alter, Robert. *The Art of Biblical Poetry.* New York: Basic Books, 1985.

Bokovoy, David. "From Distance to Proximity: A Poetic Function of Enallage in the Hebrew Bible and the Book of Mormon." *Journal of Book of Mormon Studies* 9:1 (2000): 60–63.

Rust, Richard D. *Feasting upon the Word: The Literary Testimony of the Book of Mormon.* Salt Lake City: Deseret Book and FARMS, 1997.

SKB

Nephi[1]'s vision Revelation given to Nephi in the wilderness that came in consequence of his desire to "see, and hear, and know . . . the things that [his] father had seen" (1 Ne. 10:17; 11:1; 14:29), namely, the vision of the TREE OF LIFE (1 Ne. 8). In addition to seeing the vision shown to Lehi[1], Nephi also beheld the interpretation of the vision through various segments of history, particularly as they pertained to his posterity.

Nephi's vision is a pivotal event in the Book of Mormon. Elder Jeffrey R. Holland described it as "a concise introduction to the reader of the book's central purpose in declaring that Jesus is the Christ" (42). The focus of the vision is the tree of life, a symbol of God's love (1 Ne. 11:21–23, 25). In addition and in contrast to the tree of life, Nephi's vision also described the destructive effects of the "large and spacious building," a symbol for "the pride of the world" (1 Ne. 11:35–36; 12:18–23; cf. 8:24–28, 31–34).

First Nephi 11 provides the foundation for the rest of the vision. It is here that Nephi learned of the "condescension of God" manifested through the Father and the Son (1 Ne. 11:16, 26; cf. John 3:16). The importance of this part of the vision should not be underestimated. It is the earliest known account of Christ's mortal ministry, predating the New Testament Gospels by six hundred years. Although the account is prophetic rather than historical in nature, it is a significant witness for the veracity of the New Testament. Additionally, even though chapter 11 does not contain the detail found in the Gospels, it does focus the reader's attention on the central elements of Christ's life, such as his birth (11:15–21), baptism (11:27), ministry (11:28), miracles (11:31), and death (11:33)—specific elements that bear witness of his divinity. The chapter closes with Nephi's observing multitudes within the "large and spacious building" gathered together "to fight against the apostles of the Lamb." The angel instructing Nephi said, "Behold the world and the wisdom thereof; yea, behold the house of Israel hath gathered together to fight against the twelve apostles of the Lamb" (1 Ne. 11:34–36).

Chapter 12 shifts the reader's attention geographically to the western hemisphere and also highlights the transition between Christ's mortal and resurrected ministries. In doing so, Nephi's vision teaches that the tree of life spreads forth its branches to extend God's love to all of his covenant people (cf. Jacob 4:7; 5). While chapter 11 functions as the "first" testament of Christ, witnessing of Christ's ministry in the Holy Land (as recorded in the Gospels), chapter 12 stands as "another testament" of Christ, witnessing of his ministry in the Americas (as recorded in the Book of Mormon). In chapter 12 Nephi saw the condescension of God among his own people when Christ, as a resurrected being, would visit them (1 Ne. 12:6; cf. 3 Ne. 11–28). Just as he did in the eastern hemisphere, Christ chose twelve disciples to minister unto his people (1 Ne. 12:8–10; cf. 3 Ne. 11:19–22; 18:36–37; 19:4). Nephi saw that the fruit of Christ's visit for Lehi's descendants was that they would live in righteousness for three generations (and many of the fourth generation also) and that they "are made white in the blood of the Lamb, because of their faith in him"

(1 Ne. 12:11; cf. 2 Ne. 26:9; 4 Ne. 1:1–22). Nephi also beheld their subsequent destruction because of pride, represented by "the large and spacious building," and "the temptations of the devil," represented by "the mists of darkness" (1 Ne. 12:17–19; cf. 8:21–23, 26–27).

Chapters 13 and 14 detail the Lord's response to the apostasy found in both eastern and western hemispheres at the end of chapters 11 and 12. The "great and spacious building" of LEHI[1]'S DREAM (1 Ne. 8:26–27), which works to entice people away from the tree of life, is represented in these chapters by the "great and abominable church" (1 Ne. 13:4–9). Nephi was shown that this "great and abominable church" contributed to the apostasy by removing or holding back many plain and precious gospel truths and covenants (1 Ne. 13:26, 34). This, Nephi saw, would cause "an exceedingly great many [to] stumble, . . . insomuch that Satan [would have] great power over them" (1 Ne. 13:29).

Chapter 13 describes two major acts of God intended to counteract the work of the "great and abominable church" and deliver his people—Jew, Gentile, and descendant of Lehi (1 Ne. 13:32, 39)—out of this apostasy. First,

OUTLINE OF NEPHI[1]'S VISION

I. Spirit of the Lord appears to Nephi (11:1–11)
   - A. Nephi is caught away in the Spirit while pondering the things of his father (11:1)
   - B. The Spirit questions Nephi concerning his desires and belief (11:2–11)

II. Prophecy of Christ in the eastern hemisphere (11:12–36)
   - A. Christ's birth in Nazareth (11:12–23)
   - B. Christ's baptism and mortal ministry (11:24–31)
   - C. Christ's trial and crucifixion (11:32–33)
   - D. Apostasy, the house of Israel fights against the Twelve Apostles (11:34–36)

III. Prophecy of Christ in the western hemisphere (12:1–23)
   - A. Wars and rumors of wars between the Lamanites and Nephites (12:1–3; cf. Alma 43–61; 3 Ne. 2–4)
   - B. Cataclysmic physical events prior to the coming of Christ (12:4–5; cf. 2 Ne. 26:5–6; 3 Ne. 8)
   - C. Christ ministers as a resurrected being in the western hemisphere (12:6–10; cf. 2 Ne. 26:9; 3 Ne. 9–28:12)
   - D. Three generations of righteousness (and many of the fourth generation) in the western hemisphere (12:11–12; cf. 2 Ne. 26:9; 4 Ne. 1:1–18)
   - E. Apostasy; Nephites and Lamanites battle each other (12:13–20; cf. 2 Ne. 26:10; 3 Ne. 27:32; 4 Ne. 1:20–45; Morm. 1–6)
   - F. Degenerate conditions among the Lamanites (12:21–23; cf. Morm. 8:8–10)

IV. Prophecy of Gentile nations and kingdoms (13:1–42)
   - A. The formation and characteristics of the "great and abominable church" (13:1–9)
   - B. Columbus discovers America; its colonization; and war for independence (13:10–19)
   - C. The loss of gospel truths and covenants and the subsequent effect of that loss upon the Gentiles (13:20–33)
   - D. The coming forth of "other books," including the Book of Mormon, to restore precious gospel truths, verify biblical records, and testify of Christ (13:34–42)

V. Prophecy of the last days (14:1–30)
   - A. Blessing extended to the Gentiles if they give heed to the Restoration (14:1–7)
   - B. Two churches: "the church of the Lamb of God, and . . . the church of the devil" (14:8–17)
   - C. Differentiation between the stewardship of Nephi and John the Revelator in regards to the recording of their visions of the last days and the end of the world (14:18–30)

Nephi saw the Spirit of God working upon the Gentiles to establish the Americas. Specifically, Nephi saw COLUMBUS crossing the Atlantic ocean (13:12), other Gentiles arriving to colonize the Americas (13:13–16), and the subsequent war for independence (13:17–19). These providential events were necessary for the establishment of a free nation (3 Ne. 21:4). Second, in this free nation the Lord would "work a great and a marvelous work among the children of men" (1 Ne. 14:7). A principal part of this work would be the coming forth of the Book of Mormon and "other books" (e.g., the Doctrine and Covenants and Pearl of Great Price) (1 Ne. 13:34–42). Together these books would do three things: they would "establish the truth" of the Bible; "make known the plain and precious things which have been taken away"; and convince all that "the Lamb of God is the Son of the Eternal Father, and the Savior of the world; and that all men must come unto him, or they cannot be saved" (1 Ne. 13:39–40). Moreover, Nephi was told that the Savior's words contained in both the Nephite records and the writings of the Twelve Apostles were destined to become one (1 Ne. 13:41).

In chapter 14 Nephi was reminded by the angel of the "covenants of the Father unto the house of Israel" (1 Ne. 14:8, 17), and he was taught concerning the Gentiles' opportunity to participate in those covenants (1 Ne. 14:1–2, 5–6). Within this context the chapter shows the alternative consequences for the children of men if they hearken to the Lamb of God or if they become ensnared by the wiles of the great and abominable church. God would "work a great and a marvelous work among the children of men." This work, the restoration of the Church of Jesus Christ through the Prophet Joseph Smith, would "be everlasting" and either convince them of "peace and life eternal" or deliver them into "captivity, and also into destruction, both temporally and spiritually, according to the captivity of the devil" (1 Ne. 14:7; cf. 22:8–12). Nephi also beheld that the Lamb of God would not allow the great and abominable church, as powerful as it would become, to be victorious (1 Ne. 14:3–4, 8–17). The "covenant people of the Lord" would be armed with righteousness and the power of God (1 Ne. 14:14), and the "wrath of God" would be poured out upon the great and abominable church: "Then, at that day, the work of the Father shall commence, in preparing the way for the fulfilling of his covenants, which he hath made to his people who are of the house of Israel" (1 Ne. 14:17; cf. 3 Ne. 21:25–28).

Even though Nephi was shown much more than he described in these chapters (1 Ne. 14:28), he was told that the responsibility for writing "concerning the end of the world," the ultimate victory over Satan lay with John the Revelator and others (1 Ne. 14:22, 25–26; cf. 2 Ne. 27:10–11; Ether 3:21–27).

In summary, Nephi's vision provides latter-day people with another testament of the divinity of Jesus Christ. Moreover, it gives additional testimony of a universal apostasy and subsequent restoration of gospel truths. Nephi's vision reminds readers that despite the seemingly pervasive power of Satan and the great and abominable church, God and his Saints will ultimately triumph. It also teaches latter-day readers that they can have confidence in the prophecies of the Lord's anointed servants. Much of what was prophecy for Nephi is now history for people living in modern times.

See also Book of Mormon: Another Testament of Jesus Christ; Condescension of God; Great and abominable church; Israel, covenants unto; John the Beloved/Revelator; Plain and precious things, loss of and restoration of; Tree of life in ancient cultures.

BIBLIOGRAPHY

Holland, Jeffrey R. *Christ and the New Covenant.* Salt Lake City: Deseret Book, 1997.

GS

Nephite civilization Civilization is the sum of a society's conventional art, culture, language, literature, and literacy, as well as government, law, ethics, morality, and economics. Reading between the lines in the Book of Mormon, one can discover many clues concerning the nature of Nephite civilization.

Historical overview

As reflected in the Book of Mormon, Nephite civilization changed dramatically during the course of its thousand-year history. The Nephite records reflect four distinct eras. During the first era (ca. 580–200 B.C.), the primarily agrarian Nephite culture was centered on the city of Nephi and the temple that Nephi[1] built there in the sixth century B.C. (2 Ne. 5:16–17). The relatively small group of Nephites attempted to establish a foothold in their new world and struggled to maintain their religious and cultural heritage in a new setting. During these years being a Nephite stood mainly in contrast with being a Lamanite. The posterity of Lehi[1] was divided into seven tribes (2 Ne. 1:28–4:11; Jacob 1:13), and these seven groups persisted to the end of Nephite history (4 Ne. 1:36–38; Morm. 1:8). Tribal wars soon plagued the small population (Jacob 7:26; Jarom 1:7; Omni 1:3, 10), which polarized into two main bodies. After an initial burst of creativity and formative efforts by Nephi and Jacob[2], Nephite civilization appears to have stagnated, receiving as far as is known no new revelation and producing few noteworthy achievements in their second through fourth centuries (Jarom 1:2; Omni 1:11).

The second era began when king Mosiah[1], following the Lord's guidance, led his people out of the land of Nephi and moved the center of Nephite civilization down to the city of Zarahemla, where they were welcomed as effective leaders by the indigenous Mulekites (Omni 1:12–16). Here the Nephites experienced a century of innovation, rejuvenation, growth, expansion, inventions, development, and inspiration. The Zarahemla era (ca. 200 B.C. to A.D. 17) was characterized by religious and cultural diversity, group fragmentation, and efforts to establish citizen equality while still retaining Nephite religious and political control. Several important contacts continued between the land of Zarahemla and the land of Nephi, involving diplomatic investigation and record exchange (Mosiah 7–8), missionary work (Alma 17–26; Hel. 5), and occasional commercial activity (Hel. 6:8), as well as resettlements (Mosiah 22–24; Alma 27) and considerable warfare (W of M 1:13; Alma 16; 28; 43–62; Hel. 4). Eventually, political rivalries in the land of Zarahemla degenerated into corruption, assassinations, and lawlessness at the hands of several robber bands and secret combinations (Hel. 1–2; 6; 11; 3 Ne. 2–4).

The third era began when Nephite civilization removed its center from the city of Zarahemla (3 Ne. 3:22), eventually ending up in a new temple city at Bountiful[2], seventeen years after the signs of Christ's birth. From this strategic location at the isthmus separating the land northward from the land southward (Alma 22:27–33), the Nephites anticipated and witnessed the coming of Christ in the year A.D. 34. Nephite civilization then enjoyed four generations of glorious peace and righteousness (4 Ne.).

The fourth and final era commenced around the end of the second century A.D., when privatization and fractionalization again fragmented Nephite civilization. Wickedness and secret combinations led to two hundred years of decline and destruction from which Nephite civilization never recovered (Morm. 2–7; Moro. 9).

Inclusion and membership

Belonging to the Nephite civilization was based fundamentally on family and lineage. Descendants of Nephi[1], Jacob[2], Joseph[2], and at different times, Zoram[1], were counted as Nephites (Jacob 1:13). Other peoples, however, were also numbered among the Nephites through a process of making covenants and taking down names (Mosiah 6:1–2; 3 Ne. 2:14). For example, the Lamanite converts brought to Zarahemla by Ammon[2] became Nephites when they were given the land of Jershon by the Nephites as the land of their inheritance within the Nephite hegemony (Alma 27:21–25). Conversely, some groups, such as the Zoramites[2], disassociated themselves from the Nephite culture (Alma 31:2–3; 43:13). Geographical proximity, too, played a role in defining group membership, as when king Benjamin numbered all the people within the land of Zarahemla as his people (Mosiah 1:10). Similarly, converted Lamanites united with the Nephites in the days of Lachoneus to defend themselves against the Gadianton robbers (3 Ne. 2:12).

Nephite civilization was closely connected with the lineage-based history kept by the descendants of Jacob[2] and Alma[1] that recorded their interactions with other groups. For the most part, however, the Nephites remained separate, lonely, and isolated. Mobility appears to have been limited, indicating that they lived in areas of broken terrain. Transportation was difficult enough that long-range communication was limited, and great joy and relief were expressed when groups reunited after long periods of separation (Mosiah 21:25–22:14; Alma 26). Relocations of population groups proved problematical on several occasions (Omni 1:28; Mosiah 21–22; Alma 50:31–33). Nephites also strongly discouraged marriage outside of appropriate Nephite circles; differences in skin color served to distinguish their seed "from the seed of their brethren . . . that they might not mix and believe in incorrect traditions" (Alma 3:8; 2 Ne. 5:23). These social and religious conditions contributed to the rise of marginalized social elements on the fringes of Nephite civilization who harbored resentment and hostility (Mosiah 10:12–18), often forming secret combinations and dissenting groups (Alma 9–16; 46; Hel. 2).

Material and social culture

The Book of Mormon mentions many details indicative of the material culture underlying Nephite civilization. Their foods, crafts, metal working, tools, markets, symbols, and other elements of daily life compare favorably with what is known about ancient Mesoamerican civilization generally; for example, trees served important symbolic functions in both Nephite and Mesoamerican civilizations (Sorenson, *Images*, 182–83). Wealth was readily gained and lost in Nephite civilization, indicating a relatively simple agricultural economy vulnerable to weather and many other factors causing large economic fluctuations. Not land but tangible personal property, especially "costly apparel" and jewelry, was the main outward indicator of wealth in this society (Jacob 2:13; Alma 1:27, 29; 5:53). Clothing distinguished social classes; pride and costly apparel contributed to social barriers and conflicts (e.g., Alma 4:6–10; 31:28; Hel. 13:28).

Educational instruction is mentioned in the Book of Mormon (Mosiah 24:1–4; 3 Ne. 6:12), and fathers and mothers apparently taught or personally saw to the academic and spiritual education of their children, presumably at home (1 Ne. 1:1; Enos 1:1; Mosiah 1:2–3). Literacy levels and regard for record keeping among the Nephites always remained fairly high and appears to have received increased emphasis (Mosiah 1:2–4) after they encountered the Mulekites, who had brought no records with them and whose language "had become corrupted" (Omni 1:17). While retaining an interest in Hebrew language and Egyptian script, the Nephite vernacular changed significantly over its thousand-year span (Morm. 9:33–34). Language was largely functional, useful for record keeping, law giving, speech recording, and military communications. Several Nephite writers were skillful and creative in the use of various literary forms, notably CHIASMUS. Women in this society apparently spent most of their time rearing children and performing domestic duties.

Nephite political culture was based on the LAW OF MOSES, as found on the PLATES OF BRASS and modified by Nephite revelation and legal innovations. The monarchy of the first era was transformed into a more democratic system of judges during the second era, although in both systems the chief officer was installed for life, preferred on the basis of heredity, and functioned as a single head of state (Mosiah 29). Under the reign of the judges, freedom of belief was legally protected (Alma 1:17; 30:11), but that did not necessarily extend to complete freedom of speech (Alma 30:30). The Nephite polity was composed of several loosely affiliated and largely autonomous cities, with ethnic groups tending to cluster in their own lands or areas, such as the Zoramites[2] in the land of Antionum (Alma 31), the Ammonites in the land of Jershon (Alma 27), the Nehorites in the land of Ammonihah (Alma 9–16), and the Limhites apparently in the land of Gideon (Gideon had been an important member of Limhi's colony in the land of Nephi; Alma 6:7–8).

Although not always righteous, Nephite society was thoroughly religious. Until the coming of Christ, faithful Nephites were strict in their observance of the law of Moses and other laws given by God to their Israelite forefathers (2 Ne. 5:10; Jarom 1:5; Alma 30:3): the righteous adhered to the TEN COMMANDMENTS

(Mosiah 13:15–24), offered burnt sacrifices (Mosiah 2:3), observed the Sabbath (Jarom 1:5), refrained from eating blood (Jarom 1:6), and prayed morning, noon, and night (Alma 34:21). The lack of any identifiable Nephite art may be due in part to the prohibition under the law of Moses that forbids the making of any graven images. Looking forward to the coming of Christ, the Nephites also gathered regularly at their main temples in the cities of Nephi, Zarahemla, and Bountiful[2], as their law required (Deut. 31:12). As religious groups proliferated, they gathered at other places of assembly or worship, sometimes building unconventional synagogues (e.g., Alma 31:12).

World view

Ultimately, civilization is a composite of attitudes and practices that reflect how a group of people defines the place of mankind in the world. Nephite civilization saw humanity collectively. Group well-being and survival usually dominated over individual rights. An individual remained an enemy to God so long as he or she remained unrepentant and lived out of harmony with the religious order (Mosiah 2:36–37; 3:19).

The Nephite civilization, as portrayed in the Book of Mormon, viewed history providentially. God was close to his people, looking after their welfare, giving them victories, or inflicting divine judgment and punishment (Jacob 6:5). God, as creator of heaven and earth, continued to maintain life's order from day to day, giving breath (Mosiah 2:21) and speaking to his prophets (Jacob 4:6). OATHS sworn in the name of God were taken seriously, in fear of his wrath (Alma 44:8). Those who kept their covenants with God became his sons and daughters and were sealed his (Mosiah 5:7, 15).

In response to life's ultimate questions, Nephite civilization understood the purpose of this existence and the fall of Adam and Eve in a positive sense, that all people might have joy (2 Ne. 2:25). The possibility of pain and destruction, however, was equally evident (Mosiah 2:38; Alma 12:11). Life was a time "for men to prepare to meet God" (Alma 34:32). After death, resurrection would allow all mankind to stand before God in their bodies to be judged by him (Alma 33:22). The purpose of human life was essentially to allow people to choose between good and evil (2 Ne. 2:26–27), and all human choices were reduced to these alternatives (Moro. 7:12). Good was defined as coming unto Christ, repenting, being baptized, keeping his commandments, and enduring to the end (3 Ne. 11:36–39; Moro. 7:13; 10:6).

Not unlike Christian nations today, Nephite civilization experienced contradictions. Essentially a faithful people, they were also often forgetful. Constant in their main worldview, the Nephites experienced repeated cycles of righteousness, prosperity, pride, and wickedness. They were often hardworking, humble, and longsuffering; but at the same time, they were proud, stubborn, and uncooperative. Remarkably, Nephite civilization existed without slavery, an almost universal practice in ancient civilizations. Equality before God translated fundamentally into social equality for the Nephites, leading at times to deep concern for the poor and needy (Mosiah 4:16–27). Yet, social stratification and class distinctions were also frequently evident (e.g., Alma 2:9; 4:6; 45:24; Hel. 3:36). While often presenting themselves as a peace-loving people, waging no offensive wars and willing to relocate in order to avoid hostilities, the Nephites still expended great energy on the production of weapons and the construction of fortifications. Moreover, Nephite civilization thought of itself as an open society, welcoming converts and allies; however, strongly held religious principles impeded or precluded extensive collaboration, compromise, or reconciliation (e.g., with the apostate Zoramites[2]; Alma 31).

Nephite civilization was particularly self-conscious. The faithful among the Nephites never forgot that they had been scattered from Israel onto the islands of the sea, had been brought to a promised land given to them on condition of obedience to certain covenants, and were anticipating the coming of the Messiah. They knew that the Messiah would be rejected (1 Ne. 11:32) and their own civilization would not survive (1 Ne. 12:22) but that their words would survive to come forth through the hands of the Gentiles (1 Ne. 13:35) to bring about a reunification of all of Israel (1 Ne. 14:17; 2 Ne. 29:13–14).

NEPHITE WEIGHTS AND MEASURES

Despite watching the collapse of Nephite civilization, Mormon and his people knew Nephi's prophecies that God's purposes would ultimately prevail over evil (1 Ne. 14; 2 Ne. 30). Ancient covenants also assured them that the Nephite records would come forth to be used at the final day of judgment (Mosiah 3:24; Moro. 10:27). These eternal perspectives added an enduring quality to much of Nephite civilization.

See also Agriculture in the Book of Mormon; Book of Mormon, selected themes of, cycles of prosperity and destruction; Government, principles of; Jaredite civilization; Judges, reign of; Kings; Lamanite civilization; Law, civil; Warfare in the Book of Mormon.

BIBLIOGRAPHY

Sorenson, John L. *Images of Ancient America: Visualizing Book of Mormon Life*. Provo, Utah: Research Press, 1998.

———. *An Ancient American Setting for the Book of Mormon*. Salt Lake City: Deseret Book and FARMS, 1985.

Welch, John W. "The Temple in the Book of Mormon: The Temples at the Cities of Nephi, Zarahemla, and Bountiful." *Temples of the Ancient World: Ritual and Symbolism*. Edited by Donald W. Parry. Salt Lake City: Deseret Book and FARMS, 1994.

JWW

Nephite weights and measures Nephite system of monetary exchange for goods and services. The Nephite system of weights and measures at the time of Mosiah[2] is specifically outlined in Alma 11:5–19, presumably to underscore the high value of a bribe that Zeezrom offered to Amulek while Amulek was preaching in Ammonihah. Zeezrom offered six onties of silver, or the equivalent of 42 measures of grain (also equal to 42 days of pay for a Nephite judge; Alma 11:3, 13; *see* accompanying table), to Amulek if he would "deny the existence of a Supreme Being" (Alma 11:22).

The system of weights and measures known in the Book of Mormon is not a continuation of the system known in the Old Testament. According to the Book of Mormon, names, weights, and values of the pieces of gold and silver were not reckoned "after the manner of the Jews" but were altered "according to the minds and the circumstances of the people, in every generation, until the reign of the judges" (Alma 11:4). Thus, the origination of a general system of weights and measures could have begun shortly after Lehi[1] and his family left Jerusalem or arrived in the promised land, and continued to develop to the time of Mosiah[2].

According to the "law of Mosiah . . . every man who was a judge of the law, or those who were appointed to be judges, should receive wages according to the time which they labored to judge" (Alma 11:1). Apparently there was some problem in Nephite society with debtors

Nephite Weights and Measures According to Alma 11:5–19				
MEASURES	RATIO	BARLEY/GRAIN	SILVER	GOLD
42		84 shiblon	6 onti (bribe)	6 limnah
7	1:56	14 shiblon	onti	limnah
4	1:32	8 shiblon	ezrom	shum (Alma 11:9) / shun (Alma 11:5)
2	1:16	4 shiblon	amnor	seon
1½	1:12	3 shiblon	3 shiblon	antion
1	1:8	2 shiblon (measure)	senum	senine
½	1:4	shiblon (=½ measure)	shiblon	
¼	1:2	shiblum	shiblum	
⅛	1:1	leah	leah	

FARMS Staff

reneging on their obligations, and judges were the arbiters of such disputes. Judges had the authority to send enforcement officers to individuals who would not pay and bring them to a court where evidence was presented against them. If an individual was found guilty, the judge could force payment (Alma 11:2). In payment for his service the judge would receive "a senine of gold" or "senum of silver" per day, which were equivalent in value (Alma 11:3). By ca. 82 B.C. some of the legal experts had devised ways to enhance the profit they could make from these legal suits by stirring "up the people to riotings, and all manner of disturbances and wickedness, that they might have more employ, that they might get money according to the suits which were brought before them" (Alma 11:20). Verses 5–19 of Alma 11 list various kinds of gold and silver measures, presumably designated by weights and their relative values. Mosiah assigned these values relative to certain amounts of grains (*see* accompanying table).

As one source on the subject indicates, it is not possible to "be altogether confident about the meanings of terms in the weights and measures system or their possible etymologies" ("Weights," 2). A few terms, however, such as "shum," "shiblom," and "limnah," bear some resemblance to Jaredite, Sumerian, and Akkadian words ("Weights," 1–3).

Systems of weights and measures are known from Mesopotamia and Egypt from the third millennium B.C., but coinage proper was not invented until the sixth century B.C. by the Lydians. The Book of Mormon says nothing about coins. Instead, the word *money* is used, which may indicate that pieces of metal of different shapes and sizes could be assigned a value through weighing (Nibley, 224). Richard Smith suggests that the Nephite "system was a peculiarly efficient one. The selection of 1, 2, 4, and 7 for the values of the larger coins [metal pieces] seems particularly wise. . . . In every case it turns out that the '1–2–4–7' system has an edge over . . . other systems from the standpoint of number of coins [metal pieces] required for a purchase" (316).

BIBLIOGRAPHY

Nibley, Hugh. *Since Cumorah.* 2d ed. Vol. 7 of *The Collected Works of Hugh Nibley.* Edited by John W. Welch. Salt Lake City: Deseret Book, 1988.

Smith, Richard Pearson. "The Nephite Monetary System." *Improvement Era* 57 (May 1954): 316–17.

"Weights and Measures in the Time of Mosiah II." Provo, Utah: Foundation for Ancient Research and Mormon Studies, 1983.

BMH

Nephites, the Three Three of the twelve Nephite disciples who were granted permission to remain on the earth as translated beings until the "judgment day of Christ" (3 Ne. 28:40). Bringing his personal ministry to the Nephites to an end, Jesus bestowed desired blessings on each of his twelve disciples, and "then he departed" (3 Ne. 28:12). Three of the disciples, the Three Nephites, feared to express their desires. Jesus knew their thoughts and said, "Ye have desired the thing which John, my beloved, who was with me in my ministry, before that I was lifted up by the Jews, desired of me" (3 Ne. 28:6–9). Modern revelation states that John "desired of [Christ] that he might bring souls unto [him]," or "that he might do more, or a greater work yet among men than what he has before done" (D&C 7:4–5). Answering Peter's question about what John would do, Jesus said, "If I will that he tarry till I come, what is that to thee?" (John 21:20–23). John was made "as flaming fire and a ministering angel" to "minister for those who shall be heirs of salvation who dwell on the earth" (D&C 7:6).

Granted a similar mission, the Three Nephites "were caught up into heaven, and saw and heard unspeakable things" (3 Ne. 28:13); they were made "as the angels of God" (3 Ne. 28:30). Jesus declared that a change was "wrought upon their bodies, that they might not suffer pain nor sorrow save it were for the sins of the world" (3 Ne. 28:38). Further, they were changed so that "Satan could have no power over them . . . and they were sanctified in the flesh, that they were holy, and that the powers of the earth could not hold them" (3 Ne. 28:38–39). In the final rebellion of the Nephites, to erase the memory of the teachings of Christ, the people tried to destroy the Three Nephites. They cast them into prisons, which crumbled. They buried them in the earth, but no pit could hold them. Three times they were cast into furnaces and twice into dens of wild beasts, but they were never harmed (3 Ne. 28:18–22; 4 Ne. 1:30–37).

Mormon had a record of their ministering unto "all the people," uniting and baptizing as many as would believe into the Church (3 Ne. 28:18). Three centuries after the Lord blessed them, they ministered to Mormon and Moroni[2] (3 Ne. 28:26; Morm. 8:11). Though the Lord took them away from the Nephites because of prevailing wickedness (Morm. 1:13), Mormon prophesied that before the Judgment Day, great and marvelous works would be wrought by the Three Nephites among the Gentiles, the Jews, all the scattered tribes of Israel, and "all nations, kindreds, tongues and people." They "shall bring out of them unto Jesus many souls, that their desire may be fulfilled, and also because of the convincing power of God which is in them" (3 Ne. 28:27–29). Mormon said that "they are as the angels of God, and if they shall pray unto the Father in the name of Jesus they can show themselves unto whatsoever man it seemeth them good" (3 Ne. 28:30). Their desire was to bring the souls of men unto Christ "while the world shall stand" (3 Ne. 28:9). Their blessing included his promise that when that time ended, they would be resurrected: "When I shall come in my glory ye shall be changed in the twinkling of an eye from mortality to immortality; and then shall ye be blessed in the kingdom of my Father" (3 Ne. 28:8).

See also Sanctified in the flesh; Taste of death; Translation.

AKP

Nethermost *See* Appendix C.

Neum An Israelite prophet known only from Nephi[1]'s reference in 1 Nephi 19:10. Neum foretold the crucifixion of the God of Israel, a prophecy that was presumably cited from the brass plates of Laban and appears in Nephi's writings with additional prophecies by Zenock, Zenos, and an unnamed angel, all of whom related specific details concerning the future mortal ministry of the Holy One of Israel. Neum's prophecy was confirmed by Nephi's own vision of the crucifixion (1 Ne. 11:33).

RAC

Never-ending torment *See* Endless torment, eternal torment, never-ending torment.

New Jerusalem In the Book of Mormon "New Jerusalem" has at least two meanings: (1) a holy city to be built in the latter days "upon this land [America]" (Ether 13:4–7; 3 Ne. 21:23–24; A of F 10); and (2) a heavenly city "which should come down out of heaven" at the beginning of the MILLENNIUM, when the Savior returns to the earth, to join the earthly New Jerusalem (Ether 13:3; cf. Moses 7:60–64).

The earthly New Jerusalem

The Savior said that the converted Gentiles, the descendants of Lehi[1], and "as many of the house of Israel as shall come" would all participate in building the New Jerusalem (3 Ne. 21:22–23), that it would be a gathering place for the Lord's people, notably the seed of Joseph (3 Ne. 21:24; Ether 13:6–8), and that the power of heaven and the Savior himself would be there (3 Ne. 20:22; 21:25). Joseph Smith learned that the New Jerusalem was to be "called Zion" (D&C 45:67), a place of gathering, peace, and protection for the Lord's people (D&C 45:64–71). The Lord also revealed that "the land of Missouri . . . [is] the place for the city of Zion," Independence being "the center place" (D&C 57:1–3).

The heavenly New Jerusalem at the beginning of the Millennium

In summarizing the words of Ether, Moroni[2] told of "the New Jerusalem, which should come down out of heaven" (Ether 13:3), descriptive of the City of Enoch coming to earth at the beginning of the Millennium to meet the people of the Lord, the elect who have been gathered "from the four quarters of the earth, unto . . . an Holy City, . . . called Zion, a New Jerusalem" (Moses 7:62–64; cf. Ether 13:8–10; JST Gen. 9:21–23). Isaiah foresaw that ZION (the New Jerusalem) would be one of two world capitals during the Millennium, from which "shall go forth the law" (2 Ne. 12:3 // Isa. 2:3).

LED

Night of darkness That point in time when one's probationary opportunities come to an end and the inevitable consequences of previous choices and behavior ensue. Amulek warned the apostate Zoramites[2], "I beseech of you that ye do not procrastinate the day of your repentance until the end; for after this day of life, which is given us to prepare for eternity, behold, if we do not improve our time while in this life, then cometh the night of darkness wherein there can be no labor performed" (Alma 34:33). Similarly, the Savior charged his Nephite disciples to follow the narrow path and enter the strait gate that leads to life, rather than choose the broad way and wide gate that leads to death, the path many travel "until the night cometh, wherein no man can work" (3 Ne. 27:33). Alma[2] taught his son Corianton the principle of restoration: evil for evil, good for good (Alma 41:4, 13). He said that if one "desired to do evil all the day long even so shall he have his reward of evil when the night cometh," while "if he hath repented of his sins, and desired righteousness until the end of his days, even so he shall be rewarded unto righteousness . . . delivered from that endless night of darkness" (Alma 41:5–7).

By using the phrases "this life," "the end," "until the end," "this day of life" (Alma 34:32–33), and "all the day long" (Alma 41:5), both Alma and Amulek clearly seem to have been warning their hearers not to procrastinate repentance until they leave their mortal probation through death. Both also associated this "night of darkness," this "awful crisis," and the point at which "there can be no labor performed" with the time of resurrection: Amulek declared, "That same spirit which doth possess your bodies at the time that ye go out of this life, that same spirit will have power to possess your body in that eternal world" (Alma 34:33–34), and Alma testified of all being raised from mortality to immortality, the righteous to endless happiness, and the wicked to endless misery "when the night cometh" (Alma 41:4–5).

Other than Alma's brief commentary, little is said in the Book of Mormon about what happens between death and resurrection. Alma explained that at death the righteous are received into a state of happiness and peace; the wicked, on the other hand, "shall be cast into outer darkness," where there "shall be weeping, and wailing, and gnashing of teeth." What is meant by "righteous" is not discussed. The "wicked," however, are described as those who "chose evil works rather than good; therefore the spirit of the devil did enter into them, and take possession of their house." Alma said the wicked remain in this state of misery, "as well as the righteous in paradise, until the time of their resurrection." At the resurrection, the righteous shall "shine forth in the kingdom of God," and the wicked will suffer "an awful death . . . for they die as to things pertaining to things of righteousness; for they are unclean, and no unclean thing can inherit the kingdom of God" (Alma 40:11–15, 25–26).

It is helpful to consider carefully what the Book of Mormon says about a "night of darkness" in light of latter-day scripture and prophetic commentary. Following are some conclusions that may be drawn:

1. The night of darkness occurs for sons of perdition when they commit the unpardonable sin, the sin against the Holy Ghost. The devil enters into them and takes "possession of their house" (Alma 40:13), having power also to "possess [their] body in that eternal world." The devil seals them his permanently and has all power over them, "and this is the final state of the wicked" (Alma 34:34–35).

2. Those who do not sin to the point of becoming sons of perdition but who procrastinate repentance until mortal death also experience a night of darkness "wherein there can be no labor performed." Nothing can be done to avoid the consequences of their earthly wickedness (Alma 34:33). Yet, this night of darkness is not permanent. By virtue of the atonement of Christ, "the dead who repent will be redeemed, through obedience to the ordinances of the house of God, And after they have paid the penalty of their transgressions, and are washed clean, shall receive a reward according to their works, for they are heirs of salvation" (D&C 138:58–59).

See also Hell; Judgment, the; Spiritual death.

LED

Nimrah *See* Jared[1], posterity of.

Nimrod[1] *See* Nimrod[1], valley of.

Nimrod[2] *See* Jared[1], posterity of.

Nimrod[1], valley of A valley north of Babel in the Old World named after "the mighty hunter" (cf. Gen. 10:8–10), where Jared[1], his brother, their families, and friends, gathered before their exodus to a land "choice above all the lands of the earth" (Ether 1:41–42). Here the Lord talked with the brother of Jared "in a cloud, . . . [and] commanded them that they should go forth into the wilderness" (Ether 2:1–5).

Noah[1] Old World patriarch at the time of the Flood, son of Lamech, and father of Shem, Ham, and Japheth (Gen. 5:30–32; 6:11–14; 7). The Book of Mormon contains three references to Noah and thus confirms the historicity of this biblical character: the ark he built (Ether 6:7), the covering of the earth by water, and the "utter" destruction of all life by the Flood. Noah is mentioned twice in connection with the Lord's promise not to destroy the earth again by water (Alma 10:22; 3 Ne. 22:9).

Noah[2] *See* Jared[1], posterity of.

Noah[3] Son of Zeniff, father of Limhi, and second king (succeeding Zeniff) of the Nephite colony that left Zarahemla and returned to the land of Lehi-Nephi. Unlike his faithful and even at one time "over-zealous" father (Mosiah 7:21), Noah lived a life full of "whoredoms and all manner of wickedness" (Mosiah 11:2). Noah replaced the priests whom his father had consecrated with those who joined him in setting their hearts upon riches and spending their "time in riotous living" (Mosiah 11:14). Noah's self-indulgent lifestyle necessitated his placing a heavy tax upon his people, which amounted to "one fifth part of all they possessed" (Mosiah 11:3, 6).

Noah rejected God and the prophet Abinadi and the warning that he and his people must repent or be taken in bondage (Mosiah 11:23, 27). Although he nearly released Abinadi because of his fear "that the judgments of God would come upon him" (Mosiah 17:11), in the end Noah hearkened to his wicked priests and had Abinadi put to death by fire (Mosiah 17:12, 20). Before his death, Abinadi prophesied of a similar fate for his executioners: "Ye shall be hunted, and ye shall be taken by the hand of your enemies, and then ye shall suffer, as I suffer, the pains of death by fire" (Mosiah 17:18). Scripture records that the unrepentant Noah was indeed killed by fire at the hands of his own people (Mosiah 19:20), a sobering illustration of the consequences of placing self before God and family (Mosiah 19:10–11, 20).

See also Noah[3], priests of.

DKJ

Noah, land of and city of Nephite region and city in the land of Zarahemla, near Ammonihah. Previously "the weakest part of the land," Moroni[1] strengthened its defenses greatly against an expected Lamanite attack. The Lamanite armies decided not to attack neighboring Ammonihah because of the manner in which Moroni had fortified the city. Supposing the city of Noah to be an easy target, the chief captains made an oath to attack the city and destroy its people. The Lamanites thus played into Moroni's hands, for on arriving, they were astonished to find Noah more heavily fortified than Ammonihah. Nevertheless, having sworn an oath to attack, the Lamanites fought but in vain. They were not able to penetrate the heavily fortified city. In the Lamanites' effort to tear down the city's fortifying banks of earth, many were slain. The record makes the ironic observation that the strategic ditches surrounding Noah became filled not with earth from the protective banks but with the bodies of the Lamanite dead and wounded. The city was spared without one Nephite casualty (Alma 49:12–25; 72 B.C.).

Noah[3], priests of A group of men who attended king Noah[3] in Lehi-Nephi after Zeniff, in his old age, conferred the Nephite kingdom upon his son Noah[3]. The wicked Noah had dismissed his father's priests and replaced them with men who would support him in his sinful lifestyle.

Described as being "lifted up in the pride of their hearts," these priests were lazy, idolatrous whoremongers who used "vain and flattering words" (Mosiah 11:5–7). Moreover, they lived off the high taxation of Noah's people, set a bad example for the citizenry, and proved to be a plague to the Nephites long after the death of king Noah.

When the Lord sent the prophet Abinadi to call Noah's people to repentance, Noah called him up before his priests. The record of that encounter is one of the most powerful moments in the Book of Mormon. Noah's wicked priests sought to "cross [Abinadi], that thereby they might have wherewith to accuse him; but he answered them boldly, and withstood all their questions, yea, to their astonishment; for he did withstand them in all their questions, and did confound them in all their words" (Mosiah 12:19). After one of the priests asked Abinadi a question from the scriptures, he chided them for their lack of knowledge and pretentiousness. "What teach ye this people?" Abinadi inquired of the priests. Their response, "We teach the law of Moses," brought Abinadi's stinging rebuke, "If ye teach the law of Moses why do ye not keep it?" (Mosiah 12:27–29). Frightened by Abinadi's preaching, Noah was ready to release him, but his priests (with one exception) appealed to his vanity, and he condemned Abinadi to death by fire (Mosiah 17:11–12). The one priest who believed Abinadi, Alma[1], spoke up in his defense but then had to flee for his own life (Mosiah 17:2–4). As Abinadi's sentence was being carried out, he prophesied that destruction would come upon the king and all of the evil priests (Mosiah 12:27–29; 17:14–18).

When king Noah was later put to death by fire, his priests escaped into the wilderness, where they endangered their former countrymen by kidnapping twenty-four Lamanite daughters and making them their wives (Mosiah 20:1–5, 18, 23). Discovered by Lamanite armies, the priests were spared through the pleas of their wives in their behalf (Mosiah 23:33–34). The priests then joined with the Lamanites (Mosiah 23:35). Their leader Amulon and the other priests were appointed to teach the Lamanites the Nephite language (Mosiah 24:4). Relishing his newfound clout, Amulon "began to exercise authority over Alma and his brethren," abusing and persecuting them, even refusing to let them pray (Mosiah 24:8, 11). There were no converts among the seed of Noah's priests (Alma 24:29), and eventually their seed were hunted and destroyed by the Lamanites for their evil as Abinadi had prophesied (Alma 25:4, 9–12).

See also Lamanites, twenty-four daughters of.

CDT

Noised *See* Appendix C.

And now behold, Ammon, and Aaron, and **Omner**, and Himni, and their brethren did rejoice exceedingly, for the success which they had had among the Lamanites, seeing that the Lord had granted unto them according to their prayers, and that he had also verified his word unto them in every particular. ALMA 25:17

Oaths Solemn statements, often sworn as part of rituals, used to establish covenants or promises or to strengthen declarations. Oaths were an important part of Near Eastern and biblical culture (Lev. 19:12; Num. 30:2). Oaths first appear in the Book of Mormon with Nephi[1] and Zoram[1] swearing to each other (1 Ne. 4:32–37). King Benjamin appointed priests to "stir [his people] up in remembrance of the oath which they had made" to keep the commandments (Mosiah 6:1–3). Instances of oath swearing can also be seen in warfare. For example, invading Lamanites swore an oath to destroy the city of Ammonihah (Alma 49:13) which Moroni[1] had sworn an oath to defend (Alma 48:13). Conversely, the Ammonites swore an oath of peace (Alma 24:18; 53:11–14; 56:8). Evidently, public officials were sworn in by oaths; Nephihah took an "oath and sacred ordinance" of judgeship (Alma 50:39). The seriousness of oaths and their associated covenants is demonstrated by the Lamanite leader Zerahemnah's refusal to swear a false oath to Moroni to surrender with a pledge of peace, even while surrounded by Nephite armies (Alma 44:1–20). Yet, Mormon "repent[ed]" of an oath not to lead his people (Morm. 5:1; 3:11). The oath "as the Lord liveth," or a form of it, appears frequently in the Book of Mormon and is used to strengthen solemn declarations. For example, Nephi asserted to his brethren that "as the Lord God liveth, there is none other name given under heaven save it be this Jesus Christ, of which I have spoken, whereby man can be saved" (2 Ne. 25:20; Omni 1:26; Alma 23:6). This type of oath is also found in the Old Testament where its use is similar (e.g., 2 Sam. 12:5; 1 Kgs. 17:1). Unfortunately, powerful oaths also made the Gadianton tradition possible (Hel. 6:21–24), and the "oath of the ancients" handed down from Cain helped destroy Jaredite civilization (Ether 9:5; 8:15, 20–21). In fulfilling the law of Moses, Jesus taught concerning oaths: "And again it is written, thou shalt not forswear thyself, but shalt perform unto the Lord thine oaths; but verily, verily, I say unto you, swear not at all; . . . but let your communication be Yea, yea; Nay, nay; for whatsoever cometh of more than these is evil" (3 Ne. 12:33–37). Christ was enjoining the Nephites to forgo the use of oaths as a means of guaranteeing their integrity: they were to follow a higher standard of personal honesty.

TLS

Obedience *See* Book of Mormon, selected themes of, obedience.

Offerings *See* Sacrifices.

Oft *See* Appendix C.

Ogath An area near the hill Ramah and south of the waters of Ripliancum, to which the Jaredite armies of Shiz fled before the forces of Coriantumr[2]. Presumably it was there that Shiz spent four years gathering all his people for the final conflict with the armies of Coriantumr (Ether 15:8–10, 14).

Old Testament, historical narrative referred to The expression "Old Testament" is not found in the Book of Mormon, but the PLATES OF BRASS obtained by Nephi[1] included records contained in the present Old Testament up to 600 B.C. For example, the plates of brass contained the five books of Moses and a "record of the Jews," as well as "prophecies of the holy prophets" from the beginning down to the time of Zedekiah, a contemporary of Lehi[1] (1 Ne. 5:5–13). From the plates of brass, Book of Mormon prophets, teachers, and writers were familiar with the same historical narratives preserved in the Old Testament records and often made reference to these narratives. Throughout the Book of Mormon, references are found to the account of the Creation, Adam and Eve, the Fall, the Flood, the Abrahamic covenant, Joseph in Egypt, the Exodus, and the history of Israel up to 600 B.C.

The Nephites might be thought of as an Old Testament people. Lehi[1] (1 Ne. 1:4) and Ishmael (1 Ne. 7:2) were descendants of Jacob[1] and Abraham through Manasseh and Ephraim, the sons of Joseph[1]. Later, the people of Mulek, son of king Zedekiah, joined them in the "new" land (Omni 1:15; Hel. 6:10). All had come from "the land of Jerusalem" (1 Ne. 2:11) and were politically "descendants of the Jews" (2 Ne. 30:4). As

BOOK OF MORMON REFERENCES THAT REFLECT HISTORICAL INFORMATION IN THE OLD TESTAMENT

OLD TESTAMENT SOURCE	NARRATIVE	B OF M REFERENCES
	Nephites take "Old Testament" records with them on plates of brass obtained from Laban	1 Ne. 5:10–14; 2 Ne. 5:12; Mosiah 2:3; 3:14–15
Gen. 1:1 ff.	"all things . . . from the beginning"	3 Ne. 26:2–3
Gen. 1:1–2:25	"all things . . . from the creation"	2 Ne. 6:3; Ether 1:3; Moro. 10:3
JST Gen. 3:4; Moses 4:3–4	Satan's fall	2 Ne. 2:17
Gen. 2:7–3:24	Adam, Eve, and the Fall	1 Ne. 5:11; 2 Ne. 2:15–25; Alma 22:12–14
Gen. 3:22–24	tree of life	Alma 12:21; 42:5
Gen. 6–9	Noah and the Flood	Alma 10:22; Ether 6:7
Gen. 11:3–9	tower of Babel	Omni 1:22; Ether 1:33
Gen. 14:18–20	Melchizedek	Alma 13:14–18
Gen. 17:2–8	covenant people	1 Ne. 15:18; 3 Ne. 15:5
Gen. 22	Abraham and Isaac	2 Ne. 8:2; Jacob 4:5
Gen. 35:9–12; 36:31	children of Israel / house of Israel	1 Ne. 15:14; 19:24
Gen. 37:31–33	"coat of Joseph"	Alma 46:24
Gen. 49	"words of Jacob"	Alma 46:24–26
Gen. 50:24–25	"covenants . . . made unto Joseph"	2 Ne. 3:4
JST Gen. 50:24–37	prophecies of latter days and choice seer to be raised up	2 Ne. 3:6–21
Ex. 13:20–22	Israel led out of Egypt	1 Ne. 17:33–35; Alma 36:28
Ex. 14:15–31	crossing the Red Sea	1 Ne. 17:23–35; Alma 36:28
Ex. 20	the Ten Commandments	Mosiah 13:12–24
Ex. 21:1 ff.	law of Moses	1 Ne. 4:15–16; 2 Ne. 5:10; Jarom 1:11
Lev. 1–7	"sacrifice and burnt offerings"	1 Ne. 7:22
Num. 21:8–9	Moses and the serpent	Alma 33:19–20
Deut. 9:13	Jews' stiffneckedness	Jacob 4:14
Deut. 18:15	a prophet like unto Moses	3 Ne. 20:23
2 Sam. 11:4; 1 Kgs. 11:1	David and Solomon's whoredoms	Jacob 1:15; 2:23–24
1 Kgs. 6	Solomon's temple	2 Ne. 5:16
2 Kgs. 24:14	the Babylonian captivity	2 Ne. 25:10–11
Ps. 107:4	the scattered tribes	1 Ne. 22:4; 3 Ne. 21
Isa. 2–14; 48–52:2; 53–54	Isaiah and Isaiah chapters quoted in the Book of Mormon	1 Ne. 20–21; 2 Ne. 6:4; 7–8, 12–24; Mosiah 14; 3 Ne. 20, 22, 23:1–3
Jer. 11:16	the olive tree	Jacob 5
Jer. 24:9	the scattering of Israel	1 Ne. 19:13–14
Jer. 39:6	times of Zedekiah	1 Ne. 5:10–13; Omni 1:14–15
Mal. 4:5	reference to Malachi and Elijah	3 Ne. 24; 25

the plates of brass were the only scriptures the Nephites possessed, they often made reference to their contents in their sermons and writings, as did the resurrected Christ during his Nephite ministry in the land Bountiful (e.g., 3 Ne. 20:23–24; 23:1). The Savior also revealed writings that were not available when they left Jerusalem (3 Ne. 24; 25), but which were later added to the Nephite canon of scripture. These writings from the prophet Malachi also became part of the Old Testament canon. The accompanying table illustrates references in the Book of Mormon that reflect historical information in the Old Testament.

Additional allusions to the Old Testament account provide evidence that the Nephites were familiar with Old Testament sources and drew heavily from them for their discourses and writings. For example, Book of Mormon prophets, teachers, and record keepers used their Old World scriptures to help emphasize their goals, which included the following:

To show what great things the Lord had done for their fathers, to reveal the Lord's covenants, and to convince their audience that Jesus is the Christ (Title Page; 1 Ne. 19:23).

To recognize that they (Lehi's posterity) were of the house of Israel, the covenant people, and to know Christ's doctrines (1 Ne. 15:14; 19:24; 2 Ne. 6:5).

To emphasize that all the prophets taught of Christ (Jacob 4:4; 7:10–11).

To show that the plan of redemption came through Christ (Alma 22:13).

To enlarge the memory of their people, convince them of their errors, cause them to repent, and bring them to a knowledge of their God (Alma 37:3–8).

In his concluding testimony, Mormon said if people believe the other sacred writings, they will believe the Book of Mormon, and vice versa (Morm. 7:8–9).

See also Book of Mormon, selected purposes of, to prove to the world that the holy scriptures are true; Book of Mormon, what it says about the Bible; Moses, five books of.

GAH

Olive trees The olive was an important plant during biblical times and olive trees are frequently mentioned in the scriptures. In addition to being used for fruit, olives also supplied oil that filled basic needs of the people. Olive oil was used for cooking, healing, lighting, anointing, and many other purposes. Although there are thirty-five to forty species of olive (*Olea*), the cultivated or tame olive (*Olea europaea* L.) and the *oleaster,* or wild olive (*Olea europaea* var. *oleaster*), are the only ones of concern from a scriptural point of view. The tame plants probably originated in the eastern Mediterranean and spread westward. Tame trees were cultivated for their desirable growth patterns and fruit quality. The tame olive has larger fruits with a smaller amount of the bitter glucoside, oleuropein than wild olives. Because tame plants readily hybridize with wild plants, producing seeds of uncertain genetic makeup, it is not desirable to grow new trees from seeds. Desirable plants are therefore usually propagated from cuttings taken from tame trees.

The allegory of Zenos (Jacob 5) relies upon imagery of olive culture. The author of the ALLEGORY was well versed in olive tending. For example, it might seem odd from a traditional botanical perspective that the Lord of the vineyard in the allegory had his servant graft wild branches onto the rootstock of a tame tree (Jacob 5:9–10). Wild branches are usually not used in fruit tree grafting because the wild material retains its wild characteristics even when grafted onto tame root stock. Yet, olive trees often live for centuries, and in ancient olive culture, productive rootstock was sometimes rejuvenated by grafting wild branches, which grow vigorously, onto the rootstock. As the Lord stated in the allegory, this was the reason for grafting in the wild branches, "that perhaps I might preserve the roots thereof that they perish not, that I might preserve them unto myself, I have done this thing" (Jacob 5:11).

Furthermore, more than fifty botanical and cultural principles of olive care can be found in Zenos' allegory of the olive tree (Hess et al., 479–555; Hess, 87–102). Examples include the following: The benefits of being nourished (Jacob 5:3–5, 11, 20, 22–23, 25, 27–28, 31, 34, 47, 58, 63, 71, 75–76), which may include

Olive tree in the garden of Gethsemane; courtesy D. Kelly Ogden.

Olive fruit; courtesy D. Kelly Ogden.

Younger branches growing out of an old olive tree trunk; courtesy Wilford M. Hess.

Olive tree trunk with grafted branches; courtesy Wilford M. Hess.

being dunged (Jacob 5:47, 64, 76) for nutritional purposes. Proper pruning contributes to general tree health and fruit production (Jacob 5:4–5, 11, 27). Young, tender branches will form with proper care (Jacob 5:4, 6). Branches can be grafted (Jacob 5:8–10, 17–18, 30, 34, 52, 54–57, 60, 63–65, 67–68) or planted (Jacob 5:23–25, 43) for new growth. Root and foliage tissue need to be balanced (Jacob 5:37, 48, 65–66). Fruit can be wild (bad or evil) or good (Jacob 5:17–18, 20, 25–27, 30, 32–33, 35–40, 42, 45–46, 52, 54, 60–61, 65, 77). Land for growing trees can be poor or good (Jacob 5:21–23, 25, 43). The roots may perish if the foliage of an otherwise healthy tree is removed or reduced below the ability of the tree to provide photosynthate to the roots (Jacob 5:8, 18, 34, 36, 54, 60, 65–66).

The remarkable detail concerning olive culture in the allegory supports the text's claim of ancient Old World authorship (Jacob 5:1). It is untenable to ascribe its authorship to Joseph Smith. While he probably knew how to prune, dig about, dung, and nourish fruit trees, and perhaps he knew the principles of grafting, he would have known very little about the unique aspects of olive culture found in the allegory because domesticated olives cannot grow in his native northeastern United States. Moreover, it is not likely that an author of the Book of Mormon period would have known enough about olives to compose this remarkable allegory. Olive culture does not appear to have been practiced by Book of Mormon peoples. It is possible that Lehi's family attempted to bring cuttings with them on their journey to establish olive yards in their new promised land, but cuttings would not normally survive the long journey. Moreover, olives require specific ecological conditions to grow and reproduce. Only four limited areas in the New World—California, Arizona, Chile, and Argentina—fit these specific growing conditions. At the time Jacob 5 was recorded on the plates of Nephi (ca. 544 to 521 B.C.) it is probable that only a few dozen people present had ever seen an olive tree. After Jacob 6, olive is not mentioned again in the Book of Mormon.

The most plausible way the Nephites could have known the specific details about olive tending was from the records which they brought with them. As the text testifies, Jacob[2] quoted Zenos, an Old World prophet known to the Nephites from the brass plates (Jacob 5:1). Zenos' writings were not included in the Old Testament.

While the botanical information used in the allegory is very detailed and accurate, there are two startling exceptions that seemingly defy botanical principles: First, if a wild olive branch is grafted onto a tame olive tree, that branch, and all tissue which grows from it, will be genetically different from the tame tree and the fruit. The grafted wild branch should still produce wild olives. Yet surprisingly, in the allegory wild branches grafted into the tame roots began to produce tame fruit (Jacob 5:9, 17–18). This anomaly, wherein the grafted wild branches became tame and bore good fruit, is symbolic of the miraculous conversion that occurs when one is "grafted in" or comes unto Christ and the covenant: one's very nature is changed. Second, a desirable rate of growth will not occur from either wild or tame plants in poor soil, even with tending and digging. Moreover, with an equal amount of effort, the growth in good soil will normally be far superior to growth in poor soil. Yet in the allegory olives growing in poor soil became more productive than those grown in good soil, even though both received equal care (Jacob 5:20–25). Here again the anomaly teaches a gospel truth. It illustrates that regardless of the "soil" or circumstances in which God's children are placed, they can still bring forth "good fruit" if they will respond to the nurturing of the Master (Hess et al., 479–555).

See also Trees; Zenos, allegory of.

BIBLIOGRAPHY

Hess, Wilford M. "Botanical Comparisons in the Allegory of the Olive Tree." *The Book of Mormon: Jacob through Words of Mormon—To Learn with Joy.* Salt Lake City: Desert Book, 1990.

Hess, Wilford M., Daniel J. Fairbanks, John W. Welch, and Jonathan K. Driggs. "Botanical Aspects of Olive Culture Relevant to Jacob 5." *The Allegory of the Olive Tree: The Olive, the Bible, and Jacob 5.* Edited by Stephen D. Ricks and John W. Welch. Salt Lake City: Deseret Book, 1994.

WMH

Omer *See* Jared[1], posterity of.

Omner A son of king Mosiah[2] (ca. 100–74 B.C.). Omner was "numbered among the unbelievers," but after the appearance of an angel, he labored to rectify the damage he had caused endeavoring to destroy the Church (Mosiah 27:8–10, 32–36). Like his brothers, he elected not to succeed his father as king but rather set out with them on what was to be a challenging and ultimately successful fourteen-year Lamanite mission in the land of Nephi (Mosiah 28:1–10; Alma 17:2–18; 23:1–3; 25:17; 26:29–30). Omner, along with his brothers, was described as a man of God (Alma 48:18). He was a man who had a "sound understanding" of the gospel, who had the "spirit of prophecy, and the spirit of revelation" and who taught with power. These qualities are credited to his diligent scripture study and to his "much prayer, and fasting" (Alma 17:2–3). Omner later accompanied Alma[2] on a mission to the Zoramites[2] (Alma 31:6–7).

See also Mosiah[2], sons of.

Omner, city of Strongly fortified Nephite city on the east borders by the seashore (Alma 51:26–27; ca. 67 B.C.). While Moroni[1] was busy subduing the king-men, Amalickiah and his Lamanite army captured many coastal cities, including Omner, which temporarily gave them strongholds in Nephite territory (Alma 51:21–27).

Omni Son of Jarom who made a brief entry on the small plates of Nephi before passing them to his son Amaron. Omni characterized himself as an unrighteous man and acknowledged that he had not kept the commandments "as I ought to have done." Nonetheless, he "fought much with the sword" to preserve the Nephites during "seasons of serious war" (Omni 1:1–3; ca. 361–317 B.C.).

See also Omni, book of.

Omni, book of The final book recorded on the small PLATES OF NEPHI, written by a series of five record keepers—Omni, Amaron, Chemish, Abinadom, and Amaleki[1]—between 361 B.C. and ca. 130 B.C.

OUTLINE OF OMNI

- I. The record of Omni (1:1–3)
  - A. Omni's introduction (1:1–2)
  - B. Many seasons of peace and war between Nephites and Lamanites (1:3)
  - C. Transmission of the plates to Omni's son Amaron (1:3)
- II. The record of Amaron (1:4–8)
  - A. Destruction of wicked Nephites; a verification of the Lord's words (1:4–7)
  - B. Transmission of the plates to Amaron's brother Chemish (Omni 1:8–9)
- III. The record of Chemish (1:9)
  - A. Reception of the plates from Amaron (1:9)
  - B. The manner of record keeping (1:9)
- IV. The record of Abinadom (1:10–11)
  - A. Extensive war between the Nephites and Lamanites (1:10)
  - B. No new revelation or prophecy known (1:10–11)
- V. The record of Amaleki (1:12–30)
  - A. The inspired departure of Mosiah[1] and believers from the land of Nephi (1:12)
  - B. The discovery of the land and people of Zarahemla, and commentary on their origins and struggles (1:13–18)
  - C. Mosiah interprets Jaredite engravings (1:20–22)
  - D. The rule of Mosiah[1] and Benjamin (1:19, 23–24)
  - E. Amaleki's testimony, counsel, and transmission of the plates to Benjamin (1:25–26)
  - F. Nephite excursions to the land of Nephi (1:27–30)

Content and message

The book of Omni reports wars between Nephites and Lamanites, the flight of Mosiah[1] from the land of Nephi with "as many as would hearken unto the voice of the Lord," the discovery of the people of Zarahemla, and the establishment of a new Nephite center in the land of Zarahemla. While Omni is the first to write in the book, Amaleki is the main author. Amaleki recorded that Mosiah's exodus was prompted and guided by revelation (Omni 1:12–13). He wrote that Zarahemla's ancestors had also journeyed to the land with divine assistance, but their language and religion became corrupted because they had no written records. Consequently, they received with joy the "record of the Jews" which Mosiah brought with him to their land. The people of Zarahemla subsequently united with the Nephites, learned their language, and accepted Mosiah as their king (Omni 1:14–19). Amaleki further told how Mosiah exercised divine gifts to interpret engravings on a "large stone" that told of the Jaredites (Omni 1:20–22).

Mosiah's son Benjamin succeeded him as king. During Benjamin's just reign, two groups of Nephites tried to return to the land of Nephi (Omni 1:27–30). The first group failed due to contention among themselves. Amaleki had no knowledge of the fate of the second group, whose history is later recorded in the book of Mosiah (Mosiah 7–22).

The book of Omni shows the fulfillment of prophetic warnings: unrighteous Nephites did not prosper in their land (Omni 1:5–7; cf. 2 Ne. 1:20; Jarom 1:9); God led righteous Nephites out of the land of Nephi (Omni 1:12) to escape Lamanite conquest (Jacob 3:4; cf. 1 Ne. 17:38); and the unrepentant Jaredites were utterly destroyed, their bones heaped on the earth and their land inherited by another people (Omni 1:20–22; cf. Ether 11:6, 20–21; 13:20–21).

See also Zarahemla, people of (Mulekites).

JCT

One eternal round An expression used to testify of God's constancy. Alma[2] testified that God "cannot walk in crooked paths; neither doth he vary from that which he hath said; neither hath he a shadow of turning from the right to the left, or from that which is right to that which is wrong; therefore, his course is one eternal round" (Alma 7:20; cf. 37:12). Therefore, his law operates without variance from all eternity to all eternity. For example, concerning the consistent pattern the Lord has set for receiving revelation, Nephi[1] proclaimed, "He that diligently seeketh shall find; and the mysteries of God shall be unfolded unto them, by the power of the Holy Ghost, as well in these times as in times of old, and as well in times of old as in times to come; wherefore, the course of the Lord is one eternal round" (1 Ne. 10:19).

Mormon testified that "God is not a partial God, neither a changeable being; but he is unchangeable from all eternity to all eternity" (Moro. 8:18). According to Elder Bruce R. McConkie, "when our revelations say of Christ, 'From eternity to eternity he is the same, and his years never fail' (D&C 76:4), they mean that from one preexistence to the next he does not vary, his course is one eternal round. They mean, for instance, that from our premortal or preexistent state to the day when the exalted among us provide a preexistence for our spirit children, he is the same" (McConkie, 166).

See also God, nature of.

BIBLIOGRAPHY

McConkie, Bruce R. *The Promised Messiah*. Salt Lake City: Deseret Book, 1978.

RDD

One God The Father and the Son, resurrected beings with immortal bodies of flesh and bone, together with the Holy Ghost, a "personage of Spirit," constitute the one God of scripture (D&C 130:22; 2 Ne. 31:21; Alma 11:44; 3 Ne. 11:27, 36; The Testimony of the Three Witnesses). This definition of the GODHEAD, known as tritheism, is in contradistinction to the doctrine of trinitarianism, which is one god existing in three coequal, coeternal, and indivisible persons of identical immaterial substance. The unity of the Godhead in the Book of Mormon has been misinterpreted by some as trinitarianism.

Although Christ is a separate and distinct member of the triad Godhead, in the Book of

Mormon he is declared to be "God himself" (Mosiah 13:28, 34; 15:1) who fulfills dual roles, as "the Father and the Son" (Mosiah 15:2–3; Ether 3:14). As the incarnate Son of God he "subjected the flesh to the will of the Father" (Mosiah 15:2–3; cf. D&C 93:3–4; Luke 22:41–42; Philip. 2:5–9). But as the risen Lord, possessing his Father's powers in perfection (3 Ne. 12:48; John 10:36; 14:10), he is the spiritual (not *spirit*) Father of the redeemed. "Born of him," such become "the children of Christ, his sons, and his daughters" (Mosiah 5:7; cf. 27:25; D&C 25:1). Thus Christ is "Son" to his Father, and "Father" to mankind.

Further, a literal rendering of the expression "one God" led some Nephites to the erroneous assumption that there cannot be a *Son* of God (Alma 11:28–35; 14:5). But the oneness of the Godhead is spiritual, not physical, a unity of holiness, minds, and purposes. Thus Jesus, referring to those who believed in him, prayed "that I may be in them as thou, Father, art in me, that we may be one" (3 Ne. 19:23; cf. John 17:21).

The Father, the "most high God" (1 Ne. 11:6), the source of all truth, brought forth the spirits of mankind and presides as Patriarch of the human family. The Son is, by divine investiture, the Creator, "the Father of heaven and of earth" (2 Ne. 25:12; Mosiah 7:27), the "Holy One of Israel" (2 Ne. 6:9), the Messiah, Savior, and Redeemer (1 Ne. 10:4–5), who atoned for all sin, conquered death, and will yet come to his temple in Zion (Alma 34:8; 3 Ne. 24:1–4 // Mal. 3:1–4). In sum, he is "the Lord God Omnipotent" (Mosiah 5:15; cf. Rev. 19:6).

The HOLY GHOST testifies of God the Father and his Only Begotten Son (2 Ne. 31:18; 3 Ne. 11:32). He is the Comforter (Moro. 8:26) and a revelator (2 Ne. 32:5; Moro. 10:4–5). He justifies (2 Ne. 2:5; Moses 6:60), sanctifies (Alma 13:12; 3 Ne. 27:20), and, as the Holy Spirit of promise, seals up the righteous (D&C 88:3–4; 132:7, 9). The distinct, individual members of the Godhead act in concert in bringing to pass the salvation of mankind (3 Ne. 11:32–33). Their combined efforts constitute the labors of the one God.

See also Children of Christ; God the Father; Jesus Christ; Jesus Christ, role of, as Father and Son.

RT

Onidah Called "the place of arms," Onidah was where "the more part" of the Lamanites fled from their king's command to go up to battle against the Nephites (Alma 47:1–5; ca. 72 B.C.).

Onidah, hill A hill in the land of Antionum from which Alma[2] preached to the humbler of the apostate Zoramites[2] (Alma 32:4; ca. 74 B.C.).

Onihah, city of Following his crucifixion, Christ caused waters to cover Onihah and its inhabitants to hide their wickedness that the blood of martyred prophets and Saints would cease to testify against them (3 Ne. 9:7).

Onti *See* Nephite weights and measures.

Opposition in all things The existence of opposing alternatives. For AGENCY to exist (2 Ne. 2:16) and the eternal purposes of God to be fulfilled (2 Ne. 2:12, 15), "it must needs be, that there is an opposition in all things" (2 Ne. 2:11). One could not be righteous and receive the consequence of happiness unless he or she had the alternative to be wicked and receive the consequence of misery (2 Ne. 2:11–13). Lehi[1] taught that without such opposing alternatives or distinctions, "all things must needs be a compound in one," leaving no real choices and thus "destroy[ing] the wisdom of God and his eternal purposes, and also the power, and the mercy, and the justice of God" (2 Ne. 2:11–12).

DLL

Opposition to the Book of Mormon *See* Book of Mormon, opposition to.

Orihah *See* Jared[1], posterity of.

Other sheep Term used by the Savior to describe members of the house of Israel, such as the Nephites and the lost tribes of Israel, who were scattered or separated from their brethren in the Holy Land (3 Ne. 15:15–21; 16:1–3; 17:4). During his mortal ministry Christ referred to himself as the Good Shepherd and the house

OUTER DARKNESS

of Israel as his sheep (John 10:11, 14). Continuing the metaphor, he explained to the Jews in the eastern hemisphere that he had "other sheep . . . which are not of this fold: them also I must bring, and they shall hear my voice; and there shall be one fold, and one shepherd" (John 10:16). Because of "stiffneckedness and unbelief" among the Jews they did not understand Jesus' words (3 Ne. 15:18), and they mistakenly assumed that the "other sheep" to which Jesus referred were the Gentiles (3 Ne. 15:21–22). During his ministry among the Nephites, however, the resurrected Savior revealed that they, as well as other Israelites not living in the Holy Land, were his "other sheep" who were to hear his voice and be part of his fold (3 Ne. 15:15–17, 21; 16:1–3). He also clarified that he would not manifest himself to the Gentiles through a personal ministry but that the Gentiles would learn of Jesus through the preaching of the Jews and the witness of the Holy Ghost (3 Ne. 15:22–23; cf. Matt. 10:5–6; 15:24).

See also Israel, lost tribes of.

RH

Outer darkness Used but once in the Book of Mormon (Alma 40:13) to refer to the state of sons of perdition, a particular group of spirits in the SPIRIT WORLD between death and resurrection. They are the spirits of those who "chose evil works rather than good" during their mortal lives, to the extent that "the spirit of the devil did enter into them, and take possession of their house" (Alma 40:13). Their state is one of "weeping, and wailing, and gnashing of teeth," in "awful, fearful looking for the fiery indignation of the wrath of God upon them" (Alma 40:13–14). Alma[2] explained that "they remain in this state . . . until the time of their resurrection" (Alma 40:14). Alma also affirmed that these spirits will be reunited with their bodies in the resurrection but will then suffer "an awful death . . . for they die as to things pertaining to things of righteousness" (Alma 40:18, 23, 26). Being yet unclean, they cannot enter into the kingdom of God, but inherit the kingdom of the devil (Alma 40:26; 41:1–5). The Doctrine and Covenants uses the term "outer darkness" twice (D&C 101:91; 133:73). Both instances refer to the punishment of the "wicked," or those who "believed not my servants" and "obeyed not my voice," but do not label such punishment as perdition. Doctrine and Covenants 101:90–91 states they will receive "their portion among hypocrites, and unbelievers; even in outer darkness," apparently indicating that when "their portion" has been received (i.e., justice has been satisfied), they will be freed from the sufferings of outer darkness at the last resurrection (D&C 76:85), unlike the sons of perdition who remain with the devil and his angels after the resurrection.

See also Hell; Paradise.

LED

And then shall it come to pass, that the spirits of those who are righteous are received into a state of happiness, which is called **paradise**, a state of rest, a state of peace, where they shall rest from all their troubles and from all care, and sorrow. ALMA 40:12

Paanchi A son of Pahoran[1] who, following the death of his father, contended with two of his brothers, Pahoran[2] and Pacumeni, for the JUDGMENT-SEAT (Hel. 1:2–4; ca. 52 B.C.). When the popular voice chose Pahoran, Pacumeni acceded to the people's will, but Paanchi and his supporters planned a rebellion (Hel. 1:5–7). Before he could carry out his scheme, however, Paanchi was arrested, tried, and condemned to death for rebelling and for seeking "to destroy the liberty" of the Nephites. His followers then engaged "one Kishkumen" to assassinate Pahoran (Hel. 1:8–9).

Pachus King of Nephite DISSENTERS who drove chief judge Pahoran[1] and many freemen out of Zarahemla and also prevented supplies from being sent to afflicted Nephite armies (Alma 61:3–5; ca. 62 B.C.). Pachus made an alliance with the king of the Lamanites that would have granted him continued kingship over the people of Zarahemla had the Lamanites conquered the remainder of the Nephite lands (Alma 61:8). Moroni[1] joined forces with Pahoran at Gideon and defeated the men of Pachus at Zarahemla. Pachus was killed in this battle, and the remaining rebels who "would not take up arms in the defence of their country . . . were put to death" (Alma 62:6–9).

Pacify To calm (1 Ne. 15:20); to alleviate anger or distress (Mosiah 20:19–20); to lull, appease, or tranquilize. For example, while SATAN stirs up anger in some, "others will he pacify, and lull them away into carnal security, that they will say: All is well in Zion; yea, Zion prospereth, all is well—and thus the devil cheateth their souls, and leadeth them away carefully down to hell" (2 Ne. 28:20–21).

See also All is well in Zion.

RHC

Pacumeni Son of Pahoran[1] who, following the death of his father, contended with two of his brothers, Pahoran[2] and Paanchi, for the JUDGMENT-SEAT (Hel. 1:2–4; ca. 52 B.C.). When the popular voice chose Pahoran, Pacumeni united with the people's will, but Paanchi and his supporters rebelled (Hel. 1:5–7). After one of them, a man named Kishkumen, murdered Pahoran, Pacumeni was chosen by the people to be chief judge (Hel. 1:9, 13). This civil unrest allowed the Lamanites to conquer Zarahemla, and their military leader Coriantumr[3] killed Pacumeni (Hel. 1:18–21).

Pagag The firstborn son of the brother of Jared[1], Pagag was chosen king by the people but refused the position. When the people wanted his father to prevail upon him, the brother of Jared "commanded" that they "constrain no man to be their king" (Ether 6:25).

Pahoran[1] Third chief judge of the Nephites (ca. 68 B.C.), Pahoran succeeded his father Nephihah to the judgment-seat (Alma 50:40). Although Pahoran began his rule in a time of relative peace, that peace soon gave way to internal strife. A segment of Nephite society began agitating for a monarchy to replace the government of judges elected by the people. The KING-MEN, as the dissenters were called, were defeated in a general election and then, because of the critical state of affairs (Alma 51:7, 9, 13), they were compelled to defend Nephite liberty and lands or be killed or imprisoned (Alma 51:19). The struggle of Pahoran to maintain his seat as chief judge had nothing to do with a personal desire for power. Rather, the struggle came from his commitment to maintain the rights and freedoms of the people he served (Alma 51:3–7).

Mormon elected to include in his abridgment the full text of three important EPISTLES exchanged during Pahoran's rule. These letters, taken as a whole, illustrate Pahoran's incredible magnanimity and forgiving nature. The letters were written in the midst of warfare with the external and internal enemies of the Church and state. The first letter, from Helaman[2] to Moroni[1], details victories, defeats, and sufferings attributed to the apparent neglect of Pahoran and his government to send provisions and reinforcements to the battlefront (Alma 58:3–9, 34–36). Moroni sent an epistle to Pahoran requesting more men for Helaman's army, but it was not included in the record and Pahoran may have never received it (Alma 59:3). The second epistle included was again from Moroni to Pahoran (Alma 60), and the third is from Pahoran to

Moroni (Alma 61). Angered at the circumstances and at Pahoran's failure to answer his first request, Moroni sent a scathing letter to the chief judge. He went so far as to accuse Pahoran of being a traitor, and he threatened to march on Zarahemla and make war on him (Alma 60:27–30).

Pahoran's reply is an example of Christ's injunction to turn the other cheek, and it teaches the modern reader the appropriate way to respond to false accusations (3 Ne. 12:11; Matt. 5:11). Rather than responding angrily, Pahoran quietly explained that he had been driven out of Zarahemla and his government taken over by dissenters. Then he wrote, "In your epistle you have censured me, but it mattereth not; I am not angry, but do rejoice in the greatness of your heart" (Alma 61:9). That Pahoran did not take offense when wrongly accused, that he did not return the wrong but instead absorbed it, defines the man. Understanding now that the government would have to be won back, Pahoran took heart and, with Moroni, defeated the enemies of liberty. Having been restored to the judgment-seat, he marched with Moroni to retake the fallen city of Nephihah (Alma 62:18–26). After a series of wars, peace was established, and Pahoran returned to the judgment-seat (Alma 62:44). The father of many sons, Pahoran died in about 52 B.C. (Hel. 1:2–4).

MA

Pahoran[2] Fourth chief judge of the Nephites (ca. 52 B.C.), Pahoran succeeded his father, Pahoran[1], to the JUDGMENT-SEAT. One of three sons who sought the position, he was elected by the people. Those who favored the election of his brother Paanchi sent Kishkumen to murder him "as he sat upon the judgment-seat" (Hel. 1:9).

MA

Paradise The state of happiness, peace, and rest enjoyed by the spirits of the righteous in the interval between death and resurrection (Alma 40:12). In the Book of Mormon the term "paradise," or an extended phrase, "paradise of God" is used by Jacob[2] (2 Ne. 9:13), Alma[2] (Alma 40:12,14), Mormon (4 Ne. 1:14), and Moroni[2] (Moro. 10:34). The term is used in other scriptures with a different or broadened meaning. It sometimes refers to HEAVEN or the rewards of the righteous (D&C 77:2, 5; 2 Cor. 12:4; Rev. 2:7). In regard to the Savior's words to the thief on the cross in Luke 23:43, Joseph Smith explained that the meaning was "This day thou shalt be with me in the world of spirits" (309).

See also Outer darkness; Spirit world.

BIBLIOGRAPHY

Smith, Joseph. *Teachings of the Prophet Joseph Smith.* Selected by Joseph Fielding Smith. Salt Lake City: Deseret Book, 1976.

LED

Parallelism A poetic device used commonly in ancient Hebrew literature. There are literally hundreds of parallelisms in both the Bible and the Book of Mormon. Parallelisms consist of short, balanced lines of text (phrases or sentences) with words or thoughts in one line that parallel or correspond with those in a subsequent line or lines. The words or thoughts in the later instances repeat, echo, build upon, or are symmetrical counterparts of earlier lines. In contrast to English poetry, parallelisms rarely feature rhymes of consonance or assonance (repeated vowel sounds), rather, they present a repetition of two ideas, or a rhyming of thought. The thoughts may "rhyme" or correspond in a number of ways, including the following:

Identical words or phrases, such as "light–light" and "cry unto him–cry unto him."

Antonyms, such as "holy–unholy," "poor–rich," and "grievous words–soft answer."

Synonyms or near synonyms, such as "heart–soul" and "statutes–commandments."

Gradations, an increase or decrease of the sense or idea, such as "the prince became king," and "forget God–sin against the Lord."

Complementaries, such as "bows–arrows" and "river–sea."

Different inflections of the same root, such as "to judge," "a judge," "judgment," and "judgment-seat."

Superordinates, such as "breastplates–shields," "wine–drink," and "gold–metal."

Reciprocals, such as "to retire–to sleep," "to eat–to be full," and "to sin–pain of conscience."

Parallelism appears to have been used for two chief purposes: emphasis and clarification. For example, Nephi[1] used a two-line parallelism not only to emphasize the sorrow that comes because of iniquity but also to clarify and teach about how such sorrow affects one and what may be the cause or source of iniquity:

> Yea, my heart sorroweth because of my flesh;
> my soul grieveth because of mine iniquities. (2 Ne. 4:17)

Several terms from the first line have corresponding elements in the second. The expression "my heart" parallels "my soul" suggesting that sorrow for sin is felt both in one's "heart," or thoughts and feelings, and in one's "soul," or body and spirit. The terms "sorroweth" and "grieveth" are synonymous, both emphatic and descriptive of the anguish associated with sin. The words "because of mine iniquities" of line two parallel "because of my flesh" of line one, suggesting that there is a connection between sin and the flesh or "natural man" (cf. Mosiah 3:19). Thus the parallelisms here convey the prophetic word with great clarity, permitting the reader who will recognize and ponder them to obtain new levels of knowledge and greater insights.

There are many types of parallelistic structures in the Book of Mormon, including CHIASMUS, synonymous, antithetical, repeating, and extended alternate. These may consist of two lines, four lines, six lines, or more (Parry, "Reformatted" 1992).

An example of a ten-line parallelism is found in Alma 5:28–29 (*see* fig. 1).

The bolded words of the two "a" lines correspond with each other, creating parallel lines. The same is true of the "b" lines, the "c" lines, and so on. Both of the "a" lines form an interrogative sentence, both begin with the exclamation "behold," and both have the parallel phrase "stripped of pride//stripped of envy." The "b" lines feature the synonymous phrases "ye are not prepared//such an one is not prepared." The "c" lines have the identical phrase "prepare quickly." "Soon at hand" harmonizes with "close at hand" in the "d" lines, and "one hath not eternal life" corresponds with "one is not found guiltless" in the "e" lines. Thus in several aspects the parallelism is found to possess corresponding elements, the lower half of the parallelism representing a counterpart or near mirror image of the upper half. The use of parallelism here emphasizes and invites the reader to evaluate the state of his or her soul and to prepare to meet God.

An eight-line parallelism in 1 Nephi 19 alternates four truths about Jesus Christ's atoning sacrifice (in the four lines labeled "a") with four attributions (in the four lines labeled "b"), emphasizing that these truths were revealed and known of old (*see* fig. 2).

Many other truths are set forth in parallelisms. In Helaman 12:9–15 fourteen lines are alternated to emphasize and teach about the omnipotence of God (*see* fig. 3).

The seven lines marked "a" pertain to God's commands to the earth (represented by "his voice" four times, "if he say" twice, and "his word" once); the seven lines marked "b" deal with the earth's obedience to his commands by its moving "hither and thither" (represented

a Behold, are ye **stripped of pride?**
  b I say unto you, if ye are not **ye are not prepared** to meet God.
    c Behold ye must **prepare quickly;**
      d for the kingdom of heaven is **soon at hand,**
        e and such an **one hath not eternal life.**
a Behold, I say, is there one among you who is not **stripped of envy?**
  b I say unto you that **such an one is not prepared;**
    c and I would that he should **prepare quickly,**
      d for the hour is **close at hand,** and he knoweth not when the time shall come;
        e for such an **one is not found guiltless.**

Fig. 1

a the God of Jacob, yieldeth himself,
 b according to the words of the angel,
a as a man, into the hands of wicked men, to be lifted up,
 b according to the words of Zenock,
a and to be crucified,
 b according to the words of Neum,
a and to be buried in a sepulchre,
 b according to the words of Zenos. (1 Ne. 19:10)

Fig. 2

a Yea, behold at **his voice**
 b do the hills and the mountains **tremble and quake.**
a And by the power of **his voice**
 b they are **broken up**, and become smooth, yea, even like unto a valley.
a Yea, by the power of **his voice**
 b doth the whole earth **shake**;
a Yea, by the power of **his voice**,
 b do the foundations **rock**, even to the very center.
a Yea, and if **he say** unto the earth—
 b Move—it is **moved.**
a Yea, if **he say** unto the earth—
 b Thou shalt **go back**, that it lengthen out the day for many hours—it is done;
a And thus, according to **his word**
 b the earth **goeth back.**

Fig. 3

by "tremble and quake," "broken up," "shake," "rock," "moved," "go back," and "goeth back"). The particle "yea" begins five of the "a" lines, while synonymous elements in the "b" lines present geographical terms: "hills," "mountains," "valley," "whole earth," "foundations" of the earth, and "earth," repeated three times.

Alma[2] taught the "meaning of the word restoration" to his son by using a parallelistic pattern called climax ("climax occurs when the same word or words are found in successive clauses or sentences"; Parry, 296). Alma said, "The meaning of the word restoration is to bring back again

evil for
evil, or
carnal for
carnal, or
devilish for
devilish—
good for that which is
good;
righteous for that which is
righteous;
just for that which is
just;
merciful for that which is
merciful. (Alma 41:13)

Note the repetition of seven different words in this parallelism. This climactic pattern is followed immediately by additional teachings on restoration as Alma further used parallelism to emphasize and clarify to his son that God deals with his children as they deal with others (*see* fig. 4).

In this extended parallelism the "a" lines are parallel, as are the "b" lines, the "c" lines, and so forth through the "f" lines. Alma balanced the top half of the parallelism (the first six lines) with the bottom half (the lower six lines) by repeating the key words (*mercy, justice, righteous judgment, good,* etc.).

Such use of parallelism by Book of Mormon authors confirms the ancient origin of the text.

a Therefore, my son, see that you are **merciful** unto your brethren;
  b deal **justly**,
    c **judge righteously**,
      d and do **good** continually;
        e and if **ye do** all these things
          f then **shall ye receive** your reward;
a yea, ye shall have **mercy** restored unto you again;
  b ye shall have **justice** restored unto you again;
    c ye shall have a **righteous judgment** restored unto you again;
      d and ye shall have **good** rewarded unto you again.
        e For that which **ye do** send out
          f **shall return unto you** again, and be restored. (Alma 41:14–15)

Fig. 4

See also Book of Mormon, as literature; Book of Mormon, poetry in; Nephi[1]'s psalm.

BIBLIOGRAPHY

Parry, Donald W. *The Book of Mormon Text Reformatted According to Parallelistic Patterns.* Provo, Utah: FARMS, 1992.

———. "Power through Repetition: The Dynamics of Book of Mormon Parallelism." *Book of Mormon Authorship Revisited: The Evidence for Ancient Origins.* Edited by Noel B. Reynolds. Provo, Utah: FARMS, 1997.

DWP

Parenting Throughout the Book of Mormon, principles of good parenting are demonstrated by God, the Father of all spirits, as well as Jesus Christ, the Father of salvation. Book of Mormon fathers and mothers also provide positive examples of parenting.

The account in the Book of Mormon of God's dealings with his children illustrates his loving and nurturing disposition. He knows them individually (Morm. 6:22), wants their happiness, and provides a way for them to achieve it (2 Ne. 2:24–25; Morm. 7:7). He sets reasonable expectations and rules for his children which, if followed, will protect, bless, and help them progress (1 Ne. 3:7; 2 Ne. 2:5; Mosiah 2:22). He gives his rules or commandments after explaining the larger plan into which they fit (Alma 12:32). He allows his children to make choices (2 Ne. 2:16), and by providing means for them to be "instructed sufficiently that they know good from evil," he ensures that they understand the consequences of those choices (2 Ne. 2:5, 27).

He encourages ingenuity within designated boundaries, allowing his children to grow through their own efforts to solve problems that arise (Ether 2:22–25). He is consistent (1 Ne. 10:18), fair with his discipline, and applies appropriate principles of justice and mercy (2 Ne. 9:17, 19; Jacob 4:10; Alma 41:3). He is honest in keeping his promises and covenants with his children (Enos 1:6, 16–17; 3 Ne. 16:11; 21:4). He warns them when they are in danger (2 Ne. 1:3; 5:5; Mosiah 23:1), forgives them when they repent (Enos 1:5; Mosiah 26:22; 3 Ne.13:14–15), consoles and supports them when they experience trials (2 Ne. 8:12; Jacob 3:1; Alma 17:10; 36:3), and is willing to assist them when they ask for help (2 Ne. 4:35; 3 Ne. 14:7–11). In all things he is perfect in his response with his children and thus he is a perfect model to emulate (3 Ne. 12:48).

Book of Mormon fathers and mothers were exemplary as parents in teaching their children gospel principles. President Ezra Taft Benson observed that Book of Mormon parents taught their children the plan of salvation. He stated that the "overarching message" of righteous Book of Mormon fathers was "'the great plan of the Eternal God'—the Fall, rebirth, Atonement, Resurrection, Judgment, [and] eternal life" (36). As Alma[2] rehearsed the plan of salvation to his wayward son Corianton, he reminded him that his ministry was to teach the great plan, or "glad tidings," to the people that they might "prepare the minds of their children to hear the word at the time of his coming" (Alma 39:16).

The Book of Mormon record keepers often

attributed their success to parents who taught them. Nephi[1] declared that "having been born of goodly parents, therefore I was taught somewhat in all the learning of my father" (1 Ne. 1:1). Enos also declared that his father "taught [him] in his language, and also in the nurture and admonition of the Lord—and blessed be the name of my God for it" (Enos 1:1). Alma the Younger was saved from despairing over his sins when he "remembered also to have heard [his] father prophesy unto the people concerning the coming of one Jesus Christ, a Son of God, to atone for the sins of the world" (Alma 36:17).

The importance of mothers teaching their children is also illustrated in the Book of Mormon. As Helaman[2] related to Moroni[1] the bravery of the young warriors he called his sons, he stated: "Now they never had fought, yet they did not fear death; and they did think more upon the liberty of their fathers than they did upon their lives; yea, they had been taught by their mothers, that if they did not doubt, God would deliver them. And they rehearsed unto me the words of their mothers, saying: We do not doubt our mothers knew it" (Alma 56:47–48). These young men attributed the faith that preserved them in battle to the righteous teachings of their mothers.

Parental lessons can also be gleaned from the emphasis given to teaching children gospel doctrine. King Benjamin taught his sons the "language of his fathers" that they might understand the "prophecies which had been spoken by the mouths of their fathers" (Mosiah 1:2). In an effort to penetrate the rationalizations of his sinful son Corianton, Alma[2] taught him important gospel doctrines concerning the afterlife, including the resurrection, the Judgment, and the relationship between justice and mercy (Alma 40–42). Nephi[2] and Lehi[4], just prior to their challenging mission to Nephite apostates and Lamanites, remembered important doctrinal teachings that their father Helaman[3] quoted from king Benjamin and Amulek (Hel. 5:9–19).

In his address at the temple in Zarahemla, king Benjamin taught Nephite parents concerning the true source of strength and motivation to accomplish their parental duties. He enumerated the attitudes and actions that characterize those who have tasted the love of God and who have received a remission of their sins (Mosiah 4:11–13). Parents thus empowered would "not suffer [their] children that they go hungry, or naked; neither [would they] suffer that they transgress the laws of God, and fight and quarrel one with another, and serve the devil. . . . But [they would] teach them to walk in the ways of truth and soberness; [they would] teach them to love one another, and to serve one another" (Mosiah 4:14–15).

Although some in the Book of Mormon were prompted to faithfulness because of parental teachings, others were led to apostasy and wickedness because of the "traditions of their fathers," which were "incorrect" (Mosiah 1:5; Alma 3:8; 9:16; 17:15). The teaching of Lamanite traditions by Lamanite parents instilled in their children a desire to destroy the Nephites, their records, and their traditions (Enos 1:14, 20; Mosiah 10:12–17). Thus the influence of parents, whether righteous or wicked, can have an enduring influence upon their posterity.

See also Stripling warriors.

BIBLIOGRAPHY

Benson, Ezra Taft. "Worthy Fathers, Worthy Sons." *Ensign* 15 (November 1985): 35–37.

GLD

Parents, goodly *See* Goodly parents.

Past feeling Expression used by Nephi[1] (1 Ne. 17:45), Mormon (Moro. 9:20), and Paul (Eph. 4:19) to describe an individual's inability to perceive spiritual things as a result of personal unrighteousness. The ability to recognize spiritual impressions that come to one's mind and heart through the HOLY GHOST depends on righteous living and adherence to God's laws. When Nephi used this expression to describe his rebellious brothers he added, "Ye could not feel [the angel's] words" (1 Ne. 17:45). Reference was made not to their ability to hear the message with their ears but to feel it in their hearts. Elder Boyd K. Packer stated, "I have come to know that inspiration comes more as a feeling than as a sound" (20). Paul wrote to the Corinthians that the "natural man receiveth not the things of the Spirit of God: for they are foolishness unto him: neither can he know them, because they are spiritually discerned" (1 Cor. 2:11–14). The LIGHT OF CHRIST that proceeds forth from the presence of God to fill the immensity of space enlightens people's minds and quickens their understanding (D&C 88:11–13). This light forsakes the adversary and is diminished through disobedience (D&C 93:37, 39). Through righteous living, a person gains more and more spiritual light. Through unrighteousness, light progressively decreases until a person is past the ability to feel or perceive it (Alma 12:9–11; D&C 50:24; 88:67; JST Matt. 13:10–11; Smith, 94–95).

See also Revelation.

BIBLIOGRAPHY

Packer, Boyd K. "Prayers and Answers." *Ensign* 9 (November 1979): 19–21.

Smith, Joseph. *Teachings of the Prophet Joseph Smith.* Selected by Joseph Fielding Smith. Salt Lake City: Deseret Book, 1976.

TBP

Patience Calm endurance; bearing such things as provocation, annoyance, misfortune, pain, or delay without complaint. Patience is an attribute of God (Mosiah 4:6; Alma 9:26) as well as an attribute of one who has yielded "to the enticings of the Holy Spirit," has put off the "natural man," and has become a "saint through the atonement of Christ" (Mosiah 3:19; Alma 13:28).

Many noteworthy examples of patience are found in the Book of Mormon, including Alma[1] and his followers, who did "submit cheerfully and with patience to all the will of the Lord" even when in bondage to the Lamanites (Mosiah 24:15); the Nephite Saints, who at the time of Nehor "bore with patience the persecution which was heaped upon them" (Alma 1:25); and the brethren of Ammon[2], who as missionaries patiently endured being bound naked in a Lamanite prison, suffering "hunger, thirst, and all kinds of afflictions" (Alma 20:29). The foremost example of this godly attribute is Jesus Christ, whom Alma[2] described as being "full of patience" (Alma 9:26).

God wants his children to develop and demonstrate patience. Thus, Alma[2] entreated the people to be "full of patience" (Alma 7:23). Amulek exhorted the people to patience and warned that lacking it leads to sin (Alma 34:40–41). Alma, recognizing that God can bless a person with patience, pled with the Lord to give him this virtue (Alma 31:31). Later Alma praised his son Shiblon for his patience among the Zoramites[2] and acknowledged that he, Shiblon, was able to endure adversity patiently "because the Lord was with" him (Alma 38:3–4).

The Lord tries the patience of his children and rewards those who exercise it (Mosiah 23:21). He lightened the burdens of the people of Alma[1] while they were in bondage to the Lamanites, and because of their faith and patience he eventually delivered them from that bondage (Mosiah 24:15–16). The Lord admonished Ammon[2] and the other sons of Mosiah[2] to be patient in LONG-SUFFERING and afflictions as missionaries among the Lamanites, in order that they "show forth good examples." Then, the Lord pronounced, "I will make an instrument of thee in my hands unto the salvation of many souls" (Alma 17:11). Later Ammon[2] testified that their patience did indeed contribute to their great success (Alma 26:27–31). Alma[2] identified patience as a key element in acquiring spiritual truths through faith on the "word" (Alma 32:22–42). He taught, "Because of your diligence and your faith and your patience with the word in nourishing it, that it may take root in you, behold, by and by ye shall pluck the fruit thereof, which is most precious, . . . and ye shall feast upon this fruit even until you are filled, that ye hunger not, neither shall ye thirst" (Alma 32:42).

MMM

Peace The Book of Mormon teaches about two types of peace: civil and spiritual. Civil peace, the absence of physical and social conflict, was sought after and prized by the righteous in the Book of Mormon. Kings established it (Mosiah 29:14), and at times armies enforced it (Alma 3:23–24). Throughout the Book of Mormon martial force was legitimately invoked for the preservation of civil peace (e.g., Alma 43:45–47; 44:1–7; 48:21–25).

Nephi[1] prophesied that the Nephites would enjoy three generations of peace after the Savior's advent (2 Ne. 26:9; cf. 1 Ne. 12:11–12). This peace was both civil and spiritual. Indeed, the Nephite society flourished in righteousness: "There were no contentions and disputations among them, and . . . [there was] peace in the land" (4 Ne. 1:2, 4, 15). As "prosperity in Christ" led to material prosperity, pride led to apostasy, which eventually resulted in the total destruction of an entire people (4 Ne.; Morm. 6).

The Book of Mormon illustrates repeatedly, however, that even when civil peace does not exist, the righteous may find peace within themselves (e.g., 1 Ne. 20:18 // Isa. 48:18). This spiritual peace is a "peace of conscience" granted by the Spirit to the faithful, through the application of the atonement of Jesus Christ (Mosiah 4:1–3). Alma[2] taught that the "peace of God" is bestowed "according to [one's] faith and good works" (Alma 7:27; cf. D&C 19:23).

Peace is the correlative of "life eternal" (1 Ne. 14:7), and the antitheses of hardness of heart and blindness of mind: "There is no peace, saith the Lord, unto the wicked" (1 Ne. 20:22 // Isa. 48:22).

Jesus is the "founder" of "the peace of God, which passeth all understanding" (Philip. 4:7). Because of his atonement, people can be redeemed from sin and death (Mosiah 15:17–19) and "partake of the goodness of God, that they might enter into his rest" (Jacob 1:7; cf. Alma 40:12). Hence, "how beautiful upon the mountains are the feet of him that bringeth good tidings; that publisheth peace" (Mosiah 12:21; 15:14–18).

For the penitent, peace is the fruit of the mercy of the Prince of Peace, as Alma testified: "Never, until I did cry out unto the Lord Jesus Christ for mercy, did I receive a remission of my sins. But behold, I did cry unto him and I did find peace to my soul" (Alma 38:8).

Joseph[1] prophesied that in the latter days the Book of Mormon and the Bible would "grow together" and help to establish peace among his descendants (2 Ne. 3:12).

Concerning those who seek to establish peace, both civil and spiritual, Jesus proclaimed in his sermon at the temple in Bountiful, "Blessed are all the peacemakers, for they shall be called the children of God" (3 Ne. 12:9).

CG

Pearl of Great Price, what it says about the Book of Mormon The Pearl of Great Price gives an account of how Joseph Smith received the gold plates from the angel Moroni (JS–H 1:29–59) as well as a description of two important events that occurred as the Book of Mormon was being translated. These include Martin Harris's encounter with Professor Charles Anthon (JS–H 1:63–65) in fulfillment of the prophecy of Isaiah (Isa. 29:11; cf. 2 Ne. 27:15–17), and the restoration of the Aaronic Priesthood by John the Baptist (JS–H 1:68–72). Other insights about the Book of Mormon from the pages of the Pearl of Great Price include Moroni's testimony to Joseph Smith that the gold plates contained the fulness of the gospel of Jesus Christ, as well as an account of the former inhabitants of the American continent and "the source from whence they sprang" (JS–H 1:34); the Lord's promise to Enoch that in the last days "truth will I send forth out of the earth, to bear testimony of mine Only Begotten" (Moses 7:62), a clear reference to the Book of Mormon and its important role as another testament of Jesus Christ; and the eighth Article of Faith which explicitly states that the Church accepts the Book of Mormon as the word of God (A of F 8).

See also The Coming Forth of the Book of Mormon, 9; Anthon transcript; Book of Mormon, and Article of Faith 8; Moroni[2], visits of, to Joseph Smith.

MDR

> **62 And [a]righteousness will I send down out of heaven; and truth will I send forth out of the earth, to bear [b]testimony of mine Only Begotten; his [c]resurrection from the dead; yea, and also the resurrection of all men; and righteousness and truth will I cause to sweep the earth as with a flood...**

Moses 7:62

Penitent *See* Appendix C.

People, voice of *See* Voice of the people.

Peradventure *See* Appendix C.

Perdition, son of *See* Son of perdition.

Perfection A state of consummate excellence, being all-powerful, all-knowing, possessing every virtue, lacking nothing. God the Father and Jesus Christ are perfect, and all mankind are enjoined to become perfect as they are (3 Ne. 12:48; cf. 27:27). Achieving such perfection during mortality, however, is not possible. Joseph Smith encouraged his hearers to "go on to perfection," explaining: "When you climb up a ladder, you must begin at the bottom, and ascend step by step, until you arrive at the top; and so it is with the principles of the Gospel—you must begin with the first, and go on until you learn all the principles of exaltation. But it will be a great while after you have passed through the veil before you will have learned them. It is not all to be comprehended in this world; it will be a great work to learn our salvation and exaltation even beyond the grave" (364, 348).

Although ultimate perfection is not possible in mortality, mankind may enjoy elements of perfection on earth through the GRACE of Christ and by the power of the HOLY GHOST. Moroni[2] exhorted all to "come unto Christ, and be perfected in him, and deny yourselves of all ungodliness; and if ye shall deny yourselves of all ungodliness, and love God with all your might, mind and strength, then is his grace sufficient for you, that by his grace ye may be perfect in Christ . . . then are ye sanctified in Christ by the grace of God, through the shedding of the blood of Christ, which is in the covenant of the Father unto the remission of your sins, that ye become holy, without spot" (Moro. 10:32–33). Though lacking complete knowledge, understanding, power, and other elements of perfection, such covenant people are perfectly justified, perfectly cleansed from their sins. Similarly, Book of Mormon prophets speak of men having "perfect faith" (2 Ne. 9:23), "a perfect brightness of hope" (2 Ne. 31:20), "perfect knowledge" of certain principles (Jacob 4:12; Alma 32:26–35; Ether 3:20; Moro. 7:15–17), "perfect understanding" (Alma 48:11), and "perfect love" (Moro. 8:16–17, 26), all of which are made possible through the ATONEMENT of Christ and the power of the Comforter, the Holy Ghost (Jacob 4:8, 13; Moro. 8:26). Attaining Godlike perfection is thus a long-term, step-by-step process with rewards along the way. Joseph Smith explained that "God has created man with a mind capable of instruction, and a faculty which may be enlarged in proportion to the heed and diligence given to the light communicated from heaven to the intellect; and that the nearer man approaches perfection, the clearer are his views, and the greater his enjoyments, till he has overcome the evils of his life and lost every desire for sin. . . . But we consider that this is a station to which no man ever arrived in a moment" (51).

See also Merits of Christ.

BIBLIOGRAPHY

Smith, Joseph. *Teachings of the Prophet Joseph Smith*. Selected by Joseph Fielding Smith. Salt Lake City: Deseret Book, 1976.

LED

Performances and ordinances Commandments given under the LAW OF MOSES to help the children of Israel come to Christ. Nephi[1], Abinadi, and Alma[2] reminded the Nephites that observance of these "performances and ordinances" pointed them toward the coming of the Messiah but would be fulfilled after his coming (2 Ne. 25:30; Mosiah 13:30; Alma 25:15). From this one can deduce that the performances and ordinances were that part of the law of Moses referred to in Hebrews 7:16 as "carnal commandment[s]," perhaps referring to the SACRIFICES, rituals of purification, or festivals that were a part of the law of Moses fulfilled in Christ. Lehi[1] and his descendants lived the gospel, following the law of Moses until the coming of Christ (2 Ne. 25:23–24; Jacob 4:5; Mosiah 13:27–28). While the phrase does not occur in the KJV, it is probably the equivalent of such biblical phrases as "a statute and an ordinance" (Ex. 15:25), "ordinances and laws" (Ex. 18:20), "statutes and . . . judgments" (Lev. 18:26; 2 Ne. 5:10). Korihor ridiculed these commandments, calling them "foolish" (Alma 30:23), and Mormon noted after the coming of Christ the people no longer followed them (4 Ne. 1:12).

DRS

Persecute, persecution To oppress, harass, or ill-treat another because of his or her beliefs, social status, or religious practices. Alma[2] and his followers, for example, were persecuted "with all manner of words" because of their "humility . . . and because they did impart the word of God . . . without money" (Alma 1:20). The Book of Mormon describes various sources of persecution that led to division and strife: prideful individuals who taught false doctrine (Alma 1:16, 19; Jacob 7:2–3; cf. 2 Ne. 28:3–4, 13–14), unbelievers (1 Ne. 16:37–38; 17:18; Mosiah 27:1; 3 Ne. 1:5–9), and apostate dissenters who left the Church (Hel. 4:1). But the chief cause of persecution was PRIDE, engendered by RICHES (3 Ne. 6:10, 12–13; Hel. 3:34–36; Jacob 2:13). Those who were rich as to things of the world, who were puffed up in the pride of their hearts, despised the poor and persecuted the meek supposing they were better (2 Ne. 9:30; Jacob 2:13, 20; Alma 5:53–54; 32:2–3; cf. 2 Ne. 28:13; Alma 4:8; Morm. 8:36).

The main target of persecutors were members of the Church of God (Mosiah 26:38; Alma 1:19; 4 Ne. 1:29). Alma the Elder and his followers were persecuted by Amulon, even to the point of Amulon's causing "that his children should persecute [Alma's] children" (Mosiah 24:8–9). Likewise, after his conversion Alma the Younger preached the word of God despite much tribulation, "being greatly persecuted by those who were unbelievers, being smitten by many of them" (Mosiah 27:32).

In an effort to stop persecution of believers in his day, king Mosiah[2] sent a proclamation throughout the land that unbelievers should not persecute any who belonged to the church of God (Mosiah 27:3), a measure that evidently had little effect, at least in regard to the newly converted Alma[2] and the four sons of king Mosiah (Mosiah 27:32). There was also "a strict law among the people of the church" not to persecute one another or those who did not belong to the Church (Alma 1:21). When the righteous ruled, laws prohibited persecution and required tolerance for believers in Christ (Mosiah 27:2–3; Alma 30:7). When the wicked ruled, believers were persecuted (Alma 14:6–9; 3 Ne. 1:5–9). Occasionally, this persecution led to armed conflict (Alma 2:1–4, 10–12).

The Saints, "steadfast and immovable in keeping the commandments of God," bore with patience the persecution heaped upon them (Alma 1:25). Only the humble and penitent before God would not revile at the persecution they received (3 Ne. 6:13). Saints were commanded to pray for those who persecuted them (3 Ne. 12:44). Persecution caused some church members to suffer greatly (Mosiah 24:10), and others were led by persecuting unbelievers to commit sin (Mosiah 27:1, 8–9).

The righteous who "hearken unto the words of the prophets . . . notwithstanding all persecution" will not perish (2 Ne. 26:8). Those persecuted for the Savior's name's sake will inherit the "kingdom of heaven" and "great shall be [their] reward in heaven; for so persecuted they the prophets" (3 Ne. 12:10–12).

WJM

Persons, respecter of *See* Respecter of persons.

Pharaoh The supreme and absolute ruler of ancient Egypt. The destruction of Pharaoh's armies in the RED SEA, an example of God's strength and power to deliver his people, was recalled twice by Nephi[1] to motivate his family to trust in God (1 Ne. 4:2; 17:27; Ex. 14:26–30).

Pickets *See* Appendix C.

Pillar of fire The Lord has often used a pillar of fire to symbolize his glory and power, such as with the children of Israel in the wilderness (Ex. 13:21–22), the call of Lehi[1] (1 Ne. 1:6–8), and the ministry of Nephi[2] and Lehi[4], sons of Helaman[3] (Hel. 5:24, 43–44). These occurrences attest to the outpouring of the Spirit and power of the Almighty.

JFM

Pit, the A state of suffering, ignorance, or bondage brought about by the wickedness of

PLAIN AND PRECIOUS THINGS

men and devils. Nephi[1] wrote of a "great pit" of false religion designed to produce the spiritual destruction of mankind (1 Ne. 14:3; 22:14). He prophesied that in the latter days many who justified themselves in "a little sin" would say, "Dig a pit for thy neighbor; there is no harm in this" (2 Ne. 28:8). Joseph Smith prayed that "he who diggeth a pit" for the Lord's people "shall fall into the same himself" (D&C 109:25). Isaiah employed the term to characterize the physical and spiritual bondage from which scattered Israel would be delivered in latter days (2 Ne. 8:14; cf. D&C 113:7–10) and described Lucifer's eventual exile in hell as being "to the sides of the pit" (2 Ne. 24:15).

RT

Plain and precious things, loss of and restoration of Nephi[1] learned in vision that at one time the scriptural records that would eventually become the Bible "contained the fulness of the gospel of the Lord" and went forth "from the Jews in purity unto the Gentiles." He saw, further, "the formation of [a] great and abominable church, which is most abominable above all other churches; for behold, they have taken away from the gospel of the Lamb many parts which are plain and most precious; and also many covenants of the Lord have they taken away" (1 Ne. 13:24–26). These excisions from the gospel of Jesus Christ were intentional and purposeful. The angel who appeared to Nephi explained, "All this have they done that they might pervert the right ways of the Lord, that they might blind the eyes and harden the hearts of the children of men" (1 Ne. 13:27). This extraction of gospel truth extended to the scriptural records. Nephi saw that "after the book [had] gone forth through the hands of the great and abominable church . . . there [were] many plain and precious things taken away from the book" (1 Ne. 13:28).

The book that the angel described to Nephi is clearly the Bible, including the Old and New Testaments. The angel described it as a book that "proceeded forth from the mouth of a Jew" (1 Ne. 13:24), consisting of "a record of the Jews, which contains the covenants of the Lord" and "many of the prophecies of the holy prophets . . . like unto the engravings which are upon the plates of brass" (1 Ne. 13:23). In addition, "when it proceeded forth from the mouth of a Jew . . . [it] contained the fulness of the gospel of the Lord, of whom the twelve apostles bear record" (1 Ne. 13:24). References to "the book" Nephi was shown are to both the Bible, with which modern readers are familiar (1 Ne. 13:20, 29, 38), and to the early scriptural records from which the Bible would be compiled (1 Ne. 13:24–28). The book (biblical source records) would suffer omissions at the hand of the GREAT AND ABOMINABLE CHURCH "after they go forth by the hand of the twelve apostles of the Lamb" (first and second century), and the resulting book (the Bible that Nephi saw centuries later among the Gentiles) would reflect those omissions.

In the light of the Restoration and with the help of modern biblical scholarship, it is possible to observe, describe, and discuss three different ways in which biblical truths were lost as described in the Book of Mormon: (1) the removal of texts or portions of texts from biblical records, (2) the corruption of texts through translation and transmission, and (3) the corruption of the meaning of biblical texts through faulty interpretation.

Plain and precious texts or portions of texts removed

It seems evident that the great and abominable church did its work in extracting precious truths from the scriptural records early in the New Testament era after the coming of Christ. For it was after gospel truth went forth "by the hand of the twelve apostles" that Nephi saw the "formation of [the] great and abominable church" (1 Ne. 13:26; cf. 13:39–41), and it was before the scriptural records went "forth unto all the nations of the Gentiles" that the mishandling occurred (1 Ne. 13:29).

One evidence of plain and precious truth being taken from scripture is documented in the writings of Justin Martyr, an early Church apologist who lived during this critical time in early Christian history (ca. A.D. 100–165). In his work, *Dialogue with Trypho,* Justin cited a document that he maintained had been deleted from the book of Jeremiah but was still to be found in some synagogue copies of the text: "The Lord God remembered His dead people of Israel who lay in the graves; and He descended to preach to them His own salvation" (*Ante-Nicene Fathers*, 1:235). Thus, evidence suggests that the doctrine of salvation for the dead was known and understood by the ancient Christian communities.

To what extent plain and precious things were taken from Old Testament records during this New Testament time is unclear. It is clear, however, from the Restoration as well as biblical scholarship that much has been lost from the writings from the Old Testament period. For example, the Joseph Smith Translation of the early chapters of Genesis (what is now the book of Moses in the Pearl of Great Price) shows that much has been lost from Genesis as originally recorded by Moses. The Lord anciently informed Moses about such deletions but assured him that these sacred truths would be restored: "And in a day when the children of men shall esteem my words as naught and take many of them from the book which thou shalt write, behold, I will raise up another like unto thee; and they shall be had again among the children of men—among as many as shall believe" (Moses 1:41). These particular deletions must have happened anciently, because the oldest manuscripts of the Bible do not reflect the doctrinal content of the present book of Moses. Likewise, the book of Abraham restores much important information about the life of Abraham and the Abrahamic covenant (Abr. 1–2). Additionally, the Book of Mormon provides the names and writings of prophets from the Old Testament period—Zenos, Zenock, Neum, and Ezias—that were part of the brass plates but not of the Old Testament (1 Ne. 19:10; Hel. 8:19–20), and the Bible includes lists of books from this period that are no longer extant (Num. 21:14; Josh. 10:13; 1 Kgs. 11:41; 1 Chr. 29:29; 2 Chr. 20:34; 2 Chr. 33:19). That important matters had indeed been taken from scripture before the time of Jesus is indicated by the Savior's chastisement of Jewish leaders: "Woe unto you, lawyers! For ye have taken away the key of knowledge, the fulness of the scriptures; ye enter not in yourselves into the kingdom; and those who were entering in, ye hindered" (JST Luke 11:53). Again, it is not clear when these plain and precious parts were lost or even if they were once part of the particular biblical records that Nephi saw going "forth from the Jews in purity unto the Gentiles" (1 Ne. 13:25). Nevertheless, there is evidence that Old Testament period records have suffered in the loss of plain and precious truths.

Concerning the New Testament, it is impossible to know what entire books are missing, but the New Testament does mention that Paul wrote an epistle to the Corinthians that is unavailable (1 Cor. 5:9), as well as one to the Laodiceans (Col. 4:16). One example of apparent tampering with a portion of a New Testament text concerns Luke 22:43–44 wherein Luke wrote of Jesus' agony in Gethsemane: "And there appeared an angel unto him from heaven, strengthening him. And being in an agony he prayed more earnestly: and his sweat was as it were great drops of blood falling down to the ground." The earliest manuscripts now available of the gospel of Luke contain these two verses, but some later manuscripts omit them. Because of the later omissions some translations exclude the two verses (e.g., RSV), but they note that other translations include them; others include the verses, but they note that some ancient manuscripts omit them. While it is unclear why or how the two questioned verses were omitted from Luke's Gospel in some manuscripts, it is clear that there were divergent beliefs about the nature of Christ and that some early Christian groups such as the Docetists (ca. A.D. 70–?) and the Marcionites (ca. 150–?) opposed the concept of a mortal Messiah sweating blood, instead believing that Christ only *appeared* to be human. Many scholars have argued that these verses were either added to, or excised from, the gospel of Luke in efforts to support or discredit a particular theological bias (Ehrman and Plunkett).

In the Book of Mormon, king Benjamin, an earlier source than Luke, speaking the prophetic words he had received from an angel, confirmed in his address to his people that as part of Jesus' infinite atonement for the sins of all people the Savior would bleed from every pore (Mosiah 3:7; cf. D&C 19:16–19; Isa. 63:1–3; ca. 124 B.C.).

PLAIN AND PRECIOUS THINGS

King Benjamin's statement provides another witness of the historicity of the event and its sacred meaning.

Corruption of the Bible through translation and transmission

The removal of precious truths took place in the process of the translation of the biblical text, as well as through the process of transmission. Joseph Smith wrote to John Wentworth, "We believe the Bible to be the word of God as far as it is translated correctly" (A of F 8). He further explained, "From sundry revelations which had been received, it was apparent that many important points touching the salvation of men, had been taken from the Bible, or lost before it was compiled" (Smith, 9–10).

To be sure, translation, or the transition from one language to another, is a potentially serious barrier to the communication of sacred truths. In the words of Elder Bruce R. McConkie, as the words of scripture "fell from seeric lips and flowed from prophetic pens," they made known the mind and will of God. "Since then there have been additions and deletions, editorial and other changes, and translations into tongues that oftentimes have no equivalent words or phrases to convey the original and precise meaning" of the Spirit-breathed word. He went on to explain that "aside from the sorry state of the text due to scholastic incompetence, there was a far more serious problem, namely, the theological bias of the translators. This caused them to change the meaning or paraphrase texts that were either unclear or embarrassing to them" (*New Witness,* 401, 403). Thus the understanding of doctrines was influenced by the process of translation.

Elder Orson Pratt observed that many of the differences between New Testament manuscripts "are of no particular consequence, as they do not materially alter the sense. But there are many thousands of differences wherein the sense is entirely altered. How are translators to know which of the manuscripts, if any, contain the true sense? They have no original copies with which to compare them—no standard of correction. No one can tell whether even one verse of either the Old or New Testament conveys the ideas of the original author" (7:28). The Prophet Joseph thus declared, "I believe the bible, as it ought to be, as it came from the pen of the original writers" (Ehat and Cook, 256). That the prophet should be "appointed" by God (D&C 42:56; 76:15) and called to undertake a "new translation" of the Bible implies of itself that the message of the Bible, though essentially true, needed clarification, correction, and supplementation at the hands of an inspired translator. Indeed, the early Latter-day Saints exulted in the fact that the Bible was "undergoing the purifying touch by a revelation of Jesus Christ" (*Messenger and Advocate,* 2:229).

It appears that from the angel's perspective, however, far more critical than translation was *transmission,* the movement of the texts through the hands of people. Most biblical scholars acknowledge that scribal errors inevitably took place in the transmission of the Bible and even that thousands of errors were introduced purposefully by scribes adding to or taking from the manuscripts (see, e.g., Metzger, 280–81). But because the Bible is all that many in the Christian world have, because it is the only sacred scripture in their possession, they feel the need to make statements like the following from J. Harold Greenlee: "We must trust that the same Holy Spirit who inspired the original text was able to protect it through the centuries of handwritten copying." Greenlee acknowledged that although the secular Greek classics, for example, were generally copied by professional scribes "and checked against accepted copies or originals by professional proofreaders," the New Testament texts were probably copied "mostly by ordinary Christians who were not professional scribes but who wanted a copy of a New Testament book or books for themselves or for other Christians." These did not have "the same opportunity as the secular copyists to compare their manuscripts with other manuscripts." Greenlee observed that "as scribes copied these copies, and other scribes copied their copies, they continued to make changes through the centuries. Most of these changes were insignificant; those that were of importance . . . were introduced during the first two centuries after the New Testament was written. . . . The textual variants that concern us, of course, are those that affect the meaning of the New Testament in

PLAIN AND PRECIOUS THINGS

some way. There are a few thousand of these," he stated, and then he hastened to add, "but we should be clear on the fact that they affect only a small portion of the New Testament text" (35–38).

One New Testament scholar, Bart Ehrman, has suggested that the theological debates during the first few centuries of the Christian church impacted the biblical texts in a major way: "The New Testament manuscripts were not produced impersonally by machines capable of flawless reproduction. They were copied by hand, by living, breathing human beings who were deeply rooted in the conditions and controversies of their day. Did the scribes' polemical contexts influence the way they transcribed their sacred Scriptures?" He contended that "they did, that theological disputes, specifically disputes over Christology, prompted Christian scribes to alter the words of Scripture in order to make them more serviceable for the polemical task. Scribes modified their manuscripts to make them more patently 'orthodox' and less susceptible to 'abuse' by the opponents of orthodoxy" (Ehrman, 3–4).

The loss or corruption of meaning through faulty interpretation

The third way in which plain and precious things were lost was through a tampering with meaning or interpretation. This usually results when things are taken from the gospel, thus making what were once simple doctrines appear uncertain or unclear. For example, in the first few centuries of the Christian era there grew up, especially among Hellenized Christians, what came to be known as the allegorical interpretation of scripture. Many who subscribed to this approach began to discount the literal meaning of scripture or actual historical events and to stress instead a "deeper" or symbolic interpretation of the events. As a result many concluded that any scriptural references to God having body, parts, and passions, or to God revealing himself to man were not to be taken literally. Fundamental truths were reduced to metaphor, and sacred words no longer meant what they said. What does it mean, for example, to state that Jesus Christ was the "only begotten" of the Father? What does it mean to say that God is the Father of man's spirit? Was the bodily resurrection of Jesus an actual historical event? Did it truly take place, or does it in reality symbolize mankind's rise to higher and purer understanding? In the process, something very important, plain and most precious, was lost—namely, the nature of the Being to be worshipped and how he may be approached.

A day of restoration

How, then, is it possible to know what was taken away or kept back? In general, the depth and breadth of the Restoration bear witness of the depth and breadth of the Apostasy. The Lord told Nephi, "I will be merciful unto the Gentiles in that day, insomuch that I will bring forth unto them, in mine own power, much of my gospel, which shall be plain and precious" (1 Ne. 13:34). And because the angel explained that "when [the Bible] proceeded forth from the mouth of a Jew it contained the fulness of the gospel of the Lord" (1 Ne. 13:24), it is possible to suggest what might have been taken away by comparing the gospel of the Restoration revealed by modern prophets and latter-day scripture with prevailing Christian views.

Examples of plain and precious truths that were lost through time—either through deletion from the biblical texts, faulty copying, deliberate alteration, or through incorrect and uninspired interpretation—might include the following:

1. The nature of God the Father—that he is an exalted Man of Holiness, a corporeal being;
2. The truth that God the Father and Jesus Christ are two separate and distinct beings;
3. Christ's eternal gospel, the knowledge that Christian prophets have declared Christian doctrines and administered Christian ordinances since the days of Adam, and that the ancient prophets in the Old Testament were acquainted with the plan of salvation and of the redemptive role of Jesus Christ;
4. The infinite and eternal nature of Christ's atonement;
5. The premortal existence of men and women;
6. The knowledge that all men and women are literally the children of God, spirit sons and daughters of the same Eternal Father;
7. The truth that men and women have

PLAIN AND PRECIOUS THINGS

within them the capacity, through the transforming powers of Jesus Christ and by the proper exercise of their moral agency, to become even as God is;

8. The truth that God has a plan, a great plan of happiness, a system of salvation in place whereby his children may advance and progress in light and truth;

9. The postmortal spirit world;

10. The kingdoms of glory hereafter;

11. The necessity of priesthood authority and saving ordinances;

12. The importance of the Church of Jesus Christ, and so forth.

To be sure, many of these truths can be found in the Bible, but they are not amplified or explained there, and thus some of their meanings and doctrinal implications remain unclear, especially without the aid of the light and knowledge that have come through the Restoration of the gospel of Jesus Christ through the Prophet Joseph Smith.

Another important consideration when discussing the loss of plain and precious truth is the insight from the Doctrine and Covenants that there are some truths that the ancients never possessed but were reserved to be revealed in the last dispensation: The Lord promised that "things which never have been revealed from the foundation of the world, but have been kept hid from the wise and prudent, shall be revealed unto babes and sucklings in this, the dispensation of the fulness of times" (D&C 128:18; cf. 121:26; 124:41).

Plain and precious gospel parts restored by the Book of Mormon

The visionary scene for Nephi was not, however, all bleak, for he also beheld a time of renewal, a time wherein many of the plain and precious truths that had been taken away or kept back would be revealed anew. First of all, many of these truths would be restored through the Book of Mormon itself. The Lord explained, "I will manifest myself unto thy seed, that they shall write many things which I shall minister unto them, which shall be plain and precious" (1 Ne. 13:35). In addition, Nephi saw that "other books" would come forth by the power of the Lamb of God, "unto the convincing of the Gentiles and the remnant of the seed of my brethren, and also the Jews who were scattered upon all the face of the earth, that the records of the prophets and of the twelve apostles of the Lamb are true." These last records, Nephi added, "shall establish the truth of the first," meaning the Bible. These "other books"—surely including the Doctrine and Covenants, Pearl of Great Price, Joseph Smith Translation of the Bible, and teachings of latter-day prophets—would "make known to all kindreds, tongues, and people, that the Lamb of God is the Son of the Eternal Father, and the Savior of the world" (1 Ne. 13:39–40). In a future day, God will see fit to deliver to his people such scriptural records as the brass plates (1 Ne. 5:17–19; Alma 37:4), the record of the ten tribes (2 Ne. 29:13), the sealed portion of the Book of Mormon containing the panoramic vision of the brother of Jared (2 Ne. 27:10–11; Ether 4:7), and the remainder of the Book of Mormon, including many sacred truths delivered by the risen Lord to the Nephites (3 Ne. 26:6–12).

Consider, for example, what the Book of Mormon itself does to clarify, expand, and broaden the doctrinal base of understanding, in short, what it does to restore plain and precious truths of the Lord. Of the hundreds of verities that might be brought forward as examples, the following are twelve central truths:

1. The gospel of Jesus Christ, including the doctrines of salvation, did not originate in the first century Christian church but rather were known from the beginning. Lehi[1] and Jacob[2] knew concerning the coming of the Messiah and his mortal ministry, suffering, death, atonement, and resurrection (1 Ne. 10:4–11; 2 Ne. 9:4).

2. The Lord God Omnipotent, the Lord Jehovah, the God of ancient Israel, would come to earth as Jesus of Nazareth, and that he would be scourged and crucified by wicked men (1 Ne. 19:7–10).

3. Jesus Christ, though separate and distinct from God the Father, will serve in the role of both Father and Son (Mosiah 15:1–4).

4. The fall of Adam and Eve was as much a part of the foreordained plan of salvation as the atonement of Christ (2 Ne. 2:25). In addition,

PLAIN AND PRECIOUS THINGS

the Book of Mormon teaches that had there been no fall, Adam and Eve would have remained in the Garden of Eden forever in their innocent, paradisiacal, childless, and nonprogressing condition (2 Ne. 2:22–23).

5. Unless fallen men and women put off the natural man and put on Christ (Mosiah 3:19), they remain "without God in the world" and thus in "a state contrary to the nature of happiness" (Alma 41:11). At the same time, men and women are not depraved creatures and therefore have the capacity, because of the Atonement, to choose good or evil, captivity and death or liberty and eternal life (2 Ne. 2:27; 10:23; Hel. 14:30).

6. The suffering of the Lord Jesus during the hours of Atonement caused blood to come from every pore (Mosiah 3:7; cf. Luke 22:44).

7. The people of Israel are scattered whenever they reject the true Messiah and his gospel. They are gathered when they receive the Lord, his gospel, the "very points of his doctrine," and come into his church. In addition, the Book of Mormon consistently affirms that the gathering process is first spiritual, to the Lord, and secondly temporal, to the lands of their inheritance (1 Ne. 15:14; 10:14; 2 Ne. 6:8–11; 10:3–8).

8. The Lord has a plan for his chosen people, the house of Israel, and that his patience, love, and tender regard for them are endless and eternal (Jacob 5). Further, the restoration of the gospel in the last days is in reality a restoration of the Abrahamic covenant and a significant part of the realization of God's promise to Abraham (1 Ne. 22:7–12).

9. All mortals lived before they came into mortality, and men are foreordained to receive the Holy Priesthood (2 Ne. 2:17–18; Alma 13).

10. One must have proper authority to officiate in the ordinances of the Church of Jesus Christ, and those ordinances are required for salvation (2 Ne. 31:5; Mosiah 18:13; Alma 5:3; 3 Ne. 27:19–20).

11. Jesus Christ visited his "other sheep" on the American continent and elsewhere after his resurrection from the dead (3 Ne. 15:16–24; 16:1–3; cf. John 10:14–16).

12. God is indeed the same yesterday, today, and forever, and he reveals himself through prophets to all nations, if they seek him earnestly (1 Ne. 10:17–19; 2 Ne. 29:1–14).

In a day when men and women have begun to doubt the historicity of scripture, to question what Jesus of Nazareth really said or did, the scriptures of the Restoration stand as a second witness of the essential truthfulness of the Bible. Even with all that is known about the loss of plain and precious truths, "we cannot avoid the conclusion," Elder McConkie stated, "that a divine providence is directing all things as they should be. This means that the Bible, as it now is, contains that portion of the Lord's word" that the world is prepared to receive (*Doctrines*, 280). President J. Reuben Clark testified that "notwithstanding the corruptions themselves, the Good Old Book stands as a record of God's dealings with and commandments and promises to his children, in their days of righteousness and in their generations of sin. It still, though corrupted, points out the way of righteousness to the man of faith seeking to serve God. It contains some of God's counsel to his children" (210).

Just as the angel told Nephi, "These last records [the Book of Mormon and 'other books'], which thou hast seen among the Gentiles, shall establish the truth of the first [the Bible], which are of the twelve apostles of the Lamb, and shall make known the plain and precious things which have been taken away from them; and shall make known to all kindreds, tongues, and people, that the Lamb of God is the Son of the Eternal Father, and the Savior of the world; and that all men must come unto him, or they cannot be saved" (1 Ne. 13:40).

See also Book of Mormon, what it says about the Bible.

BIBLIOGRAPHY

The Ante-Nicene Fathers. Edited by the Rev. Alexander Roberts and James Donaldson. Grand Rapids, Mich.: Eerdmans, 1981.

Clark, J. Reuben. *On the Way to Immortality and Eternal Life.* Salt Lake City: Deseret Book, 1961.

Ehat, Andrew F., and Lyndon W. Cook, eds. *The Words of Joseph Smith.* Provo, Utah: Religious Studies Center, Brigham Young University, 1980.

Ehrman, Bart D. *The Orthodox Corruption of Scripture.* New York: Oxford University Press, 1993.

Ehrman, Bart D., and Mark A. Plunkett. "The Angel and the Agony: The Textual Problem of Luke 22:43–44." *Catholic Biblical Quarterly* 45 (1983): 401–16.

Greenlee, J. Harold. *Scribes, Scrolls, and Scripture.* Grand Rapids, Mich.: Eerdmans, 1985.

McConkie, Bruce R. *Doctrines of the Restoration.* Edited by Mark L. McConkie. Salt Lake City: Bookcraft, 1989.

———. *A New Witness for the Articles of Faith.* Salt Lake City: Deseret Book, 1985.

Messenger and Advocate 2 (December 1835).

Metzger, Bruce M. *The New Testament: Its Background, Growth, and Content.* 2d ed. Nashville, Tenn.: Abingdon, 1983.

Pratt, Orson. *Journal of Discourses.* 26 vols. London: Latter-day Saints' Book Depot, 1851–86.

Smith, Joseph. *Teachings of the Prophet Joseph Smith.* Selected by Joseph Fielding Smith. Salt Lake City: Deseret Book, 1976.

RLM

Plainness Unadulterated truth, purity, clarity, and simplicity; that which is free from complication, ornamentation, obstruction, or extraneous embellishment. The Book of Mormon is full of plainness because many of the prophets (including Nephi[1], Jacob[2], Enos, and Alma[2]) spoke or wrote in plainness. Nephi declared that he delighted in plainness and felt the need to speak in plainness because the Lord does all things in plainness (2 Ne. 31:2–3; cf. 26:33). Jacob felt compelled to speak the truth "according to the plainness of the word of God" (Jacob 2:11). Nephi also indicated that he spoke plainly so that his brethren could not err (2 Ne. 25:20). Likewise, Enos said he wrote in plainness because there was nothing except plainness which would keep his people "from going down speedily to destruction" (Enos 1:23). King Benjamin spoke plainly that his people might understand (Mosiah 2:40). Yet, Alma's experience in the wicked city of Ammonihah demonstrates that prophets sometimes suffer at the hands of those they are called to serve for speaking the words of plainness (Alma 14:2–14).

Plainness is also associated with the most basic, essential, and core doctrine of the gospel as taught in the Book of Mormon: Christ was sent by the Father to make an atonement for all humankind (3 Ne. 27:13–14). Nephi related plainness and truth to Christ's redemption and gloried in all three (2 Ne. 33:5–6) because plainness and truth are embodied in the Lamb of God (1 Ne. 13:29). Jacob spoke of the prophecies about Christ's atonement as "things [which] are manifested unto us plainly" (Jacob 4:11–13). But, he continued, the Jews "despised the words of plainness, and killed the prophets." Therefore, God took "away his plainness from them" and gave them many things which they could not understand (Jacob 4:14). Because the basic message of all the prophets from the beginning centered on the coming of the Messiah (Jacob 4:4–5; Mosiah 13:33), Jewish rejection of the words of plainness was a rejection of the Messiah (Jacob 4:12–17). Those who are filled with the spirit of prophecy understand words of plainness uttered by prophets (2 Ne. 25:4).

ACS

Plan Although there are a few references to the plans of men or of Satan in the Book of Mormon (e.g., 2 Ne. 9:28; Alma 12:4–5), most references are to God's "great and eternal plan of redemption" (Alma 34:16), also called "the merciful plan of the great Creator" (2 Ne. 9:6), "the great and eternal plan of deliverance from death" (2 Ne. 11:5), "the great plan of redemption" (Jacob 6:8; cf. Alma 42:13), "the plan of restoration" (Alma 41:2), "the plan of salvation" (Alma 42:5), "the great plan of happiness" (Alma 42:8), and "the plan of mercy" (Alma 42:15). The purpose of the plan, made possible through the atonement of Christ, is "to bring to pass the immortality and eternal life of man" (Moses 1:39).

The Lord knows all things from the beginning and therefore, having anticipated humankind's situations and needs (Smith, *Church*, 4:597), has prepared a way to accomplish all his saving works among the children of men (1 Ne. 10:18), having power to fulfill all his words (1 Ne. 9:6; Morm. 8:22; D&C 3:1, 3). This plan was presented in the premortal world, in the great council of heaven, where all those to be born on the earth accepted it (Smith, *Teachings*, 181). The plan included the begetting of the spirit children of God and their preparation to descend to a fallen world (Alma 13:3; D&C 138:56); to receive a physical body and to be tested (Smith, *Teachings,* 181; 2 Ne. 2:21; Abr. 3:22–26); the CREATION and peopling of the world (1 Ne. 17:36); the fall of man (2 Ne. 2:15–26); the ATONEMENT of Jesus Christ (Alma 22:14); the teaching of the fulness of the plan which is the GOSPEL of Jesus Christ with all its laws, ordinances, doctrines, and principles by which man could be redeemed (Alma 12:32–33, 37); and the orchestration of events on the racial or national level (Morm. 5:23; Moses 6:32; D&C 117:6) as well as on a personal level for the eternal benefit of all (2 Ne. 26:24). With one's repentance, the great plan begins to operate immediately (Alma 34:31). The purpose of missionary work is to teach the great plan of redemption to the inhabitants of the earth (Alma 17:16; 29:2; 42:31).

See also Fall of Adam and Eve, the; Life, purpose of.

BIBLIOGRAPHY

Smith, Joseph. *History of The Church of Jesus Christ of Latter-day Saints.* Edited by B. H. Roberts. 7 vols. 2d ed. rev. Salt Lake City: The Church of Jesus Christ of Latter-day Saints, 1932–51.

———. *Teachings of the Prophet Joseph Smith.* Selected by Joseph Fielding Smith. Salt Lake City: Deseret Book, 1976.

MCT

Plates of brass The standard works or the basic scriptures of the Nephites. The plates of brass were like the Old Testament but more extensive (1 Ne. 13:23). They contained the Law (the five books of Moses), a history of God's dealings with ancient Israel, and the prophecies of many of the prophets, down to and including many prophecies of Jeremiah[1] (1 Ne. 5:10–14). The Nephites made repeated reference to Old World peoples and events, many of which they would have known through their study of the brass plates.

Sometime after leaving Jerusalem, Nephi[1] and his brothers were commanded to return to the city to obtain the brass plates from Laban, a descendant of Joseph of old (1 Ne. 5:14–16). The family of Lehi[1] were commanded to take the brass plates with them to America to maintain both scriptural and intellectual literacy (1 Ne. 3:2–4, 19–20; 4:13–16; cf. Omni 1:17; Mosiah 1:3).

It is uncertain how the brass plates came into Laban's possession. The discovery of a scriptural text in the days of king Josiah (ca. 620 B.C.), the excitement with which that discovery was received, and the reforms in society that resulted from Josiah's search of the holy word (2 Kgs. 22–23), suggest that scriptural records were not accessible to all people at the time of Lehi and Laban. Prior to the Assyrian captivity in 722 B.C., the brass plates may have been kept by the northern tribes, from whom Lehi and Laban descended (Millet, 208–9). Perhaps the records were carried by Lehi and Laban's ancestors who escaped the Assyrian deportation and settled in Jerusalem.

When and by whom the writing on the brass plates was begun is not stated in the Book of Mormon. The record does state, however, that they were written in Egyptian (Mosiah 1:4), perhaps attesting to the influence of such notable prophets as Joseph and Moses, both of whom had spent many years in Egypt.

Some of the prophets from the brass plates who are quoted or cited (in addition to ones known already, such as Isaiah) include Zenos, Zenock, Neum, and Ezias. Their oracles are gospel-centered and Christ-centered, straightforward and specific as to the sufferings, death, and atoning work of the Messiah, as well as the separate and distinct natures of God the Father and his beloved Son (1 Ne. 19:7–12; Alma 33:3–17; Hel. 8:18–20; 3 Ne. 10:15–16). Because the Nephite prophets sought earnestly to point their people toward the coming of the Redeemer and the destiny of the house of Israel, they quoted extensively from the writings of Isaiah and Zenos, as contained on the brass plates, and offered prophetic commentary upon those writings (1 Ne. 19:23; 2 Ne. 11–25; Jacob 5–6). The brass plates also contained insights unknown to the readers of the present Bible, including prophecies of Joseph of old, of which there are not many greater (2 Ne. 3; 4:1–2). Perhaps the best source for understanding the doctrines and central teachings of the brass plates, other than the Book of Mormon itself, is Joseph Smith's

Translation of the Bible. By revelation the Prophet Joseph Smith restored plain and precious truths that were once part of the biblical record, many of which were also contained in that ancient collection known as the brass plates.

The brass plates served to enlarge the memory of a people, convince many of their errors, and lead them to the Father unto the salvation of their souls (Alma 37:8). Lehi and Alma[2] rejoiced in the timeless teachings of the brass plates. They prophesied of a time when these records would "go forth unto every nation, kindred, tongue, and people, that they shall know of the mysteries contained thereon" (Alma 37:4; 1 Ne. 5:18). To some degree, of course, this prophecy is fulfilled as missionaries flood the earth with the Book of Mormon. Further, Elder Bruce R. McConkie suggested that in a future day "the Lord will raise up a prophet, who will also be a seer and a translator, to whom he will give the brass plates that they may be translated for the benefit and blessing of those in all nations" (16).

See also Joseph Smith Translation and the Book of Mormon; Laban, slaying of; Moses, five books of.

BIBLIOGRAPHY

McConkie, Bruce R. "The Doctrinal Restoration." *The Joseph Smith Translation: The Restoration of Plain and Precious Things*. Provo, Utah: Religious Studies Center, Brigham Young University, 1985.

Millet, Robert L. "The Influence of the Brass Plates on the Teachings of Nephi." *The Book of Mormon: Second Nephi, the Doctrinal Structure*. Provo, Utah: Religious Studies Center, Brigham Young University, 1989.

RLM

Plates of Ether Twenty-four gold plates, inscribed by the prophet Ether, which contained a secular and religious history of the JAREDITE CIVILIZATION from their inception at the "great tower" to their destruction (Mosiah 28:17). After witnessing the fulfillment of the prophecy concerning the destruction of his people, Ether finished his record and hid the plates (Ether 15:33). These plates were later found by a group on an expedition sent by king Limhi to find Zarahemla (Mosiah 8:9–11; Ether 1:1–2; ca. 123 B.C.). King Mosiah[2] obtained the plates from Limhi's people and then translated them into the Nephite language (Mosiah 28:11–13). The plates of Ether were subsequently passed down through the prophets with the plates of brass and the plates of Nephi until Moroni[2] received them and made an abridgment (Mosiah 28:20; Ether 1:1–2). The plates of Ether contained a lengthy history of a mighty nation of which Moroni[2] noted, "the hundredth part I have not written" (Ether 15:33). The language of the plates of Ether is unknown.

See also Ether, book of.

DLL

Plates of Jacob That part of the small plates of Nephi written by Jacob[2]. Jacob refers to these plates as the plates of Jacob but acknowledges that "they were made by the hand of Nephi" (Jacob 3:13–14). Before his death Jacob passed them to his son Enos (Jacob 7:27).

Plates of Mormon Commentators have described the plates of Mormon in at least two ways: (1) the plates of Mormon are specifically the plates made by Mormon with his "own hands" (3 Ne. 5:10–11) upon which he inscribed his ABRIDGMENT of the large PLATES OF NEPHI; Mormon's son Moroni made some additions to the plates of Mormon, which include Mormon 8 and 9, the books of Ether and Moroni, the title page, and the sealed portion of the plates; (2) the plates of Mormon comprise not only Mormon's abridgment of the large plates of Nephi, and Moroni's additions but also, as part of his compilation, the small plates of Nephi. In speaking about the plates of Mormon in this general way, the plates of Mormon include everything Joseph Smith received from the angel Moroni. This article will speak of the plates of Mormon in the limited specific sense described first.

The principal Nephite record was kept on a collection of metal plates known as the large plates of Nephi. Mormon, at the age of twenty-four, received these plates and began to record on them a detailed account of his people that he had observed during his own time (Morm. 1:1–3; 2:16–18). Mormon later made a new set of plates (the plates of Mormon) and abridged the whole of the large plates onto them (3 Ne. 5:8–19). This abridgment included the books known today as the books of Lehi, Mosiah, Alma, Helaman, 3 Nephi, 4 Nephi, and Mormon. He also included an abridgment of his own writings (Morm. 1–7) from the "full account" he had inscribed on the large plates (Morm. 2:18; 5:9).

Mormon's inspired abridgment is shaped by his perspective of the whole of Nephite history. It includes commentaries in which he identified himself as the author (3 Ne. 5:8–26; 26:6–12; 28:24; 4 Ne. 1:23) and a series of anonymous interpolations introduced by such phrases as "and thus we see," all of which emphasize important spiritual lessons to be drawn from the narrative (e.g., Alma 24:19, 27; 50:19–23; Hel. 3:27–30; 12:1–2).

The part of the GOLD PLATES Joseph Smith translated and published as the Book of Mormon consisted of Mormon's abridgement of the large plates of Nephi recorded on the plates of Mormon (except the book of Lehi), Moroni's additions to the plates of Mormon (except the sealed portion of the plates), and the small plates of Nephi.

When Joseph Smith translated the Book of Mormon, he started with the plates of Mormon, which began with the book of Lehi. This translation consisted of 116 pages of handwritten manuscript. When these pages were lost by Martin Harris (D&C 3; 10), the Lord instructed Joseph Smith to translate the small plates "to the reign of king Benjamin" and include it in place of the lost manuscript (D&C 10:38–42). Therefore, the Book of Mormon in its published form has no book of Lehi but begins with the small plates (1 Nephi through Omni) and then after brief explanatory comments by Mormon (the Words of Mormon) continues with the plates of Mormon (Mosiah through Mormon) followed by Moroni's additions.

See also The Structure of the Book of Mormon, 17; And thus we see; Book of Mormon, lost manuscript of (116 pages); Lehi, book of; Sealed portion of the gold plates.

DRS

Plates of Nephi Nephi[1] made two sets of metal plates—the plates which have come to be known as the large plates of Nephi (Jacob 3:13) and the small plates of Nephi (Jacob 1:1)—on which he kept two records of his people. It is not clear whether the designations "large" and "small" had to do with the actual size of the plates or with their length. Both of these records are termed the plates of Nephi (1 Ne. 9:2; D&C 10:38–42), and both records were kept by Nephi's successors. Nephi first made the large plates and recorded on them the record of his father Lehi[1] and continued with a more full account of Nephite secular history. Because Nephi wrote on the large plates first he spoke of them as the "first plates" (1 Ne. 19:2). Later Nephi fashioned the small plates for the specific purpose of recording the ministry of his people (1 Ne. 9:2–6; 19:1–6; 2 Ne. 5:28–33; Jacob 1:2–4). Many generations later, by the time of Amaleki[1], the small plates were full (Omni 1:30). Amaleki "deliver[ed] up" the small plates to king Benjamin (Omni 1:25), who thereafter recorded both spiritual and secular matters as one account on the large plates (W of M 1:10). The merged record was continued on the large plates throughout Nephite history until Mormon received them (W of M 1:11).

Large plates

The large plates were to contain a "full account of the history" of the Nephites, including "an account of the reign of the kings, and the wars and contentions of [the] people" (1 Ne. 9:2–6). The large plates were passed from king to king from Nephi until Mosiah[2], who entrusted them to the prophet Alma[2] (Mosiah 28:20). From that time they were kept by the prophets up to and including Mormon (Morm. 2:17–18). The large plates consisted of the books of Lehi, Mosiah, Alma, Helaman, 3 Nephi, 4 Nephi, and Mormon. Mormon wrote a history of his people in his day on the large plates and then, "according to the will of God," abridged the whole of the large plates from the time of Lehi to his own (3 Ne. 5:8–19; 600 B.C.–A.D. 385). The PLATES OF MORMON, made by Mormon, contained his complete abridgment of the large plates of Nephi. Unfortunately, the portion of the translation of Mormon's abridgment of the large plates

PLATES OF NEPHI

that covered the period from Lehi to the time of king Benjamin (about 470 years) was lost by Martin Harris. As a result, the Book of Mormon today does not contain Mormon's abridgment of the large plates for that time period. Fortunately, as the Lord foresaw (W of M 1:7), Nephi's record on the small plates helps to fill that gap.

When Nephi began the record on the large plates after his arrival in the promised land, he did not know that he would later be instructed to make a second set of plates that would be reserved specifically for spiritual matters (1 Ne. 19:1–7). Thus he began his record on the large plates merging both spiritual and secular histories, including his father Lehi's record, an account of his family's "journeyings in the wilderness," his father's prophecies, and his own prophecies (1 Ne. 19:1).

Small plates

Nephi was commanded by the Lord to begin a second record of his people thirty years after they left Jerusalem (2 Ne. 5:28–33; ca. 570 B.C.). This record, the small plates of Nephi, was to contain "the more sacred things" in Nephite history (1 Ne. 19:5), including the "ministry of my people" (1 Ne. 9:3) and accounts of preaching, revelation, and prophesying (Jacob 1:2–4). Nephi stated his purpose for the small plates: "For the fulness of mine intent is that I may persuade men to come unto the God of Abraham, and the God of Isaac, and the God of Jacob, and be saved" (1 Ne. 6:4). He also gave a commandment to future record keepers: "Wherefore, I shall give commandment unto my seed, that they shall not occupy these plates with things which are not of worth unto the children of men" (1 Ne. 6:6). Authors of the small plates were Nephi, Jacob², Enos, Jarom, Omni, Amaron, Chemish, Abinadom, and Amaleki (ca. 570–130 B.C.), but only Nephi and his brother Jacob wrote at any length. As the small plates were passed down, so was Nephi's commandment concerning them (e.g., Jacob 1:1–4; 7:27), thus their contents reflect careful attention to their sacred purposes. Amaleki appropriately

PLATES OF NEPHI

SMALL PLATES OF NEPHI RECORD KEEPERS	LARGE PLATES OF NEPHI RECORD KEEPERS
Nephi¹	Nephi¹
Jacob², brother of Nephi¹	Succession of unnamed Nephite Kings
Enos, son of Jacob²	Mosiah¹
Jarom, son of Enos	Benjamin, son of Mosiah¹
Omni, son of Jarom	Mosiah², son of Benjamin
Amaron, son of Omni	Alma², son of Alma¹
Chemish, brother of Amaron	Helaman², son of Alma²
Abinadom, son of Chemish	Shiblon, son of Alma²
Amaleki, son of Abinadom	Helaman³, son of Helaman²
	Nephi², son of Helaman³
	Nephi³, son of Nephi²
	Nephi⁴, son of Nephi³
	Amos¹, son of Nephi⁴
	Amos², son of Amos¹
	Ammaron, brother of Amos²
	Mormon², son of Mormon¹
	Moroni², son of Mormon²

concluded the small plates when he admonished, "And now, my beloved brethren, I would that ye should come unto Christ, who is the Holy One of Israel, and partake of his salvation, and the power of his redemption" (Omni 1:26).

The small plates consist of the books of 1 Nephi, 2 Nephi, Jacob, Enos, Jarom, and Omni. Following the book of Omni, Mormon added a short explanation (Words of Mormon), that "the workings of the Spirit of the Lord" prompted him to include the small plates with the plates of Mormon (W of M 1:3–7; D&C 10:38–46). It was after the loss of the 116 pages of translation of Mormon's abridgment of the book of Lehi that the Lord told Joseph Smith to translate the small plates of Nephi. Thus the Book of Mormon contains the whole of the unabridged small plates—no part of them was lost.

See also The Structure of the Book of Mormon, 17; Book of Mormon, lost manuscript of (116 pages); Lehi, book of; Gold plates.

DRS

Plates of Zeniff The record of the people of Zeniff from the time they left Zarahemla until the time Ammon[1] discovered them. King Limhi brought the plates before Ammon to be read (Mosiah 8:5). And later, when Limhi and his people returned to Zarahemla, Mosiah[2] received the plates (Mosiah 22:14).

Plural marriage The practice of having more than one wife. The Book of Mormon prophet Jacob[2] condemned the unauthorized practice of plural marriage among his own people. He stated that the Lord had specifically commanded that they were to "have save it were one wife, and concubines they should have none, and there should not be whoredoms committed among them" (Jacob 3:5; cf. 2:34). In testifying against the immoral and wicked practices of many of his people, Jacob explained that these wicked Nephites "understand not the scriptures, for they seek to excuse themselves in committing WHOREDOMS, because of the things which were written concerning David, and Solomon his son" (Jacob 2:23). Implicit in this passage is that plural marriage did exist, with God's approval, among the ancient patriarchs, such as Abraham and Jacob[1] (e.g., Gen. 16:2–3; 29–30; D&C 132:37). If plural marriage was always viewed as an abomination in the sight of God, there would be no justification or excuse for Nephites living it. The Book of Mormon, however, teaches that the Nephites were using David and Solomon as their justification for plural wives: "Behold, David and Solomon truly had many wives and concubines, which thing was abominable before me, saith the Lord" (Jacob 2:24). Having more than one wife is not an abomination unto the Lord in and of itself, as seen in the lives of the Old Testament patriarchs. What was abominable unto the Lord in the cases of David and Solomon was that they, like the Nephites whom Jacob[2] was rebuking, took additional wives whom the Lord did not give unto them or authorize them to take (2 Sam. 11; 1 Kgs. 11:1–12). In modern revelation the Lord explained that he had authorized David and Solomon to take plural wives as many others had done before them, "and in nothing did they sin save in those things which they received not of me" (D&C 132:38). The Nephites had been commanded not to live plural marriage but had taken it upon themselves so they could commit adultery and whoredoms. They sought to justify their disobedience and immorality by using Old Testament precedent. It is this that Jacob condemned. The Book of Mormon explains that monogamy is the rule; plural marriage, the exception: "For if I will, saith the Lord of Hosts, raise up seed unto me, I will command my people; otherwise they shall hearken unto these things" (Jacob 2:30). When the commandment to live plural marriage was given in the latter days, it came from the Lord through the established order and authority of the Church and kingdom of God on earth—through the prophets who held the keys of such power (cf. D&C 132:40–48). "I hold the keys of this power in the last days"; the Prophet Joseph Smith taught, "for there is never but one on earth at a time on whom the power and its keys are conferred; *and I have constantly said no man shall have but one wife at a time, unless the Lord directs otherwise*" (324; emphasis in original). Today Latter-day Saints live the law of marriage as taught by Jacob in the Book of Mormon. Although there have been times in the past when plural marriage was commanded and authorized of God, monogamy is the commandment and practice of today. Any practice contrary to this command, without explicit authorization and commandment of God through the prophet-president of his Church today, is akin to the Nephite immorality, which Jacob condemned in no uncertain terms.

See also Chastity; Concubines.

BIBLIOGRAPHY

Smith, Joseph. *Teachings of the Prophet Joseph Smith*. Selected by Joseph Fielding Smith. Salt Lake City: Deseret Book, 1976.

BLT

Poetry *See* Book of Mormon, poetry in.

Points of doctrine Fundamental truths of the gospel of Christ that one must know and abide in order to obtain salvation. "Doctrine" is more than mere teaching or discourse; it is basic, revealed, indispensable gospel law and principle. A "point of doctrine" is a precise, focused concept, as opposed to a vague approximation. If true points of DOCTRINE are known and followed, peace and harmony exist; if they are not, controversy and contentions arise. Because contention is of the devil (3 Ne. 11:29), he is opposed to the true points of Christ's doctrine (2 Ne. 28:19–28; 33:5).

The term "points of doctrine" occurs in variation six times in the Book of Mormon (1 Ne. 15:14; Alma 41:9; Hel. 11:22, 23; 3 Ne. 11:28; 21:6). The only other times it appears in scripture are twice in the Doctrine and Covenants (D&C 10:62–63). Though the term "points of doctrine" does not occur in the Bible, Isaiah (Isa. 8:19–20) and Paul (2 Tim. 3:15–16) taught that the scriptures (the word of God through the prophets and apostles) are the source of sound doctrine, which concept is in harmony with how "points of doctrine" is used in the Book of Mormon and in the Doctrine and Covenants.

"Points of doctrine" is used in several contexts in the Book of Mormon:

1. An integral part of the restoration of the gospel in the latter days. The coming forth of the Book of Mormon would serve to bring the descendants of Lehi[1] and the Gentiles to an understanding of the "very points," the "true points" of Christ's doctrine (1 Ne. 15:14; 3 Ne. 21:6; cf. D&C 10:62).

2. A standard to prevent justification for sin. Alma[2] warned his son Corianton, "And now behold, my son, do not risk one more offense against your God upon those points of doctrine, which ye have hitherto risked to commit sin" (Alma 41:9). From Alma's instruction to his son, it seems clear that Corianton was struggling with, rationalizing, and twisting the plain meaning of points of doctrine concerning sexual morality, the principle of restoration, and the justice of God (Alma 39–42).

3. A criterion to settle doctrinal disputations. Nephi[2] and Lehi[4], who "knew concerning the true points of doctrine," were able to quell the strife created by "a few contentions" over doctrinal issues (Hel. 11:22–23). Similarly, Jesus taught the Nephites the correct purpose and procedure for baptism, and said, "According as I have commanded you thus shall ye baptize. And there shall be no disputations among you, as there have hitherto been; neither shall there be disputations among you concerning the points of my doctrine, as there have hitherto been" (3 Ne. 11:28; cf. D&C 10:63).

All of the foregoing passages hold the Book of Mormon as a repository of the "true points" of the Savior's doctrine. There are, of course, additional true points of doctrine in the other scriptures on topics not covered in the Book of Mormon.

RJM

Polygamy *See* Plural marriage.

Ponder To think deeply, reflect, reason, contemplate, dwell upon, or meditate. Pondering, accompanied by sufficient desire, faith, sincerity, and earnest intent, is a prelude to revelation and understanding (1 Ne. 11:1; Hel. 10:2–3; 3 Ne. 17:3; Moro. 10:3; D&C 138:1). Often "ponder" is used in connection with the study of scriptures. Nephi[1] professed that his soul delighted in the scriptures, and his heart "pondereth" them (2 Ne. 4:15). Pondering is an essential element in Moroni[2]'s formula for discovering the truth of the Book of Mormon (Moro. 10:3).

SAJ

Power The possession and execution of authority, control, or influence over people, things, and circumstances. In this regard, the Book of Mormon reveals two predominant motifs of power: the power of God and the power of the devil.

The power of God

The power of God is possessed, manifested, and exercised by each member of the GODHEAD. Thus the Book of Mormon speaks not only of "the power of God" or the "Lord" in general terms (e.g., 1 Ne. 13:18–19; 2 Ne. 1:26; 3:15; Mosiah 27:20), but also of "the power of the Father" (e.g., 3 Ne. 27:15; Morm. 7:5), "the power of Christ" (e.g., 2 Ne. 27:11; Mosiah 18:2; Alma 15:6; cf. 1 Ne. 11:31; 13:35; Hel. 5:11), and "the power of the Holy Ghost" (e.g., 1 Ne. 10:17, 19; 2 Ne. 26:13; Jacob 7:17; cf. 2 Ne. 2:8).

The power of God is both "matchless" (1 Ne. 17:42; Mosiah 1:13; 4:6; Alma 9:11) and absolute (1 Ne. 9:6; Alma 7:8; 44:5; Morm. 5:23; Ether 3:4). By it God created the earth (Jacob 4:9; Morm. 9:17) and controls the elements (e.g., 1 Ne. 17:46; 19:11; Hel. 12:10–12). It has dominion over all the inhabitants of the earth (1 Ne. 1:14). Through it God delivers his people (e.g., 1 Ne. 13:18–19; Mosiah 23:13; 25:10) and destroys their enemies (2 Ne. 6:14). By it he leads his children (1 Ne. 17:42; Jacob 2:25; Omni 1:13; Alma 36:28) and establishes nations (e.g., 1 Ne. 17:35; 2 Ne. 1:11; 3 Ne. 21:4). Prophets speak on behalf of God through this power (e.g., 1 Ne. 3:20; Enos 1:26) and "every thing which inviteth to do good, and to persuade to believe in Christ, is sent forth" by this power (Moro. 7:16). The Book of Mormon was brought forth and witnesses were established by this power (2 Ne. 26:16; 27:12; Ether 5:3–4; Morm. 8:16). Truth is learned and men are converted by this power (2 Ne. 33:1; Alma 19:6; 3 Ne. 7:21; Moro. 10:4–6). It is the power through which Christ was conceived (Mosiah 15:3), ministered in mortality (Mosiah 3:5), and will resurrect and redeem humankind (2 Ne. 2:8; 9:25; Jacob 4:11; 6:9; Omni 1:26; Mosiah 15:8; Alma 4:14; 7:13; Hel. 5:11; Morm. 9:13; Moro. 8:22).

Individuals may be allowed to exercise some of God's power. Ammon[1] testified, "a man may have a great power given him from God" (Mosiah 8:16; cf. Jacob 4:6–7; Alma 5:3; Hel. 8:13; 11:18). Thus God's power is a gift to the faithful. To be "armed . . . with the power of God" (1 Ne. 14:14), one must exercise faith (1 Ne. 1:20; 10:17; 2 Ne. 1:10; Alma 57:26) and "diligently seek [God]," striving to do his work in righteousness (1 Ne. 10:17, 19; 13:37; cf. Mosiah 18:26; Alma 17:3; Hel. 10:4–7; Moro. 10:25).

The great promise that comes with such faith and diligence is that once one has the power of God, nothing is impossible. For example, Alma[2] and Amulek "could not be confined in dungeons; neither was it possible that any man could slay them" (Alma 8:31; cf. 14:24–28; Hel. 10:16). Nor could the three remaining Nephite disciples be harmed by flames and wild beasts or be held captive by walls and pits (3 Ne. 28:19–22; cf. 4 Ne. 1:30; Morm. 8:24). Those possessing God's power were able to confound the wicked (e.g., 1 Ne. 2:14; 17:48, 55; Alma 12:7; 30:52) and control the elements (e.g., 1 Ne. 17:29; 2 Ne. 25:20; Hel. 8:11). They could interpret engravings (Omni 1:20), bring men to the faith (e.g., Alma 53:10; 62:45; Hel. 6:5), perform ordinances (e.g., 3 Ne. 18:5; Moro. 3:4), and establish God's church (Mosiah 21:30).

The power of the devil

Unlike the power of God which is evidenced in good works and light, the power of the devil is shown in evil works and darkness. Satan's power especially flourishes in absence of gospel truths (e.g., 1 Ne. 13:29). The adversary's evil power deceives people (e.g., Jacob 7:18) and stirs them to iniquity, pride, greed, and worldliness (e.g., 3 Ne. 6:15; cf. Jacob 7:4; Alma 30:42). Ultimately it leads them to captivity, death, damnation, and everlasting destruction (2 Ne. 2:27; Alma 9:28; 12:6–7).

Satan is able to exercise his power upon individuals and peoples when they "yield themselves unto" it (3 Ne. 7:5) by persisting in their "carnal nature" and the "ways of sin and rebellion against God" (Mosiah 16:5). As they so "put off the Spirit of God" and harden their hearts, the devil's power takes over (Alma 30:42; 3 Ne. 2:1–2; Ether 15:19). As agents of Satan's power they become self-oriented and motivated by the desire for personal gain and the praise of the world. Consequently they seek to destroy others and use priestcraft, violence, deception, flattery, evil oaths, and secret combinations to accomplish their intent (e.g., Jacob 7:1–5; Mosiah 27:9; Alma 1:12, 16; 30:42–45; Hel. 2:3–4).

Unlike God's power, the devil's power is not absolute. Helaman[3] taught his sons that the devil would have "no power over" them if they would "build" their foundation on Christ (Hel. 5:12). Likewise, Mormon testified that if all men were as righteous as Moroni[1], "the devil would never have power over the hearts of the children of men" (Alma 48:17). Indeed, during the millennial day, the righteousness of the people will render Satan powerless (1 Ne. 22:26; 2 Ne. 30:18; cf. 1 Ne. 22:15; Ether 8:26).

The Book of Mormon uses the term "power" in two other contexts as well: one to refer to military might (e.g., Jacob 7:24; Alma 25:5; 50:12; 52:13), and the other to refer to the authority to rule and exercise law (e.g., Alma 1:17; 8:12; 14:19; 48:7; 51:8).

See also Priesthood among the Nephites; Sealing power.

MMM

Prayer The act through which mortals communicate with God. God commands his people to pray (Mosiah 26:39; D&C 19:28) and he is displeased when they fail to "call upon [his] name." The brother of Jared[1] was chastised for three hours by the Lord for failing to pray, after which he "repented of the *evil* which he had done" (Ether 2:14–15; italics added).

The Book of Mormon repeatedly witnesses that God hears and answers prayers. Jesus issued an invitation with a promise: "Ask, and it shall be given unto you; seek, and ye shall find; knock, and it shall be opened unto you" (3 Ne. 14:7). Then to build faith in prayer Jesus reasoned that if mortal fathers, notwithstanding their imperfections, "know how to give good gifts unto [their] children, how much more shall your Father who is in heaven give good things to them that ask him?" (3 Ne. 14:11).

Many such truths concerning prayer can be gleaned from the Book of Mormon.

Proper prayer

In the course of his sermon to the multitude gathered at the temple in Bountiful[2], Jesus gave the people an example of how to pray. He said, "After this manner therefore pray ye" (3 Ne. 13:9). What followed was not a set prayer that should be repeated, but a pattern for acceptable and effective prayer, representing important attitudes and acknowledgments by the one saying the prayer. Christ's prayer showed recognition and reverence for God's name (3 Ne. 13:9), acceptance of God's will (3 Ne. 13:10), and a genuine sincerity, represented by a willingness to do for others as one would have God do for them (3 Ne. 13:11).

Furthermore, prayers are to be said to the Father in the name of Jesus Christ (3 Ne. 18:19). In 3 Nephi 19 there is an occasion where the disciples prayed to Jesus. This variation is a singular experience apparently allowed because, as Jesus explained to his Father, "they pray unto me because I am with them" (3 Ne. 19:22). The practice taught by Christ and followed by the disciples was to pray to the Father in Christ's name (3 Ne. 18:19; 19:6–7).

Kneeling when praying is also an important part of prayer as it shows reverence to God. Christ exemplified this when he commanded the multitude to kneel down. He then knelt and prayed (3 Ne. 17:15–17). Prayers, as in this instance, may be vocalized, but prayers may also be offered in the heart (Alma 34:21, 27; Mosiah 24:11–12; D&C 19:28).

Where to pray

Alma[2] quoted Zenos to the poor among the Zoramites[2] to teach that worship should not be restricted to the synagogue. Prayer is acceptable and can be effective in the wilderness, or in one's house, or closet, or field (Alma 33:3–9; cf. 34:20–26; 3 Ne. 13:6). Moreover, Jesus taught the Nephites to "pray in your families" (3 Ne.

18:21). The admonition to "let your hearts be . . . drawn out in prayer unto him continually" teaches that prayer is appropriate wherever one may be (Alma 34:27).

What to pray for

Christ taught the challenging principle that "whatsoever ye shall ask the Father in my name, which is right, . . . shall be given unto you" (3 Ne. 18:20). Nephi[1] reflected an understanding of this teaching when he testified, "I know that God will give liberally to him that asketh. Yea, my God will give me, if I ask not amiss" (2 Ne. 4:35; cf. D&C 88:63–65). Latter-day revelation affirms that "he that asketh in the Spirit asketh according to the will of God; wherefore it is done even as he asketh" (D&C 46:30). The Nephite disciples enjoyed this type of inspired prayer. The record states that "they did not multiply many words, for it was given unto them what they should pray" (3 Ne. 19:24). To Nephi[2], the son of Helaman[3], the Lord promised "all things shall be done unto thee according to thy word, for thou shalt not ask that which is contrary to my will" (Hel. 10:5). In latter-day revelation the Lord has said that such a promise is given to those who are "purified and cleansed from all sin" (D&C 50:28–29).

The Book of Mormon is instructive concerning what is "right" to pray about. Prayers are to be said for one's own personal welfare, "and also for the welfare of [others]" (Alma 34:27). Alma the Elder prayed in faith for his wayward son (Mosiah 27:14). Alma the Younger prayed mightily that the hard-hearted in Ammonihah might feel the Spirit, "that he might baptize them unto repentance" (Alma 8:10). The brother of Jared[1] petitioned the Lord not to confound the language of his people (Ether 1:35, 37). The Lord taught the Nephites to pray for their enemies, and he taught the fathers in the Nephite multitude to pray for their wives and their children that they might be blessed (3 Ne. 18:21). He also instructed his disciples to pray for the unconverted, or the unrepentant (3 Ne. 12:44; 18:23, 30).

Amulek recommended prayer for a variety of personal concerns: He taught that the Nephites should pray for their "crops," their "flocks," and their "household," as well as for protection "against the power of [their] enemies" and "against the devil" (Alma 34:18–27; cf. 3 Ne. 18:18). Nephi[1] prayed for strength to bear his personal trials (2 Ne. 4:30–35), and Alma[2] prayed for strength to be delivered from prison in Ammonihah (Alma 14:26).

Additionally, the Book of Mormon contains instances in which individuals sought in prayer to gain a personal testimony of some point of religious truth. For example, Nephi[1] prayed that he might know the truth of his father's revelations (1 Ne. 2:16); Alma[2] recounted many days of prayer as he sought to know the truth of the gospel for himself (Alma 5:45–46); and king Lamoni's father prostrated himself on the ground and cried to the Lord in prayer desiring that God would make himself known unto him (Alma 22:17–18). The invitation to pray for religious understanding was given by Jesus himself. Perceiving that the people could not understand fully the doctrines he had taught them, Jesus instructed the people to ponder his teachings and to pray unto the Father for understanding (3 Ne. 17:3). When questioned by Laman[1] and Lemuel about the doctrines taught by their father Lehi[1], Nephi[1] simply responded, "Have ye inquired of the Lord?" (1 Ne. 15:8). Moroni[2]'s closing words contain a promise that if one reads the Book of Mormon and prays with faith in Christ, God "will manifest the truth of it unto [him], by the power of the Holy Ghost" (Moro. 10:4).

Most important is the truth taught repeatedly concerning the role of prayer in personally applying the Atonement. Amulek exhorted, "Cry unto him for mercy; for he is mighty to save" (Alma 34:18). Without exception throughout the Book of Mormon narrative the plea for mercy or forgiveness through Christ was granted by God. Enos (Enos 1:4), king Benjamin's people (Mosiah 4:2–3), Zeezrom (Alma 15:10), Lamoni (Alma 18:41), and Alma[2] (Alma 36:16–21) all experienced the joy resulting from true repentance and humble prayer that the Atonement would be applied to their lives.

In summary, the answer to the question of what to pray for, or what to pray about, was given by Alma: "Counsel with the Lord in all thy doings" (Alma 37:37; cf. 2 Ne. 32:9).

Frequency of prayer

As the Savior personally ministered to his people he told them to "watch and pray always lest ye enter into temptation" (3 Ne. 18:18; cf. Alma 13:28). Nephi[1] also told his brethren to "pray always" (2 Ne. 32:8–9), a practice he exemplified in his own life. Laden with the responsibility to build a ship and lead his family to the promised land, Nephi recorded, "And I, Nephi, did go into the mount oft, and I did pray oft unto the Lord; wherefore the Lord showed unto me great things" (1 Ne. 18:3).

Amulek taught the Zoramites[2] to pray morning, midday, and evening, and when one is not "cry[ing] unto the Lord, let your hearts be full, drawn out in prayer unto [God] continually" (Alma 34:27; cf. 2 Ne. 9:52; D&C 19:28).

Nephi taught that diligence to or neglect of prayer is influenced by the spirit one hearkens to: "For if ye would hearken unto the Spirit which teacheth a man to pray ye would know that ye must pray; for the evil spirit teacheth not a man to pray, but teacheth him that he must not pray" (2 Ne. 32:8).

Proper attitude and effort in prayer

Prayer must be sincere, from the heart, and offered with real intent. Enos wrote, "My soul hungered; . . . and I cried unto [God] in mighty prayer and supplication" (Enos 1:4). Mormon admonished, "Pray unto the Father with all the energy of heart" (Moro. 7:48). And Moroni[2] stipulated that to know the truth of the Book of Mormon one must "ask with a sincere heart, [and] with real intent" (Moro. 10:4).

The Lord promised serious consequences for those who do not pray with "real intent." He not only stated that the prayer "profiteth him nothing," but warned that it is "counted evil unto a man, if he shall pray and not with real intent of heart" (Moro. 7:6, 9). Alma[2] lamented the case of the apostate Zoramites who had given themselves over to repetitious and self-righteous prayers (Alma 31). His strong words, "Do not pray as the Zoramites do, for . . . they pray to be heard of men" (Alma 38:13) resemble closely the Savior's warning, "And when thou prayest thou shalt not do as the hypocrites, for they love to pray . . . that they may be seen of men" (3 Ne. 13:5).

Prayers are not to become vain (i.e., ineffectual) repetitions, for God already knows what one needs before one prays. Amulek taught the proud Zoramites another way that prayers can become vain. He taught the principle that prayers are only effective if they are coupled with charitable works toward the needy. If not, he testified, "your prayer is vain, and availeth you nothing, and ye are as hypocrites who do deny the faith" (Alma 34:28).

Prayers must be said with faith (Jacob 3:1); one must believe in God and that he hears and answers prayers (JST Mark 11:26). The Book of Mormon gives examples of successful prayers offered by individuals who prayed with great faith, such as the brother of Jared (Ether 3:5, 9, 15), Enos (Enos 1:8), and Alma[1] (Mosiah 27:14). Even a "particle of faith," or a "desire to believe" (Alma 32:27), is recognized by God and can bring answers to prayer, as was the case in the conversion of king Lamoni's father (Alma 22:17–18).

Prayer is strengthened and deepened through FASTING. Various Book of Mormon passages link prayer with fasting (Omni 1:26; Alma 17:3; 28:6; 3 Ne. 27:1; 4 Ne. 1:12). Of righteous Nephite church members during the time of Nephi[2], Mormon recorded that "they did fast and pray oft, and did wax stronger and stronger in their humility, and firmer and firmer in the faith of Christ, . . . even to the purifying and the sanctification of their hearts" (Hel. 3:35).

See also Revelation.

KJW

Precept(s) Commandments, principles, or orders prescribed as general rules for behavior. Divine precepts leading to exaltation are revealed as mortals become willing and prepared to receive them. The Lord said that he "will give unto the children of men line upon line, precept upon precept, here a little and there a little; and blessed are those who hearken unto my precepts, and lend an ear unto my counsel, for they shall learn wisdom." Those who accept will receive more; those who claim to "have enough, from them shall be taken away even that which they have" (2 Ne. 28:30).

Worship of God must be by his precepts and not by the precepts of men (2 Ne. 27:25). Following the false precepts of men is a major stumbling block for humanity, proud or humble (2 Ne. 28:14).

RLB

Premortal existence Existence as spirit offspring of God prior to being born into mortality on earth. The Book of Mormon does not extensively discuss the doctrine of premortality, but two important scriptural passages refer to it. Important implications may be drawn from those two passages. First, the appearance of the premortal Christ to the brother of Jared[1] teaches that the Savior's earthly body would be in the likeness of his premortal spirit body (Ether 3:15–16). Being created "in the image of God" (Gen. 1:26–27; Moses 6:8–9) applies both to premortal spirit bodies as well as earthly physical bodies. The First Presidency's statement entitled "The Origin of Man" reiterates this truth: "'God created man in His own image.' This is just as true of the spirit as it is of the body, which is only the clothing of the spirit, its complement; the two together constituting the soul. The spirit of man is in the form of man, and the spirits of all creatures are in the likeness of their bodies" (*Messages*, 4:203).

Second, the premortal existence is alluded to in the words of Alma[2] concerning the Nephite priests who had been "called and prepared from the foundation of the world according to the foreknowledge of God, on account of their exceeding faith and good works; in the first place being left to choose good or evil; therefore they having chosen good, and exercising exceedingly great faith, are called with a holy calling" (Alma 13:3; cf. Jer. 1:5; 1 Pet. 1:19–20). Foreordination is the premortal selection of individuals to fulfill predesignated responsibilities. Alma taught that the foreordination of these Nephite high priests was due to their great faith and righteous works in the "first place" or the premortal world. Accordingly, the premortal existence was an environment wherein agency was fully operative. Although "in the first place they were on the same standing [at least in innocence, opportunity, and agency] with their brethren" (Alma 13:5), individuals progressed differently resulting in varying levels of faithfulness and obedience. That some were called to holy callings on earth because of premortal faith and righteousness, would also imply that others exercised less faith, were less righteous, and were thereby not foreordained to such priesthood callings (Abr. 3:22–23). The Prophet Joseph Smith taught that "every man who has a calling to minister to the inhabitants of the world was ordained to that very purpose in the Grand Council of heaven before this world was" (Smith, 365).

See also Chosen; First place.

BIBLIOGRAPHY

Messages of The First Presidency of The Church of Jesus Christ of Latter-day Saints. Compiled by James R. Clark. 6 vols. Salt Lake City: Bookcraft, 1965–75.

Smith, Joseph. *Teachings of the Prophet Joseph Smith.* Selected by Joseph Fielding Smith. Salt Lake City: Deseret Book, 1976.

BLT

Preparatory redemption Redemption through Christ which was "prepared from the foundation of the world" for all mankind (Mosiah 4:6–7). The doctrine of salvation centers in the redemptive role of Jesus Christ; he alone has the power to save mankind from the effects of Adam's fall. And this redemption "through the Atonement of Christ," made possible "by obedience to the laws and ordinances of the Gospel," was prepared from the foundation of the world (A of F 3; Moses 4:1–4; Abr. 3:22–28; Rev. 12:7–11). Alma[2] affirmed that foreordinations and mortal callings exist in accordance with this preordained gospel plan of redemption for such as will choose good and exercise great faith and good works (Alma 13:3).

JFM

Pride "The central feature of pride is enmity—enmity toward God and enmity toward our fellowmen," declared President Ezra Taft Benson, and he characterized enmity as "hatred toward, hostility to, or a state of opposition" and said, "it is the power by which Satan wishes to reign over us" ("Beware," 4).

The sin of pride has been called the Nephite disease. Mormon recorded, "Behold, the pride of this nation, or the people of the Nephites, hath proven their destruction" (Moro. 8:27; cf. 1 Ne. 12:19; 2 Ne. 26:10). Then, to ensure that modern readers did not miss that momentous Book of Mormon message from "a fallen people" (D&C 20:9), the Lord warned, "Beware of pride, lest ye become as the Nephites of old" (D&C 38:39).

Pride, the seedbed of all iniquity, is "the universal sin," the great vice (Benson, "Cleansing," 6). The "great and spacious building" (1 Ne. 8:26) which Lehi[1] saw in his dream was "the pride of the world" (1 Ne. 11:35–36) and "great was the multitude that did enter" (1 Ne. 8:33).

C. S. Lewis wrote: "It is the comparison that makes you proud: the pleasure of being above the rest. Once the element of competition has gone, pride has gone" (110). Hence, the proud turn every man into an adversary by competing and comparing. For example, an Amalekite demanded of Aaron[3]: "Why do not the angels appear unto us? Behold are not this people as good as thy people?" (Alma 21:5). The wicked who opposed Nephi[3], just prior to the coming of Christ, were angry with Nephi because they saw that "he had greater power than they" (3 Ne. 7:18). In the premortal council it was pride, the first sin, that felled "Lucifer, son of the morning" (2 Ne. 24:12). Desiring to exalt his "throne above the stars of God" (2 Ne. 24:13), he placed his plan in competition with the Father's plan (Moses 4:1–3)—it was the "my will, not thy will" attitude of those who suffer from pride. Samuel the Lamanite challenged the wicked Nephites of his time for their support of false prophets who would say, "Walk after the pride of *your* own hearts; yea, walk after the pride of *your* eyes, and do whatsoever *your* heart desireth" (Hel. 13:27; cf. D&C 1:16; italics added).

The enmity of the proud toward God and others is described numerous times in the Book of Mormon, in terms such as "hard-hearted" (Alma 9:5), "high heads" (2 Ne. 28:14), "stiff necks" (Jacob 2:13), "deafness of . . . ears" (Jarom 1:3), "blindness of mind" (Ether 4:15), "puffed up" (Alma 5:53), and willful rebellion (3 Ne. 6:18).

Pride, if not repented of, can be the root cause and the first step to more grievous sin. Samuel the Lamanite condemned Nephites whose hearts swelled with "great pride, unto boasting, and unto great swelling, envyings, strifes, malice, persecutions, and murders, and all manner of iniquities" (Hel. 13:22).

The proud, like Laman[1] and Lemuel, would have no one "rule over" them, not even God (2 Ne. 5:3). "Behold," Mormon observed, the proud "do not desire that the Lord their God, who hath created them, should rule and reign over them; notwithstanding his great goodness and his mercy towards them, they do set at naught his counsels, and they will not that he should be their guide" (Hel. 12:6). The proud are not easily taught (Hel. 12:5). Nephi[1], for example, "truly spake many great things unto [his brothers], which were hard to be understood, save a man should inquire of the Lord; and they being hard in their hearts, therefore they did not look unto the Lord as they ought" (1 Ne. 15:3). Pride is a damning sin in that it limits or stops progression: "They that will harden their hearts, to them is given the lesser portion of the word until they know nothing concerning his mysteries" (Alma 12:11). Jacob[2] warned that pride could destroy the soul (Jacob 2:16).

The proud fear the judgments of men more than the judgments of God. King Noah[3] is an example of this. Fearing "the judgments of God," he was about to release Abinadi, but an appeal to Noah's pride that he had been "reviled" sent Abinadi to the flames (Mosiah 17:11–12). The proud king was more concerned about saving his face than saving his soul.

The Nephites were taught "that every man should esteem his neighbor as himself" (Mosiah 27:4) and "not think himself above another" (Mosiah 23:7), yet their history shows times of "great inequality among the people, some lifting themselves up with their pride" (Alma 4:12). Jacob spoke bluntly to the Nephites of his age about this enmity of pride: "Because some of you have obtained more abundantly than that of your brethren ye are lifted up in the pride of your hearts . . . because ye suppose that ye are better than they" (Jacob 2:13). A classic example of the enmity of the prideful is the prayer of the haughty Zoramites[2] at their Rameumptom: "Thou hast elected us that we shall be saved, whilst all around us are elected to be cast by thy wrath down to hell" (Alma 31:17). Surely pride was the foundation of Nephite prejudice against the Lamanites (Jacob 3:9; Hel. 14:10). Further, the "pride of those people who professed the blood of nobility" (Alma 51:21) had to be toppled by captain Moroni (Alma 51:17) to preserve liberty among the Nephites of his day.

The Book of Mormon demonstrates that the rich and the learned, in whatever time or place, are particularly guilty of elevating themselves above others by making prideful comparisons. In his study of the Nephite records, Mormon saw this destructive effect of pride repeated time and again. Blessed by the Lord "with the riches of the world," the Nephites "began to set their hearts upon their riches; yea, they began to seek to get gain that they might be lifted up one above another" (Hel. 6:17). "And the people began to be distinguished by ranks, according to their riches and their chances for learning" (3 Ne. 6:12).

Nephi[1] foresaw the affliction of pride manifesting itself in modern times, as he lamented the prevalence of "the wise, and the learned, and the rich, that are puffed up in the pride of their hearts" (2 Ne. 28:15). Nephi also foresaw churches who, because of pride, would "grind upon the face of the poor" (2 Ne. 26:20) and rob them because of "their fine sanctuaries" and their "fine clothing" (2 Ne. 28:12–13; Morm. 8:36–39; cf. Alma 4:12). The wearing of "fine" or "costly apparel," too, was a sign of a proud people—"and in all these things were they lifted up in the pride of their eyes, for they began to wear very costly apparel" (Alma 4:6; 1:6; 5:53; 4 Ne. 1:24).

Although pride could easily be observed among the wealthy and learned, others of Nephite society were not immune to it by any means, suffering from such things as coveting (Mosiah 4:25), envying (Alma 5:29), and murmuring (1 Ne. 2:11).

Even those "who professed to belong to the church of God" did not escape the plague of pride (Hel. 3:33–34). At one point, their pride even "exceed[ed] the pride of those who did not belong to the church of God" (Alma 4:9). Alma[2] strove to "pull down, by the word of God, all the pride . . . [of] his people, seeing no way that he might reclaim them save it were in bearing down in pure testimony against them" (Alma 4:19). Speaking to the members of the Church, he asked a crucial question: "Behold, are ye stripped of pride? I say unto you, if ye are not ye are not prepared to meet God" (Alma 5:28). Those church members who did not repent, "who were lifted up in the pride of their hearts—the same were rejected, and their names were blotted out" (Alma 6:3).

The consequences of pride were far-reaching and dire among the Nephites, and they were foreseen to be dire in modern times as well. The proud were easily lured into SECRET COMBINATIONS as Satan puffed "them up with pride, tempting them to seek for power, and authority" (3 Ne. 6:15). The objective of secret combinations was "to help such as sought power to gain power" (Ether 8:16, 23). Pride, manifest through secret combinations, resulted in the downfall of the Jaredites and in "the destruction of the people of Nephi" (Ether 8:21). During the Nephite Zion following the Savior's ministry, it was pride, too, that brought the law of consecration to an end among the Nephites: "There began to be among them those who were lifted up in pride. . . . And from that time forth they did have their goods and their substance no more common among them" (4 Ne. 1:24–25).

Nephi[1], the first prophet-writer of the Book of Mormon, witnessing the present day, lamented, "And the Gentiles are lifted up in the pride of their eyes, and have stumbled, . . . and preach up unto themselves their own wisdom and their own learning" (2 Ne. 26:20; 3 Ne. 16:10). Moroni[2], the last prophet-writer, also viewing the latter days, declared, "And I know that ye do walk in the pride of your hearts; and there are none save a few only who do not lift themselves up in the pride of their hearts, unto the wearing of very fine apparel, unto envying, and strifes, and malice, and persecutions, and all manner of iniquities; and your churches, yea, even every one, have become polluted because of the pride of your hearts" (Morm. 8:36).

It was the proud that were singled out for destruction in the last days: "The day cometh that shall burn as an oven; and all the proud, yea, and all that do wickedly, shall be stubble" (3 Ne. 25:1).

The antidote for pride is to become "humble, meek, submissive, patient, full of love and all long-suffering" (Alma 13:28; 7:23; cf. Mosiah 11:19; Alma 39:2). To overcome the sin of pride requires the new sacrifice of "a broken heart and a contrite spirit" (3 Ne. 9:20).

See also Broken heart and contrite spirit; Costly apparel; Hard-heartedness; Humility; Lowliness of heart; Meekness; Stiffnecked, stiffneckedness.

BIBLIOGRAPHY

Benson, Ezra Taft. "Cleansing the Inner Vessel." *Ensign* 16 (May 1986): 4–7.

———. "Beware of Pride." *Ensign* 19 (May 1989): 4–7.

Lewis, C. S. *Mere Christianity*. New York: Macmillan, 1952.

RAB

Priestcraft Preaching with the intent of setting oneself up to be a "light unto the world," in order to "get gain and praise" without concern for the welfare of Zion (2 Ne. 26:29; cf. Alma 1:16; 3 Ne. 18:24). The Lord forbade priestcraft and commanded men to have charity and labor for the welfare of others, not for money (2 Ne. 26:30–31). Priestcraft was first introduced among Alma's people by Nehor who taught flattering and false doctrine as he tried to convince the people that priests should be "popular" and supported by the people rather than laboring with their hands (Alma 1:2–6, 12). Although Nehor was executed for murder, his practice of priestcraft was perpetuated by "many who loved the vain things of the world" including the wicked leaders of Ammonihah, the Amalekites, and the Amulonites (Alma 1:16; 14:16; 21:4; 24:28–29). The motives and methods of priestcraft are contrary to true priesthood service (cf. Alma 1:19–20, 26–30).

Priestcraft is destructive (Alma 1:12). It contributed to wars among the people (e.g., Alma 24:28–29), the downfall of the Nephite Zion (4 Ne. 1:26), and the rejection and crucifixion of Christ (2 Ne. 10:5; cf. John 11:47–53). Moroni[2] prophesied that priestcraft would be prevalent in the last days and condemned the practice (Morm. 8:31–40). Nephi[1] prophesied that those guilty of the practice would be "brought low in the dust" and consumed as stubble (1 Ne. 22:23; cf. 2 Ne. 26:20).

TBB

Priesthood among the Nephites From Lehi[1] to the coming of Christ, the Nephite people had the Melchizedek Priesthood. During this period they did not hold the Aaronic Priesthood, inasmuch as they were not descendants of Aaron[1] and there were no Levites among them. Nonetheless, the Nephites observed the LAW OF MOSES with all its rites, rituals, and ordinances, looking "forward with steadfastness unto Christ, until the law [should] be fulfilled" (2 Ne. 25:24–25; 5:10). This was done by the authority of the Melchizedek Priesthood, which embraces the right to do all that the Aaronic Priesthood can do (D&C 107:4–10). Attendant to his ministry among them, Christ established the same system of Church government had by those in the New Testament Church. Joseph Smith testified that when the "Savior made His appearance upon this continent after His resurrection . . . He planted the Gospel here in all its fulness, and richness, and power, and blessing; that they had Apostles, Prophets, Pastors, Teachers, and Evangelists; the same order, *the same priesthood,* the same ordinances, gifts, powers, and blessings, as were enjoyed on the eastern continent" (4:538; italics added). This evidently included the Aaronic or lesser priesthood. President Joseph Fielding Smith wrote that Christ "gave the Nephites all the authority of the priesthood which we exercise today. Therefore we are justified in the belief that not only was the fulness of the Melchizedek Priesthood conferred, but also the Aaronic, just as we have it in the Church today; and this Aaronic Priesthood remained with them from this time until, through wickedness, all priesthood ceased. We may be assured that in the days of Moroni[2] the Nephites did ordain teachers and priests in the Aaronic Priesthood" (1:126; Moro. 3).

When the law of Moses was fulfilled in Christ, those duties associated with the carnal law were no longer performed. But the Aaronic Priesthood possesses keys to more than the rites and rituals associated with the law of Moses. This lesser priesthood holds "the keys of the ministering of angels, and to administer in outward ordinances, the letter of the gospel, the baptism of repentance for the remission of sins, agreeable to the covenants and commandments" (D&C 107:20).

The priesthood administers the gospel in all dispensations (D&C 84:17–19). It is only under the direction of the priesthood that the gospel can legally be taught. Thus, Nephi[1] consecrated his brothers Jacob[2] and Joseph[2] "that they should be priests and teachers" (2 Ne. 5:26). In the days of king Benjamin "there were many holy men in the land, and they did speak the word of God with power and with authority" (W of M 1:17). It was from king Mosiah[2] that Alma the Elder received "power to ordain priests and teachers over every church" established throughout the land of Zarahemla (Mosiah 25:19). Alma the Younger testified that he was consecrated by his father "to be a high priest over the church of God, he having power and authority from God to do these things" (Alma 5:3). Similarly, Aaron[3] and "his brethren went forth from city to city, and from one house of worship to another, establishing churches, and consecrating priests and teachers throughout the land among the Lamanites, to preach and to teach the word of God among them" (Alma 23:4). As to obtaining membership in the Church, the record states that "whosoever was baptized by the power and authority of God was added to his church" (Mosiah 18:17). Alma[2] preached of an earlier people of God, including Melchizedek and his city, who possessed "the high priesthood of the holy order of God" (Alma 13:6). Through the ordinances of this priesthood they were cleansed from sin and "entered into the rest of the Lord their God" (Alma 13:12). He assured the people of Ammonihah that if they would humble themselves before God and "bring forth fruit meet for repentance" (Alma 13:13), they could enjoy the same blessings (Alma 13:1–20).

When Christ introduced a new dispensation of the gospel as recorded in 3 Nephi, he called the twelve disciples and gave them "power and authority to baptize" (3 Ne. 12:1), to confer the Holy Ghost, to ordain others, and to do all else that they did in his name (3 Ne. 11:21–25; 18:37; 27:7; Moro. 2; 3). This was a re-conferral of priesthood as "old things are done away, and all things have become new" (3 Ne. 12:47; 15:2–9).

Evidences of the priesthood or its fruits were present everywhere among the Nephites. They were seen in the manner in which the gospel was preached, scriptures recorded, and ordinances performed, including all ritual associated with the temple and the law of Moses. People were baptized into the Church, and when necessary cast out (Moro. 6:1–8). Fathers blessings were given (2 Ne. 1–4), the Holy Ghost conferred (Moro. 2), and the sick healed (4 Ne. 1:5). Nephi[1]'s confidence in the power and authority that God had given him was such that he said, "If God had commanded me to do all things I could do them. If he should command me that I should say unto this water, be thou earth, it should be earth; and if I should say it, it would be done" (1 Ne. 17:50; cf. Jacob 4:6). His namesake Nephi[3], the son of Nephi[2], ministered "with power and with great authority" (3 Ne. 7:17). So great was the power with which he spoke that his enemies "could [not] disbelieve his words" (3 Ne. 7:18). Angels ministered to him daily, and "in the name of Jesus did he cast out devils and unclean spirits; and even his brother did he raise from the dead, after he had been stoned," and he worked "many more miracles, in the sight of the people, in the name of Jesus" (3 Ne. 7:19–20).

See also Chosen; Church of God (Christ) in ancient America; Elder(s); High priest(s); Holy order of God; Premortal existence; Priest(s); Sealing power; Teacher(s).

BIBLIOGRAPHY

Smith, Joseph. *History of The Church of Jesus Christ of Latter-day Saints*. Edited by B. H. Roberts. 7 vols.

2d ed. rev. Salt Lake City: The Church of Jesus Christ of Latter-day Saints, 1932–51.

Smith, Joseph Fielding. *Answers to Gospel Questions.* Compiled by Joseph Fielding Smith Jr. 5 vols. Salt Lake City: Deseret Book, 1957–66.

JFM

Priest(s) An ecclesiastical or priesthood office among the Nephites. Before the coming of Christ, the Nephites did not have the Aaronic Priesthood (Smith, 3:87), therefore it should not be confused with the office of priest as found in the Church today. References to priests before Christ's coming are to high priests holding the Melchizedek Priesthood. Because there were no Aaronic priests, they did not need to distinguish between the two different kinds of priests (McConkie, 599). Nephi[1] consecrated his brothers Jacob[2] and Joseph[2] as priests and teachers (2 Ne. 5:26). That the priest was a Melchizedek Priesthood office is made clear by Jacob's stating that he had been "ordained after the manner of his holy order" (2 Ne. 6:2). The term "high priest" is used explicitly in a few passages—for example, Helaman[2] and "his brethren" are so designated (Alma 46:6). In the time of Helaman[3] the text mentions high priests and teachers together as Church leaders (Hel. 3:25). Alma[1], as high priest of the Church, ordained other priests (Mosiah 18:18; 25:19), as did his successors Alma[2] (Alma 4:7) and Helaman[2] (Alma 45:22). After the coming of Christ, the disciples of Christ also ordained priests (Moro. 3:1–3). Whether these were high priests or priests of the Aaronic order is not explicitly stated.

See also Church of God (Christ) in ancient America; Elder(s); High priest(s); Priesthood among the Nephites; Teacher(s).

BIBLIOGRAPHY

Smith, Joseph Fielding. *Doctrines of Salvation.* Compiled by Bruce R. McConkie. 3 vols. Salt Lake City: Bookcraft, 1954–56.

McConkie, Bruce R. *Mormon Doctrine.* 2d ed. Salt Lake City: Bookcraft, 1966.

MDR

Priests of king Noah[3] *See* Noah[3], priests of.

Printing and publication of the Book of Mormon *See* Book of Mormon, printing and publication of.

Privily *See* Appendix C.

Probation, probationary *See* Life, purpose of.

Profaned *See* Appendix C.

Promised land, land of promise Land settled and inhabited by the Nephites, Lamanites, and Jaredites. This area was "a land which is choice above all other lands" (2 Ne. 1:5; Ether 1:42), a "holy land" (Enos 1:10) that the Lord "had preserved for a righteous people" (Ether 2:7) ever since "the waters had receded from off the face" of it (Ether 13:2). In fulfillment of his promise to Joseph of Egypt that he, Joseph, would be a "fruitful bough . . . whose branches run over the wall" (Gen. 49:22), the Lord covenanted with Lehi[1]—descendant of Joseph—that this land would be an everlasting land of inheritance for his seed, and also others "who should be led out of other countries by the hand of the Lord" (2 Ne. 1:5). Having learned of the land's sacred nature and destiny, Lehi prophesied that "there shall none come into this land save they shall be brought by the hand of the Lord" (2 Ne. 1:6). Moreover, the promised land would be "a land of liberty" and prosperity to those that "shall serve him according to the commandments which he hath given" (2 Ne. 1:7; cf. Enos 1:10; Alma 36:1), and "whatsoever nation shall possess it shall be free from bondage, and from captivity, and from all other nations under heaven, if they will but serve the God of the land, who is Jesus Christ" (Ether 2:12). Furthermore, those who would not serve him on such a blessed land would be "swept off . . . when they are ripened in iniquity" (Ether 2:8–9), and "other nations" will "cause them to be scattered and smitten" (2 Ne. 1:10–11).

The Book of Mormon also speaks of the establishment of the latter-day GENTILES upon the promised land, and the role they would play in redeeming Israel in the last days. In his vision of what the future held for the land of promise, Nephi[1] witnessed the eventual discovery and colonization of the Americas by explorers and settlers, and their "deliver[ance] by the power of God out of the hands of all other nations" (1 Ne. 13:12–19). This would prepare the way, Nephi continued, for the Lord to "raise up a mighty nation among the Gentiles, yea, even upon the face of this land" (1 Ne. 22:7). This promise of a mighty nation refers to the establishment of the United States in North America. Furthermore, the Lord told Jacob[2] he would "fortify this land against all other nations" (2 Ne. 10:12), and that "this land shall be a land of liberty unto the Gentiles, and there shall be no kings upon the land, who shall raise up unto the Gentiles" (2 Ne. 10:11). The Savior also taught the Nephites that the Holy Ghost would be poured out "upon the Gentiles" living in the promised land, "which blessing upon the Gentiles shall make them mighty above all" (3 Ne. 20:27).

The founding of a mighty nation in the promised land was prerequisite to the fulfillment of the prophecy regarding the Gentiles' role in bringing the gospel to the latter-day descendants of Lehi (1 Ne. 13:38–39; 15:13–14; 2 Ne. 30:3–5; 3 Ne. 21:3). Much had to be accomplished before this promise could be fulfilled, for although the Gentiles would "humble themselves before the Lord" (1 Ne. 13:16), they would initially lack important gospel truths and covenants removed from the Bible by the great and abominable church (1 Ne. 13:24–33). God intended to restore a knowledge of those truths and covenants to the Gentiles through the Book of Mormon (1 Ne. 13:34–35). It was only after the Gentiles were "established in this land, and . . . set up as a free people by the power of the Father" that the Book of Mormon could be brought forth and carried to the Nephites and Lamanites—as well as the rest of Israel—in fulfillment of "the covenant of the Father . . . which he hath covenanted with his people" (3 Ne. 21:4). Brigham Young taught: "There is not another nation under heaven but this, in whose midst the Book of Mormon could have been brought forth. The Lord has been operating for centuries to prepare the way for the coming forth of the contents of that Book from the bowels of the earth. . . . It was the Lord who directed the discovery of this land to the nations of the old world, and its settlement, and the war for independence, and the final victory of the colonies, and the unprecedented prosperity of the American nation, up to the calling of Joseph the Prophet. The Lord has dictated and directed the whole of this, for the bringing forth, and establishing of his Kingdom in the last days" (11:17).

In addition to receiving the fulness of the gospel through the Book of Mormon, the Gentiles in the promised land were assured that they too would be blessed in the land (2 Ne. 10:10), "numbered among the house of Israel" (2 Ne. 10:18), and receive the land as an inheritance (2 Ne. 10:19), but only upon conditions of righteousness (3 Ne. 16:13; 21:6). Righteous Gentiles would also be privileged to "assist . . . the remnant of Jacob, and also as many of the house of Israel as shall come, that they may build a city, which shall be called the New Jerusalem," on this continent (3 Ne. 21:23; cf. Ether 13:3–10). Should the Gentiles not repent after receiving the fulness of the gospel, however, the Lord promised to "bring the fulness of my gospel from among them" (3 Ne. 16:10). Moreover, he would "execute vengeance and fury upon them, even as upon the heathen" (3 Ne. 21:21), by allowing the house of Israel to "go through among them, and . . . tread them down" (3 Ne. 16:15) like "a lion among the beasts of the forest, and as a young lion among the flocks of sheep" (3 Ne. 20:16).

See also Columbus, Christopher; Decrees of God.

BIBLIOGRAPHY

Young, Brigham. *Journal of Discourses*. 26 vols. London: Latter-day Saints' Book Depot, 1854–86.

AHH

Prophecy in the Book of Mormon Any inspired utterance, prediction, or foreshadowing of divine will. The title page of the Book of Mormon declares that it was "written . . . by the spirit of prophecy." Thus, the essence of the Book of Mormon is prophecy and the prophets' witnesses of Jesus Christ, "for the testimony of Jesus is the spirit of prophecy" (Rev. 19:10). Jacob[2] stated, "And we also had many revelations, and the spirit of much

PROPHECY IN THE BOOK OF MORMON

prophecy; wherefore, we knew of Christ and his kingdom, which should come" (Jacob 1:6). Accordingly, much of Book of Mormon prophecy is centered in the life and mission of Jesus Christ. Nephi[1] said, "We prophesy of Christ, and we write according to our prophecies, that our children may know to what source they may look for a remission of their sins" (2 Ne. 25:26). Through the teachings of their prophets Book of Mormon people knew when and where Jesus would be born, the name of his mother (1 Ne. 10:4; Hel. 14:2; Alma 7:10), and what signs would be given to verify that Christ had indeed come into the world (Hel. 14:2–5). They also knew details concerning his earthly ministry: the mighty miracles he would perform (Mosiah 3:5–6), his tremendous suffering for the sins of the world (Mosiah 3:7; Alma 7:11–12), his death by crucifixion, and his resurrection on the third day (2 Ne. 10:5; Mosiah 3:10). Moreover, the people would know of these culminating events in Christ's life through observance of the prophesied signs: darkness for three days, great thunderings, lightnings, and mighty earthquakes (1 Ne. 19:10–13; Hel. 14:20–21). The ultimate verification of the prophetic utterances of Book of Mormon prophets concerning Jesus Christ was the personal appearance of the resurrected Christ to their people some time after his ascension in the Old World (1 Ne. 12:6; 2 Ne. 26:9; 3 Ne. 11).

Although the main purpose of prophecy is to reveal Jesus Christ, prophecy also includes inspired descriptions of the past, present, or future events. Elder Bruce R. McConkie explained, "In their most dramatic form [such prophecies] are declarations of things to come, things which no mortal power could have made manifest" (602).

The Book of Mormon illustrates several ways prophecy can be received. Most prophecy comes through the promptings of the Spirit, "for by the Spirit are all things made known unto the prophets" (1 Ne. 22:2). Jacob[2] explained that "the Spirit speaketh . . . of things as they really are, and of things as they really will be" (Jacob 4:13). Dreams are another important means whereby prophecy is received. For example, Lehi[1]'s prophetic dream showed that while part of his family would partake of the tree of life, Laman[1] and Lemuel would not (1 Ne. 8:35), a truth verified through the later division of his family according to those who believed in "the revelations of God" and those who did not (2 Ne. 5:6). Often divine messengers deliver prophetic knowledge. For example, an angel foretold that Laban would be delivered into the hands of Nephi[1] (1 Ne. 3:29), and angels foretold the coming of Christ (Mosiah 3:2–23; Hel. 13:5–9).

Prophecies may be conditional or unconditional, and they may have more than one application, interpretation, or fulfillment. Conditional prophecies, for example, often involve the foretelling of punishment and destruction for wickedness that can be averted through repentance, as in the case of the Babylonian destruction of Jerusalem, which was fulfilled in 586 B.C. (1 Ne. 1:4; 2:13; 10:3; 2 Ne. 1:4; Hel. 8:21). A recurring phrase in the Book of Mormon underscores the notion of conditional prophecy: "Inasmuch as ye shall keep the commandments of God ye shall prosper in the land; and ye ought to know also, that inasmuch as ye will not keep the commandments of God ye shall be cut off from his presence" (Alma 36:30; cf. 1 Ne. 2:20–24; Alma 9:13).

The prophet Abinadi first declared his prophecies to be conditional by using the phrase "except they repent" (Mosiah 11:20–25). Then, when he saw that his wicked audience refused to repent, his prophecy became unconditional, promising, "It shall come to pass" (Mosiah 12:2–8). Other examples of unconditional prophecy include Lehi[1]'s revelation that the brass plates will one day go forth to all nations (1 Ne. 5:18); the angel's words to Nephi[1] concerning the corruption of the Bible (1 Ne. 13:23–27), and his promise that other holy books would come forth to restore the plain and precious truths that had been taken or held back (1 Ne. 13:39–40); Joseph[1]'s description of a book (the Book of Mormon) that together with the Bible would confound false doctrine, lay down contention, and make known the covenants of the Lord (2 Ne. 3:12); Mormon's foretelling that the Book of Mormon would go "unto the unbelieving of the Jews" to persuade them "that Jesus is the Christ" (Morm. 5:14); and Moroni[2]'s detailed description of the world at the time of the coming forth of the Book of Mormon (Morm. 8:26–41).

Prophecies may also have more than one application or fulfillment. A good example of this is Nephi[1]'s quoting Isaiah concerning the fate of the king of Babylon. Isaiah's prophecy of the downfall of Babylon's powerful king also serves to foretell the downfall of Lucifer, the king of spiritual Babylon (2 Ne. 24).

Other important prophecies in the Book of Mormon include NEPHI[1]'S VISION of events that would serve as a prelude to the restoration of the gospel on the American continent—COLUMBUS, migrations to the PROMISED LAND, and the Revolutionary War (1 Ne. 13:12–19; cf. 3 Ne. 21:4); prophecies that reveal the location of the NEW JERUSALEM and who will participate in its construction (2 Ne. 1:5–6; 3 Ne. 21:22–23; Ether 13:4–7); and prophecies foretelling blessings to Gentiles, Jews, Lamanites, and all the house of Israel if they come unto Christ (1 Ne. 15:13–16; 2 Ne. 29:14; 30:2–7; 3 Ne. 20:29–37).

See also (for additional Book of Mormon prophecies) Gentiles, Book of Mormon message concerning; Jesus Christ, second coming of; Jews, Book of Mormon message concerning; Lamanites, Book of Mormon message concerning; Millennium, the.

BIBLIOGRAPHY

McConkie, Bruce R. *Mormon Doctrine.* 2d ed. Salt Lake City: Bookcraft, 1966.

FEW

Prophetic speech forms Brief statements attached to revelations from God. The speech forms frequently contain the name of God, are often located at the beginning or end of a revelation, and function in prophetic writings to indicate prophetic authority and prerogative. They belong to the world of prophets and prophecy and are well attested in the scriptures, including the Book of Mormon. Individuals who are not prophets cannot use the forms with power and authority, for the power and authority attached to the forms originate from God (Jer. 28:10–17).

The following five prophetic speech forms are found in the Book of Mormon:

1. Proclamation formula. "Hearken to the word of the Lord" (Jacob 2:27; cf. 2 Kgs. 7:1; Isa. 1:10); "Hear the words of Jesus Christ" (3 Ne. 30:1). This formula frequently introduces prophetic language with the words "hearken" or "hear," serving as a summons to give heed to God's word as revealed through the prophet.

2. Messenger formula. "Thus saith the Lord of Hosts." This formula, well attested throughout the Book of Mormon (1 Ne. 21:7–8, 22, 25; Jacob 2:25, 28–30, 32–33; Mosiah 11:20, 25; Alma 8:17, 29; Hel. 10:11, 14; 3 Ne. 24:1; cf. Ex. 5:1; Josh. 24:2), introduces prophetic language and is therefore regularly located at the beginning of a revelatory unit. God through his prophet is the ultimate source of the formula, hence its purpose is to set forth both the source as well as the divine authority of the revelation.

3. Oath formula. "As the Lord liveth" (1 Ne. 3:15; 2 Ne. 9:16; 25:20; Omni 1:26; Alma 10:10; Hel. 13:26; 3 Ne. 3:15, 21; cf. Judg. 8:19; 1 Sam. 25:26). The declaration is a solemn promise uttered by a prophet that serves to accentuate the revelation by calling upon the existence of the Lord. In another form of the oath formula, God swears by his own name, "the Lord of Hosts hath sworn" (2 Ne. 24:24; 3 Ne. 29:8; cf. Judg. 2:15; Jer. 51:14). *See* Oaths.

4. Wo oracle. The wo oracle is an accusation form that features the term "wo" in the revelation, and is located within a judgment speech or a prophecy of judgment against a person or people (1 Ne. 1:13; 2 Ne. 9:30–38; Morm. 8:31; Ether 8:24; Moro. 10:25–26; cf. Isa. 3:11; Ezek. 16:23). On occasion the wo is repeated twice ("wo, wo"; Jacob 3:3; Mosiah 3:12) or three times ("wo, wo, wo"; 2 Ne. 28:15; 3 Ne. 9:2) for emphasis.

5. Revelation formula. "The Lord spake unto me" (1 Ne. 2:19; 17:8; 2 Ne. 18:5, 11 // Isa. 8:5, 11; Ether 12:26; Ex. 7:8; Num. 13:1), and "the Spirit of the Lord . . . spake unto me" (1 Ne. 11:11). The revelation formula emphasizes the fact that God is the source of the revelation, that he "speaks" to his prophets, and therefore they have the authority to write or speak his words.

BIBLIOGRAPHY

Aune, David E. *Prophecy in Early Christianity and the Ancient Mediterranean World.* Grand Rapids, Mich.: Eerdmans, 1983. 88–100.

DWP

Prophetic tense, prophetic perfect Using past tense verbs for future events in prophetic literature or, "speaking of things to come as though they had already come" (Mosiah 16:6; cf. Jarom 1:11; Mosiah 3:13). This past tense (prophetic perfect) is often employed in prophecy "to express facts which are undoubtedly imminent, and, therefore, in the imagination of the speaker, already accomplished" (Gesenius, 312). For example, Isaiah 53 (cited by Abinadi in Mosiah 14) prophesied of Jesus' future atoning sacrifice using past tense verbs: "He has borne our griefs, and carried our sorrows; . . . he was wounded for our transgressions, he was bruised for our iniquities. . . . for the transgressions of my people was he stricken" (Mosiah 14:4–8; cf. 2 Ne. 31:6–8).

BIBLIOGRAPHY

Gesenius, Wilhelm. *Hebrew Grammar.* Oxford: Clarendon Press, 1970. Quoted by Stephen D. Ricks in "I Have a Question." *Ensign* 18 (August 1988): 27–28.

DWP

Prophets, false Preachers or teachers who claim to speak for God but have received neither authorization nor message from him. Under the law of Moses, false prophecy was a capital offense (Deut. 18:20). The law specified a test: if a person prophesied a thing that did not come to pass, he was judged to have spoken presumptuously (Deut. 18:22). Even if a person's prophecy did come to pass, he was to be rejected and executed if he led the people after false gods (Deut. 13:1–11). When Jesus Christ visited the Nephites and Lamanites, he warned of false prophets in sheep's clothing who inwardly are ravening wolves. The test was similar: "Ye shall know them by their fruits" (3 Ne. 14:15–20). In a wider sense, a false prophet is anyone who promulgates false or deceptive teachings to lead people astray. Often they are learned men who substitute their own wisdom for the counsel of God (2 Ne. 9:28). False prophets cycle through the entirety of Book of Mormon history. Some are named, such as the anti-Christs Korihor, Nehor, and Sherem. Kishkumen and Gadianton counterfeited the prophetic role by administering signs, secret words, and covenants obtained from Satan rather than from God (Hel. 6:22, 26). Zeezrom taught lying words and exemplified the pride and materialism of many false prophets (Alma 11:24–25). Zoram[3] led his followers "to bow down to dumb idols" (Alma 31:1). Some false prophets are unnamed, such as the host of false prophets who undermined the nearly two-hundred-year peace after Christ's visit (4 Ne. 1:34). Such righteous leaders as king Benjamin dealt with false prophets according to their crimes (W of M 1:16). Wicked people accused true prophets of false prophecy (Mosiah 12:9–15; Hel. 8:25- 9:41). Samuel the Lamanite condemned the Nephites for rejecting true prophets because they testified of their "sins and iniquities" while accepting and supporting false prophets, "blind guides," who justified them in their sins (Hel. 13:26–29). Some of his listeners used the law of Moses test to declare Samuel a false prophet when his prophecies did not come to pass according to their reckoning (3 Ne. 1:5–9). Similarly, the wicked subjects of king Noah[3] accused Abinadi of being a false prophet to legitimize his trial and execution (Mosiah 12:14).

See also Churches, false.

RAC

Prophets, records of the *See* Records of the prophets.

Prophets, rejection of A major theme throughout the Book of Mormon, beginning with the rejection of Lehi[1]'s message and voice of warning (1 Ne. 1:18–20) and concluding with the destruction of the Nephite people after ignoring Mormon's cry to repent (Morm. 2:2–3; 6:17–22). The people of Noah[3] killed Abinadi and consequently "brought down the wrath of God upon them" (Mosiah 7:26–29). Samuel the Lamanite warned of a curse to come upon the Nephites and prophesied that they would eventually lament because they mocked and stoned the prophets (Hel. 13:23–24; 32–33). In the great destruction before the coming of the resurrected Savior, only those Nephites were spared "who received the prophets and stoned them not" (3 Ne. 10:12; 9:10; cf. 2 Ne. 26:3–5). During the rapid demise of the Nephite Zion, attempts were made to kill the three translated Nephites who dwelt among them (4 Ne. 1:30–33), leading the Lord to "take away his beloved disciples" (Morm. 1:13). The Jaredites exemplified the same proclivity to reject and mock their prophets (Ether 7:24; 9:29; 11:22), resulting in their total annihilation (Alma 37:30–31; Ether 13:20–22; 15:29–33).

In testifying to a largely hostile Nephite audience, Samuel the Lamanite gave a fundamental reason for people's rejection of true prophets: "If a prophet come among you and declareth unto you the word of the Lord, which testifieth of your sins and iniquities, ye are angry with him, and cast him out and seek all manner of ways to destroy him; yea, you will say that he is a false prophet, and that he is a sinner, and of the devil, because he testifieth that your deeds are evil" (Hel. 13:26; cf. Mosiah 11:20–26; 12:1–8; 17:7– 13; Alma 8:9–13; Hel. 7:12–28; 8:1–8; 16:2; 3 Ne. 6:20–23; 7:16–20).

This same warning regarding the consequences of rejecting the Lord's servants applies today. A latter-day apostle, Harold B. Lee, testified that "those who criticize the leaders of this Church are showing signs of a spiritual sickness which, unless curbed, will bring about eventually spiritual death. . . . those who in public seek by their criticism, to belittle our leaders or bring them into disrepute, will bring upon themselves more hurt than upon those whom they seek thus to malign" (Lee, 67; cf. 1 Ne. 11:35– 36; Alma 30:27–31, 60; Mosiah 27:9–16; Jacob 7:1–20; D&C 1:14).

Conversely the Lord extends great blessings to those who receive his servants, such as the ANTI-NEPHI-LEHIES (Alma 23–27; cf. Matt. 10:40–41; D&C 84:36–38).

BIBLIOGRAPHY

Lee, Harold B. Conference Report, October 1947.

CF

Prophets, role of A prophet is a man called of God by revelation to be his servant, his mouthpiece, his messenger. The prophet may be called through a vision (1 Ne. 1), by a personal appearance of the Lord (1 Ne. 2:16), or through another of God's servants (Jacob 1:18). His authority is given him through the laying on of hands (Alma 6:1; A of F 5). Prophets possess the power of God—in some cases, power over the elements to cause famine, pestilence, and destruction, as well as the power to bring an end to such conditions. They have power to seal and loose on earth and in heaven (Hel. 10:6–12; 11:4–17). God manifests his power through his servants in miraculous ways. Nephi[1] was able to burst the bands on his hands and feet (1 Ne. 7:17–18). Alma[2] and Amulek broke the cords that bound them, and the prison walls fell to the earth, slaying all but them (Alma 14:26–28). Nephi[2], son of Helaman[3], was protected and conveyed by the Spirit out of the midst of those who sought to cast him into prison (Hel. 10:16). Nephi[3], son of Nephi[2], had "greater power" than his enemies and performed great miracles, even raising his brother from the dead (3 Ne. 7:15–20). The Three Nephites were delivered from pits, furnaces, and wild beasts (3 Ne. 28:19–22; 4 Ne. 1:30–33).

Each prophet has been foreordained to a specific mission (Alma 13:1–6; Smith, 365) and will be protected by the Lord until his mission is completed (1 Ne. 1:20; Mosiah 13:3; Alma 14:13).

Because the testimony of Jesus is in fact the spirit of prophecy (Rev. 19:10; Smith, 119), a prophet will always testify of the Savior (Jacob 4:4; 7:11; Mosiah 13:33–35; Moro. 7:22–23, 29–32), and his oracles will be consistent with the thrust of other messianic prophecies (Hel. 8:13–20; Luke 24:27). The prophet's message will not be his own but what the Lord wants him to say (Alma 5:44–46; 8:14–17; Hel. 7:29; 13:2–5). Prophets are sent to publish peace and settle disputations by setting forth the true points of doctrine—to teach the gospel of Jesus Christ, which is the gospel of peace (W of M 1:12–18; Mosiah 15:13–14; Hel. 11:22–23; Ether 7:23–27).

Prophets are called of God to see things "afar

off" (D&C 101:54), to envision the truth and to speak of the truth—"things as they really are, and of things as they really will be" (Jacob 4:13; cf. D&C 93:24). The spirit of prophecy and revelation enables them, when needed and appropriate, to foresee and speak of coming events. Lehi[1] was shown the destruction of Jerusalem, the future of the Jews, and the coming of the Messiah in the meridian of time (1 Ne. 1:13; 10:2–14). Because of his desire to understand the mysteries of God, Nephi[1] was shown the same vision (1 Ne. 2:16; 10:17–22; 11–14). Jacob[2] was also shown the future scattering and gathering of the house of Israel (2 Ne. 6:8–13). Alma[2] foretold the destruction of the city of Ammonihah (Alma 10:23; 16:9–10).

A prophet can also function as a SEER, revealing "secret" or "hidden" things "which are not known" (Mosiah 8:15–17). Ammon[2] "perceived the thoughts" of king Lamoni (Alma 18:16) and knew by the voice of the Lord concerning his brethren being in prison in the land of Middoni (Alma 20:2). Jacob[2] was able to confound the anti-Christ Sherem through the Spirit of the Lord (Jacob 7:8). Amulek exposed the evil intentions of Zeezrom (Alma 11:22–25; 12:3–4). Nephi[2] told of the murder of the chief judge (Hel. 8:27–28) and gave the people a sign indicating the very words Seezoram's brother, the murderer, would use when accused (Hel. 9:25–37).

A basic role of a prophet is to declare repentance and invite all to come unto Christ and be saved (1 Ne. 16:35–39; Jacob 3:3–12; Mosiah 11:20–26; Alma 5:49; Hel. 7:17; 13:10–14). Because his message is from the Lord, the prophet will generally be unpopular with the wicked. People reject the prophets for many reasons but usually because the prophets will not tolerate sin (Hel. 13:24–29). President Spencer W. Kimball pointed out that "so often the prophets have been rejected because they first rejected the wrong ways of their own society" (116).

Because the prophet is the spokesman for God, what the prophet speaks is in fact the word of God. To reject the prophet is therefore to reject God (Hel. 13:21; D&C 1:38; 21:5). Thus those who follow the prophets will be blessed, while those who cast out or reject them will be damned (2 Ne. 26:3; 3 Ne. 9:10; 10:12).

See also Prophecy in the Book of Mormon; Prophetic speech forms; Prophetic tense, prophetic perfect; Prophets, false; Prophets, rejection of.

BIBLIOGRAPHY

Kimball, Spencer W. Conference Report, April 1978.

Smith, Joseph. *Teachings of the Prophet Joseph Smith.* Selected by Joseph Fielding Smith. Salt Lake City: Deseret Book, 1976.

MSN

Prosper, prosperity Terms used in at least three ways in the Book of Mormon:

1. Temporal blessings generally referred to as riches (e.g., Mosiah 27:7; Alma 1:30–31; 9:22).

2. Spiritual blessings granted to the Church and its members, including growth (e.g., Mosiah 26:37; 27:9; Alma 49:30; Hel. 3:24–26).

3. Success in times of war (e.g., Jarom 1:9; Mosiah 2:31; Alma 48:14–16; 59:3).

4. Nonspecific references (the writer did not designate specific blessings). The Lord's promise to his covenant people that "inasmuch as ye shall keep my commandments, ye shall prosper" is given throughout the Book of Mormon (1 Ne. 2:20; 4:14; Omni 1:6; Mosiah 1:7; 2:22; Alma 9:13; 48:25).

Mormon lamented that one of the great tragedies of human nature is that people generally begin to forget God as soon as he blesses or prospers them (Hel. 12:1–2; cf. 13:22).

See also All is well in Zion; Book of Mormon, selected themes of, obedience; Riches.

KDB

Provocation, first and last Transgression of law, which brings divine justice. The first provocation, which was the transgression of Adam and Eve in partaking of the FORBIDDEN FRUIT, resulted in their being cut off from God's presence. The last provocation, which is willful, unrepentant disobedience of mankind, will result in their suffering an "everlasting destruction"—being eternally cut off from God's presence (Alma 12:36).

Alma[2] taught that because Adam and Eve "transgressed the first commandments," they fell, bringing about the conditions of mortality

(Alma 12:31). After their expulsion from the Garden of Eden, God gave them additional commandments. These "second commandments" included "that they should not do evil," and that they must "repent, and harden not [their] hearts" (Alma 12:32–33, 37). Obedience would qualify them and their posterity to receive God's mercy through his Only Begotten Son (Alma 12:33; cf. Moses 5:4–11); disobedience would bring a "second death" (Alma 12:32).

Just as Adam and Eve were cut off from God's presence through transgression (the "first provocation"), so likewise all who harden their hearts against God, persisting in iniquity, receive a similar but eternal fate, a "last" or second death ("the last provocation"), the consequence for breaking the second commandment (Alma 12:35–37).

Another view is to consider the "first provocation" (Alma 12:36) as the rebellion of the children of Israel in the wilderness (Jacob 1:7; Heb. 3:8; D&C 84:24). In either case, Alma's teaching about the first and last provocations bringing SPIRITUAL DEATH applies.

DLL

Puffed *See* Appendix C.

And now I bid unto all, farewell. I soon go to rest in the paradise of God, until my spirit and body shall again reunite, and I am brought forth triumphant through the air, to meet you before the pleasing bar of the great Jehovah, the Eternal Judge of both quick and dead. Amen. MORONI 10:34

Quarters *See* Appendix C.

Quetzalcoatl Name of a prominent deity and king of ancient Mexico (Parkes, 16–17). It is derived from two words in the Nauhtl (Aztec) language, *quetzal* and *coatl. Quetzal* means "feathers" and is the name of a beautiful Guatemalan bird with long tail feathers. *Coatl* means "serpent." The word *kukulcan* in the Maya Yucatec language has the same meaning as Quetzalcoatl in Aztec (Parkes, 18). The symbolism of the quetzal bird and the serpent goes back to Olmec times (ca. 1000–500 B.C.).

There are several variants and interpretations of Quetazalcoatl (Brown, 126–41). Many Latter-day Saints see evidence for the origin of one of the Quetzalcoatl traditions in the visit of Jesus Christ to the Book of Mormon people. The name Quetzalcoatl seems to have originated in Mesoamerica (southern Mexico and northern Central America) about the time of Christ's visit to the Nephites (Allen, 146, v. 43 of Ixtlilxochitl as translated by Allen). The sixteenth-century writer Don Fernando de Alva de Ixtlilxochitl wrote: "Quetzalcoatl was a man of comely appearance and serious disposition. His countenance was white, and he wore a beard. His manner of dress consisted of a long, flowing robe" (Allen, 147, v. 45). Such other sixteenth-century writers as Bernardino de Sahagun, Diego Duran, and Juan de Torquemada also wrote of the white god Quetzalcoatl. Similarities between the Mexican tradition of Quetzalcoatl and Book of Mormon statements about Christ include the following:

Both were recognized as the creator of all things (Mosiah 4:2; Saenz, 19, 40).

Both were born of virgins (Alma 7:10; Gamiz, 95).

Both are described as being white or wearing a white robe (3 Ne. 11:8; 19:25; Torquemada, 48).

Both performed miracles (3 Ne. 26:15; Sejourne, 136–37).

Both taught the ordinance of baptism (3 Ne. 11:23–26; Irwin, 170).

Both prophesied of future events (3 Ne. 16; Allen, 146, v. 40).

Both were associated with the cross (3 Ne. 27:14; Irwin, 165).

Both sent out disciples to preach their word (3 Ne. 12:1; Wirth, 55).

Both promised they would come a second time (2 Ne. 6:14; Sahagun, 1:40).

Both were associated with a new star (3 Ne. 1:21; Anales de Cauhtitlan, 7).

The children of both will become lords and heirs of the earth (3 Ne. 12:5; 4 Ne. 1:17; Allen 146, v. 40).

Quetzalcoatl "was representative of the wind, the whirlwind" (Sahagun, 4:101) and was called "the god of wind" because the great destruction that occurred in Mesoamerica ca. A.D. 34 was attributed to him (Allen, 140, 146, v. 16, 42–43). Ixtlilxochitl wrote about this incident, saying, "It had been 166 years since they had adjusted their calendar with the equinox and 270 years since the giants had been destroyed when the sun and the moon eclipsed and the earth quaked and rocks were broken into pieces and many other signs that had been given came to pass, although man was not destroyed. This was in the year Ce Calli, which, adjusted to our calendar, happened at the same time that Christ, our Lord, was crucified. And they say that this destruction occurred in the first few days of the year" (Allen, 140, v. 16; cf. Brown, 163). The Book of Mormon records the same date for the great destruction at the time of the crucifixion of Christ (3 Ne. 8:5).

The A.D. 300 Temple of Quetzalcoatl at Teotihuacan, Mexico, represents the white god as both a deity (by a serpent motif with quetzal feathers) and as the rain god, Tlaloc. Teotihuacan was abandoned in the seventh century A.D., and the Toltecs of Tula, located north of Mexico City, carried on the great tradition of the white god Quetzalcoatl. Many people, including priests, took upon themselves the name or title of Quetzalcoatl. One such person was Topiltzin Quetzalcoatl, who was born ca. A.D. 1040 and became a folk hero. Many historians suggest that when Cortez conquered Mexico, the people thought he was Topiltzin Quetzalcoatl returning (Parkes, 57–58 n. 1).

Today the legend of the white god Quetzalcoatl continues. Schoolchildren study

A portrayal of Quetzalcoatl by Diego Rivera; courtesy Instituto Nacional de Bellas Artes y Literatura.

the lives of the deity and of the men who took upon themselves the name of Quetzalcoatl. Their lives and teachings are widely recognized for their high moral qualities and timeless character.

BIBLIOGRAPHY

Allen, Joseph L. *Exploring the Lands of the Book of Mormon*. Orem, Utah: S. A. Publishers, 1989.

Anales de Cauhtitlan y Leyenda de los Soles en Codice Chimalpopoca. Edited and translated by Primo F. Velazquez. Mexico, D.F.: Institute of Historic Investigations, National University, 1945.

Brown, Harold, Bruce W. Warren, and Blaine M. Yorgason. *New Evidences of Christ in Ancient America*. Arlington, Va.: Stratford Books, 1999.

Coe, Michael D. *Mexico*. 3d ed. London: Thames and Hudson, 1984.

Gamiz, Abel. *Quetzalcoatl*. Sociedad Folklorica de Mexico, 1941. 91–107.

Irwin, Constance. *Fair Gods and Stone Faces: Ancient Seafarers and the New World's Most Intriguing Riddle*. New York: St. Martin's Press, 1963.

Parkes, Henry Bramford. A *History of Mexico*. Boston: Houghton Mifflin, 1969.

Saenz, Caesar A. *Quetzalcoatl*. Mexico, D.F.: Instituto Nacional de Antropologia e Historia, 1962.

Sahagun, Fray Bernardino de. *Historia General de las Cosas de Nueva Espana: Florentine Codex*. 12 vols. Edited and translated into English by Arthur J. O. Anderson and Charles E. Dibble. Santa Fe, N.M.: The School of American Research and the University of Utah, 1950–82.

Sejourne, Laurette. *El Universo de Quetzalcoatl*. Mexico, D.F.: Fondo de Cultura Economica, 1962.

Torquemada, Juan de. *Monarchia Indiana*. Vol. 1, as translated and condensed in Hubert Howe.

Bancroft, A. L. *Myths and Languages*. Vol. 3 of *The Native Races*. San Francisco: A. L. Bancroft, 1883.

Wirth, Diane E. *A Challenge to the Critics: Scholarly Evidences of the Book of Mormon*. Bountiful, Utah: Horizon Publishers, 1986.

JLA

Quick *See* Appendix C.

And no unclean thing can enter into his kingdom; therefore nothing entereth into his rest save it be those who have washed their garments in my blood, because of their faith, and the **repentance** of all their sins, and their faithfulness unto the end.

3 NEPHI 27:19

Rabbanah Term of respect given to Ammon[2] by one of king Lamoni's servants after he defeated the Lamanites at the waters of Sebus. Mormon interpreted it as "powerful or great king" (Alma 18:13). The title is related to ancient Near Eastern cognates designating "greatness," such as "Rabboni" (John 20:16) and Rabbi.

GS

Raca A transliteration of *reqa*, an Aramaic word meaning "empty, void; worthless man" (*Dictionary*, 1476). Consequently, it is a term of derision (3 Ne. 12:22). Jews in Jesus' day typically spoke Aramaic.

BIBLIOGRAPHY

A *Dictionary of the Targumim, the Talmud Babli and Yerushalmi, and the Midrashic Literature*. II, 1476. Compiled by Morris Jastrow. Brooklyn: P. Shalom, 1967.

KHM

Rack *See* Appendix C.

Railing *See* Appendix C.

Ramah, hill Site where Coriantumr[2] gathered his people for four years in preparation for the final battles that ended the Jaredite civilization. Ramah was also where Mormon later hid all the sacred records, except a few which he gave to Moroni[2] (Morm. 6:6; Ether 15:11–12). The hill Ramah was the same hill that the Nephites called Cumorah.

Rameumptom Name given by the apostate ZORAMITES[2] to the "place built up in the center of their synagogue" (Alma 31:13) for worship. "Rameumptom" is interpreted as meaning "holy stand" (Alma 31:21). The Semitic root word *ram* means "high" or "high place" (cf. Ramah in the Bible and Book of Mormon). The top of the Rameumptom "would only admit one person" (Alma 31:13). From there, the Zoramites would vainly offer the "same prayers" to be heard and praised of men (Alma 31:20; 38:13).

DKJ

Reap the chaff To receive the evil or negative consequences of one's behavior. Chaff is the husk or thin outer covering of grain. It has little nutritional value and must be removed from cereal grains by threshing and winnowing before consumption. The Lord warned that those who "sow filthiness" would "reap the chaff thereof" in a whirlwind (Mosiah 7:30). The metaphor suggests that wicked actions yield only fleeting and empty rewards.

RH

Reconciled unto Christ Being brought back into a full and right relationship with Christ from a position of alienation or estrangement due to the effects of the Fall and personal sins. Nephi[1], Jacob[2], and the apostle Paul all taught that individuals are reconciled to God through the atonement of his Only Begotten Son (2 Ne. 25:23; Jacob 4:11; 2 Cor. 5:18, 20). Nephi implored both Jew and Gentile to be thus reconciled (2 Ne. 33:8–9). Because the Father and the Son are one God in purpose and attributes (Mosiah 15:4), being reconciled to one is the same as being reconciled to the other.

ACS

Record of the Jews Initially, Nephi[1] used this term to describe the brass plates of Laban (1 Ne. 3:3; 5:6). Later, an angel used this description for the book latter-day Gentiles would possess. This record (the Bible) would be similar to the brass plates but not as complete (1 Ne. 13:23). Nephi also used this phrase to describe the more historical parts of the brass plates, as compared to the books of Moses, the prophetic books, and the genealogies (1 Ne. 5:11–12; cf. Omni 1:14).

VLL

Records, last *See* Last records.

Records of the prophets The writings of the prophets. Nephi[1] beheld in a vision that "other books" (i.e., the scriptures that came forth as part of the Restoration) would be brought forth in a future day to confirm the truth of the records of the prophets (e.g., Old Testament prophets) (1 Ne. 13:39).

See also Last records; Records of the Twelve Apostles.

TBP

Records of the Twelve Apostles The writings of Christ's New Testament apostles, from which plain and precious things have been taken. Nephi[1] learned in a vision that the Lord would bring forth "other books" (i.e., the scriptures that came forth as part of the Restoration) to confirm the truth of the records of the Twelve Apostles and also to "make known the plain and precious things which have been taken away from them" (1 Ne. 13:39–40). In the same vision an angel testified to Nephi that the words of Jesus Christ would be manifest through both the records of his posterity (the Book of Mormon), and the records of the Twelve Apostles: "Wherefore they both shall be established in one" (1 Ne. 13:41; cf. 2 Ne. 3:12).

See also Last records; Records of the prophets.

TBP

Red Sea The large sea, more than 1,000 miles in length, that divides Arabia from northeast Africa. The Book of Mormon confirms the historicity of Moses' parting the waters of the sea, allowing the Israelites to pass on dry ground, and drowning Pharaoh's armies (1 Ne. 4:2; 17:26–27; Mosiah 7:19; Alma 36:28; Hel. 8:11). Nephi[1] referred to a fertile wilderness near the shores of the Red Sea (1 Ne. 2:5; 16:14), and to a river emptying into it (1 Ne. 2:8–9). The reason for rendering the text of Isaiah 9:1 to read "by the way of the *Red* Sea" is not known (2 Ne. 19:1; italics added; *see* map, page 412).

DKO

Redemption "To redeem" is to repurchase something previously possessed and subsequently lost by paying all indemnities associated with its repossession. "Redemption" is thus God's way of reclaiming his children from the fall of man by sacrificing Christ's redeeming blood as reparation for their repossession: "By Adam came the fall of man," accordingly, and "because of the fall of man came Jesus Christ," and "because of Jesus Christ came the redemption of man" (Morm. 9:12). All Book of Mormon terms for redemption reflect ancient backgrounds

The Red Sea; courtesy S. Kent Brown.

denoting "the return [of something] to a former state or condition" (Nibley, 581; cf. 558).

Redemption as repossession

Redemption as repossession is implicit in *redemptio,* the nominal derivative of *redimo,* a Latin verb combining *re* ("back, again") with *emo* ("buy, purchase") and meaning "to buy back or repurchase something by paying what is owed." Thus, Lehi[1] knew that "all mankind were in a lost and in a fallen state, and ever would be save they should rely on this Redeemer," who was the "Messiah, or . . . Savior of the world" (1 Ne. 10:4–6). He prophesied that "the Messiah cometh . . . [to] redeem the children of men from the fall" (2 Ne. 2:26), and testified that "the Lord hath redeemed"—repossessed—"my soul from hell" (2 Ne. 1:15). The heart-cries of Nephi[1] were similar: "I glory in my Jesus, for he hath redeemed my soul from hell" (2 Ne. 33:6; cf. Mosiah 16:2, 4–5; Alma 21:9; Hel. 14:15–18; 3 Ne. 9:21–22; 20:38; Morm. 7:7).

Redemption as deliverance from bondage

The concept of redemption as deliverance from bondage may be seen in *lytrosis* ("the process of loosing or releasing something"), a Greek actional noun stressing the deliverance of captives from imprisonment by someone who pays their *lytron* ("ransom"—everything they owe to anybody). Likewise, Nephi[1] yearned for deliverance from sin: "O Lord, wilt thou redeem my soul? Wilt thou deliver me out of the hands of mine enemies? Wilt thou make me that I may shake at the appearance of sin? . . . Wilt thou make a way for mine escape. . . . Wilt thou . . . clear my way before me, and hedge not up my way, but the ways of mine enemy" (2 Ne. 4:31, 33). Jacob[2] rejoiced in this deliverance: "O how great the goodness of our God, who prepareth a way for our escape from . . . death and hell" (2 Ne. 9:10). Others followed suit, like Alma[2] who testified that he was delivered or "snatch[ed] . . . out of an everlasting burning" and "redeemed from the gall of bitterness and bonds of iniquity" (Mosiah 27:24–29; cf. 2 Ne. 9:26; Mosiah 15:12; Alma 5:7, 9–10, 21, 27; 11:40–41; 12:6; 26:13–14, 17; 36:16–20; 41:7; Hel. 5:10–12; 13:36–37).

Redemption as protective coverings of atonement

A Hebrew correlate of *redemptio* and *lytrosis* is *KPhRM* ("atonement"), a plural noun referring to protective "coverings" (its literal meaning) for human lives. The major symbols of protection are regal robes and royal embraces. Lehi[1], when redeemed by Christ, was therefore "encircled about eternally in the arms of his love" (2 Ne. 1:15). "O Lord," implored Nephi[1], "wilt thou encircle me around in the robe of thy righteousness!" (2 Ne. 4:33); and Jacob[2] envisioned the redeemed as "clothed with purity . . . [in] the robe of righteousness" (2 Ne. 9:14). The Lord "sendeth an invitation unto all men, for the arms of mercy are extended towards them" (Alma 5:33), thus bringing sinners lost in darkness into "his everlasting light" to be embraced "with the matchless bounty of his love" (Alma 26:15). Mercy, according to Amulek, enfolds repentant sinners "in the arms of safety," whereas the unrepentant are "exposed to the whole law of the demands of justice" (Alma 34:16). This Semitic concept of redemption as protective coverings of atonement is also ritualized in the sacred garments of Adam and Eve. In their innocence before the Fall they were naked, clothed only in light, and "were not ashamed" of their nakedness in the presence of God or of each other (Gen. 2:25). Shamed by their nakedness after the Fall, they tried unsuccessfully to cover their shame with garments of their own devising, aprons made of fig leaves (Gen. 3:7). God made them "coats of skins," which involved the sacrifice of life—something they could never forget—"and clothed them" with redemptive garments that covered their shame and allowed them to come into his presence without fear (Gen. 3:21). Mormon, accordingly, warned the unrepentant that "when ye shall . . . see your nakedness before God" vis-à-vis "the glory of God, and the holiness of Jesus Christ, it will kindle a flame of unquenchable fire upon you" (Morm. 9:5).

See also Atonement, the.

BIBLIOGRAPHY

Nibley, Hugh W. *Approaching Zion.* Salt Lake City: Deseret Book, 1989.

Wright, Herbert C. "The Garment of Adam," chap. 8 of an unpublished master's thesis entitled "A Study of Certain Typological References to the Atonement found in Genesis, Exodus, and Numbers." Brigham Young University, 1955.

HCW

Reformed Egyptian Term used to describe the characters Mormon and Moroni[2] used to write their record on the GOLD PLATES (Morm. 9:32). Nephi[1], the first record keeper, described the language he used as a combination of elements from the Jews and from the Egyptians: "I make a record in the language of my father, which consists of the learning of the Jews and the language of the Egyptians" (1 Ne. 1:2; cf. Mosiah 1:4). Moroni used the term "reformed Egyptian" when he said that he and his father wrote "this record . . . in the characters which are called among us the reformed Egyptian" (Morm. 9:32). Moroni noted that the reformed Egyptian was "handed down and altered by us, according to our manner of speech" (Morm. 9:32). Moroni also said that "if our plates had been sufficiently large we should have written in Hebrew; but the Hebrew hath been altered by us also; and if we could have written in Hebrew, behold, ye would have had no imperfection in our record" (Morm. 9:33). Thus Mormon and Moroni were conversant with some form of Hebrew, but they used a different system of writing, reformed Egyptian, because it occupied less space on the plates. From this limited information it is not clear whether the language of the Book of Mormon plates was some form of Egyptian or simply a form of Hebrew written with Egyptian-like characters.

See also Book of Mormon, language of the translated text of; Hebrew language.

MDR

Rely To rely upon Christ is to depend upon him, to TRUST him, to exercise FAITH in him, to move forward on the GOSPEL path because of confidence in who he is and what he has done. Aaron[3] taught that "since man had fallen he could not merit anything of himself" (Alma 22:14). That is, one's own good works or merits are insufficient to save one; one must, therefore, rely wholly upon the merits and MERCY of the Holy Messiah (1 Ne. 10:6; 2 Ne. 2:3, 8; 4:19; 31:19; Moro. 6:4).

See also Merits of Christ.

RLM

Remnant A piece or part of something. In the Book of Mormon the term is usually used to refer to that portion or part of a people that persist, especially through their descendants, after the general populace has been smitten and/or scattered. It occurs in the following phrases:

1. "Remnant of the house of Israel," "remnant of Israel," and "remnant of Jacob." The title page of the Book of Mormon testifies that one purpose of the book is "to show unto the remnant of the House of Israel what great things the Lord hath done for their fathers; and that they may know the covenants of the Lord." The Savior explained that the faithful latter-day GENTILES would bring the gospel taught in the Book of Mormon to this remnant and thereby bring them to a knowledge of their Redeemer (3 Ne. 16:4). This understanding and acceptance of the Lord and his covenants by the remnant of Jacob[1] constitutes an important part of the latter-day gathering of Israel of which the prophets testified (2 Ne. 20:20–22; 21:11–12; 3 Ne. 5:24–26). Faithful Gentiles are to be numbered among the remnant of the house of Israel and are to assist them in building the NEW JERUSALEM (3 Ne. 21:6, 22–23). Unrighteous Gentiles were warned that if they did not accept the gospel, then the remnant of Jacob would come among them like a "lion among the flocks of sheep" (3 Ne. 20:15–16; 21:12; see Micah).

2. "Remnant of the seed of Joseph," "remnant of the house of Joseph." The Joseph[1] spoken of in this context is the son of Jacob[1], he who was sold into Egypt (Gen. 37:23–36). This remnant is therefore a part of the remnant of the house of Israel, and the prophecies concerning the house of Israel apply to them. In addition, some specific promises have been made to the remnant of Joseph. Jacob received a promise that a remnant of his son Joseph would be preserved just as a remnant of Joseph's coat of many colors was preserved (Alma 46:24). Ether prophesied

that a remnant of Joseph would be brought to the Americas, that it would be a land of inheritance for them, and that they would build the New Jerusalem (Ether 13:6–8, 10).

3. "Remnant of the seed of my brethren," and "remnant of our seed." These phrases refer to the descendants of Lehi[1] (1 Ne. 13:38–39; 15:13–14). This remnant is also a remnant of the house of Israel and of Joseph[1] (Title Page; 1 Ne. 13:34; 2 Ne. 28:2; Alma 46:23–24; 3 Ne. 10:17; 15:12; 20:10; 21:2; Morm. 7:10), and as such is included in the prophecies made to the remnant of the house of Israel and the remnant of Joseph. In addition, the remnant of Lehi is given some specific promises. Lehi's descendants are told that although they will dwindle in unbelief (1 Ne. 15:13) and be smitten and scattered by the latter-day Gentiles (1 Ne. 13:33–34; 3 Ne. 21:2), eventually through the ministry of the faithful Gentiles and the coming forth of the Book of Mormon they will arrive at a knowledge of their forefathers, of the fulness of the gospel, of their redeemer, and of his covenants (1 Ne. 13:34–39; 15:13–14; 2 Ne. 30:3–4; 3 Ne. 21:4; Morm. 5:9). Mormon taught that this remnant will "be judged by the twelve whom Jesus chose in this land [the Americas]" (Morm. 3:19).

4. Other remnants. Several other remnants of peoples are mentioned in the Book of Mormon, including the remnant of Babylon that will be cut off (2 Ne. 24:22), the remnant of the Philistines that will be slain (2 Ne. 24:29–30), the remnant of the Jaredites who were destroyed (Mosiah 8:12) the remnant of the Amlicites pursued by the spies of Alma[2] (Alma 2:21), and the remnant of the Amulonites pursued by the Lamanites (Alma 25:7–9).

In addition, Isaiah taught that the king of Babylon, like Lucifer, would be cast off in disgust like "the remnant [// Isa. 14:19 'raiment'] of those that are slain, thrust through with a sword" (2 Ne. 24:19).

See also Israel, gathering of; Israel, house of; Israel, numbered among; Joseph[1], covenants unto.

MSN

Rend, rent To tear (rip); a tear or split. The rending of clothing—and, metaphorically, of one's heart—was usually associated with mourning, often because of a broken covenant (e.g., 1 Kgs. 11:11; 13:2–3; Joel 2:12–13; 1 Ne. 17:47). In the instance of Moroni[1]'s "title of liberty" (Alma 46:13), rending one's garment betokened the penalty for breaking a covenant: "The people came running . . . rending their garments . . . as a covenant, that they would not forsake the Lord their God . . . [and] if they should transgress . . . the Lord should rend them even as they had rent their garments" (Alma 46:13, 21). Mormon mourned, and his "soul was rent with anguish, because of the slain of [his] people" (Morm. 6:16).

These terms appear likewise in descriptions of natural and spiritual disasters. Of the former, one reads of the disaster following the death of Jesus that among other natural catastrophes, "the rocks were rent in twain . . . upon all the face of the land" (3 Ne. 8:18; cf. Hel. 14:22). In the case of spiritual reverses, Mormon recounted the loss of spiritual and civil freedoms under the Gadianton robbers (ca. 24 B.C.) by observing that these people "did obtain the sole management of the government, insomuch that they did . . . rend and turn their backs upon . . . the humble followers of God" (Hel. 6:39).

SKB

Repentance A principal component of the GOSPEL or "doctrine of Christ" that literally means to "change"—to turn away from sin by turning to Christ—a "mighty change" (Alma 5:14). A central message of the Book of Mormon is that through the ATONEMENT of Christ, one can be forgiven, "cleansed" from sin, "washed white" and "purified" (Alma 5:21, 24, 27; 1 Ne. 12:10–11; Morm. 9:6). As an essential part of the plan of salvation (Alma 42:4–13) and a prerequisite to the ordinance of BAPTISM (Moro. 6:2), repentance is absolutely necessary in the process of being forgiven of sins (2 Ne. 2:21; 9:23; 30:2; 31:11–17; Mosiah 4:10; Alma 9:12; Hel. 5:11; 12:23; 3 Ne. 9:22; 27:16, 19–20). Inasmuch as "all mankind [are] in a lost" and in a "fallen state" (Mosiah 16:4; 1 Ne. 10:6; Alma 12:22; 22:14) and "no unclean thing can inherit the kingdom of God" (Alma 40:26), all accountable individuals need to repent and be forgiven

REPENTANCE

(Moro. 8:10–11). Through repentance God's "mercy can satisfy the demands of justice," which requires a punishment for broken law (Alma 34:16; 42:12–26; 2 Ne. 2:5–7). The primacy of this principle is shown in Alma[1]'s command to "preach nothing save it were repentance and faith on the Lord" (Mosiah 18:18–20; 25:22; cf. D&C 6:9; 11:9) and in Amulek's warning concerning the severe consequences of procrastinating repentance until it is "everlastingly too late" (Hel. 13:38; Alma 34:31–35). Without repentance, one's sins "stand as a testimony against [one] at the last day" (Alma 39:8). The Book of Mormon narrative shows repeatedly that God blesses and prospers those persons or nations who repent (Alma 26:21–22; Hel. 4:15; Ether 7:26). Moreover, bringing others to repentance through missionary labor brings great JOY (Alma 29:9–10; D&C 18:10–16).

True repentance is a process requiring sincere FAITH, recognition of sin, "godly sorrow" (2 Cor. 7:10), confession, restitution for sin, and a forsaking or turning away from evil.

Faith in the Lord Jesus Christ

Amulek taught that "faith unto repentance" leads to FORGIVENESS through the cleansing power of the atonement of Jesus Christ (Alma 34:14–18). When Enos questioned the Lord as to how it was possible for him to be forgiven of his sins and receive peace of conscience, the Lord explained, "Because of thy faith in Christ . . . thy faith hath made thee whole" (Enos 1:4–8). Alma[2] experienced a "mighty change" of heart (Alma 5:12) through the MERCY of Christ on account of his faith in the Savior's redemptive power (Alma 36:17–20). Nephi[1] saw in vision the "twelve disciples of the Lamb," who, "because of their faith in the Lamb of God their garments are made white in his blood. . . . These are made white in the blood of the Lamb, because of their faith in him" (1 Ne. 12:8–11).

Those who possess true faith in Christ will "bring forth works which are meet for repentance" (Alma 5:54; 12:15), meaning that their lives demonstrate that in both heart and action they have eschewed evil and turned to God (Mosiah 28:3–8; Alma 5:11–15; 22:15–18; 23:5–18).

Recognition of sin and godly sorrow

True repentance requires acknowledgment of wrongdoing and "a broken heart and a contrite spirit" (2 Ne. 2:7; 3 Ne. 9:19–20; 12:19; Alma 42:18, 24; Ether 4:15; 15:3; Moro. 6:2)—a feeling of genuine sorrow for sins. This kind of sorrow is much more than remorse or regret over the consequences of sin, which Mormon called "the sorrowing of the damned, because the Lord would not always suffer them to take happiness in sin" (Morm. 2:12–14). Rather, it is a "godly sorrow" that "worketh repentance to salvation" (2 Cor. 7:10). The ANTI-NEPHI-LEHIES became "convinced of [their] sins" through the preaching of the Nephites (Alma 24:9). Their sorrow for their sins was an important component in their remarkable conversion and subsequent commitment not to sin (Alma 24:10–19). Alma[2] taught his son Corianton the seriousness of the sin of immorality in an effort to help him feel the necessary contrition that would lead to sincere repentance (Alma 39:3–5): "I would to God that ye had not been guilty of so great a crime. I would not dwell upon your crimes, to harrow up your soul, if it were not for your good" (Alma 39:7). A godly sorrow for past sins brings one "down to the dust in humility," awakening a "sense of . . . nothingness" in a "fallen state." Such recognition of one's spiritual state leads to a stripping away of all rationalization and self-justification and implants in the heart a yearning to be cleansed, to stand approved before the Lord (Alma 42:29–30; Mosiah 4:1–2, 5).

Recognition of sin and the accompanying sorrow produces mental and spiritual pain. When Alma the Younger recognized his sins, he experienced the "pains of hell," which pains drove him to plead for mercy (Alma 36:12–18; Mosiah 27:29–30). Similarly, Zeezrom experienced "great tribulations of his mind on account of his wickedness" and was "scorched with a burning heat" in the process of his repentance (Alma 15:3; 14:6).

Confession of sin

The Lord instructed Alma[1] that "whosoever transgresseth against me, him shall ye judge according to the sins which he has committed; and if he confess his sins before *thee* and *me,* and repenteth in the sincerity of his heart, him shall ye forgive, and I will forgive him also" (Mosiah 26:29–30, 35–36; italics added). Commenting on the principle contained in these verses, Elder Bruce R. McConkie explained: "There are . . . two confessions and two sources of forgiveness. A sinner must always confess all sins, great and small, to the Lord; in addition, any sins involving moral turpitude and any serious sins for which a person might be disfellowshipped or excommunicated must also be confessed to the Lord's agent, who in most instances is the bishop. The bishop is empowered to forgive sins as far as the Church is concerned, meaning that he can choose to retain the repentant person in full fellowship and not impose court [disciplinary council] penalties upon him. Ultimate forgiveness in all instances and for all sins comes from the Lord and from the Lord only" (236).

By the power of their preaching, the four sons of Mosiah[2] brought many "before the altar of God, to call on his name and confess their sins before him" (Alma 17:4; cf. Jacob 7:19; Hel. 5:17). Moroni[2] wrote that the Church in his day was "strict to observe that there should be no iniquity among them; and whoso was found to commit iniquity . . . if they repented not, and confessed not, their names were blotted out, and they were not numbered among the people of Christ" (Moro. 6:7).

Restitution for sin

Acknowledgment, sorrow, and confession of sin leads an offender to make efforts to restore or make right, as far as possible, the wrongs committed. For example, following their conversions Alma[2] and the four sons of king Mosiah[2] "traveled throughout all the land of Zarahemla, and among all the people . . . zealously striving to repair all the injuries which they had done to the church" (Mosiah 27:35). Similarly, Zeezrom acknowledged his lying words, sought to undo the damage he had done, and pleaded for the lives of Alma[2] and Amulek (Alma 14:6–7). The powerful preaching of Nephi[2] and Lehi[4] to Nephite dissenters caused the repentant dissenters to "immediately [return] to the Nephites to endeavor to repair unto them the wrongs which they had done" (Hel. 5:17), and their ministering to the Lamanites caused the repentant Lamanites to "yield up unto the Nephites the lands of their possession" (Hel. 5:50–52).

Forsaking or turning away from evil

A sign of true repentance is abandonment of sin: To repent, one must "forsake" the sin (Mosiah 4:10; Alma 39:9; 3 Ne. 5:3; Ether 11:1; D&C 58:43). The Book of Mormon gives numerous examples of how forsaking sin in the truest sense requires a comprehensive transformation of life, not merely the abandonment of a specified sin. One who is BORN AGAIN demonstrates the fruits of true repentance in his or her continuing obedience, SERVICE, CHARITY, and DISPOSITION (Enos 1:2–13; Mosiah 4:1–3; 5:2–7; 27:25, 32–37; 28:1–9; Alma 17:1–16; 27:27–28; 36:24).

See also Demands of justice; Faith unto repentance; Fruit meet for repentance; Justice, law of; Justification; Sin, transgression.

BIBLIOGRAPHY

McConkie, Bruce R. *A New Witness for the Articles of Faith.* Salt Lake City: Deseret Book, 1985.

BLT

Repentance, fruit meet for *See* Fruit meet for repentance.

Respecter of persons An individual who gives special privilege to a person or group as a result of wealth, prestige, social position, or ethnic background. The scriptures declare categorically that God is "no respecter of persons" (e.g., Acts 10:34; D&C 38:16), especially in terms of opportunities for salvation (2 Ne. 26:24–27, 33), because he "esteemeth all flesh in one" (1 Ne. 17:35) and "all are alike unto God" (2 Ne. 26:33). He exhibits this attribute in three major ways:

1. The fruits of Christ's resurrection are available for all people (Alma 11:42–45).

2. The fruits of Christ's atoning sacrifice are available to all who take advantage of it through application of the gospel (3 Ne. 27:13–21) or who are not accountable (Moro. 8:12).

3. Missionary work is extended to all, both Jew and Gentile (2 Ne. 26:33; 3 Ne. 18:25; cf. Matt. 28:19–20; Acts 10:34–48), and both the dead and living (D&C 138; 1 Pet. 3:18–20; 4:6).

The Book of Mormon teaches that God's righteous people should reflect a similar attitude in their relationships with others. They are to be no respecter of persons when it comes either to sharing their prosperity (Alma 1:30) or to preaching the gospel (Alma 16:14).

GS

Rest of the Lord The state of peace that comes with redemption; spiritual enjoyment resulting from the power or presence of the Lord. Ultimately, it is the fulness of God's glory (D&C 84:24). Prophets labor diligently to persuade their people to enter into this rest (Jacob 1:7; cf. Alma 13:6; D&C 84:23–24). The Book of Mormon refers to three degrees of divine rest: the rest available in mortality, in PARADISE, and in the kingdom of God after resurrection.

1. Mortality. Divine rest in this life begins with humbling oneself, repenting (Alma 13:12–13), having one's garments washed in the Savior's blood through faith and repentance (3 Ne. 27:19)—that is, obtaining the remission of sins (Alma 12:34; 13:16)—and coming unto Christ (Jacob 1:7; Alma 16:17). Personal revelation brings rest to the soul (Enos 1:17). Those who are meek and lowly of heart find rest to their souls (Alma 37:34). Even in the midst of trials one can experience a degree of rest, bearing one's afflictions with patience and a firm hope of rest one day from all affliction (Alma 34:41).

2. Paradise. At death righteous spirits enter this state of rest from all trouble, care, and sorrow (Alma 40:11). When the righteous die in battle or at the hands of the wicked, they enter into the rest of the Lord (Alma 57:36; 60:13; cf. 14:11). Moroni bade farewell saying he was going to rest in the paradise of God until the resurrection and the Judgment (Moro. 10:34).

3. Kingdom of God. Enos anticipated rest with and in his Redeemer in the mansions of the Father (Enos 1:27). Alma[2] listed the divine attributes people must have to "be lifted up at the last day and enter into his rest" (Alma 13:27–29). The Savior promised the Three Nephites that they would have rest with him in his kingdom (3 Ne. 28:3).

At least one reference includes all three realms. Moroni wrote, "Wherefore, I would speak unto you . . . the peaceable followers of Christ . . . that have obtained a sufficient hope by which ye can enter into the rest of the Lord, from this time henceforth until ye shall rest with him in heaven" (Moro. 7:3).

MCT

Restoration, plan of The plan of restoration is that "all things should be restored to their proper order" (Alma 41:2). Alma[2] speaks of the plan of restoration in two dimensions. First, "it is requisite and just, according to the power and resurrection of Christ, that the soul of man should be restored to its body, and that every part of the body should be restored to itself." And second, "it is requisite with the justice of God that men should be judged according to their works; and if their works were good in this life, and the desires of their hearts were good, that they should also, at the last day, be restored unto that which is good" (Alma 41:2–3). Alma[2] sought to impress this doctrine upon his wayward son Corianton that he might humble himself and repent, and not "excuse" himself because of his sins, "by denying the justice of God" (Alma 42:30).

Judgment Day will be the ultimate verification of the eternal law that "that which ye do send out shall return unto you again" (Alma 41:15). Accordingly, "the meaning of the word restoration is to bring back again evil for evil, or carnal for carnal, or devilish for devilish—good for that which is good; righteous for that which is righteous; just for that which is just; merciful for that which is merciful" (Alma 41:13; cf. Hel. 14:31). Thus, all of God's children are their "own judges," for to choose desires and actions that are either good or evil is to choose also the commensurate rewards or consequences that follow (Alma 41:7). Inasmuch as "wickedness never was happiness," one cannot be "restored from sin to happiness." Such a thing "is contrary to the nature of that righteousness which is in our great and Eternal Head" (Alma 41:10–11; Hel. 13:38). Sin and happiness are eternal opposites.

Being saved *in* sin would counter God's justice, but one can be saved *from* sin (Alma

11:34–37). If one has "repented of his sins, and desired righteousness until the end of his days, even so he shall be rewarded unto righteousness" (Alma 41:6).

Although both Book of Mormon and biblical teachings affirm a judgment restoring people to rewards based upon works (Rev. 20:12–13), the Book of Mormon illuminates with clarity the doctrinal truth that judgment will also be based on the desires of one's heart (Alma 41:3–6).

See also Desire(s); Judgment, the; Justice, law of; Resurrection, the.

DLL

Resurrection, the Permanent reunion of the spirit and the physical body after separation by death, made possible only by the resurrection of Jesus Christ. The resurrection, a principal doctrine of the GOSPEL of Jesus Christ (3 Ne. 27:13–15)—God's "plan of redemption" (Alma 42:11–13; Hel. 14:15–19; Morm. 9:13)—is discussed in the Book of Mormon in context with other essential gospel principles.

The plan of restoration

Book of Mormon prophets did not treat the resurrection as an isolated philosophical thesis. Rather, the CREATION, the Fall, birth, death, the ATONEMENT, the resurrection, and the JUDGMENT are interrelated, necessary components of God's plan of restoration. The prophets presented the doctrine of resurrection as the means by which man overcomes the two types of death occasioned by the fall of Adam. As Adam's fall brought both a physical death of the body and a spiritual death that cuts man off from the presence of the Lord, the "plan of restoration" through Christ will reunite the body and the spirit and return the resurrected person to the presence of God for judgment (Alma 11:43–45; 41:2–4; 42:23). Just how the resurrection is accomplished has not been revealed. It remains one of the "many mysteries which are kept, that no one knoweth . . . save God himself," and "no man knoweth of his ways save it be revealed unto him" (Alma 40:3; Jacob 4:8).

Alma[2] taught that resurrection is "the reuniting of the soul [spirit] with the body" (Alma 40:18). "The soul shall be restored to the body, and the body to the soul; . . . every limb and joint . . . even a hair of the head shall not be lost; but all things shall be restored to their proper and perfect frame" (Alma 40:23; 41:2). Amulek affirmed that after the resurrection "they can die no more; their spirits uniting with their bodies, never to be divided; thus the whole becoming spiritual and immortal, that they can no more see corruption" (Alma 11:45).

An indisputable demonstration of bodily resurrection is Jesus Christ, who showed his resurrected body to a multitude and permitted each person individually to touch the nail holes in his hands and feet and the wound in his side (3 Ne. 11:13–17). These scars were retained for a special purpose. The nail holes and wound in his side left no doubt that this resurrected body before them was the same body Jesus inhabited while living on earth, the same body that was nailed to the cross. Though others will not retain their mortal scars in the resurrection, every person will receive the same "fundamental parts," or "fundamental principle," of the body that was his or her mortal body (Smith, *Church*, 5:339; Alma 11:45; Morm. 6:21; D&C 88:28). Otherwise, it would not be a "restoration" but a "replacement." The doctrine of the Book of Mormon is not replacement but restoration.

All will be resurrected

Everyone who ever has lived or ever will live and die on earth will be resurrected. Amulek proclaimed, "The day cometh that all shall rise from the dead and stand before God, and be judged" (Alma 11:41). "This restoration shall come to all," old, young; bond, free; male, female; wicked, righteous (Alma 11:44). Alma added his witness: "There is a time appointed that all shall come forth from the dead" (Alma 40:4, 9–10).

Many other Book of Mormon prophets taught that all mortals who suffer death, which is all mankind, will be resurrected. Notable among these prophets were Lehi[1] (2 Ne. 2:8–10), Jacob[2] (2 Ne. 9:6, 13–16, 21–22), Abinadi (Mosiah 16:7–11), Samuel the Lamanite (Hel. 14:15–16), and Moroni[2] (Morm. 9:12–13).

If even one person were not to be resurrected, Christ's victory over death would not be complete. Victory over the grave must be as wide and as deep as is death. Just as no one escapes death, no one will be denied resurrection. Even translated beings will eventually die and experience a change equal to resurrection (3 Ne. 28:36–40; D&C 133:54–55).

The Book of Mormon deals specifically with the resurrection of mankind and not of other forms of life. Other forms of life are referred to in 2 Nephi 2:22, in connection with the Creation and the Fall, but the concept of resurrection of animals is not developed; however, latter-day revelation explains that animals will be resurrected (D&C 29:23–25; 77:2–3).

The Atonement makes the resurrection possible

The Book of Mormon makes it abundantly clear that by virtue of the atonement of Jesus Christ resurrection is made possible (Alma 42:23). "Since man had fallen he could not merit anything of himself" (Alma 22:14; 1 Ne. 10:6; Mosiah 16:4). Therefore, Jesus did for all mankind what they could not do for themselves. He performed an infinite atonement, assuring the resurrection of all (Mosiah 3:5–15; 13:33–35; Alma 34:9–12; 42:15; 3 Ne. 27:13–15). Abinadi declared, "If Christ had not risen from the dead, or have broken the bands of death . . . there could have been no resurrection. But there is a resurrection, therefore the grave hath no victory, and the sting of death is swallowed up in Christ" (Mosiah 16:7–8).

When mankind will be resurrected

Book of Mormon prophets proclaim that the resurrection began with Jesus, he being the first to rise, three days after his death (2 Ne. 2:8; 25:13; Mosiah 3:10; Hel. 14:20). Subsequently, came the "first resurrection," beginning with the righteous from Adam until Christ (Mosiah 15:21–25; Alma 40:16). Abinadi taught that "little children" and those who die in ignorance, "not having salvation declared unto them," have part in the first resurrection (Mosiah 15:24–25). Because all will be resurrected and the righteous are "first," the unrighteous will come forth at a later time (Mosiah 15:26; Alma 40:19–20). In either resurrection, the first resurrection or a later one, all do not come forth at the same time. Alma explained that this doesn't matter because all do not die at the same time. He assured his readers that "there is a time appointed" for all to rise and that "God knoweth all the times which are appointed unto man" (Alma 40:8–10).

Latter-day revelation adds detail not found in the Book of Mormon concerning the resurrection, specifying that the first resurrection includes celestial and terrestrial beings, whereas the later resurrection is for telestial beings and sons of perdition (D&C 88:21–24, 97–102; cf. D&C 76). Also, the Book of Mormon does not

Jesus Christ Visits the Americas; *painting by John Scott; courtesy VRL.*

distinguish between the "kind[s]" of resurrected bodies and the "glory" that attends them, as do both the Bible and the Doctrine and Covenants (1 Cor. 15:39–44; D&C 88:21–24).

Resurrection necessary for fulness of joy

Book of Mormon prophets insisted that the physical body is restored from the grave as part of the "plan of restoration," "the great plan of happiness" (Alma 41:2–11; 42:5, 8). Jacob[2] explained that without Christ's infinite atonement and the bodily resurrection, the spirits of all mankind, being stricken by the fall of Adam, would be miserable forever, becoming "devils, angels to a devil, to be shut out from the presence of our God" (2 Ne. 9:5–10). Such "death and hell" are an "awful monster," from which Jesus rescued all mankind (2 Ne. 9:26). Lehi[1] stated that "men are, that they might have joy" (2 Ne. 2:25). Without the resurrection there would be no eternal joy, but everlasting misery.

Latter-day revelation affirms the relationship between resurrection and receiving a fulness of joy: "Spirit and element [spirit and the physical body], inseparably connected, receive a fulness of joy; and when separated, man cannot receive a fulness of joy" (D&C 93:33–34). The Prophet Joseph Smith elaborated, "We came to this earth that we might have a body and present it pure before God in the celestial kingdom. The great principle of happiness consists in having a body. The devil has no body, and herein is his punishment" (Smith, *Teachings,* 181).

The resurrection focuses on the body, but it is evident that it is also of special value to the happiness of the spirit. This realization gives added meaning to the words of Adam and Eve (Moses 5:10–11), of Job (Job 19:26), and of Jacob[2] (2 Ne. 9:4).

These revealed truths indicate that neither man's spirit nor his body can be saved separately: They form a unit complementary to one another. Both are affected by the fall of Adam; both are benefited by the atonement of Christ; both need the resurrection. The ultimate miracle of Jesus Christ is his triumph over physical and spiritual death through the resurrection (Hunter, 18).

Conclusion

Book of Mormon prophets leave no doubt that the resurrection is real and that it is a gift from Jesus Christ to man, part of "the merciful plan of the great Creator" (2 Ne. 9:6). The writings of these prophets fulfill the Lord's promise to Enoch: "And righteousness will I send down out of heaven; and truth will I send forth out of the earth, to bear testimony of mine Only Begotten; his resurrection from the dead; yea, and also the resurrection of all men" (Moses 7:62).

See also Book of Mormon: Another Testament of Jesus Christ; Fall of Adam and Eve, the; Firstfruits, first-fruits, first fruits; Life, purpose of; Restoration, plan of; Spiritual; Translation.

BIBLIOGRAPHY

Hunter, Howard W. Conference Report, April 1986.

Smith, Joseph. *History of The Church of Jesus Christ of Latter-day Saints.* Edited by B. H. Roberts. 7 vols. 2d ed. rev. Salt Lake City: The Church of Jesus Christ of Latter-day Saints, 1932–51.

———. *Teachings of the Prophet Joseph Smith.* Selected by Joseph Fielding Smith. Salt Lake City: Deseret Book, 1976.

RJM

Revelation *Reveal,* from the Latin, means "to draw back the veil." Because of the veil that covers the understanding of men, the things of God are hidden from view unless they are revealed from heaven (Jacob 4:8). Book of Mormon prophets made clear what would be revealed, why such revelation is critical to gaining salvation, how such revelations come, and principles and practices which govern and influence the receipt of revelation. They also exposed and warned readers against false doctrine that would be taught in the latter days concerning revelation, as well as false revelation that would come from the devil.

What is to be revealed

The principal revelation of God to man is that "there is no flesh that can dwell in the presence of God, save it be through the merits, and mercy, and grace of the Holy Messiah" (2 Ne. 2:8). The Book of Mormon as a whole is a revelation concerning Christ and his role in the plan of salvation, as well as a record containing many other revealed doctrines associated with this plan.

Concerning revelation in general, God reveals anything he deems necessary. The Book of Mormon narrative is replete with examples of individuals who were guided by revelation. Revelation warned Lehi[1] to flee Jerusalem (1 Ne. 2:1–4), Nephi[1] to escape with his followers from his brothers Laman[1] and Lemuel (2 Ne. 5:5), and Mosiah[1] to travel to Zarahemla (Omni 1:12–13). Revelation was also given to Amulek to discern the evil intents of Zeezrom (Alma 12:3–4), to Ammon[2] so he could perceive the thoughts of king Lamoni (Alma 18:16–18; cf. Jacob 2:5; D&C 6:16), and to Alma[2] to know specifics concerning Lamanite battle plans (Alma 43:23–24).

Alma[2] taught that the MYSTERIES OF GOD will be revealed in full to the faithful (Alma 12:9–11). The mysteries of God may include important information about the future and the past. For instance, the sealed portion of the gold plates contains the revelation the brother of Jared[1] received when he beheld "all the inhabitants of the earth which had been, and also all that would be . . . even unto the ends of the earth" (Ether 3:25; cf. 2 Ne. 27:10).

A preeminent revelation was the appearance of the Lord himself to the righteous Nephites and Lamanites in America (ca. A.D. 34). He showed them the prints of the nails in his hands and feet and allowed them to thrust their hands into his side. Thus they "did know of a surety and did bear record, that it was he, of whom it was written by the prophets, that should come" (3 Ne. 11:15). While Jesus was with them they saw and heard things which "cannot be written," but which they understood in their hearts (3 Ne. 17:15–17; 19:32–34).

Revelation is critical to salvation

The Prophet Joseph Smith taught that "salvation cannot come without revelation" (160), and the apostle John taught that "the testimony of Jesus is the spirit of prophecy" (Rev. 19:10; cf. Alma 6:8). This testimony of Christ, which comes through revelation, is essential because "there is no other name given whereby salvation cometh" (Mosiah 5:8), and each individual must come unto Christ to be saved (3 Ne. 12:20). In addition, ministers of the gospel, whether they lived before or after the time of the Christ, had to teach with the "spirit of revelation" to be able to convey the spirit and power of the gospel and build faith in things unseen, like the Creation, the Fall, and the divine mission of Jesus Christ (e.g., Alma 17:3–4).

Revelations from God come in many forms

A universal source of personal revelation is the light or Spirit of Christ "given to every man, that he may know good from evil" (Moro. 7:16–19). Those who "enter in by the way" (i.e., baptism) are promised the gift of the HOLY GHOST through which they can know "all things what [they] should do" (2 Ne. 32:3, 5; cf. Moro. 10:5). The Book of Mormon records instances of prophets and other holy men being "led on by the Spirit" to prophesy (e.g., Jacob 4:15), or to preach to select groups of people (e.g., Alma 21:16). When Nephi set out alone to retrieve the brass plates from Laban he acknowledged that he "was led by the Spirit, not knowing beforehand the things which [he] should do" (1 Ne. 4:6). This revelation comes by the Spirit's influencing one's feelings (Hel. 13:5; 3 Ne. 11:3; cf. D&C 8:2). Joseph Smith taught that by noticing "sudden strokes of ideas" which are "presented unto your minds by the Spirit of God" and witnessing their fulfillment, a person "may grow into the principle of revelation" (151).

Lehi was given another means of revelation: the LIAHONA, "a round ball of curious workmanship . . . of fine brass," having spindles which pointed the direction his family was to travel in the wilderness. Upon the Liahona appeared writings which were "plain to be read, which did give [Lehi's family] understanding concerning the ways of the Lord." These writings were "changed from time to time, according to the faith and diligence which [they] gave unto it" (1 Ne. 16:10, 25–29). The Book of Mormon also illustrates revelation that comes through dreams (1 Ne. 8:2), visions (1 Ne. 11–14), the Lord's voice speaking words to the mind (Enos 1:10), and angels bringing messages to faithful servants of the Lord (e.g., Jacob 7:5; Mosiah 3:2; Alma 8:14–17; 10:7–10).

Principles and practices that govern and influence the receipt of revelation

Alma[2] taught Zeezrom that the mysteries of God are revealed "in full" to anyone who "will not harden his heart" but will give "heed and diligence" unto God (Alma 12:9–11). Ammon[2] rejoiced in the truth that to those who repent, exercise faith, bring forth good works, and pray without ceasing, "it is given to know the mysteries of God" and even "to reveal things which never have been revealed" (Alma 26:22; cf. Ether 4:13–15). Such knowledge, Nephi[1] taught, is imparted "line upon line, precept upon precept, here a little and there a little." To those who receive what the Lord imparts, the Lord promises to "give more" (2 Ne. 28:30).

An incident in the life of Nephi[1] illustrates another principle concerning revelation: submitting oneself to the direction of those whom the Lord has placed in leadership roles, even though those leaders may have some imperfections. Nephi sought and received direction about where to hunt for food through his murmuring father (1 Ne. 16:23–25). Joseph Smith similarly taught that God follows the order of the priesthood to reveal his will and thus will not reveal instructions to any member of the Church for those in authority over that member (21).

PRAYER is instrumental in receiving revelation. The Lord promised, "Ask, and it shall be given unto you; seek, and ye shall find; knock, and it shall be opened unto you" (3 Ne. 14:7–8). The verification of the truthfulness of this promise is demonstrated throughout the Book of Mormon. Nephi inquired about the truth of his father's words and received a revelatory confirmation (1 Ne. 2:16); Enos, after receiving forgiveness of his sins, wanted to know how his guilt was swept away, and he received a revelation that it was because of his faith in Christ (Enos 1:8); Alma[1] prayed to know how to handle the problem of transgression in the Church, and the Lord answered his prayer by giving him specific guidelines to implement (Mosiah 26:14–33). Mormon's doctrinal questions about the Three Nephites and the baptism of little children brought forth important revelations concerning these subjects (3 Ne. 28:36–40; Moro. 8:7–23).

The story of the brother of Jared[1] illustrates how faith, repentance, obedience, and ingenuity relate to receiving revelation. He first repented of failing to call upon the Lord and then sought to know his will (Ether 2:14–15). He followed the Lord's commandments precisely (Ether 2:20–21) and then, as the Lord instructed, he formulated a plan to provide light for the vessels he had been commanded to build (Ether 2:25–3:1; cf. D&C 9:7–9). His humble proposal to the Lord, offered with great faith, was met with divine approval and with further revelation that exceeded his expectations (Ether 3).

Other principles that influence receiving revelation include a sincere desire for spiritual knowledge, a belief that the Lord is able to impart that knowledge, and pondering or thinking deeply about the particular subject or concern. Nephi[1] desired, believed, and "sat pondering in [his] heart" just prior to receiving the knowledge he sought from the Lord (1 Ne. 11:1; cf. Moro. 10:3–5).

False doctrine and false revelation

Nephi[1], Mormon, and Moroni[2] each denounced false teachings that deny revelation. Nephi foresaw that in the latter days some people would supplant the revelations of God with the learning of men (2 Ne. 28:4). False teachers would say, "There is no God today, for the Lord . . . hath done his work" (2 Ne. 28:5). Nephi issued a stern warning: "Wo be unto him that . . . denieth the power of God, and the gift of the Holy Ghost! Yea, wo be unto him that saith: We have received [i.e., the revelations in the Bible], and we need no more! [i.e., the revelations in the Book of Mormon]" (2 Ne. 28:26–27). Concerning the reason for new revelation (the Book of Mormon) being added to former revelation (the Bible), the Lord taught that his words are not restricted to just one nation. He "created all men," and his "work is not yet finished" (2 Ne. 29:7–9). Mormon warned his latter-day audience, "Wo unto him that shall deny the revelations of the Lord, and that shall say the Lord no longer worketh by revelation" (3 Ne. 29:6). Moroni contended that those who deny the revelations of God "knoweth not the gospel of Christ," or they are ignorant of the scriptural teaching that God is an unchangeable being. If revelation ceases it is because of unbelief, not because God has altered his ways (Morm. 9:7–26).

Revelation can come not only from God but also from the devil. He appears to mortals, "transform[ing] himself nigh unto an angel of light, and stirreth up the children of men unto secret combinations of murder and all manner of secret works of darkness" (2 Ne. 9:9; Alma 30:53). He prompts people to anger against that which is good, pacifies them with feelings of carnal security, and flatters them with false doctrine (2 Ne. 28:20–22). He teaches men not to pray and inspires contention (2 Ne. 32:8; 3 Ne. 11:29). When his teachings are removed from a society, he reveals them anew to those who are willing to follow him (Hel. 6:26).

Prayer and righteousness are critical safeguards against being deceived by the devil's false revelation (Alma 34:23, 39; 48:17; Hel. 5:12).

See also Angels, ministry of; Light of Christ; Past feeling; Ponder.

BIBLIOGRAPHY

Smith, Joseph. *Teachings of the Prophet Joseph Smith.* Selected by Joseph Fielding Smith. Salt Lake City: Deseret Book, 1976.

ALW

Revelation, book of The Apocalypse or last book in the New Testament. Since the second century A.D., the Christian world has debated the authorship of Revelation; the Book of Mormon confirms the ancient tradition that it was written by the apostle John. God opened a grand vision to Nephi[1] but commanded him not to record the latter portion of it, explaining that "one of the twelve apostles of the Lamb" would do it and would include the events associated with the end of the world (1 Ne. 14:20–22; cf. Rev. 1:11, 19). Nephi learned that "the name of the apostle of the Lamb was John" (1 Ne. 14:27).

Like Nephi and John, the brother of Jared[1] also saw a vision of "all that would be" (Ether 3:25). He was commanded to write and seal up the vision until the Lord's "own due time" (Ether 3:27).

Christ invited the house of Israel and the Gentiles alike to come unto him, and he promised that when they did so they would understand the revelations written by John and know that the "time is at hand" when they should be fulfilled (Ether 4:13–16).

RDD

Revelator One who receives, makes known, or reveals the mind and will of God to the people (Mosiah 8:16). Revelators receive such knowledge through inspiration (e.g., 1 Ne. 4:6; 3 Ne. 6:20), dreams (e.g., 1 Ne. 2:1–2), the still small voice (e.g., 1 Ne. 17:45), an audible voice (e.g., Jacob 7:5), and visions (e.g., 1 Ne. 1:8; 3:29; 2 Ne. 11:2–3; Alma 36:22; Ether 3:13).

See also Prophets, role of; Revelation; Seer.

RT

Revile *See* Appendix C.

Reynolds, George Church leader and scripture scholar who provided some of the earliest helps and commentaries on the Book of Mormon. Born 1 January 1842 in Marylebone, London, England, George Reynolds joined the Church on 14 May 1856 and traveled to Utah in 1865. He served on the Deseret Sunday School General Board, as associate editor of the *Deseret News* and the *Juvenile Instructor,* and as a member of the First Seven Presidents of the Seventy (1890–1909). During the last decades of the nineteenth century he became one of the most important Book of Mormon scholars in the Church. By 1886, he was considered a leading authority on the Book of Mormon. In 1880 he began working on the *Concordance to the Book of Mormon,* which was eventually published in 1900. This comprehensive work listed nearly every word found in the Book of Mormon, including adverbs, conjunctions, and articles. He noted: "Had I known the vast amount of labor, patience and care it would take to prepare it I should, undoubtedly have hesitated before commencing so vast, so tedious and so costly a work" (Reynolds, 3).

In 1883 he published the *Myth of the Manuscript Found,* a discussion of the Spaulding manuscript and its relationship to the Book of Mormon (*see* Spaulding theory). In late October

George Reynolds (1842–1909); courtesy LDS Family and Church History Archives. Image of Complete Concordance of the Book of Mormon *courtesy Brent F. Ashworth.*

1883 and throughout 1884, Reynolds published an important series in the *Contributor,* entitled "The History of the Book of Mormon" (vol. 5). A second series, "Evidences of the Book of Mormon; Some External Proofs of Its Divinity" was also published in the *Contributor* several years later (vol. 17). In 1888 he published *The Story of the Book of Mormon,* the first complete commentary on the Book of Mormon text. The volume also included the first illustrations depicting events and personalities in the book. He published *Chronological Chart of Nephite and Lamanite History* in 1898. His chronology was later used by Elder James E. Talmage to provide dates for the 1921 edition of the Book of Mormon. In another book, *Dictionary of the Book of Mormon* (1891), Reynolds identified and commented upon every land, hill, river, city, and person mentioned in the book.

After his death, material from his lifelong study of the Book of Mormon was edited and arranged by one of his sons, Philip C. Reynolds, into the seven-volume *Commentary on the Book of Mormon* (1955). The compiler also used material by his father-in-law, Janne M. Sjodahl, editor and associate editor of the *Deseret News* (1890–1913).

Although major advances in Book of Mormon studies have occurred after his monumental works were completed in the late 1800s, George Reynolds laid a foundation that students and scholars of the book have enlarged upon since his death in 1909.

BIBLIOGRAPHY

Reynolds, George. "Preface." *A Complete Concordance of the Book of Mormon.* Salt Lake City: Deseret Book, 1968.

RNH

Riches The Book of Mormon teaches that riches can be either a blessing or a curse. The prophet Jacob[2] gave the most clear and complete view in scripture of the Lord's position on obtaining and using wealth: "But before ye seek for riches, seek ye for the kingdom of God. And after ye have obtained a hope in Christ ye shall obtain riches, if ye seek them; and ye will seek them for the intent to do good—to clothe the naked, and to feed the hungry, and to liberate the captive, and administer relief to the sick and the afflicted" (Jacob 2:18–19).

The Lord promised Lehi's family and their posterity that "inasmuch as ye shall keep my commandments, ye shall prosper" (1 Ne. 2:20; 4:14; 2 Ne. 1:20; Jarom 1:9; Omni 1:6; Alma 9:13). Obedience brought spiritual blessings to Book of Mormon peoples and often material blessings as well. When they arrived in the promised land, they found that their crops "did grow exceedingly" and that there was an abundance of animals, gold, silver, and copper (1 Ne. 18:24–25). During a particularly peaceful time, characterized by humility and equality among the Nephites, "they did abound in the grace of God. . . . And the Lord did visit them and prosper them, and they became a large and wealthy people" (Mosiah 27:5–7; cf. 2 Ne. 5:10–11; Alma 1:29; 62:48–49). During the zenith of righteousness, after the appearance of

Jesus Christ, Mormon observed "that [the people] had become exceedingly rich, because of their prosperity in Christ" (4 Ne. 1:23).

Conversely, riches also became a source of pride and wickedness and brought upon the Nephites the judgments of God (Hel. 12:1–3). Jacob denounced the behavior and attitudes riches can engender: "But wo unto the rich, who are rich as to the things of the world. For because they are rich they despise the poor, and they persecute the meek, and their hearts are upon their treasures; wherefore, their treasure is their god" (2 Ne. 9:30; cf. 3 Ne. 13:19–21). Jacob continued in this same vein in his sermon at the temple to the Nephite rich: "And the hand of providence hath smiled upon you most pleasingly, that you have obtained many riches; and because some of you have obtained more abundantly than that of your brethren ye are lifted up in the pride of your hearts, and wear stiff necks and high heads because of the costliness of your apparel, and persecute your brethren because ye suppose that ye are better than they. . . . If ye persist in these things his judgments must speedily come unto you" (Jacob 2:13–14). Similarly, Samuel the Lamanite cried from the walls of Zarahemla, "Ye are cursed because of your riches, and also are your riches cursed because ye have set your hearts upon them, and have not hearkened unto the words of him who gave them unto you" (Hel. 13:21; cf. Alma 45:24). Furthermore, Samuel taught that pride leads to other iniquities including boasting, swelling, envyings, strifes, malice, persecutions, and murders (Hel. 13:22), all of which can trace their roots to improper attitudes and actions concerning the acquisition, possession, and use of wealth.

In addition to being a source of pride (2 Ne. 28:15; Alma 4:6; Hel. 3:36; 7:26; 3 Ne. 6:10, 12), riches are also used to support wickedness (Mosiah 11:13–14); they are a motivation for priestcraft (Alma 1:16); they can divide societies into classes and ranks (3 Ne. 6:12; 4 Ne. 1:24–26); they are the foundation of materialism (Alma 31:24, 27–28; Hel. 7:21); and they lead to secret combinations (Hel. 6:17). The Book of Mormon attributes the temptation to seek riches for unrighteous purposes to Satan (3 Ne. 6:15).

King Benjamin testified that the obedient "are blessed in all things, both temporal and spiritual" (Mosiah 2:41). Riches can be both a reward for righteousness and also a test to see if those so blessed will remember the Lord and thank him for their success and continue in righteousness (Hel. 13:22). To those who have prospered materially, the Book of Mormon admonition is to "think of your brethren like unto yourselves, and be familiar with all and free with your substance, that they may be rich like unto you" (Jacob 2:17).

See also Prosper, prosperity.

RCR

Righteous, the/righteousness Those who believe in and follow Christ, the Holy One of Israel (2 Ne. 9:18; 31:6–10); love and hearken to the truth and are not shaken by it (1 Ne. 16:3; 2 Ne. 9:40); endure the crosses of the world and despise the shame of it (2 Ne. 9:18); observe and keep the commandments and statutes of the Lord (Alma 25:14; Ether 10:2); remain firm and steady in the faith (Hel. 6:1); hearken to the words of the prophets (2 Ne. 26:8; 3 Ne. 10:12); and serve God (3 Ne. 24:18). Significant blessings are promised to the righteous. Among those blessings are promises that the righteous will be favored of God (1 Ne. 17:35), have their prayers remembered by the Lord (Morm. 5:21), be justified by God (1 Ne. 16:2), and be spared at the second coming of Christ (3 Ne. 24:17–18; 25:2–3). The righteous "saints" will be "armed with righteousness" (1 Ne. 14:14), protected from the wicked, and preserved by God. "Wherefore," Nephi[1] taught, "the righteous need not fear; for . . . they shall be saved" (1 Ne. 22:16–19). Furthermore, upon death, the spirits of the righteous will rest in paradise (Alma 40:11–12), have a righteous judgment restored to them (Alma 41:13–15), come forth in the first resurrection (Alma 40:16–20; Mosiah 15:20–25), and have their names recorded in the book of life (Alma 5:58; 3 Ne. 24:16–17).

The Spirit of the Lord dwells in the hearts of the righteous and their garments are made white through Christ (Alma 34:36). The righteous will ultimately "shine forth" in the kingdom of God (Alma 40:25), where they will experience a perfect knowledge of their enjoyment and righteousness (2 Ne. 9:14).

Because of the prayers of the righteous, the wicked are often spared from destruction (Alma 10:22; 62:40; Hel. 13:12–14). Conversely, there are times when the Lord permits the righteous to be slain in order "that his justice and judgment may come upon the wicked" (Alma 60:13; 14:11). Moreover, when the wicked cast out the righteous, then is the time the judgments are poured out upon the wicked (Alma 10:23).

In the Book of Mormon, "righteousness" generally pertains to a state of living characterized by faithfulness or obedience to God's eternal laws. Nephi[1] had great hopes that his brethren would "walk in the paths of righteousness" (1 Ne. 16:5; cf. Alma 7:19). Various Book of Mormon kings reigned and executed "judgment in righteousness" (Ether 7:11, 27; W of M 1:17). Jesus invited people to come unto him and "bring forth works of righteousness" (Alma 5:35–36), though nations would turn away from righteousness (Hel. 6:31; 3 Ne. 7:8, 15). Alma[2] taught that being "born of God" is changing from a "carnal" state to "a state of righteousness" (Mosiah 27:25).

Righteousness refers to the things of God by which one can be nourished (Mosiah 23:18), instructed concerning (Alma 21:23; 35:16), or cut off from (1 Ne. 15:33; Alma 5:42; 40:26). Jesus admonished his disciples to "seek ye first the kingdom of God and his righteousness" (3 Ne. 13:33), and promised the Holy Ghost to those who "hunger and thirst after righteousness" (3 Ne. 12:6; cf. 2 Ne. 4:33; 9:49). Righteousness, which brings happiness, stands opposite wickedness, which brings misery (2 Ne. 2:11–13). And if a man repents of his sins and desires "righteousness until the end of his days, even so he shall be rewarded unto righteousness" (Alma 41:6; D&C 76:5).

Righteousness is spoken of as both a protection (2 Ne. 1:23) and a weapon (1 Ne. 14:14) against Satan, who is the "enemy to all righteousness" (Alma 34:23; Moro. 9:6). During the Millennium, one reason Satan will have "no power" is because of the "righteousness of [the Lord's] people" (1 Ne. 22:26).

Christ is the embodiment of all righteousness, the very "fountain of all righteousness" (Ether 8:26; 12:28; 1 Ne. 22:21; 2 Ne. 1:19; 8:8; 30:11; 31:5–9). Righteousness may also be an appropriate title referring to God the Father inasmuch as Jesus is called the "Son of righteousness" (2 Ne. 26:9; 3 Ne. 25:2; Ether 9:22; McConkie, 654–55). The righteousness of Jesus Christ, demonstrated in his perfect obedience to his father's will, is not only the path his disciples must follow (2 Ne. 31:5–21) but is the very source of their salvation. Lehi[1] testified to Jacob[2], "I know that thou art redeemed, because of the righteousness of thy Redeemer" (2 Ne. 2:3).

See also Wicked, the/wickedness.

BIBLIOGRAPHY

McConkie, Bruce R. *Mormon Doctrine.* 2d ed. Salt Lake City: Bookcraft, 1979.

RH

Righteousness, fulfill all *See* Fulfill all righteousness.

Ripe To become developed to the full extent necessary, either in goodness or in evil. For example, in Alma 26:5, "ripe" is used in the metaphor the "field was ripe" to indicate that the people were ready to receive the gospel. It also expresses the level of iniquity in a society that leads to its destruction (2 Ne. 28:16; Mosiah 12:12; Alma 10:19; 45:16; Hel. 13:14; Ether 2:15).

PYH

Riplah, hill A hill near the river Sidon and the land Manti (Alma 43:31, 32) which Moroni[1] used to conceal a part of his army during a battle with the Lamanites. As the Lamanites passed the hill Riplah, Moroni brought his men out from the hill's south side and encircled the Lamanites (Alma 43:33–36). Ultimately, the victorious Moroni compelled his foes to enter a covenant of peace (Alma 44:20).

Riplakish *See* Jared[1], posterity of.

Ripliancum, waters of Waters by which the Jaredite armies of Coriantumr[2] and Shiz pitched tents in preparation for further battle. The interpretation of the term "Ripliancum" is given in the text as "large, or to exceed all" (Ether 15:8).

River of water "River of water" is an example of Semitic phraseology called a construct state, translated into English as a phrase consisting of two nouns joined by the word "of." Other Book of Mormon examples include "mist of darkness," meaning "dark mist," and "words of plainness," meaning "plain words" (*see* Hebraisms). "River of water" simply means a riverbed that has water in it.

In the Book of Mormon the phrase is used in two contexts:

1. It is used by Nephi[1] to indicate a river flowing through a valley beside which Lehi[1] and his family camped after traveling three days from Jerusalem. Lehi named the river Laman and the valley Lemuel (1 Ne. 2:5–10). Several LDS scholars have argued that this "river of water" was a streambed in the dry country where rivers run primarily during the spring runoff, commonly referred to in Arabic as a "wadi." A spring runoff in the riverbed would indicate that the exodus of Lehi and his family occurred during the late winter or spring rainy season (Nibley, 76, 78–80; Hilton and Hilton, 62–75). But there is another possibility. Lehi spoke to his son Laman[1] and admonished him to "be like unto this river, continually running into the fountain of all righteousness" (1 Ne. 2:9). This suggests that Lehi was comparing his son to a "continually running" body of water. Such a river has been discovered in the desert of Saudi Arabia in the vicinity of the wilderness where Lehi likely sojourned that apparently flows year round through a valley into the Red Sea (Potter).

2. Lehi saw a "river of water" in his vision of the tree of life (1 Ne. 8:13, 26; 12:16).

Nephi explained to his brothers that the river of water was a representation of the "awful hell . . . prepared for the wicked" (1 Ne. 15:26–29).

See also Gulf.

BIBLIOGRAPHY

Hilton, Lynn M., and Hope A. Hilton. *In Search of Lehi's Trail.* Salt Lake City: Deseret Book, 1976.

Nibley, Hugh. *Lehi in the Desert; The World of the Jaredites; There Were Jaredites.* Vol. 5 of *The Collected Works of Hugh Nibley.* Edited by John W. Welch, Darrell L. Matthews, and Stephen R. Callister. Salt Lake City: Deseret Book and FARMS, 1988.

Potter, George D. "A New Candidate in Arabia for the Valley of Lemuel." *Journal of Book of Mormon Studies* 8:1 (1999): 54–63.

BMH

Robe of righteousness *See* Righteous, the/righteousness.

Rock A symbol implying the steadiness, strength, and sustaining power provided by the Lord and his gospel. Following are four ways the Book of Mormon uses "rock" symbolically:

1. The fulness of the gospel. The Lord declared to Nephi[1] that in the latter days the Nephite writings would come forth containing the "plain and precious" truths of his gospel that were "taken" from the Bible. These truths he called "my rock" (1 Ne. 13:28, 36; cf. D&C 11:24). The term refers to the spiritual safety afforded by the completeness of the truth versus the hazards of relying on an incomplete canon (1 Ne. 13:29, 34; cf. 2 Ne. 28:28–29).

2. The Lord. This is the most frequent use in the Book of Mormon. Nephi, like the biblical psalmist, praised the Lord by calling him "my God, and the rock of my salvation" (2 Ne. 4:30; cf. Ps. 18:46; cf. 1 Ne. 15:15; 2 Ne. 4:35; 9:45; Jacob 7:25; Hel. 5:12). This expresses the Savior's saving acts in sure and dependable terms. On the other hand, the wicked cannot progress without the Lord. Instead, he becomes to them "a stone of stumbling, and . . . a rock of offense" (2 Ne. 18:14; cf. 4:33). Further, the Jews' rejection of Jesus is symbolized as the rejection of a building's cornerstone; ultimately, he is "the only sure foundation" upon which the Jews must build (Jacob 4:15–17).

3. A secure FOUNDATION. Having rock for a foundation portrays the ultimate safety and stability that come to those who found their lives upon the gospel. The sermon on the mount reference to this analogy clearly likens building on the rock to heeding Christ's teachings (Matt. 7:24–27). Yet, in the 3 Nephi account, the Savior also connects ordinances to this analogy: baptism and confirmation (3 Ne. 11:33–40) and the sacrament (3 Ne. 18:5–13). Thus, securing oneself to the "rock of our Redeemer" requires both

following Jesus' teachings (Hel. 5:12; 2 Ne. 28:28; 3 Ne. 14:24–27) and participating in his ordinances (cf. 3 Ne. 27:13–22; D&C 33:11–13).

4. An object of a miracle during the biblical Exodus from Egypt. Several times Nephi rehearsed the incident when Moses struck a rock and it became the source of water for the wandering Israelites. This water-giving rock is a symbol of the sustaining powers of the Lord (1 Ne. 17:29; 20:21; 2 Ne. 25:20; cf. 1 Cor. 10:4).

See also Jesus Christ, names of; Types.

PAA

Rod A stick, staff, or pole usually cut from the stem or branch of a tree. In the Book of Mormon, "rod" is used 22 times in 1 and 2 Nephi, often as a tool of punishment or correction. Thus, Laman[1] and Lemuel "smote" Nephi[1] and Sam "with a rod," precipitating the intervention of an angel (1 Ne. 3:28–29; cf. 2 Ne. 19:4), and figuratively, the Lord "straitened" the children of Israel "in the wilderness with his rod" (1 Ne. 17:41; cf. 2 Ne. 20:5, 15, 24, 26; 21:4). In addition to being a tool of chastisement and correction, the rod can also be a sign of divine authority and power. For example, Joseph[1] prophesied of "a Moses" to whom the Lord would "give power . . . in a rod" (2 Ne. 3:17; cf. 20:26). In the Old Testament, the staff of Moses and Aaron[1] was used as a sign of divine investiture of authority to demonstrate God's power to the king of Egypt (e.g., Ex. 4:2, 4, 17, 20; 7:9–10, 12, 15, 17, 19–20).

In Lehi[1]'s vision of the tree of life a "rod of iron" represented the "word of God" (1 Ne. 11:25; cf. 8:20, 24, 30; 15:23–24).

"Rod," meaning a branch or descendant, is also found in 2 Nephi 21:1 // Isaiah 11:1, "And there shall come forth a rod out of the stem of Jesse" (*see* Isaiah chapter reviews, 2 Ne. 22 // Isa. 11, definitions, s.v. "rod").

SDR

Rod of iron *See* Lehi[1]'s dream.

Rooted *See* Appendix C.

Nevertheless they did fast and pray oft, and did wax stronger and stronger in their humility, and firmer and firmer in the faith of Christ, unto the filling their souls with joy and consolation, yea, even to the purifying and the **sanctification** of their hearts, which sanctification cometh because of their yielding their hearts unto God. HELAMAN 3:35

Sabbath Blessed and hallowed day set apart to remember God's rest on the seventh day of creation (Ex. 20:10–11) and, later, to remember God's redemption of Israelites from Egyptian bondage (Deut. 5:15). The commandment to keep the Sabbath day holy was perpetuated among descendants of Lehi[1] (Jarom 1:5; Mosiah 18:23). Two specific instructions are inherent in this commandment: People should not do any work on the Sabbath, and they should do all of their work during the other six days (Mosiah 13:16–19).

DKO

Sackcloth and ashes Symbols that ancient Semitic cultures associated with penitence and mourning. Sackcloth translates Hebrew *saq* (cf. Akkadian *šaqqu*), dark fabric woven of thread spun from goat hair or camel hair. Haircloth was used for coarse items—tents, rugs, and sacks (Gen. 42:25; 2 Sam. 21:10; Isa. 58:5). Unrefined and inexpensive, its use as clothing denoted abasement or abjection (2 Ne. 13:24 // Isa. 3:24; Jer. 6:26; 48:37). Even the color of sackcloth bespoke deprivation (parallel with blackness in the dearth context of 2 Ne. 7:3 // Isa. 50:3). Stripping off accustomed clothing, girding the loins with sackcloth, and soiling oneself with ashes or dust are also symbols of worthlessness and a ritual demonstration of utter humiliation and desire for mercy or reconciliation (2 Ne. 13:24; Mosiah 11:25). This ancient clothing ritual for repentance contrasts starkly with the wearing of costly apparel in times of prosperity and pride.

RAC

Sacrament, the A sacred gospel ordinance and covenant that commemorates the atoning sacrifice of the Lord Jesus Christ. The sacrament was first instituted in the Book of Mormon during the Savior's ministry among the Nephites. As recorded in 3 Nephi 18, Christ broke and blessed bread, a symbol of his broken body, and gave it to his disciples with a commandment to eat (3 Ne. 18:3, 7; 20:8); he then commanded them to administer the bread to the multitude (3 Ne. 18:4). After they had eaten of the bread, he commanded his disciples to drink of "the wine of the cup," which was a symbol of his blood which was shed for the sins of the world, and also to administer the wine to the multitude (3 Ne. 18:8, 11; 20:8). This, the Lord said, "shall ye always observe to do, even as I have done" (3 Ne. 18:6, 11). Jesus further taught that the sacrament must be administered by one ordained and given power to perform the ordinance and that it was to be given "unto the people of my church, unto all those who shall believe and be baptized in my name" (3 Ne. 18:5). He stated, "This is fulfilling my commandments, and this doth witness unto the Father that ye are willing to do that which I have commanded you" (3 Ne. 18:10). In addition to giving commandments about the sacrament on the first day of his visit to the Nephites, Christ miraculously provided the bread and wine for the multitude on his second day among them (3 Ne. 20:3–7). Subsequently, he "did show himself unto them oft, and did break bread oft, and bless it, and give it unto them" (3 Ne. 26:13).

The partaking of the sacrament is a covenant renewal of the promises entered into at baptism: promises to keep all of the Lord's commandments and to always remember the Savior (Mosiah 18:8–10; 3 Ne. 18:7–11). In turn, the Lord promises to bless Church members with his Spirit (3 Ne. 18:7, 11), a blessing the Nephite multitude experienced in a marvelous way (3 Ne. 20:9).

Obedience to the commandment to "always do these things" (i.e., partake of the sacrament frequently) would bring blessings and the promise that one is then built on the "rock," meaning that one's obedience has placed him or her on a firm gospel foundation that cannot be shaken (cf. Hel. 5:12). Doing "more or less" (i.e., adding to or taking away) from Jesus' instructions regarding the sacrament would bring condemnation (3 Ne. 18:12–13).

Though the Nephites were told to partake of the sacrament often, they were instructed to partake of it only if they were worthy. Jesus turned to his leaders, the disciples, and instructed them not to allow "any one knowingly to partake of my flesh and blood unworthily . . . ; for whoso eateth and drinketh my flesh and blood unworthily eateth and drinketh damnation to his soul" (3 Ne. 18:28–29).

The sacrament was initially introduced by Christ to his Twelve Apostles in Jerusalem at the Last Supper, the Passover meal immediately before his death (Matt. 26:26–28). For centuries, the Passover supper had celebrated the Lord's angel of death passing over the families of the ancient Israelites when he slew the firstborn of the Egyptians prior to the Exodus under Moses. It also served as a type of the Savior's coming redemption. By introducing the sacrament at the Last Supper, the Lord replaced the Passover meal with the new emblems of his universal atoning sacrifice, the bread and wine, emblematic of his body and blood. The Book of Mormon clearly indicates that these sacramental emblems are received in "remembrance" of Christ (3 Ne. 18:7, 11), clarifying the biblical phrases "this is my body" or "this is my blood" (Matt. 26:26, 28) which are interpreted by some Christians to mean that the emblems are his actual flesh and blood.

Centuries after the Lord's visit to the Nephites, Moroni[2] confirmed that the Nephite church members "did meet together oft to partake of bread and wine, in remembrance of the Lord Jesus" (Moro. 6:6). He included in his final writings the specific sacramental prayers used for the bread and wine (Moro. 4; 5). He also added a reminder of the Lord's warning against improper participation in the sacred ordinance in these words: "See that ye partake not of the sacrament of Christ unworthily" (Morm. 9:29). This verse is the only place in the Book of Mormon where "sacrament" actually appears.

See also Sacrament prayers.

BRM

Sacrament prayers Two of only three public prayers (the other being for baptism) for which exact wording has been revealed. As part of his

The Sacrament; *painting by Minerva Teichert; courtesy MOA.*

last writings, Moroni included information on the manner in which the sacrament was administered unto the Church of Christ, and he included the sacrament prayers (Moro. 4–5; cf. D&C 20:76–79). The wording of these prayers is closely linked with the covenants made at baptism (cf. 2 Ne. 31:7–9; Mosiah 18:8–10; D&C 20:37). Hence, in a very direct way Latter-day Saints renew baptismal covenants when they thoughtfully and worthily partake of the sacrament.

Two of the Gospels quote the Savior at the Last Supper as saying "This is my body" and "This is my blood" as he blessed the bread and wine, respectively (Matt. 26:26, 28; Mark 14:22, 24). Therefore, some have come to believe in a doctrine of "transubstantiation," in which the sacramental emblems, when blessed, actually become the Savior's body and blood. The Joseph Smith Translation of these verses, however, renders a different interpretation: "Take, eat; this is in remembrance of my body" (JST Matt. 26:22, 24; JST Mark 14:21–22). Luke's account (22:19–20) and an epistle of Paul (1 Cor. 11:24–25) clearly teach that the emblems were to be regarded as symbols. This interpretation is confirmed in the sacrament prayers' direction that one partakes "in remembrance" of the Savior's body and blood.

In 1830 the Lord warned the Saints not to buy wine from their enemies, explaining that "it mattereth not" what they should eat or drink as long as they did so "with an eye single to my glory" (D&C 27:2–4). In time, water has replaced wine as the symbol of Christ's blood. Because clear water is a cleansing and life-giving element, it is an appropriate symbol for the Savior's sanctifying blood.

See also Sacrament, the.

ROC

Sacrifice, great and last *See* Great and last sacrifice.

Sacrifices To sacrifice is to give up something as an offering or donation to God. Adam and Eve and their posterity were commanded to offer "the firstlings of their flocks, for an offering unto the Lord" as a "similitude of the sacrifice of the Only Begotten of the Father" (Moses 5:5–7). Under the Mosaic law, the Israelites were commanded to make a variety of complex sacrifices and offerings of agricultural produce or animals (Lev. 1–7). "Sacrifice" and "offering" are used in four different contexts within the Book of Mormon: the sacrifices and offerings of the LAW OF MOSES, the sacrifice of the Son of God, the sacrifice of a BROKEN HEART AND CONTRITE SPIRIT; and the human sacrifices of the wicked Lamanites.

Sacrifices and offerings of the Mosaic law

On at least three occasions Lehi[1] offered sacrifices on an altar near the Red Sea apparently after the manner of the Mosaic law (1 Ne. 2:7; 5:9; 7:22). Even though 1 Nephi and Mosiah 2:3 contain the only accounts of actual sacrifices being performed by Book of Mormon peoples, it is assumed the Nephites practiced the law of sacrifice because, as Nephi[1] stated, they "did observe to keep the . . . commandments of the Lord in all things, according to the law of Moses" (2 Ne. 5:10; cf. 25:25). As a complement to keeping the Mosaic law and having a place to give their offerings, the Nephites constructed a temple "after the manner of the temple of Solomon" (2 Ne. 5:16). This temple would have included an altar on which sacrifices could be performed. At the beginning of Jesus' ministry among the Nephites, he commanded them to cease their blood sacrifices and burnt offerings, which instruction implies that they had continued until that time (3 Ne. 9:19).

The sacrifice of the Son of God

Lehi[1], Jacob[2], Abinadi (quoting Isaiah), and Amulek all spoke of the sacrifice or offering of the Son of God in reference to the ATONEMENT. They taught that Christ's sacrifice was necessary to satisfy the law of justice and to fulfill the law of Moses (2 Ne. 2:7; Jacob 4:5; Mosiah 14:10; Alma 34:10–15).

The sacrifice of a broken heart and a contrite spirit

In 3 Nephi 9:19–20, the resurrected Christ commanded the Nephites to "offer for a sacrifice unto me a broken heart and a contrite spirit." In this sacrifice one offers to God a humble and repentant attitude, a necessary component of true REPENTANCE. This particular sacrifice is a prerequisite for baptism, reception of the Holy Ghost, and forgiveness through the Atonement (Moro. 6:2–4; 3 Ne. 9:20; 2 Ne. 2:7). It involves a spirit of covenant and commitment. As a higher law, beyond giving fruits and animals, one offers oneself to God. Amaleki[1] urged readers of the Book of Mormon to "offer your whole souls as an offering" unto Christ (Omni 1:26).

The human sacrifice of the Lamanites

The degenerate practice of human sacrifice was mentioned by Mormon as he recounted how the Lamanites offered their prisoners, including women and children, as sacrifices to their idol gods (Morm. 4:14–15). Thus, in the Book of Mormon, the references to sacrifices and offerings range from heaven to hell—from the divine atoning sacrifice of the Son of God to the devilish human sacrifices of the wicked.

See also Altar of stones; Temples.

VLL

Saint(s) The Saints of God are those numbered with the church of the Lamb of God (1 Ne. 14:12); they are the righteous, "they who have believed in the Holy One of Israel, they who have endured the crosses of the world, and despised the shame of it" (2 Ne. 9:18). People become Saints through the atonement of Christ. They put off the natural man, they yield to the enticings of the Holy Spirit, and they become, "as a child, submissive, meek, humble, patient, full of love, willing to submit to all things which the Lord seeth fit to inflict upon him, even as a child doth submit to his father" (Mosiah 3:19). Saints are baptized and receive a remission of sins. They are meek and lowly of heart and are visited of the Holy Ghost, "which Comforter filleth with hope and perfect love" (Moro. 8:25–26). They are covenant people of the Lord, armed with righteousness and the power of God (1 Ne. 14:14). God delivers "his saints from that awful monster the devil, and death, and hell, and that lake of fire and brimstone, which is endless torment" (2 Ne. 9:19). "All the saints shall dwell with God" (Moro. 8:26) and "shall inherit the kingdom of God, which was prepared for them from the foundation of the world, and their joy shall be full forever" (2 Ne. 9:18). Because of wickedness and abominations in the last days, the number of Saints of the church of the Lamb of God will be comparatively few and their dominions small, although they will be upon all the face of the earth (1 Ne. 14:12).

RDA

Salem Melchizedek was king in a land called "Peace," or *Salem* (Hebrew), which is traditionally equated with Jerusalem (Gen. 14:18; Heb. 7:1–2; Alma 13:17–18). The people of Salem were extremely wicked, but responding to Melchizedek's teaching and repenting of their abominations (Alma 13:17), they became righteous enough to be taken up to join the translated City of Enoch (JST Gen. 14:32–34).

DKO

Sally *See* Appendix C.

Salt A healing, flavoring, and preserving agent used as a symbol for disciples of Jesus Christ and the covenants they make with God (3 Ne. 12:13; 16:15; D&C 101:39; Num. 18:19; 2 Chr. 13:5). Covenant-keeping disciples provide healing savor when they "succor the weak, lift up the hands which hang down, and strengthen the feeble knees" (D&C 81:5). They flavor and improve those around them when they share the gospel, set righteous examples, and act as a "light" unto the world (3 Ne. 12:14–16). They preserve the purity of the word of God when they stand as "witnesses of God at all times and in all things, and in all places" (Mosiah 18:9). If disciples should "lose [their] savor" or dishonor their covenants, they are "cast out . . . to be trodden under foot of men" (3 Ne. 12:13).

CF

Salvation Everlasting or eternal life, redemption, the state of being saved in the highest kingdom of God (Mosiah 5:15; Alma 11:40; 32:41; 2 Ne. 2:3). As the Book of Mormon authors use the term, there is no middle ground, consisting of varying levels of glory, between salvation and damnation. Such insight concerning kingdoms of glory is found in Doctrine and Covenants 76 and 131. The only possibilities spoken of in the Book of Mormon include the following: "liberty and eternal life" or "captivity and death" (2 Ne. 2:27–29), "the way of everlasting death or the way of eternal life" (2 Ne. 10:23), "salvation" or "endless torment" (Mosiah 28:3), "salvation" or the "chains of hell" (Alma 5:10), "the kingdom of God" or being "cast out, and consigned to . . . drink the dregs of a bitter cup" (Alma 40:25–26), "salvation" or "destruction" (Alma 29:4), "everlasting life" or "everlasting damnation" (Hel. 12:26; cf. Alma 9:28).

Book of Mormon prophets discuss three categories of people who will receive salvation or eternal life:

1. Those who "trust in the Lord," are "diligent in keeping his commandments," and "continue in the faith even unto the end" of their lives (Mosiah 4:6–8). Faith, repentance, baptism, and remission of sins through the "baptism of fire and of the Holy Ghost" are necessary to enter the "gate" to "the strait and narrow path which leads to eternal life" (2 Ne. 31:13–18; 9:23–24; Mosiah 3:12; Alma 26:35). Thereafter, one must "press forward with a steadfastness in Christ, having a perfect brightness of hope, and a love of God and of all men," and "endure to the end," in order to receive the Father's promise, "Ye shall have eternal life" (2 Ne. 31:19–20). Further, Alma[2] taught that to receive salvation, or to inherit the kingdom of God, one must be "born of God," (Mosiah 27:25). By contrast, those "that rebel against him and die in their sins," who "have known the commandments of God, and would not keep them" will be denied salvation (Mosiah 15:26–27).

2. Those who die "without the law" or "in their ignorance, not having salvation declared unto them" (Moro. 8:22; Mosiah 15:24). Some in this category are spoken of by Abinadi as "they that have died before Christ came" (Mosiah 15:24), but modern revelation makes it clear that the principle extends to all who have lived or will yet live on the earth "who have died without a knowledge of this gospel," and "who would have received it with all their hearts" had they been given the opportunity to hear it. Such are heirs of the celestial kingdom of God (D&C 137:1–9). They will hear and accept the GOSPEL in the postmortal spirit world and become heirs of all its blessings (D&C 138).

3. Little children who die before they become accountable before God (Moro. 8:11–12; Mosiah 15:25; cf. D&C 29:46–47; 137:10). Salvation is dependent on Christ through his atoning blood: "No flesh . . . can dwell in the presence of God, save it be through the merits, and mercy, and grace of the Holy Messiah" (2 Ne. 2:8; 31:21; Mosiah 3:17–18; 4:7; 5:15; 13:28; Alma 11:40). Christ is therefore spoken of as the ROCK of salvation (2 Ne. 4:30; 9:45; Jacob 7:25; cf. 1 Ne. 15:15). He is "a sure foundation, a foundation whereon if men build they cannot fall" (Hel. 5:12). And the salvation he offers is "free"; it cannot be purchased with money (2 Ne. 2:4; 9:50; 26:25; 3 Ne. 20:38).

The "plan of salvation" is a manifestation of God's love (Alma 24:14) and the way to "never-ending happiness" (Mosiah 2:41); thus "the Lord worketh in many ways to the salvation of his people" (Alma 24:27).

See also Atonement, the; Born again; Children, salvation of little; Jesus Christ; Salvation is free.

CF

Salvation is free Salvation is free (2 Ne. 2:4). It cannot be purchased with money (2 Ne. 9:50–51) nor, strictly speaking, can it be earned. It is the greatest of all the gifts of God (D&C 6:13; 14:7). The aspect of salvation known as resurrection from the dead is a free gift to all who have received a mortal body (2 Ne. 9:7, 10–11; Alma 11:41). Salvation, meaning exaltation or eternal life, is freely available to those who come unto Christ, deny themselves of ungodliness, repent, and thereby partake of the powers of the Atonement (2 Ne. 2:4; 26:25–28; Moro. 10:32).

RLM

Sam Third son of Lehi[1] and older brother of Nephi[1], Sam is an example of a successful follower. Sam had two important qualities of any righteous follower: faith and humility. The Book of Mormon does not say that Sam experienced visions comparable to those of Nephi, but rather that when Nephi told Sam what the Spirit had made known unto him, Sam believed in his words (1 Ne. 2:17). Though Sam was older, he humbly followed his younger brother Nephi instead of murmuring and rebelling, as did Laman[1] and Lemuel. In this regard Sam seems to have resembled Hyrum Smith, who was faithful to his younger brother Joseph to the end. The lives of Sam and Hyrum illustrate the Lord's pattern of declaring the word of Christ to chosen vessels (Nephi, Joseph Smith) who testify to "the residue of men" (Sam, Hyrum) that they "may have faith in Christ" (Moro. 7:31–32).

Sam married one of Ishmael's daughters (1 Ne. 16:7) and reared a family (2 Ne. 5:6). Not surprisingly, when the great division of the family occurred at Lehi's death, Sam and his family followed Nephi (2 Ne. 5:6). Most certainly, Sam was greatly blessed for his faithfulness and righteousness. In Lehi's dream of the tree of life, Sam, along with Sariah and Nephi, partook of the fruit of the tree of life (1 Ne. 8:14–16). When Lehi blessed his children before his death, he promised Sam that his seed, like the seed of his brother Nephi, would inherit the land and that he would be blessed all the days of his life (2 Ne. 4:11).

TLS

Samuel[1] Last of the judges in ancient Israel. Samuel was also the prophet who, at the people's instigation and with the Lord's approbation, instituted the Israelite monarchy and anointed its first two kings, Saul and David (1 Sam. 1–16). During his ministry in the western hemisphere, Christ affirmed that "all the prophets from Samuel . . . have testified of me" (3 Ne. 20:24; cf. Acts 3:24).

Samuel[2] the Lamanite Courageous Lamanite prophet sent among the Nephites to preach repentance and the coming of the Lord shortly before Christ's birth (6 B.C.). Chapters 13 through 15 of the book of Helaman contain a partial account of Samuel's preaching to the Nephites (Hel. 14:1), some of which was given to Samuel by an angel (Hel 13:7; 14:9, 26, 28). Samuel is one of the most colorful figures in the Book of Mormon, and few readers can forget the image of this fearless servant of God announcing the dramatic signs of Christ's birth and death, crying repentance from the walls of Zarahemla. The proud, wicked, and prejudiced Nephites were offended by the presence of a Lamanite reproving them for their sins (Hel. 14:10). Historically, that was a Nephite prerogative, but now the roles were reversed.

The Book of Mormon is silent as to Samuel's background, but perhaps he was one of the 8000 Lamanites converted by the powerful preaching of Nephi[2] and Lehi[4] "in the land of Zarahemla and round about" (Hel. 5:19), or one of the 300 Lamanites who were converted after witnessing the miraculous intervention of God in saving Nephi and Lehi in the Lamanite prison (Hel. 5:21–49). He could have been one of the many Lamanites converted by the 300 as they declared "throughout all the regions round about all the things which they had heard and seen" (Hel. 5:50). Nevertheless, he lived at a time when the Lamanites "did observe strictly to keep the commandments of God," while the Nephites "remain[ed] in wickedness, yea, in great wickedness" (Hel. 13:1).

Notwithstanding that Samuel was divinely commissioned to declare to the Nephites the "glad tidings" that he had personally received from an angel (Hel. 13:7), and that he preached earnestly for "many days," he was soundly rejected (Hel. 13:2; 14:10). About to return to his own land, he was stopped by "the voice of the Lord," which instructed him to return and prophesy "whatsoever things should come into his heart" (Hel. 13:3). Barred from entering the city of Zarahemla, the resourceful Samuel climbed upon the city's wall and began to prophesy from there (Hel. 13:4). He boldly announced the four-fold purpose of his message: "For this intent have I come up upon the walls of this city, that ye might [1] hear and know of the judgments of God which do await you because of your iniquities, and also that ye might [2] know the conditions of repentance; and also that ye might [3] know of the coming of Jesus Christ . . . and that ye might [4] know of the signs of his coming, to the intent that ye might believe on his name" (Hel. 14:11–12).

SAMUEL[2] THE LAMANITE

The judgments of God

Samuel was blunt and forthright in his prophetic announcement of Nephite doom, declaring that God's judgments would bring "heavy destruction" (Hel. 13:6). He said that the Nephites had become a hard-hearted and stiff-necked people, rejecting God's prophets (Hel. 13:26), following "foolish and blind guides," and choosing "darkness rather than light" (Hel. 13:29). In four hundred years, Samuel warned, the "sword of justice" would fall: The Lord would "suffer them no longer"—that is, he would take away his word, withdraw his Spirit, "turn the hearts of their brethren against them," and visit them with sword, famine, pestilence, and "utter destruction" (Hel. 13:5, 8–10). Yet, this generation of Nephites would not have to wait four centuries before reaping the harvest of their wickedness. Samuel announced: "Yea, behold, the anger of the Lord is already kindled against you; behold, he hath cursed the land because of your iniquity" (Hel. 13:30). He foretold that this curse would cause their riches to "become slippery" that they could not hold them (Hel. 13:17, 35–36). Speaking by revelation, Samuel told why the Nephites were cursed in this manner: "Ye are cursed because of your riches, and also are your riches cursed because ye have set your hearts upon them" (Hel. 13:21). Further denouncing Nephite wickedness, the Lord informed the Nephites through Samuel that it was only because there were still righteous people in the city of Zarahemla that he refrained from sending fire to destroy it (Hel. 13:13).

The conditions of repentance

Samuel's message was initially intended to be one of "glad tidings," but the Nephites rejected and expelled him (Hel. 13:7). Upon his return he prophesied dire consequences if the people persisted in their wickedness. All of these consequences could be averted if the people would repent. "Nothing," Samuel testified, could "save this people save it be repentance and faith on the Lord Jesus Christ" (Hel. 13:6, 13). The Lord promised to "turn away" his anger if they would "repent and turn unto" him (Hel. 13:11; cf. 14:13); otherwise, he would "utterly destroy them" (Hel. 15:17).

Samuel taught that Adam's fall brought SPIRITUAL DEATH to all mankind and that redemption, conditional upon REPENTANCE, was made possible because of the death of Christ: "For behold, he surely must die that salvation may come. . . . Yea, and it [Christ's death] bringeth to pass the condition of repentance, that whosoever repenteth the same is not hewn down and cast into the fire; but whosoever repenteth not is hewn down and cast into the fire; and there cometh upon them again a spiritual death, yea, a second death, for they are cut off again as to things pertaining to righteousness" (Hel. 14:15, 18). Thus Samuel's teachings on repentance gave the Nephites instructions not only for escaping temporal destruction but also for avoiding spiritual death. "And if ye believe on his name," Samuel taught, "ye will repent of all your sins, that thereby ye may have a remission of them through his merits" (Hel. 14:13).

The coming of Jesus Christ

As other New World prophets before him had done (Mosiah 3:3–11; Alma 13:21–25), Samuel announced the glad tidings of Christ's coming: "The Lord Jesus Christ . . . surely shall come into the world, and shall suffer many things and shall be slain for his people" (Hel. 13:6). Like John the Baptist, Samuel was sent to cry, "Repent and prepare the way of the Lord" (Hel. 14:9; cf. Matt. 3:1–2). Moreover, he declared, "Five years more cometh, and behold, then cometh the Son of God to redeem all those who shall believe on his name" (Hel. 14:2). This precise date of the Savior's coming should not have been new information to the Nephites. From the beginning of Nephite history, prophecy held that the Messiah would come 600 years from the time Lehi[1] left Jerusalem (1 Ne. 10:4; 19:8; 2 Ne. 25:19).

The signs of Christ's coming

After prophesying of God's impending judgments, warning that only sincere repentance could avert those judgments, and then declaring the coming of Christ, Samuel revealed specific signs that would occur at the birth and the death of the Savior. At the birth of Christ there would be "one day and a night and a day, as if it were

 SAMUEL[2] THE LAMANITE

Samuel the Lamanite; *painting by Jerry Thompson; courtesy VRL.*

one day and there were no night"; a "new star" would arise, and there would also be "many signs and wonders in heaven." These cosmic phenomena would cause the people to "be amazed" and to "fall to the earth" (Hel. 14:3–7). At Christ's death, the signs would be of a different sort. There would be "no light upon the face of [the] land" for three days until his resurrection (Hel. 14:20), and "thunderings and lightnings" would shake the heavens. Earthquakes would destroy highways and cities, changing the face of the land (Hel. 14:21–24). Also, "many graves" would yield up their dead, and resurrected Saints would "appear unto many" (Hel. 14:25; 3 Ne. 23:9–11).

Samuel declared that the angel told him that these signs would be given "to the intent that there should be no cause for unbelief among the children of men—and this to the intent that whosoever will believe might be saved, and that whosoever will not believe, a righteous judgment might come upon them; and also if they are condemned they bring upon themselves their own condemnation" (Hel. 14:28–29).

Samuel concluded his address from the wall by explaining that because of the great faithfulness of the Lamanite people following their conversion (Hel. 15:4–16), the Lord would "prolong their days . . . even if they should dwindle in unbelief" until they would be restored "again to the knowledge of the truth" (Hel. 15:10–11; cf. 1 Ne. 15:13–16). The Nephites' failure to repent, however, would bring destruction "because of their unbelief notwithstanding the many mighty works . . . done among them" (Hel. 15:17).

After Samuel finished his message, those who believed sought out Nephi[2] and were baptized (Hel. 16:1). Others were angered and threw stones or shot arrows at him. When they saw that they could not hit Samuel because he was divinely protected, many more believed and sought out Nephi for baptism (Hel. 16:2–3). But the "more part" of the Nephites did not believe, attributing his protection to the "power of the devil" (Hel. 16:6). Samuel's violent rejection and expulsion from the Nephite society proved prophetic, for he had told the Nephites earlier, "As the Lord liveth, if a prophet come among you and declareth unto you the word of the Lord, which testifieth of your sins and iniquities, ye are angry with him, and cast him out and seek all manner of ways to destroy him; yea, you will say that he is a false prophet, and that he is a sinner, and of the devil, because he testifieth that your deeds are evil" (Hel. 13:26).

Samuel was pursued but he escaped, fleeing back to his own country where he continued his ministry among his own people. Samuel was "never heard of more among the Nephites" (Hel. 16:1–8).

Summary of major teachings

1. The JUDGMENTS OF GOD which would come upon wicked Nephites if they failed to repent (Hel. 13:5, 9–10).

2. The conditions of repentance and the necessity of belief in Christ (Hel. 14:8, 13, 15–19).

3. The redemption of all mankind from the fall of Adam through the ATONEMENT of Jesus Christ (Hel. 14:15–18).

4. The coming of Jesus Christ (Hel. 13:6; 14:2).

5. The signs in the New World that would attend the birth and death of Jesus Christ (Hel. 14:2–7; 14:20–27), and the purpose of these signs (Hel. 14:28–31).

6. The casting out of the righteous from among a people makes them "ripe for destruction" (Hel. 13:14; cf. Alma 10:20–23).

7. The freedom to choose "life or death" (Hel. 14:30–31).

8. The restoration of the Lamanites to the truth in the "latter times" (Hel. 15:11–13, 16; cf. Alma 9:16–17).

9. The propensity of the wicked to accept false prophets who justify them in their iniquity (Hel. 13:27–28).

10. The truth that HAPPINESS cannot be obtained in doing iniquity (Hel. 13:38; cf. Alma 41:10).

11. ACCOUNTABILITY for sinning against knowledge (Hel. 15:14–15, 17; cf. Alma 9:18–24).

See also Lamanites, Book of Mormon message concerning; Signs.

DLL

Sanctification Becoming pure, holy, free of sin. Sanctification occurs by the power of the HOLY GHOST and is only possible through the ATONEMENT of Jesus Christ (Alma 13:11–12; Moro. 10:33; Moses 6:60). Obedience to the first principles and ordinances of the GOSPEL is an integral part of the process of sanctification. Jesus said, "Now this is the commandment: Repent, all ye ends of the earth, and come unto me and be baptized in my name, that ye may be sanctified by the reception of the Holy Ghost, that ye may stand spotless before me at the last day" (3 Ne. 27:20; cf. A of F 4). Mormon included fasting, praying, and yielding one's heart to God as factors leading to sanctification (Hel. 3:35). Alma[2] taught that individuals who are sanctified cannot "look upon sin save it were with abhorrence" (Alma 13:11–12). The Lord promised those who exercise great faith in him and become sanctified the privilege of spiritual manifestations, even seeing those things which the brother of Jared[1] saw (Ether 4:7; 3:25). In the case of the Three Nephites who were "sanctified in the flesh, that they were holy," the Lord "wrought [a change] upon them, insomuch that Satan could have no power over them, . . . that the powers of the earth could not hold them" (3 Ne. 28:39).

"Sanctify" is applied differently in two Isaiah passages. The phrases "sanctify the Lord of Hosts" and "sanctify my name" express the idea of perceiving the Lord as holy, and they are used in context with both trusting the Lord (2 Ne. 18:13) and revering his name (2 Ne. 27:34). Sanctify is also used in the sacrament prayers recorded in Moroni 4 and 5. In these prayers the congregation asks God to bless and sanctify the bread or wine (water). To sanctify means the making of these sacramental emblems holy or sacred. The emblems of the sacrament remind one of the Savior and his atonement, and by partaking of the sanctified emblems of the sacrament, a person covenants to do those things that will further his own process of sanctification.

See also Forgiveness; Justification; Sanctified in the flesh.

RLH

Sanctified in the flesh To be made holy through the blood of Christ and by the power of the Holy Ghost (Alma 5:54; 13:11–12; 3 Ne. 27:19–20; Moses 6:60), to be freed from the pulls of Satan and the buffetings of this fallen world. Mormon explained that the Three Nephite disciples who desired to remain on earth and continue their ministry were "sanctified in the flesh" (3 Ne. 28:6–9, 39). At Christ's coming in glory they will be transformed from their translated or terrestrial (yet mortal) state to resurrected, celestialized immortality (3 Ne. 28:8–9, 37–40; Smith, 170–71, 191).

BIBLIOGRAPHY

Smith, Joseph. *Teachings of the Prophet Joseph Smith.* Selected by Joseph Fielding Smith. Salt Lake City: Deseret Book, 1976.

RLM

Sanctuary Term used in the Book of Mormon with at least two meanings.

1. A physical structure used for religious worship (e.g., 2 Ne. 28:13; Alma 15:17; 16:13; 21:6; Hel. 3:9,14).

2. A place usually made holy by the presence of God. The word *sanctuary* in Hebrew means "holy place." In 2 Nephi 18:14 // Isaiah 8:14 the word is a metaphor used by Isaiah to indicate that the Lord is the protector of his people: "And he shall be for a sanctuary."

Moroni[2], reflecting the teachings of Ether, wrote that "this land" (the Americas) would be "the place of the New Jerusalem, which should come down out of heaven, and the holy sanctuary of the Lord" (Ether 13:2–4). In this context, "sanctuary" may refer to both the protection of the Lord and a physical structure, such as a temple.

RNH

Sarah Wife of Abraham. Isaiah is quoted as ascribing to her the role of mother of those who "follow after righteousness" (2 Ne. 8:1–2). Her name means "princess."

Sariah Wife of Lehi[1] and matriarch of the Nephite and Lamanite civilizations. Sariah resided in Jerusalem for many years before the Lord directed Lehi in a dream to take his family into the wilderness (1 Ne. 2:2). As the family journeyed, Sariah faced challenges that included the birth of two sons, perils inherent to isolated desert travel, and family strife.

Perhaps her greatest wilderness challenge was the delayed return of her sons from their errand to acquire the brass plates from Laban[1]. Sariah mourned their prolonged absence and imagined that they had perished (1 Ne. 5:2), blaming her husband for exposing them to danger. Lehi's assurances failed to ease her concerns, and only after her sons' safe return did Sariah speak with conviction of Lehi's prophetic calling (1 Ne. 5:8).

This conviction was portrayed later in Lehi's revelatory dream of the tree of life. In the dream, Sariah willingly responded to her husband's call to come to the tree and partake, thus enjoying the blessings of the love of God (1 Ne. 8:14–16). On the long voyage to the New World, an aging Sariah was brought near death because of the cruel mistreatment of Nephi[1] at the hands of Laman[1] and Lemuel (1 Ne. 18:17–18). Her death is not mentioned in the record.

SB

Satan Also known as Lucifer (meaning "shining one" or "lightbringer"). Satan was a "son of the morning," among the early born spirit children of God the Father (2 Ne. 24:12 // Isa. 14:12; D&C 76:26–27; McConkie, 461), who was an angel "in authority in the presence of God" (D&C 76:25), who "fell" (2 Ne. 9:8) and was thrust out of the Father's presence for rebellion (2 Ne. 2:17). He became the devil (2 Ne. 9:8); he was perdition being lost forever (D&C 76:26). The devil is commonly referred to as Satan, a Hebrew term meaning adversary or slanderer. In order of frequency in the Book of Mormon, he is referred to as the devil (e.g., 1 Ne. 22:22–23; 2 Ne. 2:17; 9:8–9; Alma 12:4), Satan (e.g., 1 Ne. 22:15, 26; Alma 8:9), evil one (e.g., 2 Ne. 9:28; Hel. 16:21), enemy (e.g., Mosiah 4:14; Alma 34:23; Moro. 7:12), evil spirit (e.g., Mosiah 2:32; 4:14), father of lies (e.g., 2 Ne. 9:9; Ether 8:25), adversary (e.g., Alma 12:5), old serpent (e.g., 2 Ne. 2:18), awful monster (e.g., 2 Ne. 9:19), master of sin (Mosiah 4:14), author of all sin (Hel. 6:30), Lucifer (2 Ne. 24:12), father of contention (3 Ne. 11:29), and cunning one (2 Ne. 9:39).

Among the plain and precious truths that the Book of Mormon restores is a clearer understanding of Satan, his role in premortality, and his efforts to make mankind share in his misery. By reading only the Old Testament, one is left with a very limited and incomplete view of Satan. In the Old Testament the word devil is never used and yet it is found nearly 100 times in the Book of Mormon. As one non-LDS scholar wrote, "Nowhere in the [Old Testament] does Satan appear as a distinctive demonic figure, opposed to God and responsible for all evil" (Gaster, 4:224). Yet another scholar after discussing the depiction of Satan in the Old Testament acknowledged, "Admittedly we have not yet the fully developed doctrine" concerning Satan (Morris, 1074). Part of Satan's plan has been to use flattery and whisper that there is no devil (2 Ne. 28:22). The knowledge of Satan and his plan was originally had among Old World prophets, for Lehi[1] likely learned from the PLATES OF BRASS much of what he knew about the fall of Lucifer in premortality and his subsequent design for all mankind (2 Ne. 2:17–18). In the words of President Ezra Taft Benson, "The Book of Mormon exposes the enemies of Christ. . . . It fortifies the humble followers of Christ against the evil designs, strategies, and doctrines of the devil in our day" (94).

Satan's objectives are expressly stated in the Book of Mormon. He desires "that all men might be miserable like unto himself," being permanently cut off from the presence of God (2 Ne. 2:27). He strives continually to have mankind subjected to him rather than submitting to God (2 Ne. 2:18; 3 Ne. 18:15, 18; 9:46; Alma 34:35). And he endeavors to destroy the souls of men (Hel. 8:28; 13:37; D&C 10:27).

The Book of Mormon details many of the tactics that Satan uses to obtain the above objectives. Anything evil ultimately comes from or is promoted by the devil (Omni 1:25; Alma 5:40). He entices and invites mankind to do evil, "for he persuadeth no man to do good, no, not one" (Moro. 7:12, 17). Satan uses his "cunning plans" to "ensnare the hearts of men" (Alma 28:13). He continually tempts people to "do great wickedness" (3 Ne. 2:3; 6:16–17; Hel. 16:22). He promotes the pursuit of pride, power, riches (3 Ne. 6:15), idolatry (2 Ne. 9:37), immorality, murder, lying (Ether 8:16), sorceries, witchcraft, and magic (Morm. 1:19). Another powerful tactic Satan uses is to "stir [people] up to anger against that which is good" (2 Ne. 28:20; cf. Alma 27:12). He fosters anger against the Book of Mormon (2 Ne. 33:5). He teaches men they "must not pray" (2 Ne. 32:8). By sending forth lies and false doctrine, Satan strives to deceive and mislead mankind (Jacob 7:18; Alma 12:4–5; 3 Ne. 1:22; 2:2). Furthermore, he tempts people to sin in order that he might blind the eyes and harden the hearts of the children of men (1 Ne. 12:17; Alma 10:25). Satan can use man's ability to acquire learning and wisdom to his advantage, causing some to "think they are wise, and they hearken not unto the counsel of God" (2 Ne. 9:28). A very subtle technique of Satan is to "pacify" or "lull" people into "carnal security," causing them to feel that "all is well in Zion," when indeed, it is not (2 Ne. 28:21). Associated with this apathetic attitude is Satan's promotion of procrastinating one's day of repentance, which ultimately leaves one "subjected" to him (Alma 34:34–35).

The Book of Mormon explains how Satan introduces evil oaths and covenants to form SECRET COMBINATIONS, their ultimate purpose being to "combine against all righteousness" (3 Ne. 6:28–29; 2 Ne. 26:22; Hel. 6:26). As the "founder" of the "great and abominable church," Satan will gather "multitudes" to "fight against the Lamb of God" (1 Ne. 13:6; 14:9, 13, 17). On some occasions Satan appears "in the form of an angel" to deceive and mislead those who are unrighteous (Alma 30:53; 2 Ne. 9:9; D&C 129:8). He has the ability to enhance the capacities of the wicked in their efforts to promote his plans (Jacob 7:4; Alma 11:21). The Book of Mormon confirms Joseph Smith's assertion that "the devil has no power over us only as we permit him. The moment we revolt at anything which comes from God, the devil takes power" (Smith, 181; 2 Ne. 2:28–29; Alma 37:15). Satan gains power as individuals "yield" themselves to him (2 Ne. 4:27; 3 Ne. 7:5). He leads people by a "flaxen cord, until he bindeth them with his strong cords forever" (2 Ne. 26:22). When the Spirit of the Lord departs because people have hardened their hearts, Satan has full power over them (Alma 34:35; Ether 15:19).

Mormon recorded that Satan "will not support his children at the last day, but doth speedily drag them down to hell" (Alma 30:60). The Book of Mormon shows that the consequences of following Satan are tragic: famine, physical and spiritual captivity, and utter destruction all follow in his wake (1 Ne. 14:3–4, 7; 2 Ne. 1:18; Alma 12:11, 17; 30:42). Satan rejoices with his angels and laughs at those who have fallen victim to his cunning plan (3 Ne. 9:2; Moses 7:26).

In addition to exposing the tactics and plans of Satan, the Book of Mormon gives clear and direct counsel on how to overcome him. First and foremost it is through the atonement of

Christ that one can escape from Satan and the SPIRITUAL DEATH he promotes (2 Ne. 9:7–10, 19, 26). By building a sure foundation on Christ one can withstand the temptations of the devil and overcome his mighty winds, so "they cannot fall" (Hel. 5:12; Alma 37:33). The Book of Mormon emphasizes the importance of holding to the word of God in overcoming "all the cunning and the snares and the wiles of the devil" (Hel. 3:29; 1 Ne. 15:24). The resurrected Savior admonished his people in the New World to "watch and pray always, lest ye be tempted by the devil" (3 Ne. 18:15, 18; cf. Alma 13:28; 15:17; 34:39). King Benjamin taught that righteous parents would "not suffer" their children to "transgress the laws of God, and fight and quarrel one with another, and serve the devil, who is the master of sin" (Mosiah 4:14). Nephi[1] declared that it would be the righteousness of the people that would leave Satan with no power as the Millennium is ushered in, during which time Satan will not be loosed for "many years" (1 Ne. 22:26; cf. 22:15). Afterwards, his ultimate fate is to suffer the second death, which torment is "as a lake of fire . . . whose flame ascendeth up forever and ever" (2 Ne. 9:16; Jacob 3:11; Mosiah 26:27; Rev. 20:10). Lehi[1] summarily declared the ultimate decision facing mankind: "[Men] are free to choose liberty and eternal life, through the great Mediator of all men, or to choose captivity and death, according to the captivity and power of the devil" (2 Ne. 2:27). Christ is the great preparer of mansions for the faithful in the kingdom of his Father (Ether 12:32–34), and Satan is the "preparator" of a place for the wicked in that awful HELL, the kingdom of the devil (1 Ne. 15:35; 2 Ne. 2:29; Alma 41:4).

See also Book of Mormon, selected purposes of, to reveal the enemies of Christ; Flaxen cord; Great and abominable church.

BIBLIOGRAPHY

Benson, Ezra Taft. Conference Report, April 1975.

Gaster, Theodor H. *Interpreter's Dictionary of the Bible.* Edited by George A. Buttrick. Nashville: Abingdon Press, 1990.

Largey, Dennis L. "Enemies of Righteousness." *Ensign* 19 (December 1989): 6–11.

McConkie, Bruce R. *Mormon Doctrine.* 2d ed. Salt Lake City: Bookcraft, 1966.

Morris, L. L. "Satan." *New Bible Dictionary.* Edited by J. D. Douglas. 2d ed. Wheaton, Ill.: Tyndale House Publishers, 1982.

Smith, Joseph. *Teachings of the Prophet Joseph Smith.* Selected by Joseph Fielding Smith. Salt Lake City: Deseret Book, 1976.

CJW

Satisfy To answer, meet, fulfill, APPEASE, or comply with. Amulek used this term in explaining the relationship between God's mercy and justice to the Zoramites[2]. Because of the Atonement, mercy can satisfy the demands or requirements of broken law, if one repents (Alma 34:15–16; cf. 2 Ne. 2: 5–7; Alma 42:15).

See also Demands of justice; Justice, law of; Law, answer the ends of.

DLL

Saved *See* Salvation.

Scourge A form of corporal punishment. The term is used metaphorically to describe afflictions and punishments placed upon the wicked and rebellious by the hand of God or his agents (1 Ne. 2:24; 19:13; 2 Ne. 5:25; 20:26; Jacob 3:3; 3 Ne. 20:28), or the harassment of an individual or people (Alma 52:10). Prophets foretold of Christ's scourging prior to his crucifixion (1 Ne. 19:9; Mosiah 3:9; 14:4–5; 15:5). The prophet Abinadi was scourged unto death by fire (Mosiah 17:12–13).

In the Mosaic law scourging is specifically prescribed for sexual offenses (Lev. 19:20). The law limited the number of lashes to forty (Deut. 25:2–3), but by New Testament times that number was reduced to thirty-nine in case of any miscalculation (2 Cor. 11:24). The historian Livy reported that in Roman times scourging was a precursor to crucifixion (22:13:9; 28:37:3), hence Jesus' experience at the hands of Pilate (Matt. 27:26).

See also Crucify, crucified.

BIBLIOGRAPHY

Livy. *History of Rome.* 14 vols. *Loeb Classical Library.* Translated by B. O. Foster. New York: G. P. Putnam, 1919–59.

GS

Scriptures, additional, to come forth Throughout the ages, it has been the divine trust and obligation of prophets to record revelations from God (3 Ne. 23:6, 11, 13; Amos 3:7; 2 Pet. 1:20–21). Extant records thus represent only a small portion of scripture which has and will be given over the history of mankind (2 Ne. 29:11–14; A of F 9). There are numerous references in the Book of Mormon to sacred records which would come forth over time. These include the following:

1. The sealed portion of the Book of Mormon record which the Prophet Joseph Smith received but did not translate (2 Ne. 27:7–11, 21; Ether 5:1) which contain the magnificent visions of the brother of Jared[1] when the Lord showed him "all things" regarding past and future inhabitants of the earth (Ether 3:25–27; 4:4–5).

2. The writings of "others," similar to the brother of Jared[1], Nephi[1] and John the Revelator, who saw "all things." In Nephi's vision he learned that these writings are "sealed up to come forth in their purity . . . in the own due time of the Lord, unto the house of Israel" (1 Ne. 14:26).

3. Records of the lost tribes of Israel and "all nations" to whom the Lord has spoken (2 Ne. 29:12–13).

4. A more complete record of the Savior's teachings to the Nephites after his resurrection (3 Ne. 26:6–11).

5. "Other books" that would come forth after the Bible (1 Ne. 13:39). Such books would certainly include the Book of Mormon, Doctrine and Covenants, Pearl of Great Price, and Joseph Smith's translation of the Bible.

These additional scriptures will help establish the truthfulness of the Bible, restore plain and precious parts of the gospel lost from the Bible (1 Ne. 13:34–40), and be part of the books out of which mankind will be judged (2 Ne. 29:11; 3 Ne. 27:25–26; 28:33–34).

6. The PLATES OF BRASS (Alma 37:3–5), which include the Christ-centered prophecies of Old World prophets such as Zenos, Zenock, and Neum which are not found in the Bible (1 Ne. 19:10–12; 3 Ne. 10:15–17), as well as prophetic writings of Joseph who was sold into Egypt (2 Ne. 3:4–18). Alma[2] told his son Helaman[2] that "our fathers" prophesied that the plates of brass would "go forth unto every nation, kindred, tongue, and people, that they shall know the mysteries contained thereon" (Alma 37:4; cf. 1 Ne. 5:18). This prophecy is fulfilled, in part, by the going forth of the Book of Mormon to the peoples of the world.

The advent of additional scripture will be based on divine timing (2 Ne. 27:7–11, 21; Ether 3:21–24), and people's faith and repentance (Ether 4:5–7). The Lord invited, "Come unto me, O ye Gentiles, and I will show unto you the greater things, the knowledge which is hid up because of unbelief. Come unto me, O ye house of Israel, and it shall be manifest unto you how great things the Father hath laid up for you, from the foundation of the world" (Ether 4:13–14).

The Lord declared it expedient for his children to receive the Book of Mormon record first to try their faith, and if it "so be that they shall believe these things then shall the greater things be made manifest unto them. And if it so be that they will not believe these things, then shall the greater things be withheld from them, unto their condemnation" (3 Ne. 26:9–11).

See also Last records.

TES

Scriptures, Book of Mormon message concerning The Book of Mormon affirms that God reveals his words to men and that he commands them to write his words, "notwithstanding [their] weakness" (2 Ne. 33:11; cf. Mosiah 26:14–33). It teaches the purposes of scripture, testifies to the truth of ancient and modern scripture, and combats false ideas regarding scripture.

The title page of the Book of Mormon declares that the book was written by divine command and "by the spirit of prophecy and of revelation," to reveal to the remnant of Israel "the covenants of the Lord" and "what great things" God did for their forefathers, and to convince "Jew and Gentile that JESUS is the CHRIST, the ETERNAL GOD, manifesting himself unto all nations" (cf. 2 Ne. 26:12–13; Jacob 7:10–11, 19; Alma 33:14). Book of Mormon prophets identified additional purposes for scripture, both ancient and modern:

1. To teach that all people must believe in Christ and come unto him to be saved (1 Ne. 6:4; 13:40; 19:23; 3 Ne. 27:5–6; Morm. 7:5–7; Ether 12:41).

2. To show people how to come unto Christ (2 Ne. 31:10–21; Enos 1:2–8; Alma 22:15–18; 3 Ne. 9:20; 27:16–20; Morm. 7:8).

3. To "preserve the commandments of the Lord" for future generations (1 Ne. 5:21; 4:13–16; Mosiah 1:3–5).

4. To remind people of the "marvelous works . . . wrought by the power of God" among his people in the past (Morm. 7:9), as well as the "doings of the Lord in other lands" (1 Ne. 19:22).

5. To "show forth [God's] power" (Alma 37:19; cf. Ether 5:4).

6. To serve as a standard against which nations and individuals are judged (2 Ne. 25:18; 29:11; 33:14–15; 3 Ne. 27:23–26; Moro. 8:21).

7. To enlarge a people's memory and convince them of the "error of their ways" (Alma 37:8).

8. To confound "false doctrines," overcome "incorrect tradition," and replace "contentions" with peace (2 Ne. 3:12; Alma 37:9).

9. To test people's willingness to receive divine "counsel," whereby the faithful receive greater knowledge while the proud lose knowledge (2 Ne. 28:28–30; Alma 12:9–11; Morm. 8:12; cf. 3 Ne. 26:8–11).

10. To signal and aid the gathering of Israel (3 Ne. 16:4–5; 21:2–7; Morm. 5:12–15).

Nephi[1] foresaw that in the latter days "other books" with "convincing" power would help "establish the truth" of the Bible (1 Ne. 13:39–40; cf. 2 Ne. 3:11). Mormon said the Book of Mormon was intended to build belief in the Bible (Morm. 7:9). The Book of Mormon and modern scripture quote, explain, and show the fulfillment of biblical prophecy (e.g., 2 Ne. 11:2–3; 25:7–8; Alma 12:21–22; 15:15–24). They also restore "plain and precious things which have been taken away" from the Bible (1 Ne. 13:40). Important examples of the Book of Mormon's restorative roles include the following:

1. Its emphasis on the "great plan of . . . God" (Alma 34:9).

2. Its plain recitation of the "doctrine of Christ" or gospel of Jesus Christ (2 Ne. 31:1–21; 3 Ne. 11:32–39; 27:13–22).

3. Its teaching that the law of Moses "and all things which have been given of God from the beginning of the world, unto man" point to Jesus Christ (2 Ne. 11:4; cf. Mosiah 13:31–33; Alma 34:6–7; Hel. 8:13–22).

Just as the Bible and the Book of Mormon were destined to "grow together" (2 Ne. 3:12), other scriptural records, written by divine command as God "[brought] forth [his] word unto the children of men" in many nations and times, will yet be made available when God's "word . . . shall be gathered in one" (2 Ne. 29:7–8, 11–14).

The Book of Mormon warns against those who "wrest" the scriptures (Alma 13:20), and it combats false ideas regarding the scriptures. It plainly refutes the widespread notion that the Bible contains all revealed truth (2 Ne. 29:3–10) by demonstrating that the writings of some ancient prophets were not included in the Bible (1 Ne. 13:23; cf. 1 Ne. 19:10–21; 2 Ne. 3; Alma 33); teaching that apostates excised many of the Bible's "plain and most precious" things, causing "an exceedingly great many [to] stumble" (1 Ne. 13:24–29); and attesting that revelation continues as long as God's work continues (2 Ne. 29:9).

See also Plain and precious things, loss of and restoration of; Scriptures, use of, by Book of Mormon peoples.

JCT

Scriptures, use of, by Book of Mormon peoples Book of Mormon prophets prized "holy writ" (Alma 37:5, 8). God commanded Lehi[1] to retrieve a "record of the Jews" on PLATES OF BRASS, which contained the books of Moses and "the prophecies of the holy prophets, from the beginning" to the day of Jeremiah[1], along with historical and genealogical writings (1 Ne. 3:1–4; 5:10–16). Lehi and his successors searched and pondered the record (1 Ne. 5:10, 21; 2 Ne. 4:15), and quoted or "read" from it when teaching (1 Ne. 19:23–24; 2 Ne. 3:5–22;

4:1–2; 6:4; Mosiah 1:3–4). When Nephi[1] was commanded to make a set of "small plates" (Jacob 1:1; 1 Ne. 9:2–5; 2 Ne. 5:29–32) to preserve "plain and precious" prophecies and "the more sacred things . . . for the knowledge of [his] people" (1 Ne. 19:3–5), he included several selections from "the scriptures which are engraven upon the plates of brass," most notably some of Isaiah's prophecies (2 Ne. 4:15; 11:2, 8; 12–24).

Lehi, Nephi, and subsequent Book of Mormon prophets also wrote their own prophecies, inspired teachings, and sacred history (1 Ne. 1:16; 19:1–6; 2 Ne. 25:26; Mosiah 1:2–7; 26:14–33; Alma 37:1–2). Although Nephites kept "many books and many records of every kind" (Hel. 3:13–15), a select line of Nephite men safeguarded the "sacred records" (4 Ne. 1:48) to preserve their religious and linguistic heritage (1 Ne. 3:19–20; 5:21; 19:4–6; Jacob 4:1–4; Mosiah 1:1–7; 28:11–12, 20; Alma 37:1–2; 63:1, 13; cf. Omni 1:14–19). Belief in the words of the brass plates and in other records of their forefathers distinguished the Nephites from the Lamanites (Alma 3:11–12; Hel. 3:15–16), as did their commitment to preserving the records (Enos 1:12–14; Morm. 6:6).

In addition to the repository of engraved records, other copies of scripture circulated widely. At least as early as the time of Jacob[2], teachers referred their listeners to specific writings available for their study (Jacob 5:1; Mosiah 12:20–25; 14; Alma 33:2–3; Hel. 5:6–13; 8:11; 3 Ne. 20:11; 27:3–5). After the anti-Christ Sherem confessed his lies and died, former followers "searched the scriptures" (Jacob 7:23), and king Benjamin's prophetic discourse was "written and sent forth" to those beyond earshot at the time he delivered it (Mosiah 2:8). These writings were evidently copied on a different material subject to "perish and vanish away" (Jacob 4:2). Thus, in Ammonihah, both believers and their "records which contained the holy scriptures . . . [were] burned and destroyed by fire" (Alma 14:8).

Some time after 145 B.C., the language of the Nephites was taught "among all the people of the Lamanites" (Mosiah 24:3–6). This eventually enabled missionaries to read scriptures with them, resulting in unprecedented numbers of Lamanite converts (Alma 18:36, 38; 22:12–13; 23:4–6; 37:8–9, 18–19). A generation later, copies of the engraved records "were written and sent forth . . . throughout all the land," perhaps facilitating the widespread conversions that soon followed (Alma 63:12; Hel. 3:24–32). On the other hand, dissenters and some believers misunderstood or misused ("wrested") the scriptures to which they had access (Alma 41:1; 21:11; Jacob 7:6–11; 3 Ne. 1:24–25). Wicked Jaredites also drew upon written records to establish and justify secret combinations, a danger Alma[2] tried to avert among the Nephites (Ether 8:9; Alma 37:27; Hel. 6:25–27).

When Christ visited the people after his resurrection, he told the disciples to record his words (3 Ne. 16:4; 23:4), which included his quotations of Isaiah (3 Ne. 16:17–20; 20:36–45; 22). He told the people to "search . . . diligently" the words of Isaiah and other prophets (3 Ne. 23:1, 5), and he "expounded all the scriptures . . . which they had received" (3 Ne. 23:6). He also revealed "other scriptures" not included in their records (3 Ne. 23:6). He asked Nephi[3] to add to the account of events at the Resurrection (3 Ne. 23:9–13), and he quoted revelations of the prophet Malachi, "expounded them," then told his disciples to write the words for the benefit of "future generations" (3 Ne. 26:1–2; 24–25). Then the Savior "expound[ed] all things, even from the beginning until the time that he should come in his glory" (3 Ne. 26:3). Mormon was forbidden from including much of Christ's teaching in his abridged record (3 Ne. 26:7–11). When Christ later appeared to his disciples, he again commanded them to write down things they had "seen and heard, save it be those which are forbidden" (3 Ne. 27:23).

When the Nephites sank into their final state of apostasy, Ammaron was inspired to "hide up . . . all the sacred records" (4 Ne. 1:48). Mormon retrieved these records and abridged them on metal plates which he had made (Morm. 1:2–4; 2:17–18; 3 Ne. 5:8–18; W of M 1:3–9). Except for a few instances (e.g., Moro. 8, 9), his writings were directed to latter-day readers rather than to his contemporaries (3 Ne. 29–30; Morm.

3:16–22; 5:8–15; 7). Moroni[2], who also wrote for a latter-day audience, then hid the record "unto the Lord," to come "out of the earth . . . by the hand of the Lord" (Morm. 8:14–16, 26).

See also Scriptures, Book of Mormon message concerning.

JCT

Scriptures in one, expounded all the *See* Expounded all the scriptures in one.

Sealed portion of the gold plates The portion of the GOLD PLATES that Joseph Smith was not allowed to translate. While Joseph Smith left an accurate description of the plates as a whole, he did not indicate the size or percentage that composed the sealed portion, only to say that "a part of which was sealed" (Smith, "History," 707; Smith, *Papers,* 1:431). On one occasion David Whitmer, one of the three witnesses, stated that about half the plates were sealed, while on another occasion he said that "one-third . . . appeared to be loose," or in other words, two-thirds were sealed (Cook, 21, 75). In 1856, Orson Pratt stated that "about two-thirds were sealed up" (3:347). Although Pratt was not an eyewitness concerning the plates, he was a contemporary and close associate of Joseph Smith and also the Whitmers and likely learned many things about the plates and the coming forth of the Book of Mormon from them.

The sealed portion of the plates contains "a revelation from God, from the beginning of the world to the ending thereof" (2 Ne. 27:7). This was the marvelous revelation the Lord gave to the brother of Jared[1] wherein he saw "all the inhabitants of the earth which had been, and also all that would be . . . even unto the ends of the earth" (Ether 3:25). The brother of Jared wrote "the things which he had seen," but "they were forbidden to come unto the children of men until after [Christ] should be lifted up upon the cross." Therefore, the record of this sacred vision was not made available to the Nephites until the Savior's appearance and ministry as a resurrected being among them, at which time he instructed that it "should be made manifest" (Ether 4:1–2; 3 Ne. 26:1–6). After nearly two centuries of peace, the people "dwindled in unbelief," and eventually Moroni[2] was commanded to "hide" up the records containing the vision of the brother of Jared "again in the earth" (Ether 4:3). Before doing so, however, he was to transcribe onto other plates the things which the brother of Jared had seen and to "seal them up" with the interpreters (Ether 4:4–5). Moroni instructed the future translator of the plates (Joseph Smith) that he was not to translate the sealed portion "except by and by it shall be wisdom in God" (Ether 5:1).

The sealed portion of the plates will yet be revealed but not "until the own due time of the Lord" (2 Ne. 27:10). The Lord told Moroni that the sealed record would be revealed when the people repented of their iniquity, became clean, and exercised faith in the Lord like unto that of the brother of Jared (Ether 4:6–7). The manner in which these plates were sealed is not made clear in the text of the Book of Mormon or in the accounts of those who were privileged to view the plates.

See also Scriptures, additional, to come forth.

BIBLIOGRAPHY

Cook, Lyndon W., ed. *David Whitmer Interviews: A Restoration Witness.* Orem, Utah: Grandin Book Company, 1991.

Pratt, Orson. *Journal of Discourses.* 26 vols. London: Latter-day Saints' Book Depot, 1854–86.

Smith, Joseph. *Papers of Joseph Smith.* Vol. 1, *Autobiographical and Historical Writings.* Edited by Dean C. Jessee. Salt Lake City: Deseret Book, 1989.

———. "Church History." *Times and Seasons* 3 (1 March 1842).

ALB

Sealing power The power to seal or bind on earth and have such action be valid in eternity. To Nephi[2], the Lord said, "Whatsoever ye shall seal on earth shall be sealed in heaven; and whatsoever ye shall loose on earth shall be loosed in heaven" (Hel. 10:7). The wording is similar to when Jesus promised Peter the "keys of the kingdom" and the accompanying power to "bind" and "loose" (Matt. 16:19; cf. D&C 50:26–29). Elder Bruce R. McConkie taught: "Christ, some twenty or more years before his birth into mortality, conferred these same keys upon Nephi the son of Helaman" (1:383).

There are no references in the Book of Mormon to the use of sealing power to perform marriages, but the description of the Nephites marrying and being blessed "according to the multitude of the promises which the Lord had made" may allude to it (4 Ne. 1:11).

Other references to sealing refer to the aspect of recording a permanent witness. For instance, Nephi[1] declared, "What I seal on earth, shall be brought against you at the judgment bar" (2 Ne. 33:15; cf. D&C 1:8–10; 133:72).

BIBLIOGRAPHY

McConkie, Bruce R. *Doctrinal New Testament Commentary.* 3 vols. Salt Lake City: Bookcraft, 1965–73.

BRM

Seantum Member of a secret combination who murdered his brother Seezoram, chief judge in Zarahemla (Hel. 8:27–28; ca. 23 B.C.). After Nephi[2] proclaimed the death of Seezoram and corrupt Nephite judges accused him of conspiring in the crime (Hel. 9:16), Nephi instructed his accusers to go to the house of Seantum and inquire concerning the murder. He prophesied that Seantum would first proclaim his innocence but eventually confess the crime after those sent to investigate would find blood on his cloak and fear in his countenance (Hel. 9:25–37).

Sebus, waters of Area in the land of Ishmael where Lamanites watered their flocks (Alma 17:26). King Lamoni had previously executed shepherds who lost his flocks to Lamanite marauders at Sebus (Alma 17:28; ca. 90 B.C.). When troublemakers again scattered Lamoni's flocks, Ammon[2], a son of the Nephite king Mosiah[2] and servant to Lamoni, encouraged his fellow shepherds to retrieve the flocks to avoid the king's punishment. The animals were returned to "the place of water," but the marauders also returned to again scatter the flocks. Ammon routed them single-handedly (Alma 17:27–39; 19:21).

Second coming *See* Jesus Christ, second coming of.

Second death *See* Spiritual death.

Second time Refers to the second gathering and restoration of Israel in the last days. The first occurred when the Lord brought Israel out of Egypt, re-established his covenant with them, and led them into the promised land. Many years later the Israelites were taken by Assyrians, and later Babylonians, from their homelands and scattered among the nations. Nephi, referring to a prophecy of Isaiah, taught that "the Lord will set his hand again the second time to restore his people from their lost and fallen state" (2 Ne. 25:17; cf. 2 Ne. 21:11). To make this possible, "he shall set up an ensign for the nations, and shall assemble the outcasts of Israel, and gather together the dispersed of Judah from the four corners of the earth" (2 Ne. 21:12 // Isa. 11:12; 6:14; 25:17; 29:1; Jacob 6:2; D&C 137:6). This ENSIGN that all people would gather to is the restored gospel of Jesus Christ.

As with the first, the second gathering would be two-fold in nature—back to the Lord and back to their lands of inheritance. The Book of Mormon—"his words" (2 Ne. 25:18)—would be the means he would use to "restore his people" (2 Ne. 25:17). It would "hiss forth unto the ends of the earth, for a standard unto . . . the house of Israel" (2 Ne. 29:2). It would accomplish a "marvelous work" in restoring the Jews "from their lost and fallen state" by "convincing them of the true Messiah" (2 Ne. 25:17–18; cf. 26–27), helping persuade them "to believe in Christ, the Son of God, and the atonement" (2 Ne. 25:16; cf. Morm. 5:12–14). And its appearance would herald the arrival of this *second time* when the Lord would "gather in, from their long dispersion [his] people" and "establish again" Zion among them (3 Ne. 21:1–7). Moreover, Mormon taught that when the Book of Mormon "shall come unto the Gentiles . . . then ye may know that the covenant which the Father hath made with the children of Israel, concerning their restoration to the lands of their inheritance, is already beginning to be fulfilled" (3 Ne. 29:1).

Moses, who held the keys of the first gathering, bestowed on Joseph Smith "the keys of the [second] gathering of Israel from the four parts of the earth" (D&C 110:11).

See also Book of Mormon, selected purposes of, to be a sign of the Father's work; Israel, gathering of.

KHM

Second trump As used in the Book of Mormon, the second trump has reference to those who on the Day of Judgment will be found on the left hand of the Lord (Mosiah 26:25–28; 5:10). The sounding of a trumpet represents a summons to an event of great importance. Michael the archangel will sound the trumpet that will call forth all who are in the grave to the judgment of God. The righteous will stand on the right hand of God, the wicked on his left (D&C 29:26–27). Modern revelation makes it clear that the second trump will call forth those who will inherit the terrestrial kingdom, the third trump those who are telestial, and the fourth those who are sons of perdition (D&C 88:99–102).

See also I never knew them; Judgment, the.

JFM

Secret combinations Oath-bound conspiracies of a quasireligious character. The earliest mention of secret combinations, chronologically, occurs in the book of Ether, in the account of a prince, Jared[2], who sought to murder his father and seize the throne. His daughter, reminding him of the secret conspiracies and plots mentioned in the records their ancestors had brought with them from the Old World, suggested that he use the same techniques (Ether 8:9–10). Thus was born a conspiracy that successfully placed Jared in the kingship. Strikingly, its oath of secrecy and mutual protection, transmitted from Cain, was not secular—participants swore "by the God of heaven, and also by the heavens, and also by the earth, and by their heads" (Ether 8:14–15, 18; cf. Moses 5:29–31, 49–55).

Subsequent Jaredite leaders frequently resorted to the ancient principles of secret conspiratorial oaths and covenants, leading to rebellions, wars, thefts, murders, social and economic breakdown, and the rejection and killing of the Lord's prophets (e.g., Ether 9:26, 29; 10:3, 33; 11:7, 15, 22; 13:15, 18, 25–26; 14:8–10; Alma 37:30). Indeed, secret combinations were the primary factor leading to the extinction of the Jaredites (Alma 37:22, 25–27, 29–31; Ether 8:21).

The prophet Alma[2] encouraged his son Helaman[2] to warn the Nephites about the sins, evils, and sufferings that attended secret combinations among their Jaredite predecessors, and to emphasize their destructiveness. But he urged him to withhold any specific data about their oaths, covenants, and plans, evidently fearing their seductive power (Alma 37:21–27, 29–32; cf. Ether 8:17). Helaman obeyed (Alma 63:12). Moroni[2], the abridger of the Jaredite record, also declined to detail precisely "the manner of their oaths and combinations," but for a different reason: "For," he wrote, "it hath been made known unto me that they are had among all people, and they are had among the Lamanites" (Ether 8:20).

Nephite secret combinations arose in their classic form about 50 B.C., once again involving a political crisis within the ruling family and an assassination. When a later attempt failed, the conspirators were obliged to flee (Hel. 1:1–12; 2:1–11). They reemerged periodically, however, to carry out other assassinations and revolutionary acts (Hel. 3:23; 6:15). By this time, the Nephite secret combination had begun to be known—at least, among those who disliked them—as "Gadianton's robbers and murderers" (Hel. 6:18–19).

Mormon explained that secret combinations took root among both Lamanites and Nephites at this period because, amidst peace and prosperity, they began to be consumed by greed and ambition, and saw such conspiracies as an effective means to wealth (Hel. 6:17; cf. 7:21, 25). He ascribed their popularity to Satan (Hel. 6:20–21).

By the latter part of the first century B.C., most Nephites had embraced the Gadianton program and the government itself came under Gadianton control (Hel. 6:38–41; 10:3). Although they were gradually induced to repent and to eliminate the Gadianton movement from among them (Hel. 11:1–10), within only a few years a group of Nephite dissenters resurrected it and launched a destructive series of guerrilla wars from their mountain bases (Hel. 11:25–33; 3 Ne. 1:27–29; 2:11–13, 17–19). After great difficulty, they were defeated (3 Ne. 3:11, 13–14, 20–21; 4:1–7, 12–14, 16–28; 5:4–6; 6:3). Less than a decade later, though, ambitious lawyers and judges resuscitated the principles of the Gadiantons anew, hoping thereby both to silence the prophets and to establish a monarchy. But they only managed to plunge the Nephite nation into bloody and destructive tribal anarchy (3 Ne. 6:20–30; 7:1–3, 6–7, 9–13). Gadiantonism again played a major role in the final collapse of the Nephite civilization (4 Ne. 1:42, 46; Hel. 2:13–14; cf. Ether 8:21).

The fundamentals of Gadiantonism involved unspecified covenants and oaths of mutual protection, as well as secret signs and passwords to facilitate acts of criminal conspiracy. The strict secrecy of the movement was ensured by the Gadiantons' willingness to punish anybody guilty of breaching it (Hel. 6:21–24).

But this picture is probably, and not surprisingly, an oversimplification. The Nephite prophets themselves expressly told readers that they withheld important data about secret combinations. It seems apparent that Gadiantonism was an ideological movement, and not, or not merely, a criminal conspiracy. The letter sent to the Nephite governor Lachoneus[1] by Giddianhi, the leader of the Gadianton organization at the time, is highly instructive in this context. Politically, it refers to alleged "wrongs" inflicted upon the Gadiantons by the Nephite state, and asserts their right to rule, although it acknowledges the Nephites' perspective (3 Ne. 3:2–11). Furthermore, Giddianhi testified to the goodness and venerability of "the secret society of Gadianton" (3 Ne. 3:9), having already, by implication, indicated his skepticism about traditional Nephite religion (3 Ne. 3:2). Finally, the epistle invites the Nephites to "yield yourselves up unto us, and unite with us and become acquainted with our secret works, and become our brethren that ye may be like unto us—not our slaves, but our brethren and partners of all our substance" (3 Ne. 3:7)—an invitation that, because thieves need victims, makes sense only if the Gadiantons were more than simple criminals.

What one sees in the Gadianton movement and, by extension, in the secret combinations among the Jaredites with their theologically laden oaths, is an evil distortion, a mirror image, of true religion and its sacred covenants. For example, when at one point they were under military pressure, the last remnants of the Gadianton organization sealed their records up in the earth in a striking parallel to the story of the Book of Mormon itself, presumably to come forth at some later, more favorable time (Hel. 11:10).

And there was, unquestionably, something spiritual, though certainly not divine, about the secret combinations depicted in the Book of Mormon. The prophet Mormon stressed that the Gadianton robbers did not obtain their oaths and practices from the record of the Jaredites, but by direct inspiration from Satan (Hel. 6:25–30; cf. 8:28; Moses 5:29–31, 49–55), the ultimate author of secret combinations (2 Ne. 9:9; 26:22; 3 Ne. 6:28; Ether 8:16, 25). The Lord has expressly condemned such evils (2 Ne. 10:15; 26:23; cf. 3 Ne. 9:9; Ether 8:18–19, 22–23), and Moroni and his prophet-colleagues, aware that secret combinations would exist in the latter days, "even as in times of old," warned strictly against them (2 Ne. 26:22; Morm. 8:27, 40; Ether 8:22–25). Indeed, the Book of Mormon says that the New World ought to be particularly free of them (Alma 37:31; cf. 37:27–28). "Wherefore, O ye Gentiles," wrote Moroni, "it is wisdom in God that these things should be shown unto you, that thereby ye may repent of your sins, and suffer not that these murderous combinations shall get above you, which are built up to get power and gain—and the work, yea, even the work of destruction come upon you, yea, even the sword of the justice of the Eternal God shall fall upon you, to your overthrow and destruction if ye shall suffer these things to be" (Ether 8:23).

See also Gadianton robbers.

DCP

Secreted *See* Appendix C.

Seed Term used in the Book of Mormon with at least four meanings, as follows:

1. Posterity or descendants. Prophets frequently spoke of future events concerning their lineal descendants in terms such as "the seed of

my brethren did contend against my seed" (1 Ne. 12:19). In this sense, seed is equated with "the fruit of the loins" (2 Ne. 3:12).

2. The righteous, symbolically called the SEED OF CHRIST (Mosiah 15:10–13).

3. That from which plants may be produced. For instance, the family of Lehi and the Jaredites carried seeds with them to the promised land (1 Ne. 18:24; Ether 2:3).

4. The word of God (Alma 32:28); belief in the Son of God; the gospel (Alma 33:22–23).

BRM

Seed of Christ All the faithful Saints of every gospel dispensation. In his last powerful discourse, as he stood before king Noah[3] and his wicked priests, Abinadi invoked the testimony of the prophet Isaiah to teach about the nature and ministry of the Messiah, and to identify the seed of Christ (Mosiah 14–15; cf. Isa. 53). Abinadi provided inspired commentary on the symbols, allusions, and images used by Isaiah centuries earlier, explaining that the seed of Christ are "all the holy prophets ever since the world began," as well as "all those who have hearkened unto their words, and believed that the Lord would redeem his people, and have looked forward to that day for a remission of their sins," thus becoming "heirs of the kingdom of God" (Mosiah 15:10–18).

The seed of Christ look to the Redeemer as the father of their salvation. They become his "children" by being "born of him," born into a new realm or kingdom, the kingdom of God, by commitment to Christ's atonement through the covenant and ordinance of baptism. This rebirth involves the same elements which made birth into this mortal realm possible. Thus, Adam was instructed to teach his children that "inasmuch as ye were born into the world by water, and blood, and the spirit . . . even so ye must be born again into the kingdom of heaven, of water, and of the Spirit, and be cleansed by blood, even the blood of mine Only Begotten" (Moses 6:59; cf. Mosiah 5:7; 27:24–26). Because there is "no other name given whereby salvation cometh," all who are to enjoy eternal life must take upon them the name of Christ, and become his seed (Mosiah 5:8–11).

See also Born again; Children of Christ; Isaiah chapter reviews (Mosiah 14 // Isa. 53); Seed.

ACS

Seer "A seer is a revelator and a prophet also; and a gift which is greater can no man have, except he should possess the power of God" (Mosiah 8:16; cf. Moses 6:35–36). Thus a seer is the most inspired of men, having visual revelations of things past, present, and future pertaining to both heaven and earth. These visions are not mere dreams; they may be experienced while in a waking state. Lehi[1], Nephi[1], and the brother of Jared[1] are notable seers in the Book of Mormon.

Lehi "was carried away in a vision" and beheld God and angels, including Christ and "twelve others" (1 Ne. 1:8–10; cf. Alma 36:22). Nephi was also "caught away in the Spirit of the Lord" (1 Ne. 11:1) and beheld a series of remarkable visions of the future pertaining to Israel and the Gentiles spanning some two thousand years (1 Ne. 11–14). In doing so, he wrote of another seer, John the Revelator (1 Ne. 14:18–25). The brother of Jared's seeric revelations, first revealed to the Nephites following Christ's resurrection, and not translated by Joseph Smith, are yet to come forth (Ether 3:21; 4:1–7).

The translation of ancient records is another aspect of seership (Mosiah 8:13). In that connection ancient Joseph[1] foretold the scriptural labors of Joseph Smith (2 Ne. 3:6–9, 11–15). Mosiah[2] had "two stones" which were "handed down from generation to generation, for the purpose of interpreting languages" (Mosiah 28:13–15). One possessing them "is called seer" (Mosiah 28:16). They also constituted the URIM AND THUMMIM Joseph Smith used to translate the Book of Mormon, a product of the greatest manifestation of the power of God granted unto men (D&C 17:1).

See also Choice seer; Prophets, role of; Revelator; Seer stone.

RT

Seer, choice *See* Choice seer.

Seer stone Statements by a number of Joseph Smith's associates indicate that the Prophet had in his possession a stone, later referred to as a seer stone. That it was called a seer stone denotes that it was a medium that could be used to help in receiving revelation. According to Willard Chase, a resident of the Palmyra area, Joseph Smith found the stone in 1822 while digging a well on the Chase property (Howe, 241–42; Tiffany, 163).

Some contemporaries of Joseph Smith claimed that he used the seer stone to translate portions of the Book of Mormon (Cook, 3, 12, 53–54, 55–56, 72, 156, 157, 200, 230; Bidamon, letter). Such claims have received varied responses (Roberts, 1:129–30; Smith, *Doctrines,* 3:225–26). Neither Joseph Smith nor his principal scribe, Oliver Cowdery, mentioned a "seer stone" in their translation work, but they did repeatedly indicate the use of the Urim and Thummim. Joseph Smith declared that he translated the Book of Mormon "through the medium of the Urim and Thummim . . . by the gift and power of God" (Smith, *Church,* 4:537). Oliver Cowdery wrote, "Day after day I continued, uninterrupted, to write from his mouth, as he translated, with the *Urim* and *Thummim,* or, as the Nephites whould [*sic*] have said, 'Interpreters,' the history, or record, called 'The book of Mormon'" (*Messenger and Advocate,* 14). When asked to explain the details of the translation process, the Prophet Joseph Smith told the Saints at a conference in Ohio in 1831, "that it was not intended to tell the world all the particulars of the coming forth of the book of Mormon, & also said that it was not expedient for him to relate these things" (Cannon and Cook, 23).

Joseph Smith gave the seer stone to Oliver Cowdery (Whitmer, 32). David Whitmer stated that following Oliver's death in 1848, Phineas Young, brother to Brigham Young, visited Cowdery's widow in Missouri and from her received the seer stone. He returned to Salt Lake City and presented the stone to President Young (Cook, 200). The stone has remained in the possession of the Church since that time. On 18 May 1888, following a private dedication of the Manti Temple, President Wilford Woodruff wrote that he "Consecrated upon the Altar the seers [*sic*] Stone that Joseph Smith found by Revelation some 30 feet under the Earth" (Woodruff, 8:500). Former Assistant Church Historian Andrew Jenson described the stone as an "ovalshaped, chocolate colored stone, about the size of an egg but more flat" (Jenson, 3:623; cf. Van Wagoner and Walker, 59).

See also The Coming Forth of the Book of Mormon, 9; Book of Mormon, translation of; Seer.

BIBLIOGRAPHY

Bidamon, Emma H. Smith, to Mrs. Pilgrim, 27 March 1876, manuscript, Community of Christ Archives, Independence, Missouri.

Cannon, Donald Q., and Lyndon W. Cook, eds. *Far West Record: Minutes of The Church of Jesus Christ of Latter-day Saints, 1830–1844.* Salt Lake City: Deseret Book, 1983.

Cook, Lyndon W. ed., *David Whitmer Interviews: A Restoration Witness.* Orem, Utah: Grandin Book, 1991.

Howe, E. D. *Mormonism Unvailed.* Painesville, Ohio: Eber D. Howe, 1834.

Jenson, Andrew. *Historical Record.* 5 vols. Salt Lake City: Andrew Jenson, 1888.

Messenger and Advocate, 1 (October 1834).

Roberts, B. H. *A Comprehensive History of The Church of Jesus Christ of Latter-day Saints, Century One.* 6 vols. Provo, Utah: Corporation of the President, The Church of Jesus Christ of Latter-day Saints, 1965.

Smith, Joseph. *History of The Church of Jesus Christ of Latter-day Saints.* Edited by B. H. Roberts. 7 vols. 2d ed. rev. Salt Lake City: The Church of Jesus Christ of Latter-day Saints, 1932–51.

Smith, Joseph Fielding. *Doctrines of Salvation.* Compiled by Bruce R. McConkie. 3 vols. Salt Lake City: Bookcraft, 1954–56.

Tiffany, Joel. "Mormonism—II." *Tiffany's Monthly* 5 (May 1859).

Van Wagoner, Richard, and Steven C. Walker. "Joseph Smith: 'The Gift of Seeing.'" *Dialogue* 15 (Summer 1982).

Whitmer, David. *An Address to All Believers in Christ.* Richmond, Mo.: N.p., 1887.

Woodruff, Wilford. *Wilford Woodruff's Journal, 1833–1898.* Edited by Scott G. Kenney. 9 vols. Midvale, Utah: Signature Books, 1983–84.

ALB

Seezoram A chief judge of the Nephites and a member of the Gadianton band (Hel. 8:28; ca. 26 B.C.). Nothing is known of Seezoram's activities during his judgeship, but he was esteemed as "great" by the people (Hel. 9:10). Nephi[2] prophesied Seezoram's murder by his brother Seantum as a sign to the rebellious Nephites (Hel. 8:27; ca. 23–20 B.C.). When Nephi was himself accused of confederacy in the deed, he again demonstrated his prophetic gifts by revealing specifics as to how his accusers could determine Seantum's guilt (Hel. 9:23–36).

Selfsame *See* Appendix C.

Senine *See* Nephite weights and measures.

Sensual *See* Carnal, sensual, and devilish.

Senum *See* Nephite weights and measures.

Seon *See* Nephite weights and measures.

Sermon at Bountiful and Sermon on the Mount During the first day of the resurrected Lord's visit to the Nephites at the temple in Bountiful[2], he taught a sermon (3 Ne. 12–14; these chapters are part of a larger sermon reported in 3 Ne. 11–18) that parallels the biblical sermon known as the sermon on the mount (Matt. 5–7). Jesus may have taught variations of this sermon more than once in the Holy Land before the Nephites heard it (3 Ne. 15:1; Matt. 5–7; Luke 6). The central message of the sermon identifies what is essential to be a true disciple of Christ in any society or age. Worthy of comparison are the few yet meaningful differences between the sermon at Bountiful and the sermon on the mount. Most variations and modifications in the two sermons can be understood by recognizing differences in audience, culture, and time.

1. Audience. The biblical sermon addressed a small number of disciples, primarily the Twelve Apostles, who had separated themselves from the multitudes to come "up" to Jesus (Matt. 5:1). Furthermore, Jesus "was set down" when he gave the sermon, suggesting a smaller, more intimate setting (JST Matt. 5:1). Consequently, one important purpose of the sermon on the mount appears to be missionary-oriented, to prepare the Twelve to be sent forth to preach the gospel to the house of Israel. The Joseph Smith Translation (JST) further establishes this missionary-preparation theme in the biblical sermon with instructions to the disciples when going "house to house," a caution to keep "the mysteries of the kingdom . . . within yourselves," and an appropriate response when self-righteous Pharisees opposed them (JST Matt. 6:25–27; 7:10–11; 14–17).

The sermon to the Nephites, on the other hand, was given to a multitude of the righteous, including the Twelve disciples chosen by the Lord, because the more wicked descendants of Lehi[1] were killed in the destruction that preceded Christ's arrival in America. That multitude consisted of at least 2,500 persons (3 Ne. 17:25). Only a portion of the Nephite sermon addressed the Twelve specifically, reassuring them that the Lord would care for their daily needs (3 Ne. 13:25–34). In brief, the biblical sermon presupposes a minority of righteous individuals living in a predominantly wicked world while the Nephite audience represented a "more righteous" population prepared to receive his teachings as a covenant people.

Therefore, when Jesus taught the cluster of missionaries in Galilee about doing alms, he said, "Do not sound a trumpet before thee, *as the hypocrites do* in the synagogues and in the streets" (Matt. 6:2; italics added), but to the Nephite Saints he said, "*as will hypocrites do* in the synagogues" (3 Ne. 13:2; italics added). Religious hypocrisy was a current condition in Galilee and Jerusalem; it was temporarily eliminated from the Nephite nation with the destruction of the most wicked but would reemerge nearly two-hundred years later to contribute to their eventual downfall.

Similarly, when Jesus instructed his disciples on the mount concerning prayer, the prayer included a petition to the Father to "give us this day our daily bread" (Matt. 6:11). This phrase was omitted when teaching the Nephites. While most annotated translations of this phrase suggest it is a plea for "tomorrow's" bread today, there is confusion among scholars as to whether the plea has reference to receiving continual physical sustenance or, eschatologically speaking,

SERMON AT BOUNTIFUL

the heavenly blessings of the future. If the prayer has reference to physical sustenance, the omission in the Book of Mormon may be explained by different audiences. Because the Twelve in Galilee were soon to depart on missions and discontinue their normal livelihoods, they needed the Lord to supply them with daily physical nourishment. Conversely, the Nephite multitude was not called, as were the Twelve, to full-time missionary service, but they were expected to live the gospel while earning a temporal living to satisfy daily physical needs (Matthews, 116).

Difference in audience would also explain why Jesus told the New Testament disciples that they were the "light of the world" (Matt. 5:14) while telling the Nephites they were to be "the light of this people" (3 Ne. 12:14). The biblical sermon prepared the Twelve to be "sent forth," to take his gospel first to the house of Israel, and after Christ's resurrection, to "the uttermost part of the earth" (Acts 1:8). The Nephite audience was to spread their witness to their own people who had been spared during the destruction.

2. Culture. Lehi[1] and his family departed from Jerusalem 600 years before Jesus was born in Bethlehem. Although some elements of Old Testament Jewish culture were evidenced in Nephite culture, later cultural developments in Jerusalem were naturally absent in ancient America. In other words, the cultural milieu in New Testament times was significantly different from Nephite society at the time of Christ's ministry. These differences are apparent when comparing the two sermons. For example, there is no mention of Pharisees, scribes, or publicans in the Book of Mormon sermon, as is found in the sermon on the mount (Matt. 5:20, 46–47; 7:28–29). This should be expected because such designations within Jewish society likely began after the Babylonian captivity, decades *after* Lehi left that society. The Nephites knew the term *Gentiles* from their world before they left Jerusalem and from the words of the prophets; however, it was not used to describe any faction of the Nephite population, because all were identified as a "remnant of the house of Israel" (2 Ne. 28:2). This may explain why the Savior did not refer to Gentiles in his sermon among the Nephites but did use the term in speaking to his disciples in Galilee (Matt. 6:32). Likewise, reference to swearing by Jerusalem is not included in the Savior's sermon to the Nephites as is found in the biblical sermon, likely because the holy city of Jerusalem was only a historical memory for the Nephites, but it was the center of society for those hearing the biblical sermon (Matt. 5:35; 3 Ne. 12:35).

The Lord directed the Nephites to pay the "uttermost senine" (3 Ne. 12:26; cf. Alma 11:3); however, the disciples on the mount were told to pay "the uttermost farthing" (Matt. 5:26), reflecting two different monetary systems. A more elaborate legal process, including a judge and an officer, is described in the biblical account to sentence an offender to prison than is depicted in the Nephite sermon, suggesting a simpler judicial system among the Nephites (Matt. 5:25; 3 Ne. 12:25). Again, the Lord reminded the Nephites and the New Testament disciples that it is "your Father who is in heaven [who] maketh his sun to rise on the evil and on the good" (3 Ne. 12:45; Matt. 5:45), but only in the biblical sermon did he add "and sendeth rain on the just and on the unjust" (Matt. 5:45). Perhaps this had reference to the Jews' concern for rainfall in the deserts of the Holy Land in contrast to the land of the Nephites where rain may have been plentiful.

3. Time. Jesus taught the Sermon on the Mount *before* his atonement and the fulfillment of the LAW OF MOSES; the sermon at Bountiful was delivered *after* his atonement when the law of Moses had been fulfilled. Therefore, in the Matthew account, he taught that the law of Moses would be fulfilled in him but that time was not yet come, adding strict charges to observe the law of Moses until that time came (Matt. 5:18–19); however, the Savior told the Nephites that the law of Moses had already been fulfilled in him (3 Ne. 12:18, 46–47). In addition, he reminded the Nephites of "the law and the commandments of my Father" given them "at this time" (3 Ne. 12:19–20), referring to new commandments that make up the gospel of Christ, or higher law, taught earlier that same day to preempt the law of Moses (3 Ne. 11:31–40). It was to the Nephites, not to his New Testament disciples, that he specified

Other Sheep: The Savior's Visit to the People in America; *painting by Glen S. Hopkinson; courtesy Glen S. Hopkinson.*

The Sermon on the Mount; *painting by Carl Heinrich Bloch; courtesy DNMF.*

SERMON AT BOUNTIFUL

coming to him "with a broken heart and a contrite spirit" (3 Ne. 12:19), and "with full purpose of heart" (3 Ne. 12:24), reinforcing the focus for sacrifice required of his disciples *after* the Mosaic law was fulfilled. Similarly, bringing a gift to the altar is only mentioned in the biblical account (Matt. 5:23–24) because such sacrifices were no longer required after the law of Moses was fulfilled.

In the biblical sermon, Jesus explained that "the kingdom of heaven has come nigh unto you" (JST Matt. 7:9) and consequently taught his disciples in Galilee to pray that "thy kingdom come" (Matt. 6:10). That phrase was omitted when instructing the Nephites (3 Ne. 13:9–10), perhaps because Christ, their King, had come and they submitted themselves to him as a willing and obedient people.

Finally, before his resurrection, Jesus commanded his disciples on the mount to be perfect, "even as your Father which is in heaven is perfect" (Matt. 5:48). After his resurrection, he taught the Nephites to be perfect "even as I, or your Father who is in heaven is perfect" (3 Ne. 12:48), evidencing that the full measure of perfection comes through resurrection even for the morally perfect Jesus who never committed sin (2 Cor. 5:21; 1 Pet. 2:22).

In addition to considering audience, culture, and time, differences between the two sermons may be explained by modern revelation. There are instances in which the JST and the Nephite sermons are alike, but the King James Version (KJV) is different. Such agreement is not surprising when it is recognized that the JST is a restoration of the sermon, whether it be a restoration of the text, or a restoration of interpretation and meaning. Specific cases include the following:

It is immediately obvious that the Nephite sermon began with beatitudes not mentioned in the KJV that deal with the first principles and ordinances of the gospel, the need for the multitude to heed the words of the Twelve chosen to minister among them, and the need for others to heed the words of the multitude (3 Ne. 12:1–2). The JST adds two verses at the beginning of the biblical sermon which confirm the first principles and ordinances of the gospel and recognize the blessings of those who heed the words of the Twelve Apostles to whom Christ spoke: "Blessed are they who shall believe on me; and again, more blessed are they who shall believe on your words, when ye shall testify that ye have seen me and that I am. Yea, blessed are they who shall believe on your words, and come down into the depth of humility, and be baptized in my name; for they shall be visited with fire and the Holy Ghost, and shall receive a remission of their sins" (JST Matt. 5:3–4). Similarly, additions to the eight commonly known beatitudes found in the Nephite sermon are also included in the JST account of the Sermon on the Mount (in each case italics are added to indicate text not found in the KJV but found in both the JST and the Book of Mormon). Both accounts read: "Blessed are the poor in spirit *who come unto me*" (3 Ne. 12:3; JST Matt. 5:5), and "blessed are *all* they who do hunger and thirst after righteousness, for they shall be filled *with the Holy Ghost*" (3 Ne. 12:6; JST Matt. 5:8). Furthermore, like in the Book of Mormon sermon, "in the JST the word *and* occurs at the beginning of each of the beatitudes, giving the impression they are in a series rather than simply a collection of separate unrelated statements" (Matthews, 117). Finally, both the Nephite account and the JST account include "*all* they who do hunger and thirst after righteousness," "*all* the pure in heart," "*all* the peacemakers," and "*all* they who are persecuted for *my name's sake*" (3 Ne. 12: 6, 8, 9, 10; JST Matt. 5:8, 10, 11, 12). Both versions end the account of the beatitudes the same way: "*For ye shall have great joy* and be exceedingly glad, for great *shall be* your reward in heaven" (3 Ne. 12:12; JST Matt. 5:14).

Additional similarities between the JST account of the biblical sermon and the Nephite sermon are found in verses that follow the beatitudes: "*Verily, verily, I say unto you, I give unto you to be* the salt of the earth; but if the salt *shall lose its savor* wherewith shall the earth be salted? *The salt shall be* thenceforth good for nothing" (3 Ne. 12:13; JST Matt. 5:15); "and whosoever shall kill shall be in danger of the judgment *of God*" (3 Ne. 12:21; JST Matt. 5:23); "therefore, *if ye shall come unto me, or shall desire to come unto me*" (3 Ne. 12:23; JST Matt. 5:25).

In the context of Christ's teaching to neither commit adultery nor look "on a woman, to lust after her" (3 Ne. 12:28), two entire verses are found in both the JST and the Book of Mormon but not in the KJV: "Behold, I give unto you a commandment, that ye suffer none of these things to enter into your heart; For it is better that ye should deny yourselves of these things, wherein ye will take up your cross, than that ye should be cast into hell" (3 Ne. 12:29–30; JST Matt. 5:31). The KJV records Jesus' words to be "O ye of little faith" (Matt. 6:30) while both the JST and the Book of Mormon record him to say, "if ye are not of little faith" (3 Ne. 13:30; JST Matt. 6:34).

Another insight from the JST, which parallels the Book of Mormon account, is the identification of the audience for whom Christ taught the final portion of his sermon (3 Ne. 14; Matt. 7). In both sermons, Christ made a point that his concluding message was intended for a general audience of believers. In the Book of Mormon account, Jesus turned from the Twelve and again addressed the multitude (3 Ne. 14:1). In the JST account, Jesus instructed his missionary-disciples concerning what they should "say unto the people" (JST Matt. 7:1).

Finally, Jesus referred to the law as it had been *heard* in times of old all six times in the KJV of the biblical sermon (Matt. 5:21, 27, 33, 38, 43), but in his sermon at Bountiful, he used "written" to describe the law's form five of those times (3 Ne. 12:27, 31, 33, 38, 43). In the JST, "heard" is used three times (JST Matt. 5:23, 40, 45) and "written" three times (JST Matt. 5:29, 35, 37). While this example indicates additional cases where the Nephite sermon and the JST version of the biblical sermon agree, more importantly, it underscores the fact that Joseph Smith did not simply copy the Book of Mormon writings in preparing the JST.

A meaningful observation is found in Jesus' teachings concerning those who are angry with their brother. The earliest Greek manuscripts of Matthew 5 do not contain the words "without a cause" (Matt. 5:22), exactly as the Nephite and JST sermons read (3 Ne. 12:22; JST Matt. 5:24). Removing all justification for anger coincides with other unequivocal statements the Savior made in the sermon, such as committing adultery in one's heart and loving one's enemy (Welch, 161–63).

When thoughtfully considered, differences and similarities between the Savior's teachings to the Nephites at the temple in Bountiful and his sermon on the mount, as recorded in Matthew, reveal teachings that are culturally appropriate and personally applicable to each audience. A careful comparison validates not only the universal power of Christ's teachings to all nations in all eras, but also his care and concern for each individual. In the eyes of the Savior, there were no nameless faces in the Nephite multitude at Bountiful, or among the small corps of missionaries on the mount.

See also Joseph Smith Translation and the Book of Mormon.

BIBLIOGRAPHY

Matthews, Robert J. *Behold the Messiah: New Testament Insights from Latter-day Revelation.* Salt Lake City: Bookcraft, 1994.

Welch, John W. *The Sermon at the Temple and the Sermon on the Mount.* Salt Lake City: Deseret Book, 1990.

CF

Serpent, brazen *See* Brazen serpent.

Serpents, fiery flying *See* Fiery flying serpents.

Service As used in the Book of Mormon, "service" is broadly associated with active devotion both to God (2 Ne. 2:3) and to one's fellow beings. It can also refer to employment, as in the case of Ammon[2]'s faithful service to king Lamoni (Alma 17:25–26; 18:8–10), which led to the conversion of many. Most often, the term is used positively, with reference to righteous duty, obedience, and usefulness. But the Book of Mormon also makes it clear that an unrighteous person serves Satan, and that a follower of Christ "cannot be a servant of the devil" (Moro. 7:11); the two are mutually exclusive (3 Ne. 13:24 // Matt. 6:24). As Mormon testified, whatever persuades mortals to "serve not God . . . is of the devil" (Moro. 7:16–17). Conversely, the Spirit of Christ invites one "to do good continually" and to serve God (Moro. 7:13).

King Benjamin spoke of his people's need to serve each other. Preliminary to making his main point, Benjamin modestly alluded to himself as an example of such service (Mosiah 2:10–16). He then emphasized that "when ye are in the service of your fellow beings ye are only in the service of your God" (Mosiah 2:17). Even so, Benjamin reminded his listeners of their great debt: "If ye should serve him with all your whole souls yet ye would be unprofitable servants" (Mosiah 2:21).

One of the important blessings of serving God promised in the Book of Mormon is liberty (2 Ne. 1:7; Mosiah 7:33). But the Lord also said concerning the promised land that failure to serve him can bring about destruction when a society becomes "ripened in iniquity" (Ether 2:8–12). Moreover, Ammon[2] extolled the great JOY of missionary service (Alma 26).

RNH

Seth *See* Jared[1], posterity of.

Sexual immorality *See* Chastity.

Shadow This term is used in the Book of Mormon in at least three ways.

1. An image of some future event. A shadow may use elements of a particular event, person, ordinance, or ritual to reflect an image of a specific future reality. For example, Abinadi admonished the priests of king Noah[3] to teach the law of Moses as a shadow of those things which were to come (Mosiah 16:14). In other words, the elements of the law of Moses were designed to point to the future reality of the great and last sacrifice of Christ (Alma 34:14). In the scriptures, shadow, type, SIMILITUDE, likeness, and figure may be used interchangeably.

2. God's absolute consistency. Mormon explained that with God "there is no variableness neither shadow of changing" (Morm. 9:9). Therefore, the ways of God are consistent and are in pure light and cast no shadows by moving off course.

3. A form of protection: "In the shadow of his hand hath he hid me" (1 Ne. 21:2).

See also Types.

RJN

Shakespeare and the Book of Mormon In his address to his sons, the aging Lehi[1] called upon them to "awake! and arise from the dust, and hear the words of a trembling parent, whose limbs ye must soon lay down in the cold and silent grave, from whence no traveler can return" (2 Ne. 1:14). From the time of Alexander Campbell to the present, critics of the Book of Mormon have pointed out the similarity in the language and imagery between Lehi's statement and the lines in Shakespeare's *Hamlet:* "But that the dread of something after death, / The undiscover'd country, from whose bourn / no traveller returns" (III.i.78–80). While there is some similarity of phrasing between 2 Nephi and the passage from Shakespeare, there are Near Eastern sources, including the Old Testament, that articulate the same idea with the same imagery and may have provided the background for this tradition. In fact there are a number of passages in Job that Lehi and Shakespeare seem to echo. For example, Job 7:9–10 states, "He that goeth down to the grave shall come up no more. He shall return no more to his house, neither shall his place know him any more." Similarly, Job 10:21 reads, "Before I go whence I shall not return," and Job 16:22 says, "When a few years are come, then I shall go the way whence I shall not return." Ancient Mesopotamian literature also speaks of death with imagery resembling that of Lehi's address as a "land without return," a land "where dust is their nourishment and mud their food" (Zandee, 7). In the Sumerian *Inanna's Descent,* the gatekeeper of the Underworld asks Inanna, "Why pray hast thou come to the land of no return? / On the road whose traveler returns not, / how hath thy heart led thee?" (*Inanna's Descent,* 82–83, in Pritchard, 54). Similar imagery appears in the Semitic version of the same story: "To the house which none leave who have entered it, / To the road from which there is no way back" (*Descent of Ishtar,* 5–6, in Pritchard, 107). Ancient Egyptian literature presents similar images of the irretrievability from death. A passage from the *Pyramid Texts,* hieroglyphic funerary inscriptions dating to the third millennium B.C., states, "Do not travel [on] those western waterways, for those who travel thereon do not return" (Utterance

698, in Faulkner, 305). According to an Egyptian song from the fourteenth century B.C., "There is none who comes back from (over) there. . . . Behold, there is not one who departs who comes back again!" (*Song of the Harper,* in Pritchard, 467). Still, the Egyptians had a decidedly positive outlook on life after death, as expressed in the *Pyramid Texts:* "Raise yourself, . . . throw off the earth from your flesh" (Utterance 373 in Faulkner, 123) and, "Raise yourself, throw off your dust, . . . loosen your bonds" (Utterance 553 in Faulkner, 213). These phrases present the same imagery as Lehi's exhortation, "Awake! and arise from the dust" (2 Ne. 1:14), although in different contexts. The Egyptian phrases refer to rising from the dead while Lehi was beseeching his sons to rise up and "shake off the chains" (i.e., of unbelief and sin) that bound them (2 Ne. 1:23).

In summary, contrary to Book of Mormon criticisms, it is questionable whether Shakespeare (himself an assiduous borrower) was the source of the ideas or imagery employed in 2 Nephi 1:14. Rather, Lehi's sentiments (and perhaps Shakespeare's) are found similarly expressed in the Old Testament and other writings of the ancient Near East, including Mesopotamian and Egyptian literature.

BIBLIOGRAPHY

Faulkner, R. O. *The Ancient Egyptian Pyramid Texts.* Oxford: Clarendon Press, 1969.

Pritchard, James B. *Ancient Near Eastern Texts.* 3d ed. Princeton, N.J.: Princeton University Press, 1969.

Shakespeare, William. *Hamlet.*

Zandee, J. *Death as an Enemy: According to Ancient Egyptian Conceptions.* Leiden: E. J. Brill, 1960.

SDR

Shared Jaredite who arose in a time of wickedness and warfare to defeat and imprison Coriantumr[2]. In turn, Coriantumr's sons defeated Shared and restored the kingdom to their father. Coriantumr's anger at Shared compelled him to battle, and after three days of intense fighting in the valley of Gilgal, Coriantumr's troops beat Shared's army and chased them to the plains of Heshlon. There Shared's men defeated Coriantumr's army and drove them back to the valley of Gilgal. In the ensuing battle Coriantumr killed Shared. Some two years later Shared's brother Gilead continued the conflict (Ether 13:22–14:3).

Shazer Place in the Arabian wilderness where Lehi[1] and his family stopped during their journey. The travelers used Shazer as a base camp for a hunting expedition to replenish their food supply (1 Ne. 16:13–14). It was a four-day journey south-southeast from the valley of Lemuel.

See also Lehi[1], journey to the promised land.

TLS

Sheaves Cut stalks of ripened grain bound together into bundles for transport to garners and threshing floors. Sheaves are used as a metaphor for souls converted to the gospel (Alma 26:5; 3 Ne. 20:18).

ALB

Sheep, other *See* Other sheep.

Shelem, mount Old World mountain called Shelem "because of its exceeding height" (Ether 3:1). Here Christ touched the sixteen stones that would light the Jaredite vessels, revealed himself to the brother of Jared[1], and showed him a vision of all things (Ether 3:4–6, 13, 25).

Shem Nephite military leader killed with his ten thousand troops in the last battle between the Nephites and Lamanites (Morm. 6:14; A.D. 385).

See also Cumorah, battle of.

Shem, land of and city of Nephite land north of Jashon and Antum to which Mormon and his people fled from the Lamanites (A.D. 345). Mormon and others fortified the city and gathered as many Nephites as possible to save them from destruction. Rallying his faithless countrymen to fight for their families and homes, Mormon motivated them to stand against the Lamanites and defeat them (Morm. 2:20–26).

Shemlon, land of Area bordering the land of Lehi-Nephi, not mentioned before that land came under Lamanite control. Because the land of

Shemlon bordered the cities Lehi-Nephi and Shilom, given by the Lamanites to king Zeniff's colony (ca. 200 B.C.), references to Shemlon are intermingled with the narrative concerning these people and their descendants. For example, Zeniff sent "spies out round about the land of Shemlon" to observe Lamanite military preparations (Mosiah 10:7). Much later, king Noah[3] saw from his tower in Shilom the Lamanite army approaching from Shemlon (Mosiah 19:6; ca. 145 B.C.). Still later, the priests of Noah abducted several Lamanite daughters from "a place in Shemlon" where they habitually gathered to enjoy themselves (Mosiah 20:1–5). Pacified by Amulon, leader of these priests, the Lamanite king eventually appointed them teachers in Shemlon and throughout his lands. (Mosiah 24:1).

The Lamanites in the land of Shemlon were among those converted by Ammon[2] and his brethren (Alma 23:8, 12).

Shemnon *See* Disciples, twelve Nephite.

Sherem An ANTI-CHRIST who confronted Jacob[2], the brother of Nephi[1], and accused him of BLASPHEMY for transforming the LAW OF MOSES into a worship of Christ (Jacob 7:1, 7). His principal objective was to "overthrow the doctrine of Christ" and to shake Jacob and others from their faith in Christ and his prophesied coming (Jacob 7:2). He was learned and expert in the language of the Nephites and used his rhetorical skills to lead away many (Jacob 7:4). Sherem made specific charges from the law of Moses against Jacob, accusing him of blasphemy, false prophecy, and causing public apostasy (Welch). All three crimes were punishable by death under the law of Moses (Lev. 24:10–16; Deut. 18:20–22; 13:1–18). There were two separate and distinct ways to view the law of Moses. One way was to see Christ as the central focus of the law, which Jacob taught (Jacob 4:5). The other way was to see the law entirely without Christ as Sherem did. According to Sherem, no one could know the future, so no one could know that there would be a Christ (Jacob 7:7; cf. Alma 30:13). He contradicted his own premise, however, in contending that "there is no Christ, neither has been, nor ever will be" (Jacob 7:9). It becomes obvious that Sherem himself was guilty of the three charges that he had made against Jacob.

In the course of his confrontation with Jacob, Sherem mockingly asked Jacob to show him a sign. For this request Sherem was smitten by the Lord. He then admitted that he was deceived by the devil, that he had lied, that he knew the scriptures testified of Christ, and that he feared he had committed the UNPARDONABLE SIN. After confessing his efforts of deception and testifying to the power of the Holy Ghost and the ministering of angels, Sherem died (Jacob 7:13–20). Perhaps insight into Sherem's character can be drawn from Jesus' words to those who tempted him desiring "that he would shew them a sign from heaven" (Matt. 16:1). He said, "a wicked and adulterous generation seeketh after a sign" (Matt. 16:4).

Several important truths concerning Christ and the scriptures are substantiated in Jacob's confrontation with Sherem:

1. Satan makes every effort to strip Christ out of the lives of God's children, including removing Christ from the very types, shadows, and likenesses that are designed to draw God's children to him.
2. The Lord gave the law of Moses as a type to cause the children of Israel to look forward to the redemption of Christ.
3. The existence of Christ, the power of the Holy Ghost, and the ministering of angels are confirmed to be true (Jacob 7:5, 17).
4. The scriptures and all the holy prophets have taught of Christ (Jacob 7:10–11, 19).
5. Sherem was able to deceive the people because their love of God and understanding of the scriptures was seriously deficient (Jacob 7:10–11, 23; Alma 33:14).

BIBLIOGRAPHY

Welch, John W. "Sherem's Accusation against Jacob." *FARMS Update* 74 (January 1991).

RJN

Sherrizah During the final hostilities between the Nephite and Lamanite nations, the Lamanites are said to have taken men, women, and children prisoner from the tower of Sherrizah (Moro. 9:7). The record does not say whether the tower was an architectural structure or a feature of the landscape. In an epistle to Moroni[2], Mormon described the grisly horrors to which the prisoners were subjected. The men, he wrote, were killed, and the women and children were fed the flesh of their husbands and fathers (Moro. 9:8). Many widows and their daughters "remain[ed] in Sherrizah" and were forced to scavenge for food, because what provisions the Lamanites left, Zenephi's Nephite army took (Moro. 9:16). Mormon indicated that the Lamanite armies were positioned between his weakened army and Sherrizah (Moro. 9:17).

Sheum *See* Agriculture in the Book of Mormon.

Shez[1] *See* Jared[1], posterity of.

Shez[2] *See* Jared[1], posterity of.

Shiblom[1] or Shiblon *See* Jared[1], posterity of.

Shiblom[2] Nephite military leader killed with his ten thousand troops in the last battle between the Nephites and Lamanites (Morm. 6:14; A.D. 385).

See also Cumorah, battle of.

Shiblon Second son of Alma the Younger, first mentioned when he accompanied his father and others on a mission to the Zoramites[2] in about 74 B.C. (Alma 31:7). In individual counsel to his sons, Alma commended Shiblon's steadiness, faithfulness, patience, diligence, and long-suffering. Shiblon had not faltered even though he had been imprisoned and stoned by the apostate Zoramites (Alma 38:2–4). Alma promised his son, who had been faithful since his youth (Alma 38:2), that if he would continue trusting in God, he would "be delivered out of [his] trials" and "be lifted up at the last day" (Alma 38:5). Alma bore testimony to Shiblon that only "in and through Christ" can one "be saved," that is, saved from spiritual bondage (Alma 38:9). These words to Shiblon echo Alma's words to another son, Helaman[2], whom he reminded of the physical "bondage" of their "fathers" (Alma 36:2). Alma cautioned Shiblon against pride and boasting, against "overbearance" and "idleness," and against public display of religiosity (Alma 38:10–14). Alma also admonished this son to "bridle all [his] passions, that [he] may be filled with love" (Alma 38:12).

The record does not mention any political or military responsibility, but Shiblon was to continue teaching the word of God (Alma 38:10, 15). A subsequent reference indicates that in 72 B.C. he was preaching successfully to the Church (Alma 49:30). His valor in the faith was confirmed when in 56 B.C. he was given custody of the sacred Nephite records (Alma 63:1). Three years later, after turning the records over to his nephew Helaman[3], Shiblon died (Alma 63:10–11).

ROC

Shiblon *See* Nephite weights and measures.

Shiblum *See* Nephite weights and measures.

Shilom, land of and city of Locale in the land of Nephi, near Lehi-Nephi and Shemlon. Shilom was peacefully ceded by the Lamanite king Laman[2] to Zeniff, who repaired the walls of the city and began to till the land (Mosiah 9:6–9; ca. 200 B.C.). Laman's ulterior motive was to bring Zeniff's people into bondage so that Laman's people might "glut themselves with the labors of [their] hands" (Mosiah 9:12). Thirteen years later the Lamanites attacked the southern part of Shilom, but were repulsed by Zeniff, as were they again nine years later when they attacked in the north (Mosiah 9:14–19; 10:8–10, 20; ca. 178 B.C.). After Zeniff's death his corrupt and vain son Noah[3] became king and constructed many buildings in Shilom. But another attack by the Lamanites led to the demise of his kingdom, and Shilom fell under Lamanite rule with Noah's son Limhi as the puppet king (Mosiah 11:13; 19:6–28; ca. 145 B.C.). After the escape of Limhi's people to Zarahemla, Shilom reverted to the Lamanites. Later, the king of the Lamanites appointed the wicked Amulon and his fellow priests as teachers in Shilom (Mosiah 24:1–2). The Lamanites in the land of Shilom were eventually converted by Ammon[2] and his brethren (Alma 23:8, 12).

Shim, hill Nephite locale, in the land of Antum (Morm. 1:3). In A.D. 321 Ammaron deposited all of the sacred records of the Nephites in the hill Shim (4 Ne. 1:48). He instructed young Mormon that when he turned twenty-four he should take from these records the plates of Nephi and continue the record (Morm. 1:2–4). This Mormon did (Morm. 2:17–18), but about A.D. 375 he was forced by Lamanite advances to remove all the records from Shim (Morm. 4:23).

A "hill of Shim" is mentioned once in the Jaredite abridgment by Moroni[2]. Omer passed by the hill after the overthrow of his kingdom (Ether 9:3).

Shimnilom, city of One of the Lamanite cities whose inhabitants were converted to Christ by Ammon[2] and his fellow missionaries. The people of Shimnilom were among those who adopted the name ANTI-NEPHI-LEHIES (Alma 23:8–17).

Shiz Commander of a large Jaredite army during the last battle of that people. He assumed command of the army at the death of his brother Lib[2] who was slain in battle against the army of Coriantumr[2]. Shiz pursued Coriantumr and his army slaying both women and children, and burning cities (Ether 14:16–17). The reason for his obsessive pursuit of Coriantumr was to avenge the blood of his brother and to disprove the prophecy that Coriantumr would not be slain by the sword (Ether 14:24). He met in battle against Coriantumr several times in which millions of people were slaughtered. Consequently, the Jaredites were facing annihilation. On two separate occasions Coriantumr wrote Shiz an epistle offering the rule of the kingdom to him, if he would spare the lives of the people. Shiz refused these offers, demanding that Coriantumr give himself up that Shiz "might slay him with his own sword" (Ether 15:4–5, 18). Only upon those conditions would Shiz spare the people. Shiz "swore in his wrath that he would slay Coriantumr or he would perish by the sword" (Ether 15:28). Shiz and his army pursued Coriantumr and his army in battle until only the two commanders remained alive. A most graphic passage in scripture is recorded regarding the death of Shiz by decapitation (see Hadfield, 324–25, for the medical implications of Shiz's rising up on his hands after decapitation). The death of Shiz fulfilled the word of the Lord through the prophet Ether that if Coriantumr and his household did not repent, all of his household, save it were himself, would be destroyed (Ether 13:20–21). The story of Shiz highlights the truth taught throughout the Book of Mormon that God's words to his prophets will all be fulfilled.

BIBLIOGRAPHY

Hadfield, M. Gary. "Neuropathology and the Scriptures." *Brigham Young University Studies* 33:2 (1993): 313–28.

CJO

Shule Early Jaredite king and great-grandson of Jared[1] (Ether 1:31–32). Born while his elderly father, Kib, was living "in captivity . . . under Corihor his son" (Ether 7:7), Shule grew to be a "mighty" man in physical strength and "in judgment" (Ether 7:8). Full of righteous purpose, he forged steel swords and, arming himself and his followers, defeated his brother Corihor[1] and restored the kingdom to his father (Ether 7:9). For this, Kib passed the kingdom on to him (Ether 7:10), and he ruled justly. But eventually, Noah[2], son of the repentant Corihor, in turn started another insurrection, captured Shule, and cast him into prison (Ether 7:15–17). When Shule was about to be executed, his sons came by night, killed Noah, released their father, and restored him to his throne (Ether 7:18). Conflict between the two rival kingdoms of Shule and Cohor, the son of Noah, continued for much of Shule's reign. After Cohor's death in battle, his son Nimrod voluntarily relinquished the kingdom to Shule, thereby winning Shule's favor (Ether 7:21–22). Also during Shule's reign, the Lord sent prophets to warn the people to repent or "be destroyed" for their "wickedness and idolatry" (Ether 7:23). Shule punished those who persecuted the prophets and passed a law allowing the prophets to preach freely (Ether 7:24–25). Thus, the people were brought to repentance. Shule was a righteous king, a wise lawgiver, and a mighty warrior. By the end of his reign, Shule had established peace and righteousness among his people (Ether 7:27).

See also Jared[1], posterity of.

MDR

Shum *See* Nephite weights and measures.

Shurr, valley of Jaredite valley where Coriantumr[2] and his armies pitched their tents before proceeding to the hill Comnor to resume battle with the armies of Shiz (Ether 14:28).

Sidom, land of Nephite region to which Alma[2] and Amulek journeyed after being rejected at Ammonihah. Here they discovered the believers who had been driven out of the land of Ammonihah and had found refuge in Sidom. They also found Zeezrom, a former adversary, on his sickbed, wracked with guilt for his sins and for his opposition to Alma and Amulek. The repentant Zeezrom was healed and then baptized. In Sidom Alma preached the gospel, established a church, and consecrated priests and teachers to baptize (Alma 15:1–14; ca. 81 B.C.).

Sidon, river A prominent river in Nephite territory originating in the vicinity of the south wilderness and the land of Manti (Alma 16:6; 22:27). The Sidon apparently flowed north to the sea, passing just east of the city of Zarahemla (Alma 3:3; 6:7; 44:22). The river is mentioned most frequently as a landmark and strategic site in military confrontations among Nephites, Amlicites, and Lamanites (e.g., Alma 2–3; 16; 43–44). The "waters of Sidon" are mentioned at least once in a more peaceful context as the site of many baptisms (Alma 4:4).

ROC

Siege A military blockade of a city or other fortification with the intent of forcing it to surrender. In ancient times, capture of a stronghold or fortified position (outpost, town, or city) was usually accomplished by encircling it with a powerful armed force and preventing either escape or importation of supplies. This often hastened disease, starvation, or social disintegration. Examples of siege warfare in the ancient Near East are numerous. In Israelite territory they include Jericho (Josh. 6), Samaria (2 Kgs. 17:5), Lachish (2 Chr. 32:9), and Jerusalem (2 Kgs. 24:10). Patterns of warfare in the Book of Mormon fit perfectly within this authentic milieu, especially the great Gadianton siege of Nephite lands, including Zarahemla (3 Ne. 4:16–17, 23). This siege, led by Zemnarihah, failed because of Nephite counter measures, for "it was impossible for the robbers to lay siege sufficiently long to have any effect upon the Nephites, because of their much provision which they had laid up in store" (3 Ne. 4:18).

ACS

Signs Observable manifestations, something perceived or seen. The Book of Mormon records several reasons for the use of signs. Signs mark the timing of prophesied events (e.g., 1 Ne. 19:10), providing evidence of God's existence, and serving to encourage people to repent and turn to the Lord (e.g., Hel. 14:12–13; 15:1–3; 16:4–5). After prophesying of the signs that would accompany the birth and death of Jesus Christ (Hel. 14:1–27), Samuel the Lamanite taught that God gives signs "to the intent that there should be no cause for unbelief among the children of men—and this to the intent that whosoever will believe might be saved, and that whosoever will not believe, a righteous judgment might come upon them; and also if they are condemned they bring upon themselves their own condemnation. . . . for behold, ye are free; ye are permitted to act for yourselves" (Hel. 14:28–30). Thus, signs afford an opportunity to exercise personal agency (Hel. 14:30).

To a believer signs confirm and elicit faith in God the Father and Jesus Christ (e.g., 1 Ne. 11:6–7; Hel. 14:12; 16:4; 3 Ne. 5:1–2; 7:22). On the other hand, unbelievers often reject signs and harden their hearts (Mosiah 3:15; Hel. 9:24–25; 16:13–15; 3 Ne. 1:4–22), bringing serious consequences (1 Ne. 19:13). Sometimes people seek signs because they lack faith. Such persons say they will believe if they see a sign (Alma 32:16–18). In reality, however, the opposite is true—"faith cometh not by signs, but signs follow those that believe" (D&C 63:9). Sign-seeking angers God: "Wherefore, unto such he showeth no signs, only in wrath unto their condemnation" (D&C 63:11). The stories of Sherem and Korihor provide classic examples of what happens to those who seek after signs (Jacob 7:1–20; Alma 30:12–21, 30–60). Alma[2], in responding to Korihor's request for a sign, replied by identifying signs that were already available. Such signs included God's creations, the earth, its motion, and the movement of the planets throughout the solar system (Alma 30:43–44; cf. Gen. 1:14).

Among numerous other signs mentioned in the Book of Mormon, the night before Jesus' birth, there appeared "one day and a night and a day, as if it were one day" as a sign that the Savior of the world had been born into mortality (Hel. 14:2–4; 3 Ne. 1:13–15; Moro. 10:1); according to the prophet Zechariah, a similar sign will occur when Christ comes again (Zech. 14:6–7). Another sign of Jesus' birth included a new star and "signs and wonders in heaven" (Hel. 14:5–6). Signs accompanying the Savior's death included thunderings, lightnings, earthquakes, destructions (Hel. 14:14, 20–24), and three days of darkness "to the time that he shall rise again from the dead" (Hel. 14:20). "And many graves shall be opened, and shall yield up many of their dead; and many saints shall appear unto many" (Hel. 14:25).

The Book of Mormon, New Testament, and Doctrine and Covenants all teach that signs follow belief. Christ instructed his disciples in the New World, "And these signs shall follow them that believe—in my name shall they cast out devils; they shall speak with new tongues; they shall take up serpents; and if they drink any deadly thing it shall not hurt them; they shall lay hands on the sick and they shall recover" (Morm. 9:24; cf. 3 Ne. 7:22; D&C 84:65–73; Mark 16:17–18). The sign of the Savior's birth in the Americas—"one day and a night and a day" of light (Hel. 14:4)—was so profound that it became a focal point for generations to come (3 Ne. 2:7–8).

In the New World, Christ announced a sign that would mark the time when the gathering of Israel and the establishment of Zion would "be about to take place" (3 Ne. 21:1): the coming forth of the Book of Mormon. When the Book of Mormon would come forth to the Gentiles and the Gentiles would take the Book of Mormon to the latter-day descendants of Lehi[1], "it shall be a sign unto them, that they may know that the work of the Father hath already commenced unto the fulfilling of the covenant which he hath made unto the people who are of the house of Israel" (3 Ne. 21:7, 2–6; cf. 29:1–4).

Signs are frequently mentioned in conjunction with wonders (e.g., 1 Ne. 19:13; Mosiah 3:15; Hel. 14:28). Satan, in his efforts to dissuade people from accepting the truth, seeks to diminish the importance of signs (3 Ne. 1:22; 2:1–3; cf. Hel. 16:23; 3 Ne. 8:3–4). In his attempts to deceive, he may even manifest his own signs (e.g., Alma 30:53; cf. Mark 13:22; JST 2 Thes. 2:7–9).

Another type of sign identified in the Book of Mormon are those associated with SECRET COMBINATIONS (Alma 37:27; Hel. 2:7; 6:22).

See also Book of Mormon, selected purposes of, to be a sign of the Father's work.

DMW

Silk A fine, lustrous cloth. The word "silk" or "silks" occurs six times in the Book of Mormon, always together with "fine" or "fine-twined linen." Among the Nephites and Jaredites silk was a sign of prosperity (Alma 1:29; Ether 9:17; 10:24), and along with Nephite COSTLY APPAREL, a symbol of pride and worldliness (Alma 4:6; cf. Jacob 2:13; Alma 5:53; 4 Ne. 1:24). Silk is also listed as one of the lustful desires of the great and abominable church (1 Ne. 13:7, 8).

Usually "silk" refers to fabric woven in East Asia from fibers spun by worms fed on mulberry leaves. Scholars believe this kind of silk was brought from East Asia to Europe by Marco Polo in the thirteenth century A.D. There is currently no evidence that this specific kind of silk was known in the Americas before the Europeans came. The term may be used to describe a number of different cloths known in the New World. It is likely that "silk" in the Book of Mormon refers to a fine cloth made from materials native to the New World. For example, early Spanish explorers recorded that the natives in Mexico gathered fibers from wild cocoons, a fiber from the pod of a tree (kapok), and a fiber of a wild pineapple plant, all of which were spun into fabrics described by the Spaniards as "silk" or "silk like."

The word *silk* is used twice in the King James Version of the Old Testament, once to translate the Hebrew word *sheshee,* which was likely a fine

LINEN (Prov. 31:22), and the other to translate the Hebrew word *meshee,* which likely refers to traditional silk (Ezek. 16:10).

BIBLIOGRAPHY

Sorenson, John L. "Possible 'Silk' and 'Linen' in the Book of Mormon." *Reexploring the Book of Mormon.* Edited by John W. Welch. Salt Lake City: Deseret Book and FARMS, 1992.

DRS

Similitude A visual likeness, representing something that is similar to something else. In the scriptures, similitude, likeness, type, figure, and SHADOW may be used interchangeably. In Jacob 4:5, Jacob[2] referred to the offering of Isaac by Abraham, as a similitude of God's offering of his Only Begotten Son.

See also Types.

RJN

Sin, transgression Terms used in the Book of Mormon to designate the breaking of the commandments of God; they seem to be used synonymously. For example, "sin" is used in Moroni 8:10 to refer to "those who are accountable and capable of committing sin" (cf. Mosiah 2:33; 3:11; 3 Ne. 6:18). "Transgression" is used in reference to those who knowingly break the commandments (2 Ne. 9:27; Mosiah 2:36), those who act "contrary to the light and knowledge which they do have" (Alma 9:23), or those who "believeth" or have "cause to believe" and then fail to keep the commandments (Alma 32:19). In several places "sin" and "transgression" form a parallel pair to describe those who "have been once enlightened by the Spirit of God, and have had great knowledge of things pertaining to righteousness, and then have fallen away" (Alma 24:30; cf. 9:19; 28:13).

The Book of Mormon makes a distinction in regards to culpability for sin or transgression based upon the knowledge one has. For example, the discourse of Jacob[2] on the ATONEMENT in 2 Nephi 9 makes the distinction between the ACCOUNTABILITY of "those who have not the law given to them" and "him that has the law given, yea, that has all the commandments of God . . . and that transgresseth them" (2 Ne. 9:26–27; cf. 2:22–23; Mosiah 15:24–26; Alma 32:19; Moro. 8:22). Contemporary LDS thought distinguishes between "sin" and "transgression" in regard to the FALL OF ADAM AND EVE (Smith, *Words,* 63; Smith, *Doctrines,* 1:114; Packer, 49). Adam and Eve did not sin. By partaking of the FORBIDDEN FRUIT, they transgressed the conditions, or the law God gave them for remaining in the Garden of Eden, and were thus cast out. Interestingly, in light of this distinction, the Book of Mormon itself never refers to the cause of the fall of Adam as a "sin," but consistently uses the term "transgression" (2 Ne. 2:22; 9:6; Alma 12:31; Mosiah 3:11), which is consonant with other latter-day scripture (e.g., D&C 20:20; 29:40–41; Moses 5:11; 6:53, 59; A of F 2).

The Book of Mormon clarifies many issues regarding sin. For example, the Lord cannot look on sin with the least degree of allowance (Alma 45:16). Sin that is not repented of inevitably leads to a loss of hope (Moro. 7:41) and ensuing despair (Moro. 10:22). The devil is the author of sin (Hel. 6:30). He invites and entices to sin (Moro. 7:12). He and his angels rejoice when they succeed in tempting people to succumb to sin (3 Ne. 9:2). The Book of Mormon provides many examples of the devastating consequences of sin when it is allowed to flourish unchecked in society. Two entire Book of Mormon civilizations were destroyed because the people refused to repent of their iniquities. Also specifically pointed out are the evils that result when a sinful person is allowed to rule over the people (Mosiah 11:2; 29:17–18). The Book of Mormon makes the point that sin is the cause of the inequality seen among the people of the earth (Alma 28:13).

All individuals born on this earth are taught sufficiently to recognize some good from some evil (2 Ne. 2:5). It is because of this knowledge of good and evil that mortals can act in compliance with or contrary to the laws and will of God, that is, to perform good works or to sin (2 Ne. 2:23). Perhaps that is why, as the Book of Mormon teaches, little children and others who have not reached the age of accountability, and thus cannot have been taught sufficiently, cannot sin (Mosiah 3:16; Moro. 8:8). They are, rather, redeemed by the atonement of Christ without the need of REPENTANCE or BAPTISM (Moro. 8:8–11).

All others who have reached the age of accountability and have been taught sufficiently have need of repentance (Mosiah 3:12) and the saving ordinances. When they have repented of their sins, they are cleansed by the atonement of Christ (Mosiah 3:21), who offered himself as a sacrifice for sin (2 Ne. 2:7; Mosiah 15:10). On the other hand, those who continue in willful sin against God and, in rebellion against the knowledge they have received here on earth, refuse to repent, will in the end not enjoy the full fruits of the Atonement but will become as if there had been no redemption made for them (Mosiah 16:5). Individuals who deny the Holy Ghost and know it have committed the unpardonable sin (Alma 39:6).

See also Forgiveness.

BIBLIOGRAPHY

Packer, Boyd K. *The Things of the Soul.* Salt Lake City: Bookcraft, 1996.

Smith, Joseph. *The Words of Joseph Smith.* Edited by Andrew F. Ehat and Lyndon W. Cook. Salt Lake City: Bookcraft, 1980.

Smith, Joseph Fielding. *Doctrines of Salvation.* Compiled by Bruce R. McConkie. 3 vols. Salt Lake City: Bookcraft, 1954–56.

PYH

Sinai, mount The mount where the Lord delivered unto Moses the commandments of God (Mosiah 12:33). Moses' face shone with exceeding luster while speaking with the Lord on the mount, because the Spirit of the Lord was upon him (Mosiah 13:5). Though its location is disputed, it is commonly thought to be in the southern part of the Sinai peninsula between the gulfs of Suez and Aqaba. Tradition marks the site with one of the peaks of Jebel Musa. Another name for Mt. Sinai is Mt. Horeb (cf. 3 Ne. 25:4; Bible Map 2).

RDA

Siron, land of Mentioned only once in the Book of Mormon, this land was located near the "borders of the Lamanites" (Alma 39:3). Alma[2] chastised his son Corianton for going to the land of Siron "after the harlot Isabel" (Alma 39:3). Elder George Reynolds described Siron as "the land of the deserters, or apostates." He described how typical it is for the unrighteous "to draw off to remote corners, where they fancy the reproofs of the priesthood are the least likely to be heard" (298).

BIBLIOGRAPHY

Reynolds, George. *The Story of the Book of Mormon.* 3d ed. Chicago: Henry C. Etten & Co., 1888.

DKJ

Slippery Term used by Samuel the Lamanite to describe the consequences of a curse that would come upon Nephite lands and riches because of iniquity. To humble, encourage to repentance, and remind the materialistic Nephites of the source of their blessings, the curse would cause their treasures, tools, and weapons to become "slippery," so they could not "hold them," or keep them from being lost or stolen (Hel. 13:31–36). Mormon recorded a fulfillment of this prophecy in his time (Morm. 1:18; 2:10). The Jaredites experienced a similar curse (Ether 14:1).

TBB

Small plates of Nephi *See* Plates of Nephi.

Smith, Hyrum Book of Mormon witness and martyr, Hyrum Smith was born on 9 February 1800 at Tunbridge, Orange County, Vermont, second child of Joseph Sr. and Lucy Mack Smith. His younger brother Joseph was called by God to obtain, protect, translate, and publish the Book of Mormon. Sometime in May 1829 Hyrum went to visit Joseph who was living in Harmony, Pennsylvania. While he was there, Hyrum received a revelation through his brother which included the phrase: "Behold thou art Hyrum, my son; seek the kingdom of God, and all things shall be added according to that which is just. Build upon my rock, which is my gospel" (D&C 11:23–24). After this revelation, Hyrum became increasingly involved in his brother's mission and was baptized in early June 1829. Later in the month he was chosen to be one of the Eight Witnesses. Along with his father and his brother Samuel, Hyrum saw the plates and provided his testimony, which is published in the Book of Mormon.

Hyrum was intimately involved in the publication of the Book of Mormon in March 1830, and in the organization of the Church in April 1830. He moved to Ohio in 1831 and helped establish the Church in Kirtland. He participated in the building of the Kirtland Temple as a member of the temple building committee and worker. Hyrum served as an Assistant Counselor to the First Presidency beginning on 3 September 1837; and in November of that same year, was appointed Second Counselor in the First Presidency. After the death of his wife, Jerusha Barden, Hyrum married Mary Fielding on 24 December 1837. He and his family moved to Missouri when the Church was forced from Kirtland in 1838. Their stay in Missouri was not long, as the Saints were again driven from their homes during the winter of 1838–39. This time, Hyrum, as well as other Church leaders, was unable to help his family seek a new place of asylum. He remained in Missouri and was eventually incarcerated in Liberty Jail. State officials later allowed Hyrum and those with him to escape on 16 April 1839. They traveled to Illinois, where their families and Church members had found refuge from the persecution in Missouri.

In January 1841 Hyrum was called to be the Church Patriarch, succeeding his father, who had died. Additionally, he was called as Assistant President of the Church, replacing Oliver Cowdery, who had left the Church (D&C 124:91–95). During this period, Hyrum pronounced hundreds of patriarchal blessings upon the Saints in Nauvoo, acted as chairman of the Nauvoo Temple building committee, and served as one of Joseph's closest advisors. Hyrum also held various city government and social positions in Nauvoo.

Continued misunderstandings and suspicions, political and economic competition in the region, and religious intolerance brought the Saints and their neighbors once again into conflict. Often this hostility was focused on Joseph and Hyrum as leaders of the Church. By June 1844, a conspiracy of the leading citizens in Hancock County and dissidents from the Church had planned to murder Joseph and Hyrum. Enemies of the Smith brothers used legal and extralegal means to place Joseph and Hyrum in a vulnerable position, beyond the protecting hands of friends and supporters. These enemies found an opportunity when the city council, which included Joseph and Hyrum, decided to suppress a Nauvoo dissident newspaper, the *Nauvoo Expositor,* which they believed encouraged increased violence against the Latter-day Saints.

Joseph and Hyrum, as well as other city officials, were charged with riot and ordered to appear at the Hancock County seat in Carthage. A few days before their murders, Hyrum read an excerpt from the Book of Mormon and turned down the leaf upon it: *"And it came to pass that I prayed unto the Lord that he would give unto the Gentiles grace, that they might have charity. And it came to pass that the Lord said unto me: If they have not charity it mattereth not unto thee, thou hast been faithful; wherefore thy garments shall be made clean. And because thou hast seen thy weakness, thou shalt be made strong, even unto the sitting down in the place which I have prepared in the mansions of my Father. And now I . . . bid farewell unto the Gentiles; yea, and also unto my*

Statue of Joseph and Hyrum Smith; sculpture by Dee Jay Bawden; courtesy John Telford.

brethren whom I love, until we shall meet before the judgment-seat of Christ, where all men shall know that my garments are not spotted with your blood" (D&C 135:5; italics in original; // Ether 12:36–38).

As ordered by the Illinois state governor, Thomas Ford, Joseph and Hyrum traveled to Carthage to submit to arrest. After their arrival on 24 June 1844, the mood of the prisoners remained sober and foreboding. During the evening before their deaths, Hyrum, presumably trying to buoy up the feelings of the group, "read and commented upon extracts from the Book of Mormon, on the imprisonments and deliverance of the servants of God for the Gospel's sake" (Smith, 6:600).

On 27 June, "Hyrum bore a faithful testimony to the Latter-day work, and the coming forth of the Book of Mormon" (Smith, 6:610). It proved to be his last, as an armed mob rushed the jail and within a few minutes Joseph and Hyrum lay dead in Carthage, both men martyred for their testimonies and religious beliefs.

John Taylor wrote: "To seal the testimony of [the Doctrine and Covenants] and the Book of Mormon, we announce the martyrdom of Joseph Smith the Prophet, and Hyrum Smith the Patriarch" (D&C 135:1). He added: "Like most of the Lord's anointed in ancient times, [Joseph] has sealed his mission and his works with his own blood; and so has his brother Hyrum." John Taylor concluded: "The testators are now dead, and their testament is in force" (D&C 135:3, 5).

See also Book of Mormon, printing and publication of; Smith, Joseph, Jr.; Witnesses of the Book of Mormon.

BIBLIOGRAPHY

Smith, Joseph. *History of The Church of Jesus Christ of Latter-day Saints.* Edited by B. H. Roberts. 7 vols. 2d ed. rev. Salt Lake City: The Church of Jesus Christ of Latter-day Saints, 1932–51.

RNH

Smith, Joseph, Jr. The translator of the Book of Mormon into English and the first prophet-president of The Church of Jesus Christ of Latter-day Saints. He was foreordained to be the Lord's instrument in bringing forth the restoration of the fulness of the gospel of Jesus Christ—the full and final establishment of the kingdom of God on earth before the second coming of Jesus Christ. Cardinal events pertaining to the restoration of the ancient Church of Jesus Christ and its doctrines in their purity include the many revelations given to the Prophet Joseph Smith, the restoration of the priesthood, and the coming forth of the Book of Mormon.

Joseph Smith was born on 23 December 1805 in Sharon, Windsor County, Vermont, the son of Joseph Sr. and Lucy Mack Smith. After several financial setbacks in New England, the Smith family moved from Norwich, Vermont, to western New York in 1816 in search of a new beginning. In the Palmyra-Manchester area, many of the important founding events of the Restoration occurred as Joseph grew to maturity. The visitation of the Father and the Son to Joseph Smith in the early spring of 1820, known as the First Vision, was the first of many spiritual experiences that eventually led to the publication of the Book of Mormon in March 1830 and to the establishment of the Church in April 1830. After the First Vision in 1820, Joseph received no heavenly manifestation until the fall of 1823. The angel Moroni appeared to him in the family's log house in Palmyra Township on the night of 21 September 1823 and informed him that there was a book "written upon gold plates" (JS–H 1:34), deposited in a nearby hill, containing the fulness of the gospel. When he visited the hill on 22 September, he was informed by Moroni that it was not yet time for him to receive the plates. Joseph visited the hill on the same date each year for the next four years (1824–27), where he was instructed by the same heavenly messenger.

On 18 January 1827 Joseph married Emma Hale of Harmony, Pennsylvania, at South Bainbridge, New York, and the couple took up residence in Manchester with Joseph's parents. Eight months later, on 22 September 1827, he received the plates from Moroni. Because of mounting persecution, Joseph and Emma moved from Manchester to Harmony, Pennsylvania, in December 1827. With divine assistance, Joseph began translating the Book of Mormon on 12 April 1828, Martin Harris acting as his scribe

SMITH, JOSEPH, JR.

(*see* Book of Mormon, translation of). In the course of three months, 116 manuscript pages were produced, but they were subsequently lost or stolen (*see* Book of Mormon, lost manuscript of [116 pages]). Eventually, after a period of repentance because of the loss of the manuscript, Joseph began translating the plates with Oliver Cowdery as his scribe on 7 April 1829.

A necessary part of the restoration of the gospel was the restoration of the ancient priesthood with its authority to direct the affairs of the Church of Jesus Christ and to perform the necessary ordinances of salvation. On 15 May 1829 Joseph Smith and Oliver Cowdery "went into the woods" near Joseph's home in Harmony, Pennsylvania, "to pray and inquire of the Lord respecting baptism for the remission of sins, that [they] found mentioned in the translation of the plates" (JS–H 1:68). In answer to their prayer, John the Baptist appeared and conferred upon them the Aaronic Priesthood and instructed Joseph and Oliver to baptize each other and to confer upon each other the "same Priesthood" (JS–H 1:70–71). Within a short period after their reception of the Aaronic Priesthood and baptism they received the Melchizedek Priesthood by angelic administration from Peter, James, and John along the banks of the Susquehanna River between Harmony, Pennsylvania, and Colesville, New York.

Joseph and Oliver moved to Peter and Mary Whitmer's farm in Fayette, New York, by 1 June 1829 because of increased persecution in the Harmony region. In Fayette, Joseph and Oliver completed the translation of the Book of Mormon in June 1829. During the next few months, Joseph made arrangements for E. B. Grandin to print the Book of Mormon with Martin Harris's guarantee of financial security. Oliver Cowdery and Hyrum Smith were eventually given supervisory capacity for the publication of the Book of Mormon during the late fall and winter of 1829–1830. Meanwhile, the Prophet returned to his home in Harmony (*see* Book of Mormon, printing and publication of).

The Book of Mormon was published on 26 March 1830 in Palmyra, New York, and the Church was organized on 6 April 1830 in Fayette, New York. Joseph began working on the inspired translation of the Bible (Joseph Smith Translation, or JST) in June 1830. Six months later, in December 1830, the Lord commanded the Saints to gather in Ohio (D&C 37:1; 38:31–32). Joseph and Emma were among the first members of the Church to move to the Kirtland, Ohio, area in early 1831.

As the Church continued to grow in Ohio, Joseph Smith and other leading elders traveled to Independence, Missouri, in June and July 1831. The Lord identified this area as the site of the New Jerusalem and the spot for a temple (D&C 57:1–5). New converts began to make their way to Missouri; others continued to build up the Church center in Kirtland, Ohio, where a temple was built under Joseph's direction (1833–1836).

Persecution eventually forced the Saints from Jackson County, Missouri, in 1833, but work continued in Ohio, where a second edition of the Book of Mormon was published, along with other LDS scriptures (e.g., the Doctrine and Covenants, which contains many of the revelations given to Joseph Smith). On 27 March 1836, Joseph Smith presided at the dedication of the Kirtland Temple (D&C 109). While in the temple on 3 April 1836, one week after the dedication, the Lord appeared to Joseph Smith and Oliver Cowdery, accepting "this house" as his own. Moses, Elias, and Elijah also appeared in succession, conferring priesthood keys (D&C 110).

Joseph and the Saints enjoyed this temple only briefly. They were driven by persecution from Kirtland (1838) and moved to northwestern Missouri, where they joined the Saints who had been driven earlier from Jackson County, Missouri. In Far West, Missouri, Joseph settled with his family and continued to lead the Saints who were gathering to the region in large numbers. After only a brief respite from persecution, the Saints were again driven from their homes in the fall of 1838. Joseph Smith and other Church leaders were left behind, arrested, and imprisoned. While the Saints made their way to Iowa and Illinois to escape the "extermination order" issued by Missouri governor Lilburn W. Boggs, Joseph was imprisoned, first

SMITH, JOSEPH, JR.

at Richmond and then finally in Liberty Jail from 1 December 1838 to 6 April 1839. During a change of venue, guards permitted Joseph and other Church leaders to escape on 16 April, allowing them to reunite with their families and other Church members who had found refuge in western Illinois by 22 April 1839.

Joseph moved his family to Commerce, Illinois, a small village on a bend of the Mississippi River in Hancock County on 10 May 1839. By June, he was organizing and supervising the gathering of the Saints to their new home, which was later called Nauvoo.

Joseph was busily engaged in almost every aspect of life in Nauvoo: social, political, economic, and religious. During the building of the Nauvoo House, he placed the original manuscript of the Book of Mormon in the cornerstone on 2 October 1841. His activities during this period included correcting proofs for the third edition of the Book of Mormon in January 1842, organizing the Relief Society on 17 March 1842, and introducing the temple ordinances on 4 May 1842. Additionally, he was elected the mayor of Nauvoo on 19 May 1842.

During the last years of his life (1840–44), Joseph found numerous opportunities to teach the Saints and to reveal the word of the Lord to an ever-increasing number of members of the Church, including the doctrine of eternal marriage (D&C 131:1–3).

Intolerance by some local citizens of Hancock County and dissent from some within the Church led to increasing confrontations between the Saints and their neighbors. This hostility generally focused on Joseph Smith, and in April 1844 his life was threatened by Church dissenters, who, with enemies outside the Church, became increasingly concerned about his growing influence and the distinctive religious beliefs he was teaching in Nauvoo. After the suppression of a libelous paper, the *Nauvoo Expositor,* which the city council believed would inflame the already tense situation, Joseph Smith and his brother Hyrum and other city officers were charged with riot for destroying the press. Eventually, they surrendered at the county seat in Carthage, at the behest of the Illinois governor, Thomas Ford. Though they answered the arrest warrant on the charge of riot and posted bail, they were rearrested on a false mittimus charging them with treason; they were remanded to jail. Some of the leading citizens of Hancock County conspired to place Joseph and Hyrum in a relatively unprotected situation in order to kill them.

The evening before his murder, "Joseph bore a powerful testimony to the guards of the divine authenticity of the Book of Mormon" (Smith, 6:600). On the following day, 27 June 1844, Joseph and Hyrum Smith, along with fellow Church leaders John Taylor and Willard Richards, remained in the Carthage jail. About 10:00 A.M., "both Joseph and Hyrum bore a faithful testimony to the latter-day work, and the coming forth of the Book of Mormon" (Smith, 6:610). Later in the afternoon, around 5:00 P.M., an armed mob of about two hundred persons rushed the county jail, and in "a few short minutes of scuffling, shouts, and shots the deed was done": Joseph and Hyrum were dead (Bitton, xvi).

An eyewitness to the events of that hot, muggy, overcast day on the western Illinois frontier, Elder John Taylor wrote: "To seal the testimony of [the Doctrine and Covenants] and the Book of Mormon, we announce the martyrdom of Joseph Smith the Prophet, and Hyrum Smith the Patriarch" (D&C 135:1). He added: "Like most of the Lord's anointed in ancient times, [Joseph] has sealed his mission and his works with his own blood; and so has his brother Hyrum." He concluded: "The testators are now dead, and their testament is in force" (D&C 135:3, 5).

Later, Brigham Young, second president of the Church, received a revelation explaining Joseph's death and reinforcing John Taylor's earlier statement: "Many have marveled because of his death; but it was needful that he should seal his testimony with his blood, that he might be honored and the wicked might be condemned. Have I not delivered you from your enemies, only in that I have left a witness of my name?" (D&C 136:39–40).

See also The Coming Forth of the Book of Mormon, 9; Smith, Hyrum; Choice seer; Smith, Joseph, Jr., Book of Mormon prophecies of.

BIBLIOGRAPHY

Bitton, Davis. *The Martyrdom Remembered: A One-Hundred-Fifty-Year Perspective on the Assassination of Joseph Smith.* Salt Lake City: Aspen Books, 1994.

Smith, Joseph. *History of The Church of Jesus Christ of Latter-day Saints.* Edited by B. H. Roberts. 7 vols. 2d ed. rev. Salt Lake City: The Church of Jesus Christ of Latter-day Saints, 1932–51.

RNH

Smith, Joseph, Jr., Book of Mormon prophecies of From the days of Joseph of Egypt it was known that a prophet bearing his name would come forth in the last days to restore the covenants God made with Abraham. This prophecy, restored to the Old Testament in the Joseph Smith Translation (JST Gen. 50:24–38), was brought to the New World by Lehi[1] and his family on the brass plates. Father Lehi quoted much of it in a blessing given to his youngest son Joseph[2], recorded in 2 Nephi 3. In this prophecy, which likens the latter-day Joseph to his ancient namesake, it is made known that the Lord appeared to Joseph of Egypt and gave him the promise of a righteous posterity in the last days. Before that day came he was told that his father's family would be taken into bondage in Egypt, but that they would be delivered by a prophet bearing the name Moses. Thereafter he was told that they would be scattered throughout the nations of the earth and that a branch of his own family would be "carried into a far country" (JST Gen. 50:25). Nevertheless, he was assured that the Messiah would manifest himself to his seed in great power in the last days to bring them out of darkness into light and out of captivity unto freedom. This great latter-day gathering was to be accomplished under the direction of one of Joseph's descendants, who was to bear his name and, like him, be "a choice seer" (2 Ne. 3:7).

This prophecy also foreshadows the coming forth of the Book of Mormon at the hands of Joseph Smith. The Lord told Joseph of Egypt that "a seer will I raise up out of the fruit of thy loins; and unto him will I give power to bring forth my word unto the seed of thy loins" (2 Ne. 3:11–12). It is a companion prophecy to that of Isaiah who foretold the coming forth of a book at the hands of an unlearned man, which book was to be sealed to the learned (Isa. 29 // 2 Ne. 27). A more complete account of Isaiah's prophecy was found on the brass plates, foreshadowing the role of the Three Witnesses and the Eight Witnesses to the Book of Mormon (2 Ne. 27:12–13). And, as with Isaiah 29, the account on the brass plates contained some of the words that would yet be spoken to Joseph Smith by the Savior in the first vision (2 Ne. 27:25 // Isa. 29:13; JS–H 1:19).

Second Nephi 21 also includes a prophetic reference to Joseph Smith. In this prophecy Isaiah described the Messiah as both the "stem of Jesse" (mortal Messiah; 2 Ne. 21:1) and the righteous judge (millennial Messiah; 2 Ne. 21:4). He further spoke of a rod and root of Jesse (Joseph Smith), "a servant in the hands of Christ, who is partly a descendant of Jesse as well as of Ephraim, or of the house of Joseph, on whom there is laid much power," a man "unto whom rightly belongs the priesthood, and the keys of the kingdom, for an ensign, and for the gathering of [the Lord's] people in the last days" (D&C 113:1–2, 4–6; cf. 86:8–10). Paradoxically, Joseph Smith is also identified as a Gentile. It is clear that the Book of Mormon was to come forth "by way of the Gentile" (Title Page). Nephi[1] wrote, "They [the Gentiles] shall carry them [the words of the book] forth unto the remnant of our seed" (2 Ne. 30:3; Morm. 5:12–15). The Book of Mormon came forth at the hand of the Gentiles in that Joseph Smith and those who labored with him were citizens of a Gentile nation, as is the army of missionaries who are destined to go forth to testify of it. Thus, in a cultural/political context Joseph Smith could be considered a Gentile, even though he was of Israelite ancestry (cf. 2 Ne. 33:8; D&C 109:60).

In his visit to the Nephites, the Savior also foreshadowed Joseph Smith's ministry. Isaiah had spoken of a servant of the Lord who would be exalted and extolled, yet whose "visage" would be more marred than that of any man. This prophecy, which applied to Christ and the manner in which he would be sustained and exalted by his Father, on the one hand, and maligned and disparaged, "marred, more than any man," on the other, was applied anew by the Savior to Joseph Smith (3 Ne. 20:43–45 // Isa.

52:13–15). Similarly, Moroni[2] told the youthful Joseph that his name would be had for good and evil among every nation, kindred, tongue, and people (JS–H 1:33). And again, while a captive in the Liberty Jail, the Lord told him, "The ends of the earth shall inquire after thy name, and fools shall have thee in derision, and hell shall rage against thee; while the pure in heart, and the wise, and the noble, and the virtuous, shall seek counsel, and authority, and blessings constantly from under thy hand" (D&C 122:1–2). The Savior also quoted some text from the book of Habakkuk that speaks of Israel scattered among the heathen and of a servant of the Lord who would "work a work, which shall be a great and a marvelous work among them; and there shall be among them those who will not believe it, although a man shall declare it unto them" (3 Ne. 21:9; Hab. 1:5). The man, or servant of the Lord, as he is called, is to enjoy the protection of heaven and though he would be "marred," the Lord said he would "heal him." The Lord further said, "Whosoever will not believe in my words, who am Jesus Christ, which the Father shall cause him to bring forth unto the Gentiles . . . shall be cut off from among my people who are of the covenant" (3 Ne. 21:9–11).

In addition to these prophecies, the Book of Mormon contains Moroni[2]'s testimony of Joseph Smith and his work. Moroni wrote that the coming forth of the Book of Mormon could only be "done by the power of God" and, he declared, "blessed be he that shall bring this thing to light" (Morm. 8:14–16). Moroni also explained that the prayers of the faithful Saints among Book of Mormon peoples "were also in behalf of him that the Lord should suffer to bring these things forth" (Morm. 8:23–25). Further, he gave instructions directly to Joseph Smith regarding the sealed portion of the record and the three special witnesses to whom he would be permitted to show the plates (Ether 5).

Clearly, Joseph Smith and his work as the prophet of the Restoration was known, prophesied of, and prayed for by prophets and faithful Saints in Book of Mormon times.

See also Bible, what it says about the Book of Mormon; Choice seer; Isaiah chapter reviews (2 Ne. 21 // Isa. 11; 2 Ne. 26:6, 15–18; 27 // Isa. 29); Smith, Joseph, Jr.

JFM

Snare *See* Appendix C.

Snatch *See* Appendix C.

Sojourn *See* Appendix C.

Solomon Son and successor of the biblical king David (1 Kgs. 1:30). Solomon was born to Bathsheba after the death of the child of David's adultery with her (2 Sam. 12:24). Solomon reigned over united Israel (ca. 971–931 B.C.). The military campaigns of David allowed Solomon to rule in relative peace, and his reign became legendary as a golden age in Israel's history (3 Ne. 13:29). When the Lord appeared to Solomon in a dream and offered to bless him with whatever he asked, Solomon requested "an understanding heart to judge thy people" (1 Kgs. 3:9). The Lord granted him an understanding heart plus riches and honor (1 Kgs. 3:12–13). The Lord also granted Solomon the privilege of building the temple in Jerusalem (2 Sam. 7:12–13; 1 Kgs. 5:5). Solomon's temple was sumptuous in every respect: formed of cut stone with cedar walls, all overlaid with gold (1 Kgs. 6; the temple of Nephi[1] was "after the manner of the temple of Solomon save it were not built of so many precious things"; 2 Ne. 5:16; *see* model of Solomon's temple, page 753). The Lord accepted Solomon's temple and promised Solomon a long posterity on the throne if he lived uprightly. If he abandoned the commandments and served other gods, his kingdom would be cut off (1 Kgs. 9:1–9). Solomon had a royal harem with seven hundred wives and three hundred CONCUBINES, following the custom of his time (1 Kgs. 11:3). The Lord approved of the plural marriages of Solomon and others "from the beginning of creation," except when they received wives not given by him (D&C 132:38). Solomon "loved many strange women," including the daughter of Pharaoh and women of other nations forbidden to Israelites for marriage: Moabites, Ammonites, Edomites, Zidonians, and Hittites. The Lord had warned that "surely they will turn away your heart after their gods"

(1 Kgs. 11:1–2). These wives brought their idolatries into Solomon's household and turned his heart from the Lord. Undoubtedly, the Lord referred to such when he said that the marriages of David and Solomon were abominable before him (Jacob 2:24). For the Book of Mormon peoples, monogamy was the Lord's law given through Lehi[1] (Jacob 2:34), but certain wicked Nephites justified whoredoms by recalling the many wives and concubines of David and Solomon (Jacob 1:15; 2:23). The prophet Jacob[2] told them that they had "broken the hearts of [their] tender wives, and lost the confidence of [their] children" (Jacob 2:35).

See also Plural marriage; Temples.

RAC

Son of perdition There are two references to "the son of perdition": one, pointing to Judas Iscariot (3 Ne. 27:32; Matt. 26:14–16; John 17:12); the other, a more vague reference indicating that those who, "to get gain," claim "there can be no miracle wrought by Jesus Christ" will "become like unto the son of perdition, for whom there was no mercy" (3 Ne. 29:7). In this instance "the son of perdition" could again refer to Judas, or it may refer to the devil himself (2 Thes. 2:3; D&C 76:25–35).

Although the phrase "sons of perdition" is not used in the Book of Mormon, the concept that there are "children of the devil" who choose to follow him completely and permanently, and who will suffer the same ultimate fate, is well represented (e.g., 1 Ne. 14:3; 2 Ne. 9:15–16; 28:22–23; Mosiah 2:36–38; 3:23–27; Alma 12:12–18; 40:13–14; Hel. 14:17–18; cf. D&C 76:31–48).

LED

Song of redeeming love Phrase used to describe the joy of redemption through Christ. Singing is such a natural expression of inner feeling that often it bursts forth spontaneously. Thus Alma[2] asked his hearers if they "have felt to sing the song of redeeming love" (Alma 5:26).

Singing is an effective form of communicating gratitude, praise, worship, and adoration of man for God. The Lord said his "soul delighteth in the song of the heart; yea, the song of the righteous is a prayer unto me, and it shall be answered with a blessing" (D&C 25:12). Because of their repentance, Ammon[2]'s converts, by the thousands, were "loosed from the pains of hell" and were "brought to sing redeeming love" (Alma 26:13). After defeating the Gadianton robbers, a multitude of Nephites "did break forth, all as one, in singing, and praising their God for the great thing which he had done for them" (3 Ne. 4:31; cf. 1 Ne. 1:8; 21:13; 2 Ne. 8:11; Mosiah 2:28; Alma 26:8; Ether 6:9; Rev. 5:9; D&C 84:98–102; 133:56).

RJM

Sorcery, witchcraft, magic Methods to gain supernatural powers or knowledge, to know the future or gain control over events, from sources other than the Lord, particularly from Satan. In the Book of Mormon "sorceries, and witchcrafts, and magics" are used to describe these practices (Morm. 1:19). The Bible describes many categories of those who pursue these activities, including one "that useth divination," "observer of times," "enchanter," "witch," "charmer," "consulter with familiar spirits," "wizard," and "necromancer." The law of Moses condemned such as an "abomination unto the Lord" (Deut. 18:9–14) and defined witchcraft as a capital offense (Ex. 22:18).

There are three references to sorcery in the Book of Mormon: nonmembers of the Church who practiced sorcery in the days of Alma the Younger (Alma 1:32); the sorcerers in the last days against whom God will be a swift witness (3 Ne. 24:5 // Mal. 3:5); and the sorceries, witchcrafts, and magics in Mormon's day that manifested "the power of the evil one" (Morm. 1:19). There are many examples of sorcery in the Bible, such as Pharaoh's sorcerers who turned rods into snakes (Ex. 7:11–12) and the sorcerers Nebuchadnezzar called on to interpret his dream (Dan. 2:2). The Canaanites were destroyed for fostering certain kinds of sorcery (Deut. 18:9–12), and Isaiah prophesied that abundant sorceries would contribute to Babylon's fall (Isa. 47:9, 12–14). At the Second Coming sorcerers will be destroyed (3 Ne. 24:5 // Mal. 3:5), will be cast into hell (D&C 63:17), and will eventually inherit the telestial kingdom (D&C 76:103).

There are two references to witchcraft in the Book of Mormon. Jesus foretold of a latter-day destruction of wickedness including "witchcrafts" (3 Ne. 21:16 // Micah 5:12–13), and Mormon said that in his day "sorceries, and witchcrafts, and magics; and the power of the evil one was wrought upon all the face of the land" (Morm. 1:19). Witchcraft is also attested in the Old Testament. Saul visited the witch of Endor, a woman that had a "familiar spirit" (1 Sam. 28:7–25); Jehu slew Joram for perpetuating the witchcrafts of his mother Jezebel (2 Kgs. 9:22–24); and king Manasseh was condemned for using witchcraft (2 Chr. 33:6). In the New Testament, witchcraft is included as one of the "works of the flesh" (Gal. 5:19–20).

Magic is specifically mentioned in the Book of Mormon in two passages in the writings of Mormon. He recorded that in his time "there were sorceries, and witchcrafts, and magics" (Morm. 1:19) and that "no man could keep that which was his own, for the thieves, and the robbers, and the murderers, and the magic art, and the witchcraft which was in the land" (Morm. 2:10–11). Mormon noted that the people of his day experienced the fulfillment of the prophecy of Samuel the Lamanite (Morm. 2:10) that they would hide up their treasures in the earth and not be able to find them again (Hel. 13:17–23; cf. 12:18–20). In the Old Testament, Pharaoh summoned his magicians at the time of Joseph[1] (Gen. 41:8, 24), Pharaoh and his magicians contested against Moses (Ex. 7:11, 22; 8:7, 18–19; 9:11), and Nebuchadnezzar called for his magicians to interpret his dream (Dan. 2:2, 27; 4:7, 9).

See also Familiar spirit.

KHM

Soul Used in several contexts in the Book of Mormon, *soul* in general refers to an individual person, as in "every soul had cause to mourn" (Alma 4:3), or "there had not one soul of them fallen to the earth" (Alma 56:56). *Soul* also appears to refer to one's innermost self or the very center of one's being, as in "my soul will rejoice in thee, my God" (2 Ne. 4:30), "my soul grieveth because of mine iniquities" (2 Ne. 4:17), "my soul hungered" (Enos 1:4), or "I did pour out my whole soul unto God" (Enos 1:9). Both Nephi[1] and Alma[2] in some instances used the words *soul* and *spirit* synonymously, as in "for the things which some men esteem to be of great worth, both to the body and soul" (1 Ne. 19:7; 15:31; cf. 2 Ne. 20:18), or, "I admit it may be termed a resurrection, the raising of the spirit or the soul and their consignation to happiness or misery" (Alma 40:15, 18, 21, 23; 41:2; 29:16).

In a more technical sense, the Lord revealed through the Prophet Joseph Smith that "the spirit and the body are the soul of man" (D&C 88:15). In Book of Mormon references that do not specify otherwise, the word *soul* can be understood in light of this truth.

DAW

Spaulding theory A belief promoted by some critics of Joseph Smith that an early nineteenth-century unpublished novel, "Manuscript Found," by Solomon Spaulding, is a source for the Book of Mormon.

Solomon Spaulding of Connecticut (1761–1816) was a Revolutionary War veteran, a graduate of Dartmouth College, and a former minister. In 1812 he drafted a story about a group of Romans who arrived in North America in the fourth century A.D. The story tells that in an attempt to sail from Italy to England they were blown off course to the shores of the New World. Their first encounters with Native Americans are described, as are their early efforts to organize themselves and settle into their new life with no hope of ever returning home. The story soon shifts its emphasis from the Roman colony to the natives, discussing many of their institutions and customs and giving an overview of their history. It tells of two friendly nations whose peace was shattered by the (voluntary) abduction of a beautiful princess by a foreign prince and the efforts of her father and villainous fiance to bring her home. At the end of the manuscript, the villain is dead and the heroes are vindicated.

Spaulding's manuscript is a first and only draft that was not published in his lifetime.

While it has some charm and wit, it has never been considered to have much literary merit. Its claim to fame comes solely from the fact that in 1834 a disaffected and excommunicated Latter-day Saint, Philastus Hurlbut, invented the "Spaulding theory," the idea that Joseph Smith obtained the story line of the Book of Mormon from Spaulding's novel. Hurlbut's theory was published that year in *Mormonism Unvailed,* by E. D. Howe.

The manuscript was lost from public view in the 1830s when Howe's papers were purchased by L. L. Rice. For the next fifty years, the Spaulding theory was a common anti-Mormon idea. Its popularity waned, however, when the manuscript resurfaced in 1884 in Honolulu, and readers were able to observe that Spaulding's novel had nothing in common with the Book of Mormon. It has almost no religious content, the language is utterly unlike that of the Book of Mormon, the story lines bear no resemblance, and no historical connection can be established between Joseph Smith and the manuscript. Today, the Spaulding theory has been all but abandoned, and very few critics of the Latter-day Saint faith view it as a plausible explanation for the origin of the Book of Mormon.

The manuscript is housed in the archives at Oberlin College in Oberlin, Ohio. It was published in 1885 by the RLDS Church (now known as Community of Christ) and in 1886 by The Church of Jesus Christ of Latter-day Saints. An unedited facsimile transcription was published in 1996 by the Religious Studies Center at Brigham Young University.

BIBLIOGRAPHY

Spaulding, Solomon. *Manuscript Found: The Complete Original "Spaulding Manuscript."* Edited by Kent P. Jackson. Provo, Utah: BYU Religious Studies Center, 1997.

KPJ

Spirit, body of my *See* Body of my spirit.

Spirit of Christ *See* Light of Christ.

Spirit of prophecy and the spirit of revelation The Spirit of God bearing witness of the truth and inspiring one's thoughts, feelings, words, and actions. The terms "spirit of revelation" and "spirit of prophecy" are often linked, primarily as an affirmation that the revelatory gifts of God rest upon his servants and his work (e.g., Alma 4:20; 8:24; 9:21; 23:6; 43:2). The title page of the Book of Mormon declares that the book was written "by the spirit of prophecy and of revelation." The Lord's servants taught "according to the spirit of revelation and prophecy" and righteous military leaders led according to that same spirit (Alma 8:24; 23:6; 43:2; 3 Ne. 3:19). Through prayer and fasting, the four sons of Mosiah[2] obtained "the spirit of prophecy, and the spirit of revelation," which they exercised by teaching "with power and authority of God" (Alma 17:3). When righteous, the Nephites as a people enjoyed "the spirit of prophecy, and the spirit of revelation," but when their hearts became set on riches, pride and wickedness caused them to "disbelieve" and deny these gifts (Alma 9:21; Hel. 4:12; 4:23).

Although at times referred to individually, the "spirit of revelation" and the "spirit of prophecy" are inseparably linked, as prophecy is one of the manifestations of REVELATION. It was by the "spirit of revelation" that Alma[2] prophesied the Nephites' eventual apostasy four hundred years after the appearance of Christ (Alma 45:10). He attributed his own conviction of the gospel's truth to the "spirit of revelation," and his testimony concerning the words spoken "by our fathers concerning the things which are to come" (i.e., the coming of Christ) to the "spirit of prophecy" (Alma 5:44–48; cf. 13:26). Through "the spirit of prophecy," the gospel was taught (Alma 6:8), testimonies were strengthened (Jacob 4:6), and future events were foretold—including the coming of Christ (Jacob 1:6; Alma 4:13; 13:26; 25:16), the restoration of Israel (2 Ne. 25:4), the movements of Lamanite armies (Alma 16:5–6), and the consequences awaiting the obedient and disobedient (Alma 3:26–27; 37:15–17). It also enabled Alma and Amulek to discern the thoughts and intents of Zeezrom's heart (Alma 12:7).

Book of Mormon teachings are in harmony with those of John the Revelator and Joseph Smith, who asserted that "the testimony of Jesus is the spirit of prophecy" (Rev. 19:10; Smith,

119, 160, 265, 269, 300, 312, 315). They also illustrate the Lord's definition of the spirit of revelation: "Yea, behold, I will tell you in your mind and in your heart, by the Holy Ghost, which shall come upon you and which shall dwell in your heart. Now, behold, this is the spirit of revelation" (D&C 8:2–3).

See also Prophecy in the Book of Mormon.

BIBLIOGRAPHY

Smith, Joseph. *Teachings of the Prophet Joseph Smith.* Selected by Joseph Fielding Smith. Salt Lake City: Deseret Book, 1976.

BAV

Spirit of the Lord Term used in reference to (1) the power of God and (2) the HOLY GHOST as a personage of spirit. Other terms that mean essentially the same as "Spirit of the Lord" include "the Spirit" (1 Ne. 1:7–8; 22:2; Jacob 4:13, 15, 18; Alma 22:1; Hel.10:16–17; Moro. 6:9; 8:28); "the Holy Spirit" (2 Ne. 33:2; Jacob 6:8; Mosiah 3:19; Alma 7:16; 11:44); "the Spirit of God" (1 Ne. 13:12–13; 17:47, 52; 19:12; Alma 5:47; 24:30; 38:6; 3 Ne. 7:21–22); "his Spirit" (1 Ne. 20:16; Jacob 7:8; Mosiah 4:20; 5:3; 18:10; Alma 8:10; 12:3; 16:16; Hel. 6:36; Moro. 4:3; 5:2); "his Holy Spirit" (1 Ne. 2:17; 2 Ne. 2:28; Alma 5:46; Moro. 8:23); "Holy Spirit of God" (Alma 5:46; Hel. 5:45); "my Spirit" (Hel. 13:8; 3 Ne. 18:7, 11; Ether 2:15; 4:11); "the spirit of revelation," "the spirit of prophecy" (e.g., Alma 9:21; 17:3); "light of Christ" (Moro. 7:18–19); and "the Spirit of Christ" (Moro. 7:16; 10:17).

The power of God

Generally, "the Spirit of the Lord" and the other terms meaning the same thing refer to the "power of God" that "proceedeth forth from the presence of God to fill the immensity of space" by which God brings about his eternal purposes—the power by which he creates, governs, gives light and life, and enlightens minds (D&C 88:6–13). It is the power used by the Holy Ghost in carrying out his role of testifying of the Father and the Son and dispensing the gifts of the Spirit (2 Ne. 31:18; Moro. 10:17; Smith, 1:50–54; Talmage, 159–63; McConkie, 69–70). The Spirit of the Lord is manifested in many ways and at many levels to mankind on the earth: a measure of the Spirit of the Lord is given to all men to help them discern good from evil and draw them toward God (Moro. 7:12–19). Those who seek, ponder, and pray will receive a testimony of Christ and his gospel by this power (Moro. 10:3–5). Those who repent and are baptized will be forgiven of their sins, spiritually quickened, and receive the right to the companionship of the Holy Ghost and the gifts of the Spirit on a regular basis (2 Ne. 31:12–17; 3 Ne. 27:20; Morm. 9:7–8, 23–24). The Spirit of the Lord gives God's servants power to see visions (1 Ne. 1:8), preach the truth (Alma 43:2), know the thoughts of others (Alma 12:3), and be protected from their enemies (Hel. 16:2).

The Holy Ghost as a personage of spirit

In at least one instance, the "Spirit of the Lord" refers to a spirit personage. Nephi[1] told of seeing the Spirit of the Lord and conversing with him: "For I spake unto him as a man speaketh; for I beheld that he was in the form of a man; yet nevertheless, I knew that it was the Spirit of the Lord; and he spake unto me as a man speaketh with another" (1 Ne. 11:11). After explaining that "the Spirit of the Lord" and "the Holy Ghost" are synonyms, Elder James E. Talmage wrote of Nephi's experience: "That the Spirit of the Lord is capable of manifesting Himself in the form and figure of man, is indicated by the wonderful interview between the Spirit and Nephi, in which He revealed Himself to the prophet, questioned him concerning his desires and belief, instructed him in the things of God, speaking face to face with the man. . . . However, the Holy Ghost does not possess a body of flesh and bones, as do both the Father and the Son, but is a personage of spirit" (159–60; cf. Romney, 131).

See also Light of Christ; Spirit of prophecy and the spirit of revelation.

BIBLIOGRAPHY

McConkie, Bruce R. *A New Witness for the Articles of Faith.* Salt Lake City: Deseret Book, 1985.

Romney, Marion G. Conference Report, April 1974.

Smith, Joseph Fielding. *Doctrines of Salvation.* Compiled by Bruce R. McConkie. 3 vols. Salt Lake City: Bookcraft, 1954–56.

Talmage, James E. *Articles of Faith.* London: The Church of Jesus Christ of Latter-day Saints, 1924.

LED

Spirit world Although the term "spirit world" is not used in the Book of Mormon, the concept of spirits living in some state between death and resurrection is contained therein (2 Ne. 9:12–13; Moro. 10:34). Alma[2] affirmed that at death "the spirits of all men, whether they be good or evil, are taken home to that God who gave them life" (Alma 40:11). Joseph Fielding Smith explained that "'taken home to God,' simply means that their mortal existence has come to an end, and they have returned to the world of spirits" (2:85), or the postearth spirit world to which all go at death. Alma said the righteous spirits are received into a "state of happiness" called "paradise," whereas the spirits of the wicked are cast into "outer darkness," in which states they remain "until the time of their resurrection" (Alma 40:12–14). According to Alma's record, at the resurrection the righteous will "shine forth in the kingdom of God," and the wicked will be "cast out . . . and they drink the dregs of a bitter cup" (Alma 40:25–26). The Book of Mormon does not speak of degrees of peace and happiness in PARADISE before the resurrection or in the kingdom of God after the resurrection, nor does it speak of degrees of suffering in HELL, or OUTER DARKNESS, in the spirit world or after the resurrection. The Book of Mormon consistently speaks of just two options: Christ or Satan; freedom or captivity; paradise or outer darkness; saved or damned. With the restoration of the gospel through the Prophet Joseph Smith, the Lord has given added light on these matters. Though the wicked will indeed be consigned to hell between death and the resurrection, the light of the gospel of Jesus Christ will be available to them there: "The dead who repent will be redeemed, through obedience to the ordinances of the house of God, and after they have paid the penalty of their transgressions, and are washed clean, shall receive a reward according to their works, for they are heirs of salvation" (D&C 138:58–59). All except the sons of perdition will be delivered from hell and darkness and received into a kingdom of glory—telestial, terrestrial, or celestial, depending upon what law they have proven willing and able to abide (D&C 76; 88:22–32; 138).

BIBLIOGRAPHY

Smith, Joseph Fielding. *Answers to Gospel Questions.* Compiled by Joseph Fielding Smith Jr. 5 vols. Salt Lake City: Deseret Book, 1957–66.

LED

Spiritual Term used in several contexts in the Book of Mormon, all referring to a realm or condition distinct from TEMPORAL, or worldly, or natural. Several references point to this general distinction (1 Ne. 6:3–6; 15:32–33; 22:3; Jacob 4:8; Alma 26:21–22; Hel. 14:16).

A most significant use of the term "spiritual" has to do with the nature of the resurrected physical body in contrast to that of the mortal body. After stating that the physical body will rise from the dead with every limb and joint, without so much as the loss of one hair of the head (Alma 11:43–44), Amulek explained the resurrected state: "This mortal body is raised to an immortal body, that is from death, even from the first death unto life, that they can die no more; their spirits uniting with their bodies, never to be divided; thus the whole becoming spiritual and immortal" (Alma 11:45). Latter-day revelation affirms that resurrected personages have "bodies of flesh and bones" (D&C 129:1) and that those bodies are "as tangible as man's" (D&C 130:22). Joseph Smith explained, however, that resurrected bodies are "quickened by the Spirit" and that "there will be no blood" in them (Smith, 367). Resurrected, immortal bodies quickened by spirit rather than by blood are therefore said to be "spiritual." This specialized usage is confirmed in Doctrine and Covenants 88:27–28 and clarifies Paul's use of "spiritual" when he wrote of the resurrection (1 Cor. 15:42–45). It also clarifies Paul's statement that "flesh and blood cannot inherit the kingdom of God" (1 Cor. 15:50). Without the help of the Book of Mormon and Doctrine and Covenants, Paul's words might be mistaken to mean that a resurrected body lacks physical properties.

"Spiritual" is also used to designate a change

from "natural man" status to becoming sons and daughters of Jesus Christ, being spiritually born of him because of their faith, repentance, and baptism (Mosiah 3:19; 5:7; 27:25–28; Alma 5:14). This spiritual birth overcomes a sinful condition designated as "spiritual death," meaning being dead "as to things pertaining unto righteousness" (Alma 12:16, 32; 40:26). One who is spiritually dead is in a condition of sinfulness, "cut off from the presence of the Lord" (2 Ne. 9:6; Alma 42:9), in a "state of nature, . . . without God in the world," having "gone contrary to the nature of God" (Alma 41:11). This condition is also spoken of as "hell" (2 Ne. 9:12), and as the "chains of hell" (Alma 5:7, 9–10). That part of mankind's SPIRITUAL DEATH that resulted from the Fall is covered fully by the Atonement. That part of spiritual death brought about by man's own disobedience can also be overcome through the Atonement, "by obedience to the laws and ordinances of the Gospel" (A of F 3). Those who ultimately refuse to repent, rejecting the cleansing power of the Atonement, will suffer a permanent spiritual death, sometimes called a "second death," having "suffered themselves through the power of the devil to be overcome" (Hel. 14:18; D&C 76:31; 2 Ne. 9:10–19, 22–26; Mosiah 2:36–41; Alma 11:40–41; 12:12–18; 40:26; 42:7–24; Hel. 14:16–19; Morm. 9:12–14; cf. D&C 29:41–45; 76:30–49). They are known as "sons of perdition" (D&C 76:32).

BIBLIOGRAPHY

Smith, Joseph. *Teachings of the Prophet Joseph Smith*. Selected by Joseph Fielding Smith. Salt Lake City: Deseret Book, 1976.

RJM

Spiritual death To die as to "things pertaining unto righteousness," to be "cut off from the presence of the Lord," to experience HELL (Alma 12:12–18; 40:26; 2 Ne. 9:6–12; cf. D&C 29:41).

By virtue of Adam's fall, all his posterity are subject to spiritual death—"the first death" (Hel. 14:16), being separated from their divine Father. This spiritual death would have been endless were it not for Christ and his atoning sacrifice. Jacob[2] explained, "Because man became fallen they were cut off from the presence of the Lord. Wherefore, it must needs be an infinite atonement—save it should be an infinite atonement . . . our spirits must become subject to that angel who fell from before the presence of the Eternal God. . . . And our spirits must have become like unto him, and we become devils, angels to a devil, to be shut out from the presence of our God, and to remain with the father of lies, in misery, like unto himself" (2 Ne. 9:6–9). Because of Christ's atonement, however, "hell must deliver up its captive spirits, and the grave must deliver up its captive bodies, and the bodies and the spirits of men will be restored one to the other" (2 Ne. 9:12). Jacob, Alma[2], Samuel the Lamanite, and Moroni[2] all taught that "the resurrection of the dead bringeth back men into the presence of God; and thus they are restored into his presence, to be judged according to their works" (Alma 42:23; cf. 2 Ne. 2:10; 9:15, 26; Alma 40:21; Hel. 14:15–17; Morm. 9:13). Hence, the atonement of Christ overcomes the spiritual death which came as a result of the Fall, leaving mankind responsible for whatever measure of spiritual death they brought upon themselves through their own sins (A of F 2). At the time of final judgment, those who are free from sin, by virtue of the atonement of Christ and compliance with the laws of God, will be rewarded according to their works. Those who are "filthy still," those who utterly refuse to submit to Christ, and insist on being a law unto themselves, will suffer "again a spiritual death, yea, a second death, for they are cut off again as to things pertaining to righteousness" (Hel. 14:18–19). They will be cast out of the presence of the Lord to dwell with the devil and his angels, "chained down to an everlasting destruction" (Alma 12:12–18, 32; 2 Ne. 9:16; Jacob 3:11; Alma 13:30; 40:26; D&C 88:34–35). In the vision of the degrees of glory, Joseph Smith learned, "These are they who shall go away into the lake of fire and brimstone, with the devil and his angels," for they are "the only ones on whom the second death shall have any power" (D&C 76:36–38).

See also Cut off; Damnation; Fall of Adam and Eve, the; Judgment, the; Lake of fire and brimstone; Night of darkness.

JFM

Spiritual gifts Spiritual abilities, powers, or qualities given by the grace of God to receptive individuals for the blessing and benefit of all humanity. The gifts of the Spirit include, but are not limited to, the gifts of teaching wisdom and knowledge, great FAITH, healings, MIRACLES, prophecy, beholding of angels and MINISTERING SPIRITS, tongues, interpretation of tongues, and CHARITY (Moro. 10:8–21; 7:48; cf. D&C 46:12–16; 1 Cor. 12:4–10). In a broader application "fruit of the Spirit" as listed by Paul in his letter to the Galatians (Gal. 5:22–23), as well as the many spiritual blessings evident in the lives of those who have been BORN AGAIN, may also be considered gifts of the Spirit (Mosiah 4:2–3; 5:2–5; Alma 5:12–14, 26; 58:11; Moro. 10:20–23).

The Book of Mormon teaches about spiritual gifts through a discourse by Moroni[2] (Moro. 10:8–25) and through numerous examples of individuals who possessed and used these gifts in their ministries. Moroni's teachings parallel both the apostle Paul's writings in 1 Corinthians 12:4–12 and the revelation in Doctrine and Covenants 46:8–29. Moroni taught that spiritual gifts are conveyed by "the Spirit of God unto men, to profit them" (Moro. 10:8), that "there are different ways that these gifts are administered" to various individuals according to the will of God (Moro. 10:8–17; cf. D&C 46:11–25), that individuals should "deny not the gifts of God" (Moro. 10:8), that those who do deny these gifts know "not the gospel of Christ" (Morm. 9:8; cf. 3 Ne. 29:6), and that one should "lay hold upon every good gift, and touch not the evil gift, nor the unclean thing"—a warning against accepting the offerings or enticements of Satan and his followers (Moro. 10:30; cf. Alma 5:57; 3 Ne. 20:41). Paul taught similar truths and further exhorted all to seek "earnestly the best gifts" (1 Cor. 12:31). It was revealed to Joseph Smith that as one asks for spiritual gifts according to the will of God, he will receive them, and that "unto some it may be given to have all those gifts, that there may be a head" (D&C 46:26–30).

Moroni chose to emphasize the importance of the gift of charity, which he defined as "the pure love of Christ" (Moro. 7:47; cf. 1 Cor. 13), a gift without which, "ye can in nowise be saved in the kingdom of God" (Moro. 10:21). The gift of "the beholding of angels and ministering spirits" (Moro. 10:14)—a gift exhibited abundantly in the dramatic unfolding events of the Restoration (e.g., D&C 13; 27; 110; Rev. 14:6)—is unique to the Book of Mormon list of spiritual gifts.

Examples of the manifestation of spiritual gifts can be seen throughout the Book of Mormon narrative. For example, Ammon[2], being "wise, yet harmless," demonstrated the gift of wisdom as he instructed king Lamoni (Alma 18:22; cf. 1 Kgs. 3:9, 15); the brother of Jared[1] had the gift of great faith as he saw first the finger of the Lord and then the Lord himself (Ether 3:9, 15; cf. Alma 14:26–27); Alma[2] exhibited the gift of healing as he raised Zeezrom from a burning fever and restored him to health (Alma 15:10; cf. Acts 3:1–7); Nephi[2] used the gift of prophecy as he foretold the murder of the chief judge and the sequence of events that would follow (Hel. 8:27; cf. Acts 11:27–30; D&C 87:1–2); the Nephite faithful at the temple in Bountiful[2] had the gift of the beholding of angels as their children received heavenly visitors during Christ's ministry (3 Ne. 17; cf. John 20:11–13; Morm. 8:11); and Mormon illustrated the gift of charity as he loved his people so deeply that he pleaded for them before the Lord, even though they themselves refused to repent (Morm. 3:12; cf. 1 Ne. 7:21; Mosiah 28:3).

KJW

Spokesman One who would assist in proclaiming God's word in the latter days. The Lord told Joseph[1] who was sold into Egypt that he would raise up a "CHOICE SEER" from among his descendants, and that he would provide a "spokesman" to assist him (2 Ne. 3:6, 18). Latter-day Saints traditionally have identified Joseph Smith as this choice seer and either of two of his close associates as the prophesied spokesman: Sidney Rigdon, whom the Lord called as "a spokesman unto this people" (D&C 100:9–11), or perhaps Oliver Cowdery (D&C 21:12; 28:3). Elder Bruce R. McConkie taught that the Prophet Joseph Smith functioned as a latter-day spokesman (425–26).

BIBLIOGRAPHY

McConkie, Bruce R. *A New Witness for the Articles of Faith.* Salt Lake City: Deseret Book, 1985.

ROC

Spurn *See* Appendix C.

Standard *See* Ensign.

Steadfastness *See* Appendix C.

Steel *See* Metals of the Book of Mormon.

Stela 5 Carved stone monument (stela) containing one of the most complex depictions of the tree of life/world tree ever discovered and one of the earliest in Mesoamerica. Stela 5 is one of 164 sculptures discovered at Izapa, an ancient temple center located near the Pacific coast on the southern tip of Mexico. It was first reported in 1943 following a Smithsonian–National Geographic expedition in 1941. Stela 5 belongs to a new culture that emerged in the Guatemala highlands and nearby Pacific coast during the Late Formative era between about 300 B.C. and the time of Christ, after the Olmec civilization. Izapa is the only temple center of the time with most of its monuments still intact. Thus it assumes great importance for research in Izapan culture. Stela 5 (fig. 1) is the optimum achievement of some 34 related Izapan style carvings at this site, composed in a sophisticated narrative style with a wealth of ideographic symbols in complex relations, comparable to ancient Egyptian art. Latter-day Saint interest in Stela 5 began in the 1950s when Brigham Young University archaeology professor M. Wells

Fig. 1. Izapa Stela 5; 1964 photograph by V. Garth Norman; © V. Garth Norman. The features of figures in the line drawing (fig. 2) are visible in this photo and other early New World Archaeological Foundation project photos as analyzed by Norman (1973, 1976) and Lowe (1982). Decades of weathering have obscured some fine details that are now hard to distinguish on the stone.

STELA 5

Jakeman ("Unusual"; "Stela 5") compared it to Lehi[1]'s vision of the tree of life (1 Ne. 8).

From 1961 to 1982 the BYU New World Archaeological Foundation's Izapa project produced photos and drawings of thirty-five major sculptures. Full analytical descriptions and interpretive reports were completed about the ruins and related antiquities (Norman, "Izapa, Part 1"; "Izapa, Part 2"; "Astronomical"; Lowe et al.). From these studies scholars have concluded that Izapa was one of the earliest Mesoamerican ceremonial centers with a recognizable priesthood and a formalized religion (Bernal, 34) and that the Izapa priesthood served the philosophical and religious needs of the region that included calendrical ritual and lunar worship for productivity (Adams, 88–93).

Stela 5 was set up along with other stelae and altars at the base of earthen mounds in plaza arrangements for temple instruction and worship. The plazas, mounds, and sculptures were oriented astronomically on sun, moon, and Venus cycles for symbolic and calendric functions. Each monument is dedicated to a different lunar month in the yearly life cycle, with the full cycle recreated on Stela 5 in the twelfth month. The annual calendar cycle can be compared to the human life cycle on the monuments, expressing man's creation origin, mortal road of life, and immortal destiny—themes similar to those taught in Lehi's vision of the tree of life.

An inventory of Stela 5 reveals the complex quality and quantity of narrative relationships in this masterwork. There are more than a hundred items, including gods, humans, animals, plants, tools, and compound ideographic symbols. The chiastic composition on Stela 5 centers on the great tree of life/world tree with twenty-two figures, including thirteen humans composed in parallel fashion on opposite sides of the tree. Six humans seated on the ground panel compare to the ancestral family of Izapan civilization as related in the *Popol Vuh,* sacred book of the Quiche Maya, and have been compared to Lehi's family in the Book of Mormon account. They are engaged in worshipful instruction. A sacrifice and burnt offering on the left is presided over by a high priest (a figure which has been compared to Lehi) who instructs an initiate over an incense burner. The parallel priest-king on the right (a figure which has been compared to Nephi) similarly instructs an initiate.

The subjects of instruction are found in the complicated highly symbolic and imaginative scenes above that center on two floating gods or angels with bird masks. These appear to be guardian spirits of the tree of life—a theme common in the ancient Near East that was perpetuated in Mayan sculpture at Palenque and in Mayan and Mixtec codices. Like Stela 5, at least six other Izapa stelae are oriented northward and show winged gods symbolically descending from and ascending to the imposing Tacana mountain top that symbolizes the heavenly realm of the gods in Mesoamerican tradition. The ultimate focus of the creation, road-of-life story on Stela 5 is the man brought to the tree center (fig. 2, no. 13) by two gods. Here he partakes of the fruit and appears to be figuratively reborn from the tree of life like a human branch (cf. Alma 32).

In a broader sense, the Izapa temple appears to be a cosmological model of the universe, also characteristic of ancient temples in the Old World. Stela 5 is set at the center of the universe, so to speak, oriented with Stela 23 to sunrise on the horizon zenith date of August 13 (related to the base date of the Mesoamerican calendar), and also set on a line of sculptures between the winter solstice sunrise (December 21) and summer solstice sunset (June 21). Accordingly, the seed of life planted at new year (autumn equinox, September 21) germinates and progresses through the yearly life cycle to reach its ultimate maturity through the tree of life bearing fruit on Stela 5, starting the last month of the year on the zenith date. This symbolized the ultimate destiny of the human spirit reborn from the tree of life as man (no. 13) partakes of the divine fruit and ascends up the tree of life into the heavenly Tamoanchan-Tulan paradise of Mesoamerican tradition signified by the upper break of the tree trunk.

The accompanying table lists possible cognates between Stela 5 and Lehi's vision of the tree of life from the author's studies. The main features (tree, river, path, and rod) along with Lehi's family were first analyzed by Jakeman ("Unusual"; "Stela 5"). Alhough such tentative

Fig. 2. Izapa Stela 5; 1999 update of New World Archaeological Foundation photograph line drawing by V. Garth Norman (1973); © V. Garth Norman. See accompanying table for numbered possible parallels to Lehi's vision of the tree of life. Thirteen new carved details confirmed by studies since 1976 by G. Norman (5), P. Culbert (2), R. Williams (1), and Clark-Moreno (5) have been added.

STELA 5

parallels between the vision of the tree of life and Stela 5 are interesting, as yet published data have been inconclusive and will continue to be until researchers gain a more complete picture of Izapan culture. Since Jakeman, other studies have been made, some supportive of the tree of life/Lehi's dream thesis (e.g., Wirth, 65–75), and others divergent (e.g., Clark, 22–33).

See also Archaeology; Quetzalcoatl; Transoceanic crossings, pre-Columbian.

BIBLIOGRAPHY

Adams, Richard E. W. *Prehistoric Mesoamerica.* Rev. ed. Norman, Okla.: University of Oklahoma Press, 1991.

Clark, John E. "A New Artistic Rendering of Izapa Stela 5." *Journal of Book of Mormon Studies* 8:1 (1999): 22–33.

Bernal, Ignacio. *The Mexican National Museum of Anthropology.* Translated by Carolyn B. Czitrom. Mexico: Panorama Editorial, S.A., 1984.

Jakeman, M. Wells. "Stela 5, Izapa Chiapas, Mexico; A Major Archaeological Discovery of the New World." In *University Archaeological Society Special Publications,* no. 2. Provo, Utah: Brigham Young University, 1958.

———. "An Unusual Tree-of-Life Sculpture from Ancient Central America." *Bulletin of the University Archaeological Society,* no. 4. Provo, Utah: Brigham Young University, 1953.

Lowe, Gareth W., Thomas A. Lee Jr., and Eduardo Martinez E. "Izapa: An Introduction to the Ruins and Monuments." *Papers of the New World Archaeological Foundation,* no. 31. Provo, Utah: Brigham Young University, 1982.

Norman, V. Garth. "Critical Review of the Clark-Moreno Drawing of Izapa Stela 5." *Papers of the Ancient America Foundation,* No. 00–1. Orem, Utah, 2000.

———. "Izapa Sculpture, Part 1: Album." *Papers of the New World Archaeological Foundation,* no. 30. Provo, Utah: Brigham Young University, 1973.

———. "Izapa Sculpture, Part 2: Text." *Papers of the New World Archaeological Foundation,* no. 30. Provo, Utah: Brigham Young University, 1976.

———. "Astronomical Orientations of Izapa Sculptures." Master's thesis, Department of Anthropology. Provo, Utah: Brigham Young University, 1980.

POSSIBLE PARALLELS BETWEEN STELA 5 AND LEHI'S VISION OF THE TREE OF LIFE (Numbers correspond to those in fig. 2)

FEATURE IN TREE OF LIFE VISION	STELA 5 PARALLELS
1. Tree of Life	1. Tree of Life/World Tree with guardian spirits
2. River of water	2. River flows down from rain into water panel
3. Straight and narrow path	3. Path lines from river head go to tree
4. Rod of iron	4. Broad line next to path goes to tree
5. Spacious field/dark wasteland	5. Open field at head of river by dark mist glyph (#8)
6. Multitudes of people	6. Generic figure comes from field
7. People fill spacious building high up	7. "Boxed man" symbol is the most elevated
8. Mists of darkness	8. Eb glyph with "dark mist" bands blind eyes (#6)
9. Heavenly messenger or guide	9. Bird-serpent god (QUETZALCOATL) leads to tree
10. Person being led from dark field	10. Traveler led by god (#9) as extension from arm of (#6)
11. Lehi's family in dream (a) Lehi, (b) Sariah (c) Nephi, (d) Sam (e) Laman, (f) Lemuel	11. Six figures; ancestral family of Quiche Maya first parents of migration two younger brothers; king-scribe and attendant two older brothers subdued by younger brothers
12. Some who reach tree are blinded	12. Person at tree blinded by hood
13. Some reach tree and receive fruit	13. Figure born of tree receives fruit from goddess
14. Lehi observed law of Moses	14. High priest attends incense burner
15. Child "god" image (1 Nephi 11)	15. Priest-king (#11c) directs worship to child image

———. "What Is the Current Status of Research concerning the 'Tree of Life' Carving from Chiapas, Mexico?" *Ensign* 15 (June 1985): 55–56.

Parrish, Alan K. "Stela 5, Izapa: A Layman's Consideration of the Tree of Life Stone." *The Book of Mormon: First Nephi—The Doctrinal Foundation*. Provo, Utah: Religious Studies Center, Brigham Young University, 1988.

Wirth, Diane E. *A Challenge to the Critics*. Bountiful, Utah: Horizon Publishers, 1986.

VGN

Stick of Ephraim *See* Ephraim, stick of/Joseph, stick of.

Stick of Joseph *See* Ephraim, stick of/Joseph, stick of.

Stiffnecked, stiffneckedness Term describing the stubbornness, pride, rebellion, and disobedience of persons or nations (1 Ne. 2:11; Jacob 4:14; Omni 1:28; Alma 15:15; Hel. 4:21; 5:3; 9:21). The prophet Isaiah described Israel's stubborn disobedience with the image of a neck like "an iron sinew" (1 Ne. 20:4). This image perhaps comes from agricultural animals such as oxen or donkeys, whose necks are so stiff and strong that they will not respond to the master's prodding and turning. In addition, the term is employed to describe a heart or spirit that, because of wickedness, has difficulty understanding the plainness of God's word (2 Ne. 32:7; Jacob 4:14) or responding to the promptings of the Holy Ghost (Jarom 1:3–4; 1 Ne. 17:45). The law of Moses was given to ancient Israel on account of their stiffneckedness, which was manifest by their slowness to obey God but quickness to sin (Mosiah 13:29–30). Such stubbornness is antithetical to true discipleship which requires a heart and a will that yield to the mind and will of the Lord (Mosiah 3:19; Hel. 3:35).

See also Hard-heartedness.

BLT

Still small voice Generally refers to one of the ways that God communicates with his children. The expression "still small" carries the connotation of quiet and calm. Although the voice is a "voice of perfect mildness" (Hel. 5:30–31) and a "pleasant voice, as if it were a whisper" (Hel. 5:46), it is also associated with great power insomuch that it can shake the earth, cause walls to tremble, pierce souls, and cause hearts to burn (3 Ne. 11:3). Joseph Smith declared, "Often times it maketh my bones to quake" (D&C 85:6). Moreover, this peaceful voice evidenced the presence of God to Elijah on Mt. Horeb (1 Kgs. 19:12–13). Despite the power of this form of revelation, the brethren of Nephi[1] were unable to feel an angel's words spoken in a still small voice. Being "swift to do iniquity but slow to remember the Lord," they were "past feeling" (1 Ne. 17:45).

See also Past feeling; Revelation.

BRM

Stone boxes, burial of documents in The plates of the Book of Mormon were retrieved from a stone box like those commonly found in the ancient world. Containers of ancient buried documents include a bronze sphere bearing inscribed Semitic plates (ca. 625–600 B.C.), sarcophagi, mummies, incantation bowls, door pivot boxes, plaster boxes, brick boxes, brick chambers, false bricks, chests, coffers, earthen vessels (pots, jars, etc.), foundation holes, recesses in walls, cavities in wells, and the "mouths and 'other cavities'" of crocodiles. Stone boxes, associated with ancient writing for at least three millennia, include a granite library-box from Alexandria, stone chests and writing on bronze and silver tablets attested from ca. 1400 B.C. to A.D. 68, a stone box discovered twenty feet underground whose book roll was lost in a manure pile, three golden plates from Pyrgi concealed in a stone niche between two temples, a Roman legal agreement on bronze tablets discovered in a box made of roofing tiles, and the golden "Torah" of Pali Buddhism concealed in a bricked rock chamber. Numerous exemplars are also attested by foundation deposits from three Neo-Sumerian kings (ca. 2100–2000 B.C.), eight post-Sumerian kings (nineteenth to seventh centuries B.C.), and five Persian kings (seventh to fourth centuries B.C.; Wright, 273–332; *Encyclopedia*, 359; Evans, 106–10; Marinatos, 223).

Stone boxes were often covered with top stones for protection against burial damage. The

STONE BOXES, BURIAL OF DOCUMENTS IN

earliest stone box known (ca. 3100–2900 B.C.) was constructed from precut stone slabs "riveted together and stuck with white lime mortar" (Wright, 315). The Book of Mormon plates were "deposited in a stone box" and buried "under a stone of considerable size" that was "thick and rounding in the middle on the upper side, and thinner towards the edges," said Joseph Smith, "so that the middle part of it was visible above the ground" whereas "the edge all around was covered with earth" (JS–H 1:51). This top stone resembles the convex torus covering a limestone box interred with gold and silver plates beneath the Persepolis palace in the sixth century B.C.

A Greek invention used by Persians for securing an Ionic column to its base, this torus protected a stone box and its plates against the weight of a building. Although "a roughly squared stone lay on top of . . . [another] foundation box" (Schmidt, 79) containing identical gold and silver plates, its lid and sides were broken by the weight of the same building (*see* photo, page 538), just as Sargon's stone box, which also contained metal documents, was crushed by the weight of a wall 26 feet thick (Wright, 293–94). Thus, only the stone box "covered with a . . . limestone torus" was retrieved intact (Schmidt, 79). This torus, designed to underlie a "small" column several feet in diameter, and the topstone described by Joseph Smith, although assigned dissimilar protective functions, both did exactly what they were intended to do.

On viewing the Book of Mormon plates, Joseph noted that "the box in which they lay was formed by laying stones together in some kind of cement" (JS–H 1:52). This box was not hollowed out of stone but assembled from components made of rock by a stonecutter and stuck together with an adhesive sealant. Adhesion techniques are extremely ancient, for in addition to various mortars, brick boxes which were "laid flat in bitumen" (Wright, 286)—an asphaltic putty used by Noah to waterproof the ark—were also "coated inside with bitumen" (ca. 3500–3400 B.C.); a clay box containing a temple endowment was hidden under a bitumen floor to protect it

Stone box; courtesy Oriental Institute of the University of Chicago. This box, with its cargo of inscribed gold and silver plates, was retrieved intact from the southeast corner of the Apadana in Persepolis (in modern Iran) because it was protected against the weight of the building by the round concave limestone torus, pictured here.

against moisture, and a late Neo-Babylonian inscription (555–539 B.C.) was built into a wall "in a box of burnt bricks lined with bitumen" (Wright, 326). Mortars, bitumen, ductile metals, and similar adhesives for constructing and protecting containers of buried documents are thus fully compatible with stone boxes, earthenware vessels, waxed cords, linen wrappings, cedar and citrus oils, lead seals, and sealed lids in classical and Egypto-Mesopotamian cultures.

See also The Coming Forth of the Book of Mormon, 9; Metals, ancient writing on.

BIBLIOGRAPHY

Evans, Sir Arthur. *Scripta Minoa: The Written Documents of Minoan Crete with Special Reference to the Archives of Knossos.* Vol. 1. Oxford: Clarendon Press, 1909.

Marinatos, Spyridon. "Verlust einer Handschrift in Messenien." Gnomon 33 (1961): 223.

Oxford Encyclopedia of Archaeology in the Near East. Vol. 5. Edited by Eric M. Meyers. New York: Oxford University Press, 1997.

Schmidt, Erich F. *Persepolis.* Vol. 1. Chicago: University of Chicago Press, 1970.

Wright, H. Curtis. "Ancient Burials of Metal Documents in Stone Boxes." Chapter 10 in *By Study and Also by Faith,* vol. 2. Edited by John M. Lundquist and Stephen D. Ricks. Salt Lake City: Deseret Book, 1990. Consult this chapter for sources.

HCW

Stout *See* Appendix C.

Straight, make his paths *See* Make his paths straight.

Strait, straight *Strait,* meaning narrow; *straight,* meaning not crooked. In contemporary English, *straight* means "not crooked." The main meaning of the somewhat archaic word *strait* is narrow, as in the Straits of Gibraltar. Thus, the "strait gate" is a narrow gate. Jesus clearly contrasts the narrow gate with its opposite, the broad gate and large and spacious way (3 Ne. 14:13–14; Matt. 7:13–14). It is not always obvious which meaning is intended in certain scriptural passages.

In the 1829 printer's manuscript of the Book of Mormon, the word "straight" was never used. When Joseph Smith said the word "strai[gh]t," Oliver Cowdery apparently always preferred to spell it "s-t-r-a-i-t," which was, in the early nineteenth century, an acceptable spelling for either meaning. Indeed, spellings varied from one early edition of the Book of Mormon to the next; thus, one must consider the word in context to determine its meaning. Based on dictionary definitions and scriptural usage, the word *strai[gh]t* may have any of the following meanings when used in the phrase "strai[gh]t and narrow":

1. "Narrow," being an emphatic redundancy or parallelism typical of Hebrew literary style (that is, "narrow and narrow," meaning "very narrow").

2. "Not crooked," affirming that God does not walk in crooked paths (Alma 7:20).

3. "Difficult or stressful," indicating that the path of righteousness is not easy (2 Ne. 31:19–20), and is full of tribulation (Matt. 7:13–14; also "straiten" in 1 Ne. 17:41).

4. "Rigorous," "tight" or "crowded" (1 Ne. 8:21).

5. "Upright," "righteous," or "morally straight," admonishing people to walk "uprightly" before the Lord (1 Ne. 16:3).

Jesus Christ and a number of prophets used the terms *strait* and *straight,* all with the ultimate end of portraying the strict path that leads back to God's presence. Nephi[1] pointed out that the gate to the straight and narrow path consists of repentance and baptism, "and then cometh a remission of . . . sins by fire and by the Holy Ghost" (2 Ne. 31:17–18). The gospel announces the good news that such a path exists, which one can follow to eternal life by "press[ing] forward, feasting upon the word of Christ, and endur[ing] to the end" (2 Ne. 31:17–20).

JWW

Strait and narrow path *See* Lehi[1]'s dream.

Strait gate *See* Gate(s).

Stripes *See* Appendix C.

Stripling *See* Appendix C.

Stripling warriors Two thousand, plus an additional sixty, sons of the people of Ammon (ANTI-NEPHI-LEHIES) who were initially called "two thousand stripling soldiers" (Alma 53:22;

57:6, 19–20, 25), or the "sons" of Helaman[2] (Alma 56:10, 17; ca. 64 B.C.). Because of their great faith and obedience, they were all delivered from death on the battlefield (Alma 53, 56–58).

The parents of these young men were Lamanites who, upon their conversion to Christ, had settled among the Nephites and had entered into a covenant never again to participate in bloodshed (Alma 24–27). When they were threatened by renewed Lamanite aggression, their sons, who had not taken that vow, entered into a covenant to fight for liberty. They armed themselves under the leadership of Helaman to defend their own people and their Nephite neighbors, thereby enabling their parents to keep their sacred oath (Alma 53:10–22).

In the twenty-sixth year of the reign of the judges (66 B.C.) these youthful soldiers reinforced the Nephite army led by Antipus in the city of Judea. In the following year they, with the forces of Antipus, engaged a Lamanite army in a fierce battle in which they fought with such miraculous strength that the Lamanites surrendered (Alma 56:20–56). Helaman recorded, "To my great joy, there had not one soul of them fallen to the earth; yea, and they had fought as if with the strength of God" (Alma 56:56). The stripling warriors showed themselves to be "exceedingly valiant" and courageous men who were "true at all times in whatsoever thing they were entrusted. Yea, they were men of truth and soberness, for they had been taught to keep the commandments of God and to walk uprightly before him" (Alma 53:20–21). They exhibited remarkable faith in that, although "they never had fought, yet they did not fear death," for "they had been taught by their mothers, that if they did not doubt, God would deliver them." They were more concerned for "the liberty of their fathers" than for their own lives (Alma 56:47).

In the twenty-ninth year of the reign of the judges (63 B.C.), when the additional sixty sons of the Ammonites joined them, the young warriors took the city of Cumeni (Alma 57:12). Afterward there was an intense battle to retain their position (Alma 57:17–23). Although there were heavy losses among the Lamanites and every one of the 2060 stripling warriors was wounded, including two hundred that fainted from loss of blood, "there was not one soul of them who did perish" (Alma 57:25). Helaman and his "sons" also took control of the city of Manti by strategy (Alma 58).

The success of these valiant young men was attributed to the fact that "they did obey and observe to perform every word of command with exactness" (Alma 57:21) and to their maintaining "exceeding faith in that which they had been taught to believe," for "their minds [were] firm, and they [did] put their trust in God continually" (Alma 57:26–27). The stripling warriors of Helaman are a prime example of the blessings of strength and courage that are visited upon those who have unwavering faith in the Lord and whose lives are characterized by strict obedience and self-sacrificing service. They are also a witness to the powerful influence of diligent teaching by righteous mothers.

JHS

Stubble *See* Appendix C.

Stumble Term that refers primarily to one who trips or falters doctrinally or spiritually because of ignorance, spiritual blindness, or sin. For example, Nephi[1] was shown that the latter-day Gentiles would stumble because of the "plain and precious" truths that would be lost or "kept back" from the biblical record (1 Ne. 13:29, 34; 2 Ne. 26:20). The ancient Jews "sought for things that they could not understand," which caused them to stumble (Jacob 4:14). This stumbling would eventually lead them to reject Christ, the "stone" of Israel (Jacob 4:15–16). He would become to them as a "stone of stumbling" (2 Ne. 18:14–15). In Alma[2]'s day, the wickedness of Church members "was a great stumbling-block to those who did not belong to the church; and thus the church began to fail in its progress" (Alma 4:10).

Additionally, the word *stumble* is used to refer to physically stumbling (2 Ne. 15:26; i.e., to falter in advancing swiftly), to one stumbling in his communication or words (Ether 12:25; i.e., having a difficult time writing), and to fail to achieve a desired goal (Jacob 4:18; i.e., to falter).

SER

Stupor *See* Appendix C.

Succor *See* Appendix C.

Suffer *See* Appendix C.

Suffer his cross Undertaking the Lord's will in spite of the shame, opposition, and travails of the world. Suffering his cross is one of the requirements for coming unto him, partaking of his goodness, entering into his rest (Jacob 1:7–8), and becoming his disciple (Luke 14:26–27), or one of the "saints of the Holy One of Israel" (2 Nephi 9:18). This "fellowship of his sufferings" (Philip. 3:10), which may constitute the loss of all things, makes possible the "excellency of the knowledge of Christ Jesus" (Philip. 3:8). In the context of losing one's life to save it, the Lord taught that one must take up his cross daily (Luke 9:23–24). He explained, "For a man to take up his cross, is to deny himself all ungodliness, and every worldly lust, and keep my commandments" (JST Matt. 16:26; cf. Alma 39:9; 3 Ne. 12:30).

MCT

Sway *See* Appendix C.

Sword of Laban One of the sacred objects passed down among the Nephites, first mentioned in connection with Lehi[1]'s departure from Jerusalem in about 600 B.C. (1 Ne. 4:9). Laban had in his possession the brass plates, which contained a record similar to the Old Testament. After Laban refused to give up these records and other attempts to secure them had failed, Nephi[1] was "constrained by the Spirit" to slay him (1 Ne. 4:10). Nephi instinctively shrank from carrying out this directive, but after the Spirit instructed him about why he must slay Laban and obtain this vital scriptural record, he took Laban's sword and killed him (1 Ne. 4:10–18). Nephi, who retained the sword, wrote, "I drew it forth from the sheath thereof; and the hilt . . . was of pure gold, and the workmanship . . . was exceedingly fine, and I saw that the blade . . . was of the most precious steel" (1 Ne. 4:9).

After arriving in the New World, Nephi used the sword of Laban as a pattern to produce other swords for the defense of his people, and he used Laban's sword itself for that purpose (2 Ne. 5:14; Jacob 1:10). King Benjamin also used the sword of Laban in battle (W of M 1:13). He subsequently gave the sword, together with the Liahona and the sacred records, to his son Mosiah[2] (Mosiah 1:16). This sword must have served as a continual reminder of the Lord's deliverance of his people (Jacob 1:10).

In modern times the Lord promised the Three Witnesses that they would see the sword of Laban together with other sacred objects (D&C 17:1). In June of 1829, the Three Witnesses saw the plates, the sword of Laban, and the Liahona (D&C 17:1; Roberts, 1:143).

Brigham Young stated that on another occasion Joseph Smith and Oliver Cowdery saw the sword of Laban when they entered a large room full of plates in the interior of the Hill Cumorah: "The first time they went there the sword of Laban hung upon the wall; but when they went again it had been taken down and laid upon the table across the gold plates; it was unsheathed, and on it was written these words: 'This sword will never be sheathed again until the kingdoms of this world become the kingdom of our God and his Christ'" (19:38).

BIBLIOGRAPHY

Roberts, Brigham H. *A Comprehensive History of The Church of Jesus Christ of Latter-day Saints.* 6 vols. Provo, Utah: Brigham Young University Press, 1965.

Young, Brigham. *Journal of Discourses.* 26 vols. London: Latter-day Saints' Book Depot, 1854–86.

ROC

Synagogue(s) The word synagogue is of Greek origin (*synagōgē*) meaning "assembly" or "gathering." In early Jewish tradition, the building where one worshipped, prayed, and studied in a communal gathering was usually identified in Hebrew as a "house of assembly" (*beth-knesset*). One could go to the house of assembly or synagogue to hear the word of God and to discuss its meaning in open dialogue. For example, Jesus and Paul taught openly in synagogues (e.g., Matt. 13:54; Luke 4:16–21; John 6:59; Acts 13:14–16; 17:1–2). Nephi[1]'s use of the phrase "houses of worship" as a synonym for synagogues seems appropriate (2 Ne. 26:26).

Scholars are uncertain exactly when formal places of regular or weekly assembly developed in Jewish worship. Some Jewish traditions point to temple worship and the public assemblies of the early prophets as prototypes (e.g., Deut. 1:1–5; Josh. 24:1; 1 Sam. 7:5–7). Others see the communal practices beginning with the religious reforms of Jeremiah[1] (627–585 B.C.) and king Josiah (640–609 B.C.) as a time when groups of Jews outside Jerusalem would gather for study, prayer, and worship. Some scholars believe the reference to the "houses of the people" in Jeremiah 39:8 to be a form of synagogue. There is an early reference in Psalms to an enemy burning "all the synagogues of God in the land" (Ps. 74:8).

Although some types of communal worship in buildings other than the temple may have been practiced while Lehi lived near Jerusalem, most scholars suggest that the use of synagogues became institutionalized in the Jewish community during and after the Babylonian captivity. This was about the same time that early Nephite synagogues are first mentioned (2 Ne. 26:26). Perhaps the appearance of synagogue worship among these two widely divided peoples, the people of Lehi and the Jews of the Babylonian captivity, suggests that some types of assembly buildings were in use among the Jews before they both left Jerusalem.

The term "synagogue" (or "synagogues") is found throughout the Book of Mormon, with 26 references ranging from 2 Nephi 26:26 to Moroni 7:1, although most are in chapters 16–33 of Alma. Synagogues are often mentioned alongside temples and sanctuaries. It is not clear what distinctions existed between the buildings, either in use or design. It is clear that the temple was used as a place of instruction from as early as Jacob[2] (Jacob 1:17) and at least down to Christ (3 Ne. 11:1–10), but how this use differed from that of a synagogue or a sanctuary is not specified. Perhaps the synagogues were used more for regular study and worship (e.g., 2 Ne. 26:26; Alma 16:13; 21:20), whereas temples were used for larger gatherings on special occasions (e.g., Jacob 1:17; Mosiah 1:18; 2:5–7; 3 Ne. 11:1–10).

Synagogues were used both among the faithful Nephites and their Lamanite converts, as well as among the apostate Amalekites and Zoramites[2], but their purposes appear to have been very different. Some Nephite synagogues were apparently built "after the manner of the Jews" (Alma 16:13) and used for similar purposes, such as reading the scriptures, praying, and giving sermons. Thus, the Nephites did "humble themselves before God, and began to assemble themselves together at their sanctuaries to worship God" (Alma 15:17). Alma[2] reminded the poor and humble of the Zoramites that such worship was not limited to a physical structure (Alma 32:10). Aaron[3] and his brethren preached their gospel message in the Lamanite synagogues (Alma 21:4–6). That Nephites were allowed to speak in Amalekite and Lamanite assemblies suggests that the custom of open dialogue was a part of synagogue practice in the Book of Mormon (Welch, 193–95).

As a contrast, the Amalekites and Zoramites assembled in synagogues as places of vain public worship and social prominence (Alma 21; 31; 32). Their apostate practices followed the order of Nehor, and they rejected the study of the scriptures (Alma 14:8; 21:4, 12). They adapted the synagogue to their own purposes and through these people, the synagogue was introduced to the Lamanites. It is clear from Alma 23:2 that the Lamanites knew of synagogues and perhaps even attended the Amalekite synagogues from time to time. Alma 21:16 suggests that they also met in their own assemblies, perhaps in homes or outdoors.

See also Anachronisms, alleged.

BIBLIOGRAPHY

Welch, John W. "Synagogues in the Book of Mormon." *Reexploring the Book of Mormon*. Salt Lake City: Deseret Book and FARMS, 1997.

VLL

Syria A name of Greek origin designating a loosely defined region to the northeast of Israel, occupying approximately the same area as the modern nation of Syria (Bible Maps 4, 6, 8, 9). Apparently Herodotus (ca. 450 B.C.) first applied the name Syria to this area, perhaps as a shortened form of the name "Assyria," which historically refers to a separate and distinct geographic, cultural, and political entity. The King James Version (KJV) employs the anachronistic terms *Syria* and *Syrian(s)* to render the terms for *Aram, Aramean(s),* and *Aramaic* in the Old Testament. Aram/Syria consisted of a number of small national states during the time of the united and divided monarchies in Israel.

Little is known historically concerning the Arameans before ca. 1200 B.C., although traditions about their origins are preserved in Genesis 10:22 and 22:21. Arameans were tribally organized Semites, perhaps related to the earlier Amorites. According to the Bible the Israelites were related to the Arameans. Haran, the ancestral homeland of the Patriarchal families, was in northern Aram, and Bethuel, Laban, and even Jacob[1] are referred to as Arameans (Gen. 25:20; 31:20; Deut. 26:5). The Aramean states most often mentioned in the Bible are Zobah and Damascus (2 Sam. 8:5–6; Isa. 7:8 // 2 Ne. 17:8). The Israelites gained control of Aram during the reign of David (2 Sam. 8:3–12) but lost control of it by the end of Solomon's reign (1 Kgs. 11:23–25). The Bible depicts relations between the northern kingdom of Israel and the Arameans as generally antagonistic during the period of the Israelite Divided Monarchy (931–722 B.C.).

Book of Mormon usage follows the KJV in employing *Syria* and *Syrians* to designate *Aram. Syrians* occurs in 2 Nephi 19:12 // Isaiah 9:12, while *Syria* occurs in 2 Nephi 17:1–8 // Isaiah 7:1–8. This latter passage recounts an attempt by Pekah, king of Israel, and Rezin, king of Damascus, the most powerful state in southern Aram (2 Ne. 17:8), to force Ahaz, king of JUDAH, to join them in an anti-Assyrian coalition (ca. 735 B.C.). They besieged Jerusalem and threatened to dethrone Ahaz if he did not join them (2 Kgs. 15:37; 16:5). Isaiah prophesied that patient faith in the Lord would ensure the continued rule of Ahaz over Judah (2 Ne. 17:9–18:22 // Isa. 7:9–8:22). Ahaz, however, procured the services of the king of ASSYRIA to deliver him from this coalition (2 Kgs. 16:7–9). In partial response to the invitation of Ahaz, the Assyrians invaded and conquered the area of

SYRIA AT THE TIME OF ISAIAH

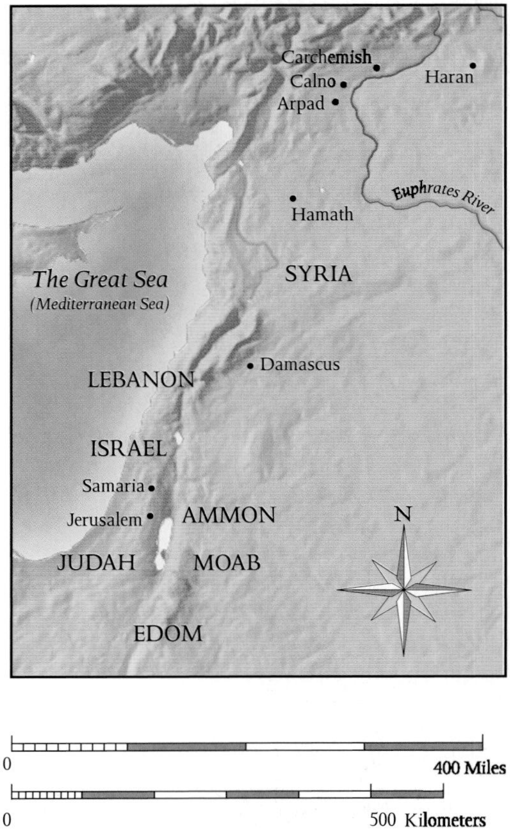

Aram, along with the northern portion of Israel, in 732 B.C. A decade later (722 B.C.), the Assyrians completely conquered the northern kingdom of Israel and deported thousands of Israelites, who became known as the ten lost tribes.

See also Chronology, Bible; Isaiah chapter reviews (2 Ne. 17 // Isa. 7); Israel, historical background of; Israel, kingdom of.

DMP

And now, O my son Helaman, behold, thou art in thy youth, and therefore, I beseech of thee that thou wilt hear my words and learn of me; for I do know that whosoever shall put their **trust** in God shall be supported in their trials, and their troubles, and their afflictions, and shall be lifted up at the last day. ALMA 36:3

Tabernacle Term used in at least two senses in the Book of Mormon.

1. A synonym for the mortal body. The phrase "tabernacle of clay" is used twice in the Book of Mormon, once to underscore the truth that Christ will become like humankind possessing a mortal body (Mosiah 3:5; cf. Alma 7:8; D&C 93:4), and the other in a letter Mormon wrote to his son Moroni[2] encouraging him to continue to labor while yet in mortality (Moro. 9:6).

2. A tent or covering—a shelter. In this context the term *tabernacle* is used as a metaphor for the peace and protection to be enjoyed by the faithful in millennial Zion: "And there shall be a tabernacle for a shadow in the daytime from the heat, and for a place of refuge, and a covert from storm and from rain" (2 Ne. 14:6 // Isa. 4:6).

RNH

Taste of death To experience the natural process of physical or mortal death, often accompanied by pain and difficulties. All who enter mortality must die (2 Ne. 9:6; 1 Cor. 15:22). A few, however, such as the three Nephite disciples, will escape the normal course of death. Their bodies have been changed (translated) permitting them to pass from mortality to immortality, without tasting death (3 Ne. 28:7–8, 37–38). In another sense, all faithful Saints, though they may suffer when they die, do not taste of death in that their departure from this life is "sweet," knowing they will stand approved by the Lord (D&C 42:46–47).

CJW

Teacher(s) An ecclesiastical office in the Nephite Church. It should not be confused with the Aaronic Priesthood office of teacher because before the coming of Christ the Nephites did not have the Aaronic Priesthood (Smith, 3:87). Nephi[1] consecrated Jacob[2] and Joseph[2] as PRIESTS and teachers (2 Ne. 5:26). Alma[1], as high priest of the Church, consecrated teachers (Mosiah 23:17), as did his successors Alma[2] (Alma 4:7) and Helaman[2] (Alma 45:22).

The duties of teachers included leadership within individual congregations and teaching the gospel (Mosiah 25:19–22). Moroni[2] described the manner in which teachers (and priests) were ordained by the disciples of Christ after the coming of Christ (Moro. 3:1–3). It is not known whether these teachers held the Aaronic or the Melchizedek Priesthood.

See also Church of God (Christ) in ancient America; Elder(s); Priesthood among the Nephites; Priest(s).

BIBLIOGRAPHY

Smith, Joseph Fielding. *Doctrines of Salvation.* Compiled by Bruce R. McConkie. 3 vols. Salt Lake City: Bookcraft, 1954–56.

MDR

Teancum Nephite military leader (ca. 67 B.C.) who played a major role in the execution and outcome of the Nephite-Lamanite wars which began with the dissension of Amalickiah and concluded with the defeat of the Lamanites in 60 B.C. Teancum led the army sent by Moroni[1] to head off the contentious people of Morianton[2] in their ambitious quest for possession of northern lands. In the ensuing battle he killed Morianton and defeated his army (Alma 50:35; 51:29). In the second campaign Amalickiah conducted against the Nephites, ca. 67 B.C., the apostate captured many Nephite cities on the east by the sea (Alma 51:26–27), but his intention to capture the land of Bountiful[2] and the land northward was "repulsed by Teancum and his men" (Alma 51:30–32). When night came, Teancum stole into the Lamanite camp and killed Amalickiah instantly with the thrust of a javelin into his heart (Alma 51:33–34). Teancum's assassination of Amalickiah caused the Lamanites to abandon their intent to march into the land northward. They retreated to the city of Mulek, and Ammoron, the brother of Amalickiah, then became king (Alma 52:1–3). In 65 B.C. Teancum received orders to retake the city of Mulek if possible, but such an action offered no hope of success. Teancum withdrew from his intention and awaited the arrival of Moroni. The two Nephite leaders then lured the Lamanite forces out of Mulek and defeated them (Alma 52:15–40). Acting under orders from Moroni, Teancum used Lamanite prisoners to fortify the city of Bountiful, making it "an exceeding stronghold ever after" (Alma 53:3–5).

These Nephite conflicts, internal and external,

dragged on for several years, with Teancum as one of the key Nephite military figures. Then in about 60 B.C., when all the Lamanite armies and king Ammoron had fled to the land of Moroni and camped for the night, Teancum again acted on his own. Angry at the bloodshed and destruction wrought by Amalickiah and Ammoron, he slipped into the Lamanite camp and found Ammoron. His javelin killed Ammoron, but not before Ammoron woke his servants, who pursued and killed Teancum (Alma 62:35–36). Mormon paid high tribute to this brave and faithful Nephite patriot. Teancum, he said, "had been a man who had fought valiantly for his country, yea, a true friend to liberty; and he had suffered very many exceedingly sore afflictions" (Alma 62:37).

TLG

Teancum, city of Nephite coastal city near the city Desolation (Morm. 4:3). In A.D. 364 the Nephites successfully defended the city of Teancum against a Lamanite invasion, only to be driven out a short time later (A.D. 367). The Lamanite victors offered Nephite women and children prisoners "as sacrifices unto their idol gods" (Morm. 4:6–14).

Temples Holy places where God may dwell. Individuals typically go to temples to communicate with God, receive instruction from God,

Model of Solomon's Temple; courtesy VRL. "And I, Nephi, did build a temple; and I did construct it after the manner of the temple of Solomon save it were not built of so many precious things" (2 Ne. 5:16).

make covenants with God, and participate in ordinances required by God.

The Book of Mormon identifies six types of temples:

1. Temple buildings. The Book of Mormon speaks of temples at the Nephite chief cities of Nephi, Zarahemla, and Bountiful[2], and it mentions Lamanite temples (Alma 23:2; 26:29) and other temples in the land of Zarahemla (Alma 16:13). "The manner of the construction [of the temple of Nephi] was like unto the temple of Solomon" (2 Ne. 5:16). The people of God offered sacrifices in these temples (Mosiah 2:1–3; cf. 2 Ne. 5:10; Alma 30:3) and made covenants (Mosiah 2–6). Prophets preached repentance and taught the gospel (Jacob 2:2; Alma 16:13), kings sent proclamations "throughout all the land" inviting people to gather at the temple to hear their words (Mosiah 2:1, 5; 1:18; 7:17), and Jesus appeared to the Nephites at the Bountiful temple (3 Ne. 11).

2. Mountains as temples. The "high mountain" of Nephi[1] (1 Ne. 11:1) and mount Shelem of the brother of Jared[1] (Ether 3:1) can be viewed as natural temples, resembling such other temple mountains as Sinai, Moriah, and the Mount of Transfiguration, all places where prophets received sacred theophanic experiences.

3. Lehi[1]'s altar as a temple. Lehi's "altar of stones" was a temporary place of worship that can be considered a temple. Here Lehi "made an offering" (Hebrew *mizbach,* "altar," means "a place of sacrifice") and "gave thanks unto the Lord" (1 Ne. 2:7).

4. The heavenly temple. The dwelling place of God in heaven is mentioned in the Book of Mormon (2 Ne. 16:1 // Isa. 6:1; cf. 1 Ne. 1:8; Ps. 11:4; 102:19; Heb. 9; Rev. 14:17; 16:17).

5. Temple of our bodies. The Bible clearly teaches that men and women can be viewed as temples of God insofar as they are holy, and the Spirit of God dwells in them (1 Cor. 3:16–17; 6:13–20; 2 Cor. 6:16). The Book of Mormon adds, "The Lord hath said he dwelleth not in unholy temples, but in the hearts of the righteous doth he dwell" (Alma 34:36; 7:21; Mosiah 2:37); also, the Lord "dwelleth not in unholy temples," such as those who "obey the evil spirit" and become "an enemy to all righteousness" (Mosiah 2:37; Hel. 4:24).

6. Temple of Christ's body. Isaiah's phrase "sanctify the Lord" in the Hebrew reads "make him a temple, the Lord of Hosts," meaning let the Lord be your temple, your place of holiness (2 Ne. 18:13–14 // Isa. 8:13–14). The idea is continued in the following sentence: The Lord "shall be for a sanctuary." Other prophets have also identified the Lord as a "sanctuary" or "temple" (Ezek. 11:16; Ps. 90:1; John 2:18–21; Rev. 21:22). In addition, Jesus Christ is both the temple's "chief corner stone" (Eph. 2:20; Ps. 118:22) and its "sure foundation" (Jacob 4:16; Hel. 5:12).

BIBLIOGRAPHY

Welch, John W. "The Temples in the Book of Mormon: The Temples at the Cities of Nephi, Zarahemla, and Bountiful." *Temples of the Ancient World: Ritual and Symbolism.* Edited by Donald W. Parry. Salt Lake City: Deseret Book, 1994. 297–387.

DWP

Temporal Pertaining to things physical, earthly, or temporary in nature (1 Ne. 15:32). The Lord blesses the faithful temporally and spiritually (Mosiah 2:41; Alma 7:23). Alma[2] explained that he had come to know the things of God, "not of the temporal" or by reason alone, but by the Spirit of God (Alma 36:4).

See also Law, temporal; Temporal death.

CJW

Temporal death The temporary separation of the mortal body from the spirit. Temporal death was introduced into the world when Adam and Eve partook of the FORBIDDEN FRUIT (Alma 12:22–24). The "sting" or effect of temporal death is "swallowed up in Christ" through the RESURRECTION (Mosiah 16:7–8; Alma 22:14; 27:28; Morm. 7:5). Adam and Eve were not allowed to circumvent death by partaking of the tree of life for, as Alma taught, "it was not expedient that man should be reclaimed from this temporal death, for that would destroy the great plan of happiness" (Alma 42:4–9; cf. 2 Ne. 9:6).

See also Fall of Adam and Eve, the.

RDD

Ten Commandments The Ten Commandments were given by the Lord on Sinai and epitomized the whole of the LAW OF MOSES in the Bible (Ex. 20; Deut. 5). They were preserved on the brass plates as Abinadi "read" them to the priests of Noah[3] in their entirety (Mosiah 12:33–13:24). The Ten Commandments were fundamental to the religion of the Book of Mormon, both before and after the coming of Christ. They were central to the preaching of the Book of Mormon prophets, and the breaking of these commandments—particularly MURDER, adultery, and stealing—is cited as the reason for the destruction of the covenant people in the Book of Mormon (Mosiah 2:13; Alma 16:18; 50:21; Hel. 6:23; 7:21–22; 13:22), just as in the Old Testament (Hosea 4:1–2; Jer. 7:9; Ezek. 18; 22). Book of Mormon prophets often reminded their audiences of the Ten Commandments. Nephi[1] warned that those who failed to obey the commandments not to murder, lie, steal, envy, commit whoredoms, and take the name of the Lord in vain, would perish (2 Ne. 26:32; cf. 3 Ne. 16:10; Morm. 8:31). Abinadi introduced the Ten Commandments in Mosiah 12 thus: "I know if ye keep the commandments of God ye shall be saved; yea, if ye keep the commandments which the Lord delivered unto Moses in the mount of Sinai" (Mosiah 12:33).

1. "Thou shalt have no other gods before me" (Ex. 20:3). Allegiance only to God was essential for the survival of the Nephites. Similarly Moroni[2] admonished latter-day readers to "love God with all your might, mind and strength" (Moro. 10:32; cf. 7:13).

2. "Thou shalt not make unto thee any graven image. . . . Thou shalt not bow down thyself unto them" (Mosiah 13:12–13). One of the signs of Lamanite degradation and apostasy was IDOLATRY (Enos 1:20; Mosiah 9:12; Alma 17:15; Morm. 4:14, 21). It was also a sign of apostasy among the Jaredites (Ether 7:23), the Nephites (Mosiah 11:6–7), and the Zoramites[2] who were led "to bow down to dumb idols" (Alma 31:1). Jacob[2] warned, "Wo unto those that worship idols, for the devil of all devils delighteth in them" (2 Ne. 9:37); and, the Lord warned those living in the latter days to "repent of your evil doings, of your lyings and deceivings, and of your whoredoms, and of your secret abominations, and your idolatries" (3 Ne. 30:2).

3. "Thou shalt not take the name of the Lord thy God in vain" (Mosiah 13:15). In the Bible and the Book of Mormon solemn OATHS were sworn invoking the name of the Lord. The sacredness of such oaths is well illustrated in the Book of Mormon in the case of Nephi[1] and Zoram[1]. Nephi swore "as the Lord liveth" that Zoram would be spared and be a free man if he would leave Jerusalem with the family of Lehi[1] (1 Ne. 4:32–33; cf. 3:15). An oath that was made falsely or without righteous intent would be categorized as taking the name of the Lord in vain (cf. Alma 49:27; Hel. 1:11).

4. "Remember the sabbath day, to keep it holy" (Mosiah 13:16). There are two references to this commandment in the Book of Mormon: Jarom said about the Nephites, "They observed to keep the law of Moses and the sabbath day holy unto the Lord" (Jarom 1:5), and Alma[1] instructed members of the Church "that they should observe the sabbath day, and keep it holy" (Mosiah 18:23).

5. "Honor thy father and thy mother, that thy days may be long upon the land which the Lord thy God giveth thee" (Mosiah 13:20). Nephi[1] quoted this commandment when he chastised Laman[1] and Lemuel (1 Ne. 17:55). Many characters illustrated this commandment through their examples, including such righteous sons as Nephi[1], Jacob[2], Enos, Mosiah[2], Helaman[2], Shiblon, the stripling warriors of Helaman[2], and Moroni[2]—all of whom honored their parents. On the other hand, the Book of Mormon provides examples of unrighteous sons who did not honor their parents, such as Laman[1] and Lemuel, who did not repent; and Alma the Younger, the sons of Mosiah[2], and Corianton, who did.

6. "Thou shalt not kill" (Mosiah 13:21). The commandment against killing is found throughout the Book of Mormon in many contexts. Satan is the author of SECRET COMBINATIONS, who "hath caused man to commit murder from the beginning" (Ether 8:25; 2 Ne. 26:22). Murder to get gain was the design of the secret combinations which led to the downfall of the Jaredites and the Nephites. Alma[2] reminded his son

Corianton that the worst two sins are "the shedding of innocent blood" and denying the Holy Ghost (Alma 39:5). The seriousness of this sin is emphasized in several passages in the Book of Mormon (Alma 1:13–14; 34:11–12; 42:19).

7. "Thou shalt not commit adultery" (Mosiah 13:22). In the Book of Mormon "adultery" is often described as "whoredoms." While the term "commit whoredoms" may cover a broad range of immorality, in many contexts it is clearly synonymous with adultery (2 Ne. 9:36; 26:32; Jacob 2:28, 33; Hel. 6:23). The deadly consequences of immorality are eloquently discussed by Jacob[2] (Jacob 2:31, 33, 35), by Abinadi (Mosiah 11:20), and by Alma[2] to his son Corianton (Alma 39:3–8, 11; 42:28). Immorality was a temptation to Book of Mormon peoples and especially characteristic of dissent and secret combinations (Hel. 4:12; 7:5; Alma 30:18; Ether 8:16). Moreover, it was prophesied as an insidious aspect of the culture of the latter days (2 Ne. 28:14–15; 3 Ne. 16:10; Morm. 8:31).

8. "Thou shalt not steal" (Mosiah 13:22). In the Book of Mormon four different English words are used for stealing: *steal, thieve, rob,* and *plunder.* Stealing was the objective of the secret combinations practiced among the Jaredites and the Nephites (for example, the GADIANTON ROBBERS) which eventually led to their destruction (Hel. 4:12; 6:23; 7:21).

9. "Thou shalt not bear false witness against thy neighbor" (Mosiah 13:23). The phrase "bearing false witness" in the Bible often refers to perjury in a formal legal proceeding. Its application was probably not confined to such formal proceedings but extended to any untruth told which would injure one's neighbor. The phrase to "bear false witness against your neighbor" is only mentioned once in the Book of Mormon (Hel. 7:21). It is likely that in the Book of Mormon the terms "lying" and "deceive" represent this commandment (2 Ne. 26:32; Alma 1:18; 16:18; Hel. 4:12; 3 Ne. 16:10; 21:19; 30:2; Ether 8:16; Morm. 8:31).

10. "Thou shalt not covet" (Mosiah 13:24). Other than Abinadi's reading of the Ten Commandments the Book of Mormon contains only one occurrence of the word "covet." King Benjamin taught that even those who had little substance should be charitable in their hearts and when asked to give to the poor should say, "I give not because I have not, but if I had I would give" (Mosiah 4:24). Otherwise, king Benjamin warned, "Ye are condemned . . . for ye covet that which ye have not received" (Mosiah 4:25). Another word in the Book of Mormon synonymous with "covet" is "envy" (2 Ne. 26:32; Alma 1:32; 5:29; 16:18; Hel. 13:22; 3 Ne. 30:2; 4 Ne. 1:16).

See also Chastity.

DRS

Teomner A Nephite military officer serving under the command of Helaman[2] (ca. 63 B.C.). To retake the city of Manti from the Lamanites, Helaman enticed the numerically superior Lamanite force to come out from the city with their army and pursue the Nephite army into the wilderness. Flanking the pursuers and hidden in the wilderness were the companies of Teomner and Gid, who slipped behind the Lamanites when they had passed and recaptured Manti (Alma 58:16–23).

That prophet A reference to Jesus Christ (3 Ne. 20:23). Moses prophesied that after his time, God would raise up a great prophet to whose words the people were to hearken (Deut. 18:15). He would speak all that God commands, and whoever would not be obedient to him, God "will require it of him" (Deut. 18:18–19). When Peter paraphrased the prophecy, he added that "every soul, which will not hear that prophet, shall be destroyed from among the people" (Acts 3:23).

The great future prophet became the object of hope and expectation. Among Jews of Jesus' day, the prophet's coming was anticipated alongside that of Elijah and the Messiah, though the relationship among the three was uncertain in their minds (Mark 6:15; John 1:21–25). Some who witnessed Jesus' ministry believed he was that prophet (John 6:14); John the Baptist and Peter made the identification explicit (JST John 1:20–29; Acts 3:18, 22–24).

The Book of Mormon adds further evidence that Jesus was the anticipated prophet. Nephi[1] stated, "And now I, Nephi, declare unto you, that this prophet of whom Moses spake was the Holy One of Israel" (1 Ne. 22:21). The Savior himself said, "Behold, I am he of whom Moses spake, saying: a prophet shall the Lord your God raise up unto you. . . . And all the prophets from Samuel and those that follow after, as many as have spoken, have testified of me" (3 Ne. 20:23–24). When Moroni[2] first appeared to Joseph Smith, he likewise identified that prophet as Christ, "but the day had not yet come when 'they who would not hear his voice should be cut off from among the people,' but soon would come" (JS–H 1:40; cf. D&C 133:63).

KPJ

Three Nephites *See* Nephites, the Three.

Timothy One of the twelve Nephite disciples called during Christ's ministry in the western hemisphere (3 Ne. 19:4). Earlier, during the great wickedness that preceded Christ's coming, Timothy was "stoned and suffered death" at the hands of the faithless Nephites, but his brother Nephi[3] miraculously raised him from the dead in the sight of the people. The miracle angered the people, for they were jealous of Nephi's power (3 Ne. 7:18–20). Timothy was baptized by Nephi, received the Holy Ghost, and was ministered to by angels and Jesus himself (3 Ne. 19:11–15).

See also Disciples, twelve Nephite.

Tire *See* Appendix C.

Tithing An offering or donation consisting of one-tenth of one's increase. That the Nephites knew of this law is evident from the teaching of Alma[2] that Abraham "paid tithes" to Melchizedek "of one-tenth part of all he possessed" (Alma 13:15; cf. D&C 119:4). Furthermore, during his ministry in the Americas, the resurrected Savior quoted Malachi's teachings on the principle (3 Ne. 24:8–12). It is not known whether or not Book of Mormon peoples lived the law of tithing. They did, however, have "all things common among them" (indicating that they were living the law of consecration) for nearly two hundred years following the Savior's appearance (4 Ne. 1:3, 25).

ALB

Title of liberty A piece of captain Moroni's coat that he fastened on the end of a pole after writing on it the words: "In memory of our God, our religion, and freedom, and our peace, our wives, and our children" (Alma 46:12). Moroni "went forth among the people, waving the rent part of his garment in the air, that all might see the writing," in an effort to rally those faithful to freedom to enter into a covenant to "maintain their rights, and their religion, that the Lord God may bless them" (Alma 46:19–20). This banner, which was later "hoisted upon every tower which was in all the land" was a call to arms to "all . . . who were desirous to maintain their liberty," to stand against the dissenter Amalickiah and his followers (Alma 46:28, 36).

Moroni's words and the rending of his coat to make the title of liberty motivated other Nephites to rend their own garments as a covenant that they would not forsake God—the penalty for so doing being that "the Lord should rend them even as they had rent their garments" (Alma 46:21). Moroni then referred to the ancient coat of Joseph[1] that was rent by his brothers and cautioned how they too, as their ancestor Joseph, would suffer at the hands of their dissident brethren if they did not keep the commandments (Alma 46:23–27).

See also Joseph[1], coat of.

DLL

Tittle *See* Jot, tittle.

Tongue of angels Speaking the words of Christ by the power of the Holy Ghost (2 Ne. 32:3). Nephi[1] explained that those who are baptized by water and by fire can "speak with the tongue of angels" (2 Ne. 31:13). They speak what angels would speak and even what the Savior and Redeemer would speak if personally present (2 Ne. 32:2–3). The reception of the Holy Ghost is, in a sense, a divine investiture that empowers and directs the utterances and quickens the understanding of those who speak and act in the name of Deity. A man or woman who speaks with the tongue of angels speaks "not as other men" (JST Matt. 3:25), but "as one having authority from God" (JST Matt. 7:37). As Jesus explained, the messengers of salvation are sent forth "in the power of my Spirit, preaching my gospel . . . in my name . . . declaring my word like unto angels of God" (D&C 42:6; cf. Alma 29:1).

RLM

Tower of Babel *See* Babel, tower of.

Traffic(k) *See* Appendix C.

Transfiguration A short-term "quickening" or spiritual transformation of the body by the power of the Holy Ghost from a lower to higher state to be able to physically abide the presence of God and behold spiritual things (D&C 67:11–13). The Book of Mormon uses the term to describe the change that came upon the Three Nephite disciples who "were changed from this body of flesh," so "that they could behold the things of God" (3 Ne. 28:15). It is not clear from the Book of Mormon text whether this term is being used synonymously with the more enduring change identified in the scriptures as TRANSLATION. Examples of transfiguration would include Moses (Ex. 34:29–35; Moses 1:11), Christ with Peter, James, and John (Matt. 17:1–13), and the apostle Paul (2 Cor. 12:1–4). In contrast, translation refers to the long-term transformation that gives one power over death for a specific period of time in order to fulfill a special mission (Smith, 170–71), such as John the Beloved and the Three Nephites (3 Ne. 28:9).

See also Nephites, the Three.

BIBLIOGRAPHY

Smith, Joseph. *Teachings of the Prophet Joseph Smith.* Selected by Joseph Fielding Smith. Salt Lake City: Deseret Book, 1976.

BLT

Transgression *See* Sin, transgression.

Translation A glorified change brought upon select mortals which lengthens their connection with mortality until the time of their resurrection. The Book of Mormon sheds greater light on this subject than any other book of scripture. Third Nephi chapter twenty-eight contains a detailed account of the Three Nephite disciples who were changed to translated beings. This account reveals many characteristics of translated beings. For example, they are not subject to pain, sorrow, or Satan (3 Ne. 28:9, 39), wicked mortal men have no power over them (3 Ne. 28:21–22), and they escape the normal process of death—they do not "taste of death" as other mortals do (3 Ne. 28:7). When their ministries as translated beings have been completed, in a "twinkling of an eye" they experience a change equivalent to death, as they go from a translated state to a resurrected state (3 Ne. 28:8, 39–40). They are "sanctified in the flesh" and "the powers of the earth [cannot] hold them" (3 Ne. 28:39).

In addition to the Three Nephite disciples, the Book of Mormon suggests the possibility of the translation of Alma[2], Nephi[2], and Ether (Alma 45:18–19; 3 Ne. 1:2–3; 2:9; Ether 15:34). In the days of Enoch and Melchizedek their respective cities were translated because of their righteousness (JST Gen. 14:32–35). Thereafter, only a few instances of translation have occurred, and most involved a specific purpose. The Prophet Joseph Smith explained that in the world "many have supposed that the doctrine of translation was a doctrine whereby men were taken immediately into the presence of God, and into an eternal fulness, but this is a mistaken idea. Their place of habitation is that of the terrestrial order, and a place prepared for such characters [God] held in reserve to be ministering angels. . . . Translated bodies are designed for future missions" (170, 191). This was the case with MOSES and ELIJAH, who were translated in order that they might bestow certain keys in the meridian of time to Peter, James, and John on the Mount of Transfiguration (Matt. 17:4).

Concerning translation in the present day Elder Bruce R. McConkie has written, "The Lord ceased translating faithful people. Rather, they were permitted to die and go into the spirit world, there to perform the ever-increasing work needed in that sphere" (285).

The doctrine of translation is one of the mysteries that has eluded humankind, but it is part of the great restoration of all things and it is found in no greater clarity than in the Book of

Mormon. The Prophet Joseph Smith taught: "The doctrine of translation is a power which belongs to [the Melchizedek] Priesthood. There are many things which belong to the powers of the Priesthood and the keys thereof, that have been kept hid from before the foundation of the world; they are hid from the wise and prudent to be revealed in the last times" (170).

See also Nephites, the Three; Sanctified in the flesh; Taste of death; Transfiguration.

BIBLIOGRAPHY

McConkie, Bruce R. *The Millennial Messiah: The Second Coming of the Son of Man.* Salt Lake City: Deseret Book, 1982.

Smith, Joseph. *Teachings of the Prophet Joseph Smith.* Selected by Joseph Fielding Smith. Salt Lake City: Deseret Book, 1976.

CJW

Translation of the Book of Mormon *See* Book of Mormon, translation of.

Transoceanic crossings, pre-Columbian

The accounts of transoceanic crossings found in the Book of Mormon are among the great seafaring tales from ancient literature. The stories of Lehi[1] and his family in their open boats (1 Ne. 17–18) and the party led by the brother of Jared[1] in their water-tight "barges" (Ether 2:6; 6:4–13) blend teachings on spiritual topics such as faith, obedience, and endurance, with vivid descriptions of ship building and seamanship that could have been written only by people who had themselves survived the trials of lengthy sea voyages.

Having spent his entire youth in the landlocked areas of Vermont and New York, Joseph Smith could hardly have invented such stories. Yet many people have wondered what archaeological or historical evidences support the reality of pre-Columbian transoceanic travel. Did groups of people actually sail from the Old World to the Americas before the first voyage of Christopher COLUMBUS in 1492?

Even before the publication of the Book of Mormon there was great interest in the young United States about the many curious artifacts settlers were finding, such as weapons, tools, small works of art, and earthen mounds arranged in ways that suggested fortifications or cities. Because these apparently had not been created by the native groups who were then living nearby, there was frequent speculation about visitors or colonists from other lands. Over the ensuing century and a half, hundreds of books and articles have been printed to try either to prove or to discredit claims that Greeks, Romans, Vikings, Phoenicians, Africans, or other peoples sailed from their homelands to the New World.

Some evidences of early contact are well documented and generally acknowledged as reliable. The Viking settlement at L'Anse aux Meadows in Newfoundland has yielded house foundations, tools, and remnants of agriculture dating to about A.D. 1000, and most archaeologists accept as fact that Norsemen were settled in the New World by this time. There is almost as much agreement, based on extensive similarities in such things as artistic representation and weaponry, that there was extensive communication between China and the northwest coast of North America from very early times.

Other claims are less widely accepted. For example, large, donut-shaped stones found along the coast of California are interpreted by some investigators as anchor stones and support the contention that Chinese ships traveled much further south. But others claim that these stones were left by nineteenth-century Portuguese whaling expeditions or are even natural rather than man-made objects. Similar disparity of opinion exists regarding the numerous stones, found widely scattered over the United States, etched with rows of short vertical lines and angular shapes. These are seen either as records in the Ogam writing system from medieval Ireland or as natural stones accidentally scratched and gouged by farmers plowing their fields.

Adventurers such as Thor Heyerdahl, with his Kon-Tiki and Ra expeditions, have demonstrated that long ocean voyages could have been made. Other researchers have studied wind and water currents looking for other routes that might have been exploited by people in drifting crafts or have reconstructed ancient ships and sailing records, seeking to explore the possibility of travel to and from distant locations.

Scholars have examined the dispersal of the sweet potato, the bottle gourd, and specific varieties of cotton, as well as the chicken, the hairless dog, and other plants and animals in hopes of understanding if their existence in widely scattered locations is due to natural causes or was the result of intervention by ancient mariners. They have asked similar questions about diseases and such human inventions as games and musical instruments. For example, tuberculosis, previously thought to be strictly an Old World ailment, has been found in Peruvian mummies buried long before the arrival of Europeans; the game of pachisi from India is remarkably like the Aztec game of patolli; the tone scales of ancient Brazilian pan pipes are almost identical to those found in Melanesia; and the poses of figures found in ancient Mayan murals bear uncanny similarities to the motions of Balinese dancers.

The pyramids found throughout Mexico are reminiscent of the pyramids and ziggurats of the ancient Near East, although the pyramids of Egypt come to an apex; those of Mexico are truncated, so they can serve as platforms for temples. Egyptian pyramids also were built of solid stone and originally had smooth, white sides; those of Mexico were built of dirt and rubble, with brightly painted sculptures on their thin stone and plaster veneers. Similarly, although the ziggurats of the Sumerians, like their visual cousins in the New World, were stepped and flattened for temples, they were not built as memorial tombs for kings, as were those of the Maya.

Among the Maya there are legends of ancestors who "came from the other side of the sea" or "from where the sun rises" (*Annals* and *Lords*, 43, 169–70), but very few other clues exist to substantiate these stories. They are examples of the problem of the "disappearing foreigners," migrating peoples who may have been assimilated so thoroughly into the extant cultures they encountered that they simply no longer are seen as a distinct group, and they left behind only the tiniest clues that they ever even existed. Such were the ancient Israelites whose sojourn in the land of Goshen is described in the scriptures but was completely ignored by contemporary Egyptian historical accounts.

Thus it can be concluded that there is ample evidence that transoceanic travel not only was possible but also probably took place on a larger scale than previously thought. Investigators no longer see the oceans as barriers to cultural contact but accept that there was at least the potential for serious, long-distance open-sea travel in pre-Columbian times by many peoples—from Africa, Asia, the Mediterranean, Scandinavia, and Polynesia.

One must be cautious, however, when trying to relate specific archaeological discoveries that suggest pre-Columbian transoceanic crossings to particulars from the Book of Mormon, lest conclusions reached exceed the strength of the evidence at hand. Two examples can illustrate this.

The first concerns the Olmec civilization that flourished along the Gulf Coast of Mexico from about 1200 B.C. (or earlier) until a few hundred years before Christ. These people constructed great earthen mounds and courtyards, often surrounded by stone pillars and maintained by carefully engineered drainage systems. They also left behind dozens of large carved stones, many of which appear to be portraits of specific individuals.

Some Latter-day Saint researchers feel that these were the Jaredites. Indeed, one sculpture (Stela 3 from the site of La Venta) shows a rather Semitic-looking man with an aquiline nose and a long, pointed beard. But excavations at the site have also revealed several sculptures of human figures that are very Negroid in appearance, with thick lips and flattened noses, and numerous small artifacts that are very Asiatic in character. Thus although one prominent Olmec art work may be interpreted to suggest contact with the ancient Near East, others may just as likely be seen as suggesting contact with Africa or Asia. But none can inform about the nature or extent of such contacts, and attempts to link specific Olmec objects to Book of Mormon events or people cannot be directly supported by any of these items alone.

The second example centers on a group of people who lived along the Pacific coast of Guatemala as early as 1400 B.C. Some suggest that the time and location make the area around the ancient city of Izapa a potential candidate for a place of occupation by Book of Mormon peoples. The site contains dozens of carved stones that portray human figures in various activities, the most famous of which is the "Tree of Life" stone (sometimes called the "Lehi Stone" but officially known as STELA 5). A similar but much less complex monument (Stela 67) shows a man in a boat that is floating on top of what appear to be large ocean waves. The man is also holding in each hand an object that resembles an "ankh," the Egyptian sign of life. While this certainly could represent a Nephite on a transoceanic voyage, it would be inappropriate to reach this conclusion without first giving additional study to all other aspects of the site in particular and of the Izapan art style in general.

The serious investigator should ask, for example, why there are at Izapa so many other monuments that depict scenes that have no parallel to Book of Mormon stories, such as the one that portrays an alligator that metamorphoses into a tree. Also, while the Olmecs often portrayed what seem to be real persons, the Izapan-style monuments almost always show people with distorted faces, long noses, animal-like lips or other nonhuman attributes. The scenes appear to be more concerned with deities or myths than with actual human events. Thus while the image of the man in the boat is certainly fascinating and suggestive, it cannot be uncritically accepted as an ocean-voyaging Nephite.

In conclusion, artifacts from sites throughout North, Central, and South America attest to numerous transoceanic contacts over hundreds, if not thousands, of years. Tying any of these specifically to the Book of Mormon may not be possible, but the reality that similar voyages were made by similar people under similar circumstances cannot be denied. That the Book of Mormon describes such voyages is not a stumbling block or even a distraction, as some have claimed, but rather is a strength, as it places the scriptural accounts squarely in line with what is known about the ancient world.

See also Archaeology.

BIBLIOGRAPHY

The Annals of the Cakchiquels, translated by Adrián Recinos and Delia Goetz, and the *Title of the Lords of Totonicapán,* translated from Quiché to Spanish by Dionisio José Chonay, English version by Delia Goetz. Bound in 1 vol. Norman: University of Oklahoma Press, 1953.

Sorenson, John L, and Martin H. Raish. *Pre-Columbian Contact with the Americas across the Oceans: An Annotated Bibliography.* 2d ed. Provo: Research Press, 1996.

MHR

Travail *See* Appendix C.

Tree of knowledge of good and evil One of two trees in the Garden of Eden specifically mentioned in the account of the Fall—the other being the TREE OF LIFE (Gen. 2:9; Moses 3:9; Abr. 5:9). The tree itself is not referred to in the Book of Mormon by name, but it is identified by the name of its fruit—the FORBIDDEN FRUIT (2 Ne. 2:15, 18–19; Mosiah 3:26; Alma 12:22; Hel. 6:26). The scriptures do not identify the nature of its fruit. God forbade Adam and Eve to eat or even touch it—warning them that if they did so, they would "surely die." "Nevertheless," he added significantly, "thou mayest choose for thyself" (Moses 3:16–17; 4:8–9). After Satan tempted Eve, she discovered the fruit was "good for food" and "pleasant to the eyes," so she ate it and gave some to Adam (Moses 4:10–12).

If Adam and Eve had not partaken, they would have remained in the Garden of Eden indefinitely, they would have had no children, and they could have known no joy (2 Ne. 2:22–23). But "Adam did fall by the partaking of the forbidden fruit" and "by his fall, all mankind became a lost and fallen people" (Alma 12:22).

See also Cherubim and a flaming sword; Fall of Adam and Eve, the.

ROC

Tree of life Term used in the Book of Mormon to represent several related ideas.

1. The LOVE OF GOD (1 Ne. 11:21–22), which is manifested in the CONDESCENSION OF GOD—the life, ministry, and atonement of Christ (1 Ne. 11). Both Lehi[1] and Nephi[1] beheld the tree of life in a "dream" or "vision" (1 Ne. 8; 11; 15). The tree is described as "precious above all" (1 Ne. 11:9) and possessing beauty that "was far beyond, yea, exceeding of all beauty; and the whiteness thereof did exceed the whiteness of the driven snow" (1 Ne. 11:8). Its FRUIT "was desirable to make one happy," "most sweet, above all," "white, to exceed all . . . whiteness" (1 Ne. 8:10–11), "most precious and most desirable above all other fruits . . . [and] the greatest of all the gifts of God" (1 Ne. 15:36; cf. Alma 5:34).

2. The tree of life in the Garden of Eden. Alma[2] spoke of this tree in explaining the need for mortals to have an opportunity to repent and prepare to meet God: "And now behold, if it were possible that our first parents could have gone forth and partaken of the tree of life they would have been forever miserable, having no preparatory state; and thus the plan of redemption would have been frustrated, and the word of God would have been void, taking none effect" (Alma 12:21–26). Later Alma testified to his son, "For behold, if Adam had put forth his hand immediately, and partaken of the tree of life, he would have lived forever, according to the word of God, having no space for repentance; yea, and also the word of God would have been void, and the great plan of salvation would have been frustrated" (Alma 42:2–6).

3. That which grows from faith. In Alma 32–33, Alma compares the word of God to a seed that is "planted" in the heart of an individual (Alma 32:28). This seed, if it is properly nourished with "faith with great diligence, and with patience" will become a "tree of life" or "everlasting life" (Alma 32:40–41; 33:23), having fruit "which is most precious, . . . And which is white above all that is white" (Alma 32:42). The description of fruit here recalls the fruit of the tree of life in Lehi's and Nephi's visions.

See also Fall of Adam and Eve, the; Lehi[1]'s dream; Stela 5; Tree of knowledge of good and evil; Tree of life in ancient cultures.

DWP

Tree of life in ancient cultures The great vision given to Lehi[1] (1 Ne. 8) and also later to Nephi[1] (1 Ne. 11–15) contained the TREE OF LIFE as one of its central features. For the righteous to partake of the fruit of the tree is to experience the LOVE OF GOD and eternal life (1 Ne. 11:21–22). The unrighteous, however, are "rejected" from the tree of life and its fruit, for they cannot enjoy the presence of God or his love in their sinful condition (1 Ne. 15:36).

The first mention of the tree of life in the scriptures is in the account of Adam and Eve in Eden. After they disobeyed God by partaking of the fruit of the TREE OF KNOWLEDGE OF GOOD AND EVIL, Adam and Eve had to leave Eden. To ensure that they did not return and partake of the fruit of the tree of life, God instructed that the way to the tree be barred from Adam and Eve and their descendants in a fallen world (Alma 12:21–26).

Nevertheless, neither the memory of the tree nor the desire to partake of its fruit was lost in the succeeding generations of mankind. Ancient cultures maintained the symbolism of the tree of life as well as an account of man's quest to obtain its fruit. In the famous Mesopotamian epic tale concerning Gilgamesh and his quest for immortality, the hero undertakes a long journey to find the plant which gives life (Pritchard, 85–97). In another Mesopotamian account, the Myth of Etana, Etana flew to heaven on an eagle to obtain the plant of life, which he brought to earth to guarantee continued procreation (Pritchard, 114–18).

Egyptian culture is likewise replete with portrayals of the tree of life. In the ancient temple of Heliopolis, a new pharaoh would bow before the sacred persea tree to receive the life and power of kingship. To each leaf on the tree was attached the name of an ancestor of the pharaoh, as well as the sacred names given to him in coronation rites, binding his life to that of his progenitors back to the gods. The lotus plant was a well-known symbol of the plant (or tree) of life, symbolizing rebirth and regeneration after each annual flood of the Nile. In the tomb

TREE OF LIFE IN ANCIENT CULTURES

The deceased receiving nourishment (food and drink) from a tree goddess growing out of the tree of life. From the Egyptian Book of the Dead, Papyrus Ani, accompanying Spell 59.

of Tuthmosis III in the Valley of the Kings, a well-known illustration of the tree of life shows the king suckling from a breast drawn on one of the branches of the tree, and the arm of a goddess grows out of the tree to embrace the king. Many ancient Egyptian coffin lids depict the goddess Nut growing out of the tree of life. She is pouring drink from a pitcher and offering food from a tray, and this is understood as the goddess offering nourishment and life from the tree of life to a person who is wandering through the dark netherworld journey to eternal life.

From the earliest artistic and literary evidence of ancient Greece, trees of life and their life-giving fruits are often encountered. Such images appear in the sacred palms on the famous Vapphio cup from ancient Crete, and scenes of Mycenaean art show dancers performing a ritual dance around an altar, out of which is growing the tree of life with fruit on its branches. Similar scenes could be illustrated over and over again. In later classical Greek sources, the olive tree is often identified as representing the tree of life given by Athena to Athens as symbol of her love for the city-state and her guardianship of its people.

The Old Testament also contains numerous references to the tree of life, most notably in the symbolism of the menorah, which is acknowledged to represent the tree of life in the tabernacle and temple of God (Ex. 25:31–40; 2 Chr. 4:7, 20; 1 Enoch 25; Goodenough, 4:72–74, 82–92).

Even the lamps of the menorah filled with olive oil represent the presence and life of God. Anointing with olive oil symbolized partaking of the tree of life, whether in anointing ancient prophets and kings, or in anointing the sick with a blessing of renewed and restored life. Moreover, the divine titles Messiah and Christ mean "anointed one" in Hebrew and Greek, respectively, indicating that the Savior is immortal and can grant eternal life. Some early Christian art depicts Jesus crucified on a tree, with living creatures (including humans) approaching to partake of the Lord, whose body and blood are depicted as the true fruit of the tree of life.

The pervasiveness and symbolism of the tree of life in ancient cultures demonstrates the compatibility of the Book of Mormon with its ancient

Two birds beneath a stylized tree of life in the form of a later menorah. Illustration on a stone vase from Khafaje, Mesopotamia, before 3000 B.C.

cultural milieu, and helps the reader appreciate the great significance of this symbol in Lehi's and Nephi's vision.

See also Fall of Adam and Eve, the; Lehi[1]'s dream; Nephi[1]'s vision.

BIBLIOGRAPHY

Goodenough, E. R. *Jewish Symbols in the Greco-Roman Era.* 13 vols. Princeton, N.J.: Princeton University Press, 1953–68.

Griggs, Wilfred C. "The Tree of Life in Ancient Cultures." *Ensign* 18 (June 1988): 26–31.

Pritchard, J. B. *Ancient Near Eastern Texts.* 3d ed. Princeton, N.J.: Princeton University Press, 1969.

Yarden, Leon. *The Tree of Light.* Uppsala: Skriv Service, 1972.

CWG

Trees Only a few references to living trees are found in the Book of Mormon. Both the Nephites and Jaredites obtained materials to build their seagoing vessels from trees available in the Old World (1 Ne. 18:1–2; Ether 2:17). Alma[1] hid in a thicket of trees near the waters of Mormon (Mosiah 18:5), and the Gadianton robber Zemnarihah was "hanged upon a tree" (3 Ne. 4:28). Apparently in the days of Helaman[3] trees were very scarce in the land northward. The people there dwelled "in tents, and in houses of cement," and they protected any tree that "should spring up" in order to have timber for future needs (Hel. 3:9–10).

Although actual living trees are mentioned infrequently in the Book of Mormon, trees are often alluded to in the context of metaphors, similes, allegories, or parables to teach gospel principles and truths.

Cedars of Lebanon; courtesy D. Kelly Ogden.

In the vision of the TREE OF LIFE that Lehi[1] and Nephi[1] saw, the tree represents the LOVE OF GOD (1 Ne. 8:10–12, 15–25; 11:4, 7–25), and its FRUIT symbolizes "the greatest of all the gifts of God" (1 Ne. 15:36; 11:21–23). Alma[2] reminded the people of Zarahemla of the Lord's invitation to all mortals to partake of the fruit of the tree of life by coming unto Christ, repenting, and being baptized (Alma 5:34–36, 62). He taught that the tree of life grows from the seed, or from the word of God, when it is planted in one's heart and nourished "with much care" in ground that is fertile (Alma 32:37–43; 33:23).

The Book of Mormon also teaches of the tree of life found in the Garden of Eden. In a blessing pronounced on his son Jacob[2], Lehi[1] explained that the tree of life existed in opposition to the tree bearing the FORBIDDEN FRUIT (2 Ne. 2:15).

In yet another metaphorical reference to trees, Jacob quoted the allegory of Zenos, in which the house of Israel was likened to an olive tree. The allegory teaches of events both past and future, in particular the scattering and gathering of the covenant people, by describing how various branches of the tree are cut off, transplanted, grafted, and restored (Jacob 5; 1 Ne. 10:12–14). Book of Mormon peoples regarded themselves as a BRANCH cut off from the house of Israel (1 Ne. 19:24; Alma 26:36). Their prophets, including Joseph of old, taught that in the latter days the Gentiles would assist them in returning to the covenant and becoming a righteous branch (1 Ne. 15:7–18; 2 Ne. 3:5–11; 9:53; 10:1–2).

Trees which bring forth good or bad fruit are also used as metaphors for peoples and individuals who bring forth good or bad works. Those bringing forth evil fruit are warned that they will eventually be hewn down and burned (Alma 5:52; 3 Ne. 14:17–19; cf. Jacob 5).

The remaining references to trees in the Book of Mormon are found in the writings of Isaiah that Nephi copied onto the small plates. Botanical metaphors are common in Isaiah's writings, and he often used trees to teach of the Messiah and his dealings with the covenant people. Isaiah prophesied that Christ would be a descendant or "stem of Jesse" (2 Ne. 21:1 // Isa. 11:1; see also D&C 113:1–2). He also likened the pride and haughtiness of men to the cedars of Lebanon and the oaks of Bashan, the tallest and the most prized trees of their respective regions, with oaks reaching heights of fifty feet and cedars 120 feet. Cedars sometimes measured eight feet in diameter.

Despite such imposing physical stature, however, Isaiah warned that in "the day of the Lord," such pride and loftiness would be brought down (2 Ne. 12:12–13).

In yet another botanical allusion, Isaiah likened the restoration of the covenant people to the oak and teil, unusually robust trees that cannot be destroyed by merely chopping them down, for their remaining stumps regenerate the tree by sending forth new shoots. Accordingly, Isaiah taught that a part of Israel would return, and like the oak and teil, which though eaten or consumed to their substance or stumps, yet contain a seed that can regenerate (2 Ne. 16:13). He indicated that this restored branch would be both beautiful and fruitful (2 Ne. 14:2). Isaiah also likened men who rejoice at the captivity of Lucifer to the fir and cedar that no longer fear being hewn down (2 Ne. 24:8). Moreover, he equated the wealth and people of treacherous Assyria to trees in a forest which, after the day of the Lord's vengeance, would be so few that even a child could count them (2 Ne. 20:18–19).

See also Zenos, allegory of.

TBB

Trial of faith A period of divine testing of one's confidence in God during which one has the opportunity to demonstrate his FAITH by obedience and good works, especially when faced with uncertainty, sacrifice, or adversity. Periods of prosperity may also serve to test faith (Hel. 12:2–3). The Lord may try the faith of his righteous children to strengthen their trust in him (Mosiah 23:21–22). Moroni[2] taught that "faith is things which are hoped for and not seen; wherefore, dispute not because ye see not, for ye receive no witness until after the trial of your faith" (Ether 12:6). Thus, God may withhold a blessing for a period of trial, or probation, until a person has proved his or her faith by obedience. Obedience and good works are an accurate measure of one's actual faith—"faith, if it hath not works, is dead" (James 2:17–22). Moroni illustrated this principle of trial before witness or blessing by repeating variations of the phrase, "until *after* they had faith in him" (Ether 12:7–22; italics added). The Savior, for example, "showed not himself [unto his people] until after their faith" (Ether 12:12). In addition, Moroni declared that the faith of Alma[2] and Amulek destroyed the prison which confined them (Ether 12:13); the faith of Nephi[2] and Lehi[4] "wrought the change upon the Lamanites" (Ether 12:14); "the faith of Ammon and his brethren" brought about a great Lamanite conversion (Ether 12:15); and the faith of the three Nephite disciples enabled the promise of their TRANSLATION (Ether 12:17). After citing these examples, Moroni made it clear that "neither at any time hath any wrought miracles until after their faith; wherefore they first believed in the Son of God" (Ether 12:18). Moroni added that the faith of some was so strong, even before Christ's earthly advent, that they gained a perfect knowledge of that which they had known only in the Spirit, or with the "eye of faith" (Ether 12:19; cf. 3; 12:20–21).

In teaching Nephite dissenters, Alma[2] also alluded to the principle of trial before blessing: "And because of your diligence and your faith and your patience with the word in nourishing it, that it may take root in you, behold, by and by ye shall pluck the fruit thereof, which is most precious, which is sweet above all that is sweet" (Alma 32:41–43).

The trial of faith is God's way of not only testing faith, but also revealing and strengthening faith (Alma 32:27–37; cf. D&C 58:2–4; James 1:3; 1 Pet. 1:7–9).

MCT

Tribes Nephite clans or groups divided according to family, kindred, and friends following the collapse of the Nephite central government (3 Ne. 7:2; A.D. 30). Just before the death and resurrection of Jesus Christ in the Old World, there was great civil unrest among the Nephites in the New World (3 Ne. 6:27–7:2), and "the regulations of the government were destroyed" by secret combinations (3 Ne. 7:6–8). The people "divided one against another" and separated into tribes (3 Ne. 7:2). Each tribe had a "chief" (3 Ne. 7:3) and the laws and government of each tribe varied according to the desires of tribal leadership (3 Ne. 7:11). The tribes came "to an agreement that they would not go to war one with another" and that "one tribe should not trespass against another" (3 Ne. 7:14).

Although the tribes were enemies "they were united in [their] hatred of those who had entered into a covenant to destroy the government" (3 Ne. 7:11). Their hearts were also turned from the Lord (3 Ne. 7:7), and "they did stone the prophets and did cast them out from among them" (3 Ne. 7:14). Nephi[3], however, enjoyed some success among the tribes, going forth exercising priesthood power and preaching "repentance and remission of sins" through Christ (3 Ne. 7:15–26).

EEV

True fold Term referring to the Church of Jesus Christ, a church that carries the Lord's name, teaches his gospel, and manifests the works of the Father (3 Ne. 27:8–10). Membership in the true fold, or Church of Christ, was one of the blessings enumerated by Nephi[1] that would come to his latter-day posterity as a result of their acceptance of the restored gospel (1 Ne. 15:15, 12–16). The gathering of the Jews and, by extension, all Israel (1 Ne. 15:17, 20; 3 Ne. 29:8; Morm. 5:14) entails coming into the "true church and fold of God" and being restored to their lands of promise (2 Ne. 9:2).

RCR

True vine Jesus Christ (John 15:1). Nephi[1] prophesied that when his latter-day posterity accepted the restored gospel they would receive "strength and nourishment" from the true vine, who is Christ (1 Ne. 15:12–16; Alma 16:17).

See also True fold.

RCR

Trump, second *See* Second trump.

Trust Term used in a number of senses in the Book of Mormon.

1. Reliance on or confidence in God. The word is used as both a noun and a verb, but with essentially the same meaning: "trust in [God] forever" (2 Ne. 4:34); "trust in God continually" (Alma 57:27); trust him to assist in overcoming weaknesses and trials: "And when I desire to rejoice, my heart groaneth because of my sins; nevertheless, I know in whom I have trusted" (2 Ne. 4:19; cf. Alma 36:3, 27); trust in his power (his arm) to help and to deliver: "On mine arm shall they trust" (2 Ne. 8:5; cf. 22:2; Mosiah 7:19; Alma 58:37). Many promises are associated with trusting in God: Alma[2] taught that "whosoever shall put their trust in God shall be supported in their trials, and their troubles, and their afflictions, and shall be lifted up at the last day" (Alma 36:3, 27–28; cf. Mosiah 4:6–7; 23:22; Alma 38:5). And Mormon stated that "the Lord in his great infinite goodness doth bless and prosper those who put their trust in him" (Hel. 12:1). After attributing the deliverance of the repentant people of king Noah[3] to the "interposition of [the] all-wise Creator," Mosiah[2] concluded, "And thus doth the Lord work with his power in all cases among the children of men, extending the arm of mercy towards them that put their trust in him" (Mosiah 29:19–20; cf. 7:33).

2. Reliance on or confidence in the power or word of man as opposed to the power or word of God. "Cursed is he that putteth his trust in man, or maketh flesh his arm, or shall hearken unto the precepts of men, save their precepts shall be given by the power of the Holy Ghost" (2 Ne. 28:31; cf. 4:34). Alma[1], when he was asked to be king, reminded the people of Helam about the iniquities of king Noah, and warned that they should "trust no man to be a king over [them]" (Mosiah 23:6, 13; cf. 29:13). Alma implied that men cannot be trusted to be as steady and reliable and just as they ought to be (Mosiah 23:7–9, 12; cf. Hel. 12:1). He went on to teach his people that they should be careful about those they trusted in other capacities: "Trust no one to be your teacher nor your minister, except he be a man of God, walking in his ways and keeping his commandments" (Mosiah 23:14).

3. Strong belief or confidence. "I trust in Christ that thou wilt be saved" (Moro. 9:22; cf. Mosiah 7:18; 21:19; Alma 7:5–6; 38:2).

TRUTH

4. Charge with possession of, entrust. "Trust not those secret plans unto this people" (Alma 37:32).

TLG

Truth The Book of Mormon speaks of truth as the way things "really" are, "in purity . . . according to the truth which is in God" (Jacob 4:13; 1 Ne. 13:24–25; 14:26; Enos 1:26). Also, Jesus Christ himself, as the embodiment of truth, is spoken of as "the word of truth" (Alma 38:9) and "the light, and the life, and the truth of the world" (Ether 4:12). Knowing the truth is assured only in and through Christ and the light of Christ.

All who have the truth about a given thing see eye to eye, be they men, angels, or gods (4 Ne. 1:17; 3 Ne. 19:23; cf. D&C 38:27; 50:21–23). On the other hand, error, which is the opposite of truth, can be infinite; the number of false conceptions possible about a particular truth is numberless. Those who subscribe to error may sometimes agree with each other, but that agreement does not establish the truth. As God is the agent of truth and oneness, Satan is the agent of error and contention (2 Ne. 2:18; 3 Ne. 11:29).

How to know truth

Through their natural mental capacities and strengthened by the light of Christ, men can learn many truths pertaining to the natural world (2 Ne. 7:11; 9:28–29; Hel. 4:13; 16:15–22). But the truth of God unto salvation can only be known by revelation through the power of the Holy Ghost (Jacob 4:8; Alma 5:45–46; 26:21–22; 36:4–5). Men begin to know the things of God when they hearken to the "Spirit of Christ [which] is given to every man, that he may know good from evil" (Moro. 7:16). Those who do not harden their hearts against such promptings are "given the greater portion of the word, until it is given unto him to know the mysteries of God until he know them in full. And they that will harden their hearts, to them is given the lesser portion of the word until they know nothing concerning his mysteries" (Alma 12:10–11; cf. D&C 84:46–48). Alma[2] assured the Zoramites[2] that if they would "exercise a particle of faith," perhaps beginning with "no more than [a] desire to believe," and "experiment" upon the word of God with faith, diligence, and patience, they would come to know the truth of God's word (Alma 32:27–43). Moroni[2] promised that anyone who would read the Book of Mormon, ponder the mercies of God unto the children of men, and pray "with a sincere heart, with real intent, having faith in Christ" would know the truth of the Book of Mormon "by the power of the Holy Ghost" (Moro. 10:3–4). He added, "And by the power of the Holy Ghost ye may know the truth of all things" (Moro. 10:5). Alma noted that "his brethren in the Lord," the sons of Mosiah[2], "waxed strong in the knowledge of the truth" because "they had searched the scriptures diligently . . . given themselves to much prayer, and fasting; therefore they had the spirit of prophecy, and the spirit of revelation" (Alma 17:2–3).

Stances concerning truth

Among the children of men there are different stances relative to truth, including (1) being in harmony with the things of God, to "love the truth" and "receive[th] it with gladness" (e.g., 2 Ne. 9:40; 28:28); (2) some others are simply ignorant of the truth and are not held accountable for what they do not know (Mosiah 15:24); (3) some are not without knowledge, but are at the moment not in harmony with the things of God, are not hearkening to heavenly promptings, and so have erroneous opinions and attitudes (e.g., Alma 10:1–10); (4) some, being wicked and "of the spirit of the devil" (2 Ne. 33:5), become angry at the truth because it exposes their wickedness and "cutteth them to the very center" (e.g., 1 Ne. 16:2; cf. 2 Ne. 9:40; Mosiah 13:4, 7); (5) some are deliberately submissive to Satan, having a sense of truth, but professing lies to others, even coming to believe those lies themselves (e.g., Alma 30:52–53). The gospel of Jesus Christ invites all men to forsake the last four of these stances and come to the first, to "come unto Christ, and be perfected in him," for "redemption cometh in and through the Holy Messiah; for he is full of grace and truth" (Moro. 10:32–33; 2 Ne. 2:6, 10).

Witnesses of the truth of the Book of Mormon

Concerning its own divine origin and truthfulness, the Book of Mormon affirms the long-standing principle that "in the mouth of two or three witnesses every word may be established" (Matt. 18:16). Very early in the record readers learn that the metal plates on which was engraved the text of the Book of Mormon would "be hid from the eyes of the world, that the eyes of none shall behold it save it be that three witnesses shall behold it, by the power of God" (2 Ne. 27:12; Ether 5:2–4). In addition to these three special witnesses who would view the plates "by the power of God," the Lord promised to provide for "a few," even "as many witnesses as seemeth him good," to also see the plates and thereafter "testify to the truth of the book and the things therein" (2 Ne. 27:12–14).

All will acknowledge the truth or be cast out

In the life to come eventually all will see the truth and acknowledge the justice and goodness of God. They will then also see the truth about Satan if they have not come to it before, and will lament any service given him in mortality. Any who absolutely refuse to acknowledge and submit to the truth will be "cast out" (Mosiah 16:1–5) and "inherit the kingdom of the devil" (Alma 41:4–5; cf. Mosiah 27:31; Alma 12:15; 34:35; 40:26).

See also Good, concept of.

CCR

Tubaloth Lamanite king and son of Ammoron (Hel. 1:16; ca. 51 B.C.). Because he wanted to gain power over the Nephites, Tubaloth incited the wrath of his armies against them and appointed Coriantumr[3], a Nephite dissenter, to lead his forces in a bold assault against Zarahemla (Hel. 1:14–17). Aided by internal discord among the Nephites, the Lamanites captured the city of Zarahemla, but then lost it to the forces of Lehi[3] and Moronihah[1] (Hel. 1:18–33).

Twelve Apostles, records of the *See* Records of the Twelve Apostles.

Twenty-four gold plates *See* Plates of Ether.

Two churches only *See* Great and abominable church.

Two rims of a bow *See* Urim and Thummim.

Types A person, thing, or event that prophetically foreshadows another person, thing, or event of greater magnitude. In the scriptures the terms *type*, SIMILITUDE, *likeness*, *figure*, and SHADOW may be used interchangeably. Nephi[1] taught that "all things which have been given of God from the beginning of the world, unto man, are the typifying of him [Christ]" (2 Ne. 11:4). Further, the Lord taught Adam at his baptism that "all things have their likeness, and all things are created and made to bear record of me" (Moses 6:63). Thus the number of types and likenesses in the gospel is inexhaustible.

Types can be seen in gospel ordinances, the LAW OF MOSES, historical events, objects, and even in the lives of people (i.e., the prophets).

Gospel ordinances as types

The ordinances of BAPTISM and the SACRAMENT are types which point to Christ and his redeeming work, the former symbolizing rebirth through the Atonement (2 Ne. 31:13, 17; Mosiah 27:25; Moses 6:59–60; Rom. 6:4), and the latter representing Christ's broken body and spilt blood in atoning for sin and overcoming death (3 Ne. 18:7, 11; Moro. 4; 5).

Law of Moses as a type

The law of Moses itself, with all of its PERFORMANCES AND ORDINANCES served as a prophetic foreshadowing of the coming atonement of Jesus Christ. Mormon wrote that the Nephites "did look forward to the coming of Christ, considering that the law of Moses was a type of his coming" (Alma 25:15). Thus, Abinadi taught, "If ye teach the law of Moses, also teach that it is a shadow of those things which are to come" (Mosiah 16:14; 13:28; cf. 2 Ne. 11:4; Jacob 4:5; Alma 34:14). An example of Mosaic ordinances was SACRIFICES, which typified or pointed to the "great and last sacrifice," Jesus Christ, who "offereth himself a sacrifice for sin" (Alma 34:14; 2 Ne. 2:7; Moses 5:5–8).

Historical events as types

The departure of Lehi[1] from the wicked city of Jerusalem, his journey in the wilderness, his dependence upon divine guidance to achieve his destination, and his being promised a land of

TYPES

inheritance "choice above all other lands" (1 Ne. 2:20; 2 Ne. 1:3–5) conditional upon obedience, can be viewed as a type of the journey all people must make to achieve the celestial kingdom (1 Ne. 17:13–14; cf. Ether 1:38–42; 2:7). To receive an inheritance in God's kingdom, one must depart or separate from wickedness and then travel the gospel path throughout life, relying upon the Lord's guidance and being obedient to his commandments (2 Ne. 31:20; Moro. 10:32).

The coming of Christ to the Nephites and Lamanites was a type, or foreshadowing, of his second coming to the world. The escalation of pride and wickedness among the Nephites before Christ's coming, the destructions that attended Christ's coming in consequence of that wickedness, and the period of peace that followed, all shadow what latter-day people can anticipate. President Ezra Taft Benson taught, "In the Book of Mormon we find a pattern for preparing for the Second Coming. A large part of the book centers on the few decades just prior to Christ's coming to America. By careful study of that time period, we can determine why some were destroyed in the terrible judgments that preceded His coming and what brought others to stand at the temple in the land of Bountiful[2] and thrust their hands into the wounds of His hands and feet" (Benson, 20–21).

The nearly two hundred years of peace among the children of Lehi following Christ's coming could be viewed as a type of the millennial reign of Christ and the peace that will attend that period of time. All social turmoil and class distinction, as well as major sins, were eliminated (4 Ne. 1:1–18). The Father and the Son rejoiced in the people of that generation, because none of them would be lost (3 Ne. 27:30–31). The people's decline after this era of peace typifies the denying of God by some and Satan's being loosed at the end of the Millennium (4 Ne. 1:24–26; D&C 29:22; cf. Jacob 5:77).

Samuel the Lamanite prophesied the sign of a "day and a night and a day" of light in the New World, heralding the birth of Christ in the Old World (Hel. 14:4, 20). This light is seen as typifying Christ, or the light of the world, coming into the world to be the Redeemer. Similarly, the sign of three days of darkness in the New World at his death could typify that Christ, the light of the world, was taken from the world because of the wickedness of men (Hel. 14:20). For additional references to historical types, see Ether 13:6–7; Exodus 12:7, 12–13; Numbers 20:8; 21:8.

Objects as types

Nephi[2] taught that the BRAZEN SERPENT was a type of the atonement of Christ. To save the people from the FIERY FLYING SERPENTS that were biting them, Moses lifted up a brazen serpent on a pole. If the people would simply look at the raised serpent they could be healed; likewise, if humankind looks to Christ, or comes unto Christ in faith, they can receive eternal life (Hel. 8:14–15; John 3:14–15).

The TREE OF LIFE was also a type for Christ (1 Ne. 11:11–33). When one partakes of the tree of life, or applies the Atonement, "it shall be a tree springing up unto everlasting life" (Alma 32:27–43). The Nephite LIAHONA was a type of the "words of Christ." In comparing the guidance of the Liahona with the words of Christ, Alma[2] said to his son Helaman[2], "These things are not without a shadow. . . . Is there not a type in this thing? For just as surely as this director did bring our fathers, by following its course, to the promised land, shall the words of Christ, if we follow their course, carry us . . . into a far better land of promise [the celestial kingdom]" (Alma 37:38–47).

ROCK, which is solid and provides a firm foundation, in contrast to sand, which can be easily washed away in a storm, serves as a type for Christ (3 Ne. 14:24–27; Moses 7:53; 1 Cor. 10:4). Helaman[3] taught his sons that Christ is the rock upon which people must build to have "a sure foundation" (Hel. 5:12).

Prophets as types

The lives of prophets can be seen as types of Christ. For example, Abinadi's arraignment before king Noah[3] and the wicked priests, and his execution following a corrupt trial wherein he denounced the people's wickedness and revealed the true role of the Messiah, was similar to, or in the likeness of, future events in the life of Christ

(Mosiah 7:26–28; Mark 14:60–64). The man Melchizedek typified Christ, the preeminent king of righteousness and prince of peace (Isa. 9:6; Luke 22:29). The name Melchizedek means "king of righteousness," and because he brought peace to his people "he was called the prince of peace" (Alma 13:18; cf. JST Gen. 14:36). Moreover, Melchizedek "did reign under his father" (Alma 13:18), just as Christ followed his father's instructions (John 5:30; 15:1). The raising of Timothy from the dead by Nephi[3] and the people's reaction to this miracle is similar to the raising of Lazarus by Jesus and the subsequent response of the Jews. This incident can be seen as typifying the power of God to raise all men from the grave (3 Ne. 7:17–20; John 12:9–11).

See also Book of Mormon, as literature.

BIBLIOGRAPHY

Benson, Ezra Taft. *A Witness and a Warning.* Salt Lake City: Deseret Book, 1988.

RJN

Typifying *See* Types.

Behold the Lord slayeth the wicked to bring forth his righteous purposes. It is better that one man should perish than that a nation should dwindle and perish in **unbelief**. 1 NEPHI 4:13

Unbelief Rejection or skepticism concerning some idea, doctrine, person, tenet, etc. Unbelief is the antithesis of BELIEF. In the Book of Mormon the term is usually used in reference to a rejection of God, his son Jesus Christ, and/or the gospel of Jesus Christ.

Such unbelief often results from pride and rebellion, and is promoted by Satan and those who follow him (e.g., Alma 30:53; 46:7; 3 Ne. 1:22; 2:2–3; 4 Ne. 1:34, 38; cf. 1 Ne. 12:17; Moro. 7:17). Frequently it is associated or in consequence of materialism and wickedness (e.g., Alma 7:6; 3 Ne. 21:5). Unbelief can also be developed gradually; for example, in Helaman[3]'s day, "the church had begun to dwindle; and they began to disbelieve" because of iniquity (Hel. 4:23). Unbelief may also be the result of false traditions and teachings of parents, as was typically the case with the Lamanites (e.g., Jacob 3:7; Mosiah 10:12–17; cf. 4 Ne. 1:38). The Lord promised to "be merciful" to the Lamanites and eventually grant them an opportunity to be restored "again to the knowledge of the truth" (e.g., Alma 9:16–17; Hel. 15:11, 15–16).

Unbelief in Christ and his gospel can lead one to commit serious sins. For example, those afflicted with this spiritual malady may reject the teachings of God's prophets and missionaries (e.g., 1 Ne. 2:13; Alma 21:6–8; Hel. 16:2, 6, 20; Ether 9:29), refuse to repent (e.g., Alma 15:15), and deny the existence of God or Christ (Alma 30:48; 31:16–17; Ether 4:12). They may be reluctant to look to God and recognize his works (e.g., Alma 33:20; 44:9; cf. 2 Ne. 32:7; Alma 32:28). They may demand signs to prove God's existence (e.g., Alma 30:48; cf. Jacob 7:13; Alma 32:17), teach their children and others to believe falsehoods (e.g., Alma 1:2–6; 30:12–53; 4 Ne. 1:38), and persecute believers (e.g., Mosiah 17:15; Alma 14:7–11; 15:1; 4 Ne. 1:29).

Such unbelief limits one's ability to understand the word of God (e.g., Mosiah 26:3; 3 Ne. 15:18; cf. 1 Ne. 15:7–11) and acts like a dark veil (e.g., Alma 19:6; cf. Ether 4:15). God's covenants, revelations, scriptures, miracles, power, and gifts may be withheld because of this kind of unbelief (2 Ne. 30:2; 3 Ne. 19:35; 26:10; Morm. 1:14; 9:20; Ether 4:3, 13–15; Moro. 10:19, 24; cf. Alma 12:9–11; 3 Ne. 16:4, 7), and thus those in such a state of "darkness" and iniquity are left to "dwindle in unbelief" (Alma 45:12; cf. 1 Ne. 10:11; 12:22–23; 2 Ne. 1:10; Alma 45:10). Ultimately, those who refuse to believe will face fear (e.g., 3 Ne. 1:16–18), destruction (e.g., Hel. 4:20–25; Ether 12:3), and damnation (2 Ne. 9:24).

See also Hard-heartedness; Stiffnecked, stiffneckedness.

TBB

Uncircumcised of heart Term used by Jacob[2] and Nephi[2] to describe those unwilling to yield their hearts in obedience to God (2 Ne. 9:33; Hel. 9:21). God gave Abraham the ordinance of circumcision as a sign of the covenant he established with him and reestablished with Moses (Gen. 17:11; Lev. 12:3). The removal of a male's foreskin was the outward sign of acceptance of, and willingness to be obedient to this covenant. Those who were circumcised in the flesh but broke the conditions of the covenant could be viewed as uncircumcised of heart (Rom. 2:25–29).

See also Law of circumcision.

RDD

Undaunted *See* Appendix C.

Unpardonable sin The sin of denying the Holy Ghost. Alma[2] taught his son Corianton that this sin is an unpardonable sin (Alma 39:5–6). Those guilty of this sin will be sons of perdition and will be cast into OUTER DARKNESS with Satan and his followers, as there is no forgiveness for them in this world nor in the world to come. They deny the truth and defy God's power after receiving it (D&C 76:25–46). Sherem, the anti-Christ, expressed concern that he had committed the unpardonable sin when he "lied unto God" by denying the Christ (Jacob 7:19). For one to deny the Holy Ghost, "he must receive the Holy Ghost, have the heavens opened unto him, and know God, and then sin against him. After a man has sinned against the Holy Ghost, there is no repentance for him. He has got to say that the sun does not shine while he sees it; he has got to deny Jesus Christ when the heavens have been opened unto him, and to deny the plan of salvation with his eyes open to the truth of it; and from that time he begins to be an enemy" (Smith, *Church,* 6:314). The Prophet Joseph Smith also taught that "a man cannot commit the unpardonable sin after the dissolution of the body" (*Teachings,* 357). This sin "requires such knowledge that it is manifestly impossible for the rank and file to commit such a sin" (Kimball, 23).

See also Spiritual death.

BIBLIOGRAPHY

Kimball, Spencer W. *Teachings of Spencer W. Kimball.* Salt Lake City: Bookcraft, 1982.

Smith, Joseph. *History of The Church of Jesus Christ of Latter-day Saints.* Edited by B. H. Roberts. 7 vols. 2d ed. rev. Salt Lake City: The Church of Jesus Christ of Latter-day Saints, 1932–51.

———. *Teachings of the Prophet Joseph Smith.* Selected by Joseph Fielding Smith. Salt Lake City: Deseret Book, 1976.

HDG

Urim and Thummim Two stones prepared by the Lord for interpreting languages (Mosiah 28:13–14) and the instrument through which Joseph Smith translated the Book of Mormon (Smith, *Church,* 4:537). In Hebrew, the term "urim and thummim" literally means "lights and perfections," referring to the stones' ability to bring to light hidden things of the past (Alma 37:23). These stones, or "interpreters," as the Book of Mormon calls them (Mosiah 8:13; 28:20; Alma 37:21; Ether 4:5), were originally given to the brother of Jared[1], who was commanded to seal them up with his record as a means of translating the same (Ether 3:23–24). The Nephite king Mosiah[2] possessed a Urim and Thummim, the origin of which is not specified in the text (Mosiah 8:13; Omni 1:20). Mosiah used them to translate the twenty-four gold plates containing the history of the Jaredites (Mosiah 28:11–13). Joseph Smith possessed the stones that had been given to the brother of Jared (D&C 17:1).

Mormon described the Urim and Thummim as "two stones which were fastened into the two rims of a bow," having been "prepared from the beginning, and were handed down from generation to generation, for the purpose of interpreting languages; and . . . discover[ing] to every creature who should possess the land the iniquities and abominations of [the Lord's] people" (Mosiah 28:13–15; cf. Alma 37:23–25). Ammon[1] taught that only select individuals, called "seers," were allowed to use these stones, lest someone "should look for that he ought not and he should perish" (Mosiah 8:13).

Joseph Smith learned of the stones' existence the night of 21 September 1823 from Moroni[2], then a resurrected being, who told him that when he should obtain them, he should show them only to those to whom he should be commanded to show them (JS–H 1:42). Joseph first saw the Urim and Thummim the following day (JS–H 1:52), and obtained them and the plates four years later (JS–H 1:59).

Joseph Smith described the Urim and Thummim as a "curious instrument . . . which consisted of two transparent stones set in the rim of a bow fastened to a breast plate" (Smith, *Church,* 4:537; cf. JS–H 1:35). Lucy Mack Smith described the instrument as "consist[ing] of two smooth three-cornered diamonds set in glass, and the glasses were set in silver bows, which were connected with each other in much the same way as old fashioned spectacles" (*Sketches,* 101). David Whitmer also compared the Urim and Thummim to a pair of eyeglasses, but noted that "the bow between the stones was more heavy, and longer apart between the stones, than we usually find it in spectacles" (Cook, 23). The breastplate upon which this was fastened, Lucy reported, "was concave on one side, and convex on the other, and extended from the neck downwards, as far as the centre of the stomach of a man of extraordinary size" (*Sketches,* 107). The "spectacles" were attached to the breastplate, according to William Smith, "by a rod which was fastened at the outer shoulde[r] edge of the breastplate. . . . This rod was just the right length so that when the Urim and thummim was removed from before the eyes it woul<d> reac<h> to a pocked [pocket?] on the left side of the breastplate where the instrument was kept when not in use" (Vogel, 1:508–9). As to the manner in which these stones were "set in two

URIM AND THUMMIM

rims of a bow," William reported that "a silver bow ran over one stone, under the other, arround [*sic*] over that one and under the first in the shape of a horizontal figure 8 much like a pair of spectacles. . . . [T]hey were much too large for Joseph and he could only see through one at a time using sometimes one and sometimes the other" (Vogel, 1:508).

Joseph used the Urim and Thummim to translate some of the characters on the plates between December 1827 and February 1828, prior to Martin Harris's taking copies of some of the characters with their translation to Professor Charles Anthon (JS–H 1:62–65). After Joseph lent Martin 116 pages of manuscript to show his wife and four others, Moroni appeared and took the instrument from Joseph "in consequence of my having wearied the Lord in asking for the privilege of letting Martin Harris take the writings" (Smith, *Church*, 1:21). Shortly after Martin lost the 116 pages, Moroni returned the Urim and Thummim to Joseph long enough for him to receive what is now Doctrine and Covenants 3, then again took the instrument into his custody. Moroni returned the stones to Joseph "in a few days" (Smith, *Church*, 1:23), after which time they remained with Joseph until the Book of Mormon was translated. *See* Book of Mormon, lost manuscript of (116 pages).

In addition to translating the Nephite record, Lucy Mack Smith reported that Joseph was able to receive visions through the Urim and Thummim, as well as "ascertain, at any time, the approach of danger, either to himself or the Record" (Smith, *Joseph Smith*, 110). Joseph also used the instrument to inquire of the Lord on behalf of various individuals (D&C 6; 11; 14; 17 headings), and to learn "whether John, the beloved disciple, tarried in the flesh or had died" (D&C 7 heading). After Joseph "had accomplished by them what was required," he again delivered the stones to Moroni (JS–H 1:60).

A Urim and Thummim was also kept in the pocket of the breastplate worn by the high priest in Old Testament Israel (Ex. 28:30; Lev. 8:8). This Urim and Thummim was also apparently used for receiving revelation from the Lord (e.g., Num. 27:21; 1 Sam. 28:6).

See also Book of Mormon, translation of; Seer stone.

BIBLIOGRAPHY

Cook, Lyndon W., ed. *David Whitmer Interviews: A Restoration Witness*. Orem: Grandin Book, 1993.

Smith, Joseph. *History of The Church of Jesus Christ of Latter-day Saints*. Edited by B. H. Roberts. 7 vols. 2d ed. rev. Salt Lake City: The Church of Jesus Christ of Latter-day Saints, 1932–51.

Smith, Lucy Mack. *Biographical Sketches of Joseph Smith, the Prophet, and His Progenitors for Many Generations*. Liverpool: S. W. Richards, 1853.

———. *History of Joseph Smith by His Mother*. Edited by Preston Nibley. Salt Lake City: Stevens & Wallis, 1945.

Vogel, Dan, ed. *Early Mormon Documents*. 3 vols. Salt Lake City: Signature Books, 1996–2000.

AHH

And he said unto me: Behold,

the **virgin** whom thou seest is

the mother of the Son of God,

after the manner of the flesh.

1 NEPHI 11:18

Vain repetitions Useless or meaningless phrases. The Savior warned against the use of vain repetitions in prayer, especially when spoken to impress others rather than to communicate with God or when repeatedly uttered in the hope that frequent repetition would cause them to be heard (3 Ne. 13:5–7). Amulek also suggested that prayers are "vain" when an individual's actions do not reflect his or her supplications (Alma 34:28). Thus Mormon taught that unless a person prays "with real intent . . . it profiteth him nothing, for God receiveth none such" (Moro. 7:9).

GS

Vale *See* Appendix C.

Verily *See* Appendix C.

Vessels of the Lord During his visit to the New World, the Savior quoted Isaiah, "Depart ye, depart ye, go ye out from thence . . . ; be ye clean that bear the vessels of the Lord" (3 Ne. 20:41; cf. Isa. 52:11). In Isaiah "vessels of the Lord" refers to the vessels of the temple which were captured by the Babylonians when they destroyed Jerusalem and the temple in 586 B.C. (2 Kgs. 25:13–16). The vessels remained in Babylon until Cyrus captured Babylon and allowed the Jews to take them back to Jerusalem and to install them in their rebuilt temple (Ezra 1:7–11). The phrase "be ye clean" refers to the necessity of those who would bear the vessels of the temple to be worthy and ritually pure. This event established a scriptural type of leaving Babylon to go to Zion which the Savior used in the Book of Mormon and in the Doctrine and Covenants to refer to the gathering of Israel in the latter days. In a revelation in the Doctrine and Covenants the Saints were called to leave Babylon and gather to Zion (D&C 133:5, 14), where they were to build a temple (D&C 84:1–5). Following the metaphor of ancient Israel leaving Babylon to rebuild their temple, the phrase "vessels of the Lord" in the context of the Restoration may be an allusion to the sacred work the Saints are called to do in building up the kingdom in the latter days (D&C 38:41–42).

Metaphorically, this phrase is also used to refer to "chosen" servants of the Lord (Moro. 7:31).

See also Isaiah chapter reviews (3 Ne. 20:32–45 // Isa. 52:1–3, 6–15); Jerusalem[1], destruction of, at 586 B.C.

DRS

View his death To visualize the atonement of Jesus Christ and ponder upon his sacrifice (Jacob 1:8). While latter-day people are admonished to "always remember" Christ, faithful Nephites were to "look forward" to his coming (Jarom 1:11) and could receive the benefits of his future Atonement "as though he had already come among them" (Mosiah 3:13). Jacob[2]'s invitation to "view his death" (Jacob 1:8) can be an antidote against sin, because of the difficulty of proceeding in sin while simultaneously visualizing the suffering of Christ for those sins.

SAJ

View of the Hebrews A book written by the Reverend Ethan Smith (1762–1849) that some since 1902 have suggested may have been a source for the Book of Mormon because it argues that the American Indians are the lost tribes of Israel. *View of the Hebrews* (1823; 2d expanded edition, 1825) was one of many books and pamphlets on religious topics published by the Reverend Smith between 1800 and 1839. He lived and ministered mostly in Vermont, New Hampshire, and Massachusetts.

The 1825 expanded second edition of *View of the Hebrews* is divided into four chapters, a conclusion, and an appendix. The first chapter, "The Destruction of Jerusalem," relies heavily on predictions of the coming destruction found in the Bible and the descriptions of its having happened found in the *Wars of the Jews* by Josephus. The second chapter, "The Certain Restoration of Judah and Israel," argues for that restoration, primarily from the Bible. In the third and longest chapter, "The Present State of the Jews, and of Israel," Reverend Smith presented ideas and information about what the American Indians said they believed about themselves, their history, language, religion, and customs. He obtained this information by reading almost everything that had been published on the subject, which was impressively broad; however, he relied most heavily on James Adair's *History of the American Indians* (1775), and Elias Boudinot's

Star in the West (1814). The fourth chapter, "An Address of the Prophet Isaiah, Relative to the Restoration of His People," is the Reverend Smith's exposition of the eighteenth chapter of Isaiah and his call to Christianity to carry the gospel of salvation to the American Indians, who he said were the lost tribes of Israel.

Parts of the third chapter are most often said to be a source for the Book of Mormon. One argument is that both books identify the American Indians as children of Israel; yet, where Reverend Smith stated that the Israelites all traveled to the American continent by migrating as a group north and east through Russia and crossing over the Bering Strait land bridge, the Book of Mormon speaks of two boat migrations under the direction of the Lord. Where Reverend Smith spoke of the American Indians as all of the lost tribes of Israel, the Book of Mormon identifies Lehi's family as stemming from Joseph[1]'s son Manasseh (Alma 10:3). Both books speak of a white leader who lived among the people, but Reverend Smith said that this leader lived with them for twenty years and called him a Moses; the Book of Mormon says that it was the resurrected Christ who visited them for a short time and then left. Where Joseph Smith, according to Emma Smith, did not know there was a wall around Jerusalem until he translated that information from the Book of Mormon plates, the Reverend Smith described Jerusalem's three walls in some detail (Briggs, 454). He also spoke of the Indian legend of a record book that was lost; Joseph Smith said the Book of Mormon is a translation of a buried record revealed by a holy angel. Both books speak of a division among the people into a good group and an evil group and note that the evil group won out over the good one. The Book of Mormon notes this is what had happened by A.D. 421; the Reverend Smith did not give a date but seemed to favor a much later time. Even in any similarities, *View of the Hebrews* and the Book of Mormon show such significant differences that it cannot be logically argued that the latter came from the former.

See also Book of Mormon, opposition to.

BIBLIOGRAPHY

Adair, James. *History of the American Indians.* 1775.

Boudinot, Elias. *Star in the West.* 1814.

Briggs, Edmond C. "A Visit to Nauvoo in 1856." *Journal of History* 9 (January 1916): 454.

Smith, Ethan. *View of the Hebrews: 1825 2d Edition.* Edited with an Introduction by Charles D. Tate Jr. Provo, Utah: Religious Studies Center, Brigham Young University, 1996.

CDT

Virgin Used in the Book of Mormon with reference to Mary, in prophecies of the birth of Christ (1 Ne. 11:13, 15, 18, 20; 2 Ne. 17:14; Alma 7:10). These passages do not define the word. The Hebrew word *'almāh* in Isaiah's IMMANUEL prophecy (Isa. 7:14), quoted in 2 Nephi 17:14, denotes a woman of marriageable age. But elsewhere in the Old Testament, "virgin" is generally translated from *betûlāh,* a woman with no sexual experience.

KPJ

Voice, still small *See* Still small voice.

Voice of the people By democratic vote, or the expressed will of the populace, the Nephites selected their kings (Mosiah 7:9; 29:2), judges (Mosiah 29:25; Hel. 1:5, 13; 2:2), and chief captains (Alma 46:34). They empowered their leaders to enact laws "and to put them in force" (Alma 4:16; cf. Hel. 5:2), settle disputes (Alma 2:3–7; 51:7), make important decisions (Alma 27:21–22), and approve of capital punishment (Hel. 1:8).

Mosiah[2] taught the cardinal principle that "it is not common that the voice of the people desireth anything contrary to that which is right . . . [but] if the time comes that the voice of the people doth choose iniquity, then is the time that the judgments of God will come upon you" (Mosiah 29:26–27; cf. Alma 10:19). The truth of these words was verified later in Nephite history during the time of Nephi[2] (Hel. 5:2), and again in the fourth generation after Christ's visitation (3 Ne. 27:32; 4 Ne. 1:45; Morm. 1:13–14).

See also Government, principles of.

DLL

Vouching *See* Appendix C.

And now behold, I say unto you that the right way is to believe in Christ, and deny him not; and Christ is the Holy One of Israel; wherefore ye must bow down before him, and **worship** him with all your might, mind, and strength, and your whole soul; and if ye do this ye shall in nowise be cast out.

2 NEPHI 25:29

Wages Reward or recompense for labor performed. "Wages" in the Book of Mormon, when not referring to a monetary reward for material labor, refers to the reward received in the eternities for doing good or evil while in mortality. For example, the Book of Mormon declares that "every man receiveth wages of him whom he listeth to obey" (Alma 3:27), that is, people will be paid by him whom they have chosen to obey, either God or Satan.

PYH

Warfare, principles governing In the Book of Mormon the Lord set forth principles by which his righteous followers could engage in warfare: "Inasmuch as ye are not guilty of the first offense, neither the second, ye shall not suffer yourselves to be slain by the hands of your enemies. . . . Ye shall defend your families even unto bloodshed" (Alma 43:46–47). Mormon explained the application of these principles by noting that "for this cause were the Nephites contending with the Lamanites, to defend themselves, and their families, and their lands, their country, and their rights, and their religion" (Alma 43:47; cf. 43:9, 26, 30, 45; 44:5; 48:24). Furthermore, "the Nephites were taught . . . never to give an offense, yea, and never to raise the sword except it were against an enemy, except it were to preserve their lives" (Alma 48:14; cf. 44:2; 61:9–10).

The Book of Mormon narrative contains evidence of the Nephites' effort to adhere to these principles. For example, amidst a conflict between the Nephites and the Gadianton robbers, "the people said unto Gidgiddoni [their chief captain]: Pray unto the Lord, and let us go up upon the mountains and into the wilderness, that we may fall upon the robbers and destroy them in their own lands" (3 Ne. 3:20). Gidgiddoni, however, knowing the consequences of staging an unprovoked offensive, replied, "The Lord forbid; for if we should go up against them the Lord would deliver us into their hands." He counseled them instead to gather in the center of their lands and prepare for when the Lamanites should come against them. Then, he promised, the Lord "will deliver them into our hands" (3 Ne. 3:21).

During the last years of the Nephite-Lamanite conflicts, the Nephites violated the law of war that required a defensive posture and swore "by the heavens, and also by the throne of God, that they would go up to battle against their enemies" (Morm. 3:10). Because of their wickedness Mormon refused to lead them into battle (Morm. 3:9–11), and he concluded when the Nephites were defeated that it was "because the armies of the Nephites went up unto the Lamanites that they began to be smitten; for were it not for that, the Lamanites could have had no power over them" (Morm. 4:4).

In a revelation to the Prophet Joseph Smith, the Lord proclaimed the law that he had given his "ancients" which justified them in going to war. It seems evident from the war narratives in the Book of Mormon that righteous Nephites understood and sought to obey this law. The law stipulated that the Lord's people should refrain from going to "battle against any nation, kindred, tongue, or people, save I, the Lord, commanded them" (D&C 98:33; cf. Alma 43:23; 60:28, 33). He also commanded, "If any nation, tongue, or people should proclaim war against them, they should first lift a standard of peace unto that people, nation, or tongue; And if that people did not accept the offering of peace, neither the second nor the third time, they should bring these testimonies before the Lord; Then I, the Lord, would give unto them a commandment, and justify them in going out to battle against that nation, tongue, or people" (D&C 98:34–36; cf. Alma 31:5; 43:46; 44:2, 6–7; 61:14; 62:15–17). Under these conditions, the Lord would justify his people in going to battle and he would "fight their battles" for them (D&C 98:37; cf. Mosiah 24:19–20; Alma 43:23–24; 56:56; 57:26). This is "an ensample unto all people, saith the Lord your God, for justification before me" (D&C 98:38).

In addition to teaching that war can be justified if it is conducted in harmony with specified conditions and purposes, the war chapters in the Book of Mormon give a view into the hearts of Christian soldiers compelled to take up arms. Although war may be necessary, one's attitude concerning it and participation in it must remain congruent with paramount Christian principles

WARFARE IN THE BOOK OF MORMON

of peace and the sanctity of life. Mormon wrote of the righteous soldiers fighting under captain Moroni's command: "They were compelled reluctantly to contend with their brethren, the Lamanites. . . . They were sorry to take up arms . . . because they did not delight in the shedding of blood; yea, and . . . they were sorry to be the means of sending so many of their brethren out of this world into an eternal world, unprepared to meet their God" (Alma 48:21–23; cf. 44:1). Consequently, whenever possible the Nephites sought opportunity to gain advantage over their enemies without the shedding of blood, and also to end conflicts with a covenant of peace, rather than seek the annihilation of their enemies when victory was assured (Alma 43:54; 44:6, 19–20; 52:37; 55:18–19; 58:28; 62:16–17). In times of Nephite wickedness attitudes about war and violence reversed. Mormon wrote of the Nephites in his day: "And every heart was hardened, so that they delighted in the shedding of blood continually" (Morm. 4:11).

HDG

Warfare in the Book of Mormon Warfare is a central and nearly constant element in the history of Book of Mormon peoples. One of the overriding themes of the Book of Mormon is the prophesied and realized destruction of the Nephites in war. War narratives form a major part of the book; several prophets and narrators of the Book of Mormon were military commanders or participated in combat. Although peace was seen as one of the major divine blessings of the gospel in the narratives of the Ammonites (Alma 23–24) and in the society of Zion founded by Christ (4 Ne. 1), warfare was more frequently the grim reality of Nephite life. War narratives in the Book of Mormon also provide a significant amount of incidental detail about warfare, reflecting broader patterns and practices of ancient war and military systems.

Ecological, social, and economic foundations of warfare

In all premodern states the military capacity of a society was limited by a wide range of natural and cultural factors, such as environment, ecology, technology, social structure, and economic capacity. These limitations are clearly reflected in Book of Mormon war narratives. Military campaigns seem to have followed seasonal patterns, based on manpower availability, labor needs for agriculture, climatic variations that affected travel, and food supply after harvests. Many of the major campaigns described in the Book of Mormon seem to have occurred between the eleventh and fourth months of the Nephite calendar (Alma 16:1; 49:1; 52:1; 62:12; Sorenson, in *Warfare,* 455), which may correlate with the seasonal aspects of warfare in the Mesoamerican post-harvest dry months between November and April (Sorenson, in *Warfare,* 445–77).

Geography played an important role in warfare by establishing ecological limitations, communication patterns, and in determining strategic and tactical use of terrain (Sorenson, in *Warfare,* 239–76).

In most Old World ancient societies, and as described in the Bible, various animals were used for three major military purposes: for chariots and cavalry, for transportation of equipment and supplies, and for food. In pre-Columbian Mesoamerican warfare, on the other hand, there is no evidence of the use of animals in combat or for military transportation (Hassig, *War and Society,* 14, 53, 59–60). Likewise, in the Book of Mormon there are no references that animals were used for military purposes (Hamblin, in *Warfare,* 486–87).

Technologically, descriptions of warfare in the Book of Mormon broadly parallel patterns of pre-gunpowder warfare. The Book of Mormon describes a number of WEAPONS which can be categorized as missile or melee weapons for use in hand-to-hand combat. A number of types of ARMOR (e.g., Alma 46:13; Hel. 1:14; Hamblin, in *Warfare,* 421), and basic forms of military engineering and FORTIFICATIONS were also used by Book of Mormon peoples (Sorenson, in *Warfare,* 425–44). The Book of Mormon describes a number of military technological innovations, including a proliferation of fortifications and the spread of Nephite styles of armor to the Lamanites (Alma 43:19; 48:9–10; 49:6, 24). Broadly speaking, the types of weapons (swords, scimitars [Book of Mormon, cimeters], bows, and arrows)

WARFARE IN THE BOOK OF MORMON

and armor (breastplates, shields, armshields, bucklers, and headplates) mentioned in the Book of Mormon find parallels in the Mesoamerican arsenal (Hassig, *Aztec,* 75–90). On the other hand, ancient Near Eastern and biblical armament such as coats of mail, helmets, battle chariots, cavalry, and sophisticated siege engines are absent from both the Book of Mormon narrative and Mesoamerican archaeological finds.

Following the pattern of the Israelites and other ancient peoples, armies of Book of Mormon peoples are described as being organized on a decimal system with units of hundreds, thousands, and ten thousands (3 Ne. 3:22; 4:21; cf. Merrill, in *Warfare,* 268–70). The Book of Mormon describes a correlation between broader demographic growth of societies and the size of armies, which numbered in the thousands in the first century B.C., increasing to the tens of thousands in the final wars in the fourth century A.D. (Morm. 2:25; 6:10–15).

The economic and social costs of warfare in ancient states were enormous, both in funding war and from the destruction caused by war. Recruiting, equipping, training, supplying, and moving thousands of soldiers often represented major economic and social undertakings for ancient peoples.

The conduct of warfare in the Book of Mormon

The Book of Mormon accurately reflects the complexities of premodern combat in a number of subtle ways. Undertaking war required complex preparations, including logistical planning. Before combat, troops needed to be recruited, equipped, trained, supplied, and moved, all aimed at focusing the largest possible amount of military power at precisely the right time and place (Hamblin, in *Warfare,* 485–91). The search for intelligence and the confusion during war is reflected in Book of Mormon combat narratives. Scouts and spies were sent to search for supplies, roads, and the position of enemy troops (e.g., Alma 43:28–30). War councils were called before battle, allowing commanders to discuss military plans and preparations, precisely as Moroni[1] did in Alma 52:19.

Formal battles could be arranged at particular times and places, as when Mormon met the Lamanites at Cumorah (Morm. 6:2). On the other hand, much of the warfare in the Book of Mormon could be described as guerrilla warfare, exemplified by numerous ambushes, stratagems, raids, and surprise attacks (e.g., Alma 52:20–40; cf. Josh. 8:1–28). The Gadianton robbers were a classic example of this type of warfare, excelling in raids and ambushes, but avoiding pitched battle (e.g., Hel. 11:25–33). Ancient armies often had special standards or banners, such as Moroni[1]'s "title of liberty" (Alma 46:13, 19–21, 36), which could be used for mobilization, command, and control.

Actual combat included an exchange of sling stones, arrows, and javelins, as well as hand-to-hand melee combat (e.g., Alma 43; 49). Defeat in battle had many causes: death of a leader, collapse of morale, or sustaining substantial casualties (Alma 49:25; 52:1–2). Defeat was often followed by the flight, pursuit, and continued destruction of the losing army (Alma 52:28; 62:31).

Religion and ethics of warfare

As in all ancient societies, the purpose of warfare among Book of Mormon peoples was intimately connected with its conduct. A close analysis of the Book of Mormon provides a reflection of ancient Israelite patterns of "holy war." Success in battle derived from the will of God and the righteousness of the people (Alma 2:28; 44:4–5; 50:21; 56:47; 57:36; 58:33; Morm. 2:26). To ensure that the war was in accord with the will of God, prophets were frequently consulted before going to battle (Alma 16:5; 43:23–24; 3 Ne. 3:19–21). Martial oaths or covenants for military purity and obedience are found in the Book of Mormon. For example, the Nephites cast their garments on the ground to signify how God would cast them at the feet of their enemies if they violated their oath (Alma 46:22; cf. 53:17).

Warfare in the Book of Mormon was also conducted in accord with traditional patterns of law and military ethics. Military oaths of surrender and nonaggression are frequently mentioned (Alma 44:6–10, 20; 50:36; 62:16; 3 Ne. 5:4–5). Organized brigands such as the Gadianton robbers were treated as military enemies rather than common thieves (Hel. 11:28). Martial law could be declared in times of military crisis, during which normal judicial processes could be suspended (Alma 46:34), and restrictions on travel imposed. Some aspects of the Book of Mormon warfare echo ancient Near Eastern practices, such as the diplomatic custom requiring warnings and offers of peace before the commencement of war (Alma 44:1–7; 54; 3 Ne. 3:6–8; cf. Deut. 20:10–13; Welch, in *Warfare,* 59–61), or the practice of providing military exemption in return for the supply of provisions and other forms of noncombat support (Alma 27:24; cf. Deut. 20:8; Babylonian Talmud, *Sotah* 43a-44a). The laws of war assumed there would be humanitarian treatment of captives and noncombatant women and children (Alma 43:54; 44:15, 20; 52:37–39; 54:2; 57:13–16; Welch, in *Warfare,* 75–82)—which was not always the case (Morm. 4:14–15; Moro. 9:7–11).

Wars in the Book of Mormon

Approximately eighty-five instances of armed conflict in varying degrees of intensity have been identified in the Book of Mormon, with the book of Alma providing the most detailed descriptions (Alma 43–63). Book of Mormon wars ranged from brief skirmishes and raids to campaigns lasting for years, including civil wars, coups, and guerilla warfare.

Conclusions

The authors of the Book of Mormon included detailed accounts of wars for a number of reasons. In one sense, they were simply recording the realities of the history of the Nephites. Mormon, who abridged and compiled the Book of Mormon, was a general as well as a prophet, and the book's emphasis on military matters probably reflects his own experiences. War was the greatest crisis faced by virtually all ancient states, because it confronted them with potential destruction. As with most civilizations, warfare and conquest were major factors in the transformation, development, and eventual destruction of Book of Mormon societies. In this regard, the Book of Mormon is relentlessly realistic. Likewise, the Book of Mormon's emphasis on warfare as a fundamentally sacred undertaking also reflects the nearly universal ancient perspective, in which warfare exhibited an intricate and complicated mixture of religious ritual and ideology with technology and tactics.

Perhaps most important, however, the prophetic authors of the Book of Mormon taught significant religious messages through their accounts of warfare. Wars were often the result of failure to heed the warnings of the Lord through prophets such as Abinadi and Samuel the Lamanite (Mosiah 12:1–2; 17:17–18; Alma 25:8–9; Hel. 15:17; cf. 4:11–26; Morm. 3:2–3; 6). Wars were also one of the instruments of God's judgment, (Morm. 4:5; cf. 2 Ne. 5:25), as well as a means by which God could deliver his people (Alma 56:46–56). The detailed military narratives were also meant to provide a message to modern readers of the Book of Mormon, warning that without repentance and righteousness, they may face the same fate as the Nephites (Morm. 9:31; Ether 2:11–12).

See also Warfare, principles governing.

BIBLIOGRAPHY

Hassig, Ross. *Aztec Warfare: Imperial Expansion and Political Control.* Norman, Okla.: University of Oklahoma Press, 1988.

———. *War and Society in Ancient Mesoamerica.* Berkeley, Calif.: University of California Press, 1992.

Sorenson, John L. *An Ancient American Setting for the Book of Mormon.* Provo, Utah: FARMS, 1985. 239–76.

———. *Images of Ancient America: Visualizing Book of Mormon Life.* Provo, Utah: FARMS, 1998. 124–33.

———. *Warfare in the Book of Mormon.* Edited by Stephen D. Ricks and William J. Hamblin. Salt Lake City: Deseret Book, 1990.

WJH

Wax *See* Appendix C.

Wealth *See* Riches.

Weapons Specially designed tools for fighting and killing. The Book of Mormon mentions a number of different types of weapons including swords, cimeters (scimitars), clubs, axes, daggers, bows and arrows, slings, spears, javelins, and darts, along with numerous generic references to "weapons of war" (Jarom 1:8).

Many of the references to swords and perhaps

other weapons are probably metaphorical rather than literal. Thus to "take my sword" (Alma 60:28) might mean simply to go to war rather than actually picking up a sword; to "fall by the sword" (2 Ne. 13:25) is probably a metaphor for dying in battle.

Most of the weapons mentioned in the Book of Mormon (clubs, axes, daggers, slings, spears, javelins, and darts) have clear parallels in the pre-Columbian Mesoamerican arsenal. Mesoamerican parallels to other weapons (swords, cimeters, and bows and arrows) are more ambiguous and have been the subject of detailed study.

Most references to swords in the New World probably refer to Mesoamerican weapons known as the *macuahuitl* or *macana*—a long narrow piece of wood embedded with obsidian or flint to form a dual cutting edge. These weapons functioned like Old World swords, and are generally called swords both by the Spanish conquistadors and by most modern scholars.

Cimeter is an archaic English spelling for *scimitar*, a type of single-edged, curved sword, known in the Near East from at least the second millennium B.C. Several Mesoamerican weapons might be related to the Book of Mormon cimeter, but limited textual evidence does not permit precise identification.

Bows and arrows were widespread in pre-Columbian America, although the date of introduction in Mesoamerica is uncertain. There is limited artistic and archaeological evidence of the bow and arrow in Book of Mormon times.

See also Armor; Fortifications; Warfare in the Book of Mormon.

BIBLIOGRAPHY

Ricks, Stephen D., and William J. Hamblin, eds. *Warfare in the Book of Mormon*. Salt Lake City: Deseret Book, 1990.

WJH

Whence *See* Appendix C.

Whit *See* Appendix C.

Whither *See* Appendix C.

Whitmer, David *See* Witnesses of the Book of Mormon.

Whore of all the earth An alternate title for Babylon, the worldwide great and abominable church described by Nephi[1] (1 Ne. 13–14) and John (Rev. 17). Babylon values money above virtue and sells what ought to be sacred; any standard is negotiable, and everything is for sale (cf. D&C 133:14).

See also Great and abominable church; Mother of abominations; Mother of harlots.

SER

Whoredoms Unchaste actions including involvement in prostitution (Mosiah 12:29) and taking unauthorized wives and concubines (Jacob 2:23–24). God views whoredoms as an abomination (Jacob 2:28; Mosiah 11:20). Practitioners are candidates for hell (2 Ne. 9:36). Secret combinations, anti-Christs, and unrighteous kings typically practice and encourage whoredoms (Hel. 6:22–23; Alma 30:18; Mosiah 11:2; 29:36; Ether 8:16; 10:7). Whoredoms contributed to the downfall of the Nephites (Alma 50:21) and will be rampant in the last days (2 Ne. 28:12–14; 3 Ne. 16:10; 30:2; Morm. 8:31). Whoredoms were absent in the Nephite Zion and will be removed in the day of the Lord (3 Ne. 21:19).

TBB

Wicked, the/wickedness Those whose character or works are an abomination to God. The wicked reject Christ, the plan of redemption, the Lord's prophets (e.g., 1 Ne. 1:19–20; 3:17–18; Alma 8:9–13; Ether 11:7, 22), and "set at defiance the commandments of God" (Alma 5:18). The wicked who fail to repent are subject to God's justice and become captive to the devil (1 Ne. 14:3–5; cf. Alma 12:11–18; 34:16). In the Book of Mormon many forms of wickedness are enumerated, including pride, idolatry, dishonesty, immorality, materialism, violent acts, secret works, and priestcrafts (e.g., Jacob 2:13–14; Alma 1:32; Hel. 10:3; 3 Ne. 30:2).

The Book of Mormon is replete with examples of "the great wickedness one very wicked man can cause to take place among the children of men" (Alma 46:9), such as iniquitous political rulers (e.g., Mosiah 11:1–2; 29:17–18, 23; Alma 2:4), corrupt religious leaders (e.g., 1 Ne. 21:1; 4 Ne. 1:27, 34), and other influential personalities (e.g., Mosiah 27:8; Alma 30:18). Wickedness is often passed on from generation to generation (e.g., Mosiah 10:17; 4 Ne. 1:39).

The Book of Mormon clearly teaches that wickedness leads to sorrow and unhappiness (1 Ne. 7:20; Alma 41:10–11; cf. Hel. 13:38), guilt and remorse (1 Ne. 16:2; Mosiah 2:38; Alma 5:18; 36:12–16). Such feelings lead to suffering and pain in both body and spirit (Alma 15:3; 38:8).

Clearly, the overriding message of the Book of Mormon is one of salvation for those who would repent of their wicked ways: "The Lord worketh in many ways to the salvation of his people" (Alma 24:27). Throughout the Book of Mormon, the Lord implored the wicked to repent (e.g., 1 Ne. 1:4; Mosiah 11:20; Alma 9:25–26; Hel. 5:29–32; Morm. 3:2). Although the Lord is long-suffering (Alma 26:16; 3 Ne. 10:4–6), eventually the time for repentance will pass (Alma 11:40–41; 34:33–35; Hel. 13:38), and those "ripe in iniquity" (e.g., 1 Ne. 17:35, 43; 2 Ne. 28:16; Hel. 11:37; 13:14) will receive their just reward, whether in this life or the next (1 Ne. 15:28–36; Mosiah 12:1–8; Morm. 3:13–15).

The land of the wicked is cursed "for their sakes" (1 Ne. 17:38; Jacob 2:29; Hel. 13:17, 30), and they are visited by famine, pestilence, war (2 Ne. 23:11, 15, 22; Hel. 10:6; Morm. 4:5; Ether 11:7), and bondage (Mosiah 11:21, 23). Indeed, "there is no peace, saith the Lord, unto the wicked" (1 Ne. 20:22). At the second coming of Jesus Christ, "they who do wickedly shall be as stubble; and the day cometh that they must be burned." The Lord will protect and preserve the righteous from the wicked, "even if it so be as by fire" (1 Ne. 22:15–17; cf. 3 Ne. 25:1).

Whether in this life or in the next, ultimately the wicked are divided from the righteous (1 Ne. 15:30; 2 Ne. 30:10; Mosiah 16:1–2; 3 Ne. 27:16–17, 19), and the wicked are destroyed (1 Ne. 3:17; Alma 12:6, 17, 36; 3 Ne. 9:12; Ether 14:25).

Upon death, the spirits of the wicked will suffer in prison (Alma 40:13–14, 26) as they await their resurrection (Alma 11:41) and the Final Judgment (Jacob 6:13; Alma 11:44). At the judgment bar, the wicked will be found in a state of filthiness and will "be cast out for they are the children of the kingdom of the devil" (Alma 5:22–25; cf. 1 Ne. 15:34–36; Alma 41:4–8).

In God's plan of salvation righteousness and happiness stand opposite wickedness and misery. To be righteous one must have the opportunity to choose to be wicked, "for it must needs be, that there is an opposition in all things." Without opposing choices, Lehi[1] taught that "righteousness could not be brought to pass, neither wickedness, neither holiness nor misery, neither good nor bad. Wherefore, all things must needs be a compound in one" (2 Ne. 2:11).

See also Hard-heartedness; Righteous, the/righteousness; Sin, transgression; Stiffnecked, stiffneckedness.

RCF

Wiles *See* Appendix C.

Wisdom, wise Understanding, knowledge, prudence, common sense; also used to suggest a correct application of knowledge or understanding (e.g., Mosiah 12:27). More than a hundred passages in the Book of Mormon use the terms "wisdom" and "wise," generally in speaking of either true wisdom, like that which God possesses, or the worldly wisdom of wicked men.

King Benjamin identified wisdom as one of God's attributes (Mosiah 4:6; cf. 29:19; Alma 26:35) and admonished his people to believe that God "has all wisdom, and all power" (Mosiah 4:9). In his wisdom God has and will do many things to bless the lives of his children, including commanding prophets to write and preserve his word through scripture (e.g., 1 Ne. 3:19–20; 5:21–22; 2 Ne. 27:22; Alma 37:2, 8, 14, 18; Morm. 5:13), allowing the fall of Adam and Eve, yet providing a redeemer (2 Ne. 2:22–26), allowing opposition so that his eternal purposes could be "brought to pass" (2 Ne. 2:11–12), providing the resurrection (2 Ne. 9:8,

10), counseling the humble (Jacob 4:10; Alma 29:8; 37:12), delivering his servants (e.g., Alma 26:29), and ultimately bringing about "everlasting salvation and eternal life" (Mosiah 5:15).

Individuals may acquire true wisdom, especially if they are willing to be humble, teachable, and obedient to God's commands (2 Ne. 28:30; Alma 32:12; cf. Mosiah 8:20; 12:27). Moroni[2] listed teaching the "word of wisdom" as a spiritual gift (Moro. 10:9; cf. D&C 46:17–18; 1 Cor. 12:8). Those possessed with true wisdom understand the importance of service (Mosiah 2:17), are prudent in their labors (Mosiah 4:27), consider the effect their desires or acts might have on others (e.g., Mosiah 29:8–10), select righteous leaders (e.g., Mosiah 29:11; Alma 4:16), appropriately teach the gospel (e.g., Alma 18:22; cf. 31:35), provide protection for those whom they love (e.g., Alma 22:33–34; 30:20; 49:5, 15), keep the commandments of God (Alma 37:35; cf. Morm 9:28), and know that salvation comes only through Christ (Alma 38:9).

Worldly wisdom, in contrast to true wisdom, is based on that which is pleasing to the natural and carnal man, rather than that which pleases God. It mistakes the mere acquisition of knowledge and its resultant pride for the wisdom which leads the humble to follow God: "O that cunning plan of the evil one! O the vainness, and the frailties, and the foolishness of men! When they are learned they think they are wise, and they hearken not unto the counsel of God, for they set it aside, supposing they know of themselves, wherefore, their wisdom is foolishness and it profiteth them not. And they shall perish" (2 Ne. 9:28; cf. 9:42; 15:21; 28:15). Those enamored with such wisdom value cunning, wickedness, and the praise of men (e.g., Mosiah 24:7; Alma 2:1; 38:11, 13; cf. 1 Ne. 11:35; Alma 10:24). Nephi[1] warned that latter-day Gentiles would be plagued with this kind of pseudo-wisdom, and under the guise of religion would use it to "get gain and grind upon the face of the poor" (2 Ne. 26:20). Such wisdom is confounded when faced with revealed truth (e.g., Alma 32:23; 37:6–7). Ultimately, the restoration of the gospel of Christ and the coming forth of the Book of Mormon would cause such vain wisdom to perish (2 Ne. 27:26).

The archaic meaning of "wise" as being a way, manner, or degree is also found in the Book of Mormon in phrases such as "he spake unto them in this wise" (e.g., Mosiah 7:18; Alma 12:2; 56:30; 3 Ne. 3:15).

RNH

Wist *See* Appendix C.

Witchcraft *See* Sorcery, witchcraft, magic.

Without *See* Appendix C.

Witnesses, law of The biblical law of witnesses reads: "One witness shall not rise up against a man for any iniquity, or for any sin, in any sin that he sinneth: at the mouth of two witnesses, or at the mouth of three witnesses, shall the matter be established" (Deut. 19:15; 17:6; Ex. 20:16; Num. 35:30; 1 Kgs. 21:10).

Nephi[1] followed this legal principle in quoting Jacob[2] and Isaiah as witnesses to corroborate his words (2 Ne. 11:2–3) and in promising three witnesses who would behold the sealed book (2 Ne. 27:12; Ether 5:3–4). God establishes his word by "as many witnesses as seemeth him good," and thus makes people accountable (2 Ne. 27:14).

Legal and ecclesiastical matters in the Book of Mormon also follow this same rule: "And three witnesses of the church did condemn them before the elders" (Moro. 6:7). As the Doctrine and Covenants clarifies, "Every word shall be established against him or her by two witnesses of the church, and not of the enemy; but if there are more than two witnesses it is better" (D&C 42:80).

In a typical Israelite community, the town elders would act as judges, prosecutors, defenders, and witnesses. Under the law of Moses, a false accuser or false witness would suffer the consequences that would have befallen the accused (Deut. 19:15–19), as the fate suffered by Sherem or the form of the punishment imposed on Abinadi illustrated (Jacob 7:19–20; Mosiah 12:3; 17:13–20). In Ammonihah, Amulek established himself as a witness by stating his genealogy and economic status in the community (Alma 10:2–4) and then proceeded to stand as a second witness in support of Alma[2].

In the biblical period, the two witness rule could be overridden in the case of a self-incriminating confession, if the confession occurred outside the court, or the will of God was evidenced in the detection of the offender, and if corroborating physical evidence was produced (Josh. 7:16–26). Seantum's self-incriminating confession was such a case (Hel. 9:14–38), and thus his execution would not have been legally problematic.

Divine evidence was invoked when no witnesses could be produced (e.g., Num. 5:11–31). The legal effect of swearing an oath, such as "as the Lord thy God liveth" (e.g., 1 Kgs. 18:10), exposed the witness to divine punishment should his testimony prove untrue (e.g., 1 Sam. 3:17; Jer. 29:20–23; cf. Falk, 60–62). In Alma 30, Alma[2] warned Korihor by naming three witnesses standing against him: Alma himself testified of the reality of both God and Christ (Alma 30:39); in addition, "all things [were] a testimony that these things are true" (Alma 30:41), and there were the testimonies "of all these thy brethren" (Alma 30:44). By contrast, Korihor lacked any witnesses (Alma 30:40), a serious deficiency, as the sign from God proved. In Mosiah 17, Abinadi asserted that if he were to die in his ordeal, two witnesses would remain against Noah[3]: Abinadi's words "shall stand as a testimony," and his innocent blood would "also stand as a testimony" (Mosiah 17:10), justifying divine punishment.

The law of witnesses can also apply when testifying of the gospel. This follows the pattern that the Godhead has established, in which the Father, Son, and Holy Ghost bear record and witness of each other (3 Ne. 11:36).

See also Witnesses of the Book of Mormon.

BIBLIOGRAPHY

Falk, Ze'ev. *Hebrew Law in Biblical Times*. Jerusalem: Wahrmann, 1964. Reprint, Provo, Utah: Brigham Young University Press, 2001.

Van Orden, Bruce. "The Law of Witnesses in 2 Nephi." *The Book of Mormon: Second Nephi, the Doctrinal Structure*. Edited by Monte S. Nyman and Charles Tate Jr. Provo, Utah: Religious Studies Center, Brigham Young University, 1989. 307–21.

Welch, John W. *Law in the Book of Mormon*. Provo, Utah: J. Reuben Clark Law School, 1996.

JWW

Witnesses of the Book of Mormon Two groups, one consisting of three men and the other of eight, whose testimonies affirm the existence of the plates from which the Book of Mormon was translated and the divine origin of the translation.

The Three Witnesses testified that an angel displayed the ancient American plates, after which the "voice of the Lord" declared "they have been translated by the gift and power of God," and commanded that the three "should bear record" of this experience (The Testimony of Three Witnesses). The Eight Witnesses reported an examination of the ancient record under more normal circumstances. Joseph Smith showed them the plates. They saw and hefted the record, and "did handle" the leaves, "which have the appearance of gold," and contained "engravings . . . of curious workmanship" (The Testimony of Eight Witnesses). These eleven men, who were respected in Mormon and non-Mormon communities, always insisted on the reality of the events reported in their published testimonies. They freely discussed these experiences, which evidence that Joseph Smith had an ancient record, and that God directed its translation into English. In addition to the formal, published testimonies of these eleven men, there were other witnesses. Joseph Smith himself was a twelfth witness. And at least three women were also witnesses of the plates themselves or other ancient objects uncovered at the hill Cumorah: Joseph showed his mother the breastplate and the Urim and Thummim, as mentioned in her original history (Smith, *Joseph Smith*, 111; 1853 ed., 101, 107); Emma Smith, the prophet's wife, dusted around the plates in her home and felt the pliable leaves through a cloth (*Saints' Herald*, 26:289–90); and Mary Whitmer was shown the plates as a reward for her willing service in having Joseph Smith, Emma, and Oliver Cowdery stay at the Whitmer home during the last few weeks of the translation (Jenson, 621).

WITNESSES OF THE BOOK OF MORMON

The eleven designated witnesses contributed significantly to establishing the Restored Church, and all faithfully endured early persecutions. Though all of the Three Witnesses disagreed with Joseph Smith's leadership in 1837–38 and were excommunicated, two returned and were rebaptized in their last years. Three of the Eight Witnesses also became disaffected, with one (John Whitmer) being excommunicated and two (Jacob Whitmer and Hiram Page) voluntarily ceasing their affiliation with the Church. Nonetheless, all eleven witnesses reiterated their convictions relative to the Book of Mormon to the end of their lives. Their united testimony is impressive, all the more so because several left, and remained outside, the Church.

Three scriptures alerted early believers that there would be witnesses of the plates (D&C 5:11–18; 2 Ne. 27:12–14; Ether 5:1–4). The first known scriptural promise came in 1829 to Martin Harris, a prominent landowner and farmer in Palmyra, New York, who devoutly believed in biblical prophecy of latter-day miracles. He investigated Joseph Smith's visions, took copies of the characters on the plates to New York linguists, and became Joseph's scribe during two months of 1828. The two produced 116 pages of manuscript, which were lost through Martin's negligence. Though not allowed to continue as scribe, this staunch supporter stood by and later financed the printing of the Book of Mormon. When Martin sought proof of the plates in March 1829, he was given a conditional promise that he might be one of three witnesses who would see the plates: "If he will go out and bow down before me, and humble himself in mighty prayer and faith, in the sincerity of his heart, then will I grant unto him a view of the things which he desireth to know" (*Book of Commandments,* 4:8).

The other two scriptures promising witnesses are in the Book of Mormon itself (2 Ne. 27; Ether 5), and would have come to the attention of Joseph and Oliver during the work of translation between April 7 and the latter part of June 1829. Oliver Cowdery's involvement began in the winter of 1828–29, when he came, providentially, into the area near Palmyra where the Prophet's parents lived. While boarding with the Smiths as a young school teacher in their district, Oliver carefully investigated what they said about their son's visions, received divine confirmation (D&C 6:22–24), and in early April traveled about 130 miles to the Prophet's small farm at Harmony, Pennsylvania, where he became Joseph's scribe. Amidst increasing persecution in the Harmony area, they moved the work to the Peter Whitmer home in Fayette, New York. David Whitmer drove his team and wagon to bring the translators to the Whitmer farm. The translation of the Book of Mormon was completed by about the end of June 1829 (Smith, *Church,* 1:48–49, 71).

The Book of Mormon texts promised that three witnesses from among "those who shall assist to bring forth this work" would be shown the "plates," or the "book," by the "power of God" (Ether 5:2–3; 2 Ne. 27:12). Inspired by the earlier revelation to Martin Harris and these divine assurances in the Book of Mormon, Oliver Cowdery, David Whitmer, and Martin Harris came to the Prophet with a driving desire to be the three witnesses—a logical hope because they had indeed assisted in making the translation possible. A revelation came to the Prophet Joseph Smith, granting their request on strict condition of faith, promising a view "with your eyes" of the ancient objects the prophet had possessed: the plates, the breastplate, and the Urim and Thummim. They were also promised a view of the sword of Laban and the "miraculous directors," called in the Book of Mormon, "Liahona" (D&C 17:1–3; Alma 37:38). Joseph Smith and his three associates went to the woods near the Whitmer home and prayed for fulfillment of these promises. After the men prayed twice, each in succession, Martin Harris withdrew, believing he was a negative influence. When Joseph and Oliver and David resumed praying, they "beheld a light above [them] in the air, of exceeding brightness; and behold, an angel stood before [them]. In his hands he held the plates. . . . He turned over the leaves one by one, so that [they] could see them, and discern the engravings thereon distinctly" (Smith, *Church,* 1:54). After the angel spoke a word on obedience to David Whitmer, a voice from heaven declared the translation to be correct,

WITNESSES OF THE BOOK OF MORMON

and commanded the witnesses to testify of what they had seen and heard. Joseph Smith immediately searched for Martin Harris, and, as Joseph reported, after the two prayed for some time, "the same vision was opened to our view, at least it was again opened to me, and I once more beheld and heard the same things; . . . Martin Harris cried out, . . . 'Tis enough; 'tis enough; mine eyes have beheld'" (Smith, *Church,* 1:55). The Prophet's mother described the emotional return of the four to the Whitmer home, noting Joseph's sense of relief and the fervent gratitude that poured from the Three Witnesses (Smith, *Joseph,* 152).

A few days after this miraculous visitation, the Whitmer family traveled some 20 miles from Fayette to the Smith farm near Palmyra. There, most of the men in the group went to "a place where the [Smith] family were in the habit of offering up their secret devotions to God" (Smith, *Joseph,* 154). Mother Smith said an angel had deposited the record there, and the Eight Witnesses lifted and examined the plates. Those who testified of handling the plates were Joseph Smith Sr., two of the prophet's brothers, and five of the Whitmer family, including Hiram Page, being the husband of David Whitmer's sister. The Eight Witnesses qualified as being among the "few" in addition to the Three Witnesses, who, "according to the will of God," would be privileged to view the ancient record (2 Ne. 27:12–13). Not only did most of the men in the Whitmer and Smith families become witnesses of the Book of Mormon but all members of both large households became devout believers in the restored Church.

The lives of the Three Witnesses undergird their testimonies. Oliver Cowdery stands out because he also testified that he was with Joseph Smith when John the Baptist restored the lesser priesthood and when the ancient apostles restored the greater priesthood (D&C 27:8–13). Oliver led the first major mission of the Church, traveling through Ohio to Missouri. His 1830–31 declarations that he saw the angel and the plates are found in writings of converts, in records of a Shaker community, and in a report of a Missouri Indian agent. Oliver served constantly as a capable clerk, editor, high councilor, and even assistant president of the Church under Joseph Smith. He married Elizabeth Ann Whitmer, whose brother David was also trusted by the prophet as a capable leader. In 1832 David was one of some two dozen elders sent to preach from Ohio to Missouri. Schoolteacher William E. McLellin, who became an apostle but later apostatized, investigated Mormonism because of the impressive testimony of David Whitmer "to having seen an Holy Angel who had made known the truth of this record to him" (Shipps and Welch, 29). After serving in leadership councils in Jackson County, David was ordained by Joseph Smith in 1834 as President of the high council in Zion (Missouri), "to be a leader, or a prophet to this Church, which (ordination) was on conditions that he (J. Smith jr) did not live to God himself" (Cannon and Cook, 72, 151). Though Oliver and David were among the early leaders of the Church and had participated in the powerful visions and endowments accompanying the dedication of the Kirtland Temple, a split developed between them and Joseph Smith. Complex emotions ran their course after the failure of the Kirtland bank in early 1837, because many members had simplistically thought the Prophet's early participation guaranteed financial success. The hard times that followed gave rise to doubts in the minds of some about Joseph Smith's leadership, and by the end of the year, a strong dissenting party developed. During the first half of 1838, most of the faithful Saints migrated from Kirtland to Missouri, where the Whitmer family supported the questionable conduct of David Whitmer's two counselors in the Missouri presidency. These leaders, John Whitmer and W. W. Phelps, had spent church funds for land in the city of Far West, then sold lots to gathering members as their own enterprise. After the two men were called to account by the Missouri high council, negotiations broke down, and the pair were excommunicated. David Whitmer and Oliver Cowdery were excommunicated soon afterward. Both David and Oliver wrote letters of resignation, regretting conflict over policies but still indicating faith in the Church as originally restored (Smith, *Church,* 3:17–19 nn). Thomas B. Marsh, President of the Twelve in 1838, later

WITNESSES OF THE BOOK OF MORMON

recalled questioning them about their views during this troubled time. Marsh, whose own faith was being tried by events in and around Far West, left the Mormon settlements and traveled to Richmond, Missouri, where Oliver and David had relocated. He bluntly asked David whether his written testimony of the Book of Mormon was true: "He replied, as sure as there is a God in heaven, he saw the angel according to his testimony in that book." Marsh then asked why "he did not stand by Joseph." David replied that the prophet was inspired in the beginning but had "now fallen." Marsh added, "I interrogated Oliver Cowdery in the same manner, who answered similarly" (*Deseret News*). Although Oliver Cowdery and David Whitmer were then filled with personal resentment toward Joseph Smith and the Church, they insisted on the divine origin of the Book of Mormon.

Martin Harris, the third of the Three Witnesses, stayed in Ohio after most of the Church moved to Missouri in 1838. He had sold a major portion of his New York farm in 1831 to pay for the publishing of the first edition of the Book of Mormon. His strong convictions cost him his reputation and his family, as well as his property. The great respect he had enjoyed in his community changed to scorn, and he suffered estrangement, and finally separation from his wife and children. Martin had loyally followed Joseph Smith in the first Ohio years, continuing to contribute money to church projects such as the first printing of the revelations known as the Book of Commandments, in 1833. Though serving for a time on the Kirtland high council, Martin later complained that he was not given high position. Martin developed a stormy alliance with the Kirtland dissenters, for which he was excommunicated at the end of 1837 (Anderson, 119 n. 13). He stayed at Kirtland for a third of a century before returning to the Church in Utah in 1870. Even though in his Ohio years Martin was often critical of church leaders, he never denied or compromised his firm testimony of the Book of Mormon. At age eighty-three he put his deepest convictions in crisp words: "I do say that the angel did show to me the plates containing the Book of Mormon. . . . I do firmly believe and do know that Joseph Smith was a prophet of God" (*Saints' Herald*, 22:630). In 1875 he bore that same testimony on his deathbed.

Oliver Cowdery returned to the Church after a decade as a respected lawyer in Ohio and Wisconsin. A prominent non-Mormon attorney who studied law with Oliver said he was "a great advocate," well informed, possessing a "friendly disposition," and was "modest" and generous in his relationships (Lang, 365). Oliver was successful in regional politics, though his detractors ridiculed his testimony which was published with the Book of Mormon. Nevertheless, Oliver did not explain away this public declaration, and private letters in this period show that he firmly accepted Joseph Smith's visions, mentioning being present at some. On rejoining the Church in 1848, Oliver spoke of the Book of Mormon before a large audience: "I beheld with my eyes, and handled with my hands, the gold plates from which it was translated. I also beheld the Interpreters. That book is true" (Anderson, 61). Oliver died a year and a half later at age forty-three. A dozen family members left memories of his last moments, when he reassured his wife, daughter, and close relatives of his love for Christ, of the truthfulness of the Book of Mormon, and of the reality of priesthood restoration.

After leaving the Church, David Whitmer lived half a century in Richmond, Missouri, where he ran a successful livery business, renting horses and rigs. He was highly respected in his community, and at his death a local editor said he was "honest, conscientious and upright in all his dealings" (Cook, 227–28). David lived until 1888, well into the era of modern journalism, and after all other ten witnesses had passed away. He was regularly sought out by reporters, curious non-Mormons, and believers traveling through the area where he lived. On scores of occasions David testified that he saw the angel with the plates and heard the divine voice declare the translation to be correct. This central message is clear, though minor variations appear in the reports of the many interviews. In his last decade, David published statements reiterating his Book of Mormon testimony, while at the same time explaining why he thought Joseph

WITNESSES OF THE BOOK OF MORMON

Smith lost the gift of inspiration he enjoyed when translating the Book of Mormon and receiving early revelations. In his last year, David corrected encyclopedia accounts alleging that the Three Witnesses renounced their written testimony. He stated, "I will say once more to all mankind, that I have never at any time denied that testimony or any part thereof" (Whitmer, 8). Like Oliver Cowdery and Martin Harris, in his final hours David Whitmer reaffirmed his testimony that the Book of Mormon was revealed by God.

Among the Eight Witnesses were both prominent and less-noted supporters of the Restored Church. The Whitmer brothers, including their brother-in-law Hiram Page, were among the first Mormons to accept the call to settle near Independence, Missouri. They endured mob violence in the 1833 expulsion of the Saints from Jackson County, Missouri. When Christian and Peter Whitmer Jr. died of illness in the mid-1830s in Missouri, Oliver Cowdery reported, "They proclaimed to their last moments, the certainty of their former testimony" (*Messenger and Advocate,* 3:426). After the 1838 excommunications of David and John Whitmer, Hiram Page and Jacob Whitmer disassociated themselves from the Church. Hiram and Jacob farmed near Richmond, Missouri, and Jacob also pursued his trade as a shoemaker. Both men passed away in the 1850s. According to their sons, these two remained firm in their testimony of seeing the plates to the end of their lives. John Whitmer lived until 1878, far beyond the others of the Eight Witnesses. He had earlier served as Church historian and editor, as well as in the Missouri presidency. Successful in farming and raising stock after his excommunication, he regularly repeated the convictions he had expressed in 1836 at the end of his editorial career in Kirtland: "I have most assuredly seen the plates from whence the book of Mormon is translated, and . . . have handled these plates, and know of a surety that Joseph Smith, jr. has translated the book of Mormon by the gift and power of God" (*Messenger and Advocate,* 2:286–87).

Joseph Smith's father and two brothers, Hyrum and Samuel, were really martyrs to the cause of the Book of Mormon and the Restoration. Joseph Smith Sr. served on the high council and in the First Presidency for a time in Ohio. He was a revered patriarch, giving nearly 400 recorded blessings. Emotionally devastated by the arrest and imprisonment of Joseph and Hyrum in Missouri in 1838, he suffered from exposure in migrating to Illinois, where he died in 1840. Hyrum Smith's Church career paralleled that of the Prophet, whom he served as counselor and then as assistant president in Nauvoo (D&C 124:94–96). He went to Carthage with Joseph, fully aware of the threat of assassination, finding solace in the Book of Mormon, in particular Moroni[2]'s farewell testimonial to the Gentiles (D&C 135:4–5; Ether 12:36–38). Earlier,

Clockwise: Oliver Cowdery (1806–1850), Martin Harris (1783–1875), and David Whitmer (1805–1888); courtesy HBLL.

after nearly six months in Missouri prisons, Hyrum Smith wrote, "I felt a determination to die, rather than deny the things which my eyes had seen, which my hands had handled, and which I had borne testimony to, wherever my lot had been cast" (*Times and Seasons*, 1:23). Samuel Smith rode hard, hoping to rescue his brothers, arriving at Carthage immediately after their murder on 27 June 1844. He himself succumbed a month later, weakened by internal injury or overexertion. Samuel was always true to his published testimony as one of the Eight Witnesses. Samuel had given copies of the Book of Mormon to a brother and sister of Brigham Young, laying the groundwork for the conversion of Joseph Smith's dynamic successor.

Moroni testified that "in the mouth of three witnesses shall these things be established." Added to the testimony of the Three Witnesses is that of the Eight Witnesses. And added to their testimony is the life and witness of the Prophet Joseph Smith himself and the work he brought forth, "in the which shall be shown forth the power of God and also his word, of which the Father, and the Son, and the Holy Ghost bear record—and all this shall stand as a testimony against the world at the last day" (Ether 5:4).

See also The Coming Forth of the Book of Mormon, 9; Book of Mormon, translation of; Gold plates; Witnesses, law of.

BIBLIOGRAPHY

Anderson, Richard L. *Investigating the Book of Mormon Witnesses*. Salt Lake City: Deseret Book, 1981.

Book of Commandments. Zion, Mo.: W. W. Phelps & Co., 1833. Reprint, Independence, Mo: Herald House, 1972.

Cannon, Donald Q., and Lyndon W. Cook, eds. *Far West Record*. Salt Lake City: Deseret Book, 1983.

Cook, Lyndon W., ed. *David Whitmer Interviews*. Orem, Utah: Grandin Book, 1991.

Deseret News 8, no. 3 (24 March 1858).

Jenson, Andrew, ed. *The Historical Record*. Salt Lake City: Andrew Jenson, 1889.

Lang, W. *History of Seneca County*. Springfield, Ohio: Transcript Printing Co., 1880.

Latter Day Saints' Messenger and Advocate 2, no. 6 (March 1836); 3, no. 3 (December 1836).

Saints' Herald 22, no. 20 (15 October 1875); 26, no. 19 (1 October 1879).

Shipps, Jan, and John W. Welch, eds. *The Journals of William E. McLellin, 1831–1836*. Provo, Utah: BYU Studies, 1994.

Smith, Joseph. *History of The Church of Jesus Christ of Latter-day Saints*. Edited by B. H. Roberts. 7 vols. 2d ed. rev. Salt Lake City: The Church of Jesus Christ of Latter-day Saints, 1932–51.

Smith, Lucy Mack. *History of Joseph Smith by His Mother, Lucy Mack Smith*. Edited by Preston Nibley. Salt Lake City: Bookcraft, 1958.

Times and Seasons 1, no. 2 (December 1839).

Whitmer, David. *An Address to All Believers in Christ*. Richmond, Mo.: David Whitmer, 1887.

RLA

Wo *See* Appendix C.

Wonderful *See* Appendix C.

Word, the This term is used in at least two ways in the Book of Mormon.

1. That which is given of God to lead one to eternal life (1 Ne. 11:25; 2 Ne. 31:20). It includes Jesus Christ (Alma 38:9; John 1:1–14) and his plan of redemption (Alma 33:22–23), scriptures (e.g., 2 Ne. 29:13–14), and truths revealed by the Holy Ghost (D&C 68:4).

Jacob[2] testified that the word is eternal (2 Ne. 9:16) and Nephi[1], drawing on the prophecies of Isaiah, warned that those who reject it would be condemned (2 Ne. 27:14). Alma[2] taught that the portion of the word a person is allowed to receive and understand is dictated by his heed and diligence to it (Alma 12:9–11). He likened the word to a seed and explained that if one would plant it in one's heart and nourish it, one's faith would grow and lead to eternal life (Alma 32:28–43). He further explained that one may plant and nourish the word through such activities as prayer, scripture study, and faith (Alma 33:1–23).

There is power in the word. God uses this power to create, control, and direct the earth, its elements, and its inhabitants (1 Ne. 17:46; Jacob 4:9). The power of the word can nourish the faithful (Moro. 6:4), heal the wounded soul (Jacob 2:8), help the righteous feel the love of God (Jacob 3:2), initiate spiritual rebirth (Alma 5:13; 26:13; 36:26), help one overcome

WORDS OF MORMON

temptations (1 Ne. 11:25; 15:24), and bring the believer to eternal life (2 Ne. 31:20). In contrast, it can also condemn the wicked (2 Ne. 1:26), expose and combat the adversary (Alma 35:3; Hel. 3:29), put down pride (Alma 4:19), destroy secret combinations (Hel. 6:37), and bring men unto repentance (Jarom 1:12; Mosiah 27:32; Alma 32:14). Alma[2] testified that the word was more powerful than even the sword in leading people to what was just (Alma 31:5; cf. D&C 11:2, 21). Accordingly the word was preached frequently to convert nonbelievers (e.g., Alma 17:4), reclaim the apostate (e.g., Hel. 5:14–17), and maintain the righteous (e.g., Mosiah 25:21). Prophets are held accountable for the sins of the people if they do not preach the word (Jacob 1:19).

2. A divine decree, prophecy, or pronouncement (e.g., 2 Ne. 5:20; Alma 8:29).

TBB

Words of Mormon The seventh division of the Book of Mormon, placed between two sets of plates: the small plates of Nephi, and Mormon's abridgment of the large plates of Nephi. Written by Mormon[2] near the end of Nephite history (ca. A.D. 385), the Words of Mormon informs readers of Mormon's discovery of the small plates and his decision to include them with his abridgment. Mormon also gave a brief summary of the reign of king Benjamin. This summary fills a historical gap between the small plates and Mormon's abridgment inasmuch as the last book of the small plates (Omni) only briefly mentions king Benjamin, and the first book of Mormon's abridgment (Mosiah) begins with the end of Benjamin's reign. It is unclear whether Mormon inscribed "The Words of Mormon" on remaining space on the small plates of Nephi, or on an additional plate(s) he inserted into his record.

Content and message

Having abridged Nephite history to the reign of king Benjamin, Mormon searched the records, possibly spurred by Benjamin's words (W of M 1:3; cf. Mosiah 1:6–7; Packer, 275), and found the small plates of Nephi. Pleased to find many prophecies concerning Jesus Christ and the Nephites on the small plates, and inspired by the whisperings of the Spirit concerning "a wise purpose," he included them with his record (W of M 1:4, 6–7). One "wise purpose" behind this inspiration, and the earlier commandment the Lord gave Nephi[1] to engrave a second record (1 Ne. 9:5–6; 2 Ne. 5:30), was revealed after 116 manuscript pages of translated material were stolen from Martin Harris in 1828. A revelation to Joseph Smith told him to replace the lost text by translating the "more particular account" found on the small plates, which in fact would "throw greater views upon" the gospel (D&C 10:38–45). This course brought forth the "choice" writings of the small plates (W of M 1:6) and also foiled any possible conspiracy to alter the stolen manuscript and then discredit a retranslated text (D&C 10:8–33). Mormon's exposure to the sacred focus of the small plates probably "greatly influenced . . .

OUTLINE OF WORDS OF MORMON

I. The discovery of the small plates of Nephi (1:1–11)
   A. Mormon's account of finding the small plates after abridging the large plates down to the reign of Benjamin (1:1–3)
   B. Mormon's account of the reasons for including the small plates with his abridgment of the large plates (1:4–9)

II. Summary of the reign of king Benjamin (1:10–18)
   A. Benjamin's reception of the small plates of Nephi (1:10–11)
   B. Contentions among Benjamin's people as well as with the Lamanites (1:12–14)
   C. The challenge of false Christs, false prophets, false teachers, and dissension (1:15–16)
   D. The restoration of peace through the efforts of Benjamin and other holy men (1:15–18)

the rest of his abridgment" of the Nephite records (Packer, 276; cf. Jacob 1:4; W of M 1:9).

Mormon wrote of dissension and contention among king Benjamin's people, stemming in part from false ideas and false teachers (W of M 1:12, 15–16), and possibly compounded by the challenge of unifying the people of Zarahemla and the Nephites under a Nephite king, and the desire of many Nephites to return to the land of Nephi (Omni 1:27–30; cf. W of M 1:16). Despite internal strife, Benjamin's forces rebuffed a Lamanite attack upon the land of Zarahemla and drove the Lamanites "out of all the lands of their inheritance" (W of M 1:12–14). Through legal means and with the help of other "holy prophets," Benjamin overcame false teachings and established peace among his people (W of M 1:15–18).

See also Book of Mormon, lost manuscript of (116 pages).

BIBLIOGRAPHY

Packer, Boyd K. "The Book of Mormon." *Let Not Your Heart Be Troubled.* Salt Lake City: Bookcraft, 1991.

JCT

World, the Term used in the Book of Mormon to refer to one or more of the following concepts.

1. The physical planet earth, as in "the creation of the world" (1 Ne. 5:11) or "from the foundation of the world" (Ether 3:14).

2. The human inhabitants of the earth, as in Christ being the Savior of the world (1 Ne. 10:5) who took upon him the sins of the world (3 Ne. 11:11).

3. This state of mortality—individuals who died "went out of the world rejoicing" (Alma 46:39).

4. The physical possessions which men and women accumulate, often referred to as the riches or things of the world (2 Ne. 9:30).

5. The pride and wisdom of the world (the learning and philosophies of men), which oppose the wisdom of God (1 Ne. 11:35–36).

CJO

Worship Genuine feelings and acts of homage; reverence; adoration. Book of Mormon prophets taught people to worship "the true and the living God" (Alma 7:6; 43:10), and warned against worshipping false Gods (2 Ne. 9:37; Mosiah 12:34–37; cf. 2 Ne. 12:8, 20; 3 Ne. 21:17). Beyond the general injunction to worship God, Nephi[1] and Jacob[2] spoke of worshipping the Father in the name of Jesus Christ (2 Ne. 25:16; Jacob 4:5), a principle Christ taught during his postresurrection ministry at Bountiful[2] (3 Ne. 18:16–23). Christ himself worshipped the Father through prayer (3 Ne. 17:13–17; 19:19–23, 27–29, 31–34). Nephi also spoke of the necessity of worshipping Christ (2 Ne. 25:29), a principle beautifully realized during the risen Lord's visit to the Americas when the multitude and the disciples worshipped at his feet (3 Ne. 11:17; 17:10; 19:15–36; cf. 1 Ne. 11:24).

True worship is more than outward acts; it emanates from sincere belief and proper intent (2 Ne. 25:16, 29; Mosiah 4:1–3; Alma 7:6; 4 Ne. 1:37). Book of Mormon prophets made it clear that the intent of the law of Moses was to lead worshippers to "look forward unto the Messiah, and believe in him" (Jarom 1:11; 2 Ne. 25:23–30; Jacob 4:5; cf. Mosiah 13:25–30; Alma 25:15–16).

Book of Mormon peoples gathered at temples, synagogues, and sanctuaries to worship, often at set times (Jacob 2:2, 11; Mosiah 1:18; 18:25; Alma 15:17; 23:4; 3 Ne. 11:1–2; Moro. 6:5–6; 7:1). When the Savior visited them after his resurrection, he taught them that giving ALMS and PRAYER, both acts of worship and devotion, were to be done "in secret," rather than in public to be seen and praised of men (3 Ne. 13:1–6, 16–18).

The ZORAMITES[2] practiced a false system of worship in place of the commandments and statutes of the law of Moses. They also failed to observe "the performances of the church, to continue in prayer and supplication to God daily, that they might not enter into temptation" (Alma 31:9–10). Once a week, one at a time, wealthy Zoramites recited loudly a rote prayer that professed belief in a "holy God," but denied the Christ. They proclaimed themselves God's "holy children" by election, but condemned to hell those who believed in Christ (Alma 31:12–18). Alma[2] marveled at the Zoramites' "wickedness and infidelity" (Alma 31:30). He observed that their hearts remained "swallowed up in their pride" and "set upon" worldly riches even while they prayed, and that they never spoke of God outside this weekly assembly (Alma 31:27–28, 23–24). When the less affluent Zoramites complained that their exclusion from the synagogue left them "no place to worship" (Alma 32:5), Alma and Amulek taught them they could worship God "in whatsoever place ye may be in" (Alma 34:38) through honest prayer (Alma 32:10–11; 33:2–12; 34:17–31, 37–39).

True Christian worship is the opposite of Zoramite attitudes and beliefs. It is characterized by sincerity (Alma 33:11; cf. 2 Ne. 31:13), HUMILITY (Alma 32:12–16; cf. Alma 34:38), love for one's neighbor (Alma 34:28–29; cf. Moro. 7:48; 1 Jn. 4:20), and obedience to God's commandments (Alma 34:32–37; cf. 2 Ne. 31:10). Paramount is the acknowledgment that redemption comes through Jesus Christ (Alma 34:8; cf. Mosiah 3:17).

JCT

Wrapt *See* Appendix C.

Wrest *See* Appendix C.

Wrestle Word used by Enos to describe his personal spiritual struggle as he sought to overcome his sins and communicate with the Lord. To wrestle as Enos includes such aspects of personal effort as penetrating reflection, deep desire for forgiveness, mighty prayer, and the exercise of abiding faith in Christ (Enos 1:2–8).

KJW

Writing of divorcement A legal document formally repudiating any covenant or connection between a husband and wife. Under the law of Moses, a man wishing to "put away" or divorce his wife was required to give her a writing or "bill" of divorcement, thereby establishing her legal right to remarry (3 Ne. 12:31 // Matt. 5:31; Deut. 24:1–3).

The law of Moses specified that a man might divorce his wife if she found "no favour in his eyes" because he found in her "some uncleanness" (Deut. 24:1), but Christ, emphasizing the sanctity of marriage, taught that a man who "shall put away his wife" for any reason other than "fornication" would cause her as well as anyone she subsequently married to commit adultery (3 Ne. 12: 32 // Matt. 5:32; cf. Mark 10:1–12). It is unclear whether the term "put away" as used in this context refers to all divorce, or simply those not legalized through a writing of divorcement. Today Latter-day Saints understand that in addition to infidelity in a marriage, there may be other serious sins and violations of covenants, such as those associated with abuse, in which divorce might be considered. Elder Bruce R. McConkie explained, "At this time divorces are permitted in the Church for a number of reasons other than sex immorality, and divorced persons are permitted to marry again and enjoy all of the blessings of the gospel" (1:548–49).

The Lord used the imagery of divorce to emphasize to ancient Israel that though he had never put away his people or initiated a "bill" of divorcement, they had chosen to divorce themselves from him and broken sacred covenants through their iniquities (2 Ne. 7:1 // Isa. 50:1).

BIBLIOGRAPHY

McConkie, Bruce R. *Doctrinal New Testament Commentary.* 3 vols. Salt Lake City: Bookcraft, 1965–73.

SER

Wroth *See* Appendix C.

Wrought *See* Appendix C.

Wrought on or upon *See* Appendix C.

My brother has called upon the words of **Zenos**, that redemption cometh through the Son of God, and also upon the words of Zenock; and also he has appealed unto Moses, to prove that these things are true. And now, behold, I will testify unto you of myself that these things are true. Behold, I say unto you, that I do know that Christ shall come among the children of men, to take upon him the transgressions of his people, and that he shall atone for the sins of the world; for the Lord God hath spoken it. ALMA 34:7-8

Zarahemla A descendant of Mulek, the son of Zedekiah[1], who was king of Judah at the time of Lehi[1]'s departure from Jerusalem[1] (Mosiah 25:2; 1 Ne. 1:4). Zarahemla was leader of "the people of Zarahemla," or the Mulekites in "the land of Zarahemla," when they were discovered by the Nephites. He rejoiced when the people of Mosiah[1] arrived with the plates of brass in their possession (Omni 1:13–14). Zarahemla recounted his genealogy for the Nephites, but it was not recorded on "these" plates, the small plates of Nephi (Omni 1:18). Among his descendants were Ammon[1] and Coriantumr[3] (Mosiah 7:3, 13; Hel. 1:15).

Zarahemla, land of and city of Mulekite-Nephite region, as well as the capital city in that land. The land of Zarahemla was located in the northern portion of the land southward. The river Sidon "ran by the land of Zarahemla" (Alma 2:15). The original settlement was founded by a people (Mulekites) who left the Old World some time in the sixth century B.C. (Omni 1:15). The Mulekites had apparently wandered from their original landing spot in the land of Mulek, located in the land northward, southward to the land of Zarahemla (Alma 22:29–31; Omni 1:14–17; Hel. 6:10).

In roughly 200 B.C. Mosiah[1] led a group of Nephites northward and downward as they fled out of the land of Nephi. Being "led by the power of [the Lord's] arm" through the wilderness they eventually came to a land called Zarahemla and discovered the people of Zarahemla. Mosiah caused that these people be taught the language of the Nephites. The people of Mosiah and the people of Zarahemla, who were led by a man named Zarahemla, united and Mosiah was appointed to be king (Omni 1:12–19). During Mosiah's reign a man named Zeniff led a group of Nephites back up to the land of Nephi to dwell in their original homeland (Mosiah 9:1–7). Thus there were two Nephite groups: one group in the land of Zarahemla and a Nephite colony living in Lamanite territory in the land of Nephi.

Mosiah's son Benjamin succeeded him as king in Zarahemla, led his people into victory against the Lamanites, and ruled the Nephites in peace and righteousness (W of M 1:12–18). At about 124 B.C. Benjamin turned the kingdom over to his son Mosiah[2] (Mosiah 6:4). Some four years later, the descendants of Zeniff's earlier group of Nephites—the people of Alma[1] and the people of Limhi—arrived in the land of Zarahemla and were reunited into the kingdom. Under Mosiah's direction Alma established churches in the land of Zarahemla. Originally there were seven congregations (Mosiah 25:15–23).

Over the next two generations (120–75 B.C.), the land of Zarahemla grew rapidly in population. It extended its borders and contained multiple cultures (e.g., Mosiah 25:2–3; 27:6). The city of Zarahemla became the hub for sophisticated religious and mercantile systems (Sorenson, 190–97). Under Mosiah the kingdom was abolished and a system of judgeships elected by the people was created in every city with the chief judge residing in the city of Zarahemla (Mosiah 29). The prophet Alma[2], who was the son of Alma[1], was the first chief judge (Mosiah 29:42). When he became "sorrowful" because of the wickedness of his people, he resigned his judgment-seat and went on a circuit throughout the land of Zarahemla preaching repentance and the pure doctrines of Jesus Christ (Alma 4–15). His reform effort was mostly successful, but in Ammonihah in the northern reaches of the land, Alma and his companion Amulek were rejected and nearly assassinated (Alma 14).

From 73–60 B.C. the Lamanites from the land of Nephi engaged the Nephites in a massive war throughout the entire land of Zarahemla, with the Lamanites finally being expelled from the land (Alma 43–62). Toward the end of this period the city of Zarahemla was seized by Nephite rebels (the KING-MEN) who drove out chief judge Pahoran[1] and appointed one of their number, Pachus, as king. With the intent of securing his position, the new king entered an alliance with the Lamanites agreeing to maintain control of Zarahemla while the Lamanites conquered the remainder of Nephite territory. Captain Moroni rallied Nephites against the traitors and won back Zarahemla and restored Pahoran to his office (Alma 61–62:9).

About 51 B.C. a bold Nephite dissenter named Coriantumr[3] marched Lamanite troops through the heart of Nephite territories and took control of the city of Zarahemla. Moronihah[1] soon recaptured the city (Hel. 1:14–33).

A few years later (ca. 36–34 B.C.) Nephites who dissented to the Lamanites incited the Lamanites to war against the Nephites and captured the land of Zarahemla, as well as many other lands, driving the Nephites northward to the land of Bountiful[2] (Hel. 4:1–6). Parts of the land were subsequently won back by the Nephites under the spiritual and military leadership of Moronihah (Hel. 4:9–17).

At about 30 B.C. Nephite dissenters and eight thousand Lamanites in the land of Zarahemla were converted to Christ through the preaching of Nephi[2] and Lehi[4] (Hel. 5:16–19). Moreover, many other Lamanite conversions took place as Nephi and Lehi extended their ministry to the Land of Nephi, and as their converts preached the word "throughout all the regions round about" (Hel. 5:50). These Lamanites gave back to the Nephites lands they had taken, presumably including the land of Zarahemla (Hel. 5:52).

In 6–5 B.C. Samuel the Lamanite preached in the city of Zarahemla to the wicked Nephites who dwelt there (Hel. 13–16). In the days of chief judge Lachoneus[1], the land of Zarahemla was designated as the central gathering place for Nephites preparatory to war with the Gadianton robbers (3 Ne. 3:22–23). After Nephite victories, first over Giddianhi, and then Zemnarihah, Nephites in Zarahemla enjoyed peace and prosperity until pride, secret combinations, and the killing of the Lord's prophets led to destruction (3 Ne. 4–8). In the great destructions that accompanied the death of Jesus Christ, the city of Zarahemla and its inhabitants were burned (3 Ne. 8:8, 24; 9:3). The city of Zarahemla was rebuilt in the first century A.D. (4 Ne. 1:8). Mormon mentioned being taken southward by his father to the land of Zarahemla (about A.D. 322), and that "the whole face of the land had become covered with buildings, and the people were as numerous almost, as it were the sand of the sea" (Morm. 1:6–7). Mormon referred to a Nephite/Lamanite war beginning in the borders of Zarahemla (Morm. 1:10).

See also Nephite civilization; Zarahemla, people of (Mulekites).

BIBLIOGRAPHY

Sorenson, John L. *An Ancient American Setting for the Book of Mormon*. Salt Lake City: Deseret Book, 1985.

BAV

Zarahemla, people of (Mulekites) A people discovered by Mosiah[1] (Omni 1:12–14). Warned of the Lord to flee the land of Nephi, Mosiah and his followers were directed by God through the wilderness "until they came down" into a land called Zarahemla (Omni 1:13). The people of the land, then led by a man named Zarahemla, were descended from a group which had come out of the land of Jerusalem[1] at the time Zedekiah "was carried away captive into Babylon . . . and were brought by the hand of the Lord across the great waters, into the land where Mosiah discovered them" (Omni 1:15–16). Amaleki[1], who recorded these events, noted that at the time Mosiah's group discovered the city of Zarahemla, the people there had become "exceedingly numerous" and had experienced "many wars and serious contentions" (Omni 1:17). Zarahemla and his people rejoiced that Mosiah had brought "the plates of brass which contained the record of the Jews," for "they had brought no records with them." Consequently, "their language had become corrupted . . . and they denied the being of their Creator" (Omni 1:14, 17). Sometime after the people of Zarahemla were taught the language of the Nephites, they and the people of Mosiah "did unite together; and Mosiah was appointed to be their king" (Omni 1:18–19). From this time forth the people of Zarahemla were identified with the Nephites, and became an integral part of the Book of Mormon account of Nephite history.

The people of Zarahemla have come to be known as Mulekites because they were descendants of Mulek, a son of Zedekiah. Mulek appears in three Book of Mormon references. In Mosiah 25:2 it is noted that "the people of Zarahemla, who was a descendant of Mulek," had become more numerous than the Nephites. Helaman 6:10 reveals that when migrating to the promised land, Mulek was brought by the Lord "into the land north, and Lehi into the land south." In Helaman 8:21 Nephi[2] also identified Mulek as a son of Zedekiah and taught that the presence of the "seed of Zedekiah" among them was a witness that Jerusalem had been destroyed.

BMH

Zedekiah[1] King of Judah who reigned from about 600 B.C. to the fall of Jerusalem in 586 B.C. (biblical scholarship identifies the first year of the reign of Zedekiah as 597 B.C.; the Book of Mormon places the beginning of his reign at about 600 B.C.; *see* Chronology, Book of Mormon). His wicked reign is recounted in 2 Kings 24:17–25:7; 2 Chronicles 36:11–13; and in Jeremiah 21:1–25:14; 37–39; 52:1–11. Nephi[1] began his record in the "first year" of Zedekiah's reign (1 Ne. 1:4), and the commencement of his reign is recorded on the brass plates (1 Ne. 5:13). A son of the righteous king Josiah, Nebuchadnezzar placed him on the throne to replace his nephew Jehoiachin who was deported to BABYLON along with many of the leading citizens of JUDAH following a rebellion against Babylon (2 Kgs. 24:8–17). Zedekiah was a weak and vacillating king. He owed his allegiance to Babylon and yet was continuously pressured by his advisers to revolt and restore the independent Davidic empire as his father Josiah had attempted to do. On several occasions Zedekiah summoned the prophet Jeremiah[1] to ascertain the word of the Lord. Jeremiah repeatedly told him it was the Lord's will to submit to Babylonian authority to spare Jerusalem from destruction and exile (Jer. 37:1–10, 16–21; 38:14–28). Zedekiah allowed Jeremiah to be imprisoned but spared his life (Jer. 37:11–21). Eventually Zedekiah conspired with his neighbors and rebelled against Babylon. Babylon responded in 586 B.C. by destroying Jerusalem as prophesied by Jeremiah and Lehi[1] (1 Ne. 1:4) and taking many of its inhabitants into exile. They captured Zedekiah in Jericho as he fled from Jerusalem, took him to Riblah in Syria where Nebuchadnezzar had all of his captured sons killed before him, put out his eyes, and took him to Babylon in chains where he died (Jer. 39:4–7; 52:7–11).

Mulek, Zedekiah's only surviving son, escaped and journeyed with a group of people to the promised land in the Americas where they became a people named after him (Omni 1:15; Hel. 6:10; 8:21).

See also Chronology, Bible; Chronology, Book of Mormon; Jeremiah[1], prophecies of; Jerusalem[1], city of; Jerusalem[1], destruction of, at 586 B.C.

DRS

Zedekiah[2] *See* Disciples, twelve Nephite.

Zeezrom Legal official in the city of Ammonihah who argued against Alma[2] and Amulek, asserting that the divinity of Christ was not logically possible (ca. 82 B.C.) but who later converted to Christ.

Lawyers are rarely mentioned in the Book of Mormon, so it remains unclear how they functioned in the Nephite legal system. Lawyers in Ammonihah, such as Zeezrom, were officials skilled in the study of the law, hired or appointed by the people to administer the law at their times of legal trials (Alma 10:14).

When Zeezrom questioned Amulek, his scheming strategy was to require Amulek to answer specific questions regarding the nature of God. He tried to bribe Amulek to "deny the existence of a Supreme Being" (Alma 11:22) with a substantial sum of six ontis—worth forty-two days of professional labor (Alma 11:3, 5–13)—and he questioned Amulek regarding the existence of God, monotheism, the coming of the Son of God, and the salvation of sinful people (Alma 11:26–37). Amulek rejected the bribe, accused Zeezrom of lying (Alma 11:25, 36), and declared that God will redeem his people if they will "believe on his name" (Alma 11:40). Amulek's direct and penetrating response caused Zeezrom to tremble, conscious that he was guilty of lying not only to men but also to God.

Zeezrom then asked to know more about the resurrection and the Judgment (Alma 12:8). In response, Alma delivered a profound discourse on the mysteries of God, the Creation, the Fall, the plan of redemption and happiness, the priesthood, repentance, and many other sacred themes (Alma 12:9–13:20). Alma's elaborate statement strengthened Amulek and the other faithful men in the audience, instructed Zeezrom, and warned the others.

Upon hearing the people use his own arguments to condemn Alma and Amulek before the chief judge, Zeezrom became "astonished" (Alma 14:6), and he realized the stark consequences of his shrewdness. He knew that he had been manipulative in his debate with Amulek, that he had lied, and that he had been silenced by Amulek and Alma's bold responses. To his credit, Zeezrom realized he could not join the other witnesses in accusing Alma and Amulek, and instead he publicly admitted his guilt and embraced the teachings of Alma and Amulek. For this he was accused of having an evil spirit and was cast out of the city (Alma 14:7). He then went to the land of Sidom, where he fell ill and was healed miraculously by Alma (Alma 15:11), baptized (Alma 15:12), and seven years later served as a missionary in Antionum (Alma 31:6).

JWW

Zeezrom, city of One of several Nephite cities captured by the Lamanites in the days of Moroni[1] and Helaman[2] (Alma 56:13–14; ca. 66 B.C.). These cities, presumably including Zeezrom, were abandoned by the Lamanites after Helaman[2] recaptured the city of Manti (Alma 58:28–31).

Zelph The name by which Joseph Smith identified "the skeletal remains of an ancient warrior" discovered in a burial mound in western Illinois in June 1834. The remains were found by members of Zion's Camp, an LDS military group traveling to Missouri to recover lands from which some Missouri Saints had been expelled in 1833. The discovery took place near present-day Griggsville, Illinois, on the west bank of the Illinois river, Monday, 2 June 1834.

The primary source material for the Zelph story comes from the diaries kept by some members of Zion's Camp. Six men wrote diary accounts concerning Zelph: Wilford Woodruff, Heber C. Kimball, George A. Smith, Levi Hancock, Moses Martin, and Reuben McBride. Searching these accounts for evidence of what Joseph Smith said about the find reveals general agreement on the following points: (1) members of Zion's Camp, traveling through Illinois, unearthed the skeletal remains of a man, 2 June 1834 near the top of a large burial mound; (2) Joseph Smith learned what he knew about the skeletal remains by way of a vision after the discovery; (3) the man was a white Lamanite named Zelph, a man of God, and a great warrior who served under a widely known leader named Onandagus; (4) Zelph was killed by the arrow found with his remains in a battle with Lamanites.

That the Prophet Joseph Smith believed that the lands over which Zion's Camp was traveling had some connection with Book of Mormon peoples is clear from a letter he wrote to Emma, 4 June 1834, just two days after Zelph's discovery: "The whole of our journey . . . wandering over the plains of the Nephites, recounting occasionally the history of the Book of Mormon, roving over the mounds of that once beloved people of the Lord, picking up their skulls & their bones, as proof of its divine authenticity . . . all serves to pass away time unnoticed" (Smith, 324).

Interestingly, recent scientific studies of several mounds in the area, including the Zelph mound, identified as "Naples-Russell Mound Number 8," date activities there about 100 B.C. –400 A.D. (Godfrey, 54 n. 2). These dates carry obvious significance for Book of Mormon students. It has been suggested, however, that Zelph, being at the top of the burial mound, may have lived in a later time period. Elder John A. Widtsoe, in an article on Book of Mormon geography printed in the *Improvement Era* in July 1950, suggested that "Zelph probably dated from a later time when the Nephites and Lamanites had been somewhat dispersed and had wandered over the country" (qtd. in Godfrey, 48).

Though the journal accounts of members of Zion's Camp and the prophet's letter to Emma are evidence that Joseph Smith and his contemporaries believed in a North American location for at least some events related to the Book of Mormon, they do not give the time or specific historical circumstances of Zelph's death. Details were added in later historical accounts indicating that Zelph was killed in "the last great struggle of the Lamanites and Nephites" (Godfrey, 42–46).

A North American location for some Book of Mormon events does not rule out a Central American location for others. The two are not mutually exclusive. Joseph Smith's statements about Zelph are important because they expand the possible geographical setting of Book of Mormon peoples.

See also Archaeology; Geography.

BIBLIOGRAPHY

Cannon, Donald Q. "Zelph Revisited." *Regional Studies in Latter-day Saint Church History: Illinois*. Edited by H. Dean Garrett. Provo: Department of Church History and Doctrine, 1995.

Godfrey, Kenneth W. "The Zelph Story." *Brigham Young University Studies* 29:2 (1989): 31–56.

Smith, Joseph. *Personal Writings of Joseph Smith*. Compiled and edited by Dean C. Jessee. Salt Lake City: Deseret Book, 1984, 2002.

DQC

Zemnarihah The appointed leader of the GADIANTON ROBBERS following the death of Giddianhi (3 Ne. 4:14, 17; A.D. 21). Under Zemnarihah's command, the Gadianton robbers laid SIEGE to the people of Nephi in expectation that "if they should cut them off from all their outward privileges, that they could cause them to yield themselves up according to their wishes" (3 Ne. 4:16). In fact, this tactical decision played directly into the hands of the Nephites, who were well provisioned for a lengthy siege. It also operated against the robbers' best interests, because a prolonged siege resulted in the virtual destruction of their own food supply and the beginning of their starvation. Finally, Zemnarihah ordered the lifting of the siege and the withdrawal of the Gadianton robbers. Gidgiddoni, the prophet-commander of the Nephites, recognizing the difficult circumstances of the Gadianton band, ordered a night march of the Nephite army that resulted in the robbers' being surrounded (3 Ne. 4:18–26). "Many thousands" of the robbers (a type of guerrilla army) were compelled to surrender, and Zemnarihah "was taken and hanged upon a tree . . . until he was dead" (3 Ne. 4:27–28; cf. Deut. 21:23). Following Zemnarihah's execution, the Nephites "did fell the tree [where he was hanged] to the earth, and did cry with a loud voice . . . that they may cause to be felled to the earth all who shall seek to slay them because of power and secret combinations" (3 Ne. 4:28–29).

SDR

Zenephi Nephite military commander during the final Nephite-Lamanite wars. Because Zenephi's army confiscated the remaining supplies at Sherrizah, many Nephite widows and their daughters who tarried in the land were forced to wander for food. Many of the old women fainted and died (Moro. 9:16).

Zeniff Father of king Noah[3], grandfather of king Limhi, and leader of a group of Nephites who left Zarahemla in the hope of re-establishing themselves in their ancestral lands (ca. 200 B.C.). Initially, Zeniff had been part of a Nephite faction that intended to take back their former land by force. Assigned to spy on the Lamanite armies to determine an attack strategy, Zeniff saw that there was good among the Lamanites, and desired that his leader withdraw his military objectives and instead make a treaty. For advocating this alternative view, Zeniff was condemned to death. His rescue came at a terrible price, leaving the greater part of the group dead; a surviving few (fifty) returned to Zarahemla (Mosiah 9:1–2; Omni 1:27–30).

Being "over-zealous to inherit the land of [their] fathers," Zeniff returned to Lamanite territory and made a dubious covenant with king Laman[2] (Mosiah 9:3–6) in which he received the lands of Lehi-Nephi and Shilom. Zeniff was made king over this Nephite colony (Mosiah 7:21). Laman's seeming generosity was only a demonstration of his "cunning" and "craftiness" to eventually enslave these Nephites (Mosiah 9:10; 7:21–22), a plan which succeeded years later with the bondage of king Limhi's people (Mosiah 7:21–22). Under the leadership of Zeniff, the Nephites in his colony prospered as a free people for twenty-two years, constructing buildings, repairing city walls, planting and harvesting crops, spinning cloth "of every kind," and defending their lands and cities from Lamanite attacks (Mosiah 9:8–9, 17–18; 10:5, 19–21).

Zeniff's writings provide the most thorough

rendition of the Lamanite traditions that perpetuated their hatred of the Nephites (Mosiah 10:12–17). His story also illustrates how overzealousness can lead to poor decisions (Mosiah 7:21). Zeniff's conferral of his kingdom on his lazy, self-indulgent son Noah proved disastrous to later generations of Nephites, who would suffer because of the iniquities of Noah and his priests.

DLL

Zenock Prophet who lived after the days of Abraham (Hel 8:19–20) and whose teachings were apparently included on the PLATES OF BRASS (1 Ne. 19:10, 21). Mormon taught that Zenock was an ancestor of the Book of Mormon peoples (3 Ne. 10:16). Zenock's teachings are referred to five times in the Book of Mormon. In each case, his message centers on the Messiah. He taught that the Son of God would come to redeem his people (Alma 34:7; Hel. 8:18–20). He spoke of the Lord's anger with the people for their refusal to understand the mercies which had been bestowed upon them because of the Son (Alma 33:14–17). He prophesied that the Savior would be crucified (1 Ne. 19:10), and that great destruction would accompany his death (3 Ne. 10:14–16). Zenock died a martyr: "Because the people would not understand his words they stoned him to death" (Alma 33:17).

TBB

Zenos Ancient prophet whose writings and sermons were contained on the PLATES OF BRASS and whose teachings were quoted, paraphrased, and highly prized by the Nephites. Zenos lived prior to the time of Lehi[1] and Nephi[1] (600 B.C.) but "since the days of Abraham" (Hel. 8:19; ca. 1900–1800 B.C.). Mormon stated that Zenos and Zenock prophesied of the destruction accompanying the death of Christ and that "they testified particularly concerning us, who are the remnant of their seed" (3 Ne. 10:15–16). This latter statement affirms that Zenos and Zenock were both Israelite prophets and may well imply that they were of the tribe of Joseph[1], just as Lehi[1] was (1 Ne. 5:14; Alma 10:3). Zenos is cited or quoted by Nephi[1] (1 Ne. 19:10–17), Jacob[2] (Jacob 5:1–77; 6:1), Alma[2] (Alma 33:3–11, 13, 15), Amulek (Alma 34:7), Nephi[2] (Hel. 8:19), and Mormon (3 Ne. 10:14–17).

Zenos' doctrinal messages included the following:

1. Redemption in Christ. Zenos knew concerning the role of Jesus Christ as Savior. Alma[2] quoted a prayer by Zenos: "And thou didst hear me because of mine afflictions and my sincerity; and it is because of thy Son that thou hast been thus merciful unto me . . . for thou hast turned thy judgments away from me, because of thy Son" (Alma 33:11). Zenos further testified that "redemption cometh through the Son of God" (Alma 34:7).

2. Destructions at the time of Christ's death. Zenos knew concerning Christ's burial in a sepulchre and he spoke concerning the signs of the Savior's death, many of which were later repeated by Samuel the Lamanite (1 Ne. 19:10–12; cf. Hel. 14:20–28).

3. Prayer and worship. Through the prayer of Zenos cited above, Alma[2] taught the poorer Zoramites[2] that true worship is less dependent on location than on sincerity of heart. In that prayer, Zenos exulted in God's mercy and goodness and also stressed that the supplicant may call upon the Lord in any place: in the wilderness, in the field, in the closet, in congregations of the Saints and under any circumstances, even when despised and rejected by enemies (Alma 33:2–11).

4. The destiny of Israel. Zenos taught that when the people of Israel cease to turn away from the Holy One of Israel, then "will he remember the isles of the sea; yea, and all the people who are of the house of Israel, will I gather in, saith the Lord . . . from the four quarters of the earth" (1 Ne. 19:15–16). Zenos also uttered a specific prophecy concerning the restoration of the Lamanites in the last days to a knowledge of the truth and to a knowledge of their Redeemer (Hel. 15:11–13). An extensive treatise concerning God's plan to save and redeem his people Israel is contained in the allegory of Zenos (Jacob 5). The central message is clear: God will not abandon Israel! In a brief commentary on the allegory, Jacob[2] pleaded that the people of Israel would "cleave unto God as he cleaveth unto you. And while his arm of mercy is

extended towards you in the light of the day, harden not your hearts" (Jacob 6:5). It may be that the apostle Paul also drew upon the allegory of Zenos in calling the early Christians to faithfulness (Rom. 11:17–21).

5. The destruction at the time of the Savior's second advent. Nephi[1] relayed that "the day soon cometh that all the proud and they who do wickedly shall be as stubble; and the day cometh that they must be burned" (1 Ne. 22:15, 23). Nephi also stated that after Christ's crucifixion "and after he is laid in a sepulchre for the space of three days he shall rise from the dead, with healing in his wings; and all those who shall believe on his name shall be saved in the kingdom of God" (2 Ne. 25:13; 26:9). This language is unmistakably similar to that of Malachi (4:1–2), who prophesied some time between 500 and 400 B.C., more than a century after Lehi's colony left the Old World. Because Malachi's words would not have been available to Nephi, one could conclude that God saw fit to reveal the very same language to Nephi that he did to Malachi. Or, as Elder Bruce R. McConkie has suggested, these later prophets found a common source in a more ancient prophet, namely Zenos. "Once the Lord has revealed his doctrine in precise language to a chosen prophet," he observed, "there is no reason why he should inspire another prophet to choose the same words in presenting the same doctrine on a subsequent occasion. It is much easier and simpler to quote that which has already been given in perfection" (McConkie, 18).

Zenos was true and faithful to the end, and like many of the Lord's anointed, he sealed his testimony of Christ with his life (Hel. 8:19). Elder McConkie has declared, "I do not think I overstate the matter when I say that next to Isaiah himself—who is the prototype, pattern, and model for all the prophets—there was not a greater prophet in all Israel than Zenos. And our knowledge of his inspired writings is limited to the quotations and paraphrasing summaries found in the Book of Mormon" (McConkie, 17). In a future day the faithful will, like Lehi[1] and Alma[2], be able to search the brass plates (1 Ne. 5:17–18; Alma 37:4) and study many remarkable oracles of the prophet Zenos. His words are plain and profound, his testimony sure and certain.

See also Zenos, allegory of.

BIBLIOGRAPHY

McConkie, Bruce R. "The Doctrinal Restoration." *The Joseph Smith Translation: The Restoration of Plain and Precious Things*. Edited by Monte S. Nyman and Robert L. Millet. Provo, Utah: Religious Studies Center, Brigham Young University, 1985.

RLM

Zenos, allegory of The allegory of Zenos, through metaphors, outlines various aspects of the history of the house of Israel from its beginnings to the end of the world.

The Book of Mormon prophet Jacob[2] employed the ALLEGORY to explain to his people (and indirectly to the latter-day readers of the Book of Mormon) how those who have rejected Jesus Christ as their foundation stone can return and build on him. In retelling the allegory in the Book of Mormon, Jacob most likely relied on the brass plates account originally given by the Israelite prophet Zenos, who lived between the days of Joseph[1], the son of Israel, and the time Lehi[1] left Jerusalem (Ludlow, 1623). Although no record of Zenos or his allegory exists from the ancient biblical world, elements of the allegory, or a similar one, are recorded in Romans 11:16–27 (cf. Isa. 5:1–7; Matt. 13:24–30; D&C 86:1–7).

One approach to interpreting the allegory is to divide it into seven parts, each part representing sequential periods in the history of the world. A short interpretation of each part is offered parenthetically in the accompanying outline (for other studies, see Jackson, 190–94; Nyman, 24–34; McConkie et al., 46–82; Crowley, 150–52; *Living*, 119–26).

Though an allegory can have multiple interpretations, at least four main lessons are taught in the allegory of the olive tree: (1) how anyone can make Christ their foundation after they have once rejected him; (2) why Israel was scattered; (3) why the apostasy happened; and (4) how Israel will be gathered and purified in the latter days. The various metaphors used in the allegory correspond to concepts and ideas connected

OUTLINE OF THE ALLEGORY OF ZENOS

I. The founding and aging of the house of Israel (Jacob 5:3)
   A. The tree was planted (the founding of the house of Israel) (Jacob 5:3).
   B. The tree had grown old and parts had begun to decay (the house of Israel had existed for quite some time and had begun to go into apostasy) (Jacob 5:3).

II. The scattering of the house of Israel (Jacob 5:4–14)
   A. The Lord of the vineyard came to the vineyard and noticed the decay (God saw the state of apostasy among the house of Israel) (Jacob 5:4).
   B. The Lord of the vineyard acted to stem the decay by pruning, digging about, and dunging the tree (God did what he could do to eliminate apostasy among the house of Israel) (Jacob 5:4–5).
   C. Part of the tree recovered but the top began to perish (some of the house of Israel began to look promising but the leadership was going bad) (Jacob 5:6).
   D. The Lord of the vineyard took measures to save the tree (God scattered Israel) (Jacob 5:7–14).
      1. He had the worst branches cut out and burned (God destroyed the more apostate parts of the house of Israel) (Jacob 5:7, 9).
      2. He had wild olive branches grafted into the mother tree (non-Israelites were mixed with the house of Israel) (Jacob 5:7–10).
      3. He had NATURAL BRANCHES of the mother tree grafted into other parts of his vineyard and natural branches planted in the nethermost parts of his vineyard (some of the house of Israel were scattered among non-Israelite people and some were taken as an Israelite entity to other parts of the world) (Jacob 5:8, 13–14). For example, Lehi and his people were settled in the Americas as a group. In addition, the land was prepared for the planting of the natural tree, Lehi and his descendants, by being cleared of previous growth, the Jaredite nation (Jacob 5:44).

III. The day of the former-day Saints (Jacob 5:15–28)
   A. The Lord of the vineyard returns after a long time (Jacob 5:15).
   B. The mother tree with wild branches produced good FRUIT (Israel with non-Israelites grafted in produced good works) (Jacob 5:16–18).
   C. The mother tree and all the transplanted branches of the mother tree bore nothing but good fruit, except the last one, half of which bore good fruit and the other half bad fruit (Israel in its scattered places had produced gospel fruit, except the last planting, the Nephites and Lamanites, which produced respectively good and bad fruit) (Jacob 5:19–25).
   D. The Lord wanted to destroy the bad part of the last planting, but the servant counseled to try one more time to save the tree (God did not give up on the Lamanites, but continued to work with them) (Jacob 5:26–28).

IV. The Great Apostasy (Jacob 5:29–49)
   A. After a long time, the Lord of the vineyard came back to the vineyard and found that the mother tree bore nothing but bad fruit (a long time after the close of the New Testament period, God found nothing but apostasy in the Old World) (Jacob 5:29–37).
   B. The other natural trees also bore nothing but bad fruit, and the bad part of the last transplanted tree had overcome the good part (all of scattered Israel had also gone into complete apostasy, and the Lamanites had destroyed the Nephites) (Jacob 5:38–49).

V. The gathering of the house of Israel (Jacob 5:50–74)
   A. The Lord determined to make one last effort to save his trees by GRAFTING back into the natural tree the natural branches he had grafted into the wild trees (after a long period of

continued

continued

apostasy, God will make one more last effort to gather Israel in from among the non-Israelites) (Jacob 5:50–74).

B. At the same time, the Lord will cut out of the natural trees the branches that produce wild fruit, beginning with the worst, as the newly grafted natural branches begin to grow strong (God will gather scattered Israel to the gospel, while at the same time those parts of Israel that produce evil works will be cut off, beginning with the worst parts) (Jacob 5:57–69).

C. In this last effort to produce good fruit, a few other servants will be brought into the work (as God for the last time prepares the earth for the Millennium, he will call a small number to help, including the prophets of the latter days) (Jacob 5:61–63 and 70–71).

VI. The Millennium (Jacob 5:74–76)

The pruning and grafting of the natural trees will continue until there is no more wild fruit on the natural trees (God will continue to work with those who have gathered to the gospel until they produce nothing but good fruit).

VII. The end of the world (Jacob 5:77)

After a long time, the trees of the vineyard will again begin to produce wild fruit. When that happens, the Lord of the vineyard will destroy the vineyard by fire (the Millennium will end as people again begin to produce evil works; this will continue until God destroys the earth by fire).

with the house of Israel. The accompanying table presents a few of these correspondences.

Jacob retold Zenos' allegory to explain to his brethren, the Nephites, how the Jews (the only political remnant of the house of Israel left in the Holy Land), after they have rejected the "stone upon which they might build [Jesus Christ] . . . the only sure foundation" (Jacob 4:15–16), can yet build on Christ, that he "may become the head of their corner" (Jacob 4:17). That is, Jacob explains how those who have rejected Christ can make him the point of alignment for their house of faith. The allegory explains this "mystery" (Jacob 4:18) by giving a history of the house of Israel from its inception with Abraham, Isaac, Jacob, and Jacob's sons to the end of the world, including the restoration of the gospel and the gathering thereunto of the house of Israel in the latter days. It is through this restoration, after a long period of apostasy, that Israel again accepts Christ by repenting and coming unto him.

The allegory makes clear that Israel was scattered to preserve Israel. The house of Israel had begun to go into apostasy. If apostasy had been allowed to continue, it would have destroyed the tree, and the covenants and teachings would have been lost. Without the covenants and teachings, the house of Israel would not have been able to survive. Therefore, God took measures to ensure that Israel would survive. He grafted non-Israelites into the house of Israel to stimulate growth, while at the same time, he took parts of the house of Israel and scattered them around the world to be fed and nourished by the Gentiles.

After the house of Israel had been pruned and nurtured and non-Israelites had been grafted in, all except one branch of scattered Israel brought forth good fruit. Not long afterwards, however, apostasy again set in, so that eventually no good fruit was produced, either on the mother tree or on the transplanted branches. Why did this turn of events take place? In the allegory, the Lord of the vineyard asks the same question, using slightly different words: "What could I have done more for my vineyard?" (Jacob 5:41). The answer is that he had done everything he possibly could have done to prevent apostasy in the house of Israel (Jacob 5:42–46). If the apostasy was not caused by God's neglect, what did cause it? The allegory explains that parts of the house of Israel, because of pride, began to take "strength unto themselves" and thereby they did "overcome the roots which [were] good" (Jacob 5:48). They amassed their own covenants and doctrines (Jacob 5:48). In other words, short of interfering in their agency, there was nothing God could have done to prevent prideful people from self-willing the apostasy.

In the latter days that precede the Millennium, God will again, for the last time, work to restore the house of Israel to the gospel of Jesus Christ. The gathering of Israel will proceed in the reverse order of the scattering of Israel (Jacob 5:63). The process is described in the allegory as a pruning out of the branches that do not produce good fruit, and a grafting into the house of Israel of natural descendants. As the natural branches begin to grow, flourish, and produce good fruit, the less desirable parts of the house of Israel will be cut out (Jacob 5:65–66). As an example of this process in these days, many people will be converted to the gospel of Jesus Christ and will join the Church. As they grow in the gospel and begin to produce good fruit they will prosper, but those members who do not produce good fruit in the gospel will begin to fall away. This process will continue until the Church becomes clean and pure, and obedient to the "principles of the law of the celestial kingdom" (D&C 105:5).

The allegory also makes clear how merciful, tender, long-suffering, and loving God is in his efforts to help Israel reach its potential: "How merciful is our God unto us, for he remembereth the house of Israel, both roots and branches" (Jacob 6:4). For over three thousand years he worked to bless and strengthen Israel and did everything in his power to help them produce good works (Jacob 5:41). In these the latter days he is again working to gather, instruct, and purify the house of Israel.

In this setting, Jacob's application of the allegory to his people is equally apropos today for those who are of the house of Israel. Every detail of the allegory will "surely come to pass" (Jacob 6:1). God will do everything in his power, including nourishing them "by the good word of God all the day long" (Jacob 6:7) to help them produce good works that they might "be saved in the kingdom of God" (Jacob 6:4). Therefore, there is not much more that can be said to the house of Israel in these days, except to "be wise" (Jacob 6:12).

SYMBOLISM IN THE ALLEGORY

METAPHOR	MEANING
vineyard	this world
tame olive tree	the house of Israel
wild olive tree	non-Israel
branches	different parts of the house of Israel
grafting	being joined to the house of Israel
pruning, digging, and dunging	nurturing the house of Israel
fruit	works
the main top of the tree	the leaders of the house of Israel
decay	apostasy
roots	the good word of God, including covenants and teachings
the servant	the Savior (others equate the servant with the prophets)
lord of the vineyard	God the Father (others equate Lord of the vineyard with Christ)

See also Israel, gathering of; Israel, historical background of; Israel, scattering of; Jews, Book of Mormon message concerning; Jews, history of; Olive trees (including photographs).

BIBLIOGRAPHY

Crowley, Ariel. *About the Book of Mormon.* Salt Lake City: N.p., 1961.

Ludlow, Daniel H. "Zenos." *Encyclopedia of Mormonism.* Edited by Daniel H. Ludlow et al. 4 vols. New York: Macmillan, 1992.

Jackson, Kent P. "Nourished by the Good Word of God (Jacob 4–6)." *1 Nephi to Alma 29.* Edited by Kent P. Jackson. Vol. 7 of *Studies in Scripture* series, edited by Robert L. Millet and Kent P. Jackson. Salt Lake City: Deseret Book, 1987.

Living Truths from the Book of Mormon. Salt Lake City: Deseret Sunday School Union, 1970.

McConkie, Joseph Fielding, Robert L. Millet, and Brent L. Top. *Doctrinal Commentary on the Book of Mormon.* 4 vols. Salt Lake City: Bookcraft, 1987–92.

Nyman, Monte. *An Ensign to the People.* Salt Lake City: Deseret Book, 1987.

PYH

Zerahemnah Lamanite military commander who, with his armies, was defeated by captain Moroni and Lehi[3] in a fierce battle at the river Sidon (ca. 74 B.C.). Zerahemnah assembled a massive coalition of Lamanites and Nephite dissenters to assist him in subjugating the Nephites to bondage. Aware of the bitter animosity and "murderous disposition" of the Amalekites and Zoramites[2], he cunningly appointed his chief captains from among them (Alma 43:5–8, 13).

Zerahemnah, however, could not withstand the power of the Nephites' faith in Christ (Alma 44:3); the advantages that armor accorded the Nephite soldiers (Alma 43:19–22, 38); the revelation to Alma[2] of Lamanite battle plans (Alma 43:23–24); captain Moroni's strategic placement of his soldiers (Alma 43:27, 31–33); and the "better cause" of troops "fighting for their homes and their liberties, their wives and their children, and their all, yea, for their rites of worship and their church" (Alma 43:45).

Although an immense slaughter occurred on both sides, Moroni's strategy to surround the Lamanites was successful. Seeing the "terror" this entrapment created, Moroni called a halt to the conflict, and demanded their weapons and a covenant of peace as terms to stop the bloodshed (Alma 43:53–54; 44:6). Moroni credited the Nephite victory to God, while Zerahemnah attributed his defeat to Nephite armor.

Though Zerahemnah was willing to surrender, he would not agree to permanent peace. When Moroni restated his position, an angered Zerahemnah rushed at him, only to lose his scalp at the hand of one of Moroni's men. Many of Zerahemnah's soldiers surrendered with a "covenant of peace," yet he again incited the remainder to further combat. Finally, at the point of annihilation, Zerahemnah surrendered, covenanting never again to make war against the Nephites (Alma 44:3–19).

An important contribution of the Zerahemnah narrative is the contrast it illustrates between righteous and evil purposes for war (Alma 43:8–9, 29–30, 45–47).

DLL

Zeram *See* Amnor.

Zerin, mount A mountain of unknown location to which the brother of Jared[1] said, "Remove—and it was removed" (Ether 12:30).

Ziff *See* Metals of the Book of Mormon.

Zion The Book of Mormon discusses Zion in several different contexts. Zion is considered a favored community of the people of the Lord characterized by unity and brotherly kindness. Sometimes, Zion refers to the restoration of the church and kingdom of God in the latter days. Zion is also identified as the New Jerusalem to be built in the western hemisphere in preparation for the Savior's second coming. In Isaiah's writings Zion often refers to Jerusalem and the mount upon which it is built (e.g., 2 Ne. 14:5; 18:18; 20:12, 24; cf. Isa. 30:19).

Nephi[1] quoted Isaiah concerning Zion. As a favored people of the Lord, it was Zion that the Lord loved (1 Ne. 21:14–16; 2 Ne. 8:16), would comfort (2 Ne. 8:3), and would defend (1 Ne. 22:14; 2 Ne. 14:5; 20:24). He also warned that the apostate daughters of Zion would be purged and punished (2 Ne. 13:16–26; 14:4). Nephi included the promised blessings of the Lord to those who would seek to establish Zion (1 Ne.

13:37) and warned those who "fight against Zion" (2 Ne. 6:12–13; 10:16), labor for money rather than for Zion (2 Ne. 26:29–31), or who are "at ease in Zion" (2 Ne. 28:21–25).

No group of people in the Book of Mormon better satisfied the characteristics of Zion than those living after the Savior's visit to the western hemisphere (4 Ne. 1:1–18; cf. D&C 97:21; 105:5). While the Book of Mormon does not specifically use the term Zion to refer to these converted descendants of Lehi[1], they satisfied the criteria of being a righteous and holy people. They eliminated contention "because of the love of God which did dwell in [their] hearts" (4 Ne. 1:15). Further, they were a people without envy, strife, whoredoms, murders, and lasciviousness (4 Ne. 1:16). They enjoyed a social harmony that eliminated poverty and inequality, for they had "all things common among them," and "every man did deal justly one with another" (4 Ne. 1:2–4). Of these covenant people, Mormon recorded, "Surely there could not be a happier people among all the people who had been created by the hand of God" (4 Ne. 1:16). The Nephite Zion lasted nearly two hundred years before the people abandoned the sustaining principles of righteousness, returned to traditional rivalries, and lost their favored status (4 Ne. 1:24–45).

The Book of Mormon prophesies of the time when the Lord would again establish Zion by gathering his people and restoring his church and kingdom (3 Ne. 21:1, 6–9, 22; cf. D&C 6:6; 21:7). A "choice seer" (2 Ne. 3:6–7) raised up by God in the latter days would bring about "a great and a marvelous work" (3 Ne. 21:9), prompting the righteous to respond to gospel truth and gather as a covenant people. The Lord declared, "I . . . shall establish again among them my Zion" (3 Ne. 21:1), and "I will establish my church among them" (3 Ne. 21:22; 1 Ne. 22:8–11; 2 Ne. 27:26).

Zion is also a holy city to be built on the American continent in the last days. This will be the New Jerusalem which will complement the original Jerusalem existing in the eastern hemisphere. It will be a place of gathering for the faithful as they prepare for Christ's second coming and will serve as a governing center for his kingdom after his return (D&C 45:64–71; 57:2–3; 2 Ne. 12:3; 3 Ne. 20:22; 21:23; Ether 13:1–12; Moses 7:62).

DAW

Zion, all is well in *See* All is well in Zion.

Zoram[1] Servant of Laban who, after surrendering the plates of brass to a disguised Nephi[1], was persuaded to join the group leaving Jerusalem (1 Ne. 4:20–37; ca. 600 B.C.). Zoram was a trusted man holding Laban's treasury keys. Still, he was a slave, and he accepted the freedom Nephi offered him (1 Ne. 4:33–35). Being a slave whose tribal lineage is never given, he may not have been an Israelite. Nephi told him he would nevertheless "have place" with the family (1 Ne. 4:34). Zoram's marriage to Ishmael's oldest daughter (1 Ne. 16:7) may indicate that he was older than Lehi[1]'s sons. In blessing him, Lehi commended his faithfulness and called him "a true friend unto my son, Nephi, forever." Lehi also promised Zoram that because of his faithfulness his seed would prosper with the seed of Nephi "upon the face of this land forever" (2 Ne. 1:30–32). When Nephi and his followers split from Laman[1] and his followers, Zoram was numbered among the believers who accompanied Nephi (2 Ne. 5:6).

See also Zoramites[1].

TLS

Zoram[2] Chief captain over Nephite armies (ca. 81 B.C.). After the Lamanites had destroyed the people of Ammonihah in fulfillment of the prophecy of Alma[2] (Alma 9:18–19), the Lamanites took nearby residents captive into the wilderness (Alma 16:2–3). Wishing to liberate them, Zoram and his sons, Lehi[2] and Aha, importuned Alma to ask God where they should conduct their search. Following Alma's inspired instructions, Zoram and his sons crossed to the east side of the river Sidon, entered the south wilderness, scattered the Lamanite army, and rescued all the captives (Alma 16:4–8).

Zoram[3] Nephite apostate and leader of the ZORAMITES[2] who "separated themselves from the Nephites" and gathered into the land of

Antionum. There Zoram led "the hearts of the people to bow down to dumb idols" (Alma 30:59–31:3; ca. 74 B.C.).

Zoramites[1] The descendants of Zoram[1], who were numbered among the Nephites (Jacob 1:13; 4 Ne. 1:36–37; Morm. 1:8) and to whom "the knowledge of a Savior" was to come in the latter-days "through the testimony of their fathers" (i.e., through the testimonies of Christ recorded in the Book of Mormon) (D&C 3:16–17).

Zoramites[2] An apostate sect of Nephite dissenters led by Zoram[3] (ca. 74 B.C.). The focus of the Zoramite story is the Nephite mission to reclaim them (Alma 31–35), for they had "fallen into great errors" (Alma 31:9). They worshipped idols, were disobedient to the law of Moses, and failed to "observe the performances of the church, to continue in prayer" (Alma 31:10, 1, 9). Their perverted style of worship included a set prayer offered weekly which declared God to be a spirit and belief in Christ to be a foolish tradition. The prayer also reinforced their arrogance by declaring God's predetermination to save them while damning the remainder of humanity (Alma 31:15–17). The Zoramite people were proud and materialistic, and their religion pretentious, vain, and exclusive (Alma 31:24–25, 27–28).

The central theme of the Zoramite account is the answer to the "great question"—"whether the word be in the Son of God, or whether there shall be no Christ" (Alma 34:5). Therefore, these chapters (Alma 31–34) are vital to the divine design of the Book of Mormon as another testament of Jesus Christ. Speaking to the Zoramite poor, who had been cast out of the synagogues by their prideful neighbors, Alma[2] proposed a formula by which one might know the truth about Christ and his gospel. Alma challenged his Zoramite listeners to "experiment" upon the word (Alma 32). He then quoted the prophets Zenos (Alma 33:3–13) and Zenock (Alma 33:15–17) and referred to an event in the ministry of Moses to further support his testimony concerning Christ (Alma 33:19–21). When Alma concluded, Amulek arose and added his witness concerning the reality of the coming of Christ (Alma 34:8, 37) and the infinite nature of the Atonement (Alma 34:10–14).

Alma and his companions left the Zoramite city of Antionum and went to Jershon. The converts they had made in Antionum were expelled by the Zoramite rulers, teachers, and priests who were angered by the Nephite teachings. It also angered the ruling Zoramites that the refugees were warmly received in Jershon by the people of Ammon. This event became the catalyst for the Zoramite-Lamanite alliance and the war that soon followed (Alma 35:8–13).

One purpose of the Book of Mormon is to confound false doctrine (2 Ne. 3:12). Both in matters of doctrine and in religious practice the Zoramite narrative offers many lessons for latter-day people, including the following: Christ is a reality and this truth can be known, God is not solely a spirit, and religion devoid of charity is vain. The Zoramite story also confounds the mere recitation of creeds; the declaring of one's predestined status as "chosen," "elect," or "saved," and the hypocrisy of the heartless profession of God on the Sabbath, but then never thinking or speaking of him again during the week. One need only reverse the false religious practices of the Zoramites to identify essential elements of genuine worship. True worship centers in Christ, requires obedience to the commandments, and is neither exclusively a Sabbath day nor a synagogue (church) activity. In addition, worship must be of God, not wealth or material possessions, and prayer must be sincere and humble, not vainly repetitious and arrogant. In Alma 31 the juxtaposition of the Zoramites' prideful prayer and Alma's humble prayer teaches that lesson, and is reminiscent of a parable in which Jesus contrasted the prayer of a proud Pharisee with that of a humble publican (Luke 18:9–14). Typically the proud separate themselves from others, supposing a superior status, as the wealthier Zoramites did (Alma 31:16–17). This deliberate separation makes it impossible to keep the second great commandment, which is to love one's neighbors as oneself (Matt. 22:34–40; cf. 1 Jn. 2:9).

The Zoramite account also provides a valuable lesson on apostasy. Those who are disobedient

ZORAMITES[2]

and who fail to pray properly and frequently lose the Spirit and become susceptible to false revelation and perverted doctrines and practices. It appears, too, that the Zoramites had neglected or misread the scriptures. Alma inquired, "I would ask if you have read the scriptures?" He then concluded, "If ye have, how can ye disbelieve on the Son of God?" (Alma 33:14). Alma's appeal to the written word, to correct errors and testify of Christ, highlights and models the importance of the scriptures in this regard (Alma 33:2, 11–20).

In effect, the apostate Zoramites became Lamanites (Alma 43:4ff.), and later "some who were Zoramites" led away Lamanite children "by their lyings and their flattering words, to join [the] Gadianton robbers" (3 Ne. 1:29).

See also Book of Mormon, selected purposes of, to confound false doctrine.

DLL

APPENDIXES

Appendix A
Study Guide to the Book of Mormon

This study guide is divided into two sections. The first section matches topics in the *BMRC* with readings in the Book of Mormon. The second section matches topics in the *BMRC* with subject groupings. For additional information, use the cross-referencing system within the individual articles: SMALL CAPITALS, *see,* and *See also*. Articles marked with an asterisk are suggested under more than one heading.

Readings in the Book of Mormon

Introduction

The Book of Mormon: An Overview and Introduction
The Coming Forth of the Book of Mormon
The Structure of the Book of Mormon
And thus we see
Book of Mormon: Another Testament of Jesus Christ
Book of Mormon, condemnation for treating lightly
Book of Mormon, early conversions through
Book of Mormon, title page of
Book of Mormon, selected purposes of
Book of Mormon, selected themes of
Statements on the Book of Mormon from LDS Church leaders (Appendix B)

1 Nephi 1–7

Nephi, first book of
Lehi[1]
Nephi[1]
Laban
Laban, slaying of
Plates of brass
Plates of Nephi
Laman[1]
Lehi[1], journey of, to the promised land
Jerusalem[1], city of

1 Nephi 8–15

Lehi[1]'s dream
Gentile(s)
Nephi[1]'s vision
Condescension of God
Columbus, Christopher
Plain and precious things, loss of and restoration of
Great and abominable church
*Plates of Nephi

1 Nephi 16–22

Liahona
Israel, historical background of
Isaiah, life and ministry of
Isaiah, understanding of
Isaiah, purposes for quoting
Isaiah in the Book of Mormon
Isaiah chapter reviews: 1 Nephi 20 // Isaiah 48
Isaiah chapter reviews: 1 Nephi 21 // Isaiah 49
Israel, gathering of
Zenos

2 Nephi 1–5

Nephi, second book of
Promised land, land of promise
Fall of Adam and Eve, the
Agency

STUDY GUIDE: READINGS

Choice seer
Nephi[1]'s psalm
Joseph[1], covenants unto

2 Nephi 6–10

* Isaiah, life and ministry of
* Isaiah, understanding of
* Isaiah, purposes for quoting
* Isaiah in the Book of Mormon

Jews, history of
Isaiah chapter reviews: 2 Nephi 7 // Isaiah 50
Isaiah chapter reviews: 2 Nephi 8 // Isaiah 51:1–52:2
Atonement, the
Judgment, the
Hell

2 Nephi 11–25:8

* Isaiah, life and ministry of
* Isaiah, understanding of
* Isaiah, purposes for quoting
* Isaiah in the Book of Mormon

Isaiah chapter reviews: 2 Nephi 12–24 // Isaiah 2–14

2 Nephi 25:9–30:18

Jews, Book of Mormon message concerning
Lamanites, Book of Mormon message concerning
Gentiles, Book of Mormon message concerning
Isaiah chapter reviews: 2 Nephi 26:6, 15–18; 27 // Isaiah 29
Priestcraft
Book of Mormon, selected purposes of, to reveal the enemies of Christ

2 Nephi 31–33

Baptism
Fulfill all righteousness
Gospel, the
Endurance to the end
Holy Ghost, the
Millennium, the

Jacob 1–4

Jacob, book of
Jacob[2]
Looking beyond the mark
Pride
Riches
Plural marriage
Chastity

Jacob 5–7

Allegory
Zenos, allegory of
Olive trees
Sherem
Antichrist

* Zenos
* Book of Mormon, selected purposes of, to reveal the enemies of Christ

Enos, Jarom, Omni, Words of Mormon

Enos, book of
Enos
Prayer
Repentance
Forgiveness
Jarom, book of
Omni, book of
Words of Mormon
Amaleki[1]
Mosiah[1]
Zarahemla, people of (Mulekites)

Mosiah 1–6

Mosiah, book of
Benjamin, king
Children of Christ
Born again
Kings
Natural man
Service

* Book of Mormon: Another Testament of Jesus Christ

Mosiah 7–8; 18–24

Mosiah[2]
Ammon[1]
Alma[1]
Noah[3]
Noah[3], priests of
Church of God (Christ) in ancient America
Amulon
Limhi
Book of Mormon, selected themes of, bondage and deliverance

* Baptism
* Mosiah, book of

Mosiah 9–17

Zeniff
Abinadi
Law of Moses
Isaiah chapter reviews: Mosiah 14 // Isaiah 53
Seed of Christ
Resurrection, the
Jesus Christ, role of, as Father and Son
*Mosiah, book of
*Noah[3]

Mosiah 25–29

Alma[2]
Church discipline
Mosiah[2], sons of
Government, principles of
Judges, reign of
*Born again
*Church of God (Christ) in ancient America
*Repentance

Alma 1–4

Alma, book of
Nehor
Priestcraft
Amlici
Pride

Alma 5–16

Zarahemla, land of and city of
Gideon
Melek, land of
Jerusalem[1], land of
Ammonihah, land of and city of
Amulek
Zeezrom
Mysteries of God, the
Spiritual death
Cherubim and a flaming sword
Premortal existence
Chosen
Priesthood among the Nephites
Preparatory redemption
*Born again
*Alma[2]
*Resurrection, the

Alma 17–29

Aaron[3]
Ammon[2]

STUDY GUIDE: READINGS

Anti-Nephi-Lehies
Lamoni
Lamoni, father of
Abish
Missionary service
Joy
*Alma[2]
*Mosiah[2], sons of

Alma 30–35

Korihor
Zoramites[2]
Faith
Zenock
Moses
Justice, law of
Mercy
Night of darkness
*Amulek
*Zenos
*Atonement, the
*Book of Mormon, selected purposes of, to reveal the enemies of Christ

Alma 36–39

Chiasmus
Helaman[2]
Shiblon
Corianton
Scriptures, Book of Mormon message concerning
Gazelem
*Liahona
*Book of Mormon, selected themes of, bondage and deliverance
*Book of Mormon, selected themes of, come unto Christ
*Repentance
*Forgiveness
*Chastity

Alma 40–42

Spirit world
Outer darkness
Paradise
Restoration, plan of
Plan
*Mercy
*Justice, law of
*Atonement, the
*Resurrection, the

STUDY GUIDE: READINGS

* Fall of Adam and Eve, the
* Hell

Alma 43–63

Moroni[1]
Warfare in the Book of Mormon
Pahoran[1]
Amalickiah
Warfare, principles governing
Stripling warriors
Teancum
Lehi[3]
Epistles
* Alma, book of
* Helaman[2]

Helaman 1–16

Helaman, book of
Helaman[3]
Gadianton robbers
Secret combinations
Nephi[2]
Lehi[4]
Book of Mormon, selected themes of, cycles of prosperity and destruction
Book of Mormon, selected themes of, remember, remembrance
Samuel[2] the Lamanite
Signs
* Pride
* Spiritual death

3 Nephi 1–10

Nephi, third book of
Lachoneus[1]
Giddianhi
Nephi[3]
* Epistles
* Signs
* Gadianton robbers
* Pride

3 Nephi 11–19

Jesus Christ
Sermon at Bountiful and Sermon on the Mount
Other sheep
Sacrament, the
Christ, in the name of
* Baptism
* Gospel, the
* Nephi, third book of
* Book of Mormon: Another Testament of Jesus Christ

3 Nephi 20–30

Book of Mormon, selected purposes of, to be a sign of the Father's work
Isaiah chapter reviews: 3 Nephi 20:32–45 // Isaiah 52:1–3, 6–15
Isaiah chapter reviews: 3 Nephi 22 // Isaiah 54
Micah
New Jerusalem
Malachi chapter review: 3 Nephi 24–25 // Mal. 3–4
Nephites, the Three
Translation
Israel, numbered among
* Israel, gathering of
* Gospel, the

4 Nephi

Nephi, fourth book of
* Book of Mormon, selected themes of, cycles of prosperity and destruction

Mormon

Mormon, book of
Mormon[2]
Cumorah, battle of
Moroni[2]
Ether
Ether, book of

Ether

Jaredite civilization
Fulness of iniquity
Jared[1], brother of
Jesus Christ, premortal appearances of
Scriptures, additional, to come forth
Witnesses of the Book of Mormon
Jared[1], posterity of
Trial of faith
Coriantumr[2]
Shiz
* Faith
* New Jerusalem
* Secret combinations

Moroni

Moroni, book of
Evil, concept of

Subject Groupings

Old Testament Background

Book of Mormon as Literature

The Coming Forth of the Book of Mormon

Doctrines

Isaiah

Appendix B
Statements about the Book of Mormon by LDS Church Leaders

Benson, Ezra Taft

Some of the early missionaries, on returning home, were reproved by the Lord in section 84 of the Doctrine and Covenants because they had treated lightly the Book of Mormon. As a result, their minds had been darkened. The Lord said that this kind of treatment of the Book of Mormon brought the whole Church under condemnation, even all of the children of Zion. And then the Lord said, "And they shall remain under this condemnation until they repent and remember the new covenant, even the Book of Mormon." (See D&C 84:54–57.) Are we still under that condemnation?—*Ensign* 5 (May 1975): 65.

We are to use the Book of Mormon as the basis for our teaching. . . . As we read and teach, we are to liken the Book of Mormon scriptures unto us "that it might be for our profit and learning." (1 Ne. 19:23.)—*Ensign* 5 (May 1975): 64.

Every Latter-day Saint should make the study of this book a lifetime pursuit. Otherwise he is placing his soul in jeopardy and neglecting that which could give spiritual and intellectual unity to his whole life. There is a difference between a convert who is built on the rock of Christ through the Book of Mormon and stays hold of that iron rod, and one who is not. . . . It will hold us as close to the Spirit of the Lord as anything I know.—*Ensign* 5 (May 1975): 65.

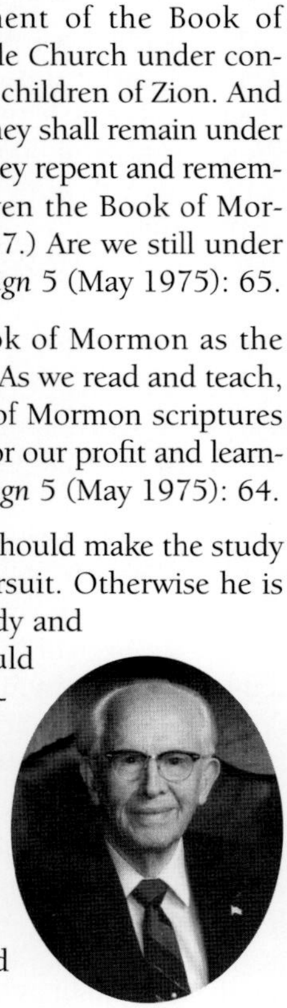

Ezra Taft Benson

The Book of Mormon was written for us today. God is the author of the book. It is a record of a fallen people, compiled by inspired men for our blessing today. Those people never had the book—it was meant for us. Mormon, the ancient prophet after whom the book is named, abridged centuries of records. God, who knows the end from the beginning, told him what to include in his abridgment that we would need for our day.—*Ensign* 5 (May 1975): 63.

The Book of Mormon brings men to Christ through two basic means. First, it tells in a plain manner of Christ and his gospel. . . . Second, the Book of Mormon exposes the enemies of Christ. It confounds false doctrines and lays down contention. (See 2 Ne. 3:12.)—*Ensign* 5 (May 1975): 64.

Members of the Church everywhere should know the Book of Mormon better than any other book. . . . I have noted within the Church the difference in discernment, in insight, conviction, and spirit between those who know and love the Book of Mormon and those who do not. That book is a great sifter.—*New Era* 5 (May 1975): 19.

Now, we have not been using the Book of Mormon as we should. Our homes are not as strong unless we are using it to bring our children to Christ.—*Ensign* 5 (May 1975): 65.

Reading the Book of Mormon is one of the greatest persuaders to get men on missions. —*Ensign* 5 (May 1975): 65.

STATEMENTS: BENSON, EZRA TAFT

Combined with the Spirit of the Lord, the Book of Mormon is the greatest single tool which God has given us to convert the world.—*Ensign* 14 (November 1984): 7.

We do not have to prove the Book of Mormon is true. The book is its own proof. All we need to do is read it and declare it! The Book of Mormon is not on trial—the people of the world, including the members of the Church, are on trial as to what they will do with this second witness for Christ.—*Ensign* 14 (November 1984): 8.

I bless you with increased *understanding* of the Book of Mormon. I promise you that from this moment forward, if we will daily sup from its pages and abide by its precepts, God will pour out upon each child of Zion and the Church a blessing hitherto unknown—and we will plead to the Lord that He will begin to lift the condemnation—the scourge and judgment. Of this I bear solemn witness.

I testify that the Book of Mormon is the word of God.—*Ensign* 16 (May 1986): 78.

Young men, the Book of Mormon will change your life. It will fortify you against the evils of our day. It will bring a spirituality into your life that no other book will. It will be the most important book you will read in preparation for a mission and for life. A young man who knows and loves the Book of Mormon, who has read it several times, who has an abiding testimony of its truthfulness, and who applies its teachings will be able to stand against the wiles of the devil and will be a mighty tool in the hands of the Lord. —*Ensign* 16 (May 1986): 43.

The Lord inspired His servant Lorenzo Snow to reemphasize the principle of tithing to redeem the Church from financial bondage. In those days the General Authorities took that message to the members of the Church.

Now, in our day, the Lord has revealed the need to reemphasize the Book of Mormon to get the Church and all the children of Zion out from under condemnation—the scourge and judgment. (See D&C 84:54–58.) This message must be carried to the members of the Church throughout the world.—*Ensign* 16 (May 1986): 78.

There are three ways in which the Book of Mormon is the keystone of our religion. It is the keystone in our witness of Christ. It is the keystone of our doctrine. It is the keystone of testimony.—*Ensign* 16 (November 1986): 5.

I would like to speak about one of the most significant gifts given to the world in modern times. The gift I am thinking of is more important than any of the inventions that have come out of the industrial and technological revolutions. This is a gift of greater value to mankind than even the many wonderful advances we have seen in modern medicine. It is of greater worth to mankind than the development of flight or space travel. I speak of the gift of the Book of Mormon, given to mankind 156 years ago.

This gift was prepared by the hand of the Lord over a period of more than a thousand years, then hidden up by Him so that it would be preserved in its purity for our generation. —*Ensign* 16 (November 1986): 4.

If they [the Book of Mormon writers] saw our day, and chose those things which would be of greatest worth to us, is not that how we should study the Book of Mormon? We should constantly ask ourselves, "Why did the Lord inspire Mormon (or Moroni or Alma) to include that in his record? What lesson can I learn from that to help me live in this day and age?" —*Ensign* 16 (November 1986): 6.

It is not just that the Book of Mormon teaches us truth, though it indeed does that. It is not just that the Book of Mormon bears testimony of Christ, though it indeed does that, too. But there is something more. There is a power in the book which will begin to flow into your lives the moment you begin a serious study of the book. You will find greater power to resist temptation. You will find the power to avoid deception. You will find the power to stay on the strait and narrow path.—*Ensign* 16 (November 1986): 7.

The Book of Mormon must be reenthroned in the minds and hearts of our people. We must honor it by reading it, by studying it, by taking its precepts into our lives and transforming them into lives required of the true followers of Christ. —*Ensign* 16 (November 1986): 80.

We are not required to prove that the Book of Mormon is true or is an authentic record through external evidences—though there are many. It never has been the case, nor is it so now, that the studies of the learned will prove the Book of Mormon true or false. The origin, preparation, translation, and verification of the truth of the Book of Mormon have all been retained in the hands of the Lord, and the Lord makes no mistakes. You can be assured of that.

God has built in His own proof system of the Book of Mormon as found in Moroni, chapter 10, and in the testimonies of the Three and the Eight Witnesses.—*Ensign* 17 (May 1987): 83–84.

Now, what is the instrument that God has designed for this gathering? It is the same instrument that is designed to convince the world that Jesus is the Christ, that Joseph Smith is His prophet, and that The Church of Jesus Christ of Latter-day Saints is true. It is that scripture which is the keystone of our religion.—*Ensign* 17 (May 1987): 85.

I do not know fully why God has preserved my life to this age, but I do know this: That for the present hour He has revealed to me the absolute need for us to move the Book of Mormon forward now in a marvelous manner. You must help with this burden and with this blessing which He has placed on the whole Church, even all the children of Zion.

Moses never entered the promised land. Joseph Smith never saw Zion redeemed. Some of us may not live long enough to see the day when the Book of Mormon floods the earth and when the Lord lifts His condemnation. (See D&C 84:54–58.) But, God willing, I intend to spend all my remaining days in that glorious effort.—*Ensign* 18 (November 1988): 6.

Presently the Book of Mormon is studied in our Sunday School and seminary classes every fourth year. This four-year pattern, however, must *not* be followed by Church members in their personal study of the standard works. All scripture is not of equal value. The book that is the "keystone of our religion" and that will get a man "nearer to God by abiding by its precepts, than by any other book" needs to be studied constantly. (*History of the Church* 4:461.)—*A Witness and a Warning* (Salt Lake City: Deseret Book, 1988), vii.

Hanks, Marion D.

The lessons of life in the Book of Mormon are based on sound eternal principles as they apply to and affect our lives. . . . The basic decisions about how we choose to live—the kind of people we are—can be materially influenced if we will comprehend and apply the great lessons which spring from the revealed truths so forcefully and plainly taught in the Book of Mormon.—*Book of Mormon Symposium Speeches 1986* (Salt Lake City: The Church of Jesus Christ of Latter-day Saints, 1987), 8.

Marion D. Hanks

Hinckley, Gordon B.

As has been demonstrated for a hundred and fifty years, the truth of the book will not be determined by literary analysis or by scientific research, although these are reassuring and most welcome. The truth will be determined today and tomorrow, as it has been throughout the yesterdays, by the reading of it in a spirit of reverence and respect and prayer. . . .

. . . To think that anyone less than one inspired could bring forth a book which should have so profound an affect for good upon others is to imagine that which simply cannot be. The evidence for the truth of the Book of Mormon is found in the lives of the millions, living and gone, who have read it, prayed about it, and received a witness of its truth.—*Teachings of Gordon B. Hinckley* (Salt Lake City: Deseret Book, 1997), 38–39.

Gordon B. Hinckley

Without reservation I promise you that if you will prayerfully read the Book of Mormon, regardless of how many times you previously have read it, there will come into your hearts an added measure of the Spirit of the Lord. There will come a strengthened resolution to walk in obedience to his commandments, and there will come a stronger testimony of the living reality of the Son of God.—*Teachings of Gordon B. Hinckley,* 41.

Each time we encourage a man to read the Book of Mormon we do him a favor. If he reads it prayerfully and with a sincere desire to know the truth, he will know by the power of the Holy Ghost that the book is true. And from that knowledge there will flow a conviction of the truth of many other things.—*Teachings of Gordon B. Hinckley,* 39.

Hunter, Howard W.

To those who may not be familiar with the Book of Mormon but are sincerely seeking truth, reading it will have a profound effect on your life. It will expand your knowledge of the way God deals with man and will give you a greater desire to live in harmony with his gospel teachings. It will also provide for you a powerful testimony of Jesus. —*Ensign* 13 (May 1983): 16.

Howard W. Hunter

Kimball, Spencer W.

It is not the [Book of Mormon's] dramatic crises, its history, its narrative that are so important, but its power to transform men into Christlike beings worthy of exaltation.

It is the word of God. It is a powerful second witness of Christ. And, certainly, all true believers who love the Redeemer will welcome additional evidence of his divinity. —CR (April 1963): 67.

Spencer W. Kimball

In the final chapter of the book [of Mormon] is the never-failing promise that every person who will read the book with a sincere, prayerful desire to know of its divinity shall have the assurance. Aside from all other interest that the Book of Mormon holds, this reason for our prayerfully studying it remains prominent: through it we can obtain true knowledge of God and what he wishes of us.—*Faith Precedes the Miracle* (Salt Lake City: Deseret Book, 1972), 337.

Lee, Harold B.

There is nothing better that we can do to prepare ourselves spiritually than to read the Book of Mormon. Many doctrines of the Bible that are only partially covered there are beautifully explained in the Book of Mormon, the Doctrine and Covenants, and the Pearl of Great Price. —*The Teachings of Harold B. Lee,* ed. Clyde J. Williams (Salt Lake City: Bookcraft, 1996), 155.

Harold B. Lee

The witness of the Book of Mormon is not found in the ruins of Central and South America. They may be outward evidences of a people long since disappeared. The real witness is that which is found in the Book of Mormon itself.

The Book of Mormon ought to be to you one of the most prized books you have. —*Teachings of Harold B. Lee,* 156.

Maxwell, Neal A.

The concepts in the Book of Mormon are a constant source of inspiration, if we will but contemplate them. There, more abundantly than in any other volume, the Lord opens the windows of heaven, not only to pour out blessings, but to let us look in.—*All These Things Shall Give Thee Experience* (Salt Lake City: Deseret Book, 1980), 35.

The density of the spiritual truths of the Book of Mormon is especially impressive. Indeed, the doctrinal density of the Book of Mormon clearly overshadows the portion that is given over to history or to details such as the description of Nephite money. The book's structure is clearly and intentionally secondary to its substance, and its plot to its principles. The Book of Mormon's innumerable insights and doctrinal declarations constitute their own witness. Clearly, this book came *through* but not *from* Joseph Smith. It is translated language, but its substance is of the Savior. —*Plain and Precious Things* (Salt Lake City: Deseret Book, 1983), 14.

Neal A. Maxwell

The Book of Mormon will be with us "as long as the earth shall stand." We need all that time to explore it, for the book is like a vast mansion with gardens, towers, courtyards, and wings. There are rooms yet to be entered, with flaming fireplaces waiting to warm us. The rooms glimpsed so far contain further furnishings and rich detail yet to be savored, but decor dating from Eden is evident. There are panels inlaid with incredible insights, particularly insights about the great question [the reality of Jesus Christ]. Yet we as Church members sometimes behave like hurried tourists, scarcely venturing beyond the entry hall.—*Not My Will but Thine* (Salt Lake City: Bookcraft, 1988), 33.

McConkie, Bruce R.

The Book of Mormon is a definitive, all-embracing, comprehensive account. Our scripture says it contains the fulness of the everlasting gospel. What that means is that it is a record of God's dealings with a people who had the fulness of the gospel. It means that in it are recorded the basic principles which men must believe to work out their salvation. After we accept and believe and comprehend the principles therein recorded, we are qualified and prepared to take another step and to begin to acquire a knowledge of the mysteries of godliness.—*The Foolishness of Teaching* (Salt Lake City: The Church of Jesus Christ of Latter-day Saints, 1981), 7.

Bruce R. McConkie

There is another and simpler test that all who seek to know the truth might well take. It calls for us simply to read, ponder, and pray—all in the spirit of faith and with an open mind. To keep ourselves alert to the issues at hand—as we do read, ponder, and pray—we should ask ourselves a thousand times, "Could any man have written this book?"

And it is absolutely guaranteed that sometime between the first and thousandth time this question is asked, every sincere and genuine truth seeker will come to know by the power of the Spirit that the Book of Mormon is true, that it is the mind and will and voice of the Lord to the whole world in our day. . . .

It is the divine evidence, the proof, that God has spoken in our day. Its chief purpose is to convince all men, Jew and Gentile alike, that Jesus is the Christ, the Eternal God, who manifests himself, by faith, in all ages and among all peoples. . . .

It is the book that will save the world and prepare the sons of men for joy and peace here and now and everlasting life in eternity.—*Ensign* 13 (November 1983): 73–74.

What then is the power of the Book of Mormon? It will proclaim the everlasting gospel; it will gather Israel; it will build the New Jerusalem; it will prepare a people for the Second Coming; it will usher in the Millennium—at least it will play such an important part in all of these that its value and power can scarcely be overstated.—*The Millennial Messiah: The Second Coming of the Son of Man* (Salt Lake City: Deseret Book, 1982), 171.

Pratt, Orson

I am fully aware that there are in the Church of Latter-day Saints many persons who are very careless about reading the "Book of Mormon." It is one of the greatest treasures, so far as books are concerned, that has been given to mankind for almost 1,800 years. It contains the things of God in great plainness, so easy of comprehension that the child who reads can understand it. And yet, how many there are of the Latter-day Saints who suffer this book to remain upon their shelves, week after week, without ever reading a page of these precious things.—*Journal of Discourses,* 26 vols. (London: Latter-day Saints' Book Depot, 1854–86), 19:213.

Orson Pratt

Roberts, B. H.

In common with all books the Book of Mormon has its spirit, produces its effects upon the minds of men; and as it claims to be a work originally written and also translated through the inspiration of God, and deals primarily with sacred things, it is to be expected that the spirit of this book will have not only a good, but even a divine influence; that it will be of a faith-promoting, doubt-dispersing, comfort-bringing character. Its effects upon the minds of men, therefore, may be another test of its claims to a divine origin; and to that test I now submit it. . . . Men have gone to the Book of Mormon in despondency, and have come away cheered; they have gone to it in sorrow, and have come away comforted; they have gone to it at times when overwhelmed for the moment by the mists which the speculations of men sometimes throw over truth, and have come away from it enlightened—with faith and hope and charity renewed. It created for them a firmer faith in God. In the presence of its spirit doubt took wings. Its moral and spiritual standards they find to be the highest and noblest. Indeed so perfect is its morality that no one has yet been able to bring a complaint against it on the ground of moral defect. . . . Whatever power it possesses to cheer, comfort and encourage men; whatever power to build up hope, create faith or promote charity, exists not by virtue of its human excellencies, but in spite of their absence; therefore such influence for good as it possesses must be attributed to the Spirit of God in which it was written, and by which it is permeated; and by reason of the presence of that spirit in it, the book itself must be accorded a divine origin.—*New Witnesses for God* (Salt Lake City: Deseret Book, 1951), 3:325–27, 331.

B. H. Roberts

Romney, Marion G.

A few years ago as I began to practice law, members of my family were a little uneasy. They were afraid I would lose my faith. I wanted to practice law, but I had an even greater desire to keep my testimony, and so I decided upon a little procedure which I recommend to you. For thirty minutes each morning before I began the day's work I read from the Book of Mormon . . . and in just a few minutes a day I read the Book of Mormon through, every year, for nine years. I know that it kept me in harmony, so far as I did keep in harmony, with the Spirit of the Lord. —CR (April 1949): 36.

I urge you to get acquainted with this great book. Read it to your children; they are not too young to understand it. I remember reading it with one of my lads when he was very young. On one occasion I lay in the lower bunk and he in the upper bunk. We were each reading aloud alternate paragraphs of those last three marvelous chapters of Second Nephi. I heard his voice breaking and thought he had a cold, but we went on to the end of the three chapters. As we finished he said to me, "Daddy, do you ever cry when you read the Book of Mormon?"

Marion G. Romney

"Yes, Son," I answered. "Sometimes the Spirit of the Lord so witnesses to my soul that the Book of Mormon is true that I do cry."

"Well," he said, "that is what happened to me tonight."

I know not all of them will respond like that,

but I know that some of them will, and I tell you this book was given to us of God to read and to live by, and it will hold us as close to the Spirit of the Lord as anything I know. Won't you please read it?—CR (April 1949): 41.

I am persuaded, my brethren and sisters, that it is irrational to hope to escape the lusts of the world without substituting for them as the subjects of our thoughts the things of the spirit, and I know that the things of the spirit are taught with mighty power in the Book of Mormon. I believe with all my heart, for example, that if our young people could come out of our homes thoroughly acquainted with the life of Nephi, imbued with the spirit of his courage and love of truth, they would choose the right when a choice is placed before them.—CR (April 1960): 112.

If our young folks are traditioned in the teachings of the Book of Mormon, they will not only be inspired with righteous courage to choose the right . . . they will also be so schooled in the principles of the gospel of Jesus Christ that they will know what is right.

From almost every page of the book, there will come to them a moving testimony that Jesus is indeed the Christ, the Son of the Living God, our Redeemer and Savior. This witness alone will be a sustaining anchor in every storm.—CR (April 1960): 112.

And so, I counsel you, my beloved brothers and sisters and friends everywhere, to make reading in the Book of Mormon a few minutes each day a lifelong practice. All of us need continuing close contact with the Spirit of the Lord. We need to take the Holy Spirit for our guide that we be not deceived. I am persuaded by my own experience and that of my loved ones, as well as by the statement of the Prophet Joseph Smith, that one can get and keep closer to the Lord by reading the Book of Mormon than by reading any other book. Don't be content with what someone else says about what is in it. Drink deeply from the divine fountain itself.

I feel certain that if, in our homes, parents will read from the Book of Mormon prayerfully and regularly, both by themselves and with their children, the spirit of that great book will come to permeate our homes and all who dwell therein. The spirit of reverence will increase, mutual respect and consideration for each other will grow. The spirit of contention will depart. Parents will counsel their children in greater love and wisdom. Children will be more responsive and submissive to that counsel. Righteousness will increase. Faith, hope, and charity—the pure love of Christ—will abound in our homes and lives, bringing in their wake peace, joy, and happiness.—CR (April 1960): 112–13.

Scott, Richard G.

Richard G. Scott

It is not sufficient that we should treasure the Book of Mormon, nor that we testify that it is of God. We must know its truths, incorporate them into our lives, and share them with others.—*Ensign* 18 (November 1988): 76.

Smith, Joseph, Jr.

Joseph Smith, Jr.

I told the brethren that the Book of Mormon was the most correct of any book on earth, and the keystone of our religion, and a man would get nearer to God by abiding by its precepts, than by any other book.—*History of The Church of Jesus Christ of Latter-day Saints,* ed. B. H. Roberts, 2d ed. rev., 7 vols. (Salt Lake City: The Church of Jesus Christ of Latter-day Saints, 1932–51), 4:461.

The fact is, that by the power of God I translated the Book of Mormon from hieroglyphics, the knowledge of which was lost to the world, in which wonderful event I stood alone, an unlearned youth, to combat the worldly wisdom and multiplied ignorance of eighteen centuries, with a new revelation, which (if they would receive the everlasting Gospel,) would open the eyes of more than eight hundred millions of people, and make "plain the old paths," wherein if a man walk in all the ordinances of God blameless, he shall inherit eternal life.—*History of the Church,* 6:74.

Smith, Joseph F.

I have read it many times since, and I have asked myself scores of times, have you ever discovered one precept, doctrine, or command within the lids of that book that is calculated to injure anybody, to do harm to the world, or that is in contradiction to the word of God as contained in the Bible? And the answer invariably came, No, not one solitary thing; every precept, doctrine, word of advice, prophecy, and indeed every word contained within the lids of that book relating to the great plan of human redemption and salvation is calculated to make bad men good, and good men better.—*Journal of Discourses,* 26 vols. (London: Latter-day Saints' Book Depot, 1854–86), 24:14.

Joseph F. Smith

Smith, Joseph Fielding

I started to read the Book of Mormon before I was old enough to be a deacon, and I have been reading it ever since, and I know that it is true. Every member of the Church ought to know that it is true, and we ought to be prepared with an answer to all of these critics who condemn it. . . . It seems to me that any member of this Church would never be satisfied until he or she had read the Book of Mormon time and time again, and thoroughly considered it so that he or she could bear witness that it is in very deed a record with the inspiration of the Almighty upon it, and that its history is true. . . . I want to address myself to the men holding the priesthood, particularly, and to their wives and to all other members of the Church. No member of this Church can stand approved in the presence of God who has not seriously and carefully read the Book of Mormon.—CR (October 1961): 18.

Now the Lord has placed us on probation as members of the Church. He has given us the Book of Mormon, which is the lesser part, to build up our faith through our obedience to the counsels which it contains, and when we ourselves, members of the Church, are willing to keep the commandments as they have been given to us and show our faith as the Nephites did for a short period of time, then the Lord is ready to bring forth the other record and give it to us, but we are not ready now to receive it. Why? Because we have not lived up to the requirements in this probationary state in the reading of the record which had been given to us and in following its counsels.—CR (October 1961): 20.

Joseph Fielding Smith

See also The Book of Mormon: An Overview and Introduction, page 1; Book of Mormon, early conversions through.

Appendix C
Definitions from Webster's 1828 *American Dictionary of the English Language*

For the Lord God giveth light unto the understanding;
for he speaketh unto men according to their language, unto their understanding.
—*2 Nephi 31:3*

Abbreviations

a.	stands	for adjective.
adv.	"	for adverb.
def.	"	for definition.
defs.	"	for definitions.
n.	"	for name or noun.
obs.	"	for obsolete.
pp.	"	for participle passive.
ppr.	"	for participle of the present tense.
prep.	"	for preposition.
pret.	"	for preterit tense.
v.i.	"	for verb intransitive.
v.t.	"	for verb transitive.

The number associated with each definition coincides with that found in Webster's 1828 *American Dictionary of the English Language.*

Definitions

Accursed, *pp.* or *a.* [as in Hel. 12:18–20] 1. Doomed to destruction or misery. 2. Separated from the faithful; cast out of the church; excommunicated. 3. Worthy of the curse; detestable; execrable.

Admonish, *v.t.* [defs. 1, 2, 4 as in Mosiah 26:6; def. 3 as in Omni 1:13] 1. To warn or notify of a fault; to reprove with mildness. 2. To counsel against wrong practices; to caution or advise. 3. To instruct or direct. 4. In *ecclesiastical affairs,* to reprove a member of the church for a fault, either publicly or privately.

Against, *prep.* [as in Alma 43:26; 58:17] 8. In provision for; in preparation for.

Amiss, *adv.* [as in 2 Ne. 4:35] 2. In a faulty manner; contrary to propriety, truth, law or morality.

Aright, *adv.* [as in Hel. 8:8] Rightly; in a right form; without mistake or crime.

Artificer, *n.* [as in 2 Ne. 13:3] 1. An artist; a mechanic or manufacturer; one whose occupation requires skill or knowledge of a particular kind; as a silversmith or sadler.

Asunder, *adv.* [as in Mosiah 27:18] Apart; into parts; separately; in a divided state.

Bade, the past tense of *bid.* BID, *v.t.* [as in 1 Ne. 1:11] 1. To ask; to request; to invite. 2. To command; to order or direct.

Barren, *a.* [def. 1 as in 3 Ne. 22:1; def. 2 as in Alma 32:39] 1. Not producing young, or offspring. 2. Not producing plants; unfruitful; steril; not fertile; or producing little; unproductive.

Baseness, *n.* [as in Alma 17:9] 1. Meanness; vileness; worthlessness.

Beguiled, *pp.* [as in 2 Ne. 9:9] Deluded; misled by craft; eluded by stratagem.

Behoove[th], *v.t.* [as in 2 Ne. 9:5] To be necessary for; to be fit for; to be meet for, with respect to necessity, duty, or convenience.

Beset, *v.t.* [as in 2 Ne. 4:18] 1. To surround; to inclose; to hem in; to besiege. 2. To press on all sides, so as to perplex; to entangle, so as to render escape difficult or impossible. 3. To waylay.

Besom, *n.* [as in 2 Ne. 24:23] a broom; a brush of twigs for sweeping.

Besought, *pp.* [as in Alma 15:5] Entreated; implored; sought by entreaty.

Bestead, *pp.* [as in 2 Ne. 18:21] 2. Distressed; perplexed.

Bestir, *v.t.* [as in Alma 60:29] To put into brisk or vigorous action; to move with life and vigor.

Betwixt, *prep.* [as in Alma 35:13] 1. Between; in the space that separates two persons or things.

Bittern, *n.* [as in 2 Ne. 24:23] a fowl of the grallic order, the *Ardea stellaris,* a native of Europe. This fowl has long legs and neck, and stalks among reeds and sedge, feeding upon fish.

Bowels, *n.* [def. 1 as in 1 Ne. 21:1; def. 3 as in Alma 34:15] 1. The intestines of an animal; the entrails. 3. The seat of pity or kindness; hence, tenderness, compassion.

Bridle, *v.t.* [as in Alma 38:12] 2. To restrain, guide or govern; to check, curb or control.

Buckler[s], *n.* [as in 3 Ne. 3:26] a kind of shield, or piece of defensive armor, anciently used in war.

By and By [as in Alma 55:14] a phrase denoting nearness in time; in a short time after; presently; soon.

Caul[s], *n.* [as in 2 Ne. 13:18] 2. a kind of net in which females inclose their hair.

Chasten, *v.t.* [def. 1 as in Mosiah 23:21; def. 2 as in 1 Ne. 16:39] 1. To correct by punishment; to punish; to inflict pain for the purpose of reclaiming an offender. 2. To afflict by other means.

Check, *v.t.* [as in Alma 57:18] 1. To stop; to restrain; to hinder; to curb.

Check, *n.* [as in Alma 15:17] a stop; sudden restraint, or continued restraint; curb; control.

Circumspectly, *adv.* [as in Mosiah 26:37] Cautiously; with watchfulness every way; with attention to guard against surprise or danger.

Cite, *v.t.* [as in Alma 13:1] 2. To enjoin; to direct; to summon; to order or urge.

Clapped, *pp.* [as in Alma 31:36] Thrust or put on or together; applauded by striking the hands together.

Confounded, *pp.* [as in 2 Ne. 4:22] Mixed or blended in disorder; perplexed; abashed; dismayed; put to shame and silence; astonished.

Consign, *v.t.* [as in Alma 26:19] 1. To give, send or set over; to transfer or deliver.

Constrain, *v.t.* [as in Ether 6:25] In *a general sense,* to strain; to press; to urge; to drive; to exert force, physical or moral, either in urging to action or in restraining it.

Constrained, *pp.* [as in 1 Ne. 4:10] Urged irresistibly or powerfully; compelled;

Cross, *v.t.* [def. 5 as in Alma 39:9; def. 6 as in Alma 10:16] 5. To thwart; to obstruct; to hinder; to embarrass. 6. To counteract; to clash or interfere with; to be inconsistent with; as, natural appetites may cross our principles.

Cross[es], *n.* [as in 2 Ne. 9:18] 6. Any thing that thwarts, obstructs, or perplexes; hindrance; vexation; misfortune; opposition; trial of patience.

Cumber, v.t. [def. 1 as in Jacob 5:30; def. 4 as in Jacob 5:9] 1. To load, or crowd. 4. To trouble; to be troublesome to; to cause trouble or obstruction in, as anything useless.

Cunning, *a.* [def. 1 as in 2 Ne. 13:3; def. 4 as in 2 Ne. 9:28] 1. Knowing; skilful; experienced; well-instructed. 3. Artful; shrewd; sly; craft; astute; designing; as a *cunning* fellow. 4. Deceitful; trickish; employing strategems.

Cunning, *n.* [as in Mosiah 7:21] 2. Art; artifice; artfulness; craft; shrewdness; the faculty or act of using stratagem to accomplish a purpose.

Curious, *a.* [def. 1 as in Alma 63:5; def. 3 as in Hel. 6:11; defs. 5, 7, 10 as in 1 Ne. 16:10] 1. Strongly desirous to see what is novel, or to discover what is unknown; solicitous to see or to know; inquisitive. 3. Accurate; careful not to mistake; solicitous to be correct. 5. Nice; exact; subtile; made with care. 7. Wrought with care and art; elegant; neat; finished. 10. Rare; singular.

Dash, *v.t.* [def. 1 as in Ether 2:24; def. 9 as in 2 Ne. 23:18] 1. To strike suddenly or violently. 9. To break; to destroy; to frustrate.

Daunted, *pp.* [as in Alma 61:4] Checked by fear; intimidated.

Dearth, *n.* [as in Ether 9:30] Scarcity. 2. Want; need; famine. 3. Barrenness; sterility.

Dim, *v.t.* [as in 1 Ne. 5:19] 4. To make less bright; to obscure. 5. To render less bright; to tarnish or sully.

Disannul, *v.t.* [as in 2 Ne. 24:27] To annul; to make void; to deprive of authority or force; to nullify; to abolish.

Divers, *a.* [as in Mosiah 4:29] 1. Different; various. 2. Several; sundry.

Dregs, *n.* [as in 2 Ne. 8:22] 1. The sediment of liquors; lees; grounds; feculence; any foreign matter of liquors that subsides to the bottom of a vessel.

Dross, *n.* [def. 1 as in Alma 34:29; def. 3 as in Alma 32:3] 1. The scum or extraneous matter of metals, thrown off in the process of melting. 3. Waste matter; refuse; any worthless matter separated from the better part.

Durst, *pret.* of *dare.* DARE, *v.i.* [as in 1 Ne. 17:52] To have courage for any purpose; to have strength of mind or hardihood to undertake any thing; to be bold enough; not to be afraid; to venture; to be adventurous.

Dwindle, *v.i.* [as in Alma 45:12] 2. To degenerate; to sink; to fall away.

Effectual, *a.* [as in Mosiah 7:18] Producing an effect, or the effect desired or intended; or having adequate power or force to produce the effect.

Entreated, *pp.* [as in Alma 7:23] Earnestly supplicated, besought or solicited; importuned; urgently requested. 2. Prevailed on by urgent solicitation; consenting to grant what is desired.

Esteem, v.t. [def. 1 as in 2 Ne. 33:2–3; def. 2 as in Mosiah 29:40] 1. To set a value on, whether high or low; to estimate; to value. 2. To prize; to set a high value on; to regard with reverence, respect or friendship.

Exalt, *v.t.* [def. 4 as in 2 Ne. 24:13; def. 6 as in 2 Ne. 23:2] 4. To raise with pride; to make undue pretensions to power, rank or estimation. 6. To raise, as the voice; to raise in opposition.

Exhort, *v.t.* [as in Moro. 10:3] 1. To incite by words or advice; to animate or urge by arguments to a good deed or to any laudable conduct or course of action. 2. To advise; to warn; to caution. 3. To incite or stimulate to exertion.

Exhortation, *n.* [as in Moro. 10:2] The act or practice of exhorting; the act of inciting to laudable deeds; incitement to that which is good or commendable. 2. The form of words intended to incite and encourage. 3. Advice; counsel.

Expedient, *a.* [def. 1 as in 2 Ne. 3:19 and Alma 34:9; def. 2 as in 1 Ne. 10:15] 1. Literally, hastening; urging forward. Hence, tending to promote the object proposed; fit or suitable for the purpose; proper under the circumstances. 2. Useful; profitable.

Extolled, *ppr.* [as in 3 Ne. 20:43] Exalted in commendation; praised; magnified.

Fagot[s], *n.* [spelled "faggots" as in Mosiah 17:13] 1. a bundle of sticks, twigs or small branches of trees, used for fuel, or for raising batteries, filling ditches, and other purposes in fortification.

Fain, *adv.* [as in Alma 12:14] Gladly; with joy or pleasure.

Fair, *a.* [as in 1 Ne. 11:13] 3. Pleasing to the eye; handsome or beautiful in general.

Fatness, *n.* [as in 2 Ne. 9:51] 4. That which gives fertility. 5. The privileges and pleasures of religion; abundant blessings.

Fine, *In fine.* [as in 1 Ne. 10:14] In the end or conclusion; to conclude; to sum up all.

Firebrand[s], *n.* [as in 2 Ne. 17:4] 2. An incendiary; one who inflames factions, or causes contention and mischief.

Forswear, *v.t.* [as in 3 Ne. 12:33] 1. To reject or renounce upon oath. 2. To deny upon oath. *To forswear one's self,* is to swear falsely; to perjure one's self.

Fro, *adv.* [as in 1 Ne. 22:4] From; away; back or backward; as in the phrase, *to* and *fro,* that is, *to* and *from,* hither and thither.

Gainsaying, *ppr.* [as in Jacob 6:4] Contradicting; denying; opposing.

Garner[s], *n.* [as in Alma 26:5] a granary; a building or place where grain is stored for preservation.

Gird, *v.t.* [def. 1, 6 as in 2 Ne. 18:9; defs. 2, 4 as in 1 Ne. 4:19] 1. To bind by surrounding with any flexible substance, as with a twig, a cord, bandage or cloth. 2. To make fast by binding; to put on. 4. To clothe; to dress; to habit. 6. To surround; to encircle; to inclose; to encompass.

Glut, *v.i.* [as in Mosiah 9:12] 1. To swallow, or to swallow greedily; to gorge. 2. To cloy; to fill beyond sufficiency; to sate; to disgust. 3. To feast or delight even to satiety.

Gnashing, *ppr.* [as in Alma 14:21] Striking the teeth together, as in anger, rage or pain.

Gnashing, *n.* [as in Alma 40:13] a grinding or striking of the teeth in rage or anguish.

Go To [as in Jacob. 5:61, 71; Enos 1:8] come, move, begin; a phrase of exhortation.

Goodly, *a.* [as in 1 Ne. 1:1] Being of a handsome form; beautiful; graceful. 2. Pleasant; agreeable; desirable.

Guile, *n.* [as in Alma 18:23] Craft; cunning; artifice.

Halt, *a.* [as in 3 Ne. 17:7] Lame; that is, holding or stopping in walking.

Harrow, *v.t.* [as in Alma 15:3] 3. To tear; to lacerate; to torment.

Haughty, *a.* [as in 2 Ne. 20:33] 1. Proud and disdainful; having a high opinion of one's self, with some contempt for others; lofty and arrogant; supercilious. 3. Proud and imperious.

Hearken, *v.i.* [as in 1 Ne. 20:1] 1. To listen; to lend the ear; to attend to what is uttered, with eagerness or curiosity. 2. To attend; to regard; to give heed to what is uttered; to observe or obey. 3. To listen; to attend; to grant or comply with.

Hedge, *v.t.* [as in Mosiah 7:29] 2. To obstruct with a hedge, or to obstruct in any manner. 4. To inclose for preventing escape.

Heed, *v.t.* [as in 1 Ne. 16:28] To mind; to regard with care; to take notice of; to attend to; to observe.

Heed, *n.* [def. 2 as in 2 Ne. 17:4; def. 3 as in 1 Ne. 15:25] 2. Caution; care; watch for danger; notice; circumspection; usually preceded by *take.* 3. Notice; observation; regard; attention; often preceded by *give.*

Hiss, *v.i.* [as in 2 Ne. 29:2] 3. To whiz, as an arrow or other thing in rapid flight.

Hiss, *n.* [as in 1 Ne. 19:14] 2. An expression of contempt or disapprobation, used in places of public exhibition.

Ignominious, *a.* [as in Alma 1:15] 2. Very shameful; reproachful; dishonorable; infamous.

Indolence, *n.* [as in Alma 47:36] 2. Habitual idleness; indisposition to labor; laziness; inaction or want of exertion of body or mind, proceeding from love of ease or aversion to toil. *Indolence,* like *laziness,* implies a constitutional or habitual love of ease.

Insurrection[s], *n.* [as in Alma 60:27] 1. a rising against civil or political authority; the open and active opposition of a number of persons to the execution of law in a city or state.

Intercourse, *n.* [as in Hel. 6:8] 1. Communication; commerce; connection by reciprocal dealings between persons or nations, either in common affairs and civilities, in trade, or correspondence by letters.

Interposition, *n.* [as in Mosiah 29:19] 1. a being, placing or coming between; intervention.

Intrigue, *n.* [as in Alma 53:8, 9] 1. a plot or scheme of a complicated nature, intended to effect some purpose by secret artifices.

Lasciviousness, *n.* [as in Jacob 3:12] Looseness; irregular indulgence of animal desires; wantonness; lustfulness.

List, *v.t.* [as in Mosiah 2:32] 6. To hearken; to attend.

Loathsome, *a.* [as in 1 Ne. 12:23] Disgusting; exciting disgust. 2. Hateful; abhorred; detestable.

Lucre, *n.* [as in Mosiah 29:40] Gain in money or goods; profit; usually in an ill sense, or with the sense of something base or unworthy.

Mar, *v.t.* [as in Ether 6:10] 2. To injure; to hurt; to impair the strength or purity of. 3. To injure;
to diminish; to interrupt. 4. To injure; to deform; to disfigure.

Meet, *a.* [as in 1 Ne. 7:1] Fit; suitable; proper; qualified; convenient; adapted, as to a use or purpose.

Mete, *v.t.* [as in 3 Ne. 14:2] To measure; to ascertain quantity, dimensions or capacity by any rule or standard.

Methought, *pret.* of *methinks.* [As in 1 Ne. 8:4] It seemed to me; I thought.

Molder, *v.i.* [as in Morm. 6:15] 1. To turn to dust by natural decay; to crumble; to perish; to waste away by a gradual separation of the component particles, without the presence of water.

More, *adv.* [as in Alma 53:11; 63:8] 4. a second or another time; again.

Narrowly, *adv.* [as in 2 Ne. 24:16] 3. Closely; accurately; with minute scrutiny.

Nethermost, *a.* [as in Jacob 5:13] Lowest.

Noised, *pp.* [as in 3 Ne. 19:2–3] Spread by report; much talked of.

Oft, *adv.* [as in Alma 6:6] Often; frequently; not rarely.

Penitent, *a.* [as in Alma 26:21] Suffering pain or sorrow of heart on account of sins, crimes or offenses; contrite; sincerely affected by a sense of guilt and resolving on amendment of life.

Peradventure, *adv.* [as in Alma 37:27] By chance; perhaps; it may be.

Picket[s], *n.* [as in Alma 50:3–4] a stake sharpened or pointed; used in fortification and encampments. 2. a narrow board pointed; used in making fence.

Privily, *adv.* [as in Alma 51: 34] Privately; secretly.

Profane[d], *v.t.* [as in Jarom 1:5] To violate anything sacred, or treat it with abuse, irreverence, obloquy or contempt; as, to *profane* the name of God; to *profane* the sabbath; to *profane* the Scriptures or the ordinances of God.

Puffed, *pp.* [as in 2 Ne. 9:42] Blown up; swelled with air; inflated with vanity or pride.

Quarter[s], *n.* [def. 5 as in 1 Ne. 19:16; def. 6 as in Ether 2:5] 5. a region in the hemisphere or great circle; primarily, one of the four cardinal points; as the four *quarters* of the globe. 6. a particular region of a town, city or country; as all *quarters* of the city; in every *quarter* of the country or of the continent.

Quick, *n.* [as in Moro. 10:34] 2. The living flesh.

Rack, *v.t.* [as in Alma 36:14] 2. To torment; to torture; to affect with extreme pain or anguish.

Railing, *n.* [as in 3 Ne. 6:13] Reproachful or insolent language.

Revile, *v.t.* [as in Alma 30:29] To reproach; to treat with opprobrious and contemptuous language.

Root[ed], *v.t.* [as in Alma 22:15] *To root up or out,* to eradicate; to extirpate; to remove or destroy root and branch; to exterminate.

Sally, *v.i.* [as in Alma 56:29] 1. To issue or rush out, as a body of troops from a fortified place to attack besiegers.

Secreted, *pp.* [as in Alma 43:27] Concealed.

Selfsame, *a.* [as in Alma 31:22] The very same; identical.

Snare, *n.* [as in Alma 12:6] 2. Any thing by which one is entangled and brought into trouble.

Snare, *v.t.* [as in 2 Ne. 18:15] To catch with a snare; to ensnare; to entangle; to bring into unexpected evil, perplexity or danger.

Snatch, *v.t.* [as in Mosiah 27:28] 1. To seize hastily or abruptly. 3. To seize and transport away.

Sojourn, *v.i.* [as in 1 Ne. 17:3] To dwell for a time; to dwell or live in a place as a temporary resident, or as a stranger, not considering the place as his permanent habitation.

Spurn, *v.i.* [as in 3 Ne. 29:4–5] To manifest disdain in rejecting any thing. 2. To make contemptuous opposition; to manifest disdain in resistance.

Steadfastness, *n.* [as in 2 Ne. 31:20] Firmness of standing; fixedness in place. 2. Firmness of mind or purpose; fixedness in principle; constancy; resolution.

Stout, *a.* [def. 4 as in 2 Ne. 20:12; def. 5 as in 3 Ne. 24:13] 4. Proud; resolute; obstinate. 5. Strong; firm.

Stripe[s], *n.* [as in 2 Ne. 28:8] 4. a stroke made with a lash, whip, rod, strap or scourge. 5. Affliction; punishment; sufferings.

Stripling, *n.* [as in Alma 53:22] a youth in the state of adolescence, or just passing from boyhood to manhood; a lad.

Stubble, *n.* [as in 1 Ne. 22:15] The stumps of wheat, rye, barley, oats or buckwheat, left in the ground; the part of the stalk left by the sythe or sickle.

Stupor, *n.* [as in Alma 60:7] Great diminution or suspension of sensibility; suppression of sense; numbness. 2. Intellectual insensibility; moral stupidity; heedlessness or inattention to one's interests.

Succor, *v.t.* [as in Alma 7:12] Literally, to run to, or run to support; hence, to help or relieve when in difficulty, want or distress; to assist and deliver from suffering.

Suffer, *v.t.* [as in Jacob 2:32] 3. To allow; to permit; not to forbid or hinder.

Sway, *n.* [as in Alma 42:30] 5. Influence; weight or authority that inclines to one side.

Tire, *n.* [as in 2 Ne. 13:18] 2. a head dress; something that encompasses the head.

Traffick, *v.i.* [spelled "traffic" as in 4 Ne. 1:46] 1. To trade; to pass goods and commodities from one person to another for an equivalent in goods or money; to barter; to buy and sell wares; to carry on commerce. 2. To trade meanly or mercenarily.

Travail, *n.* [as in Mosiah 27:33] Labor with pain; severe toil.

Undaunted, *a.* [as in Alma 57:20] Not daunted; not subdued or depressed by fear; intrepid.

Vale, *n.* [as in Alma 37:45] 1. a tract of low ground or of land between hills; a valley.

Verily, *adv.* [as in 2 Ne. 11:2] In truth; in fact; certainly. 2. Really; truly; with great confidence.

Vouch[ing], *v.i.* [as in Alma 24:18] To bear witness; to give testimony or full attestation.

Wax, *v.i.* [def. 1 as in Mosiah 24:7; def. 2 as in 2 Ne. 7:9] 1. To increase in size; to grow; to become larger. 2. To pass from one state to another; to become.

Whence, *adv.* [def. 1 as in 2 Ne. 6:8; def. 2 as in 1 Ne. 8:14; def. 4 as in 2 Ne. 28:23] 1. From what place. 2. From what source. 4. How; by what way or means.

Whit, *n.* [as in Alma 34:14] a point; a jot; the smallest part or particle imaginable.

Whither, *adv.* [as in Alma 22:29] To what place, interrogatively. 2. To what place. 5. Whithersoever.

Wile[s], *n.* [as in Hel. 3:29] a trick or stratagem practiced for ensnaring or deception; a sly, insidious artifice.

Wis, *v.t.* [as in Hel. 9:30] To think; to suppose; to imagine.

Wist, *pret.* of *wis. Obs.*

Without, *adv.* [as in Mosiah 7:10; 21:19] Not on the inside; not within. 2. Out of doors.

Wo, *n.* [as in 2 Ne. 15:21; 16:5] 1. Grief; sorrow; misery; a heavy calamity. 2. a curse. 3. *Wo* is used in denunciation, and in exclamations of sorrow.

Wonderful, *a.* [as in Alma 2:5] Adapted to excite wonder or admiration; exciting surprise; strange; astonishing.

Wrapt, *pp.* [as in 3 Ne. 26:3] Wound; folded; inclosed.

Wrest, *v.t.* [as in Alma 13:20] 3. To distort; to turn from truth or twist from its natural meaning by violence; to pervert.

Wroth, *a.* [as in Mosiah 10:14] Very angry; much exasperated.

Wrought, *pret.* and *pp.* of *work.* [def. 1 as in Ether 10:7; def. 2 as in 1 Ne. 17:51; def. 3 as in Mosiah 5:2] 1. Worked; formed by work or labor; as *wrought* iron. 2. Effected; performed. 3. Effected; produced.

Wrought on or upon, [as in 1 Ne. 19:12] influenced; prevailed on.

INDEX

C

D

INDEX

E

F

INDEX

G

H

I

INDEX

J

INDEX

K

L

M

N

INDEX

O

P

INDEX

Q

R

S

INDEX

T

U

V

W

INDEX

Z